the BIG
selection
2015

over 1000 independent reviews

the best campsites
in Europe

Compiled by: Alan Rogers Travel Ltd

Designed by: Vine Design Ltd

Additional photography: T Lambelin, www.lambelin.com
Maps created by Customised Mapping (01769 540044)
contain background data provided by GisDATA Ltd

Maps are © Alan Rogers Travel Ltd and GisDATA Ltd 2014

© Alan Rogers Travel Ltd 2015

Published by: Alan Rogers Travel Ltd,
Spelmonden Old Oast, Goudhurst, Kent TN17 1HE
www.alanrogers.com Tel: 01580 214000

British Library Cataloguing-in-Publication Data:
A catalogue record for this book is available
from the British Library.

ISBN 978-1-909057-67-8

Printed in Great Britain by Stephens & George Print Group

Contents

Alan Rogers in search of 'the best'

Alan Rogers Guides were first published over 40 years ago. Since Alan Rogers published the first campsite guide that bore his name, the range has expanded and now covers 27 countries in six separate guides. No fewer than 20 of the campsites selected by Alan for the first guide are still featured in our 2015 editions.

There are many thousands of campsites in Europe of varying quality: this guide contains impartially written reports on over 1,000, including many of the very finest, in no less than 22 countries. Each one is individually inspected and selected. This guide does not include sites in Britain and Ireland, for which we publish a separate guide, and it contains only a limited selection of sites in France, Italy, Spain and Portugal as we also publish separate guides for these destinations. We aim to provide you with a selection of the best, rather than information on all – in short, a more selective, qualitative approach. New, improved maps and indexes are also included, designed to help you find the choice of campsite that's right for you.

Finally, in 2013 we launched the new Alan Rogers Travel Card. Free to readers, it offers exclusive online extras, money saving deals and offers on many campsites. Find out more on page 14.

We hope you enjoy some happy and safe travels – and some pleasurable 'armchair touring' in the meantime!

How do we find the best?

The criteria we use when inspecting and selecting campsites are numerous, but the most important by far is the question of good quality. People want different things from their choice of site so we try to include a range of campsite 'styles' to cater for a wide variety of preferences: from those seeking a small peaceful campsite in the heart of the countryside, to visitors looking for an 'all singing, all dancing' site in a popular seaside resort. Those with more specific interests, such as sporting facilities, cultural events or historical attractions, are also catered for.

The size of the site, whether it's part of a chain or privately owned, makes no difference in terms of it being required to meet our exacting standards in respect of its quality and it being 'fit for purpose'. In other words, irrespective of the size of the site, or the number of facilities it offers, we consider and evaluate the welcome, the pitches, the sanitary facilities, the cleanliness, the general maintenance and even the location.

" ...the campsites included in this book have been chosen entirely on merit, and no payment of any sort is made by them for their inclusion."

Alan Rogers, 1968

Expert opinions

We rely on our dedicated team of Site Assessors, all of whom are experienced campers, caravanners or motorcaravanners, to visit and recommend campsites. Each year they travel some 100,000 miles around Europe inspecting new campsites for the guide and re-inspecting the existing ones. Our thanks are due to them for their enthusiastic efforts, their diligence and integrity.

We also appreciate the feedback we receive from many of our readers and we always make a point of following up complaints, suggestions or recommendations for possible new campsites. Of course we get a few grumbles too – but it really is a few, and those we do receive usually relate to overcrowding or to poor maintenance during the peak school holiday period. Please bear in mind that, although we are interested to hear about any complaints, we have no contractual relationship with the campsites featured in our guides and are therefore not in a position to intervene in any dispute between a reader and a campsite.

Independent and honest

Whilst the content and scope of the Alan Rogers guides have expanded considerably since the early editions, our selection of campsites still employs exactly the same philosophy and criteria as defined by Alan Rogers in 1968.

'telling it how it is'

Firstly, and most importantly, our selection is based entirely on our own rigorous and independent inspection and selection process. Campsites cannot buy their way into our guides – indeed the extensive Site Report which is written by us, not by the site owner, is provided free of charge so we are free to say what we think and to provide an honest, 'warts and all' description. This is written in plain English and without the use of confusing icons or symbols.

Looking for the best

Highly respected by site owners and readers alike, there is no better guide when it comes to forming an independent view of a campsite's quality. When you need to be confident in your choice of campsite, you need the Alan Rogers Guide.

- Sites only included on merit
- Sites cannot pay to be included
- Independently inspected, rigorously assessed
- Impartial reviews
- Over 40 years of expertise

Written in plain English, our guides are exceptionally easy to use, but a few words of explanation regarding the layout and content may be helpful. This guide is divided firstly by country, subsequently (in the case of larger countries) by region. For a particular area the town index at the back provides more direct access.

Maps, campsite listings and indexes

For this 2015 guide we have changed the way in which we list our campsites and also the way in which we help you locate the sites within each region.

We have changed the maps at the back of the guide to show the towns near which one or more of our featured campsites are located.

Within each country section of the guide, we list these towns and the site(s) in that vicinity in alphabetical order.

You will certainly need more detailed maps for navigation, for example the Michelin atlas. We provide GPS coordinates for each site to assist you. Our three indexes will also help you to find a site by its reference number and name, by region and site name, or by the town where the site is situated.

Index town
Site name
Postal address (including region) T: telephone number. E: email address
alanrogers.com web address (including Alan Rogers reference number)

A description of the site in which we try to give an idea of its general features – its size, its situation, its strengths and its weaknesses. This section should provide a picture of the site itself with reference to the facilities that are provided and if they impact on its appearance or character. We include details on pitch numbers, electricity (with amperage), hardstandings etc. in this section as pitch design, planning and terracing affects the site's overall appearance. Similarly we include reference to pitches used for caravan holiday homes, chalets, and the like. Importantly at the end of this column we indicate if there are any restrictions, e.g. no tents, no children, naturist sites.

Facilities
Lists more specific information on the site's facilities and amenities and, where available, the dates when these facilities are open (if not for the whole season). Off site: here we give distances to various local amenities, for example, local shops, the nearest beach, plus our featured activities (bicycle hire, fishing, riding, boat launching). Where we have space we listsuggestions for activities and local tourist attractions.

Open: Site opening dates.

Directions
Separated from the main text in order that they may be read and assimilated more easily by a navigator en-route. Bear in mind that road improvement schemes can result in road numbers being altered.

GPS: references are provided in decimal format. All latitudes are North. Longitudes are East unless preceeded by a minus sign e.g. 48.71695 is North, 0.31254 is East and -0.31254 is West.

Charges 2015 (or a general guide)

Understanding the entries

Facilities

Toilet blocks: Unless we comment otherwise, toilet blocks will be equipped with WCs, washbasins with hot and cold water and hot showers with dividers or curtains, and will have all necessary shelves, hooks, plugs and mirrors. We also assume that there will be an identified chemical toilet disposal point, and that the campsite will provide water and waste water drainage points and bin areas. If not the case, we comment. We do mention certain features that some readers find important: washbasins in cubicles, facilities for babies, facilities for those with disabilities and motorcaravan service points. Readers with disabilities are advised to contact the site of their choice to ensure that facilities are appropriate to their needs.

Shop: Basic or fully supplied, and opening dates.

Bars, restaurants, takeaway facilities and entertainment: We try hard to supply opening and closing dates (if other than the campsite opening dates) and to identify if there are discos or other entertainment.

Children's play areas: Fenced and with safety surface (e.g. sand, bark or pea-gravel).

Swimming pools: If particularly special, we cover in detail in our main campsite description but reference is always included under our Facilities listings. We will also indicate the existence of water slides, sunbathing areas and other features. Opening dates, charges and levels of supervision are provided where we have been notified. There is a regulation whereby Bermuda shorts may not be worn in swimming pools (for health and hygiene reasons). It is worth ensuring that you do take 'proper' swimming trunks with you.

Leisure facilities: For example, playing fields, bicycle hire, organised activities and entertainment.

Dogs: If dogs are not accepted or restrictions apply, we state it here. Check the quick reference list at the back of the guide.

Off site: This briefly covers leisure facilities, tourist attractions, restaurants etc. nearby.

Charges

These are the latest provided to us by the sites. In those cases where 2015 prices have not been provided to us by the sites, we try to give a general guide.

Reservations

Necessary for high season (roughly mid-July to mid-August) in popular holiday areas (i.e. beach resorts). You can reserve many sites via our own Alan Rogers Travel Service or through other tour operators. Or be wholly independent and contact the campsite(s) of your choice direct, using the phone or e-mail numbers shown in the site reports, but please bear in mind that many sites are closed all winter.

Telephone Numbers: The numbers given assume you are actually IN the country concerned. If you are phoning from the UK remember that the first '0' is usually disregarded and replaced by the appropriate country code. For the latest details you should refer to an up-to-date telephone directory.

Opening dates

These are advised to us during the early autumn of the previous year – sites can, and sometimes do, alter these dates before the start of the following season, often for good reasons. If you intend to visit shortly after a published opening date, or shortly before the closing date, it is wise to check that it will actually be open at the time required. Similarly some sites operate a restricted service during the low season, only opening some of their facilities (e.g. swimming pools) during the main season; where we know about this, and have the relevant dates, we indicate it – again if you are at all doubtful it is wise to check.

Sometimes, campsite amenities may be dependent on there being enough customers on site to justify their opening and, for this reason, actual opening dates may vary from those indicated.

Some campsite owners are very relaxed when it comes to opening and closing dates. They may not be fully ready by their stated opening dates – grass and hedges may not all be cut or perhaps only limited sanitary facilities open. At the end of the season they also tend to close down some facilities and generally wind down prior to the closing date. Bear this in mind if you are travelling early or late in the season – it is worth phoning ahead.

The Camping Cheque low season touring system goes some way to addressing this in that many participating campsites will have all key facilities open and running by the opening date and these will remain fully operational until the closing date.

Taking a tent?

In recent years, sales of tents have increased dramatically. With very few exceptions, the campsites listed in this guide have pitches suitable for tents, caravans and motorcaravans. Tents, of course, come in a dazzling range of shapes and sizes. Modern family tents with separate sleeping pods are increasingly popular and these invariably require large pitches with electrical connections. Smaller lightweight tents, ideal for cyclists and hikers, are also visible on many sites and naturally require correspondingly smaller pitches. Many (but not all) sites have special tent areas with prices adjusted accordingly. If in any doubt, we recommend contacting the site of your choice beforehand.

You're on your way!

Whether you're an 'old hand' in terms of camping and caravanning or are contemplating your first trip, a regular reader of our Guides or a new 'convert', we wish you well in your travels and hope we have been able to help in some way.

We are, of course, also out and about ourselves, visiting sites, talking to owners and readers, and generally checking on standards and new developments.

We wish all our readers thoroughly enjoyable Camping and Caravanning in 2015 – favoured by good weather of course! The Alan Rogers Team

Countries of Europe

Sweden
page 462

Finland
page 114

Norway
page 354

Denmark
page 102

Netherlands
page 322

Germany
page 182

Slovakia
page 384

Belgium
page 56

Luxembourg
page 312

Czech Republic
page 92

Austria
page 24

Hungary
page 242

Portugal
page 370

France
page 120

Slovenia
page 390

Croatia
page 76

Andorra
page 20

Italy
page 254

Greece
page 232

Switzerland
page 478

Spain
page 398

The Alan Rogers awards

The Alan Rogers Campsite Awards were launched in 2004 and have proved a great success. Our awards have a broad scope and before committing to our winners, we carefully consider more than 2,000 campsites featured in our guides, taking into account comments from our site assessors, our head office team and, of course, our readers.

Our award winners come from the four corners of Europe, from Spain to Croatia, and this year we are making awards to campsites in 12 different countries.

Needless to say, it's an extremely difficult task to choose our eventual winners, but we believe that we have identified a number of campsites with truly outstanding characteristics.

In each case, we have selected an outright winner, along with two highly commended runners-up. Listed below are full details of each of our award categories and our winners for 2014.

Our warmest congratulations to all our award winners and our commiserations to all those not having won an award on this occasion. **The Alan Rogers Team**

Alan Rogers Progress Award 2014
This award reflects the hard work and commitment undertaken by particular site owners to improve and upgrade their site.

Winner	IT60450	Camping Marina di Venezia	*Italy*
Runners-up	NL6160	Camping Landclub Ruinen	*Netherlands*
	BE0760	Goolderheide Vakantiepark	*Belgium*

Alan Rogers Welcome Award 2014
This award takes account of sites offering a particularly friendly welcome and maintaining a friendly ambience throughout readers' holidays.

Winner	FR24090	Domaine de Soleil Plage	*France*
Runners-up	BE0670	Camping Parc la Clusure	*Belgium*
	ES90290	Kawan Village El Astral	*Spain*

Alan Rogers Active Holiday Award 2014
This award reflects sites in outstanding locations which are ideally suited for active holidays, notably walking or cycling, but which could extend to include such activities as winter sports or watersports.

Winner	FR83170	Camping Domaine de la Bergerie	*France*
Runners-up	AU0100	Camping Seeblick Toni	*Austria*
	DK2010	Hvidbjerg Strand	*Denmark*

Alan Rogers Innovation Award 2014

Our Innovation Award acknowledges campsites with creative and original concepts, possibly with features which are unique, and cannot therefore be found elsewhere. We have identified innovation both in campsite amenities and also in rentable accommodation.

Winner	ES82000	Camping Cala Llevadó	*Spain*
Runners-up	FR24010	Kawan Village Château le Verdoyer	*France*
	DE28990	Camping Stover Strand International	*Germany*

Alan Rogers Small Campsite Award 2014

This award acknowledges excellent small campsites (less than 75 pitches) which offer a friendly welcome and top quality amenities throughout the season to their guests.

Winner	UK0745	Riverside Caravan and Camping Park	*England*
Runners-up	NL5715	Camping WeidumerHout	*Netherlands*
	DE36420	Lech Camping	*Germany*

Alan Rogers Seaside Award 2014

This award is made for sites which we feel are outstandingly suitable for a really excellent seaside holiday.

Winner	CR6782	Zaton Holiday Resort	*Croatia*
Runners-up	ES84830	Camping Tamarit Park Resort	*Spain*
	FR29180	Camping les Embruns	*France*

Alan Rogers Country Award 2014

This award contrasts with our former award and acknowledges sites which are attractively located in delightful, rural locations.

Winner	IT62030	Caravan Park Sexten	*Italy*
Runners-up	FR74140	Camping Les Dômes de Miage	*France*
	DE32540	Camping Harfenmühle	*Germany*

Alan Rogers Family Site Award 2014

Many sites claim to be child friendly but this award acknowledges the sites we feel to be the very best in this respect.

Winner	IT60200	Camping Union Lido Vacanze	*Italy*
Runners-up	CH9890	Camping Campofelice	*Switzerland*
	NL6480	Camping De Molenhof	*Netherlands*

Alan Rogers Readers' Award 2014

We believe our Readers' Award to be the most important. We simply invite our readers (by means of an on-line poll at www.alanrogers.com) to nominate the site they enjoyed most. The outright winner for 2014 is:

Winner	FR24060	Camping le Paradis	*France*

Alan Rogers Special Award 2014

A Special Award is made to campsites which have suffered a significant setback, but have coped admirably in difficult circumstances.

For 2014, we wish to acknowledge a top quality Slovenian campsite, which suffered extensive storm damage but, thanks to a very great deal of hard work, soon reverted to its normal high standard.

Winner	SV4210	Camping Šobec	*Slovenia*

The Alan Rogers
Travel Card

At Alan Rogers we have a network of thousands of quality inspected and selected campsites. We also have partnerships with numerous organisations, including ferry operators and tourist attractions, all of whom can bring you benefits and save you money.

Our **FREE** Travel Card binds all this together at

alanrogers.com/travelcard

So register today...and start saving.

![alan rogers logo]

Benefits that add up

- Offers and benefits on many Alan Rogers campsites across Europe

- Save up to 60% in low season on over 600 campsites

- Free cardholders' magazine

- Big savings on rented accommodation and hotels at 400 locations

- Discounted ferries

- Savings on Alan Rogers guides

- Vote for your favourite campsite in the Alan Rogers Awards

Register today... and start saving

Carry the Alan Rogers Travel Card on your travels through Europe and save money all the way.

You'll enjoy exclusive deals with ferry operators, continental partners, tourist attractions and more. Even hotels, apartments, mobile homes and other campsite accommodation.

We've teamed up with Camping Cheque, the leading low season discount scheme, to offer you the widest choice of quality campsites at unbelievable prices. Simply load your card with Cheques before you travel.

Step 1
Register at **www.alanrogers.com/travelcard**

Step 2
You'll receive your activated card, along with a Welcome email containing useful links and information.

Step 3
Start using your card to save money or to redeem benefits during your holiday.

alanrogers.com/travelcard

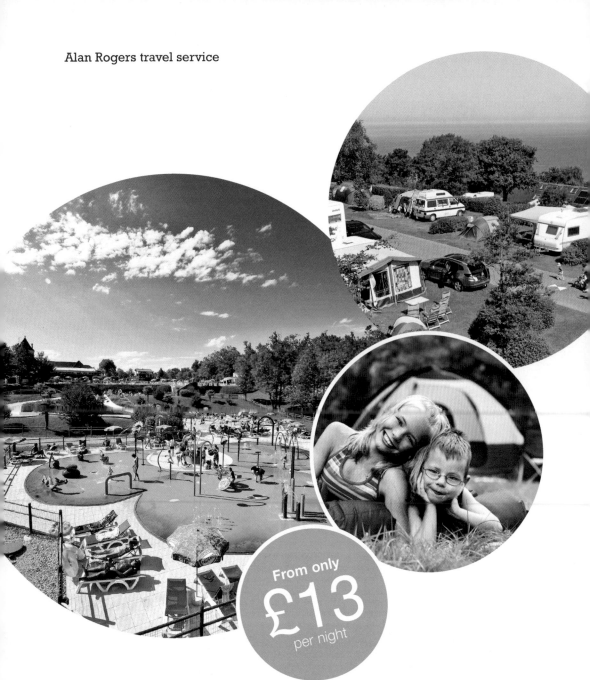

From only
£13
per night

essentials

All you need for a fantastic holiday
on an Alan Rogers inspected and
selected campsite.

Narrowing down the campsite choices can be one of the hardest parts. Modern campsites have so much to offer, from great facilities to well-run activity clubs for children. Whether you're looking to stay by the beach in Spain or in the Austrian mountains, there are always plenty of options.

The Alan Rogers Travel Service has made life a little easier with an exciting **essentials** brochure - over 160 of Europe's finest campsites in 11 countries, all independently inspected and selected by Alan Rogers inspectors for our market leading guide books. So all you need do is make your choice, call us to make arrangements and start looking forward to your well-earned holiday. We'll do the rest.

The Alan Rogers Travel Service was originally set up to provide a low cost booking service for readers. We pride ourselves on being able to put together a bespoke holiday, taking advantage of our experience, knowledge and contacts. You'll get convenience, peace of mind, a friendly, efficient service - and amazing value for money.

It's our biggest ever choice of campsites, with even more coming soon online, and we can arrange more ferry crossings at incredible prices too. So order a copy today and take a look at our **essentials** programme for your next holiday.

FREE brochure

- 168 campsites in 11 countries

- Ideal for tents, caravans, motorhomes - and everything in between

- Travel Card benefits at many sites

- More ferry routes at seriously reduced prices - call us for a quote and see for yourself!

Order your **FREE** brochure
01580 214000

Don't miss out on your
essentials
alanrogers.com/brochure

alan rogers ◗ travel

17

Getting the most from off peak touring

£14.95 night
outfit +
2 people

There are many reasons to avoid high season, if you can. Queues are shorter, there's less traffic, a calmer atmosphere and prices are cheaper. And it's usually still nice and sunny!

And when you use Camping Cheques you'll find great quality facilities that are actually open and a welcoming conviviality.

Did you know?

Camping Cheques can be used right into mid-July and from late August on many sites. Over 90 campsites in France alone accept Camping Cheques from 20th August.

Save up to 60% with Camping Cheques

Camping Cheque is a fixed price scheme allowing you to go as you please, staying on over 600 campsites across Europe, always paying the same rate and saving you up to 60% on regular pitch fees. One Cheque gives you one night for 2 people + unit on a standard pitch, with electricity. It's as simple as that.

Special offers mean you can stay extra nights free (eg 7 nights for 6 Cheques) or even a month free for a month paid! Especially popular in Spain during the winter, these longer-term offers can effectively halve the nightly rate. See Site Directory for details.

Check out our amazing Ferry Deals!

Why should I use Camping Cheques?

- It's a proven system, recognised by all 600+ participating campsites
  - so no nasty surprises.

- It's flexible, allowing you to travel between campsites, and also countries, on
  a whim - so no need to pre-book. (It's low season, so campsites are rarely full,
  though advance bookings can be made).

- Stay as long as you like, where you like - so you travel in complete freedom.

- Camping Cheques are valid at least 2 years - so no pressure to use them up.
  (If you have a couple left over after your trip, simply keep them for the following
  year, or use them up in the UK).

Tell me more... (but keep it brief!)

Camping Cheques was started in 1999 and has since grown in popularity each
year (nearly 2 million were used last year). That should speak for itself. There
are 'copycat' schemes, but none has the same range of quality campsites that
save you up to 60%.

The independent principality of Andorra is situated high in the Pyrenees between France and Spain. It has a contrasting landscape of rugged mountains, lush valleys, forests and lakes, and its winter and summer resorts and duty-free shopping make it a popular holiday destination.

With tourism as its main source of income, Andorra has plenty to offer the visitor in terms of leisure activities. There are endless opportunities to explore the rugged mountain passes and spectacular landscape, on foot, by mountain bike and even on horseback. There are a number of protected areas, including La Vall de Sorteny Nature Park with its outstanding variety of plants, many known for their medicinal properties. In between shopping and skiing, discover the history and culture of Andorra in its many museums and Romanesque churches; Sant Joan de Caselles, Canillo is a popular example. Village festivals are common in high season with many Andorran towns and hamlets celebrating their heritage with music, dancing, wine and feasts. An ideal way to see it all is on the tourist bus that offers numerous guided routes. The Principality of Andorra can be accessed by road from France through Pas de la Casa and the Envalira Pass and from Spain via Sant Julià de Lòria. The nearest main cities are Barcelona (185 km) and Lleida (151 km) on the Spanish side, and Toulouse (187 km) and Perpignan (169 km) on the French side.

CAPITAL: Andorra La Vella

Tourist Office
Embassy of the Principality of Andorra
63 Westover Road, London SW18 2RF
Tel: 020 8874 4802 (visits by appointment only)
Internet: www.andorra.com

Population
85,000

Climate
The climate is temperate, with cold winters
with a lot of snow and warm summers.
The country's mountain peaks often remain
snowcapped until July.

Language
The official language is Catalan, with French
and Spanish widely spoken.

Telephone
The country code is 00 376.

Money
Currency: The Euro
Banks: Mon-Fri 09.00-13.00 and
15.00-17.00, Sat 09.00-12.00.

Shops
Mon-Sat 09.00-20.00, Sun 09.00-19.00.

Public Holidays
New Year's Day; Epiphany; Constitution Day, Mar
14; Holy Thursday to Easter Monday; Labour Day;
Ascension; Whit Sunday; Whit Monday; St John's
Day Jun 24; Assumption Aug 15; National Day
Sep 8; All Saints' Day Nov 1; St Charles' Day
Nov 4; Immaculate Conception Dec 8; Christmas
Dec 24-26; New Year's Eve.

Motoring
There are no motorways in Andorra. Main roads
are prefixed 'N' and side roads 'V'. Certain
mountain passes may prove difficult in winter
and heavy snowfalls could cause road closures.
Expect traffic queues in the summer, with a high
volume of motorists coming to and from France.

Andorra-la-Vella

Camping Valira

Avenida Salou s/n, AD500 Andorra-la-Vella (Andorra) T: 722 384. E: campvalira@andorra.ad

alanrogers.com/AN7145

This compact, terraced site is named after the river in the town of Andorra-la-Vella. It has a steep curving entrance directly off the N145, which can become congested at peak times. You pass the pleasant restaurant and heated indoor pool as you enter the site. Maximum use has been made of the space here and it is worth looking at the picture of the site in reception as it was in 1969. The 150 medium sized pitches are mostly level on terraces with some shading. All pitches have access to electricity (3-10A), although some may need long leads, and there are drinking water points around the site.

Facilities

The facilities (heated in winter) are modern and clean, with provision for disabled campers. Room with toddlers' toilet and good baby room. Three washing machines and a dryer. Well stocked small shop. Bar/restaurant with good menu at realistic prices. Small heated indoor pool. Jacuzzi. Play area. Pétanque. Picnic area. Free WiFi over site. Barbecue. Barrier closed 23.00-07.00. Off site: Town shops 10 minutes walk.

Open: All year.

Directions

Site is on the south side of Andorra-la-Vella, on left travelling south behind sports stadium. It is well signed off the N145. Watch signs carefully – an error with a diversion round town will cost you dear at rush hour. GPS: 42.50249, 1.51493

Charges guide

Per unit incl. 2 persons and electricity	€ 27.00 - € 31.10
extra person	€ 5.85 - € 6.10
child (1-10 yrs)	€ 4.85 - € 4.95
dog	€ 2.00 - € 2.10

La Massana

Camping Xixerella

Ctra de Palamos, Xixerella, AD400 La Massana (Andorra) T: 738 613. E: info@xixerellapark.com

alanrogers.com/AN7143

Andorra is a country of narrow valleys with pine and birch forested mountains. Xixerella is attractively situated in just such a small valley below towering mountains and beside a river. The site is made up of several sections of gently sloping grass, accessed by tarmac or gravel roads which lead to informal pitching. Electricity (3/6A) is available to all of the 80 pitches. There are barbecues and a picnic area with bridge access to walks in the woods, and a pleasant bar and restaurant with a poolside terrace. The site can be very busy from mid July to mid August, but otherwise it is usually peaceful.

Facilities

The satisfactory main sanitary building is fully equipped, including British style WCs, some washbasins in cabins, showers with dividers. Laundry facilities. Further facilities in a round building by the pool. Small shop, bar and restaurant (closed Nov). Swimming and paddling pools (15/6-15/9). Play area. Minigolf. Pitch and putt course. Electronic games. Disco in season. Torch useful. Off site: Riding 3 km. Skiing at Arinsal (5 km) and Pal (6 km).

Open: All year excl. October.

Directions

Site is 8 km. from Andorra-la-Vella on the road to Pal (this road can only be accessed on the north side of town), via La Massana. GPS: 42.55324, 1.48884

Charges guide

Per unit incl. 2 persons and electricity	€ 32.60
extra person	€ 6.60
child	€ 5.20
dog	€ 4.40

For latest campsite news, availability and prices visit

alanrogers.com

Leading Camping in Europe

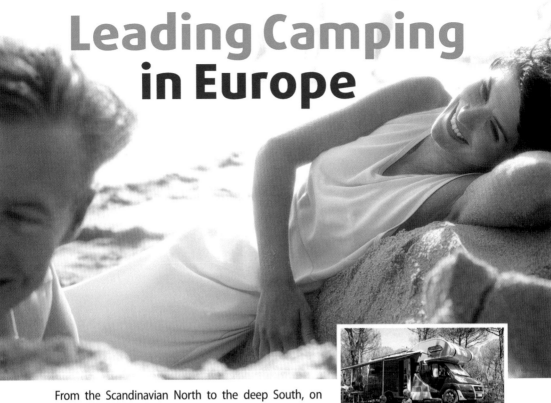

From the Scandinavian North to the deep South, on white sandy beaches or in the mountains – you'll find **LeadingCampings** always at the nicest spots in continental Europe.

LeadingCampings means **first class camping** and it shows: spacious pitches, fully equipped. Flawless sanitary blocks at highest level. Pools, wellness and sports facilities. Well trained animation teams, gastronomy and leisure programs: all leading.

And, well, children are especially welcome.

In this camping guide all entries of LeadingCampings are highlighted as 'member of the LeadingCampings'. We are looking forward welcoming you.

Austria is primarily known for two contrasting attractions: the capital Vienna with its cathedral, wine bars and musical events, and the skiing and hiking resorts of the Alps. It is an ideal place to visit all year round, for the Easter markets, winter sports and the many cultural and historical attractions, as well as the breathtaking scenery.

The charming Tirol region in the west of Austria is easily accessible, and popular with tourists who flock to its ski resorts in winter. In the summer months, it is transformed into a verdant landscape of picturesque valleys dotted with wild flowers, a paradise for walkers. Situated in the centre are the Lake District, and Salzburg, city of Mozart, with its wealth of gardens, churches and palaces. Vienna's iconic ferris wheel is a must for taking in the beautiful parks and architecture from 200 ft. The neighbouring provinces of Lower Austria, Burgenland and Styria, land of vineyards, mountains and farmland, are off the tourist routes, but provide good walking territory. Further south, the Carinthia region enjoys a mild, sunny climate and is dominated by crystal clear lakes and soaring mountains, yet has plenty of opportunities for winter sports. There are numerous monasteries and churches, and the cities of Villach and Klagenfurt, known for its old square and attractive Renaissance buildings.

CAPITAL: Vienna

Tourist Office
Austrian National Tourist Office
9-11 Richmond Buildings, London W1D 3HF
Tel: 020 7440 3830
Fax: 020 7440 3848
Email: holiday@austria.info
Internet: www.austria.info/uk

Population
8.5 million

Climate
Temperate, with moderately hot summers,
cold winters and snow in the mountains.

Language
German

Telephone
The country code is 00 43.

Money
Currency: The Euro
Banks: Mon, Tues, Wed and Fri 08.00-12.30
and 13.30-15.00. Thurs 08.00-12.30 and
13.30-17.30.

Shops
Mon-Fri 08.00-18.30, some close 12.00-14.00;
Sat 08.00-17.00.

Public Holidays
New Year; Epiphany; Easter Mon; Labour Day;
Ascension; Whit Mon; Corpus Christi; Assumption
15 Aug; National Day 26 Oct; All Saints 1 Nov;
Immaculate Conception 8 Dec; Christmas 25,
26 Dec.

Motoring
Visitors using Austrian motorways and 'A' roads
must display a Motorway Vignette on their vehicle
as they enter Austria. Failure to have one will
mean a heavy, on-the-spot fine. Vignettes are
obtained at all major border crossings into Austria
and at larger petrol stations. All vehicles above
3.5 tonnes maximum permitted laden weight are
required to use a small device called the 'GO
Box' – visit the website at http://www.austria.info

see campsite map 4

Döbriach

Camping Brunner am See

Glanzerstrasse 108, Millstätter See, A-9873 Döbriach (Carinthia) T: 042 46 7189.

E: office@camping-brunner.at **alanrogers.com/AU0475**

This well appointed site at the eastern end of the Millstätter See is the only one in the area with direct access to its own private beach. Consisting of fairly coarse sand, it is regularly cleaned. The 214 marked pitches (60-107 sq.m), all for touring units, are all serviced with water, drainage and 6A electricity hook-ups, and are in rows on level grass with tarmac access roads. The site is fairly open with some shade from bushes and trees. The site owns land on the opposite side of the road, which includes forest walks, a dog walk, a parking area and one of the playgrounds.

Facilities

Well appointed sanitary unit behind reception with good facilities for disabled campers, especially disabled children, plus a children's room with low level showers, washbasins, baby baths, changing deck etc. Family bathrooms (some for rent), all washbasins in cubicles, laundry facilities. Motorcaravan services. Site owned supermarket adjacent (May-Sept). Communal barbecue. New indoor playground for children (up to 10 yrs). Internet access. WiFi over site (charged). Fishing. Watersports. Off site: Supermarket. Several restaurants (some open all year). Bicycle hire 100 m.

Open: All year.

Directions

Döbriach is at eastern end of Millstätter See, 15 km. southwest of Spittal. Leave A10, exit 139 (Spittal, Millstätter), proceed alongside northern shore of lake through Millstatt towards Döbriach. Just before Döbriach turn right and after 1.5 km. turn right at roundabout. Site is on right after 100 m. GPS: 46.76768, 13.64850

Charges guide

Per unit incl. 2 persons and electricity	€ 26.50 - € 39.00
extra person	€ 7.20 - € 9.50
child (4-14 yrs)	€ 5.20 - € 8.50

Eberndorf

Rutar Lido FKK Naturist See-Camping

A-9141 Eberndorf (Carinthia) T: 042 362 2620. E: fkkurlaub@rutarlido.at

alanrogers.com/AU0360

This site is affiliated to the International Naturist Federation (INF) and is in a peaceful location adjacent to both open countryside and forested hills. The 365 pitches (300 for touring units) are either on an open area of grass marked out by low hedges or in a more established area of pine trees. There are 10A electrical connections throughout and some pitches have their own water supply and waste point. One area is set aside for those with dogs. There are three lakes within the site, one for swimming and dinghies, whilst the other two provide pleasure for those who enjoy fishing.

Facilities

Four sanitary blocks with some private cabins and free controllable showers. Facilities for disabled visitors. Laundry facilities. Well stocked small supermarket (1/4-30/9). Two bar/restaurants (one all year). Outdoor pools (1/4-30/9). Indoor pools (all year). Two saunas. Play area, club and activities for children (July/Aug). Fitness room. Disco. Bowling alley. Live music evenings and dances (high season). Chapel. Fishing. WiFi (charged).

Open: All year.

Directions

From A2 (Graz-Klagenfurt) road, take B82 south at Volkermarkt to roundabout at Eberndorf and follow signs to site. GPS: 46.588, 14.627

Charges guide

Per unit incl. 2 persons and electricity	€ 22.80 - € 31.80
extra person	€ 7.00 - € 9.50
child (3-12 yrs)	€ 4.60 - € 7.80
dog	€ 3.00 - € 5.00

Eberndorf

Sonnencamp Gösselsdorfer See

Seestrasse 21-33, A-9141 Gösselsdorf (Carinthia) T: 042 362 168. E: office@goesselsdorfersee.com

alanrogers.com/AU0384

Sonnencamp Gösselsdorfer See is a quiet, attractive site in a natural setting, bordering a small stretch of water connected to the Gösseldorfer See and its lakeside bathing facility (entry is free to campers). They are also joined through the woods by a 600 m. long path. The site has 300 mostly large, numbered pitches, they are level and nicely grassed, with tree shade in places. All have 10A electricity. The site is surrounded by mature trees and woodland, beyond which there are views of the mountains that separate Carinthia (Kärnten), an attractive region of mountains and lakes, from Italy and Slovenia to the south.

Facilities

Two well maintained sanitary blocks have free hot water. Laundry room with sinks, washing machines and dryer. Shop (July/Aug). Restaurant with breakfast menu. Bar with takeaway. Play area. Organised activities for children in summer. WiFi (charged). Accommodation to rent. Off site: Beach swimming pool (free entry to campers) at Gösselsdorfer See 600 m. Bicycle hire 3 km. Golf 5 km. Burg Hochosterwitz 20 km. Karnten card (from reception) gives free/reduced price entry to local attractions.

Open: 1 May - 3 October.

Directions

Leave autobahn A2 at Volkermarkt West exit 288 and head east for 3 km. then south on the 82 for 10 km. through Eberndorf to Gösselsdorf. In Gösselsdorf right. Site is a few hundred metres on the left. GPS: 46.57499, 14.62456

Charges guide

Per unit incl. 2 persons and electricity	€ 19.90 - € 23.50
extra person	€ 5.90 - € 7.10
child (3-18 yrs)	€ 3.00 - € 5.20

For latest campsite news, availability and prices visit

alanrogers.com

Döbriach

Komfort-Campingpark Burgstaller

Seefeldstrasse 16, A-9873 Döbriach (Carinthia) T: 042 467 774. E: info@burgstaller.co.at

alanrogers.com/AU0480

This is one of Austria's top sites in a beautiful location and with all the amenities you could want. You can always tell a true family run site by the attention to detail and this site oozes perfection. This is an excellent family site with a very friendly atmosphere, particularly in the restaurant in the evenings. Good English is spoken. The 590 pitches (540 for tourers) are on flat, well drained grass, backing onto hedges on either side of access roads. All fully serviced (including WiFi), they vary in size (45-120 sq.m) and there are special pitches for motorcaravans. One pitch actually rotates and follows the sun during the course of the day! The latest sanitary block warrants an architectural award; all toilets have a TV, and a pirate ship on the first floor of the children's area sounds its guns every hour. The site entrance is directly opposite the park leading to the bathing lido, to which campers have free access. There is also a heated swimming pool. Much activity is organised here, including games and competitions for children and there are special Easter and autumn events.

Facilities

Three exceptionally good quality toilet blocks include washbasins in cabins, facilities for children and disabled visitors, dishwashers and underfloor heating for cool weather. Seven private rooms for rent (3 with jacuzzi baths). Motorcaravan services. Bar. Good restaurant with terrace (May-Oct). Shop (May-Sept). Bowling alley. Disco (July/Aug). TV room. Sauna and solarium. Two play areas (one for under 6s, the other for 6-12 yrs). Bathing and boating on lake. Special entrance rate for lake attractions. Fishing. Bicycle hire. Mountain bike area. Riding. Comprehensive entertainment programmes. Covered stage and outdoor arena for church services (Protestant and Catholic, in German) and folk and modern music concerts. Off site: Mountain walks, climbing and farm visits all in local area.

Open: 27 March - 1 November.

Directions

Döbriach is at the eastern end of the Millstätter See, 15 km. southeast of Spittal. Leave A10 at exit 139 (Spittal, Millstätter) then proceed alongside northern shore of lake through Millstätter towards Döbriach. Just before Döbriach turn right and after 1 km. site is on left. GPS: 46.77151, 13.64918

Charges guide

Per unit incl. 2 persons	
and electricity	€ 19.10 - € 34.00
extra person	€ 7.00 - € 10.00
child (4-14 yrs)	€ 5.00 - € 8.00
dog	€ 3.00 - € 4.00

Discounts for retired people in low season.

Faak am See
Camping Arneitz
Seeuferlandesstrasse 53, A-9583 Faak am See (Carinthia) T: 042 542 137. E: camping@arneitz.at

alanrogers.com/AU0400

Directly on Faakersee, Camping Arneitz is one of the best sites in this area, central for the attractions of the region, watersports and walking. Family run, Arneitz leads the way with good quality and comprehensive facilities. A newly built reception building at the entrance reflects the quality of the site and, separate from reception facilities, has a good collection of tourist literature and two desks with computers for guests to use. The 420 level, marked pitches are mainly of gravel, off hard roads, all with 16A electricity, TV, water and waste water connections. Some have good shade from mature trees. There is a delightfully appointed restaurant at the entrance where there is entertainment in high season.

Facilities
Splendid family washroom, large, heated and airy, with family cubicles around the walls and in the centre, washbasins at child height in a circle with a working carousel in the middle. Extra, small toilet block nearer the lake. Laundry facilities. Motorcaravan services. Supermarket. Self-service restaurant, bar and terrace. General room with TV. Small cinema for children's films. Well equipped indoor playground. Fishing. Dogs are not accepted in July/Aug. WiFi over site (charged).

Open: 23 April - 30 September.

Directions
Site is southeast of Villach, southwest of Velden. Follow signs for Faakersee and Egg rather than for Faak village. From A11 take exit 3 and head towards Egg, turn left at T-junction and go through Egg village. Just after leaving village, site is on right. GPS: 46.57768, 13.93775

Charges guide
Per unit incl. 2 persons and electricity	€ 27.50 - € 46.00
extra person	€ 7.00 - € 8.00

Hermagor
Schluga Camping Hermagor
Vellach 15, A-9620 Hermagor (Carinthia) T: 042 822 051. E: camping@schluga.com

alanrogers.com/AU0440

Schluga Camping is under the same ownership as Schluga Seecamping, some 4 km. to the west of that site in a flat valley with views of the surrounding mountains. The 213 touring pitches are of varying size, 122 with water, drainage and satellite TV connections. Electricity connections are available throughout (10-16A). Mainly on grass covered gravel on either side of tarmac surfaced access roads, they are divided by shrubs and hedges. The site is open all year, to include the winter sports season, and has a well kept, tidy appearance, although it may be busy in high season. English is spoken. The site reports a new artificial swimming lake and 23 new pitches for motorcaravans.

Facilities
Four sanitary blocks (a splendid new one, plus one modern and two good older ones) are heated in cold weather. Most washbasins in cabins and good showers. Family washrooms for rent. Baby rooms and suite for disabled visitors. Washing machines and dryers. Drying rooms and ski rooms. Motorcaravan services. Well stocked shop (1/5-30/9). Bar/restaurant with terrace (closed Nov). Heated indoor and outdoor pools. New natural swimming pond (500 sq.m). Playground. Youth games room. Bicycle hire. Fitness. WiFi (charged).

Open: All year.

Directions
Site is on the B111 Villach-Hermagor road (which is better quality than it appears on most maps) just east of Hermagor town. GPS: 46.63141, 13.39598

Charges guide
Per unit incl. 2 persons and electricity	€ 21.90 - € 38.30
extra person	€ 6.75 - € 9.70
child (5-14 yrs)	€ 4.00 - € 6.40
dog	€ 2.50 - € 3.10

Hermagor
Naturpark Schluga Seecamping
A-9620 Hermagor (Carinthia) T: 042 822 051. E: camping@schluga.com

alanrogers.com/AU0450

This site is pleasantly situated on natural wooded hillside. It is about 300 m. from a small lake with clean water, where the site has a beach of coarse sand and a large grassy meadow where inflatable boats can be kept. There is also a small bar and a sunbathing area for naturists, although this is not a naturist site. The 250 pitches for touring units are on individual, level terraces, many with light shade and all with 8/16A electricity. There are 154 pitches that also have water, drainage and satellite TV. A further 47 pitches are occupied by a tour operator. English is spoken.

Facilities
Four heated modern toilet blocks with some washbasins in cabins and family washrooms to hire. Facilities for disabled campers. Washing machines and dryer. Motorcaravan services. Shop (20/5-10/9). Bar/restaurant and takeaway (20/5-10/9). Playground. Films. Kiosk and bar with terrace at beach. Surf school. Pedalo and canoe hire. Pony rides. Bicycle hire. Activity programme. WiFi.

Open: 10 May - 20 September.

Directions
Site is on the B111 road (Villach-Hermagor) 6 km. east of Hermagor town. GPS: 46.63184, 13.44654

Charges guide
Per unit incl. 2 persons and electricity	€ 25.65 - € 36.90
extra person	€ 6.75 - € 9.70
child (5-14 yrs)	€ 4.00 - € 6.40
dog	€ 2.50 - € 3.10

For latest campsite news, availability and prices visit
alanrogers.com

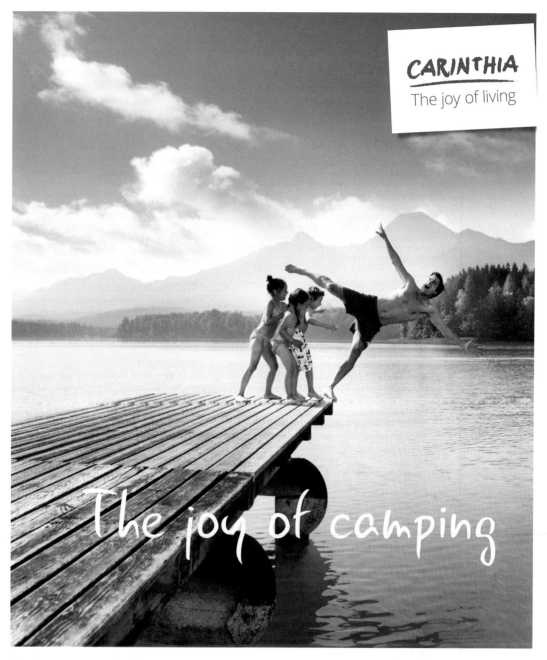

CARINTHIA
The joy of living

The joy of camping

This is what it looks like. The zest for life that I experience when camping and caravanning. On the southern side of the Alps. Between gentle hills and warm lakes. An invitation to cycle, hike or swim. Happy moments that I cherish back home. Feels like the joy of living.

Free camping and caravanning magazine

You can get the free camping and caravanning magazine
and further information from:
Urlaubsinformation Kärnten (Carinthia Holiday Information):
Tel.: +43 (0)463 3000, Fax: +43 (0)463 3000-50
E-mail: info@kaernten.at

Austria's south
www.camping.at

Austria
arrive
and revive

Keutschach am See
FKK Kärntner Lichtbund Turkwiese

Dobeinitz 32, A-9074 Seental Keutschach (Carinthia) T: 042 732 838. E: office@klb.at

alanrogers.com/AU0416

Turkwiese is a tranquil naturist campsite, attractively located on the southern banks of the Keutschacher See, with its own secluded beach. There are 116 pitches here, around 56 of which are available for touring units. Many of these have views across the lake. Pitches are grassy and generally well shaded by mature trees. The site's bar/restaurant is a convivial place for a drink or meal, and there are many other cafés and restaurants in the vicinity. Other amenities include a children's playground and sports field, as well as a giant chess board. The lake offers some excellent opportunities for watersports including sailing, canoeing and windsurfing.

Facilities

One modern sanitary building has controllable showers with sliding door (token) and open style washbasins. Washing machine and dryer. Bar/restaurant. Takeaway. Lake beach. Play area. Giant chess. Sports field. Please note that this is a naturist site. Dogs are not accepted. Off site: Walking and mountain biking in the Carinthian mountains. Golf. Watersports.

Open: 1 June - 30 September.

Directions

Approaching on A10 motorway (from Salzburg), leave at Villach exit and continue east on A2 towards Klagenfurt. Follow signs to Keutschach on southern side of Wörther See. At Keutschach, head west on L97 to Keutschacher See, from where site is well signed. GPS: 46.5836, 14.1679

Charges guide

Per unit incl. 2 persons and electricity	€ 20.80 - € 24.30
extra person	€ 6.70 - € 7.20

Keutschach am See
FKK Naturist Camping Müllerhof

Dobein 10, A-9074 Keutschach-am-See (Carinthia) T: 042 732 517. E: muellerhof@fkk-camping.at

alanrogers.com/AU0420

Müllerhof is an excellent naturist site, very well run, with families in mind, by its owners, the Safron family. Backed by a pine forest, on the southern side of the Keutschacher lake in Carinthia, the gently sloping site of almost six hectares provides 270 touring units, all with 6/10A electricity (Europlug) and TV connections. Manicured grass with neat rows of varied, mature trees, light coloured compacted gravel access roads and a security barrier at the entrance indicates that this is a well maintained site. Three grass sunbathing areas (one large, two small), each have direct access to the crystal clear waters of the lake which are edged with flowering lilies and rushes.

Facilities

Two large, fully equipped toilet blocks are of the highest order and kept very clean. Some private cabins. Washing machine, dryer and ironing facilities. The block at the centre of the site has a really high quality baby room. Sauna and massage. Small shop. Restaurant with waiter service and comprehensive menu, also takeaway (May-Sept). Large play room and well appointed play area. WiFi. Mobile homes and cabins to rent. No dogs.

Open: 1 May - 30 September.

Directions

From A2 motorway take exit 335 signed Velden West. Follow signs for Keutschach (or Keutschacher See). 4 km. after village of Schiefling, turn right at signs for FKK Centre. Site is on left in just over 1 km. GPS: 46.57795, 14.150583

Charges guide

Per unit incl. 2 persons and electricity	€ 20.00 - € 27.40
extra person	€ 7.35 - € 9.40

No credit cards.

Keutschach am See
Camping Hafnersee

Plescherken 5, A-9074 Keutschach (Carinthia) T: 042 732 375. E: info@hafnersee.at

alanrogers.com/AU0421

Set within the well maintained grounds of the hotel of the same name, Camping Hafnersee combines the best of a rural lakeside campsite with the facilities of a very well appointed hotel. The 212 pitches, mostly on level grass, are well defined in rows separated by low hedges, with 88 currently available for touring units (6A electricity). The others are used by seasonal units. The site is set on the gently sloping grass banks of the lake and there are pontoons for swimming and boating. There is some shade from mature trees around the site.

Facilities

Two traditional toilet blocks have very good WCs, washbasins and showers and ample hot water. Facilities for disabled visitors. Drinking water points. Washing machine, dryer. Hotel bar and separate restaurant (all season). Jacuzzi and sauna. Internet at hotel. Fishing (with permit). Bicycle hire. Off site: Riding 1 km. Golf 5 km.

Open: 1 May - 30 September.

Directions

From A2 motorway take exit 335 (Velden). Follow signs for Keutschach. Just past village of Schiefling look for sign to Seehotel Hafnersee and Camping. GPS: 46.588966, 14.136808

Charges guide

Per unit incl. 2 persons and electricity	€ 27.40 - € 32.40
extra person	€ 7.20 - € 8.70
child (6-16 yrs)	€ 4.10 - € 5.10

For latest campsite news, availability and prices visit

alanrogers.com

Malta

Terrassen Camping Maltatal

Malta 6, A-9854 Malta (Carinthia) T: 047 332 34. E: info@maltacamp.at

alanrogers.com/AU0490

Situated between two national parks in a valley between the mountains, this four hectare site offers spectacular views over the surrounding area, especially from the pool which is over 300 sq.m. with a grassy sunbathing area and is open to all (free for campers). There are 220 grass pitches on narrow terraces (70-100 sq.m) and mostly in rows on either side of narrow access roads. Numbered and marked, some separated with low hedges, all have electricity and 160 have water and drainage (the electric boxes are often inconveniently located on the next terrace). The Kärnten-card is available to purchase from the site which gives free travel on public transport and free entry to many attractions.

Facilities

Two toilet blocks, one new for 2011, have about half the washbasins in cabins and ten family wash cabins. Facilities for babies and children. Laundry facilities. Motorcaravan services. Fridge hire. Shop, restaurant, bar. Heated outdoor swimming pool (1/6-1/9). Sauna. Playground. Bicycle hire. Entertainment programme and many walks and excursions. WiFi over site (charged). Gas. Electric barbecues are not permitted. Off site: Village 500 m. Fishing and golf 6 km. Riding 10 km. Malta High alpine road, Reisseck mountain railways and The Porsche Museum in Gmund are all nearby.

Open: 30 April - 11 October.

Directions

Site is 15 km. north of Spittal. Leave A10 at exit 130 Gmund. Pass through Gmund towards Malta. Site is on right 6 km. from autobahn exit.
GPS: 46.949724, 13.509606

Charges guide

Per unit incl. 2 persons	
and electricity	€ 23.50 - € 33.50
extra person	€ 5.70 - € 8.20
child (2-14 yrs)	€ 3.70 - € 5.60
dog	€ 2.50 - € 3.80

Less for longer stays.

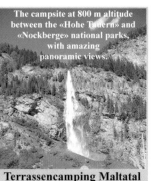

The campsite at 800 m altitude between the «Hohe Tauern» and «Nockberge» national parks, with amazing panoramic views.

Terrassencamping Maltatal

A-9854 Malta 5-6, Kärnten • Tel. 0043-4733-234 • Fax 0043-4733-23416 • www.maltacamp.at • info@maltacamp.at

---

Keutschach am See

Camping Reichmann

Reauz 5, A-9074 Keutschach (Carinthia) T: 046 328 1452. E: info@camping-reichmann.at

alanrogers.com/AU0422

This is a very basic, rural site at the eastern end of the Rauschelesee lake. The 180 pitches are all on grass, some close to the lake and some on a gentle slope. All have 16A electricity supply available (long cables may be required). There is a very pleasant restaurant and bar with outside terrace, where traditional local meals can be sampled at reasonable prices. Very little English is spoken, but the owner and his staff are keen to ensure that all visitors have an enjoyable stay.

Facilities

One large block, built on a slope, houses the restaurant and bar at the higher level with the toilets and other facilities on the lower level. Water points at toilet blocks. Washing machine, dryer. Bar, restaurant and takeaway. Swimming in lake. Fishing with permit. Bicycle hire. Boat launching. Dogs accepted in designated area. WiFi throughout (charged). Off site: Riding 1 km. Golf 10 km.

Open: 1 May - 30 September.

Directions

From A10 take road towards Veldon and follow signs to Keutschach am See. Continue past the Keutschachersee lake for 7 km. to Rauschelesee. At eastern end of lake turn right into Reauz. Site is on right. GPS: 46.58296, 14.228384

Charges guide

Per unit incl. 2 persons	
and electricity	€ 24.30 - € 25.30
extra person	€ 7.90

Klagenfurt

Camping Klagenfurt Wörthersee

Metnitzstrand 5, A-9020 Klagenfurt (Carinthia) T: 0463 287 810. E: info@campingfreund.at

alanrogers.com/AU0370

Set in the picturesque region of Carinthia, Camping Klagenfurt is located near the east bay of Lake Wörthersee across the road from the public beach, Strandbad Klagenfurt. The site is in a green area of more than 400 acres and has 350 pitches for mobile homes, caravans, and tents. There are three different sizes of plot ranging from standard to over 100 sq.m. with electricity (10A) and showers included in the price. The main attraction is Strandbad Klagenfurt, a sandy beach with an especially long water slide, a 'beer island' and an area of nearly 40 acres for sunbathing. The beach is just a short walk from the campsite (less than one minute). Access is with a chip card available from reception.

Facilities

Two modern and clean sanitary buildings with en-suite facilities for disabled visitors. Family shower rooms. Baby room. Laundry facilities. Motorcaravan services. Mini shop in reception (1/5-15/9). Small restaurant with beer garden (15/5-15/9). Cinema. Video arcade. Unfenced play area. Bicycle hire. Entertainer offering many fun activities, reading and play. Free WiFi throughout. Off site: A wide range of trips, boat trips on lake Wörthersee, guided tours through Klagenfurt. Fishing 1 km. Golf and riding 5 km.

Open: 17 April - 30 September.

Directions

The site is at the east side of the Wörthersee. From A2/E55 exit Klagenfurt West/Zentrum/Worthersee, merge onto A2, take exit Klagenfurt-Wörthersee towards Wien/Flughafen Graz/B83/Wörthersee, merge onto Sudring, turn right onto Villacher Str. (B83), then slight left onto Metnitzstrand and site. GPS: 46.61858, 14.25742

Charges guide

Per unit incl. 2 persons and electricity	€ 19.90 - € 32.70
extra person	€ 5.50 - € 8.90

Kötschach Mauthen

Alpencamp Kärnten

Kötschach 284, A-9640 Kötschach Mauthen (Carinthia) T: 04715 429. E: info@alpencamp.at

alanrogers.com/AU0445

Materials hundreds of millions of years old, centuries old crafts and practices, together with the very latest technology have been combined in the construction of this environmental award-winning site. Four years in the planning, Alpencamp showcases comfortable, attractive and environmentally friendly accommodation set against an impressive panorama of mountains in the beautiful Lesachtal. This quiet family run site has 80 pitches, all with 13/16A electricity; they are level and on grass with some shade.

Facilities

Modern well maintained sanitary facilities. Free hot showers, washbasins in cabins. Laundry. Motorcaravan services. Shop with fresh bread each morning. Comfortable and bright restaurant with bar. Playground and playroom for children. Free Internet terminal in reception, WiFi over site (charged). Off site: Walking, cycling, mountain bike trails, climbing, riding, geological trails to follow. Free entry to Aquarena, swimming pool, wellness centre. Rafting, canoeing, fishing. During winter, skiing and other winter sports. Golf 25 km.

Open: All year excl. 1 November - 14 December.

Directions

Coming from Villach on the 111, in town at the junction with the 110 turn left then after 200 m. turn right and continue along the 111 towards Lesachtal. After 500 m. site is to the left. GPS: 46.6698184, 12.9909468

Charges guide

Per unit incl. 2 persons and electricity	€ 22.10 - € 33.30
extra person	€ 4.90 - € 7.80
child (3-13 yrs)	€ 3.10 - € 4.90

Camping Cheques accepted.

Ossiach

Terrassen Camping Ossiacher See

Ostriach 67, A-9570 Ossiach (Carinthia) T: 042 434 36. E: martinz@camping.at

alanrogers.com/AU0460

This gently terraced site is protected by rising hills and enjoys lovely views across the lake to the mountains beyond. Trees, flowers, hedges and bushes abound, adding atmosphere to this neat and tidy site. The 530 level pitches, all with electricity, are in rows on the level grass terraces, separated by hard roads and some divided by hedges. A separate area (25 pitches only) is provided for campers with dogs. Good English is spoken.

Facilities

Five well maintained sanitary blocks, one new in 2011, are heated in cool weather, and some with washbasins in cabins. Ten family washrooms (charged), baby rooms and facilities for disabled campers. Laundry facilities. Motorcaravan services. Restaurant (15/5-15/9). Well stocked supermarket. ATM. High season entertainment. Beach volleyball. Trampoline. Playgrounds, games rooms and disco courtyard. Water-skiing and windsurfing schools. Tennis. Bicycle and moped hire. Fishing. Riding.

Open: 1 May - 30 September.

Directions

Site is directly on the lake shore, 1.5 km. southwest of Ossiach village. Leave the A10 at exit 178 for Ossiacher See, turn left on road B94 towards Feldkirchen and shortly right to Ossiach Sud. The site is just before Ossiach. GPS: 46.66371, 13.9748

Charges guide

Per unit incl. 2 persons and electricity	€ 20.60 - € 31.90
extra person	€ 6.20 - € 9.30
child (3-12 yrs)	free - € 6.30

For latest campsite news, availability and prices visit

alanrogers.com

Ossiach

Ideal Camping Lampele

Alt Ossiach 57, A-9570 Ossiach (Carinthia) T: 0424 3529. E: camping@lampele.at

alanrogers.com/AU0404

Ideal Camping Lampele can be found on the banks of the Ossiacher See, the third largest lake in Carinthia. Pitches (80-120 sq.m) are grassy and semi-shaded, all with 8A electrical connections. Forty-five mobile homes are available for hire. The site has its own private beach and a grassy sports field adjacent. There is also a children's play area and bouncy castle. The restaurant (with a pleasant covered terrace) is popular with campers and local people and offers a range of local and international cuisine, including pizzas. There is also a takeaway food service.

Facilities
The modern, well maintained, heated sanitary block at the top of the site has all facilities including free, controllable showers, private cabins, a baby room, facilities for disabled visitors and a dog shower. Washing machine and dryer. Motorcaravan services. Shop. Bar/restaurant. Takeaway. Direct lake access with small jetty. Fishing. Playground. Trampoline. Activity programme. WiFi over site (charged). Dogs are not accepted in the lake area. Off site: Adventure sports. Minigolf. Tennis.

Open: 1 May - 30 September.

Directions
Site is 10 km. southwest of Klagenfurt. Approaching from north (Salzburg) head south on A10 as far as Villach/Ossiacher See exit. Leave motorway here and head east on L49 towards Ossiach and then follow signs to the site. GPS: 46.682664, 13.998519

Charges guide
Per unit incl. 2 persons and electricity	€ 22.10 - € 31.90
extra person	€ 5.70 - € 8.50
child (3-16 yrs)	free - € 7.90

Rennweg

Sommer & Winter Camping Ramsbacher

Gries 53, A-9863 Rennweg (Carinthia) T: 047 346 63. E: camp.ram@utanet.at

alanrogers.com/AU0405

This is a beautiful small site set in a high alpine valley with great views in every direction. With 72 touring pitches, all with electricity, this is a great site for those seeking peace and quiet and the opportunity to explore the local area either by bike or on foot. The site is well placed in the Katschberg Mountains and close to the Pölital Nature Reserve. Cars are not allowed in the national park in the summer so entry is via a small train. In winter, of course, the site is very well placed for local skiing.

Facilities
Toilet facilities are clean, heated and modern with free showers but a communal changing area. Washing machine, dryer and drying area. Attractive bar/restaurant. Small play area. WiFi (charged). Off site: Swimming pool, minigolf, tennis, rollerskating and play area 25 m. Winter skiing with free shuttle bus.

Open: All year.

Directions
From A10 take exit 113 (south of Katschberg toll tunnel) and turn towards Rennweg. Turn right later into the village, then right again towards Oberdorf where site is well signed. Alternatively from A10 exit, climb hill from the junction then turn left down towards Oberdorf. GPS: 47.01499, 13.61498

Charges guide
Per unit incl. 2 persons and electricity	€ 24.40 - € 25.30
extra person	€ 5.80 - € 6.00

St Kanzian

Camping Süd

Südpromenade 57, Unterburg am Klopeiner See, A-9122 St Kanzian (Carinthia) T: 042 392 322.

E: office@feriensued.com **alanrogers.com/AU0383**

Camping Süd is a small quiet site which, together with a family run restaurant, makes it a site for those who appreciate a few days spent in peaceful surroundings with lakeside views, and who enjoy regional specialities, fresh water fish and game, freshly prepared by the restaurant's owner. The homely restaurant has been in the family for almost 50 years and the wood carvings by the present owner's father are worth a close look. Many of the site's 105 fairly level, grassy pitches are taken by permanent campers, all have 8A electricity and the practical sanitary facilities are well maintained.

Facilities
One well maintained sanitary block with free hot showers and the usual facilities. Small shop. Swimming in the lake. Breakfast can be served in the part of the restaurant overlooking the lake. Off site: Bicycle hire 500 m. Golf 1.5 km. Riding 2 km.

Open: 1 May - 30 September.

Directions
Site is 8 km. SSE of Völkermarkt. From the 70 road follow signs for Klopeiner See. In St Kanzian fork right (opposite Penny supermarket) and after 500 m. straight ahead at roundabout. Site is 1 km. beside the lake on the left low down. GPS: 46.59913, 14.58258

Charges guide
Per unit incl. 2 persons and electricity	€ 18.70 - € 22.00
extra person	€ 4.40 - € 6.00

FREE Alan Rogers Travel Card
Extra benefits and savings - see page 14

St Margareten im Rosental

Camping Rosental Roz

Gotschuchen 34, A-9173 St Margareten im Rosental (Carinthia) T: 042 268 1000.

E: camping.rosental@roz.at **alanrogers.com/AU0415**

In the picturesque Drau valley, southeast of Flagenfurt, Rosental Roz has magnificent views along the valley and of the cliffs that form the Austrian southern border with Slovakia. The site is also close to Italy. There are 430 pitches (all for touring) and 16 mobile homes to rent around a small swimming lake with water slide. All pitches have 16A electricity and 50 pitches also have water and drainage. An active children's club provides lots to occupy the youngsters and guided walks for adults are organised from the campsite. This attractive, family run site caters for all members of the family.

Facilities

Toilet facilities are clean and modern with free showers, ten family washrooms and a large shower facility with fun mirrors for young children. Washing machine and dryer. Facilities for disabled visitors. Restaurant/bar (1/5-30/9). Shop (1/6-15/9). Children's club (1/6-30/8). Playgrounds and large games area. WiFi. Spring drinking water. Dog exercise area. Off site: Fishing 1 km. Riding 2 km. Many walks to suit all levels of fitness. Cycle tracks.

Open: Easter - 15 October.

Directions

Site is southeast of Klagenfurt. From 91 road turn onto the 85 towards Feriach. Before St Margareten, in centre of small hamlet of Gotschuchen turn left towards site. It is 1.5 km. but well signed (watch the overhanging gutters especially when passing another vehicle). GPS: 46.54363, 14.39088

Charges guide

Per unit incl. 2 persons and electricity	€ 28.90
extra person	€ 8.90
child (under 18 yrs)	€ 6.10 - € 7.20

St Primus

Strandcamping Turnersee Breznik

A-9123 St Primus (Carinthia) T: 042 392 350. E: info@breznik.at

alanrogers.com/AU0410

This neat and tidy site is situated in a valley with views of the surrounding mountains. The 225 marked and numbered pitches for touring units vary in size, on level grass terraces. Although there are many trees, not all parts have shade. All pitches have 6A electricity and 55 also have water, drainage, TV and phone connections. At the lakeside is a large, well kept grass area for sunbathing, with a wooden deck area right next to the water providing steps for swimming in the lake. It is very much a site for families where children really are catered for and it has a pleasant atmosphere.

Facilities

Four sanitary blocks renovated in 2010 include provision for young children and babies in the largest block. Facilities for disabled visitors. Large, central building housing well stocked shop (24/4-18/9). Pleasant restaurant with terrace, takeaway (9/5-12/9) and play room for small children. Good play areas and small zoo with goats and rabbits. Topi club and organised activities for adults and children. Games room. Bicycle hire. Watersports. Internet access. Off site: Golf 1.5 km. Fishing and riding 3 km. Boat launching 5 km.

Open: 17 April - 3 October.

Directions

Site is 20 km. east-southeast of Klagenfurt. Leave A2 motorway at exit 298 signed Grafenstien. Go east on road 70 for 5 km. and turn right for Tainach and St Kanzian. In St Kanzian keep bearing to the right, St Primas is signed. Site is on left before St Primus. GPS: 46.58569, 14.56598

Charges guide

Per unit incl. 2 persons and electricity	€ 18.40 - € 29.30
extra person	€ 5.50 - € 9.10

Camping Cheques accepted.

Villach Landskron

Seecamping Berghof

Ossiachersee Süduferstrasse 241, A-9523 Villach Landskron (Carinthia) T: 042 424 1133.

E: office@seecamping-berghof.at **alanrogers.com/AU0425**

This surely must be the ultimate camping experience: a perfect location, excellent facilities, great pitches and a welcome to match. The Ertl family and their staff manage this 460 pitch site to perfection. Use of the natural topography leads you to think that you are in a small site wherever you camp. With lovely lake views from almost every spot, this is a great site to stop for short or long stays. There are now 190 pitches with water, electricity and drainage and all pitches have WiFi.

Facilities

Five modern toilet blocks spread around the site, provide the usual facilities including special provision for young children and babies in two blocks. Facilities for disabled visitors. Well stocked supermarket. Pleasant restaurant with terrace, takeaway and games room for older children. TV room. Good play area and daily club (4-11 yrs). Car hire. Bicycle hire. Minigolf. Swimming possible in the lake. Skateboard park. Tennis. Volleyball. Fishing with permit. WiFi. Dogs accepted (July/Aug, limited area).

Open: Easter - mid October.

Directions

From A10 take exit 178, which travelling south is just after the tunnel. Head towards Ossiacher See and after 1 km. turn right towards Ossiacher See Sud. At traffic lights turn left and site is 3.5 km. on the left just after entering hamlet of Heiligengestade. GPS: 46.65305, 13.93360

Charges guide

Per unit incl. 2 persons and electricity	€ 20.80 - € 35.40
extra person	€ 6.20 - € 9.60
child (2-13 yrs)	€ 3.90 - € 8.70

For latest campsite news, availability and prices visit

alanrogers.com

Schönbühel

Camping Stumpfer

A-3392 Schönbühel (Lower Austria) T: 027 528 510. E: office@stumpfer.com

alanrogers.com/AU0280

This small, well appointed site with just 60 pitches is directly on the River Danube, near the small town of Schönbühel, and is a convenient night stop being near the Salzburg-Vienna autobahn. The 50 unmarked pitches for touring units, all with 16A electricity, are on flat grass and the site is lit at night. There is shade in most parts and a landing stage for boat trips on the Danube. The main building also houses a Gasthof, with a bar/restaurant of the same name. This is very much a family run site. The Danube cycle track runs past the site.

Facilities

Part of the main building, the toilet block is of good quality with hot water on payment. Facilities for disabled visitors include ramps by the side of steps up to the block. Washing machine and dryer. Motorcaravan services. Small shop. Playground. Fishing. WiFi. Off site: Swimming pool, bicycle hire and riding within 5 km. Golf 25 km. Day trips to Vienna.

Open: 1 April - 31 October.

Directions

Leave Salzburg-Vienna autobahn at Melk exit. Drive towards Melk, then Melk Nord. Just before bridge turn right (Schönbühel, St Polten), at T-junction turn right again and go downhill. Turn right just before BP filling station (Schönbühel) and site is 3 km. on left with narrow entrance. GPS: 48.254, 15.37106

Charges guide

Per unit incl. 2 persons and electricity	€ 15.50 - € 20.00

Tulln

Donaupark Camping Tulln

Donaulande 76, A-3430 Tulln (Lower Austria) T: 022 726 5200. E: camptulln@oeamtc.at

alanrogers.com/AU0290

Donaupark Camping, owned and run by the Austrian Motor Club (OAMTC), is imaginatively laid out, village style, with unmarked grass pitches grouped around six circular gravel areas. Further pitches are to the side of the hard road which links the circles and these include some with grill facilities for tents; 100 of the 120 touring pitches have electricity (3/6A) and cable TV sockets. Tall trees surrounding the site offer shade in parts. Tucked neatly away at the back of the site are 120 long stay caravans. Activities are organised in high season with guided tours around Tulln on foot, by bike and on the river by canoe.

Facilities

Three identical, modern, octagonal sanitary blocks can be heated. One is at reception (next to the touring area), the other two are at the far end of the site. Facilities for disabled visitors. Washing machines and dryers. Cooking rings. Gas supplies. Bar and restaurant (1/5-15/9). Shop (1/5-30/9). Play areas. Tennis. Bicycle and canoe hire. Excursion programme. Internet access. Off site: Lake swimming in adjacent park (entry free for campers). Fishing 500 m. Bus service into Vienna (May-Sept). Train service to Vienna. Steamer excursions.

Open: 15 April - 15 October.

Directions

From Vienna follow south bank of the Danube on B14; from the west, leave the A1 autobahn at either St Christophen or Altenbach exits and go north on B19 to Tulln. Site is on the east side of Tulln and well signed. GPS: 48.33239, 16.07275

Charges guide

Per unit incl. 2 persons and electricity	€ 25.00 - € 29.50
extra person	€ 7.00
child (5-14 yrs)	€ 3.50

Abtenau

Oberwötzlhof Camp

Erlfeld 37, A-5441 Abtenau (Salzburg) T: 062 432 698. E: oberwoetzlhof@sbg.at

alanrogers.com/AU0262

High up in the Lammertal Valley is this small, hilltop farm site with attractive views of the surrounding mountains. Part of a working farm, it has a total of 70 pitches, of which 40 are for touring units. All are serviced with 10A electricity, water and drainage. The site is quiet at night, and dark, so a torch would be useful. The small, fenced swimming pool (10x5 m) is unheated, and has paved surrounds. The site has attractive sanitary facilities, completed in 2010, and together with its rural location and a friendly atmosphere is a good site for those seeking some peace and quiet. No English is spoken.

Facilities

Sanitary building. Laundry facilities and drying room. Solarium. Swimming pool. Internet. WiFi throughout (free). Charcoal barbecues not permitted. Off site: Abtenau 2.5 km. (about 25 minutes walk). Skiing 2.5 km. Riding 8 km. Hallstättersee and salt mines 30 km. The Panorama Strasse.

Open: All year.

Directions

Abtenau is 34 km. southeast of Salzburg. From A10 exit 28 (Golling), take B162 east for 14 km. and site is signed to the left 2.5 km. before Abtenau (sat nav is unreliable). GPS: 47.585704, 13.324635

Charges guide

Per unit incl. 2 persons (electricity on meter)	€ 20.80 - € 29.80
extra person	€ 7.00 - € 8.00
child (3-15 yrs)	€ 4.00 - € 4.50
No credit cards.	

FREE Alan Rogers Travel Card

Extra benefits and savings - see page 14

Maishofen

Camping Bad Neunbrunnen am Waldsee

Neunbrunnen 56, A-5751 Maishofen (Salzburg) T: 065 426 8548. E: camping@neunbrunnen.at
alanrogers.com/AU0267

This site has been recommended to us and will be inspected in 2015. Surrounded by fields on one side and woods on the other, Camping Neunbrunnen is in the north of Austria close to the mountainous border with Germany. Its own small lake offers opportunities to swim and fish; it even has its own fresh water spring. There are around 250 pitches, of which 60 are for touring units, all with electricity (max: 16A); the rest are occupied on a permanent basis, including just five for hire. The site is open all year, with skiing attracting visitors in winter whilst during the rest of the year guided walks and cycle tracks cater for the needs of the energetic. The small town of Maishofen and the popular lake-side resort of Zell am See lie just to the south and offer a wide choice of shops, bars and restaurants and numerous sporting and water-based activities, whilst a short distance to the north is the town and ski-resort of Saalfelden. The surrounding countryside provides ample opportunities for walking and cycling, with numerous forests and lakes to visit. Car outings could include visits to the Hohe Tauern National Park to the south or across the border into Bavaria to the Berchtesgarden National Park.

Facilities

Modern sanitary block with provision for children and disabled visitors, baby room and hot and cold water to dishwashing and laundry sinks. Washing machine and dryer. Bread and limited groceries. Restaurant with takeaway. Small playground. Games room. Children's entertainment programme (7-21/6 and 1/7-31/8). Guided walks. Swimming, fishing and boat-launching. Pedal boats. Grass beach. Off site: Cycle routes and cross-country skiing from site entrance. Maishofen 3 km. Zell am See 7 km. Saalfelden 8 km. National Parks 50 km. Salzburg 80 km.

Open: All year.

Directions

From A12/E60 (Innsbuck/Germany) motorway at exit 17 Worgl-Ost follow B178 east for 30 km. to Sankt Johann, turn south then southeast on B164 to Saalfelden and finally head south on B311 towards Zell am See. After 8 km. turn west at Mittenhofen and follow signs for Neunbrunnen and campsite. GPS: 47.37745, 12.79549

Charges guide

Per unit incl. 2 persons	
and electricity	€ 15.70 - € 20.20
extra person	€ 4.50 - € 5.50
child (2-7 yrs)	€ 3.00 - € 3.50

The campsite in beautiful natural surroundings with a fishing and bathing lake and its own natural spring is located very near to all the sights and destinations for excursions. The possibilities for hikes practically start on your doorstep.
The winter sports enthusiasts among you will be pleased that the ski re-sorts of the Europe Sports Region and Ski Circus Saalbach-Hinterglemm are only a short distance away. Cross-country skiers can set off on the ski runs right from the campsite. We really take care of your physical well-being. In the restaurant, you'll be served culinary delights from our local cuisine. Comfort rooms with a bal-cony, bath/shower, WC and cable TV as well as pleasant apartments are also available.

Camping Bad Neunbrunnen
Neunbrunnen 60
A-5751 Maishofen b. Zell am See
Tel. 0043-6542-68548 Fax DW 8
www.camping-neunbrunnen.at
E-mail: camping@neunbrunnen.at

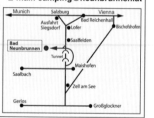

Salzburg

Panoramacamping Stadtblick

Rauchenbichl, Rauchenbichler Strasse 21, A-5020 Salzburg (Salzburg) T: 066 245 0652.
E: info@panorama-camping.at alanrogers.com/AU0212

Salzburg and Panoramacamping Stadtblick are a superb combination. From this 70 pitch site with excellent new sanitary facilities, there are views over the city to Salzburg's hilltop castle beyond. The city is easily reached, either from a bus stop only a few minutes walk away, or tours can be arranged departing directly from the site. All the 70 level pitches are on grass-gravel with 6A electricity and are arranged on shallow terraces with a separate area for tents. The site's restaurant is extremely good value. Each morning, from 08.00, fresh bread and breakfast are available, and in the evening, 18.00-21.00, there is a comprehensive menu; do try the regional specialities.

Facilities

Excellent sanitary facilities include six spacious wash rooms with shower and washbasin. Facilities for disabled visitors. Laundry. Motorcaravan services. Shop for basic supplies, gas and souvenirs. Restaurant (May-Sept). TV lounge. Small playground. WiFi (charged). Apartments for hire. Off site: Bus stop to city centre five minutes' walk (every 10 mins). Bicycle hire and swimming pool 3 km.

Open: 20 March - 5 November; 5-15 December and 28 December - 10 January.

Directions

From A1 exit 288 (Salzburg-Nord) turn south towards city. Approaching the first set of traffic lights get into the right hand lane, turn right here on a minor road (site signed) and continue to top of hill, and follow site signs. GPS: 47.81664, 13.05232

Charges guide

Per unit incl. 2 persons	
and electricity	€ 30.00 - € 34.00
extra person	€ 9.00 - € 10.00

For latest campsite news, availability and prices visit
alanrogers.com

Bruck

Sportcamp Woferlgut

Kroessenbachstraße 40, A-5671 Bruck an der Glocknerstraße (Salzburg)

T: 065 457 3030. E: info@sportcamp.at alanrogers.com/AU0180

LeadingCampings

The village of Bruck lies at the northern end of the Grossglocknerstrasse spectacular mountain road in the Hohe Tauern National Park, very near the Zeller See. Sportcamp Woferlgut, a family run site, is one of the very best in Austria. Surrounded by mountains, the site is quite flat with pleasant views. The 520 level, grass pitches (300 for touring units) are marked out by shrubs and each has 16A electricity (Europlug), water, drainage, cable TV socket and gas point. A high grass bank separates the site from the road. The site's own lake, used for swimming, is surrounded by a landscaped sunbathing area. A free activity and entertainment programme is provided all year round, but especially during the summer. This includes live music evenings, a club for children, weekly barbecues and guided cycle and mountain tours. The fitness centre has a fully equipped gym, whilst another building contains a sauna and cold dip, Turkish bath, solarium (all free), massage (charged), and a bar. In winter, a cross-country skiing trail and toboggan run lead from the site and a free bus service is provided to nearby skiing facilities. With Salzburg to the north and Innsbruck to the northwest, the management is pleased to advise on local attractions and tours, making this a splendid base for a family holiday. Excellent English is spoken. Used by tour operators (45 pitches) and a popular rally venue. A member of Leading Campings group.

Facilities

Three modern sanitary blocks (the newest in a class of its own) have excellent facilities, including private cabins, underfloor heating and music. Washing machines and dryers. Facilities for disabled visitors. Family bathrooms for hire (some with bathtubs). Motorcaravan services. Well stocked shop. Bar, restaurant and takeaway. Small, heated outdoor pool and children's pool (1/5-15/10). Fitness centre. Two playgrounds, indoor play room and children's cinema. Tennis. Bicycle hire. Watersports and lake swimming. Children's farm and pony rides. New crazy golf course. WiFi over site (charged). Off site: ATM 500 m. Fishing 100 m. Riding 1.5 km. Golf 3 km. Boat launching and sailing 0.5 km. Hiking and skiing (all year) nearby. Dry toboggan run at Kaprun 4 km.

Open: All year.

Directions

Site is southwest of Bruck. From road B311, Bruck bypass, take southern exit (Grossglockner) and site is signed from the junction of B311 and B107 roads (small signs). Note: 3.4 m. height restriction if you go through village. GPS: 47.2838, 12.81694

Charges guide

Per unit incl. 2 persons and electricity (plus meter)	€ 23.80 - € 45.10
extra person	€ 5.60 - € 9.20
child (2-10 yrs)	€ 4.40 - € 6.80
dog	€ 3.40 - € 4.70

Special offers for longer stays in low season.

St Martin bei Lofer

Park Grubhof

Grubhof Nr. 39, A-5092 St Martin bei Lofer (Salzburg) T: 065 888 237. E: home@grubhof.com

alanrogers.com/AU0265

Park Grubhof is a well organised, level and spacious site set in the former riding and hunting park of the 14th-century Schloss Grubhof. The 200 pitches all with 12A electricity, have been carefully divided into separate areas for different types of visitor – dog owners, young people, families and groups, and a quiet area. There are 150 very large pitches, all with electricity, water and drainage, many along the bank of the Saalach river. Although new, the central building has been built in traditional Tirolean style using, in part, materials hundreds of years old, reclaimed from old farmhouses. The result is most attractive. On the ground floor you will find reception, a cosy café/bar and a small shop and, on the first floor, a super sauna and wellness suite, two apartments and a relaxation room. Some areas are wooded with plenty of shade, others are more open and there are some very attractive log cabins which have been rescued from the old logging camps. Many of the possible activities are based around the river, where you will find barbecue areas, canoeing and white-water rafting, fishing and swimming (when the river level reduces). The ski resort of Lofer Alm is only 2 km. away (free ski shuttle). A cross-county track is 300 m. away and snow cleared winter walks start directly from the site. Excellent English is spoken.

Facilities

Three attractive, modern sanitary units built with plenty of glass and wood, give good provision of all facilities. The newest (2013) includes large family bathrooms (free with certain pitches, to rent in the winter), a recreation and conference room and a fitness centre. Saunas, steam bath, massage, fitness room. Separate drying facilities for canoeists. Ski and equipment room. Motorcaravan services. Shop, restaurant and bar. WiFi throughout (charged). Playground. Games room. Children's playroom. Watersports. Bicycle hire. Cabins to rent. Hotel and B&B.

Open: All year excl. November.

Directions

From A12 exit 17 (south of Kufstein) take B178 east to St Johann in Tyrol, then on B178 to Lofer, then south on B311 towards Zell am See. Site is 200 m. after Lagerhaus filling station on left. GPS: 47.57427, 12.70602

Charges guide

Per unit incl. 2 persons and electricity	€ 19.00 - € 32.50
extra person	€ 6.30 - € 8.50
child (under 15 yrs)	€ 5.00 - € 8.50

No credit cards.

Zell am See

Seecamp Zell am See

Thumersbacherstrasse 34, A-5700 Zell am See (Salzburg) T: 065 427 2115. E: zell@seecamp.at

alanrogers.com/AU0160

The Zeller See, delightfully situated in the south of Salzburg province and near the start of the Grossglocknerstrasse, is ideally placed for enjoying the splendid southern Austrian countryside. Seecamp is right by the water, less than two kilometres from the town of Zell and with fine views to the south end of the lake. Stretching along the waterfront, the site has 160 good level, mainly grass and gravel pitches of average size, 147 with 16A electricity. About half have water, drainage and TV connections. Units can be close together in peak season. Good English is spoken.

Facilities

Excellent, heated sanitary facilities include facilities for disabled visitors and a baby room. Washing machines, dryers and irons. Motorcaravan services. Bar, restaurant and takeaway (all 20/12-Easter; Mother's day-October). Shop. Play area. Play room. Fishing. Bicycle hire. Canoe and kayak hire. Topi Club and summer entertainment for children. Activity programme. Winter ski packages and free ski bus. Glacier skiing possible in summer. Free WiFi.

Open: All year.

Directions

From the north on B311 go through short 600 m. tunnel, take Thumersbach exit just before long tunnel entrance (2 km. north of Zell am See town). After 500 m. turn left and site entrance is 750 m. on right. Signed from B311. GPS: 47.339925, 12.809141

Charges guide

Per unit incl. 2 persons	€ 28.80 - € 35.80
extra person	€ 8.35 - € 10.35
electricity (per kWh)	€ 0.80

Bairisch Kölldorf

Camping Im Thermenland

Bairisch Kölldorf 240, A-8344 Bairisch Kölldorf (Steiermark) T: 031 593 941. E: camping.bk@aon.at

alanrogers.com/AU0502

Camping Im Thermenland is tucked quietly away in the hills of eastern Steiermark, 45 km. southeast of Graz and close to the borders of Slovenia and Hungary. It is a modern, well maintained site with 70 level touring pitches, with some hedge separation, all with 16A electricity, water and drainage. As the name suggests, the site is situated close to numerous spas and thermal baths including Bad Gleichenberg, which dates back to Roman times. Nearby Bairisch Kölldorf is a town of only 1,000 inhabitants; it does however boast the world's largest fire engine!

Facilities
Excellent toilet facilities are clean, well maintained and include free showers. Facilities for disabled visitors. Dog shower. Washing machine and dryer. Restaurant with terrace adjoining small play area. Unheated outdoor swimming pool with cover (May-Sept). Off site: Fishing 100 m. Small shop with essentials and local produce 500 m. Golf 3 km. Styrassic Park 4 km.

Open: All year.

Directions
Southeast of Graz, Bairisch Kölldorf is unlikely to appear on any map. Leave A2 at exit 157 and head towards Feldbach on 68. Continue on 66 to Bad Gleichenberg, go straight over first roundabout and turn left at second (supermarket). After 2.8 km. (past fire station) turn left by a chapel and immediately right to site in 600 m. GPS: 46.875583, 15.93445

Charges guide
Per unit incl. 2 persons and electricity	€ 20.60
extra person	€ 6.20

Graz

Camping Central

Martinhofstrasse 3, A-8054 Graz (Steiermark) T: 067 637 85102. E: office@campingcentral.at

alanrogers.com/AU0330

Although not as well known as Vienna, Salzburg and Innsbruck, Graz in the southern province of Styria, is Austria's second largest city. Camping Central is a quiet site, which makes a good night stop when travelling between Klagenfurt and Vienna or as a base from which to explore the region. The site's name is misleading as it is situated in the southwest of the town in the Strassgang district, some 6 km. from the centre. The 60 level touring pitches are either in regular rows either side of tarmac roads under a cover of tall trees or on an open meadow where they are not marked out. All have 6A electricity. There is a bus every 15 minutes to the city centre.

Facilities
The new, well built toilet block is of good quality and the other two blocks have been refurbished. Each can be heated in cool weather. Facilities for disabled visitors. Washing machines and dryer. Swimming pool with facilities including a special entry to the water for disabled campers. Small restaurant at the pool. Tennis. Playground. Jogging track. Limited animation during high season. Off site: Two restaurants within 300 m. Good shop 400 m.

Open: 1 April - 31 October.

Directions
From the west take Graz-west exit, from Salzburg the Graz-sud exit and follow signs to Central and Strassgang and turn right just past traffic lights for site (signed). GPS: 47.02045, 15.39253

Charges guide
Per unit incl. 2 persons and electricity	€ 32.00 - € 50.00
extra person	€ 10.00
No credit cards.	

Leibnitz

Camping Leibnitz

Rudolf Hans Bartsch-Gasse 33, A-8430 Leibnitz (Steiermark) T: 034 528 2463. E: camping@leibnitz.at

alanrogers.com/AU0505

Near the Slovenian border, close to the small town of Leibnitz, this site is set in the rolling wine growing countryside of southeast Austria. A small site with only 61 pitches, it is set in a lovely park area, close to an excellent swimming pool complex (some noise can be heard), which is available for campers' use (with access arrangements for disabled visitors). A sports centre and facilities for minigolf and tennis are nearby. All the pitches are of a good size, level and with 16A electricity connections, and most have some shade. The town has shops and restaurants with weekly events held, for example, at the Jazz Club. There are marked footpaths and cycle ways to allow you to explore.

Facilities
Excellent toilet facilities are clean and well maintained with free showers. Facilities for disabled visitors. Washing machine. Small restaurant (15/5-31/8) but many more within walking distance. Small play area. Off site: Leibnitz 500 m. Leisure centre with two heated outdoor swimming pools 100 m. (15/5-15/9).

Open: 1 May - 15 October.

Directions
From A9 take Leibnitz exit, go straight over two roundabouts (through factory outlet centre), over traffic lights and after 300 m. turn left (site signed). Go straight over roundabout and enter Leibnitz, turn right and site is 500 m. on left, in park next to pool complex. GPS: 46.77888, 15.52900

Charges guide
Per unit incl. 2 persons and electricity	€ 21.90 - € 26.90

Peterdorf
Camping Bella Austria
Peterdorf 100, A-8842 Sankt Peter am Kammersberg (Steiermark) T: 035 367 3902.
E: info@camping-bellaustria.com **alanrogers.com/AU0515**

This newly renovated campsite now with some 200 pitches is ideally located for exploring southwest Styria, the beautiful Mur valley, and the Niedere Tauern alps (highest point Greimberg 2,472 m). To the north, snow-capped Greimberg sits high above the site whilst in other directions you can see pine clad slopes and alpine pastures. Not too far away is the small ski resort of Turracher Hohe. Bella Austria is an ideal base for discovering traditional Austria by bicycle, on foot or in a horse-drawn carriage. The site also offers a unique range of workshops. The level, unmarked pitches all have access to 16A electricity, water and drainage.

Facilities
The modern sanitary blocks provide ample and clean facilities including toilets, hot showers and washbasins. Washing machine. Bar and restaurant. Wellness centre. Heated swimming pool (11/6-23/9). Play area. Volleyball. Basketball. 5-a-side football. Electric bicycles for hire.
Open: 28 March - 27 October.

Directions
From the Murau-Scheifling no. 96 road, turn north towards Katsch just west of Frojach. Follow this road up the valley towards and through Peterdorf to the site on the right set back from the road but clearly signed. GPS: 47.1808, 14.2157

Charges guide
Per unit incl. 2 persons and electricity	€ 20.00 - € 24.00
extra person	€ 5.00 - € 8.00

Weisskirchen
50plus Campingpark Fisching
Fisching 9, A-8741 Weisskirchen (Steiermark) T: 035 778 2284. E: campingpark@fisching.at
alanrogers.com/AU0525

This small site is unusual in that it only accepts clients over 50 years of age. It is a high quality site with an attractive setting in the Steiermark region, west of Graz. There are 50 large, level pitches of 100-130 sq.m, all equipped with 6A electricity, water, drainage and cable TV connections. Most pitches are on hardstanding. A number of chalets and holiday apartments are also available for rent. There is a small swimming lake which is surrounded by an attractive garden and sunbathing area. The site's bar/snack bar is inviting with a selection of homemade dishes on offer.

Facilities
Two excellent modern toilet blocks were very clean, with free controllable showers. No facilities for children or disabled visitors. Laundry room. Bar, snack bar and shop (all 1/4-30/10). Outdoor swimming pool (1/5-30/9). Swimming lake. Tennis. Bicycle hire. Activity programme. Chalets and apartments for rent. WiFi (charged).
Off site: Walking and cycle tracks. Fishing 1 km. Riding 2 km. Golf (Murtal) 8 km. Graz 70 km.
Open: 1 April - 30 October.

Directions
From north (A9 motorway), head for Graz and join westbound S36 at Sant Michael in Obersteiermark. Continue to Aichdorf then head south on B78 to Weisskirchen, then follow signs to Fisching, from where site is signed. GPS: 47.163189, 14.738281

Charges guide
Per unit incl. 2 persons and electricity	€ 20.50
extra person	€ 7.50

Achenkirch
Alpen Caravanpark Achensee
Achenkirch 17, A-6215 Achenkirch (Tirol) T: 052 466 239. E: info@camping-achensee.com
alanrogers.com/AU0098

Three thousand feet above sea level, alongside the Achensee lake and surrounded by wooded hills and mountains, this impressive site has been redesigned and extended to exceptional standards. Easily accessible from Munich, Salzburg and Innsbruck, it offers everything needed for an active family holiday and for exploring the lake and its surroundings. There are 210 pitches, 110 for tourers, all with 16A electricity. Forty new all-weather comfort pitches are close to the restaurant and bar, which overlook the site and the lake. There has been camping here since 1961, but imaginative management is now taking Alpen Caravanpark to a new level.

Facilities
New heated sanitary block has free showers, a baby room and facilities for disabled visitors. Bathrooms for hire. Washing machine and dryer. Drying room. Motorcaravan services. Freezer for ice packs. Shop for basics. Restaurant and bar. Playroom, activity room and youth room with games (charged). Large lakeside playground. Football pitch and beach volleyball court. WiFi (charged). Lake swimming and boat launching.
Open: All year.

Directions
From A12 take junction 39 on to B181 northbound signed Achensee. Pass end of lake and turn left into Achenkirch. Follow road through village to site. GPS: 47.49958, 11.70643

Charges guide
Per unit incl. 2 persons and electricity	€ 32.00 - € 48.50
extra person	€ 7.00 - € 10.50
child (0-13 yrs)	€ 5.00 - € 6.50
dog	€ 4.50 - € 5.00

For latest campsite news, availability and prices visit
alanrogers.com

Aschau im Zillertal
Erlebnis-Comfort-Camping Aufenfeld

Aufenfeldweg 10, A-6274 Aschau im Zillertal (Tirol) T: 052 822 9160.
E: info@camping-zillertal.at **alanrogers.com/AU0120**

LeadingCampings

This outstanding site is situated in a wide mountain valley with fine views and first class facilities. The main area of the site itself is flat with pitches up to 100 sq.m. on grass and gravel, between hard access roads, with further pitches on terraces at the rear. There are 350 pitches (240 for touring units with 6A electricity) including 40 with private bathrooms. The site can become full mid July until mid August and at Christmas. A splendid indoor swimming pool has been added and there is a heated outdoor pool, paddling pool, and tennis courts for summer use, as well as a play and activity centre.

Facilities
Five well kept, heated sanitary blocks of excellent quality and size, each with a few washbasins in cabins for each sex, baby rooms and nine units for disabled visitors. Four additional units provide 40 private bathrooms for luxury pitches and several family bathrooms for rent. Laundry and drying rooms. Ski room. Motorcaravan services. Supermarket. Restaurant. General room. TV. Indoor pool, sauna and sun beds. Wellness centre. Outdoor pool. Playground. Multisports court. Tennis. Riding. Skateboard and rollerblade facilities. Bicycle hire. WiFi (charged). ATM.

Open: All year excl. 3 November - 8 December.

Directions
From A12 Inntal motorway, take Zillertal exit 39, 32 km. northeast of Innsbruck. Follow road 169 to the village of Aschau from which site is well signed. GPS: 47.263333, 11.899333

Charges guide
Per unit incl. 2 persons, (electricity on meter)	€ 26.50 - € 43.90
incl. private sanitary cabin	€ 35.10 - € 57.50
extra person	€ 6.70 - € 12.10
child (2-12 yrs)	€ 5.10 - € 8.30

Winter prices are higher.

Ehrwald
Ferienanlage Tiroler Zugspitze

Obermoos 1, A-6632 Ehrwald (Tirol) T: 056 732 309. E: welcome@zugspitze-resort.at
alanrogers.com/AU0040

Although Ehrwald is in Austria, it is from the entrance of Tiroler Zugspitze that a cable car runs to the summit of Germany's highest mountain. Standing at 1,200 feet above sea level at the foot of the mountain, the 200 pitches (120 for touring), mainly of stones over grass, are on flat terraces with fine panoramic views in parts. All have 16A electricity connections. The modern reception building at the entrance also houses a fine restaurant with a terrace which is open to those using the cable car, as well as those staying on the site. There are 30 pitches outside the barrier for late arrivals and overnighters.

Facilities
A good sanitary block provides some washbasins in cabins and 20 private bathrooms for rent. Separate baby and toddler unit. Facilities for disabled visitors. Laundry facilities. Drying rooms. Motorcaravan services. Shop. Bar. Restaurant. Indoor pool with sauna, whirlpool and fitness centre. Outdoor pool and children's pool. Internet access. Bicycle loan and motor scooters for hire. Play area.

Open: 1 January - Easter, 28 May - 31 October, mid - end December.

Directions
Carefully follow signs in Ehrwald to Tiroler Zugspitzbahn and then signs to site. GPS: 47.42521, 10.93809

Charges guide
Per person	€ 8.00 - € 18.00
child (4-15 yrs)	€ 5.00 - € 12.00
pitch	€ 10.00 - € 19.00
electricity per kWh.	€ 0.80
dog	€ 4.00

Fieberbrunn
Tirol Camp

Lindau 20, A-6391 Fieberbrunn (Tirol) T: 053 545 6666. E: office@tirol-camp.at
alanrogers.com/AU0110

This is one of many Tirol campsites that cater equally for summer and winter (here seemingly more for winter, when reservation is essential and prices are 50% higher). Tirol Camp is in a quiet and attractive mountain situation on sloping ground and has 240 touring pitches all on wide flat terraces, plus 26 deluxe pitches with their own bathroom at the pitch. Marked out mainly by the electricity boxes or low hedges, they are 80-100 sq.m. and all have 10A electricity, gas, water/drainage, TV and telephone connections. There is a fitness centre, a wellness centre (free to campers) with indoor/outdoor pool complex, sauna, steam room, solarium and aromatherapy massage.

Facilities
The newly upgraded toilet block in the main building has some washbasins in cabins and some private bathrooms (on payment). A modern heated block at the top end of the site has spacious showers and washbasins in cabins. Facilities for disabled visitors. Washing machines, dryers and drying room. Motorcaravan services. Shop and snacks. Restaurant (closed Oct, Nov and May). Outdoor pool (12x8 m). Indoor pool and wellness. Sauna. Outdoor chess. Playground. Activity programmes (July/Aug). WiFi.

Open: 19 May - 2 November and 2 December - 21 April.

Directions
Site is on the B164, 2 km. to the east of Fieberbrunn. Turn south at the clear green sign and site entrance is 500 m. on the left. Look for the flags. GPS: 47.468368, 12.554739

Charges guide
Per unit incl. 2 persons (electricity on meter)	€ 34.50 - € 48.00
with individual sanitary facility	€ 50.00 - € 69.00

No credit cards.

Fügen

Hells Ferienresort Zillertal

Gageringer Strasse 1, A-6263 Fügen (Tirol) T: 052 886 2203. E: info@zillertal-camping.at

alanrogers.com/AU0090

The village of Fügen lies about six kilometres from the A12 autobahn at the start of the Zillertal, so is well placed for exploring the valley and the area around Schwaz. Easy to reach, Camping Zillertal is a very attractive site with excellent facilities and 190 marked pitches (170 for touring units) on flat grass and gravel. All have 16A electricity, water and drainage and there are some hardstandings for motorcaravans. The site is a good overnight stop and useful for a longer stay but, being on a main road, there is a little daytime road noise.

Facilities

New modern, attractive heated sanitary block of top quality has some washbasins in cabins, a children's wash room, and private bathrooms for hire. Unit for disabled campers. Laundry facilities. Drying room. Drive over motorcaravan service point. Attractive bar and small restaurant. Small shop. Heated swimming pool (20x10 m, 1/5-15/10). Solarium, sauna and steam room. Games room with TV. Playground. WiFi over site (charged). Organised games and entertainment. Bicycle hire.

Open: All year.

Directions

Site is 30 km. east of Innsbruck. From the A12 motorway take exit 39 and turn south on B169 towards Mayrhofen for 5 km. Site signed to right Camping Hell. Turn in and immediately left to site. GPS: 47.3596, 11.8521

Charges guide

Per unit incl. 2 persons and electricity	€ 25.00 - € 41.00
extra person	€ 6.50 - € 8.00

Grän

Comfort Camp Grän

Engetalstrasse 13, A-6673 Grän (Tirol) T: 056 756 570. E: info@comfortcamp.at

alanrogers.com/AU0227

In a village location in the Tannheimer Tal, with panoramic mountain scenery, Comfort Camp Grän is a family run site with excellent heated sanitary facilities and a stylish, modern indoor pool complex. It makes a good base for exploring this border region of Austria and Germany. The site has 190 pitches of 80-100 sq.m. (160 for touring units), all with 16A electricity, water (only for summer use) and waste water on fairly level grass, over gravel terrain with some shallow terraces. Gas connections are available in winter. There are 14 private sanitary cabins for rent. The main services are grouped near the entrance. These include a hotel, restaurant, bar and a mini-market.

Facilities

The main sanitary unit is impressive with superb facilities: controllable hot showers, washbasins in cubicles, a children's section in the ladies', a baby room and many family bathrooms for rent. The second smaller unit at one end of the site is equally good. Indoor pool complex (access with key card) with relaxation areas, sauna and steam room. Solarium. Shop. Restaurant and bar. Small playground and indoor playroom for under 12s. WiFi (charged). Teenagers' room. No dogs in high season.

Open: 25 May - 2 November, 15 December - 25 April.

Directions

Grän is close to the German border, southwest of Füssen. From Germany on autobahn A7, turn off at exit 137, and turn south on road 310 to Oberjoch, then take road 308 (road 199 in Austria) east to Grän. Turn north on L261 signed Pfronten, and site is 1.5 km. on left. GPS: 47.50996, 10.55603

Charges guide

Per person	€ 8.00 - € 11.00
pitch (electricity on meter)	€ 8.00 - € 13.00
electricity	€ 0.75

Huben

Ötztaler Naturcamping

Huben 241, A-6444 Huben (Tirol) T: 052 535 855. E: info@oetztalernaturcamping.com

alanrogers.com/AU0078

Four thousand feet above sea level, Ötztaler Naturcamping is set in a clearing among the pines and towering mountains of the Ötz valley. Mostly level, but with some terraces, the 100 touring pitches (60-110 sq.m) are marked out by stone and timber features. All have now been equipped with water (warm in winter), 16A electricity, gas and TV connections, plus individual drains. A stream of mountain water runs through the site and also powers the wheel of a newly restored Tirolean flour mill. The flour is used for a weekly bake of delicious bread in the campsite's own wood-fired oven. The site closes for two weeks in May and October.

Facilities

Heated sanitary block with showers (token). Washing machine and dryer (token). Dishwasher. Baby changing table. Drying room. Motorcaravan services. No shop, but bread to order. Bar, restaurant and takeaway (1/4-7/9). Common room with TV. Bicycle hire. Restored flour mill and own bread weekly. WiFi over site (charged). Off site: Shops and restaurants in Huben and Sölden.

Open: All year (excl. 2 weeks in May and October).

Directions

From A12 trunk road, take exit 123 onto the 186 towards Solden. Pass Langenfeld and turn right to Huben. Follow the green camping signs. GPS: 47.037468, 10.975881

Charges guide

Per unit incl. 2 persons and electricity (plus meter in winter)	€ 19.60 - € 22.10
extra person	€ 6.30 - € 6.70

For latest campsite news, availability and prices visit

alanrogers.com

Innsbruck

Camping Innsbruck Kranebitterhof

Kranebitterallee 216, A-6020 Innsbruck (Tirol) T: 051 227 9558. E: info@camping-kranebitterhof.at

alanrogers.com/AU0165

Opened in 2009, this site, set on steep terraces, is easily reached from the A12 and being only 5 km. west of Innsbruck is good for overnight stays, as well as a base from which to visit the city. The 70 level pitches are 80 to 120 sq.m. and all have 16A electricity, water and waste water connections and their terracing and southerly aspect make most use of the sunshine, allowing unobstructed views of the valley and mountains. A large, two-storey, air-conditioned sanitary block is at the top of the site. Lower down are reception, further WCs (including disabled facilities), the Italian bar/restaurant and shop, all housed in a modern building with large glass windows.

Facilities

Two new heated sanitary facilities, large block at top of site and smaller one in reception building. Free hot showers, three family shower rooms, one with bath. Facilities for disabled visitors in lower block. Kitchen with hotplates, dishwashing and laundry. Small shop (bread can be ordered). Italian restaurant, bar. Play area. WiFi over site (free). Bicycle hire. Off site: Skiing in winter 5 km. Touring in this beautiful mountain region. Innsbruck 5 km.

Open: All year.

Directions

Site is 5 km. west of Innsbruck. Leave A12, Arlberg tunnel-Innsbruck autobahn at exit 83 (Innsbruck Kranebitten). Follow signs for airport/Kranebitten. After a few hundred metres keep left under main road then very sharp right onto N171 Kranebitter Allee. Site is a few hundred metres on right. GPS: 47.26382, 11.32622

Charges guide

Per unit incl. 2 persons, electricity, water and waste water	€ 25.00 - € 30.00
extra person	€ 4.50 - € 5.00

Itter bei Hopfgarten

Terrassen-Camping Schlossberg Itter

Brixentaler Strasse 11, A-6305 Itter bei Hopfgarten (Tirol) T: 053 352 181. E: info@camping-itter.at

alanrogers.com/AU0130

This well kept site with 150 touring pitches and good facilities is suitable both as a base for longer stays and also for overnight stops, as it lies right by a main road west of Kitzbühel. It is on sloping ground, but most of the pitches are on level terraces. Some pitches are individual and divided by hedges and most have 8/10A electricity, cable TV connections, water and drainage. Space is usually available. There is a toboggan run from the site in winter. Good walks and a wealth of excursions by car are available nearby. There is some daytime road noise. Good English is spoken.

Facilities

The main sanitary facilities are heated and of very high standard. The newest section has a large room with private cubicles, some with vanity style washbasins, others with baths. Facilities for disabled visitors. Washing machines and dryers. Motorcaravan services. Cooking facilities. Fridge. Small shop, bar-restaurant (both closed Nov). Heated swimming pool (16x8 m) and paddling pool (1/5-30/9). Sauna and solarium. Playground and indoor playroom. Entertainment. WiFi over site (charged).

Open: All year excl. 16-30 November.

Directions

From A12 exit 17 towards Wörgl Ost and Brixental. After 4 km. at roundabout turn right on B170 (Brixental). Site is 2 km. before Hopfgarten on left. Sat nav can be unreliable. GPS: 47.46699, 12.13979

Charges guide

Per unit incl. 2 persons and electricity (meter in winter)	€ 28.00 - € 38.00
extra person	€ 6.50 - € 9.00
child (1-13 yrs)	€ 3.50 - € 7.00

No credit cards.

Jerzens

Mountain Camp Pitztal

Niederhof 206, A-6474 Jerzens (Tirol) T: 054 148 7571. E: info@mountain-camp.at

alanrogers.com/AU0085

This is a small, unspoiled family run site set among the mountains in the Pitztal. It is an ideal base for walks in the Tirolean mountains and for mountain bike tours on the numerous paths through the woods and on the Schotterpiste and Wildspitze, the highest mountain in the Tirol. Each of the 38 open plan pitches has 13A electricity, water, waste water and gas points. The pitches are laid out on level, rectangular fields on a grass and gravel base, with gravel access roads. There are beautiful views of the mountains on all sides and an Alpine stream feeds the lake and fish ponds.

Facilities

One new, centrally located toilet block (heated) with toilets, washbasins (open style and in cabins) and free, controllable hot showers. Bathroom. Washing machine. Dryer. Bar/restaurant with takeaway and covered terrace (closed May and Nov). Fishing. Skate ramp. Swimming pond with small beach. Full activity programme for all in high season. WiFi over site (charged).

Open: All year.

Directions

From the A12 motorway, take exit 132 at Imst and continue south to Arzl and Wenns; continue toward St. Leonhard. Site is signed to the right 4 km. south of Wenns. (NB: set sat nav to Wenns not Jerzens). GPS: 47.14253, 10.746483

Charges guide

Per unit incl. 2 persons and electricity	€ 19.00 - € 27.00
extra person	€ 6.50 - € 7.50

FREE Alan Rogers Travel Card
Extra benefits and savings - see page 14

Kössen

Euro Camp Wilder Kaiser

Kranebittau 18, A-6345 Kössen (Tirol) T: 053 756 444. E: info@eurocamp-koessen.com

alanrogers.com/AU0140

This well run site lies near the A8 and A12 autobahns, which offer easy access to this attractive location. The site sits at the foot of the Unterberg with views of the Kaisergebirge (the Emperor's mountains) and is surrounded by forests. Being about 2 km. south of the village, it is a quiet location away from main roads. Some 190 of the 290 pitches (grass over gravel) are available for touring units, plus an area for late arrivals. With a second restaurant across the road, there may be a little evening noise.

Facilities

The heated, central sanitary block is of good quality with spacious showers, some washbasins in cubicles and a baby room. Facilities for disabled visitors. Washing machines and dryers. Motorcaravan services. Shop. Large restaurant/bar (closed 18/10-15/11). Second restaurant by play area. Snack bar (high season). Club room with TV and Play Station. Heated swimming pool (May-Sept). Youth room. Sauna and solarium. Beach volleyball. Tennis. Large imaginative adventure playground. Club for children and activities for all (high season). Covered play area. Car hire. WiFi over site (charged). Off site: Bicycle hire 1 km. Golf 2 km. Fishing and riding 4 km. Beach 6 km.

Open: All year excl. 4 November - 7 December.

Directions

Site is 18 km. northeast of Kufstein. From A8 (München-Salzburg), take Grabenstatt exit 109 and go south on B307/B176 to Kössen. Cross river and at roundabout follow signs for Bergbahnen and Euro Camp. After 600 m. follow signs to site. From A93 (Rosenheim-Innsbruck) take exit 59 and go east on B172 to Walchsee and Kössen. Follow green signs. GPS: 47.65388, 12.41544

Charges guide

Per unit incl. 2 persons and electricity (plus meter)	€ 22.30 - € 33.90
extra person	€ 6.50 - € 9.00
child (5-14 yrs)	free - € 5.50

Kramsach

Camping & Appartements Seehof

Reintalersee, Moosen 42, A-6233 Kramsach (Tirol) T: 053 376 3541. E: info@camping-seehof.com

alanrogers.com/AU0065

Camping Seehof is a family run site and excellent in every respect. It is situated in a marvellous sunny and peaceful location on the eastern shores of the Reintalersee. The site's comfortable restaurant has a terrace with lake and mountain views and serves local dishes as well as homemade cakes and ice cream. The site is in two areas: a small one next to the lake is ideal for sunbathing, the other larger one adjoins the excellent sanitary block. There are 170 pitches, 140 of which are for touring (20 tent pitches), served by good access roads and with 16A electricity (Europlug) and TV points; 100 pitches are fully serviced, with more being upgraded every year. Seehof provides an ideal starting point for walking, cycling and riding (with a riding stable nearby) and skiing in winter. The Alpbachtal Seenland card is available without cost at reception and allows free bus transport and free daily entry to many worthwhile attractions in the region. With easy access from the A12 autobahn, the site is also a useful overnight stop. Bread is available each morning from 07.00 without pre-ordering. An extensive lakeside playground has just been added.

Facilities

The sanitary facilities are first class and include ten bathrooms to rent for private use. Baby room. Facilities for disabled visitors. Dog shower. Washing machine and dryer. Ski room. Motorcaravan services. Small shop. Good value restaurant. Playground. Bicycle hire. Fishing. WiFi over site (charged). Apartments to rent. Renovated fitness and play rooms. Off site: Riding 200 m. Tiroler farmhouse museum 1 km. Kramsach 3 km. Rattenberg 4 km.

Open: All year.

Directions

From A12 take Kramsach exit and follow signs for Zu den Seen past Camping Krummsee and Stadlerhof along north shore of lake, then right at crossroads. All clearly signed. GPS: 47.46196, 11.90713

Charges guide

Per unit incl. 2 persons and electricity	€ 18.00 - € 26.50
extra person	€ 4.80 - € 6.90
child (2-14 yrs)	€ 3.20 - € 4.80

Kramsach

Camping Seeblick Toni

Moosen 46, am Reintalersee, A-6233 Kramsach (Tirol) T: 053 376 3544.

E: info@camping-seeblick.at **alanrogers.com/AU0100**

Austria has some of the finest sites in Europe. In a quiet, rural situation on the edge of the small Reintaler See lake, Seeblick Toni is well worth considering for holidays in the Tirol with many excursions possible. The surrounding mountains give scenic views and the campsite has a neat and tidy appearance. The 243 level pitches (215 for touring units) are in regular rows off hard access roads and are of a good size with firm grass and gravel. All pitches have 10A electricity, 150 are fully serviced including cable TV and phone connections. This is a family run site where good English is spoken and there is a warm welcome.

Facilities

Two outstanding sanitary blocks (heated in cool weather). One includes en-suite toilet/basin/shower rooms, the other also has individual bathrooms to rent. Facilities for disabled visitors in second block. New facilities for children. Baby room. Laundry facilities. Drying rooms. Freezer. Motorcaravan services. Restaurant. Bar. Snack kiosk. Shop. Playground. New indoor play area. Topi club, kindergarten and organised activities for children in high season. Youth room. Fishing. Bicycle hire. WiFi (charged).

Open: All year.

Directions

Take exit 32 for Kramsach from A12 autobahn and turn right at roundabout, then immediately left following signs for Camping in village. After 3 km. turn right at site sign. GPS: 47.46109, 11.90647

Charges guide

Per unit incl. 2 persons	
and electricity	€ 24.50 - € 39.50
extra person	€ 6.00 - € 10.50

Camping Cheques accepted.

Kramsach

Seen Camping Stadlerhof

Seebühel 14, A-6233 Kramsach (Tirol) T: 053 376 3371. E: camping.stadlerhof@chello.at

alanrogers.com/AU0102

This child friendly, family run site is in a beautiful location near the Krummsee. There are 130 pitches (80-120 sq.m; 99 for touring units) all with 6-12A electricity (Europlug) and TV connection. Many are individual and divided by hedges and shrubs, and some mature fruit trees offer shade in parts. Fifty multi-serviced pitches are available. The site has a heated outdoor pool complex with café and wellness centre, in addition to a small lake and a dog walk. Excellent English is spoken. A Stellplatz facility with grassy pitches and electric hook-up for quick overnight stays is also offered.

Facilities

Spacious sanitary facilities include showers, some washbasins in cubicles, and five family bathrooms for rent. Laundry facilities. No dedicated facilities for disabled visitors. Small restaurant and bar. Basic provisions available. Wellness centre. Outdoor heated stainless steel swimming pool (12.5x6 m; open in winter) with spa pool and children's pool, and a café. Comprehensive playground. TV room. Drying room, ski room. Bicycle hire. WiFi over site (charged). Off site: Reintaler See 500 m.

Open: All year.

Directions

From A12 exit 32 turn right at roundabout and immediately left following green signs to site, just outside village on left. GPS: 47.4567, 11.88084

Charges guide

Per unit incl. 2 persons	
and electricity	€ 19.80 - € 31.80
extra person	€ 4.90 - € 7.30
child (under 14 yrs)	€ 3.20 - € 4.90

No credit cards.

Landeck

Camping Riffler

Bruggenfeldstrasse 2, A-6500 Landeck (Tirol) T: 054 426 4898. E: lorenz.schimpfoessl@aon.at

alanrogers.com/AU0150

This very friendly 35 pitch site has easy access from the A12/E60 Arlberg-Innsbruck autobahn and being in a small town with numerous supermarkets, restaurants and bars makes it a good stopover point as well as a comfortable base from which to tour this interesting region through which the Via Claudia Augusta, the Roman route linking Venice with Germany, once passed. The pitches (40-70 sq.m) are grassed, accessed by hard roads and all have 10A electricity. Established by the present owners in 1956, much care and attention has gone into a fairly small plot, but there are no on-site refreshments or activities.

Facilities

The small toilet block has been rebuilt to a good standard. Washing machine and spin dryer. Fridge for campers' use. Ski and boot storage. Small general room with TV. Fishing. Off site: Bicycle hire and swimming pool 500 m. Reschen (just down the glorious Via Claudia valley) and Arlberg mountain passes within easy driving distance. Lots of walking. Mountain biking. Paragliding. Rafting (including family rafting on the quieter stretches). Canyoning.

Open: All year excl. May.

Directions

Site is at the western end of Landeck. Take exit for Landeck-West from the A12 and turn right towards Landeck. Site is on the left after the roundabout. It is situated beside a shopping area. GPS: 47.14253, 10.56124

Charges guide

Per unit incl. 2 persons	
and electricity	€ 22.80 - € 33.70
extra person	€ 5.70 - € 8.30

No credit cards.

FREE Alan Rogers Travel Card
Extra benefits and savings - see page 14

Längenfeld

Camping Ötztal Längenfeld

Unterlangenfeld 220, A-6444 Längenfeld (Tirol) T: 052 535 348. E: info@camping-oetztal.com

alanrogers.com/AU0045

Camping Ötztal Längenfeld, a family run site, is situated some 400 metres from the pretty village of Längenfeld, at the edge of a forest. Next door are the local sports centre and swimming pool, and a restaurant. In summer, the campsite is ideal for walking and cycling, as well as mountaineering tours. In the winter you can enjoy cross-country skiing right from the doorstep and a free bus shuttle operates to the Ötztal Ski arena. The site provides 200 level grass pitches of which 150 are for tourers. All pitches have electricity and 100 also have gas, water, drainage and a TV point.

Facilities

Excellent sanitary facilities include four bathrooms to rent for private use. Baby room. Facilities for disabled visitors. Female hairdressing room. Dog shower. Washing machines and dryer. Ski room. Motorcaravan services. Restaurant serves breakfast and takeaway. Sauna and solarium. WiFi. Off site: Sports centre and swimming pool adjacent (reduced prices for campers). Längenfeld and Aqua Dome thermal spa facility. Bicycle hire 500 m.

Open: All year.

Directions

From A12 take exit 123 and follow 186 along Ötztal Valley towards Sölden for 20 km. On entering Längenfeld, continue up hill into town and shortly after tourist information office on right there are signs for site. Enter through yard and follow lane past sports centre to entrance. GPS: 47.07229, 10.96431

Charges guide

Per unit incl. 2 persons and electricity (plus meter)	€ 22.40 - € 31.80
extra person	€ 6.40 - € 7.80

No credit cards.

Lienz

Campingplatz Seewiese

Tristachersee 2, A-9900 Lienz-Tristach (Tirol) T: 048 526 9767. E: seewiese@hotmail.com

alanrogers.com/AU0185

High above the village of Tristach and 5 km. from Lienz, this is a perfect location for a peaceful and relaxing holiday or as a base for exploring the Dolomite region. Situated amongst giant conifers and surrounded by snow-capped mountains, the site offers everyone a view of the volcanic Lake Tristachsee. The 110 pitches all have 6A electricity (long leads necessary for some) and 14 pitches for motorcaravans near reception each have electricity, water and drainage. Caravans are sited on a gently sloping field which has level areas although pitches are unmarked and unnumbered. At the bottom of this field is the lake which is used for swimming.

Facilities

Toilet facilities are clean, heated and modern with free showers. No facilities for disabled visitors. Washing machines and dryers. Motorcaravan services. Shop (July/Aug). Excellent restaurant/bar (1/6-1/9). Small play area. WiFi (charged). Swimming in adjoining lake. Lakeside games field. Off site: The historic town of Lienz 5 km. Plenty of things to do in the area (information found in a copy of the Osttirol brochure supplied to all visitors).

Open: 20 May - 14 September.

Directions

Site is 5 km. east of Lienz. Take the B100 and the B318. 1.5 km. past Tristach, turn right (signed) and climb the steep (1:10) hill for 1 km. to the site. GPS: 46.80601, 12.80307

Charges guide

Per unit incl. 2 persons and electricity	€ 30.00 - € 34.50
extra person	€ 8.00

No credit cards.

Lienz

Dolomiten-Camping Amlacher Hof

Seestraße 20, A-9908 Amlach (Tirol) T: 048 526 62317. E: info@amlacherhof.at

alanrogers.com/AU0186

The small hamlet of Amlach is south of the busy town of Lienz, in the eastern Tirol, and is surrounded by mountain peaks. Dolomiten-Camping is located around the old Amlacher Hof, a former manor house and hotel. Restoration of the villa is almost complete, but parts of the campsite still need attention. The camping areas are pleasant and peaceful, but other parts are somewhat unkempt. The surrounding area and views are very attractive. There are 84 level and numbered pitches, all with 16A electricity, and many with water and drainage to hand. A kitchen and toilets for disabled visitors are behind the villa in a modern building, with all other facilities in the basement of the villa.

Facilities

Modern sanitary facilities with ample and clean toilets, hot showers (token) and washbasins. Facilities for disabled campers. Washing machines and dryers. Kitchen facilities. Motorcaravan services. Bar and takeaway (1/5-30/9). Small swimming pool (1/5-30/9). Play areas. Minigolf. Games/TV room. WiFi over site (charged). Bicycle hire. Off site: Riding stables adjacent. Fishing 200 m.

Open: 15 December - 31 October.

Directions

The small hamlet of Amlach is 2 km. south of Lienz. You need to turn south at traffic lights near railway station, go under the railway and over the river then straight on to site. GPS: 46.81338, 12.76328

Charges guide

Per unit incl. 2 persons and electricity	€ 18.70 - € 23.40
extra person	€ 4.60 - € 5.90

Camping Cheques accepted.

For latest campsite news, availability and prices visit

alanrogers.com

Nassereith

Romantik Camping Schloss Fernsteinsee

Am Fernpass Tirol, A-6465 Nassereith (Tirol) T: 052 655 210. E: hotel@fernsteinsee.at

alanrogers.com/AU0225

This is a secluded, attractive woodland site in a sheltered location in the protected area of the Fernstein Lakes and part of the Schloss Fernsteinsee estate. There are 100 pitches for touring units, 80 of which have 4/13A electricity, and 39 also have water and drainage. The pitches are on slightly sloping grass in front of the reception and services building, on four shallow terraces divided by low rails or shrubs. A new area with flat, gravel pitches and all services has been developed in the lower part of the site. There is plenty of shade here and it provides a most relaxing atmosphere in natural surroundings.

Facilities
Modern heated facilities with a generous supply of controllable hot showers, washbasins (open style and in cabins) and facilities for disabled visitors. Laundry room. Boules. Small playground. Games/TV room. Football field. Volleyball court. Drinks machine. Communal barbecue facility. Sauna and solarium. Fishing and boating on the lake (500 m). WiFi (charged). Off site: Hotel with bar and restaurant 500 m. right by a busy main road. Nassereith village, shops and indoor swimming pool 1.5 km.

Open: 1 May - 15 October.

Directions
Leave A12 at exit 132. From Imst take road 189 north for 13 km, then left on road 179 and continue past Nassereith. Follow Fern Pass signs on 179 and watch for green signs to site, then take tarmac entry road. GPS: 47.342318, 10.81565

Charges guide
Per unit incl. 2 persons	€ 27.00 - € 34.00
extra person	€ 4.00 - € 5.00
child (5-15 yrs)	€ 3.00
dog	€ 2.00

Pettneu am Arlberg

Arlberg Panorama Camping

Dorfstrasse 58c, A-6574 Pettneu am Arlberg (Tirol) T: 054 488 352. E: info@arlberg-panoramacamping.at

alanrogers.com/AU0025

Owned and run by the Grobner family, this informal little site nestles between wooded mountains with wonderful views along the valley. A crystal clear mountain stream runs down along one side. There are 40 touring pitches on a level terrace overlooking grassy meadows. They vary in size, all have electricity and easy access to water (heated in winter) and five also have drainage and TV points. The main service can be found on the upper terrace, but due to the steep access, it is not suitable for disabled visitors. A ski and boot hire centre is attached to the site, making it a very popular winter destination.

Facilities
Heated sanitary facilities in the main block are clean and well maintained. Showers token operated. Indoor sinks for dishwashing. Washing machine and dryer. No shop but bread, milk and essentials available to order. Cosy bar with limited menu, snacks and takeaway. Large drying room for ski clothing and equipment. Ski and boot hire and maintenance. Games room and TV room with library and children's games. Large indoor caravan storage garage. Water supply to pitches is heated in winter. WiFi over site (small charge).

Open: All year.

Directions
From the A12/S16 take the L68 for 6.5 km. towards Pettneu. On arriving at the village, keep left at the chapel. The entrance to the site is signed in 100 m. on the left, by the fire station. GPS: 47.14802, 10.34646

Charges guide
Per unit incl. 2 persons and electricity (plus meter)	€ 18.50 - € 30.50
extra person	€ 5.00 - € 8.50
child (0-14 yrs)	free - € 6.00

No credit cards. Prices higher in winter.

Pettneu am Arlberg

Camping Arlberg

A-6574 Pettneu am Arlberg (Tirol) T: 054 482 22660. E: info@camping-arlberg.at

alanrogers.com/AU0055

This is an unusual site, located alongside, and lower than, the S16 autobahn, just a few kilometres to the east of the 13 km. long Arlberg tunnel. Inevitably there is some traffic noise. The site is unusual because it offers 145 pitches that are provided with an on-pitch wooden cabin housing the sanitary facilities, TV connection and 16A electricity. The grass and hardcore pitches are of medium size, fairly level and offer some views of the surrounding mountains. The other 40 pitches are near the reception building and offer electricity with a pre-payment meter only (€ 1 coins).

Facilities
145 private bathrooms in wooden cabins, electrically heated with WC, washbasin and shower (electricity is metered). Motorcaravan services. Shop. Bar. Restaurant. Indoor pool. Spa. Play area. Fishing. Bicycle hire. WiFi throughout (charged). Off site: Pettneu, swimming pool and the Tirol. Skiing; ski bus operates in the season. Golf and riding 10 km.

Open: 4 December - 30 April and 10 June - 15 October.

Directions
From S16 (B316) take exit to Pettneu (not St Anton). Just at the end of the slip road between a swimming complex and a play area is the site entrance. If travelling to Pettneu on L68, access is best from marked turning to west of the village. GPS: 47.14495, 10.3388

Charges guide
Per unit incl. 2 persons and electricity	€ 23.00 - € 42.00

No credit cards.

Natters

Ferienparadies Natterer See

Natterer See 1, A-6161 Natters (Tirol) T: 051 254 6732. E: info@natterersee.com

alanrogers.com/AU0060

In a quiet location arranged around two lakes and set amidst beautiful alpine scenery, this site founded in 1930 is renowned as one of Austria's top sites. Over the last few years many improvements have been carried out and pride of place goes to the innovative, award-winning, multifunctional building at the entrance to the site. This contains all of the sanitary facilities expected of a top site, including a special section for children, private bathrooms to rent and also a dog bath. The reception, shop, café/bar/bistro and cinema are on the ground floor, and on the upper floor is a panoramic lounge. Almost all of the 235 pitches are for tourers. They are terraced, set on gravel/grass, all have electricity and most offer a splendid view of the mountains. The site's lakeside restaurant with bar and large terrace has a good menu and is the ideal place to spend the evening. With a bus every hour and the city centre only 19 minutes away this is also a good site from which to visit Innsbruck. The Innsbruck Card is available at reception and allows free bus transport in the city, including a sightseeing tour, free entry to museums and one cable car trip.

Facilities

The large sanitary block has underfloor heating, some private cabins, plus excellent facilities for babies, children and disabled visitors. Laundry facilities. Motorcaravan services. Fridge box hire. Bar. Restaurant and takeaway with at least one open all year. Pizzeria. Good shop. Playgrounds. Children's activity programme. Day nursery (high season). Sports field. Archery. Youth room with games, pool and billiards. TV room with Sky. Open-air cinema. Mountain bike hire. Aquapark (1/5-30/9). Surf bikes and pedaloes. Canoes and mini sailboats for rent. Fishing. Extensive daily entertainment programme (mid May-mid Oct). No dogs in high season. WiFi (charged).

Open: All year.

Directions

From Inntal autobahn (A12) take Brenner autobahn (A13) as far as Innsbruck-sud/Natters exit (no. 3). Turn left by Shell petrol station onto B182 to Natters. At roundabout take first exit and immediately right again and follow signs to site 4 km. Do not use sat nav for final approach to site, follow camping signs. GPS: 47.23755, 11.34201

Charges guide

Per unit incl. 2 persons	
and electricity	€ 28.85 - € 49.85
extra person	€ 6.30 - € 9.30
child (under 13 yrs)	€ 4.90 - € 6.70

Prutz

Aktiv-Camping Prutz Tirol

Pontlatzstrasse 22, A-6522 Prutz (Tirol) T: 054 722 648. E: info@aktiv-camping.at

alanrogers.com/AU0155

Aktiv-Camping is a long site which lies beside, but is fenced off from, the River Inn. The 115 touring pitches, mainly gravelled for motorcaravans, are on level ground and average 80 sq.m. They all have 6A electrical connections, adequate water points, and in the larger area fit together somewhat informally. As a result, the site can sometimes have the appearance of being quite crowded. This is an attractive area with many activities in both summer and winter for all age groups. You may well consider using this site not just as an overnight stop, but also for a longer stay.

Facilities

The sanitary facilities are of a very high standard, with private cabins and good facilities for disabled visitors. Baby room. Washing machine. Dog shower. Small shop (all year). Bar, restaurant and takeaway (15/5-30/9; Christmas to Easter). Play room. Ski room. Play area. Children's entertainment. Guided walks. Free shuttle bus to ski slopes. Bicycle hire. Slipway for canoes/kayaks. WiFi over site. Off site: Riding 1 km. Indoor pool at Feichten. Pilgrim's Church at Kaltenbrunn. Kaunertaler Glacier.

Open: All year.

Directions

From E60/A12 exit at Landeck and follow the B315 (Reschenpass) turn south onto the B180 signed Bregenz, Arlberg, Innsbruck and Fern Pass for 11 km. to Prutz. Site is signed to the right from the B180 over the bridge. GPS: 47.08012, 10.6594

Charges guide

Per unit incl. 2 persons	
and electricity	€ 22.00 - € 31.60
extra person	€ 4.20 - € 7.50
child (5-17 yrs)	€ 3.00 - € 6.20
dog	€ 2.00 - € 3.50

For latest campsite news, availability and prices visit

alanrogers.com

full of life

Natterer See
★ ★ ★ ★ ★

The holiday paradise near Innsbruck

Tirol

Luxury Camping · Mobile Homes · Apartments · Guest Rooms

Restaurant with lakeside terrace · Pizzeria · Café-Bar-Bistro with lounge · Mini-Market
Ultra-modern sanitary facilities · Private family bathrooms · Children's bathrooms · Kid's Club
Entertainment program · Swimming lake with Aquapark · Deluxe panorama pitches up to 155m²

www.natterersee.com

Ferienparadies Natterer See
Natterer See I · A-6161 Natters/Tirol/Austria · Tel.+43 (0)512 / 54 67 32 · Fax +43 (0)512 / 54 67 32 -16
E-mail: info@natterersee.com

Seefeld

Camp Alpin Seefeld

Leutascherstrasse 810, A-6100 Seefeld (Tirol) T: 052 124 848. E: info@camp-alpin.at

alanrogers.com/AU0035

Camp Alpin Seefeld is a beautifully laid out, modern campsite with first class facilities in an attractive setting some 1,200 metres above sea level. With excellent views of the surrounding mountains and forests there are 140 large, individual pitches mainly on flat grass (plus a few hardstandings). All have 16A electricity, gas and TV connections (metered), with ten well placed water points. Some pitches at the back and edge of the site are terraced. This is a good base for both summer and winter activity, whether you wish to take a gentle stroll or participate in something more demanding, including skiing direct from the site.

Facilities

Excellent heated sanitary facilities include nine private bathrooms for hire, some private cabins. Washing machines and dryer. Sauna, Turkish bath and solarium. Sun bed cabin. Shop. Bar. Cosy restaurant with a limited menu and takeaway. Play area. Bicycle hire. Apartments to rent. Off site: Sports centre with heated indoor and outdoor pools and restaurant are nearby. The popular Tirolean village of Seefeld 1 km. Golf 1.5 km. Free shuttle to town centre.

Open: All year.

Directions

From the A12 motorway, take the 67 (87) exit to the B177, signed Seefeld (steep climb). Take slip road on right, signed Seefeld and Alpin Camping. Follow green signs through village to site. GPS: 47.33735, 11.1786

Charges guide

Per unit incl. 2 persons and electricity	€ 23.20 - € 45.80
extra person	€ 6.00 - € 11.50
child (3-14 yrs)	€ 3.00 - € 8.50

Umhausen

Camping Ötztal Arena

Mühlweg 32, A-6441 Umhausen (Tirol) T: 052 555 390. E: info@oetztal-camping.at

alanrogers.com/AU0220

This is a delightful site with lovely views, in the beautiful Ötz valley, on the edge of the village of Umhausen. Situated on a gentle slope in an open valley, with a river running along one side, it has an air of peace and tranquillity and makes an excellent base for mountain walking in spring, summer and autumn, skiing in winter or a relaxing holiday. The 98 pitches, some on individual terraces, are all marked and numbered and have 12A electrical connections; charges relate to the area available, long leads may be necessary. The reception building houses an attractive bar/restaurant, a TV room, a new, fully equipped sauna, solarium and gym and a ski drying room.

Facilities

With underfloor heating, open washbasins and showers on payment, the toilet facilities are of the highest quality. A small toilet/wash block at far end of site is used in summer. Baby room. Washing machine and dryer. Drying room. Motorcaravan services. Fridge hire. Bar/restaurant (May-Oct, Dec-March). No shop, but bread can be ordered at reception. Sauna. Solarium. TV room. Ski room. Fishing. Bicycle hire. Basic playground. Climbing wall. Dining hut with coffee machine. WiFi (charged).

Open: All year.

Directions

Site is 60 km. west of Innsbruck. Take Ötztal Valley exit 123 from Imst-Innsbruck A12 motorway, and Umhausen is 13 km. towards Solden on the B186; site is well signed to south of village (follow green camping signs NOT sat nav). Some signs say Camping Krismer. GPS: 47.13452, 10.93147

Charges guide

Per unit incl. 2 persons and electricity (plus meter)	€ 18.90 - € 21.60

No credit cards.

Volders

Schloss-Camping

A-6111 Volders (Tirol) T: 052 245 2333. E: info@schlosscamping.com

alanrogers.com/AU0080

The Inn valley is a very beautiful and popular part of Austria. Volders, some 15 km. from Innsbruck, is one of the little villages on the banks of the Inn river and is perhaps best known for its 17th-century Baroque Servite Church and monastery. It is home to the most attractive Schloss-Camping, overlooked by the castle from which it gets its name, and which towers at the back of the site with views of the mountains across the Inn valley. The 160 numbered grass pitches (80-100 sq.m) are on level or slightly sloping ground, with electricity connections throughout (16A, long leads may be necessary).

Facilities

New modern sanitary block to left of entrance has washbasins in cabins and facilities for disabled visitors. Laundry room. Motorcaravan services. New attractive bar/restaurant, snack bar with terrace (all open to public). Bread and milk available. Heated swimming pool (mid May-mid Sept). Playground. Games and entertainment for children (high season). Free WiFi over site. Off site: Supermarket 400 m. Bicycle hire 500 m.

Open: 1 May - 20 September.

Directions

From A12 motorway take exit 61 (Wattens) and follow B171 and signs for Volders. Pass Spar on right and site is signed to left. GPS: 47.28714, 11.57259

Charges guide

Per unit incl. 2 persons and electricity	€ 19.80 - € 25.40
extra person	€ 5.10 - € 7.20
child (3-14 yrs)	€ 3.20 - € 4.50
dog	€ 2.00 - € 2.50

Sölden

Camping Sölden

Wohlfahrtstrasse 22, A-6450 Sölden (Tirol) T: 052 542 6270. E: info@camping-soelden.com

alanrogers.com/AU0053

This campsite has been recommended to us and we plan to undertake an inspection. Camping Sölden is a well equipped family site located deep within the Ötztaler Alps, and open for both summer and winter seasons. This site celebrated its 50th anniversary in 2013. Pitches are grassy and are all equipped with electricity (10A), as well as TV and telephone connections. A number of caravans are available for rent. The site boasts an excellent spa/wellness centre with a Finnish sauna, steam bath, infra-red cabin and comfortable relaxation room. Spa facilities are free to campers during the winter season. Other amenities include an excellent 85 m. indoor climbing wall. Ötztal is a superb centre for active holidays in summer and winter. There are miles of waymarked trails for walkers and mountain bikers, and all manner of other activity sports are on offer in the area. This is an important winter sports destination with a wide range of amenities. Sölden is a delightful village with many good restaurants, cafés and shops. Further afield, Innsbruck is the region's capital and has plenty to offer the visitor.

Facilities

Heated sanitary facilities have some individual cabins and facilities for children and disabled visitors. Motorcaravan services. Washing machine and dryer. Shop. Fresh bread. Restaurant, pizzeria and takeaway. Spa and wellness centre. TV room. Play area. Bicycle hire. Caravans for rent. Fishing. WiFi over most of site (charged). Off site: Shops and restaurants in Sölden. Riding and skiing 200 m. Cycle and walking tracks. Golf. Innsbruck (80 km).

Open: All year excl. 15 April - 22 June and 23 September - 11 October.

Directions

Approaching from the north (Munich or Salzburg) take A93 to Kufstein, then A12 past Innsbruck to Ötztal. Head south on B186 for 35 km. to Sölden, and follow signs to the site.
GPS: 46.95785, 11.011933

Charges guide

Per unit incl. 2 persons	
and electricity (plus meter)	€ 23.00 - € 28.80
extra person	€ 6.90 - € 8.30
child (4-15 yrs)	€ 4.20 - € 5.80
dog	€ 3.00 - € 3.50

ÖTZ TAL · Campingeldorado Ötztal

ÖTZTAL ARENA CAMPING
6441 Umhausen
www.oetztal-camping.at

CAMPING ÖTZTAL längenfeld
6444 Längenfeld
www.camping-oetztal.com

ÖTZTALER NATURCAMPING
6444 Huben bei Längenfeld
www.oetztalernaturcamping.com

CAMPING SÖLDEN
6450 Sölden
www.camping-soelden.com

Weer

Alpencamping Mark

Bundesstrasse 12, A-6114 Weer bei Schwaz (Tirol) T: 052 246 8146. E: alpencampingmark@gmail.com

alanrogers.com/AU0250

This pleasant Tirol site is neat and friendly with family owners who offer a warm welcome and a variety of outdoor activities. Formerly a farm, they now breed horses, giving free horse and carriage rides to youngsters as well as organising mountain treks. Courses, run by qualified instructors, are available for individuals or groups in climbing (there are practice climbing walls on site), rafting, mountain biking, trekking, hiking, etc. Set in the Inn valley, with wonderful mountain views, the site has 96 flat, firm, grass pitches, all with 10A electrical connections (2-pin sockets). The site is close to the Inn Valley cycle track.

Facilities

Good quality, modern, heated sanitary facilities are provided in the old farm buildings. Washing machines and dryer. Freezer. Motorcaravan services. Shop (1/6-1/9). Small, cheerful bar/restaurant (1/6-1/9). Small heated pool (5/5-15/9). Free activity programme with instruction. Bicycle hire. Riding (free for children). Trekking for experienced riders. Glacier tours. Play area. Climbing wall. Barn for use by children in wet weather. WiFi over site (charged). Off site: Swarovski Kristallwelten 2 km.

Open: 1 April - 31 October.

Directions

Site is 20 km. east of Innsbruck. From A12 exit at junction 61 to Wattens, then east on B171, signed Schwaz. Site is 200 m. east of the village of Weer, on Wattens-Schwaz road no. B171. Look for the flags. GPS: 47.30663, 11.64925

Charges guide

Per unit incl. 2 persons and electricity	€ 17.70 - € 26.90
extra person	€ 4.50 - € 7.50
child (under 14 yrs)	€ 3.00 - € 5.00

Zell-am-Ziller

Campingdorf Hofer

Gerlosstrasse 33, A-6280 Zell-am-Ziller (Tirol) T: 052 822 248. E: info@campingdorf.at

alanrogers.com/AU0070

Zell-am-Ziller is in the heart of the Zillertal valley, about as far as is comfortable for caravans, and centred around an unusual 18th-century church noted for its paintings. Campingdorf Hofer, owned by the same family for over 50 years, is on the edge of the village, just five minutes walk from the centre, on a quiet side road. The 100 pitches, all with electricity (6A in summer, 16A in winter; watertight 2-pin adapters and long leads required) are grass on firm gravel. A few trees decorate the site and offer some shade. Adjoining the reception area are the bar/restaurant and terrace, games and TV room, a small heated pool with sliding cover, and a sun deck.

Facilities

Good quality, heated sanitary provision is on the ground floor of the apartment building and has some washbasins in cabins. Baby room. Washing machines and dryers. Gas supplies. Motorcaravan services. Restaurant with bar. Shop opposite. Swimming pool (1/4-31/10). Free activities in high season. Bicycle hire. Guided walks, cycle tours, barbecues, biking, skiing. Free ski bus service (every 20 mins). Ski room and ski boot dryer. Apartments to rent. B&B and half-board accommodation. WiFi over site (charged). Off site: Town and supermarket 300 m.

Open: All year.

Directions

Site is well signed from the main B169 road at Zell-am-Ziller. Site is at the southern end of town, close to the junction of the B169 and B165. GPS: 47.22862, 11.88603

Charges guide

Per unit incl. 2 persons and electricity (plus meter in winter)	€ 27.90 - € 36.50
extra person	€ 6.00 - € 8.70
child (under 14 yrs)	€ 3.70 - € 5.70

No credit cards (debit cards accepted).
Camping Cheques accepted.

Au an der Donau

Camping Au an der Donau

Hafenstrasse 1, A-4332 Au an der Donau (Upper Austria) T: 072 625 3090. E: info@camping-audonau.at

alanrogers.com/AU0332

You can be sure of a friendly welcome, in English, at this attractive site on the Danube cycle route. Reception, bar, restaurant and flowered terrace are located on the dam top from where there are views of the Danube and surrounding countryside – an ideal place to try out the local drink, cider, and home smoked trout. The 45 touring pitches are in a protected area behind the dam, all with 13A electricity, and a separate area accommodates 30 tents; each area has its own well maintained sanitary facility. The pitches are grassy and separated by hedges.

Facilities

Two modern sanitary units, with hot water, free controllable showers and facilities for disabled visitors. Laundry room with washing machine and dryer. Motorcaravan services. Small bar/restaurant (1/5-15/9) serving local specialities (breakfast and fresh bread available). Playground. Regular entertainment on site's own stage. Access to Danube beach and small motorboat to hire. Small boat (Tille) on lake (free). Bicycle hire. Barbecue and campfire areas. Free WiFi over site.

Open: 1 April - 15 October.

Directions

Site is 20 km. east of Linz. From Autobahn 1, take Asten or St Valentin exit and head for Mauthausen. Follow signs for Au an der Donau where site is well signed. It is the orange building on top of the dam. GPS: 48.227778, 14.57912

Charges guide

Per unit incl. 2 persons and electricity	€ 29.00
extra person	€ 8.00
child (4-14 yrs)	€ 4.00

No credit cards.

For latest campsite news, availability and prices visit

alanrogers.com

Mondsee

Camping MondSeeLand

Punzau 21, A-5310 Mondsee, Tiefgraben (Upper Austria) T: 062 322 600. E: austria@campmondsee.at

alanrogers.com/AU0350

MondSeeLand is a well established campsite that first opened in 1970. It is set in a delightful location and offers excellent facilities in a pleasant part of Austria, to the east of Salzburg, between the lakes of Mondsee and Irrsee. There are 60 good sized, level touring pitches (80 long stay), set amongst the trees at a lower level and on terraces, each with water, waste water and 16A electricity. The heated swimming pool is covered and has a sunbathing terrace. There is a small fishing lake (unfenced) and a small playground. During summer there is an entertainment programme for children. Good English is spoken.

Facilities

The sanitary facilities are in the reception and pool complex and offer first class facilities including some washbasins in cabins and a suite for disabled visitors. Laundry with washing machines and dryer. Kitchen with cooking and dishwashing. Motorcaravan services. Shop and restaurant. Swimming pool (free). Playground. Fishing and riding. WiFi over site (charged). Off site: Adjoining restaurant offers local and other dishes served in a traditional setting. Sailing 3 km. Golf 5 km.

Open: 1 April - 4 October.

Directions

From A1/E55 exit 264 (signed Straßwalchen) turn north onto B154. In 1.5 m. turn left at crossroads (by glassworks) and then 2 km. to site (signed). NB: signs can be difficult to spot. GPS: 47.86655, 13.306567

Charges guide

Per unit incl. 2 persons	
and electricity	€ 25.00 - € 27.50
extra person	€ 5.80 - € 6.40
child (6-15 yrs)	€ 4.10 - € 4.50

Nussdorf am Attersee

Seecamping Gruber

Dorfstrasse 63, A-4865 Nussdorf am Attersee (Upper Austria) T: 076 668 0450. E: office@camping-gruber.at

alanrogers.com/AU0345

The Attersee is the largest of a group of lakes just to the east of Salzburg, in the very attractive Salzkammergut area. Seecamping Gruber is a small, often crowded site halfway up the western side of the lake. There are 150 individual pitches, with an increasing number of seasonal units taking the larger pitches. There are some 70 pitches for tourers, all with 16A electricity and many with shade. Pitches tend to be small to medium size and the access roads are narrow making entrance and exit difficult.

Facilities

Modern sanitary facilities, now with a children's area, offer some private cabins, washing machine and dryer, good unit for disabled visitors, and baby room. Bar, restaurant, shop and takeaway (all 15/4-15/10). TV room. Play area. Swimming, paddling pools, sauna, solarium and gym (all 1/5-30/9). Fishing. Bicycle hire. Free WiFi over site. Accommodation to rent. Off site: Windsurfing and sailing, both with courses. Mountain bikes, diving and balloon rides all available locally. Tennis, golf, rambling, cycling and mountain bike tracks nearby.

Open: 15 April - 15 October.

Directions

From the A1/E55/E60 between Salzburg and Linz, take exit 243 to Attersee and then south on the B151 to Nussdorf. Site is on the southern edge of the village. GPS: 47.87965, 13.52444

Charges guide

Per unit incl. 2 persons	
and electricity	€ 21.00 - € 33.00
extra person	€ 5.50 - € 8.00
child (6-13 yrs)	€ 3.00 - € 6.00
dog	€ 2.50 - € 4.00

Obertraun

Camping Am See

Winkl 77, A-4831 Obertraun (Upper Austria) T: 061 312 65. E: camping.am.see@chello.at

alanrogers.com/AU0340

It is unusual to locate a campsite so deep in the heart of spectacular mountain scenery, yet with such easy access. Directly on the shores of Halstattersee, near Obertraun and the Dachstein range of mountains, this 2.5 hectare, flat site, with 70 pitches is an excellent, peaceful holiday base which has been upgraded. The grass site is basically divided into two, with tents in a shady area, whilst caravans and motorcaravans are more in the open. There are no specific pitches although the owners, within reason, control where you place your unit. At the time of our visit there were only 36 electricity hook-ups.

Facilities

Completely refurbished, fully equipped and modern, the toilet block includes a small baby room. Washing machine. Open barn-style area with purpose built barbecues, seating and tables. Bar and limited restaurant with hot meals and fine wines available to order. Basic daily provisions kept such as bread and milk. Small playground. Off site: Activities nearby include walking for all ages and abilities, birdwatching, fishing, mountain biking, rock climbing, scuba diving and much more.

Open: 1 May - 30 September.

Directions

Due south from Bad Ischl on road B145, take road B166 to Hallstatt. After single carriageway tunnel, site is 4 km. on left on entering village of Winkle. Note: Road is narrow in places so care is needed. GPS: 47.54897, 13.67422

Charges guide

Per unit incl. 2 persons	
and electricity	€ 29.90 - € 31.10
extra person	€ 7.80

No credit cards.

St Wolfgang

Camping Appesbach

Au 99, A-5360 St Wolfgang (Upper Austria) T: 061 382 206. E: camping@appesbach.at

alanrogers.com/AU0240

Saint Wolfgang, a pretty little village on the lake of the same name which was made famous by the operetta, White Horse Inn, is ringed by hills in a delightful situation. Camping Appesbach has an attractive lakeside location with a small boat jetty and offers views over this most attractive lake. The site has 170 pitches, with 100 for touring units (including 20 tent pitches), with some in regular rows and the rest on open meadows that could become full in high season. Pitches near the lakeside have higher charges. All have electricity (10A) with a mix of German and European sockets.

Facilities

The two toilet blocks have been combined into one, extended and refurbished to a good standard. Motorcaravan services. Good shop. Bar (1/5-31/8). Restaurant with TV (Easter-30/9). Snack bar with terrace (Easter-30/9). Small playground. WiFi. Off site: Tennis nearby. Village 1 km. Many excursions possible including Salzburg 50 km.

Open: Easter - 31 October.

Directions

Site is 30 km. east-southeast of Salzburg. From B158 Salzburg-Bad Ischl road, just east of Stobl turn north to St Wolfgang. Site is on the left 1 km. before St Wolfgang. GPS: 47.73254, 13.463756

Charges guide

Per person	€ 4.90 - € 6.40
pitch acc. to position and size of unit	€ 5.00 - € 14.50
electricity	€ 3.30

Wien

Aktiv Camping Wien Neue Donau

Am Kaisermuhlendamm 119, A-1220 Wien-Ost (Vienna) T: 012 024 010. E: neuedonau@campingwien.at

alanrogers.com/AU0302

This is a very good site from which to visit Vienna. It is easily accessible from the autobahn system and the city centre is quickly reached from the site by the efficient Vienna U-bahn system, line U2; tickets for which can be purchased at reception. There is some traffic and train noise as is found on most city sites. With 254 level touring pitches with electricity and a further 12 with water and drainage, the site has a large and changing population. The site is close to the Donauinsel, a popular recreation area. The Neue Donau (New Danube), a 20 km. long artificial side arm of the Danube provides swimming, sports and play areas, while the Danube bicycle trail runs past the site. This is a useful location for an overnight stop or a short break to visit old Vienna and the Danube.

Facilities

Modern toilet facilities are clean, and well maintained with free showers. Facilities for disabled visitors. Washing machines and dryers. Motorcaravan services. Campers' kitchen with cooking facilities, fridges, freezers and TV. Shop. Small restaurant. Play area. Barbecue areas. Bicycle hire and free guided bicycle tours. WiFi. Off site: Vienna city centre 5 km. Prater Park 1 km.

Open: Easter - 15 September.

Directions

Site is close to the A23 and A22. From A23 heading east turn off at first exit after crossing the Donau (signed Lobau). At first traffic lights, near Shell station, turn left and after 200 m. turn right into site. GPS: 48.20848, 16.44733

Charges guide

Per unit incl. 2 persons and electricity	€ 25.50 - € 34.00
extra person	€ 6.50 - € 7.50
child (5-14 yrs)	€ 4.00 - € 5.00

Wien

Camping Wien West

Hüttelbergstrasse 80, A-1140 Wien (Vienna) T: 019 142 314. E: west@campingwien.at

alanrogers.com/AU0306

Opera, classical music, museums, shopping and the Danube; whatever it is you want in Vienna you are spoilt for choice. Wien West is an all-year-round site with good transport links to the city centre. It is the parent site of Wien Sud and Neue Donau and is inevitably busier. The site is located on the edge of the Vienna Woods with direct access to walking and mountain bike trails. There are 202 level and numbered pitches, all with 13A electricity. Buses to the metro stop right outside the gates and you can be in the centre in 35 minutes.

Facilities

Three modern toilet blocks provide ample and clean toilets, hot showers and washbasins. Washing machine and dryer. Kitchen facilities. Motorcaravan services. Small shop for essentials, bar and restaurant (all 15/4-1/10). Games room. Playground. Bicycle hire. WiFi (free) and Internet point. Off site: Vienna centre 8 km. Schönbrunn palace. Bicycle and walking trails. Tennis.

Open: All year excl. February.

Directions

From the city centre follow signs to autobahn west and Linz. Site is well signed from the main roads. Coming from the A1 (Salzburg-Vienna) drive over the Bergmillergasse (bridge). Stay on this road to Huttelbergstraße after the first traffic lights. GPS: 48.21433, 16.25018

Charges guide

Per unit incl. 2 persons and electricity	€ 25.50 - € 31.50
extra person	€ 6.50 - € 7.50

For latest campsite news, availability and prices visit

alanrogers.com

Nenzing

Alpencamping Nenzing

Garfrenga 1, A-6710 Nenzing (Vorarlberg) T: 055 256 2491. E: office@alpencamping.at

alanrogers.com/AU0010

LeadingCampings

Only a short drive from the A14 autobahn, Alpencamping is a well run and comfortable, all-year-round site, set in a natural bowl from which there are splendid mountain views. All 165 level pitches are for touring with 16A electricity; 105 also have fresh and waste water, gas, TV and telephone connections. Most are set on neat terraces. At the centre of the site is the well appointed restaurant, built in a traditional style with lots of atmosphere and its tables lit by lamps hanging on meter long ropes attached to beams in the massive wooden roof. The restaurant with its bar and terrace understandably attracts a lot of local custom and can be quite busy at weekends. A member of Leading Campings group.

Facilities
The newer facilities are state of the art and have 20 private bathrooms (some free, others for rent). The two older blocks still provide good facilities. Excellent washroom for children. Baby room. Facilities for disabled visitors. Motorcaravan services. Small shop. Bar. Restaurant with terrace. New heated indoor and outdoor swimming complex. Paddling pool. Small play area with another larger one on the top terrace. Practice climbing wall. Sauna, solarium, massage room. WiFi over site (charged).

Open: All year excl. week after Easter - 1 May.

Directions
Site is 15 km. southeast of Feldkirk. From the E60, A12/14 Bregenz-Innsbruck motorway take exit 50 for Nenzing (green camping sign) on B190 road and then follow small green camping signs which have the site's butterfly logo. GPS: 47.18233, 9.68227

Charges guide
Per unit incl. 2 persons	€ 19.00 - € 35.90
extra person	€ 6.50 - € 9.50
child (acc. to age)	€ 5.00 - € 7.00
electricity per kWh	€ 0.65

Nüziders

Panorama Camping Sonnenberg

Hinteroferst 12, A-6714 Nüziders bei Bludenz (Vorarlberg) T: 055 526 4035. E: sonnencamp@aon.at

alanrogers.com/AU0232

A friendly welcome awaits at this well equipped, family run site delightfully located at the junction of five Alpine valleys. From this hillside site there are magnificent, ever-changing views along and across the mountains. Very easily reached from the A14 autobahn and located on the outskirts of a large village with all facilities, the site is not only ideal as a stopover but also as a base from which to tour in this spectacular alpine region. All of the 120 generously sized, terraced pitches have 13A electricity, 60 are fully serviced and most are hard enough for motorcaravans. Two terraces for caravans are car free with a separate car parking area.

Facilities
A superb new building contains high quality facilities. On the lower floor are WCs, spacious hot showers, and washbasins (some in cubicles), and a baby room. No facilities for disabled visitors. Drying room, laundry and dishwashing room upstairs. Motorcaravan services. Small shop (break to order). Gas supplies. TV and cinema room with tourist information. Playground. Only one dog per unit is allowed. WiFi over site (charged). Two chalets to rent. Off site: Village with shops and ATM 500 m. Free entrance to the large outdoor swimming pool, Val Blu 3 km.

Open: 1 May - 27 September.

Directions
Nüziders is 25 km. southeast of Feldkirch. From A14 exit 57 (Bludenz-Nüziders) turn north on road 190 and left at roundabout into village. Follow green camping signs through village turning right at church then fork left to site. GPS: 47.170147, 9.807677

Charges guide
Per unit incl. 2 persons and electricity	€ 20.00 - € 31.00
extra person	€ 6.00 - € 7.50
child (2-17 yrs)	free - € 4.00

No credit cards.

Raggal

Camping Grosswalsertal

Plazera 21, A-6741 Raggal (Vorarlberg) T: 055 532 09. E: info@camping-austria.info

alanrogers.com/AU0015

Climbing up the newly rebuilt road alongside the green valley, we reach the pretty village of Raggal. Grosswalsertal lies just beyond the village on a small plateau. From almost every pitch there are the most fantastic views down the valley. On open grass, there are 55 slightly sloping, un-numbered and unmarked pitches all with 16A electricity. Plenty of sporting activities are available locally and there are many places to visit, as well as walks and bike rides in the immediate area. Alternatively, just rest on the site and watch the clouds roll by. The site is very popular with Dutch visitors.

Facilities
The modern sanitary block has ample and clean toilets, hot showers and washbasins. Washing machine and dryer. Small shop with essential supplies. Swimming pool (1/6-15/9). Play area. Bicycle hire. WiFi over site (charged). Off site: Fishing and riding 2 km. Golf 14 km.

Open: 1 May - 30 September.

Directions
From the A14 take exit 57 for Nuziders and follow signs to 193 and Ludesch. Turn right towards Raggal and site is on the left, just past the village. GPS: 47.21585, 9.8537

Charges guide
Per unit incl. 2 persons and electricity	€ 20.00 - € 23.00

No credit cards.

Belgium

A small country divided into three regions, Flanders in the north, Wallonia in the south and Brussels the capital. Belgium is rich in scenic countryside, culture and history, notably the great forest of Ardennes, the historic cities of Bruges and Gent, and the western coastline with its sandy beaches.

Brussels is at the very heart of Europe and is a must-see destination with its heady mix of shops, bars, nightlife, exhibitions and festivals – a multi-cultural and multi-lingual city that is a focal point of art, fashion and culture. In the French-speaking region of Wallonia lies the mountainous Ardennes, home to picturesque villages rich in tradition and folklore. It is a favourite of nature-lovers and walkers who enjoy exploring its many castles and forts.

The safe, sandy beaches on the west coast run for forty miles. The cosmopolitan resort of Ostend with its yacht basin and harbour offers year round attractions including a carnival weekend and a Christmas market, and the myriad seafood restaurants will suit every taste. Bruges is Europe's best preserved medieval city, criss-crossed by willow-lined canals, where tiny cobbled streets open onto pretty squares. After visiting the many museums and art galleries, why not sample some of the delicious chocolate for which the city is famous.

CAPITAL: Brussels

Tourist Office

Belgian Tourist Office Brussels & Wallonia,
Unit 6, Cumbrian House,
217 Marsh Wall, London E14 9FJ
Tel: 020 7537 1132 Fax: 020 7531 0393
Email: info@belgiumtheplaceto.be
Internet: www.belgiumtheplaceto.be

Tourism Flanders-Brussels,
Flanders House, 1a Cavendish Square,
London W1G 0LD
Tel: 020 7307 7738
Email: info@visitflanders.co.uk

Population
11 million

Climate
Temperate climate similar to Britain.

Language
There are three official languages. French
is spoken in the south, Flemish in the north,
and German is the predominant language in the
eastern provinces.

Telephone
The country code is 00 32.

Money
Currency: The Euro
Banks: Mon-Fri 09.00-15.30.
Some banks open Sat 09.00-12.00.

Shops
Mon-Sat 09.00-17.30/18.00 – later on Thurs/Fri;
closed Sundays.

Public Holidays
New Year's Day; Easter Mon; Labour Day;
Ascension; Whit Monday; Flemish Day
11 July; National Day 21 July; Assumption
15 Aug; French Day 27 Sept; All Saints
1, 2 Nov; Armistice Day 11 Nov; King's Birthday
15 Nov; Christmas 25, 26 Dec.

Motoring
For cars with a caravan or trailer, motorways are
toll free except for the Liefenshoek Tunnel in
Antwerp. Maximum permitted overall length of
vehicle/trailer or caravan combination is 18 m.
Blue Zone parking areas exist in Brussels, Ostend,
Bruges, Liège, Antwerp and Gent. Parking discs
can be obtained from police stations, garages,
and some shops.

see campsite map 1

Gierle

Camping De Lilse Bergen

Strandweg 6, Gierle, B-2275 Lille (Antwerp) T: 014 557 901. E: info@lilsebergen.be

alanrogers.com/BE0655

This attractive, quietly located holiday site has 513 shady pitches, of which 238 (all with 10A Europlug electricity) are for touring units. Set on sandy soil among pine trees and rhododendrons and arranged around a large lake, the site has a Mediterranean feel. It is well fenced, with a night guard and comprehensive, well labelled, fire-fighting equipment. Cars are parked away from units. The site is really child friendly with each access road labelled with a different animal symbol to enable children to find their own unit easily. An entertainment programme is organised in high season. The lake has marked swimming and diving areas (for adults), a sandy beach, an area for watersports, plus a separate children's pool complex (depth 50 cm) with a most imaginative playground. There are lifeguards and the water meets Blue Flag standards. A building by the lake houses changing rooms, extra toilets, showers and a baby room. There are picnic areas and lakeside and woodland walks.

Facilities

One of the six heated toilet blocks has been fully refitted to a good standard. Some washbasins in cubicles and good hot showers (on payment). Well equipped baby rooms. Facilities for disabled campers. Laundry. Barrier keys can be charged up with units for operating showers, washing machine etc. First aid post. Motorcaravan services. Restaurant (all year, weekends only in winter), takeaway and well stocked shop (Easter-15/9; weekends only). Tennis. Minigolf. Boules. Climbing wall. Playground, trampolines and skateboard ramp. Pedalos, kayaks and bicycles for hire. Children's electric cars and pedal kart tracks (charged). Free WiFi over site. Off site: Golf 1 km.

Open: All year.

Directions

From E34 Antwerp-Eindhoven take exit 22. On the roundabout take the exit for De Lilse Bergen and follow forest road to site entrance.
GPS: 51.28908, 4.85508

Charges guide

Per unit incl. 4 persons and electricity	€ 20.00 - € 26.50
dog	€ 4.50

Lichtaart

Camping Floreal Kempen

Herentalsesteenweg 64, B-2460 Lichtaart (Antwerp) T: 014 556 120. E: kempen@florealgroup.be

alanrogers.com/BE0665

This is an attractive woodland site and a member of the Floreal group. It is located close to the well known Purperen Heide, a superb nature reserve with 15 scenic footpaths leading through it. There are 228 pitches, of which only 32 are reserved for touring units. These are of a good size (100 sq.m. or more), all with 16A electricity and most with their own water supply. Two simple cabins are available for hikers, as well as fully equipped mobile homes. There are some good leisure facilities, including tennis and a multisports pitch, as well as a popular bar and restaurant.

Facilities

Three modern, heated toilet blocks are well equipped with some washbasins in cabins and have facilities for disabled visitors. Hairdryer. Laundry facilities. Motorcaravan services. Washing machine. Bar. Restaurant. TV room. Tennis. Play area. Multisports terrain. Pétanque. Bicycle hire. Mobile homes for rent (one adapted for disabled users). Free WiFi over site. Off site: Walking and cycling tracks. Golf. Antwerp. Bobbejaanlaand amusement park.

Open: All year.

See advertisement on pg 69.

Directions

Approaching from Antwerp, head east on A21/E34 motorway as far as exit 24 (Turnhout). Leave here and head south on N19 to Kasterlee, and then west on N123 to Lichtaart. Follow signs to the site.
GPS: 51.21136, 4.90298

Charges guide

Per unit incl. 2 persons	€ 13.95 - € 19.90
extra person	€ 4.70
child (3-11 yrs)	€ 3.30
dog (max. 1)	€ 3.80

For latest campsite news, availability and prices visit

alanrogers.com

Sint-Job-in't-Goor

Camping Floreal Het Veen

Eekhoornlaan 1, B-2960 Sint-Job-in't-Goor (Antwerp) T: 036 361 327. E: het.veen@florealgroup.be

alanrogers.com/BE0650

Floreal Het Veen can be found 20 km. north of Antwerp in a woodland area, and has many sports facilities. There are 305 marked pitches (65 for touring units) on level grass, most with some shade and 10A electricity (long leads in some places) and also five hardstandings. Amenities include an indoor sports hall (hourly charge), while tennis courts, football, basketball and softball are outside. Good cycling and walking opportunities exist in the area. English is spoken. The site is alongside a canal with good cycle and walking routes.

Facilities

Four spacious toilet blocks include a few washbasins in cubicles (only two are close to touring pitches). Facilities for disabled visitors. Laundry facilities. Motorcaravan services. Shop. Restaurant, bar, café and takeaway (daily July/Aug. weekends only at other times). Tennis. Badminton. Boules. Playgrounds. Children's entertainment in season. Fishing. Canoeing. Bicycle hire. WiFi (free). Wooden chalets for rent. Off site: Riding and golf 8 km.

Open: All year.

See advertisement on pg 69.

Directions

Sint-Job-in't-Goor is northeast of Antwerp. From A1 (E19) exit 4, turn southeast towards Sint-Job-in't-Goor, straight on at traffic lights and, immediately after canal bridge, turn left at campsite sign. Continue straight on for 1.5 km. to site.
GPS: 51.30513, 4.58622

Charges guide

Per unit incl. 2 persons and electricity	€ 17.45 - € 23.40
extra person	€ 4.70

Turnhout

Camping Baalse Hei

Roodhuisstraat 10, B-2300 Turnhout (Antwerp) T: 014 448 470. E: info@baalsehei.be

alanrogers.com/BE0660

The Campine is an area covering three quarters of the Province of Antwerp, noted for its nature reserves, pine forests, meadows and streams and is ideal for walking and cycling, while Turnhout itself is an interesting old town. Baalse Hei, a long established, friendly site, has 469 pitches including a separate touring area of 71 large grass pitches (all with 16A electricity, TV connections and shared water point), thoughtfully developed with trees and bushes. Cars are parked away from, but near the pitches. Large motorcaravans can be accommodated (phone first to check availability). There is also accommodation to rent. It is 100 m. from the edge of the field to the modern, heated, sanitary building. There is a small lake for swimming with a beach, a boating lake and a large fishing lake (on payment). Entertainment and activities are organised in July and August. Follow the walking trails in the woods (and you will undoubtedly come across some of the many red squirrels) and the nature reserves, or take the pleasant 1.5 km. riverside walk to the next village.

Facilities

Three toilet blocks provide hot showers on payment (€ 0.50), some washbasins in cabins and facilities for disabled visitors. Dishwashing (hot water € 0.20). Launderette. Motorcaravan services. Shop (1/4-30/9). Café/restaurant (daily 1/4-30/9, w/ends only other times, closed 16/11-25/1). Breakfast served in high season. Club/TV room. Lake swimming. Fishing. Tennis. Boules. Volleyball. Basketball. Adventure play area. Bicycle hire. English is spoken. Overnight pitches for vehicles under 3.5t. In low season reception opens for limited hours (14.00-17.00). WiFi over site (free). Off site: Riding 1.5 km.

Open: 16 January - 15 December.

Directions

Site is northeast of Turnhout off the N119. Approaching from Antwerp on E34/A12 take Turnhout ring road to the end (not a complete ring) and turn right. There is a small site sign to right in 1.5 km. then a country lane.
GPS: 51.35757, 4.95896

Charges guide

Per unit incl. 2 persons and electricity	€ 19.00 - € 25.00
dog	€ 1.50

Visa cards accepted.

FREE Alan Rogers Travel Card
Extra benefits and savings - see page 14

Grimbergen

Camping Grimbergen

Veldkantstraat 64, B-1850 Grimbergen (Brabant) T: 022 709 597. E: camping.grimbergen@telenet.be

alanrogers.com/BE0630

A popular little site with a friendly atmosphere, Camping Grimbergen has 90 pitches on fairly level grass, of which around 50 have 10A electricity. The site is not really suitable for large units, although some hardstandings for motorcaravans have been added. The municipal sports facilities are adjacent and the site is well placed for visiting Brussels. The bus station is by the traffic lights at the junction of N202 and N211 and buses run into the city centre every hour, 200 m. from the site, excluding Sunday mornings. In Grimbergen itself visit Norbertine Abbey, Saint Servaas church, and the Sunday morning market.

Facilities

Immaculate new sanitary facilities are heated in colder months. Separate facilities for disabled visitors. Motorcaravan services. Shop (with milk and bread) and bar (July/Aug). Off site: Restaurant 100 m. Fishing 2 km. Riding 5 km.

Open: 1 April - 25 October.

Directions

From Brussels ring road take exit 7 (N202) to Grimbergen. After 2.5 km, turn right at lights on N211 towards Vilvoorde (site signed), then left at second set of lights (slight oblique turn). Entrance is on right in 500 m. GPS: 50.93486, 4.38257

Charges guide

Per unit incl. 2 persons and electricity	€ 23.00
extra person	€ 5.50

No credit cards.

Deinze

Camping Groeneveld

Groenevelddreef 14, Bachte-Maria-Leerne, B-9800 Deinze (East Flanders) T: 093 801 014.

E: info@campinggroeneveld.be alanrogers.com/BE0600

Quiet and clean is how Marc Gysemberg describes his campsite. Groeneveld is a traditional site in a small village within easy reach of Gent. It has a friendly atmosphere and is also open over a long season. Although this site has 98 pitches, there are a fair number of seasonal units, leaving around 50 large touring pitches with 10A electricity. Hedges and borders divide the grassy area, access roads are gravel and there is an area for tents. Family entertainment and activities organised in high season include themed, musical evenings, barbecues, pétanque matches, etc.

Facilities

Two fully updated toilet blocks provide British style WCs, washbasins and free hot showers. Motorcaravan services. Washing machine. Freezer (free). Traditional Flemish style bar (July/Aug; Thurs-Sun low season) with comprehensive range of speciality and local beers. Small coarse fishing lake. Floodlit pétanque court. Adventure play area. TV room. Pool. Internet (at reception) and WiFi (€ 1.50 per stay). Bicycles on loan from reception (free). Max. 2 dogs. Off site: Shops and restaurants nearby. Golf 3 km.

Open: 1 April - 30 September.

Directions

From A10 (E40) exit 13, turn south on N466. After 3 km. go straight on at roundabout and site is on left on entering village (opposite large factory). NB: the yellow signs are very small. GPS: 51.00509, 3.57229

Charges guide

Per unit incl. 2 persons and electricity	€ 21.00 - € 25.00
extra person	€ 3.00 - € 4.00
child (0-13 yrs)	€ 2.00 - € 3.00

No credit cards.

Gent

Camping Blaarmeersen

Zuiderlaan 12, B-9000 Gent (East Flanders) T: 092 668 160. E: camping.blaarmeersen@gent.be

alanrogers.com/BE0610

Blaarmeersen is a comfortable, well managed municipal site in the west of the city. It adjoins a sports complex and a fair sized lake which together provide facilities for a variety of watersports, tennis, squash, minigolf, football, athletics track, roller skating and a playground. There are 238 pitches for touring units, these are flat, grassy, individually separated by hedges and mostly arranged in circular groups, all with electricity. There are 43 hardstandings for motorcaravans, plus a separate area for tents with barbecue area. There is noise from the nearby city ring road. There is a good network of paths and cycle routes around the city.

Facilities

Five sanitary units of a decent standard vary in size. Showers and toilets for disabled visitors. Laundry. Motorcaravan services. Shop, café/bar (both daily March-Oct). Takeaway. Sports facilities. Playground. Fishing. Bicycle hire. Lake swimming. Communal barbecue. WiFi by restaurant, whole site planned for 2014. Off site: Riding and golf 10 km.

Open: 1 March - 31 October.

Directions

From E40 take exit 13 (Ghent-West) and follow dual carriageway for 5 km. Cross second bridge and look for Blaarmeersen sign, turning sharp right and following signs to leisure complex. In city avoid overpasses – most signs are on the lower levels. GPS: 51.04722, 3.68333

Charges guide

Per unit incl. 2 persons and electricity (plus meter)	€ 15.00 - € 18.25
extra person	€ 4.50 - € 5.50
child (5-12 yrs)	€ 1.75 - € 2.50

For latest campsite news, availability and prices visit

alanrogers.com

Odrimont

Camping Gossaimont

Gossaimont 1, B-4990 Odrimont (Liège) T: 080 319 822. E: camping.gossaimont@florealgroup.be

alanrogers.com/BE0701

Located in beautiful countryside on the southern slope of one of the Belgian Ardennes' highest hills, this relaxing site of 295 pitches has direct access to the forest for hikers and cyclists. Under the new ownership of the Floreal group, there is a warm welcome from the managers. The 133 spacious touring pitches are set alongside mature trees, and all have 10A electricity. Mobile homes and tents can be rented from April to October. An indoor games room, a cosy café, and outdoor playgrounds for young children are provided. The campsite is open over the winter season, when sledging and snowman building are popular. There is a ski slope just 4 km. away and its café has a welcoming log fire.

Facilities

Three heated toilet blocks are well spaced around the site. Facilities for disabled visitors in two blocks. Laundry. Shop, bar and café (all year). Play areas. Games room. Pétanque. Accommodation for rent. WiFi (charged). Off site: Walking and mountain biking. Fishing and riding 2 km. Bicycle hire 5 km. Local market towns. Swimming pool. Waterfalls and caves.

Open: All year (accommodation 1 April - 15 October).

See advertisement on pg 69.

Directions

From A26 autoroute take exit 49 and follow N651 northeast towards Lierneux. Turn right on N645 then left on local road for Odrimont. Follow signs to site. GPS: 50.32103, 5.81857

Charges guide

Per unit incl. 2 persons and electricity	€ 17.05 - € 23.05
extra person	€ 3.60
child (3-11 yrs)	€ 2.60
dog	€ 3.25

Stavelot

Camping l'Eau Rouge

Cheneux 25, B-4970 Stavelot (Liège) T: 080 863 075. E: fb220447@skynet.be

alanrogers.com/BE0740

A popular, lively and attractively situated site, l'Eau Rouge is in a sheltered valley close to Spa and the Grand Prix circuit. There are 140 grassy pitches of 110 sq.m. on sloping ground either side of a central road (speed bumps) – 120 for touring units, 80 with 10A electricity (70 with water and waste water), the remainder for static units. The main building houses the busy reception, shop, bar and the main sanitary facilities. There are plenty of sporting activities in the area including skiing and luge in winter. The site is close to the motor race circuit at Spa-Francorchamps and is within walking distance for the fit. The site's Dutch owners have completed a five year programme upgrading the infrastructure and have other ideas in the pipeline. This is an excellent site, planned and run with passion by the owners.

Facilities

A brand new environmentally friendly toilet block has showers (on payment), private cubicles, and facilities for babies and children. Motorcaravan services. Washing machine. Shop. Baker calls daily at 08.30 (in season). Takeaway (in summer). Bar. Boules. Archery (free lessons in high season). Playground. Entertainment in season. WiFi over part of site (charged). Max. 2 dogs. Off site: Bicycle hire 1.5 km. Riding 10 km. Spa-Francorchamps motor racing circuit.

Open: All year.

Directions

Site is 1 km. east of Stavelot on the road to the race circuit. Leave E42 exit 11 Malmédy, at roundabout follow signs for Stavelot. At end of road at T-junction turn right, then first right. Do not follow sat nav, which will take you down narrow roads. GPS: 50.41203, 5.95317

Charges guide

Per unit incl. 2 persons and electricity	€ 19.00
extra person	€ 3.50
child (4-15 yrs)	€ 2.50
dog	€ 1.00

Sart-lez-Spa

Camping Spa d'Or

Stockay 17, B-4845 Sart-lez-Spa (Liège) T: 087 474 400. E: info@campingspador.be

alanrogers.com/BE0700

Camping Spa d'Or is set in a beautiful area of woodlands and picturesque villages, 4 km. from the town of Spa (Pearl of the Ardennes). The site is on the banks of a small river and is an ideal starting point for walks and bicycle trips through the forests. With 310 pitches in total, 240 are for touring, and all have 10A electricity (40 places are reserved for tents). The touring pitches have an open aspect, most are slightly sloping and all have 10A electricity connections. This is an acceptable campsite within easy reach of many tourist attractions.

Facilities

One new large, bright and cheerful sanitary block and one new smaller, prefabricated block, both with all the usual facilities. Room for visitors with disabilities. Laundry. Shop. Bar, restaurant (weekends only in low season) and takeaway. Outdoor heated swimming pool (1/5-15/9). Play area with good equipment. TV in bar. Goal posts and two boules courts. Entertainment during July/Aug. Mountain bike hire. Maps for mountain biking and walking on sale at reception. WiFi over site (charged). Off site: Fishing 2 km. Golf and riding 5 km. Spa 4 km.

Open: 1 April - 7 November.

Directions

From E42 take exit 9 and follow the signs to Spa d'Or. GPS: 50.50758, 5.91952

Charges guide

Per unit incl. 2 persons	
and electricity	€ 20.00 - € 31.50
extra person	€ 4.25 - € 5.50
dog	€ 4.00 - € 5.00

Camping Cheques accepted.

Bocholt

Goolderheide Vakantiepark

Bosstraat 1, B-3950 Bocholt (Limburg) T: 089 469 640. E: info@goolderheide.be

alanrogers.com/BE0760

A large family holiday site with 900 individual pitches, Goolderheide has been owned and operated by the same family for many years and has an excellent pool complex and playgrounds. There are many seasonal and rental units, plus around 300 touring pitches with 4/6A electricity, all in a forest setting. The pitches are of variable size and access roads are quite narrow. The outdoor pool complex has two large pools (one of Olympic size), a slide and a paddling pool. There is also a fishing lake, and a lake with a small sandy beach. An enormous area is devoted to a comprehensive play area with a vast range of equipment. During the main season there is also a weekly supervised assault course with aerial ropeways etc, a soundproofed over-16s disco, plus a younger kids' disco and an extensive programme of varied activities to keep children and adults occupied. There are no extra charges for most of these activities.

Facilities

Four sanitary buildings provide an ample supply of WCs and washbasins in cabins, but rather fewer preset showers. Baby areas. Two en-suite units for disabled visitors (key access). Laundry facilities. Shop, bar and takeaway (daily in July/Aug, w/ends and public holidays in low season). Takeaway. Swimming pools. Tennis. Fishing. Boules. Minigolf. Play area and assault course. Children's discos. Programme of activities (July/Aug). Off site: Bicycle hire 1 km.

Open: 1 April - 30 September.

Directions

From A13 (E313, Antwerp-Liege) take exit 25 and N141 to Leopoldsburg, then N73 through Peer, to outskirts of Bree (35 km). Take N76 north for 3 km, turn left at large roundabout into Bocholt, and towards Kaulille. Site road is on left towards edge of town. GPS: 51.17343, 5.53902

Charges guide

Per unit incl. 2 persons and electricity	€ 30.00
extra person	€ 5.00
dog	€ 5.00

No credit cards.

Hechtel

Vakantiecentrum De Lage Kempen

Kiefhoekstraat 19, B-3941 Hechtel-Eksel (Limburg) T: 011 402 243. E: info@lagekempen.be

alanrogers.com/BE0796

This is a small, good quality site of which the owners are rightly proud. There are 100 pitches with 70 available for touring units. The pitches are large, all with 6/10A electricity, and are laid out in rows. A pleasant swimming pool complex has three heated pools, two for children and one with a large slide, and they are supervised in high season. A new bar and restaurant building opened in July 2012 and a shop is open in high season. Entertainment is provided daily in high season. This is a friendly and welcoming site with a good atmosphere. The owners have found the right balance of entertainment and time for relaxation.

Facilities

Single, high quality toilet block providing very good facilities including free hot showers, washbasins in cabins and good facilities for babies and disabled visitors. Laundry facilities. Motorcaravan services. Small shop with fresh bread (high season). Bar/restaurant and takeaway (all 15/5-1/9). Outdoor heated pool complex (May-Sept). Large adventure playground. Magical minigolf. Bicycle hire. WiFi over most of site (charged). Max. 1 dog. Off site: Riding 3 km. Fishing 5 km.

Open: Easter - 30 October.

Directions

From the E314/A2 motorway take exit for Houthalen and follow signs to Hechtel. Shortly after passing through Hechtel, on Kiefhoekstraat, site is 3.5 km. on the right. GPS: 51.16092, 5.31433

Charges guide

Per unit incl. 2 persons and electricity	€ 24.00
extra person	€ 4.00
child (0-2 yrs)	free
dog (max. 1)	€ 2.00

Houthalen

Oostappen Vakantiepark Hengelhoef

Tulpenstraat 141, B-3530 Houthalen-Helchteren (Limburg) T: 089 382 500.

E: info@vakantieparkhengelhoef.be **alanrogers.com/BE0788**

This attractive and well cared for site would suit families with younger children. Situated in a forest it has 478 pitches of which 368 are for touring units. The pitches are large and laid out in avenues with plenty of shade and all have 10A electricity, water and drainage. At the centre of the site is a large, man-made lake surrounded by sand which is safe for children. A good sub-tropical style pool complex offers a range of slides and water based activities. With a range of activities on offer there is little need to leave the site. There is a large supermarket and a good restaurant and bars.

Facilities

Several good quality toilet blocks throughout the site provide very good facilities including hot showers, washbasins in cabins and good facilities for babies and disabled visitors. Laundry facilities. Motorcaravan services. Supermarket. Restaurant. Bar. Takeaway. Lake with beach. Indoor pool complex. Multisports court. Max. 1 dog accepted in certain areas. Off site: Bicycle hire 1 km. Riding 3 km.

Open: All year.

Directions

From the E314/A2 motorway take exit towards Houthalen Centrum Zuid. The site is well signed from the centre. GPS: 51.01439, 5.46655

Charges guide

Per unit incl. 2 persons and electricity	€ 16.00 - € 32.00

Houthalen

Camping De Binnenvaart

Binnenvaartstraat 49, B-3530 Houthalen-Helchteren (Limburg) T: 011 526 720. E: info@debinnenvaart.be

alanrogers.com/BE0793

De Binnenvaart is a well equipped family site north of Hasselt, open all year. This is a very well equipped holiday centre with a good range of leisure amenities including minigolf and a sports field. The site has been developed alongside a small lake, with its own sandy beach, and is surrounded by woodland. Of the 180 pitches, 34 are for touring, all are of a good size and equipped with electricity (16A Europlug). Many pitches here are reserved all year. The site is part of the same group as BE0792 and BE0780, both of which are nearby, and guests are able to use amenities at these sites too.

Facilities

Two sanitary blocks, one being upgraded, have facilities for disabled visitors. Motorcaravan services. Cafeteria and bar. Lake (swimming, fishing and windsurfing) with sandy beach. Tennis. Sports field. Minigolf. Play area. Animal park. Activity and entertainment programme. Free WiFi over site. No charcoal barbecues. Off site: Walking and cycle routes. Riding. Paintball. Hot-air ballooning. Golf 5 km.

Open: All year.

See advertisement on pg 65.

Directions

Leave the A2 motorway at the Houthalen-Helchteren exit (number 29) and join the northbound N715 to the town. The site is clearly signed from here. GPS: 51.032158, 5.415949

Charges guide

Per unit incl. 2 persons and electricity	€ 26.00
extra person	€ 8.00
child	€ 4.00
dog	€ 4.00

Lommel

Oostappen Vakantiepark Blauwe Meer

Kattenbos 169, B-3920 Lommel (Limburg) T: 011 544 523. E: info@blauwemeer.be

alanrogers.com/BE0785

Surrounded by woodland, and with shade from tall pines, this large site has 976 pitches, of which 277 are for touring units. The touring pitches are attractively arranged around a large man-made lake with a fence surrounding it (safe for children). Each pitch has 10A electricity, water, drainage and television connections. There is a whole range of activities including a disco and a heated outdoor pool with a slide. There are two additional small pools for children. A bar offers takeaway food and a good supermarket is on the site. This is a popular and lively site with an extensive entertainment programme which is varied to suit all age groups.

Facilities

Good clean toilet blocks are located throughout the site. Free hot showers, washbasins in cabins. Facilities for babies and children. Good facilities for disabled visitors. Laundry room. Supermarket, bar and takeaway (July/Aug; weekends in low season). Heated outdoor swimming pool, two smaller ones for children (May-Aug). Several adventure style playgrounds. Children's zoo. Minigolf. Bicycle hire. WiFi over most of site (charged). Max. 1 dog. Off site: Forest Park adjacent for walking and cycling. Riding 7 and 12 km. Golf 10 km.

Open: Easter - 30 October.

Directions

Lommel is 35 km. north of Hasselt. From the N71 at Lommel, turn south at traffic lights on N746 (signed Leopoldsburg), for 2 km. to Kattenbos, and site entrance is on southern side of village on left. GPS: 51.19407, 5.30322

Charges guide

Per unit incl. up to 4 persons   € 31.00 - € 33.00

Minimum stays apply (1 week in high season, 3 or 4 nights on public holidays. American RVs, 12 m. max. in high season, larger at other times).

Lommel

Oostappen Vakantiepark Parelstrand

Luikersteenweg 313A, B-3920 Lommel (Limburg) T: 011 649 349. E: info@vakantieparkprinsenmeer.nl

alanrogers.com/BE0790

This large, attractive site is situated alongside the Bocholt-Herentals canal and the Lommel yacht marina. It has 800 pitches of which 250 are for touring units. Each pitch has 10A electricity, water and drainage. The site fronts onto a large lake with a safe beach and there are three smaller lakes within the site, one of which is used for fishing (well stocked but all fish must be returned). There is an Olympic-size, outdoor pool with a large slide and a small pool for children (not supervised). Several good quality play areas are spread throughout the site. This site is ideal for relaxing or enjoying the canal and other water-based activities. There is a good, well stocked supermarket and a snack bar also offers a takeaway service. A pleasant terrace by the bar is used for evening entertainment. A good entertainment programme is organised in high season.

Facilities

All the facilities that one would expect from a large site are available. Free hot showers, some washbasins in cabins. Facilities for babies and children. Good facilities for disabled visitors. Laundry room. Supermarket. Bar. Takeaway. Outdoor swimming pools (July/Aug), one for children. Bicycle hire. Fishing. WiFi over part of site (charged). Max. 1 dog per pitch. Off site: Boat launching 1 km. Riding 5 km.

Open: Easter - 30 October.

Directions

Take the N712 from Lommel and after 3 km. turn left on the N715. After a further 3 km. the site is on the right hand side. It is well signed from Lommel. GPS: 51.2431, 5.3791

Charges guide

Per unit incl. 2 persons and electricity   € 13.00 - € 25.00

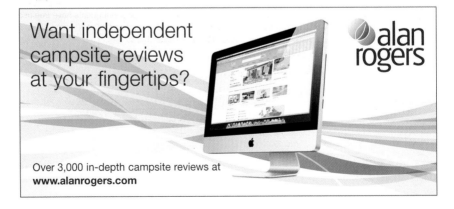
For latest campsite news, availability and prices visit

alanrogers.com

Opglabbeek

Family Camping Wilhelm Tell

Hoeverweg 87, B-3660 Opglabbeek (Limburg) T: **089 810 014**. E: *receptie@wilhelmtell.com*

alanrogers.com/BE0780

Wilhelm Tell is a family run site that caters particularly well for children with its indoor and outdoor pools and lots of entertainment throughout the season. There are 128 pitches with 70 available for touring units, some separated, others on open fields and 60 electricity connections (10A). The super bar/restaurant has access for wheelchair users. M. Lode Nulmans has a very special attitude towards his customers and tries to ensure they leave satisfied and want to return. For example, in his restaurant he says 'it serves until you are full'. The Limburg region is a relaxing area with much to do, including shopping or touring the historic towns with a very enjoyable choice of food and drink!

Facilities

Toilet facilities are adequate, but might be under pressure in high season. Facilities around the pool supplement at busy times. Baby room in reception area. Two en-suite units for disabled visitors. Laundry facilities. Motorcaravan services. Fridge hire. Bar/restaurant and snack bar (times vary acc. to season). Outdoor heated pool with slide and wave machine (July/Aug) and indoor pool (all year), both well supervised. Play area. WiFi. No charcoal barbecues. Off site: Riding 1 km. Fishing 6 km. Golf 10 km.

Open: All year.

Directions

From E314 take exit 32 for Maaseik and follow 730 road towards As. From As follow signs to Opglabbeek. In Opglabbeek take first right at roundabout (Weg van Niel) then first left (Kasterstraat) to site. GPS: 51.02852, 5.59813

Charges guide

Per unit incl. 2 persons and electricity	€ 32.00
extra person	€ 8.00
child (0-12)	€ 4.00
dog	€ 4.00
Less 30% in low season.	

Opoeteren

Camping Zavelbos

Kattebeekstraat 1, B-3680 Opoeteren (Limburg) T: **089 758 146**. E: *receptie@zavelbos.com*

alanrogers.com/BE0792

Camping Zavelbos lies between woodland and moorland in a nature park of 2,000 hectares. It is a pleasant spot for nature lovers and those who love peace and quiet. There are many cycling and walking routes to enjoy in this beautiful region, alternatively you can simply relax in the peaceful campsite grounds complete with a large fishpond. There is no swimming pool but guests have free use of the pool complex at Wilhelm Tell Holiday Park (6 km). The 60 touring pitches (100-120 sq.m) all have 16A electricity (Europlug) and water. Bungalows and chalets are available to rent.

Facilities

New sanitary facilities include family bathrooms, baths with jacuzzi and jet stream (key access € 50 deposit). Provision for disabled visitors. Laundry facilities. Dog shower. Motorcaravan services. Bar and snack bar. Tavern. Fishpond. Playground. Boules. Bicycle hire and free recharging of electric bikes. Free WiFi over site. No charcoal barbecues. Off site: Riding 6 km. Golf 10 km. Shops. Cycling and walking routes. National Park Hoge Kempen. Bobbejaanland. Maastricht. Hasselt. Genk.

Open: All year.

Directions

Take the Maaseik exit from the A2 (Eindhoven-Maastricht) motorway and drive via Neerpoeteren to Opoeteren. The site is on the right heading to Opglabbeek. GPS: 51.0583, 5.6288

Charges guide

Per unit incl. 2 persons and electricity	€ 21.00 - € 30.00
extra person	€ 8.00
child (under 12 yrs)	€ 4.00
dog	€ 4.00
No credit cards.	

Zonhoven

Camping Holsteenbron

Hengelhoefseweg 9, B-3520 Zonhoven (Limburg) T: 011 817 140. E: camping.holsteenbron@telenet.be

alanrogers.com/BE0786

Situated in the heart of the Park Midden-Limburg, this is a delightful site. There are 91 pitches with 60 for touring units, numbered and arranged in rows that are separated by hedges. All have easy access and 6A electricity. Water is provided by a single supply at the toilet block, but being such a small site, this is not a problem. A pretty lake is at the centre of the site and is well stocked with fish for the exclusive use of the camping guests. The site is situated only 500 m. from the start of a network of cycle tracks that stretches for 1,600 km. throughout the National Park. The site is highly recommended.

Facilities

One single well equipped toilet block with large token operated showers. Laundry room. Excellent bar and restaurant with limited but good menu (all season). Playground. Sports field. Fishing. TV in bar. Free WiFi over site. Off site: Riding 3 km.

Open: 1 April - 11 November.

Directions

Site is situated on the N29 Eindhoven-Hasselt road and is well signed from Zonhoven.
GPS: 50.99826, 5.42451

Charges guide

Per unit incl. electricity	€ 19.00 - € 24.00
dog	€ 6.00

Amberloup

Camping Tonny

Rue des Rainettes 1, B-6680 Sainte-Ode (Luxembourg) T: 061 688 285. E: info@campingtonny.be

alanrogers.com/BE0720

The Dutch owners here are rightly proud of their site. With a friendly atmosphere, it is an attractive, small campsite in a pleasant valley by the River Ourthe. A family site, there are 75 grass touring pitches, with wooden chalet buildings giving a Tirolean feel. The pitches (80-100 sq.m) are separated by small shrubs and fir trees, 4/6A electricity is available. Cars are parked away from the units and there is a separate meadow for tents. Surrounded by natural woodland, Camping Tonny is an ideal base for outdoor activities.

Facilities

A new sanitary unit (heated in cool weather) includes showers (now free). Baby area and laundry. Freezer for campers' use. TV lounge and library. Sports field. Boules. Games room. Playgrounds. Fishing. Bicycle hire. Cross-country skiing. WiFi (free by reception).

Open: 30 March - 2 November.

Directions

From N4 take exit for Libramont at km. 131 (N826), then to Amberloup (4 km) where site is signed just outside of the southwest town boundary.
GPS: 50.02657, 5.51283

Charges guide

Per unit incl. 2 persons and electricity	€ 18.00 - € 26.00
extra person	€ 4.50
child (3-12 yrs)	€ 2.50

Arlon

Camping Officiel Arlon

Route de Bastogne 373, B-6700 Arlon (Luxembourg) T: 063 226582. E: campingofficiel@skynet.be

alanrogers.com/BE0684

An attractive and well maintained, family owned site situated close to Belgium's largest forest. There are 80 grassy touring pitches (100 sq.m) with 6A electricity. The excellent on-site amenities include a clean sanitary block, a bar and restaurant and a pleasant terrace and swimming pool. This is an ideal stopover site when travelling north or south, with good access from the E411. However, the Roman city of Arlon has many interesting sights, and a large flea market is held on the first Sunday of the month from March until October, so you may be tempted to linger. Luxembourg is just 4 km. away for cheaper fuel.

Facilities

One clean, well maintained sanitary block by the entrance has free, controllable, hot showers and some washbasins in cubicles. Facilities for disabled visitors (key access). Dishwashing area and washing machine. Motorcaravan services. Bar/restaurant/takeaway (April-Oct; limited menu). Spring water swimming pool (15/6-31/8). Free WiFi over site. Off site: Shops, bars, restaurants and market (Thu) in Arlon 2 km. Riding 4 km. Golf 6 km.

Open: All year.

Directions

From E41 exit at junction 31 towards Arlon. Follow signs for Bastogne. Continue on N82 for 4 km. before merging onto N4. Site is just after the bend, 200 m. on right. GPS: 49.702009, 5.806765

Charges guide

Per unit incl. 2 persons and electricity	€ 20.40
extra person	€ 4.00
child (4-9 yrs)	€ 2.50
dog	€ 2.00

No credit cards.

For latest campsite news, availability and prices visit

alanrogers.com

Attert

Camping Sud

Voie de la Liberté 75, B-6717 Attert (Luxembourg) T: 063 223 715. E: info@campingsudattert.com

alanrogers.com/BE0680

This is a pleasant, family run site which would make a good base for a short stay and is also well situated for use as an overnight halt. The 86 touring pitches are on level grass, all with 6A electricity. There are 11 drive-through pitches especially for stopovers, plus four hardstandings for motorcaravans and a tent area. The far end of the site is close to the N4 and may suffer from some road noise. On-site facilities include a small, but welcoming restaurant/bar with takeaway facility, a shop for basics, an outdoor swimming pool (12x6 m) with paddling pool and a sports field.

Facilities

A single building provides modern sanitary facilities including some washbasins in cubicles and baby areas. Showers are free in low season (€ 0.50 July/Aug). No facilities for disabled campers. Small shop (July/Aug). Pleasant bar/restaurant and takeaway (1/4-15/10). TV in bar. Swimming and paddling pools (June-Sept). Small playground. Children's entertainment (4-12 yrs) three afternoons per week during July/Aug. Free WiFi in reception. Dogs are not accepted. Off site: Supermarket 5 km.

Open: 1 April - 15 October.

Directions

Attert is 8 km. north of Arlon. From E25/E411 from Luxembourg take exit 31 and follow signs for Bastogne to join N4 north; take Attert exit, continue east for 1 km. to Attert village, site entrance is immediately on your left as you join the main street. GPS: 49.74833, 5.78698

Charges guide

Per unit incl. 2 persons and electricity	€ 20.50
extra person	€ 4.50
child (2-11 yrs)	€ 2.25

No credit cards.

Auby-sur-Semois

Camping Maka

Route du Maka 100, B-6880 Auby-sur-Semois (Luxembourg) T: 061 411 148. E: info@campingmaka.be

alanrogers.com/BE0716

Camping Maka is a delightful, rural site on the banks of the River Semois, reputedly Belgium's cleanest river. Fifty touring pitches, with 10A electricity and water, are sited close to the water, allowing everyone access to the river and its banks and there is space for 30 tents. Forty-eight private mobile homes are hidden on two higher terraces. Two fully equipped wooden cabins and two tents are for rent. The river is popular for swimming, fishing and canoeing. Canadian canoes, mountain bikes, barbecues and outdoor cooking equipment are available for hire. Facilities include a bar with a terrace overlooking the water and a shop. Not suitable for large units (over 8 m. long).

Facilities

A modern, heated toilet block includes facilities for babies and for disabled campers (key access). Pub/café with takeaway and terrace, shop. Play area. Fishing. Games area. Direct river access. Campfire area. Canoe and mountain bike hire. Occasional activities and entertainment. Tents and cabins for rent. WiFi over site (charged). No electric barbecues. Off site: Walking. Mountain biking. Canoeing. Bouillon, Bertrix, Bastogne.

Open: 1 April - 19 September.

Directions

Site is close to the village of Auby-sur-Semois, east of Bouillon. Approaching from the east on N89, leave at N853 exit and follow signs to Bertrix. Before reaching the centre of Bertrix, follow signs to Auby-sur-Semois to the southwest, and then signs to site. GPS: 49.808842, 5.164824

Charges guide

Per unit incl. 2 persons and electricity	€ 30.35
extra person	€ 4.95

Bertrix

Ardennen Camping Bertrix

Route de Mortehan, B-6880 Bertrix (Luxembourg) T: 061 412 281. E: info@campingbertrix.be

alanrogers.com/BE0711

Bertrix is located at the heart of the Belgian Ardennes, between the towns of Bastogne and Bouillon and overlooking the hills of the Semois valley. Part of a Dutch chain, the site has 498 terraced pitches of which 303 are for touring, all with 10A electricity, and 43 also have water and drainage. A variety of seasonal caravans are sited among them and there is a friendly feel to the area. Some pitches are available with children's play huts on stilts! A wide range of imaginative activities are organised in the holidays, including some exciting excursions on horseback to the nearby working slate mine.

Facilities

Five well appointed toilet blocks, one with facilities for disabled visitors. The central one has a large laundry. Motorcaravan services. Shop for basics and bread. Excellent restaurant and bar (closed low season on Tues. and Thurs) has satellite TV, Internet access and a terrace overlooking the large, heated swimming and paddling pools (27/4-16/9, supervised high season). Tennis. Bicycle hire. Children's games room. Woodland adventure trail. WiFi in part of the site (charged). Max. 1 dog in July/Aug.

Open: 28 March - 12 November.

Directions

Take exit 25 from the E411 motorway and take the N89 towards Bertrix. After 6.5 km. join N884 to Bertrix then follow yellow signs to site south of town. GPS: 49.83861, 5.25122

Charges guide

Per unit incl. 2 persons and electricity	€ 20.00 - € 34.00
extra person (over 2 yrs)	€ 4.00 - € 6.00

Camping Cheques accepted.

FREE Alan Rogers Travel Card
Extra benefits and savings - see page 14

Bomal-sur-Ourthe

Camping International

Pré Cawai 3, B-6941 Bomal-sur-Ourthe (Luxembourg) T: 049 8629 079. E: info@campinginternational.be

alanrogers.com/BE0718

Camping International is a small site in the Belgian Ardennes, located on the banks of the River Ourthe. Although in a French-speaking area, it has a very Dutch ambience. The 60 pitches (20 for seasonal caravans) are of a good size and most have (metered) electrical connections. A central area is available for groups. The campsite tavern, which also houses reception, serves a selection of bar meals to eat in or take away. A wide range of activities are on offer in the area, including canoeing on the Ourthe, raft building, abseiling and mountain biking. There is occasional railway noise.

Facilities

The basic sanitary facilities are adjacent to the tavern and have preset showers, cold water to washbasins (cabins in ladies). No facilities for disabled visitors. Bar. Snack bar. Takeaway. Play area. Bicycle hire. Canoeing. Activity and entertainment programme. Direct river access. Fishing (licence needed). WiFi in reception area (charged). Off site: Adventure sports and canoeing 200 m. Bar and restaurants 200 m. Shops and bicycle hire in Bornal-sur-Ourthe 500 m. Walking and mountain biking. Riding 8 km.

Open: 4 March - 13 November.

Directions

From E411 Brussels/Luxembourg motorway leave at exit 18 for Assesse. Head south on N4 as far as Sinsin and turn east on N929 and N933 as far as Le Petit Han. Then take N983 to Barvaux-sur-Ourthe and N86 to Bomal. Turn west on N683 to site on left after bridge. GPS: 50.374925, 5.519439

Charges guide

Per unit incl. 2 persons and electricity (plus meter)	€ 15.50 - € 19.50
extra person	€ 4.50

Dochamps

Panoramacamping Petite Suisse

Al Bounire 27, B-6960 Dochamps (Luxembourg) T: 084 444 030. E: info@petitesuisse.be

alanrogers.com/BE0735

This quiet site is set in the picturesque countryside of the Belgian Ardennes, a region in which rivers flow through valleys bordered by vast forests where horses are still usefully employed. Set on a southerly slope, the site is mostly open and offers wide views of the surrounding countryside. The 193 touring pitches, all with 10A electricity, are either on open sloping ground or in terraced rows with hedges in between, and trees providing some separation. Gravel roads provide access around the site. To the right of the entrance barrier a large wooden building houses reception, a bar and a restaurant.

Facilities

All the facilities that one would expect of a large site are available. Showers are free, washbasins both open and in cabins. Baby room. Laundry room with washing machines and dryers. Shop, restaurant, bar and takeaway (4/4-2/11). Heated outdoor swimming pool (1/5-1/9), paddling pool and slide. Sports field. Tennis. Bicycle hire. Playground and club for children. Entertainment programme during school holidays. Varied activity programme. WiFi (charged).

Open: All year.

Directions

From E25/A26 autoroute (Liège-Luxembourg) take exit 50 then the N89 southwest towards La Roche. After 8 km. turn right (north) on N841 to Dochamps where site is signed. GPS: 50.23127, 5.62583

Charges guide

Per unit incl. 2 persons and electricity	€ 21.50 - € 37.50
extra person (over 4 yrs)	€ 3.00 - € 6.00
dog (high season max. 1)	€ 2.00 - € 4.00

Camping Cheques accepted.

Erezée

Camping le Val de l'Aisne

Rue du TTA 1 A, B-6997 Erezée (Luxembourg) T: 086 470 067. E: info@levaldelaisne.be

alanrogers.com/BE0725

From a nearby hill, Château de Blier overlooks Camping le Val de l'Aisne, a large site attractively laid out around a 1.5-hectare lake in the Belgian Ardennes. The site has 450 grass pitches with 150 for touring units, on level ground and with 16A electricity. Tarmac roads circle the site providing easy access. Trees provide some shade although the site is fairly open allowing views of the surrounding hills and the château. Activities play a large part on this site, ranging from quiet fishing in the lake to hectic quad bike tours in the surrounding hills. To the left of the entrance a building houses reception and the bar/restaurant.

Facilities

Three toilet blocks provide showers (paid for by sep key) and mainly open washbasins. Facilities for disabled visitors. Baby room. Washing machines and dryers. Motorcaravan services. Bar/restaurant and snack bar with takeaway. Bread can be ordered in reception. On the lake: fishing, swimming, kayaks (to hire). Quad bike hire and tours arranged. Mountain bike hire. Play area. WiFi. Entertainment (summer). Activities team arrange a range of adventure activities including paintball, canyoning, etc.

Open: All year.

Directions

From E411/A4 (Brussels-Luxembourg) take exit 18 (Courière, Marche), then southeast on N4 to Marche. At Marche head northeast on N86 to Hotton, crossing river bridge. In Hotton follow signs for Soy and Erezée. Just west of Erezée at roundabout follow signs for La Roche. Site is 900 m. on left. GPS: 50.2815, 5.5505

Charges guide

Per unit incl. 2 persons and car	€ 18.00
extra person (over 3 yrs)	€ 3.00

No credit cards.

For latest campsite news, availability and prices visit

alanrogers.com

La Roche-en-Ardenne

Camping Floreal La Roche

Route de Houffalize 18, B-6980 La Roche-en-Ardenne (Luxembourg) T: 084 219 467.

E: camping.laroche@florealgroup.be alanrogers.com/BE0732

Maintained to very high standards, this site is set in a beautiful wooded valley bordering the Ourthe river. Open all year, the site is located on the outskirts of the attractive small town of La Roche-en-Ardenne, in an area understandably popular with tourists. The site is large with 587 grass pitches (min. 100 sq.m), of which 290 are for touring units. The pitches are on level ground and all have 10/16A electricity and water connections. Amenities on site include a well stocked shop, a bar, a restaurant and takeaway food. In the woods and rivers close by, there are plenty of opportunities for walking, mountain biking, rafting and canoeing. For children, there is a large adventure playground, which is very popular, and entertainment programmes are organised during the summer. The Ardennes region is rightly proud of its cuisine in which game, taken from the forests that cover the area, is prominent; for those who really enjoy eating, a visit to a small restaurant should be planned. English, French, Dutch and German are spoken in reception.

Facilities

Six modern, well maintained sanitary blocks provide washbasins (open and in cabins), free preset showers. Facilities for disabled visitors. Baby room. Washing machines and dryers (token from reception). Motorcaravan services. Well stocked shop (with fresh bread, pastries and newspapers in July/Aug). Bar, restaurant, snack bar and takeaway. At Camping Floreal 2: heated outdoor swimming pool (1/7-31/8). New wellness facilities with sauna and jacuzzi (all year). Professional entertainment team (during local school holidays). Sports field. Volleyball. Tennis. Minigolf. Pétanque. Dog shower. WiFi. Mobile homes to rent.

Open: All year.

Directions

From E25/A26 take exit 50 and follow the N89 southwest to La Roche. In La Roche follow signs for Houffalize (beside Ourthe river). Floreal Group Camping 1 is 1.5 km. along this road. Note: go to camping 1 not 2. GPS: 50.17600, 5.58600

Charges guide

Per unit incl. 2 persons	
and electricity	€ 17.15 - € 23.15
extra person	€ 3.60
child (3-11 yrs)	€ 2.60
dog (max. 1)	€ 3.25

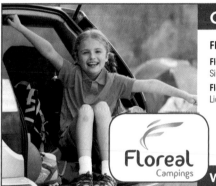
Manhay

Camping Domaine Moulin de Malempré

Rue Moulin De Malempré No 1, B-6960 Manhay (Luxembourg) T: 086 455 504.

E: info@camping-malempre.be alanrogers.com/BE0730

This pleasant countryside site, very close to the E25, is well worth a visit and the owners will make you very welcome (English is spoken). The reception building houses the office and a small shop, above which is an attractive bar and restaurant with open fireplace. The 140 marked touring pitches are separated by small shrubs and gravel roads on sloping terrain. All have 10A electricity, 90 have water and drainage as well and the site is well lit. There is a little traffic noise from the nearby E25 (not too intrusive).

Facilities

Modern toilet facilities include some washbasins in cubicles and family bathrooms on payment. The unisex unit can be heated and has a family shower room. Unit for disabled visitors. Baby room. Laundry. Motorcaravan services. Shop for basic provisions. Baker calls daily 08.30-09.15. Bar, restaurant and takeaway (July/Aug and weekends). Heated swimming and children's pools (28/5-30/9). TV. Boules. Playground. WiFi over site (free).

Open: 1 March - 11 November.

Directions

From E25/A26 (Liege-Bastogne) exit 49. Turn onto N651 (southwest) towards Manhay. After 220 m. turn sharp left (east) towards Lierneux. Follow signs for Malempré and site. GPS: 50.29498, 5.72317

Charges guide

Per unit incl. 2 persons	
and electricity	€ 20.00 - € 30.00
extra person	€ 3.75
child (to 14 yrs)	free

Belgium

Neufchâteau

Camping Spineuse

Rue de Malome 7, B-6840 Neufchâteau (Luxembourg) T: 061 277 320. E: info@camping-spineuse.be

alanrogers.com/BE0675

This delightful Dutch owned site lies about 2 km. from the town centre. It is on low lying, level grass, bordered by a river, with trees and shrubs dotted around the 87 pitches. Seasonal units take just 14 pitches leaving 73 for touring units, all with 10/16A electricity. One corner of the site is particularly secluded, but the whole place has the feel of a peaceful garden. There is unfenced water on site and a footbridge over the river with no guard rails. The attractive main building houses reception, and a pleasant bar/bistro with a friendly, family atmosphere.

Facilities

Toilet facilities in the central building and in a new block (open mid May to Sept) are neat and clean with preset showers, open washbasins in main block, cubicles with shower and washbasin in new block. Very limited facilities for disabled campers (none for wheelchair users). Washing machine and dryer. Motorcaravan services. Small shop for basics (July/Aug). Bistro/bar and takeaway (April-Oct). Large inflatable pool (June-Sept). Tennis. Boules. Two playgrounds and playing field with volleyball court. Fishing. Mobile homes to rent. WiFi (free).

Open: All year.

Directions

Neufchâteau is just off E25/E411 (Luxembourg-Liège-Brussels) at exits 26-28. Site is 2 km. southwest of Neufchâteau on the N15 towards Florenville. There are three sites fairly close together, this is the last one on the left hand side. GPS: 49.83287, 5.41743

Charges guide

Per unit incl. 2 persons and electricity	€ 20.00
extra person	€ 3.50
child (0-6 yrs)	€ 2.00
dog	€ 1.25

Rendeux

Camping Floreal le Festival

89 route de la Roche, B-6987 Rendeux (Luxembourg) T: 084 477 371. E: camping.festival@florealgroup.be

alanrogers.com/BE0733

Floreal le Festival is a member of the Floreal group, attractively located in the wide wooded valley of the River Ourthe. There are 360 pitches here and the site is open all year. Pitches are of a good size and each is surrounded by hedges. Most have electrical connections. On-site amenities include a small supermarket, a bar (which also provides takeaway meals) and a restaurant. Sports amenities are good and include a football field, volleyball and tennis. Furthermore, the region is ideal for walking and mountain biking, and the site's managers will be pleased to recommend routes.

Facilities

Three traditional toilet blocks have washbasins (open style and in cabins), free showers, baby bath and facilities for disabled visitors. Washing machines and dryers. Supermarket. Bar. Takeaway meals. Restaurant. Play area. Tennis. Volleyball. Football. Mobile homes for rent. WiFi. Off site: Walking and cycle tracks. Riding 500 m. Bicycle hire 1 km. Grottes de Hotton. La Roche-en-Ardennes.

Open: All year.

See advertisement on pg 69.

Directions

Approaching from Namur, head south on N4 as far as Marche-en-Famenne. Here, join the westbound N86 to Hotton and then the southbound N822 to Rendeux. From here follow signs to the site. GPS: 50.22469, 5.52603

Charges guide

Per unit incl. 2 persons and electricity	€ 13.95 - € 19.90
extra person	€ 3.60

Tellin

Camping Parc la Clusure

Chemin de la Clusure 30, B-6927 Bure-Tellin (Luxembourg) T: 084 360 050.
E: info@parclaclusure.be **alanrogers.com/BE0670**

A friendly and very well run site, Parc la Clusure is highly recommended. Set in a river valley in the lovely wooded uplands of the Ardennes, known as the l'Homme Valley touring area, the site has 438 large, marked, grassy pitches (320 for touring). All have access to electricity, cable TV and water taps and are mostly in avenues off a central, tarmac road. There is some noise from the nearby railway. There is a very pleasant riverside walk; the river is shallow in summer and popular with children (caution in winter). The site's heated swimming pool and children's pool have a pool-side bar and terrace.

Facilities

Three excellent sanitary units, one heated in winter, include some washbasins in cubicles, facilities for babies and children. Facilities for disabled campers. Motorcaravan services. Shop, bar, restaurant, snack bar and takeaway (all Easter-1/11). Swimming pools (1/5-13/9). Bicycle hire. Tennis. New playgrounds. Organised activity programme including canoeing, archery, abseiling, mountain biking and climbing (summer). Caving. Fishing (licence essential). WiFi over site (free). Barrier card deposit (€ 20). Max. 1 dog in July/Aug.

Open: All year.

Directions

Site is signed north at the roundabout off the N803 Rochefort-St Hubert road at Bure, 8 km. southeast of Rochefort. GPS: 50.09647, 5.2857

Charges guide

Per unit incl. 2 persons and electricity	€ 20.00 - € 37.00
extra person (over 2 yrs)	€ 4.00 - € 7.00
dog (max. 1)	€ 4.00 - € 5.00
Camping Cheques accepted.	

For latest campsite news, availability and prices visit

alanrogers.com

Tintigny

Camping De Chênefleur

Norulle 16, B-6730 Tintigny (Luxembourg) T: 063 444 078. E: info@chenefleur.be

alanrogers.com/BE0715

Camping De Chênefleur is an excellent family run site situated beside the Semois river. With a total of 223 pitches (196 for touring), it would make an ideal site for a stopover or equally for a longer stay. It is attractively laid out in an informal, park-like style with 6A electricity available to all pitches. Some are separated by hedges, others are arranged in more open space and a few are available along the river bank. Fred Lemmers, the owner, has developed a generally peaceful and quiet environment with entertainment organised for children in high season.

Facilities

Two new fully refurbished sanitary blocks, one with facilities for children. Washing machine and dryer. Shop. Bar. Restaurant. Heated outdoor swimming pool (25/4-15/9). Two play areas with beach volleyball court. Full entertainment programme in season. Bicycle hire. Max. 2 dogs. WiFi (charged). Off site: Riding 17 km. Luxembourg City 40 km.

Open: 1 April - 1 October.

Directions

From Liège follow E25 towards Luxembourg and continue on E411. Take exit 29 (Habay-La-Neuve) and continue to Etalle. From Etalle follow N83 to Florenville. Drive through Tintigny and follow site signs. GPS: 49.68497, 5.52050

Charges guide

Per unit incl. 2 persons and electricity	€ 19.50 - € 32.00
extra person (over 3 yrs)	€ 4.00 - € 5.50
dog	€ 4.00 - € 5.00

Camping Cheques accepted.

Virton

Camping Colline de Rabais

Clos des Horles 1, B-6760 Virton (Luxembourg) T: 063 422 177. E: info@collinederabais.be

alanrogers.com/BE0710

Colline de Rabais is a large site on a hill top looking out over the surrounding wooded countryside. The Dutch owners offer a warm welcome and are slowly making improvements to the site while maintaining its relaxed atmosphere. There are around 217 pitches for touring units, all with 16A electricity (some long leads needed), plus 37 mobile homes and bungalows for rent and a few tour operator tents. Various activities are organised throughout the season.

Facilities

Three toilet blocks, one modernised with shower/washbasin cubicles and an en-suite room for disabled visitors. Cleaning and maintenance can be variable and not all blocks are open in low season. Washing machines and dryers. Shop (1/4-31/8). Bar/restaurant and takeaway (Apr-Oct). Small outdoor swimming pool (15/5-15/9) with wood decking for sunbathing. Bicycle hire. Free WiFi over site. Off site: Fishing 1 km. Shops, bars and restaurants in Virton 2 km. Riding 3 km.

Open: All year.

See advertisement on pg 69.

Directions

Virton is 39 km. southwest of Arlon on E25/E411 Luxembourg-Brussels/Liège motorway. From exit 29 head for Virton. After Etalle, turn west for Vallée de Rabais, right at sports complex and at crossroads turn right up hill to site at end of road. From exit 31 take N82 for 22 km, then turn right for Vallée de Rabais and left to site. GPS: 49.58015, 5.54773

Charges guide

Per unit incl. 2 persons	€ 18.50 - € 25.00
extra person (over 2 yrs)	€ 3.00 - € 4.50
dog	€ 4.00 - € 5.00

Ave-et-Auffe

Camping Le Roptai

Rue du Roptai 34, B-5580 Ave-et-Auffe (Namur) T: 084 388 319. E: info@leroptai.be

alanrogers.com/BE0850

This family site in the heart of the Ardennes, within easy reach of Dinant and Namur was established in 1932. In a rural wooded setting with its own adventure playground in the trees, it is a good site for an active holiday, especially in high season when there is a weekly programme, including rock climbing, abseiling, mountain biking and potholing. There are 108 good sized, grassy, touring pitches on sloping ground, most with 6A electricity. A programme of activities is organised for adults and children in high season. Other amenities include a swimming pool, a well stocked shop and a bar/snack bar. There are excellent footpaths around the site and the owner and staff will be pleased to recommend routes. The pretty little village of Ave is just 1 km. from le Roptai, and the larger village of Han-sur-Lesse is around 4 km. away. There is an evening market at Han, as well as world famous caves. The village is also home to the interesting Maison de la Vie Paysanne.

Facilities

Sanitary facilities below reception include an excellent suite for babies and disabled visitors. Five other blocks of varying styles are kept clean and offer basic facilities. Shop (1/7-31/8). Bar/snack bar with takeaway (1/7-31/8). Swimming pool and paddling pool (1/7-31/8). Play area. Activity programme (July/Aug). Bicycle hire. WiFi over part of site (charged). Mobile homes for rent. Off site: Fishing 6 km. Riding 10 km. Golf 16 km. Skiing 25 km. Cycling and walking tracks. Canoeing. Caves at Han-sur-Lesse.

Open: 1 February - 31 December.

Directions

From E411 (Brussels-Luxembourg) motorway take exit 23 (Wellin-Han-sur-Lesse) and follow signs for Han-sur-Lesse. Continue 1 km. to Ave and turn left at the church, following signs to the site (1 km. further). GPS: 50.11128, 5.13376

Charges guide

Per unit incl. 2 persons	
and electricity	€ 25.00 - € 33.00
extra person	€ 3.00 - € 4.00
child (5-15 yrs)	€ 2.00 - € 3.00
dog	€ 2.00 - € 3.00

Rochefort

Camping les Roches

Rue du Hableau, 26, B-5580 Rochefort (Namur) T: 084 211 900. E: campingrochefort@lesroches.be

alanrogers.com/BE0845

Camping les Roches has been recently renovated and can be found close to the centre of Rochefort, in the heart of the Ardennes. Despite its proximity to the town centre, this is a tranquil site, close to the large Parc des Roches. The 76 grassy touring pitches all have 16A electricity, water and drainage. They are of a good size on sloping ground. The adjacent tennis courts and municipal swimming pool are free to campers. During peak season, an entertainment team organises a range of activities for adults and children, including archery and accompanied cycle tours.

Facilities

Two modern, well maintained toilet blocks, heated when required, have washbasins in cabins and preset showers. Family room with shower, children's bath and WC. Excellent unit for disabled visitors. Bar with basic snacks (July/Aug). Games/TV room. Playground. Activity and entertainment programme (July/Aug). Free Internet access and WiFi (charged) in reception. Off site: Swimming pool and tennis (free). Minigolf. Bicycle hire, shops and restaurants in Rochefort 500 m. Caves at Han-sur-Lesse 6 km. Golf 20 km. Walking and cycle tracks.

Open: Easter - All Saints' week.

Directions

Rochefort is 50 km. southeast of Namur. From E411 motorway leave at exit 22 for Rochefort and continue east on N911 to Rochefort. Cross the river and take the first road on the left (rue au Bord de l'Eau) and follow signs to the site. GPS: 50.159585, 5.226185

Charges guide

Per unit incl. 2 persons	
and electricity	€ 22.50 - € 25.00
extra person	€ 4.00
child (4-11 yrs)	€ 3.00

For latest campsite news, availability and prices visit

alanrogers.com

De Haan

Camping Ter Duinen

Wenduinsesteenweg 143, B-8420 De Haan (West Flanders) T: 050 413 593. E: info@campingterduinen.be

alanrogers.com/BE0578

Ter Duinen is a large, seaside holiday site with 120 touring pitches and over 700 privately owned static holiday caravans. The pitches are laid out in straight lines with tarmac access roads and the site has three immaculate toilet blocks. Other than a bar and a playing field, the site has little else to offer, but it is only a 600 m. walk to the sea and next door to the site is a large sports complex with a sub-tropical pool and several sporting facilities. Opportunities for riding and golf (18-hole course) are close by. It is possible to hire bicycles in the town. Access to the beach is via a good woodland footpath. There is a main road and tramway to cross, but there are designated pedestrian crossings. Cycling is very popular in this area and there are numerous good cycle paths, including one into the centre of De Haan (1.5 km). The best places to visit for a day trip are Ostend with the Atlantic Wall from WWII, Knokke (which holds many summer festivals) and Bruges.

Facilities

Three modern toilet blocks have good fittings, washbasins in cubicles (hot and cold water) and showers (€ 1.20). Baby bath. Facilities for disabled visitors. Laundry facilities with two washing machines and a dryer, irons and ironing boards. Motorcaravan services. Shop. Snack bar and takeaway. Internet room (charged). Off site: Bicycle hire and sea with sandy beach 600 m. Golf 3 km. Riding 1 km. Golf 3 km. Boat launching 6 km. A bus for Bruges stops 200 m. from the site, a tram for the coast 400 m.

Open: 15 March - 15 October.

Directions

On E40/A10 in either direction take exit 6 for De Haan/Jabbeke. Follow N377 towards Haan-Bredene, at roundabout head towards Vlissegem. After 4 km. go straight on at junction. Turn right after a further 1.5 km. Site is 750 m. on right. GPS: 51.28318, 3.05753

Charges guide

Per unit incl. 4 persons and electricity	€ 19.00 - € 28.00
extra person	€ 3.50
child (under 10 yrs)	€ 3.00
dog	€ 3.50

Camping Cheques accepted.

Jabbeke

Recreatiepark Klein Strand

Varsenareweg 29, B-8490 Jabbeke (West Flanders) T: 050 811 440. E: info@kleinstrand.be

alanrogers.com/BE0555

In a convenient location just off the A10 motorway and close to Bruges, this site is in two distinct areas divided by an access road. The main part of the site offers a lake with a marked off swimming area, a sandy beach, water slides and boating (no fishing). The touring section has 137 large pitches on flat grass separated by well trimmed hedges; all have electricity and access to water and drainage. Some leisure facilities for children are provided on this part of the site, along with a spacious bar and snack bar with takeaway (seasonal). The main site with all the privately owned mobile homes is closer to the lake, so has most of the amenities. These include the main reception building, restaurants, bar, minimarket, and sports facilities. This is a family holiday site and offers a comprehensive programme of activities and entertainment in July and August. Klein Strand is an ideal base from which to visit Bruges (by bus, every 20 minutes) and Gent (by train from Bruges); or why not head for the coast and pick up the delightful KustTram which runs from De Panne near the French border to Knokke?

Facilities

Single modern, heated, toilet block includes good sized showers (charged) and vanity style washbasins. Baby room. Basic facilities for disabled campers. Washing machines and dryer. Additional toilet facilities with washbasins in cubicles are located behind the touring field reception building (open July/Aug). Motorcaravan services. Bar and snack bar. Play area. Fun pool for small children. In main park: European and Chinese restaurants, bar and snack bar, takeaways (all year). Shop (Easter-end Aug). Tennis courts and sports field. Water-ski school; water-ski shows (Sun. in July/Aug). Bicycle hire. WiFi (free).

Open: All year.

Directions

Jabbeke is 12 km. southwest of Bruges. From A18/A10 motorways, take exit 6/6B (Jabbeke). At roundabout take first exit (site signed). In 650 m. on left-hand bend, turn left to site in 600 m. Main reception is on left but in high season continue to touring site on right in 200 m.
GPS: 51.18448, 3.10445

Charges guide

Per unit incl. up to 4 persons and electricity	€ 22.00 - € 39.00
dog	€ 2.00

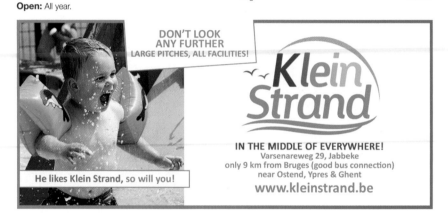

DON'T LOOK ANY FURTHER
LARGE PITCHES, ALL FACILITIES!

Klein Strand

He likes Klein Strand, so will you!

IN THE MIDDLE OF EVERYWHERE!
Varsenareweg 29, Jabbeke
only 9 km from Bruges (good bus connection)
near Ostend, Ypres & Ghent

www.kleinstrand.be

Lombardsijde

Camping De Lombarde

Elisabethlaan 4, B-8434 Lombardsijde Middelkerke (West Flanders) T: 058 236 839. E: info@delombarde.be

alanrogers.com/BE0560

De Lombarde is a spacious, good value holiday site between Lombardsijde and the coast. It has a pleasant atmosphere and modern buildings. The 380 pitches (150 for touring) are set out in level, grassy bays surrounded by shrubs, all with 16A electricity, long leads may be needed. Vehicles are parked in separate car parks. There are many seasonal units and 21 holiday homes, leaving 170 touring pitches. There is a range of activities and an entertainment programme in season. This is a popular holiday area and the site becomes full at peak times. A pleasant stroll of one kilometre takes you into Lombardsijde. There is a tram service from near the site entrance to the town and the beach.

Facilities

Three heated sanitary units are of an acceptable standard, with some washbasins in cubicles. Facilities for disabled visitors. Large laundry. Motorcaravan services. Shop, restaurant/bar and takeaway (1/4-31/8 and school holidays). Tennis. Boules. Fishing lake. TV lounge. Entertainment for children. Outdoor fitness equipment. Playground. WiFi in bar. ATM. Torch useful. Max. 1 dog. Off site: Beach 400 m. Golf 500 m. Bicycle hire 1 km.

Open: All year.

Directions

Coming from Westende, follow the tramlines. From the traffic lights in Lombardsijde, turn left following tramlines into Zeelaan. Continue following tramlines until crossroads and tram stop, turn left into Elisabethlaan. Site is on right after 200 m.
GPS: 51.15644, 2.75329

Charges guide

Per unit incl. 1-6 persons and electricity	€ 18.40 - € 33.20

No credit cards.

For latest campsite news, availability and prices visit

alanrogers.com

Nieuwpoort

Kompas Camping Nieuwpoort

Brugsesteenweg 49, B-8620 Nieuwpoort (West Flanders) T: 058 236 037.

E: nieuwpoort@kompascamping.be alanrogers.com/BE0550

Not far from Dunkerque and Calais and convenient for the A18 motorway, this large, well equipped and well run site with 1056 pitches caters particularly for families. There are many amenities including a heated pool complex, a range of sporting activities, play areas and a children's farm. The 469 touring pitches, all with 10A electricity, are in regular rows on flat grass in various parts of the site; 120 also have a water point and waste water drainage. With many seasonal units and caravan holiday homes, the site becomes full during Belgian holidays and in July and August. A network of footpaths links all areas of the site. Gates to the rear lead to a reservoir reserved for sailing, windsurfing and canoeing (canoes for hire) during certain hours only. Although the site is vast, there is a sense of spaciousness thanks to the broad stretch of landscaped leisure areas. The site is well fenced with a card-operated barrier and a night guard. The whole area is a paradise for cyclists with access to over 200 km. of cycle-friendly paths and roads. Possible days out include to Ypres and the First World War battlefields, Bruges and Ghent.

Facilities

Five modern, clean and well maintained toilet blocks have washbasins in cubicles, controllable showers and great facilities for families, young children and disabled visitors. Dishwashing and laundry rooms. Washing machines and dryers. Motorcaravan services. Supermarket, bakery, restaurant, takeaway and café/bar (all daily; w/ends in low season). Swimming pools (heated and supervised) with slide, paddling pool and pool games (17/5-14/9). Bicycle hire. Tennis. Extensive adventure playgrounds. Multisports court. Entertainment programme in July/Aug. WiFi over site (charged). Off site: Nearest village 2 km. Riding 3 km.

Open: 28 March - 12 November.

Directions

From Dunkerque on A18 (E40) take exit 3. At roundabout take fourth exit (small road, easily missed). At junction turn left on N356. At end of this road at T-junction, turn right on N367. Site is on the left in 300 m. GPS: 51.12965, 2.77222

Charges guide

Per unit incl. 4 persons and electricity	€ 25.90 - € 39.90
dog	€ 2.90

Largest unit accepted 2.5x8 m.

Camping Cheques accepted.

Amidst Flanders battlefields and significant sites and monuments of the Great War

BELGIAN COAST — WESTENDE • NIEUWPOORT — KOMPAS camping

TEL. WESTENDE: +32 (0)58-22 30 25
TEL. NIEUWPOORT: +32 (0)58-23 60 37

HOLIDAY ... EXPERIENCE IT AT KOMPAS CAMPING

W W W . K O M P A S C A M P I N G . B E

Westende

Kompas Camping Westende

Bassevillestraat 141, B-8434 Westende (West Flanders) T: 058 223 025. E: westende@kompascamping.be

alanrogers.com/BE0565

Camping Westende is a large holiday site near the sea. The beach is only a short walk away and there is easy access to the coastal tram service. Of the 435 pitches, half are taken by seasonal caravans plus 43 rental units, leaving some 100 touring pitches on grass with 10A electricity, plus a group of 77 large (150 sq.m) serviced pitches with water and electricity. The site is well cared for with a range of amenities for children, including a play barn. The shop, bar and restaurant are grouped around reception. One end of the site is leased to a firm providing rental accommodation in mobile homes. Adjacent are a large holiday rental complex and a barrier operated motorcaravan area. Ostend is only 15 km. away and offers a wide variety of activities. Day trips could include Ypres and the First World War battlefields, Bruges and even Ghent. There is easy access to the cycle path network.

Facilities

Four toilet blocks are modern, recently renovated and very clean. One block is due for refurbishment. Good facilities for children and disabled visitors in one block. Shop, bar, restaurant and takeaway (high season and w/ends). Adventure playground. Play barn. Sports area. Boules. Entertainment and activities programme for children (July/Aug). Bicycle hire. WiFi throughout (charged). Off site: Fishing and golf adjacent. Beach 800 m.

Open: 28 March - 11 November.

Directions

From the E40 take exit 4 to Middelkerke (3-4 km). At the church turn left on N318 to Westende. After Westende church take the fourth turn right to the site (signed). GPS: 51.15787, 2.7606

Charges guide

Per unit incl. 4 persons and electricity	€ 25.90 - € 39.90
dog	€ 2.90

Camping Cheques accepted.

Croatia has developed into a lively and friendly tourist destination, while retaining the unspoilt beauty and character of its coastal ports, traditional towns and tiny islands with their secluded coves. Its rich history is reflected in its Baroque architecture, traditional festivals and two UNESCO World Heritage sites.

The most developed tourist regions in Croatia include the peninsula of Istria, where you will find the preserved Roman amphitheatre in Pula, the beautiful town of Rovinj with cobbled streets and wooded hills, and the resort of Umag, with a busy marina, charming old town and an international tennis centre. The coast is dotted with islands, making it a mecca for watersports enthusiasts, and there is an abundance of campsites in the area.

Further south, in the province of Dalmatia, Split is Croatia's second largest city and lies on the Adriatic coast. It is home to the impressive Diolectian's Palace and a starting point for ferry trips to the islands of Brac, Hvar, Vis and Korcula, with their lively fishing villages and pristine beaches. The old walled city of Dubrovnik is 150 km. south. A favourite of George Bernard Shaw, who described it as 'the pearl of the Adriatic', it has a lively summer festival, numerous historical sights and a newly restored cable car to the top of Mount Srd.

CAPITAL: Zagreb

Tourist Office
Croatian National Tourist Office
2 The Lanchesters
162-164 Fulham Palace Road
London W6 9ER
Tel: 020 8563 7979 Fax: 020 8563 2616
Email: info@cnto.freeserve.co.uk
Internet: www.croatia.hr

Population
4.4 million

Climate
Predominantly warm and hot in summer
with temperatures of up to 40°C.

Language
Croatian

Telephone
The country code is 00 385.

Money
Currency: Kuna (Kn)
Banks: Mon-Fri 08.00-19.00.

Shops
Mainly Mon-Sat 08.00-20.00, although some
close on Monday.

Public Holidays
New Year's Day; Epiphany 6 Jan; Good Friday;
Easter Monday; Labour Day 1 May; Parliament
Day 30 May; Day of Anti-Fascist Victory 22 June;
Statehood Day 25 June; Thanksgiving Day 5 Aug;
Assumption 15 Aug; Independence Day 8 Oct;
All Saints 1 Nov; Christmas 25, 26 Dec.

Motoring
Croatia is proceeding with a vast road
improvement programme. There are still some
roads which leave a lot to be desired but things
have improved dramatically. Roads along the
coast can become heavily congested in summer
and queues are possible at border crossings.
Tolls: some motorways, bridges and tunnels.
Cars towing a caravan or trailer must carry two
warning triangles. It is illegal to overtake
military convoys.

see campsite map 9

Plitvicka Jezera
Camping Korana

Eatrnja bb, HR-47245 Rakovica (Central) T: 053 751 888. E: info@np-plitvicka-jezera.hr

alanrogers.com/CR6650

This is the perfect site for a visit the Plitvice Lakes National Park (over 100 sq.km), deservedly one of Croatia's most famous attractions with its waterfalls vegetation and lakes. This 35-hectare site has a large, park-like environment and 550 unmarked pitches. Tourers can choose between the tarmac hardstandings close to the entrance and open grass plots with spectacular views towards the rear of the site. All have 16A electricity. The site has a good information centre and planning a visit to the park is well worthwhile. We took Tour E, down the waterfalls, which takes two and a half hours.

Facilities
The well maintained toilet blocks include facilities for disabled visitors. Washing machines. Motorcaravan services. Large restaurant. Shop is opened in the morning and afternoon and a dedicated information office with details about the National Park is open all day. No charcoal barbecues. WiFi (free in information office). 47 furnished cabins for hire. Off site: The wonderful National Park with its spectacular lakes and waterfalls (1- and 2-day visitors' tickets available). Walking. Cycling.

Open: 1 April - 31 October.

Directions
Take road from Karlovac to Plitvicka. Camp Korana is on the left, just past village of Grabovac. Site is north of the park area just before the village of Seliste and is signed. GPS: 44.95043, 15.64114

Charges guide
Per person	€ 7.00 - € 9.00
child (7-12 yrs)	€ 5.00 - € 6.50
pitch incl. electricity	€ 6.00
dog	€ 3.00

Camping Cheques accepted.

Dubrovnik
Camping Solitudo

Vatroslava Lisinskog 17, HR-20000 Dubrovnik (Dalmatia) T: 020 448 686.

E: camping-dubrovnik@valamar.com **alanrogers.com/CR6890**

Solitudo is located on the north side of Dubrovnik. There are 238 pitches, all for touring units, all with 12A electricity and 30 with water, arranged on four large fields that are opened according to demand. Field D is mainly used for tents and pitches here are small. Field A has pitches of up to 120 sq.m. and takes many motorcaravans (long leads required). From some pitches here there are beautiful views of the mountains and the impressive Dr. Franjo Tudman Bridge. All pitches are numbered, some are on terraces and most are shaded by a variety of mature trees.

Facilities
Attractively decorated, clean and modern toilet blocks have British style toilets, open washbasins and controllable, hot showers. Good facilities for disabled visitors. Laundry. Motorcaravan services. Shop. Attached restaurant/bar. Snack bar. Tennis. Minigolf. Fishing. Bicycle hire. Beach with pedalo, beach chair, kayak and jet ski hire. Excursions organised to Elafiti Islands. WiFi. Off site: Outdoor pool, disco and restaurant 500 m.

Open: 1 April - 1 November.

Directions
From Split follow no. 8 road south towards Dubrovnik. Site is very well signed, starting 110 km. before reaching Dubrovnik, and throughout the city. GPS: 42.661883, 18.07135

Charges guide
Per unit incl. 2 persons and electricity	€ 32.90 - € 49.30
extra person	€ 8.20 - € 11.20

Camping Cheques accepted.

Nin
Zaton Holiday Resort

Draznikova ulica 76 t, HR-23232 Nin (Dalmatia) T: 023 280 215.

E: camping@zaton.hr **alanrogers.com/CR6782**

Zaton Holiday Resort is a modern family holiday park with a one and a half kilometre private sandy beach. It is close to the historic town of Nin and just a few kilometres from the ancient city of Zadar. This park itself is more like a large village and has every amenity one can think of for a holiday on the Dalmatian coast. The village is divided into two areas separated by a public area with reception, bakery, shops, restaurant and a large car park, one for campers close to the sea, the other for a complex with holiday apartments. Zaton has 1,030 mostly level pitches for touring units, all with electricity, water and waste water. A member of Leading Campings group.

Facilities
Five modern and one refurbished toilet blocks with washbasins (some in cabins) and controllable hot showers. Child-size washbasins. Family shower rooms. Facilities for disabled visitors. Outdoor grill station. Motorcaravan services. Car wash. Shopping centre. Restaurants (self-service one has breakfast, lunch and evening menus). Several bars and kiosks. Water play area for children. Heated outdoor pools. Mini-car track. Riding. Tennis centre. Trim track. Scuba diving. Professional entertainment team. Teen club. Games hall. WiFi. New (2014) beach extension with climbing pyramids.

Open: 25 April - 30 September.

Directions
From Rijeka take no. 2 road south or A1/E65 Autobahn leave at exit for Zadar. Drive north towards Nin, Zaton Holiday Resort is signed a few kilometres before Nin. GPS: 44.234767, 15.164367

Charges guide
Per unit incl. 2 persons and electricity	€ 23.70 - € 55.90
extra person	€ 6.00 - € 11.90
child (1-11 yrs acc. to age)	€ 3.30 - € 9.40
dog	€ 5.00 - € 9.90

For latest campsite news, availability and prices visit

alanrogers.com

Pakostane

Camping Kozarica

Brune Busica 43, HR-23211 Pakostane (Dalmatia) T: 023 381 070. E: kozarica@adria-more.hr

alanrogers.com/CR6928

Camp Kozarica is situated directly by the sea. It has 325 well shaded touring pitches set on fairly level ground on the upper part of the site, and on terraces towards the water's edge. All have 6A electricity and 56 are fully serviced. The small town of Pakostane is is only a short, attractive walk from the site and has shops, restaurants, bars and watersports facilities. It is in a picturesque setting among the 100 small islands that comprise The Kornaten National Park. There is easy access from the coastal road, which makes this a convenient site to rest up for a few days and enjoy what this particular part of the coast has to offer.

Facilities
Very good toilet blocks with facilities for children and bathrooms for disabled visitors. Controllable showers and washbasins in cabins. Family shower rooms. Bathrooms to rent. Laundry room. Dog washing area. Motorcaravan services. Mini-market. Pâtisseries. Bars, restaurant, takeaway (20/5-15/9). Outdoor paddling pool (1/5-15/10). Play area. Miniclub. Entertainment (high season). Beach volleyball. Windsurf school. Diving lessons. Boat and bicycle hire. Accommodation for hire. WiFi throughout (charged). Off site: Fishing 0.5 km. Riding 5 km.

Open: 5 April - 31 October.

Directions
The site is 30 km. south of Zadar on road to Sibenic. It is very well signed with a right turn just after yellow 'Pakostane' sign. GPS: 43.91107, 15.49968

Charges guide
Per unit incl. 2 persons	
and electricity	€ 17.90 - € 37.70
extra person	€ 4.90 - € 8.90
child (3-12 yrs)	€ 3.10 - € 6.20
dog	€ 3.10 - € 6.10

Primosten

Camp Adriatic

Huljerat 1/a, HR-22202 Primosten (Dalmatia) T: 022 571 223. E: camp-adriatic@adriatic.com

alanrogers.com/CR6845

As we drove south down the Dalmatian coast road, we looked across a clear turquoise bay and saw a few tents, caravans and motorcaravans camped under some trees. A short distance later we were at the entrance of Camp Adriatic. With 530 pitches that slope down to the sea, the site is deceptive and enjoys a one kilometre beach frontage which is ideal for snorkelling and diving. Most pitches are level and have shade from pine trees. There are 212 numbered pitches and 288 unnumbered, all with 10/16A electricity. Close to the delightful town of Primosten, (with a taxi boat service in high season) the site boasts good modern amenities and a fantastic location.

Facilities
Four modern and well maintained sanitary blocks provide clean toilets, hot showers and washbasins. Facilities for disabled visitors. Bathroom for children. Washing machine and dryer. Kitchen facilities. Small supermarket (15/5-30/9). Restaurant, bar and takeaway (all season). Sports centre. Miniclub. Beach. Diving school. Sailing school and boat hire. Entertainment programme in July/Aug. WiFi in reception area (charged). Off site: Primosten 2.5 km. Riding 15 km. Sibenic 25 km.

Open: 1 May - 31 October.

Directions
Take the A1 motorway south and leave at the Sibenik exit. Follow the 33 road into Sibenik and then go south along the coast road (no. 8), signed Primosten. Site is 2.5 km. north of Primosten. GPS: 43.606517, 15.92095

Charges guide
Per person	Kn 37 - 68
child (3-12 yrs)	Kn 26 - 49
pitch incl. car and electricity	Kn 69 - 95
dog	Kn 34 - 50

FREE Alan Rogers Travel Card
Extra benefits and savings - see page 14

Split

Camping Stobrec Split

Sv. Lovre 6, Stobrec, HR-21311 Split (Dalmatia) T: 052 132 5426. E: camping.split@gmail.com

alanrogers.com/CR6855

Camping Stobrec is a new site which is still being developed, and is ideally located for those visiting Croatia and travelling down the coastal road or visiting Split – a must! The site, with 400 partially grassed pitches all with electricity and 200 also with water connections, is located on a small peninsula. From the level pitches, which have ample shade from trees, there are views over the sandy beach and across the bay. Set on top of rocks at the point of the peninsula is a small, comfortable restaurant with terrace and wonderful views – an ideal place for a quiet drink or evening meal. Split, with its squares, streets and narrow alleys worn smooth by almost 2,000 years of continuous use (wear shoes with a good grip), really must not be missed. The campsite can organise trips and at reception there is plenty of tourist information as well as good, personal advice available. Being close to the coastal road there is some traffic noise, especially during the day; however, it is not too obtrusive.

Facilities

Toilet blocks include facilities for disabled visitors. Free hot water, controllable showers and some washbasins in cabins. Laundry facilities. Motorcaravan services planned. Bar/restaurant. Supermarket at entrance. Play area. Children's club and entertainment programme (July/Aug). Bicycle hire. Fishing. Internet access and WiFi. Off site: Shops, cafés and restaurants within easy walking distance. Boat trips. Rafting on the River Cetina. Split city centre 5 km.

Open: All year.

Directions

Site is 7 km. southeast of Split city centre close to No. 8 coastal road. Travelling north to south, bypass Split on No. 8 road, at bottom of hill on the descent to Stobrec, site is signed to right. Turn right and site entrance is almost immediately on left.
GPS: 43.50333, 16.5275

Charges guide

Per unit incl. 2 persons and electricity	Kn 104 - 182
extra person	Kn 26 - 40
child (5-12 yrs)	Kn 17 - 24

Camping Cheques accepted.

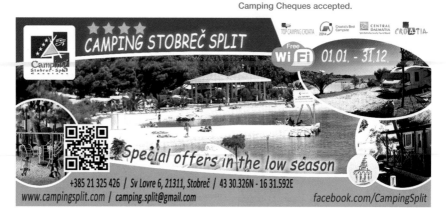

Fazana

Camping Bi-Village

Dragonja 115, HR-52212 Fazana (Istria) T: 052 300 300. E: info@bivillage.com

alanrogers.com/CR6745

Camping Bi-Village is a large holiday village in an attractive location close to the historic town of Pula and opposite the islands of the Brioni National Park. From the beach superb sunsets can be observed as the sun sinks below the sea's horizon. The site is landscaped with many flowers, shrubs and rock walls and offers over 1,000 pitches for touring units (the remainder taken by bungalows and chalets). The campsite is separated from the holiday bungalows by the main site road which runs from the entrance to the beach. Pitches are set in long rows accessed by gravel lanes, slightly sloping towards the sea, with only the bottom rows having shade from mature trees and good views over the Adriatic.

Facilities

Four modern toilet blocks with toilets, open plan washbasins and controllable hot showers. Child-size washbasins. Baby room. Facilities for disabled visitors. Washing machine. Shopping centre (1/5-11/10). Bars (1/5-30/9) and restaurants. Bazaar. Gelateria. Pastry shop. Three swimming pools. Playground on gravel. Playing field. Trampolines. Motorboats and pedaloes for hire. Boat launching. Games hall. Sports tournaments and entertainment organised. Massage. WiFi in some areas (charged). Dogs are not permitted on the beach.

Open: 16 April - 13 October.

Directions

Follow no. 2 road south from Rijeka to Pula. In Pula follow site signs. Site is close to Fazana.
GPS: 44.91717, 13.81105

Charges guide

Per unit incl. 2 persons and electricity	€ 18.00 - € 40.00
extra person	€ 5.00 - € 11.00
dog	€ 3.00 - € 6.00

Camping Cheques accepted.

Funtana

Naturist Camping Istra

Grgeti 35, HR-52452 Funtana (Istria) T: 052 465 010. E: camping@valamar.com

alanrogers.com/CR6726

Located in the tiny and picturesque village of Funtana, this peaceful naturist site is part of the Camping on the Adriatic group. Istra has a fine array of facilities and, although there is no pool, it is surrounded by sparkling sea on three sides. The formally marked pitches ring the peninsula and some are directly at the water's edge giving great views of the island off to the south (early booking is advised). There are 1,000 pitches on site with 904 for touring, most with ample shade and varying in size from about 90 sq.m. All have 10A electricity and water points are scattered around the site. The ground is undulating and some areas have been cut into low terraces.

Facilities

Three old and three new sanitary buildings provide toilets, washbasins, showers (hot and cold), hairdryers and some facilities for disabled campers. Laundry facilities. Small supermarket. Restaurant and bars. Play areas. Entertainment for children in high season. Organised sport. Minigolf. Tennis. Massage. WiFi near reception (free). Dogs are allowed in some areas. Charcoal barbecues are not permitted. Off site: Shops and restaurants in Funtana, a short walk from the gate.

Open: April - October.

Directions

Site is signed off Porec-Vrsar road 6 km. south of Porec in Funtana. Access for large units could be difficult turning off main road from Porec. If so, go past the signed turning and turn around in the night club car park a few metres further on.
GPS: 45.17464, 13.59869

Charges guide

Per unit incl. 2 persons	
and electricity	€ 17.50 - € 32.90
extra person	€ 4.20 - € 8.00

Labin

Camping Marina

Sveta Marina bb, HR-52220 Labin (Istria) T: 052 879 058. E: camping@valamar.com

alanrogers.com/CR6747

Camping Marina is a very quiet site with a somewhat steep approach. It is overlooked by high, tree clad hills and adjoins a small bay. The 267 touring pitches, all with electricity, are either centred around the site's facilities or set on a new level terrace on the cliff top. Many of these have superb views over the sea and to the island of Cres. The site has a new café and a sunbathing area from where you can relax and enjoy the views. A stairway leads down to the crystal clear water's edge, an ideal place for snorkelling and a haven for divers.

Facilities

The single, well maintained toilet block houses British style toilets, free controllable showers and washbasins. Toilet for children and a baby room. Facilities for disabled visitors. Washing machine and ironing area. Motorcaravan services and points for washing diving/snorkelling equipment. Restaurant/bar. Church. Play area. Dog shower and garden. WiFi on part of site. Off site: Well stocked supermarket at start of the entrance road to site.

Open: 12 April - 1 November.

Directions

From E751/21 Pula-Opatija road turn off to Labin and follow signs towards Rabac. On outskirts of Labin, site is signed sharp right and up a climbing cobbled road. Follow signs for Marina SV. Turn off country road for site. GPS: 45.033391, 14.157976

Charges guide

Per unit incl. 2 persons	
and electricity	€ 24.30 - € 34.00
extra person	€ 4.60 - € 7.30

No credit cards.

Novigrad

Camping Mareda

Mareda, HR-52466 Novigrad (Istria) T: 052 858 680. E: camping@laguna-novigrad.hr

alanrogers.com/CR6713

Backed by oak woods and acres of vineyards, Camping Mareda is in a quiet coastal location 4 km. north of the small picturesque town of Novigrad. The site slopes down to a half bay and has 600 touring pitches, all with 16A electricity, either set on shallow terraces or slightly sloping gravel/grass. Mature trees provide shade and many pitches have views over the sea; 95 pitches are fully serviced. The site has an attractive, rocky sea frontage with areas for sunbathing, a good sized swimming pool, a restaurant bar and a café, all with sea views. This site is an ideal base for day trips to Novigrad, Pula or Rovinj.

Facilities

Five modern toilet blocks, one excellent one refurbished in 2013, have British and Turkish style toilets, washbasins in cabins and hot showers. Family shower room. Child-size toilets and washbasins. Laundry with sinks and washing machine. Motorcaravan services. Supermarket. Beach restaurant, coffee bar and bar with terrace. Seawater swimming pool. Play area. Tennis. Fishing. Boats, kayaks, canoes and pedaloes for hire. Bicycle hire. Games hall with video games. Organised entertainment. Free WiFi.

Open: 1 May - 30 September.

Directions

From Novigrad travel north towards Umag. After 4 km. the site is signed to the left.
GPS: 45.34363, 13.54815

Charges guide

Per unit incl. 2 persons	
and electricity	€ 17.50 - € 42.50
extra person	€ 5.00 - € 8.50
child (5-9 yrs)	€ 3.00 - € 4.50
dog	€ 3.50 - € 5.50

Porec

Camping Lanterna

Lanterna 1, Tar-Vabriga, HR-52465 Porec (Istria) T: 052 465 010.

E: camping@valamar.com **alanrogers.com/CR6716**

LeadingCampings

This is a well organised site and one of the largest in Croatia with high standards and an amazing selection of activities, and is part of the Camping Adriatic by Valamar group. Set in 80 hectares with over 3 km. of beach, there are 3000 pitches, of which 1,886 are for touring units. All have 16A electricity and fresh water, and 255 also have waste water drainage. Pitches are 60-120 sq.m. with some superb locations right on the sea, although these tend to be taken first so it is advisable to book ahead. There are wonderful coastal views from some of the well shaded terraced pitches. A member of Leading Campings group.

Facilities

The sixteen sanitary blocks are clean and good quality. Facilities for children and baby care areas, some Turkish style WCs, hot showers, with some blocks providing facilities for disabled visitors. Three supermarkets sell most everyday requirements. Fresh fish shop. Four restaurants, bars and snack bars and fast food outlets. Swimming pool and two paddling pools. Sandpit and play areas, with entertainment for all in high season. Tennis. Bicycle hire. Watersports. Boat hire. Minigolf. Riding. Internet café. Jetty and ramp for boats. WiFi (free).

Open: 3 April - 3 October.

Directions

The turn to Lanterna is well signed off the Novigrad to Porec road 8 km. south of Novigrad. Continue for 2 km. along the turn off road towards the coast and the campsite is on the right hand side. GPS: 45.29672, 13.59442

Charges guide

Per unit incl. 2 persons	
and electricity	€ 19.30 - € 38.30
extra person	€ 5.00 - € 9.90
child (under 4yrs)	free

Prices for pitches by the sea are higher.

Porec

Naturist Resort Solaris

Lanterna bb, HR-52465 Porec (Istria) T: 052 465 010. E: camping@valamar.com

alanrogers.com/CR6718

This naturist site is part of the Camping on the Adriatic group and has a most pleasant atmosphere. When we visited in high season there were lots of happy people having fun. A pretty cove and lots of beach frontage with cool pitches under trees makes the site very attractive. Of the 1,448 pitches, 550 are available for touring, with 600 long stay units. There are 145 fully serviced pitches (100 sq.m) available on a 'first come, first served' basis, with an ample supply of electricity hook-ups (10/16A) and plentiful water points. As this is a naturist site, there are certain rules that must be followed.

Facilities

Eleven excellent, fully equipped toilet blocks provide toilets, washbasins and showers. Some blocks have facilities for disabled visitors. Washing machines and ironing facilities. Restaurants, grills and fast food, and supermarkets. Swimming pool. Tennis. Bicycle hire. Riding. Play areas. Boat launching. Car wash. Entertainment. WiFi over site (free). Dogs are allowed in certain areas, but not on the beach. Off site: Excursions.

Open: May - October.

Directions

Site is 12 km. south of Novigrad on Novigrad-Porec road. Turn towards the coast signed Lanterna. Continue straight on down this road and after passing the security barrier, turn left to Solaris. GPS: 45.29126, 13.5848

Charges guide

Per unit incl. 2 persons	
and electricity	€ 17.50 - € 45.40
extra person	€ 4.60 - € 8.00

Porec

Autokamp Zelena Laguna

HR-52440 Porec (Istria) T: 052 410 101. E: mail@plavalaguna.hr

alanrogers.com/CR6722

Zelena Laguna (green lagoon) is a well run and long established site with 540 touring pitches, all with 10A electricity, 42 being fully serviced. Access to the pitches is by hard surfaced roads with gravel side roads. There are many mature trees providing plenty of shade and hedges separate most pitches. Part of the site is on a peninsula with terraced pitches and the remainder are either on level or slightly sloping ground. A path circles the peninsula, below which are paved waterside sunbathing areas. Those to the right of the site are within easy reach of the cocktail bar. Further to the right is a small harbour, attractive restaurant and swimming pool.

Facilities

Six modern and well maintained sanitary blocks. The washbasins have hot water and there are free hot controllable showers. Toilets are mostly British style and there are facilities for disabled campers. Supermarket and shop. Several restaurants and snack bars. Swimming pool. Tennis (instruction available). Bicycle hire. Boat hire (motor and sailing). Boat launching. Riding. Entertainment.

Open: One week before Easter - 7 October.

Directions

Site entrance is 2 km. south of Porec on the Vrsar-Porec coastal road. It is very well signed and part of a large multiple hotel complex. GPS: 45.19529, 13.58927

Charges guide

Per unit incl. 2 persons	
and electricity	€ 19.20 - € 34.50
extra person	€ 4.40 - € 8.40
child (4-10 yrs)	free - € 5.70

For latest campsite news, availability and prices visit

alanrogers.com

Porec

Camping Bijela Uvala

Bijela Uvala, Zelena Laguna, HR-52440 Porec (Istria) T: 052 410 551. E: mail@plavalaguna.hr

alanrogers.com/CR6724

Bijela Uvala is a large friendly campsite with an attractive waterside location and an extensive range of facilities. The direct sea access makes the site very popular in high season. The 2,000 pitches, 1,476 for touring, are compact and due to the terrain some have excellent sea views and breezes, however as usual these are the most sought after, so book early. They range from 60-120 sq.m. and all have electricity and water connections. Some are formal with hedging, some are terraced and most have good shade from established trees or wooded areas. There are also very informal areas where unmarked pitches are on generally uneven ground.

Facilities

Eight sanitary blocks are clean and well equipped with mainly British style WCs. Free hot showers. Washing machines. Facilities for disabled visitors. Motorcaravan services. Gas. Fridge boxes. Three restaurants, three fast food cafés, two bars and a bakery. Large well equipped supermarket and a shop. Two swimming pool complexes, one with a medium size pool and the other larger, lagoon-style with fountains. Tennis. Playground. Amusements. TV room. Entertainment for children. WiFi (charged).

Open: 19 March - 7 October.

Directions

The site adjoins Zelena Laguna. From the main Porec to Vrsar coast road turn off towards coast and the town of Zelena Laguna 4 km. south of Porec and follow campsite signs. GPS: 45.19149, 13.59686

Charges guide

Per unit incl. 2 persons	
and electricity	€ 19.20 - € 34.50
extra person	€ 4.40 - € 8.40
child (4-10 yrs)	free - € 5.70

Rovinj

Camping Amarin

Monsena bb, HR-52210 Rovinj (Istria) T: 052 802 000. E: info@maistra.hr

alanrogers.com/CR6730

Situated 4 km. from the centre of the lovely old port town of Rovinj, this site has much to offer. The complex is part of the Maistra group. It has 12.6 hectares of land and is adjacent to the Amarin bungalow complex. Campers can take advantage of the facilities afforded by both areas. There are 650 pitches for touring units on various types of ground, all between 70-100 sq.m. Most are separated by foliage, and 10A electricity is available. A rocky beach backed by a grassy sunbathing area is very popular, but the site has its own superb, supervised round pool with corkscrew slide plus a splash pool for children. Boat owners have a mooring area and launching ramp and a breakwater is popular with sunbathers. The port of Rovinj contains many delights, particularly if you are able to contend with the hundreds of steps which lead to the church above the town from where the views are well worth the climb.

Facilities

Thirteen respectable toilet blocks have a mixture of British and Turkish toilets. Half the washbasins have hot water. Some showers have hot water, the rest have cold and are outside. Some blocks have a unit for disabled visitors. Fridge box hire. Laundry service. Motorcaravan services. Supermarket. Small market. Two restaurants, taverna, pizzeria and terrace grill. Swimming pool. Flume and splash pool. Watersports. Bicycle hire. Fishing (permit). Daily entertainment. Hairdresser. Massage. Barbecues not permitted. Dogs are not allowed on beach. Free WiFi over part of site. Off site: Hourly minibus service to Rovinj. Excursions including day trips to Venice. Riding 2 km.

Open: 25 April - 23 September.

Directions

Site is 2 km. north of Rovinj. Follow signs for campsite from main road. GPS: 45.10876, 13.61988

Charges guide

Per unit incl. 2 persons	
and electricity	€ 16.00 - € 34.00
extra person	€ 4.50 - € 9.00
child (5-11 yrs)	€ 3.00 - € 6.00
dog	€ 4.00 - € 7.00

For stays less than 3 nights in high season add 10%.

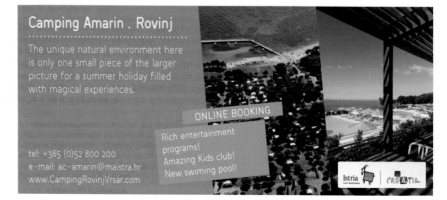

For latest campsite news, availability and prices visit

alanrogers.com

Pula

Camping Brioni

Puntizela 155, HR-52100 Pula (Istria) T: 052 517 490. E: camping@valamar.com

alanrogers.com/CR6744

Situated on a small peninsula overlooking the Brioni archipelago (a National Park comprising 14 islands) and within easy reach of Pula, Camping Brioni is a quiet and useful base from which to tour in a scenically attractive and historically interesting region. The site has 420 touring pitches under ample shade, all with 10A electricity and 272 with fresh water taps. On mainly level grass and gravel, the pitches are numbered with some terracing. Part of the site is devoted to a youth hostel which shares the site facilities. A diving club is based on the site, the clear seawater being ideal for snorkelling.

Facilities

Three sanitary blocks, one with facilities for disabled visitors. Cleaning and maintenance needed some attention when we visited. Baby room. Laundry room. Small supermarket and kiosk selling fruit, vegetables and bread (10/5-15/9). Restaurant. Beachside snack bar. Play area. Boat rental. Internet access. Off site: Pula, Brioni National Park.

Open: All year.

Directions

Site is 7 km. northwest of Pula. Heading north on the road running alongside the harbour in Pula (Trscanska ulinka) turn left at the roundabout towards Rijeka. After 800 m. site is signed to the left (west). GPS: 44.89812, 13.80833

Charges guide

Per unit incl. 2 persons and electricity	€ 15.70 - € 38.30
extra person	€ 3.75 - € 6.80

No credit cards.

Rovinj

Camping Polari

Polari bb, HR-52210 Rovinj (Istria) T: 052 801 501. E: polari@maistra.hr

alanrogers.com/CR6732

This 60-hectare site has excellent facilities for both textile and naturist campers, the latter in an area of 12 hectares to the left of the main site. Most parts of the site have good shade cover provided by mature trees. There are 1,650 level pitches for touring units on grass/gravel, terraced in places; many have open views over the sea to the islands. All have access to 10A electricity. An impressive swimming pool complex is child friendly with large paddling areas, and there is a new (2013) aquapark. The ancient town of Rovinj is well worth a visit, and is best reached via the 4.5 km. coastal cycle path or by bus from the campsite. Part of the Maistra group, a massive improvement programme has been undertaken and the result makes it a very attractive site. Enjoy a meal in one of the two restaurants with panoramic views of the sea.

Facilities

The sanitary facilities are well maintained with plenty of hot water. Washing machines and dryers. Motorcaravan services. Bar/snack bar. Takeaway food (17/4-3/10). Pool bar. Two restaurants. Aquapark with slide (17/4-3/10). Tennis. Minigolf. Children's entertainment with all major European languages spoken. Bicycle hire. Watersports. Windsurfing school. Trampoline. Miniclub. Games room. Live music (June-Sept). WiFi (charged). Off site: Riding 1 km. Rovinj 3 km. (five buses daily 15/6-15/9). Golf 30 km.

Open: 17 April - 3 October.

Directions

From any access road to Rovinj look for blue signs to AC Polari (amongst other destinations). The site is 3 km. south of Rovinj. GPS: 45.06286, 13.67489

Charges guide

Per unit incl. 2 persons and electricity	€ 18.00 - € 56.20
extra person (18-64 yrs)	€ 5.40 - € 10.60
child (5-17 yrs)	free - € 9.00
dog	€ 3.10 - € 8.00

For stays less than 3 nights in high season add 20%.

Camping Polari . Rovinj

A picturesque cove, ideal for all those who relish the pleasant shade of olive trees and the cleanest sea in the Mediterranean.

ONLINE BOOKING

Mobile homes with a whirlpool! Children's clubs and playgrounds! Pitch with water supply and drain! Wi-Fi !

tel: +385 (0)52 800 200
e-mail: polari@maistra.hr
www.CampingRovinjVrsar.com

Istria   CROATIA

Rovinj
Camping Vestar

Vestar bb, HR-52210 Rovinj (Istria) T: 052 803 700. E: vestar@maistra.hr

alanrogers.com/CR6733

Camping Vestar is a quiet site just 5 km. from the historic harbour town of Rovinj, and is one of the rare sites in Croatia with a partly sandy beach. Right behind the beach is a large area, attractively landscaped with young trees and shrubs, with grass for sunbathing. The site has 650 large pitches, of which 500 are for touring units, all with 6/10A electricity (the rest being taken by seasonal units and 60 pitches for tour operators). It is largely wooded with good shade and from the bottom row of pitches there are views of the sea. Pitching is on two separate fields, one for free camping, the other with numbered pitches. The pitches at the beach are in a half circle around the shallow bay, making it safe for children to swim. Vestar has a small marina and a jetty for mooring small boats and excursions to the islands are arranged. There is a miniclub and live music with dancing at one of the bars/restaurants in the evenings. The restaurants all have open-air terraces, one covered with vines to protect diners from the hot sun.

Facilities
Six modern and one refurbished toilet blocks with British style toilets, open washbasins and controllable hot showers. Child size facilities. Baby rooms. Family bathroom. Facilities for disabled visitors. Laundry service. Fridge box hire. Motorcaravan services. Shop. Three bars. Two restaurants. Large swimming pool. Playground. Fishing. Boat and pedalo hire. Miniclub (5-11 yrs). Excursions. Internet access in reception. WiFi (charged). Off site: Riding 2 km. Rovinj 5 km.

Open: 21 April - 1 October.

Directions
Site is on the coast 4 km. southeast of Rovinj. From Rovinj travel south towards Pula. After 4 km. turn right following campsite signs.
GPS: 45.05432, 13.68568

Charges guide
Per person	€ 5.00 - € 10.80
child (5-18 yrs)	free - € 9.20
pitch incl. electricity	€ 7.00 - € 30.00
dog	€ 3.10 - € 7.20

Camping Veštar . Rovinj

This campsite has a special charm – a warm welcome is guaranteed, in a stunning beachside setting.

tel: +385 (0)52 800 200
e-mail: vestar@maistra.hr
www.CampingRovinjVrsar.com

ONLINE BOOKING

Modern sanitary facilities!
Pitch with water supply
and drain! Wi-Fi !

Istria | CROATIA

Rovinj
Camping San Polo & Colone

Predio Longher bb, HR-52211 Bale (Istria) T: 052 824 338. E: reservations@camping-monperin.hr

alanrogers.com/CR6740

San Polo and Colone are two sister campsites with a number of shared amenities, including reception. They are located mid-way between Pula and Rovinj and have direct access to the sea. There are 800 pitches, many near the sea, including 500 for touring, well shaded and of a good size (100-120 sq.m), most with 16A electrical connections. Sixty mobile homes and chalets are available for rent. The beach here is long and pebbly, with a degree of natural shade. At Colone, a restaurant with a terrace serves delicious pizzas and other dishes prepared over a wood-fired grill. A great site, popular with families with young children and equally suitable for those seeking a relaxing beachside holiday.

Facilities
Eight, well maintained, prefabricated sanitary blocks provide free hot showers and open style washbasins. A new block will include facilities for disabled visitors. Laundry facilities. Mini market with fruit and vegetables. Three restaurants. Bar. Beach bar. Takeaway meals. Aquapark. Sports area. Playground. Volleyball. Direct beach access. Boat hire. Communal barbecue. WiFi on part of site (free). Off site: Walking and mountain bike trails. Bale town. Pula, Rovinj and Brijuni National Park.

Open: 27 March - 12 October.

Directions
Site is on the coast 18 km. south of Rovinj and is well signed on the Rovinj-Pula road at Bale.
GPS: 45.01986, 13.72275

Charges guide
Per unit incl. 2 persons and electricity	€ 17.20 - € 34.70
extra person	€ 4.40 - € 8.00
child (5-11 yrs)	free - € 4.30
dog	€ 2.60 - € 4.70
Camping Cheques accepted.	

For latest campsite news, availability and prices visit

alanrogers.com

Rovinj

Camping Valdaliso

Monsena bb, HR-52210 Rovinj (Istria) T: 052 800 200. E: ac-valdaliso@maistra.hr

alanrogers.com/CR6736

Camping Valdaliso has its affiliated hotel in the centre of the site. The 315 pitches are mostly flat with shade from pine trees and the site is divided into three sections, all with 16A electricity. The choice of formal numbered pitches, informal camping or proximity to the sea impacts on the prices. The kilometre plus of pebble beach has crystal clear water. The entertainment programme is extremely professional and there is a lot to do at Valdaliso, which is aimed primarily at families. The variety of activities here and the bonus of the use of the hotel make this a great choice for campers. The fine Barabiga restaurant within the hotel offers superb Istrian and fish cuisine and the pool is also within the hotel. You are close to the beautiful old town of Rovinj and parts of this site enjoy views of the town. A water taxi makes exploring Rovinj very easy, compared with the impossible parking for private cars. A bus service is also provided but this involves considerable walking. Alternatively it is a 3 km. cycle ride.

Facilities

Two large, clean sanitary blocks have hot showers. The northeastern block has facilities for disabled campers. Hotel facilities. Shop. Pizzeria. Restaurant. Tennis. Fitness centre. Bicycle hire. Games room. Children's games. Summer painting courses. Exchange. Boat rental. Watersports. Boat launching. Fishing. Diving school. Internet in both receptions. WiFi (charged). Water taxi. Bus service. Dogs are not accepted. Off site: Town 1 km.

Open: 6 April - 13 October.

Directions

Site is 7 km. north of Rovinj on the local road between Rovinj and Monsena.
GPS: 45.104267, 13.625183

Charges guide

Per unit incl. 2 persons	
and electricity	€ 18.00 - € 41.20
extra person	€ 4.50 - € 9.60
child (5-11 yrs)	free - € 5.90

Camping Valdaliso . Rovinj

A green and, for the most part, forested peninsula is situated just in front of the old Rovinj's town centre and is a place of perfect peace and quiet.

ONLINE BOOKING

Mobil Homes!
Diving center!
Children's playgrounds!

tel: +385 (0)52 800 200
e-mail: ac-valdaliso@maistra.hr
www.CampingRovinjVrsar.com

Istria   CROATIA

Savudrija

CampingIN Pineta Umag

Istarska bb, HR-52475 Savudrija (Istria) T: 052 709 550. E: camp.pineta@istraturist.hr

alanrogers.com/CR6711

This pleasant, quiet site is set under tall pines and has direct access to the sea over fairly level rocks. It is of medium size (17 hectares) and gets its name from its setting amongst a forest of fully mature pine trees around two sides of a coastal bay. There are 460 pitches of which 160 are occupied on a long stay basis. Pitches are numbered and are 50-120 sq.m, all with access to electricity (10A). This is a site for those who prefer cooler situations as the dense pines provide abundant shade. Those who like the peaceful life will enjoy this site. Sea bathing is easy from the site and sunbathing areas are on the rocks the whole length of the site.

Facilities

Toilet blocks have been refurbished to a high standard. Hot and cold showers (plus showers for dogs). Mostly British style WCs and a few Turkish style. Excellent facilities for disabled campers. Fresh water at toilet blocks only. Motorcaravan services. Supermarket. Six bars, three restaurants and snack bar. Tennis. Fishing (permit). Bicycle hire. Boat launching. Activities centre. Evening music. WiFi in some areas (charged). Off site: Gas is available in local garage 500 m. from the site entrance. Riding 6 km. Sailing 9 km. Golf 12 km.

Open: 22 April - 25 September.

Directions

Site is 6 km. north of Umag. From Umag travel north following signs for Savundrija signs. In the village of Basanija, at the tourist office, turn left. Reception is 500 m. on the left. GPS: 45.48674, 13.49246

Charges guide

Per unit incl. 2 persons	
and electricity	€ 14.60 - € 27.70
extra person	€ 3.70 - € 7.00
child (5-11 yrs)	€ 2.20 - € 4.40
dog	€ 2.20 - € 3.70

For stays less than 3 nights in high season add 10%.

Umag

CampingIN Stella Maris Umag

Savudrijska cesta bb, HR-52470 Umag (Istria) T: 052 710 900. E: camp.stella.maris@istraturist.hr

alanrogers.com/CR6712

This extremely large, sprawling site of 4.5 hectares is split by the Umag - Savudrija road. The camping site and reception is to the east of the road and the amazing Sol Stella Maris leisure complex, where the Croatian open tennis tournament is held (amongst other competitions), is to the west and borders the sea. Located some 2 km. from the centre of Umag, the site comprises some 575 pitches of which 60 are seasonal and 20 are for tour operators. They are arranged in rows on gently sloping ground, some are shaded. The pitches all have 10A electricity. The site's real strength is its attachment to the leisure complex, with numerous facilities available to campers.

Facilities

Three sanitary blocks of a very high standard. Hot water throughout. Excellent facilities for disabled visitors. Large supermarket. Huge range of restaurants, bars and snack bars. International tennis centre with pools and beach area. Watersports. Fishing (permit required from Umag). Entertainment programme for children. Communal barbecue areas. Excursions organised. Off site: Land train every 15 minutes into Umag and a local bus service to towns further along the coast. Riding 500 m. Golf 1 km.

Open: 23 April - 26 September.

Directions

Site is 2.5 km. north of Umag. On entering Umag look for signs on the main coast road to all campsites and follow the Stella Maris signs. GPS: 45.450417, 13.5222

Charges guide

Per unit incl. 2 persons	
and electricity	€ 10.10 - € 30.50
extra person	€ 2.80 - € 7.50
child (5-12 yrs)	free - € 4.50
dog	€ 1.70 - € 3.70

For stays less than 3 nights in high season add 10%.

Vrsar

Camping Porto Sole

Petalon 1, HR-52450 Vrsar (Istria) T: 052 426 500. E: petalon-portosole@maistra.hr

alanrogers.com/CR6725

Located near the pretty town of Vrsar and its charming marina, Porto Sole is a spacious and comfortable campsite with a long water frontage and two tiny bays that provide rocky swimming areas. The site has good facilities, including a large and attractive first floor swimming pool and sunbathing area above the shopping arcade, restaurant, pizzeria and pub. There are 730 grassy touring pitches, most in front of the reception area. They are reasonably level and fairly open, with 6-10A electricity, but have hardly any views of the sea. In a separate area, there are a few pitches for tourers set on terraces looking out over a small bay. In peak season the site is buzzing with activity and the hub of the site is the pool and shopping arcade area where there is also a pub and both formal and informal eating areas. The food available is varied but simple with a tiny terrace restaurant by the water.

Facilities

The five toilet blocks (one refurbished in 2014) have mostly British style WCs and are very clean and well maintained. Facilities for disabled visitors and children. Washing machines and dryers. Large well stocked supermarket (1/5-15/9). Small shopping centre. Pub. Pizzeria. Formal and informal restaurants. Swimming pools (1/5-29/9). Play area. Boules. Tennis. Minigolf. Massage. Entertainment in season. Miniclub. Scuba diving courses. Boat launching. Free WiFi. Off site: Vrsar 500 m. Marina and sailing 1 km. Riding 3 km.

Open: All year.

Directions

Site is on the coast 500 m. south of Vrsar. From main road take turning for Koversada then follow site signs. GPS: 45.142117, 13.602267

Charges guide

Per unit incl. 2 persons	
and electricity	€ 17.90 - € 38.00
extra person	€ 5.20 - € 9.20
child (5-12 yrs)	free - € 6.20
dog	€ 3.10 - € 6.50

Camping Porto Sole . Vrsar

A hidden oasis with clear seas and amazing underwater world. This is a true discovery for all lovers of active holidays.

tel: +385 (0)52 800 200
e-mail: portosole@maistra.hr
www.CampingRovinjVrsar.com

ONLINE BOOKING

Amazing sport centre, various entertainment programmes, diving centre! The campsite is open throughout the year!

Istria

CROATIA

For latest campsite news, availability and prices visit

alanrogers.com

Umag

CampingIN Park Umag

Karigador bb, HR-52470 Umag (Istria) T: 052 725 040. E: camp.park.umag@istraturist.hr

alanrogers.com/CR6715

This extremely large site is very well planned in that just 60% of the 127 hectares is used for the pitches, resulting in lots of open space around the pitch area. It is the largest of the Istraturist group of sites. Of the 2,090 pitches, 1,800 are for touring units, all with 10A electricity. Some pitches have shade. There are around 300 mobile homes, 70 for rent. Some noise is transmitted from the road alongside the site. The site is very popular with Dutch campers and a friendly and happy atmosphere prevails, even in the busiest times. The very long curved beach is of rock and shingle with grassy sunbathing areas. There are many watersports on offer and a new swimming pool complex has four pools, cascades and fountains. Several of the restaurant/bars offer excellent views over the sea.

Facilities

Ten toilet blocks include two bathrooms with deep tubs. Two blocks have children's WCs and there are facilities for disabled campers. The site has plans to update these facilities. Fresh water and waste water points only at toilet blocks. Motorcaravan services. Shops and supermarket. Bars, snack bars and restaurant (musical entertainment some evenings) all open early morning, one until the small hours. Swimming pool complex. Tennis. Fishing. Minigolf.

Open: 23 April - 26 September.

Directions

Site is on the Umag-Novigrad road 6 km. south of Umag. Look for large signs.
GPS: 45.36707, 13.54716

Charges guide

Per unit incl. 2 persons

and electricity	€ 19.00 - € 48.40
extra person	€ 4.90 - € 9.40
child (5-12 yrs)	€ 2.60 - € 5.20

For stays less than 5 nights in high season add 20%.

Vrsar

Camping Valkanela

Valkanela, HR-52450 Vrsar (Istria) T: 052 445 216. E: valkanela@maistra.hr

alanrogers.com/CR6727

Camping Valkanela is located in a beautiful green bay, right on the Adriatic Sea, between the villages of Vrsar and Funtana. It offers 1,300 pitches, all with 10A electricity. Pitches near the beach are numbered, have shade from mature trees and are slightly sloping towards the sea. Those towards the back of the site are on open fields without much shade and are not marked or numbered. Unfortunately, the number of pitches has increased dramatically over the years, many are occupied by seasonal campers and statics of every description, and these parts of the site are not very attractive. Most numbered pitches have water points close by, but the back pitches have to go to the toilet blocks for water. Access roads are gravel. For those who like activity, Valkanela has four gravel tennis courts, beach volleyball and opportunities for diving, water-skiing and boat rental. There is a little marina for mooring small boats and a long rock and pebble private beach with some grass lawns for sunbathing. It is a short stroll to the surrounding villages with their bars, restaurants and shops. There may be some noise nuisance from the disco outside the entrance and during high season the site can become very crowded.

Facilities

Fifteen toilet blocks provide toilets, open style washbasins and controllable hot showers. Child size toilets, basins and showers. Bathroom (free). Facilities for disabled visitors. Laundry. Dog showers. Two supermarkets. Fish market (08.00-14.00). Souvenir shops and newspaper kiosk. Bars and restaurants (25/4-30/9). Pâtisserie. Tennis. Minigolf. Fishing (with permit). Bicycle hire. Games room. Daily entertainment under 12s. WiFi.

Open: 19 April - 12 October.

Directions

Site is 2 km. north of Vrsar. Follow campsite signs from Vrsar. GPS: 45.16522, 13.60723

Charges guide

Per unit incl. 2 persons

and electricity	€ 17.50 - € 44.40
extra person	€ 4.50 - € 9.20
child (5-17 yrs)	free - € 7.30
dog	€ 2.50 - € 6.50

Vrsar

Naturist Park Koversada

Koversada, HR-52450 Vrsar (Istria) T: 052 441 378. E: koversada-camp@maistra.hr

alanrogers.com/CR6729

Reputedly, the first naturist on Koversada was the famous adventurer Casanova. Today Koversada is a first class enclosed naturist camping holiday park with bungalows. There are 1,700 pitches (all with 10A electricity), a shopping centre and its own island, which is reached by a narrow bridge; the island is suitable only for tents and has a restaurant and two toilet blocks. Between the island and the mainland is an enclosed, shallow section of water for swimming. The site is surrounded by a long beach, part sand, part paved. The pitches are of average size on grass and gravel ground and slightly sloping. Pitches on the mainland are numbered and partly terraced beneath mature pine and olive trees. Pitches on the island are unmarked and have shade from mature trees. The bottom row of pitches on the mainland enjoy views over the island and the sea.

Facilities

Seventeen toilet blocks provide British and Turkish style toilets, washbasins and controllable hot showers. Child size toilets and washbasins. Facilities for disabled visitors. Laundry service. Motorcaravan services. Supermarket. Kiosks with newspapers and tobacco. Several bars and restaurants. Tennis. Minigolf. Surf boards, canoes and kayaks for hire. Tweety Club for children. Live music. Sports tournaments. Internet access in reception and WiFi on part of site (charged). Communal barbecue. Off site: Fishing and riding 8 km.

Open: 26 April - 28 September.

Directions

Site is just south of Vrsar. From Vrsar, follow site signs. GPS: 45.14288, 13.60527

Charges guide

Per unit incl. 2 persons	
and electricity	€ 18.00 - € 36.00
extra person	€ 5.50 - € 10.00
child (5-18 yrs acc. to age)	free - € 6.20
dog	€ 3.20 - € 6.60

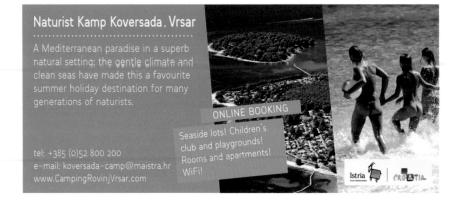

Naturist Kamp Koversada. Vrsar

A Mediterranean paradise in a superb natural setting; the gentle climate and clean seas have made this a favourite summer holiday destination for many generations of naturists.

tel: +385 (0)52 800 200
e-mail: koversada-camp@maistra.hr
www.CampingRovinjVrsar.com

ONLINE BOOKING

Seaside lots! Children's club and playgrounds! Rooms and apartments! WiFi!

Istria CROATIA

Vrsar

Camping Orsera

Sv. Martin 2/1, HR-52450 Vrsar (Istria) T: 052 465 010. E: camping@valamar.com

alanrogers.com/CR6728

This is a very attractive site with a 900 m. shoreline from which there are stunning views over the sea to the islands and very often there are spectacular sunsets. This 30-hectare site with direct access to the old fishing port of Vrsar has 575 pitches of which 433 are available to touring units. Marked and numbered, the pitches vary in size with 90 sq.m. being the average. There is some terracing but the pitches to the north of the site are on level ground and offer better views. Ample shade is provided by mature pines and oak trees. All pitches have 10/16A electricity.

Facilities

The modern and well maintained sanitary blocks are distributed over the site and have mainly British style WCs. Free showers, hot and cold water to washbasins. Some have facilities for disabled visitors. Facilities for babies and children. Motorcaravan services. Laundry. Supermarket (1/5-15/9). Bar/restaurant and takeaway (1/5-15/9). Sports centre. Cinema. Bicycle hire. Fishing. Watersports (no jet skis). Only electric barbecues are permitted. Free WiFi throughout. Off site: Shops in Vrsar, although the nearest large shopping centre is at Porec. Riding 3 km. Golf 7 km. Excursions.

Open: 1 April - 8 October.

Directions

Site is on the main Porec (7 km) to Vrsar (1 km) road, well signed. GPS: 45.15548, 13.61032

Charges guide

Per unit incl. 2 persons	
and electricity	€ 18.50 - € 35.30
extra person	€ 4.50 - € 8.70
child (4-9 yrs)	free - € 6.10
dog	€ 4.00 - € 6.10

Prices for pitches by the sea are higher.

For latest campsite news, availability and prices visit

alanrogers.com

Cres
Camping Kovacine

Melin I/20, HR-51557 Cres (Kvarner) T: 051 573 150. E: campkovacine@kovacine.com

alanrogers.com/CR6765

Camping Kovacine is located on a peninsula on the beautiful Kvarner island of Cres, just 2 km. from the town of the same name. The site has just under 1000 pitches for touring units, most with 16A electricity (from renewable sources) and a water supply. On sloping ground, partially shaded by mature olive and pine trees, pitching is on the large, open spaces between the trees. From the waterside pitches there are far reaching views over the sea to the coast beyond. Kovacine is partly an FKK (naturist) site, which is quite common in Croatia, and has a pleasant atmosphere. The site has its own beach (Blue Flag), part concrete, part pebbles, and a jetty for mooring boats and fishing.

Facilities

Seven modern, well maintained toilet blocks (water heated by solar power) with open plan washbasins (some cabins for ladies) and free hot showers. Private family bathrooms for hire. Facilities for disabled visitors and children. Laundry sinks and washing machine. Motorcaravan services. Electric car/scooter charging point. Car wash. Mini-marina and boat crane. Supermarket. Bar. Restaurant and pizzeria (May-18/10). Playground. Daily children's club. Evening shows with live music. Boat launching. Fishing. Diving centre. Motorboat hire. WiFi (free). Airport transfers. Off site: Cres 2 km.

Open: 27 March - 18 October.

Directions

From Rijeka take the coast road E65 towards Senj and Split. After 20 km. follow signs for Krk island (reached over bridge). Continue on the 102 for 20 km. then the 104 to Valbiska-Merag ferry. From Merag drive to Cres where, at beginning of town, site is signed to right. A ferry runs from Brestova to Porozina but the road onto Cres is only suitable for smaller units. GPS: 44.96346, 14.39747

Charges guide

Per unit incl. 2 persons	
and electricity	€ 18.20 - € 37.20
extra person	€ 6.20 - € 12.50

Krk
Camping Jezevac

HR-51500 Krk (Kvarner) T: 051 221 081. E: jezevac@valamar.com

alanrogers.com/CR6757

Camping Jezevac is an excellent and well maintained seaside site, within walking distance of the pretty town of Krk. It is a large site extending to over 11 hectares and is built on a hillside at the western side of the town. The 550 pitches, all for touring, are mainly on level terraces, separated by hedges with some shade and a number enjoy views of the bay below. All have 10A electricity, 120 are fully serviced. Some premium beachside pitches are available, with water and electricity. The 800 m. private beach is the focal point and in high season the atmosphere can be very lively.

Facilities

Six modern, well maintained toilet blocks with free hot showers. Washing machines. Facilities for disabled visitors and children. Motorcaravan services. Shops (1/4-15/10). Restaurants (1/5-1/10) and bars. Takeaway (1/5-30/9). Tennis. Playground. Activity and entertainment programmes and children's club (May-Sept). Fishing. Bicycle hire. Boat launching and sailing. Max. 1 dog. Communal barbecue area. WiFi over site.

Open: 13 April - 7 October.

Directions

From the toll bridge onto Krk, follow signs to Krk town and the town centre. Take the second right turn and continue ahead for 2.2 km. At the first roundabout take the second exit. Continue for 600 m. following signs to Camp Jezevac. GPS: 45.01964, 14.57072

Charges guide

Per unit incl. 2 persons	
and electricity	€ 25.20 - € 36.30
extra person	€ 5.90 - € 8.80

Krk
Camping Krk

Politin bb, HR-51500 Krk (Kvarner) T: 051 221 351. E: camping@valamar.com

alanrogers.com/CR6758

LeadingCampings

This is an excellent, attractive and well maintained site in a secluded hillside setting with views over the sea and close to the centre of Krk. On arrival you are assured of a good welcome from the staff who speak good English. There are 361 clearly defined and well spaced out touring pitches, mostly on level sandy terraces, all with 10A electricity, and ranging in size from 70-120 sq.m. Of these, 130 plots are fully serviced and include 96 with satellite TV connection. There are also 55 seasonal pitches that do not impinge on the touring units.

Facilities

Two excellent sanitary blocks are clean and well decorated and provide hot showers. Facilities for disabled visitors. Laundry facilities. Restaurant, bar and shop (all 1/5-30/9). Tennis. Playground. Activity programme for children. Fishing. Boat launching. Sailing. New, spacious mobile homes for rent. Payphones at reception. Outdoor pool. Children's pool. Saunas. Free WiFi to most of site.

Open: April - September.

Directions

Cross toll bridge to island of Krk, head for island's capital, Krk (28 km). On arrival head to second traffic junction and turn right. After 500 m. turn left (beyond petrol station). Continue for 800 m. to site. Site is well signed. GPS: 45.02440, 14.59280

Charges guide

Per unit incl. 2 persons	
and electricity	€ 23.60 - € 39.50

No credit cards.

FREE Alan Rogers Travel Card
Extra benefits and savings - see page 14

The Czech Republic, once known as Bohemia, is a land of fascinating castles, romantic lakes and valleys, picturesque medieval squares and famous spas. It is divided into two main regions, Bohemia to the west and Moravia in the east.

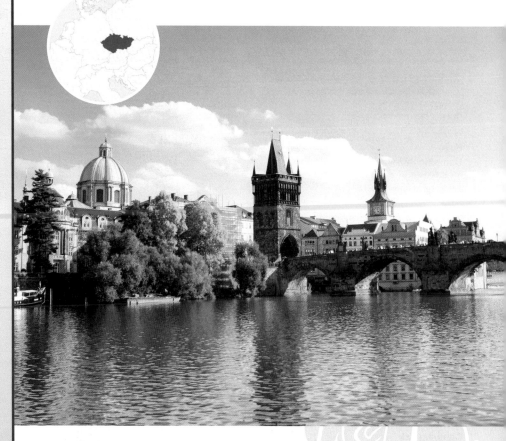

Although small, the Czech Republic has a wealth of attractive places to explore. The historic city of Prague is the hub of tourist activity and a treasure trove of museums, historical architecture, art galleries and theatres, as well as the annual 17-day beer festival!

The beautiful region of Bohemia, known for its Giant Mountains, is popular for hiking, skiing and other sports. West Bohemia is home to three renowned spas: Karlovy Vary, Mariánské Lázně and Františkovy Lázně, which have developed around the hundreds of mineral springs which rise in this area, and offer a wide variety of restorative treatments.

Brno is the capital of Moravia in the east, lying midway between Prague, Vienna and Budapest. Visitors will admire its beautiful architecture, notably Mies van der Rohe's Villa Tugendhat. North of Brno is the Moravian Karst, where the underground Punkya River has carved out a network of caves, some open to the public and connecting with boat trips along the river.

CAPITAL: Prague

Tourist Office

Czech Tourist Authority

13 Harley Street, London W1G 9QG

Tel: 020 7631 0427 Fax: 020 7631 0419

Email: info-uk@czechtourism.com

Internet: www.visitczech.cz

Population

10.5 million

Climate

Temperate, continental climate with four distinct seasons. Warm in summer with cold, snowy winters.

Language

The official language is Czech.

Telephone

The country code is 00 420.

Money

Currency: The Koruna

Banks: Mon-Fri 08.30-16.30.

Shops

Mon-Fri 08.00-18.00, some close at lunchtime. Sat 09.00 until midday.

Public Holidays

New Year; Easter Mon; May Day; Prague Uprising 5 May; National Day 8 May; Saints Day 5 July; Festival (John Huss) Day 6 July; Independence Day 28 Oct; Democracy Day 17 Nov; Christmas 24-26 Dec.

Motoring

There is a good and well signposted road network throughout the Republic and, although stretches of cobbles still exist, surfaces are generally good. An annual road tax is levied on all vehicles using Czech motorways and express roads, and a disc can be purchased at border crossings, post offices and filling stations. Do not drink any alcohol before driving. Dipped headlights are compulsory throughout winter months. Always give way to trams and buses.

see campsite map 8

Cerná v Posumavi
Camping Olsina
CZ-38223 Cerna v Posumavi (Jihocesky) T: 608 029 982. E: info@campingolsina.cz

alanrogers.com/CZ4725

Camping Olsina is a part wooded site, with direct access to Lake Lipno, and within walking distance of the pretty lakeside village of Cerná v Posumavi, in southern Bohemia. This is a tranquil site with splendid views across the lake to the hills beyond. There are 180 grassy pitches (150 with electrical connections), and many have lake front positions. There are also 15 chalets (for four people) and six mobile homes (six people). On-site amenities include a shop and restaurant, as well as cycle and boat hire. Cerná v Posumavi has a yacht club and a windsurfing school with rental facilities.

Facilities
Two modern sanitary buildings, one serving the camping area, the other serving the rented accommodation. Both are well maintained with open style washbasins and controllable hot showers with sliding doors. Facilities for disabled visitors. Laundry room. Small shop. Restaurant. Bar. Direct lake access. Fishing. Play area. Boat hire. Bicycle hire. Free WiFi over site. Accommodation for rent. Off site: Cycle and walking tracks. Riding. Cesky Krumlov. Sumava National Park.

Open: 1 April - 31 October.

Directions
From Ceské Budejovice, head south on E55 and road 39 to Cesky Krumlov and continue to Cerná v Posumavi. The site is clearly signed 1 km. before reaching town. GPS: 48.746115, 14.116911

Charges guide
Per unit incl. 2 persons	
and electricity	CZK 330 - 440
extra person	CZK 80
child (under 14 yrs)	CZK 50
dog	CZK 60

Ceské Budejovice
Camping Dlouhá Louka
Stromovka 8, CZ-37001 Ceské Budejovice (Jihocesky) T: 387 203 601. E: motel@dlouhalouka.cz

alanrogers.com/CZ4770

The medieval city of Ceské Budejovice is the home of Budweiser beer and is also an industrial centre. It lies on the River Vltava with mountains and pleasant scenery nearby. Dlouhá Louka is a motel and camping complex two kilometres south of the town on the Ceské Budejovice - Cesky Krumlov road. The camping part is a flat, rectangular meadow surrounded by trees which give some shade around the edges. There are some marked, hedged pitches and hardstanding, but many of the grass pitches are not marked or numbered so pitching can be rather haphazard. In total, 100 units are taken and there are 50 electricity connections (10A) and ten pitches with electricity and waste water.

Facilities
The single sanitary block, with British style WCs, is at one end making a fair walk for some. Washing machine and irons. Kitchen with electric rings. Playground. Tennis. Volleyball. Football. Bicycle hire. Off site: Shops 200 m. Bicycle hire 2 km. Fishing and golf 10 km.

Open: All year.

Directions
From town follow signs for Cesky Krumlov. After leaving ring road, turn right at motel sign. Take this small road and turn right 60 m. before Camp Stromovky. Campsite name cannot be seen from the entrance, only the word Motel. GPS: 48.96640, 14.46050

Charges guide
Per unit incl. 2 persons	
and electricity	CZK 450
extra person	CZK 100

No credit cards.

Cesky Krumlov
Camping Paradijs
Rájov 26, CZ-38101 Cesky Krumlov (Jihocesky) T: 776 898 022. E: jakesova.jana@centrum.cz

alanrogers.com/CZ4705

Camping Paradijs is a small, quiet, family run site in a natural setting beside the River Vltava. It has several stone-ringed fireplaces for camp fires (wood available at reception) and a fairly large building with tables and benches plus an open fireplace - useful in bad weather. There are 60 pitches on grass (20 for touring), near or bordering the tree-lined river, with a separate area of 12 pitches with electricity (6A). Reception and the sanitary facilities are housed together in one building raised above site level. This is essentially a site for those who enjoy and like to live close to nature.

Facilities
The very limited number (2 each) of toilets and showers, with changing/shower compartments separated by a sliding door, are well maintained and very clean. Reception stocks essential items, drinks and tourist information. Bar. Play area. Fishing. Bicycle hire. Free WiFi. Off site: Canoeing on the Vltava. Cesky Krumlov. Ceské Budejovice. Nature reserves. Castles at Hluboka and Vltavou. Walking routes.

Open: 17 April - 12 October.

Directions
Site is 5 km. north of Cesky Krumlov on the 39 road between Cesky Krumlov and Ceské Budejovice. Site is signposted at the bottom of a hill. Follow 'camping by the river' signs for 900 m. Follow site directions rather than GPS when nearing site. GPS: 48.839639, 14.375184

Charges guide
Per unit incl. 2 persons	
and electricity	CZK 280 - 370

No credit cards.

Chvalsiny

Camping Chvalsiny

Chvalsiny 321, CZ-38208 Chvalsiny (Jihocesky) T: 380 739 123. E: info@campingchvalsiny.nl

alanrogers.com/CZ4710

Camping Chvalsiny is Dutch owned and has been developed from an old farm into real camping fields which are terraced and level. The 200 pitches are of average size but look larger because of the open nature of the terrain which also means there is little shade. Chvalsiny is a real family site and children are kept occupied with painting, crafts and stories. Older youngsters take part in soccer, volleyball and rafting competitions. The location in the middle of the Blanky Les nature reserve, part of the vast Sumava forest, provides excellent opportunities for walking, cycling and fishing.

Facilities
Modern, clean and well kept toilet facilities include washbasins in cabins and controllable showers (coin operated). Family showers and baby room. Laundry. Kiosk (1/6-13/9) with bread and daily necessities. Snack bar (1/6-15/9). Motorcaravan services. Play attic. Lake swimming. Outdoor pool. Climbing equipment and swings. Crafts, games and soccer. Recreation hall (used in bad weather and for film nights). Animal farm. Torches useful. WiFi. Off site: Village restaurants nearby. Riding 10 km.

Open: 25 April - 15 September.

Directions
Take exit 114 at Passau in Germany (near the Austrian border) towards Freyung in the Czech Republic. Continue to Philipsreut and take no. 4 road (Vimperk). Turn right on no. 39 road to Horni Plana and Cesky Krumlov. Turn left 4 km. before Cesky Krumlov on no. 166 to Chvalsiny and follow site signs through village. GPS: 48.85583, 14.20850

Charges guide
Per unit incl. 2 persons and electricity	CZK 400
extra person	CZK 115

No credit cards.

Frymburk

Camping Frymburk

Frymburk 184, CZ-38279 Frymburk (Jihocesky) T: 380 735 284. E: info@campingfrymburk.cz

alanrogers.com/CZ4720

Camping Frymburk is beautifully located on the Lipno lake in southern Bohemia and is an ideal site. From this site, activities could include walking, cycling, swimming, sailing, canoeing or rowing, and afterwards you could relax in the small, cosy bar/restaurant. You could enjoy a real Czech meal in one of the restaurants in Frymburk or on site. The site has 170 level pitches on terraces (all with 6A electricity, some with hardstanding and four have private sanitary units) and from the lower terraces on the edge of the lake there are lovely views over the water to the woods on the opposite side.

Facilities
Three immaculate toilet blocks with washbasins, preset showers (charged) and an en-suite bathroom with toilet, basin and shower. Facilities for disabled visitors. Launderette. Shop, restaurant and bar, takeaway (1/5-15/9). Motorcaravan services. Playground. Canoe, bicycle, pedalos, rowing boat and surfboard hire. Kidstown. Volleyball competitions. Rafting. Bus trips to Prague. Torches useful. WiFi. Off site: Shops and restaurants in the village 900 m. from reception.

Open: 25 April - 21 September.

Directions
Take exit 114 at Passau in Germany (near the Austrian border) towards Freyung in the Czech Republic. Continue to Philipsreut, from there follow road 4 towards Vimperk. Turn right a few kilometres after border towards Volary on road 141. From Volary follow the road 163 to Horni Plana, Cerna and Frymburk. Site is on 163 road, right after village. GPS: 48.655947, 14.170239

Charges guide
Per unit incl. 2 persons and electricity	CZK 484 - 834

No credit cards.

Trebon

Autocamp Trebon

Libusina 601, CZ-37901 Trebon (Jihocesky) T: 384 722 586. E: info@autocamp-trebon.cz

alanrogers.com/CZ4765

Autocamp Trebon offers a happy Czech atmosphere especially around the bar/restaurant and is located on a lake where swimming, surfing and boating (the site rents out canoes) are possible. Being next to a large forest, it also makes a great location for walking and cycling. The site has 200 pitches, all for touring units and with 7A electricity, plus 35 cabins. Pitching is off tarmac access roads in two areas and there are some hardstandings for motorcaravans. The lower field is a single large, grassy area with a circular road around it and pitches on both sides of the road. The front pitches look out over the lake which is not fenced. The top field is smaller and more cramped.

Facilities
An older toilet building has some old and some new facilities, including British style toilets, open washbasins and controllable hot communal showers (token from reception, cleaning variable). Washing machine. Kiosk for bread and drinks. Bar with terrace. Self-service restaurant. Play area. Basketball. Fishing. Canoe rental. Boat launching. Beach. Off site: Bicycle hire 100 m.

Open: May - 30 September.

Directions
Take no. 34 road to Trebon; and in town follow the site signs. GPS: 48.992683, 14.767483

Charges guide
Per person	CZK 60
child (5-18 yrs)	CZK 45
pitch incl. car and electricity	CZK 180 - 250
dog	CZK 60

FREE Alan Rogers Travel Card
Extra benefits and savings - see page 14

Bojkovice
Eurocamping Bojkovice S.R.O.
Stefanikova ATC, CZ-68771 Bojkovice (Jihomoravsky) T: 604 236 631. E: info@eurocamping.cz

alanrogers.com/CZ4890

This family site in Bojkovice, close to the Slovak border and with views across the valley to the white castle Novy Svetlo, is attractive and well managed. It is on hilly ground with tarmac access roads connecting the 40 pitches. These are all for touring units on grassy fields taking six or eight units. Mostly on terraces in the shade of mature birch trees, all have 6A electricity. A footpath connects the three toilet blocks which offer a more than adequate provision. It also leads to the bar/restaurant and the centrally located outdoor pool.

Facilities
Three good toilet blocks (one refurbished) are clean and include British style toilets, open washbasins and controllable hot showers (free). Washing machine. Campers' kitchen. Bar/restaurant with open-air terrace (breakfast and dinner served, open 1/7-30/8). Outdoor swimming pool (15x8 m, unfenced). Fishing. Bicycle hire. WiFi. Off site: Riding 10 km.

Open: 1 May - 30 September.

Directions
From Brno take E50 road southeast towards the Slovakian border. Exit onto the 495 road towards Uhersky Brod and follow signs for Bojkovice. In town, turn left uphill and follow the green signs. GPS: 49.0398, 17.79993

Charges guide
Per unit incl. 2 persons	
and electricity	CZK 450 - 530
extra person	CZK 75 - 90
child (3-15 yrs)	CZK 60 - 75

Hluboke Masuvky
Camping Country
Hluboke Masuvky 257, CZ-67152 Hluboke Masuvky (Jihomoravsky) T: 515 255 249.

E: camping-country@cbox.cz **alanrogers.com/CZ4896**

Camping Country is a well cared for and attractively landscaped site close to the historical town of Znojmo. It is a rural location, in a wine growing region close to a national park, and with its small wine cellar, wine tasting evenings, small stables and riding school, barbecue and campfire areas, is an ideal site for a longer stay. Visitors will enjoy the new cycling routes which have been set out in the national park. Camping Country has 50 pitches (all for touring units), 30 with 16A electricity, on two fields – one behind the main house taking six or eight units, the other one larger with a gravel access road.

Facilities
Modern and comfortable toilet facilities provide British style toilets, open washbasins (cold water only) and free, controllable hot showers. Campers' kitchen. Bar/restaurant with one meal served daily. Play area. Tennis. Minigolf. Riding. Some live music nights in high season. Internet and WiFi (charged). Only gas and electric barbecues allowed on pitches. Tours to Vienna, Brno and wine cellars organised. Torch useful. Off site: Fishing and boat launching 2 km. Beach 10 km.

Open: 1 May - 31 October.

Directions
Coming from the northwest on the E59 road exit to the east at Kasarna onto the 408 road and continue north on the 361 road towards Hluboke Masuvky. Site is well signed. GPS: 48.9192, 16.0256

Charges guide
Per unit incl. 2 persons	
and electricity	CZK 410 - 490
extra person	CZK 120
child (3-12 yrs)	CZK 60
dog	CZK 50

Veverska Bityska
Camping Hana
Dlouha 135, CZ-66471 Veverska Bityska (Jihomoravsky) T: 607 905 801. E: camping.hana@seznam.cz

alanrogers.com/CZ4895

The caves of the Moravian Karst, the site of the battle of Austerlitz and the castles of Veveri, Pertstejn and Spillberk are all within easy reach of this pleasant, small and quiet campsite. Hana Musilova runs the site to very high standards, speaks excellent English and Dutch and provides lots of local information. There are 55 level, numbered pitches with 10A electricity. Brno, the capital of Moravia and the Czech Republic's second largest city, is a short boat or bus ride away and the village of Veverska Bityska has shops, restaurants, bars and an ATM plus a reasonable, small supermarket.

Facilities
The modernised sanitary block provides ample and clean toilets, hot showers (token, 1st free per person then CZK 10), washbasins and baby changing. Washing machine and dryer. Kitchen and dishwashing facilities. Small shop with essential supplies. Bicycle hire. Free WiFi throughout. Charcoal and gas barbecues allowed. Off site: Boat cruise to Brno 500 m. Veverska Bityska village and fishing 1 km. Riding 4 km. Golf 10 km. Fitness centre.

Open: 20 April - 30 September.

Directions
From D1 Prague-Brno autoroute, turn off at Ostrovacice and head towards Tisnov. The site is at Veverska Bityska on the road to Chudcice. From 43 turn off south of Lipuvka towards Kurim, then follow signs to Veverska Bityska where site is on right before entering village. GPS: 49.276567, 16.452633

Charges guide
Per unit incl. 2 persons	
and electricity	CZK 410 - 430
extra person	CZK 90
child (4-12 yrs)	CZK 40

For latest campsite news, availability and prices visit

alanrogers.com

Praha
Camp Drusus

K Reporyjim 4, CZ-15500 Praha 5 Trebonice (Prague) T: 235 514 391. E: drusus@drusus.com

alanrogers.com/CZ4785

Camp Drusus is a friendly, family site on the western edge of Prague. It provides a good base from which to explore this beautiful city, with the metro station only 15 minutes walk away. The site has 70 level pitches (all for touring units), with 16A electricity and varying in size (60-90 sq.m), with access off a circular, grass and gravel road. There is no shop here but basics can be ordered at reception and one of the biggest shopping areas in Prague is only 2 km. away. You could enjoy a real Czech breakfast in the restaurant which also opens for dinner and serves as a bar. A small, fenced pond bordered with flowers is attractive. This is a pleasant and well kept site with good connections to the Czech capital.

Facilities
Modern sanitary facilities. Laundry. Kitchen. Motorcaravan services. No shop, but basics to order at reception. Bar/restaurant. Small fitness centre. Playground. Games room with billiards. WiFi throughout (free). Off site: Bus 200 m. Shops 2 km. Metro station for Prague (15 minutes). Golf 6.5 km.

Open: 1 April - 5 October.

Directions
The site is not far from the junction of the D5 and the Prague ring road R1/E48/E50 (Prazsky Okruh) to the west of the city. From the ring road take exit 21 and follow signs to Trebonice and the camp for 2 km. GPS: 50.044083, 14.284217

Charges guide
Per unit incl. 2 persons and electricity	CZK 500 - 640
extra person	CZK 100 - 120

Praha
Triocamp Praha

Ustecka Ul., CZ-18400 Praha 84 (Prague) T: 28 385 0795. E: triocamp.praha@telecom.cz

alanrogers.com/CZ4815

This site on the northern edge of Prague is a great place to stay for a few days to visit the city. It has 70 pitches (all for touring units) with electricity (6/15A; half with Europlugs). Most are in the shade of mature trees, which can be very welcoming after a hard day sightseeing. The ground is slightly sloping but most pitches are level and access is off one circular, tarmac road, with cabins and pitches on both sides. There is one hardstanding for a motorcaravan. Triocamp has a bar/restaurant with a comprehensive menu and covered terrace attractively decorated with a variety of flowers.

Facilities
Modern, comfortable toilet facilities provide British style toilets, open washbasins and free, preset hot showers. Facilities for disabled campers. Laundry with washing machine. Motorcaravan services. Shop. Attractive bar/restaurant. Play area and children's pool. Off site: Prague is a few kilometres by public transport (bus/tram or Metro).

Open: All year.

Directions
On E55 in either direction, take exit 1 towards Zdiby and continue straight ahead on 608 road. Site is on right after 3 km. GPS: 50.152283, 14.450317

Charges guide
Per unit incl. 2 persons and electricity	CZK 450 - 730
extra person	CZK 140 - 180
child (5-15 yrs)	CZK 80 - 100

Praha
Camping Oase Praha

Libenska, CZ-25241 Zlatniky (Prague) T: 241 932 044. E: info@campingoase.cz

alanrogers.com/CZ4840

Camping Oase Praha is an exceptional site, only five kilometres from Prague and with easy access. You can take the bus (from outside the site) or drive to the underground stop (10 minutes). The site has 120 pitches, all around 100 sq.m, with 6/10A electricity and 55 with water and drainage, on level, well kept fields. The site is very well kept and has just about everything one may expect, including a new Western style toilet block, a well maintained outdoor and a new indoor swimming pool with separate paddling pool, a restaurant and a bar. Children can amuse themselves with trampolines, the new playground, a roofed miniclub, volleyball and basketball.

Facilities
An outstanding, new toilet block includes washbasins, controllable showers and child sized toilets. Facilities for disabled visitors. Family showers. Jacuzzi with sauna and massage (30/4-15/9). Laundry facilities. Campers' kitchen. Motorcaravan services. Restaurant and bar. Basic groceries are available in the shop. Outdoor pool (9x15 m; open July/Aug), indoor pool (10x4 m; all season) and separate paddling pool with slide. New adventure style playgrounds and roofed miniclub for children. Trampolines. Football. Minigolf. WiFi. TV and video. Board games. Closed circuit security cameras.

Open: 26 April - 15 September.

Directions
Go south from Prague on the R1 (Prazsky okruh) and take exit 82 to Jesenice. At Jesenice turn left, following camping signs to the site in Zlatniky where you turn left at the roundabout. Site is 700 m. after the village. GPS: 49.95145, 14.47517

Charges guide
Per unit incl. 2 persons and electricity	CZK 340 - 1030
extra person	CZK 120 - 140
child (under 11 yrs)	CZK 60 - 90

Less 3% discount for payment in cash.

FREE Alan Rogers Travel Card
Extra benefits and savings - see page 14

Praha
Camping Busek Praha

U parku 6, CZ-18200 Praha 8 Brezineves (Prague) T: 283 910 254. E: campbusekprag@volny.cz

alanrogers.com/CZ4845

No trip to the Czech Republic would be complete without a visit to the capital, Prague. At this site you can do just that without getting tangled up with the city traffic. Just about 8 km. from the centre, there is an excellent bus link from the site to the new metro station at Ladvi that is a part of the new integrated transport system. The site is part of a small motel complex and provides 20 level and unnumbered pitches, all with 10A electricity. It is on the edge of a small, rural village, which offers peace and quiet at the end of a long day's sightseeing.

Facilities
Older style sanitary block with clean toilets, hot showers and washbasins. Washing machine and dryer. Kitchen and dishwashing facilities. Small restaurant (all year). WiFi (free). Off site: Prague city centre only a bus and metro ride away. Outdoor swimming pool.

Open: All year.

Directions
From the Prague-Teplice (Dresden) motorway, the D8/E55, take exit to Brezineves and head towards the village. The site is 200 m. after the village sign on the right. Turn towards the small fire station and the site is on the right. GPS: 50.164716, 14.485578

Charges guide
Per unit incl. 2 persons and electricity	CZK 480 - 610
extra person	CZK 140

No credit cards.

Praha
Camp Sokol Troja

Trojská 171A, CZ-17100 Praha (Prague) T: 233 542 908. E: info@camp-sokol-troja.cz

alanrogers.com/CZ4850

This site is very close to the Vltava river although you cannot see it. It was subject to heavy flooding in 2002 and some of the facilities were washed away. There are 75 touring pitches (10 with 16A electricity). The pitches are small (80-90 sq.m) and about half are on hardstanding. The grass pitches can become muddy with rain. The access road is narrow and manoeuvring space is limited so the site may be less suitable for large caravans and motorcaravans. Nevertheless, it is only a 15 or 20 minute journey to the centre of the city by bus. There is a bus stop in front of the site and a tram (no. 17) a 300 m. walk away.

Facilities
The single, refurbished toilet block has toilets, washbasins with hot and cold water and preset showers in cabins without curtain or door. Cleaning can be variable. Facilities for disabled visitors. Motorcaravan services. Campers' kitchen with hob. Good restaurant. Off site: Fishing 1 km.

Open: All year.

Directions
From Dresden or Teplice, follow signs to the centre and turn right before the first bridge over the Moldau into the Kozlovka Pátkova, in the Troja district. Site is well signed from here. GPS: 50.11683, 14.42500

Charges guide
Per person	CZK 70 - 150
child (under 18 yrs)	CZK 50 - 90
caravan	CZK 140 - 300
motorcaravan	CZK 140 - 300
electricity	CZK 100

Januv Dul
Camping 2000

Janov Dul 15, CZ-46352 Januv Dul (Severocesky) T: 485 179 621. E: camping2000@online.nl

alanrogers.com/CZ4695

Created from pleasant farm buildings and the fields behind them, Camping 2000 is especially popular with Dutch visitors. It is a good base for exploring Northern Bohemia with Prague (90 km) and the Krkonose mountains (50 km) from a pleasant, rural location. Most of the pitches are of average size (up to 100 sq.m) and numbered, all with 6A electricity. There is little shade and cars parked on the pitches make the curved rows feel a bit crowded during high season. Further off, however, there are a few larger pitches catering for larger units.

Facilities
Until an extra new block is built, in high season prefabricated units are used next to the main toilet block. Facilities for disabled visitors. Washing machine and dryer. Shop (July/Aug). Bar and takeaway (May-Sept). Swimming and paddling pools. Bicycle hire. TV room. Five wooden cottages (fully equipped) for hire. WiFi. Off site: Golf 3 km. Fishing and riding 5 km. Jested Mountain (1012 m) with restaurant can be reached by road or cable car. Bezdez Castle. Bus excursions to Prague in high season. Liberec 15 km.

Open: 15 April - 15 September.

Directions
From E65/E442 (Prague-Liberec) motorway take exit 35 for Hodkovicevia Ceske Dub and on to Osecna, then to Januv Dul hamlet where site is signed. GPS: 50.7043, 14.93898

Charges guide
Per unit incl. 2 adults, 2 children (under 18 yrs) and electricity	€ 33.72 - € 36.72
extra person	€ 4.25
dog	€ 3.00

For latest campsite news, availability and prices visit
alanrogers.com

Litomerice

Slavoj Autocamp Litomerice

Strerelecky Ostrov, CZ-41201 Litomerice (Severocesky) T: 416 734 481. E: kemp.litomerice@post.cz

alanrogers.com/CZ4685

Slavoj is a pleasant, small site with a friendly atmosphere and welcoming people. The site was totally destroyed during the flood of 2002 and has been rebuilt with help from many camp guests from all over Europe. For example, an American visitor painted the little landscape on the outer wall of the restaurant. Located centrally, the bar/restaurant is the main focus on the site and here you can enjoy a good value breakfast, as well as lunch and dinner. The site is on level ground, with 50 unmarked pitches, all for touring units. Some look out over the River Laba (Elbe) which is well fenced. Around 24 electricity connections (8/16A) are available. In high season the site can become rather crowded.

Facilities
The well maintained toilet block has British style toilets, open washbasins and free, controllable hot showers. Laundry facilities. Kitchen. Motorcaravan services. Basics from restaurant. Bar/restaurant with covered and open-air terrace. River fishing. Canoeing. WiFi throughout (charged). Off site: Tennis adjacent. Boat launching 500 m. Golf 4 km. Beach 5 km. Boat trips are possible and a meal can be included. Bus trips into Prague.

Open: 1 May - 30 September.

Directions
On E55 from either direction, take exit 45 towards Litomerice. Cross the river, the railway bridge and turn left. Take first left and go left again. Cross under railway bridge and continue to site. GPS: 50.532, 14.13867

Charges guide
Per unit incl. 2 persons and electricity	CZK 345 - 395
extra person	CZK 85 - 90

Benesov u Prahy

Autocamping Konopiste

CZ-25601 Benesov u Prahy (Stredocesky) T: 317 722 732. E: konopiste@amberhotels.cz

alanrogers.com/CZ4780

Benesov's chief claim to fame is the Konopiste Palace, the last home of Archduke Franz Ferdinand whose assassination in Sarajevo sparked off the First World War in 1914. Autocamp Konopiste, now under new ownership, is part of a motel complex with excellent facilities situated in a very quiet, tranquil location south of Prague. On a hillside, rows of terraces separated by hedges provide 65 grassy pitches of average size, 50 with electricity (10A). Konopiste has many different varieties of trees and much to offer. A fitness centre and heated swimming pool are shared with motel guests.

Facilities
The good quality sanitary block is central to the caravan pitches. Washing machine and irons. Kitchen. Site's own bar/buffet (high season) with simple meals and basic food items. Motel bar and two restaurants (all year). Swimming pool (1/6-31/8). Tennis. Minigolf. Bicycle hire. Badminton. Fitness centre. Playground. Club room with TV. Château and park. WiFi. Off site: Shop 200 m. Fishing 1.5 km.

Open: 1 May - 30 September.

Directions
Site is signed near the village of Benesov on the main Prague-Ceske Budejovic road no. 3/E55. GPS: 49.776, 14.669

Charges guide
Per person	CZK 70
child (6-15 yrs)	CZK 50
pitch	CZK 150

Electricity included.

Lodenice

Caravan Camp Valek

Chrustenice 155, CZ-26712 Lodenice (Stredocesky) T: 311 672 147. E: info@campvalek.cz

alanrogers.com/CZ4820

Only 2.5 km. from the E50 motorway, this well maintained site creates a peaceful, friendly base enjoyed by families. It has been family owned for 21 years. Surrounded by delightful countryside, it is possible to visit Prague even though it is about 28 km. from the city centre. The site is well grassed and most of the pitches are on level ground to one side of the pool. The other part of the site is on sloping ground and more suitable for tents. Most of the 50 pitches are in the open and not specifically marked. However this does not appear to cause overcrowding and there is plenty of space. Electricity (10A) is available to all. Some places have pleasant views of the sunbathing area in front of the pool with a pine forested hillock as a backdrop.

Facilities
The single extremely well maintained toilet block has limited numbers of toilets and showers, but during our visit in high season coped well. Small shop with fresh rolls daily. Waiter service restaurant with terrace has an extensive menu. Communal grill on the terrace. Natural swimming pool (20x60 m; June-Sept) with constantly changing water checked regularly by the authorities to ensure its purity. Extensive games room with arcade machines and Internet. Live musical nights on Saturdays. Tennis. Off site: Riding 3 km. Golf 8 km. Prague 28 km.

Open: 1 May - 30 September.

Directions
From E50 (D5) motorway take exit 10 for Lodenice. Follow camping signs and for Chrustenice. Site is 300 m. on right 1 km. north of Chrustenice. GPS: 50.011517, 14.150217

Charges guide
Per unit incl. 2 persons and electricity	CZK 435 - 515
extra person	CZK 115
child (6-14 yrs)	CZK 55
dog	CZK 45

FREE Alan Rogers Travel Card
Extra benefits and savings - see page 14

Nové Straseci

Camping Bucek

Trtice 170, CZ-27101 Nové Straseci (Stredocesky) T: 313 564 212. E: info@campingbucek.cz

alanrogers.com/CZ4825

Camping Bucek is a pleasant, Dutch-owned site 30 km. west of Prague. Its proprietors also own Camping Frymburk (CZ4720). Bucek is located on the edge of woodland and has direct access to a small lake with a private beach. Here you can enjoy canoes and rowing boats which are available to guests free of charge. There are 100 pitches here, many with pleasant views over the lake, and all with electrical connections (6A). Four pitches have private sanitary facilities. Shade is quite limited. On-site amenities include an indoor swimming pool, play equipment and there is an animation programme.

Facilities

Renovated toilet blocks with free hot showers. Washing and drying machine. Restaurant, takeaway and bar. Direct lake access with rowing boats and canoes. Heated indoor swimming pool with paddling pool (all season). Minigolf. Play area. Trampolines. Activity programme. Walking and cycling opportunities. WiFi throughout (free). Bicycle hire. Off site: Revnicov 2 km. with shops (including a supermarket), bars and restaurants. Fishing 3 km. Riding 4 km. Karlovy Vary 10 km. Prague 40 km. Koneprusy caves.

Open: 25 April - 15 September.

Directions

From the west, take no. 6/E48 express road towards Prague. Site is close to this road, 3 km. after the Revnicov exit and is clearly signed from this point. Coming from the east, ignore other camping signs and continue until Bucek is signed (to the north). GPS: 50.1728, 13.8348

Charges guide

Per unit incl. 2 persons and electricity	CZK 460 - 880
extra person	CZK 75 - 100

No credit cards.

Vrchlabi

Holiday Park Lisci Farma

Dolni Branna 350, CZ-54362 Vrchlabi (Vychodocesky) T: 499 421 473. E: info@liscifarma.cz

alanrogers.com/CZ4590

This is truly an excellent site that could be in Western Europe considering its amenities, pitches and welcome. However, Lisci Farma retains a pleasant Czech atmosphere. In the winter months, when local skiing is available, snow chains are essential. The 260 pitches are fairly flat, although the terrain is slightly sloping and some pitches are terraced. There is shade and some pitches have hardstanding. The site is well equipped for the whole family with its adventure playground offering trampolines for children, archery, beach volleyball, Russian bowling and an outdoor bowling court for older youngsters. A beautiful sandy, lakeside beach is 800 m. from the entrance.

Facilities

Two good sanitary blocks near the entrance and another modern block next to the hotel, both include toilets, washbasins and spacious, controllable showers (on payment). Child size toilets and baby room. Toilet for disabled visitors. Sauna and massage. Launderette. Shop (15/6-15/9). Bar/snack bar with pool table. Games room. Swimming pool (6x12 m). Adventure style playground on grass with climbing wall. Trampolines. Tennis. Minigolf. Archery. Russian bowling. Paragliding. Rock climbing. Bicycle hire. Entertainment. Excursions to Prague.

Open: All year.

Directions

Follow road no. 14 from Liberec to Vrchlabi. At the roundabout turn towards Prague and site is 1.5 km. on the right. GPS: 50.61036, 15.60264

Charges guide

Per unit incl. 2 persons and electricity	CZK 390 - 475
extra person	CZK 55 - 65
child (4-15 yrs)	CZK 35 - 40
dog	CZK 25

Various discounts available in low season.

Cheb

Camping Václav

Jesenická prehrada, CZ-35002 Cheb - Podhrad (Zapadocesky) T: 354 435 653. E: info@kempvaclav.cz

alanrogers.com/CZ4645

Camping Václav is situated close to the German border on the banks of the Jesenice Lake. The site is on two levels – the lower one, which is slightly sloping, has beautiful views over the lake; the upper level, which is newer and has an excellent new toilet block, offers less shade. The 150 touring pitches are generous (80-150 sq.m), all have 6/10A electricity and ten also have water and drainage. Václav is in the 'spa triangle' giving visitors a choice of three different spas – Karlovy Vary, Mariánské Lázné and Frantiskovy Lázné. Guests at Camping Václav can take advantage of discounts for Frantiskovy Lázné.

Facilities

Excellent modern toilet block with open style washbasins, controllable hot showers and facilities for disabled visitors. Washing machine and dryer. Motorcaravan services. Bar/restaurant. Small shop for drinks and ice-creams. Internet access. Football field. Tennis. Fishing. Play area. Lake for swimming and boating. WiFi (free). Off site: Sailing 1 km. Bicycle hire 4 km. Riding 5 km. Golf 10 km.

Open: 28 April - 14 September.

Directions

Coming from the west on the 21 road, follow the signs Centrum-Cheb and then Podhrad. From there follow signs for Kemp Václav. On the motorway take exit 146 Podhrad. GPS: 50.04997, 12.41183

Charges guide

Per unit incl. 2 persons and electricity	CZK 510 - 790
extra person	CZK 100 - 125

No credit cards.

For latest campsite news, availability and prices visit

alanrogers.com

Velká Hled'sebe

Autocamping Luxor

Plzenska, CZ-35301 Velká Hled'sebe (Zapadocesky) T: 354 623 504. E: autocamping.luxor@seznam.cz

alanrogers.com/CZ4650

An orderly site, near the German border, Luxor is adequate as a stopover for a couple of days. Now under new management, it is in a quiet location by a small lake on the edge of the village of Velká Hled'sebe, 4 km. from Marianbad. The 100 pitches (60 for touring units) are in the open on one side of the entrance road (cars stand on a tarmac park opposite the caravans) or in a clearing under tall trees away from the road. All pitches have access to electricity (10A) but connection in the clearings section may require long leads. Forty bungalows occupy one side of the site. There is little to do here but it is a good location for visiting the spa town of Marianbad.

Facilities

Toilet buildings have been refurbished and the provision is more than adequate. Showers are on payment. No chemical disposal point. Restaurant with self-service terrace (1/5-30/9). Rest room with TV, kitchen and dining area. Small playground. Fishing. Bicycle hire. Internet access. Off site: Very good motel restaurant and shops in village 500 m. Riding 5 km. Golf 8 km.

Open: 1 May - 30 September.

Directions

Site is directly by the Stribo-Cheb road no. 21, 500 m. south of Velká Hled'sebe.
GPS: 49.95242, 12.66833

Charges guide

Per unit incl. 2 persons and electricity	CZK 180 - 360

No credit cards.

Want independent campsite reviews at your fingertips?

alan rogers

Over 3,000 in-depth campsite reviews at
www.alanrogers.com

Denmark offers a diverse landscape all within a relatively short distance.

The countryside is green and varied with flat plains, rolling hills, fertile farmland, many lakes and fjords, wild moors and long beaches, interrupted by pretty villages and towns.

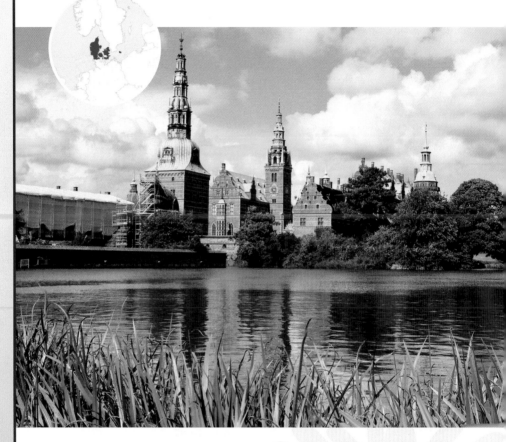

Denmark is the easiest of the Scandinavian countries to visit, and distances are short so it is easy to combine the faster pace of the city with the tranquillity of the countryside and the beaches. It comprises the peninsula of Jutland and the larger islands of Zeeland and Funen, in addition to hundreds of smaller islands, many uninhabited. Zeeland is home to the climate-friendly capital city, Copenhagen, with its relaxing, waterside cafés, vibrant nightlife, 13 Michelin Star restaurants and the stunning Frederiksborg Castle. Funen is Denmark's second largest island, linked to Zeeland by the Great Belt Bridge. Known as the Garden of Denmark, its gentle landscape is dotted with orchards and pretty thatched, half-timbered houses. It also has plenty of safe, sandy beaches. Jutland's flat terrain makes it ideal for cycling, and its long beaches are popular with windsurfers. It's also home to one of the most popular attractions in Denmark, Legoland, and the oldest town in Scandinavia, Ribe.

CAPITAL: Copenhagen

Tourist Office
Danish Tourist Board
55 Sloane Street, London SW1X 9SY
Tel: 020 7259 5958
Fax: 020 7259 5955
Email: london@visitdenmark.com
Internet: www.visitdenmark.com

Population
5.6 million

Climate
Generally mild although changeable throughout
the year.

Language
Danish, but English is widely spoken.

Telephone
The country code is 00 45.

Money
Currency: Danish Krone (DKK).
Banks: Mon-Wed & Fri 09.30-16.00,
Thurs to 18.00. Closed Sat. In the provinces
opening hours vary.

Shops
Hours may vary in the main cities.
Regular openings are Mon-Thu
09.00-17.30, Fri 09.00-19.00/20.00,
and Sat 09.00-13.00/14.00.

Public Holidays
New Year's Day; Three Kings Day 6 Jan; April
Fools Day 1 April; Maundy Thursday; Good Friday;
Easter Monday; Queen's Birthday 16 April; Flag
Day 18 April; Ascension; Whit Mon; Constitution
Day 5 Jun; Valdemars 15 June; Mortens Day
11 Nov; Christmas 24-26 Dec; New Year's Eve

Motoring
Driving is much easier than at home as roads
are much quieter. Driving is on the right. Do not
drink and drive. Dipped headlights are compulsory
at all times. Strong measures are taken against
unauthorised parking on beaches, with
on-the-spot fines.

see campsite map 2

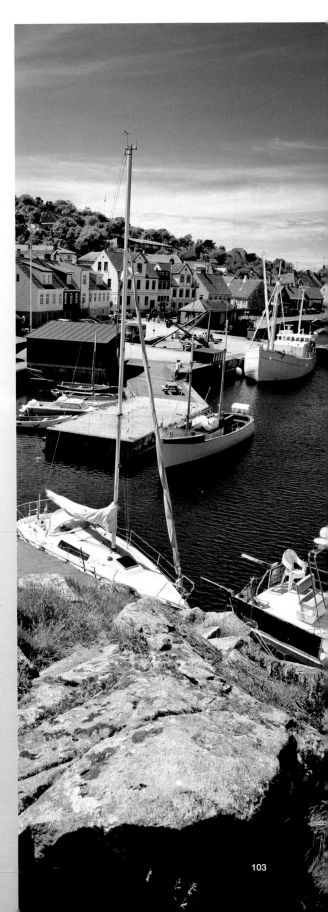

Ebeltoft

Blushoj Camping-Ebeltoft

Elsegårdevej 55, DK-8400 Ebeltoft (Århus) T: 86 34 12 38. E: camping@blushoj.com

alanrogers.com/DK2100

This is a traditional type of site where the owners are making a conscious effort to keep mainly to touring units – there are only six seasonal units and four rental cabins. The site has 250 pitches on levelled grassy terraces surrounded by mature hedging and shrubs. Some have glorious views of the Kattegat and others overlook peaceful rural countryside. Most pitches have electricity (10A), but long leads may be required. There is a heated and fenced swimming pool (14x7 m) with a slide and a terrace. The beach below the site provides opportunities for swimming, windsurfing and sea fishing.

Facilities

One toilet unit includes washbasins with dividers and showers with divider and seat (charged; cleaning can be variable). The other unit has a new kitchen with electric hobs, sinks, dining/TV room, laundry and baby facilities. A heated extension provides six very smart family bathrooms, and additional WCs (including one for disabled visitors) and washbasins. Motorcaravan services. Shop. Swimming pool (20/5-20/8). Minigolf. Play area. Games room. Beach. Fishing. Internet access. Free WiFi over site. Off site: Riding, bicycle hire and golf all 5 km.

Open: 1 April - 14 September.

Directions

From road 21 northwest of Ebeltoft turn off at junction where several sites are signed towards Dråby. Follow signs through the outskirts of Ebeltoft turning southeast to Elsegårde village. Turn left for Blushøj and follow site signs. GPS: 56.16773, 10.73067

Charges guide

Per unit incl. 2 persons and electricity	DKK 195 - 225
extra person	DKK 80 - 95

No credit cards.

Grenå

Fornæs Camping

Stensmarkvej 36, DK-8500 Grenå (Århus) T: 86 33 23 30. E: info@fornaescamping.dk

alanrogers.com/DK2070

In the grounds of a former farm, Fornæs Camping is about 5 km. from Grenå. From reception, a wide gravel access road descends through a large grassy field to the sea. Pitches to the left are mostly level, to the right slightly sloping with some terracing and views of the Kattegat. The rows of pitches are divided into separate areas by colourful bushes and each row is marked by a concrete tub containing a young tree and colourful flowers. Fornæs has 320 pitches of which 240 are for tourers, the others being used for seasonal visitors. All touring pitches have 10A electricity. At the foot of the site is a pebble beach and there is also an attractive outdoor pool near the entrance.

Facilities

Two partly refurbished toilet blocks have British style toilets, washbasins in cabins and controllable hot showers. Children's section and baby room. Family shower rooms. Facilities for disabled visitors. Laundry. Campers' kitchen. Motorcaravan services. Shop. Café with bar and takeaway (evenings). Swimming pool (80 sq.m) with paddling pool. Sauna and solarium. Play area and adventure playground. Games room with satellite TV. Minigolf. Fishing. Watersports.

Open: 15 March - 20 September.

Directions

From Århus follow the 15 road towards Grenå and then the 16 road towards town centre. Turn north and follow signs for Fornæs and the site. GPS: 56.45602, 10.94107

Charges guide

Per person	DKK 85
child (1-12 yrs)	DKK 45
electricity (10A)	DKK 35

Credit cards 5% surcharge.

Ry

Holmens Camping

Klostervej 148, DK-8680 Ry (Århus) T: 86 89 17 62. E: info@holmenscamping.dk

alanrogers.com/DK2080

A warm welcome awaits you at Holmens Camping, which lies between Silkeborg and Skanderborg in a very beautiful part of Denmark. The site is close to the waters of the Gudensø and Rye Møllesø lakes which are used for boating and canoeing, and fishing is a speciality of the site (it has its own pond). Holmens has 225 grass touring pitches, partly terraced and divided by young trees and shrubs. The site itself is surrounded by mature trees. Almost all the pitches have 6A electricity and vary in size between 70-100 sq.m. The lake is suitable for swimming but the site also has an attractive pool complex.

Facilities

One traditional and one modern toilet block have washbasins (open and in cabins) and controllable hot showers (on payment). En-suite facilities with toilet, basin, shower. Baby room. Facilities for disabled visitors. Laundry. Campers' kitchen. Small shop. Covered pool and paddling pool. Wellness facilities (charged). Pool bar. Games room. Playground. Pétanque. Pony rides. Minigolf. Fishing. Bicycle hire. Boat rental. Some activities incur a charge. WiFi (charged). Off site: Riding 2 km. Golf 14 km.

Open: 1 April - 30 September.

Directions

Going north on E45, take exit 52 at Skanderborg turning west on 445 road towards Ry. In Ry follow the site signs. GPS: 56.07607, 9.76549

Charges guide

Per person	DKK 73 - 83
child (3-11 yrs)	DKK 40 - 45
pitch	DKK 26
electricity (6A)	DKK 30

For latest campsite news, availability and prices visit
alanrogers.com

Silkeborg

Terrassen Camping

Himmelbjergvej 9A, Laven, DK-8600 Silkeborg (Århus) T: 86 84 13 01. E: info@terrassen.dk

alanrogers.com/DK2050

Terrassen Camping is a family run site arranged on terraces, overlooking the lovely Lake Julso and the countryside. It is open and spacious, and when we visited was lively with people enjoying themselves. There are 220 touring pitches, many with good views, all with electricity (10/16A). The solar heated swimming pool has a paved terrace and is well fenced. This is a comfortable base from which to explore this area of Denmark where a warm welcome, real enthusiasm for making your holiday enjoyable, and good English will greet you.

Facilities

Modern heated sanitary unit. Showers on payment. Family bathrooms. Baby room. Kitchen with hobs, ovens. Refurbished unit contains another kitchen and four shower cubicles, external access. All facilities clean and well maintained. Motorcaravan services. Shop (11/4-14/9). Takeaways from town (by arrangement). Swimming pool (mid May-31/8). Games/TV rooms with Internet. Adventure playground. Indoor play room. Pets' corner. Covered barbecue. Canoe hire. WiFi (free). Bicycles and riding can be ordered. Off site: Fishing 200 m.

Open: 11 April - 14 September.

Directions

From the harbour in the centre of Silkeborg follow signs and minor road towards Sejs (5 km) and Ry (20 km). Site is on the northern side of the road at village of Laven (13 km). Height restriction of 3 m. on railway bridge over this road.
GPS: 56.12409, 9.71037

Charges guide

Per unit incl. 2 persons and electricity	DKK 242 - 382
extra person	DKK 100
child	DKK 50

Ebberup

Helnæs Camping

Strandbakken 21, Helnæs, DK-5631 Ebberup (Fyn) T: 64 77 13 39. E: info@helnaes-camping.dk

alanrogers.com/DK2220

Helnæs Camping is on the remote Helnæs peninsula to the southeast of Fyn, connected to the mainland by a small road. The site is adjacent to a nature reserve making it ideal for walkers, cyclists and birdwatchers, or for those who enjoy sea fishing (this is a great location for sea trout). Helnæs Camping has 160 pitches, some terraced, on grassy fields sloping down towards the sea. Almost all the pitches have beautiful views of Helnæs Bugt and the site is only 300 m. from the beach. Low rock walls and different types of newly planted trees and low shrubs separate pitches. All have 6A electricity.

Facilities

Two toilet blocks include washbasins in cabins and controllable showers. Baby room (heated). Family shower rooms. Facilities for disabled visitors. Laundry with washing machines and dryers. Campers' kitchen. Shop. Takeaway. Playground. Minigolf. Bicycle and canoe hire. Watersports. In high season small circus for children. TV lounge. Internet access. Covered barbecue area.

Open: 15 March - 1 September.

Directions

From Nørre Åby follow 313 road south to Ebberup. In Ebberup turn south to Helnæs and follow signs for Helnæs Strand. GPS: 55.13254, 10.03622

Charges guide

Per person	DKK 69
child	DKK 40
electricity	DKK 30

No credit cards.

Fåborg

Bøjden Strand Ferie Park

Bøjden Landevej 12, Bøjden, DK-5600 Fåborg (Fyn) T: 63 60 63 60. E: info@bojden.dk

alanrogers.com/DK2200

Bøjden is located in one of the most beautiful corners of southwest Fyn (Funen in English), known as the Garden of Denmark, and may well be considered one of the most complete campsites in the country. With just a hedge separating it from the beach, it is suitable for an entire holiday, while remaining a very good centre for excursions. Arranged in rows on mainly level, grassy terraces and divided into groups by hedges and some trees, many pitches have sea views as the site slopes gently down from the road. The 295 pitches (210 for touring) all have electricity (10A) and include 65 new, fully serviced pitches (water, drainage and TV aerial point).

Facilities

Superb central toilet block includes washbasins in cubicles, controllable showers, family bathrooms, baby room and excellent facilities for disabled visitors. Excellent kitchen and laundry. Additional facilities to the far end of the site. Motorcaravan services. Supermarket. Restaurant. Takeaway. Indoor and outdoor swimming pools with flumes and slides. Solarium. Well equipped, fenced toddler play area and separate adventure playground. TV and games rooms. Internet café and WiFi. Barbecue area. Fishing. Minigolf. Off site: Beach adjacent.

Open: 14 March - 20 October.

Directions

From Fåborg follow 8 road to Bøjden and site is on right 500 m. before ferry terminal (from Fynshav). GPS: 55.105289, 10.107808

Charges guide

Per unit incl. 2 persons, 1 child and electricity	DKK 225 - 385
extra child	DKK 65

Credit cards accepted with 5% surcharge.

Hårby

Løgismosestrand Camping

Løgismoseskov 7, DK-5683 Hårby (Fyn) T: 64 77 12 50. E: info@logismose.dk

alanrogers.com/DK2205

A countryside site with its own beach and pool, Løgismosestrand is surrounded by picturesque villages and the owners are a friendly young couple. The pitches here are arranged in rows and groups divided by hedges and small trees which provide some shade. All the 221 pitches for touring units have 6/10A electricity points and ten comfort pitches (up to 140 sq.m) are fully serviced. A barbecue area has been developed with gas grills and there are swimming (8x14 m) and paddling pools for which there is a small charge. Recent additions include an Asian restaurant, a new football pitch and ten cabins to rent.

Facilities

Clean and heated toilet units include washbasins in cubicles, roomy showers (on payment), fairytale-themed facilities for children, bathrooms for families and disabled visitors. Good laundry. Excellent kitchen (cooking charged). Motorcaravan services. Shop. Asian restaurant. Takeaway (high season). Swimming pool (1/6-1/9) with paddling area. Minigolf. Bicycle and boat hire. Adventure playground. Large undercover games room. Play field. Free WiFi over part of site. Off site: Riding 2 km. Golf 8 km. Odense, the birth city of Hans Christian Andersen.

Open: 20 March - 22 September.

Directions

Southwest of Hårby via Sarup and Nellemose to Løgismoseskov, site is well signed. Lanes are narrow, large units should take care.
GPS: 55.17938, 10.07390

Charges guide

Per unit incl. 2 persons and electricity	DKK 237 - 342
extra person	DKK 85
child (0-11 yrs)	DKK 58
dog	DKK 20

Credit cards accepted with 4% surcharge.

Hesselager

Bøsøre Strand Feriepark

Bøsørevej 16, DK-5874 Hesselager (Fyn) T: 62 25 11 45. E: info@bosore.dk

alanrogers.com/DK2210

A themed holiday site on the eastern coast of Fyn, the tales of Hans Christian Andersen are evident in the design of the indoor pool complex, the minigolf course and the main outdoor play area. The former has two pools on different levels, two hot tubs, a sauna and features characters from the stories; the latter has a fairytale castle with a moat as its centrepiece. There are 300 pitches in total (some up to 150 sq.m), and with only 25 seasonal units there should always be room for touring units out of the main season. All have 10A electricity, there are 124 multi-serviced pitches and 20 hardstandings.

Facilities

Sanitary facilities provide all the usual facilities plus some family bathrooms, special section for children, baby rooms and facilities for disabled campers. They could be stretched in high season. Basic wellness facility. Laundry. Motorcaravan services. Shop, bar/restaurant, pizzeria, takeaway (all open all season). Kitchen (water charged). Solarium. Indoor pool complex. Games and TV rooms. Indoor playroom for toddlers. Playground with moat. Animal farm. Internet access and WiFi (charged). Bicycle hire. Entertainment (main season). Boat launching with jetty. Communal barbecue. Off site: Golf 10 km.

Open: 11 April - 19 October.

Directions

Site is on the coast midway between Nyborg and Svendborg. From 163 road just north of Hesselager, turn towards coast signed Bøsøre Strand (5 km).
GPS: 55.19287, 10.80530

Charges guide

Per unit incl. 2 persons and electricity	€ 32.19 - € 46.95
extra person	€ 10.73
child (0-11 yrs)	€ 7.24
dog	€ 2.68

Odense

DCU Odense City Camp

Odensevej 102, DK-5260 Odense (Fyn) T: 66 11 47 02. E: odense@dcu.dk

alanrogers.com/DK2215

Although within the confines of the city, this site is hidden away amongst mature trees and is therefore fairly quiet and an ideal base from which to explore the fairytale city of Odense. The 225 pitches, of which 200 have electricity (10A), are on level grass with small hedges and shrubs dividing the area into bays. There are a number of seasonal units on site, together with 13 cabins. Eight overnight pitches and minigolf are recent additions. A good network of cycle paths lead into the city. The Odense Adventure Pass (available at the site) allows unrestricted free travel on public transport within the city limits.

Facilities

Large sanitary unit provides modern facilities including washbasins in cubicles, family bathrooms, baby room and excellent suite for disabled visitors. Well equipped kitchen with gas hobs. Laundry facilities. Motorcaravan services. Shop. Small swimming and paddling pools. Games marquee. TV room. Large playground. Minigolf. WiFi over site (charged). Off site: Cycle track to city centre. Bicycle hire 700 m. Golf 4 km. Fishing 10 km.

Open: All year.

Directions

From E20 exit 50, turn towards Odense Centrum, site entrance is 3 km. on left immediately beside the UnoX petrol station. GPS: 55.3697, 10.3929

Charges guide

Per person	€ 10.20 - € 10.70
child (0-11 yrs)	€ 5.37 - € 6.71
pitch	€ 2.95 - € 6.44
electricity	€ 1.08

For latest campsite news, availability and prices visit

alanrogers.com

Sakskøbing

Sakskøbing Camping

Saxes Allé 15, DK-4990 Sakskøbing (Lolland) T: 54 70 47 57. E: info@saxcamping.dk

alanrogers.com/DK2235

This small, traditional-style site provides a useful stopover on the route from Germany to Sweden, within easy reach of the Puttgarden - Rødby ferry. There are 100 level grass pitches (90 for tourers), most with electricity (10A Europlug) and, although there are a fair number of seasonal units, one can usually find space. There is a pool at a nearby sports centre. The site has a well stocked shop, which is open long hours, but the attractive town centre is semi-pedestrianised, and has a good range of shops and a supermarket. The town is noted for its unusual 'smiling' water tower, which you pass on the way to the site. Sakskøbing is a quiet little town with museums and two mediaeval castles.

Facilities
Two sanitary units provide basic, older style facilities, including pushbutton free hot showers, some curtained washbasin cubicles and a baby room. Cooking and laundry facilities. Motorcaravan services. Shop. New covered grill area. Full information centre with interactive screen. Play area. Bicycle hire. Free WiFi over site. Off site: Town and fishing 100 m. Golf and riding 10 km.

Open: 1 April - 30 September.

Directions
From E47, exit 46, turn towards town on 9 road. Turn right at crossroads towards town centre (site is signed), cross railway and then turn right again, and site entrance is 250 m. on left.
GPS: 54.79842, 11.64093

Charges guide
Per unit incl. 2 persons and electricity	DKK 170
extra person	DKK 70
child (0-14 yrs)	DKK 35

Aalbæk

Skiveren Camping

Niels Skiverenrej 5-7, DK-9982 Skiveren/Aalbæk (Nordjylland) T: 98 93 22 00. E: info@skiveren.dk

alanrogers.com/DK2165

This friendly, family run seaside site, a member of the Danish TopCamp organisation, is adjacent to a beautiful, long sandy beach. Skiveren Camping has 595 pitches (496 for touring units), all with 10/16A electricity and generally separated into named areas. Around the site are different varieties of low spruce and fir which give the site a pleasing appearance and atmosphere. There is an excellent, large indoor play area as well as many outdoor amenities. A horse and cart can take campers for rides around the site, which has an excellent supermarket and restaurant (high season).

Facilities
Three toilet blocks include free family showers and private facilities with shower, toilet and basin for rent (DKK 40-70). Facilities for disabled visitors. Laundry. Campers' kitchens. Motorcaravan services. Supermarket. Strand Café for meals, drinks and takeaway (27/3-15/9). Outdoor pool (17/5-1/9) with whirlpool and sauna. Playground. New large indoor play hall. Multisports court. Tennis. Games room with machines and wide screen TV. Bicycle hire. Minigolf (charged). Fishing. Horse and cart rides. Children's club daily (from 16.00). Live music and dancing.

Open: Weekend before Easter - 30 September.

Directions
From the 40 road going north from Ålbæk, turn left at sign for 'Skiveren'. Follow this road all the way to the end. GPS: 57.61611, 10.27908

Charges guide
Per unit incl. 2 persons and electricity	€ 27.62 - € 50.33
extra person	€ 9.12 - € 11.97
child (0-11 yrs)	€ 5.85 - € 8.84
dog	€ 1.36
Credit cards 2.75% surcharge.	

Aalbæk

Bunken Strand Camping

Ålbekvej 288, DK-9982 Aalbæk (Nordjylland) T: 98 48 71 80. E: info@bunkenstrandcamping.dk

alanrogers.com/DK2378

Ideal for families, Bunken Strand is located in natural surroundings between forest and sand dunes, by the safe, gently shelving sea. Most of the 700 pitches are for tourers, arranged in tree-lined avenues and bordered on three sides by mature hedges and trees, providing peace and privacy for each unit. Closer to the dunes and the beach, an open area is just the place for those who wish to enjoy more of the sunshine on this coast, which experiences the very best of Denmark's climate. Conveniently located close to the ports of Fredrickshavn and Hirtshals, it would make a good stopover or short stay, but has everything necessary for a longer summer stay by the sea.

Facilities
Four sanitary units with family and baby rooms, kitchens and dishwashing. Modern central unit with large laundry. En-suite unit for disabled campers (key access). Motorcaravan services. Well stocked shop (27/03-27/09). Snack bar and takeaway. Good play areas. Games room. Minigolf. Free one-hour use of pedal cars. Football/games field. Organised activities in high season. Bicycle hire. Free WiFi. Accommodation to rent. Off site: Riding 2 km.

Open: 27 March - 27 September.

Directions
From Fredrickshavn travel north on road 40. Site is on right and signed 3 km. north of Ålbæk. GPS: 57.6442, 10.46157

Charges guide
Per unit incl. 2 persons and electricity	DKK 189 - 239
extra person	DKK 75 - 89
child (under 13 yrs)	DKK 49 - 56
dog	DKK 15

FREE Alan Rogers Travel Card
Extra benefits and savings - see page 14

Fjerritslev

Klim Strand Camping

Havvejen 167, Klim Strand, DK-9690 Fjerritslev (Nordjylland) T: 98 22 53 40. E: ksc@klim-strand.dk

alanrogers.com/DK2170

A large family holiday site right beside the sea, Klim Strand is a paradise for children. It is a privately owned TopCamp site with a full complement of quality facilities, including its own fire engine and trained staff. The site has 460 numbered touring pitches, all with electricity (10A), laid out in rows, many divided by trees and hedges, with shade in parts. Some 220 of these are extra large (180 sq.m) and fully serviced with electricity, water, drainage and TV hook-up. On-site activities include an outdoor water slide complex, an indoor pool, tennis courts and pony riding. A wellness spa centre including a pirate-themed indoor play hall is a recent addition. Cabins are also available to rent.

Facilities

Two good, large, heated toilet blocks are central, with spacious showers and some washbasins in cubicles. Separate room for children. Baby rooms. Bathrooms for families (some charged) and disabled visitors. Laundry. Kitchens and barbecue areas. TV lounges. Motorcaravan services. Pizzeria. Supermarket, restaurant and bar. Pool complex. Wellness centre with sauna, solariums, whirlpool bath, fitness room and indoor play hall. TV rental. Play areas. Crèche. Bicycle hire. WiFi over part of site (charged).

Open: 30 March - 21 October.

Directions

Turn off Thisted-Fjerritslev 11 road to Klim from where site is signed. GPS: 57.133333, 9.166667

Charges guide

Per unit incl. 2 persons and electricity	€ 26.42 - € 42.25
extra person	€ 8.72
child (1-11 yrs)	€ 7.11

Frederikshaven

Nordstrand Camping

Apholmenvej 40, DK-9900 Frederikshaven (Nordjylland) T: 98 42 93 50. E: info@nordstrand-camping.dk

alanrogers.com/DK2180

An excellently positioned site, Nordstrand is 2 km. from Frederikshaven and the ferries to Sweden and Norway. It is a TopCamp site and provides very good facilities with all the attractions of the nearby beach, town and port. The 440 large pitches, of which 350 are for tourers, mostly with electricity (10/13A), are attractively arranged in small enclosures of 9-13 units surrounded by hedges and trees. Many hedges are of flowering shrubs and this makes for a very pleasant atmosphere. A major attraction for families is the modern fun house with many indoor activities.

Facilities

Centrally located, large toilet blocks provide spacious showers (on payment) and washbasins in cubicles, together with some family bathrooms, rooms for disabled visitors and babies. All are spotlessly clean. Laundry. Good kitchens at each block. Motorcaravan services. Supermarket (1/4-15/9). Café and pizza service. Indoor swimming pool. Sauna. Solarium. 'Short' golf course. Minigolf. Tennis. Bicycle hire. Play areas. WiFi (charged). Separate Fun House (charged). Off site: Beach 200 m.

Open: 1 April - 2 October.

Directions

Turn off the main 40 road 2 km. north of Frederikshaven at roundabout just north of railway bridge. Site is signed. GPS: 57.46422, 10.52755

Charges guide

Per unit incl. 2 persons and electricity	DKK 370 - 505
extra person	DKK 80
child (1-12 yrs)	DKK 58 - 64
dog	DKK 12

Nibe

Nibe Camping

Logstorvej 2, DK-9240 Nibe (Nordjylland) T: 98 35 10 62. E: info@nibecamping.dk

alanrogers.com/DK2150

Nibe Camping is a family run site with welcoming, enthusiastic and hardworking owners. It is next to the peaceful waters of Limfjord and a 15 minute walk from the old town centre of Nibe. There are 170 numbered pitches, of which 120 are for tourers. All have electricity (13A) and are arranged in rows separated by hedges. The pitches are spacious (100-140 sq.m), and those next to the fjord have uninterrupted views. There are watersports and swimming in the fjord. The site has a heated swimming pool (8x16 m), slide and splash pool, a children's pool, all with paved sunbathing area. The new sanitary block, covered barbecue, kitchen/laundry and outside area add to the site's features.

Facilities

New sanitary block. A second central sanitary unit includes washbasins in cubicles, four family bathrooms, a baby room and facilities for disabled visitors. Kitchen and small dining area. Laundry facilities. Hot water (except in washbasins) is charged for. Motorcaravan services. Shop. Café/takeaway (main season). Swimming pool (June-Aug). Solarium. Play area. Minigolf. Boules. TV room. Games room. Fishing. Bicycle hire. Boat launching. Beach. Communal barbecue area. WiFi (charged).

Open: All year.

Directions

Site is clearly signed from the 187 road west of Nibe town, with a wide entrance. GPS: 56.9722, 9.6245

Charges guide

Per person	€ 9.50 - € 10.50
child (under 12 yrs)	€ 6.00 - € 6.20
pitch	€ 1.40 - € 5.60
electricity	€ 5.00

For latest campsite news, availability and prices visit

alanrogers.com

Saltum

Jambo Vesterhav Camping

Solvejen 60, DK-9493 Saltum (Nordjylland) T: 98 88 16 66. E: info@jambo.dk

alanrogers.com/DK2160

Jambo Vesterhav is reported to be one of the best sites in Denmark and the sanitary facilities here are certainly some of the best we have seen. It offers 660 attractive, level pitches, landscaped with a variety of bushes. Of these, 200 are fully serviced. Some pitches also have TV connections and private Internet point. There are some newer fields to the rear of the site with very limited shade. With children in mind, the on-site facilities include a huge play castle, sports hall, outdoor pool with slide and imaginative minigolf. Member of Leading Campings group.

Facilities
Three superb toilet blocks with card operated hot showers and washbasins in cabins. Good facilities for children with baby room. Family showers. Facilities for disabled visitors. Shop. Bar/restaurant. Snack bar. Ice cream bar. Outdoor pool with slide and jacuzzi. Sauna. Sports hall. Large play castle. Indoor play room. Games room. Minigolf. Full entertainment programme in high season. Off site: Fårup Sommerland 3 km.

Open: 8 April - 16 October.

Directions
From the south on the 55 road, drive through Saltum and turn left onto the 543 Saltum Strandvej road. Follow signs to site. GPS: 57.278461, 9.661118

Charges guide
Per unit incl. 2 persons	
and electricity	€ 29.50 - € 52.00
extra person	€ 12.00
child (0-11 yrs)	€ 9.25
dog	€ 2.75

Blavand

Hvidbjerg Strand Camping

Hvidbjerg Strandvej 27, DK-6857 Blavand (Ribe) T: 75 27 90 40.

E: info@hvidbjerg.dk **alanrogers.com/DK2010**

A family owned TopCamp holiday site, Hvidbjerg Strand is on the west coast near Blåvands Huk, 43 km. from Esbjerg. It is a high quality, seaside site with a wide range of amenities including a large wellness facility. Most of the 570 pitches have electricity (6/10A) and the 130 'comfort' pitches also have water, drainage and satellite TV. To the rear of the site, 70 new, fully serviced pitches have been developed, some up to 250 sq.m. and 44 with private sanitary facilities. Most pitches are individual and divided by hedges, in rows on flat sandy grass, with areas also divided by small trees and hedges. A member of Leading Campings group.

Facilities
Five superb toilet units include washbasins, roomy showers, spa baths, suites for disabled visitors, family bathrooms, kitchens and laundry facilities. Bathroom for children and baby baths. Motorcaravan services. Supermarket. Café/restaurant. TV rooms. Pool complex, solarium and sauna. Wellness facility. Western-themed indoor play hall. Play areas. Supervised play rooms (09.00-16.00 daily). Barbecue areas. Minigolf. Riding (Western style). Fishing. Dog showers. Free WiFi.

Open: 20 March - 18 October.

Directions
From Varde take roads 181/431 to Blåvand. Site is signed left on entering the town. GPS: 55.54600, 8.13507

Charges guide
Per unit incl. 2 persons	
and electricity	€ 35.62 - € 74.62
extra person	€ 11.31
child (0-11 yrs)	€ 8.55
dog	€ 4.14

Esbjerg

Esbjerg Camping

Gudenåvej 20, DK-6710 Esbjerg V-Sædding (Ribe) T: 75 15 88 22. E: info@esbjergcamping.dk

alanrogers.com/DK2015

Owned and run by Britta and Peter Andersen, this superb site is in the northeast of Esbjerg and is a great starting point from which to tour the city with its harbour, museums and sea water aquarium. It is also convenient for those arriving on the ferry from Harwich (16 hours). From the attractive, tree lined drive, gravel lanes lead to large fields with well mown grass and good services. The site has 193 pitches for touring visitors (some with hardstanding) and there are 30 seasonal places. The pitches are split into groups of five or ten by mature trees that provide some shade. There are 16 concrete hardstandings for large caravans or motorcaravans, 4 of which are fully serviced. Everything on this site is in pristine order.

Facilities
Two very clean toilet blocks with free hot showers. Special section for children in bright colours and family shower rooms (for rent). Excellent facilities for disabled visitors. Baby room. Laundry. Campers' kitchen. Motorcaravan services. Basics from reception (bread to order). Outdoor pool (15x10 m) with slide, waterfall, flume and paddling pool (1/6-1/9). Two new playgrounds. Animal farm. Giant chess. Minigolf. WiFi. TV room with library. Off site: Fishing, golf and bicycle hire 5 km.

Open: All year.

Directions
From Esbjerg, take the 447 road northeast and continue along the coast. Turn right at sign for site and follow the signs. GPS: 55.51302, 8.38778

Charges guide
Per unit incl. 2 persons	
and electricity	€ 30.43 - € 34.51
extra person	€ 9.39
child (1-11 yrs)	€ 5.58
dog	€ 1.40

FREE Alan Rogers Travel Card
Extra benefits and savings - see page 14

Charlottenlund
Camping Charlottenlund Fort
Strandvejen 144B, DK-2920 Charlottenlund (Sjælland) T: 39 62 36 88. E: info@campingcopenhagen.dk
alanrogers.com/DK2265

On the northern outskirts of Copenhagen, this unique site is within the walls of an old fort, which still retains its main armament of twelve 29 cm. howitzers (disabled, of course). There are 65 pitches on grass, all with 10A electricity. The obvious limitation on the space available means that pitches are relatively close together, but many are quite deep. The site is very popular and is usually full every night, so reservation is necessary. The site is only 6 km. from the centre of Copenhagen, with a regular bus service from just outside the site.

Facilities
Sanitary facilities located in the old armoury are newly rebuilt, well maintained and heated. Free showers. Kitchen facilities include gas hobs and a dining area. Laundry. Motorcaravan services. Small café in reception. Restaurant with terrace and views. Bicycle hire. Free WiFi over site. Beach. Off site: Riding 1.5 km. Golf 2 km. Copenhagen town centre 20 minutes by bus.

Open: 7 March - 19 October.

Directions
Leave E47/E55 at exit 17, and turn southeast on Jægersborgvej. After a short distance turn left (east) on Jægersborg Allé, following signs for Charlottenlund (5 km) and follow all the way to the end. Finally turn right (south) on to Strandvejen, and site entrance is on left after 500 m. GPS: 55.74480, 12.58538

Charges guide

Per unit incl. 2 persons and electricity	DKK 245 - 260
extra person	DKK 100
electricity (per kWh)	DKK 5

Faxe
TopCamp Feddet
Feddet 12, DK-4640 Faxe (Sjælland) T: 56 72 52 06. E: info@feddetcamping.dk
alanrogers.com/DK2255

This interesting, spacious site with ecological principles is located on the Baltic coast. It has a fine, white, sandy beach (Blue Flag) which runs the full length of one side, with the Præstø fjord on the opposite side of the peninsula. There are 413 pitches for touring units, generally on sandy grass, with mature pine trees giving adequate shade. All have 10A electricity and 20 are fully serviced (water, electricity, drainage and sewerage). The sanitary buildings have been specially designed, clad with larch panels from sustainable local trees and insulated with flax mats.

Facilities
Both sanitary buildings are equipped to high standards. Family bathrooms (with twin showers), complete suites for children and babies. Facilities for disabled visitors. Laundry. Kitchens, dining room and TV lounge. Excellent motorcaravan service point. Well stocked licensed shop. Licensed bistro and takeaway (1/5-20/10; weekends only outside peak season). Large, indoor swimming pool and paddling pool (charged). Minigolf. Games room. Indoor playroom and several playgrounds. Event camp for children. Pet zoo. Massage. Watersports. Fishing. WiFi.

Open: All year.

Directions
From south on E47/55 take exit 38 towards Præsto. Turn north on 209 road towards Faxe and from Vindbyholt follow site signs. From the north on E47/55 take exit 37 east towards Faxe. Just before Faxe turn south on 209 road and from Vindbyholt, site signs. GPS: 55.17497, 12.10203

Charges guide

Per unit incl. 2 persons and electricity	DKK 265 - 340
extra person	DKK 75

Føllenslev
Vesterlyng Camping
Ravnholtvej 3, DK-4591 Føllenslev (Sjælland) T: 59 20 00 66. E: info@vesterlyng-camping.dk
alanrogers.com/DK2257

Vesterlyng is a pleasant, quiet site, close to Føllenslev and Havnsø on Sjælland. The ground slopes towards the sea and there are views from some pitches. It is an open site but some mature trees provide shade. Vesterlyng has 181 mostly level touring pitches, 150 with 6/13A electricity. A further 100 pitches are used by mostly elderly, seasonal units. The pitches are on long, grassy meadows each taking 16-20 units, off tarmac access roads. Facilities on this site are basic, but clean. The local beaches are ideal for swimming and a relaxing beach holiday.

Facilities
Two traditional style toilet blocks (maintenance can be variable) include washbasins (open style and in cabins) and controllable hot showers. Family shower rooms. Basic facilities for disabled visitors. Washing machine and dryer. Small shop. Bar/restaurant. Swimming pool complex (charged). Minigolf. Riding. Bicycle hire. Games room with air hockey. Watersports. WiFi over site (charged). Boules. Animal enclosure. Live music nights. Off site: Fishing and boat launching 1 km. Golf 15 km.

Open: 22 March - 21 October.

Directions
From Kalundborg follow 23 road east and exit on 155 road (Svinninge). At Snertinge, continue north on 255 road for 2 km. Follow signs to site (6 km). From the west exit on 255 road towards Snertinge and follow signs after 2 km. GPS: 55.7417, 11.309

Charges guide

Per person	€ 10.20
pitch	€ 2.68 - € 5.90
electricity	€ 4.56

No credit cards.

Hillerød

Hillerød Camping

Blytækkervej 18, DK-3400 Hillerød (Sjælland) T: 48 26 48 54. E: info@hillerodcamping.dk

alanrogers.com/DK2250

The northernmost corner of Sjælland is packed with interest, based not only on fascinating periods of Denmark's history but also its attractive scenery. Hillerød is also a fine base for visiting Copenhagen and is only 25 km. from the ferries at Helsingør and the crossing to Sweden. Centrally situated, the town is a hub of main roads from all directions, with this neat campsite clearly signed. It has a park-like setting in a residential area with five acres of well kept grass, colourful flowers and some attractive trees. There are 107 pitches for tourers, of which 90 have electricity (13A) and these are marked. You are assured of a warm welcome here by enthusiastic couple, Annette and Taco.

Facilities

The smart, new toilet block behind reception includes washbasins in cabins, free hot showers, facilities for disabled visitors and a baby room. Campers' kitchen adjoins the club room and includes free electric hot plates and coffee making machine. Laundry room (free iron). Motorcaravan services. Small shop. Comfortable club room with TV. Play area. Bicycle hire. WiFi over site (charged). Off site: Indoor pool 1 km. Riding 2 km. Golf 3 km. New electric train service to Copenhagen.

Open: 12 April - 28 September.

Directions

Follow road no. 6 bypassing road to south until sign for Hillerød S. Turn towards town at sign for 'Centrum' on Roskildvej road no. 233 and site is signed to the right. GPS: 55.924144, 12.294522

Charges guide

Per unit incl. 2 persons	
and electricity	DKK 210 - 240
extra person	DKK 85 - 100
child (1-11 yrs)	DKK 40 - 50
dog	DKK 10

Broager

Gammelmark Strand Camping

Gammelmark 20, DK-6310 Broager (Sønderjylland) T: 74 44 17 42. E: info@gammelmark.dk

alanrogers.com/DK2036

This was the first Scandinavian site to achieve Ecocamp status, showing commitment to the environment. Gammelmark has 289 level, grass pitches (200 for tourers), all with 10-13A electricity. Many have great views of the Baltic sea. This site combines Danish hospitality with historical interest and various family activities are available, many involving nature and the history of the area when war was waged over the Bay of Sønderborg. It is useful as a stopover on your way north, but is also a good choice for active campers. The site is close to the war museum in Dybbøl Banke.

Facilities

Modern, heated sanitary facilities include toilets, washbasins (open and in cabins), controllable showers. Facilities for children and disabled visitors. Baby room. Private facilities to rent. Laundry facilities. Motorcaravan services. Shop. Snacks (high season). Heated swimming pool. Play area. Children's farm. Fishing. Riding. Sailing and boat launching. Diving. Beach. Activity programme (high season). TV room. WiFi (charged). Torches advised. English spoken. Off site: Bar and restaurant 2 km.

Open: Easter - 22 October.

Directions

From Flensburg take no. 7 road north and at exit 75 turn east towards Sønderborg. Take Dynt exit and follow site signs. Do not turn into house at 16 Gammelmark, but continue 200 m. down small road to reception. GPS: 54.88545, 9.72876

Charges guide

Per person	€ 10.50
child (1-11 yrs)	€ 5.55
pitch (high season)	€ 5.55
electricity (per kWh)	€ 3.50

Haderslev

Sandersvig Camping & Tropeland

Espagervej 15-17, Espagervej 15, DK-6100 Haderslev (Sønderjylland) T: 74 56 62 25.
E: camping@sandersvig.dk **alanrogers.com/DK2030**

An attractively laid out, family run site, Sandersvig offers the very best of modern facilities in a peaceful and beautiful countryside location, 300 metres from the beach. The 470 large grassy pitches (270 for tourers) are divided by hedges, shrubs and small trees into small enclosures, many housing only four units, most with electricity (10A). The site is well lit, very quiet at night and there are water taps close to most pitches. The playground boasts Denmark's largest bouncing cushion! Five hundred metres from the site a seven-hectare park has a thriving herd of red deer. A very comfortable base for excursions.

Facilities

Four heated sanitary blocks offer washbasins in cubicles and roomy showers (on payment). Suites for disabled visitors, 14 family bathrooms and baby rooms. Children's section in one block. Excellent kitchens. Laundry. Fish cleaning area. Motorcaravan services. Supermarket and fast food service, with dining room adjacent (Easter-20/9). Takeaway (15/6-15/8). Indoor heated pool with sauna, solarium, jacuzzi, whirlpool and slide. Playground. Games room. TV lounge. Tennis. Boat launching. WiFi throughout (charged). Off site: Riding 4 km. Bicycle hire 6 km.

Open: 27 March - 20 September.

Directions

Leave E45 at exit 66 and turn towards Errested and then left towards Christianfeld. Turn right onto 170 and follow signs for Fjelstrup and Knud village, turning right 1 km. east of the village from where site is signed. GPS: 55.33424, 9.63152

Charges guide

Per unit incl. 2 persons	
and electricity	DKK 198 - 228
extra person	DKK 75
child (0-11 yrs)	DKK 45

FREE Alan Rogers Travel Card
Extra benefits and savings - see page 14

Tonder

Møgeltønder Camping

Sønderstregsvej 2, Møgeltønder, DK-6270 Tønder (Sønderjylland) T: 74 73 84 60.

E: info@mogeltondercamping.dk alanrogers.com/DK2020

This site is only five minutes walk from one of Denmark's oldest villages and ten minutes drive from Tønder with its well preserved old buildings and interesting pedestrian shopping street. A quiet family site, Møgeltønder is well maintained with 285 large, level, numbered pitches on grass, with electricity (10A), of which 250 are for tourers. They are divided up by shrubs and hedges. The site has an excellent outdoor heated swimming pool and children's pool, a good playground with bouncy cushion and a range of trolleys, carts and tricycles. There are two good free kitchens for campers' use, and fishing is available next to the site.

Facilities

Two heated sanitary units include roomy showers (on payment), washbasins with either divider/curtain or in private cubicles, plus bathrooms for families and disabled visitors. Baby room. Two kitchens with hobs (free). Laundry. Motorcaravan services. Shop (bread ordered daily, 1/4-1/10). Outdoor heated swimming pool (10x5 m) with chute and paddling pool (June-Sept). Minigolf. Playground. TV and games rooms. WiFi (charged).

Open: All year.

Directions

Turn left off no. 419 Tønder-Højer road, 4 km. from Tønder. Drive through Møgeltønder village and past the church where site is signed. The main street is cobbled so drive slowly. GPS: 54.93826, 8.7994

Charges guide

per unit incl. 2 person and electricity	DKK 206
extra person	DKK 68
child (0-12 yrs)	DKK 38
dog	DKK 10

Fredericia

Mycamp Trelde Næs

Trelde Næsvej 297, Trelde, DK-7000 Fredericia (Vejle) T: 75 95 71 83. E: trelde@mycamp.dk

alanrogers.com/DK2046

Trelde Næs is a busy and lively site next to a beach. It is one of Denmark's larger sites with 500 level and numbered pitches. The 350 touring pitches all have 10A electricity and there are 37 fully serviced pitches with electricity, water, drainage and Internet access. Seasonal units take up the remaining pitches. Pitches are mainly in rows off tarmac access roads on well kept, grassy fields with some shade from bushes at the rear. At the front of the site is a heated, open-air, fun pool with large slide, jacuzzi and play island. This is connected to a room with a sauna, Turkish baths and massage chairs, with play stations for children.

Facilities

Four traditional toilet blocks have washbasins in cabins and controllable hot showers (card operated). Child size toilets and washbasins. Family shower room. Baby room. Laundry. Fun pool (10x20 m) with island, large slide, Turkish bath, solarium and sauna. Shop. Takeaway. Several playgrounds. Minigolf. Fishing. Bicycle hire. Watersports. Full entertainment programme for children (high season). TV room. WiFi (charged). Cabins and rooms to rent. Off site: Riding 1 km. Golf 6 km. Sailing 7 km.

Open: 1 April - 23 October.

Directions

From Fredericia follow road 28 north and take Trelde exit. Follow signs for Trelde and Trelde Næs. GPS: 55.62489, 9.83333

Charges guide

Per unit incl. 2 persons and electricity	DKK 184 - 277
extra person	DKK 66
child (3-11 yrs)	DKK 38
dog	DKK 20

Give

TopCamp Riis Feriepark

Osterhovedvej 43, DK-7323 Give (Vejle) T: 75 73 14 33. E: info@topcampriis.dk

alanrogers.com/DK2040

TopCamp Riis is a good quality touring site ideal for visiting Legoland and Lalandia Billund (18 km), and Givskov Zoo (3 km). It is a friendly, family run site with 150 large touring pitches on sheltered, gently sloping, well tended lawns surrounded by trees and shrubs. Electricity (13A) is available to all pitches, and 15 comfort pitches also have water and drainage. The outdoor heated pool and water slide complex, and the bar that serves beer, ice cream, soft drinks and snacks, are only open in the main season. The excellent indoor kitchen facilities and an attractive, covered barbecue area are very useful. This is a high-class site suitable for long or short stays in this very attractive part of Denmark.

Facilities

Two excellent sanitary units (the older one now refurbished) include washbasins with divider/curtain and controllable showers (on payment). Suites for babies and disabled visitors, family bathrooms (one with whirlpool bath, on payment) and solarium. Laundry. Motorcaravan services. New kitchen. Sitting room with TV, plus new barbecue grill house. Shop. Pool complex (2/6-4/9). Café/bar (25/5-11/8). Minigolf. New playground. Train ride for children. Animal farm. Bicycle hire. WiFi.

Open: 31 March - 30 September.

Directions

Turn onto Osterhovedvej southeast of Give town centre (near Shell garage) at sign to Riis and site. After 4 km. turn left onto tarmac drive which runs through the forest to the site. Alternatively, turn off the 442 Brande-Jelling road at Riis village north of Givskud. GPS: 55.83116, 9.30076

Charges guide

Per unit incl. 2 persons and electricity	DKK 235 - 285
extra person	DKK 80

For latest campsite news, availability and prices visit

alanrogers.com

Jelling

Fårup Sø Camping

Fårupvej 58, DK-7300 Jelling (Vejle) T: 75 87 13 44. E: faarupsoecamp@firma.tele.dk

alanrogers.com/DK2048

Fårup Sø Camping is a friendly and welcoming family run site next to the beautiful Fårup Lake, a good location for visiting some of Denmark's best known attractions such as Legoland and the Lion Park. There are 250 grassy pitches, mostly on terraces (from top to bottom the height difference is 53 m). Some have beautiful views of the Fårup Lake. There are 200 pitches for touring units, all with 16A electricity, and some tent pitches without electricity. A heated swimming pool (min. 25°C), a whirlpool and an indoor play area are popular, as are the available activities, many associated with the lake.

Facilities
One modern and one older toilet block have British style toilets, open style washbasins and controllable hot showers. Family shower rooms. Baby room. Facilities for disabled visitors. Laundry. Campers' kitchen. Motorcaravan services. Shop (bread to order). Heated swimming pool and whirlpool. Indoor play area. Playgrounds. Lake with fishing, watersports and Viking ship. Three play areas. Activities for children (high season). WiFi (charged). Off site: Golf and riding 2 km.

Open: 28 March - 13 September.

Directions
From Vejle take the 28 road towards Billund. In Skibet turn right towards Fårup Sø, Jennum and Jelling and follow the signs to Fårup Sø. GPS: 55.73614, 9.41777

Charges guide
Per unit incl. 2 persons and electricity	DKK 232 - 257
extra person	DKK 75
child (1-11 yrs)	DKK 45
dog	DKK 15

Vestbirk

Vestbirk Camping

Møllehøjvej 4, Brædstrup, DK-8752 Østbirk (Vejle) T: 75 78 12 92. E: info@vestbirk.dk

alanrogers.com/DK2045

This small family site with 260 pitches (170 for tourers) is close to a small lake where boating (no motor boats or sailing boats), swimming or just relaxing on the beach are possible. Vestbirk also has a heated swimming pool (16x8 m) with paddling pool and small slide. One area of the site has pitches in long lanes off gravel access roads on fields taking six to ten units, and there is one large field to the right. All the pitches are on grass with 10A electricity and some of the larger fields are terraced. The groups are separated by high and low bushes.

Facilities
Heated toilet block with washbasins (open style and cabins), controllable hot showers (DKR 5), family showers and facilities for children. Baby room. Laundry. Campers' kitchen. Motorcaravan services. Shop with bread to order. Takeaway (24/5-31/8). Heated outdoor pool with slide and paddling pool (14/05-30/08). Solarium and Sauna. Whirlpool. Play area. Minigolf. Fishing. Boules. Bicycle hire. Canoe hire. Games room. Children's entertainment (high season). WiFi throughout (charged).

Open: 28 April - 20 September.

Directions
From the E45 in either direction take exit 55 onto the 461 road towards Østbirk. Drive through Østbirk towards Vestbirk and follow the site signs. GPS: 55.96397, 9.69967

Charges guide
Per unit incl. 2 persons and electricity	€ 30.20 - € 32.95
extra person	€ 11.40

Credit cards 5% surcharge.

Nykobing Mors

Jesperhus Feriecenter & Camping

Legindvej 30, DK-7900 Nykobing Mors (Viborg) T: 96 70 14 00. E: jesperhus@jesperhus.dk

alanrogers.com/DK2140

Jesperhus is an extensive, well organised and busy site with many leisure activities, adjacent to Blomsterpark (Northern Europe's largest flower park). This TopCamp site has 662 numbered pitches, mostly in rows with some terracing, divided by shrubs and trees and with shade in parts. Many pitches are taken by seasonal, tour operator or rental units, so advance booking is advised for peak periods. Electricity (6A) is available on all pitches and water points are in all areas. There are 300 pitches available with full services. With all the activities at this site, an entire holiday could be spent here regardless of the weather, although Jesperhus is also an excellent centre for touring.

Facilities
Four good sanitary units are cleaned three times daily. Facilities include washbasins in cubicles or with divider/curtain, family and whirlpool bathrooms (on payment), suites for babies and disabled visitors. Free sauna. Superb kitchens. Laundry facilities. Supermarket (1/4-1/11). Restaurant. Bar. Café, takeaway. Pool complex with spa facilities. Bowling. Minigolf. Tennis. Go-karts and other outdoor sports. Children's 'playworld'. Playgrounds. Pets corner. Golf. Fishing pond. Practice golf (3 holes).

Open: All year.

Directions
From south or north, take road 26 to Salling Sund bridge, site is signed Jesperhus, just north of the bridge. GPS: 56.75082, 8.81580

Charges guide
Per person	DKK 80
child (1-11 yrs)	DKK 60
pitch	free - DKK 50
electricity	DKK 40

FREE Alan Rogers Travel Card
Extra benefits and savings - see page 14

Finland

Finland is one of the world's most northerly countries. Long and generally flat, it comprises thousands of lakes and islands, with three quarters covered by dense forest. Finland is ideal for a relaxing holiday in natural, peaceful surroundings with an extensive and diverse range of wildlife.

Finland is a landscape of contrasts, with the undulating, rural landscape of the south giving way to hills and forests in the north. The southeast is the country's lake district, with thousands of post-glacial lakes and islands, and endless opportunities for fishing, swimming and sailing. In the south, the coastal capital, Helsinki, has open-air cafés, green parks, waterways and a busy market square amid beautiful Art Deco architecture. Close to the Arctic Circle are the treeless fells and peat-lands of Lapland. Here visitors can enjoy outdoor pursuits in summer and snowmobiling and husky safaris in winter. The flat western coastal regions with their distinctive wooden towns are popular with fishermen, in particular the coast and rivers of Ostrobothnia.

CAPITAL: Helsinki

Tourist Office
Finnish Tourist Board
PO Box 33213, London W6 8JX
Tel: 020 7365 2512
Fax: 020 8600 5681
Email: finlandinfo.lon@mek.fi
Internet: www.visitfinland.com/uk

Population
5.4 million

Climate
Temperate climate, but with considerable
variations. Summer is warm, winter is very cold.

Language
Finnish

Telephone
The country code is 00 358.

Money
Currency: The Euro
Banks: Mon-Fri 09.15-16.15
(regional variations may occur).

Shops
Mon-Fri 09.00-17.00/18.00.
Sat 09.00-14.00/15.00, department stores usually
remain open to 18.00. Supermarkets are usually
open to 20.00 Mon-Fri.

Public Holidays
New Year; Epiphany; Saints Day 16 Mar;
Language Day 9 April; Good Friday; Easter Mon;
May Day 30 Apr/1 May; All Saints Day 1 Nov;
Independence Day 6 Dec; Christmas 25, 26 Dec.

Motoring
Main roads are excellent and relatively uncrowded
outside city limits. Traffic drives on the right. Horn
blowing is frowned upon. There are many road
signs warning motorists of the danger of elk
dashing out on the road. If you are unfortunate
enough to hit one, it must be reported to the
police. Do not drink and drive, penalties are
severe if any alcohol is detected.

see campsite map 3

Ruovesi
Camping Haapasaaren Lomakylä

Haapasaarentie 5, FIN-34600 Ruovesi (Häme) T: 044 080 0290. E: lomakyla@haapasaari.fi

alanrogers.com/FI2840

Haapasaaren is located on Lake Näsijärvi, around 70 km. north of Tampere in south western Finland. This is a well equipped site with a café and restaurant, a traditional Finnish outside dancing area and, of course, plenty of saunas! Rowing boats, canoes, cycles and, during the winter months, sleds are all available for rent. Fishing is very popular here. Pitches are grassy and of a good size. There is also a good range of accommodation to rent, including holiday cottages with saunas. The cosy restaurant, Jätkäinkämppä, has an attractive terrace and fine views across the lake. Alternatively, the site's café, Portinpieli, offers a range of snacks as well as Internet access.

Facilities
Sanitary facilities include toilets and showers. Laundry facilities. Campers' kitchen. Shop. Café. Restaurant (all year). Bar (1/5-30/9). Takeaway (1/5-30/9). Direct lake access. Saunas. Fishing. Minigolf. Boat and canoe hire. Bicycle hire. Guided tours. Play area. Chalets for rent. Off site: Walking and cycle routes. Golf 30 km. Boat trips. Helvetinjärvi National Park.

Open: All year.

Directions
From Helsinki, head north on the E12 motorway to Tampere and then northeast on N63-9 to Orivesi. Then, continue north on route 66 to Ruovesi and follow signs to the site. GPS: 61.99413, 24.069843

Charges guide

Per unit incl. 2 persons and electricity	€ 31.00
extra person	€ 5.00
child (under 15 yrs)	€ 2.00

Tampere
Tampere Camping Härmälä

Leirintäkatu 8, FIN-33900 Tampere (Häme) T: 020 719 9777. E: harmala@suomicamping.fi

alanrogers.com/FI2820

Härmälä is a lively campsite near Lake Pyhäjärvi. It is situated only 4 km. from Tampere city centre. You can choose from a large, unspecified number of unmarked pitches (about 180). The site has 111 cabins of various sizes and facilities. Amenities include a beach, saunas, playgrounds for children, a small shop and a pizzeria. The site seems a little run down but is acceptable for a couple of nights. Tampere is beautifully situated beside Lake Näsijärvi. A stroll along the harbour with its yachts and through the parks is a pleasant experience. Another must is the Sänkänniemi Adventure Park with its 168 m. high tower and revolving restaurant, children's zoo, aquarium and amusements.

Facilities
Four sanitary blocks, one is new, three are rather basic. Washbasins and showers have free hot water. Facilities for disabled visitors. Laundry room. Campers' kitchen with cooking rings, microwave. Motorcaravan services. Small shop. Pizzeria. Off site: Golf and riding 5 km.

Open: 15 May - 30 August.

Directions
Turn off the E12 and follow signs. GPS: 61.471967, 23.73945

Charges guide

Per unit incl. 2 persons and electricity	€ 30.00 - € 31.50
per person	€ 5.00
child (4-14 yrs)	€ 5.00
child (0-3 yrs)	free

Virrat
Camping Lakari

Lakarintie 405, FIN-34800 Virrat (Häme) T: 034 758 639. E: lakari@virtainmatkailu.fi

alanrogers.com/FI2830

The peace and tranquillity of the beautiful natural surroundings are the main attractions at this vast campsite (18 hectares), which is located on a narrow piece of land between two lakes. This site is a must if you want to get away from it all. There are a variety of cabins to rent, some with their own beach and jetty! Marked pitches for tents and caravans are beside the beach or in little meadows in the forest. You pick your own place. Site amenities include a café and a beach sauna. This is a spectacular landscape with deep gorges and steep lakeside cliffs. Facilities at the site are rather basic but very clean and well kept. This is a glorious place for a nature loving tourist looking to relax.

Facilities
Two toilet blocks, basic but clean and well kept, include toilets, washbasins and showers. Free hot water. Motorcaravan services. Covered campers' kitchen with fridge, cooking rings and oven. Washing machine. Small shop and café. TV. Fishing. Bicycle hire. Off site: Golf 1 km. Riding 5 km.

Open: 1 May - 30 September.

Directions
Site is 7 km. south of Virrat on road 66. Follow signs. GPS: 62.209817, 23.837767

Charges guide

Per unit incl. 2 persons and electricity	€ 24.50
extra person	€ 3.50
child	€ 1.50

For latest campsite news, availability and prices visit
alanrogers.com

Iisalmi

Koljonvirta Camping

Ylemmäisentie 6, FIN-74160 Iisalmi (Kuopio) T: 017 825 252. E: koljonvirta@koljonvirta.fi

alanrogers.com/FI2960

Koljonvirta Camping is a large but quiet site located about five kilometres from the centre of Iisalmi. There are 200 marked grass pitches, 120 with electricity (16A). The site adjoins a lake and has a small beach and facilities for boating and fishing. Iisalmi town itself is on the northern edge of the Finnish Lake District and provides a good variety of shops, including some factory outlets, and an interesting variety of events during June, July and August. These vary from the world famous 'Wife Carrying' World Championships to the Lapinlahti 'Cattle Calling' Competition and the International Midnight Marathon.

Facilities
The sanitary blocks provide showers, toilets and a sauna in one block. Launderette. Shop. Snack bar. Fully licensed restaurant. Motorcaravan services. Lake and small beach with facilities for boating and fishing. The site exhibits large wooden sculptures of animals, plus they now have a new beach, volleyball field and minigolf. Off site: Riding 100 m.

Open: May - September.

Directions
From road 5 turn onto the 88 (towards Oulu) just north of Iisalmi. Go straight over the roundabout and the site is 1 km. on the left. Follow signs. GPS: 63.59462, 27.16084

Charges guide
Per unit incl. 2 persons and electricity	€ 25.00

Ivalo

Ukonjärvi Camping

Ukonjärventi 141, FIN-99801 Ivalo (Lapland) T: 016 667 501. E: nuttu@ukolo.fi

alanrogers.com/FI2995

Ukonjärvi Camping lies on the banks of Lake Inari, situated in a forested area alongside a nature reserve. It is a quiet, peaceful site, ideal for rest and relaxation. Thirty touring pitches have electricity and are surrounded by pine and beech trees. Cottages are available to rent. A bar and restaurant are located at reception; a range of local dishes are produced including reindeer casserole. There is also a barbecue hut located in the centre of the site if you prefer to cook your own food. A climb up to the nearby viewpoint offers spectacular views over the lake – you can even see over to Russia. The lake also provides plenty of opportunities for boating and fishing.

Facilities
Sanitary block includes toilets and showers. Laundry and campers' kitchen. Lakeside sauna (charged). Bar and restaurant. Charcoal barbecues are not permitted. Barbecue hut with logs. Small beach. Fishing and boating on lake. TV room. WiFi. Off site: Tankavaaran Kansainvalinen Kulamuseo, a gold mining experience where you can try gold panning, keeping what you find! The Northern Lapland Centre and the Sami Museum, displaying cultural and natural history exhibitions.

Open: 15 May - 15 September.

Directions
Ukonjärvi Camping is 11 km. north of Ivalo on road 4. Look for signs to Lake Inari viewpoint; site is 1 km. down a narrow road (signed). GPS: 68.73687, 27.47687

Charges guide
Per unit incl. 2 persons and electricity	€ 23.50
extra person	€ 4.00
child	€ 2.50

Karigasniemi

Camping Tenorinne

Ylatenontie 55, FIN-99950 Karigasniemi (Lapland) T: 016 676 113. E: camping@tenorinne.com

alanrogers.com/FI2990

This is probably the most northerly campsite in Finland and makes an excellent stopover en route to North Cape. This is a small site with space for 30 units, on three levels with a small access road sloping down to the river. Electricity points (16A) are available throughout the site but the pitches are unmarked. This area is still largely unpopulated, scattered with only small Sami communities and herds of reindeer. Karigasniemi is a slightly larger town as it is a border post with Norway and is close to both the Kevo Nature reserve and the Lemmenjoki National Park. The campsite is on the banks of the Tenojoki River and is an excellent base for walking and bird watching. A little further north you will find Nuvvus-Ailigas, the holy fell of the ancient Sami, which rises to a height of 400 m. above the level of the Teno river.

Facilities
Sanitary block includes showers, toilets and sauna. Launderette. Kitchen. Reception with TV.

Open: 5 June - 15 September.

Directions
If travelling south on the 970, site is on right as you enter town. If travelling west on the 92, turn right immediately before Norwegian customs point. Site is shortly on left past petrol station. Entrance is quite steep. GPS: 69.40033, 25.84450

Charges guide
Per unit incl. 2 persons and electricity	€ 24.00
extra person	€ 3.00
child (0-16)	€ 1.00

Rovaniemi

Ounaskoski

Jäämerentie 1, FIN-96200 Rovaniemi (Lapland) T: 16 345 304. E: ounaskoski-camping@windowslive.com

alanrogers.com/FI2980

Ounaskoski Camping is situated almost exactly on the Arctic Circle, 66 degrees north and just 8 km. south of the Santa Claus post office and village, on the banks of the Kemijoki river. The site has 153 marked touring pitches, 72 with 10A electricity, plus a further small area for tents. Rovaniemi attracts many visitors each year, especially in the weeks leading up to Christmas, who fly direct to the local airport and pay Santa Claus a visit. The town has much to offer with a good selection of shops and some restaurants. Slightly further afield you can visit Vaattunkiköngäs and enjoy one of the many walks, which are suitable for everyone, from the 1 km. walk to the most challenging 9 km. path.

Facilities

There are two sanitary buildings each providing toilets, showers, laundry and kitchen. One also houses a sauna. Facilities for disabled visitors. Motorcaravan services. Café. Small kiosk. Playground. Fishing. Organised coach trips. WiFi throughout (charged). Off site: Ranua Zoo. The Kemijoki, Finland's largest river, offers numerous opportunities for sightseeing by boat. Santa Claus village and Santa Park.

Open: 22 May - 20 September.

Directions

Ounaskoski Camping is on the banks of the Kemijoki river in the middle of Rovaniemi. From the 4/E75 go via the centre across the river and turn right. Site is between the Jatkankynttilasilta Bridge and the Rautatiesilta Bridge. GPS: 66.49748, 25.743504

Charges guide

Per unit incl. 2 persons and electricity	€ 35.50

Sodankylä

Camping Sodankylä Nilimella

Kelukoskentie 4, FIN-99600 Sodankylä (Lapland) T: 16 612 181. E: info@nilimella.fi

alanrogers.com/FI2985

Camping Sodankylä Nilimella is a small, quiet site situated alongside the Kitinen river, just one kilometre from the centre of Sodankylä. The site is split into two areas by a small, relatively quiet, public road. The good sized pitches (100 in total) are clearly marked with hedges and 80 have 16A electricity. The reception area also serves drinks and snacks. Sodankylä town itself, at the junction of routes 4 and 5, is home to a small Sami community and is an important trading post, so you will find a variety of shops including supermarkets. The town is also home to the Geophysical Observatory, which constantly surveys the earth's magnetic field and measures earthquakes using seismic recordings.

Facilities

Two good sanitary blocks with toilets, hot showers and saunas. Facilities for disabled visitors. Campers' kitchen. Motorcaravan services. Playground. Bicycle hire. River swimming, canoeing and water-skiing. Free WiFi. Off site: Shops and supermarkets in Sodankylä town.

Open: 1 June - 30 September.

Directions

Turn off road 4 onto road 5. Site is on the left just after crossing the river. It is well signed and easy to find. GPS: 67.41755, 26.60803

Charges guide

Per unit incl. 2 persons and electricity	€ 20.00 - € 24.00
extra person	€ 4.00
child	€ 2.00

Manamansalo

Manamansalo Camping

Teeriniemientie 156, FIN-88340 Manamansalo (Oulu) T: 088 741 38. E: manamansalo@kainuunmatkailu.fi

alanrogers.com/FI2975

Manamansalo is a top class, 'wild north' tourist centre on the island of Manamansalo in Lake Oulojärvi. You come by ferry or via a bridge from the mainland. This site is a real find if you are looking for peace and quiet and is also very good for families. It has 200 pitches, 140 with electricity, very attractively laid out in the forest with natural dividers of pine trees. The site stretches along the lake and has a long, narrow sandy beach. Nature lovers will appreciate the network of trails in the pine forest. Choose between walking and cycling or even skiing in spring. For fishermen the lake is a paradise with an enormous range of fish – salmon, pike, trout. The site's marina has 12 guest places for boats. There is a fully licensed restaurant and a small shop on the site.

Facilities

Three toilet blocks have toilets, washbasins and showers in cubicles with free hot water. Washing machines and dryers. Kitchen with sinks, cooking rings and ovens. Motorcaravan services. Fully licensed restaurant and small shop (from May). Playground. Canoes, pedaloes and rowing boats for hire. Fishing. WiFi.

Open: 1 March - 30 September.

Directions

Coming from the south on road 5/E63 turn at Mainau on road 28. At Vuottolahti turn on road 879 and follow signs to Manamansalo and site. From road 22 turn at Liminpuro or Melaillahti and follow signs. GPS: 64.389417, 27.026083

Charges guide

Per unit incl. 2 persons and electricity	€ 28.50
extra person	€ 5.50
child (0-15 yrs)	€ 1.00

For latest campsite news, availability and prices visit

alanrogers.com

Oulu

Nallikari Camping

Leiritie 10, FIN-90510 Oulu (Oulu) T: 044 703 1353. E: nallikari.camping@ouka.fi

alanrogers.com/FI2970

This is probably one of the best sites in Scandinavia, set in a recreational wooded area alongside a sandy beach on the banks of the Baltic Sea, with the added bonus of the adjacent Eden Spa complex. Nallikari provides 200 pitches, 176 with 16A electricity (seven also have water supply and drainage), plus an additional 78 cottages to rent, 28 of which are suitable for winter occupation. Oulu is a modern town, about 100 miles south of the Arctic Circle, that enjoys long, sunny and dry summer days. The Baltic, however, is frozen for many weeks in the winter and then the sun barely rises for two months. In early June the days are very long with the sun setting at about 23.30 and rising at 01.30! Nallikari, to the west of Oulu, is 3 km. along purpose-built cycle paths and the town has much to offer.

Facilities

The modern shower/WC blocks also provide male and female saunas, kitchen and launderette facilities. Facilities for disabled visitors. Motorcaravan services. Playground. Reception with café/restaurant (June-Aug), souvenir and grocery shop. TV room. Free WiFi over site. Bicycle hire. Communal barbecues only. Off site: The adjacent Eden Centre provides excellent modern spa facilities where you can enjoy a day under the glass-roofed pool with its jacuzzis, saunas, Turkish baths and an Irish bath. Riding 2 km. Fishing 5 km. Golf 15 km.

Open: All year.

Directions

Leave road 4/E75 at junction with road 20 and head west down Kiertotie. Site well signed, Nallikari Eden, but continue on, just after traffic lights, cross a bridge and take the second on the right. Just before the Eden Centre turn right towards Leiritie and reception. GPS: 65.02973, 25.41793

Charges guide

Per unit incl. 2 persons	€ 27.00 - € 31.00
extra person	€ 4.00
child (under 15 yrs)	€ 2.00
electricity	€ 6.00 - € 7.00

Helsinki

Rastila Camping Helsinki

Karavaanikatu 4, FIN-00980 Helsinki (Uusimaa) T: 093 107 8517. E: rastilacamping@hel.fi

alanrogers.com/FI2850

No trip to Finland would be complete without a few days stay in Helsinki, the capital since 1812. This all year round site has exceptional transport links, with the metro only five minutes walk from the campsite gates. It provides 165 pitches with electrical hook-ups, plus an additional small field for tent campers. Shrubs have been planted between the tarmac and grass pitches. All visitors will want to spend time in the capital and a 24-hour bus, tram and metro pass can be bought at the metro station. Once on the metro, you are in the city centre within 20 minutes on this regular, fast train service. Essential visits will include Senate Square in the heart of the city, and Suomenlinna, a marine fortress built on six islands in the 1700s. This garrison town is one of the most popular sights in Finland and is the world's largest maritime fortress. Helsinki, on the other hand, is one of Europe's smallest capitals and walking around the centre and port is popular as well as visiting the market square alongside the ferry port.

Facilities

Four sanitary blocks (two heated) provide toilets and showers. Kitchens with cooking rings and sinks. Facilities for disabled visitors and babies. Laundry room. Saunas. Motorcaravan services. Fully licensed restaurant. Playground. Games and TV room. Bicycles for hire. Free WiFi over part of the site. Off site: Small beach adjacent. Golf 5 km. Tallinn the capital of Estonia is only 90 minutes away from Helsinki by fast Jetliner ferry.

Open: All year.

Directions

Well signed from 170 or Ring I. From the 170, turn at Itakeskus shopping complex towards Vuosaari. After crossing bridge go up slip road to Rastila. At top of road turn left. Site is directly ahead. GPS: 60.206667, 25.121111

Charges guide

Per unit incl. 2 persons and electricity	€ 29.00 - € 38.00
extra person	€ 5.00
child (0-15 yrs)	€ 1.00

Discounts for weekly or monthly bookings.

France

From the hot sunny climate of the Mediterranean to the more northerly and cooler regions of Normandy and Brittany, with the Châteaux of the Loire and the lush valleys of the Dordogne, and the mountain ranges of the Alps, France offers holidaymakers a huge choice of destinations to suit all tastes.

France boasts every type of landscape imaginable, ranging from the wooded valleys of the Dordogne to the volcanic uplands of the Massif Central, the rocky coast of Brittany to the lavender-covered hills of Provence and snow-capped peaks of the Alps. The diversity of these regions is reflected in the local customs, cuisine, architecture and dialect. Many rural villages hold festivals to celebrate the local saints and you can also find museums devoted to the rural arts and crafts of the regions.

France has a rich cultural heritage with a wealth of festivals, churches, châteaux, museums and historical monuments to visit. The varied landscape and climate ensure many opportunities for outdoor pursuits from hiking and cycling, wind- and sand-surfing on the coast and rock climbing and skiing in the mountains. And no trip to France is complete without sampling the local food and wine.

CAPITAL: Paris

Tourist Office
French Government Tourist Office
Maison de la France
178 Piccadilly, London W1J 9AL
Tel: 090 682 44123
Fax: 020 7493 6594
Email: info.uk@franceguide.com
Internet: www.franceguide.com

Population
65.8 million

Climate
France has a temperate climate but this varies
considerably from region to region.

Language
French

Telephone
The country code is 00 33.

Money
Currency: The Euro
Banks: Mon-Fri 09.00-12.00 and
14.00-16.00.

Shops
Mon-Sat 09.00-18.30. Some are closed
between 12.00-14.30. Food shops are open
07.00-18.30/19.30. Some food shops
(particularly bakers) are open Sunday
mornings. Many shops close Mondays.

Public Holidays
New Year; Easter Mon; Labour Day; VE Day
8 May; Ascension; Whit Mon; Bastille Day 14 July;
Assumption 15 Aug; All Saints 1 Nov; Armistice
Day 11 Nov; Christmas Day.

Motoring
France has a comprehensive road system from
motorways (Autoroutes), Routes Nationales
(N roads), Routes Départmentales (D roads) down
to purely local C class roads. Tolls are payable
on the autoroute network which is extensive but
expensive, and also on certain bridges.

see campsite map 5

Biscarrosse

Camping Resort la Rive

Route de Bordeaux, F-40600 Biscarrosse (Landes) T: 05 58 78 12 33. E: info@larive.fr

alanrogers.com/FR40100

Surrounded by pine woods, la Rive has a superb beach-side location on Lac de Sanguinet. With a total of 800 pitches, it provides 250 mostly level, numbered and clearly defined touring pitches of 100 sq.m. all with electricity connections (10A), 100 also with water and waste water. The swimming pool complex is wonderful with pools linked by water channels and bridges. There is also a jacuzzi, paddling pool and two large swimming pools all surrounded by sunbathing areas and decorated with palm trees. An indoor pool is heated and open all season. This is a friendly site with a good mix of nationalities. The latest additions are a super children's aquapark with various games, and a top quality bar/restaurant complex where regular entertainment is organised. There are plans to extend the outdoor pools with the addition of new slides more than 200 m. long. The beach is excellent, shelving gently to provide safe bathing for all ages. There are windsurfers and small craft can be launched from the site's slipway.

Facilities

Three good clean toilet blocks have washbasins in cabins and mainly British style toilets. Facilities for disabled visitors. Baby baths. Motorcaravan services. Shop with gas. New bar/restaurant complex with entertainment. Swimming pool complex (supervised July/Aug) with aquapark for children. Games room. Play area. Tennis. Bicycle hire. Boules. Fishing. Water-skiing. Watersports equipment hire. Tournaments (June-Aug). Skateboard park. Trampolines. Miniclub. No charcoal barbecues on pitches. Communal barbecue areas. WiFi (charged). Off site: Riding 2 km. Golf 8 km. Beach 18 km.

Open: 4 April - 30 August.

Directions

Take D652 from Sanguinet to Biscarrosse and site is signed on the right in 6 km. Turn right and follow tarmac road for 2 km. GPS: 44.46052, -1.13065

Charges guide

Per unit incl. 2 persons and electricity	€ 27.50 - € 54.00
extra person	€ 5.30 - € 10.60
child (3-7 yrs)	€ 3.80 - € 8.70
dog	€ 6.20 - € 11.30

No credit cards.
Camping Cheques accepted.

Allés-sur-Dordogne

Camping le Port de Limeuil

F-24480 Allés-sur-Dordogne (Dordogne) T: 05 53 63 29 76. E: didierbonvallet@aol.com

alanrogers.com/FR24170

At the confluence of the Dordogne and Vézère rivers, opposite the picturesque village of Limeuil, this delightful family site exudes a peaceful and relaxed ambience. There are 75 marked touring pitches on grass, some spacious and all with electricity (6/10A). The buildings are in traditional Périgourdine style and surrounded by flowers and shrubs. A sports area on a large, open, grassy space between the river bank and the main camping area adds to the feeling of space and provides an additional recreation and picnic area (there are additional unmarked pitches for tents and camper vans along the bank here).

Facilities

Two clean, modern toilet blocks provide excellent facilities. Bar. Restaurant with snacks and takeaway (15/5-15/9). Small shop. Swimming pool with jacuzzi, paddling pool and children's slide (1/5-30/9). Badminton. Tennis. Volleyball. Football. Boules. Trampoline. Mountain bike hire. Canoe hire, launched from the site's own pebble beach. Free WiFi in bar area. Off site: The pretty medieval village of Limeuil 200 m. Riding 1 km. Golf 10 km.

Open: 1 May - 30 September.

Directions

Site is 7 km. south of Le Bugue. From D51/D31E Le Buisson-Le Bugue road turn west towards Limeuil. Just before bridge into Limeuil, turn left (site signed), across another bridge. Site shortly on the right. GPS: 44.87977, 0.88587

Charges guide

Per unit incl. 2 persons and electricity	€ 14.50 - € 29.50
extra person	€ 4.00 - € 7.50
child (under 10 yrs)	€ 2.50 - € 4.90
dog	€ 2.00

For latest campsite news, availability and prices visit

alanrogers.com

Belvès

RCN le Moulin de la Pique

Le Moulin de la Pique, F-24170 Belvès (Dordogne) T: 05 53 29 01 15. E: moulin@rcn.fr

alanrogers.com/FR24350

This high quality campsite set in the heart of the Dordogne has fine views looking up to the fortified town of Belvès. It is a splendid rural estate where there is plenty of space and a good mixture of trees and shrubs. Set in the grounds of a former mill, the superb traditional buildings date back to the 18th century. There are 219 level pitches with 159 for touring units, all with 10A electricity, a water point and drainage. The remainder are used for mobile homes to rent. The site is ideally suited for families with young and teenage children as there is so much to do, both on site and in the surrounding area.

Facilities

Three modern sanitary blocks include facilities for disabled visitors. Launderette. Shop (bread to order), bar, restaurant, snack bar and takeaway (all open all season). Swimming pools (two heated). Recreational lake. Playgrounds. Outdoor fitness area. Library. Fossil field. Sports field. Tennis. Minigolf. Boules. Satellite TV. Games room. Bicycle hire. Internet facilities. WiFi (charged). Off site: Bars, restaurants and shops in the village of Belvès 2 km. Canoeing 2 km. Riding 5 km. Golf 7 km.

Open: 20 April - 28 September.

Directions

Site is 35 km. southwest of Sarlat on the D710 road, 7 km. south of Siorac-en-Périgord. GPS: 44.76228, 1.01412

Charges guide

Per unit incl. 2 persons, electricity and water	€ 16.50 - € 49.00
extra person (over 3 yrs)	€ 2.60 - € 5.50
dog (max. 1)	€ 7.00

Camping Cheques accepted.

Bidart

Camping le Pavillon Royal

Avenue du Prince de Galles, F-64210 Bidart (Pyrénées-Atlantiques) T: 05 59 23 00 54.

E: info@pavillon-royal.com alanrogers.com/FR64060

Le Pavillon Royal has an excellent situation on raised ground overlooking the sea (100 m. from the beach), with good views along the coast to the south and to the north coast of Spain beyond. There is a large heated swimming pool and sunbathing area in the centre of the site. The camping area is divided up into 325 marked, level pitches, many of a good size. Seventy-five are reserved for tents and are only accessible on foot. The remainder are connected by asphalt roads. All have electricity. Much of the campsite is in full sun, although the area for tents is shaded. Beneath the site – and only a very short walk down – stretches a wide sandy beach where the Atlantic rollers provide ideal conditions for surfing. A central, marked out section of the beach is supervised by lifeguards (from mid June). There is also a section with rocks and pools. Reservation in high season is advisable.

Facilities

Good quality toilet blocks with baby baths and two units for disabled visitors. Washing facilities (only two open at night). Washing machines, dryers. Motorcaravan services. Shop (including gas), restaurant and takeaway, bar, heated swimming and paddling pools, wellness facilities, fitness room (all open all season). Playground. General room, TV room, games room, films. Fishing. Surf school. Dogs are not accepted. WiFi throughout (charged). Off site: Golf 500 m. Bicycle hire 2 km. Riding 3 km. Sailing 5 km. New oceanographic centre at Biarritz.

Open: 15 May - 30 September.

Directions

From A63 exit 4, take the N10 south towards Bidart. At roundabout after the Intermarché supermarket turn right (signed for Biarritz). After 600 m. turn left at site sign. GPS: 43.45458, -1.57649

Charges guide

Per unit incl. 2 persons, electricity and water	€ 33.00 - € 58.00
tent pitch	€ 27.00 - € 48.00
extra person (over 4 yrs)	€ 8.00 - € 14.00

For latest campsite news, availability and prices visit

alanrogers.com

Duras

Le Cabri Holiday Village

Route de Savignac, F-47120 Duras (Lot-et-Garonne) T: 05 53 83 81 03. E: holidays@lecabri.eu.com

alanrogers.com/FR47110

This countryside site of 5.5 hectares is divided into three areas: camping, chalets and open fields. It is on the border of the Dordogne and the Lot-et-Garonne departments. Le Cabri Holiday Village is an English owned and run, small holiday complex. The owners, Peter and Eileen Marston who are keen caravanners themselves, have developed 24 new spacious pitches (generally 150 sq.m), all with electricity (4/16A) and water. The open, level pitches are all on hardstandings surrounded by grass and separated by young trees, so with limited shade. Access for large motorcaravans using the rear entrance is possible as this was considered when the site was planned.

Facilities

A recently refurbished sanitary block is centrally located, heated in low season and includes three new private cabins. Separate cabin for disabled visitors. Washing machines, dryers and ironing board. Shop (all year) selling basics including bread. Restaurant (all year) with occasional entertainment year round and Internet access. Swimming pool (June-Sept). Large play area. Boules. Well stocked fishing pond. WiFi (charged).

Open: All year.

Directions

In Duras, look for the D203 and follow signs for site. It is less than 1 km. away. GPS: 44.68296, 0.18615

Charges guide

Per unit incl. 2 persons and 10A electricity	€ 17.00 - € 22.00
extra person	€ 4.00 - € 5.00
child (under 12 yrs)	€ 2.00 - € 3.00

Labenne-Océan

Yelloh! Village le Sylvamar

Avenue de l'Océan, F-40530 Labenne-Océan (Landes) T: 05 59 45 75 16.

E: camping@sylvamar.fr alanrogers.com/FR40200

LeadingCampings

Less than a kilometre from a long sandy beach, this campsite has a good mix of tidy, well maintained chalets, mobile homes, a tree house and touring pitches. The 289 touring pitches (592 in total) are level, numbered and mostly separated by low hedges. A number of new, less shaded pitches have recently been added. Following development, all now have electricity (10A), water and drainage. Some have additional facilities and are charged accordingly. Pitches are set around a superb pool complex with pools of various sizes (one heated, one not) with a large one for paddling, a wild water river, toboggans and slides. In a sunny setting, all are surrounded by ample sunbathing terraces and overlooked by the excellent bar/restaurant. A member of Leading Campings group.

Facilities

Four modern toilet blocks have washbasins in cabins. Excellent facilities for babies and disabled visitors. Laundry. Fridge hire. Shop, bar/restaurant and takeaway. Swimming pool complex. Play area. Games room. Cinema, TV and video room. Fitness centre. Wellness amenities. Tennis. Football pitch. Bicycle hire. Library. Entertainment programme for all ages. WiFi over site (charged). No charcoal barbecues. Off site: Beach 900 m.

Open: 27 March - 4 October.

Directions

Labenne is on the N10. In Labenne, head west on D126 signed Labenne-Océan and site is on right in 4 km. GPS: 43.59570, -1.45638

Charges guide

Per unit incl. 2 persons and electricity	€ 18.00 - € 52.00
extra person	€ 6.00 - € 9.00
child (3-6 yrs)	free - € 6.00
dog	€ 5.00

Lacanau-Océan

Yelloh! Village les Grands Pins

Plage Nord, F-33680 Lacanau-Océan (Gironde) T: 05 56 03 20 77. E: reception@lesgrandspins.com

alanrogers.com/FR33130

This Atlantic coast holiday site with direct access to a fine sandy beach, is on undulating terrain amongst tall pine trees. A large site with 576 pitches, there are 341 hardstanding pitches of varying sizes for touring units all with electricity (10A). One half of the site is a traffic free zone (except for arrival or departure day, caravans are placed on the pitch, with separate areas outside for parking). There are 71 tent pitches, those in the centre of the site having some of the best views. This popular site has an excellent range of facilities available for the whole season.

Facilities

Four well equipped toilet blocks, one heated, have baby room and facilities for disabled campers. Launderette. Motorcaravan services. Dog showers. Supermarket. Bar with TV. Restaurant and takeaway. Part-covered, heated swimming pool complex (800 sq.m; lifeguard July/Aug) with sunbathing surround and jacuzzi. Fitness activities (charged) and wellness suite. Games room. Pool tables. Multisports pitch. Boules. Tennis. Playgrounds. BMX course. Bicycle hire. Organised activities. WiFi (charged).

Open: 25 April - 29 September.

Directions

From Bordeaux take N125/D6 west to Lacanau-Océan. At second roundabout, take second exit: Plage Nord, follow signs to 'campings'. Les Grand Pins signed to right at the far end of road. GPS: 45.01107, -1.19337

Charges guide

Per unit incl. 2 persons and electricity	€ 18.00 - € 50.00
extra person	€ 6.00 - € 9.00
child (3-12 yrs)	free - € 7.00

France

Hourtin-Plage

Airotel Camping de la Côte d'Argent

F-33990 Hourtin-Plage (Gironde) T: 05 56 09 10 25. E: info@cca33.com

alanrogers.com/FR33110

Côte d'Argent is a large, well equipped site for leisurely family holidays. It makes an ideal base for walkers and cyclists with over 100 km. of cycle lanes in the area. Hourtin-Plage is a pleasant invigorating resort on the Atlantic coast and a popular location for watersports enthusiasts. The site's top attraction is its pool complex, where wooden bridges connect the pools and islands, and there are sunbathing and play areas plus an indoor heated pool. The site has 600 touring pitches (all with 10A electricity), not always clearly defined, arranged under trees with some on sand. High quality entertainment takes place at the impressive bar/restaurant near the entrance. Spread over 20 hectares of undulating sand-based terrain and in the midst of a pine forest, the site is well organised and ideal for children.

Facilities
Very clean sanitary blocks include provision for disabled visitors. Washing machines. Motorcaravan services. Large supermarket, restaurant, takeaway, pizzeria and bar. Four outdoor pools with slides and flumes (20/5-10/9). Indoor pool (all season). Fitness room. Massage (Institut de Beauté). Tennis. Play areas. Miniclub, organised entertainment in season. Bicycle hire. WiFi over site (charged). ATM. Charcoal barbecues are not permitted. Hotel (12 rooms). Off site: Path to the beach 300 m. Fishing and riding. Golf 30 km.

Open: 13 May - 13 September.

Directions
Turn off D101 Hourtin-Soulac road 3 km. north of Hourtin. Then join D101E signed Hourtin-Plage. Site is 300 m. from the beach. GPS: 45.22297, -1.16465

Charges guide
Per unit incl. 2 persons

and electricity	€ 30.00 - € 58.00
extra person	€ 5.00 - € 10.00
child (3-9 yrs)	€ 4.00 - € 9.00
dog	€ 3.00 - € 7.00

Camping Cheques accepted.

Messanges

Camping le Vieux Port

Plage Sud, F-40660 Messanges (Landes) T: 558 482 200. E: contact@levieuxport.com

alanrogers.com/FR40180

A well established destination appealing particularly to families with teenage children, this lively site has 1,546 pitches (975 for touring) of mixed sizes, most with electricity (6A). The camping area is well shaded by pines and pitches are generally of a good size, attractively grouped around the toilet blocks. There are many tour operators here and well over a third of the site is taken up with mobile homes and chalets. An enormous 7,000 sq.m. aquatic park is now open and is the largest on any French campsite. This heated complex is exceptional, boasting five outdoor pools (all 25ºC), three large water slides plus waves and a heated spa. There is also a heated indoor pool. At the back of the site a path leads across the dunes to a good beach (400 m).

Facilities
Nine well appointed, recently renovated toilet blocks with facilities for disabled visitors. Motorcaravan services. Good supermarket and various smaller shops in high season. Several restaurants, takeaway and three bars (all open all season). Large pool complex (no Bermuda shorts; open all season) including new covered pool and Polynesian themed pool. Tennis. Multisports pitch. Minigolf. Outdoor fitness area. Fishing. Bicycle hire. Riding centre. Organised activities including frequent discos and karaoke evenings (1/4-12/9). Spa, massages and beauty area. Only communal barbecues are allowed. WiFi over site (charged). Off site: Beach 400 m. Sailing 2 km. Golf 8 km.

Open: 28 March - 27 September.

Directions
Leave RN10 at Magescq exit heading for Soustons. Pass through Soustons following signs for Vieux-Boucau. Bypass this town and site is clearly signed to the left at second roundabout. GPS: 43.79778, -1.40111

Charges guide
Per unit incl. 2 persons

and electricity	€ 21.55 - € 61.80
extra person	€ 4.85 - € 9.10
child (under 13 yrs)	€ 3.85 - € 6.25
dog	€ 3.10 - € 5.85

Camping Cheques accepted.

For latest campsite news, availability and prices visit

alanrogers.com

Moliets-Plage
Camping le Saint-Martin

Avenue de l'Océan, F-40660 Moliets-Plage (Landes) T: 05 58 48 52 30. E: contact@camping-saint-martin.fr

alanrogers.com/FR40190

A family site aimed mainly at couples and young families, le Saint-Martin offers 383 touring pitches and 173 mobile homes and chalets available for rent. First impressions are of a neat, tidy, well cared for site and the direct access to a wonderful fine sandy beach is an added bonus. The pitches are mainly typically French in style with low hedges separating them, and with some shade. Electricity hook ups are 10/15A and a number of pitches also have water and drainage. Entertainment in high season is low key (with the emphasis on quiet nights) – daytime competitions and a miniclub, plus the occasional evening entertainment, well away from the pitches and with no discos or karaoke. With a top-class pool complex and an 18-hole golf course 700 m. away (special rates negotiated), this would be an ideal destination for a golfing weekend or longer stay.

Facilities

Seven toilet blocks of a high standard and very well maintained, have washbasins in cabins, large showers, baby rooms and facilities for disabled visitors. Motorcaravan services. Washing machines and dryers. Fridge rental. Supermarket. Bars, restaurants and takeaways. Indoor pool, jacuzzi and sauna (charged July/Aug). Outdoor pool area with jacuzzi and paddling pool (15/6-15/9). Multisports pitch. Play area. Bicycle hire. Beach access. WiFi throughout (charged). Off site: Fishing and beach 300 m. Golf and tennis 700 m. Sailing 6 km.

Open: Easter - 1 November.

Directions

From the N10 take D142 to Lèon, then D652 to Moliets-et-Mar. Follow signs to Moliets-Plage, site is well signed. GPS: 43.85242, -1.38732

Charges guide

Per unit incl. 2 persons	
and electricity	€ 22.70 - € 50.00
extra person	€ 6.00 - € 8.90
child (under 13 yrs)	€ 4.00 - € 6.30
dog	free - € 5.30

Prices are for reserved pitches.

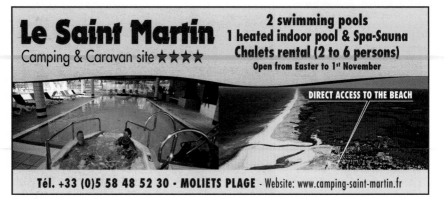

Saint Avit-de-Vialard
Castel Camping Caravaning Saint-Avit Loisirs

Le Bugue, F-24260 Saint Avit-de-Vialard (Dordogne) T: 05 53 02 64 00. E: contact@saint-avit-loisirs.com

alanrogers.com/FR24180

Although Saint-Avit Loisirs is set amidst rolling countryside, far from the hustle and bustle of the main tourist areas of the Dordogne, the facilities are first class, providing virtually everything you could possibly want without the need to leave the site. This makes it ideal for families with children of all ages. The site is in two sections. One part is dedicated to chalets and mobile homes which are available to rent, whilst the main section of the site contains 199 flat and mainly grassy, good sized pitches, 99 for touring, with electricity (6/10A). With a choice of sun or shade, they are arranged in cul-de-sacs off a main access road and are easily accessible.

Facilities

Three modern unisex toilet blocks provide high quality facilities, but could become overstretched (particularly laundry and dishwashing) in high season. Motorcaravan services. Shop, bar, good quality restaurant, cafeteria. Outdoor swimming pool, children's pool, water slide, crazy river, heated indoor pool with jacuzzi. Fitness room. Soundproofed disco. Minigolf. Boules. BMX track. Tennis. Quad bikes. Play area. Bicycle hire. Canoe trips on the Dordogne and other sporting activities organised. Good walks and cycle routes from site. Additional charge for some activities. WiFi over site (charged).

Open: 28 March - 27 September.

Directions

Site is 6 km. north of Le Bugue. From D710 Le Bugue-Périgueux road, turn west on narrow and bumpy C201 towards St Avit-de-Vialard. Follow road through St Avit, bearing right and site is 1.5 km. GPS: 44.95161, 0.85042

Charges guide

Per unit incl. 2 persons	
and electricity	€ 20.90 - € 46.20
extra person	€ 4.10 - € 11.60
child (under 4 yrs)	free
dog	€ 2.30 - € 5.60

For latest campsite news, availability and prices visit

alanrogers.com

Saint Geniès-en-Périgord

Camping Caravaning la Bouquerie

F-24590 Saint Geniès-en-Périgord (Dordogne) T: 05 53 28 98 22. E: labouquerie@wanadoo.fr

alanrogers.com/FR24310

La Bouquerie is situated within easy reach of the main road network in the Dordogne, but without any associated traffic noise. Recent new owners here are investing in new amenities. The main complex is based around some beautifully restored traditional Périgord buildings. There is a bar and restaurant that overlook the impressive pool complex, with a large outdoor terrace for fine weather. The excellent restaurant menu is varied and reasonably priced. Of the 185 pitches, 58 are used for touring units and these are of varying size (80-120 sq.m), flat and grassy, some with shade, and all with 10A electrical connections. The majority of the remainder are for mobile homes and chalets for rent.

Facilities
Three toilet blocks with facilities for disabled visitors and baby rooms. Washing machines and covered drying lines. Shop (15/5-15/9). New bar and restaurant (12/5-15/9). Takeaway. Heated swimming pool complex including water slides, paddling pool and sunbathing areas with loungers (all season). Carp fishing in lake. Multisports area. Boules. Gym. Paintball. WiFi (charged).
Off site: Shops, restaurants and Sunday market in the nearby village of St Geniès. Prehistoric caves at Lascaux.

Open: 7 April - 15 September.

Directions
Site is signed on east side D704 Sarlat-Montignac, 500 m. north of junction with D64 St Geniès road. Turn off D704 at campsite sign and take first left turn signed La Bouquerie. Site is straight ahead. GPS: 44.99865, 1.24549

Charges guide
Per unit incl. 2 persons and electricity	€ 22.80 - € 37.50
extra person	€ 5.80 - € 9.50
child (1-6 yrs)	free - € 7.50

Saint Girons-Plage

Camping Club International Eurosol

Route de la Plage, F-40560 Saint Girons-Plage (Landes) T: 05 58 47 90 14.

E: contact@camping-eurosol.com **alanrogers.com/FR40060**

Privately owned, Eurosol is an attractive, friendly and well maintained site extending over 15 hectares of undulating ground amongst mature pine trees giving good shade. Of the 356 touring pitches, 231 have electricity (10A) with 120 fully serviced. A wide range of mobile homes and chalets, which are being updated, are available for rent. This is very much a family site with multi-lingual entertainers. Many games and tournaments are organised and a beach volleyball competition is held regularly in front of the bar. The adjacent boules terrain is floodlit. An excellent sandy beach 700 metres from the site has supervised bathing in high season and is ideal for surfing. The landscaped swimming pool complex is impressive with three large pools, one of which is covered and heated, and a large children's paddling pool. There is a convivial restaurant and takeaway food service. A large supermarket is well stocked with fresh bread daily and international newspapers. A number of cycle trails lead from the site through the vast forests of Les Landes, and a riding centre is located just 500 m. from Eurosol. To the south, the Basque country and Biarritz are within easy access.

Facilities
Four main toilet blocks and two smaller blocks are comfortable and clean with facilities for babies and disabled visitors. Motorcaravan services. Fridge rental. Well stocked shop and bar (all season). Restaurant, takeaway (1/6-7/9). Stage for live shows arranged in July/Aug. Outdoor swimming pool, paddling pool (all season) and heated, covered pool (May-July). Tennis. Multisports court. Bicycle hire. WiFi (charged). Charcoal barbecues are not permitted. Off site: Beach 700 m.

Open: 12 May - 13 September.

Directions
Turn off D652 at St Girons on D42 towards St Girons-Plage. Site is on left before coming to beach (4.5 km). GPS: 43.95166, -1.35212

Charges guide
Per unit incl. 2 persons and electricity	€ 20.00 - € 39.00
extra person (over 5 yrs)	€ 6.00
dog	€ 4.00

Saint Martin-de-Seignanx

Sites et Paysages Caravaning Lou P'tit Poun

110 avenue du Quartier Neuf, F-40390 Saint Martin-de-Seignanx (Landes) T: 05 59 56 55 79.

E: contact@louptitpoun.com alanrogers.com/FR40140

The manicured grounds surrounding Lou P'tit Poun give it a well kept appearance, a theme carried out throughout this very pleasing site which celebrated its 20th anniversary in 2009. It is only after arriving at the car park that you feel confident it is not a private estate. Beyond this point an abundance of shrubs and trees is revealed. Behind a central sloping flower bed lies the open plan reception area. The avenues around the site are wide and the 168 pitches (142 for touring) are spacious. All have 10A electricity, many also have water and drainage and some are separated by low hedges. The jovial owners not only make their guests welcome, but extend their enthusiasm to organising weekly entertainment (at the café/restaurant) for young and old during high season.

Facilities

Two unisex sanitary blocks, maintained to a high standard and kept clean, include washbasins in cabins, a baby bath and provision for disabled visitors. Laundry facilities with washing machine and dryer. Motorcaravan services. Shop, bar and café/restaurant (all 7/7-31/8). Outdoor swimming pool (15/6-13/9). Play area. Games room, TV. Half-court tennis. No charcoal barbecues. WiFi on part of site (charged). Off site: Bayonne 6 km. Fishing and riding 7 km. Golf 10 km. Sandy beaches of Basque coast ten minute drive. Trips to the Pyrenees.

Open: 14 June - 13 September.

Directions

Leave A63 at exit 6 and join D817 towards Pau. Site is signed at Leclerc supermarket. Continue for 3.5 km. and site is clearly signed on right. GPS: 43.52406, -1.41196

Charges guide

Per unit incl. 2 persons

and electricity	€ 24.45 - € 36.50
extra person	€ 7.90 - € 8.40
child (under 7 yrs)	€ 5.85 - € 6.45
dog	€ 4.65 - € 5.65

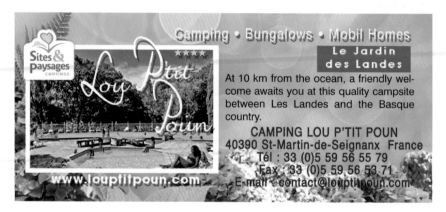

Camping • Bungalows • Mobil Homes

Le Jardin des Landes

At 10 km from the ocean, a friendly welcome awaits you at this quality campsite between Les Landes and the Basque country.

CAMPING LOU P'TIT POUN
40390 St-Martin-de-Seignanx France
Tél : 33 (0)5 59 56 55 79
Fax : 33 (0)5 59 56 53 71
E-mail : contact@louptitpoun.com

www.louptitpoun.com

Saint Pardoux-la-Rivière

Kawan Village Château le Verdoyer

Champs Romain, F-24470 Saint Pardoux-la-Rivière (Dordogne) T: 05 53 56 94 64.

E: chateau@verdoyer.fr alanrogers.com/FR24010

alan rogers

Runner up 2014 Awards

This 22-hectare estate has three lakes, two for fishing and one with a sandy beach and safe swimming area. There are 135 good sized touring pitches, level, terraced and hedged. With a choice of wooded area or open field, all have electricity (5/10A) and most share a water supply between four pitches. There is a swimming pool complex and high season activities are organised for children (5-13 yrs) but there is no disco. This site is well adapted for those with disabilities, with two fully adapted chalets, wheelchair access to all facilities and even a lift into the pool.

Facilities

Well appointed toilet blocks include facilities for disabled visitors and baby baths. Serviced launderette. Motorcaravan services. Fridge rental. Shop and takeaway (15/5-15/9). Bar (15/5-30/9). Restaurant (25/4-30/9). Bistro (July/Aug). Two pools, slide, paddling pool. Play areas. Tennis. Minigolf. Bicycle hire. Fishing. Small library. Kids' club (July/Aug). WiFi (free in courtyard). Computer in reception for Internet access. Off site: Golf 3 km. Riding 12 km. 'Circuit des Orchidées' (22 species of orchid). Vélo-rail at Bussière Galant. Market (Wed) in Piegut.

Open: 19 April - 30 September.

Directions

Site is 2 km. from the Limoges (N21)-Chalus (D6bis-D85)-Nontron road, 20 km. south of Chalus and is well signed from main road. Site on D96 4 km. north of village of Champs Romain. GPS: 45.55035, 0.7947

Charges guide

Per unit incl. 2 persons

and electricity	€ 22.00 - € 37.00
extra person	€ 5.00 - € 7.00
child (6-11 yrs)	€ 4.00 - € 5.00
dog	€ 3.00

Camping Cheques accepted.

For latest campsite news, availability and prices visit

alanrogers.com

Sarlat-la-Canéda

Domaine de Soleil Plage

Caudon par Montfort, Vitrac, F-24200 Sarlat-la-Canéda (Dordogne) T: 05 53 28 33 33.

E: info@soleilplage.fr alanrogers.com/FR24090

This site is in one of the most attractive sections of the Dordogne valley, with a riverside location. There are 218 pitches, in three sections, with 118 for touring units. Additionally, there are 53 recently purchased mobile homes and 27 fully renovated chalets for rent. The site offers river swimming from a sizeable sandy bank or there is a very impressive heated pool complex. A covered, heated pool has been added. All pitches are bound by hedges and are of adequate size, 79 with 16A Europlug, 44 also have water and a drain. Most pitches have some shade. If you like a holiday with lots going on, you will enjoy this site. Various activities are organised during high season including walks and sports tournaments, and daily canoe hire is available from the site. Once a week in July and August there is a 'soirée' (charged for) usually involving a barbecue or paella, with a band and some free wine – and lots of atmosphere! The site is busy and reservation is advisable. English is spoken. You pay more for a riverside pitch, but these have fine river views. There is some tour operator presence.

Facilities

Toilet facilities are in three modern unisex blocks. One has been completely renovated to a high standard with heating and family shower rooms. Washing machines and dryer. Motorcaravan services. Well stocked shop, pleasant bar with TV and attractive, newly refurbished restaurant with local menus and a pleasant terrace (all 7/5-16/9). Picnics available to order. Very impressive heated main pool, new covered pool, paddling pool, spa pool and two slides. Tennis. Minigolf. Three play areas. Fishing. Canoe and kayak hire. Bicycle hire. Currency exchange. Small library. WiFi throughout (charged). Activities and social events (high season). Max. 2 dogs. Off site: Golf 1 km. Riding 5 km. Many attractions of the Dordogne are within easy reach.

Open: 11 April - 30 September.

Directions

Site is 6 km. south of Sarlat. From A20 take exit 55 (Souillac) towards Sarlat. Follow the D703 to Carsac and on to Montfort. After Montfort castle site is signed on left. Continue for 2 km. down to the river and site. GPS: 44.825, 1.25388

Charges guide

Per unit incl. 2 persons	
and electricity	€ 23.90 - € 39.90
incl. full services	€ 26.00 - € 47.30
extra person	€ 5.20 - € 8.20
child (2-8 yrs)	€ 3.10 - € 4.90
dog (max. 2)	€ 2.60 - € 3.60

Camping Cheques accepted.

Sanguinet

Camping les Grands Pins

1039 avenue de Losa, F-40460 Sanguinet (Landes) T: 05 58 78 61 74. E: info@campinglesgrandspins.com
alanrogers.com/FR40250

Approached by a road alongside the lake, this Airotel group site is surrounded by tall trees. Of the 345 pitches, the 80 sand/gravel pitches are of average size, mostly level with varying degrees of shade. All have 6A electricity connections. Low hedges and young trees divide those available for tourers and most are set away from the mobile homes and chalets. An impressive central pool complex is open all season and includes a covered heated indoor pool, an outdoor pool, water slide and flume, children's pool and jacuzzi. There are plenty of walks, cycle rides and the lake to enjoy. The poolside bar and restaurant are open all season and the shop is open in July and August when the site becomes busier. The site offers watersports, minigolf, a children's club, boat trips and organised activities. Volleyball, tennis and boules are available all season. Fishing is also available. The charming small village of Sanguinet is 2 km. away, with a supermarket, shops, bank, restaurants and archaeological museum.

Facilities

Four toilet blocks include washbasins in cabins, showers and British style toilets (not all open in low seasons). Provisions for disabled visitors. Laundry facilities. Motorcaravan services. Shop, bar, restaurant and takeaway (July/Aug). Indoor and outdoor pool complex with jacuzzi. Play area. Games room and TV in bar. Tennis, volleyball, boules. Sports equipment to hire. Bicycle hire. Club for children. Dogs are not accepted in July/Aug. Gas barbecues only. Off site: Fishing 200 m. Boat launching 1 km. Riding 1.5 km. Golf 17 km. Beach and windsurfing 20 km.

Open: 4 April - 27 September.

Directions

Enter Sanguinet from the north on the D46. At one way system turn right. Do not continue on one way system but go straight ahead toward lake (signed) on Rue de Lac. Site is 2 km. on left.
GPS: 44.48396, -1.089716

Charges guide

Per unit incl. 2 persons	
and electricity	€ 20.00 - € 46.50
extra person	€ 6.90 - € 10.00
child (3-7 yrs)	€ 5.20 - € 7.20
dog	€ 4.00

Sarlat-la-Canéda

Camping les Grottes de Roffy

Sainte Nathalène, F-24200 Sarlat-la-Canéda (Dordogne) T: 05 53 59 15 61. E: contact@roffy.fr
alanrogers.com/FR24130

About 5 km. east of Sarlat, les Grottes de Roffy is a pleasantly laid out, family site. There are 162 clearly marked pitches, some very large, set on very well kept grass terraces. They have easy access and good views across an attractive valley. Some have plentiful shade, although others are more open, and all have 6A electricity. Those with very large units are advised to check availability in advance. The reception, bar, restaurant and shop are located within converted farm buildings surrounding a semi-courtyard. The site shop is well stocked with a variety of goods and a tempting épicerie. A good heated outdoor pool complex is open all season and is popular with visitors.

Facilities

Two toilet blocks with modern facilities are more than adequate. Well stocked shop. Bar and gastronomic restaurant with imaginative and sensibly priced menu. Takeaway. Good swimming pool complex comprising two deep pools (one heated), a fountain, paddling pool and heated jacuzzi. All amenities are available all season. Tennis. Games room. Room for teenagers. Play area. Bicycle hire. Entertainment and activities for all ages. Internet access. WiFi in courtyard area (free). Off site: Fishing 2 km. Riding 10 km. Golf 15 km.

Open: 18 April - 21 September.

Directions

Take D47 east from Sarlat to Ste Nathalène. Just before Ste Nathalène the site is signed on the right hand side of the road. Turn here and the site is 800 m. along the lane. GPS: 44.90404, 1.2821

Charges guide

Per pitch incl. 1-6 persons	
and electricity	€ 10.80 - € 23.10
with full services	€ 12.80 - € 25.10

For latest campsite news, availability and prices visit
alanrogers.com

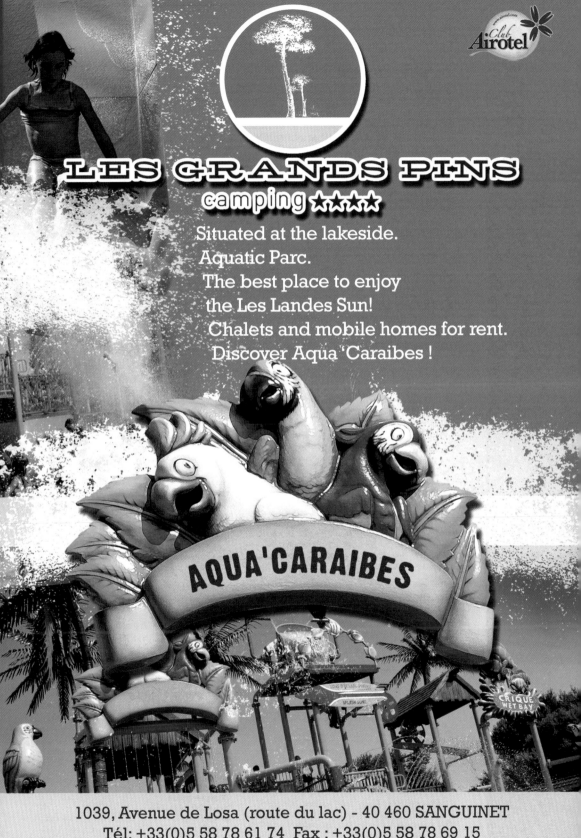

LES GRANDS PINS
camping ★★★★

Situated at the lakeside.
Aquatic Parc.
The best place to enjoy
the Les Landes Sun!
Chalets and mobile homes for rent.
Discover Aqua'Caraibes !

AQUA'CARAIBES

Club Airotel

1039, Avenue de Losa (route du lac) - 40 460 SANGUINET
Tél : +33(0)5 58 78 61 74 Fax : +33(0)5 58 78 69 15
info@campinglesgrandspins.com
www.campinglesgrandspins.com

Sarlat-la-Canéda

Camping la Sagne

Lieu-dit Lassagne, Vitrac, F-24200 Sarlat (Dordogne) T: 05 53 28 18 36. E: info@camping-la-sagne.com

alanrogers.com/FR24940

Camping la Sagne is a family run site and was significantly rebuilt for the 2012 season. The rebuilding programme includes a new reception, bar and snack bar complex and a covered swimming pool and paddling pool with jacuzzi. There are 100 large, level pitches with 65 for touring, all with 16A electricity but long leads are required. Trees and hedges separating the pitches have been planted in the new area, which has little shade as yet, while pitches in the older section are separated by hedges and mature trees providing good shade. The site is close to the Dordogne river and access is available via a track down through the trees.

Facilities

The old toilet block has been refurbished and a new one built with family bathroom, child size toilet, baby bath and facilities for disabled visitors. Washer/dryers. Small shop. Bread service daily. Bar with TV, snack bar and takeaway (July/Aug). Library. Games room. Covered, heated swimming pool, paddling pool and jacuzzi. Playground. River fishing and bathing. Bicycle hire. WiFi over site (charged). Accommodation to rent.

Open: 12 April - 28 September.

Directions

Site is 6 km. south of Sarlat. Leave autoroute A20, exit 55 (Souillac) towards Sarlat. Take D703 to Montfort, turn left following site signs. Site entrance on right in 1 km. GPS: 44.825452, 1.242346

Charges guide

Per unit incl. 2 persons and electricity	€ 15.70 - € 31.00
extra person	€ 4.70 - € 6.70
child (2-13 yrs)	€ 3.10 - € 4.10

Sauveterre-la-Lemance

Flower Camping Moulin du Périé

F-47500 Sauveterre-la-Lemance (Lot-et-Garonne) T: 05 53 40 67 26. E: moulinduperie@wanadoo.fr

alanrogers.com/FR47010

Set in a quiet area and surrounded by woodlands, this peaceful little site is well away from much of the tourist bustle. It has 95 reasonably sized, grassy touring pitches, all with 6A electricity, divided by mixed trees and bushes with most having good shade. All are extremely well kept, as indeed is the entire site. The attractive front courtyard is complemented by an equally pleasant terrace at the rear. Two small, clean swimming pools overlook a shallow, spring water lake, ideal for inflatable boats and paddling, and bordering the lake, a large grass field is popular for games. The picturesque old mill buildings, adorned with flowers and creepers, now house the reception, bar and restaurant.

Facilities

Two clean, modern and well maintained toilet blocks include facilities for disabled visitors. Motorcaravan services. Fridge, barbecue. Basic shop. Bar/reception, restaurant and takeaway. Two small swimming pools (no Bermuda-style shorts). Boules. Outdoor chess. Playground. Small indoor play area. Bicycle hire. Organised activities in high season include canoeing, riding, wine tasting visits, sightseeing trips, barbecues, gastronomic meals. Internet access should be available using cable connection to your own equipment.

Open: 12 May - 18 September.

Directions

From D710, Fumel-Périgueux, turn southeast into Sauveterre-la-Lemance. Turn left (northeast) at far end on C201 signed Château Sauveterre and Loubejec (site also signed). Site is 3 km. on right. GPS: 44.59016, 1.04761

Charges guide

Per unit incl. 2 persons and electricity	€ 16.00 - € 34.10
extra person	€ 4.00 - € 7.30
child (2-7 yrs)	€ 2.00 - € 3.85

Camping Cheques accepted.

Urrugne

Sunêlia Col d'Ibardin

220 route d'Olhette, F-64122 Urrugne (Pyrénées-Atlantiques) T: 05 59 54 31 21. E: info@col-ibardin.com

alanrogers.com/FR64110

This family owned site at the foot of the Basque Pyrenees is highly recommended and deserves praise. It is well run with emphasis on personal attention, the friendly family and their staff ensuring that all are made welcome, and is attractively set in the middle of an oak wood with a mountain stream cascading through it. Behind the forecourt, with its brightly coloured shrubs and modern reception area, various roadways lead to the 203 pitches. These are individual, spacious and enjoy the benefit of the shade (although a more open aspect can be found). There are electricity hook-ups (6/10A) and water points.

Facilities

Two toilet blocks, one rebuilt to a high specification, are kept very clean. WC for disabled visitors. Laundry facilities. Motorcaravan services. Shop for basics and bread orders (15/6-15/9). Restaurant, takeaway service and bar (1/6-15/9). Heated swimming pool and paddling pool (with water games). Playground and club (adult supervision). Tennis. Boules. Video games. Multisports area. Free WiFi on part of site. Not suitable for American-style motorhomes. Off site: Shopping centre 5 km.

Open: 1 April - 30 September.

Directions

Leave A63 at St Jean-de-Luz sud, exit no. 2 and join RN10 towards Urrugne. Turn left at roundabout (Col d'Ibardin) on D4. Site on right after 5 km. Do not turn off to the Col itself, carry on towards Ascain. GPS: 43.33376, -1.68458

Charges guide

Per unit incl. 2 persons and electricity	€ 17.50 - € 41.00
extra person	€ 3.50 - € 6.50
child (2-7 yrs)	€ 2.50 - € 4.00

For latest campsite news, availability and prices visit

alanrogers.com

Baguer-Pican

Camping Caravaning le Vieux Chêne

Baguer-Pican, F-35120 Dol-de-Bretagne (Ille-et-Vilaine) T: 02 99 48 09 55. E: vieux.chene@wanadoo.fr

alanrogers.com/FR35000

This attractive, family owned site is situated between Saint-Malo and le Mont Saint-Michel. Developed in the grounds of a country farmhouse dating from 1638, its young and enthusiastic owner has created a really pleasant, traditional atmosphere. In spacious, rural surroundings it offers 199 good sized pitches on gently sloping grass, most with 10A electricity, water tap and a light. They are separated by bushes and flowers, with mature trees for shade. A very attractive tenting area (without electricity) is in the orchard. The site is used by a Dutch tour operator (20 pitches).

Facilities

Three very good, unisex toilet blocks, which can be heated, include washbasins in cabins, a baby room and facilities for disabled visitors. Small laundry. Motorcaravan services. Shop, bar, takeaway and restaurant (1/6-4/9). Heated swimming pool, paddling pool, slides (17/5-11/9; lifeguard July/Aug). TV room (satellite). Games room. Tennis. Minigolf. Giant chess. Play area. Riding in July/Aug. Fishing. WiFi (charged). Off site: Beach 20 km.

Open: 17 May - 25 September.

Directions

Site is by the D576 Dol-de-Bretagne-Pontorson road, just east of Baguer-Pican. It can be reached from the new N176 taking exit for Dol-Est and Baguer-Pican. GPS: 48.54924, -1.684

Charges guide

Per unit incl. 2 persons and electricity	€ 18.00 - € 30.00
extra person	€ 8.00 - € 10.00
child (4-13 yrs)	€ 3.00 - € 5.00

Bénodet

Camping du Letty

Chemin de Creisanguer, F-29950 Bénodet (Finistère) T: 02 98 57 04 69. E: reception@campingduletty.com

alanrogers.com/FR29030

The Guyader family have ensured that this excellent and attractive site has plenty to offer for all the family. With a charming ambience, the site on the outskirts of the popular resort of Bénodet spreads over 22 acres with 542 pitches, all for touring units. Groups of four to eight pitches are set in cul-de-sacs with mature hedging and trees to divide each group. All pitches have electricity (10A), water and drainage. As well as direct access to a small sandy beach, with a floating pontoon (safe bathing depends on the tides), the site has a grand aquatic parc, with heated open-air and indoor pools including children's pools, jacuzzi, and slides.

Facilities

Six well placed toilet blocks are of good quality and include washbasins in large cabins and controllable hot showers. One block includes a separate laundry and dog washing enclosures. Baby rooms. Separate facility for disabled visitors. Launderette. Motorcaravan services. Shop. Snack bar and takeaway. Bar with games room and night club. Library with four computer stations. Entertainment room with satellite TV. Pool complex with indoor and outdoor pools, children's pool, jacuzzi and slide. Fitness centre. Sauna (charged). Tennis and squash (charged). Boules. Entertainment (July/Aug). WiFi.

Open: 20 June - 4 September.

Directions

From N165 take D70 Concarneau exit. At first roundabout take D44 to Fouesnant. Turn right at T-junction. After 2 km. turn left to Fouesnant (still D44). Continue through La Forêt Fouesnant and Fouesnant, picking up signs for Bénodet. Shortly before Bénodet at roundabout turn left (Le Letty). Turn right at next mini-roundabout and site is 500 m. on left. GPS: 47.86700, -4.08783

Charges guide

Per unit incl. 2 persons and electricity	€ 24.00 - € 43.00
extra person	€ 5.00 - € 10.00

Concarneau

Flower Camping le Cabellou Plage

Avenue du Cabellou, F-29185 Concarneau (Finistère) T: 02 98 97 37 41. E: info@le-cabellou-plage.com

alanrogers.com/FR29520

Le Cabellou Plage is a very pleasant, well maintained site located close to Concarneau. The large, grassy pitches are divided by young hedges, all have 10A electricity and some also have water and drainage. Many have fine views to the nearby beach and the old walled town beyond. The enthusiastic owner has tastefully landscaped many areas of the site with a profusion of shrubs and flowers. A large swimming pool on site is overlooked by a terrace and bar, and the beach is just 25 m. away. The wide and attractive bay is ideal for canoeing and canoes are available for hire from the site. The area for mobile homes is most attractive and cars are parked in an adjacent parking area.

Facilities

One modern toilet block is bright and cheerful and provides mainly open style washbasins and preset showers. Baby room. Facilities for disabled visitors. Laundry room. Motorcaravan services. Shop (July/Aug). Bar with television and Internet (July-Aug). Outdoor heated pool. Play area. Sea fishing. Scuba lessons and water gymnastics. Bicycle hire. Free WiFi over part of site.

Open: 25 April - 15 September.

Directions

Site is just south of Concarneau. Take the D783 towards Tregunc. Turn right onto Avenue Cabellou. Site is well signed from here. GPS: 47.85616, -3.90005

Charges guide

Per unit incl. 2 persons and electricity	€ 15.00 - € 30.00
extra person	€ 3.00 - € 5.50

FREE Alan Rogers Travel Card
Extra benefits and savings - see page 14

Le Pouldu

Camping les Embruns

2 rue du Philosophe Alain, le Pouldu Plages, F-29360 Clohars-Carnoët (Finistère)

T: 02 98 39 91 07. E: camping-les-embruns@orange.fr alanrogers.com/FR29180

This site is unusual in that it is located in the heart of a village, yet is only 250 metres from a sandy cove. The entrance with its code operated barrier and wonderful floral displays, is the first indication that this is a well tended and well organised site, and the owners have won numerous regional and national awards for its superb presentation. The 176 pitches (100 occupied by mobile homes) are separated by trees, shrubs and bushes, and most have electricity (16A Europlug), water and drainage. There is a covered, heated swimming pool, a circular paddling pool and a water play pool and slide. A recent addition is the wellness centre with sauna and massage facilities. It is only a short walk to the village centre with all its attractions and services. It is also close to beautiful countryside and the Carnoët Forest which are good for walking and cycling.

Facilities

Two modern sanitary blocks, recently completely renewed and heated in winter, include mainly British style toilets, some washbasins in cubicles, baby baths and good facilities for disabled visitors. Family bathrooms. Laundry facilities. Motorcaravan services. Shop. Restaurant by entrance, bar and terrace, takeaway (11/4-13/9). Covered, heated swimming and paddling pools (1/7-26/8). New wellness centre with sauna, steam room and fitness. Large games hall. Play area. Football field. Minigolf. Communal barbecue area. Daily activities for children and adults organised in July/Aug. Bicycle hire. Internet access and WiFi in reception area (charged). Off site: Sea and river fishing and watersports. Beach 250 m. Riding 2 km.

Open: 10 April - 19 September.

Directions

From N165 take either exit for Kervidanou, Quimperlé Ouest or Kergostiou, Quimperlé Centre, Clohars Carnoët exit and follow D16 to Clohars Carnoët. Then take D24 for Le Pouldu and follow site signs in village. GPS: 47.76867, -3.54508

Charges guide

Per unit incl. 2 persons	
and electricity	€ 16.50 - € 39.50
extra person	€ 4.00 - € 6.50
child (under 7 yrs)	€ 2.85 - € 4.00
dog	€ 2.80
Less in low seasons.	
Use of motorcaravan services € 4.	

Locunolé

Castel Camping le Ty-Nadan

Route d'Arzano, F-29310 Locunolé (Finistère) T: 02 98 71 75 47. E: info@camping-ty-nadan.fr

alanrogers.com/FR29010

Castel Camping le Ty-Nadan is a well organised site set in wooded countryside in southern Brittany, along the bank of the River Elle (renowned for fishing). There are 183 grassy pitches for touring units, many with shade, and 99 fully serviced. A variety of outdoor family pursuits is on offer, including canoeing, horse riding, walking, mountain biking, rock climbing. An interesting option is excursions on Segway electric vehicles. All activities are supervised by qualified staff. The pool complex with slides and paddling pool is very popular as are the large indoor pool complex and indoor games area. There is an adventure play park and another play park for 5-8 year olds.

Facilities

Three sanitary blocks are equipped with showers, private washing cubicles and facilities for babies. Washing machines and dryers. Well stocked shop. Bar. Restaurant and takeaway. Heated outdoor pools. Indoor pool with changing rooms. Small river beach (unfenced). Indoor badminton. Activity and entertainment programmes (school holidays). Riding centre. Bicycle hire. Canoe trips. Fishing. Segway and electric quad bikes for children. WiFi (charged). Shuttle service to beaches.

Open: 1 May - 1 September.

Directions

Make for Arzano which is northeast of Quimperlé on the Pontivy road and turn off D22 just west of village at site sign. Site is 3 km. GPS: 47.90468, -3.47477

Charges guide

Per unit incl. 2 persons	
and electricity	€ 20.80 - € 47.50
extra person	€ 4.45 - € 9.10
child (2-6 yrs)	€ 2.10 - € 5.60
dog	€ 2.20 - € 6.10
Camping Cheques accepted.	

For latest campsite news, availability and prices visit

alanrogers.com

Névez

Camping le Raguénès-Plage

19 rue des Iles, F-29920 Névez (Finistère) T: 02 98 06 80 69. E: info@camping-le-raguenes-plage.com

alanrogers.com/FR29090

Mme. Guyader and her family will ensure you receive a warm welcome on arrival at this well kept and pleasant site. Le Raguénès-Plage is an attractive and well laid out campsite with many shrubs and trees. The 287 pitches are a good size, flat and grassy, separated by trees and hedges. All have electricity (6/10/15A), water and drainage. The site is used by two tour operators (51 pitches), and has 60 mobile homes of its own. A pool complex complete with heated indoor pool and water toboggan is a key feature and is close to the friendly bar, restaurant, shop and takeaway. From the far end of the campsite a delightful five minute walk along a path and through a cornfield takes you down to a pleasant, sandy beach looking out towards the Ile Verte and the Presqu'île de Raguénès.

Facilities

Two clean, well maintained sanitary blocks include mixed style toilets, washbasins in cabins, baby baths and facilities for disabled visitors. Laundry. Motorcaravan services. Small shop, bar and takeaway (from 1/5). Restaurant (from 14/9). Reading and TV room. Heated indoor and outdoor pools with sun terrace and paddling pool. Sauna (charged). Play areas. Games room. Organised activities (July/Aug). Internet access. Bicycle hire. WiFi over site (charged). Off site: Beach, fishing and watersports 300 m. Supermarket 3 km. Riding 10 km.

Open: 11 April - 27 September.

Directions

From N165 take D24 Kerampaou exit. After 3 km. turn right towards Nizon and bear right at church in village following signs to Névez (D77). Continue through Névez, following signs to Raguénès. Continue for 3 km. to site entrance on left (entrance is quite small and easy to miss). GPS: 47.79337, -3.80049

Charges guide

Per unit incl. 2 persons	
and electricity	€ 21.90 - € 39.10
extra person	€ 4.60 - € 6.20
child (under 7 yrs)	free - € 3.90
dog	€ 1.50 - € 3.20

Plobannalec-Lesconil

Yelloh! Village l'Océan Breton

Lieu-dit le Manoir de Kerlut, F-29740 Plobannalec-Lesconil (Finistère) T: 02 98 82 23 89.

E: info@yellohvillage-loceanbreton.com alanrogers.com/FR29120

LeadingCampings

L'Océan Breton is a comfortable site in the grounds of a manor house on a river estuary near Pont l'Abbé. The campsite itself has neat, modern buildings and is laid out on flat grass providing 220 pitches (60 for touring units). All have electricity connections (6/10A), some also have water and drainage and around ten pitches have hardstanding. One area is rather open with separating hedges planted, the other part being amongst more mature bushes and some trees which provide shade. Site amenities are of excellent quality. The old Manoir is still open to the public and is used during the high season as a crêperie.

Facilities

New sanitary facilities including washbasins all in cabins, and facilities for babies and disabled visitors. Laundry. Small shop. Restaurant. Takeaway. Large modern bar with TV (satellite) and entertainment all season. Large aquapark with slides and children's pool. Covered, heated swimming pool. Sauna, solarium and small gym. Fitness centre. Play area. Tennis. Pétanque. Games room. Bicycle hire. Off site: Riding 1 km. Beach and fishing 2 km. Golf 15 km.

Open: 12 April - 15 September (with all services).

Directions

From Pont l'Abbé, on D785, take D102 road towards Lesconil. Site is signed on the left, shortly after the village of Plobannalec. GPS: 47.81234, -4.22105

Charges guide

Per unit incl. 2 persons	
and electricity	€ 17.00 - € 42.00
extra person	€ 6.00 - € 8.00
child (under 10 yrs)	free
dog	€ 4.00

Pénestin-sur-Mer

Domaine d'Inly

Route de Couarne, B.P. 24, F-56760 Pénestin-sur-Mer (Morbihan) T: 02 99 90 35 09. E: inly-info@wanadoo.fr

alanrogers.com/FR56240

This very large site is mainly taken up with mobile homes and cottages, some belonging to the site owner, some private and some belonging to tour operators. Most of these pitches are arranged in groups of 10 to 14 around a central stone circle with a water point in the centre. The many large trees have been sensibly pruned to provide an acceptable level of shade. Of the 500 pitches, 80 are for touring units and all are large (100 sq.m) with 10A electrical connections (Europlug). Most are level and are situated by the attractive lake at the bottom of the site where one can fish or canoe. Pony rides are possible around the lake. The heated indoor pool, the outdoor pool with its slide and the bar and restaurant area, form two sides of an attractive courtyard. There is a variety of sporting and leisure activities, including a fishing lake.

Facilities

Two toilet blocks include facilities for disabled visitors, and a baby room. Laundry. Shop. Small, comfortable bar with large screen satellite TV, attractive restaurant and takeaway (all season). Heated indoor and outdoor pool complex with slide (outdoor 15/5-20/9, indoor all season). Games room. Play areas. Football pitch (weekly games organised in July/Aug). Lake for fishing/canoeing. Pony rides. Bicycle hire. Sports and activities. WiFi (free). Off site: Supermarket 1.5 km. Pénestin town centre 2 km. Beach 1.7 km. Sailing and boat launching 4 km. Golf 25 km.

Open: 10 April - 20 September.

Directions

On D34 from La Roche-Bernard, at roundabout just after entering Pénestin, take D201 south signed Assérac. After 100 m. turn left (site signed) opposite Carrefour supermarket. After 650 m. turn right, again signed, and campsite is 400 m. on left. GPS: 47.471483, -2.467267

Charges guide

Per unit incl. 2 persons	
and electricity	€ 18.00 - € 42.00
extra person	€ 6.00 - € 7.00
child (3-7 yrs)	free - € 6.00
dog	€ 5.00

Quimper

Castel Camping l'Orangerie de Lanniron

Château de Lanniron, F-29000 Quimper (Finistère) T: 02 98 90 62 02. E: camping@lanniron.com

alanrogers.com/FR29050

L'Orangerie is a beautiful and peaceful family site set in ten acres of a 17th-century, 38-hectare country estate on the banks of the Odet river, formerly the home of the Bishops of Quimper. There are 199 grassy pitches (156 for touring units) of three types varying in size, services and price. They are on flat ground, laid out in rows alongside access roads with shrubs and bushes providing separation. All have electricity and 88 have three services. The original outbuildings have been attractively converted around a walled courtyard. Used by tour operators (30 pitches). There are lovely walks within the grounds and in spring the rhododendrons and azaleas are magnificent – the gardens and the restaurant are open to the public.

Facilities

Excellent heated block in the courtyard and second modern block serving the top areas of the site. Facilities for disabled visitors and babies. Washing machines and dryers. Motorcaravan services. Shop (15/5-10/9). Gas supplies. Bar (23/5-7/9). Restaurant and takeaway (open daily). Swimming and paddling pool. Aquapark with waterfall, Balnéo, spa, jacuzzi, fountains and water slides. Small play area. Tennis. Minigolf. Golf course (9 holes), driving range, two putting greens, training bunker and pitching area (weekly green fee package available). Fishing. Archery. Bicycle hire. Reading, games and billiards rooms. TV/video room. Karaoke. Outdoor activities. Large room for indoor activities. Pony rides and tree climbing (high season). Internet access and WiFi throughout (charged). Off site: Two hypermarkets 1 km. Historic town of Quimper under 3 km. Golf, cycling, walking, fishing, surfing and sailing. Beach 15 km.

Open: 28 March - 15 November.

Directions

From Quimper follow Quimper Sud signs, then Toutes Directions and general camping signs, finally signs for Lanniron. GPS: 47.97685, -4.11102

Charges guide

Per unit incl. 2 persons	
and electricity	€ 23.60 - € 63.40
extra person	€ 4.10 - € 8.50
child (2-9 yrs)	€ 3.10 - € 5.50
dog	€ 3.40 - € 5.10

For latest campsite news, availability and prices visit

alanrogers.com

Saint Cast-le-Guildo

Castel Camping le Château de Galinée

La Galinée, F-22380 Saint Cast-le-Guildo (Côtes d'Armor) T: 02 96 41 10 56. E: chateaugalinee@wanadoo.fr

alanrogers.com/FR22090

Situated a few kilometres back from Saint Cast and owned and managed by the Vervel family, Galinée is in a parkland setting on level grass with numerous and varied mature trees. It has 273 pitches, all with electricity, water and drainage and separated by many mature shrubs and bushes. The top section is mostly for mobile homes. An attractive outdoor pool complex has swimming and paddling pools and two pools with a water slide and a stream. A new indoor complex has now also been added and includes a swimming pool, bar, restaurant and large entertainment hall.

Facilities

The large modern sanitary block includes washbasins in private cabins, facilities for babies and a good unit for disabled visitors. Laundry room. Shop for basics, bar and excellent takeaway menu (all 25/5-4/9). Attractive outdoor heated pool complex with swimming and paddling pools. Covered complex with heated swimming pool, bar, restaurant, entertainment hall and outside terrace with large play area. Tennis. Fishing. Field for ball games. Internet access. WiFi throughout (charged).

Open: 14 May - 10 September.

Directions

From D168 Ploubalay-Plancoet road turn onto the D786 towards Matignon and St Cast. Site is very well signed 1 km. after leaving Notre Dame de Guildo. GPS: 48.58475, -2.25656

Charges guide

Per unit incl. 2 persons and electricity	€ 26.40 - € 65.20
extra person	€ 4.20 - € 7.10
child (under 7 yrs)	€ 2.70 - € 5.00

Camping Cheques accepted.

Telgruc-sur-Mer

Sites et Paysages le Panoramic

Route de la Plage-Penker, F-29560 Telgruc-sur-Mer (Finistère) T: 02 98 27 78 41.

E: info@camping-panoramic.com alanrogers.com/FR29080

This medium sized, traditional site is situated on quite a steep, ten-acre hillside with fine views. It is personally run by M. Jacq and his family who all speak good English. The 200 pitches are arranged on flat, shady terraces, in small groups with hedges and flowering shrubs, and 23 pitches have services for motorcaravans. Divided into two parts, the main upper site is where most of the facilities are located, with the swimming pool, its terrace and a playground located with the lower pitches across the road.

Facilities

The main site has two well kept toilet blocks with another very good block opened for main season across the road. All three include showers, washbasins in cubicles, facilities for disabled visitors, baby baths, plus laundry facilities. Motorcaravan services. Small shop (July/Aug). Refurbished bar/restaurant with takeaway (1/5-31/8). Barbecue area. Heated pool, paddling pool and jacuzzi (15/5-15/9). Playground. Games and TV rooms. Tennis. Bicycle hire. Free WiFi. Off site: Beach and fishing 700 m.

Open: 1 May - 15 September.

Directions

Site is just south of Telgruc-sur-Mer. On D887 pass through Ste Marie du Ménez Horn. Turn left on D208 signed Telgruc-sur-Mer. Continue straight on through town and site is on right within 1 km. GPS: 48.22409, -4.37186

Charges guide

Per unit incl. 2 persons and electricity (10A)	€ 26.50
extra person	€ 5.00
child (under 7 yrs)	€ 3.00
dog	€ 3.00

Palinges

Camping du Lac

Le Fourneau, F-71430 Palinges (Saône-et-Loire) T: 03 85 88 14 49. E: camping.palinges@gmail.com

alanrogers.com/FR71110

Camping du Lac is a very special campsite and it is all due to M. Labille and his wife, the owners, who think of the campsite as their home and every visitor as their guest. The campsite has 40 touring pitches in total, of which 32 have 10A electricity and 16 are fully serviced. There are also seven chalets to rent. The site is adjacent to a lake with a beach and safe bathing. Set in the countryside yet within easy reach of many tourist attractions, especially Cluny, the local Château de Digoine and Mont Saint Vincent with distant views of Mont Blanc on a clear day. Opened in July 2014, a new restaurant serves local Charolais beef and Burgundy wines.

Facilities

The central sanitary block provides all necessary facilities including those for campers with disabilities. Site is particularly well adapted for disabled visitors. Motorcaravan services. Washing machine and fridge. Bread and croissants to order. Boules. Play area. TV room. Sports field. Lake beach, swimming and fishing adjacent. Simple locally sourced food from the 'resto-bus' (1/5-30/9). WiFi over part of site (free). Off site: Snack bar outside entrance (1/7-31/8). Riding 8 km.

Open: 1 April - 30 October.

Directions

Palinges is midway between Montceau-les-Mines and Paray-le-Monial. From Montceau take N70, then turn left onto D92 to Palinges. Follow campsite signs. Site is also well signed from D985 Toulon-sur-Arroux to Charolles road. GPS: 46.56095, 4.22492

Charges guide

Per unit incl. 2 persons and electricity	€ 23.00
extra person	€ 4.10
child	€ 1.80
dog	€ 1.90

No credit cards.

FREE Alan Rogers Travel Card
Extra benefits and savings - see page 14

Gigny-sur-Saône

Castel Camping Château de l'Epervière

6 rue du Château, F-71240 Gigny-sur-Saône (Saône-et-Loire) T: 03 85 94 16 90.

E: **domaine-de-leperviere@wanadoo.fr alanrogers.com/FR71070**

This popular and high quality site is peacefully situated in the wooded grounds of a 16th-century château, close to the A6 and near the village of Gigny-sur-Saône. It is within walking distance of the river where you can watch the cruise boats on their way to and from Châlon-sur-Saône. There are 160 pitches in two separate areas, of which 120 are used for touring, all with 10A electricity. Some are on hardstanding and 30 are fully serviced. Some pitches, close to the château and fishing lake, are hedged and have shade from mature trees; another area has a more open aspect. Red squirrels, ducks and the occasional heron can be found on the campsite and the pitches around the periphery are good for birdwatchers. The château's main restaurant serves regional dishes and there is a good range of takeaway meals. Gert-Jan and her team enthusiastically organise many activities, mainly for younger children, but including wine tasting in the cellars of the château from mid May to mid September. Don't forget, here you are in the Maconnais and Châlonnaise wine regions, so arrange some visits to the local caves.

Facilities

Two well equipped, very clean toilet blocks with all necessary facilities including those for babies and campers with disabilities. Washing machine/dryer. Motorcaravan services. Basic shop (26/4-30/9). Restaurant with good menu and takeaway (26/4-30/9). Cellar with wine tasting. Converted barn with bar, large TV. Heated outdoor swimming pool and new heated paddling pool with slides (26/4-20/9) partly enclosed by old stone walls and updated for 2014. Smaller indoor heated pool (1/4-30/9). Play areas and open field. Fishing. Bicycle hire. Free WiFi in bar area. Off site: Boat launching 500 m. Riding 15 km. Golf 20 km. Historic towns of Châlon and Tournus, both 20 km. The Monday market of Louhans, to see the famous Bresse chickens 26 km.

Open: 1 April - 30 September.

Directions

From A6 heading south, take exit 26 Châlon-Sud, or from A6 heading north take exit 27 Tournus. Then D906 to Sennecey-le-Grand, turn east D18, signed Gigny. Follow site signs to site (6.5 km). GPS: 46.65485, 4.94463

Charges guide

Per unit incl. 2 persons	
and electricity	€ 25.90 - € 39.90
extra person	€ 6.20 - € 8.90
child (2-9 yrs)	€ 4.00 - € 6.50
dog	€ 2.40 - € 3.00

Châlon-sur-Saône

Camping du Pont de Bourgogne

Rue Julien Leneveu, Saint Marcel, F-71380 Châlon-sur-Saône (Saône-et-Loire) T: 03 85 48 26 86.

E: **campingchalon71@wanadoo.fr alanrogers.com/FR71140**

This is a well presented and cared for site, useful for an overnight stop or for a longer stay to explore the local area. It is close to the A6 autoroute, and the interesting market town of Châlon-sur-Saône is only 2 km. away There are 100 slightly sloping pitches (90 sq.m) all with 10A electricity, most on grass, but 30 have a gravel surface. They are separated by beech hedging, and a variety of mature trees gives varying amounts of shade. Many pitches overlook the river, a good spot to watch the passing boats. Access is easy for large outfits. The new central toilet block is of the highest standard and kept very clean. The bar, restaurant and terrace, close to the entrance and overlooking the river, have been recently extended. Takeaway meals are available from the bar all season but the restaurant is open only in July and August. The site gets crowded in the third week of July during the Châlon street theatre festival. Across the river is a large municipal swimming pool. It is possible to walk or cycle alongside the river for several kilometres. A golf club and sailing club are within 1 km.

Facilities

Three toilet blocks, two are brand new, kept very clean and have high quality fittings including a children's bathroom, disabled bathroom and family shower. Motorcaravan services. Laundry facilities. Essential items sold in the bar (bread to order). Modern bar/restaurant (July/Aug). Simple play area. Bicycle hire arranged. WiFi. Off site: Fishing and boat ramp 200 m. Municipal swimming pool 300 m. Golf 2 km. Riding 10 km. Châlon-sur-Saône with many shops, bars, banks etc.

Open: 1 April - 30 September.

Directions

From A6 exit 26 (Châlon-Sud), take N80 (signed Dôle) to second roundabout. Take fourth exit (signed Roseraie) and fork right (les Chavannes). At traffic lights turn right (signed Roseraie) under bridge to site entrance 500 m. GPS: 46.78448, 4.87295

Charges guide

Per unit incl. 2 persons	
and electricity	€ 21.50 - € 28.70
extra person	€ 5.30 - € 7.00
child (under 7 yrs)	€ 3.70 - € 5.20
dog	€ 2.20 - € 2.60

Camping Cheques accepted.

For latest campsite news, availability and prices visit

alanrogers.com

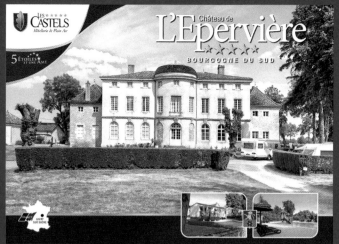

Tournus
Camping de Tournus

14 rue des Canes, F-71700 Tournus (Saône-et-Loire) T: 03 85 51 16 58. E: reception@camping-tournus.com

alanrogers.com/FR71190

This very well maintained, pleasant site is just 1.5 km. from exit 27 of the A6 'Autoroute du Soleil'. It is therefore an ideal stop en route to and from the south of France, and reservation may be necessary in high season. The site is 200 metres from the River Saône and 1 km. from the centre of the interesting old market town of Tournus. All the 90 pitches are for touring and are equipped with 6A electricity, 27 have hardstanding. A few trees give some pitches varying amounts of shade. Access is very easy for large units. A municipal outdoor swimming pool is adjacent to the site and open for the high season.

Facilities
Two clean toilet blocks near the entrance provide all necessary facilities, including those for disabled visitors. Motorcaravan services. Small bar and shop in the reception area where bread can be ordered daily and light snacks purchased. Small play area. Bicycle hire. WiFi near the bar (free). Off site: Municipal pool next door. Fishing 100 m. Riding 10 km. Golf 15 km.

Open: 1 April - 30 September.

Directions
From the A6 take exit 27 for Tournus and the N6 south for just over 1 km. In Tournus (opposite railway station), turn left signed camping and follow signs to site, 1 km. GPS: 46.57372, 4.909349

Charges guide
Per unit incl. 2 persons
and electricity	€ 21.50 - € 26.80
extra person	€ 4.90 - € 6.20

Camping Cheques accepted.

Langres
Kawan Village Lac de la Liez

Peigney, F-52200 Langres (Haute-Marne) T: 03 25 90 27 79. E: campingliez@free.fr

alanrogers.com/FR52030

Managed by the enthusiastic Baude family, this excellent lakeside site is near the city of Langres. Only twenty minutes from the A5/A31 junction, Camping Lac de la Liez provides an ideal spot for an overnight stop en route to the south of France. However, there is also a lot on offer for a longer stay. The site provides 131 fully serviced pitches, some with panoramic views of the 250 hectare lake with its sandy beach and small harbour where boats and pedaloes may be hired. Ideal for swimming and watersports, access to the lake is down steps and across quite a fast road.

Facilities
Two older heated toilet blocks (one closed in low season) have all facilities including washbasins in cabins, controllable showers, and facilities for disabled campers and babies. A new block for 2013 has 8 en-suite units, along with new, large pitches with private sanitary facilities. Laundry facilities. Motorcaravan services. Shop (from 1/5). Bar and restaurant with takeaway (from 15/4). Indoor pool complex (water slides 15/6-15/9) with spa and sauna. Heated outdoor pool (15/6-15/9). Games room. Playground. Extensive games area. Tennis (free in low season). Bicycle hire. WiFi.

Open: 29 March - 29 September.

Directions
From A5/A31 motorways follow signs for Langres. From Langres via N19 towards Vesoul. After 3 km. turn right, straight after the large river bridge, then follow site signs. Also signed from D74 (Neufchâteau). GPS: 47.87317, 5.38069

Charges guide
Per unit incl. 2 persons
and electricity	€ 23.50 - € 34.00
extra person	€ 6.00 - € 8.00
child (2-12 yrs)	€ 3.00 - € 4.50

Camping Cheques accepted.

Agay
Camping Caravaning Esterel

Avenue des Golfs, Agay, F-83530 Saint Raphaël (Var) T: 04 94 82 03 28. E: contact@esterel-caravaning.fr

alanrogers.com/FR83020

Esterel is a quality, award-winning caravan site east of Saint Raphaël, set among the hills beyond Agay. The site is 3.5 km. from the sandy beach at Agay, where parking is perhaps a little easier than at most places on this coast, but a shuttle runs from the site to and from the beach several times daily in July and August (€ 1). There are 164 touring pitches for caravans but not tents; all have 10A electricity and a water tap; 18 special ones have their own en-suite washroom adjacent whilst others also have a washing machine, a dishwasher, a jacuzzi, 16A electricity and free WiFi. Pitches are on shallow terraces, attractively landscaped with good shade and flowers, giving a feeling of spaciousness.

Facilities
Excellent refurbished, heated toilet blocks. Facilities for disabled visitors. Laundry room. Motorcaravan services. Shop. Gift shop. Takeaway. Bar/restaurant. Five circular pools (two heated), one for adults, one for children (covered and heated), three arranged as a waterfall. Spa with sauna, etc. Disco. Archery. Minigolf. Tennis. Pony rides. Pétanque. Squash. Playground. Nursery. Bicycle hire. Organised events in season. WiFi over site.

Open: 28 March - 26 September.

Directions
From A8, exit Fréjus, follow signs for Valescure, then for Agay, site is on left. The road from Agay is the easiest to follow but it is possible to approach from St Raphaël via Valescure. Look carefully for site sign, which is difficult to see. GPS: 43.453775, 6.832817

Charges guide
Per unit incl. 2 persons
and electricity	€ 18.00 - € 38.00
extra person	€ 9.00 - € 10.00

For latest campsite news, availability and prices visit

alanrogers.com

Bormes-les-Mimosas

Camp du Domaine

B.P. 207 La Favière, 2581 route de Bénat, F-83230 Bormes-les-Mimosas (Var)

T: 04 94 71 03 12. E: mail@campdudomaine.com alanrogers.com/FR83120

LeadingCampings

Camp du Domaine, 3 km. south of Le Lavandou, is a large, attractive beachside site with 1,320 pitches set in 45 hectares of pinewood, yet surprisingly it does not give the impression of being so big. The pitches are large and most are reasonably level; 800 have 10A electricity. The most popular pitches are beside the beach, but those furthest away are generally larger and have more shade. Amongst the trees, many pitches are more suitable for tents. The price for each pitch is the same – whether smaller but near the beach, or larger under shade. The beach is the attraction and everyone tries to get close. American motorhomes are not accepted. A member of Leading Campings group.

Facilities

Ten modern, well used but clean toilet blocks. Mostly Turkish WCs. Facilities for disabled visitors (but steep steps). Baby room. Washing machines. Fridge hire. Well stocked supermarket, bars, pizzeria (all open all season). No swimming pool. Several excellent play areas for all ages. Activities and entertainment for children and teenagers (July/Aug). Tennis. Boats, pedaloes for hire. Wide range of watersports. New water games and fitness area. Multisports courts. Gas and electric barbecues only. Direct beach access. WiFi (free at the Tennis Bar).

Open: 28 March - 31 October.

Directions

From Bormes-les-Mimosas, head east on D559 to Le Lavandou. At roundabout, turn off D559 towards the sea on road signed Favière. After 2 km. turn left at site signs. GPS: 43.11779, 6.35176

Charges guide

Per unit incl. 2 persons	
and electricity	€ 31.00 - € 49.00
extra person	€ 6.50 - € 11.50
child (2-7 yrs)	free - € 5.60
dog (not 13/7-17/8)	free

Cavalaire-sur-Mer

Camping Cros de Mouton

F-83240 Cavalaire-sur-Mer (Var) T: 04 94 64 10 87. E: campingcrosdemouton@wanadoo.fr

alanrogers.com/FR83220

Cros de Mouton is an attractive and reasonably priced campsite in a popular area. High on a steep hillside, about 2 km. from Cavalaire and its popular beaches, the site is a calm oasis away from the coast. There are stunning views of the bay but, due to the nature of the terrain, some of the site roads are very steep – the higher pitches with the best views are especially so. There are 199 large, terraced pitches (electricity 10A) under cork trees with 126 available for touring. Half of these are more suitable for tents with parking close by. A range of languages is spoken by the welcoming and helpful owners.

Facilities

Clean, well maintained toilet blocks have all the usual facilities including those for disabled customers (although site is perhaps a little steep in places for wheelchairs). Washing machine. Shop (1/4-15/10). Bar/restaurant with reasonably priced meals and takeaway (1/4-30/9). Swimming and paddling pools with many sunbeds on the terrace and small bar for snacks and cold drinks. Small play area. Games room. Bicycle hire. No charcoal barbecues on pitches. WiFi. Off site: Beach 1.8 km.

Open: 22 March - 31 October.

Directions

Take the D559 to Cavalaire (not Cavalière 4 km. away). Site is 1.5 km. north of Cavalaire-sur-Mer, very well signed from the approach to the town. GPS: 43.18247, 6.5161

Charges guide

Per unit incl. 2 persons	
and electricity	€ 26.70 - € 38.00
extra person	€ 7.20 - € 9.50
child (under 7 yrs)	€ 4.50 - € 5.20

Fréjus

Camping Caravaning les Pins Parasols

3360 rue des Combattants d'Afrique du Nord, F-83600 Fréjus (Var) T: 04 94 40 88 43.

E: lespinsparasols@wanadoo.fr alanrogers.com/FR83010

Les Pins Parasols with its 200 pitches is a comfortably sized site, which is quite easy to walk around. It is family owned and run. Although on very slightly undulating ground, all of the pitches (all have 6A electricity) are levelled or terraced and separated by hedges or bushes with pine trees for shade. There are 48 pitches equipped with their own fully enclosed, sanitary unit, with WC, washbasin, hot shower and dishwashing sink. These pitches naturally cost more but may well be of interest to those seeking a little bit of extra comfort.

Facilities

Good quality toilet blocks (one heated) providing facilities for disabled visitors. Small shop with reasonable stock, restaurant, takeaway (15/4-20/9). Heated swimming pool with attractive rock backdrop, separate long slide with landing pool and small paddling pool. Half-court tennis. General room, TV. Volleyball. Basketball. Play area. Internet in reception and WiFi (charged). Off site: Bicycle hire and riding 2 km. Bus from the gate into Fréjus 5 km.

Open: 4 April - 26 September.

Directions

From A8 take exit 38 for Fréjus Est. Turn right immediately on leaving pay booths on a small road which leads across to D4, then right again and under 1 km. to site. GPS: 43.46290, 6.72570

Charges guide

Per unit incl. 2 persons	
and electricity	€ 19.50 - € 30.70
pitch with sanitary unit	€ 24.10 - € 38.00
extra person	€ 4.65 - € 6.65
child (under 7 yrs)	€ 3.10 - € 4.10

FREE Alan Rogers Travel Card

Extra benefits and savings - see page 14

Fréjus

Camping Resort la Baume-la Palmeraie

3775 rue des Combattants d'Afrique du Nord, F-83618 Fréjus (Var) T: 04 94 19 88 88.

E: reception@labaume-lapalmeraie.com alanrogers.com/FR83060

La Baume is a large, busy site about 5.5 km. from the long sandy beach of Fréjus-Plage, although with its fine and varied selection of swimming pools many people do not bother to make the trip. The pools, with their palm trees, are remarkable for their size and variety (water slides, etc) – the very large feature pool being a highlight. There is also an aquatic play area and two indoor pools with a slide and a spa area. The site has 240 adequately sized, fully serviced pitches with some separators and most have shade. Although tents are accepted, the site concentrates on caravanning. It becomes full in season.

Facilities
Five toilet blocks. Supermarket, several shops. Two bars, terrace overlooking pools, TV. Restaurant, takeaway, pizzeria. Six swimming pools (heated all season), one aquatic playground for children up to four years, two covered, plus steam room and jacuzzi, seven slides. Fitness centre. Tennis. Archery (July/Aug). Skateboard park. Organised events, day and evening entertainment, some in English. Amphitheatre. Discos all season. Children's club (4-11 yrs). Two renovated play areas. WiFi (charged).

Open: 28 March - 26 September (with full services).

Directions
From west on A8, exit 38 'Fréjus centre' and right at first roundabout onto D4a, right at second roundabout, right at the crossroads onto D4 and site is 1 km. on the left. GPS: 43.45998, 6.72048

Charges guide

Per unit incl. 2 persons, electricity, water and drainage	€ 19.00 - € 51.00
extra person	€ 5.00 - € 14.00
child (under 7 yrs)	free - € 8.00
dog	€ 5.00

Min. stay for motorcaravans 2 nights.

Grimaud

Domaine des Naïades

655 chemin des Mûres, F-83310 Grimaud (Var) T: 04 94 55 67 80. E: info@lesnaiades.com

alanrogers.com/FR83640

Les Naïades is a well equipped site with an enviable setting close to the modern resort of Port Grimaud and the Gulf of Saint Tropez. The 470 pitches (226 are used for mobile homes for rent) are of a good size and well shaded, most have 10A electricity. The site boasts an Olympic sized pool and two water slides, as well as a separate pool for children and there is a restaurant. Les Naïades becomes lively in high season with a full activity and entertainment programme, as well as a miniclub for children. Port Grimaud is a stylish resort, built in the 1960s in the marshy delta of the Giscle. It is modelled on Venice and is a car-free environment.

Facilities
Four basic but adequate toilet blocks. Facilities for disabled visitors, but access can be difficult. Laundry facilities. Supermarket. Bar. Restaurant. Swimming pool with water slides. Play area. Motorcaravan services. Mobile homes for rent. Off site: Port Grimaud. St Tropez. Fishing. Watersports.

Open: 11 April - 3 October.

Directions
The site is slightly to the north of Port Grimaud. From D98 head north to N98, Pons-les-Mûres and site is clearly signed. GPS: 43.285278, 6.579722

Charges guide

Per unit incl. 2-3 persons and electricity	€ 26.00 - € 60.00
extra person (over 7 yrs)	€ 4.00 - € 8.00

Mandelieu-la-Napoule

Camping Caravaning les Cigales

505 avenue de la Mer, F-06210 Mandelieu-la-Napoule (Alpes-Maritimes) T: 04 93 49 23 53.

E: campingcigales@wanadoo.fr alanrogers.com/FR06080

It is hard to imagine that such a quiet, peaceful site could be in the middle of such a busy town and so near Cannes. The entrance (quite easily missed) has large electronic gates that ensure that the site is very secure. There are only 68 pitches (35 mobile homes) so this is quite a small, personal site. There are three pitch sizes, from small ones for tents to pitches for larger units and 33 have electricity (6A), 17 fully serviced. All are level with much needed shade in summer, although the sun will get through in winter when it is needed. English is spoken.

Facilities
Well appointed, clean toilet blocks. Attractive swimming pool, heated according to the weather conditions, and large sunbathing area (April-Oct). Play area. River fishing. WiFi (free). Only gas barbecues allowed. Max 1 dog per pitch. Off site: Beach 800 m. The town is an easy walk. Two golf courses within 1 km. Railway station 1 km. for trains to Cannes, Nice, Antibes, Monte Carlo. Hypermarket 2 km. Bus stop 30 m.

Open: 15 December - 15 November.

Directions
From A8, exit 40, bear right. Remain in right-hand lane, continue right signed Plages-Ports, Creche-Campings. Casino supermarket on right. Continue under motorway to T-junction. Turn left, site is 60 m. on left opposite Chinese restaurant. Some other approaches have a 3.3 m. height restriction. GPS: 43.5391, 6.94275

Charges guide

Per unit incl. 2 persons and electricity	€ 35.20 - € 58.20
extra person	€ 8.60
child (under 5 yrs)	€ 4.00

For latest campsite news, availability and prices visit

alanrogers.com

Roquebrune-sur-Argens

Camping Caravaning Leï Suves

Quartier du Blavet, F-83520 Roquebrune-sur-Argens (Var) T: 04 94 45 43 95.

E: camping.lei.suves@wanadoo.fr alanrogers.com/FR83030

This quiet, pretty site is a few kilometres inland from the coast, 2 km. north of the N7. Close to the unusual Roquebrune rock, it is within easy reach of Saint Tropez, Sainte Maxime, Saint Raphaël and Cannes. The site entrance is appealing – wide and spacious, with a large bank of well tended flowers. Mainly on a gently sloping hillside, the 310 pitches are terraced with shade provided by the many cork trees which give the site its name. All pitches have electricity and access to water. There is a pleasant pool and a new children's pool beside the bar/restaurant and entertainment area. It is possible to walk in the surrounding woods. There are 150 mobile homes available to rent.

Facilities

Modern, well kept toilet blocks include facilities for disabled visitors, washing machines and dryers. Shop (2/4-30/9). Good sized swimming pool, paddling pool. Bar, terrace, snack bar, takeaway (all 30/3-15/10). Outdoor stage near the bar for evening entertainment in high season. Excellent play area. Table tennis, tennis, sports area. WiFi over whole site. Only gas barbecues are permitted. Off site: Bus stop at site entrance. Riding 1 km. Fishing 3 km. Bicycle hire 5 km. Golf 7 km. Beach at St Aygulf 15 km.

Open: 30 March - 15 October.

Directions

Leave autoroute at Le Muy and take the N7 towards St Raphaël. Turn left at roundabout onto D7 heading north signed La Bouverie (site also signed). Site on right in 2 km. GPS: 43.47793, 6.63881

Charges guide

Per unit incl. 2 persons and electricity	€ 23.00 - € 46.50
incl. 3 persons	€ 25.00 - € 50.00
child (under 7 yrs)	free - € 7.60
dog	€ 2.00 - € 3.50

Roquebrune-sur-Argens
Castel Camping Domaine de la Bergerie

Vallée du Fournel, route du Col-du-Bougnon, F-83520 Roquebrune-sur-Argens (Var)

T: 04 98 11 45 45. E: info@domainelabergerie.com alanrogers.com/FR83170

alan rogers
Runner up 2014 Awards

This excellent site near the Côte d'Azur will take you away from all the bustle of the Mediterranean to total relaxation amongst the cork, oak, pine and mimosa in its woodland setting. The 60-hectare site is well spread out with semi-landscaped areas for mobile homes and 200 separated pitches for touring caravans and tents. All pitches average over 80 sq.m. and have electricity, with those in one area also having water and drainage. The restaurant/bar, a converted farm building, is surrounded by shady patios, whilst inside it oozes character with high beams and archways leading to intimate corners.

Facilities
Four new toilet blocks are kept clean and include washbasins in cubicles, facilities for babies and disabled visitors. Supermarket (5/4-30/9). Bar/restaurant/takeaway, pool complex with indoor pool (all 5/4-15/10) and fitness centre (body building, sauna, gym, etc). Tennis. Archery. Roller skating. Minigolf. English-speaking children's club. Mini-farm for children. Fishing. WiFi throughout (charged). Only gas barbecues permitted. Off site: Riding and golf 2 km. Bicycle hire 7 km. Beach, St Aygulf and Ste Maxime 7 km. Water-skiing and rock climbing nearby.

Open: 27 April - 30 September.

Directions
Leave A8 at Le Muy exit on D7 towards Roquebrune. At Roquebrune proceed for a further 9 km. then at roundabout turn right on D8 signed St Aygulf. Continue for 2 km. to site on the right. GPS: 43.3988, 6.675417

Charges guide
Per unit incl. 2 persons	€ 21.50 - € 43.50
incl. electricity, water and drainage	€ 22.50 - € 57.00
extra person	€ 6.10 - € 12.10
child (under 7 yrs)	€ 4.50 - € 8.40

Roquebrune-sur-Argens
Camping les Pêcheurs

F-83520 Roquebrune-sur-Argens (Var) T: 04 94 45 71 25. E: info@camping-les-pecheurs.com

alanrogers.com/FR83200

Les Pêcheurs will appeal to families who appreciate natural surroundings with many activities, cultural and sporting. Interspersed with mobile homes, the 110 good sized touring pitches (10A electricity) are separated by trees or flowering bushes. The Provençal-style buildings are delightful, especially the bar, restaurant and games room with its terrace down to the river and the site's own canoe station (locked gate). Across the road is a lake with a sandy beach and restaurant. Enlarged spa facilities include a swimming pool, a large jacuzzi, massage, a steam pool and a sauna (some charges apply).

Facilities
Modern, refurbished, well designed toilet blocks, baby baths, facilities for disabled visitors. Washing machines. Shop. Bar and restaurant. Heated outdoor swimming pool (09.00-19.00, lifeguard in July/Aug, no Bermuda shorts), separate paddling pool, ice-cream bar. Games room. Separate adults-only pool and spa facilities. Playing field. Fishing. Minigolf. Miniclub (July/Aug). Activities for children and adults (high season), visits to local wine caves. Only electric barbecues allowed. WiFi throughout (charged). Security bracelets for all guests. Spring and late summer French courses (3 levels). Off site: Bicycle hire 1 km.

Open: 5 April - 30 September.

Directions
From A8 take Le Muy exit, follow N7 towards Fréjus for 13 km. bypassing Le Muy. After crossing A8, turn right at roundabout towards Roquebrune-sur-Argens. Site is on left after 1 km. just before bridge over river. GPS: 43.450783, 6.6335

Charges guide
Per unit incl. 2 persons and electricity	€ 23.00 - € 47.50
extra person	€ 4.00 - € 9.00
child (acc. to age)	free - € 6.80
dog (max. 1)	€ 3.20

La Tour-du-Meix
Camping de Surchauffant

Le Pont de la Pyle, F-39270 La Tour-du-Meix (Jura) T: 03 84 25 41 08. E: info@camping-surchauffant.fr

alanrogers.com/FR39020

With only 200 pitches, this site may appeal to those who prefer a more informal atmosphere, however it can be lively in high season. It is pleasantly situated above the beaches bordering the Lac de Vouglans, which can be reached quickly on foot directly from the site. The 157 touring pitches are of a reasonable size and are informally arranged, some are fully serviced and most have electricity (10A). They are divided by hedges and there is some shade. The lake offers a variety of watersports activities, boat trips, etc. and is used for fishing and swimming (guarded in high season as it shelves steeply).

Facilities
The sanitary facilities are older in style and adequate rather than luxurious, but reasonably well maintained and clean when we visited. They include some washbasins in private cabins. Laundry. Heated swimming pool (200 sq.m), paddling pool and surround (15/6-15/9). Three playgrounds. Entertainment (July/Aug). Bicycle hire. Safety deposit boxes. Off site: Riding 5 km. Restaurant, takeaway and shops adjacent.

Open: 24 April - 14 September.

Directions
From A39 take exit 7 and N1082 to Lons-le-Saunier. Continue south on D52 for 20 km. to Orgelet. Site is by the D470, at La Tour-du-Meix, 4 km. east of Orgelet. GPS: 46.5231, 5.67401

Charges guide
Per unit incl. 2 persons and electricity	€ 14.00 - € 24.00
extra person	€ 3.00 - € 6.00
dog	free - € 2.00

For latest campsite news, availability and prices visit
alanrogers.com

Canet-en-Roussillon

Yelloh! Village le Brasilia

2 avenue Anneaux du Roussillon, F-66141 Canet-en-Roussillon (Pyrénées-Orientales)

T: 04 68 80 23 82. E: info@lebrasilia.fr alanrogers.com/FR66070

LeadingCampings

Situated across the yacht harbour from the resort of Canet-Plage, le Brasilia is an impressive, well managed family site directly beside the beach. Although large, it is pretty, neat and well kept with an amazingly wide range of facilities – indeed, it is camping at its best. There are 421 neatly hedged touring pitches, all with electricity (6-10A) and 304 with water and drainage. They vary in size from 80 to 120 sq.m. and some of the longer pitches are suitable for two families together. There is a variety of shade from pines and flowering shrubs, with less on pitches near the beach. There are 288 pitches with mobile homes and chalets to rent (the new ones have their own gardens). The sandy beach here is busy, with a beach club and a naturist section to the west of the site. An exciting pool complex with pools catering for all ages and hydrotherapy facilities for adults is overlooked by its own snack bar and restaurant. The village area of the site offers a good range of shops, a busy restaurant and bar, entertainment (including a nightclub) and clubs for children of all ages. In fact you do not need to stir from the site which is almost a resort in itself. A free tourist train runs to Canet-Plage in summer. A new state-of-the-art reception and information centre was completed in 2012. A member of Yelloh! Village and Leading Campings group.

Facilities

Nine modern sanitary blocks are very well equipped and maintained, with British style WCs and washbasins in cabins. Good facilities for children and for disabled campers. Laundry room. Motorcaravan services. Range of shops. Gas supplies. Bars and restaurant. New pool complex (heated). Play areas. Sports field. Tennis. Sporting activities. Library, games and video room. Hairdresser. Internet café and WiFi. Daily entertainment programme. Bicycle hire. Fishing. ATM. Exchange facilities. Post office. Weather forecasts. Free WiFi in bar. Only gas or electric barbecues are allowed. Off site: Boat launching and sailing 500 m. Riding 5 km. Golf 12 km.

Open: 11 April - 3 October.

Directions

From A9 exit 41 (Perpignan Centre, Rivesaltes) follow signs for Le Barcarès and Canet on D83 for 10 km. then for Canet (D81). At first Canet roundabout, turn fully back on yourself (Ste Marie) and watch for Brasilia sign almost immediately on right.
GPS: 42.70467, 3.03483

Charges guide

Per unit incl. 2 persons

and electricity (6A)	€ 24.00 - € 61.00
extra person	€ 6.50 - € 9.00
child (3-6 yrs)	free
dog (max. 2)	€ 5.00

No credit cards.

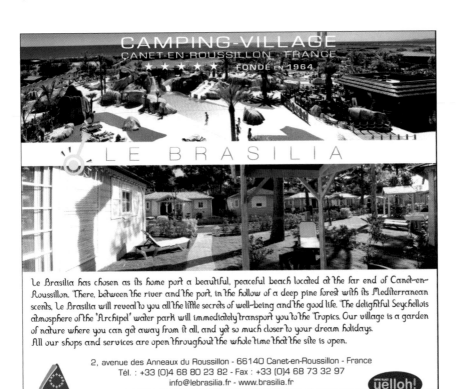

CAMPING-VILLAGE
CANET-EN-ROUSSILLON · FRANCE
★ ★ ★ ★ ★ FONDÉ en 1964

LE BRASILIA

Le Brasilia has chosen as its home port a beautiful, peaceful beach located at the far end of Canet-en-Roussillon. There, between the river and the port, in the hollow of a deep pine forest with its Mediterranean scents, Le Brasilia will reveal to you all the little secrets of well-being and the good life. The delightful Seychellois atmosphere of the 'Archipel' water park will immediately transport you to the Tropics. Our village is a garden of nature where you can get away from it all, and yet so much closer to your dream holidays. All our shops and services are open throughout the whole time that the site is open.

2, avenue des Anneaux du Roussillon - 66140 Canet-en-Roussillon - France
Tél. : +33 (0)4 68 80 23 82 - Fax : +33 (0)4 68 73 32 97
info@lebrasilia.fr - www.brasilia.fr

yelloh! VILLAGE

The Leading Campings of Europe

Argelès-sur-Mer

Camping Club la Sirène

Route de Taxo à la Mer, F-66702 Argelès-sur-Mer (Pyrénées-Orientales) T: 04 68 81 04 61.

E: contact@camping-lasirene.fr alanrogers.com/FR66560

From the moment you step into the hotel-like reception area you realise that this large site offers the holidaymaker everything they could want, including a super pool complex, in a well managed and convenient location close to Argelès-sur-Mer and the beaches. There are 740 pitches over the 17-hectare site, and 520 mobile homes and chalets. They are modern in design, all less than five years old, and laid out in pretty avenues with flowering shrubs and shade from tall trees. There are now just ten touring pitches, with 16A electricity and water, and some 200 taken by tour operators. All the shops and amenities are near reception making the accommodation areas quite peaceful and relaxing.

Facilities

Two well equipped toilet blocks with facilities for babies and disabled visitors (key access). Laundry. Traditional restaurant and fast food bar, bar and takeaway, large shop and bazaar, large aqua park, paddling pools, slides, jacuzzi. Games room. Two play areas. Multisports field. Four tennis courts. Archery. Minigolf. Football. Theatre, evening entertainment, discos, show time spectacular. Riding. Bicycle hire. Watersports. WiFi in bar area. Off site: Resort of Argelès-sur-Mer 2 km.

Open: 20 April - 28 September.

Directions

Leave A9 motorway at exit 42, take D114, towards Argelès. Leave D114, exit 10 and follow signs for Plage Nord. Site signed after first roundabout and is on right 2 km. after last roundabout.
GPS: 42.57093, 3.02906

Charges guide

Per unit incl. 1-3 persons	
and electricity	€ 26.00 - € 43.00
extra person	€ 6.00 - € 9.00
child (under 5 yrs)	€ 4.00 - € 6.00

Crespian

Kawan Village le Mas de Reilhe

Chemin du Mas de Reilhe, F-30260 Crespian (Gard) T: 04 66 77 82 12. E: info@camping-mas-de-reilhe.fr
alanrogers.com/FR30080

This is a pleasant family site in the heart of the Gard region with a favourable climate. There are 92 pitches, 66 for tourers, 41 have electricity (10A), 25 also have water and waste water and some of the upper ones may require long leads. The large lower pitches are separated by tall poplar trees and hedges, close to the main facilities but may experience some road noise. The large terraced pitches on the hillside are scattered under mature pine trees, some with good views, more suited to tents and trailer tents but with their own modern sanitary facilities.

Facilities

Excellent, very clean toilet blocks with facilities for disabled visitors. Laundry. Motorcaravan services. Limited shop (bread to order). Bar, takeaway, restaurant (1/5-14/9). Heated swimming pool and paddling pool. Multisports area with trampolines, bouncy castle and outdoor fitness equipment. TV room. Trampolines. Fitness area. Multisports court. Pétanque. Bicycle hire. Only gas or electric barbecues on pitches. Communal barbecue area. Internet access. WiFi over site (charged).

Open: 26 April - 14 September.

Directions

From the A9 take exit 25, Nîmes-ouest signed Alès, then D999 towards Le Vigan (about 23 km). Turn north on the D6110, site shortly on right at southern edge of Crespian. GPS: 43.87931, 4.09637

Charges guide

Per unit incl. 2 persons	
and electricity	€ 23.00 - € 30.00
extra person	€ 5.50 - € 6.50

Camping Cheques accepted.

Font-Romeu

Huttopia Font-Romeu

Route de Mont-Louis, F-66120 Font-Romeu (Pyrénées-Orientales) T: 04 68 30 09 32.

E: font-romeu@huttopia.com alanrogers.com/FR66250

This is a large, open site of some seven hectares, with 126 touring pitches (72 with 10A electricity), nestling on the side of the mountain at the entrance to Font-Romeu. This part of the Pyrenees offers some staggering views and the famous Mont Louis is close by. An ideal base for climbing, hiking and cycling, it would also provide a good stopover for a night or so whilst travelling between Spain and France, or to and from Andorra. The terraced pitches are easily accessed, with those dedicated to caravans and motorcaravans at the top of the site, whilst tents go on the lower slopes. Trees provide shade to many of the pitches from the sun, which can be quite hot at this altitude.

Facilities

Three bright and clean toilet blocks, one behind reception, the other in the centre of the tent pitches. Toilet for children and excellent facilities for disabled visitors. Laundry facilities at each block. Shop (for basics). Bar, restaurant and takeaway service (weekends only outside July/Aug). Outdoor heated swimming pool. Large games hall. No charcoal barbecues. Max. 1 dog. Off site: Bicycle hire 300 m. Golf and riding 2 km. Beach 8 km.

Open: 19 June - 14 September.

Directions

Font-Romeu is on the D118, some 12 km. after it branches off the N116 heading west, just after Mont Louis. The site is just before the town, on the left and accessed before the public car park.
GPS: 42.50593, 2.04564

Charges guide

Per unit incl. 2 persons	
and electricity	€ 16.00 - € 33.70
extra person	€ 5.60 - € 7.50

For latest campsite news, availability and prices visit

alanrogers.com

Narbonne

Yelloh! Village les Mimosas

Chaussée de Mandirac, F-11100 Narbonne (Aude) T: 04 68 49 03 72. E: info@lesmimosas.com

alanrogers.com/FR11070

Six kilometres inland from the beaches of Narbonne and Gruissan, this family owned site benefits from a less hectic situation than others by the sea. Set amongst the vineyards, it is welcoming, peaceful in low season, but lively in July and August with plenty to amuse and entertain the younger generation whilst offering facilities for the whole family. A free club card is available in July/August for use at the children's club, gym, sauna, tennis, minigolf, billiards etc. There are 266 pitches, 153 for touring, hedged and on level grass, and of a very good size, most with 6/10A electricity. There are a few 'grand confort' pitches with reasonable shade, mostly from two-metre-high hedges. There are also some 113 mobile homes and chalets to rent. This could be a very useful site offering many possibilities to meet a variety of needs, on-site entertainment (cabarets, karaoke, shows, dances etc), and easy access to popular beaches. Nearby Gruissan is a fascinating village with its wooden houses on stilts, beaches, ruined castle, port and salt beds. Narbonne has Roman remains and inland Cathar castles are to be found perched on rugged hill tops.

Facilities

Sanitary buildings refurbished to a high standard include a baby room. Washing machines. Shop and restaurant (all season, incl. breakfast). Takeaway. Bar (low season only at w/e). Small lounge, amusements (July/Aug). Landscaped heated pool with slides and islands (open 12/4-mid October), plus the original large pool and children's pool (high season). Play area. Minigolf. Mountain bike hire. Tennis. Wellness area with massage, beauty treatments and sauna. Gym. Children's activities, sports and entertainment (high season). Bicycle hire. Multisports ground. WiFi over site (charged).

Open: 30 March - 1 November.

Directions

From A9 exit 38 (Narbonne Sud) take last exit on roundabout, back over the autoroute (site signed from here). Follow signs for La Nautique and then Mandirac and site (6 km. from autoroute). Also signed from Narbonne centre.
GPS: 43.13662, 3.02562

Charges guide

Per unit incl. 2 persons and electricity	€ 16.00 - € 46.00
extra person	€ 5.00 - € 8.00
child (3-6 yrs)	free - € 7.00

Narbonne

Camping la Nautique

Chemin de la Nautique, F-11100 Narbonne (Aude) T: 04 68 90 48 19. E: info@campinglanautique.com

alanrogers.com/FR11080

This well established site is owned and run by a friendly Dutch family. It is an extremely spacious site situated on the Etang de Bages, where flat water combined with strong winds make it one of the best windsurfing areas in France. La Nautique has 390 huge, level pitches, 270 for touring, all with 10A electricity and fully equipped individual sanitary units. Six or seven overnight pitches with electricity are in a separate area. A range of mobile homes are available to rent. The flowering shrubs and trees give a pleasant feel while providing some shade. Hedges separate the pitches making some quite private and providing shade. The ground is quite hard and stony. English is spoken in reception.

Facilities

Each pitch has its own fully equipped sanitary unit. Specially equipped facilities for disabled visitors. Laundry. Motorcaravan services. Shop. Bar/restaurant with terrace, TV, and takeaway (all 1/5-30/9). Snack bar (July/Aug). Outdoor heated swimming pool, water slide and paddling pool (1/5-30/9). Play areas. Tennis. Minigolf. Pétanque. Bicycle hire. Miniclub (high season). Games room. WiFi (charged). Torch useful. Off site: Narbonne 4 km.

Open: 1 March - 31 October.

Directions

From A9 take exit 38 (Narbonne Sud). Go round roundabout to last exit and follow signs for la Nautique and site, then further site signs to site on right in 2.5 km. GPS: 43.14696, 3.00439

Charges guide

Per unit incl. 2 persons, electricity, water and sanitary unit	€ 21.00 - € 46.00
extra person	€ 5.00 - € 8.50
child (2-12 yrs)	free - € 7.50

Sérignan-Plage

Yelloh! Village le Sérignan-Plage

Le Sérignan Plage, F-34410 Sérignan-Plage (Hérault) T: 04 67 32 35 33. E: info@leserignanplage.com

alanrogers.com/FR34070

A lively and vibrant site with direct access onto a superb 600 m. sandy beach (including a naturist section), plus two swimming pool complexes and an indoor pool, this is a must for a Mediterranean holiday. It is a busy, friendly, family orientated site with a very comprehensive range of amenities and activities for children. There are now over 1,200 pitches with 260 for touring units. They are fairly level, on sandy soil and all have 10A electricity. The collection of spa pools (balnéo) built in Romanesque style with colourful terracing and columns is overlooked by a very smart restaurant, Le Villa, available to use in the afternoons (used by the adjacent naturist site in the mornings). The owners, Jean-Guy and Catherine, continually surprise us with their flair and unique style in developing and organising the site. Their latest project is a shallow fun pool with colourful play equipment (watch out for the buckets of water!). There are over 300 mobile homes and chalets to let, plus some 400 privately owned units and a good number of tour operator pitches. The busy heart of the site is some distance from reception, a busy and informal area with shops, another good restaurant, the Au Pas d'Oc, an indoor pool and a super roof-top bar. There is a range of sporting activities, children's clubs and evening entertainment, indeed something for all the family – a good holiday choice.

Facilities

Seven modern blocks of individual design with good facilities including showers with washbasin and WC. Facilities for disabled visitors. Baby bathroom. Launderette. Motorcaravan services. Supermarket, bakery and newsagent. Other shops (2/6-14/9). ATM. Restaurants, bars and takeaway. Hairdresser. Balnéo spa (afternoons). Gym. Heated indoor pool. Outdoor pools (all season). Tennis courts. Multisports courts. Play areas. Trampolines. Children's clubs. Evening entertainment. Sporting activities. Bicycle hire. Bus to Sérignan village (July/Aug). Beach (lifeguards 15/6-15/9). WiFi over site (charged). Gas barbecues only. Off site: Fishing 1 km. Riding 1.5 km. Golf 15 km. Sailing and windsurfing school on beach. Local markets. Ferry to Valras Plage.

Open: 23 April - 28 September

Directions

From A9 exit A75 (Béziers Centre) and exit 64 towards Sérignan, D64 (9 km). Before Sérignan, turn left, Sérignan-Plage (4 km). At small sign (blue) turn right. At T-junction turn left over small road bridge and after left hand bend. Site is 100 m. GPS: 43.26308, 3.31976

Charges guide

Per unit incl. 2 persons and electricity	€ 19.00 - € 65.00
extra person	€ 6.00 - € 10.00
child (3-7 yrs)	free - € 9.00
dog	€ 5.00

Low season offers. Discounts in low season for children under 7 yrs.

Sérignan-Plage

Camping le Sérignan-Plage Nature

Route de l'Orpellière, F-34410 Sérignan-Plage (Hérault) T: 04 67 32 09 61. E: info@leserignannature.com

alanrogers.com/FR34080

Sérignan-Plage Nature benefits from the same 600 m. of white, sandy beach as its sister site next door but being a naturist site, it actually abuts the naturist section of the beach with direct access to it. It also has the use of the Sérignan-Plage balnéotherapy pool in the mornings, an excellent facility with spa and jacuzzi pools in a Romanesque-style setting for those over 16 years of age. The site has 286 good sized pitches on level sandy grass of which 99 are available for touring (6A electricity). There is plenty of shade except on the pitches beside the beach. Eighty-three mobile homes and chalets are available to rent. A friendly bar and shop serve the site although visitors may also use the facilities at le Sérignan-Plage. In recent years both Sérignan-Plage and Sérignan-Plage Nature have been developed by Jean-Guy and Catherine. The original work was done by Jean-Guy's father who loved his Romanesque columns, arches and pillars which give both sites a degree of individuality. It was his foresight that masterminded the award-winning, environmentally friendly irrigation system that reuses waste water which serves both this site and Camping Sérignan-Plage. This allows colourful shrubs and trees to grow providing shade and a very pleasant environment ensuring a comfortable site suitable for young and old. After crossing the Orb by a ferry boat, it is possible to cycle a round trip taking in Valras and Sérignan, and even Béziers and the 'Neuf Ecluses' (nine locks) via the towpath of the Canal du Midi.

Facilities

Two toilet blocks of differing designs offer modern facilities with some washbasins in cabins. All clean and well maintained. Washing machines. Supermarket, fresh fruit and vegetables, newsagent/souvenir shop and ice-cream kiosk. Small bar/café. Evening entertainment. Play area, miniclub and disco for children. Facilities and pools at Sérignan-Plage. Only gas barbecues are permitted. WiFi on part of site (charged). Off site: Bicycle hire 200 m. Fishing 500 m. Riding 800 km. Golf 2 km.

Open: 25 April - 30 September.

Directions

From A9 exit 35 (Béziers Est) towards Sérignan, D64 (9 km). Before Sérignan, take road to Sérignan-Plage. At small sign (blue) turn right for 500 m. At T-junction turn left over bridge, site is 75 m. immediately after left-hand bend (the second naturist site). GPS: 43.263409, 3.320148

Charges guide

Per unit incl. 2 persons and electricity	€ 17.00 - € 54.00
extra person	€ 6.00 - € 10.00
child (1-7 yrs)	free - € 10.00
dog	€ 5.00

Special discounts in low season. No credit cards.

For latest campsite news, availability and prices visit

alanrogers.com

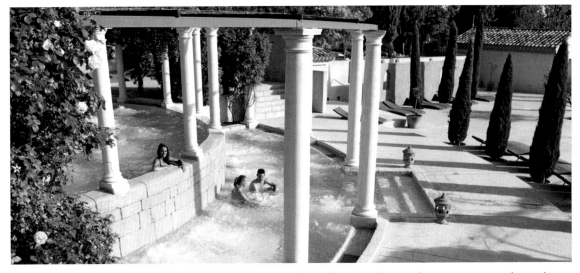

Imagine - hot sunshine, blue sea, vineyards, olive and eucalyptus trees, alongside a sandy beach - what a setting for a campsite - not just any campsite either ! With three pool areas, one with four toboggans surrounded by sun bathing areas, an indoor pool for baby swimmers plus a magnificent landscaped, Romanesque spa-complex with half Olympic size pool and a superb range of hydromassage baths to let you unwind and re-charge after the stresses of work. And that's not all - two attractive restaurants, including the atmospheric "Villa" in its romantic Roman setting beside the spa, three bars, a mini-club and entertainment for all ages, all add up to a fantastic opportunity to enjoy a genuinely unique holiday experience.

★★★★★
Le Sérignan Plage
The Mediterranean
The place for your holidays

34410 Sérignan France - Tel : +33 4 67 32 35 33 Fax : +33 4 67 32 68 39
info@leserignanplage.com   www.leserignanplage.com

Portiragnes-Plage
Camping Caravaning les Mimosas

Port Cassafières, F-34420 Portiragnes-Plage (Hérault) T: 04 67 90 92 92.
E: les.mimosas.portiragnes@wanadoo.fr alanrogers.com/FR34170

Les Mimosas is quite a large site with 400 pitches – 200 for touring units, the remainder for mobile homes – in a rural situation. The level, grassy pitches are of average size, separated and numbered in regular avenues, all with 6A electricity (long leads may be required), some have good shade, others have less. The pool area, a real feature of the site, includes a most impressive wave pool, various toboggans, the 'Space Hole' water slide, a large swimming pool and a super paddling pool (nine pools in all) with lots of free sun beds. This is a friendly, family run site with families in mind, with something new for each year. Les Mimosas has a less hectic situation than sites closer to the beach. However, it is possible to walk to a lovely sandy beach (1.2 km). There is lots going on and many day trips and excursions are arranged all season, from canoeing to visiting castles. Portiragnes-Plage is about 2 km. away and can be reached by cycle tracks. The Canal du Midi runs along the edge of the site (no access), providing another easy cycle route.

Facilities
Good, modern toilet blocks include baby rooms, toilets for children, facilities for disabled visitors (whole site wheelchair friendly). En-suite facilities on payment. Washing machines and dryers. Motorcaravan services. Fridge hire. Large well stocked shop. Bar, restaurant and takeaway. Swimming pool complex (lifeguards all season). Good play area. Miniclub (4-8 yrs). Boules. New gym with sauna, games room, beauty salon and massage. Multisports court. Bicycle hire. Games/TV room. Variety of evening entertainment. WiFi throughout (charged). Communal barbecue (only gas and electric on pitches). Off site: Portiragnes-Plage with bars and restaurants 2 km.

Open: 30 May - 5 September.

Directions
From A9 exit 35 (Béziers Est) take N112 south towards Sérignan (1 km). Large roundabout follow signs for Cap d'Agde, watch carefully for the D37, Portiragnes (1-2 km), follow signs for Portiragnes-Plage. Site well signed before Portiragnes-Plage (5 km). GPS: 43.29153, 3.37348

Charges guide
Per unit incl. 2 persons	
and electricity	€ 21.00 - € 46.00
extra person	€ 5.00 - € 10.50
child (under 4 yrs)	free - € 5.00
dog	€ 2.00 - € 6.00
private sanitary unit	€ 8.50 - € 11.00

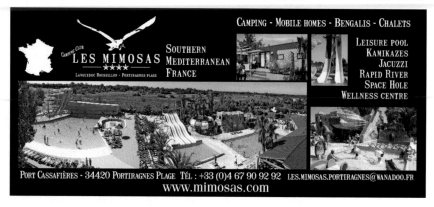

CAMPING - MOBILE HOMES - BENGALIS - CHALETS

LES MIMOSAS ★★★★ LANGUEDOC ROUSSILLON · PORTIRAGNES PLAGE — SOUTHERN MEDITERRANEAN FRANCE

LEISURE POOL
KAMIKAZES
JACUZZI
RAPID RIVER
SPACE HOLE
WELLNESS CENTRE

PORT CASSAFIÈRES - 34420 PORTIRAGNES PLAGE TÉL : +33 (0)4 67 90 92 92 LES.MIMOSAS.PORTIRAGNES@WANADOO.FR
www.mimosas.com

Boussac
Castel Camping le Château de Poinsouze

Route de la Châtre, B.P. 12, F-23600 Boussac-Bourg (Creuse) T: 05 55 65 02 21.
E: info.camping-de.poinsouze@orange.fr alanrogers.com/FR23010

Le Château de Poinsouze is a well established site arranged on an open, gently sloping, grassy park with views over a small lake and château. It is an attractive, well maintained, high quality site situated in the unspoilt Limousin region. The 116 touring pitches, some with lake frontage, have electricity (6-20A Europlug), water and drainage, and 68 have sewerage connections. The site has a friendly family atmosphere with many organised activities in main season including dances, children's games and crafts. There are marked walks around the park and woods. All facilities are open all season.

Facilities
High quality, sanitary unit, washing machines, dryer, ironing, suites for disabled visitors. Motorcaravan services. Well stocked shop. Takeaway. Bar, two satellite TVs, library. Restaurant with new mini-bar for low season. Heated swimming pool, slide, children's pool and new water play area with fountains (June-Sept). Fenced playground. Pétanque. Bicycle hire. Free fishing in the lake, boats and lifejackets can be hired. Sports facilities. WiFi over site (charged). No dogs in high season.

Open: 15 May - 16 September.

Directions
Boussac is 35 km. west of Montluçon, between the A20 and A71 autoroutes. Site is 2.5 km. north of Boussac on D917 (towards La Châtre). GPS: 46.37243, 2.20268

Charges guide
Per unit incl. 2 persons	
and full services	€ 19.00 - € 36.00
extra person	€ 3.00 - € 6.00
child (2-7 yrs)	€ 2.00 - € 5.00
dog (not 14/7-18/8)	€ 3.00

For latest campsite news, availability and prices visit
alanrogers.com

Sanchey

Kawan Village Club Lac de Bouzey

19 rue du Lac, F-88390 Sanchey (Vosges) T: 03 29 82 49 41. E: lacdebouzey@orange.fr

alanrogers.com/FR88040

Open all year, Camping Lac de Bouzey is 8 km. west of Épinal, at the start of the Vosges Massif. The 134 reasonably level grass pitches are separated by tall trees and neat hedging giving varying amounts of shade. There are 100 for touring, all with access to electricity (6-10A) and water. They are on a gently sloping hillside above the lake with its sandy beaches. In high season there is an extensive timetable of activities for all ages, especially teenagers, and the site will be very lively. Golf can be arranged at a local course with discounted rates. English is spoken.

Facilities

The toilet block includes a baby room and one for disabled visitors (there are some gradients). Small, heated section in the main building with toilet, washbasin and shower is used in winter. Family shower room and facilities for children. Laundry facilities. Motorcaravan services. Shop (all year), bar (1/5-1/11), restaurant and takeaway (1/3-1/11). Heated pool (1/5-30/9). Fishing. Riding. Games room. Archery. Bicycle hire. Soundproofed room for cinema shows and discos (high season). WiFi.

Open: All year.

Directions

Site is 8 km. west of Épinal on the D460. From Épinal follow signs for Lac de Bouzey and Sanchey. At western end of Sanchey turn south, site signed. GPS: 48.16692, 6.35990

Charges guide

Per unit incl. 2 persons	
and electricity	€ 27.00 - € 32.00
extra person	€ 7.00 - € 11.00
child (4-12 yrs)	€ 5.00 - € 8.00

Camping Cheques accepted.

Argelès-Gazost

Kawan Village du Lavedan

Lau-Balagnas, 44 route des Vallees, F-65400 Argelès-Gazost (Hautes-Pyrénées) T: 05 62 97 18 84.

E: contact@lavedan.com alanrogers.com/FR65080

Camping du Lavedan is a well established, family owned site set in the Argelès-Gazost valley south of Lourdes, where a warm welcome and an impressive mountain view await you. There are 60 level touring pitches, all with electricity (3-10A) and most have shade from trees. They are set away from the 48 mobile homes, of which 12 are for rent. Planting of bushes and trees has been carefully considered. The large, well designed restaurant and bar area is the scene of some lively evening entertainment in the summer. It is beside the main road so there is some daytime road noise.

Facilities

Recent well maintained toilet block. Baby room. Facilities for disabled visitors. Washing machines and dryer in a separate block heated in winter. Shop, bread delivery (1/5-15/9). Restaurant with terrace, pizzeria and snacks (1/5-15/9). Bar, TV (all year). Swimming pool (15/5-15/9; can be covered). Paddling pool. Play area. Boules. WiFi over site (charged). Off site: Trout fishing and bicycle hire 1 km. Supermarket 2 km. Riding 5 km. Golf 15 km.

Open: All year.

Directions

From Lourdes take the N21 (Voie rapide) south. This becomes the N821/N821A. Take exit 3 for Argelès-Gazost. Take D921 then D921B to Lau-Balagnas. Site is on right at southern edge of town. GPS: 42.98822, -0.089

Charges guide

Per unit incl. 2 persons	
and electricity	€ 19.30 - € 32.70
extra person	€ 5.10 - € 10.05

Camping Cheques accepted.

Estaing

Camping Pyrénées Natura

Route du Lac, F-65400 Estaing (Hautes-Pyrénées) T: 05 62 97 45 44.

E: info@camping-pyrenees-natura.com alanrogers.com/FR65060

Pyrénées Natura, at an altitude of 1,000 m. on the edge of the national park, is the perfect site for lovers of nature. The 66 pitches (47 for touring units), all with electricity (3/10A), are in a landscaped area with 75 varieties of trees and shrubs – but they do not spoil the fantastic views. A traditional-style building houses the reception, bar and indoor games/reading room. There is a small, well stocked shop in the former watermill. Prices are very reasonable and homemade bread can be purchased. On the river there is a small beach belonging to the site for supervised water play.

Facilities

First class toilet blocks. Facilities for disabled visitors and babies. Washing machine and airers (no lines allowed). Motorcaravan services. Bar and small shop (all season). Takeaway 1/5-1/10). Lounge, library, TV, upstairs games/reading room. Birdwatching is a speciality of the site and equipment is available. Infrared sauna and jacuzzi. Play area for the very young. Small beach beside river. Boules. Giant chess. Weekly evening meal in May, June and Sept. Internet. Wine tasting and barbecues with Pyrennean singers (July/Aug). WiFi over site (free in bar).

Open: 20 April - 10 October.

Directions

At Argelès-Gazost, take D918 towards Aucun. After 8 km. turn left on D13 to Bun, cross the river, then right on D103 to site (5.5 km). Narrow road, few passing places. GPS: 42.94152, -0.17726

Charges guide

Per unit incl. 2 persons	
and electricity	€ 20.60 - € 47.00
extra person	€ 6.00
child (under 8 yrs)	€ 3.90
dog	€ 3.00

FREE Alan Rogers Travel Card

Extra benefits and savings - see page 14

France

Figeac
Kawan Village Le Domaine du Surgié
Domaine du Surgié, F-46100 Figeac (Lot) T: 05 61 64 88 54. E: contact@marc-montmija.com
alanrogers.com/FR46320

Very conveniently placed, this rural site is only 2 km. from the centre of the interesting old town of Figeac. There are 193 pitches, of which 103 are for touring, the remaining 90 are split between mobile homes and gîtes, all of which are for rent. The grass pitches are level with a mixture of shade and sun, and all have 10A electricity. Access is easy for large outfits. The site is split into different areas with the aquatic centre next to the camping area. There are many organised activities both on site and in the surrounding area making it an ideal choice for an active family, including teenagers.

Facilities
Three modern toilet blocks include facilities for babies and disabled visitors. Laundry. Shop, bar, restaurant and takeaway. Swimming pool complex adjacent (15/5-15/9, open to the public). Sports competitions and party nights with themed dining. Children's clubs. Canoeing. Fishing. Minigolf. Boules. Bicycle hire. WiFi near reception (charged). Off site: Riding 2 km. Figeac with shops, bars, restaurants and museums 2 km.
Open: 1 April - 30 September.

Directions
From the west, enter Figeac on the D802 and then turn right across river, signed Base de Loisirs. Shortly turn left at small roundabout and then, at traffic lights, branch left uphill to site. Well signed from the centre of Figeac. GPS: 44.60989, 2.05015

Charges guide
Per unit incl. 2 persons and electricity	€ 19.00 - € 26.00
extra person	€ 5.00 - € 7.50

La Bastide-de-Sérou
Flower Camping l'Arize
Lieu-dit Bourtol, F-09240 La Bastide-de-Sérou (Ariège) T: 05 61 65 81 51. E: mail@camping-arize.com
alanrogers.com/FR09020

The site sits in a delightful, tranquil valley among the foothills of the Pyrenees and is just east of the interesting village of La Bastide-de-Sérou, beside the River Arize (good trout fishing). The river is fenced for the safety of children on the site, but may be accessed just outside the gate. The 71 large touring pitches are neatly laid out on level grass within the spacious site. All have 6/10A electricity and are mostly separated into bays by hedges and young trees. Full services are available to some pitches with access to a small toilet block.

Facilities
Toilet block includes facilities for babies and disabled visitors. Laundry room. Motorcaravan services. Shop. Bar (1/7-31/8). Takeaway (5/7-30/8) Small swimming pool (1/6-30/9) and sunbathing area. Entertainment in high season. Weekly barbecues and welcome drinks on Sundays. Fishing. Bicycle hire. WiFi (charged). Off site: The nearest restaurant is located at the national stud for the famous Merens horses just 400 m. away.
Open: 4 April - 30 October.

Directions
Site is southeast of the village La Bastide-de-Sérou. Take the D15 towards Nescus and site is on right after 1 km. GPS: 43.00182, 1.44538

Charges guide
Per unit incl. 2 persons and electricity	€ 15.60 - € 28.60
extra person	€ 4.30 - € 6.40
child (2-13 yrs)	€ 2.30 - € 5.00
dog	€ 1.20 - € 2.60

Martres-Tolosane
Sites et Paysages le Moulin
Lieu-dit le Moulin, F-31220 Martres-Tolosane (Haute-Garonne) T: 05 61 98 86 40.
E: info@campinglemoulin.com alanrogers.com/FR31000

With attractive, shaded pitches and many activities, this family run campsite incorporates 12 hectares of woods and fields beside the River Garonne. It is close to Martres-Tolosane, an interesting medieval village. Some of the 60 level and grassy pitches are super-size and all have 6/10A electricity. There are 24 chalets to rent. Summer brings opportunities for guided canoeing, archery and walking. A large sports field is available all season, with tennis, volleyball, basketball, boules and birdwatching on site. The site is very child friendly and provides many amenities to occupy and entertain young visitors. There is slight road noise.

Facilities
Large sanitary block with separate toilets for men and women. Communal area with showers and washbasins in cubicles. Separate heated area for disabled visitors, with shower, WC and basin. Baby bath. Laundry facilities. Motorcaravan services. Outdoor bar. Restaurant (1/7-20/8). Snack bar and takeaway (1/6-15/9). Bread to order. Heated swimming and paddling pools (1/6-15/9). Fishing. Tennis. Canoeing. Archery. Fitness area. Two playgrounds. Games room. Bouncy castle. Entertainment programme and children's club (high season). Massage (charged). Car rental service. WiFi throughout (charged).
Open: 1 April - 30 September.

Directions
From the A64 motorway (Toulouse-Tarbes) take exit 21 (Boussens) or exit 22 (Martres-Tolosane) and follow signs to Martres-Tolosane. Site is well signed from village. GPS: 43.19048, 1.01788

Charges guide
Per unit incl. 2 persons and electricity	€ 18.90 - € 31.90
extra person	€ 5.00 - € 7.00
child (under 7 yrs)	€ 3.00 - € 5.00
dog	€ 3.00

La Romieu

Castel Camping Le Camp de Florence

Route Astaffort, F-32480 La Romieu (Gers) T: 05 62 28 15 58. E: info@lecampdeflorence.com

alanrogers.com/FR32010

Camp de Florence is an attractive and very well equipped site on the edge of an historic village in pleasantly undulating Gers countryside. The 197 large, part terraced pitches (100 for touring units) all have 10A electricity, 20 with hardstanding and 16 fully serviced. They are arranged around a large field with rural views, giving a feeling of spaciousness. The 13th-century village of La Romieu is on the Santiago de Compostela pilgrims' route. The Pyrenees are a two hour drive, the Atlantic coast a similar distance. The site has been developed by the friendly Mijnsbergen family. They have sympathetically converted the old farmhouse buildings to provide facilities for the site. The Collegiate church, a UNESCO World Heritage monument, is visible from the site and well worth visiting (the views from the top of the tower are magnificent). The local arboretum has the biggest collection of trees in the Midi-Pyrénées.

Facilities

Three toilet blocks provide all the necessary facilities. Washing machines and dryers. Motorcaravan services. Restaurant (1/5-27/9, also open to the public). Takeaway. Bread. Swimming pool area with water slide (1/5-30/9). Bubble bath. Protected children's pool (open to public in afternoons). New playgrounds, games and animal park. Bouncy castle. Trampoline. Outdoor fitness machines. Games room. Tennis. Pétanque. Bicycle hire. Discos, picnics, musical evenings. WiFi over site (charged, free in bar). Max. 2 dogs. Off site: Shop 500 m. in village. Fishing 5 km. Riding 10 km. Walking tours. Walibi theme park.

Open: 1 April - 10 October.

Directions

Site signed from D931 Agen-Condom road. Small units turn left at Ligardes (signed), follow D36 for 1 km, turn right at La Romieu (signed). Otherwise continue to outskirts of Condom and take D41 left to La Romieu, through village to site.
GPS: 43.98299, 0.50183

Charges guide

Per unit incl. 2 persons	
and electricity	€ 17.00 - € 41.00
extra person	€ 3.90 - € 8.00
child (4-17 yrs)	free - € 7.60
dog (max. 2)	€ 2.00 - € 3.00

Special prices for groups, rallies, etc.

Le Camp de Florence - 32480 La Romieu

Sun * Comfort * Nature * Water
The Gers - A region waiting to be discovered, an unspoilt landscape of rolling hills, sunflowers and historic fortified villages and castles. Peace, tranquillity, the home of Armagnac, Fois Gras and Magret de Canard. A 4* site with an excellent restaurant, spacious pitches, panoramic views and luxury mobile homes for hire.

Tel: 0033 562 28 15 58
E-mail: info@lecampdeflorence.com - www.lecampdeflorence.com

Nant

Sites et Paysages les 2 Vallées

Route de l'estrade basse, F-12230 Nant (Aveyron) T: 05 65 62 26 89. E: contact@lesdeuxvallees.com

alanrogers.com/FR12420

Les 2 Vallées is an attractive site with very welcoming and informative young owners. It is located in a valley at the confluence of the Dourbie and the Durzon, deep in the countryside south of Millau. There are 80 pitches in total, extending over two hectares. The 64 touring pitches are of a good size and all are equipped with electrical connections (6A Europlug). Sixteen fully equipped mobile homes and chalets are available for rent. The site is situated around 800 m. from the pretty village of Nant with shops and restaurants. One side of the site runs along the Durzon and fishing is popular here (particularly trout).

Facilities

Heated sanitary block is very clean and well maintained and includes some washbasins in cubicles, hot showers and facilities for disabled visitors. Small laundry. Motorcaravan services. Basic shop. Bar and takeaway (15/6-15/9). Heated swimming pool (30/5-30/9). Fishing. Bicycle hire. Play area. Games room. Activity and entertainment programme. Fitness equipment. No electric or charcoal barbecues on pitches. New communal barbecue area. Mobile homes for rent. WiFi over site.

Open: 23 April - 12 October.

Directions

Nant is southeast of Millau. Leave the A75 motorway at exit 47 (La Cavalerie) and head east on D999 to Nant. From here, follow signs to the site.
GPS: 44.01702, 3.30162

Charges guide

Per unit incl. 2 persons	
and electricity	€ 15.00 - € 20.00
extra person	€ 4.00
child (under 7 yrs)	€ 2.00
dog	€ 1.00

Souillac

Castel Camping le Domaine de la Paille Basse

F-46200 Souillac-sur-Dordogne (Lot) T: 05 65 37 85 48. E: info@lapaillebasse.com

alanrogers.com/FR46010

Set in a rural location some 8 km. from Souillac, this family owned site is easily accessible from the A20 and well placed to take advantage of excursions into the Dordogne. It is part of a large domaine of 80 hectares, all available to campers for walks and recreation. The site is quite high up and there are excellent views over the surrounding countryside. The 262 pitches are in two main areas – one is level in cleared woodland with good shade, and the other on grass with limited shade. Of these, 169 are available for touring units. Numbered and marked, the pitches are a minimum 100 sq.m. and often considerably more. All have electricity (10A) with 80 fully serviced.

Facilities

Three main toilet blocks all have modern equipment and are kept very clean. Laundry. Small shop with a large selection of wine (from 1/7). Restaurant, bar (open until 02.00 in high season), terrace, pizza takeaway. Crêperie. Main swimming pool, a smaller one, paddling pool (unheated), water slides. Sun terrace. Soundproofed disco (three times weekly in season). TV (with satellite). Cinema below the pool area. Tennis. Play area. Library. WiFi in office/bar area (charged). Mini farm. Entertainment for all (July/Aug). Electric barbecues are not permitted. Off site: Golf 4 km.

Open: 11 May - 15 September.

Directions

From Souillac take D15 and then D62 roads leading northwest towards Salignac-Eyvignes and after 6 km. turn right at site sign and follow steep and narrow approach road for 2 km.
GPS: 44.94728, 1.43924

Charges guide

Per person incl. 2 persons	
and electricity	€ 19.00 - € 35.90
incl. water and drainage	€ 19.00 - € 39.90
extra person	€ 5.00 - € 9.50
child (2-13 yrs)	free - € 9.50
dog	€ 2.00 - € 4.00

Less 20% outside 15/6-1/9.
Camping Cheques accepted.

Eperlecques

Kawan Village Château du Gandspette

133 rue de Gandspette, F-62910 Eperlecques (Pas-de-Calais) T: 03 21 93 43 93.

E: contact@chateau-gandspette.com alanrogers.com/FR62030

This spacious family run site is set in the grounds of a 19th-century château. It is conveniently situated for the Channel ports and tunnel, providing overnight accommodation together with a range of facilities for longer stays. There are 110 touring pitches, all with 6A electric hook-ups and 21 with hardstanding. These are intermingled with 20 privately owned mobile homes and caravans and a further 18 for hire. Most pitches are delineated by trees and hedging. Mature trees form the perimeter of the site, through which there is access to woodland walks. Even when the site is busy there is still a sense of space with large green areas kept free of caravans and tents.

Facilities

Two sanitary blocks with a mixture of open and cubicle washbasins. Good facilities for disabled visitors and babies. Laundry facilities. Motorcaravan services. Bar, grill restaurant and takeaway (all 1/5-15/9). Swimming pools (15/5-15/9). Playground. Multisport court. Tennis. Pétanque. Children's room. Entertainment in season. Electric barbecues are not permitted. WiFi throughout (charged). Off site: Supermarket 1 km. Fishing 3 km. Riding and golf 5 km. Bicycle hire 15 km. Beach 40 km.

Open: 1 April - 30 September.

Directions

From Calais follow D943 (St Omer) for 25 km. Southeast of Nordausques take D221 (east). Follow site signs for 5-6 km. From Dunkirk ferry follow signs for St Omer D300. At Watten roundabout exit right (Gandspette) following site signs.
GPS: 50.81924, 2.17753

Charges guide

Per unit incl. 2 persons	
and electricity (6A)	€ 21.70 - € 32.00
extra person	€ 6.20 - € 7.20
child (3-6 yrs)	€ 4.20 - € 5.20
dog	€ 1.10

Camping Cheques accepted.

For latest campsite news, availability and prices visit

alanrogers.com

Pontorson

Kawan Village Haliotis

Chemin des Soupirs, F-50170 Pontorson (Manche) T: 02 33 68 11 59. E: camping.haliotis@wanadoo.fr

alanrogers.com/FR50080

The staff at this beautiful campsite offer a warm welcome to visitors. Situated on the edge of the little town of Pontorson, 9 km. from Le Mont Saint-Michel, the site has 152 pitches, including 118 for touring units. Most have 16A electricity and 24 really large ones also have water and drainage. Excellent private sanitary facilities are also available on 12 luxury pitches. The comfortable reception area incorporates a pleasant bar where breakfast is served. This opens onto the swimming pool terrace. The site is attractively laid out and includes a Japanese garden. Haliotis (which takes its name from a large shell) is next to the River Couesnon and it is possible to walk, cycle and canoe to Mont Saint-Michel.

Facilities

Well equipped, heated toilet block with controllable showers and washbasins in cubicles. Good facilities for disabled visitors. Baby room. Laundry facilities. Bar serving breakfast. Bread to order. Shop. Outdoor heated swimming pool (1/5-30/9) with jacuzzi and separate paddling pool. Sauna and solarium. Good fenced play areas. Pétanque. Archery. Games room. Tennis. Golf practice range. Multisports court. Outdoor fitness equipment. Bicycle hire. Japanese garden and animal park. Miniclub. Free WiFi over site.

Open: 15 March - 11 November.

Directions

Pontorson is 22 km. southwest of Avranches and bypassed by the N176. Site is 300 m. north of town centre. NB: Entrance is on rue du Général Patton. Sat nav users should follow signs!
GPS: 48.55836, -1.51429

Charges guide

Per unit incl. 2 persons and electricity	€ 19.50 - € 25.50
with individual sanitary facility	€ 25.40 - € 31.40
extra person	€ 5.00 - € 6.00

Camping Cheques accepted.

Port-en-Bessin

Camping Port'land

Chemin du Castel, F-14520 Port-en-Bessin (Calvados) T: 02 31 51 07 06. E: campingportland@wanadoo.fr

alanrogers.com/FR14150

You will be made most welcome at Port'land, now a mature site lying 700 m. to the east of the little resort of Port-en-Bessin, one of Normandy's busiest fishing ports. The 279 pitches are large and grassy with 157 available for touring units, all with 16A electricity. There is a separate area for tents without electricity. The camping area has been imaginatively divided into zones, some overlooking small fishing ponds and another radiating out from a central barbecue area. An attractive modern building houses reception and the good amenities which include a shop and a bar/restaurant with fine views over the Normandy coastline. There are 98 site-owned mobile homes for rent.

Facilities

The two sanitary blocks are modern and well maintained. Special facilities for disabled campers. Two heated swimming pools, one with slides (indoor pool all season, outdoor July/Aug) and paddling pool. Shop, bar, restaurant, takeaway (all open all season). Large TV and games room. Multisports pitch. Fishing. Play area. Free WiFi over part of site. Off site: Nearest beach 4 km.

Open: 1 April - 1 November.

Directions

Site is clearly signed off the D514, 4 km. west of Port-en-Bessin. GPS: 49.3463, -0.7732

Charges guide

Per unit incl. 2 persons and electricity	€ 27.00 - € 43.00
extra person	€ 6.00 - € 10.00
child (2-10 yrs)	€ 3.00 - € 6.00
dog	€ 5.00

Ravenoville-Plage

Kawan Village le Cormoran

2 le Cormoran, F-50480 Ravenoville Plage (Manche) T: 02 33 41 33 94. E: lecormoran@wanadoo.fr

alanrogers.com/FR50050

This welcoming, environmentally friendly, family run site, close to Cherbourg and Caen, is situated just across the road from a long sandy beach. It is also close to Utah beach and is ideally located for those wishing to visit the many museums, landing beaches and remembrance gardens of WW2. On flat, quite open ground, the site has 110 good sized pitches on level grass, all with 6/10A electricity (Europlug). Some extra large pitches are available. The well kept pitches are separated by mature hedges and the site is decorated with flowering shrubs. A covered pool, a sauna and a gym are among recent improvements. These facilities, plus a shop, comfortable bar and takeaway are open all season.

Facilities

Four toilet blocks, three heated, are of varying styles and ages but all are maintained to a good standard. Laundry facilities. Shop. Bar and terrace. Snacks and takeaway. Outdoor pool (30/6-1/9, unsupervised). New covered pool, sauna and gym. Play areas. Tennis. Boules. Entertainment, TV and games room. Billiard golf. Playing field with archery (July/Aug). Bicycle and shrimp net hire. Riding (July/Aug). BMX park for children. WiFi (charged).

Open: 5 April - 30 September.

Directions

From N13 take Ste Mère-Eglise exit and in centre of town take road to Ravenoville (6 km), then Ravenoville-Plage (3 km). Just before beach turn right and site is 500 m. GPS: 49.46643, -1.23533

Charges guide

Per unit incl. 2 persons and electricity	€ 23.00 - € 35.00
extra person	€ 4.70 - € 8.20

Camping Cheques accepted.

FREE Alan Rogers Travel Card

Extra benefits and savings - see page 14

Les Andelys
Sites et Paysages l'Ile des Trois Rois

1 rue Gilles Nicolle, F-27700 Les Andelys (Eure) T: 02 32 54 23 79. E: campingtroisrois@aol.com

alanrogers.com/FR27070

One hour from Paris, on the banks of the Seine and overlooked by the impressive remains of Château Gaillard (Richard Coeur de Lion), this attractive and very spacious ten-hectare site will appeal to couples and young families. There is easy access to the 115 level, grassy touring pitches in a well landscaped setting, all with electricity (6A), although some long leads may be required. Many pitches back onto the River Seine where you can watch the barges, and most have views of the château. Of the 80 mobile homes, there are seven for rent, leaving lots of space to enjoy the surroundings, including the large lake full of perch and bream for those eager fishermen. Others can try their luck in the Seine. A nearby station will whisk you to Paris for the day, while a short drive will bring the delights of Monet's house and garden. A Medieval Festival is held in Les Andelys in the last weekend of June. Walk along the banks of the Seine and watch the huge passenger boats cruising there, or stroll into the main town for shopping and restaurants.

Facilities
Four small, unheated toilet blocks have showers and washbasins in cubicles. One has facilities for disabled visitors, one with laundry facilities. Motorcaravan services. Heated swimming and paddling pools (15/5-15/9). Bar and restaurant (1/6-15/9). Fenced play area. Adult open-air exercise area. Evening entertainment (4/7-30/8). Bicycles and barbecues for hire. Satellite TV. Internet access. WiFi throughout (charged). Off site: Cycling and walking trails. Riding and golf 5 km. Giverny 20 km.

Open: 15 March - 15 November.

Directions
Les Andelys is 40 km. southeast of Rouen. From the town centre, continue on D125 and follow signs until roundabout by bridge where second exit leads directly into site. GPS: 49.23564, 1.40005

Charges guide
Per unit incl. 2 persons	
and electricity	€ 22.00 - € 26.00
extra person	€ 6.50
child (under 3 yrs)	free
dog	€ 2.50

Camping Cheques accepted.

Crèvecoeur-en-Brie
Caravaning des 4 Vents

22 rue de Beauregard, F-77610 Crèvecoeur-en-Brie (Seine-et-Marne) T: 01 64 07 41 11. E: f.george@free.fr

alanrogers.com/FR77040

This peaceful, pleasant site has been owned and run by the same family for over 50 years. There are around 200 pitches, with a few permanent and seasonal units, however, there are 140 spacious grassy pitches for touring units, well separated by good hedges, all with 6A electricity and a water tap shared between two pitches. The whole site is very well cared for and landscaped with flowers and trees everywhere. This is a great family site with pool and games facilities located at the top end of the site so that campers are not disturbed. Some aircraft noise can be expected. Crevecoeur-en-Brie celebrates the 'feast of small villages' during the last week of June each year. Central Paris is just a 40 minute train ride from the nearest railway station in Tournan en Brie (8 km). Disneyland is just 15 minutes by road.

Facilities
Three sanitary units (two heated in cooler weather) provide British style WCs, washbasins (mainly in cubicles) and pushbutton showers. Facilities for disabled visitors. Laundry facilities. Motorcaravan services. In high season (July/Aug) a mobile snack bar and pizzeria (open 16.00-23.00), and a baker (07.30-11.00). Well fenced but unsupervised, circular swimming pool (16 m. diameter; June to Sept). Playground, games room, volleyball and boules court. Riding (high season). Free WiFi on part of site. Off site: La Houssaye 1 km. Fontenay Tresigny 5 km.

Open: 20 March - 1 November.

Directions
Crèvecoeur is just off the D231 between A4 exit 13 and Provins. From north, pass obelisk and turn right onto the C3 in 3 km. From south 19 km. after junction with N4, turn left at signs to village. Follow site signs. GPS: 48.75060, 2.89714

Charges guide
Per unit incl. 2 persons and electricity	€ 30.00
extra person (over 5 yrs)	€ 6.00
dog	€ 4.00

For latest campsite news, availability and prices visit
alanrogers.com

L'Ile des Trois Rois

The park Ile des Trois Rois is situated in the most beautiful bend of the Seine nearby Castle Gaillard in Normandy and is a haven of peace. Paris is situated of less than an hour and Rouen is half an hour driving from the campsite.

Facilities:
- Two heated swimming pools
- Ping pong
- Camper service
- Bar and restaurant (high season)
- Play Area

1, Rue Gilles Nicole - F-27700 Les Andelys - France
Tel. 0033 (0) 2 32 54 23 79 - Fax 0033 (0) 2 32 51 14 54
Email campingtroisrois@aol.com - www.camping-troisrois.com

Jablines

International de Jablines

Base de Loisirs, F-77450 Jablines (Seine-et-Marne) T: 01 60 26 09 37. E: welcome@camping-jablines.com

alanrogers.com/FR77030

Jablines is a modern site which, with the leisure facilities of the adjacent Espace Loisirs, offers an interesting alternative to other sites in the region. Man-made lakes provide opportunities for many water-based activities. The Grand Lac is said to have the largest beach on the Ile-de-France. The site itself has 154 pitches, of which 145 are for touring units. Most are of a good size (100-120 sq.m), often slightly sloping, with gravel hardstanding and grass, accessed by tarmac roads and marked by young trees. All have 10A electrical connections, 60 are fully serviced. There are nine wooden chalets for rent.

Facilities

Two toilet blocks, heated in cool weather, include pushbutton showers, some washbasins in cubicles. Facilities for disabled visitors. Laundry facilities. Motorcaravan services (charged). Shop (all season). Play area. Boules. Public telephone. Internet point in reception. Ticket sales for Disneyland and Parc Astérix. Mobile homes for rent. Off site: Bar/restaurant adjacent (500 m) at Base de Loisirs with watersports, riding, tennis and minigolf. Fishing, riding, bicycle hire, beach, boat launching all 500 m. Golf 15 km.

Open: 28 March - 31 October.

Directions

From A4 Paris-Rouen turn north on A104. Take exit 8 on D404 Meaux/Base de Loisirs Jablines. From the A1 going south, follow signs for Marne-la-Vallée using A104. Take exit 6A Clay-Souilly on N3 (Meaux). After 6 km. turn south on D404 and follow signs. At park entry keep left for campsite.
GPS: 48.91378, 2.73451

Charges guide

Per unit incl. 2 persons and electricity	€ 26.00 - € 29.00

Camping Cheques accepted.

Maisons-Laffitte

Camping Caravaning International

1 rue Johnson, F-78600 Maisons-Laffitte (Yvelines) T: 01 39 12 21 91. E: maisonslaffitte@sandaya.fr

alanrogers.com/FR78010

This site on the banks of the Seine is consistently busy, has multilingual, friendly reception staff and occupies a grassy, tree covered area bordering the river. There are 336 pitches, 111 occupied by mobile homes and tour operators, plus two areas dedicated to tents. Most pitches are separated by hedges, are of a good size with some overlooking the Seine (unfenced access), and all 225 touring pitches have electricity hook-ups (10A). The roads leading to the site are a little narrow so large vehicles need to take care. There is a frequent train and occasional noise from aircraft.

Facilities

Three sanitary blocks, two insulated for winter use and one more open (only used in July/Aug). Facilities are clean with constant supervision necessary, due to volume of visitors. Provision for disabled visitors. Motorcaravan services. Self-service shop. Restaurant/bar. Takeaway food and pizzeria (all open all season). TV in restaurant, table tennis, badminton, football area. Fishing possible with licence. Internet point and WiFi throughout (charged). Off site: Sports complex adjacent. Riding 500 m.

Open: 1 week before Easter - 3 November.

Directions

From A13 take exit 7 (Poissy) and follow D153 (Poissy), D308 (Maisons-Laffitte), then site signs on right before town centre. From A15 exit 7 take D184 towards St Germain, after 11 km. turn left on D308 (Maisons-Laffitte). Follow site signs.
GPS: 48.9399, 2.14589

Charges guide

Per unit incl. 2 persons and electricity	€ 32.50 - € 37.50
extra person	€ 6.90 - € 7.50

Pommeuse

Camping le Chêne Gris

24 place de la Gare de Faremoutiers, F-77515 Pommeuse (Seine-et-Marne) T: 01 64 04 21 80.

E: info@lechenegris.com alanrogers.com/FR77020

This site is being progressively developed by a Dutch holiday company. A principal building houses reception on the ground floor and also an airy restaurant/bar plus a takeaway. Of the 339 pitches, 48 are for touring, many of which are on aggregate stone, the rest (higher up the hill on which the site is built) being occupied by over 217 mobile homes and 79 tents belonging to a Dutch tour operator. The pitches are not suitable for larger units (over 7 m). Terraces look out onto the heated leisure pool complex and an outdoor adventure-type play area for over-fives, whilst the indoor soft play area is in a large tent at the side of the bar.

Facilities

One toilet block with pushbutton showers and washbasins in cubicles. At busy times these facilities may be under pressure. Facilities for disabled visitors and children. Laundry area. Bar, restaurant, takeaway and swimming pool complex (from Easter weekend). Indoor and outdoor play areas. WiFi (charged). Off site: Shops, bars and restaurants within walking distance.

Open: 4 April - 1 November.

Directions

From A4 at exit 16 take N34 towards Coulommiers. In 10 km. turn south for 2 km. on D25 to Pommeuse; site is on right after level-crossing.
GPS: 48.808213, 2.993935

Charges guide

Per unit incl. 2 persons and electricity	€ 25.00 - € 44.00
extra person	€ 3.50 - € 6.00
child (3-11 yrs)	€ 3.00 - € 4.50

Rambouillet

Huttopia Rambouillet

Route du Château d'Eau, F-78120 Rambouillet (Yvelines) T: 01 30 41 07 34. E: rambouillet@huttopia.com

alanrogers.com/FR78040

This pleasant site is now part of the Huttopia group whose philosophy is to rediscover the camping spirit. It is in a peaceful forest location beside a lake, with good tarmac access roads and site lighting. The 136 touring pitches, 100 with electrical connections (10A), are set among the trees and in clearings. As a result, shade is plentiful and grass sparse. The main area is kept traffic-free but there is a section for motorcaravans and those who need or prefer to have their car with them. The result is a safe, child-friendly site. There is an Espace Nature with 40 huge pitches for campers.

Facilities

The brand new sanitary block has controllable showers, some washbasins in cubicles and a number of more spacious family cubicles. Facilities for disabled visitors. Laundry facilities. Three outlying 'rondavels' each with two family rooms. Motorcaravan services. Small shop (all season) selling basics plus bar/restaurant with terrace (weekends; and daily in July/Aug). Games room with TV. Play area. Natural swimming pool (June-Sept, earlier if possible). Boules. Volleyball. Picnic area. Bicycle hire. Fishing. Children's and family activities with a nature theme (July/Aug). Off site: Large supermarket nearby.

Open: 3 April - 3 November.

Directions

Rambouillet is 52 km. southwest of Paris. Site is southeast of town: from N10 southbound take Rambouillet/Les Eveuses exit, northbound take Rambouillet centre exit, loop round (site signed) and rejoin N10 southbound, taking next exit. Pass under N10, following signs to site in 1.7 km.
GPS: 48.62638, 1.84375

Charges guide

Per unit incl. 2 persons and electricity	€ 18.30 - € 34.20
extra person	€ 5.80 - € 8.00
child (2-7 yrs)	€ 4.20 - € 5.10

Guérande

Le Domaine de Léveno

Lieu dit Léveno, F-44350 Guérande (Loire-Atlantique) T: 02 40 24 79 30. E: domaine.leveno@wanadoo.fr

alanrogers.com/FR44220

There have been many changes to this extensive site over the years and considerable investment has been made to provide a range of excellent new facilities. The number of mobile homes and chalets has increased considerably, leaving only around 76 of the 600 pitches for touring. These are in small groups or scattered among the mobiles, on pitches divided by hedges and with mature trees which offer good shade. All have electricity (6A). When we visited in mid May, they were rather overgrown. Access to some is challenging and the site is not recommended for larger units.

Facilities

Main toilet block offers preset showers, washbasins in cubicles and facilities for disabled visitors. A second, smaller block has been refurbished to a high standard. Laundry facilities. Motorcaravan services. Small shop selling basics and takeaway snacks. Restaurant. Bar with TV and games (all April-Sept). Indoor pool. Heated outdoor pool complex (15/5-15/9). Fitness room. Play areas. Multisports court, tennis and crazy golf. Activities and events (high season). WiFi in bar (free). Off site: Hypermarket 1 km.

Open: 12 April - 28 September.

Directions

From Nantes via N165/N171/D213 and from Vannes on D774 take D99E Guérande bypass. Turn east following signs for Villejames and Leclerc hypermarket and continue on D247 to site on right.
GPS: 47.33352, -2.3906

Charges guide

Per unit incl. 2 persons, electricity and water	€ 22.00 - € 40.00
extra person	€ 3.00 - € 7.00
child (1-7 yrs)	€ 2.00 - € 5.00
dog	€ 3.00 - € 6.00

La Plaine-sur-Mer

Sites et Paysages la Tabardière

2 route de la Tabardière, F-44770 La Plaine-sur-Mer (Loire-Atlantique) T: 02 40 21 58 83.
E: info@camping-la-tabardiere.com alanrogers.com/FR44150

Owned and managed by the Barré family, this campsite is pleasant, peaceful and immaculate. It will suit those who want to enjoy the local coast and towns but return to an oasis of relaxation. However, it still provides activities and fun for those with energy remaining. The pitches are mostly terraced and care needs to be taken in manoeuvring caravans into position – although the effort is well worth it. The pitches have access to electricity and water taps are conveniently situated nearby. The site is probably not suitable for people using wheelchairs.

Facilities

Two good, clean toilet blocks are well equipped and include laundry facilities. Motorcaravan services. Shop and takeaway (1/7-31/8). Bar (1/6-6/9). Good sized covered swimming pool, paddling pool and slides. Playground. Golf. Minigolf. Volleyball and basketball. Half size tennis courts. Boules. Fitness programme. Bicycle hire (July/Aug). WiFi (charged). Off site: Beach and sea fishing 3 km. Golf 4 km. Riding 5 km.

Open: 4 April - 25 September.

Directions

Site is well signed, inland off the D13 Pornic-La Plaine-sur-Mer road. GPS: 47.14111, -2.152285

Charges guide

Per unit incl. 2 persons and electricity	€ 20.00 - € 36.00
extra person	€ 4.30 - € 7.90
child (2-9 yrs)	€ 3.30 - € 5.20
dog	€ 3.70

Camping Cheques accepted.

Le Croisic

Castel Camping de l'Océan

15 route de la Maison Rouge, F-44490 Le Croisic (Loire-Atlantique) T: 02 40 23 07 69.

E: camping-ocean@wanadoo.fr alanrogers.com/FR44210

Camping de l'Océan is situated on the Le Croisic peninsula, an attractive part of the Brittany coastline. Out of a total of 400 pitches, some 50 are available for touring units with the remainder being taken by mobile homes either privately owned or for rent. The pitches are level and 80-100 sq.m. in size (they were rather worn when we visited). The leisure facilities, which include a restaurant, bar and pool complex, are of an excellent standard. This site, probably more suitable for families with young teenagers, can be very lively in high season with a wealth of activities and entertainment for all ages. Sports are well catered for and there are tournaments in high season. After an excellent meal in the restaurant you can enjoy a range of entertainment on most evenings in July and August. The site is within walking distance of the Atlantic Ocean and white sandy beaches, just 150 m. away.

Facilities

Three adequate toilet blocks with facilities for disabled visitors. Washing machines and dryers. Restaurant, bar, takeaway and shop (all season). Motorcaravan services. Swimming pool complex comprising an indoor pool, outdoor pool and paddling pool (15/5-27/9). Spa and wellness facility. Volleyball. Football. Basketball. Tennis. Bicycle hire. Charcoal barbecues are permitted. WiFi over site (charged; free in bar area). Mobile homes and maisonettes for rent. Off site: Riding, fishing and beach 150 m. Golf 400 m. Sailing 2 km. Market (most days). Shops, bars and restaurants in Le Croisic.

Open: 10 April - 27 September.

Directions

From Le Pouliguen, travel west on the N171 to Le Croisic. Site is well signed from here and found in 1.5 km. GPS: 47.29752, -2.53593

Charges guide

Per unit incl. 2 persons	
and electricity	€ 26.00 - € 54.00
extra person	€ 6.00 - € 9.00
child (2-7 yrs)	€ 4.00 - € 7.00
dog	€ 5.00 - € 7.00

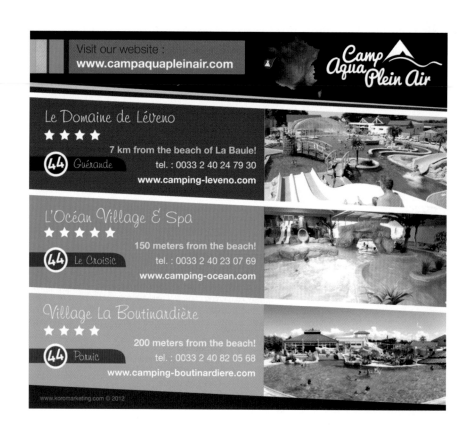
For latest campsite news, availability and prices visit

alanrogers.com

Pontchâteau

Kawan Village du Deffay

B.P. 18 Le Deffay, Sainte Reine-de-Bretagne, F-44160 Pontchâteau (Loire-Atlantique) T: 02 40 88 00 57.

E: campingdudeffay@wanadoo.fr alanrogers.com/FR44090

A family managed site, Château du Deffay is a refreshing departure from the usual formula in that it is not over organised and not supervised and has no tour operator units. The 170 good sized, fairly level pitches have pleasant views and are either on open grass, on shallow terraces divided by hedges, or informally arranged in a central, slightly sloping wooded area. All have 10A electricity. The bar, restaurant and covered pool are located within the old courtyard area of the smaller château that dates from before 1400. A significant attraction of the site is the large, unfenced lake which is well stocked for fishermen and even has free pedaloes for children.

Facilities

The main toilet block is well maintained, if a little dated, and is well equipped including washbasins in cabins, provision for disabled visitors, and a baby bathroom. Laundry facilities. Shop. Bar and small restaurant with takeaway (15/5-15/9). Heated swimming pool with sliding cover and paddling pool (all season). Play area. TV. Entertainment in season including miniclub. Fishing and pedaloes on the lake. Torches useful. WiFi (charged). Off site: Golf 7 km. Riding 10 km. Beach 20 km.

Open: 1 May - 30 September.

Directions

Site is signed from D33 Pontchâteau-Herbignac road near Ste Reine. Also signed from the D773 and N165-E60 (exit 13). GPS: 47.44106, -2.15981

Charges guide

Per unit incl. 2 persons and electricity	€ 19.08 - € 29.38
extra person	€ 3.43 - € 5.74
child (2-12 yrs)	€ 2.42 - € 4.11
dog	free

Camping Cheques accepted.

Pornic

Camping le Patisseau

29 rue du Patisseau, F-44210 Pornic (Loire-Atlantique) T: 02 40 82 10 39. E: contact@lepatisseau.com

alanrogers.com/FR44100

Just a short drive from the fishing village of Pornic, le Patisseau is a relaxed site with a large number of mobile homes and chalets, and is popular with young families and teenagers. The 67 touring pitches, all with electrical connections (10A), are in the forest with plenty of shade from mature trees. Some are on a slight slope and access to others might be tricky for larger units. A railway runs along the bottom half of the site with trains several times a day, (but none overnight) and the noise is minimal.

Facilities

Modern heated toilet block is very spacious and well fitted; most washbasins are open style, but the controllable showers are all in large cubicles which have washbasins. Also good facilities for disabled visitors and babies. Laundry rooms. Shop (27/6-29/8). Restaurant, bar and takeaway (4/4-27/9). Indoor heated pool with sauna, jacuzzi and spa (all season). Small heated outdoor pools and water slides (30/5-27/9). Play areas. Bouncy castle. Multisports court. Bicycle hire. WiFi in bar area (charged). Off site: Supermarket 1 km. Fishing and beach 2.5 km.

Open: 4 April - 27 September.

Directions

Pornic is 48 km. west of Nantes via D273/D751 and 19 km. south of the St Nazaire bridge via D213. Access to site is at junction of D751 Nantes-Pornic road with the D213 St Nazaire-Noirmoutier Route Bleue. From north take exit for D751 Nantes. At roundabout take exit for le Patisseau and follow signs to site. Avoid Pornic town centre. GPS: 47.118833, -2.072833

Charges guide

Per unit incl. 2 persons and electricity (6A)	€ 22.00 - € 39.00
extra person	€ 5.00 - € 8.00

Pornic

Camping de la Boutinardière

Rue de la Plage de la Boutinardière 23, F-44210 Pornic (Loire-Atlantique) T: 02 40 82 05 68.

E: info@laboutinardiere.com alanrogers.com/FR44180

This is truly a holiday site to suit all the family, whatever their ages, just 200 m. from the beach. It has 150 individual, good sized pitches, 90-120 sq.m. in size, many bordered by three metre high, well maintained hedges for shade and privacy. All pitches have electricity available (6/10A). It is a family owned site and part of the Airotel group. English is spoken by the helpful, obliging reception staff. There is an excellent site shop and, across the road, a water complex comprising indoor and outdoor pools, a paddling pool and a twin toboggan water slide, in addition to sports and entertainment areas.

Facilities

Toilet facilities are in three good blocks, one large and centrally situated and two supporting blocks. Washbasins are in cabins. Laundry facilities. Shop. New complex of bar, restaurant, terraces. Three heated swimming pools, one indoor (April-Sept), a paddling pool and water slides (15/5-22/9). Games room. Sports and activity area. Playground. Minigolf. Fitness equipment. Wellness suite. Maisonette accommodation for rent. WiFi throughout.

Open: 1 April - 30 September.

Directions

From north or south on D213, take Nantes D751 exit. At roundabout (with McDonalds) take D13 signed La Bernarie-en-Retz. After 4 km. site is signed to right. Note: do NOT exit from D213 at Pornic Ouest or Centre. GPS: 47.09805, -2.05176

Charges guide

Per unit incl. 2 persons and electricity	€ 36.60 - € 67.90
extra person	€ 5.50 - € 8.50
child (under 8 yrs)	€ 4.50 - € 6.50

FREE Alan Rogers Travel Card
Extra benefits and savings - see page 14

Saint Brévin-les-Pins

Camping le Fief

57 chemin du Fief, F-44250 Saint Brévin-les-Pins (Loire-Atlantique) T: 02 40 27 23 86.
E: camping@lefief.com alanrogers.com/FR44190

If you are a family with young children or lively teenagers, this could be the campsite for you. Le Fief is a well established site only 800 m. from sandy beaches on the southern Brittany coast. It has a magnificent aquapark with outdoor and covered swimming pools, paddling pools, slides, river rapids, fountains, jets and more. The site has 125 pitches for touring units, all with 8A electricity and varying slightly in size and accessibility. There are also 205 mobile homes and chalets to rent and 40 privately owned units. An impressive Taos mobile home village includes a new Sunny Club for children.

Facilities

One excellent new toilet block and three others of a lower standard. Laundry facilities. Shop (1/6-31/8). Bar, restaurant and takeaway (4/4-28/9) with terrace overlooking the pool complex. Heated outdoor pools (1/5-15/9). Covered pool (all season). Wellness centre. Play area. Tennis. Pétanque. Archery. Games room. Organised entertainment and activities (weekends April/June, daily July/Aug). Bicycle hire. WiFi (charged).

Open: 4 April - 27 September.

Directions

From the St Nazaire bridge take the fourth exit from the D213 signed St Brévin-l'Océan. Continue over first roundabout and bear right at the second to join Chemin du Fief. The site is on the right, well signed. GPS: 47.23486, -2.16757

Charges guide

Per unit incl. 2 persons and electricity	€ 25.00 - € 47.00

No credit cards.

Saumur

Sites et Paysages de Chantepie

La Croix, Saint Hilaire-Saint Florent, F-49400 Saumur (Maine-et-Loire) T: 02 41 67 95 34.
E: info@campingchantepie.com alanrogers.com/FR49020

On arriving at Camping de Chantepie with its colourful, floral entrance, a friendly greeting awaits at reception, set beside a restored farmhouse. The site is owned by a charitable organisation which provides employment for local people with disabilities. Linked by gravel roads (which can be dusty), the 120 grass touring pitches are level and spacious, with some new larger ones (200 sq.m. at extra cost – state preference when booking). All pitches have electricity (16A, 10 also with water and waste water) and are separated by low hedges of flowers and trees which offer some shade. Water points are easily accessible around the site. This is a good site for families.

Facilities

The toilet block is clean and facilities are good with washbasins in cubicles, new showers (men and women separately) and facilities for disabled visitors. Baby area. Laundry facilities. Shop, bar, terraced café and takeaway (all 21/6-31/8). Covered and heated pool, outdoor pool and paddling pool. Fitness centre. Play area with apparatus. Terraced minigolf. TV. Video games. Pony rides. Bicycle hire. Free WiFi over site.

Open: 26 April - 13 September.

Directions

St Hilaire-St Florent is 2 km. west of Saumur. Take D751 (Gennes). Right at roundabout in St Hilaire-St Florent and on until Le Poitrineau and campsite sign, then turn left. Continue for 3 km. then turn right into site road. GPS: 47.29382, -0.14285

Charges guide

Per unit incl. 2 persons and electricity	€ 20.00 - € 39.00

Camping Cheques accepted.

Miannay

Sites et Paysages le Clos Cacheleux

12, route de Bouillancourt, F-80132 Miannay (Somme) T: 03 22 19 17 47.
E: raphael@camping-lecloscacheleux.fr alanrogers.com/FR80210

Le Clos Cacheleux is a well situated campsite of eight hectares bordering woodland in the park of the Château Bouillancourt, which dates from the 18th century. The site was first opened in July 2008. It is 11 km. from the Bay of the Somme, regarded as being amongst the most beautiful bays in France. There are 90 very large, grassy pitches (230-250 sq.m) and all have electricity (10A Europlug), 5 also with water and waste water. The aim of the owners is to make your stay as enjoyable as possible by providing a high quality site, and improvements are being made each year. There is no shop or bar, but all visitors have access to the swimming pool, shop, bar and children's club of the sister site – le Val de Trie, less than five minutes' walk away.

Facilities

Two modern sanitary blocks are clean and well maintained with a baby room and facilities for disabled visitors. Laundry room with washing machine and dryer. Fridge hire. Adult fitness area. Fishing pond. Free WiFi. At the sister site: shop (all season), bar with terrace (1/4-15/10). Restaurant and takeaway (27/4-1/9). Covered pool (13/4-30/9). Library and TV room. Play area. Boules. Picnic tables. Freezer for ice packs. Tree houses to rent.

Open: 15 March - 15 October.

Directions

From the A28 at Abbeville take the D925 towards Eu and Le Tréport; do not go towards Moyenville. Turn left in Miannay village onto the D86 towards Toeufles. After 2 km. site is on right opposite road into Bouillancourt village. GPS: 50.08676, 1.71515

Charges guide

Per unit incl. 2 persons and electricity	€ 18.90 - € 27.10
extra person	€ 3.30 - € 5.60

For latest campsite news, availability and prices visit

alanrogers.com

Moyenneville

Camping le Val de Trie

Rue des Sources, Bouillancourt-sous-Miannay, F-80870 Moyenneville (Somme) T: 03 22 31 48 88.

E: raphael@camping-levaldetrie.fr alanrogers.com/FR80060

Le Val de Trie is a natural countryside site in woodland, near a small village. The 80 numbered, grassy touring pitches are of a good size, divided by hedges and shrubs with mature trees providing good shade in most areas, and all have 10A electricity, plus 11 also with water and waste water. It can be very quiet in April, June, September and October. If there is no-one on site, just choose a pitch or call at the farm to book in. This is maturing into a well managed site with modern facilities and a friendly, relaxed atmosphere. It is well situated for the coast and also the cities of Amiens and Abbeville. There are five new wooden chalets (including one for disabled visitors). There are good walks around the area and a notice board keeps campers up to date with local market, shopping and activity news. English is spoken. The owners of le Val de Trie have recently opened a new campsite nearby, le Clos Cacheleux (FR80210), where larger units can be accommodated.

Facilities

Two clean, recently renovated sanitary buildings include washbasins in cubicles, units for disabled visitors, babies and children. Laundry facilities. Microwave. Shop, bar with TV (all season), bread to order and butcher visits in season. Snack bar with takeaway (27/4-30/8). Room above bar for children. Covered heated swimming pool with jacuzzi (13/4-29/9). Outdoor pool for children (27/4-8/9). WiFi in bar area (free). Electric barbecues are not permitted. Off site: Riding 4 km. Golf 10 km. Beach 20 km.

Open: 1 April - 4 October.

Directions

From A28 take exit 2 near Abbeville and D925 to Miannay. Turn left on D86 to Bouillancourt-sous-Miannay: site is signed in village. GPS: 50.0855, 1.71492

Charges guide

Per unit incl. 2 persons	
and electricity	€ 18.90 - € 27.10
extra person	€ 3.30 - € 5.60
child (under 7 yrs)	€ 2.10 - € 3.60
dog	€ 1.80 - € 2.10

Camping Cheques accepted.

Nampont-Saint Martin

Kawan Village la Ferme des Aulnes

Fresne, F-80120 Nampont-Saint Martin (Somme) T: 03 22 29 22 69. E: contact@fermedesaulnes.com

alanrogers.com/FR80070

This peaceful site, with 144 pitches, has been developed on the meadows of a small, 17th-century farm on the edge of Fresne and is lovingly cared for by its new enthusiastic owners, Marie and Denis Lefort and their hard working team. Restored outbuildings house reception and the facilities around a central courtyard that boasts a fine heated swimming pool. A new development includes a bar and entertainment room. Outside, facing the main gate, are 20 large, level grass pitches for touring. There is also an area for tents. The remaining 22 touring pitches are in the main complex, hedged and fairly level.

Facilities

Both sanitary areas are heated and include washbasins in cubicles with a large cubicle for disabled visitors. Shop, piano bar and restaurant (3/4-1/11). Motorcaravan services. TV room. Swimming pool (16x9 m; heated and with cover for cooler weather). Jacuzzi and sauna. Fitness room. Aquagym and Balnéotherapy. Playground. Boules. Archery. Fishing. WiFi throughout (free). Shuttle service to stations and airports. Off site: Private lake fishing (free) 2 minutes away. River fishing 100 m. Golf 2 km. Riding 6 km.

Open: 3 April - 1 November.

Directions

From Calais, take A16 to exit 25 and turn for Arras for 2 km. and then towards Abbeville on N1. At Nampont-St Martin turn west on D485 and site will be found in 2 km. GPS: 50.33645, 1.71285

Charges guide

Per unit incl. 2 persons	
and electricity	€ 27.00 - € 35.00
extra person	€ 7.00
child (under 7 yrs)	€ 4.00
dog	€ 4.00

Camping Cheques accepted.

Villers-sur-Authie

Sites et Paysages le Val d'Authie

20 route de Vercourt, F-80120 Villers-sur-Authie (Somme) T: 03 22 29 92 47. E: camping@valdauthie.fr

alanrogers.com/FR80090

In a village location, this well organised site is within 12 km. of several beaches, but also has its own excellent pool complex, small restaurant and bar. The owner has carefully controlled the size of the site, leaving space for a leisure area with an indoor pool complex. There are 170 pitches in total, but with many holiday homes and chalets, there are only 60 for touring units. These are on grass, some are divided by small hedges, with 6/10A electric hook-ups, and ten have full services. Amenities on the site include a fitness trail and running track, a mountain bike circuit and plenty of paths for evening strolls.

Facilities

Good toilet facilities, some unisex, include shower and washbasin units, washbasins in cubicles, and limited facilities for disabled campers and babies. Shop. Bar/restaurant (4/4-3/10; hours vary). Swimming and paddling pools (lifeguards in July/Aug). Playground, club room with TV. Weekend entertainment in season. Multisport court, beach volleyball, football, boules and tennis court. Trampoline. Fitness room including sauna (charged). Internet access (free). WiFi over site (charged). Off site: Shops, banks and restaurants in Rue 6 km.

Open: 1 April - 3 October.

Directions

Villers-sur-Authie is 25 km. north-northwest of Abbeville. From A16 exit 24 take N1 to Vron, then left on D175 to Villers-sur-Authie. Or use D85 from Rue, or D485 from Nampont-St Martin. Site is at southern end of village at road junction. GPS: 50.31357, 1.69488

Charges guide

Per unit incl. 2 persons and electricity	€ 25.50 - € 31.00
extra person	€ 6.50

Camping Cheques accepted.

La Brée-les-Bains

Antioche d'Oléron

16 route de Proires, F-17840 La Brée-les-Bains (Charente-Maritime) T: 05 46 47 92 00.
E: info@camping-antiochedoleron.com alanrogers.com/FR17570

Close to the northern point of the Ile d'Oléron, Antioche is quietly located within a five minute walk of the beach. There are 130 pitches, of which 87 are occupied by mobile homes, half available for rent, and 43 are for touring units. The pitches are set amongst attractive shrubs and palm trees and all have electricity (16A), water and a drain. The site becomes livelier in season with regular evening entertainment and activities for all the family. A thriving market selling local produce and products is within easy reach on foot, and is held daily in high season.

Facilities

The modern sanitary block is of a good standard and is kept clean and fresh. Cubicle with controllable shower and washbasin. Facilities for babies and disabled visitors. No chemical disposal point (drains on pitches used). Laundry. Bar and snack bar with takeaway. Two heated swimming pools (one covered from 2014). Paddling pool. Jacuzzi. Play area. Children's club and evening entertainment and activities for all the family (July/Aug). WiFi over site (charged July/Aug). Bicycle hire.

Open: 6 April - 28 September.

Directions

Cross the bridge to the Ile d'Oléron and continue on the D26/D704 through St Pierre and St Georges, then turn right onto the D273E1 towards La Brée-les-Baines. Bear left at roundabout, then at T-junction turn left from where campsite is signed. GPS: 46.02007, -1.35764

Charges guide

Per unit incl. 2 persons and electricity	€ 23.10 - € 39.05
extra person	€ 7.75 - € 9.10

La Flotte-en-Ré

Camping la Grainetière

Route de Saint Martin, chemin des Essarts, F-17630 La Flotte-en-Ré (Charente-Maritime) T: 05 46 09 68 86.
E: la-grainetiere@orange.fr alanrogers.com/FR17280

A truly friendly welcome awaits you from Isabelle, Eric and Fanny at la Grainetière. It is a peaceful campsite set in almost three hectares of pine trees which provide some shade for the 51 touring pitches of various shapes and sizes. There are also 80 well spaced chalets, mobile homes and roulottes for rent. Some pitches are suitable for units up to seven metres (these should be booked in advance). There are no hedges for privacy and the pitches are sandy with some grass. Most pitches have a water point, electricity (10A) and waste water drainage. The site is well lit.

Facilities

The unisex, heated sanitary block is first class, with washbasins in cubicles, showers, British style WCs, facilities for children and disabled visitors. Laundry facilities. Shop. Takeaway. Covered swimming pool (heated all season) and jacuzzi. Bicycle hire. Fridge hire. Play area. Games room. Library. TV room. Charcoal barbecues are not permitted. Free WiFi over site. Off site: Beach, fishing, boat launching and sailing 2 km. Bar and restaurant 2 km. Riding 3 km. Golf 10 km.

Open: 4 April - 30 September.

Directions

Follow the signs for St Martin. The site is on the main road between La Flotte and St Martin. GPS: 46.18755, -1.344933

Charges guide

Per unit incl. 2 persons and electricity	€ 21.00 - € 45.00
extra person	€ 5.50 - € 9.00
child (0-7 yrs)	€ 3.50 - € 5.00
dog	€ 3.00 - € 4.50

For latest campsite news, availability and prices visit

alanrogers.com

Saint Georges-les-Baillargeaux

Kawan Village le Futuriste

RD 20, F-86130 Saint Georges-les-Baillargeaux (Vienne) T: 05 49 52 47 52.
E: camping-le-futuriste@wanadoo.fr alanrogers.com/FR86040

Le Futuriste is a neat, modern site, open all year and close to Futuroscope. Its location is very convenient for the A10 and N10 motorway network. There are 123 individual, level, grassy pitches of a generous size and divided by flowering hedges. Seventy-six have electricity (6A) and 64 also have water and waste water connections. Pitches are mostly open although some do have the benefit of shade from trees. All are accessed via tarmac roads. There are lovely panoramic views from this site and the popular attraction of Futuroscope can be clearly seen. Large units are accepted by prior arrangement. There is a pleasant restaurant on site offering good food at reasonable prices. Entertainment takes place in the daytime rather than in the evenings. This site is ideal for a short stay to visit Futuroscope, which is only 2 km. away, but it is equally good for longer stays to see the region.

Facilities

Excellent, clean sanitary facilities in two heated blocks. Good facilities for disabled visitors and babies. Laundry facilities. Shop (1/5-30/9, bread to order). Bar/restaurant snack bar and takeaway (July/Aug). Heated outdoor pool with slide and paddling pool (July/Aug). Covered pool. Games room. TV. Boules. Multisports area. Lake fishing. Daily activities in season. Youth groups not accepted. Only gas and electric barbecues allowed. WiFi (charged). Off site: Hypermarket 600 m. Futuroscope 2 km. Golf 5 km. Riding 10 km.

Open: All year.

Directions

From either A10 autoroute or N10, take Futuroscope exit. Site is east of both roads, off D20 (St Georges-les-Baillargeaux). Follow signs to St Georges. Site on hill; turn by water tower and site is on left.
GPS: 46.66447, 0.394564

Charges guide

Per unit incl. 2 persons and electricity	€ 22.20 - € 30.00
extra person (over 5 yrs)	€ 2.70 - € 3.60
dog	€ 2.60

Camping Cheques accepted.

Saint Georges-de-Didonne

Camping Bois Soleil

2 avenue de Suzac, F-17110 Saint Georges-de-Didonne (Charente-Maritime) T: 05 46 05 05 94.

E: camping.bois.soleil@wanadoo.fr alanrogers.com/FR17010

Close to the sea, Bois Soleil is a large site in three parts, with 165 serviced pitches for touring units and a few for tents. All the touring pitches are hedged and have electricity (all 10A), with water and drainage between two. The main part, Les Pins, is attractive with trees and shrubs providing shade. Opposite is La Mer with direct access to the beach, some areas with less shade and an area for tents. The third part, La Forêt, is for caravan holiday homes. It is best to book your preferred area as it can be full mid June to late August. Excellent private sanitary facilities are available to rent, either on your pitch or at a block (subject to availability). There are a few pitches with lockable gates. The areas are all well tended and are cleared and raked between visitors. This lively site offers something for everyone, whether it be a beach-side spot or a traditional pitch, plenty of activities or the quiet life. Recent additions include a new toilet block and some accommodation to rent with sea views. The wide sandy beach is popular with children and provides a pleasant walk to the pretty town of Saint Georges-de-Didonne.

Facilities

Each area has one large and one small sanitary block. Heated block near reception. Cleaned twice daily, they include facilities for disabled visitors and babies. Launderette. Supermarket, bakery and beach shop (all 15/4-15/9). Restaurant, bar and takeaway (all 15/4-15/9). Swimming pool (heated 15/6-15/9). Steam room. Tennis. Play area. TV room and library. Internet terminal. WiFi throughout (charged). Charcoal and electric barbecues are not permitted. Dogs are not accepted 29/6-25/8. Off site: Bicycle hire adjacent. Fishing 200 m. Riding 500 m. Golf 20 km.

Open: 2 April - 9 October.

Directions

From Royan centre take coast road (D25) along the seafront of St Georges-de-Didonne towards Meschers. Site is signed at roundabout at end of the main beach. GPS: 45.583583, -0.986533

Charges guide

Per unit incl. 3 persons	
and electricity	€ 16.00 - € 47.00
extra person	€ 6.00 - € 12.00
child (under 7 yrs)	free - € 8.00
dog (not 29/6-25/8)	€ 3.00 - € 5.00

Camping Cheques accepted.

Saint Just-Luzac

Castel Camping Séquoia Parc

La Josephtrie, F-17320 Saint Just-Luzac (Charente-Maritime) T: 05 46 85 55 55.

E: info@sequoiaparc.com alanrogers.com/FR17140

LeadingCampings

This is definitely a site not to be missed. Approached by an avenue of flowers, shrubs and trees, Séquoia Parc is a Castel site set in the grounds of La Josephtrie, a striking château with beautifully restored outbuildings and courtyard area with a bar and restaurant. Most of the 640 pitches are about 140 sq.m. with 6/10A electricity connections and separated by mature shrubs providing plenty of privacy. The site has 350 mobile homes and chalets, with a further 65 used by tour operators. This is a popular site and reservation is necessary in high season. Children's clubs are run all season (4-7 yrs and 7-12 yrs), with entertainment provided in high season. A member of Leading Campings group.

Facilities

Three spotlessly clean luxurious toilet blocks (one heated) include units with washbasin and shower and facilities for disabled visitors and children. Large laundry. Motorcaravan services. Gas supplies. Large supermarket. Boutique. Restaurant/bar and takeaway. Impressive swimming pool complex with water slides and large paddling pool. Massage (July/Aug). Multisports pitch. Tennis. Games and TV rooms. Bicycle hire. Updated play areas. Organised entertainment/excursions in high season. Clubs for children all season. Pony trekking. Children's farm. WiFi (charged). Off site: Supermarket and bank 5 km. Fishing 5 km. Golf 15 km. Flying trips. Ile d'Oléron. La Rochelle.

Open: 13 May - 6 September (with all services).

Directions

Site is 5 km. southeast of Marennes. From Rochefort take D733 south for 12 km. Turn west on D123 to Ile d'Oléron. Continue for 12 km. Turn southeast on D728 (Saintes). Site signed, in 1 km. on left. From A10 at Saintes take D728 and turn right shortly after St Just. Site signed. GPS: 45.81095, -1.06109

Charges guide

Per unit incl. 2 persons	
and electricity	€ 21.00 - € 55.00
extra person	€ 7.00 - € 10.00
child (3-9 yrs)	€ 3.00 - € 6.00
dog	€ 5.00

For latest campsite news, availability and prices visit

alanrogers.com

★★★★★ BOIS - SOLEIL

Half-way between Great Britain and Spain in the middle of the Romanesque Saintonge area, Bois Soleil will seduce you with its wooded parks and its direct access to a 4 km long sand beach.

Bar, restaurant, panoramic terraces, heated swimming pool 240 m² with balneo and paddling pool, hammam, fitness, internet, library.
Entertainment in July and August.

2, avenue de Suzac, 17110 Saint-Georges de Didonne
Tél. +33 (0)5.46.05.05.94
http://www.bois-soleil.com
camping.bois.soleil@wanadoo.fr

Forcalquier

Camping Indigo Forcalquier

Route de Sigonce, F-04300 Forcalquier (Alpes-de-Haute-Provence) T: 04 92 75 27 94.

E: forcalquier@camping-indigo.com alanrogers.com/FR04120

Although Camping Indigo is an urban site, there are extensive views over the surrounding countryside where there are some excellent walks. The 70 touring pitches are on grass and of a good size, all with electricity, six fully serviced (long leads may be needed). The site is secure, with an electronic barrier (card deposit required) and there is no entry between 22.30 and 07.00. This is an excellent base for visiting Forcalquier, a 15th-century fortified hill town, and the Monday market (the best in Haute-Provence). Local guides lead tours of the historic town and area. Since Camping Indigo acquired this site, an extensive modernisation programme has been put into effect.

Facilities

Three refurbished toilet blocks with washbasins in cubicles and excellent facilities for disabled visitors. Motorcaravan services. Bar (all season). Snack bar and takeaway (July/Aug). Heated swimming and paddling pools (all season). Play area. Boules. Basketball. Range of activities in high season, often involving local people, including food tasting and storytelling. Max. 1 dog. WiFi in some areas (free). Off site: Town centre for shops 200 m.

Open: 17 April - 29 September.

Directions

From town centre, follow D16 signed to Montlaux and Sigonce. Site is 500 m. on the right. Well signed from town. GPS: 43.96206, 5.78743

Charges guide

Per unit incl. 2 persons	
and electricity	€ 20.70 - € 29.00
extra person	€ 5.20 - € 6.40
child (2-7 yrs)	free - € 4.60
dog	€ 2.10 - € 4.20

Graveson-en-Provence

Camping les Micocouliers

445 route de Cassoulen, F-13690 Graveson-en-Provence (Bouches du Rhône) T: 04 90 95 81 49.

E: micocou@orange.fr alanrogers.com/FR13060

M. and Mme. Riehl started work on les Micocouliers in 1997 and they have developed a comfortable site. On the outskirts of the town, the site is only some 10 km. from Saint Rémy and Avignon. Purpose built, terracotta houses in a raised position provide all the facilities at present. The 116 pitches radiate out from here with the pool and entrance to one side. The pitches are on level grass, separated by small bushes, and shade is developing well. Electricity connections are possible (4-10A). There are also a few mobile homes. The popular swimming pool is a welcome addition. Bread can be ordered and a small shop is opened in July and August.

Facilities

Several unisex units provide toilets and facilities for disabled visitors (by key), showers and washbasins in cabins and laundry facilities. A new block has just been added. Small shop (July/Aug). Swimming pool (12x8 m; 15/05-15/9). Paddling pool (July/Aug). Play area. Gas and electric barbecues permitted. WiFi in some areas (charged). Off site: Riding and bicycle hire 1 km. Golf and fishing 5 km. Beach 60 km. at Ste Marie-de-la-Mer.

Open: 15 March - 15 October.

Directions

Site is southeast of Graveson. From the N570 at new roundabout take D5 towards St Rémy and Maillane and site is 500 m. on the left. GPS: 43.84397, 4.78131

Charges guide

Per unit incl. 2 persons	
and electricity	€ 20.90 - € 32.20
extra person	€ 5.40 - € 8.00
child (1-10 yrs)	€ 4.00 - € 5.80

Volonne

Sunêlia L'Hippocampe

Quartier la Croix, route de Napoléon, F-04290 Volonne (Alpes-de-Haute-Provence) T: 04 92 33 50 00.

E: camping@l-hippocampe.com alanrogers.com/FR04010

Sunêlia L'Hippocampe is a friendly, family run, all action, riverside site (no swimming), with families in mind, situated in a beautiful area of France. The perfumes of thyme, lavender and wild herbs are everywhere and the higher hills of Haute-Provence are not too far away. There are 447 level, numbered pitches (177 for touring units), medium to very large (130 sq.m) in size. All have 10A electricity and 140 have water and drainage, most being separated by bushes and cherry trees. Some of the best pitches border the lake or are in the centre of the site. The restaurant, bar, takeaway and shop have all been completely renewed.

Facilities

Four refurbished toilet blocks, all with good clean facilities that include washbasins in cabins. Washing machines. Motorcaravan services. Bread available (all season). Shop (July/Aug). Bar, restaurant and pizzeria (25/4-13/9). Large, heated pool complex (all season) with five waterslides, (second pool 1/5-30/9). Tennis (free in low season). Fishing. Canoeing. Boules. Bicycle hire. Several sports facilities (some with free instruction). Charcoal barbecues are not permitted. WiFi throughout (charged).

Open: 25 April - 30 September.

Directions

Approaching from the north turn off the N85 across river bridge to Volonne, then right to site. From the south right on D4 for 3 km. to site on the left. GPS: 44.10462, 6.01688

Charges guide

Per unit incl. 2 persons	
and electricity	€ 16.00 - € 36.00
extra person (over 4 yrs)	€ 3.00 - € 8.00

Credit cards not accepted in low seasons.

Camping Cheques accepted.

For latest campsite news, availability and prices visit

alanrogers.com

Castellane

Castel Camping le Domaine du Verdon

Camp du Verdon, F-04120 Castellane (Alpes-de-Haute-Provence) T: 04 92 83 61 29.

E: contact@camp-du-verdon.com alanrogers.com/FR04020

Close to the Route des Alpes and the Gorges du Verdon, le Domaine du Verdon is a large, level site, part meadow, part wooded with an attractive range of planting. There are 500 partly shaded, rather stony pitches (390 for touring units), 360 with 16A electricity and 125 also with water and drainage. Numbered and separated by bushes, they vary in size and are mostly separate from 60 mobile homes and pitches used by tour operators. Some overlook the unfenced Verdon river, so watch your children. This is a very popular holiday area, the gorge and the associated canoeing and rafting being the main attractions. Two heated pools and numerous on-site activities during high season help to keep non-canoeists here. This site is ideal for active families. One can walk to Castellane without using the main road where there are numerous shops, cafés and restaurants. Dances and discos in July and August suit all age groups. The latest finishing time is around 23.00, after which time patrols make sure that the site is quiet. The site is popular and very busy in July and August.

Facilities

Refurbished toilet blocks include facilities for disabled visitors. Washing machines and dryers. Fridge hire. Motorcaravan services. Babysitting service. Supermarket. Restaurant, terrace, log fire for cooler evenings. Pizzeria/crêperie. Takeaway. Heated swimming pools, paddling pool with fountain. All amenities are open all season. Fitness equipment. Organised entertainment (July/Aug). Play areas. Minigolf. Archery. Organised walks. Bicycle hire. Riding. Small fishing lake. Room for games and TV. Internet access. Communal barbecue (charcoal not permitted on pitches). WiFi in some parts (free). Off site: Bus stop outside main entrance (only one bus each day). Castellane and the Verdon Gorge 1 km. Riding 1.5 km. Boat launching 4.5 km. Watersports.

Open: 13 May - 15 September.

Directions

From Castellane take D952 westwards towards Gorges du Verdon and Moustiers. Site is 1 km. on left. GPS: 43.83921, 6.49396

Charges guide

Per unit (low season 2 or high season 3 persons) and electricity	€ 28.00 - € 48.00
extra person (over 4 yrs)	€ 9.00 - € 14.00
dog	€ 4.00 - € 5.00

Domaine du VERDON
Camping Caravanning
★★★★

Close to the famous Gorges du Verdon on only 1,2 kilometres distance from the typical Provence village of Castellane you will love this lovely harmonius estate with many flowers and trees. Direct access to the river Verdon.

Animation in July and August - 500 pitches
14 acres - 220 mobile homes

Castel Camping Caravanning Domaine du Verdon
04120 Castellane - Tel.: +33 492 836 129 - Fax: +33 492 836 937
E-mail: contact@camp-du-verdon.com - www.camp-du-verdon.com

LES ★★★★
CASTELS
Hôtellerie de Plein Air

Bourdeaux

Yelloh! Village les Bois du Chatelas

Route de Dieulefit, F-26460 Bourdeaux (Drôme) T: 04 75 00 60 80. E: reservation@chatelas.com

alanrogers.com/FR26210

Located in the heart of the Drôme Provençale, les Bois du Chatelas is a very high quality, family run site just 1.5 km. from the delightful village of Bourdeaux which offers some shops, cafés, etc. There are 169 level, good sized, terraced pitches, 70 for touring (rock pegs advised). They are separated by hedges, and maturing trees give some shade; all have electricity, water and drainage. There is a superb swimming pool complex with indoor and outdoor pools, toboggan, paddling pool, fitness room, jacuzzi and sauna. Overlooking the pool area is a restaurant with a full menu and superb views over the valley and mountains beyond. Les Bois du Chatelas is a good choice for those seeking an active holiday.

Facilities

Two excellent toilet blocks (one heated), on upper and lower levels, with facilities for babies and visitors with disabilities (though site is not ideal for those with mobility problems). Shop. Bar. Restaurant/takeaway/pizzeria. Indoor and outdoor pools with water slide, waterfall, sauna, aquagym and jacuzzi. Sports field. Archery. Play area. Bicycle hire. Entertainment and excursion programme (July/Aug). WiFi over site (charged).

Open: 13 April - 15 September.

Directions

Leave A7 autoroute, exit 16 (Loriol). Take D104 east to Crest. Leave Crest bypass at traffic lights, take D538 south to Bourdeaux and continue towards Dieulefit for 1.5 km. Site is on the left (well signed). GPS: 44.57825, 5.12761

Charges guide

Per unit incl. 2 persons and electricity	€ 22.00 - € 41.00
extra person	€ 6.00 - € 8.00

Bourg-Saint Maurice

Camping le Versoyen

Route des Arcs, F-73700 Bourg-Saint Maurice (Savoie) T: 04 79 07 03 45. E: leversoyen@wanadoo.fr

alanrogers.com/FR73020

Bourg-St-Maurice is on a small, level plain at an altitude of 830 m. on the River Isère, surrounded by mountains. Le Versoyen attracts visitors all year round (except for a short time when they close). The site's 160 unseparated, flat pitches (140 for touring) are marked by numbers on the tarmac roads and all have electrical connections (4/6/10A). Most are on grass but some are on tarmac hardstanding making them ideal for use by motorcaravans or in winter. Trees give shade in most parts, although some pitches have almost none. Duckboards are provided for snow and wet weather.

Facilities

Two well maintained toilet blocks can be heated and have British and Turkish style WCs. No facilities for disabled visitors. Laundry. Motorcaravan service facilities. No shop but bread available to order. Heated rest room with TV. Small bar with takeaway in summer. Play area. Free shuttle in high season to funicular railway. WiFi (charged). Off site: Cross-country ski track just behind the site. Municipal swimming pool adjacent (discounted entry).

Open: All year excl. 7/11-14/12 and 2/5-25/5.

Directions

Site is 1.5 km. east of Bourg-St-Maurice on CD119 Les Arcs road. GPS: 45.62248, 6.78475

Charges guide

Per unit incl. 2 persons and electricity (10A)	€ 18.00 - € 23.30
extra person	€ 4.40 - € 5.30
child (4-13 yrs)	€ 2.00 - € 4.90
dog	€ 0.50 - € 1.00

Darbres

Camping les Lavandes

Le Village, F-07170 Darbres (Ardèche) T: 04 75 94 20 65. E: sarl.leslavandes@online.fr

alanrogers.com/FR07140

Situated northeast of Aubenas, in a quieter part of this region, les Lavandes is surrounded by magnificent countryside, vineyards and orchards. The welcoming French owners, who speak English well, run their site in the heart of the tiny village of Darbres with dedication and enthusiasm. The 70 pitches (58 for touring) are arranged on low terraces separated by a variety of trees and shrubs that give welcome shade in summer. Electricity 6/10A is available to all. Visit at the end of May to see the trees laden with luscious cherries. Organised activities include jazz and piano musical evenings and children's games.

Facilities

Comprehensive and well maintained facilities, baby room and excellent facilities for disabled visitors. Washing machine. Small shop (July/Aug). Bar, terrace (1/6-31/8). Restaurant (15/6-31/8). Takeaway (15/4-31/8). Excellent swimming pool (30/5-31/8), paddling pool, sunbathing areas, all with super views. Three small play areas. Games room. Outdoor chess. Electric barbecues are not permitted, but gas and charcoal barbecues are allowed. Reception is happy to help arrange various activities, some with discounts. WiFi (free).

Open: 15 April - 15 September.

Directions

Site is best approached from the south. From Montélimar take N102 towards Aubenas. After Villeneuve, in Lavilledieu, turn right at traffic lights on D224 to Darbres (10 km). In Darbres turn sharp left by post office (care needed) and follow site signs. GPS: 44.64788, 4.50338

Charges guide

Per unit incl. 2 persons and electricity	€ 16.50 - € 28.50
extra person	€ 2.80 - € 4.20
child (under 8 yrs)	€ 1.50 - € 3.20

For latest campsite news, availability and prices visit

alanrogers.com

Le Grand-Bornand

Camping Caravaning l'Escale

33 chemin du Plein Air, F-74450 Le Grand-Bornand (Haute-Savoie) T: 04 50 02 20 69.

E: contact@campinglescale.com alanrogers.com/FR74070

You will receive a good welcome in English from the Baur family at this beautifully maintained and picturesque site, situated at the foot of the Aravis mountain range. There are 149 pitches with 122 for touring. Of average size, part grass, part gravel they are separated by trees and shrubs that give a little shade. All pitches have 2-10A electricity and 86 are fully serviced. Rock pegs are essential. Housed in a 200-year-old building, a bar/restaurant is decorated in traditional style and offers regional dishes in a delightful, warm ambience. The village is 200 m. away and has all the facilities of a resort with activities for both summer and winter holidays.

Facilities

Good toilet blocks (heated in winter) have all the necessary facilities for disabled campers. Drying room for skis, clothing and boots. Superb pool complex with interconnected indoor (all season) and outdoor pools and paddling pools (30/6-30/8), jacuzzi and water jets. Cosy bar/restaurant and takeaway. Play area. Tennis. Activities for adults and children. Video games. Discounts on organised walks and visits to Chamonix-Mont Blanc. Traditional chalets and mobile homes to rent. WiFi (free).

Open: 19 December - 12 April, 22 May - 27 September.

Directions

From Annecy follow D16 and D909 towards La Clusaz. At St Jean-de-Sixt, turn left at roundabout D4 signed Grand-Bornand. Just before village fork right signed Vallée de Bouchet and camping. Site entrance is on right at roundabout in 1.2 km. GPS: 45.94036, 6.42842

Charges guide

Per unit incl. 2 persons and electricity	€ 24.00 - € 34.70
extra person (over 2 yrs)	€ 5.80 - € 6.70

Matafelon-Granges

Camping des Gorges de l'Oignin

Rue du Lac, F-01580 Matafelon-Granges (Ain) T: 04 74 76 80 97.

E: camping.lesgorgesdeloignin@wanadoo.fr alanrogers.com/FR01050

This attractively landscaped, terraced site (English spoken) offers stunning views across the lake to the hills beyond. There are 130 good sized pitches, 120 for touring, which are thoughtfully laid out and separated by young trees and flowering shrubs. Most have grass and hardstanding. Forty-five have their own water point and most have 10A electricity. The reception, bar/restaurant and the pool complex are at the top of the site with a gently sloping road down to the lower terraces and lake. At the lowest part of the site is a large grassy area next to the lake for sunbathing and activities. Twin-axle caravans are not accepted.

Facilities

Two modern, well equipped and clean toilet blocks with all the usual facilities. There are no facilities for disabled visitors. Washing machine and dryer (tokens). Bar/restaurant, takeaway and TV room (July/Aug). Swimming pool, paddling pool and new lazy river (1/6-22/9). Play and sports areas. Pétanque. Swimming, fishing and boating on the lake (no motorboats). Free WiFi over part of site. Off site: Matafelon 800 m. Golf 2 km.

Open: 1 May - 20 September.

Directions

Matafelon is 40 km. east of Bourg-en-Bresse. Leave autoroute A404 at Nantua, exit 9 and turn right towards D18 road and continue to Matafelon (10 km). On entering village and opposite the Mairie turn left, signed camping, and descend to site (800 m). GPS: 46.25535, 5.55717

Charges guide

Per unit incl. 2 persons and electricity	€ 19.00 - € 29.00

Séez

Camping le Reclus

F-73700 Séez (Savoie) T: 04 79 41 01 05. E: contact@campinglereclus.com

alanrogers.com/FR73100

Bordering a fast flowing but well fenced stream, this small mountain campsite, set in the hills above Bourg-St-Maurice in the Vanoise National Park, is enthusiastically run by Mélanie Bonato. The 75 terraced pitches (45 for touring), most with electricity (4-10A), are small and uneven. The village of Séez is a few minutes' walk away. Winter sports enthusiasts are well catered for here, with a drying room and ski-shoe heating, plus discounts on ski passes and other activities. There is a free shuttle to Les Arcs and La Rosière and it is centrally situated for the Tarentaise ski lifts. This site is not recommended for larger units due to small pitches and very steep access.

Facilities

Two sanitary blocks have been renovated, the central one more modern, have small shower cubicles with preset hot water; and open style washbasins. Laundry room with washer/dryer and indoor drying area. Bar, restaurant and takeaway (1/7-31/8). Small play area. Bread, drinks and ice-cream for sale. TV room. Fishing. WiFi on part of site (free). Off site: Shops and bars in Séez.

Open: All year.

Directions

From A43 Lyon-Chambéry-Grenoble motorway take A430 to Albertville and RN90 to Moutiers and Bourg-St Maurice. Drive through town, at third roundabout follow signs for Tignes and Val d'Isère. Site is 2 km. up the hill on right on entering Séez. Access road is very steep. GPS: 45.625844, 6.792794

Charges guide

Per unit incl. 2 persons and electricity	€ 18.50 - € 24.00

Samoëns
Camping Caravaneige le Giffre

1064 route du Lacs aux Dames, La Glière, F-74340 Samoëns (Haute-Savoie) T: 04 50 34 41 92.
E: camping.samoens@wanadoo.fr alanrogers.com/FR74230

Surrounded by magnificent mountains in this lesser known Alpine area, yet accessible to major ski resorts, le Giffre could be the perfect spot for those seeking an active, yet relaxing holiday. There are 212 firm, level pitches on stony grass (rock pegs advised) with 154 for touring units. Most have electricity (6/10A) but long leads may be needed. They are spaced out amongst mature trees which give varying amounts of shade and some overlook the attractive lake and leisure park. The small winter/summer resort of Samoëns is only a 15 minute, level stroll away. There is little in the way of on-site entertainment but there are many activities available in Samoëns and the surrounding area.

Facilities
Three adequate toilet blocks, heated in winter with facilities for campers with disabilities. Games room. Play area. Boules. Fishing. Lake swimming. Accommodation for hire. WiFi throughout (free). Off site: Leisure park next to site with pool (entry free summer), ice skating (entry free winter), tennis (summer), archery, adventure park. Paragliding. Rafting, many walks and bike rides (summer) and ski runs (winter). Snack bar and baker (high season) 100 m. Samoëns with a good range of shops, bars, restaurants 1 km. Grand Massif Express cable car 150 m. Bicycle hire 200 m. Riding 2 km.

Open: All year.

Directions
Leave A40 autoroute at Cluses (exit 18 or 19). Go north on D902 towards Taninges. In Taninges turn east on D907 to Samoëns (avoiding weight and width restriction on D4). The site is signed from the village. Park outside the entrance.
GPS: 46.07731, 6.71851

Charges guide
Per unit incl. 2 persons and electricity	€ 17.55 - € 29.25
extra person	€ 4.30
child (4-12 yrs)	€ 2.95
dog	€ 2.35

Camping Caravaneige Le Giffre***

Open all year, located on the edge of the Giffre and the 'Lacs aux Dames', 700m from the town and its shops and at the heart of the leisure park, our campsite has 312 level grass pitches on a well shaded site of 6.9h.

In winter, departures for cross-country skiing from the campsite and ski lifts 150m away. Access within 8 min to 265 km of downhill slopes.

Camping Caravaneige Le Giffre • La Glière • F-74340 Samoens
www.camping-samoens.com

Vallon-Pont-d'Arc
Castel Camping Nature Parc l'Ardéchois

Route touristique des Gorges, F-07150 Vallon-Pont-d'Arc (Ardèche) T: 04 75 88 06 63.
E: ardecamp@wanadoo.fr alanrogers.com/FR07120

LeadingCampings

This very high quality, family run site is within walking distance of Vallon-Pont-d'Arc. It borders the River Ardèche and canoe trips are run, professionally, direct from the site. This campsite is ideal for families with younger children seeking an active holiday. The facilities are comprehensive and the central toilet unit is of an extremely high standard. Of the 250 pitches, there are 225 for touring units, separated by trees and individual shrubs. All have electrical connections (6/10A) and with an additional charge, 125 larger pitches have full services (22 include a fridge, patio furniture, hammock and free WiFi). Forming a focal point are the bar and restaurant (excellent menus), with an attractive terrace and a takeaway service. A member of Leading Campings group.

Facilities
Two very well equipped toilet blocks, one superb with everything working automatically. Facilities are of the highest standard, very clean and include good facilities for babies, children and disabled visitors. Laundry facilities. Four private bathrooms to hire. Well stocked shop. Excellent restaurant, bar and takeaway. Heated swimming pool and paddling pool (no Bermuda shorts). Massage. Gym. Tennis. Very good play area. Organised activities, canoe trips. Bicycle hire. Gas barbecues only. Communal barbecue. WiFi over site (charged).

Open: 1 April - 30 September.

Directions
From Aubenas take the D579 towards Ruoms. Continue south on D579 at Ruoms towards Vallon-Pont-d'Arc (western end of the Ardèche Gorge) at a roundabout go east on the D290. Site entrance is shortly on the right. GPS: 44.39804, 4.39878

Charges guide
Per unit incl. 2 persons and electricity	€ 33.00 - € 55.00
extra person	€ 6.50 - € 10.90
child (2-13 yrs)	€ 5.00 - € 8.60
dog	€ 5.00 - € 8.40

No credit cards.

For latest campsite news, availability and prices visit
alanrogers.com

Candé-sur-Beuvron

Kawan Village la Grande Tortue

3 route de Pontlevoy, F-41120 Candé-sur-Beuvron (Loir-et-Cher) T: 02 54 44 15 20.

E: grandetortue@wanadoo.fr alanrogers.com/FR41070

In the region that the Kings of France chose to build their most beautiful residences, this pleasant, shady site has been developed in the surroundings of an old 800-hectare forest, just 1 km. from the banks of the Loire river. For those seeking a relaxing holiday, it provides 169 pitches, including 111 for touring units, all with 10A electricity (119 Europlugs) and 58 with full services. The friendly family owners continue to develop the site with a multisports court and an attractive swimming pool complex. During July and August, they organise a programme of trips including canoeing and riding excursions, as well as twice weekly concerts and shows. La Grande Tortue is very well placed for visiting the châteaux of the Loire and the cities of Orléans and Tours. It is located on the long distance 'Loire à Vélo' cycle track and this leads from the site to Chaumont, Blois and Chambord, with over 300 km. of marked cycle tracks in the surrounding area. There are several good restaurants close at hand, although the site restaurant is also recommended with a range of good value meals in a pleasant environment.

Facilities

Three sanitary blocks offer British style WCs, washbasins in cabins and pushbutton showers. Facilities for disabled visitors in one block. Laundry facilities. Motorcaravan services. Shop, terraced bar and restaurant with takeaway service (open all season). Heated swimming pool covered in poor weather, shallow outdoor pools for children (1/5-22/9). Trampolines, ball crawl with slide and climbing wall, two bouncy inflatables. Club for children (July/Aug). Multisports court. Bicycle hire (13/4-22/9). WiFi over site (charged). No electric barbecues. Off site: Fishing 1 km. Riding 3 km. Golf 10 km. Châteaux at Blois (10 km), Chambord (20 km), Chenonceau (20 km).

Open: 12 April - 23 September.

Directions

Site is just outside Candé-sur-Beuvron on D751, between Amboise and Blois. From Amboise, turn right just before Candé, then left into site. GPS: 47.4900069, 1.2583208

Charges guide

Per unit incl. 2 persons

and electricity	€ 23.00 - € 35.00
extra person	€ 7.00 - € 10.00
child (5-11 yrs)	€ 4.25 - € 6.75
dog	€ 4.00

Camping Cheques accepted.

Francueil-Chenonceau
Camping le Moulin Fort

F-37150 Francueil-Chenonceau (Indre-et-Loire) T: 02 47 23 86 22. E: **lemoulinfort@wanadoo.fr**
alanrogers.com/FR37030

Camping le Moulin Fort is a tranquil, riverside site with British owners, John and Sarah Scarratt. The 130 pitches are enhanced by trees and shrubs offering plenty of shade and 110 pitches have electricity (6A). From the snack bar terrace adjacent to the restored mill building, a timber walkway over the mill race leads to the unheated swimming pool and paddling pools. The site is ideal for couples and families with young children, although the river is unfenced. There is occasional noise from trains passing on the opposite bank of the river. All over the campsite, visitors will find little information boards about local nature (birds, fish, trees and shrubs), and the history of the mill.

Facilities
Two toilet blocks are of a good standard, with washbasins in cubicles, baby baths and facilities for disabled visitors. Washing machine. Motorcaravan services. Shop (7/5-27/9). Bar, restaurant and takeaway (all 22/5-21/9). Swimming pool (23/5-26/9). Excellent play area. Minigolf. Pétanque. Games/TV room. Library. Fishing. Bicycle and canoe hire. Family activities. (July/Aug). WiFi (charged).
Open: 7 May - 27 September.

Directions
Site is 35 km. east of Tours off D976 Vierzon road. From A85 at exit 11 take D31 towards Bléré and turn east on D976 (Vierzon) for 7 km. then north on D80 (Chenonceau) to site. GPS: 47.32735, 1.08936

Charges guide
Per unit incl. 2 persons and electricity	€ 21.00 - € 27.00
extra person	€ 4.00 - € 5.00

Gien
Kawan Village les Bois du Bardelet

Le Petit Bardelet, Poilly-lez-Gien, F-45500 Gien (Loiret) T: 02 38 67 47 39. E: **contact@bardelet.com**
alanrogers.com/FR45010

This attractive, high quality site, ideal for families with young children, is in a rural setting and well situated for exploring the less well known eastern part of the Loire Valley. Two lakes (one for boating, one for fishing) and a pool complex have been attractively landscaped in 18 hectares of former farmland, blending old and new with natural wooded areas and more open grassland with rural views. There are 245 large, level grass pitches with 120 for touring units. All have at least 10A electricity, 15 have water, waste water and 16A electricity, and some 30 have hardstanding. Eight have individual en-suite sanitary units beside the pitch.

Facilities
Two heated toilet blocks have some washbasins in cubicles, controllable showers, en-suite unit for disabled visitors and a baby room. Washing machines and dryers. Minimart, bar, takeaway and restaurant (May-Sept). Heated outdoor pool (1/5-31/8). Heated indoor pool and children's pool. Wellness centre. Fitness and jacuzzi rooms. Beach on lake. Games area. Canoeing and fishing. Tennis. Minigolf. Volleyball. Pétanque. Play area with trampoline. Kids' club, sports tournaments, excursions and activities, aquagym, archery (July/Aug). Bicycle hire. Chalets/mobile homes for hire. WiFi over site.
Open: 17 April - 27 September.

Directions
Leave A77 autoroute at exit 19 and take D940 (Bourges) to bypass Gien. Continue on D940 for 5 km. At junction with D53 (no left turn) turn right and right again to cross D940 (site signed). Follow signs for 1.5 km. to site. GPS: 47.64152, 2.61528

Charges guide
Per unit incl. 2 persons and electricity	€ 21.10 - € 35.20
extra person (over 2 yrs)	€ 5.40 - € 7.20
dog	€ 4.00

Camping Cheques accepted.

Pierrefitte-sur-Sauldre
Leading Camping les Alicourts

Domaine des Alicourts, F-41300 Pierrefitte-sur-Sauldre (Loir-et-Cher) T: 02 54 88 63 34.
E: **info@lesalicourts.com** **alanrogers.com/FR41030**

LeadingCampings

A secluded holiday village set in the heart of the forest, with many sporting facilities and a super spa centre, Camping les Alicourts is midway between Orléans and Bourges, to the east of the A71. There are 490 pitches, 153 for touring and the remainder occupied by mobile homes and chalets. All pitches have 6A electricity connections and good provision for water, and most are 150 sq.m. (min. 100 sq.m). Locations vary, from wooded to more open areas, thus giving a choice of amount of shade. All facilities are open all season and the leisure amenities are exceptional. A member of Leading Campings group.

Facilities
Three modern sanitary blocks include some washbasins in cabins and baby bathrooms. Laundry facilities. Facilities for disabled visitors. Motorcaravan services. Shop. Restaurant. Takeaway in bar with terrace. Pool complex. Spa centre. Lake (fishing, bathing, canoes, pedaloes, cable-ski). 9-hole golf course. Adventure play area. Tennis. Minigolf. Boules. Roller skating and skateboarding (bring own equipment). Bicycle hire. WiFi (charged).
Open: 2 May - 5 September.

Directions
From A71, take Lamotte-Beuvron exit (no 3) or from N20 Orléans to Vierzon turn left on to D923 towards Aubigny. After 14 km. turn right at camping sign on to D24E. Site signed in 2 km. GPS: 47.54398, 2.19193

Charges guide
Per unit incl. 2 persons and electricity	€ 20.00 - € 50.00
extra person	€ 7.00 - € 12.00
child (1-17 yrs acc. to age)	free - € 10.00

For latest campsite news, availability and prices visit
alanrogers.com

Rillé

Huttopia Rillé

Lac de Rillé, F-37340 Rillé (Indre-et-Loire) T: 02 47 24 62 97. E: rille@huttopia.com

alanrogers.com/FR37140

Huttopia Rillé is a rural site ideal for tent campers seeking a more natural, environmentally friendly, peaceful campsite close to a lake. Cars are parked outside the barrier but allowed on site to unload and load. The 133 slightly uneven and sloping pitches, 80 for touring, are scattered between the pine trees. All have 10A electricity (very long leads needed) and 24 are fully serviced. They vary in size and are numbered but not marked. This site is designed for those with tents, though small caravans and motorcaravans (special area) are accepted. Several types of accommodation for hire (cabin, hut, trailer or Canadian cabin). It is not ideal for those with walking difficulties.

Facilities

Modern central toilet block with family rooms and facilities for disabled visitors (no ramps and difficult access for wheelchairs). A smaller block has separate showers, washbasins and facilities for disabled visitors. Motorcaravan services. Small heated swimming pool with paddling area (20/4-30/9). Play area. Fishing. Canoes on lake. Communal barbecue areas (no charcoal barbecues). Max. 1 dog. Off site: Small steam train passes site.

Open: 17 April - 3 November.

Directions

Rillé is 40 km. west of Tours. Leave D766 Angers-Blois road at Château la Vallière take D749 southwest. In Rillé turn west on D49. Site is on right in 2 km. GPS: 47.44600, 0.33291

Charges guide

Per unit incl. 2 persons and electricity	€ 16.10 - € 36.30
extra person	€ 5.50 - € 8.20
child (2-7 yrs)	€ 4.50 - € 5.40

Sonzay

Camping l'Arada Parc

Rue de la Baratière, F-37360 Sonzay (Indre-et-Loire) T: 02 47 24 72 69. E: info@laradaparc.com

alanrogers.com/FR37060

A good, well maintained site in a quiet location, easy to find from the motorway and popular as an overnight stop, Camping l'Arada Parc is an attractive family site nestling in the heart of the Tourangelle countryside between the Loire and Loir valleys. The 62 grass touring pitches all have 10A electricity (Europlug) and 18 have water and drainage. The clearly marked pitches, some slightly sloping, are separated by trees and shrubs, some of which are hardstanding and now provide a degree of shade. An attractive, heated pool is on a pleasant terrace beside the restaurant. Entertainment, themed evenings and activities for children are organised in July/August.

Facilities

Two modern toilet blocks provide unisex toilets, showers and washbasins in cubicles. Baby room. Facilities for disabled visitors recently improved. Laundry facilities. Shop, bar, restaurant and takeaway (all season). Motorcaravan services. Outdoor swimming pool with slide and new terrace surround (no Bermuda-style shorts; 1/5-15/9). Heated, covered pool (all season). Fitness room. Small play area. Games area. Boules. TV room. Bicycle hire. WiFi over site (charged). Footpath to village.

Open: 3 April - 11 October.

Directions

Sonzay is northwest of Tours. From the new A28 north of Tours take exit 27 to Neuillé-Pont-Pierre which is on the D938 Le Mans-Tours road. Then take D766 towards Château la Vallière and turn southwest to Sonzay. Follow campsite signs. GPS: 47.526228, 0.450865

Charges guide

Per unit incl. 2 persons and electricity (10A)	€ 22.50 - € 32.00
extra person	€ 4.20 - € 5.80

Trogues

Sites et Paysages du Château de la Rolandière

Château de La Rolandière, F-37220 Trogues (Indre-et-Loire) T: 02 47 58 53 71. E: contact@larolandiere.com

alanrogers.com/FR37090

This is a charming site set in the grounds of a château and you are assured of a very warm welcome here. There are 50 medium sized, level or gently sloping pitches, separated by hedges with a variety of trees giving some shade. Most have 6A electricity (long leads advised) with water taps nearby. There is a large chalet and mobile homes for hire, and bed and breakfast is also available. The site has a pleasant swimming pool, paddling pool, fitness room and games/TV room. The bar and restaurant have a sunny terrace overlooking the château. Minigolf, swings, slides and an area for ball games are adjacent.

Facilities

The older style toilet block has been refurbished to provide good facilities with modern showers, washbasin and laundry areas. Provision for disabled visitors and children. Small shop for basics. Bar with terrace. Snacks and takeaway (July/Aug). Swimming pool (15/5-30/9). Minigolf. Play area. Fitness room. TV lounge. WiFi. Off site: Fishing 1 km. on River Vienne. River beach and boat launching 4 km. Restaurant 4 km. Shops 6 km.

Open: 23 April - 24 September.

Directions

Trogues is 40 km. southwest of Tours on the D760 Loches-Chinon road. Site is on D760, midway between Trogues and A10 (exit 25). Entrance is signed and marked by a model of the château. GPS: 47.10767, 0.51052

Charges guide

Per unit incl. 2 persons and electricity	€ 22.90 - € 31.40
extra person	€ 4.70 - € 6.70
No credit cards.	

FREE Alan Rogers Travel Card
Extra benefits and savings - see page 14

Avrillé

Camping Domaine des Forges

Rue des Forges, F-85440 Avrillé (Vendée) T: 02 51 22 38 85. E: forges@franceloc.fr

alanrogers.com/FR85930

Arranged in the beautiful grounds of a 16th-century manor house, the 145 touring pitches here are very generous in size (100-200 sq.m) with 16A electricity, water and drainage. Some of the premium pitches with additional services such as Internet access and cable TV carry an extra charge. The owners' aim is to develop a prestige campsite with the highest quality of services and they have made a very good start. A further 120 pitches are occupied by mobile homes, chalets, roulottes and tents available to hire. A large lake is available for fishing.

Facilities

Four new, heated sanitary blocks include facilities for disabled visitors and babies. Laundry facilities. Shop. Bar and takeaway. Outdoor pool (15/5-1/9). Heated indoor pool (all season). Play area. Minigolf. Fishing lake. Multisports area. Boules. Fitness room. Bicycle hire. Gas barbecues only. Internet WiFi over site (charged). One dog per pitch. Off site: Village 400 m. Vendée beaches 7 km. Golf de la Domangère and Golf Port Bourgenay (discount) 10 km. Riding 10 km. Les Sables d'Olonne 25 km.

Open: 19 April - 28 September.

Directions

Travel south from La Roche-sur-Yon on the D747 for 21 km. At the D19, turn right for Avrillé (about 6 km). At junction with the D949 turn right and first right again into rue des Forges. Site at the end of the road. GPS: 46.47609, -1.49454

Charges guide

Per unit incl. 2 persons, electricity, water and waste water	€ 19.00 - € 33.00
extra person	€ 4.70 - € 7.00
child (2-6 yrs)	€ 3.50 - € 4.50

Brem-sur-Mer

Camping Caravaning le Chaponnet

16 rue du Chaponnet, F-85470 Brem-sur-Mer (Vendée) T: 02 51 90 55 56. E: contact@le-chaponnet.com

alanrogers.com/FR85480

This well established, family run site is within five minutes' walk of Brem village and 1.5 km. from a sandy beach. The 81 touring pitches are level with varying amounts of grass, some with shade from mature trees. Pitches are separated by tall hedges and serviced by tarmac or gravel roads and have frequent water and electricity points (long leads may be required). Premium pitches are available for an additional charge. Tour operators have mobile homes and tents on 85 pitches and there are 155 other mobile homes and chalets, over half available for rent. The swimming pool complex features heated indoor and outdoor pools with a jacuzzi, slides and a children's pool, together with a sauna and fitness centre.

Facilities

Five sanitary blocks (two open in low season) are well maintained with showers and washbasins in cubicles. Facilities for babies and disabled visitors. Laundry facilities. Motorcaravan service point. Bar, restaurant, snack bar and pizzeria (early June-late Aug). Indoor and outdoor heated pools. Waterslide, jacuzzi and sauna. Play area. Multisports area. Tennis. Bicycle hire. Indoor games room. WiFi in bar/pool area (charged). Kids' club (July/Aug, 4-14 yrs), family activities and entertainment. Free bus to beach (July/Aug). Off site: Shops 200 m.

Open: 2 April - 30 September.

Directions

From A87 at La Roche continue on D160 towards Les Sables d'Olonne. Take exit for La Mothe-Achard and Brétignolles-sur-Mer. Follow D54 to Brem-sur-Mer. Site is clearly signed, just off the one-way system in village centre. GPS: 46.60433, -1.83244

Charges guide

Per unit incl. 2 persons and electricity	€ 24.60 - € 36.80
extra person	€ 5.30 - € 7.60
child (1-10 yrs)	€ 3.10 - € 4.60

Jard-sur-Mer

Camping les Ecureuils

Route des Goffineaux, F-85520 Jard-sur-Mer (Vendée) T: 02 51 33 42 74. E: ecureuils@franceloc.fr

alanrogers.com/FR85210

Les Ecureuils is a wooded site in a quieter part of the southern Vendée. It is undoubtedly one of the prettiest sites on this stretch of coast, with an elegant reception area, attractive vegetation and large pitches separated by low hedges with plenty of shade. Of the 278 pitches, 77 are for touring units, each with water and drainage, as well as easy access to 10A electricity. Jard is rated among the most pleasant and least hectic of Vendée towns. The harbour is home to some fishing boats and rather more pleasure craft.

Facilities

One toilet block, well equipped and kept very clean, includes baby baths, and laundry rooms. Small shop (bread baked on site), snack bar and takeaway (1/6-1/9). Bar with snacks and ice-creams. Good sized swimming pool and separate paddling pool. New large flume into separate pool. Indoor pool and fitness centre. New, imaginative play area (3-10 yrs). Minigolf. Boules. Multisports pitch. Bouncy castle. Kids' club (5-10 yrs, July/Aug). Games room. Bicycle hire. WiFi (free).

Open: 11 April - 21 September.

Directions

From La Roche-sur-Yon follow D474 and D49 towards Jard-sur-Mer. Do not use sat nav for final approach. From village follow signs for Autres Campings or Camping les Ecureuils. Site is on the left. GPS: 46.4113, -1.5896

Charges guide

Per unit incl. 2 persons, and electricity	€ 16.00 - € 33.00
extra person	€ 4.70 - € 7.00
child (0-7 yrs)	€ 3.50 - € 4.50

For latest campsite news, availability and prices visit

alanrogers.com

La Tranche-sur-Mer

Camping du Jard

123 boulevard Maréchal de Lattre de Tassigny, F-85360 La Tranche-sur-Mer (Vendée) T: 02 51 27 43 79.
E: info@campingdujard.fr alanrogers.com/FR85020

Camping du Jard is a well maintained site between La Rochelle and Les Sables-d'Olonne. First impressions are good, with a friendly welcome from M. Marton and his staff. The 130 touring pitches, all with 10A electricity (Europlug) and 60 also with water and drainage, are level and grassy; many are hedged by bushes and a large variety of trees provide shade in places. A similar ratio of pitches are used by tour operators and 50 accommodation units are available to rent. An impressive pool complex has a heated outdoor pool with toboggan and paddling pool, plus an indoor pool with jacuzzi. The site is 700 m. from a sandy beach with many shops and restaurants nearby.

Facilities
Three toilet blocks (unheated, only one open in low season) provide washbasins, showers and facilities for babies and disabled visitors. Washing machines and dryers. Shop, restaurant and bar (all July/Aug). Heated outdoor pool (from 18/5); heated indoor pool (all season). Sauna, solarium and fitness room. Tennis. Minigolf. Bicycle hire. Play area, games and TV rooms. Internet point; free WiFi around bar. American-style motorhomes not accepted. No pets. Off site: Beach 700 m.

Open: 17 May - 13 September.

Directions
La Tranche-sur-Mer is 40 km. southeast of Les Sables d'Olonne. From A87 Cholet/La Roche-sur-Yon leave at exit 32 for La Tranche-sur-Mer and take D747 to La Tranche. Turn east following signs for La Faute-sur-Mer along bypass. Take exit for La Grière and then turn east to site. GPS: 46.34836, -1.38738

Charges guide
Per unit incl. 2 persons and electricity	€ 24.50 - € 33.00
extra person	€ 6.00 - € 7.00

Longeville-sur-Mer

MS Vacances Camping Club Les Brunelles

Le Bouil, F-85560 Longeville-sur-Mer (Vendée) T: 02 53 81 70 00. E: reservation@ms-vacances.com
alanrogers.com/FR85440

This is a well managed site with a wide range of facilities and a varied programme of high season entertainment for all the family. A busy site in high season, there are plenty of activities to keep younger children and teenagers happy and occupied. Les Brunelles has 607 pitches of which 121 are for touring units; all have electricity (10A) and 40 also have water and drainage. Most are 100 sq.m. to allow easier access for larger units. The touring pitches are mainly level on sandy grass and separated by hedges, away from most of the mobile homes.

Facilities
Six well maintained and modernised toilet blocks have British style toilets and washbasins/showers in cubicles. Facilities for disabled visitors. Laundry facilities. Shop, restaurant, takeaway and large modern, airy bar. Covered pool with jacuzzi. Outdoor heated pool with slides and paddling pools. Solarium. Tennis. Entertainment for all age groups. Bicycle hire. Max. 1 dog. WiFi over site (charged). Gas barbecues only. Off site: Riding 3 km. Good, supervised, sandy beach 800 m.

Open: 11 April - 20 September.

Directions
Longeville-sur-Mer is 28 km. south from the A87 exit 32 at La Roche-sur-Yon via the D747 (La Tranche), D949 (Les Sables) and in 3 km, D91. Site is 3.5 km. southwest of the village and is signed from the D21 (Jard-sur-Mer). GPS: 46.41330, -1.52313

Charges guide
Per unit incl. 2 persons and electricity	€ 25.00 - € 47.00
extra person	€ 6.20 - € 12.40
Camping Cheques accepted.	

Noirmoutier-en-l'Ile

Camping Indigo Noirmoutier

23 allée des Sableaux, Bois de la Chaize, F-85330 Noirmoutier-en-l'Ile (Vendée) T: 02 51 39 06 24.
E: noirmoutier@camping-indigo.com alanrogers.com/FR85720

Located in woodland and on dunes along a two kilometre stretch of sandy beach, just east of the attractive little town of Noirmoutier on the island of the same name, this could be paradise for those who enjoy a simple campsite in a natural setting. On land belonging to France's forestry commission, this site is operated by Huttopia whose aim is to adapt to the environment rather than take it over. The 398 touring pitches, all with electricity (10A), are situated among the pine trees and accessed along tracks. Those on the sand dunes have fantastic views across the Baie de Bourgneuf. They cost a few euros extra – if you are lucky enough to get one. Some pitches may experience noise from a nearby bar.

Facilities
Five sanitary blocks provide preset showers and washbasins in cubicles. The central one is larger and more modern. Facilities for children and disabled visitors. Motorcaravan services. Freezer service. Bread to order. Bar, snack bar and takeaway (July/Aug). Picnic tables. New play area. Boules. Volleyball. Bicycle hire. Only electric barbecues allowed. Free WiFi over part of site. Off site: Shops and restaurants 2 km. Riding 4 km.

Open: 10 April - 29 September.

Directions
At La Barre-de-Monts, take D38 across bridge to island and continue 20 km. to Noirmoutier-en-l'Ile. Go through town past three sets of traffic lights and at roundabout turn right following blue signs to Campings. Site is ahead at roundabout in 2 km. Do not use sat nav. GPS: 46.9969, -2.2201

Charges guide
Per unit incl. 2 persons and electricity	€ 20.60 - € 35.00

FREE Alan Rogers Travel Card
Extra benefits and savings - see page 14

Saint Gilles-Croix-de-Vie

Camping les Cyprès

41 rue du Pont Jaunay, F-85806 Saint Gilles-Croix-de-Vie (Vendée) T: 02 51 55 38 98.

E: contact@camping-lescypres85.com alanrogers.com/FR85495

On the edge of a pine forest and just a short walk across the dunes from a fine sandy beach, this could be an ideal spot for a seaside holiday. Les Cyprès is a very French campsite with good basic facilities and a pleasant modern pool complex. The 300 pitches are in an arc curving out towards the sea in both directions from reception; the 141 touring pitches of varying shapes and sizes occupy the southern end of the arc. All have access to electricity (10A) and water, though long leads are required in places and some are more suitable for tents because of the trees.

Facilities

Two traditional toilet blocks serving the touring areas. Baby bath in ladies' section of main block. Unit for disabled visitors opposite reception plus washing machines, dryers and ironing facilities. Small shop (Apr/Aug). Bar (July/Aug). Snack bar and takeaway with shared terrace (July/Aug and weekends). Outdoor pool (from 1/5) and heated indoor pool with jacuzzi (from 4/4) with paddling pools. Motorcaravan service point. Games room. Play area. Multisports court. Bicycle hire and children's go-karts. Free WiFi in bar area.

Open: 4 April - 20 September.

Directions

St Gilles-Croix-de-Vie is 45 km. west of La Roche-sur-Yon on the D38 coast road. From roundabout at southern end of St Gilles bypass, head towards town and take first left in 400 m. Site is signed and is in 1 km. GPS: 46.67089, -1.909132

Charges guide

Per unit incl. 2 persons and electricity	€ 21.50 - € 30.50
extra person	€ 6.10 - € 6.70
child (2-5 yrs)	€ 4.30 - € 4.70
dog (max. 1)	€ 3.60

Saint Jean-de-Monts

Camping la Yole

13 chemin des Bosses, Orouet, F-85160 Saint Jean-de-Monts (Vendée) T: 02 51 58 67 17.

E: contact@la-yole.com alanrogers.com/FR85150

La Yole is an attractive and well run site, two kilometres from a sandy beach. It offers 369 pitches, of which 76 are occupied by tour operators and 133 mobile homes are either privately owned or available to rent. There are 170 touring pitches, most with shade and separated by bushes and trees. An area at the rear of the site is a little more open. All the pitches are of at least 100 sq.m. and have electricity (10A), water and drainage. The pool complex includes an attractive outdoor pool, a paddling pool, slide and an indoor heated pool with jacuzzi. There are also gym facilities and entertainment is organised in high season. This is a clean and tidy site, ideal for families with children and you will receive a warm welcome.

Facilities

Four toilet blocks (one heated in low season) include washbasins in cabins, hot showers and facilities for disabled visitors and babies. Laundry facilities. Shop (20/5-5/9). Bar with TV, restaurant and takeaway (11/5-7/9). Outdoor pool and paddling pool. Indoor heated pool with jacuzzi (all season, no shorts). Gym centre. Play area. Tennis. Games room. Kids' club. Bicycle hire. Entertainment in high season. WiFi on part of site (charged). Gas barbecues only. Max. 1 dog.

Open: 11 April - 24 September.

Directions

Site is signed off the D38, 6 km. south of St Jean-de-Monts in the village of Orouet. Coming from St Jean-de-Monts turn right at l'Oasis restaurant towards Mouette and follow signs to site. GPS: 46.75659, -2.00792

Charges guide

Per unit incl. 2 persons, electricity, water and drainage	€ 22.00 - € 38.50
extra person	€ 4.00 - € 7.20

Camping Cheques accepted.

Talmont-Saint-Hilaire

Camping le Paradis

Route de Port Bourgenay, rue de la Source, F-85440 Talmont-Saint-Hilaire (Vendée) T: 02 51 22 22 36.

E: info@camping-leparadis85.com alanrogers.com/FR85915

Camping le Paradis can be found close to the popular seaside resort of Talmont-Saint-Hilaire, between Jard-sur-Mer and the larger resort of Les Sables-d'Olonne. Talmont makes up part of the Côte de Lumière, and its 3.5 km. sandy beach (Le Veillon) has longstanding Blue Flag accreditation. There is a free shuttle bus from the campsite to the beach. Pitches here are of average size with limited shade. A number of mobile homes are available for rent. On-site amenities include a covered, heated pool and an all-weather sports pitch (basketball, volleyball, football).

Facilities

The single toilet block provides washbasins and showers in cubicles. Laundry. Shop. Bar/snack bar and takeaway (July/Aug). Covered swimming pool. Play area. All weather sports pitch. Activity and entertainment programme (July/Aug). No charcoal barbecues. WiFi over part of site (charged). Max. 1 dog. Mobile homes and caravans for rent. Off site: Beach 1 km. Shops, cafés and restaurants in Talmont, 3 km. Fishing and bicycle hire 4 km.

Open: 1 May - 30 September.

Directions

Approaching from the north (Les Sables-d'Olonne) take the southbound D9494 towards Talmont-St Hilaire. Before reaching Talmont turn right on D4 and follow signs to the site. GPS: 46.46486, -1.65484

Charges guide

Per unit incl. 2 persons and electricity	€ 17.00 - € 26.00
extra person	€ 3.00 - € 4.50

For latest campsite news, availability and prices visit

alanrogers.com

Germany

With its wealth of scenic and cultural interests, Germany is a land of contrasts.

From the flat lands of the north to the mountains in the south, with forests in

the east and west, regional characteristics are a strong feature of German life,

and present a rich variety of folklore and customs.

Each region in Germany has its own unique identity. Home of lederhosen, beer and sausages is Bavaria in the south, with small towns, medieval castles and Baroque churches. In the southwest, Baden Württemberg is famous for its ancient Black Forest and its spas, and boasts the most hours of sunshine. Further west is the stunningly beautiful Rhine Valley, where the river winds through steep hills dotted with castles, ruins and vineyards. Eastern Germany is studded with lakes and rivers, and undulating lowlands that give way to mountains. The north has busy cities such as Bremen and Hamburg as well as traditional North Sea family resorts. The capital city of Berlin, situated in the northeast of the country, and once divided by the Berlin Wall, is an increasingly popular tourist destination, with its blend of old and modern architecture, zoos and aquariums, museums, green spaces and lively nightlife.

CAPITAL: Berlin

Tourist Office

German National Tourist Office

PO Box 2695, London W1A 3TN

Tel: 020 7317 0908

Fax: 020 7317 0917

Email: gntolon@d-z-t.com

Internet: www.germany-tourism.co.uk

Population

81 million

Climate

Temperate climate. In general, winters are
a little colder and summers a little warmer than
in the UK.

Language

German

Telephone

The country code is 00 49.

Money

Currency: The Euro

Banks: Mon-Fri 08.30-12.30 and
14.00-16.00. Late opening on Thurs until 18.00.

Shops

Mon-Fri 08.30/09.00 to 18.00/18.30.

Public Holidays

New Year's Day; Good Fri; Easter Mon; Labour
Day; Ascension; Whit Mon; Unification Day 3 Oct;
Christmas, 25, 26 Dec. In some areas: Epiphany
6 Jan; Corpus Christi 22 Jun; Assumption
15 Aug; Reformation 31 Oct; All Saints 1 Nov
(plus other regional days).

Motoring

An excellent network of (toll-free) motorways
(autobahns) exists in the West and the traffic
moves fast. Remember in the East a lot of road
building is going on, amongst other works, so
allow plenty of time when travelling and be
prepared for poor road surfaces.

see campsite map 2

Bad Wildbad

Family-Resort Kleinenzhof

Kleinenzhof 1, D-75323 Bad Wildbad (Baden-Württemberg) T: 070 813 435. E: info@kleinenzhof.de

alanrogers.com/DE34060

In the northern Black Forest, popular with walkers and cyclists alike, this large and busy site runs along the bank of a small but safe stream in a dramatic wooded valley. Of the 300 or so pitches, some 120 are for tourers, all with 16A electricity and water, and most with drainage. The four shower blocks are of the highest quality. In the middle of the site is a hotel/bar/restaurant complex which incorporates indoor and outdoor pools available free to campers. A full programme of activities is arranged, including walks, other outings, visits to the site's own distillery, films and communal barbecues at weekends, and a children's club every afternoon from May to September. A free bus runs four times a day in season to Calmbach.

Facilities

Four excellent sanitary blocks, all heated, are clean with many washbasins in cabins and showers. Facilities for disabled visitors. Baby changing. Children's bathroom. 12 family bathrooms to rent. Dog shower. Laundry facilities and dishwasher. Motorcaravan services. Gas. Shop. Bar and restaurant (at hotel). Indoor pool. Outdoor pool (May-Sept) and paddling pool. Impressive new indoor sports/games hall with toddler annexe. TV and games room. Fishing. Go-kart hire. WiFi over site (charged). Off site: Fishing 5 km. Riding, bicycle hire and skiing 8 km. Golf 25 km.

Open: All year.

Directions

Whether approaching from Pforzheim in the north or Freudenstadt in the south, stay on the 294. Do not go to Bad Wildbad. The site is on the main road just south of Calmbach, and is clearly signed. If coming from the south, the turning into the site is very sharp. GPS: 48.73807, 8.57710

Charges guide

Per unit incl. 2 persons and electricity (plus meter)	€ 24.50 - € 25.90
extra person	€ 7.10 - € 7.50
child (1-12 yrs)	€ 4.40 - € 4.80
dog	€ 2.20 - € 2.40

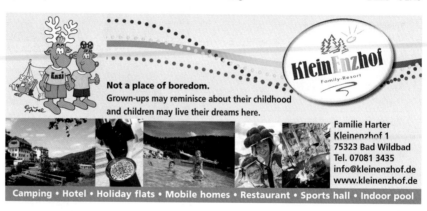
Badenweiler

Kur & Feriencamping Badenweiler

Weilertalstrasse 73, D-79410 Badenweiler (Baden-Württemberg) T: 076 321 550.

E: info@camping-badenweiler.de alanrogers.com/DE34540

Badenweiler is an attractive spa centre on the edge of the southern Black Forest, and is the site of the largest Roman baths north of the Alps. It is easily accessed from the A5 or B3, but far enough from them to be peaceful. This well kept, family run campsite with outstanding open views is on a hillside close to Badenweiler and the spa facilities. There are four terraces with 100 wide, individual grass pitches, 96 for touring, all with electricity (16A), water and drainage. The main building houses reception, a small shop and a bar/café which serves takeaway snacks in high season. Downstairs are further toilets and a well equipped playroom. This small site with superb views is ideal for exploring the local area.

Facilities

Top quality sanitary facilities are contained in two fully tiled buildings, one with toilets and the other with free, controllable hot showers with full glass dividers and washbasins (cabins and vanity style). Family washrooms, facilities for babies and disabled visitors. Laundry facilities. Motorcaravan services. Gas supplies. Shop for basics. Play area. Games room. Internet point and WiFi over site (charged). No charcoal barbecues. Off site: Bicycle hire 100 m. Municipal outdoor, heated swimming pool (free to campers, 15/5-15/9) 200 m. Restaurants 200 m. Shop 300 m. Golf 12 km.

Open: All year excl. 14 December - 16 January.

Directions

From the A5 midway between Freiburg and Basel take exit 65 onto the B378 to Müllheim, then the L131 signed to Badenweiler-Ost from where site is well signed. GPS: 47.809961, 7.676954

Charges guide

Per unit incl. 2 persons	€ 29.90
extra person	€ 8.00
child (2-15 yrs)	€ 4.00 - € 5.50
electricity (per kWh)	€ 0.70
dog	€ 3.50

Credit cards accepted (2% charge).
1% discount for cash.

For latest campsite news, availability and prices visit

alanrogers.com

Bühl

Camping Adam

Campingstrasse 1, D-77815 Bühl (Baden-Württemberg) T: 072 232 3194. E: info@campingplatz-adam.de

alanrogers.com/DE34150

This very convenient, family owned lakeside site is by the A5 Karlsruhe-Basel autobahn near Baden-Baden, easily accessed from exit 52 Bühl (also from the French autoroute A35 just northeast of Strasbourg). It is also a useful base for the Black Forest. Most of the touring pitches (160 from 490 total) have electricity connections (10A Europlug), 100 also have water and drainage. Tents are positioned along the outer area of the lake. At very busy times, units staying overnight only may be placed close together on a lakeside area of hardstanding. The site has a well tended look and good English is spoken. The lake is divided into separate areas for bathing or boating and windsurfing, with a long waterslide. The public are admitted to this on payment and it attracts many people on fine weekends. The shop and restaurant/bar remain open virtually all year (not Mondays or Tuesdays in low season), so this is a useful site to visit out of season, either as a stopover or for a relaxing break in lakeside surroundings.

Facilities

Three heated sanitary buildings. Private cabins in the new block, hot showers on payment. Facilities for babies and disabled visitors. Washing machine and dryer. Gas. Motorcaravan services. Shop (1/4-31/10). Restaurant (1/3-30/10). Takeaway (1/5-31/8). Playground. Volleyball court. Outdoor chess. Bicycle hire. Fishing. WiFi over site (charged). Off site: Riding and golf 5 km.

Open: All year (mobile homes 1/4-31/9 only).

Directions

Take A5/E35-52, exit 52 (Bühl), turn towards Lichtenau, go through Oberbruch and left to site. From French autoroute A35 take exits 52 or 56 onto D2 and D4 respectively then turn onto A5 as above. GPS: 48.72650, 8.08500

Charges guide

Per unit incl. 2 persons	
and electricity	€ 17.00 - € 28.00
extra person	€ 5.00 - € 8.50
child (3-15 yrs)	€ 3.00 - € 5.50
dog	€ 2.50 - € 3.50

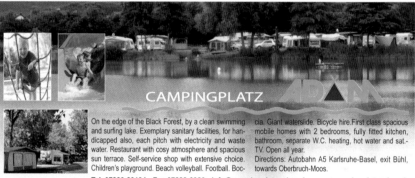

On the edge of the Black Forest, by a clean swimming and surfing lake. Exemplary sanitary facilities, for handicapped also, each pitch with electricity and waste water. Restaurant with cosy atmosphere and spacious sun terrace. Self-service shop with extensive choice. Children's playground. Beach volleyball. Football. Boc- cia. Giant waterslide. Bicycle hire. First class spacious mobile homes with 2 bedrooms, fully fitted kitchen, bathroom, separate W.C. heating, hot water and sat.-TV. Open all year.
Directions: Autobahn A5 Karlsruhe-Basel, exit Bühl, towards Oberbruch-Moos.

Tel. 07223-23194 • Fax 07223-8982 • info@campingplatz-adam.de • www.campingplatz-adam.de

Creglingen

Camping Romantische Strasse

Munster 67, D-97993 Creglingen-Münster (Baden-Württemberg) T: 079 332 0289.

E: camping.hausotter@web.de alanrogers.com/DE36020

This popular tourist area can become very busy during summer, and Romantische Strasse will be greatly appreciated for its peaceful situation in a wooded valley just outside the small village of Münster. There are 100 grass touring pitches (out of 140), many level, others with a small degree of slope. They are not hedged or fenced, in order to keep the natural appearance of the woodland. All the pitches have electricity (6A), some shade, and are situated either side of a stream (fenced off from a weir at the far end of the site). Twenty-seven fully serviced pitches are on higher ground near reception.

Facilities

The two main sanitary blocks are of good quality with free hot water. A third unit further into the site is due for refurbishment. Launderette. Motorcaravan services. Small shop (1/4-9/11). Gas supplies. Large, pleasant bar/restaurant at the entrance (1/4-9/11, closed Mon). Barbecue and covered sitting area. Heated indoor swimming pool (caps required) and sauna. Minigolf. Play area. Bicycle hire. Four mobile homes for hire. WiFi (charged). Off site: Bus service 200 m. Large lakes for swimming 100 m. and fishing 500 m. Riding 3.5 km. Rothenburg with its fortifications 16 km.

Open: 15 March - 15 November.

Directions

From the Romantische Strasse between Rothenburg and Bad Mergentheim, exit at Creglingen to Münster (3 km). Site is just beyond this village. GPS: 49.43950, 10.04211

Charges guide

Per unit incl. 2 persons	
and electricity	€ 17.80 - € 23.80
extra person	€ 5.50 - € 6.50
child (3-14 yrs)	€ 3.50 - € 4.00
dog	€ 1.00

No credit cards.

FREE Alan Rogers Travel Card
Extra benefits and savings - see page 14

Ettenheim

Campingpark Oase

Mühlenweg 34, D-77955 Ettenheim (Baden-Württemberg) T: 07822 445918. E: info@campingpark-oase.de
alanrogers.com/DE34280

This busy, pleasant family owned and managed site lies on wooded land on the western edge of the Black Forest, a very good region for walking and cycling. The main level area near the entrance holds all of the main facilities and 170 touring pitches on grass (all with 6A electricity), which include 32 very large, fully serviced pitches. On sloping land further away are 95 terraced seasonal pitches. Just outside the entrance is the family hotel/restaurant, which also has a playground, all open to campers. As well as being a convenient night stop for the main motorway, this site makes for easy exploration of the historic cities of Freiburg and Strasbourg, and the majestic Rhine.

Facilities

Two heated sanitary blocks are clean and well maintained. Many washbasins are in cabins. Showers are coin-operated. Facilities for wheelchair users. Baby room. Children's bathroom. Laundry service (no public machines). Motorcaravan services. Gas. Shop. Restaurant and takeaway (at hotel). TV and club room. WiFi over site (charged). Max. one dog per unit. Off site: Municipal pool and leisure centre adjacent. Tennis, riding and bicycle hire within 1 km. Fishing 2 km. Golf 5 km.

Open: 28 March - 4 October.

Directions

From A5/E35, exit 57A (Ettenheim), follow L103 road southeast to Ettenheim (about 2.5 km). From here site is signed, and is a further 1 km. along the same road. GPS: 48.24770, 7.82753

Charges guide

Per unit incl. 2 persons and electricity	€ 23.50 - € 31.50
extra person	€ 7.50 - € 8.50
child (1-15 yrs)	€ 3.50 - € 4.00

Freiburg

Camping Am Möslepark

Waldseestrasse 77, D-79117 Freiburg (Baden-Württemberg) T: 076 176 79333.
E: information@camping-freiburg.com alanrogers.com/DE34380

This is a small, quiet, family run site in the suburbs of Freiburg. Its grass pitches, set on small terraces, are shaded by many mature trees. Most of the 70 pitches are for touring units and have electricity (10/16A Europlug). On the upper part of the site is a long established and very attractive restaurant. Open in the evenings, the restaurant specialises in dishes freshly prepared from organic ingredients; vegetarian and local specialities are also part of the menu. Additionally a small bar and bistro is part of a wellness centre which adjoins the site.

Facilities

Well maintained sanitary facilities provide some washbasins in cabins and showers with free hot water (a new block with facilities for disabled visitors and a kitchen for tent campers is scheduled). Space for baby changing. Small dining room with metered hotplate and kettle. Motorcaravan service area. Small shop. Play area. Bicycle hire. Free WiFi over site. The adjoining wellness centre has sauna, steam bath, massage and jacuzzi plus a small swimming pool (reduced rate entrance for campers). Accommodation to rent.

Open: 1 April - 28 October.

Directions

Site is 2 km. southeast of Freiburg. Leave A5 at exit 62 (Freiburg Mitte) and take the B31A southeast, following signs for Titisee, Neustadt. After 7 km. keep left through Freiburg and do not enter tunnel. After 300 m. turn right (Stadthalle), keep straight on, then left at Waldsee sign. Continue left, and site is signed to left. GPS: 47.98064, 7.88153

Charges guide

Per unit incl. 2 persons and electricity	€ 22.80 - € 25.60
extra person	€ 7.90

Freiburg

Hirzberg Camping Freiburg

Kartäuserstrasse 99, D-79104 Freiburg (Baden-Württemberg) T: 076 135 054.
E: hirzberg@freiburg-camping.de alanrogers.com/DE34390

Hirzberg Camping is a quiet city site backing onto meadows and wooded hills, yet within easy reach of Freiburg's old town quarter. To the right of the entrance is reception, a shop, the sanitary facilities and a children's room with a play area outside. Just inside is a large convenient overnight parking area. The main part of the site is reached by a short climb passing a small reading room and flower decked sitting areas. The upper part has 76 pitches, 65 for tourers, all with 10A electricity connections. Tarmac roads lead to open grass pitches, many under mature trees. The site owners, Herr and Frau Ziegler, both speak very good English and are most helpful with tourist advice.

Facilities

Modern, heated sanitary block provides free hot water, roomy adjustable showers and some washbasins in cabins. Washing machines and dryer. Kitchen with fridge, microwave and cooking rings on payment. Small shop with essential supplies. Play room and play area. Reading room with daily weather report. Bicycle hire. WiFi over site (charged). Off site: Bus service at entrance, tram 300 m. Golf 6 km. Riding 8 km.

Open: All year.

Directions

Site is in the eastern part of the city. To reach it without having to drive through the city, from the B31 take exit Freiburg Kappel (F. Kappel) which is well to the east of the city and follow camping signs. GPS: 47.99212, 7.87392

Charges guide

Per unit incl. 2 persons and electricity	€ 21.70 - € 25.50
extra person	€ 7.50 - € 8.40

For latest campsite news, availability and prices visit
alanrogers.com

Herbolzheim

Terrassen Campingplatz Herbolzheim

Im Laue, D-79336 Herbolzheim (Baden-Württemberg) T: 076 431 460. E: s.hugoschmidt@t-online.de
alanrogers.com/DE34420

This well equipped campsite is in a quiet location on a wooded slope to the north of Freiburg. There are 70 touring pitches close to reception and all facilities. All have electricity (16A) and grass surfaces, on terraces linked by hard access roads with some shade. Pitches on the higher slopes are used by a tour operator and for long-term occupancy. This is good walking country and with only occasional entertainment, this is a very pleasant place in which to relax between daily activities. Recently installed solar panels now provide most of the site's electricity and heating.

Facilities

The main toilet facilities have just been upgraded to an exceptional standard, with new facilities for babies and disabled visitors. Laundry facilities (charged) and covered clothes line. Motorcaravan services. Bar/restaurant (Easter-Sept). Two play areas. WiFi (charged). Dogs are not accepted 15/7-15/8. Off site: Large open-air heated municipal swimming pool complex adjacent (1/5-15/9). Restaurants and shops in the village 3 km. Riding and bicycle hire 5 km. Local market Fri. mornings.

Open: 14 April - 3 October.

Directions

From A5 Frankfurt-Basel autobahn take exit 57, 58 or 59 and follow signs to Herbolzheim. Site is signed on south side of town near swimming pool. Go through pool car park and 350 m. past the pool entrance. GPS: 48.21610, 7.78857

Charges guide

Per unit incl. 2 persons and electricity	€ 23.00 - € 25.00
extra person	€ 7.00
child (0-15 yrs)	€ 3.00

Hohenstadt

Camping Waldpark Hohenstadt

Waldpark 1, D-73345 Hohenstadt (Baden-Württemberg) T: 073 356 754.
E: camping@waldpark-hohenstadt.de alanrogers.com/DE34080

Situated on a wooded hillside close to the A8 autoroute, this neat and tidy site is open all year and is an ideal stopover between Stuttgart and Ulm. The 50 good sized plots for touring units each have water and 16A electric supply and are positioned on terraces at the front of the site, with little shade. The rear of the site is used for seasonal units. The restaurant/bar provides a good selection of local food and is open every evening. For a longer stay, the towns of Ulm and Blaubeuren are worth a visit and a tour of the Laichingen Pothole (the deepest show cave in Germany) should not be missed.

Facilities

A large modern toilet block is centrally situated, containing WCs, hot showers (free tokens for touring units), washbasins and facilities for disabled visitors. A smaller modern block in the touring area provides WCs and washbasins. Washing machine and dryer. Motorcaravan services. Small shop in reception for basics (bread to order). Restaurant/bar (evenings). Swimming pool (15/5-30/9). Play area. Activity programme (5-10 yrs; high season). Electric bicycle hire. Nordic skiing in winter. WiFi. Off site: Nordic skiing from site. Riding 200 m.

Open: 1 March - 31 October.

Directions

From A8/E52 Stuttgart-Ulm, exit at exit 60, signed Behelfsausfahrt and follow signs to Hohenstadt and the site. GPS: 48.548009, 9.667245

Charges guide

Per unit incl. 2 persons and electricity	€ 16.50 - € 18.00
extra person	€ 5.00 - € 5.50
child (4-14 yrs)	€ 3.00 - € 3.50
dog	€ 1.00

Isny

Waldbad Camping Isny

Lohbauerstrasse 61-69, D-88316 Isny (Baden-Württemberg) T: 075 622 389.
E: info@waldbad-camping-isny.de alanrogers.com/DE34670

Isny is a delightful spot for families and for others looking for a peaceful stay in a very well managed environment. The site has been developed to a high standard and lies just south of the village in a wood, by a lake. In an open area there are 50 individual 100 sq.m. hardstanding pitches (all with 16A electricity) with a circular access road. A further area is on a terrace just above. A café with light snacks during the week and meals at the weekends is open long hours in high season. It has a terrace that overlooks the lake, which is used for swimming (unsupervised).

Facilities

The main sanitary unit is first class and has automatic toilet seat cleaning. There are cabins as well as vanity style washbasins, large controllable showers, with full curtain, token operated. Further facilities near the reception house showers, WCs, washbasins, and a good unit for disabled visitors. Laundry. Basic motorcaravan services. Café/bar. Reception keeps a few basic supplies. Bicycles to borrow. Free WiFi throughout. Off site: Tennis club. Recreation and play areas. Barbecue area. Restaurant and supermarket 1.5 km.

Open: 1 January - 15 November.

Directions

From the B12 between Lindau and Kempten, exit Isny-Mitte (new road) and follow signs. GPS: 47.67828, 10.03035

Charges guide

Per unit incl. 2 persons (electricity on meter)	€ 23.50 - € 26.00
extra person	€ 6.50
child per year of age	€ 0.40
dog	€ 2.00

Special rates for senior citizens (low season).

Kirchzarten

Camping Kirchzarten

Dietenbacher Strasse 17, D-79199 Kirchzarten (Baden-Württemberg) T: 076 619 040910.

E: info@camping-kirchzarten.de alanrogers.com/DE34400

Set in a green valley among the foothills of the Black Forest, this family managed site is well placed for visiting the popular Titsee, Feldberg and Totdnau areas, and is only 8 km. from Freiburg. It is divided into 486 numbered pitches, 362 of which are for touring, all with electricity (16A Europlug). Most pitches, which are side by side on gently sloping ground, are of reasonable size and clearly marked out, though there is nothing to separate them. There are increasing numbers of hardstanding pitches suitable for motorcaravans. From about late June to mid August, this site becomes very busy, and booking is advised. The fine swimming pool complex adjoining the site is free to campers, with pools for diving, water games, swimming and a separate children's pool, surrounded by sunbathing areas and a play area. It is only a short stroll to the village centre, which has supermarkets, restaurants, etc. Visitors are entitled to a Konus Card, which gives free bus and train travel throughout the Black Forest.

Facilities

The superb main sanitary building includes a large, central section for children, private cabins (some for hire) and a laundry room. The block near reception has been rebuilt to exemplary standards. Cooking stoves. Laundry facilities (all on payment by meter). Motorcaravan services. New bar/restaurant and takeaway. Shop (15/4-31/10). Swimming pool complex (15/5-15/9). Wellness. TV room, play room and youth room. Large playground. Bicycle hire (electric). WiFi over site (charged). Children's activities in season. Off site: Tennis. Adventure playground, fitness track, tennis and minigolf nearby. Riding 2 km. Golf 4 km. Steinwasen Park with zoo and chair lift.

Open: All year.

Directions

From Freiburg take B31 road signed Donaueschingen to Kirchzarten where site is signed (it is south of the village). GPS: 47.96042, 7.95083

Charges guide

Per unit incl. 2 persons	€ 8.40 - € 9.90
extra person	€ 7.70 - € 10.90
child (4-15 yrs)	€ 4.00 - € 5.90
electricity (per kWh)	€ 0.60

Every 15th day free.

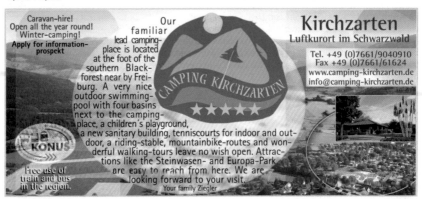

Markdorf

Camping Wirthshof

Steibensteg 12, D-88677 Markdorf (Baden-Württemberg) T: 075 449 6270.

E: info@wirthshof.de alanrogers.com/DE34650

LeadingCampings

Lying 7 km. back from the Bodensee, 12 km. from Friedrichshafen, this friendly site with excellent facilities will be of interest to Britons with young children as well as those seeking a tranquil holiday in a delightful region. The 280 individual touring pitches have electrical connections (6-12A) and are of about 80 sq.m. on well tended flat grass, adjoining access roads. There are 78 larger (120 sq.m) pitches with water, waste water and electricity and 30 hardstandings for motorcaravans. Dogs are only accepted by prior arrangement, on pitches in a reserved area.

Facilities

Three heated toilet blocks provide washbasins in cubicles, a unit for disabled visitors and two bathrooms for children. Cosmetic studio. New beauty spa. Solar heated unit for dishwashing and laundry. Gas supplies. Motorcaravan services. Shop. Restaurant/bar with takeaway. Swimming pool (25x12.5 m; 10/5-10/9). Sports field. Adventure playgrounds. Bicycle and electric bike hire. Minigolf and 'pit-pat' (crazy golf played at table height with billiard cues). Activity programme. Crafts room. WiFi (charged). Dogs are not accepted in July/Aug.

Open: 15 March - 30 October.

Directions

Site is on eastern edge of Markdorf, turn south off B33 Ravensburg road. The site is signed (but not named) from Markdorf, immediately off the main B33. GPS: 47.71459, 9.40924

Charges guide

Per unit incl. 2 persons and electricity	€ 26.00 - € 40.50
extra person	€ 8.00 - € 9.00
child (1-14 yrs)	€ 5.00
dog	€ 3.00

No credit cards.

For latest campsite news, availability and prices visit

alanrogers.com

Münstertal

Campingplatz Münstertal

Dietzelbachstrasse 6, D-79244 Münstertal (Baden-Württemberg) T: 76 367 080.

E: info@camping-muenstertal.de alanrogers.com/DE34500

Münstertal is an impressive site pleasantly situated in a valley on the western edge of the Black Forest. It has been one of the top graded sites in Germany for 25 years, and first time visitors will soon realise why when they see the standard of the facilities here. There are 305 individual pitches in two areas, either side of the entrance road on flat gravel, their size varying from 70-100 sq.m. All have electricity (16A), water, drainage, TV and radio connections. The large indoor pool and the outdoor pool, are both heated and free. The adjacent Health and Fitness Centre offers a range of treatments. Children are very well catered for here with a play area and play equipment, tennis courts, minigolf, a games room with table tennis, table football and a pool table, and fishing. Riding is popular and the site has its own stables. The site organises regular guided walks and cycle rides, plus winter sports and cross-country skiing (there are courses in winter for both children and adults, and ski hire). Visitors wanting a quiet holiday are thoughtfully pitched on one side of the site, whilst more active families and children are pitched nearer the games and sports areas. The site becomes full in season and reservations, especially in July, are necessary.

Facilities

Three toilet blocks are of truly first class quality, with washbasins, all in cabins, showers with full glass dividers, baby bath, a unit for disabled visitors and individual bathrooms, some for hire. Dishwashers in two blocks. Laundry. Drying room. Motorcaravan services. Well stocked shop (all year). Restaurant, particularly good (closed Nov). Heated swimming pools, indoor all year, outdoor (with children's area). New health and fitness centre. Sauna and solarium. Games room. Extensive playing fields. Fishing. Bicycle hire. Tennis courses in summer. Riding. WiFi over site (charged). Konus Card for free bus and train travel. Off site: Village amenities and train station next to site entrance. Golf 15 km. Freiburg and Basel easy driving distances for day trips.

Open: All year.

Directions

Münstertal is south of Freiburg. From A5 autobahn take exit 64, turn southeast via Bad Krozingen and Staufen and continue 5 km. to the start of Münstertal, where site is signed from the main road on the left. GPS: 47.85973, 7.76375

Charges guide

Per unit incl. 2 persons and services	€ 25.00 - € 28.50
extra person	€ 7.10 - € 8.70
child (2-10 yrs)	€ 4.90 - € 5.80
dog	€ 4.00

Maestro cards accepted.

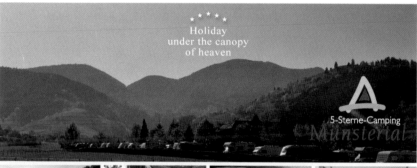

Holiday under the canopy of heaven

5-Sterne-Camping Münstertal

Enjoy our variety and comfort:

★ Sanitary facilities with private bathrooms for rent and facilities for babies and disabled
★ Heated indoor and outdoor pools
★ Wellness oasis with sauna and solarium
★ Gym, water aerobics and spinal gymnastics
★ Grocery store, gas sales
★ Cosy restaurant with garden terrace
★ Horse farm with Iceland horses and ponies
★ Adventure playground with lots of ball courts
★ Tennis court, mini golf
★ Guided mountain bike and hiking tours
★ Rental of bicycles and e-bikes
★ Supply and disposal for motorhomes
★ and much more ...

All pitches have:

★ Connection to water, sewage and electricity
★ TV connection with Sky channels including football
★ Wireless internet access with your own laptop

Since 1983 always top grade

www.camping-muenstertal.de

Telephone +49 (0) 7636 / 70 80
info@camping-muenstertal.de
Dietzelbachstraße 6 | D-79244 Münstertal
2nd campsite past Staufen

Neuenburg

Gugel's Dreiländer Camping

Oberer Wald 3, D-79395 Neuenburg am Rhein (Baden-Württemberg) T: 076 317 719.

E: info@camping-gugel.de alanrogers.com/DE34550

Set in natural heath and woodland, Gugel's is an attractive site with 220 touring pitches, either in small clearings in the trees, in open areas or on a hardstanding section used for overnight stays. All have electricity (10/16A), and 40 also have water, waste water and satellite TV connections. Opposite is a meadow where late arrivals and early departures may spend the night. There may be some road noise near the entrance. The site may become very busy in high season and on bank holidays but you should always find room. The excellent pool and wellness complex add to the attraction of this all year site. There is a social room with satellite TV where guests are welcomed with a glass of wine and a slide presentation of the attractions of the area. The Rhine is within walking distance and there is an extensive programme of activities on offer for all ages. The site is ideally placed not only for enjoying and exploring the south of the Black Forest, but also for night stops when travelling from Frankfurt to Basel on the A5 autobahn. The permanent caravans, set away from the tourist area with their well tended gardens, enhance rather than detract from the natural beauty. A doctor is on call.

Facilities

Three good quality, heated sanitary blocks include some washbasins in cabins. Baby room. Facilities for disabled visitors. Laundry facilities. Motorcaravan services. Shop. Excellent restaurant. Takeaway (weekends and daily in high season). Wellness centre. Indoor/outdoor pool. Community room with TV. Activity programme (high season). Play areas. Boules. Tennis. Fishing. Minigolf. Barbecue. Beach bar. Petting zoo and aviary. Electric go-karts. Bicycle hire. Free WiFi in central area. Off site: Riding 1.5 km. Golf 5 km. Neuenburg, Breisach, Freiburg, Basel and the Black Forest.

Open: All year.

Directions

From autobahn A5 take Neuenburg exit, turn left, then almost immediately left at traffic lights, left at next junction and follow signs for 2 km. to site (called 'Neuenburg' on most signs). GPS: 47.79693, 7.55

Charges guide

Per unit incl. 2 persons	
and electricity	€ 22.50 - € 31.50
extra person	€ 7.00
child (2-15 yrs)	€ 4.00
dog	€ 4.00

Discount every 10th night.

Rheinmunster

Freizeitcenter Oberrhein

D-77836 Rheinmunster (Baden-Württemberg) T: 072 272 500. E: info@freizeitcenter-oberrhein.de

alanrogers.com/DE34200

This large, well equipped holiday site offers a wide range of activities and is also a good base for visiting the Black Forest. Close to reception are a touring area and a section of hardstanding for 12 motorcaravans. The 285 touring pitches (out of 695 pitches overall) all have electricity connections (all 16A Euro sockets), and include 235 with water and drainage, but little shade. Two of the site's lakes are used for swimming, with roped-off areas for toddlers, and non-powered boating. The water was very clean when we visited. The third smaller lake is for fishing.

Facilities

Seven top quality, heated toilet buildings have free hot water and very smart fittings. Some have special rooms for children, babies and families. Family wash cabins to rent. Dog shower. Motorcaravan services. Gas supplies. Shop (1/4-31/10). Two restaurants (one at the lakeside), two snack bars, two beer gardens and a takeaway (1/4-31/10). Play areas. Small aviary. Tennis. Bicycle hire. Minigolf. Windsurf school. Swimming and boating lakes. Fishing (charged). Three small cars for hire (for those with motorcaravans to explore locally). WiFi (charged).

Open: All year.

Directions

Leave A5/E35-52 at exit 51 and travel west towards Iffezheim. Turn south onto B36 passing through Hügelsheim to Stollhoffen where at the roundabout site is signed. GPS: 48.77243, 8.04150

Charges guide

Per unit incl. 2 persons	
and electricity	€ 19.50 - € 31.50
extra person	€ 5.50 - € 9.00
child (2-16 yrs)	€ 2.50 - € 6.00
dog	€ 3.00 - € 5.00

Seelbach

Ferienparadies Schwarzwälder Hof

Tretenhofstrasse 76, D-77960 Seelbach (Baden-Württemberg) T: 078 239 60950. E: info@spacamping.de

alanrogers.com/DE34270

This site lies in a wooded valley, just south of the pleasant village of Seelbach in the Black Forest. The old buildings have been replaced by very attractive ones built in traditional log cabin style, but containing very modern facilities. There are 180 well drained touring pitches, either grass or hardstanding, all with electricity (10A Europlug), water supply and waste water outlet. There is also space for groups in tents. Just by the entrance is the family hotel with a restaurant and wellness centre. Besides a comprehensive general menu, there are also menus for children and older people with smaller appetites.

Facilities

Two excellent sanitary blocks, heated and well maintained, include many washbasins in cabins and free showers. Facilities for wheelchair users. Family rooms. Baby room. Superb children's bathroom. Laundry facilities. Motorcaravan services. Small shop (31/3-9/11). Restaurant, snacks and takeaway. New spa centre and swimming pools (outdoor 12/5-9/9, heated indoor all year). TV and club room. Sauna. Children's club. Riding. Bicycle and electric car hire. WiFi over site (charged). New log chalets for hire.

Open: All year.

Directions

From A5/E35 autobahn, leave at exit 56 (Lahr). Follow L36/L415 road east through Lahr, until turn south to Seelbach. Go through Seelbach and the site is 1 km. south, on the right. GPS: 48.29972, 7.94422

Charges guide

Per unit incl. 2 persons	
and electricity (plus meter)	€ 31.70 - € 35.70
extra person	€ 11.10
child (3-12 yrs)	€ 8.20

No credit cards.

Staufen

Camping Belchenblick

Münstertälerstrasse 43, D-79219 Staufen (Baden-Württemberg) T: 076 337 045.

E: info@camping-belchenblick.de   alanrogers.com/DE34450

This site stands at the gateway, via Münstertal, to the Black Forest. Not very high up itself, it is just at the start of the long road climb which leads to the top of Belchen, one of the highest summits of the forest. The site has plenty of shade for the 230 pitches (182 for touring units), all with electrical connections (10/16A, some 2-pin) and TV (100 also have water). On site is a small heated indoor swimming pool and adjacent is a municipal sports complex, including an outdoor pool and tennis courts. Reservation is necessary from early June to late August at this popular site.

Facilities

Three sanitary blocks are heated and have free hot water, individual washbasins (six in private cabins), plus 21 family cabins with WC, basin and shower (some on payment per night for exclusive use). Washing machine. Gas supplies. Motorcaravan services. Shop (1/3-31/10). Bar (all year). Snacks and takeaway (1/3-31/10). Indoor pool. Sauna and solarium. Tennis. Playground with barbecue area. Table tennis and pool room. Bicycle, fun bike and skate hire. WiFi (charged). Off site: Restaurant nearby.

Open: All year.

Directions

Take autobahn exit for Bad Krozingen, south of Freiburg, and continue to Staufen. Site is southeast of the town and signed, across an unmanned local railway crossing near the entrance. GPS: 47.87178, 7.73667

Charges guide

Per unit incl. 2 persons	
and electricity	€ 24.60 - € 27.60
extra person	€ 6.00 - € 7.50

No credit cards.

Steinach

Camping Kinzigtal

Welschensteinacherstrasse 34, D-77790 Steinach (Baden-Württemberg) T: 078 328 122.

E: webmaster@campingplatz-kinzigtal.de alanrogers.com/DE34310

Campingplatz Kinzigtal is a small, friendly campsite attractively located at the heart of the Black Forest. Pitches here are neat and grassy, and many are pleasantly situated beside a small stream. All are equipped with 16A electrical connections. There is a restaurant with friendly bar, specialising in local cuisine, such as schnitzel and locally caught trout, as well as an impressive range of pizzas and pasta dishes between Easter and September. The site shop sells a good selection of groceries and essentials, including fresh bread and local wines. Access to the adjacent swimming pool is free for campers.

Facilities

Restaurant. Bar. Shop. Takeaway. Games room. Fishing (charge made). Playground. Activity programme in season. Off site: Bus service 400 m. Trains 800 m. Swimming pool complex. Tennis. Volleyball. Riding. Cycle and walking tracks. Steinach 2 km. Haslach 5 km.

Open: All year.

Directions

The site is close to Steinach, south of Offenburg. From Offenburg take southbound B33 as far as Steinach, and then follow signs to the site. GPS: 48.295564, 8.047968

Charges guide

Per unit incl. 2 persons and electricity	€ 22.05 - € 24.05
extra person	€ 7.00 - € 7.50

Sulzburg

Terrassen-Camping Alte Sägemühle

Badstrasse 57, D-79295 Sulzburg (Baden-Württemberg) T: 076 345 51181.

E: info@camping-alte-saegemuehle.de alanrogers.com/DE34520

This site lies just beyond the beautiful old town of Sulzburg with its narrow streets, and is on a peaceful road leading only to a natural swimming pool (formerly the mill pond) and a small hotel. It is set in a tree-covered valley with a stream running through the centre and is divided into terraced areas, each enclosed by high hedges and trees. Electrical connections (16A) are available on 42 of the 45 large touring pitches (long leads may be necessary). The site has been kept as natural as possible and is perfect for those seeking peace and quiet.

Facilities

In the main building, facilities are of good quality with two private cabins, separate toilets, washing machine and dryer. Small shop for basics, beer and local wines. Torch may be useful. Motorcaravan service point. New room for tent guests. Free bus and train travel in the Black Forest for guests. Off site: Natural, unheated swimming pool adjacent (June-Aug) with discount to campers. Bicycle hire, restaurants and other shops in Sulzburg 1.5 km. Riding 3 km. Fishing 8 km. Golf 12 km.

Open: All year.

Directions

Site is easily reached from autobahn A5/E35. Take exit 64 for Bad Krozingen, south of Freiburg, onto B3 south to Heitersheim, then through Sulzburg, or if coming from south, exit 65 through Müllheim, Heitersheim and Sulzburg. Reception is to left of road. Note: arch in Sulzburg has only 3.1 m. height clearance. GPS: 47.83548, 7.72337

Charges guide

Per unit incl. 2 persons and electricity (plus meter)	€ 19.50 - € 22.50
extra person	€ 7.00

Tengen

Hegau Familien Camping

An der Sonnenhalde 1, D-78250 Tengen (Baden-Württemberg) T: 077 369 2470. E: info@hegau-camping.de

alanrogers.com/DE34900

Located in the sunny southwest corner of Germany, this site, new in 2003, must be one of the best we have seen. It is ultra modern in design and exceptionally high standards are maintained. Located in meadowland in a quiet rural valley close to the Swiss border, it provides excellent opportunities for walking, cycling and sightseeing. All 170 touring pitches have electricity (16A), water and drainage points. The pitches are grassy and level and of a good size. In the lower part of the site is an excellent indoor heated swimming pool with a children's pool, a whirlpool, a jacuzzi, a sauna and Turkish bath. A new giant indoor play room has recently been added.

Facilities

New heated sanitary facilities include private cabins, showers, facilities for disabled visitors and for children. Three family shower rooms for rent (two also have a bath). Laundry facilities. Motorcaravan services. Good value restaurant, small shop and bar (all season). Indoor swimming pool (all season), sauna and Turkish bath (charged). Three games rooms with TV and computer. Play areas. New indoor play room. Crazy golf. Communal barbecue pit. Beach volleyball court. Free WiFi over site. Bicycle hire. Car hire. Off site: Supermarket less than 1 km. Riding 10 km. Golf 20 km. Fishing 35 km.

Open: 20 March - 1 November.

Directions

From A81 take exit 42 on to B314. At roundabout in Tengen follow international camping signs. Turn right at supermarket on edge of village. From Kommingen follow camp signs turning left towards site at supermarket on edge of village. GPS: 47.8244, 8.65323

Charges guide

Per unit incl. 2 persons	€ 38.80
extra person	€ 9.90
child (4-14 yrs)	€ 6.30
electricity (per kWh)	€ 0.52

For latest campsite news, availability and prices visit

alanrogers.com

Titisee

Camping Bankenhof

Bruderhalde 31a, D-79822 Titisee (Baden-Württemberg) T: 076 521 351. E: info@camping-bankenhof.de
alanrogers.com/DE34360

This peacefully located, fairly informal woodland site, with a friendly atmosphere, is situated just beyond the western end of Lake Titisee. The 180 pitches are on sparse grass and gravel, with some shade from a variety of trees, and 30 are occupied by seasonal units. The site is generally level, although there is a separate grassy area for tents which does have a slight slope. Most pitches have electric hook-ups (16A), with gravel roads, and water taps for each area. Recent work has greatly improved the pitch layout. Although there is some site lighting a torch might be useful for the darker areas under the trees.

Facilities

Two sets of quality sanitary facilities plus three family bath/shower rooms for rent. Well equipped and heated, they include controllable hot showers and some washbasins in cubicles. Separate facilities for disabled campers, and a unit for children (under 10 yrs). Kitchen (on payment). Laundry. Motorcaravan services. Shop. Bar. Restaurant. Wellness suite. TV and cinema room. Adventure play area. Fishing. Bicycle, go-kart and buggy hire. WiFi (charged). Off site: Free bus service 300 m. Golf, riding and boat launching within 3 km.

Open: All year.

Directions

From Freiburg take road B31 east to Titisee. Pass through the town centre and continue for 2.5 km. following camping signs. The entrance to Bankenhof is on the left. GPS: 47.88598, 8.13070

Charges guide

Per unit incl. 2 persons	€ 24.00 - € 29.50
extra person	€ 8.50 - € 10.00
child (3-15 yrs)	€ 3.50 - € 4.80
electricity (per kWh)	€ 0.50
dog	€ 2.80

Todtnau

Camping Hochschwarzwald

Oberhäuserstrasse 6, D-79674 Todtnau-Muggenbrunn (Baden-Württemberg) T: 076 711 288.
E: infor@camping-hochschwarzwald.de alanrogers.com/DE34370

Hochschwarzwald is a small, peaceful, rustic site in an attractive wooded valley 3,400 feet up in the Black Forest. Of 85 marked pitches (some with shade), 50 are for tourers (all with 10A electricity) on level terraces of grass and gravel. There is an area at the entrance for overnight stays in high season. This is an extremely popular area, with many summer visitors enjoying walking and cycling, but it is also ideal for winter stays, with skiing from the site. At the back of the site, as well as being able to walk in the woods, you can paddle in a flat area of the stream, which tumbles down the hill.

Facilities

The modern, heated sanitary building has good facilities with a few private cabins, a family room and a unit for disabled campers. Washing machine and dryer. Restaurant/bar (closed Mon). Bicycle, motorbike and ski washing facilities. Konus Card with free bus and train travel. Off site: Walking and skiing directly from the site. Bus to Freiburg 50 m. Heated indoor pool, tennis court and ski school in Muggenbrunn. Todtnau waterfalls 3 km. Bicycle hire 5 km. Fishing 6 km. Riding 12 km.

Open: All year.

Directions

Site is 1 km. beyond Muggenbrunn on the road from Todtnau towards Freiburg. GPS: 47.86557, 7.91617

Charges guide

Per unit incl. 2 persons and electricity (plus meter)	€ 22.40 - € 24.80
extra person	€ 5.60 - € 6.10
child (3-12 yrs)	€ 3.20 - € 3.70
electricity (per kWh)	€ 0.50
No credit cards.	

Erlangen

Camping Rangau

Campingstrasse 44, D-91056 Erlangen-Dechsendorf (Bavaria (N)) T: 091 358 866.
E: infos@camping-rangau.de alanrogers.com/DE36050

This pleasant site makes a convenient stopover and is quickly and easily reached from either the A3 Würzburg-Nürnberg or the A73 Bamberg-Nürnberg autobahns. It has 110 pitches on flat ground which are mainly for touring units. All are numbered and partly marked but mainly between 50-70 sq.m. so it can look very cramped when busy. There are also 60 permanent units. There is usually space available, but in peak season overnight visitors can often be put on the adjacent football pitch. A large lake with access from the site through a gate, can be used for sailing or windsurfing and boats are available to hire. There is no fishing at present.

Facilities

A well maintained sanitary block, heated when cold, has well spaced washbasins (some cabins for ladies) and showers. Good facilities for disabled visitors. A new facility provides washbasins in cabins and WCs. Laundry facilities. Gas supplies. Purpose-built dog shower. Motorcaravan services. Pleasant restaurant with terrace for meals or drinks. Order bread from reception. Playground. Club/TV room Off site: Swimming 200 m. Erlangen centre 5 km.

Open: 1 April - 30 September.

Directions

Take exit for Erlangen-West from A3 autobahn, turn towards Erlangen but after less than 1 km. at Dechsendorf turn left and follow signs to site. GPS: 49.62690, 10.94100

Charges guide

Per unit incl. 2 persons and electricity	€ 19.50 - € 20.50
extra person	€ 5.50
child (6-12 yrs)	€ 3.50
dog	€ 3.00

FREE Alan Rogers Travel Card
Extra benefits and savings - see page 14

Gemünden

Spessart-Camping Schönrain

Schönrainstrasse 4-18, D-97737 Gemünden-Hofstetten (Bavaria (N)) T: 093 518 645.

E: info@spessart-camping.de alanrogers.com/DE37350

Situated 4 km. west of the town of Gemünden, with views of forested hills bordering the Main river, this is a very friendly, well organised, family run site, with excellent facilities. Frau Endres welcomes British guests and speaks a little English. There are 100 pitches, 70 of which are for touring. They vary in size (70-150 sq.m) and all have 10A electricity, 20 also with water. Another area has been developed for tents. The site has a pleasant bar with a terrace. Meals can be ordered from local restaurants for delivery or the site's bus will provide transport. The site shop sells necessities, plus local schnapps and wine.

Facilities
A superb new heated sanitary building has card-operated entry – the card is prepaid and operates the showers, washing machines and dryers, gas cooker, baby bathroom, jacuzzi etc. Two private bathrooms for rent. Motorcaravan services. Bar. Shop. Swimming pool. Beauty and wellness programme. General room with play area for very young children, games and a TV. Upstairs library and Internet café, fitness room and solarium. Playground. Bicycle hire. Excursions. Off site: Bus service 200 m. Fishing 400 m. Canoeing 10 km. Riding 12 km.

Open: 1 April - 5 October.

Directions
From Frankfurt-Würzburg autobahn, take exit for Weibersbrunn-Lohr and then B26 to Gemünden. Turn over Main river bridge to Hofstetten and follow official town camping signs. From Kassel-Wurzburg autobahn, leave at Hammelburg and take B27 to Gemünden, and as above. GPS: 50.05144, 9.65684

Charges guide
Per unit incl. 2 persons and electricity (plus meter)	€ 23.85 - € 28.65
extra person	€ 6.80
child (under 14 yrs)	€ 4.20

Issigau

Camping Schloss Issigau

Schloss Issigau, altes Schloss 3, D-95188 Issigau (Bavaria (N)) T: 092 937 173. E: info@schloss-issigau.de

alanrogers.com/DE37500

This family run site is small, attractive and well organised. On the left of the entrance courtyard, the small Schloss (c.1398) houses reception, a display of armour, a comfortable breakfast room and a restaurant serving regional and international dishes. Homemade cakes and drinks are served on the small terrace in front of the Schloss. There are 40 level pitches, all with 16A electricity and five with fresh water and drainage. They are on grass with some terracing, and in places trees offer some shade. To the rear of the site, beside a pond, is a large grass sloping area for tents.

Facilities
Modern and heated sanitary facilities are housed in a renovated old building. Showers are controllable and free, some washbasins are in cabins. Bathroom for rent. Laundry facilities. Baby room. Kitchen. The building also houses a games room and upstairs, a sauna, solarium, fitness studio, children's play room and a reading room. Café/bar and restaurant (breakfast served). Bicycle hire. Playground. Hotel accommodation. Off site: Small supermarket 300 m. Riding 1.5 km. Fishing 6 km.

Open: 15 March - 31 October, 20 December - 9 January.

Directions
The village of Issigau is between Holle and Berg. 6 km from A9 (Berlin-Nuremberg) take exit 31 Berg/Bad Steben. Turn left and follow signs for Berg and then continue straight on towards Holle. Site is signed in Issigau. Go down a small slope and to the right. GPS: 50.37418, 11.72122

Charges guide
Per unit incl. 2 persons and electricity (plus meter)	€ 18.50 - € 19.50
extra person	€ 5.50

Nürnberg

Knaus Campingpark Nürnberg

Hans Kalb Strasse 56, D-90471 Nürnberg (Bavaria (N)) T: 091 198 12717. E: nuernberg@knauscamp.de

alanrogers.com/DE36100

This is an ideal site for visiting the fascinating and historically important city of Nürnberg (Nuremberg). There are 140 shaded pitches, 118 with 10A electrical connections and with water taps in groups. On mainly flat grass among the tall trees, some pitches are marked out with ranch-style boards, others still attractively 'wild', some others with hardstanding. There is sufficient space for them to be quite big and many have the advantage of being drive through. When there is an event at the Stadion there is a lot of noise and road diversions are in place. It is well worth checking before planning an arrival.

Facilities
A brand new heated sanitary building offers first class facilities including free showers. Laundry facilities. Cooking facilities. Unit for disabled visitors. Gas supplies. Shop. Motorcaravan services. Bar/bistro area with terrace and light meals served. Play area in woodland. Off site: Swimming pool (free entry for campers) and football stadium 200 m. Boat launching and bicycle hire 2 km. City centre 4 km. (a 20 minute walk following signs takes you to the underground station).

Open: All year.

Directions
Site is 4 km. southeast of the city centre. From A9 (München-Bayreuth) east of Nürnberg, take exit 52 (Nürnberg-Fischbach). Proceed 5 km. on dual carriageway towards city turning left at first traffic lights (Burger King) under two bridges and follow road around to left and site. GPS: 49.42318, 11.12154

Charges guide
Per unit incl. 2 persons and electricity	€ 28.50 - € 32.40
extra person	€ 7.00 - € 7.70

For latest campsite news, availability and prices visit

alanrogers.com

Sommerach am Main

Camping Katzenkopf

Am See, D-97334 Sommerach am Main (Bavaria (N)) T: 093 819 215.

alanrogers.com/DE37390

Katzenkopf is quietly and attractively located in a nature protected area on the banks of the River Main and only a short walk from the small, well known wine village of Sommerach. This is an excellent family run site with 142 touring pitches, and a quick-stop area near the site entrance. The level, grass pitches are shaded, all have 16A electricity, and 29 are fully serviced; there is no extra charge for those directly bordering the river. Two protected areas of water are suitable for swimming and boating, and a sandy bay is popular for sand castle building or lazing around in what is claimed to be Germany's driest region.

Facilities

Excellent, modern toilet blocks include private cabins, free showers and facilities for disabled campers and children. Laundry facilities. Motorcaravan services. Shop selling fresh rolls, restaurant, bar and takeaway (all open all season). Fishing. Boat launching. Sailing. Bicycle hire. Dogs accepted in part of the site only. Off site: Sailing. Shops and vineyards.

Open: 28 March - 27 October.

Directions

From the A3 take Kitzingen exit and turn towards Schweinfurt. After 4 km. turn right towards Sommerach. Just before the village turn left and site is well signed. GPS: 49.82585, 10.20556

Charges guide

Per unit incl. 2 persons and electricity	€ 20.80 - € 21.60
extra person	€ 6.20

No credit cards.

Stadtsteinach

Camping Stadtsteinach

Badstrasse 5, D-95346 Stadtsteinach (Bavaria (N)) T: 092 258 00394. E: info@camping-stadtsteinach.de

alanrogers.com/DE36150

Stadtsteinach is well placed for exploring this region with its interesting towns, forest walks and the Fichtel Mountains nearby and this is a comfortable base. Occupying a quiet position in gently undulating countryside with tree-clad hills rising to the east, there are 80 static caravans and space for 100 touring units. Brick main roads give way to hard access roads with pitches on either side, all of which have 16A electricity. The site is on a gentle slope, pitches having been terraced where necessary and there are some hardstandings for motorcaravans. High hedges and trees separate pitches or groups of pitches in some areas giving the effect of camping in small clearings.

Facilities

The sanitary area is part of the administration and restaurant building, heated and of good quality. It has free hot water and some washbasins in cabins. Facilities for disabled visitors. Motorcaravan services. Cooking rings (on payment). Laundry facilities. Gas supplies. Restaurant. Bread and papers from reception. Solar heated swimming pool near the entrance is free to campers (high season). Play area. Tennis. TV. Bicycle hire. Off site: Shops 800 m.

Open: 1 March - 30 November.

Directions

Stadtsteinach is 22 km. north of Bayreuth. Take exit 39 from the A9/E51 Nürnberg-Berlin autobahn and travel north on road 303 to Stadtsteinach. Site is well signed. GPS: 50.16126, 11.51527

Charges guide

Per unit incl. 2 persons and electricity	€ 18.00 - € 21.10
extra person	€ 5.20 - € 5.70

No credit cards.

Aitrang

Camping Elbsee

Am Elbsee 3, D-87648 Aitrang (Bavaria (S)) T: 083 432 48. E: camping@elbsee.de

alanrogers.com/DE36720

This site is attractively situated in the foothills of the Alps on land sloping down to a lake with a backdrop of mountains. Together with its associated hotel, it has been developed into a first class, family run site with good, modern facilities. All of the 120 touring pitches have 16A electricity and fresh and waste water connections. The grass and gravel pitches are level, some are on terraces and some are shaded by trees. A range of interesting activities are provided, particularly for children, including painting, pony riding and entertainment programmes in summer. Next to the site is a municipal supervised lake bathing area with a kiosk selling drinks and snacks, a playground and an indoor play area.

Facilities

Two well appointed, well maintained, heated sanitary blocks include free showers, washbasins all in cabins, a children's bathroom area and family bathrooms to rent. Facilities for disabled visitors. Dog shower. Motorcaravan services. Shop (order bread for following day). New playground, indoor play area and activity rooms. TV, games and meeting rooms. Sports field. Fishing. Bicycle hire. Riding. Boat launching. Activity programme (20/7-31/8). WiFi over site (charged). Off site: At hotel: a very good restaurant, takeaway and bar. Shop 2 km.

Open: All year.

Directions

Site is 36 km. NNW of Füssen. From centre of Marktoberdorf, take minor road northwest to Ruderatshofen and from there minor road west (Aitrang/Elbsee). Just south of Aitrang, site signed to south of road. The road to site (2 km) is winding and narrow in places. GPS: 47.80277, 10.55343

Charges guide

Per unit incl. 2 persons incl. electricity (plus meter)	€ 20.00 - € 28.80
extra person	€ 6.60 - € 8.00
child (4-15 yrs)	€ 3.50 - € 4.30

FREE Alan Rogers Travel Card
Extra benefits and savings - see page 14

Augsburg

Lech Camping

Seeweg 6, D-86444 Affing-Mühlhausen bei Augsburg (Bavaria (S)) T: 082 072 200.

E: info@lech-camping.de alanrogers.com/DE36420

Situated just north of Augsburg, this beautifully run site is a pleasure to stay on. Gabi Ryssel, the owner, spends her long days working very hard to cater for every wish of her guests – from the moment you arrive and are given the key to one of the cleanest toilet blocks we have seen, and plenty of tourist information, you are in very capable hands. The 50 level, grass and gravel pitches are roomy and have shade from pine trees. Electricity connections are available (10/16A Europlug). This is an immaculate site with a separate area for disabled visitors to park near the special facilities provided.

Facilities

The new toilet block (cleaned several times daily) includes good showers with seating area and non-slip flooring. Baby room. Separate family bathroom for rent. Five star facilities for disabled visitors. Motorcaravan services. Laundry facilities. Small shop, restaurant/bar/takeaway. Small playground (partially fenced). Bicycle hire. Free WiFi. Trampolines. Pedal boats and rowing boats (free). Communal barbecue area. Off site: Football field 300 m. Bus to city. Fishing 4 km. Golf 10 km. Riding 15 km.

Open: 1 April - 30 September.

Directions

Site is 8 km. NNE of Augsburg at the border of Mühlhausen. Leave E52/A8 (Munich-Stuttgart) at exit 73 and follow signs to Neuburg/Pöttmes. After 3 km. (pass airport on right) on U49 you will see the Mühlhausen sign. Lech Camping is on right. GPS: 48.43759, 10.92937

Charges guide

Per unit incl. 2 persons and electricity	€ 28.50 - € 33.50
extra person	€ 6.50 - € 8.00

Bad Birnbach

Kur-Gutshof-Camping Arterhof

Hauptstrasse 3, Lengham, D-84364 Bad Birnbach (Bavaria (S)) T: 085 639 6130. E: info@arterhof.de

alanrogers.com/DE36960

Based around a Bavarian farmstead, Arterhof is an excellent site combining the charm of the old together with the comfort of the new. An attractive courtyard at the front of the site houses reception, a farm shop and a café with a flower decked terrace. To the rear is a tropical indoor pool containing soft water at a comfortable 30°C as well as a sauna, solarium, fitness room and much more. The 190 touring pitches with some hedge separation, on grass or pebble standing, all have TV, electricity, fresh and waste water connections, and 12 have their own pitch-side sanitary facilities. For winter camping, 50 of the pitches have a gas supply. Opposite the site entrance is Inattura, a spacious flower-filled meadow with a large, natural pool, scented garden and lots of lawn; ideal for quiet relaxation and sunbathing in the open Bavarian countryside. This is very much a site with facilities for those who feel they have earned a well deserved break. There are numerous fitness programmes to cure one's present aches and pains, as well as preventative programmes. With ample provision for children, both outdoor and traditional indoor restaurants, this is a site to suit the whole family.

Facilities

Modern, attractive, well maintained sanitary blocks with heated floor, free showers, washbasins in cabins, hairdryers and bathrooms to rent. Hairdressing salon, cosmetic studio. Laundry facilities. Motorcaravan services. Swimming pools. Wellness centre. Traditional restaurant serving southern Bavarian dishes with meat from the farm's own Aberdeen Angus cattle. Play area. Live music Fridays. WiFi. Off site: Rottal Thermal baths in Bad Birnbach (free bus from site). Cycle and mountain bike tracks. Nordic walking. Golf.

Open: All year.

Directions

Site is 12 km. east of Pfarrkirchen. Leave autobahn 3 at exit 106 and head south on B20 to Eggenfelden then east on B20 past Pfarrkirchen to Bad Birnbach where site is signed to the right opposite supermarket. GPS: 48.435176, 13.109415

Charges guide

Per unit incl. 2 persons and electricity (plus meter)	€ 29.30 - € 33.30
extra person	€ 7.70
child (2-13 yrs)	€ 4.80
with own sanitary unit	€ 43.30

For latest campsite news, availability and prices visit

alanrogers.com

Bad Griesbach

Kur & Feriencamping Dreiquellenbad

Singham 40, D-94086 Bad Griesbach (Bavaria (S)) T: 085 329 6130.

E: info@camping-bad-griesbach.de alanrogers.com/DE36970

LeadingCampings

This excellent site is part of a wellness, health and beauty spa complex where camping guests have free use of the indoor and outdoor thermal pools, sauna, Turkish bath and jacuzzi. A large selection of treatments are also available (on payment) and the complex has its own doctor. The site has 200 pitches, all with fresh and waste water, electricity and TV connections. In addition, there is a new camping car area (29 units) with its own service point. This is a site where visitors should take full advantage of the facilities, and plenty of information is available at the helpful English-speaking reception. The location of the site enables you to combine a relaxing holiday with interesting sightseeing. Regensburg, Munich, Linz and Salzburg are all within easy reach, as is Passau, which dates from Roman times and is where three rivers join to become the Danube, flowing on to the Black Sea. Passau with its cathedral, old town and the peninsula where the Danube and Inn merge are well worth visiting. Adjoining the site is Europe's largest golf centre and within walking distance are the spa facilities of Bad Griesbach. A member of Leading Campings Group.

Facilities

Excellent sanitary facilities include private cabins and free showers, facilities for disabled visitors, special child facilities and a dog shower. Two private bathrooms for rent. Laundry facilities. Bar/restaurant. Motorcaravan services. Shop. Gym. Luxury leisure complex (heated outdoor pool 1/3-15/11, indoor pool and wellness all year). Play area. Bicycle hire. Fishing. Internet. WiFi. No charcoal barbecues. Off site: Riding. Fishing.

Open: All year.

Directions

Site is 25 km. southwest of Passau. From A3 take exit 118 and follow signs for Pocking. After 2 km. turn right on B388. Site is in the hamlet of Singham. Turn right into Karpfhan then left towards site. GPS: 48.42001, 13.19261

Charges guide

Per unit incl. 2 persons and electricity	€ 26.10 - € 31.20
extra person	€ 8.40
child (0-14 yrs)	€ 5.40

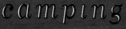

Berchtesgaden

Camping Allweglehen

Allweggasse 4, D-83471 Berchtesgaden (Bavaria (S)) T: 086 522 396. E: urlaub@allweglehen.de

alanrogers.com/DE36850

This spacious and well maintained all-year site occupies a hillside position, with spectacular mountain views. The site access road is steep in places (14%) with a sharp, steep bend about halfway up, but the proprietor will use his tractor to tow caravans if requested, especially during snowy weather. There are 130 pitches (122 for touring), all arranged on a series of level, gravel terraces, separated by hedges or fir trees and all with good views and electrical connections (16A). There is a separate area on a sloping meadow for tents. The pleasant, traditional restaurant, with terrace, offers Bavarian specialities at reasonable prices throughout the year. This is a useful base for sightseeing, relaxing or for a winter break.

Facilities

Two adjacent older style toilet blocks near the restaurant (heated in winter). A new, luxury block provides modern facilities. Bathroom. Baby room. Washing machines, dryers and iron. Motorcaravan services. Gas supplies. Restaurant/bar/takeaway. Small shop for essentials. Play area. Small heated pool. Solarium. Minigolf. Fishing. Excursions in high season. WiFi (charged). Off site: Winter sports nearby. Walks. Fishing 1 km. Riding 2 km. Bicycle hire 3 km. Golf 5 km.

Open: All year.

Directions

Site is 4 km. northeast of Berchtesgaden. Easiest access is via Austrian autobahn A10 (vignette), Salzburg Sud and follow B160 towards Berchtesgaden for 4 km. (becomes B305). Site is on left after a further 8 km. Alternatively take B305 from Ruhpolding (winding and with 4 m. height limit). GPS: 47.64489, 13.05086

Charges guide

Per unit incl. 2 persons	€ 23.95 - € 33.55
extra person	€ 7.05 - € 8.85
electricity (per kWh)	€ 0.65

Eggelstetten
Camping Donau-Lech

Campingweg 1, D-86698 Eggelstetten (Bavaria (S)) T: 090 904 046. E: info@donau-lech-camping.de

alanrogers.com/DE36300

The Haas family have developed this friendly site just off the attractive Romantische Strasse very well and run it very much as a family site, providing a useful information sheet in English for their guests. The lake provides swimming and wildlife for children and adults to enjoy. Alongside it are 50 marked touring pitches with 16A electrical connections, on flat grass arranged in rows either side of a tarmac access road. With an average of 120 sq.m. per unit, it is a comfortable site with an open feeling and developing shade. There are three flat, grass areas with unmarked pitches by the entrance, for visitors with tents.

Facilities
All amenities are housed in the main building at the entrance with reception. Sanitary facilities are downstairs with free showers and washbasins (no cabins), all of a good standard. Sauna. Washing machine and dryer. Motorcaravan services. Bar area with terrace. Small shop for basics, bread to order (1/4-31/10). General room. Youth room. Play area. Lake for swimming (at own risk). Free WiFi. Off site: Golf 300 m. Fishing 3 km.

Open: All year.

Directions
Turn off main B2 road 5 km. south of Donauwörth (site signed) at signs for Asbach, Bäumenheim Nord towards Eggelstetten, then follow signs for over 1 km. to site. GPS: 48.67590, 10.84083

Charges guide
Per unit incl. 2 persons and electricity	€ 23.00
extra person	€ 6.50
child (2-15 yrs)	€ 3.00
dog	€ 2.20

Füssen im Allgäu
Camping Hopfensee

Fischerbichl 17, D-87629 Füssen im Allgäu (Bavaria (S)) T: 083 629 17710.

E: info@camping-hopfensee.de alanrogers.com/DE36700

LeadingCampings

This exceptional, family run site is situated beside a lake in the beautiful Bavarian Alps, not far from the fairytale castle of Neuschwanstein. Although one can appreciate the mountain scenery from the 376 level, fully serviced pitches, it is more comfortably viewed whilst swimming in the 31°C swimming pool on the first floor of the wellness complex. The wellness complex, which offers a full spa programme and excellent sanitary facilities, is arranged around a large courtyard adorned with cascading flowers in summer. The site has an excellent restaurant and bar with views over the lake. A member of Leading Campings Group.

Facilities
The excellent heated sanitary facilities provide free hot water in washbasins (some in cabins) and large showers. Separate babies' and children's washrooms. Private units for rent. Motorcaravan services. Takeaway. Shop. Supervised courses of water treatments, aromatherapy, massage, etc. Sauna, solarium and steam bath. Playground and kindergarten. Pavilion for children (up to 6 yrs old, accompanied by adult) and meeting room for teenagers. Large games room. Bicycle hire. Tennis. Fishing. Ski safari in winter. Small golf academy and discounts for two local courses. No tents taken.

Open: 16 December - 4 November.

Directions
Site is 4 km. north of Füssen. Turn off the B16 to Hopfen and site is on the left through a car park. If approaching from the west on B310, turn towards Füssen at T-junction with the B16 and immediately right again for the road to Hopfen. GPS: 47.60572, 10.68052

Charges guide
Per unit incl. 2 persons and electricity (plus meter)	€ 30.65 - € 34.50
extra person	€ 8.85 - € 10.10

No credit cards.

Irring bei Passau
Dreiflüsse Camping

Am Sonnenhang 8, Donautat, D-94113 Irring bei Passau (Bavaria (S)) T: 085 466 33.

E: dreifluessecamping@t-online.de alanrogers.com/DE36950

Although the site overlooks the Danube, it is in fact some 9 km. from the confluence of the Danube, Inn and Ilz. Dreiflüsse Camping occupies a hillside position, well above high water level, to the west of Passau with pitches, flat or with a little slope, on several rows of terraces. The 180 places for touring units are not all numbered or marked, although 16A electricity connection boxes determine where units pitch, and half have water and drainage. Trees and low banks separate the terraces which are of gravel with a thin covering of grass. There is some road and rail noise (24 hrs).

Facilities
The sanitary facilities are acceptable, if a little old, with two private cabins for women, one for men. Laundry. Motorcaravan services. Gas supplies. Shop. Modern Gasthof restaurant with terrace at site entrance, where the reception, shop and sanitary buildings are also located. Small heated indoor swimming pool (1/5-15/9; charged). Play area. Bicycle hire. Aquakur wellness centre. Off site: Bus service for Passau from outside site, or from Schalding 1.5 km. Riding 3 km. Passau 9 km. Golf 10 km.

Open: 1 April - 31 October.

Directions
Site is 9 km. northwest of Passau. From autobahn A3, take exit 115 (Passau-Nord) from where site is signed. Follow signs from Passau on road to west of city and north bank of Danube towards Windorf and Irring. GPS: 48.60647, 13.34602

Charges guide
Per unit incl. 2 persons and electricity	€ 25.00
extra person	€ 5.50
child (4-14 yrs)	€ 4.00

No credit cards.

For latest campsite news, availability and prices visit

alanrogers.com

Kipfenberg

Azur Camping Altmühltal

Campingstrasse 1, D-85110 Kipfenberg (Bavaria (S)) T: 084 659 05167. E: kipfenberg@azur-camping.de

alanrogers.com/DE36320

In the beautiful Altmühltal river valley, this Azur site is in pretty woodland, with lots of shade for much of it. On flat grassland with direct access to the river, one looks from the entrance across to the old Schloss on the hill. Outside the main entrance is a large, flat, grass/gravel field for 60 overnight tourers (with electricity). The main site has 277 pitches, of which 178 are for touring, plus two small areas for tents and one large one. Ranging in size up to 90 sq.m. they are generally in small groups marked by trees or bushes. This friendly, well run site is a popular base for walking, cycling, fishing and watersports.

Facilities

The main sanitary facilities are good, with free hot water (no private cabins), baby room, unit for disabled visitors. Launderette. Kitchen. These facilities are mostly duplicated in prefabricated units at the other end of the site (toilets only in low season). Motorcaravan services. Shop combined with reception and vending machine for drinks. Beer garden with campfire and serving snacks in July/Aug. Play area. Fishing. WiFi. Off site: Supermarket 100 m. Outdoor pool 200 m. Restaurants within 300 m.

Open: 1 April - 31 October.

Directions

From the A9/E45 (Munich-Nürnberg), take exit 59 Denkendorf or 58 Eichstätt and follow the signs to Kipfenberg. Site is signed in Kipfenberg and is opposite a supermarket. GPS: 48.94840, 11.38933

Charges guide

Per unit incl. 2 persons	
and electricity	€ 22.30 - € 28.80
extra person	€ 6.50 - € 8.50
child (2-12 yrs)	€ 3.00 - € 4.50
dog	€ 3.50

Krün-Obb

Alpen-Caravanpark Tennsee

Am Tennsee 1, D-82494 Krün-Obb (Bavaria (S)) T: 088 251 70. E: info@camping-tennsee.de

alanrogers.com/DE36800

Tennsee is an excellent, friendly site in truly beautiful surroundings high up (1,000 m) in the Karwendel Alps with super mountain views, and close to many famous places of which Innsbruck (44 km) and Oberammergau (26 km) are two. Mountain walks are plentiful, with several lifts close by. It is an attractive site with good facilities including 164 serviced pitches with individual connections for electricity (up to 16A and two connections), gas, TV, radio, telephone, water and waste water. The other 80 pitches all have electricity and some of these are available for overnight guests at a reduced rate.

Facilities

The first class toilet block has underfloor heating, washbasins in cabins and private units with WC, shower, basin and bidet for rent. Unit for disabled guests. Baby bath, dog bathroom and a heated room for ski equipment. Laundry facilities. Gas supplies. Motorcaravan services. Cooking facilities. Shop. Restaurants (waiter, self-service and takeaway). Bar. Youth room. Solarium. Bicycle hire. Playground. WiFi (charged). Organised activities and excursions. Bus service to ski slopes in winter. Off site: Fishing 400 m. Riding and golf 3 km.

Open: All year excl. 6 November - 15 December.

Directions

Site is just off the main Garmisch-Partenkirchen-Innsbruck road no. 2 between Klais and Krün, 15 km. from Garmisch watch for small sign Tennsee and Barmsee and turn right there for site. GPS: 47.49066, 11.25396

Charges guide

Per unit incl. 2 persons	
and electricity	€ 27.20 - € 30.20
extra person	€ 7.50 - € 8.00
child (6-16 yrs)	€ 3.00 - € 4.00
electricity (per kWh)	€ 0.75
dog	€ 3.40

Lechbruck am See

Via Claudia Camping

Via Claudia 6, D-86983 Lechbruck am See (Bavaria (S)) T: 08862 8426. E: info@camping-lechbruck.de

alanrogers.com/DE36170

Situated between lakes and mountains, Via Claudia lies on the banks of Lech Lake and is just a few minutes walk to a second smaller lake belonging to the site, Baderwäldle Lake, which is ideal for swimming with its pleasant warm moor water. As the campsite name suggests, Via Claudia Camping is on the ancient roman road which passes through the Alps, linking the Adriatic Sea with the River Danube. The site offers lodges, Finnish wooden huts, odd pods, vats and caravans for rent. A motorcaravan area (60 pitches) with full services is also open throughout the year.

Facilities

Three sanitary buildings including facilities for disabled visitors and children. Extra bathroom for dogs. Cooking facilities. First aid room. Restaurant (27/3-7/11) and takeaway (opening times vary according to season) with summer beer garden. Shop. Large playground. Book and game rentals. Teenager's area. Beach volleyball. Bavarian curling. Cooking classes. Entertainment (high season). WiFi throughout (charged). Off site: Bicycle hire 1 km. Golf and riding 3 km. Skiing 12 km. Rafting tours. Oberammergau. Linderhof Palace and Park.

Open: All year.

Directions

Site is 21 km. from Füssen, north on B16 for 11 km. then right toward Steingaden/Lechbruck and shortly right onto St2059 for 6.7 km, left onto Flößerstraße, continue onto Schongauer Straße, turn right onto Lechwiesenstraße, slight right onto Via Claudia, keep right to stay on Via Claudia to site. GPS: 47.71169, 10.81872

Charges guide

Per unit incl. 2 persons	
and electricity	€ 25.05 - € 28.05

No credit cards.

Lindau

Camping Gitzenweiler Hof

Gitzenweiler 88, D-88131 Lindau (Bodensee) (Bavaria (S)) T: 083 829 4940. E: info@gitzenweiler-hof.de

alanrogers.com/DE36500

Gitzenweiler Hof is a really well equipped, first class site with quality amenities, close to the Swiss and Austrian borders. Set in the countryside with 620 pitches, 320 for touring units arranged in rows with access roads, all are numbered and have 6/16A electricity. A separate open area is for tents, with 30 electrical connections; 56 of the pitches have water, drainage and TV connections. A large outdoor swimming pool has attractive surrounds with seats. This is a pleasant, friendly, well run site with lots of activities for children and also space for those seeking peace and quiet.

Facilities

The toilet blocks have been beautifully renovated and include some washbasins in cabins, a children's bathroom and baby bath. Laundry facilities. Motorcaravan services. Shop (limited hours in low season). Two restaurants with takeaway. Large, heated, outdoor swimming pool in summer (33x25 m). Three playgrounds. Play room. Entertainment during the holidays. Organised activities. Small animals and ponies for children. Fishing in lake. Minigolf. Cinema. Club room with arcade games, library and WiFi (charged). American-style motorhomes accepted up to ten tonnes. Overnight parking for motorcaravans.

Open: All year.

Directions

Site is signed from the B12 4 km. north of Lindau. Also from A96 exit 3 (Weißensberg), and from in and around Lindau. GPS: 47.58331, 9.68331

Charges guide

Per unit incl. 2 persons and electricity	€ 31.00 - € 34.00
extra person	€ 9.00
child (3-15 yrs)	€ 4.50 - € 5.00
dog	€ 3.50

Discounts for stays over 14 days and in low season. Overnight hardstanding with electricity outside barrier € 15.80.

München

Camping München-Obermenzing

Lochhausenerstrasse 59, D-81247 München (Bavaria (S)) T: 089 811 2235.

E: campingplatz-obermenzing@t-online.de alanrogers.com/DE36350

On the northwest edge of Munich, this site makes a good stopover for those wishing to see the city or spend the night. The flat terrain is mostly covered by mature trees, giving shade to most pitches. Caravan owners have a special section of 130 individual drive-through pitches, mainly separated from each other by high hedges and opening off the hard site roads with easy access. These have 10A (Europlug) electricity connections and 15 have water and drainage also. About 200 tents and motorcaravans are taken on quite large, level grass areas, with an overflow section, so space is usually available.

Facilities

The central sanitary block, partially renovated in 2013, is large, having been extended, and together with a new prefabricated type unit, the provision should now be adequate. Hot showers require tokens, as do some washbasins. Cooking facilities (on payment). Laundry facilities. Gas supplies. Motorcaravan services. Shop (from May). Bar (from July). TV room. Bicycle hire. WiFi (charged). Off site: Baker and café nearby. Fishing 3 km. Riding and golf 5 km.

Open: 15 March - 31 October.

Directions

Site is 5 km. northwest of the city centre. From Stuttgart, Nürnberg, Deggendorf or Salzburg, leave A99 at Kreuz-West, exit 8 for München-Lochhausen and turn left into Lochhausener Strasse (site signed). Site is a further 1.5 km. GPS: 48.18055, 11.44032

Charges guide

Per unit incl. 2 persons	€ 20.00 - € 22.50
extra person	€ 5.50
electricity (per kWh)	€ 0.50

No credit cards.

München

Camping Municipal München-Thalkirchen

Zentralländstrasse 49, D-81379 München (Bavaria (S)) T: 089 723 1707.

E: munichtouristoffice@compuserve.com alanrogers.com/DE36400

This municipal site is pleasantly and quietly situated on the southern side of Munich in parkland formed by the River Isar conservation area, 4 km. southwest of the city centre (there are subway and bus links) and tall trees offer shade in parts. The large city of Munich has much to offer and the Thalkirchen site becomes quite crowded during the season. There are 550 touring pitches, all with 10A electricity and shared water and waste water. The pitches are of various sizes (some quite small), marked by metal or wooden posts and rails. The site is very busy (and noisy) during the Beer Festival (mid-September - early October), but is well maintained and kept clean. Like many city sites, groups are put in one area.

Facilities

Five refurbished toilet blocks, two of which can be heated, with seatless toilets, washbasins with shelf, mirror and cold water. Hot water for showers and sinks is on payment. Facilities for disabled campers. Laundry facilities. Shop. Snack bar with terrace. Drinks machine. General room with TV, pool and games. Good small playground. Bicycle hire. Dormitory accommodation for groups. Office hours 07.00-23.00. Max. stay 14 days.

Open: 15 March - end October.

Directions

From autobahns follow Mittel ring road to southeast of city centre where site is signed; also follow signs for Thalkirchen or the Zoo and site is close. Signed now from all over the City. GPS: 48.08333, 11.51665

Charges guide

Per unit incl. 2 persons and electricity	€ 26.00 - € 33.20
extra person	€ 5.50 - € 9.10

Credit cards only accepted for souvenirs.

For latest campsite news, availability and prices visit

alanrogers.com

Neureichenau

Knaus Campingpark Lackenhäuser

Lackenhäuser 127, D-94089 Neureichenau (Bavaria (S)) T: 085 833 11. E: lackenhaeuser@knauscamp.de

alanrogers.com/DE37050

This extensive site is some 40 km. from Passau, right at the southeast tip of Germany – the border with Austria runs through one side of the site and the Czech Republic is very close too. It is a very popular site and reservations may be advisable from mid-June to September and it is very busy in winter with skiing and other winter activities. Mainly on sloping ground with good views from some parts, it has 400 pitches with terracing in some areas, nearly all for touring units, and 100 seasonal pitches. Electricity connections (16A) are available and water points are fed from pure springs. A new area provides 50 pitches for motorcaravans, all with electricity and some fully serviced.

Facilities

Three sanitary buildings are of good quality with some washbasins in cabins, and underfloor heating for cool weather. Baby room. Laundry. Gas. Motorcaravan services. Cooking facilities. Supermarket (1/12-31/10). Restaurant/bar (1/12-31/10). Hairdressing salon. General room for young. Caravan shop. Heated indoor pool with child's pool, sauna and fitness room, and an outdoor spring water pool. Sauna, fitness room and massage. Small lake (ice sports in winter). Fishing. Bowling. Church. Organised activities (July/Aug. and Xmas). Ski hire.

Open: All year.

Directions

Site is 30 km. northeast of Passau. Leave the A3 at exit 114 (Aicha/Wald) and head northeast to Hutthum, Waldkirchen, Jandelsbrunn, Gsenget to Lackenhaüser. Do not go into Neureichenau. (Warning: some sat nav systems are unreliable in this area) GPS: 48.74886, 13.81723

Charges guide

Per unit incl. 2 persons,	
1 child and electricity	€ 26.40 - € 32.90
extra person	€ 6.10 - € 7.00

Pielenhofen

Internationaler Campingplatz Naabtal

Distelhausen 2, D-93188 Pielenhofen (Bavaria (S)) T: 094 093 73. E: camping.pielenhofen@t-online.de

alanrogers.com/DE37200

International Camping Naabtal is an attractive riverside site in a beautiful tree-covered valley and makes an excellent base for exploring the ancient city of Regensburg on the Danube and other areas of this interesting part of Germany. It is also a good overnight site for those wishing to visit or pass through Austria or the Czech Republic. The best 100 of the 270 pitches, all with electricity, are reserved for touring units. They are mainly located on the banks of the river on flat or gently sloping ground under willow and other trees. This is good walking and biking country with many marked trails.

Facilities

Excellent new sanitary block and two original blocks (one renovated in 2010) are part of larger buildings and there is a newer block for the tent area. Some washbasins are in cabins, showers are on payment. First class unit for disabled campers. Laundry facilities. Gas. Motorcaravan services. Sauna and solarium. Bar/restaurant (1/4-31/10 plus Xmas/New Year). Small shop (Easter-end Sept). Playground. Meeting room. Tennis. Bicycle hire. Fishing (permit required). Small boats on river. WiFi.

Open: All year.

Directions

Site is 15 km. northwest of Regensburg. From A3 (Nürnberg-Regensburg) take exit 97 (Nittendorf). Follow road to Pielenhofen and pass under the arch. Cross river and turn right to site. Site is 11 km. from autobahn exit. From A93 exit 39 onto B8 towards Nittendorf, then at Etterzhausen turn towards Pielenhofen. GPS: 49.06959, 11.96204

Charges guide

Per unit incl. 2 persons	
and electricity (plus meter)	€ 21.90
No credit cards.	

Prien am Chiemsee

Panorama Camping Harras

Harrasser Strasse 135, D-83209 Prien am Chiemsee (Bavaria (S)) T: 080 519 04613.

E: info@camping-harras.de alanrogers.com/DE36880

Panorama Harras is a popular, friendly site on a small, wooded peninsula by the Chiemsee, with good views to the mountains across the lake. With some near the lake, the pitches vary in size (40-70 sq.m) and most have electricity (6A). There are some 200 numbered pitches marked by trees, but with no hedges, the site can look and feel crowded at busy times. A separate, numbered section of gravel hardstandings is provided for motorcaravans, and an area for tents on grass and gravel. Sailing and windsurfing are very popular here and you can swim from the shingle beach.

Facilities

Toilet facilities include family shower rooms with washbasin and toilet. Pushbutton showers need a token. Baby room. Launderette. Good unit for disabled campers. Well stocked shop. Restaurant with bar and takeaway (all open for the whole season). Beach and small boat launch access from site. Off site: Bus services 1 km. in town. Boat trips on the lake (a visit to the islands is worthwhile). Bicycle hire 2 km. Golf and riding 5 km.

Open: 10 April - 2 November.

Directions

Site is 20 km. east of Rosenheim. From A8/E52 take exit 106 (Bernau) then north (Prien). After 3 km, at roundabout, turn east (Harras/Kreiskrankenhaus) following site signs. GPS: 47.84083, 12.37150

Charges guide

Per unit incl. 2 persons	
and electricity	€ 24.80 - € 31.30
extra person	€ 5.90 - € 8.40
Camping Cheques accepted.	

Waging am See

Strandcamping Waging am See

Am See 1, D-83329 Waging-am-See (Bavaria (S)) T: 086 815 52. E: info@strandcamp.de

LeadingCampings

alanrogers.com/DE36860

This is an exceptionally big site on the banks of a large lake fed by clear alpine streams. There are some 700 pitches for touring units out of a total of over 1,200. All the grass, level touring pitches have electricity (16A) with 150 also providing water and drainage and some new 150 sq.m. super comfort pitches. As you would expect with a site of this kind, there is a considerable range of sports facilities and an extensive games and entertainment programme during July and August. A small sandy beach offers facilities for swimming in the lake (lifeguards are in attendance in the high season). A member of Leading Campings group.

Facilities

Good sanitary facilities include private cabins and free showers. Facilities for disabled visitors and children in the four modern blocks. 11 private bathrooms for rent. Laundry facilities. Motorcaravan services. Shop and Internet access at reception. Very good restaurant and bar. Lake beach. Windsurfing. Tennis. Archery. Minigolf. Fishing. Bicycle and electric bike hire. WiFi over site (charged). A new 200 sq.m. indoor children's play area and a young people's games room and trampoline have been added. Off site: Golf 1 km. Berchtesgaden. Salzberg. Chiemsee palace and gardens.

Open: All year.

Directions

Site is 30 km. northwest of Salzburg. From A8 take exit 112 and head towards Traunstein. Turn right on road no. 304 then left towards Waging. Just before bridge turn right and then right towards site. GPS: 47.9434, 12.7475

Charges guide

Per unit incl. 2 persons and electricity	€ 21.50 - € 40.20
extra person	€ 6.30 - € 7.60
child (3-15 yrs)	€ 3.50 - € 5.90
dog	€ 4.90

Potsdam

Camping Sanssouci

An der Pirschheide 41, D-14471 Potsdam (Brandenburg) T: 033 195 10988. E: info@camping-potsdam.de

alanrogers.com/DE38270

Sanssouci is a good, if rather expensive, base for visiting Potsdam and Berlin, about 2 km. from Sanssouci Park on the banks of the Templiner See in a quiet woodland setting. Looking attractive, reflecting the effort which has been put into its development, it has a modern reception, shop, takeaway, restaurant and bar. There are 240 pitches in total with around 90 being used for seasonal units. All the touring pitches have 6/16A electricity, many also with their own water tap and drainage. Tall trees mark out these pitches. There is a separate area for tents by the lake.

Facilities

Top class sanitary facilities are in two excellent, modern, heated blocks containing hot showers, washbasins in cabins and facilities for babies. Useful facility for wheelchair users. Bathrooms to rent, kitchen, hairdresser and solarium. Laundry. Gas supplies. Motorcaravan services. Restaurant/bar. Shop. Rowing boats, motorboats, canoes and pedaloes for hire. Fishing. Outdoor and heated indoor pools. Swimming and sailing in the lake. Play area. Bicycle hire. Wellness. Internet café and WiFi throughout (charged). Public transport tickets and discounts for Berlin attractions. Off site: The pool, sauna, solarium and skittle alley at the nearby Hotel Semiramis (100 m.) may be used by campers at a discount. Riding 3 km. Golf 10 km.

Open: 1 April - 3 January.

Directions

From A10 take exit 22 (Gross Kreutz) and follow the B1 towards Potsdam. After 10 km. turn right (Zeppelinstrasse through woodland) just after the Potsdam sign and before the railway bridge, then follow camping signs. GPS: 52.35857, 13.00633

Charges guide

Per unit incl. 2 persons and electricity	€ 33.80 - € 56.90
dog	€ 4.90

Special low season offers.
No credit cards.

For latest campsite news, availability and prices visit

alanrogers.com

Bremen

Camping Am Stadtwaldsee

Hochschulring 1, D-28359 Bremen (Bremen) T: 042 184 10748. E: contact@camping-stadtwaldsee.de

alanrogers.com/DE30210

This well designed and purpose built campsite overlooking a lake is ideally placed for those travelling to northern Europe and for people wishing to visit Bremen and places within the region. There is a bus stop outside the site. Of the 220 level pitches 168 are for touring units, standing on grass with openwork reinforcements at the entrances. All have 16A electricity, water and drainage. The pitches are positioned around the spacious grass-roofed sanitary block and are laid out in areas separated by trees and hedges. A restaurant/cafeteria with open-air terrace overlooks the lake.

Facilities

Modern sanitary block with free hot showers, facilities for disabled visitors, five private bathrooms for rental. Washing machines and dryers. Motorcaravan services. Kitchen. Sitting/dining room with LCD projector facilities. Small supermarket (1/3-31/12). Lakeside café/restaurant with terrace. Play room. Play area. Lake swimming, windsurfing, fishing and scuba diving. Tents for hire. WiFi (charged). Bicycle and go-kart hire. Off site: Naturist beach nearby with general beach 5 minutes away.

Open: All year.

Directions

From A27 northeast of Bremen take exit 19 for Universitat and follow signs for university and camping. Site is on the left, 1 km. after leaving the university area. GPS: 53.114833, 8.832467

Charges guide

Per unit incl. 2 persons	
and electricity (plus meter)	€ 32.00 - € 35.50
extra person	€ 11.00 - € 12.00
child (3-17 yrs)	€ 5.50 - € 6.50
dog	€ 3.00 - € 4.00

Hamburg

Knaus Camping Hamburg

Wunderbrunnen 2, D-22457 Hamburg (Hamburg) T: 040 559 4225. E: hamburg@knauscamp.de

alanrogers.com/DE30050

Situated some 15 km. from the centre of Hamburg on the northern edge of the town, this is a suitable base either for visiting this famous German city, or as a night stop before catching the Harwich ferry or travelling to Denmark. There is some traffic noise because the autobahn runs alongside (despite efforts to screen it out) and also some aircraft noise. However, the proximity of the A7 (E45) does make it easy to find. The 145 pitches for short-term touring are of about 100 sq.m, on grass with access from gravel roads. All have 6A electricity and are marked out with small trees and hedges.

Facilities

A deposit is required for the key to the single sanitary block, a well constructed modern building with high quality facilities and heated in cool weather. Good facilities for disabled visitors, with special pitches close to the block. Washing machines and dryers. Motorcaravan services. Shop with essentials. Playground. Dogs are not accepted. WiFi (charged). Off site: Bus service, restaurants and shops 10 minutes' walk. Swimming pool, tennis courts, golf and fishing nearby.

Open: 1 April - 31 October.

Directions

From A7 autobahn take Schnelsen Nord exit. Stay in outside lane as you will soon need to turn back left; follow signs for Ikea store and site signs. GPS: 53.65015, 9.92927

Charges guide

Per unit incl. 2 persons	
and electricity	€ 28.90 - € 32.40
extra person	€ 7.70
child (4-14 yrs)	€ 2.50 - € 3.50
dog	€ 3.00

Geisenheim

Campingplatz Geisenheim Am Rhein

Campingplatz 1, D-65366 Geisenheim (Hessen) T: 067 227 5600. E: info@rheingaucamping.de

alanrogers.com/DE32930

Geisenheim is in a lovely position, on the north bank of the Rhine and within walking distance of the picturesque small town of Rüdesheim. There are 100, slightly sloping touring pitches each with 16A electricity plus some attractive seasonal pitches. The touring pitches are on the part of the site nearest the river and are on well maintained grass. Some have shade and some are marked out by hedges. There are four special hardstandings for long, heavy motorcaravans, but these must be booked in advance. A level pedestrian/cycle path runs alongside the river in both directions and there are many small picturesque villages in the area to visit.

Facilities

Toilet block with showers and washbasins in cubicles. Laundry. Motorcaravan services. Small shop. Separately run restaurant (all season). Fishing adjacent. WiFi throughout (charged). Off site: Two supermarkets in Rüdesheim. Shop, restaurant, swimming, tennis adjacent. Bicycle hire 2 km. Boat trips. Wine tastings.

Open: 3 March - 31 October.

Directions

Geisenheim is on the B42 north bank of the Rhine about 21 km. west of Wiesbaden. There is also a ferry from Bingen to Rüdesheim. GPS: 49.97871, 7.9554

Charges guide

Per unit incl. 2 persons	
and electricity	€ 23.90 - € 25.20
extra person	€ 5.70
child (4-14 yrs)	€ 3.50
dog	€ 2.00

Limburg an der Lahn

Lahn Camping

Schleusenweg 16, D-65549 Limburg an der Lahn (Hessen) T: 064 312 2610. E: info@lahncamping.de

alanrogers.com/DE32650

Pleasantly situated directly on the bank of the River Lahn between the autobahn and the town of Limburg, the site is a useful overnight stop for travellers along the Köln-Frankfurt stretch of the A3. The site is on level grass with 200 touring pitches, each about 50-60 sq.m. All have 6A electricity, but may need long cables, some of which may have to cross a road. A few of the larger trees have been removed, giving a pleasing mix of open and shaded pitches. The site is very popular with many nationalities and can become very crowded at peak times, so arrive early. There is some road and rail noise.

Facilities

The main sanitary block near reception is old and facilities are rather tired. A better quality, heated block at the far end of the site is a welcome addition. Showers (by token). Laundry facilities. Cookers. Gas. Motorcaravan services. Bar/restaurant (evenings and Sundays) offers simple meals and takeaway. Small shop (not Sunday p.m). Fishing (permit on payment). Play area. WiFi throughout (charged). Off site: Swimming pool opposite. Overnight motorcaravan stop adjacent. Supermarkets, shops and restaurants in town. Pleasure cruises. Riding 5 km.

Open: Easter - end October.

Directions

Leave A3 autobahn at Limburg-Nord exit and follow road towards town. Turn left into Schleusenweg at traffic lights just before the bridge over River Lahn. Site is on right, just past the swimming pool. Do not enter the Stellplatz – signs are confusing. GPS: 50.38897, 8.07388

Charges guide

Per unit incl. 2 persons and electricity	€ 22.50
extra person	€ 5.20
child (3-14 yrs)	€ 3.20

No credit cards.

Lorch

Naturpark Camping Suleika

Im Bodental 2, D-65391 Lorch am Rhein (Hessen) T: 06726 839402. E: info@suleika-camping.de

alanrogers.com/DE32250

On a steep hillside in the Rhine-Taunus Nature Park and approached by a scenic drive along a narrow system of roads through the vineyards, this site is arranged on small terraces on the side of a wooded hill with a stream flowing through – the water supply is direct from springs. The surroundings are most attractive, with views over the vineyards to the river below. Of the 60 pitches, 35 are available for touring units. These are mostly on the lower terraces, in groups of up to four units. All have electricity (16A Europlugs) and five are fully serviced. Cars are parked away from the pitches near the entrance. The site is popular for small caravan rallies.

Facilities

The excellent toilet block is heated in cool weather and provides some washbasins in cabins for each sex and a nicely furnished room for children with WC, shower and bath. Laundry service. Motorcaravan services. Gas supplies. Restaurant (closed Mon. and Thurs). Small shop (bread to order). Small play area. Some entertainment in season. WiFi on part of site. Off site: The Rheinsteig footpath passes above the site. Touring and wine tasting in the Rhine valley.

Open: 15 March - 31 October.

Directions

Site is 8 km. northwest of Rudesheim. Direct entrance road from B42 (cars only), between Rudesheim and Lorch (2.25 m. height limit under railway bridge). Higher vehicles will find site signed on south side of Lorch via a one-way system (one-way for caravans and motorcaravans only; watch out for oncoming tractors/cars!). GPS: 50.02146, 7.84579

Charges guide

Per unit incl. 2 persons and electricity	€ 24.00
extra person	€ 7.00
child (2-14 yrs)	€ 5.00
dog	€ 2.00

No credit cards.

For latest campsite news, availability and prices visit

alanrogers.com

Vöhl

Camping & Ferienpark Teichmann

Zum Träumen 1A, D-34516 Vöhl-Herzhausen (Hessen) T: 056 352 45. E: info@camping-teichmann.de

alanrogers.com/DE32800

Situated near the eastern end of the 27 km. long Edersee and the Kellerwald-Edersee National Park, this attractively set site is surrounded by wooded hills and encircles a six-hectare lake, which has separate areas for swimming, fishing and boating. Of the 500 pitches, 250 are for touring; all have 10A electricity and 50 have fresh and waste water connections. The pitches are on level grass, some having an area of hardstanding, and are separated by hedges and mature trees. At the opposite side of the lake from the entrance, there is a separate area for tents with its own sanitary block. The adjoining national park, a popular leisure attraction, offers a wealth of holiday/sporting activities including walking, cycling (there are two passenger ferries that take cycles), boat trips, cable car and much more. Full details are available at the friendly reception. For winter sports lovers, the ski centre at Winterberg is only 30 km. away from this all-year-round site. With a range of facilities for children, this is an ideal family site, as well as being suited to country lovers who can enjoy the forest and lakeside walks/cycle tracks in the park.

Facilities

Three good quality sanitary blocks can be heated and have free showers, washbasins (open and in cabins), baby rooms and facilities for wheelchair users. Laundry. Motorcaravan services. Café and shop (both summer only). Restaurant by entrance open all day (closed Feb). Watersports. Boat and bicycle hire. Lake swimming. Fishing. Minigolf. Playground. Sauna. Solarium. Disco (high season). Internet access. Off site: New national park opposite site entrance. Riding 500 m. Golf 25 km. Cable car. Aquapark. Boat trips on the Edersee.

Open: All year.

Directions

Site is 45 km. southwest of Kassel. From the A44 Oberhausen-Kassel autobahn, take exit 64 for Diemelstadt and head south for Korbach. Site is between Korbach and Frankenberg on the B252 road, 1 km. to the south of Herzhausen at the pedestrian traffic lights. GPS: 51.17550, 8.89067

Charges guide

Per unit incl. 2 persons	
and electricity	€ 26.20 - € 35.00
extra person	€ 5.90 - € 7.90
child (3-15 yrs)	€ 3.50 - € 4.60

Bad Lauterberg

Camping Wiesenbeker Teich

Wiesenbek, D-37431 Bad Lauterberg (Lower Saxony) T: 05524 2510. E: info@campingwiesenbek.de

alanrogers.com/DE30430

Camping Wiesenbeker Teich, classified in Germany as an eco campsite, is situated in the Harz National Park on the edge of the forest 2.5 kilometres from Bad Lauterberg. It is on the south western shore of the lake, which is a popular destination, with many opportunities for recreational activities. The terraced family site offers 90 touring pitches (6-16A electricity), divided into 30 for caravans, 20 for motorcaravans and 40 for tents. Almost all the pitches overlook the lake and due to its location it is quiet with no through traffic, although a walking route around the lake runs through the site. There are also 30 permanent rental units, including a wooden wigwam settlement, a biker house and caravans.

Facilities

Heated sanitary block has hot showers and some washbasins in cubicles. Washing machine and dryer. Restaurant. Motorcaravan services. Adventure playground. Trampoline. Beach volleyball. Boat hire. Fishing. Windsurfing. Diving. Archery. Entertainment for children and adults. Flight school for model helicopters and fixed wing aircraft (weekly programme). Motorcycle safety training. WiFi (charged). Off site: Kirchberg thermal baths.

Open: All year.

Directions

The site is 2 km. southeast of Bad Lauterberg. From road 27 in centre of Bad Lauterberg turn southeast onto Schanzenstrasse then shortly continue onto Butterbergstrasse for 100 m. then left again onto Wiesenbek for 2 km. to site. GPS: 51.61761, 10.48978

Charges guide

Per unit incl. 2 persons	
and electricity	€ 24.50 - € 30.20
extra person	€ 7.50 - € 8.30

Bleckede

Knaus Campingpark Elbtalaue/Bleckede

Am Waldbad 23, D-21354 Bleckede (Lower Saxony) T: 05854 311. E: elbtalaue@knauscamp.de

alanrogers.com/DE30470

This welcoming site is in the middle of the bio reserve of the Elbtalaue, an excellent area for walking and cycling. The site provides 225 pitches (142 for tourers), all with a minimum of 6A electricity. Pitching is in long lanes off hard roads on grassy fields (some slightly sloping, some on terraces). There are two fully serviced pitches. To the front of the site are a shop and a large room for activities, where you can also have breakfast. Adjacent to the site are the open-air public pool (free for campers) and tennis courts. Being in a reserve, you will find plenty of information about the local flora and fauna on and around the site, including a special 'hotel' for bees.

Facilities

Three toilet blocks (one central and refurbished to a high standard) with controllable hot showers, facilities for children and disabled visitors and a baby room. Laundry. Kitchen. Kiosk for basics. Bar/snack bar (breakfast to order). Sauna. Boules. Playground. Playing field. Bicycle hire. WiFi (on payment). Off site: Public swimming pool (free to campers). Restaurant and shopping 1 km.

Open: All year.

Directions

From Lüneburg, follow 216 east, then turn north towards Bleckede. After a few kilometres, turn right towards Alt Garge and site. Site is signed in the village. GPS: 53.25966, 10.80555

Charges guide

Per unit incl. 2 persons and electricity (plus meter)	€ 15.30 - € 25.00
extra person	€ 5.50 - € 7.50
child (4-14 yrs)	€ 2.10 - € 3.20

Camping Cheques accepted.

Drage

Camping Stover Strand International

Stover Strand 10, D-21423 Drage (Lower Saxony) T: 041 774 30. E: info@stover-strand.de

alanrogers.com/DE28990

This is a large site, part of which directly borders the River Elbe, with 500 pitches, of which 200 are for touring (all with electricity, water and drainage). The main part of the site is located behind a dyke and contains reception and the principal sanitary facilities. Pitches bordering and overlooking The Elbe are serviced by excellent, modern mobile sanitary units containing WCs and washbasins. Along the Elbe's banks there are sandy areas useful for playing and sunbathing in summer with some showers. Next to the site's main building there is a further area set aside for touring units and this has easy access to the main sanitary facilities, the bar and restaurant and children's playground. With its location some 20 km. southeast of Hamburg, Stover Strand is a useful site from which to visit the city and its attractions, which include the world famous Reeperbahn; another popular tourist attraction is the fish market. To the south of the site is the old town of Lüneburg, the Lüneburger Heide and other attractive towns. The site organises boat tours to Hamburg, including breakfast, and has won several prizes for its local dishes.

Facilities

Modern sanitary facilities with washing machines and dryer, facilities for disabled visitors, and a baby room. Kitchen with cooking facilities. Motorcaravan services. Supermarket. Bar. Restaurant. Play areas. Family entertainment (July/Aug). Bicycle hire. Fishing. Sport boat harbour with 100 moorings. Boat slipway. Car rental. WiFi (charged). Off site: New clubroom/cocktail lounge on a boat on the Elbe. Bus service to Hamburg. Golf 8 km.

Open: All year.

Directions

Site is 20 km. southeast of Hamburg on the southern banks of the River Elbe. Leave A250 at exit 3 Winsen West, travel northeast on L217 through Winsen and Drage. Site entrance is signed to left 4 km. northeast of Drage. Stover Strand is last campsite at end of entrance road. GPS: 53.424383, 10.294977

Charges guide

Per unit incl. 2 persons and electricity	€ 14.00 - € 22.00
extra person	€ 5.00 - € 6.00
child (2-12 yrs)	€ 3.00 - € 4.00

Dransfeld

Campingplatz Am Hohen Hagen

Zum Hohen Hagen 12, D-37127 Dransfeld (Lower Saxony) T: 05502 2147.

E: mail@campingplatz-dransfeld.de alanrogers.com/DE30390

This family run campsite is on the edge of the small town of Dransfeld in the heart of Lower Saxony. There are over 300 pitches of which 150 are for touring units, all with 16A electrical connections and 20 also have water and waste water connections. One touring section offers superb views over the surrounding countryside. The site is quiet and relaxing in low season, becoming more lively during the main holiday period with a range of activities and entertainment provided. Shops and restaurants are within walking distance, whilst the old town of Göttingen is an easy drive away.

Facilities
Three sanitary blocks with free hot showers. Heated outdoor swimming pool (June-Oct). Shop (mornings). Restaurant with terrace. Laundry. Kitchen. Playground. Football field. Beach volleyball. Basketball. Minigolf. Wellness and sauna. Fitness equipment. Entertainment and activities for all ages (holiday periods). Free loan of city and mountain bikes. Six caravans for hire. Motorcaravan services. WiFi throughout (charged). Off site: Shops and restaurants in Dransfeld 800 m.

Open: All year excl. November.

Directions
Dransfeld is 14 km. southwest of Göttingen and site is on southern edge of town. From A7 motorway (Hannover-Kassel) at junction 73 (Göttingen) head west for 8 km. on B3 to Dransfeld, turn south at second major crossroads just after filling station, and follow signs to campsite on right in 1 km. GPS: 51.49139, 9.76123

Charges guide
Per unit incl. 2 persons and electricity	€ 24.00
extra person	€ 6.00

Eckwarderhörne

Knaus Campingpark Eckwarderhörne

Butjadinger Strasse 116, D-26969 Eckwarderhörne (Lower Saxony) T: 04736 1300.

E: eckwarderhoerne@knauscamp.de alanrogers.com/DE28355

Knaus Campingpark Eckwarderhörne is directly on the Wadden Sea National Park. This is an excellent area to enjoy the North Sea beaches and watch the tides change. It has 180 pitches, of which just 30 are for tourers, on flat and open grassy fields right behind the dyke. There are two pitches for very large units and 16 hardstandings. All are fully serviced with water, waste water and 16A electricity. Being small, it is much quieter than many of the sites along this stretch of coast.

Facilities
One central toilet block with open style washbasins, controllable hot showers and facilities for disabled visitors. Washing machine and dryer. Playground. Playing Field. Games room with billiards, library and TV. Activity programme (July/Aug). Boat launching. WiFi (charged). Off site: Village of Eckwarden 1 km. Bicycle hire 5 km.

Open: All year.

Directions
From Oldenburg, take the A29 north towards Wilhelmshaven, and at Varel continue East on 437 road. Take exit for Stollhamm and Butjadingen (L855) and from Stollhamm follow Ulmenstrasse until crossing the L859. Turn right and continue to Eckwarden. From there follow K184 road southwest to site. Be aware that there are two no. 116s on Butjadingerstrasse. GPS: 53.52107, 8.23484

Charges guide
Per unit incl. 2 persons and electricity	€ 17.90 - € 30.90
extra person	€ 4.50 - € 7.50

Eschwege

Knaus Campingpark Eschwege

Am Werratalsee 2, D-37269 Eschwege (Lower Saxony) T: 05651 338883. E: eschwege@knauscamp.de

alanrogers.com/DE30510

This Knaus site is in beautiful natural surroundings on an idyllic peninsula between the River Werra and the Werratal Lake. It offers around 220 pitches, of which 123 are for tourers, all on level, grassy ground. To the front of the site are 12 extra large motorcaravan pitches on hardstanding with great views over the lake, plus an area for late arrivals. The lake with its sandy beach offers opportunities for swimming and boating, and the whole area is excellent for walking and biking tours. Boat tours are organised. Via a pedestrian bridge, it is an easy ten minute walk to the lovely romantic centre of Eschwege, with its restaurants, cobbled medieval streets and terraces. Close to the site are the Landgrafenschloss, a botanical garden and Climbing Forest for youngsters.

Facilities
Two excellent toilet blocks provide washbasins (open style and in cabins), controllable hot showers and facilities for children and disabled visitors. Family bathrooms for rent. Laundry and kitchen. Playground. Entertainment programme. Children's club. Football. Table tennis. Basketball. Beach volleyball. Sailing. Surfing. Fishing. Bicycle hire. Boat hire. WiFi (charged). Off site: Tennis 300 m. Minigolf 400 m. Sauna and massage 800 m.

Open: All year excl. 3 November - 20 December.

Directions
East of Kassel on A7 motorway, turn eastwards on 7 road towards Hessischs Lichtenau. Follow the 7 eastwards to junction with 27 road. Proceed north on 27 until crossing with 249 road and then follow the signs for Eschwege. Site is well signed. GPS: 51.19147, 10.06857

Charges guide
Per unit incl. 2 persons and electricity	€ 23.90 - € 34.30

FREE Alan Rogers Travel Card
Extra benefits and savings - see page 14

Fassberg

Ferienpark Heidesee

D-29328 Fassberg-Oberohe (Lower Saxony) T: 058 279 70546. E: info@campingheidesee.com

alanrogers.com/DE30750

Ferienpark Heidesee is a holiday centre surrounding a small lake in the Lünenberg Heide. The grass pitches are mostly on level ground in open areas, separated by low hedges. Some have good views over the lake. There are 250 touring pitches, all with 10A electricity connections. Private sanitary facilities are available to rent. This is an excellent site for family holidays, with a full entertainment programme in high season, an indoor play hall, skate ramp, bowling alley, and a small zoo on site. Part of the site is divided off and accommodates 120 naturist pitches.

Facilities

Heated toilet blocks provide free hot showers, a baby room and facilities for disabled visitors. Washing machine and dryer. Cooking facilities. Motorcaravan services. Bread to order. Restaurant/bar and snack bar (Wed-Sun). Outdoor swimming pool (July/Aug). Sauna. Tennis. Basketball. Beach volleyball. Fishing. In-line skating. Children's entertainment. Indoor play area. Adventure playground. Petting zoo. Bicycle hire. Go-kart hire. Free WiFi over part of site. Off site: Heide-Park Soltau 35 km.

Open: All year.

Directions

From Fassberg go eastwards towards Unterlüß and site is signed in Oberohe. The road leading to the site from the main road is rough.
GPS: 52.87583, 10.22694

Charges guide

Per unit incl. 2 persons and electricity	€ 17.00 - € 21.00
extra person	€ 4.00 - € 5.00
child (3-14 yrs)	€ 2.00 - € 3.00

Camping Cheques accepted.

Rieste

Alfsee Ferien & Erholungspark

Am Campingpark 10, D-49597 Rieste (Lower Saxony) T: 054 649 2120. E: info@alfsee.de

alanrogers.com/DE30250

Leading Campings

Alfsee has plenty to offer for the active family and children of all ages. It is a really good base for enjoying the many recreational activities available here on the lake. The smaller lake has a 780 m. water-ski cableway (on payment) and there is also a separate swimming area with a sandy beach. The Alfsee itself is now a nature reserve. Many birdwatching excursions are organised by the site. Improvements to this already well equipped site continue. There are now over 800 pitches (many long stay but with 375 for touring units) on flat grass, all with 16A electricity, with some shade for those in the original area. A new camping area provides 290 large pitches. A member of Leading Campings group.

Facilities

Five excellent sanitary blocks (two heated) with family bathrooms (to rent), baby rooms and laundry facilities. Cooking facilities. Dishwashers. Motorcaravan services. Gas supplies. Shop, restaurants and takeaway (high season). Watersports. Playground, new indoor play centre and entertainment for children. Entertainment hall. Grass tennis courts. Trampoline. Minigolf. Go-kart track. Games room. Fishing. Bicycle and E-bike hire. Safe box hire. Riding. WiFi (charged). Off site: Golf 10 km.

Open: All year.

Directions

From A1 autobahn north of Osnabrück take exit 67 for Neuenkirchen and follow signs for Rieste, Alfsee and site. GPS: 52.48597, 7.99215

Charges guide

Per unit incl. 2 persons and electricity	€ 17.50 - € 32.50
extra person	€ 3.50 - € 4.50
child (2-15 yrs acc. to age)	€ 2.00 - € 3.50
dog	€ 2.50 - € 3.50

Soltau

Röders' Park

Ebsmoor 8, D-29614 Soltau (Lower Saxony) T: 51 912 141. E: info@roeders-park.de

alanrogers.com/DE30100

Röders' Park is a most attractive site near Soltau centre (1.5 km), in a peaceful location, ideal for visits to the famous Luneburg Heath or as a stop en-route to Denmark. The site is run by the third generation of the Röders family who make their visitors most welcome (each guest receives a local information pack) and speak excellent English. There are 120 pitches (90 touring), all with 6-16A electricity and 85 with water and drainage. All pitches have satellite TV connections and WiFi. Most have hardstanding and there is reasonable privacy between pitches. The central feature of this wooded site is a small lake crossed by a wooden bridge.

Facilities

Two modern, very clean sanitary blocks (both with underfloor heating and a wood burning stove) contain all necessary facilities. Excellent, separate unit (including shower) for wheelchair users. Private bathrooms for rent. Laundry room. Motorcaravan services. Gas supplies. Simple shop. Restaurant and takeaway (all Easter-Oct). Play area. Bicycle hire. Internet (free), WiFi (on payment). Off site: Thermal swimming pool 1 km. Fishing and riding 1.5 km. Golf 3 km. 999 km. of cycle paths.

Open: All year.

Directions

From the A7 exit for Soltau Sud then on the B3 to Soltau. In Soltau travelling towards Hamburg, directly after the town's end, at the traffic island turn left into Ebsmoor Strasse. GPS: 53.00222, 9.83862

Charges guide

Per unit incl. 2 persons and electricity (plus meter)	€ 31.00
extra person	€ 8.50
child (4-13 yrs)	€ 4.00
dog	€ 3.00

For latest campsite news, availability and prices visit

alanrogers.com

Suderburg

Campingplatz am Hardausee

D-29556 Suderburg-Hosseringen (Lower Saxony) T: 058 267 676. E: info@camping-hardausee.de

alanrogers.com/DE30800

The Hardausee site is evolving from a seasonal-only site into a site for touring units. When we visited, there were 80 touring pitches, all with fresh water connections and 16A electricity, and 270 seasonal units, but as soon as a seasonal guest leaves, the pitch will be re-allocated for touring. Hardausee is on sloping ground although the grassy, marked pitches are mostly level. Some pitches are numbered and most are 100 sq.m. or larger in size. The newer pitches have hardly any shade, but mature trees surround the older field. There are 45 serviced pitches with 16A electricity, fresh water and drainage. It is an easy 300 m. walk from the site to the Hardausee.

Facilities

Three heated toilet blocks provide washbasins in cabins and free, controllable hot showers. Washing machines and dryer. Motorcaravan services. Shop (for basics). Bar, restaurant and takeaway (April-Oct, closed Mon). Large adventure playground. Cycling tours and excursions in the woods. Fishing. Lakeside beach. WiFi throughout (charged). Off site: Bus service 200 m. Bicycle hire 300 m. Riding 1 km.

Open: 1 March - 31 October.

Directions

From Uelzen, follow 4/191 road south towards Braunschweig. Take exit for Suderburg and follow signs for Hösseringen. Site signed on right 2 km. before Hösseringen. GPS: 52.86430, 10.420414

Charges guide

Per unit incl. 2 persons and electricity	€ 19.00 - € 22.00
extra person	€ 6.00

No credit cards.

Wietzendorf

Südsee-Camp

Südsee-Camp 1, D-29649 Wietzendorf (Lower Saxony) T: 051 969 80116.

E: info@suedsee-camp.de alanrogers.com/DE30700

LeadingCampings

Südsee-Camp in the Lüneburger Heide is a large, well organised holiday centre where children are especially well catered for. There are 726 touring pitches of varying types and sizes, 580 with electricity (4-10A), fresh water and drainage; 440 of these have a TV connection. Modern sanitary blocks are well maintained and contain all necessary facilities, including some areas specially built for children. Although centred around a large sandy shored lake, complete with shipwreck, the main swimming attraction is the South Sea Tropical swimming pool. A member of Leading Campings group.

Facilities

Twelve modern, well maintained sanitary blocks with all the expected facilities, including those for disabled visitors and private bathrooms to rent. Special areas for children (Kinderland), facilities for babies. Laundry rooms. Kitchens. Bar (1/4-1/11), shop, restaurants and takeaway (all year). Pool complex (on payment). Soundproofed disco. Fitness room. Bicycle and pedal car hire. Games room. WiFi over part of site (charged). High ropes adventure course. Jungle golf. Overnight parking outside site. Off site: Riding adjacent. Fishing 2 km. Golf 12 km.

Open: All year.

Directions

From A7 autobahn take exit 45 towards Bergen and Celle on the B3 (campsite is signed). After 6 km. turn left (site again signed). GPS: 52.931639, 9.965254

Charges guide

Per unit incl. 2 persons and electricity	€ 28.80 - € 53.30
extra person	€ 4.70 - € 5.70
child (2-17 yrs. acc. to age)	€ 3.20 - € 4.70
dog	€ 2.80 - € 3.80

Wilsum

Camping Wilsumer Berge

Zum Feriengebiet 1, D-49849 Wilsum (Lower Saxony) T: 05945 995 580. E: info@wilsumerberge.de

alanrogers.com/DE29400

This is a very large site (90 ha.) based around a lake, with 1,000 pitches (120 sq.m) of which over half are for touring in a separate area. They are large, level and arranged in various ways, with some in secluded areas, some with hedge separation, others in open areas and in places shaded, on sandy grass with electricity (6/16A Europlug), 150 having fresh and waste water connections. This site has good facilities and the lake, the centrepiece of the site, with its 60 m. waterslide and bridge, has separate areas for swimmers and non swimmers. A tent area for groups is located away from other pitches.

Facilities

Very good sanitary facilities. Washing machines and dryers. Shop. Restaurant, snacks and takeaway. Beach café with open-air terrace. Several playgrounds. Children's theatre. Lake swimming. Fishing pond. Volleyball. Beach volleyball. Multisports court. Basketball. Boules. Bicycle hire. WiFi throughout (charged). Off site: Walking and cycling in the surrounding countryside. Stables and riding school.

Open: 3 April - 31 October.

Directions

From A31 take exit 25 Lingen and travel west along the 213 Nordhornerstrasse to Nordhorn where north onto the 403 to Neuenhaus and Uelsen then north, still on the 403 Wilsumerstrasse to site. GPS: 52.51394, 6.86164

Charges guide

Per unit incl. 2 persons and electricity	€ 23.00
extra person	€ 2.00 - € 3.00
dog	€ 3.00

Wingst

Knaus Campingpark Wingst

Schwimmbadallee 13, D-21789 Wingst (Lower Saxony) T: 047 787 604. E: wingst@knauscamp.de

alanrogers.com/DE30000

With an impressive landscaped entrance, a shop and restaurant to one side and reception to the other, and a barrier which is closed in the evening, this is a good quality site. The heart of this site is a deep set, small fishing lake and beach. Lightly wooded, pitches are accessed by circular roadways on differing levels and terraced where necessary. Because of the design you don't realise that there are 410 pitches, nearly all with electricity (6A) and clearly defined by shrubs and trees (330 for touring units). This is a rural area with attractive villages and woodland. Dogs are accepted on part of the site.

Facilities
Two heated toilet blocks, one adjoining reception and one nearer the lake (access to this is by steps from the varying levels). The provision is good and well kept, with one block recently renovated. Motorcaravan services. Shop (7.30-22.00), restaurant, bar and takeaway. Playground. Minigolf. Beach volleyball. Fishing. Bicycle hire. Large screen TV. Barbecue facility with roof. WiFi (charged). Off site: Riding. Watersports near. Swimming pool behind the hotel opposite the site. Riding 2 km. Golf 5 km.

Open: 29 March - 2 November.

Directions
Follow the B73 north from Hamburg and take exit for Wingst (Spiel and Sportpark) signed Campingplatz. Then take first left. GPS: 53.752867, 9.0845

Charges guide
Per unit incl. 2 persons

and electricity	€ 23.40 - € 28.20
extra person	€ 6.50 - € 7.50
child (3-14 yrs)	€ 3.20 - € 3.50
dog	€ 3.20

No credit cards.

Ahrensberg

Campingplatz Am Drewensee

C10, D-17255 Ahrensberg (Mecklenburg-West Pomerania) T: 039 832 2950. E: info@haveltourist.de

alanrogers.com/DE38110

The Drewensee (2000 sq.m), popular with anglers, is connected to many waterways so this is a useful site for tourers who enjoy canoeing and motorboating. Nevertheless, boating regulations ensure that it is quiet. The site has a total of 200 level, grassy pitches, over half for use by tourers. Most are well shaded beneath mature trees and all have 16A electricity. Two jetties are provided, one for boat users, the other for swimmers, and a grassed area bordering the lake is a popular relaxation area.

Facilities
Modern, heated and well maintained sanitary building with some washbasins in cubicles and controllable showers (payment by chip key). Family rooms. Laundry facilities. Motorcaravan services. Small shop. Beach snack bar. Play area. Children's entertainment (high season). Boat launching. Boat rental. Bicycle hire. Fishing. WiFi over site (charged). Off site: Bar and restaurant within 2 km. Müritz National Park. The Baltic coast is within easy reach.

Open: 1 April - 2 November.

Directions
Leave the autobahn at exit 18 Röbel/Müritzand and take 198 east to Wesenberg, continue through Wesenberg then on the outskirts of town southeast to Ahrensberg and site. GPS: 53.2625, 13.0513

Charges guide
Per unit incl. 2 persons

and electricity	€ 13.00 - € 28.90
extra person	€ 4.50 - € 7.20
child (2-14 yrs)	€ 1.70 - € 4.80
dog	€ 1.10 - € 4.80

Boltenhagen

Regenbogen Boltenhagen

Ostseeallee 54, D-23946 Boltenhagen (Mecklenburg-West Pomerania) T: 038 825 42222.

E: boltenhagen@regenbogen.ag alanrogers.com/DE26140

Boltenhagen is a seaside resort on the Baltic Sea coast, east of Lübeck. The site has direct access (500 m.) to a long stretch of a wide, sandy beach. It is a large site with 422 pitches and is divided into two sections: one has 81 Scandinavian-style chalets for hire, the other is largely devoted to caravans and teepees for rent, and there are 86 pitches (with 10A Europlug) for tourers, divided over three grassy areas. Those at the front of the site have shade from mature trees, while two fields at the back are more open. A boardwalk along the shore takes you to restaurants and health spas. A marina with a fishing harbour has hotels and private beaches overlooking the vast Wohlenberger Wiek, a shallow bay between Boltenhagen and Wismar.

Facilities
Modern sanitary buildings with facilities for disabled visitors. Family bathrooms to rent. Bakery and supermarket. Bar and restaurant. Snack bar (daily in July/Aug). Gym. Wellness Centre with sauna, solarium, jacuzzi, steam bath and Kneipp massage, and a variety of massage and beauty treatments. Sports facilities and playgrounds. Children's entertainment. Organised excursions and walks. Bicycle and car rental. WiFi (charged), plus free loan of small laptops. Off site: Bars and restaurants along beach boardwalk. Riding 2 km.

Open: All year.

Directions
Boltenhagen is 45 km. northeast of Lübeck. From A20 Lübeck/Rostock motorway, take exit 6 for Grevesmühlen and head north on the LO3/B105 following signs to Boltenhagen. Site is to east of resort in 1.3 km. GPS: 53.98172, 11.21709

Charges guide
Per unit incl. 2 adults, all children under 13 yrs

and electricity	€ 18.50 - € 38.00
extra person	€ 4.00 - € 7.00

For latest campsite news, availability and prices visit

alanrogers.com

Flessenow

Seecamping Flessenow

Am Schweriner See 1A, D-19067 Flessenow (Mecklenburg-West Pomerania) T: **038 668 1491**.

E: **info@seecamping.de** **alanrogers.com/DE38120**

Dutch owned and in a peaceful, natural setting directly on the banks of Germany's third largest lake, Seecamping Flessenow is ideal for those seeking a relaxing holiday and also for more active campers who enjoy watersports and the many hiking and cycling routes nearby. There are 250 level, grassy pitches (170 for touring units), arranged on two rectangular fields to one side of a hardcore access lane and on a newer field to the rear of the site. Some pitches have shade from mature trees, all are numbered and separated by low wooden fences. All have 10A electricity, 45 also have water and drainage.

Facilities

Three toilet blocks with some washbasins in cabins and free controllable hot showers. Baby room with shower. Facilities for disabled visitors in one block. Washing machine and dryer. Motorcaravan services. Bar, kiosk and takeaway. New reception has fresh bread each morning and useful tourist information. Playground. TV room. Lake with beach and swimming. Fishing. Watersports. Bicycle hire. Boat launching. Sailing and windsurfing schools. Canoe hire. WiFi. Off site: Riding 1.5 km. Golf 20 km. Schwerin, Wismar and the coast.

Open: April - September.

Directions

Site is 14 km. north-northeast of Schwerin. From 8 km. east of Schwerin, take A14 (formerly 241) north along east side of lake. Exit at Schwerin Nord and turn left towards Rampe/Cambs/Güstow. After 100 m. turn left at lights towards Retendorf and Flessnow. Follow road signs rather than sat nav. GPS: 53.75175, 11.49628

Charges guide

Per unit incl. 2 persons and electricity	€ 24.00 - € 32.00
extra person	€ 4.00

Kühlungsborn

Campingpark Kühlungsborn

Waldstrasse 1B, D-18225 Kühlungsborn (Mecklenburg-West Pomerania) T: **03829 37195**.

E: **campingpark.kuehlungsborn@t-online.de** **alanrogers.com/DE38240**

Campingpark Kühlungsborn is a large, well organised site with excellent facilities and direct access to a long sandy beach. It is within easy walking distance of Kühlungsborn, Mecklenburg's largest seaside resort, a town with a long and interesting history, and where many events for visitors are to be found. The site has 550 touring pitches, 388 of which are fully serviced. They are fairly level, on grass and separated by hedges. Most are in shade and vary in size from 80-150 sq.m. The site has a very active and varied programme of activities and entertainment for both children and adults.

Facilities

Three modern, well maintained sanitary buildings have facilities for families, children and disabled visitors. Separate family shower rooms for rent. Laundry. Kitchen. Dog shower. Motorcaravan services. Small shop. Cinema. Bowling. Archery. Volleyball. Basketball. Children's clubs and entertainment. Bicycle hire. WiFi over site (charged). Off site: Large supermarket at site entrance. Rostocker Zoo. Sealife museum in Stralsund.

Open: 15 March - 15 November.

Directions

Site is on the coast just west of Kühlungsborn. Leave A20 at exit 12 for Kröpelin, then north to Kühlungsborn-Kühlungsborn West where site is signed. GPS: 54.15141, 11.7196

Charges guide

Per unit incl. 2 persons and fully serviced	€ 28.00 - € 42.00
extra person	€ 7.00 - € 9.00
child (3-12 yrs)	€ 4.00 - € 5.00
dog	€ 3.00 - € 5.00

Schillersdorf

Camping Am Leppinsee

C20, D-17252 Schillersdorf (Mecklenburg-West Pomerania) T: **039829 2500**. E: **info@haveltourist.de**

alanrogers.com/DE38210

Bordering and with direct access to the Leppinsee via a meadow, a beach and a small jetty, Am Leppinsee offers 70 well shaded, grassy pitches, all with 10A electricity, arranged amongst the trees. This is a very quiet site and borders Germany's largest national park where cranes, red deer, the white-tailed eagle, osprey and much more can be found. Close to the site is an eight-acre 'dendrologischer' garden (study of wooded plants); founded in 1906, it contains many rare examples of trees as well as 600-year-old oak and beech.

Facilities

The modern bright sanitary building is heated and well maintained. Entry and use of showers requires chip key. Washing machines and dryers. Kitchen and dishwashing facilities. Motorcaravan services. Bread to order from reception. Play area. Volleyball pitch. Boat jetty. Limited entertainment. Bicycle hire. WiFi over part of site (charged). Off site: Müritz National Park adjacent. Riding and boat launching 5 km. Müritz information centre and a 100,000-litre freshwater Aquarium (Germany's largest) at Herrensee, near Weren.

Open: 1 April - 31 October.

Directions

Leave the autobahn at exit 18 Röbel/Müritzand and take the 198 east to Mirow, then north through Granzow towards Roggentin. Continue north through Qualzow, then Shillersdorf keeping left to site (signed). Follow directions rather than sat nav in Schillersdorf. GPS: 53.34740, 12.82659

Charges guide

Per unit incl. 2 persons and electricity	€ 13.00 - € 28.90
extra person	€ 4.50 - € 7.20
child (2-14 yrs)	€ 1.70 - € 4.80

FREE Alan Rogers Travel Card
Extra benefits and savings - see page 14

Schwaan

Camping Schwaan

Sandgarten 17, D-18258 Schwaan (Mecklenburg-West Pomerania) T: 03844 813716.
E: info@campingplatz-schwaan.de alanrogers.com/DE37850

Peacefully located beside a gently flowing river, ideal for swimming and with good shade from mature trees, Camping Schwaan is a large site for those who want to relax in a natural setting. There is ample space for children to play, and being close to the Baltic coast and many interesting towns, it makes a quiet base from which to tour the area. There are 150 touring pitches, eight fully serviced, and almost all with 10/16A electricity. They are level, grassy and open, so you can spread yourself out under the tall trees. For those using the Rostock ferry service it is also a useful overnight stop.

Facilities

Three modern, well maintained sanitary blocks have some individual cabins, controllable showers (payment card), baby bath and facilities for disabled visitors. Washing machines and dryers. Motorcaravan services. Small kitchen. Fresh bread to order. Part of river partitioned off as children's swimming area. Minigolf. Play areas. WiFi over part of site (charged). Off site: Small café just outside of site selling snacks, takeaway food, ices. Beach 30 km.

Open: 1 March - 31 October.

Directions

Site is 1 km. south of Schwaan. From A20 take exit 13 and travel south 14 km. to Schwaan then towards Kassow. Site is 1 km. beyond Schwaan on the right. GPS: 53.923561, 12.10676

Charges guide

Per unit incl. 2 persons and electricity	€ 13.00 - € 20.50
extra person	€ 4.00 - € 5.00
child (3-14 yrs)	€ 2.50 - € 3.00

Strasen

Naturcamping Am Grossen Pälitzsee

C54, D-17255 Strasen (Mecklenburg-West Pomerania) T: 03981 24790. E: info@haveltourist.de
alanrogers.com/DE38190

Set in a quiet, wooded location and with direct access to the Pälitzsee, this site is covered by mature trees offering good shade mixed with some glades. The terraced ground slopes down to the water's edge, where there are views over the lake, access to boat jetties and a floating platform for swimmers. There are 40 fairly level, grassy touring pitches located amongst the trees and all have 10A electricity. The lake is connected to other lakes through a network of waterways and is popular with canoeists. The use of motorboats is permitted.

Facilities

Modern, well maintained sanitary block with clean facilities including open washbasins and toilets for children. Hot water to controllable showers (on payment). Washing machines and dryers. Small shop. Playground. Campfire. Volleyball. Fishing. Boat launching. Boat jetty. Entertainment programmes for children (high season). Bicycle hire. Off site: Bar/restaurant 3.5 km. The Müritz National Park and park centre.

Open: 1 April - 31 October.

Directions

Leave the autobahn at exit 18 Röbel/Müritzand and take the 198 east to Wesenberg then south through Wustrow, Strasen to Pelzkuhl. Site is along a 1 km. track passing through the forest.
GPS: 53.1844, 12.97795

Charges guide

Per unit incl. 2 persons and electricity	€ 13.00 - € 28.90
extra person	€ 4.50 - € 7.20

Userin

Camping & Ferienpark Havelberge am Woblitzsee

An den Havelbergen 1, Userin, D-17237 Gross Quassow (Mecklenburg-West Pomerania)
T: 039 812 4790. E: info@haveltourist.de alanrogers.com/DE38200

LeadingCampings

The Müritz National Park is a very large area of lakes and marshes, popular for birdwatching as well as watersports, and Havelberge is a large, well equipped site to use as a base for enjoying the area. It is quite steep in places with many terraces, most with shade, and views over the lake. There are 400 pitches in total with 330 good sized, numbered touring pitches (all with 16A Europlug electrical connections) and 230 pitches on a newly developed area to the rear of the site with water and drainage. Pitches on the new field are level and separated by low hedges and bushes but have no shade. A member of Leading Campings group.

Facilities

Four sanitary buildings (one new and of a very high standard) provide very good facilities, with private cabins, showers on payment and large section for children. Kitchen and laundry. Motorcaravan services. Small shop, restaurant, bar, takeaway and wellness (all 1/4-31/10). Lake for fishing, swimming from a small beach and boats can be launched (over 5 hp requires a German boat licence). Rowing boats, windsurfers and bikes can be hired. Canoe centre with beginners' courses and canoe hire. Accompanied canoe, cycle and walking tours. Play areas. Entertainment in high season. Tepee village. Tree walkway (2.5 m. high with safety wires). WiFi (charged).

Open: All year.

Directions

From A19 Rostock-Berlin road take exit 18 and follow B198 to Wesenberg and go left to Klein Quassow and follow site signs.
GPS: 53.30517, 13.00133

Charges guide

Per unit incl. 2 persons and electricity	€ 26.60 - € 31.30
extra person	€ 4.40 - € 7.10
child (2-14 yrs)	€ 1.60 - € 4.70
dog	€ 1.00 - € 4.70

For latest campsite news, availability and prices visit
alanrogers.com

Wesenberg

Camping Park Am Weissen See

C63, D-17255 Wesenberg (Mecklenburg-West Pomerania) T: 03981 24790. E: info@haveltourist.de

alanrogers.com/DE38180

The site lies just 300 metres from and overlooks the Weissen See, which is open to the public and used for swimming and boating. Of the 150 pitches, 100 are for touring units, all with 16A electricity and in an open-plan arrangement. Although the site is somewhat undulating in places, the pitches are reasonably level, with a grass/sand base and shaded by mature tall pine trees. In addition, there are overnight parking places outside of the barrier. A local train service (more a bus on rails) passes the site, allowing easy access to the towns of Mirow and Neustrelitz.

Facilities

Two traditional, well maintained sanitary blocks have open style washbasins and controllable showers (payment by token € 0.90). Facilities for disabled campers. Washing machines and dryers. Motorcaravan services. Hot plates for hire. Small shop. Fresh bread to order. Play area. Children's entertainment (high season). WiFi (charged). Off site: Bar/restaurant adjacent with swimming and boating lake and sandy beach. Waren, Neubrandenburg and Neustrelitz.

Open: 23 March - 29 September.

Directions

Site is 1 km. west of Wesenberg. Leave autobahn 19 at exit 18 Röbel/Müritz and travel westwards on 198 (Neustrelitz/Plau Am See). After 38 km, just before Wesenberg turn left (north) towards Kleiner Weiser See and follow signs to site (400 m). GPS: 53.28411, 12.94844

Charges guide

Per unit incl. 2 persons and electricity	€ 14.50 - € 31.90
extra person	€ 4.00 - € 7.20

Zierow

Ostseecamping

Strandstrasse 19c, D-23968 Zierow (Mecklenburg-West Pomerania) T: 038 428 638 20.

E: ostseecampingzierow@t-online.de alanrogers.com/DE25000

Set on top of sand dunes overlooking and with direct access to the beach, Ostseecamping is in a quiet location yet within easy reach of major towns in the region. There is good swimming from the beach, although the site does have a small swimming pool. Of the 450 level pitches, 300 are for touring units, all have electricity connections (10-16A) and 120 are fully serviced. They are set on grass and in places there is some tree shade. Outside the site there are eight quickstop facilities with electricity connections. This is a good site for families, with entertainment programmes in summer, playgrounds and a gently shelving, sandy beach. This part of Germany, formally the DDR, is not that well known to tourists, yet it has a great deal to offer in the way of sandy beaches, attractive landscapes and historic towns, cities and buildings. Anyone travelling to the Baltic coast should make a point of passing through and allowing a few hours to visit Schwerin with The Schloss and its gardens, set on an island in the Schweriner lake, the second largest in Northern Germany.

Facilities

Two modern, attractive and well maintained sanitary blocks, one completely renovated in 2013, have a special children's area, a baby bath and disabled facilities. Showers (on payment). Bathrooms to rent. Laundry room with washing machines and dryer. Shop (1/4-1/10). Bar. Restaurant. Takeaway. Indoor heated swimming pool. Sauna, massage and cosmetic studio. Bowling alley. Small zoo. Indoor playroom (free entry). Volleyball. Watersports centre with windsurfing, sailing and catamaran sailing. Go-kart and bicycle hire. WiFi over site and Internet in reception (charged). Off site: Riding 200 m. Golf 8 km. Schwerin Schloss, Wismar (can be reached by cycleway). Rostock and Lübeck.

Open: All year.

Directions

Site is on the coast 6 km. northwest of Wismar. Leave A20 at exit 8 Wismar Mitte, north to Gägelow then north on minor road to Zierow. GPS: 53.9347, 11.3718

Charges guide

Per unit incl. 2 persons and electricity	€ 20.30 - € 29.70
extra person	€ 4.50 - € 5.70
child (5-14 yrs)	free - € 3.00
dog	€ 3.00

Zwenzow

Camping Zwenzower Ufer

Am Grossen Labussee (C56), D-17237 Zwenzow (Mecklenburg-West Pomerania) T: 03981 24790.
E: info@haveltourist.de alanrogers.com/DE38150

On the edge of Zwenzower village, this is a small, attractive, well kept campsite with 75 touring pitches. It slopes gently down to the banks of Grosser Labussee which is suitable for swimming, is connected to other lakes and where motorboats are permitted. The site has direct access to the lake and a separate lakeside area is reserved for FKK guests. The pitches (60-100 sq.m) are level and all have 16A electricity and are on grass; many have views over the lake and there is good tree shade over parts of the site.

Facilities
The traditional sanitary facilities are heated and well maintained with controllable showers (payment by key). Facilities for disabled visitors. Washing machine and dryer. Motorcaravan services. Small shop/snack bar in reception. Playground. Limited entertainment. Fishing. Bicycle hire. Boat launching. WiFi over most of site (charged). Off site: Restaurant 200 m. Riding 6 km.

Open: 1 April - 2 November.

Directions
Leave the autobahn at exit 18 Röbel/Müritz and take the 198 east towards Wesenberg. In Mirow North towards Userin, through Granzow, Roggetin to Zwenzow. GPS: 53.31883, 12.94506

Charges guide

Per unit incl. 2 persons	
and electricity	€ 13.00 - € 28.90
extra person	€ 4.50 - € 7.20
child (2-14 yrs)	€ 1.70 - € 4.80
dog	€ 1.10 - € 4.80

Attendorn

Camping Hof Biggen

Finnentroperstrasse 131, D-57439 Attendorn (North Rhine-Westphalia) T: 027 229 5530. E: info@biggen.de
alanrogers.com/DE31490

Camping Hof Biggen is a well established site in the heart of the Sauerland region, close to the city of Attendorn, just 4 km. away from the Biggesee. It is set amidst beautiful green countryside and a large touring area at the top of the site offers a great view over woods, meadows and the Burg Schnellenberg castle. There are 350 pitches, 50 for tourers, all equipped with 16A electricity, in addition to 50 for tents on slightly sloping ground. There are 12 caravans for hire. The site can become a suntrap in hot weather.

Facilities
Three older style toilet blocks of varying sizes are clean and well maintained, with showers and washbasins in cubicles. Car wash area. Waste disposal station. Laundry. Camp kitchen. Self-service supermarket, restaurant with adjoining terrace (both open all year). Large screen TV. Bowling alley. Play areas. Football field. Volleyball court. Outdoor board games. Games room. Children's entertainment (July/Aug). Bicycle hire. Free cars available for motorcaravanners. Off site: Limestone cave in Attendorn. Fishing 1 km. Sailing 3 km. Golf and riding 5 km.

Open: All year.

Directions
From the A45 exit 16 join the L539 east towards Attendorn. Continue on the same road around the southern edge of the town. The site is then on your left after about 3 km. GPS: 51.13694, 7.93984

Charges guide

Per unit incl. 2 persons and electricity	€ 19.90
extra person	€ 6.00
child (2-15 yrs)	€ 2.50
dog	€ 3.00

Camping Cheques accepted.

Barntrup

Ferienpark Teutoburger Wald

4 Bade-Anstalts-Weg, D-32683 Barntrup (North Rhine-Westphalia) T: 052 632 221.
E: info@ferienparkteutoburgerwald.de alanrogers.com/DE31820

Under Dutch ownership, this site has 110 touring pitches, all with 16A electricity. Just outside the main gate there are nine fully serviced hardstanding pitches with charcoal grill, designed with motorcaravans in mind. Although the site is sloping, the pitches are 110-250 sq.m. on mainly level grassy areas with some shade. Energy saving equipment has been installed in the toilet block for the production of hot water and the site is actively promoting good environmental practices. The famous fairytale town of Hameln (20 km) is worth a visit, especially on a Sunday for the Rattenfangerspiel.

Facilities
Excellent toilet block with underfloor heating and Roman baths theme inside. Roomy showers and open washbasins. Colourful children's section. Family showers. Dog shower with hairdryer. Laundry facilities. Key system for use of hot water. Motorcaravan services. Games room with TV. Free WiFi. Play area. Electric scooters for hire. Off site: Walking in the adjacent woods. Outdoor pool next door. Bicycle hire and golf 10 km. (reduced fees). Spa town of Bad Pyrmont 12 km. Riding and fishing 20 km. The towns of Detmold, Biedefeld and Paderborn.

Open: 1 April - 1 November.

Directions
From Hanover, take the A2 west (Osnabrück). At exit 35 continue on B83 road towards Hameln. In Hameln take the B1 road south towards Barntrup and follow signs. GPS: 51.98681, 9.10842

Charges guide

Per unit incl. 2 persons	
and electricity	€ 19.50 - € 27.50
extra person	€ 5.75
child (2-15 yrs)	€ 3.25
dog	€ 2.50

For latest campsite news, availability and prices visit

alanrogers.com

Hörstel

Erholungsanlage Hertha-See

Herthaseestrasse 70, D-48477 Hörstel (North Rhine-Westphalia) T: 054 591 008. E: contact@hertha-see.de

alanrogers.com/DE31950

This campsite with 570 pitches (150 for tourers) is centred around an artificial lake which has a gently sloping sandy beach and is surrounded by a mass of tall pine trees. Under the pine trees there is room for 120 touring pitches, all with electricity (16A, long leads required), 27 also with water, cable and waste water. In this area campers can park at will, on open, sandy, grass-covered ground. From most touring pitches there are good views over the lake, and campers will enjoy the welcoming bar/restaurant with its covered terrace.

Facilities

Good sanitary facilities are in modern heated blocks. Showers on payment (€ 0.50). Facilities for disabled visitors. Laundry rooms with washing machines, dryers and ironing point. Dishwashers. Baby room. Shop, bar, restaurant and takeaway (all season). Motorcaravan services. Sports field. Minigolf. Tennis. Play area. Large chess game. Swimming in the lake. Dogs are not permitted. WiFi throughout (charged). Off site: Indoor play hall adjacent. Bicycle hire 100 m. Fishing 200 m.

Open: Easter - 30 September.

Directions

Leave A30/E30 autobahn at exit 10 and drive north towards Hopsten to stop sign. Turn left towards Rheine and after 100 m. turn right. Site is signed. GPS: 52.32753, 7.60197

Charges guide

Per unit incl. 2 persons	
and electricity	€ 21.10 - € 25.20
extra person	€ 6.30 - € 6.90
child (4-15 yrs)	€ 2.50 - € 2.90

Köln

Campingplatz der Stadt Köln

Weidenweg 35, D-51105 Köln-Poll (North Rhine-Westphalia) T: 022 183 1966.

E: die-eckardts@netcologne.de alanrogers.com/DE32050

The ancient city of Cologne offers much for the visitor. This wooded park is pleasantly situated along the river bank, with wide grass areas on either side of narrow tarmac access roads with low wire mesh fencing separating it from the public park and riverside walks. Of 140 unmarked, level or slightly undulating touring pitches, 50 have 10A electricity and there is shade for some from various mature trees. Tents have their own large area. Because of its position close to the autobahn bridge over the Rhine, there is road and river noise.

Facilities

The toilet block, which has been totally renovated, is heated with free hot water (06.00-12.00, 17.00-23.00) in washbasins and by a 50 cent coin in the showers. New facilities for disabled visitors. Large open-fronted room for cooking and eating with microwave oven. Washing machine and dryer. Small shop for bread and basic supplies (mid May-Sept). Evening snacks (March-Oct). Fishing. Bicycle hire. Drinks machine. WiFi (charged). Off site: Bar/café by entrance. Trams and buses to city centre 1 km. across the bridge. Golf 5 km. Riding 15 km.

Open: 1 April - 16 October.

Directions

Leave A4 at exit 13 for Köln-Poll (just to west off intersection of A3 and A4). Turn left at first traffic lights and follow international site signs through a sometimes fairly narrow one-way system to the riverside, back towards the motorway bridge. GPS: 50.90438, 6.99188

Charges guide

Per unit incl. 2 persons	
and electricity	€ 22.00 - € 25.00
extra person	€ 6.50
child (4-12 yrs)	€ 4.00

Lemgo

Campingpark Lemgo

Regenstorstr. 10, D-32657 Lemgo (North Rhine-Westphalia) T: 0526 114 858.

E: lemgo@meyer-zu-bentrup.de alanrogers.com/DE31290

This site is located close to the city centre of Lemgo and adjacent to the municipal leisure area, Eau Le, which offers a range of facilities to guests including a pool and sauna. There are 90 touring pitches on three grassy fields, two to the front exclusively for tourers and mainly hardstanding, one to the back with a mixture of tourers and seasonal pitches. All have 16A Europlug (long leads necessary). The well maintained city centre of Lemgo is within a ten minute walk and displays impressive Gothic and Renaissance architecture.

Facilities

Two toilet blocks, one traditional and refurbished, one modern, have excellent facilities for children. Laundry room. New play area. WiFi (free). Off site: At Eau Le: outdoor pool, indoor pool, sauna, steam room, massage. Lemgo city centre. Castle Brake.

Open: 1 March - 30 November.

Directions

From Osnabruck, follow the A30 and take exit 28 (Hiddenhausen). Continue on Bunder Strasse then the B239. Turn right onto Oerlinhauser Strasse and then third exit on roundabout to L712. Continue for 11.6 km. following B238/B66 then turn left onto Striftstrasse. Site is 900 m. GPS: 52.02446, 8.91017

Charges guide

Per unit incl. 2 persons	
and electricity	€ 19.00
extra person	€ 4.50
child (7-16 yrs)	€ 2.50

Lienen

Eurocamp

Holperdorp 4, D-49536 Lienen (North Rhine-Westphalia) T: 05483 290. E: holperdorper-tal@t-online.de

alanrogers.com/DE29500

Eurocamp is a traditional rural site in the Holperdorper Valley in North Rhine Westphalia, a short drive south from Osnabrück and conveniently located close to several motorways, including the A30 from the Netherlands. There are 250 pitches, of which about 60 are available for touring units. They are on terraces (some slightly sloping) but are not marked out, so you choose your spot either in the open or in the shade of fruit and walnut trees. Electricity connections (16A) are available. There are numerous opportunities for walkers and cyclists to enjoy the surrounding countryside and woodland. Nearby Lienen has shops and restaurants.

Facilities

Central toilet block has been renovated and provides showers (€ 0.5) open-style washbasins and facilities for children. Restaurant and bar with terrace. Fishing lakes (licence required). Walking and cycling tracks from campsite. WiFi (free). Off site: Major cycle track (Hermannsweg) 1 km. Lienen 5 km. Bad Iburg 6 km. Hagen 8 km. Osnabrück 20 km. Münster 50 km.

Open: All year.

Directions

From A30 motorway (Netherlands/Hanover) take exit 18 (Osnabrück-Nahne) and head south on B51 for 11 km. In Bad Iburg turn west on K332/K30. Site is on right in 4 km. Narrow access road. GPS: 52.16664, 7.98098

Charges guide

Per unit incl. 2 persons and electricity	€ 15.00
extra person	€ 4.00
child (0-16 yrs)	€ 2.50

Meschede

Knaus Campingpark Hennesee/Meschede

Mielinghausen 7, D-59872 Meschede (North Rhine-Westphalia) T: 029 195 2720.

E: hennesee@knauscamp.de alanrogers.com/DE31900

Camping Hennesee can be found in the 'land of the 1,000 mountains', a beautiful part of Sauerland. The site is situated on the banks of Lake Hennesee which links the nature reserves of Arnsberger Wald and Homert. The site offers 183 grassy touring pitches (some slightly sloping), all with 6A Europlug and some with great views over the lake. Twenty-five pitches have water and drainage also. Hennesee is an ideal base for all kinds of water-based activities, such as windsurfing, fishing (permit needed) and swimming. English is spoken.

Facilities

Three toilet blocks have controllable showers, some washbasins in cabins, family showers and a baby room. Washing machines and dryers. Bar. Restaurant. Takeaway. TV room. Supermarket. Indoor swimming pool. Sauna. Massage. Sunbed, infrared room. Bicycle hire. Electric cars for children. Fully equipped tents and mobile homes to rent. WiFi (charged). Off site: Tennis, volleyball, golf and minigolf. Riding 5 km.

Open: All year.

Directions

From the A46 take exit 70 (Meschede) and join the B55 towards Olpe. Follow this road along the Hennesee (lake) until Mielinghausen. Cross the bridge over the lake and turn right to the campsite. GPS: 51.29999, 8.25000

Charges guide

Per unit incl. 2 persons and electricity	€ 18.00 - € 31.20
extra person	€ 4.30 - € 7.50
child (6-14 yrs)	€ 2.20 - € 3.90
Camping Cheques accepted.	

Münster

Campingplatz Münster

Laerer Werseufer 7, Wolbecker Strasse, D-48157 Münster (North Rhine-Westphalia) T: 025 131 1982.

E: mail@campingplatz-muenster.de alanrogers.com/DE31850

This is a first class site on the outskirts of Münster. Of a total of 570 pitches, 120 are for touring units, each with electricity, water, drainage and TV socket. The pitches are level, most with partial hardstanding and others are separated into groups by mature hedges and a number of trees provide shade. The university city of Münster with its many historical buildings and over 500 bars and restaurants, many offering local traditional dishes, is only 5 km. from the site. The city is the main attraction in this region and well worth visiting, especially on market days (Wednesdays and Saturdays).

Facilities

The two toilet blocks are well designed, modern and maintained to the highest standards. Controllable showers are token operated. Two units for disabled campers. Baby room. Cooking facilities. Washing machine, dryer and ironing facilities. Sauna. Hairdressing salon. Motorcaravan services. Shop. Bar/restaurant. Minigolf. Play area. Beach volleyball. Chess. Tennis. Playroom for children under 8 yrs. Bicycle hire. Security barrier card deposit € 10. Off site: Public open-air swimming pool adjacent. Canoeing and fishing. Bus stop 100 m.

Open: All year.

Directions

Site is 5 km. southeast of Münster city centre. Leave A1 autobahn at exit 78 (Münster Süd) and take B51 towards Münster. After 2 km. stay on the B51 towards Bielefeld/Warendorf. After 5 km. turn south (right) towards Wolbeck. Follow site signs. GPS: 51.94645, 7.68908

Charges guide

Per unit incl. 2 persons and electricity	€ 28.00
extra person	€ 7.00
child (4-11 yrs)	€ 4.50 - € 5.50

For latest campsite news, availability and prices visit

alanrogers.com

Olpe

Feriencamp Biggesee – Vier Jahreszeiten

Am Sonderner Kopf 3, D-57462 Olpe-Sondern (North Rhine-Westphalia) T: 027 619 44111.

E: info@biggesee-sondern.com alanrogers.com/DE32100

Situated on a gentle, south facing slope that leads down to the water's edge of the Biggesee, Feriencamp Biggesee blends in well with its wooded surroundings. The 200 touring pitches, all with electricity, are arranged in circles at the top part of the site and on a series of wide terraces lower down. They are grassy with some hardstanding. From the lower part of the site there is access through a gate to a large open meadow that ends at the water's edge where swimming is permitted. The attractive Biggesee, with arms branching out into the surrounding hills, is a watersports paradise where virtually all forms of watersports are available.

Facilities

Excellent heated sanitary facilities are in two areas. New building with cabins to hire. Many washbasins in cabins and special showers for children. Facilities for babies and campers with disabilities. Laundry. Motorcaravan services. Cooking facilities. Shop. Restaurant. Bistro (including breakfast). Playroom and playground for smaller children. Grill hut. Fishing. Solarium and sauna. Entertainment and excursions. Dog shower. Off site: Tennis nearby. Train service 1 km. Sailing 1 km. Riding 8 km. Golf 12 km.

Open: All year.

Directions

From A45 (Siegen-Hagen) autobahn, take exit 18 to Olpe (N), and turn towards Attendorn. After 6 km. turn right signed Erholungsanlage Vier-Jahreszeiten, then after 100 m. turn right and follow site signs. GPS: 51.07529, 7.85323

Charges guide

Per unit incl. 2 persons and electricity	€ 21.25 - € 23.70
extra person	€ 4.90

No credit cards.

Tecklenburg

Regenbogen Tecklenburg

Grafenstrasse 31, D-49545 Tecklenburg-Leeden (North Rhine-Westphalia) T: 05405 1007.

E: tecklenburg@regenbogen.ag alanrogers.com/DE30300

This is a well designed and attractive countryside site with lots of trees and hedges where modern buildings have been built in keeping with the traditional, half timbered style of the region. There are 500 grass touring pitches arranged on large, open areas divided by tall hedges. Trees provide good shade and all pitches have electrical connections. Access from the A30 autobahn is convenient, although this is offset by the fact that some noise from the autobahn is evident in the touring pitch area. Facilities on this site are really good, from the modern pool complex, to the half timbered bar/restaurant with its wooden beams and adjoining beer garden.

Facilities

Four modern, heated toilet blocks have free showers and provision for disabled visitors. Family shower rooms to rent. Washing machines and dryer. Cooking facilities. Motorcaravan services. Shop. Bar and restaurant (Easter-end Oct and Christmas). Heated pool complex with indoor and outdoor pools, slide and paddling pool. Sauna, wellness, massage and cosmetic studio (charged). Play area. Minigolf. Off site: Riding 3 km. Golf 5 km.

Open: 12 February - 3 January.

Directions

Leave A30/E30 autobahn at exit 13 towards Tecklenburg. Between the autobahn exit and Tecklenburg, the site is signed at a roundabout. Leeden is a village to the east of Tecklenburg, site is 2 km. from the village. GPS: 52.22947, 7.89019

Charges guide

Per unit incl. 2 adults, all children under 13 yrs and electricity	€ 19.90 - € 39.50

Vlotho

Camping Sonnenwiese

Borlefzen 1, D-32602 Vlotho (North Rhine-Westphalia) T: 057 338 217. E: info@sonnenwiese.com

alanrogers.com/DE31800

Sonnenwiese is a first class, family run campsite where care has been taken to make everyone feel at home – there is even an insect hotel! The site is tastefully landscaped with flowers, an ornamental pond crossed by a wooden bridge and large grass areas extending to the river. Situated between wooded hills to the north and bordering the Weser river to the south, this 400 pitch site offers 100 touring pitches, all with electricity and most also having water and drainage. In addition, there are special pitches with a private shower, toilet and washbasin unit. The site is particularly geared towards families with children.

Facilities

The toilet block is modern and maintained to the highest standard. Showers are token operated. Baby room. Washing machines, dryer and ironing board. Cooking facilities. Supermarket. Panorama restaurant with good choice of dishes. Snack bar. Sauna, solarium and fitness room. Club room and room used for children's entertainment. Large adventure play area. Grass bordered lake for swimming. Fishing. Bicycle hire. WiFi (charged). Off site: Bus service from gate. Golf 4 km. Riding 5 km.

Open: All year.

Directions

Leave A2 autobahn at exit 31, 32 or 33 and head for Vlotho. In Vlotho, cross Weser river bridge and turn right towards Rinteln. After 3 km. on right are entrances to two campsites. Sonnenwiese is on left hand side at end of entrance road. GPS: 52.17083, 8.904

Charges guide

Per unit incl. 2 persons and electricity	€ 23.30
extra person	€ 5.40

No credit cards.

Wesel

Erholungszentrum Grav-Insel

Grav-Insel 1, D-46487 Wesel (North Rhine-Westphalia) T: 028 197 2830. E: info@grav-insel.com

alanrogers.com/DE32020

Grav-Insel claims to be the largest family camping site in Germany, providing entertainment and activities to match, with over 2,000 permanent units. A section for 500 touring units runs beside the water to the left of the entrance and this area has been completely renewed. These pitches, all with 10A electricity, are flat, grassy, mostly without shade and of about 100 sq.m. A walk through the site takes you past a nature reserve and to the Rhine, where you can watch the barges. Despite its size, this site is very well maintained, calm, clean and spacious.

Facilities

Excellent sanitary facilities, all housed in a modern building above which is the bar/restaurant. Touring area augmented by prefabricated units to be renewed. Facilities for disabled visitors. Baby room. Launderette. Motorcaravan services. Supermarket. Restaurant/pizzeria. Entertainment area with satellite TV. WiFi. Solarium. Large play area on sand plus wet weather indoor area. Bicycle hire. Boat park. Sailing. Fishing. Swimming. Football (international coaching in high season). Entertainment in high season. Off site: Bus service 500 m. Riding 2 km. The attractive town of Xanten 23 km.

Open: All year.

Directions

Site is 5 km. northwest of Wesel. From A3 take exit 6 and B58 towards Wesel, then right towards Rees. Turn left at sign for Flüren, through Flüren and left to site after 1.5 km. If approaching Wesel from west (B58), cross the Rhine, turn left at first traffic lights and follow signs Grav-Insel and Flüren. GPS: 51.67062, 6.55600

Charges guide

Per unit incl. 2 persons and electricity	€ 12.50 - € 18.50
extra person	€ 4.00
child (under 12 yrs)	€ 2.00

Asbacherhütte

Camping Harfenmühle

An der Deutschen Edelsteinstrasse, D-55758 Asbacherhütte (Rhineland Palatinate)

T: 067 867 076. E: mail@harfenmuehle.de alanrogers.com/DE32540

Harfenmühle is a quiet, family run and family orientated site with an excellent restaurant, set in a wooded valley on the Edelsteinstrasse (precious stone route) between the wine regions Mosel and Nahe and is a site well suited to those interested in an active outdoor holiday. Besides on-site activities for children, such as searching for gems in the gemstone river or 'gold' washing off-site, there are many interesting places to visit and things to do, such as stone breaking in search of gemstones at a nearby quarry. The 100 touring pitches are arranged in several separate areas, level, on grass and all with electricity.

Facilities

Two sanitary blocks include good shower cubicles (on payment), facilities for babies, children and disabled visitors. Launderette. Kiosk with fresh bread daily. Takeaway. Wine cellar/bar. Restaurant with terrace serving local specialities, and international cuisine with a French flavour (open daily). Sauna and solarium. Swimming lake. Play areas. Playing field. Water play area. Rental accommodation. WiFi. Off site: Walking paths directly from site. Riding 3 km and 4.5 km. Fishing 5 km. Golf 10 km.

Open: 1 March - 31 December.

Directions

Site is 12 km. north of Idar-Oberstein. From the B41 Saarbrücken-Bad Kreuznach, exit north at Fischbach signed towards Herrstein and then on through Morschied to Asbacherhütte, with site entrance on right. GPS: 49.80362, 7.26945

Charges guide

Per unit incl. 2 persons and electricity	€ 20.50 - € 22.00
extra person	€ 5.50 - € 6.00

No credit cards.

Bad Dürkheim

Knaus Campingpark Bad Dürkheim

In den Almen 1, D-67098 Bad Dürkheim (Rhineland Palatinate) T: 063 226 1356.

E: badduerkheim@knauscamp.de alanrogers.com/DE32600

This is a large, comfortable site with almost 600 pitches, half of which are for touring. Being situated in Bad Dürkheim, which claims to have the world's largest wine festival, it can understandably become quite full in high season. The site is arranged either side of a long, central arcade of growing vines and along one side of the site there is a lake. Growing trees provide some shade and electrical connections are available throughout (16A). There is some noise from light aircraft, especially at weekends.

Facilities

Three large sanitary blocks are spaced out along the central avenue. They are of a high standard (private cabins, automatic taps etc) and are heated in cool weather. Laundry facilities. Gas supplies. Motorcaravan services. Cooking facilities. Shop. Restaurant, bar and takeaway (all year excl. Nov). Sports programme. Tennis. Playground. Sauna. Swimming and non-powered boats on lake. Fishing. Riding. Bicycle hire. Activity programme (guided tours, biking and climbing). WiFi on part of site (charged). Off site: Golf 8 km.

Open: All year (reduced facilities in November).

Directions

Bad Dürkheim is 18 km. west of Ludwigshafen. Site is signed on the 37 (Ludwigshafen) road on the eastern outskirts of Bad Dürkheim at the traffic lights. GPS: 49.47380, 8.19170

Charges guide

Per unit incl. 2 persons and electricity	€ 22.30 - € 32.50
extra person	€ 5.80 - € 8.20
child (4-14 yrs)	€ 2.30 - € 4.00
dog	€ 2.00 - € 3.80

For latest campsite news, availability and prices visit

alanrogers.com

Burgen
Camping Burgen

Moselstrasse, D-56332 Burgen (Rhineland Palatinate) T: 026 052 396. E: Info@camping-burgen.de
alanrogers.com/DE32300

Camping Burgen is pleasantly situated between the road and the river on the flat, grassy bank of the Mosel between Koblenz and Cochem. The site has views with most of the pitches on the river's edge being occupied by permanent caravans and attendant boats, but there are 120 individual numbered grassy pitches for touring units, plus a meadow at one end, both with electricity (10/16A). With a railway and a road across the water, a road alongside the site and commercial boats, some noise may be expected. The site fills up for much of July and August but a few pitches are kept for short stay visitors.

Facilities
The single central toilet block is adequate, with washbasins (five in cabins), and nine showers which might be hard pressed in high season. Laundry facilities. Gas supplies. Motorcaravan services. Shop. General room with TV and games. Small swimming pool (June-Aug). Fishing (with permit). Slipway for boats. Playground. Bicycle hire. Outdoor chess. Max 2 dogs per pitch. WiFi over site (charged). Off site: Restaurant 200 m. Riding 15 km. Golf 20 km. Boat trips. Cycling tracks. Rambling. Wine tasting.
Open: 2 April - 18 October.

Directions
Site is 22 km. southwest of Koblenz bordering the Mosel on the eastern bank. Access is signed from the B49 just north of Burgen.
GPS: 50.21665, 7.39376

Charges guide
Per unit incl. 2 persons	
and electricity	€ 21.50
extra person	€ 6.00
child (1-13 yrs)	€ 4.00
dog	€ 2.00

Burgen
Knaus Campingpark Mosel/Burgen

Am Bootschafen (An du B43), D-56332 Burgen (Rhineland Palatinate) T: 02605 952176.
E: mosel@knauscamp.de alanrogers.com/DE35420

This long-established, riverside site is now part of the Knaus Camping group, and is already seeing major improvements. Extended along a kilometre of the banks of the Mosel, the site boasts its own marina for campers who enjoy boating, canoeing and other watersports. New toilet facilities are of the highest modern quality. A small swimming pool is heated in season, overlooked by the restaurant and terrace bar. Recent additions include a beach volleyball court and a small playground. Soon to be ready is a separate unit for disabled visitors and new motorcaravan services. All touring pitches have completely new 16A electricity hook-ups.

Facilities
Modern toilet facilities above the main block. Baby bath and changing room. Newly constructed facility for disabled visitors. Laundry facilities. Motorcaravan services. Friendly restaurant and bar. Small swimming pool open in season. Small playground. Beach volleyball. Boating marina. Deposit for chipcards to open barrier and toilet facilities. Special rates for overnight motorcaravan stops. WiFi throughout (charged). Off site: Most riverside villages offer river cruises. Wine tasting opportunities, ancient villages and numerous castles. Bus to Koblenz.
Open: 11 April - 19 October.

Directions
On the B49, just south of Burgen. Clearly signed from both directions, but if approaching from the south the road markings can confuse and care must be taken in turning into the site entrance. Reception hut immediately inside gate.
GPS: 50.20474, 7.38164

Charges guide
Per unit incl. 2 persons	
and electricity	€ 17.80 - € 21.10
extra person	€ 4.50 - € 5.50

Camping Cheques accepted.

Koblenz
Camping Gülser Moselbogen

Am Gülser Moselbogen 20, Güls, D-56072 Koblenz (Rhineland Palatinate) T: 026 144 474.
E: info@moselbogen.de alanrogers.com/DE32220

This site is set well above the river and has a pleasant outlook to the forested valley slopes. A large proportion of the 16-acre site is taken up by privately owned bungalows, but the touring section of 125 large individual pitches is self contained and accessed by gravel paths leading off the main tiled roads. Some pitches have little or no shade, but all have 11/16A electricity and there are water points in each section. An area of gravel hardstanding has been developed and RVs are accepted.

Facilities
Entry to the excellent, heated sanitary building is by a coded card that also operates the hot water to the showers (free to the washbasins, many of which are in cabins). Unit for disabled visitors. Baby room. Cooking rings (charged). Laundry. Gas supplies. Motorcaravan services. Shop, bar/café/takeaway (1/4-31/10). Play area. Bicycle hire. Off site: Fishing and special area for swimming in the Mosel 200 m. Restaurant 500 m. Güls village 1.5 km. Riding 3 km. Cycling.
Open: All year.

Directions
Site is 6 km. west of Koblenz. From A61 take exit 38 towards Winningen. After 1 km. right at roundabout and then straight on towards Winningen (do not follow Güls/camping sign to left) then left on B416 towards Koblenz. Site is on right after 3.5 km.
GPS: 50.33257, 7.55308

Charges guide
Per unit incl. 2 persons	
and electricity	€ 20.00 - € 27.00
extra person	€ 7.00

FREE Alan Rogers Travel Card
Extra benefits and savings - see page 14

Koblenz

Knaus Campingpark Rhein-Mosel/Koblenz

Schartwiesenweg 6, D-56070 Koblenz (Rhineland Palatinate) T: 02618 2719. E: koblenz@knauscamp.de

alanrogers.com/DE35510

One of the Knaus Group sites, Rhein-Mosel Koblenz overlooks the confluence of the Rhine and Mosel rivers where the city of Koblenz has stood since Roman times. One of the most visited cities in Germany, it is well served by this large, busy and efficient site. Unusually, there are no seasonal pitches here, leaving the whole site available for touring units and tents. All pitches have 16A electricity. There is some shade from trees, but the site has an open feel with views of the rivers, the Kaiser Wilhelm Monument and the Ehrenbreitstein Fortress. There are also twelve motorcaravan night-stop places outside the barrier at reduced rates. There is some noise from rail and river traffic, but our sleep was not disturbed.

Facilities

Two excellent toilet blocks with free showers. One block has a baby bathing and changing room, whilst the other has a suite for disabled visitors. Washing machine and dryer at each block. Electric hotplates at each block (slot meters). Motorcaravan services. Small restaurant. Small playground. Boules. Dog bath. WiFi throughout (charged). Off site: Bicycle hire, fishing, boat launching 1 km. Riding 10 km. Golf 17 km. Cable car up to the Ehrenbreitstein Fortress. Riverside cycle path adjacent.

Open: 4 April - 9 November.

Directions

From A48 autobahn, take exit 10 Koblenz North. Follow B9 into Koblenz. Take care with lanes and follow campsite signs (they are not named, just symbols). From the south on the B49, arrive in Koblenz and follow signs to B9 and then campsite signs. GPS: 50.366217, 7.603767

Charges guide

Per unit incl. 2 persons and electricity	€ 26.40 - € 31.40
extra person	€ 7.00 - € 8.50

Lahnstein

Camping Burg Lahneck

Ortsteil Oberlahnstein, D-56112 Lahnstein (Rhineland Palatinate) T: 026 212 765.

alanrogers.com/DE32200

The location of this site is splendid, well above and overlooking the Rhine valley and the town of Lahnstein – many of the pitches have their own super views. It consists partly of terraces and partly of open grassy areas, has a cared for look and all is very neat and tidy. One can usually find a space here, though from early July to mid-August it can become full. There are 80 individual touring pitches marked but not separated and mostly level, all with electricity (16A). Campers are sited by the site owner. The reception here is friendly and charges reasonable.

Facilities

The single central, heated toilet block is of a good standard, and very well maintained. There are some cabins for both sexes. Showers are on payment. Washing machine and dryer. Restaurant with terrace. Motorcaravan services. Gas supplies. Small shop. Small playground. Off site: Café/restaurant adjoining site; meals also in Burg Lahneck restaurant. Town swimming pool (15/5-31/8). Tennis nearby. Riding 500 m. Bicycle hire 2 km. Fishing 3 km. Bad Ems thermal baths 12 km.

Open: Easter/1 April - 31 October.

Directions

Travelling north on B42 from Rüdesheim towards Koblenz, after passing through Braubach, turn off to the right (Oberlahnstein, Kurzentrum, Burg Lahneck). Take second exit at roundabout, up hill and at top turn left. Follow signs to Burg Lahneck and site. GPS: 50.30527, 7.61335

Charges guide

Per unit incl. 2 persons and electricity (plus meter)	€ 21.00 - € 24.50
extra person	€ 7.00
No credit cards.	

Leiwen

Landal Sonnenberg

Sonnenberg 1, D-54340 Leiwen (Rhineland Palatinate) T: 065 079 3690. E: sonnenberg@landal.de

alanrogers.com/DE32450

Sonnenberg is a pleasant hilltop site reached from the attractive riverside wine village of Leiwen by a four kilometre twisty climb, from which there are wonderful views of the Mosel valley. It has a splendid free leisure centre incorporating an indoor activity pool with paddling pool, whirlpool, cascade and slides. Also in this building are ten-pin bowling, solarium, multi-function sport area, plus a snack bar. Combining a bungalow complex (separate) with camping, the site has 140 large, individual and numbered grass/gravel pitches on terraces with electricity (10A) and TV connections.

Facilities

The single toilet block has underfloor heating, washbasins in cabins (all for women, a couple for men). It is stretched in busy times. Separate suite for disabled visitors. Facilities for children. Laundry. Motorcaravan services. Shop. Restaurant, bistro, bar and snacks (all 20/3-9/11). Indoor leisure centre with activity pool, climbing wall, 10-pin bowling and tennis. Minigolf. Playground. Bicycle hire (high season). Disco, entertainment and excursions at various busy times. Deer park. Off site: Fishing 5 km.

Open: 20 March - 9 November.

Directions

From A48/A1 (Trier-Koblenz) take new exit 128 for Bekond, Föhren, Hetzerath and Leiwen. Follow signs for Leiwen and in town follow signs for Ferienpark, Sonnenberg or Freibad. GPS: 49.80378, 6.89257

Charges guide

Per unit incl. 2 persons and electricity	€ 20.00 - € 40.00
extra person	€ 5.25
dog	€ 5.50

For latest campsite news, availability and prices visit

alanrogers.com

Mesenich

Family Camping

Wiesenweg 25, D-56820 Mesenich bei Cochem (Rhineland Palatinate) T: 026 734 556.

E: info@familycamping.de alanrogers.com/DE32320

Family Camping is an attractive, (Dutch/German) family run site situated on a stretch of the River Mosel, with views of forest and vineyards. Most of the 100 touring pitches are separated by vines, they are mainly level, with 6/10A electricity hook-ups, and some have shade. There are 25 pitches with their own water tap and 27 tents available for rent. The site roads are relatively narrow and are not suitable for larger units especially American RVs or twin-axle caravans. On arrival you must stop in the lay-by on the approach road while booking in at reception. Good English is spoken.

Facilities
Well equipped, heated toilet facilities provide good sized showers (€ 0.50), washbasins mainly in cubicles or curtained. Baby room. Laundry facilities. Shop, bar. Takeaway (1/5-15/9). Swimming pools (1/6-15/9, weather dependent). Play area. Disco evenings and wine tours in July/Aug. River fishing (with permit). Dogs are not accepted in July/Aug. WiFi on part of site (charged). Off site: Bicycle hire 300 m. Golf 7 km. Riding 10 km.

Open: 21 April - 3 October.

Directions
Site is 40 km. southwest of Koblenz on the eastern banks of the Mosel river. It is signed in the village of Mesenich. GPS: 50.10151, 7.19391

Charges guide
Per unit incl. 2 persons and electricity	€ 16.00
extra person	€ 4.00

No credit cards.

Neuerburg

Camping In der Enz

In der Enz 25, D-54673 Neuerburg (Rhineland Palatinate) T: 065 642 660. E: info@camping-inderenz.com

alanrogers.com/DE32370

This site is just outside the town, next to the municipal swimming pool complex, and the enthusiastic Dutch owners give a very warm welcome that makes this a very pleasant place to stay. The site is bisected by the unfenced River Enz, which is little more than a stream at this point. The section nearest the road is occupied by 35 long stay units. The other half, on the other side of the river with its own access road, is solely for tourers. This has 70 very large, open grass pitches, all with 16A electricity, of which 20 are fully serviced with water and drainage.

Facilities
New sanitary block of very high quality is fully equipped and has some washbasins in cabins and controllable hot showers (€ 0.60/5 minutes). Provision for disabled visitors. Baby room. Kitchen and laundry. Heated outdoor swimming pool (May-Sept). Takeaway. Play area. WiFi over site. Off site: Swimming pool complex (May-Sept) and all-year restaurant and bar, both adjacent. Fishing and tennis within walking distance. Bicycle hire 4 km. Golf 15 km.

Open: 16 March - 31 October.

Directions
Site is 15 km. northwest of Bitburg. From the A60 (E29) take exit 6 and head south to Bitburg, then take road 50 west to Sinspelt. Finally turn north for 6 km. to Neuerburg, pass through town and follow camping signs to site 1.5 km. north of the town. GPS: 50.02852, 6.27266

Charges guide
Per unit incl. 2 persons and electricity (plus meter)	€ 23.00 - € 30.50
extra person	€ 7.00
child (0-15 yrs)	€ 4.50 - € 5.50

Oberweis

Prümtal Camping Oberweis

In der Klaus 17, D-54636 Oberweis (Rhineland Palatinate) T: 065 279 2920. E: info@pruemtal.de

alanrogers.com/DE32470

This is a most attractive and popular site set in a wooded valley alongside the River Prüm. The site has an excellent restaurant, pizzeria and takeaway and a beautiful heated swimming pool. A new, state-of-the-art toilet block was added in 2014 and 91 pitches are now fully serviced. There are 72 long stay units grouped in a separate area at the western end of the site, with the touring area stretching out alongside the river. The 130 touring pitches are on grass, mostly separated by hedging and all with 16A electricity. Pitches vary in size (from 30-110 sq.m) and price, and there is shade from mature trees in most parts.

Facilities
New exceptional toilet block, existing high quality block plus a third small block in season. Good motorcaravan service point. Small shop with a good range of food, drink and camping accessories (1/4-31/10). Restaurant, bar and pizzeria (all year). Swimming pool (1/5-7/9). Adventure style playground. Full size soccer pitch and volleyball pitch. Children's entertainment in July/Aug. River fishing. WiFi throughout (free). Free walking and cycling route guides. Off site: Golf 4 and 9 km. Riding 4.5 km. Bicycle hire 10 km.

Open: All year.

Directions
Oberweis is 35 km. northwest of Trier. From the A60 (E29) take exit 6, and head south to Bitburg, then B50 west for 8 km. to Oberweis. Immediately after sharp right hand bend at entry to town turn left before river bridge and garage (blue circle site sign). Continue to end of road and site entrance is to right of pool complex. GPS: 49.95883, 6.42385

Charges guide
Per unit incl. 2 persons and electricity	€ 21.65 - € 29.25
extra person	€ 7.50
child (4-13 yrs)	€ 4.30

FREE Alan Rogers Travel Card
Extra benefits and savings - see page 14

Pfalzfeld

Country Camping Schinderhannes

Schinderhannes 1, D-56291 Hausbay-Pfalzfeld (Rhineland Palatinate) T: 06746 800 5440.
E: info@countrycamping.de alanrogers.com/DE32420

About 30 km. south of Koblenz, between Rhine and Mosel, and an ideal base from which to visit these regions, this site is set on a south facing slope that catches the sun all day. With trees and parkland all around, it is a peaceful and picturesque setting. There are 150 permanent caravans in a separate area from 90 short stay touring pitches on hardstanding. For longer stays, an area around the lake has a further 160 numbered pitches. These are of over 100 sq.m. on grass, some with hardstanding and all with 8A electricity. The lake is used for inflatable boats and fishing. Country Camping could be a useful transit stop en route to the Black Forest, Bavaria, Austria and Switzerland, as well as a family holiday.

Facilities

The sanitary buildings, which can be heated, are of a high standard with one section in the reception/shop building for the overnight pitches, and the remainder close to the longer stay places. Laundry. Bar. Restaurant with takeaway. TV area. Skittle alley. Shop (all amenities 1/3-31/10 and Xmas). Tennis. Fishing. Play area. Rallies welcome. Torches useful. WiFi in restaurant and reception areas (charged). Some breeds of dog not accepted. Off site: Boat trips on the Rhine and Mosel.

Open: All year.

Directions

Site is 28 km. south of Koblenz. From A61 Koblenz-Ludwigshafen road, take exit 43 Pfalzfeld and on to Hausbay where site is signed. If using sat nav enter Hausbayer Strasse in Pfalzfeld.
GPS: 50.10597, 7.56822

Charges guide

Per unit incl. 2 persons and electricity	€ 19.00 - € 25.00
extra person	€ 7.00

Reinsfeld

Azur Camping Hunsrück

Parkstrasse 1, D-54421 Reinsfeld (Rhineland Palatinate) T: 065 039 5123. E: reinsfeld@azur-camping.de
alanrogers.com/DE32560

This quiet countryside site, spread over 20 hectares, is situated close to the French and Luxembourg borders. With 980 pitches (600 for touring units), the site is constructed with 29 circular grassed areas, each surrounded by trees, and containing no more than 25 pitches. This creates the impression that you are staying on a small site, although you do have the facilities provided by a larger one. A spacious central meadow opposite a lake is used for caravans and tents and is separated from a playing field by a tree-lined stream. This is a quiet and relatively unknown corner of Germany.

Facilities

Four heated sanitary buildings with free hot showers, washbasins in cabins and family bathrooms to rent. Baby rooms. Facilities for disabled visitors. Laundry facilities. Motorcaravan services. Gas and camping supplies. Shop. Bread to order. Comfortable restaurant/bar with takeaway. Swimming pool (heated June-Sept). Tennis. Large play area and new water play area. Children's entertainment (high season). Beach volleyball. Fishing. Go-kart hire. WiFi over part of site (charged).

Open: 1 April - 31 October.

Directions

Site is 20 km. southeast of Trier. Leave A1 at exit 132 (Reinsfeld) and follow sign for Reinsfeld. Continue through village and site is signed on the left just before leaving village.
GPS: 49.687053, 6.869502

Charges guide

Per unit incl. 2 persons and electricity	€ 20.80 - € 25.80
extra person	€ 5.50 - € 7.50

10% discount for online bookings.

Saarburg

Landal Warsberg

In den Urlaub 1, D-54439 Saarburg (Rhineland Palatinate) T: 065 819 1460. E: warsberg@landal.de
alanrogers.com/DE32500

From the valley a series of hairpin bends leads to this attractive hilltop site. From the site and approach road there are wonderful panoramic views of the Saar valley and the surrounding region. A large, well organised site, there are 429 numbered touring pitches of quite reasonable size on flat or slightly sloping ground, separated in small groups by trees and shrubs, all with 16A electrical connections. There are some tour operator pitches and a separate area with holiday bungalows to rent. This site should appeal to all age groups. July and August are very busy.

Facilities

Three toilet blocks of very good quality provide washbasins (many in private cabins) and a unit for disabled visitors. Family shower room. Large launderette by reception. Motorcaravan services. Gas supplies. Shop. Restaurant and takeaway, games rooms adjacent. Disco. Swimming pool. Climbing wall. Minigolf. Bicycle hire. Playground. Football field. Volleyball. Basketball. Entertainment in season. WiFi over site (charged). Off site: 530 m. Rodelbahn toboggan and cable chair lift to the valley 300 m. Riding and fishing 5 km.

Open: 20 March - 2 November.

Directions

From Trier on road 51 site is well signed in the northwest outskirts of Saarburg off the Trierstrasse (signs also for Ferienzentrum) and from all round town. Follow signs up hill for 3 km.
GPS: 49.61992, 6.54348

Charges guide

Per unit incl. 2 persons and electricity	€ 22.00 - € 37.00
extra person	€ 5.25
dog	€ 5.50

Special 5, 8 or 10 day rates.

For latest campsite news, availability and prices visit

alanrogers.com

Remagen

Camping Goldene Meile

Simrockweg 9-13, D-53424 Remagen (Rhineland Palatinate) T: 026 422 2222.

E: info@camping-goldene-meile.de alanrogers.com/DE32150

This site is on the banks of the Rhine between Bonn and Koblenz. Although there is an emphasis on permanent caravans, there are about 200 pitches for touring units (out of 500), most with 6A electricity and 100 with water and drainage. They are either in the central, more mature area or in a newer area where the numbered pitches of 80-100 sq.m. are arranged around an attractively landscaped, small lake. Just five are by the busy river and there may be some noise from the trains that run on the other side. Access to the river bank is through a locked gate (key from reception). Adjacent to the site is a large complex of open-air public swimming pools (small concession for campers). They claim always to find space for odd nights, except perhaps at Bank Holidays. This site is in a popular area and is busy at weekends and in high season.

Facilities

The main toilet block is heated and well maintained, with some washbasins in cabins, showers (token) and facilities for wheelchair users. A smaller block serves the newer pitches (no showers). Laundry and cooking facilities. Motorcaravan services. Gas. Shop, bar, restaurant and takeaway (all 1/4-30/10 and some weekends). Play areas. Entertainment for children (July/Aug). Bicycle hire. WiFi over site (charged). Main gate is closed 22.00-07.00 (also 13.00-15.00). Off site: Swimming pool complex adjacent (May-Sept). Riding 1 km. Cycling and walking in the Ahr valley. Remagen, Bonn and Cologne to visit. Boat trips on the Rhine and Mosel rivers.

Open: All year.

Directions

Remagen is 20 km. south-southeast of Bonn. Site is beside the Rhine and is signed on the N9 road just south of Remagen. GPS: 50.57428, 7.25189

Charges guide

Per unit incl. 2 persons	
and electricity	€ 23.20 - € 24.80
extra person	€ 6.00
child (6-16 yrs)	€ 5.00
dog	€ 1.70

No credit cards.

Seck

Camping Park Weiherhof am See

Campingplatz Weiherhof, D-56479 Seck (Rhineland Palatinate) T: 026 648 555.

E: info@camping-park-weiherhof.de alanrogers.com/DE35670

Camping Park Weiherhof is a family run site in the Hoher Westerwald, an attractive nature protected area of meadows forests and streams with over 250 km. of maintained trails, ideal for those who enjoy rambling or cycling, or simply to relax. Eight years ago Birgit and Helmut Stelzen took over the site and have developed it into a prize winning environmentally friendly site. Of the 340 pitches, 140 are available to visitors, all with electricity (10-16A). They are gently sloping, on grass/gravel with some tree shade and hedge separation, 80 are fully serviced and some have a lakeside location.

Facilities

Four well maintained sanitary blocks, some washbasins in cabins, showers upon payment, facilities for disabled visitors and children, baby room. Washing machine and dryers. Restaurant with terrace and lake view. Snack bar (high season). Play areas. Indoor activity room. Animation in high season. Swimming and boating on small lake. Sunbathing area beside lake and small beach. Rambling/cycling directly from site. Bicycle and E-bicycle hire (battery charging stations in Westerwald). Overnight pitches outside barrier (€ 10). Off site: Riding 1 km.

Open: 1 March - 31 October.

Directions

From the A3 eastbound take exit 40 (Montabaur) onto B255 for 33 km. towards Rennerod as far as Hellenhahn. At the roundabout turn right into Secker Strasse towards Seck. After 3 km. the site is on the right. Westbound, leave the A3 at exit 42, take B49 north, then B54 north. Turn left at Irmtraut to Seck and follow the signs. GPS: 50.58688, 8.03488

Charges guide

Per unit incl. 2 persons	
and electricity (plus meter)	€ 25.00 - € 27.00
extra person	€ 6.00

Senheim

Campingplatz Holländischer Hof

Am Campingplatz 1, D-56820 Senheim (Rhineland Palatinate) T: 026 734 660. E: holl.hof@t-online.de

alanrogers.com/DE32330

Holländischer Hof is a well run Dutch-operated site attractively situated on the banks of the Mosel, with a small boat harbour backing onto it. The well known picturesque wine village of Senheim, with its prominent church, is within easy walking distance and this and many other villages in the area are famous for their wine festivals, which take place in late summer. The site caters mostly for tourers. All 199 touring pitches are on grass with adequate shade from mature trees and all have 6/10A electricity points. Dogs are not allowed on the site, but there are a dozen pitches outside the barrier for those who have dogs. Many wine producing villages and towns are within easy reach.

Facilities

The main sanitary block includes washbasins (some in cubicles) and showers (by token € 0.85). Unit for disabled visitors. Laundry facilities. Other toilet facilities in a prefabricated unit. Motorcaravan services. Gas. Shop, restaurant, snack bar, pizzeria and takeaway with terrace. Playground. TV room. Games room. Sports field. River fishing. WiFi throughout (charged). Dogs are not accepted. Off site: Rambling, including the Bremmer Calmont path, the steepest vineyard in Europe. Cycle tracks direct from site. Tennis 300 m. Bicycle hire 2 km.

Open: 12 April - 1 November.

Directions

Site is 42 km. southwest of Koblenz on the eastern bank of the Mosel River. When travelling south on the B49 after passing Senheim, site entrance is just before the bridge, on the right. GPS: 50.08218, 7.20868

Charges guide

Per unit incl. 2 persons	
and electricity	€ 17.20
extra person	€ 4.85
child (3-10 yrs)	€ 3.55

Special offers in low season.

Stadtkyll

Landal Wirfttal

Wirftstrasse, D-54589 Stadtkyll (Rhineland Palatinate) T: 065 979 2920. E: wirfttal@landal.de

alanrogers.com/DE32120

Peacefully and attractively set in a small valley in the northern Eifel, Wirfttal is a good all-round family site with 230 numbered pitches. They mostly back onto fences, hedges etc. on fairly flat ground. The 150 touring pitches (many on gravel) are 80 sq.m. or more, and all have electricity (8A) and TV aerial points. Five individual pitches have water and waste water points. Also part of the site, but separate from the camping, is a large holiday bungalow complex. This is a good base for rambling or mountain biking in the surrounding hills. Fishing (but not swimming) is allowed in the small lake.

Facilities

One main toilet block, and two small units, all heated, some washbasins in cabins. New shop. Restaurant and snacks. Indoor pool (free) and sauna and solarium (on payment). Two indoor play areas. Tennis. Minigolf. Fishing. Bicycle hire. Large adventure playground. Sports centre adjacent. Winter sports. Bicycle and sledge hire. WiFi over site (charged). Entertainment in season. Off site: Riding 1 km. Rambling trails.

Open: All year.

Directions

Site is 1.5 km. south of Stadtkyll on road towards Schüller. Follow signs in Stadtkyll for Haus an der See. GPS: 50.33877, 6.53753

Charges guide

Per unit incl. 2 persons	
and electricity	€ 19.00 - € 36.00
extra person	€ 5.25
dog	€ 5.50

Wolfstein

Camping Am Königsberg

Am Schwimmbad 1, D-67752 Wolfstein (Rhineland Palatinate) T: 063 044 143. E: info@campingwolfstein.de

alanrogers.com/DE32550

Situated in an area between the Rhine and Mosel rivers in a nature area at the foot of the Königsberg, this is a small, attractive, well maintained site with plenty of facilities. Of the 100 pitches, 80 are reserved for touring units, all with electricity, most with fresh and waste water connections. The level, grass, mainly open pitches are easily reached by tarmac site roads. A large separate meadow is for tents and has a paddling pool, communal grill and covered eating area. Trees and hedges provide some shade and division of the site. A large, attractive swimming pool complex next to the site is free to campers.

Facilities

Modern comfortable, heated sanitary block with all usual facilities including showers, free hot water and private cabins. Facilities for disabled visitors and children. Family shower room. Laundry room. Fridge rental. Shop. Bar/restaurant (all year). Takeaway. Play cabin, play area and games room for children with entertainment daily in summer. Minigolf. Bicycle hire. Fishing. WiFi throughout (charged). Off site: Large swimming pool complex next to site (free to campers). Shops and other facilities in the village 300 m. Riding 2 km.

Open: 1 March - 31 October.

Directions

Wolfstein is 20 km. northwest of Kaiserslautern on the B270. From A6 (Ludwigshafen-Saarbrücken) take exit 15 for Kaiserslauten West and head north towards Lauterecken. In Erfenbach left on B270 towards Lauterecken and Idar-Oberstein. Stay on the B270. Site is signed 300 m. south of the village of Wolfstein. GPS: 49.58034, 7.61883

Charges guide

Per unit incl. 2 persons	
and electricity	€ 21.00 - € 27.00
extra person	€ 5.50 - € 7.50

For latest campsite news, availability and prices visit

alanrogers.com

Trippstadt

Camping-Freizeitzentrum Sägmühle

Sägmühle 1, D-67705 Trippstadt (Rhineland Palatinate) T: 063 069 2190. E: info@saegmuehle.de

alanrogers.com/DE32580

Camping Sägmühle is peacefully situated beside a lake, in a wooded valley in the heart of the Palatinate Nature Park, and there are many kilometres of walks to enjoy, as well as castles to explore. There are 303 pitches in total, of which 154 are available for touring, at least 80 sq.m. or more on flat grass, each with electricity (4/16A). Fifty of these are fully serviced and some have hardstanding. One area is close to the lake and it is a pleasant change to find a site that keeps the lakeside pitches for touring units. A first class restaurant offers local and international dishes and fine local wines, and there is plenty for younger children to enjoy with fishing, swimming and boating in the lake (pedaloes for hire), a fort, minigolf and tennis.

Facilities

Each area has its own sanitary facilities, which feature private cabins, baby bathroom, facilities for disabled visitors, launderette. Motorcaravan services. Restaurant serving local specialities and takeaway (lunchtime and evening). Bread available in high season. Solarium. Tennis. Play areas. Boules. Minigolf. Lake fishing. Beach volleyball. Entertainment daily in high season. Guided tours for ramblers and mountain bikers. Electric barbecues are not permitted. WiFi on part of site (charged). Off site: Shops and bus service 10 minutes walk in Trippstadt. Wilenstein Castle (12th-century ruin) and the famous romantic Karls Valley Gorge are nearby.

Open: All year excl. 1 November - 11 December.

Directions

Site is 14 km. SSE of Kaiserslautern. From the A6, take exit 15 (Kaiserslautern West) onto B270 towards Pirmasens. Turn left after 9 km. towards Karlstal/Trippstadt and follow site signs. GPS: 49.35174, 7.78066

Charges guide

Per unit incl. 2 persons	
and electricity	€ 21.50 - € 28.60
extra person	€ 6.90 - € 8.00
child (2-14 yrs)	€ 2.85 - € 3.70
dog	€ 2.30 - € 2.90

No credit cards.

Camping Cheques accepted.

Bosen

Camping Bostalsee

Am Campingplatz 1, D-66625 Nohfelden/Bosen (Saarland) T: 06852 92333. E: campingplatz@bostalsee.de

alanrogers.com/DE35320

Located in the beautiful Saar-Hunsrück National Park, this impressive and busy site has 444 pitches of which 100 are for touring (100 sq.m). Touring visitors are accommodated in areas between the seasonal pitches, most accessed by hard roads. All pitches have electricity. There are ten generous hardstanding pitches for motorcaravans and 24 serviced pitches with electricity, water and drain. There are five areas for tents and rental units. Two large toilet blocks offer exemplary facilities for all visitors. A sports field, play areas and a multisports court will keep active children busy. This site offers exceptional value for one of this quality.

Facilities

Heated sanitary facilities in two large blocks. Family bathrooms (charged). Facilities for disabled visitors. Sauna and solarium (charged). Motorcaravan services. Laundry facilities. Microwave and fridge. Small supermarket (15/3-15/11). Bread (1/4-1/10). Restaurant, snack bar, takeaway. Multisports field. Play areas. Recreation room. TV/video room. Library. Boules. Bicycles, mountain bikes, pedal boats, canoes, rowing boats, sailing boats, surf boards to hire. Communal barbecue pits. WiFi near reception (charged). Off site: Bostalsee with sandy beach.

Open: All year.

Directions

Take the A1 as far as the Nonnweiler crossing and then A62 as far as exit 3. Then follow signs to Bostalsee. GPS: 49.56066, 7.06118

Charges guide

Per unit incl. 2 persons	
and electricity	€ 23.00 - € 38.00
extra person	€ 4.00
child (6-17 yrs)	€ 2.50

Amtsberg

Waldcamping Erzgebirgsblick

An der Dittersdorfer Höhe, D-09439 Amtsberg (Saxony) T: 037 177 50833.

E: info@waldcamping-erzgebirge.de alanrogers.com/DE38360

The Scheibner family first thought of opening a campsite when touring Canada in 1998, so it is not surprising to find reminders of their trip appearing in the site's buildings with pictures and Canadian names. They found their spot on land once belonging to the Stasi, the East German secret police, and turned it into a well kept and welcoming campsite. It has 90 touring pitches, either under mature pine trees in the woods or on open ground, partly separated by low bushes and shrubs, in front of reception and the sanitary block. All have 16A electricity and there are 12 with electricity, water, drainage and hardstanding. This area has much to offer for sightseeing, walking and cycling.

Facilities

Excellent sanitary facilities with British style toilets, free, controllable hot showers and washbasins (1 cabin each for men and women). Washbasin and toilet for children. Baby room. Bathroom for rent. Laundry facilities. Fully equipped kitchen, including fridge and dishwasher. Small shop in reception (bread to order). Takeaway. Lounge with dining table, TV and library. Playground. Bicycle hire. Riding. Off site: Riding 2 km. Fishing and golf 5 km.

Open: All year.

Directions

Site is 11 km. southeast of Chemnitz. From A72/E41 autobahn exit 14 for Chemnitz Sud, take the B174 southeast towards Gornau, Marienberg, then Prag. Site is well signed in Amtsberg, off the B174. GPS: 50.76600, 13.01448

Charges guide

Per person	€ 6.95
pitch	€ 8.50 - € 18.00
electricity (per kWh)	€ 0.70

No credit cards.

Dresden

Camping & Freizeitpark LuxOase

Arnsdorfer Strasse 1, Kleinröhrsdorf, D-01900 Dresden (Saxony) T: 035 952 56666.

E: info@luxoase.de alanrogers.com/DE38330

LeadingCampings

This is a well organised and quiet site located just north of Dresden with easy access from the autobahn. The site has very good facilities and is arranged on grassland beside a lake. There is access to the lake through a gate. Although the site is fairly open, trees do provide shade in some areas. There are 198 large touring pitches (plus 40 seasonal in a separate area), marked by bushes or posts on generally flat or slightly sloping grass. All have 10/16A electricity and 132 have water and drainage. At the entrance is an area of hardstanding (with electricity) for late arrivals. A member of Leading Campings group.

Facilities

Two excellent buildings provide modern, heated facilities with private cabins, a family room, baby room, units for disabled visitors and eight bathrooms for hire. Special facilities for children. Jacuzzi. Kitchen. Gas supplies. Motorcaravan services. Shop and bar (1/3-31/12) plus restaurant (15/3-31/12). Bicycle hire. Lake swimming. Sports field. Fishing. Play area. Sauna. Train, bus and theatre tickets from reception. WiFi throughout (charged). Minigolf. Fitness room. Regular guided bus trips to Dresden, Prague etc. Off site: Riding next door.

Open: All year excl. February.

Directions

Site is 17 km. northeast of Dresden. From the A4 (Dresden-Görlitz) take exit 85 (Pulnitz) and travel south towards Radeberg. Pass through Leppersdorf and site is signed to the left. Follow signs for Kleinröhrsdorf and camping. Site is 4 km. from the autobahn exit. GPS: 51.120401, 13.980103

Charges guide

Per unit incl. 2 persons and electricity	€ 16.40 - € 29.90
extra person	€ 5.50 - € 8.50
child (3-15 yrs acc. to age)	€ 2.50 - € 5.00

Dresden

Camping Dresden-Mockritz

Boderitzer Str 30, D-01217 Dresden (Saxony) T: 035 147 15250. E: camping-dresden@t-online.de

alanrogers.com/DE38340

Within 15 minutes of the city centre and with a bus every 20 minutes, this family run site is ideally located for visiting one of Europe's most attractive and interesting cities. Very good English is spoken in the well organised reception, where bus tickets and plenty of tourist information are readily available. The site has 180 pitches in three areas: the main short stay section has grass pitches in rows with concrete entry roads. Here the units are packed next to each other under mature trees. For longer stays there is a fairly open grass section and adjoining is a grass area for tents.

Facilities

Three heated sanitary blocks with controllable showers (token required) and washbasins in cabins (crowded at peak periods). Facilities for disabled visitors. Laundry room. Motorcaravan services. Bar. Restaurant with terrace. Small shop with essentials and camping goods. Play area. Accommodation to rent. Off site: Dresden, with large open squares, the newly rebuilt Frauen Kirche and its visitors centre. Boat trips along The Elbe. Schloss Pilnitz and park. Meissen porcelain works and cathedral.

Open: All year excl. 20 December - 5 January.

Directions

Site is 4 km. south of city centre. Leave the A4 at Dreieck Dresden West and travel east on A17 for 11 km. Leave A17 at exit 3 (Anschlusstelle, Dresden, Südvorstadt) just after two fairly long tunnels. Head north on 170 towards city centre. After 1.5 km. site is signed to right. GPS: 51.01452, 13.74766

Charges guide

Per unit incl. 2 persons and electricity	€ 20.80 - € 23.30
extra person	€ 6.00

For latest campsite news, availability and prices visit

alanrogers.com

Leipzig

Campingplatz & Motel Auensee

Gustav-Esche-Strasse 5, D-04159 Leipzig (Saxony) T: 034 146 51600. E: info@camping-auensee.de

alanrogers.com/DE38470

It is unusual to find a good site in a city, but this large, neat and tidy site is one. It is far enough away from roads and the airport to be reasonably peaceful during the day and quiet overnight, and has 164 pitches, all for touring units. It is set in a mainly open area with tall trees and attractive flower beds, with some chalets and 'trekker' cabins for rent in the adjoining woodland, home to shoe-stealing foxes. The individual, numbered, flat grassy pitches are large (at least 100 sq.m), all with 16A electricity and five on hardstanding, arranged in several sections. There is a separate area for young people with tents.

Facilities

Five central sanitary buildings with WCs, washbasins in cabins and showers. Rooms for babies and disabled visitors (key access). Kitchen and laundry rooms. Motorcaravan services. Restaurant and snack bar (April-Oct). Entertainment rooms. Multisports court. Play area. Barbecue area. Good English spoken. Off site: Public transport to the city centre every 15 minutes from just outside the site (tickets from reception). Supermarkets 15-20 minutes walk. Fishing 500 m. Riding 4 km. Golf 11 km.

Open: All year.

Directions

Site (not well signed) is 6 km. from city centre in an area called Wahren. Best approached from A9 exit 17, turning towards Leipzig on B181 Merseberger Str. After 8 km. turn left on Ludwig Hupfeld. At T-junction, turn left across a railway and immediately right. After crossing two canals, site is on left in 100 m. GPS: 51.36975, 12.31400

Charges guide

Per unit incl. 2 persons and electricity	€ 13.00 - € 27.00
extra person	€ 5.00 - € 6.00

Augstfelde/Plön

Campingpark Augstfelde

Augstfelde, D-24306 Augstfelde/Plön (Schleswig-Holstein) T: 04522 8128. E: info@augstfelde.de

alanrogers.com/DE30230

Campingpark Augstfelde is a spacious site with plenty of good sport and leisure facilities. The site borders a lake and is next to an 18-hole golf course in this picturesque region of hills, forests and lakes. Two hundred of the 500 pitches are reserved for touring, 145 are fully serviced and all have 16A Europlug. Undulating in some areas, the grassed site offers some tree shade, with hedges and bushes providing pitch separation in places. The sandy beaches along the sites 800 m. long bank with the lake are a popular sunbathing area and playground for children.

Facilities

Sanitary blocks with showers on payment (€ 0.75) and bathrooms to rent. Laundry facilities. Restaurant. Shop. Motorcaravan services. Dog shower. Separate beach for dogs. Sauna, fitness, massage. Four playgrounds. Activity programmes. Theatre club with cinema and disco in high season. Sailing. Windsurfing. Fishing. Canoe, boat and bicycle hire. Football. Basketball. Volleyball. WiFi. Quick stop facility at entrance. Off site: 18-hole golf adjacent.

Open: 1 April - 26 October.

Directions

Site is 45 km. northwest of Lübeck. From autobahn 1 take exit 15 Eutin then B76 towards Eutin. Just before Eutin stay on B76 towards Plön. Just after Bösdorf left into Kleinmühlen towards Bosau then after 1 km. right into Augstfelder Weg. Site is signposted. GPS: 54.12923, 10.45504

Charges guide

Per unit incl. 2 persons and electricity	€ 19.30 - € 25.60
extra person	€ 3.90 - € 5.30

Camping Cheques accepted.

Basedow

Camping Lanzer See

Am Lanzer See1, D-21483 Basedow (Schleswig-Holstein) T: 04153 599171. E: info@camping-lanzer-see.de

alanrogers.com/DE29610

In the attractive countryside of Schleswig-Holstein, near the border with Lower Saxony and just 50 km. south-east of Hamburg, this pleasant rural campsite stands on the bank of the Elbe-Lübeck Canal and the shore of the lake that gives it its name. Much of the site is devoted to holiday units, but there are 25 touring pitches on hardstanding (all with 16A Europlug, water and drainage) plus 25 tent pitches. Many occupy prime locations overlooking the canal or the lake. Anglers can sit outside their van or tent and fish, while walkers and cyclists can head off on the Alte Salzstrasse cycle path.

Facilities

Two sanitary blocks (one heated) provide hot showers, washing machine and dryer and chemical disposal (eco-friendly only). Motorcaravan services. Kiosk with bread and newspapers (July/Aug). Gasthaus on lake-shore serving home-cooked meals. Football field. Play area. Wooded area. Swimming and waterslide. Fishing. Canoe and rowing boat for hire. Mobile home for rent. Torches useful. Off site: Shops, bars and restaurants in Lauenburg 8 km. Mölln and Lüneburg both 30 km.

Open: 22 March - 27 October.

Directions

Basedow is 45 km. east of Hamburg and the site is southeast of the village. From A24 (Hamburg/Berlin) at exit 6 (Schwarzenbek/Grande) take B404 southeast to Schwarzenbek and continue southeast on B209 towards Lauenburg for 9.5 km. Turn east on K70 to Basedow and continue to campsite at southern end of lake. GPS: 53.40975, 10.59736

Charges guide

Per unit incl. 2 persons and electricity	€ 16.50 - € 19.50
extra person	€ 5.00

FREE Alan Rogers Travel Card
Extra benefits and savings - see page 14

Büsum

Camping Zur Perle

Dithmarscher Strasse 43, D-25671 Büsum (Schleswig-Holstein) T: 04834 60137.

E: info@campingplatz-zur-perle.de alanrogers.com/DE30170

Camping Zur Perle is directly on the North Sea beaches, on an enclosed artificial lagoon, making it an ideal place for a family holiday. It has 260 marked and numbered pitches (203 for tourers with water, 16A Europlug and waste water) on level, grassy fields with some separation by low trees and bushes. To the front of the site is a separate area for seasonal units and motorcaravans. Pitches vary in size (75-140 sq.m) and there are 60 hardstandings for touring units. The campsite is close to the Schleswig-Holstein Wadden Sea National Park. Zur Perle is a top class site for a relaxing family holiday and part of the Premium Camps group.

Facilities
Two sanitary blocks with controllable hot showers, open style washbasins and an excellent children's area. Baby room. Facilities for disabled campers. Motorcaravan services. Laundry. Kitchen. Kiosk (daily 07.30–22.00). Full restaurant. Playing field. Basketball. Volleyball. Minigolf. Fishing. Playground. Entertainment team (July/Aug). Bicycle hire. WiFi (charged).

Open: 4 April - 31 October.

Directions
From Hamburg, follow A23 north towards Heide, turn west onto 203 road towards Büsum. At roundabout marking end of 203, turn right onto K71/Mitteldeichsweg and continue to site (signed). GPS: 54.13999, 8.84243

Charges guide
| Per unit incl. 2 persons and electricity | € 20.20 - € 26.70 |
| extra person | € 5.80 - € 6.40 |

Fehmarn

Strandcamping Wallnau

Wallnau 1, D-23769 Fehmarn (Schleswig-Holstein) T: 043 729 456. E: wallnau@strandcamping.de
alanrogers.com/DE30070

With direct beach access and protected from the wind by a dyke, this family site is on Germany's second largest island (since 1963 joined to the Baltic sea coast by a bridge). This is a quiet location on the western part of Fehmarn Island in close proximity to a large bird sanctuary. Of the 800 pitches, 400 are for touring, all with electricity (6-16A) and on level grass areas arranged in alleys and separated by hedges. The island is low lying, ideal for leisurely walking and cycling, especially along the track that runs along the top of the dyke.

Facilities
Heated sanitary blocks provide free showers. Child-size toilets and showers. Baby rooms. Facilities for disabled visitors. Laundry facilities. Motorcaravan services. Shop. Bar, restaurant and snack bar. Open-air stage and soundproofed disco. Wellness, solarium and sauna. Archery. Watersports. Minigolf. Bouncy castles. Internet café. Beach fishing. Riding. WiFi (charged). Off site: Boat launching 6 km. Golf 16 km.

Open: 1 April - 26 October.

Directions
After crossing the bridge follow road to Landkirchen and Petersdorf. From Petersdorf site is signed. It is 4 km. northwest of the town. GPS: 54.48761, 11.0186

Charges guide
| Per unit incl. 2 persons and electricity | € 18.20 - € 36.90 |

No credit cards.
Camping Cheques accepted.

Grossensee

Camping ABC am Grossensee

Trittauer Strasse 11, D-22946 Grossensee (Schleswig-Holstein) T: 04154 60642.

E: info@campingplatz-abc.de alanrogers.com/DE25480

Only thirty minutes from the centre of Hamburg in the heart of Stormarner Schweiz, ABC is a peaceful, family run campsite established in the late 1940s, with just 70 pitches, half of which are for touring units, with electrical connections (16A Europlug). The remainder are occupied by seasonal units and by chalets for rent. There is direct access to the lakeside with supervised swimming. The village has a bakery and restaurants, whilst nearby Trittau has shops, a water mill and Napoleon's Bridge. Walkers and cyclists can explore the three lakes plateau or the Hahnheide, Schleswig-Holstein's largest Nature Reserve.

Facilities
Heated sanitary block completely renovated in 2013, with modern showers (small charge) and some washbasins in cabins. Washing machine and dryer. Football field. Direct access to beach. Bicycle hire. WiFi throughout (free). Off site: Beach with supervised swimming, sunbathing, kiosk (snacks and ice creams), toilet facilities, children's playground, volleyball and restaurant with terrace. Bakery 300 m. Inn and restaurants within 600 m. Golf and riding 1 km. Tennis 3 km. Trittau 4 km. Indoor pool 10 km.

Open: 1 April - 15 October.

Directions
Grossensee is 30 km. northeast of Hamburg. From the A1 (Hamburg-Lübeck) exit 28 (Ahrensburg) head east then south on L224 for 6 km. to Grossensee. Turn east on L93 towards Trittau, site is on left in 500 m. GPS: 53.61126, 10.34449

Charges guide
| Per unit incl. 2 persons and electricity | € 22.50 - € 27.50 |
| extra person | € 5.00 - € 5.50 |

For latest campsite news, availability and prices visit
alanrogers.com

Klein Rönnau

Klüthseecamp Seeblick

Klüthseehof 2, D-23795 Klein Rönnau (Schleswig-Holstein) T: 045 518 2368. E: info@kluethseecamp.de

alanrogers.com/DE30080

Klüthseecamp Seeblick is a modern, family run site situated on a small hill between two lakes. It is an ideal location for a family holiday with activities on site for all ages and a useful base to explore the region. The large, open grass, touring part of the site has sunny, shaded and semi-shaded areas on offer. There are 120 touring pitches on fairly level ground, all with electricity (10/16A) and 30 with water and drainage, and pitches for tents in natural surroundings. Klüthseecamp offers wellness, a swimming pool, food and drink, organised entertainment for all ages, and a sandy lakeside beach.

Facilities

Two modern, heated sanitary blocks, some washbasins in cabins, five bathrooms to rent and free showers. Facilities for children and disabled visitors including electric vehicle. Baby room. Motorcaravan services. Gas. Laundry. Shop with breakfast service. Bar and café. Beer garden and restaurant by the lake. Outdoor swimming pool (heated May-Sept). Wellness. Sauna, steam bath, massage. Play room/kindergarten. Play areas. Large projected TV. Bicycle hire. Go-kart hire. Minigolf. Way-marked paths around lake. Kids' and teenagers' clubs including weekly disco. Free WiFi at small restaurant. Off site: Riding 4 km.

Open: All year.

Directions

Site is 26 km. west-northwest of Lübeck. Leave A1 at exit 27 and travel north towards Kiel on the A21 to exit 13 (Bad Segeberg Sud). Follow B432 (Hamburger Strasse) into Bad Segeberg and at T-junction with Ziegelstrasse turn left (north) and continue on B432. 300 m. after Klein Rönnau turn right into Stripsdorferweg. Site is signed. GPS: 53.96142, 10.33737

Charges guide

Per unit incl. 2 persons and electricity	€ 24.00
extra person	€ 7.50

Kleinwaabs

Ostseecamping Familie Heide

Strandweg 31, D-24369 Kleinwaabs (Schleswig-Holstein) T: 04352 2530. E: info@waabs.de

alanrogers.com/DE25730

Ostseecamping Familie Heide is an excellent family site on the East Sea coast. Most of the 400 touring pitches are set high above the beach, so have good views over the sea. Pitching is on level, grassy fields off tarmac access roads, with sizes up to 160 sq.m. All are full service with 16A Europlug, water and drainage. Amenities on this quality site include a full supermarket with separate bakery, and a butcher. Campers can enjoy many water-based activities, including diving and surfing. This is a great site for children with several adventure play areas dotted around the site, and a children's club.

Facilities

Six high class sanitary buildings with controllable hot showers, open style washbasins, nine bathrooms for rent, children's section and facilities for disabled campers. Laundry. Supermarket. Bakery. Butcher. Bar and beach bar. Full restaurant. Takeaway. Indoor pool (free in low season). Fitness. Wellness. Sports court. Fishing. Tennis. Surfing and diving school. Playgrounds. Minigolf. Cinema. WiFi (charged).

Open: 15 March - 31 October.

Directions

From A7 motorway driving north, take Rendsburg exit (AS8). Continue on B203 towards Eckernförde. Drive through town and at harbour take L26 road. In village of Klein Waabs, follow site signs. GPS: 54.53195, 9.99967

Charges guide

Per unit incl. 2 persons and electricity	€ 21.70 - € 36.70
extra person	€ 4.50 - € 7.50

Meeschendorf

Insel-Camp Fehmarn

Meeschendorfer Strand, D-23769 Meeschendorf/Fehmarn (Schleswig-Holstein) T: 04371 50300.

E: info@inselcamp.de alanrogers.com/DE25770

Insel-Camp Fehmarn was developed in 2001, but everything on this well kept site looks brand new. The site is on the East Sea coast at the southern end of the Fehmarn Island. It has 389 pitches, 304 for tourers, on grassy fields. Some are in circular bays, while others are off tarmac access lanes. All touring pitches are fully serviced with water, drainage, cable and electricity (6-16A Europlug) and vary in size from 90-200 sq.m. This is a good site both for families and couples who want to enjoy the long hours of sunshine (1,900 per year) on this bustling island. A good site for a sunny holiday on the German coast.

Facilities

Two modern toilet blocks with hot showers, open style washbasins, family shower rooms (charged), baby room and facilities for disabled visitors. Laundry. Motorcaravan services. Shop (1/5-30/9, mornings only). Modern style café/restaurant. TV room. Fitness and sauna area. Playground. Full entertainment programme (July/Aug). Boat launching. Sports organised. Kite surfing school. WiFi.

Open: 5 April - 5 October.

Directions

From Hamburg, follow the A1 north towards Puttgarden, cross the Fehmarnsund Bridge and take the second exit to the right towards Meeschendorf. From the village follow the site signs. GPS: 54.41574, 11.24461

Charges guide

Per unit incl. 2 persons and electricity	€ 26.50 - € 44.00
extra person	€ 6.00 - € 8.50
child (2-14 yrs)	€ 3.00 - € 5.00

FREE Alan Rogers Travel Card
Extra benefits and savings - see page 14

Rabenkirchen-Faulück

Camping Park Schlei-Karschau

Karschau 56, D-24407 Rabenkirchen-Faulück (Schleswig-Holstein) T: 046 429 20820.

E: info@campingpark-schlei.de alanrogers.com/DE30020

Schlei-Karschau is a pleasant, quiet site on the only Baltic Sea fjord in Germany. All you will hear is the wind from the sea and the calls of the birds. This site is ideal if you enjoy fishing or sailing, or you could visit one of the beaches on this coast, just 10 km. to the north east. The site has 160 open pitches, 60 for touring units, all with at least 6A electricity. There is no shop as yet, but bread can be ordered from a kiosk and a restaurant, with a bar and takeaway, is open in high season.

Facilities

The single sanitary block includes controllable hot showers in cabins with washbasin, child-size toilets and washbasins and facilities for disabled visitors. Washing machines and dryers. Campers' kitchen with fridge. Motorcaravan services. Shop. Restaurant and bar (daily in high season). New playground. Sports field. Children's activity programme six days a week in high season. River fishing (permits from reception). Bicycle hire. Motorboat hire. Off site: Golf 4 km. Riding 6 km.

Open: All year.

Directions

Follow the A7 from Hamburg north to Flensburg and take exit Schleswig-Schuby. Take the B201 road towards Kappeln. Drive through Süderbrarup and turn right 5 km. after village to Faulück. Follow signs to site. GPS: 54.61960, 9.88415

Charges guide

Per unit incl. 4 persons	
and electricity	€ 26.00 - € 29.00
extra person	€ 4.00 - € 5.00
child (1-16 yrs)	€ 2.20 - € 3.20

Camping Cheques accepted.

Frankenhain

Oberhof Camping

Am Stausee 09, D-99330 Frankenhain (Thuringia) T: 036 205 76518. E: info@oberhofcamping.de
alanrogers.com/DE38550

Beside a lake, at an altitude of 700 metres and quietly hidden in the middle of the Thüringer forest, Oberhof Camping has seen many changes since the departure of its former owners, the East German secret police. There are 120 touring pitches, all with electricity (10A Europlug) and 20 with water and drainage. From this fairly open site there are views of the surrounding forests and of the lake which is bordered by wide grass areas ideal for a picnic or for just lazing around and enjoying the view. The site is very quiet and has direct access to marked routes for rambling and cycling in the forest.

Facilities

New heated sanitary block with all usual facilities including free hot water, plus 15 bathrooms to rent. Facilities for disabled visitors. Baby room. Laundry. Motorcaravan services. Gas sales. Modern reception building with shop and attractive restaurant serving traditional dishes. Shop. Children's club room. Play area. On the lake: fishing (licence required), swimming and boating. WiFi (charged). Off site: Over 100 km. of waymarked paths from the site. Bus service 1.5 km. Riding 8 km.

Open: All year.

Directions

Site is 25 km. south of Gotha. From the A4 between Eisenach and Dresden take exit 42 (Gotha). Travel south on the B247 to Ohrdruf then the B88 to Crawinkel then Frankenhain. In Frankenhain follow Lütsche Stausee and Campingpark signs. GPS: 50.73367, 10.75667

Charges guide

Per unit incl. 2 persons	
and electricity	€ 22.00
extra person	€ 7.00

Camping Cheques accepted.

Gera

Camping Strandbad Aga

Reichenbacherstrasse 14, D-07554 Gera-Aga (Thuringia) T: 036 695 20209.

E: info@campingplatz-strandbad-aga.de alanrogers.com/DE38500

Strandbad Aga is a useful night stop near the A4/A9 and is within reach of the cities of Dresden, Leipzig and Meissen. It is situated in open countryside on the edge of a small lake, with 200 individual, fenced pitches, mostly fairly level, without shade. The 70 touring pitches all have 16A electricity - for stays of more than a couple of days, over-nighters being placed on an open area. The lake is used for swimming, boating and fishing (very popular with day visitors at weekends and with a separate naturist area) and there is a small playground on one side (close to a deep part).

Facilities

The sanitary building, which has been completely renovated and now includes some family rooms, is at one side, with some washbasins in cabins and hot showers on payment. Large room for wheelchair users. Washing machines and dryers. Motorcaravan services. Modern restaurant/bar open long hours. Kiosk for drinks, ice-creams, etc. (high season). Playground. Small lake used for inflatables, fishing, swimming and watersports. Entertainment (high season). Off site: Football 200 m. Shop in village 1 km. Riding and tennis 1 km.

Open: 1 April - 31 October.

Directions

Site is 8 km. north of Gera. From A4/E40 Chemnitz-Erfurt autobahn take exit 58A for Gera and Landenberg, then the B2 towards Zeitz, following Bad Köstritz signs at first, then Reichenbach and site signs. Site is on left 1 km. after passing through Reichenbach. GPS: 50.95387, 12.08683

Charges guide

Per unit incl. 2 persons	
and electricity	€ 17.50 - € 20.00
extra person	€ 5.00

No credit cards.

For latest campsite news, availability and prices visit

alanrogers.com

Wulfen
Camping Wulfener Hals

Wulfener Hals Weg 100, D-23769 Wulfen auf Fehmarn (Schleswig-Holstein)

T: 043 718 6280. E: info@wulfenerhals.de alanrogers.com/DE30030

LeadingCampings

This is a top class, all year round site suitable as a stopover or as a base for a longer stay. Attractively situated by the sea, it is large, mature (34 hectares) and well maintained. It has over 800 individual pitches (half for touring) of up to 160 sq.m. in glades. Some are separated by bushes providing shade in the older parts, less so in the newer areas nearer the sea. There are many hardstandings and all pitches have electricity, water and drainage. Some new rental accommodation has been added, including a 'honeymoon mobile home'. A separate area has been developed for motorcaravans. It provides 60 extra large pitches, all with electricity, water and drainage, and some with TV aerial points, together with a new toilet block. There is much to do for young and old alike at Wulfener Hals, with a new heated outdoor pool and paddling pool (unsupervised), although the sea is naturally popular as well. The site also has many sporting facilities including its own golf courses and schools for watersports. A member of Leading Campings group.

Facilities

Five heated sanitary buildings have first class facilities including showers and both open washbasins and private cabins. Family bathrooms for rent. Facilities for children and disabled campers. Beauty and cosmetic facilities (all year), wellness (Apr-Oct). Laundry. Motorcaravan services. Shop, bar, restaurants and takeaway (April-Oct). Swimming pool (May-Oct). Sauna. Solarium. Jacuzzi. Sailing, catamaran, windsurfing and diving schools. Boat slipway. Golf courses (18 holes, par 72 and 9 holes, par 3). Riding. Fishing. Archery. Well organised and varied entertainment programmes for all ages. Bicycle hire. Catamaran hire. WiFi over part of site (charged). Off site: Naturist beach 500 m.

Open: All year.

Directions

From Hamburg take A1/E47 north towards Puttgarden, after crossing the bridge to Fehmarn first exit to the right to Avendorf. In Avendorf turn left and follow the signs for Wulfen and the site. GPS: 54.40805, 11.17374

Charges guide

Per unit incl. 2 persons

and electricity	€ 16.20 - € 42.50
extra person	€ 5.70 - € 9.50
child (2-12 yrs)	€ 2.70 - € 5.30
dog	€ 3.00 - € 7.50

Plus surcharges for larger pitches.
Many discounts available and special family prices.

Greece

Greece is made up of clusters of islands with idyllic sheltered bays and coves, golden stretches of sand with dunes, pebbly beaches, coastal caves with steep rocks and volcanic black sand and coastal wetlands. Its rugged landscape is a monument to nature with dramatic gorges, lakes, rivers and waterfalls.

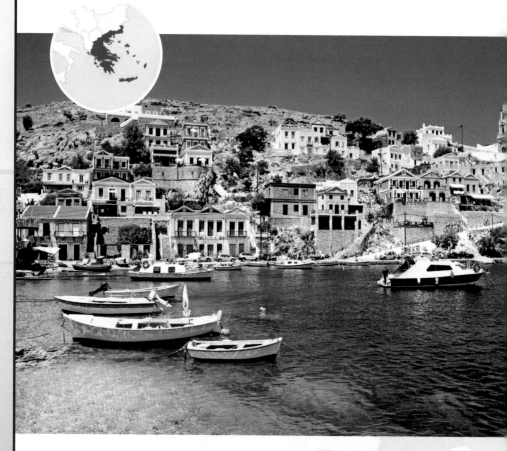

Nestling between the waters of the Aegean, Ionian and Mediterranean seas, Greece has over 13,000 km. of coastline. A largely mountainous country, its backbone is formed from the Pindus range, which extends as far as Crete, the largest of Greece's 6,000 islands, themselves peaks of the now submerged landmass of Aegeis. Mount Olympus in the north of the country, known from Greek mythology as the abode of the gods, is the highest mountain (2,917 m).

The Greek Islands have something to offer every visitor – the vibrant nightlife of Mykonos, the 'honeymoon' island of Santorini; Rhodes, where the modern city sits alongside the medieval citadel, and Corfu with its Venetian and French influences. The mainland is home to some of the most important archaeological sites, including the Acropolis, the Parthenon and Delphi.

CAPITAL: Athens

Tourist Office
Greek National Tourism Organisation
4 Conduit Street, London W1S 2DJ
Tel: 020 7495 9300
Fax: 020 7287 1369
Email: info@gnto.co.uk
Internet: www.gnto.co.uk

Population
11 million

Climate
Greece has a Mediterranean climate with plenty of sunshine, mild temperatures and a limited amount of rainfall.

Language
Greek, but most of the people connected to tourism and the younger generations currently practise English and sometimes German, Italian or French.

Telephone
The country code is 00 30.

Currency
The Euro

Time
GMT + 2 (GMT + 3 from last Sunday in March to last Sunday in October).

Public Holidays
New Year's Day 1 Jan; Epiphany 6 Jan; Shrove Monday Orth. Easter; Independence Day 25 Mar; Easter: Good Friday, Easter Sunday and Easter Monday (Orthodox); Labour Day 1 May; Whit Sunday and Monday (Orthodox); Assumption Day 15 Aug; Ochi Day (National Fest) 28 Oct; Christmas 25/26 Dec.

Motoring
Speed limits are 100-120 km/h on highways unless otherwise posted; 50 km/h in residential areas unless otherwise marked. An international driver's licence is required. Road signs are written in Greek and repeated phonetically in English. Road tolls exist on two highways in Greece, one leading to Northern Greece and the other to the Peloponnese.

see campsite map 10

Athene
Camping Athens

198-200 Leoforos Athinon, Peristeri, GR-12136 Athene (Attica) T: 210 581 4114.

E: info@campingathens.com.gr **alanrogers.com/GR8590**

Camping Athens is an all-year site, located to the west of the city and convenient for visiting Athens. The site prides itself on friendly Greek hospitality and offers 66 touring pitches, all with 16A electricity connections. The pitches are of a reasonable size and are generally well shaded. Smaller pitches are available for tents. The two toilet blocks are of modern design and well maintained. To visit the city, there is a bus stop opposite the site entrance. The site's restaurant is most welcoming after a day's sightseeing, and a selection of Greek starters, helped along by cool wine, can be thoroughly recommended. Before coming to Athens, be sure to plan your visit programme in advance. The city can be hot during mid-afternoon in summer and the traffic may be heavy. The public transport system (bus/tram/metro etc) works well, so don't plan to drive into the city yourself.

Facilities

Two modern toilet blocks. Washing machines. Shop. Bar. Takeaway food and restaurant (all May-Oct). Free WiFi over site. Excursions can be arranged. Barbecues and open fires are forbidden. Off site: Bus stop opposite site entrance with frequent service to the bus terminus at main railway station where you descend into the metro station (just in front of the bus stop) for journey to the city sites. Full travel information, including bus tickets, from reception staff (remember to validate on the bus). Bicycle hire 7 km. Beach 12 km. Golf 20 km.

Open: All year.

Directions

From north (Thessaloniki/Lamia) E75 signed Athina-Pireas, turn right for second exit towards Korinthos. Site is on right after 2.2 km. and well signed. From south (Peloponissos) take No. 8 road (Athina-Pireas). Continue towards Athens, site is 4 km. after Dafni Monastery. GPS: 38.008883, 23.6721

Charges guide

Per unit incl. 2 persons	
and electricity	€ 26.00 - € 31.00
extra person	€ 8.50
child	€ 6.00

Open all year around, is situated only 7 km from the center of Athens, connected with an excellent organised bus service, provides all necessary and high quality facilities and services for a comfortable and unforgetable stay.

198 - 200 Athinon Ave. - 121 36 Athens, Greece - Tel. 210 581 4114 - Fax 210 582 0353
E-mail: info@campingathens.com.gr - www.campingathens.com.gr

Nea Kifissia
Camping Nea Kifissia

Potamou 60 & Dimitsanas strasse, Adames, GR-14564 Nea Kifissia (Attica) T: 210 807 5579.

E: camping@hol.gr **alanrogers.com/GR8595**

Many visitors to Greece will want to spend some time in Athens, the capital. Camping Nea Kifissia offers one of the best opportunities to do that, being in a quiet location with easy access. A small site, run personally by the Komianidou family, there are 66 level pitches, some with shade, in well kept grounds. A regular bus service runs to the Kifissia metro station for fast and regular transport to all the sights. The Acropolis, Parthenon and the Porch of Caryatids are essential viewing, as are the many museums. Athens' shops and the flea market near Monastiraki also have much to offer.

Facilities

A centrally positioned toilet block includes showers, WCs and washbasins. Washing machine. Bar and coffee shop (1/6-20/9). Swimming pool (1/6-20/9). WiFi over site. Communal barbecue area. English spoken in reception. Off site: Riding 4 km. Athens 16 km. (45 minutes by bus/metro).

Open: All year.

Directions

From Athens-Thessaloniki motorway travelling north take Kifissa exit. At roundabout, site is signed. Under motorway, straight ahead site is again signed to right. Travelling south, just before Mercedes garage, turn right and immediately right again. Follow camping signs. GPS: 38.09943, 23.79175

Charges guide

Per unit incl. 2 persons and electricity	€ 31.00

For latest campsite news, availability and prices visit

alanrogers.com

Delphi

Camping Delphi

Delphi-Itea km 4, GR-33054 Delphi (Central Greece) T: 226 508 2209. E: info@delphicamping.com

alanrogers.com/GR8520

Camping Delphi enjoys a stunning location on the slopes of Mount Parnassus, just four kilometres from ancient Delphi. There are some truly outstanding views over valleys of olive groves across to the Gulf of Corinth. The site's 80 fairly level pitches all offer electrical connections (6A) and some benefit from the great views. This is a well managed and well equipped site with an attractive pool and a friendly bar featuring an exhibition of paintings by Avyeris Kanatas, a former owner of the site. The prevailing ambience here is geared towards a peaceful, relaxing stay.

Facilities
Two toilet blocks, one modern and one refurbished. Facilities for disabled visitors. Washing machine. Motorcaravan services. Shop, bar, restaurant and takeaway (all April-Oct). Swimming pool. Tennis. Play area. Max. 1 dog. WiFi throughout (charged). Off site: Bus stop opposite site entrance with regular service to Athens and other places of interest. Beach 13 km. Walking trails to Delphi and Chrisso.

Open: 1 April - 15 October.

Directions
From Delphi take the road towards Itea. Just after a bridge, 4 km. from Delphi, site is signed to the right. Site is 500 m. on the right.
GPS: 38.478533, 22.474733

Charges guide
Per unit incl. 2 persons

and electricity	€ 21.30 - € 25.60
extra person	€ 6.20 - € 6.70
child (4-10 yrs)	€ 4.00 - € 4.60

Delphi

Chrissa Camping

GR-33054 Delphi (Central Greece) T: 226 508 2050. E: info@chrissacamping.gr

alanrogers.com/GR8525

From this well kept site a free road train takes guests to Delphi which was once sacred to the god Apollo and is now the setting for some of the most important monuments of ancient Greek civilisation. The site's situation on a hill ensures stunning views across a vast olive grove to the Gulf of Corinth beyond. There are 60 pitches with electricity connections (16A). They are well shaded and mostly terraced, which means that everyone can enjoy the views. The site is attractively landscaped, with lots of flowers and round wooden cabins to rent blend in very well with the natural environment. An evening meal on the restaurant's terrace is a must.

Facilities
Modern, well maintained toilet block with British style WCs, open washbasins and controllable showers. Family shower rooms. Motorcaravan services. Laundry room with sinks, washing machine and dryer. Shop (1/4-30/10). Bar, restaurant and takeaway (weekends only in winter). Outdoor pool and paddling pool. Barbecues are not allowed. Internet point. WiFi (charged). Off site: Distance to fishing and sailing 7 km. Beach 8 km. Skiing 18 km.

Open: All year.

Directions
Site is halfway between Itea and Delphi (6 km. from each) on the E65. It is well signed and entry is via a 300 m. lane. GPS: 38.472433, 22.45915

Charges guide
Per unit incl. 2 persons

and electricity	€ 22.50 - € 25.50
extra person	€ 5.50 - € 6.50
child (4-10 yrs)	€ 4.00 - € 5.50

Camping Cheques accepted.

Neos Marmaras

Camping Areti

GR-63081 Neos Marmaras (Central Macedonia) T: 237 507 1430. E: info@areti-chalkidiki.gr

alanrogers.com/GR8145

If you imagine a typical Greek campsite as being set immediately behind a small sandy beach in a quiet cove with pitches amongst pine and olive trees that stretch a long way back to the small coast road, then you have found your ideal site. Camping Areti is beautifully located just off the beaten track on the peninsula of Sithonia. It has 130 pitches for touring units. The olive groves at the rear provide hidden parking spaces for caravans and boats, and small boats can be launched from the beach. The Charalambidi family maintain their site to very high standards and visitors will not be disappointed.

Facilities
Three excellent toilet blocks include showers, WCs and washbasins. Kitchen with sinks, electric hobs and fridges. Laundry with washing machines. Small shop and restaurant. Sandy beach. Fishing, sailing and swimming. Communal barbecues. Free WiFi over part of site. Bungalows to rent. Dogs are not allowed on the beach. Off site: Riding, golf and bicycle hire 10 km. Sithonia, Mount Athos and the nearby Spalathronisia islands.

Open: 1 May - 31 October.

Directions
Postal address is Neos Marmaras but site is 12 km. south. Stay on main coast road, past casino resort at Porto Carras and in 5 km. turn right towards site (signed). Then turn right again to coast and turn left and on for 1.5 km. Turn right into site access road. Reception is 700 m. GPS: 40.024183, 23.81595

Charges guide
Per unit incl. 2 persons

and electricity	€ 36.40 - € 40.00

No credit cards.

FREE Alan Rogers Travel Card
Extra benefits and savings - see page 14

Igoumenitsa
Camping Kalami Beach

Plataria, GR-46100 Igoumenitsa (Epirus) T: 266 507 1211. E: info@campingkalamibeach.gr

alanrogers.com/GR8235

Set in a bay, this is a colourful, attractive, family run site that leads down to a beach and the crystal clear waters of the Ionian Sea. Colour comes mainly from the beautiful bougainvillea plants that clad many site buildings, and ample shade for the 75 level, terraced pitches, all with 10A electricity, is provided by olive and eucalyptus trees. From the lower pitches there are panoramic views of the island of Corfu from which, at night, lights reflect across the open water. The construction of the site with natural stone paving and a generous display of plants is totally in keeping with its well chosen setting.

Facilities
One sanitary block with British style WCs, washbasins and large showers. Second block has showers and washbasins in cabins. Laundry room with sinks, washing machines and dryer (token operated). Shop. Bar and restaurant, takeaway. Beach.

Open: 20 March - 20 October.

Directions
Site is 6 km. south of Igoumenista on the E55 coastal road to Preveza. From port follow signs for Preveza. From A2 motorway keep to the left at the end and take Exit Preveza. Site is signed towards the bottom of an incline. Entrance is very sharp right. GPS: 39.473783, 20.240817

Charges guide
Per unit incl. 2 persons
and electricity   € 26.00 - € 32.00

Parga
Camping Valtos

Valtos Beach, GR-48060 Parga (Epirus) T: 268 403 1287. E: info@campingvaltos.gr

alanrogers.com/GR8220

Valtos Camping lies two kilometres west of the picturesque village of Parga and just 60 m. from the beautiful sandy beach at Valtos. This is a small, friendly site with a shop, bar and restaurant. The 92 touring pitches here are of various sizes, all with electrical connections (16A). There is little grass but good shade is supplied by mulberry, lemon and olive trees. Access to the site is quite narrow and owners of larger motorcaravans will need to be careful. The 35-minute walk up over the castle hill and the steep descent through the narrow, shop-lined alleys of Parga yields magnificent views, especially from the castle walls. A water taxi service connects with Parga.

Facilities
Two toilet blocks, one modern and one refurbished. Washing machine. Motorcaravan services. Shop, bar, takeaway and restaurant (all May-Sept). Caravans for rent. Off site: Beach, sailing, fishing and boat launching 60 m. Water taxi to Parga beach. Bicycle hire 2 km. Boat trips to the Ionian islands. Walking trails.

Open: 1 May - 30 September.

Directions
From Igoumenitsa head south towards Preveza (E55). Turn right to Parga, in Parga keep right and continue on the coastal road towards Anthousa. Watch out for Valdos sign to the left and descend to Valdos beach. At the end of the beach (Tango Club) turn right. site is 50 m. GPS: 39.28555, 20.389833

Charges guide
Per unit incl. 2 persons
and electricity   € 21.50 - € 24.50
child   € 4.00 - € 4.50

Parga
Camping Enjoy-Lichnos

Lichnos, GR-48060 Parga (Epirus) T: 268 403 1171. E: holidays@enjoy-lichnos.net

alanrogers.com/GR8225

This is a quiet campsite with attractive views of the Ionian Sea and the coastlines towards Preveza and Parga. The site has been created on a steep incline with wide terraces and pitches under constructed shade, all with electricity. The ground levels out in front of the beach and pitches here have sea views. The site has 180 touring pitches and a large area for tents under the shade of the 500-year-old olive trees. The sandy beach is the site's main attraction and various water-based activities are available.

Facilities
Unisex toilet blocks in small units are situated on each terrace with washbasins (cold water only) and solar-heated showers. Main sanitary facilities at base of site, two blocks, one of which has wheelchair access. Washing machine and ironing. Shop. Bar and beach bar. Restaurant with discount for campsite visitors and children's menu. English is spoken. Off site: Parga, ruins of Nekromanteio, island of Lefkada.

Open: 1 May - 31 October.

Directions
From Igoumenitsa head south (E55) towards Preveza. At sign for Parga turn right and follow the road for 7 km. At Lichnos village turn left at Lichnos Camping and Apartments. Site entrance is 500 m. down a steep slope. GPS: 39.281717, 20.43395

Charges guide
Per unit incl. 2 persons
and electricity   € 28.30 - € 37.30

For latest campsite news, availability and prices visit
alanrogers.com

Corfu

Camping Dionysus

Dassia, Dafnilas Bay, Kerkyra, GR-49083 Corfu (Ionian Islands) T: 266 109 1417. E: laskari7@otenet.gr

alanrogers.com/GR8370

The Ionian island of Corfu is known by most as a popular tourist destination but perhaps not considered by many for camping. The hourly ferry from Igoumenitsa takes 90 minutes to cross to Kerkyra. Many ferries from Italian ports now stop here en-route to either Igoumenitsa or Patras, so it is possible to break your journey to mainland Greece. The north of the island now has some good campsites and Dionysus is amongst them, with its 107 pitches of which 55 are suitable for caravans and motorcaravans. The site, south of Dassia, slightly slopes and has been terraced in part to provide grassy pitches under old olive trees, which offer some shade.

Facilities

Two excellent toilet blocks include showers, WCs and washbasins. Washing machine. Small shop, bar and restaurant (all 1/6-1/10). Swimming pool (1/6-1/10). Bicycle hire. WiFi throughout (free). Off site: Beach, boat launching and fishing 600 m. Horse riding 6 km. Kerkyra 9 km. Golf 15 km.

Open: 1 April - 15 October (depending on the weather).

Directions

Most people will arrive in Corfu on one of the many ferries from either Igoumenitsa or one of the Italian ports. So, from the ferry terminal turn right initially signed Paleokastritsa. After 8 km. turn right at traffic lights signed Dassia. Site is on the right after 1 km. GPS: 39.66440, 19.84430

Charges guide

Per unit incl. 2 persons and electricity	€ 19.30 - € 25.00
extra person	€ 5.60 - € 6.50

Corfu

Camping Karda Beach

Dassia, P.O. Box 225, GR-49100 Corfu (Ionian Islands) T: 266 109 3595. E: campco@otenet.gr

alanrogers.com/GR8375

The popular holiday island of Corfu offers many sporting and leisure activities and access to it is easy, and comparatively cheap, via one of the many ferries from either Igoumenitsa or one of the Italian ports serving the Greek mainland. Camping Karda Beach offers a quiet low season site with excellent facilities, close to the beach and the island's main town, Kerkyra. It also offers a popular high season site for families and those looking for good weather, good beaches and lots of activities close at hand. It has 101 good grassy pitches of which 70 are for touring units, all with electricity (16A Europlug), under tall trees. The beach is a two minute walk away.

Facilities

Three excellent toilet blocks include showers, WCs and washbasins. Facilities for disabled visitors. Fridges. Laundry. Bar, small shop and restaurant (open all day, 1/5-30/9). Swimming pool with sun beds (1/5-5/10). Internet access. Play area and pool. Bungalows to rent. WiFi (free). Off site: Beach 50 m. Dassia 1-2 km. Kerkyra 12 km.

Open: 25 April - 7 October.

Directions

From the ferry terminal turn right initially signed Paleokastritsa. After 8 km. turn right at traffic lights signed Dassia. Go through Dassia and site is on the right after 1 km. just after a right hand bend. GPS: 39.686272, 19.838511

Charges guide

Per person	€ 6.80 - € 7.20
pitch incl. car	€ 8.70 - € 13.70
electricity	€ 4.60

Epidavros

Camping Bekas

Gialasi, GR-21052 Ancient Epidavros (Peloponnese) T: 275 309 9930. E: info@bekas.gr

alanrogers.com/GR8625

Just 60 kilometres south of Corinth you will find the town of Ancient Epidavros, and just south of that is Camping Bekas. With 150 pitches (120 for touring) set amongst the trees there is shade and a quiet atmosphere. Arranged along a small sand and shingle beach, the site offers opportunities for swimming, sailing and fishing. The Argolid region of the Peloponnese has much to offer the inquisitive tourist. About 12 km. south is the sanctuary of Asclepios. On a hillside lies the theatre, the most famous and best preserved of all the ancient theatres in Greece.

Facilities

Three toilet blocks include the usual facilities including two shower rooms for disabled visitors. Laundry with washing machine. Shop. Bar. Restaurant (15/5-15/9). Internet access. TV room. Sand and shingle beach. Apartments to rent. Off site: Theatre of Epidavros 12 km.

Open: 1 April - 20 October.

Directions

To avoid driving right through the town of Ancient Epidavros take the southern exit towards the town. Turn inland here down a slip road, then turn under the main road above towards the town. On entering the town turn right towards Gialasi and the site is 1.6 km. on the left. GPS: 37.61855, 23.15639

Charges guide

Per person	€ 5.00 - € 6.00
child (4-10 yrs)	€ 3.00 - € 3.50
pitch incl. electricity	€ 11.00 - € 13.70

FREE Alan Rogers Travel Card
Extra benefits and savings - see page 14

Finikounda
Camping Anemomilos

GR-24006 Finikounda (Peloponnese) T: 272 307 1120. E: robakibr@otenet.gr

alanrogers.com/GR8690

Anemomilos is a small friendly site situated directly on a beautiful sandy beach, with turquoise sea and quayside fish restaurants in the nearby village. Many German campers come here for the windsurfing, sailing and beach life generally. The site offers 80 level pitches with good shade and great views. The small picturesque village, just a few minutes walk away, is at the back of the bay. Caiques and fishing boats are drawn up all along the sandy shore, while tavernas serve their fresh catch by the water's edge.

Facilities
Two good toilet blocks include showers, WCs and washbasins. Facilities for disabled visitors. Laundry with washing machines and ironing boards. Two kitchens with sinks, electric hobs for cooking, fridges and ice machines. Bar and small shop (1/5-31/10). Beach. Off site: Restaurant opposite. Riding. Finikounda and the Inouse Islands. Tractor rides around the local villages!

Open: 1 March - 31 November.

Directions
Site is just 5 minutes walk from the centre of Finikounda. From the village head west and turn left at the end of the wide pavement. The site is 300 m. ahead. GPS: 36.8054, 21.8018

Charges guide
Per unit incl. 2 persons
and electricity   € 25.00 - € 32.00

Finikounda
Camping Finikes

GR-24006 Finikounda (Peloponnese) T: 272 302 8524. E: camping-finikes@otenet.gr

alanrogers.com/GR8695

This site offers 80 level pitches with good shade and great views. It also has 16 apartments to rent. Some pitches have high reed screens that give good protection from the blazing Greek sun and the turquoise sea is great for swimming, windsurfing and sailing. The site is at the western corner of Finikounda Bay and has direct access to the sandy beach by crossing small natural dunes. The facilities are excellent and in low season, when there are 18 or less campers, each camper is given the keys to a WC and shower for their own personal use.

Facilities
The good toilet block includes showers, WCs and washbasins. Facilities for disabled visitors. Kitchen includes sinks, electric hobs and fridges. Laundry. Bar, small shop and restaurant. Accommodation to rent. Off site: Finikounda and the Inouse Islands. Distance to boat launching and sailing 3 km. Bicycle hire 25 km.

Open: All year.

Directions
Site is 3 km. from the centre of Finikounda. From the village head west and turn left into the site. GPS: 36.802817, 21.78105

Charges guide
Per unit incl. 2 persons
and electricity   € 18.50 - € 22.50
extra person   € 5.50 - € 6.00
child (4-10 yrs)   € 3.00 - € 3.50
No credit cards.

Gythion
Camping Gythion Bay

Mavrovouni Gythion, GR-23200 Gythion (Peloponnese) T: 273 302 2522. E: info@gythiocamping.gr

alanrogers.com/GR8685

Camping Gythion Bay is in the Peloponnese, three kilometres west of Gythion town on the road to Areopolis. It has 71 unmarked pitches set amongst orange, fig, olive and pine trees and all with electricity. Some trees limit access but the owner, Mr Zafirakos, is dealing with this to improve the site. Indeed he has also been busy refurbishing the toilets, showers and other facilities. With a good beach alongside the site, there are good opportunities for windsurfing and storage for boards is available. This is a good starting point for excursions to the Caves of Diros and for wider exploration of Lakonia and especially Inner and Outer Mani and Sparta.

Facilities
Four toilet blocks (totally renovated) include the usual facilities plus those for disabled visitors. Laundry with washing machines. Motorcaravan services. Small shop (1/5-30/9) including gas. Bar, restaurant and takeaway (15/6-15/9). Outdoor swimming pool (all year). Play area. Fishing, windsurfing and limited boat launching. Small beach. Free WiFi over part of site. Off site: Gythion 4 km. Bicycle hire and sailing 4 km. Water-skiing 10 km.

Open: All year.

Directions
Site is 4 km. south of the fishing port of Gythion on the road to Aeropoli. It is between two petrol stations on the left and has a wide entrance. GPS: 36.72817, 22.54614

Charges guide
Per unit incl. 2 persons
and electricity   € 19.90 - € 24.90
extra person   € 5.60 - € 6.10
child (4-10 yrs)   € 4.10 - € 4.60
dog   free
Camping Cheques accepted.

For latest campsite news, availability and prices visit

alanrogers.com

Killinis

Camping Fournia Beach

Kastro, GR-27050 Killinis (Peloponnese) T: 262 309 5095. E: fournia@otenet.gr

alanrogers.com/GR8325

The village of Kastros and the Chlemoutsi castle that towers above it can be seen for miles across the flat landscape towards the coast. Camping Fournia Beach is owned by the four Lefkaditis brothers, and their wives have ensured that this new site is awash with flowering shrubs. The site offers 90 first class pitches and modern facilities, and the bar and restaurant sit in a landscaped area high above the beach with spectacular views across the sea to Zakinthos. Steps to the beach provide private access to the sandy cove below. The brothers plan to install a swimming pool.

Facilities

Two modern toilet blocks include showers, WCs and washbasins and good facilities for disabled visitors. Laundry with washing machines, sinks and hot water. Kitchen with hobs, fridge and freezer. Shop. Restaurant and bar overlooking the sea and the island of Zakinthos. Accommodation for rent. Off site: Chlemoutsi castle.

Open: 1 April - 30 October.

Directions

Travel 61 km. south of Patras on the main road to Pyrgos. At traffic lights, turn west (Killinis and Zakinthos). Site is well signed from here, 15 km. and past village of Kastros. Descend towards thermal springs and continue on a left hand hairpin bend towards beach. GPS: 37.8992, 21.1165

Charges guide

Per unit incl. 2 persons and electricity	€ 15.60 - € 19.80
extra person	€ 4.60 - € 5.40

Camping Cheques accepted.

Nafplio

Camping Triton II

Plaka Drepano, GR-21060 Nafplio (Peloponnese) T: 27 52 09 21 28.

alanrogers.com/GR8635

What do we look for in a good campsite in Greece? Given the excellent Greek weather, the answer is probably a good, flat pitch with some shade, excellent toilets and showers that are spotlessly clean, a small shop and proximity to a beach and local tavernas. Well, here you have it all! Under the control of the owners, Mr and Mrs George Christopoulous, this is an exceptional site with 40 good sized touring pitches under high screens, just across the road from Drepano beach. Local tavernas are within strolling distance and the town's shops are about a mile away.

Facilities

Excellent refurbished toilet blocks include showers, WCs and washbasins. Baby bath. Facilities for disabled visitors. Laundry with washing machines and ironing board. Electric hobs for cooking. Fridge and freezer. Small shop (1/6-30/9). Off site: Drepano beach, local tavernas and bars. Assini.

Open: 1 April - 30 October.

Directions

From Nafplio follow the main road west and then turn right towards Drepano. In the town follow the signs Plaka Drepano and turn left towards the coast. At the beach turn right and site is just ahead. GPS: 37.53202, 22.89165

Charges guide

Per unit incl. 2 persons and electricity	€ 24.00 - € 26.00

Olympia

Camping Alphios

GR-27065 Olympia (Peloponnese) T: 262 402 2951. E: alphios@otenet.gr

alanrogers.com/GR8340

High above ancient and modern Olympia, this site enjoys spectacular views, both across the adjoining countryside and to the coast at Pyrgos. It provides 97 pitches, all have 16A electricity and many have high reed screens that provide shade. Olympia is a popular tourist destination with dozens of coaches each day bringing tourists from around the world to this small town and the adjoining archaeological sites. However, the area also offers opportunities for walking and cycling amidst some wonderful scenery and this site provides a good base for excursions to the surrounding northern Peloponnese countryside.

Facilities

Two toilet blocks include showers, WCs and washbasins. Two kitchens with sinks, electric hobs and fridges. Laundry with washing machines. Small shop. Bar and restaurant. Small swimming pool. Off site: Ancient Olympia. Town centre within walking distance.

Open: 1 April - 15 October.

Directions

Site is at a height of 400 m. to the west of the town, 1.5 km. from the centre. Go through the town and past the station. Turn right, then at back of the town follow signs up the hill to the site. GPS: 37.64317, 21.61975

Charges guide

Per unit incl. 2 persons and electricity	€ 23.30 - € 30.30

FREE Alan Rogers Travel Card
Extra benefits and savings - see page 14

Pylos

Camping Erodios

Pylos, Gialova, GR-24001 Pylos (Peloponnese) T: 272 302 3269. E: info@erodioss.gr

alanrogers.com/GR8700

Efthinios Panourgias has given great thought to what is needed, and has provided everything to the highest possible standard in an environmentally friendly way. He is constantly on the site ensuring these standards are maintained and already has plans for further improvements. The 90 pitches have high reed screens to provide shade, which is most welcome given the high temperatures, even in the low season. There is direct access to a sandy beach and the glorious turquoise sea in a sheltered bay north of the busy town of Pylos.

Facilities

Three good toilet blocks include showers, WCs and washbasins. Facilities for disabled visitors. Two kitchens include sinks, electric hobs and fridges. Laundry. Motorcaravan services. Very good shop. Bar/café with Internet access (all season). Excellent restaurant/takeaway (10/5-30/9). Play area for under 5s. Car and motorbike rental. Barbecue. Eight bungalows for rent. Free WiFi throughout. Off site: Pylos.

Open: 15 April - 15 October.

Directions

From Pylos head north on main road and fork left towards Gialova. Once in the village turn left, signed to site and Golden Beach. Site is on left in 700 m. From Gargaliari head south towards Pylos and in the village of Gialova turn right towards site.
GPS: 36.95188, 21.69561

Charges guide

Per unit incl. 2 persons	
and electricity	€ 19.00 - € 28.00
extra person	€ 5.50 - € 7.00
child	€ 3.00 - € 4.00

Pylos

Camping Navarino Beach

Gialova, GR-24001 Pylos (Peloponnese) T: 272 302 2973. E: info@navarino-beach.gr

alanrogers.com/GR8705

There are 150 pitches, most facing the beach, with 30 being directly situated alongside. All have electricity (10A) and most have good shade. The pitches are arranged in rows to ensure that all have beach access. The facilities are adequate and cleaned regularly. The staff are friendly and efficient, and there is a very good restaurant with a terrace directly by the beach. The light wind in the morning, which strengthens on some afternoons, makes it a great windsurfing location and boats can be moored by the beach. This site is highly recommended.

Facilities

The five toilet blocks are well situated and, even in high season, were kept very clean and never became overcrowded. Open washbasins, hot water to showers, and communal refrigerators and freezers. Small shop sells basic provisions (May-Oct). Other shops within walking distance. WiFi over part of site. Off site: Within walking distance of Gialova with its promenade restaurants. Pylos 6 km. Nestors Palace 12 km. Numerous places to visit. Golf 2 km. Bicycle hire 0.5 km.

Open: 1 April - 31 October.

Directions

Directly on the National Road Pylos Kyparissia. 300 m. from the village of Gialova.
GPS: 36.94764, 21.70618

Charges guide

Per unit incl. 2 persons	
and electricity	€ 20.00 - € 24.00
extra person	€ 5.50 - € 6.50
child	€ 2.50 - € 3.00

For latest campsite news, availability and prices visit
alanrogers.com

Vartholomio Ilias

Camping Ionion Beach

Glifa, GR-27050 Vartholomio Ilias (Peloponnese) T: 262 309 6395. E: ioniongr@otenet.gr

alanrogers.com/GR8330

This is a very attractive and well kept site in a beautiful location by the Ionian Sea, created from former farmland by the Fligos family. Much has changed since they welcomed their first guests in 1982, when they still left plenty of space for growing potatoes. Now it is a modern site with a large pool and a paddling pool and two blocks of apartments to rent. Separated by a variety of trees and oleander bushes, there are 235 pitches of 80-100 sq.m. with 16A electricity. Those at the front of the site enjoy views over the sea and the island of Zakinthos.

Facilities

Three excellent sanitary blocks with British style WCs and showers with washbasins in cabins. Motorcaravan services. Turkish style chemical disposal point. Laundry room. Shop, bar, restaurant (15/4-15/11). Internet access. Swimming pool (no depth markings) and paddling pool (15/4-15/11). Excellent new play area. Off site: Ferries to Zakinthos from Kilini, ancient city of Olympia, Frankish fortress of Chlemoutsi.

Open: All year.

Directions

From Patra head south on E55 towards Pyrgos. At sign for Vartholomio, turn right in town centre, then right at sign for Glyfa and Ionion Beach. In 15 km. campsite sign is on right. Coming from the north of Greece, there is a toll for the Korinthian Gulf bridge. GPS: 37.836617, 21.1338

Charges guide

Per unit incl. 2 persons	
and electricity	€ 21.10 - € 29.10
extra person	€ 6.00 - € 7.00
child (4-11 yrs)	€ 3.50 - € 4.00

Discounts for long stays.

Kato Gatzea

Camping Sikia

GR-38500 Kato Gatzea (Thessaly) T: 242 302 2279. E: info@camping-sikia.gr

alanrogers.com/GR8280

Camping Sikia is an attractive, well maintained site enthusiastically run by the Pandelfi family. The site offers 80 pitches of varying sizes all with 16A electricity. They are arranged on terraces and may become quite dusty during the dry season, but most are well shaded by olive trees. There are superb views from many pitches – the sea to the south and the mountains to the north. There are also 17 apartments to rent. The calm sea and golden beaches of the Pagasitikos Gulf make this a perfect spot for family holidays. The site is just 100 m. from a sand and shingle beach on the edge of a rocky bay.

Facilities

Two modern and one refurbished sanitary blocks with British style WCs, open washbasins and preset showers. Facilities for disabled visitors are planned. Laundry area with sinks, washing machines and ironing facilities. Shop. Bar. TV room. Internet corner. Restaurant. Communal barbecue areas. Fishing. Dogs are not allowed on the beach. WiFi over site (free). Off site: Bicycle hire 1 km. Riding and sailing 2 km. Boat trips to Skiathos.

Open: 1 April - 31 October.

Directions

Follow E75 south towards Lamia, turn left at sign for Volos onto E92. Follow coastal road towards Argalasti for 18 km. Site is off the coastal road on the right at Kato Gatzea immediately past Camping Hellas. GPS: 39.310267, 23.109783

Charges guide

Per unit incl. 2 persons	
and electricity	€ 24.00 - € 32.00

Volos

Camping Hellas International

GR-38500 Kato Gatzea (Thessaly) T: 242 302 2267. E: info@campinghellas.gr

alanrogers.com/GR8285

There is a warm welcome from the English-speaking brother and sister team who own and run Camping Hellas. The campsite has been in the family since the sixties, when tourists first asked if they could camp overnight and use the facilities of the taverna. It is in a beautiful setting in a 500-year-old olive grove, right next to the beach and the calm blue waters of the Pagasitikos gulf. There are around 100 pitches all with 16A electricity. Pitch sizes vary and some parts are more level than others, but shade is plentiful thanks to the olive trees.

Facilities

One modern and one old sanitary block, both very clean with British style toilets and open washbasins. Very good facilities for disabled visitors. Laundry room with sinks and washing machines, ironing facilities. Shop, bar, restaurant and takeaway from 1 May. TV room. Dogs are not allowed on the beach. Off site: Sailing 5 km. Riding and bicycle hire 18 km. Pelion steam railway, boat trips to Skiathos.

Open: All year.

Directions

From the north follow the E75 towards Lamia. Turn left at sign for Volos onto E92. Follow coastal road south towards Argalasti for 18 km. Site is off coastal road on right at Kato Gatzea. GPS: 39.310833, 23.1091

Charges guide

Per unit incl. 2 persons	
and electricity	€ 23.80 - € 29.50
extra person	€ 6.00 - € 7.00
child (4-16 yrs)	€ 3.50 - € 5.50

FREE Alan Rogers Travel Card
Extra benefits and savings - see page 14

Hungary

Centrally located in Europe, Hungary is a landlocked country of hills and plains divided along its length by the River Danube. Its largest mountains are in the Carpathians, lying along the border with Slovakia. It is home to ten national parks, two major rivers, Europe's largest cave system and the world's biggest thermal lake.

The Danube flows through Budapest, now one of central Europe's most visited destinations. The hills of Buda lie to the west, with the flat plain of Pest on the eastern bank. Its impressive architecture and bridges can be appreciated from one of the many boats that cruise along the river. There are plenty of opportunities to relax in the thermal spas or the botanical gardens. The Danube Bend, considered to be one of the most beautiful stretches of the river, is a popular day trip from Budapest taking in historic towns and ruins. Further afield in the north-eastern hills, the spectacular caves at Aggtelek are another firm favourite.

Lake Balaton is Central Europe's largest freshwater lake, covering an area of almost 600 sq.km, and offers all manner of watersports. The more genteel north shore has attractive towns and some historical sights, in contrast to the south with its lively beaches, restaurants and nightlife.

CAPITAL: Budapest

Tourist Office

Hungarian National Tourist Office

46 Eaton Place, London SW1X 8AL

Tel: 020 7823 1032

Fax: 020 7823 1459

Email: info@gotohungary.co.uk

Internet: www.gotohungary.co.uk

Population

9.9 million

Climate

There are four fairly distinct seasons – hot in summer, mild spring and autumn, very cold winter with snow.

Language

The official language is Magyar, but German is widely spoken.

Telephone

The country code is 00 36.

Money

Currency: Hungarian Forints (HUF).

Banks: Mon-Fri 09.00-14.00, Sat 09.00-12.00.

Shops

Mon-Fri 10.00-18.00, Sat 10.00-14.00.

Food shops open Mon-Fri 07.00-19.00, Sat 07.00-14.00.

Public Holidays

New Year; Revolution Day 15 March; Easter Mon; Labour Day; Whitsun; Constitution Day 20 Aug; Republic Day 23 Oct; All Saints Day 1 Nov; Christmas 25, 26 Dec.

Motoring

Dipped headlights are compulsory at all times but main beams should not be used in towns. Motorway stickers must be purchased for the M1 to Budapest, the M7 from Budapest to Lake Balaton and also on the M3 eastward. Also the full length of the M5 (Budapest-Kiskunfelegyhaza). Give way to trams and buses at junctions. Carrying spare fuel in a can is not permitted.

see campsite map 8

Kiskunmajsa
Jonathermál Motel-Camping
Kökút 26, H-6120 Kiskunmajsa (Bacs-Kiskun County) T: 77 481 855. E: info@jonathermal.hu

alanrogers.com/HU5260

Situated three kilometres to the north of the town of Kiskunmajsa, a few kilometres west of road 5 (E75) from Budapest (140 km) to Szeged (35 km), this is one of the best Hungarian campsites. The camping area is large, reached by tarmac access roads, with 250 unmarked pitches in several areas around the motel and sanitary buildings. Some shade is available and more trees are growing. All the 205 large touring pitches have electricity (10A) and are set on flat grass. Entrance to the impressive pool complex is charged (daily or weekly tickets are available - 40 per cent reduction for campsite guests).

Facilities
Heated sanitary block providing first class facilities including washbasins in cabins and a unit for disabled visitors. Second new block to the back with showers and toilets. Launderette. Gas supplies. Kiosk on site for bread and basics. etc. Smart bar and rest room. Restaurant by pool complex. Large swimming and thermal complex with other facilities (1/5-1/10). Massage (charged). New playground. Tennis. Minigolf. Fishing lake (day permits). Bicycle hire. Riding. WiFi in reception. German spoken. Accommodation to rent. Off site: Restaurants nearby. Riding 100 m. Shop opposite entrance 120 m.

Open: All year.

Directions
From M5 motorway (Budapest-Szeged), take exit for Kiskunmajsa and site is well signed 3 km. north of the town on road 5402. GPS: 46.52133, 19.74687

Charges guide
Per unit incl. 2 persons and electricity	HUF 2350 - 3050
extra person	HUF 600 - 800
child (6-14 yrs)	HUF 300 - 350
dog	HUF 350 - 500

Less 5-10% for longer stays. No credit cards.

Magyaregregy
Máré Vára Camping
Várvölgy utca 2, H-7332 Magyaregregy (Baranya) T: 72 420 126. E: info@camping-marevara.com

alanrogers.com/HU5320

Máré Vára takes its name from an ancient castle situated on top of a hill, two kilometres away, where the German noble family of Mariën once lived. The site is on archaeological ground: where the main house now stands, there used to be a monastery and centuries before that there was an ancient Roman settlement. Some 40 pitches (36 with 10A electricity) are on slightly sloping, well kept fields. On site is a small swimming pool. Modern toilet facilities are in an old barn and here in the walls one can see remains of the former monastery.

Facilities
Modern and clean toilet facilities (in a former barn) with British style toilets, some washbasins in cabins and controllable showers (free, hot water variable). Washing machine. Motorcaravan services. No shop, but bread to order. Small bar with terrace for drinks and ice-cream (1/5-30/9) on site. Playground. Social events organised. TV room with satellite, DVD and video. Free WiFi over site. Off site: Máré Vára Castle 2 km.

Open: 30 April - end September.

Directions
Magyaregregy is northeast of Pécs. Site is just outside Magyaregregy on the left and well signed. GPS: 46.233611, 18.308333

Charges guide
Per unit incl. 2 persons and electricity	HUF 3200 - 5100
extra person	HUF 1200
child (under 12 yrs)	HUF 900

No credit cards.

Magyarhertelend
Camping Forras
Bokréta u. 105, H-7394 Magyarhertelend (Baranya) T: 72 521 110. E: bojtheforras@freemail.hu

alanrogers.com/HU5315

Camping Forras, or 'Bij Balázc' as it is called by some Dutch guests, is close to the historic city of Pécs, in a part of Hungary with a Mediterranean style climate. It is next to the renovated thermal spa of Magyarhertelend, and close to the Mescék National Park, where there are many marked walking routes. The site has 120 pitches, all for tourers, off gravel and grass access roads. Of these, 80 are marked and have 6A electricity connections. The remaining pitches are used mainly for tents. The whole site looks well cared for with many different varieties of trees giving a pleasant atmosphere and providing useful shade in summer.

Facilities
The traditional toilet block provides basic facilities with British style toilets, some washbasins in cabins and controllable showers (free). Washing machine and spin dryer. Bar with library. Basic playground. Minigolf. Torch useful. Off site: Fishing 3 km. City of Pécs is nearby.

Open: 7 May - 30 September.

Directions
From Pécs, take no. 66 road north towards Sásd. Turn left in Magyarszék towards Magyarhertelend and follow signs. Site is just outside the village on the left. GPS: 46.190883, 18.141767

Charges guide
Per unit incl. 2 persons and electricity	HUF 3000 - 3600

No credit cards.

For latest campsite news, availability and prices visit

alanrogers.com

Tiszaújváros

Termál Camping

Szederkényi út 53, H-3580 Tiszaújváros (Borsod-Abauj-Zemplen) T: 49 542 210. E: camping@tujvaros.hu

alanrogers.com/HU5197

Termál Camping was opened in 2004 and is on the outskirts of Tiszaújváros (the former Lenin City) and not far from the River Tisza in eastern Hungary. The site has some 166 grass pitches (all for touring units), of which 16 have 25A electricity. To one end of the site are eight holiday homes and centrally located is a well equipped toilet block. The trees and bushes have not yet fully developed and the site can become a suntrap in the hot Hungarian summer. The site is next to a tributary of the River Tisza, and the area offers good opportunities for walking, cycling, boating and fishing. Some English is spoken.

Facilities

One central, modern toilet block with toilets, preset hot showers,washbasins and facilities for disabled visitors (out of order when we visited). Laundry with washing machines. Kitchen with cooking rings, oven and fridge. Communal barbecue areas. Small buffet/bar. Fishing. Bicycle hire. Torch useful. Off site: Thermal spa. Supermarket and swimming pool 300 m.

Open: All year.

Directions

From M3 motorway from Budapest to the east, take exit for Debrecen and then to Tiszaújváros. On entering town follow the signs to the Thermal Spa bath and the site. GPS: 47.9318, 21.0465

Charges guide

Per unit incl. 2 persons and electricity	HUF 5500 - 6000
extra person	HUF 1500
dog	HUF 500

Budapest

Zugligeti Niche Camping

Zugligeti út 101, H-1121 Budapest (Budapest City) T: 12 008 346. E: camping.niche@t-online.hu

alanrogers.com/HU5165

Zugligeti Niche is in the Buda Hills on the starting point of the former 58 tramline, of which the main building now houses the reception, bar and restaurant. There are 80 pitches in one long row, all for tourers, mainly suitable for camper vans and caravans, and a few pitches for tents off a tarmac and gravel access road. To the front of the site are two old tram carriages, one of which functions as a restaurant. Breakfast is included in the price at this welcoming site and in high season visitors are offered a free drink upon arrival. Zugligeti Niche is popular with Italians, who park their camper vans here to enjoy a few days sightseeing in Budapest. By bus it is an easy 20 minutes to the first metro station at Széll Kálmán tér. From here you can visit the parliament and the royal palace and enjoy the great views of the Danube from Castle Hill (UNESCO World Heritage).

Facilities

Two good refurbished toilet blocks with free, controllable hot showers, toilets and open style washbasins. Basic facilities for disabled visitors. Laundry with sinks and washing machine. Campers' kitchen. Bar/restaurant with good value meals. Torch useful. Free WiFi on part of site. Off site: Cable track. Budapest city centre 30 minutes by public transport.

Open: All year.

Directions

Site is in the Budapest district 12. Coming from the north follow signs for M1 and M7 motorways. Site is well signed from Moszkva Tér. GPS: 47.516383, 18.974617

Charges guide

Per unit incl. 2 persons and electricity	HUF 6800 - 8300
extra person	HUF 1800
child (4-14 yrs)	HUF 900
dog	free

FREE Alan Rogers Travel Card

Extra benefits and savings - see page 14

Budapest
Camping Haller

Haller utca 27, H-1096 Budapest (Budapest City) T: 14 763 418 (in season). E: info@hallercamping.hu

alanrogers.com/HU5156

Camping Haller is very much a city site, set in a park in the centre of Budapest. It has 100 pitches available for touring, on a new, open area, most with hardstanding and some in the shade of mature trees, all with 16A electricity. The site is close to buses, the metro and trams for visiting the beautiful city of Budapest. From the site it is a few hundred metres walk to the banks of the Danube where you can enjoy an evening stroll after a day visiting the town.

Facilities
Sanitary facilities are next to reception with WCs and free hot showers. Washing machine. Restaurant. Free WiFi over site. English is spoken. Off site: Bicycle hire 3 km. Budapest city centre with restaurants, shops, pools, museums.

Open: 10 May - 30 September.

Directions
Coming from Vienna via the M1 follow signs for Petofi Hid (bridge). Cross the bridge and turn immediately right. After about 1 km. turn left onto Vágóh'd utca (do not take the Haller utca). After 750 m turn left into the entrance to the Obester utca (one-way). GPS: 47.475833, 19.082916

Charges guide
Per unit incl. 2 persons and electricity	HUF 5800 - 6900
extra person	HUF 1650
child (3-14 yrs)	HUF 825

No credit cards.

Györ
Gasthof Camping Pihenö

I-es föút, H-9011 Györszentivan-Kertváros (Gyor-Moson-Sopron County) T: 96 523 008.

E: piheno@piheno.hu **alanrogers.com/HU5120**

This privately owned site makes an excellent night stop when travelling to and from Hungary as it lies close to the M1 motorway to the east of Györ. It is set amidst pine trees with pitches that are not numbered, but marked out by small shrubs, in a small clearing or between the trees (firm pegs needed). With space for about 40 touring units, all with electrical connections (6A), and eight simple, one roomed bungalows and four en-suite rooms. On one side of the site, fronting the road, is the reception and bar (hot food available for camp guests; menu in English). English is spoken.

Facilities
A single, small, basic toilet block has just two showers for each sex (on payment) and curtained, communal dressing space. Baby room. Room for washing clothes and dishes with small cooking facility. Washing machine. Order bread at reception the previous evening. Shop (1/5-30/9). Bar. Restaurant with good menu and reasonable prices. Solar heated swimming pool and children's pool (10x5 m, June-Sept). Some road noise can be heard. Off site: Györ with shops and swimming pool.

Open: 1 April - 30 October.

Directions
Coming from Austria via the M1 motorway, take the exit for Györ and continue on the no. 1 road towards Budapest. Site is 3 km. to the east of Györ on the left. GPS: 47.71664, 17.69997

Charges guide
Per unit incl. 2 persons and electricity	€ 15.73
extra person	€ 4.80
child (3-18 yrs)	€ 1.85 - € 3.70
dog	€ 3.70

Less 10% for stays over 4 days, 20% after 8.

Pannonhalma
Panoráma Camping

Fenyvesalja 4/A, H-9090 Pannonhalma (Gyor-Moson-Sopron County) T: 96 471 240.

E: info@borbirodalom.hu **alanrogers.com/HU5130**

In 1982, this became the first private enterprise campsite in Hungary. It offers a very pleasant outlook and peaceful stay at the start or end of your visit to this country, situated just 20 km. southeast of Györ, on a hillside with views across the valley to the Sokoro hills. The 70 numbered and hedged touring pitches (50 with 16A electricity, long leads necessary) are on terraces, generally fairly level but reached by fairly steep concrete access roads, with many trees and plants around. Some small hardstandings are provided. There are benches provided and a small, grass terrace below reception from where you can purchase beer, local wine and soft drinks. No English is spoken.

Facilities
Good sanitary facilities are in a small building near reception and a larger unit halfway up the site. Curtained, hot showers with curtained communal changing. Cooking facilities. Bar (1/6-31/8). Shop. Recreation room with TV and games. Small play area and small pool (cleaned once a week). No charcoal barbecues. Off site: Hourly bus service to Györ. Shop for essentials 150 m. Good value restaurant 400 m. away in the village. Riding 3 km.

Open: 1 May - 31 August.

Directions
From no. 82 Györ-Veszprém road at Ecs turn to Pannonhalma. Site is well signed. NB: the final approach road is fairly steep.
GPS: 47.54915, 17.7578

Charges guide
Per unit incl. 2 persons and electricity	HUF 4900
extra person	HUF 1000
child (2-14 yrs)	HUF 500

No credit cards.

For latest campsite news, availability and prices visit

alanrogers.com

Eger

Öko-Park Camping

9 Borsod u. Szarvaskö, H-3323 Eger-Szarvaskö (Heves County) T: 36 352 201. E: info@oko-park.hu

alanrogers.com/HU5205

Öko-Park Camping is close to the Baroque style town of Eger, on the edge of the protected Bükk National Park. Buildings on the site are all made of natural materials and there is a well used for watering the plants. Öko-Park has 45 pitches off a single gravel access lane that runs to the back of the site. The grass pitches are level, marked and numbered. All have 16A electricity and are in the shade of mature trees. There is a small adventure park on site with climbing wall, tree-path and waterfall. The disadvantages are a road running alongside, a railway to the back and pitches which may be small for larger units. A pond is at the rear of the site and a covered picnic area.

Facilities

One good toilet block to the front provides toilets, open style washbasins and preset hot showers. Baby bath and changing mat. Basic facilities for disabled visitors. Washing machine and spin dryer. Campers' kitchen. Restaurant with bar for breakfast and dinner (all year). Climbing wall. Playground on gravel. Eco tours, walks and wine cave visits organised. Bicycle hire. WiFi on part of site (free). Off site: Shop nearby. Fishing 7 km. Eger 9 km.

Open: All year.

Directions

From Budapest, follow M3 motorway east and take exit for Eger. Follow to Eger and, from there, the 25 road north towards Szarvaskö. It is the second site on the right. GPS: 47.988283, 20.331017

Charges guide

Per unit incl. 2 persons and electricity	€ 27.20
extra person	€ 4.40
child (3-15 yrs)	€ 2.90

No credit cards.

Martfü

Martfü Health & Recreation Centre

Tüzép út, H-5435 Martfü (Jász-Nagykyun-Szolnok County) T: 56 580 531. E: martfu@camping.hu

alanrogers.com/HU5255

The Martfü campsite is a modern site with 61 touring pitches on grassy terrain with rubber hardstandings. Each is around 90 sq.m. and separated by young bushes and trees. All have electricity (16/25A), waste water drainage, cable and satellite TV. There is a water tap per two pitches. There is no shade as yet, which may cause the site to become a real suntrap in summer, when temperatures may rise up to 34 degrees. A small lake and its beach on the site will cool you off. The main attraction at this site is the thermal spa, which is said to aid people with skin and rheumatic problems.

Facilities

Two modern, heated toilet blocks with British style toilets, open style washbasins, and free, controllable hot showers. Children's toilet and shower. Heated baby room. En-suite facilities for disabled visitors. Laundry. Kitchen with cooking rings. Motorcaravan services. Shop for basics. Takeaway for bread and drinks. Welcoming bar with satellite TV and WiFi. Indoor and outdoor swimming pools. Bowling. Library. Sauna. Jacuzzi. Playing field. Tennis. Minigolf. Fishing. Bicycle hire. Watersports. English is spoken. Off site: Fishing 50 m. Boat launching 1.5 km.

Open: All year.

Directions

Driving into Martfü from the north on the 442 road, take the first exit at the roundabout (site is signed). Continue for 800 m. and site is signed on the right. GPS: 47.019933, 20.268517

Charges guide

Per person	HUF 1200
child (6-14 yrs)	HUF 600
pitch	HUF 900 - 1200

No credit cards.

Dömös

Dömös Camping

Duna-Part, H-2027 Dömös (Komarom-Esztergom County) T: 33 482 319. E: info@domoscamping.hu

alanrogers.com/HU5110

The area of the Danube Bend is a major tourist attraction and here at Dömös is a lovely modern, well maintained and presented, friendly, peaceful site with large pitches and easy access. There are 107 quite large pitches, of which 80 have 6A electricity, in sections on flat grass, numbered and divided by small plants and some with little shade. At the top of the site is an inviting open-air swimming pool with a grass lying out area and tiny children's pool with a large bar with pool tables alongside. Sightseeing tours to Budapest, Esztergom and Szentendre are arranged. The Danube is just over 50 m. away and quite fast flowing.

Facilities

The modern, long, brick built sanitary building is tiled with sliding doors and includes large, preset hot showers with individual changing, and good facilities for children and disabled visitors. Cooking area. Laundry with washing machines and dryer. Motorcaravan services. Bar. Restaurant. Small café with terrace. Swimming pool (20x10 m). WiFi on part of site (charged). Small play area on grass. English is spoken. Off site: Fishing 50 m.

Open: 1 May - 30 September.

Directions

Site is between the village and the Danube, off road 11 Esztergom-Visegrad-Szentendre. GPS: 47.76545, 18.91440

Charges guide

Per unit incl. 2 persons and electricity	HUF 4660 - 5890
extra person	HUF 990 - 1150
child (2-14 yrs)	HUF 800 - 900

No credit cards (cash only).

FREE Alan Rogers Travel Card
Extra benefits and savings - see page 14

Erdötarcsa

Helló Halló Park

Falujárók út 8, H-2177 Erdötarcsa (Nograd) T: 70 321 4038. E: info@hellohallopark.eu

alanrogers.com/HU5184

Helló Halló Park is situated on the edge of the small village of Erdötarcsa and is a good base for touring the beautiful countryside and for visiting the city of Budapest. You will receive a warm welcome from the Dutch owners who will happily inform you about the activities on offer, in particular the riding facilities. The site provides just 19 touring pitches with 6-16A electricity, on large grassy fields, some on hardstandings, with access from hardcore lanes. Pitches to the front are partially terraced and shaded, whilst the newer pitches to the rear are larger and more open. This site is excellent for those seeking a peaceful and quiet holiday. Some tents and accommodation are available for rent.

Facilities

Two small toilet blocks (one heated) provide the usual facilities including those for disabled visitors and a family shower room. Private sanitary units for rent. Washing machine. Small meals and drinks served. Outdoor pool (June-Sept). Bicycle hire. Indoor play room. TV room. Play area. Fishing pond for children. Riding (including lessons). Communal barbecue area. WiFi over site.

Open: All year (telephone first 1/11 - 31/3).

Directions

From Budapest, take the M3 motorway east towards Nyiregyháza. Take the exit for Bag and Aszód and follow signs towards Aszód. From there, head northeast towards Kartal, Verseg and Erdötarcsa. Site is on the right as you enter the village. GPS: 47.759466, 19.545689

Charges guide

Per unit incl. 2 persons and electricity	€ 14.25 - € 16.50
extra person	€ 3.25 - € 4.00

No credit cards.

Törökbálint

Fortuna Camping

Dózsa György út 164, H-2045 Törökbálint (Pest County) T: 23 335 364. E: info@fortunacamping.hu

alanrogers.com/HU5150

This good site lies at the foot of a hill with views of the vineyards, but Budapest is only 25 minutes away by bus. Concrete and gravel access roads lead to terraces where there are 170 individual pitches most bordered with hedges, all with electricity (up to 16A, long leads needed), and 14 with water, on slightly sloping ground. The site is surrounded by mature trees and Mr Szücs, the owner, will proudly name the 150 varieties of bushes and shrubs that edge the pitches. An open-air swimming pool with flume will help you to cool off in summer with an indoor pool for cooler weather.

Facilities

One fully equipped sanitary block and two smaller blocks. Good facilities for disabled campers. Six cookers in sheltered area. Washing machine and dryer. Gas supplies. Motorcaravan services. Bar. Essentials from reception (order bread previous day). Outdoor swimming pool with slide (15/5-15/9). Indoor pool. Small play area. WiFi over site (charged). Excursions organised. English spoken. Off site: Close to bus terminal for city centre 1 km.

Open: All year.

Directions

From M1 (Györ-Budapest) take exit for Törökbálint following signs for town and then site. Also accessible from M7 Budapest-Balaton road. GPS: 47.43203, 18.90110

Charges guide

Per unit incl. 2 persons and electricity	€ 20.00
extra person	€ 6.00

No credit cards.

Uröm

Jumbo Camping

Budakalászi út 23-25, H-2096 Uröm (Pest County) T: 26 351 251. E: jumbo@campingbudapest.com

alanrogers.com/HU5180

Jumbo Camping is a modern, carefully developed, terraced site in the northern outskirts of Budapest. The concrete and gravel access roads lead shortly to 55 terraced pitches of varying sizes, a little on the small size for large units, and some slightly sloping. Hardstanding for cars and caravan wheels, as well as large hardstandings for motorcaravans. There is a steep incline to some pitches and use of the site's 4x4 may be required. All pitches have 6A electricity (may require long leads) and there are nine caravan pitches with water and drainage. They are mostly divided by small hedges and the whole area is fenced.

Facilities

Sanitary facilities are excellent, with large showers (communal changing). Washing machine, iron and cooking facilities on payment. Motorcaravan services. Café (where bread orders taken), milk and butter available. Attractive swimming pool (July/Aug). Playground with covered area for wet weather. Barbecue area. TV in reception. Free WiFi over site. English spoken and information sheet provided in English. Off site: Shop and restaurant 500 m. Bicycle hire and bus to city 500 m.

Open: 1 April - 31 October.

Directions

Site signed on roads to Budapest – 11 from Szentendre and 10 from Komarom. If approaching from Budapest use 11 (site sign appears quickly after sharp right bend; signs and entry are clearer on road 10). Can also approach via Györ on M1/E60 and Lake Balaton on M7/E71. Turn into site is quite acute and uphill. GPS: 47.60178, 19.01967

Charges guide

Per unit incl. 2 persons and electricity	€ 15.20 - € 18.90

No credit cards (cash only).

Visegrad
Blue Danube Camping

Fö ut 70, H-2025 Visegrad (Pest County) T: 26 398 120. E: info@hotelhonti.hu

alanrogers.com/HU5175

Just opposite a road that runs alongside the beautiful Danube river, this small site has only 40 pitches (all for tourers and with 4A electricity) and two static units. It is owned by the Honti Hotel 50 m. down the road and this is where reception is located. It is attractively landscaped with low trees, shrubs and flowers. The good sized pitches are arranged on well kept, grassy lawns, separated by hedges in the middle field. Between the hotel and the site a new pool complex has been built complete with indoor and outdoor pools, a pool for children, massage rooms, a hot tub, salt caves and infrared cabins.

Facilities
Adequate prefabricated type toilet block with British style toilets, open washbasins and controllable showers (free). A new toilet block is planned. Basic kitchen with electric cookers and fridge. Bar/restaurant to the front of the site. Fishing. Canoe hire. Off site: New indoor and outdoor pool complex (a short walk between site and hotel). Restaurants nearby. Boat launching 1 km. Riding 6 km.

Open: 1 May - 30 September.

Directions
Site is on the right of the no. 11 road running to Budapest at km. 43. GPS: 47.783083, 18.8339

Charges guide

Per person	HUF 1100
pitch incl. car	HUF 1700
electricity	HUF 850
dog	HUF 1000

No credit cards.

Balatonszemes
Balatontourist Camping & Bungalows Vadvirág

Lellei u. 1-2., H-8636 Balatonszemes (Somogy County) T: 84 360 114. E: vadvirag@balatontourist.hu

alanrogers.com/HU5000

This large Balatontourist site (16 hectares) on the southern shore of Lake Balaton has a grassy beach almost 600 metres long, which is also used by day visitors. On flat grass, the 308 touring pitches are individual ones with electricity connections (10/16A). Shade is provided by a variety of trees. Windsurfing and excellent swimming are possible in the lake and there are pedaloes for hire. There are many sporting activities available and children's entertainment. A train line runs along the back of the site.

Facilities
Two sanitary blocks with some washbasins in cabins, six private bathrooms for hire and facilities for disabled visitors. Launderette. Motorcaravan services. Shop and bar (15/5-31/8). Takeaway. Small pool (15/5-31/8). New playgrounds. Beach volleyball. Paddle boats. Three tennis courts. Minigolf. Bicycle hire. Boat launching. Fishing. Entertainment for children. WiFi over site (charged). Off site: Restaurants and gift shop nearby. Riding 2 km.

Open: 27 April - 16 September.

Directions
On the M7 coming from the north, take the exit for Balatonöszöd and then continue towards road 7. Turn towards the lake at km. 132, over the railway. GPS: 46.80092, 17.74019

Charges guide

Per unit incl. 2 persons and electricity	HUF 2900 - 4500
extra person	HUF 700 - 1150
child (2-14 yrs)	HUF 500 - 800

Zamardi
Balatontourist Camping Autós

Szent István út, H-8621 Zamárdi (Somogy County) T: 84 348 931. E: autos@balatontourist.hu

alanrogers.com/HU5040

If you have young children or non-swimmers in your party, then the southern shores of the lake where this Balatontourist site is situated are ideal as you can walk out for nearly a kilometre before the water rises to more than a metre in depth. It is a large site with its own direct access to the lake, offering 456 touring pitches with 10A electricity. There are many tall trees and the more attractive pitches are near the lake, including some unshaded ones alongside the water with views of the Tihany peninsula.

Facilities
Three modern, tiled sanitary buildings. Three en-suite private bathrooms can be rented including bath and shower. Warm water to washbasins. Showers with private changing area. Facilities for disabled visitors. Laundry. Restaurant with excellent menu. Snack bar with terrace (from June). Lake swimming. Fishing. Minigolf. Wooden play equipment on sandy grass by the lake. Bicycle hire. Free guided walks in summer. Accommodation for hire. WiFi over part of site. Off site: Restaurant and gift shop nearby. Riding 4 km.

Open: 7 May - 12 September.

Directions
Exit road no. 7/E71 between Balatonföldvár and Siófok towards Tihany, and the site is well signed. GPS: 46.88065, 17.91556

Charges guide

Per unit incl. 2 persons and electricity	HUF 3700 - 5750
extra person	HUF 900 - 1150
child (2-14 yrs)	HUF 650 - 900
dog	HUF 650 - 900

Camping Cheques accepted.

FREE Alan Rogers Travel Card
Extra benefits and savings - see page 14

Tokaj

Tiszavirág Camping

P.f. 27, H-3910 Tokaj (Szabolcs-Szatmar-Bereg Co) T: 47 352 626.

alanrogers.com/HU5220

From mid July to mid August, this site gets quite busy, but either side of these dates it is quiet and very relaxing. Set on the banks of the wide River Tisza, the level grass pitches, 120 in number, are close together and narrow but quite long, off a hard circular access road so siting should be quite easy. All the pitches have electricity (mostly 6A) and there is much shade from a variety of trees. There is a high season reception, but at other times, you site yourself and a gentleman calls during the evening to collect the fee. There may be some daytime noise from watersports on the river but it is quiet by night.

Facilities

The toilet block is basic, but clean, and has British style WCs (external entry) and curtained showers with communal undressing. Kitchen with gas hob. Kiosk and bar with covered terrace. Simple restaurant. Wine shop. Barbecue places and large outdoor grill area for baking bread and barbecues. River sports. No English spoken (German is). Off site: Shops for basics outside the main season are in the town over the bridge, 600 m. walk.

Open: 1 May - 30 September.

Directions

Tokaj is east of Miskolc and north of Debrecen. Site is just south of the river bridge on road no. 38. (Avoid the noisy campsite signed on the other side of the road). GPS: 48.12336, 21.4181

Charges guide

Per unit incl. 2 persons	
and electricity	HUF 2850 - 3050
extra person	HUF 650
child	HUF 325

Sárvár

Thermal Camping Sárvár

Vadkert u. 1, H-9600 Sárvár (Vas) T: 95 320 292. E: info@thermalcamping.com

alanrogers.com/HU5094

Thermal Camping Sárvár opened in 2006 and is the municipal site next to the impressive thermal spa. There are 89 pitches off of tarmac access lanes on hardstandings, all with 16A electricity, water, waste water and TV connections. To the back of the site there are some additional pitches for rental units on well kept grassy fields. The main attraction of this site is of course the renovated spa and if staying here, access to the spa is included in the price (some activities are charged extra). You can also enjoy a ten percent discount on meals in the restaurant. Those looking to enjoy a wellness holiday will certainly be in the right place in Sárvár.

Facilities

Two adequate, heated toilet blocks with washbasins in cabins, controllable hot showers, baby room and facilities for disabled visitors. Washing machines. Campers' kitchen. Motorcaravan services. Shop. Playground. Bicycle hire. Gym. Off site: Wellness centre with indoor and outdoor pools, sauna, jacuzzi, massage and a restaurant. Centre of Sárvár 200 m.

Open: All year.

Directions

Site is in the centre of Sárvár. From the north, follow the 84 road around town and exit towards Sótony. Drive towards Sárvár and to the pool. Site is directly next to the pool. GPS: 47.246717, 16.9473

Charges guide

Per unit incl. 2 persons	
and electricity	€ 30.50 - € 39.00
extra person	€ 12.00
child (6-16 yrs)	€ 7.00
dog	€ 2.00
Camping Cheques accepted.	

Balatonakali

Balatontourist Camping Strand Holiday

Strand út 2, H-8243 Balatonakali (Veszprem County) T: 87 544 021. E: strand@balatontourist.hu

alanrogers.com/HU5078

Balatontourist Camping Strand Holiday, formerly two separate sites, stretches for over two kilometres along the north shore of Lake Balaton. As its name suggests, this is a real beach holiday site, and most campers will find themselves within 100 metres of the water. The pitches are in lanes, five units on each side, facing towards the lake. They are on level, grassy fields, some divided by low hedges, and there are several gravel hardstandings. Drinks and snacks can be purchased on site, and there is a restaurant just outside the gate. English and German are spoken in reception.

Facilities

Four toilet blocks (maintenance variable, could be pressed in high season) with open style washbasins (cold water only) and preset hot showers. Facilities for disabled visitors. Laundry with washing machines. Kitchen and fish preparation area. Shop (1/6-30/8). Bar. Snack bar. Restaurant (1/5-31/8). Takeaway. Entertainment and excursions. Adventure playground. Beach volleyball. Basketball. Sports field. Watersports. Bicycle hire. WiFi (charged). Torch useful. Off site: Riding 1.5 km. Golf 5 km.

Open: 17 April - 30 September.

Directions

Follow the 71 road South from Balatonfüred and in Balatonakali follow the site signs.
GPS: 46.8811, 17.75409

Charges guide

Per unit incl. 2 persons	
and electricity	HUF 3600 - 7300
extra person	HUF 900 - 1250
child (2-14 yrs)	HUF 650 - 950
dog	HUF 650 - 950
Camping Cheques accepted.	

For latest campsite news, availability and prices visit

alanrogers.com

Balatonakali

Balatontourist Camping Levendula Naturist

Hókuli u. 25, H-8243 Balatonakali (Veszprem County) T: 87 544 011. E: levendula@balatontourist.hu

alanrogers.com/HU5385

Levendula is a naturist site on the north side of Lake Balaton. It has 108 level unmarked pitches, varying in size from 60-120 sq.m, and separated by low hedges. Some have views of the lake, some are in the shade of mature trees, and all have electricity (4/10A). The site is attractively landscaped with shrubs and flowers and there is direct access to the lake. As part of the Balatontourist organisation, Levendula has similar amenities to the other sites, including a full entertainment program for children in high season, but without the noise of its larger brothers.

Facilities
Two toilet blocks with modern fittings, including one washbasin in a cabin for men and women. Facilities for disabled campers. Heated baby room. Laundry. Campers' kitchen with cooking rings. Fish cleaning area. Motorcaravan service point. Dog shower. Bar/restaurant with terrace. Shop. Playground with colourful equipment. Watersports. Games room. Volleyball. Entertainment programme. Excursions. Off site: Riding 1.5 km.

Open: 7 May - 12 September.

Directions
Follow no. 71 road towards Keszthely and site is signed in Balatonakali. GPS: 46.882778, 17.755833

Charges guide
Per unit incl. 2 persons

and electricity	HUF 3500 - 7900
extra person	HUF 850 - 1250
child (2-14 yrs)	HUF 650 - 950
dog	HUF 650 - 950

Camping Cheques accepted.

Balatonfüred

Balatontourist Camping & Bungalows Füred

Széchenyi út 24., H-8230 Balatonfüred (Veszprem County) T: 87 580 241. E: fured@balatontourist.hu

alanrogers.com/HU5090

This is a large international holiday village rather than just a campsite. Pleasantly decorated with flowers and shrubs, it offers a very wide range of facilities and sporting activities. All that one could want for a family holiday can be found here. The 890 individual pitches (60-120 sq.m), all with electricity (6/10A), are on either side of hard access roads on which pitch numbers are painted. Many bungalows are for rent. Mature trees cover about two thirds of the site giving shade, with the remaining area being in the open. Directly on the lake with 800 m. of access for boats and bathing, there is a large, grassy area for relaxation, a small beach area for children and a variety of watersports.

Facilities
Five fully equipped toilet blocks around the site include hot water for dishwashing and laundry. Baby rooms. Private cabins for rent. Laundry service. Numerous bars, restaurants, cafés, and a supermarket (15/5-15/9). Stalls and kiosks with wide range of goods and souvenirs. Excellent swimming pool (1/6-31/8). Sandy beach. Large free water chute. Animation for adults and children. Sports activities organised for adults. Sauna. Massage. Fishing. Water-ski lift. Windsurf school. Sailing. Pedalos. Play area. Bicycle hire. Tennis. Minigolf. Video games. WiFi over site (charged). Dogs are not accepted.

Open: 24 April - 27 September.

Directions
Site is just south of Balatonfüred, at the traffic circle on Balatonfüred-Tihany road and well signed. GPS: 46.94565, 17.87709

Charges guide
Per unit incl. 2 persons

and electricity	HUF 3600 - 9900
extra person	HUF 800 - 1600
child (2-14 yrs)	HUF 500 - 1200

Camping Cheques accepted.

Balatonszepezd

Balatontourist Camping Venus

Halász ut. 1., H-8252 Balatonszepezd (Veszprem County) T: 87 568 061. E: venus@balatontourist.hu

alanrogers.com/HU5380

For those who want to be directly beside Lake Balaton and would like a reasonably quiet location, Camping Venus would be a good choice. Apart from the rather noisy train that regularly passes the site, this is a quiet setting with views of the lake from almost all the pitches. From the front row of pitches you could almost dangle your feet from your caravan in the warm water of the lake. There are 120 flat pitches all with at least 4/10A electricity. Varying in size (70-100 sq.m), almost all have shade.

Facilities
Two acceptable sanitary blocks provide toilets, washbasins (open style and in cabins) with hot and cold water and preset showers. Facilities for disabled campers. Toilets and washbasins for children. Launderette. Motorcaravan services. Shop for basics. Bar. Restaurant. Snack bar. Playground. Daily activity programme with pottery, fairy tale reading, horse shows, tournaments in Sümeg, trips over the lake and to Budapest. Pedalo and rowing boats for hire. WiFi over site (charged).

Open: 14 May - 5 September.

Directions
On the 71 road between Balatonfüred and Keszthely, site is in Balatonszepezd on the lake side of the road. GPS: 46.861051, 17.673368

Charges guide
Per unit incl. 2 persons

and electricity	HUF 2900 - 6100
extra person	HUF 750 - 1000
child (2-14 yrs)	HUF 600 - 800
dog	HUF 600 - 800

FREE Alan Rogers Travel Card

Extra benefits and savings - see page 14

Révfülöp

Balatontourist Camping Napfény

Halász ut. 5, H-8253 Révfülöp (Veszprem County) T: 87 563 031. E: napfeny@balatontourist.hu

alanrogers.com/HU5370

Camping Napfény, an exceptionally good site, is designed for families with children of all ages looking for an active holiday, and has a 200 m. frontage on Lake Balaton. The site's 370 pitches vary in size (60-110 sq.m) and almost all have shade – very welcome during the hot Hungarian summers – and 6-10A electricity. As with most of the sites on Lake Balaton, a train line runs just outside the site boundary. There are steps to get into the lake and the canoes, boats and pedaloes for hire. An entertainment programme is offered for all ages and there are several bars and restaurants.

Facilities

The three excellent, well equipped sanitary blocks have child-size toilets and washbasins. Two bathrooms (hourly charge). Heated baby room. Facilities for disabled campers. Launderette. Dog shower. Motorcaravan services. Supermarket, souvenir shop and several bars (all 1/6-31/8). Restaurants. Children's pool (1/6-31/8). Massage. Hairdresser. Sports field. Minigolf. Fishing. Bicycle hire. Canoe, rowing boat and pedalo hire. Extensive entertainment programme for all ages. WiFi throughout (one free zone, elsewhere charged).

Open: 25 April - 28 September.

Directions

Follow road 71 from Veszprém southeast to Keszthely. Site is in Révfülöp.
GPS: 46.829469, 17.640164

Charges guide

Per unit incl. 2 persons and electricity	HUF 3750 - 7300
extra person	HUF 900 - 1250
child (2-14 yrs)	HUF 550 - 1000
dog	HUF 550 - 1000

Camping Cheques accepted.

Cserszegtomaj

Panoráma Camping

Panoráma Köz 1, H-8372 Cserszegtomaj (Zala County) T: 83 330 215. E: matuska78@freemail.hu

alanrogers.com/HU5030

Campsites around Lake Balaton generally have the disadvantage of being close to the main road and/or the railway, as well as being extremely busy in high season. Panoráma is popular too, but is essentially a quiet site inland from the western end of the lake. It also has the benefit of extensive views from the flat, grass terraces. Only the young or very fit are advised to take the higher levels with the best views of all. The original 50 pitches vary in size from fairly small to quite large (100 sq.m), all with electricity (10A), with the lower terraces having fairly easy access. The lower part of the site is a suntrap, but the top part is shaded by mature trees. This site is for those who prefer a quiet holiday, yet still being close to the major attractions.

Facilities

Two satisfactory heated sanitary blocks (hot water variable) contain curtained, controllable showers (communal changing). Washing machine. Ladies' hairdresser. Massage. Small swimming pool. Free WiFi over site. Off site: Many walking and cycling opportunities. Riding, bicycle hire and tennis 3 km. Fishing and boat launching 6 km. Lake Balaton 7 km. Héviz is the famous, large, thermal lake and there are castles to visit.

Open: 1 April - 31 October.

Directions

Site is 2 km. north of Héviz. From the 71 road initially follow the signs for Héviz, then take road to Sümeg. Entering Cserszegtomaj, site is off to the left via a long, hard access road with a large sign.
GPS: 46.80803, 17.21248

Charges guide

Per unit incl. 2 persons	€ 14.00 - € 20.00
tent (2 persons)	€ 14.00

No credit cards.

Keszthely

Castrum Camping Keszthely

Mora Ferenc út 48, H-8360 Keszthely (Zala County) T: 83 312 120. E: info@castrum.eu

alanrogers.com/HU5035

Castrum Keszthely is a three-hectare site on the southwest corner of Lake Balaton. Although it is next to the main road and a railway, and there is a disco nearby, we found it surprisingly quiet at night. It is a real family site with 176 pitches, all for tourers and with electricity (6/12A). The level pitches of up to 90 sq.m. are numbered on a grass and gravel surface (firm tent pegs necessary) and are separated by hedges with shade from a variety of mature trees. It is on the wrong side of the railway that runs along the north side of Lake Balaton and therefore has no direct access to the lake or the beach. However, this is compensated for by a large, well kept outdoor pool in the centre of the site.

Facilities

Traditional toilet blocks with British style toilets, open washbasins and preset, hot showers (free, hot water variable). Laundry. Small shop for basics. Bar/restaurant. Swimming pool (25x10 m) with oval paddling pool (daily charge). Indoor playroom with arcade games. Tennis. Minigolf. Daily activity programme for children in high season. Bus service to Thermal Spa. Bicycle hire. WiFi.

Open: 15 April - 15 October.

Directions

Follow no. 71 road along Lake Balaton to Keszthely and then follow signs 'Castrum 2,900 metres'. Continue straight on for exactly 2,900 metres and turn right towards site. GPS: 46.768117, 17.25955

Charges guide

Per unit incl. 2 persons and electricity	HUF 4300 - 6500

Camping Cheques accepted.

For latest campsite news, availability and prices visit

alanrogers.com

Lenti

Castrum Thermal Camping Lenti

Tancsics M.U. 18-20, H-8960 Lenti (Zala County) T: 92 351 368. E: info@lentikemping.hu

alanrogers.com/HU5024

Camping Lenti is one of a series of thermal spa campsites in the Hungarian-Slovenian-Austrian border region. It is a well established, well kept site with friendly management, ideal for those seeking peace and quiet in combination with the healing thermal waters of the Lenti spa (free access for campers). There are 146 numbered and fenced pitches (40-80 sq.m) with 6A electricity connections and 40 with hardstanding. Pitching is in rows, off gravel access roads mostly in the shade of mature trees. The site provides a good base for visiting the neighbouring thermal baths or just staying the night en-route to further destinations.

Facilities

The modern, heated toilet block is clean and well equipped with some washbasins in cubicles and hot showers. Washing machine and spin dryer. Restaurant (breakfast and dinner to order) and rooms housed in a modern main building. Free WiFi over site. Free entry to spa. Off site: Thermal baths. Bars, takeaways and restaurants available inside the thermal bath complex. Shop 500 m.

Open: All year.

Directions

From roundabout in centre of Lenti, go west towards Rédics for a little under 1 km. Site is on the left (big blue sign) just before the railway station.
GPS: 46.61764, 16.53155

Charges guide

Per unit incl. 2 persons and electricity	HUF 4190 - 5990
extra person	HUF 1000 - 1300
child (4-12 yrs)	HUF 700 - 900
dog	HUF 700 - 900

Zalakaros

Balatontourist Camping Termál

Gyógyfürdö Ter 6, H-8749 Zalakaros (Zala County) T: 93 340 105. E: termal@balatontourist.hu

alanrogers.com/HU5025

Balatontourist Camping Termál in Zalakaros has 280 attractively laid out, level pitches, all with 10A electricity and varying in size from 50-100 sq.m. (the larger pitches need to be reserved). There are 280 for touring units on grass and gravel (firm tent pegs may be needed), with around ten hardstandings for larger units and motorcaravans. Mature trees provide useful shade and access roads are gravel. This site attracts many elderly people who spend their days at the thermal spa 200 m. down the road – the waters are reputed to be beneficial for rheumatism and other joint problems.

Facilities

Comfortable toilet facilities have been updated and have British style toilets, some washbasins in cubicles and controllable, hot showers (free). Facilities for disabled visitors. Full service laundry including ironing. Campers' kitchen. Motorcaravan services and car wash. Shop and restaurant (1/4-30/9). Small playground. WiFi over site (charged). Massage, acupuncture and pedicure. Sauna. Hairdresser. Bicycle hire. Off site: Golf 500 m. Riding 2 km. Fishing and beach 3 km.

Open: 1 April - 31 October.

Directions

On the M7/E71 travelling southwest, take exit 191 for Zalakomár and then Zalakaros. Follow good site signs in Zalakaros. GPS: 46.552267, 17.125933

Charges guide

Per unit incl. 2 persons and electricity	HUF 4330 - 5430
extra person	HUF 1300
child (2-14 yrs)	HUF 600

Italy

Italy, once the capital of the Roman Empire, was unified as recently as 1861, thus regional customs and traditions have not been lost. Its enviable collections of art, literature and culture have had worldwide influence and continue to be a magnet for visitors who flock to cities such as Venice, Florence and Rome.

In the north, the vibrant city of Milan is the fashion capital of the world, and home to the famous opera house, La Scala, as well as Da Vinci's 'The Last Supper'. It is also a good starting-off point for the Alps; the Italian Lake District, incorporating Lake Garda, Lake Como and Lake Maggiore; the canals of Venice and the lovely town of Verona. The hilly towns of central Italy are especially popular, with Siena, San Gimignano and Assisi among the most visited. The historic capital of Rome with its Colosseum and Vatican City is not to be missed. Naples is an ideal base for visiting Pompeii and the breathtaking scenery of the Amalfi coast, but the city also has a charm of its own – winding narrow streets and crumbling façades inset with shrines sit alongside boutiques, bars and lively street markets, amid chaotic traffic and roaring scooters.

CAPITAL: Rome

Tourist Office

Italian State Tourist Office (ENIT)

1 Princes Street, London W1B 2AY

Tel: 020 7408 1254

Fax: 020 7399 3567

Email: italy@italiantouristboard.co.uk

Internet: www.enit.it

Population

60.5 million

Climate

The south enjoys extremely hot summers and mild, dry winters, whilst the mountainous regions of the north are cooler with heavy snowfalls in winter.

Language

Italian. There are several dialect forms and some German is spoken near the Austrian border.

Telephone

The country code is 00 39.

Money

Currency: The Euro.

Banks: Mon-Fri 08.30-13.00 and 15.00-16.00.

Shops

Mon-Sat 08.30/09.00-13.00 and 15.30/16.00-19.30/20.00, with some variations in larger cities.

Public Holidays

New Year; Easter Mon; Liberation Day 25 Apr; Labour Day; Republic Day 2 June; Assumption 15 Aug; All Saints 1 Nov; Unity Day 4 Nov; Immaculate Conception 8 Dec; Christmas 25, 26 Dec; plus some special local feast days.

Motoring

Tolls are payable on the autostrada network. If travelling distances, save time by purchasing a 'Viacard' from pay booths or service areas. An overhanging load, e.g. a bicycle rack, must be indicated by a large red/white hatched warning square. Failure to do so will result in a fine.

see campsite map 7

Roseto degli Abruzzi

Camping Village Eurcamping

Lungomare Trieste Sud, I-64026 Roseto degli Abruzzi (Abruzzo) T: 085 899 3179.

E: eurcamping@camping.it alanrogers.com/IT68040

Eurcamping is about 2 km. south of the small town of Roseto degli Abruzzi, at the end of the coastal road which runs parallel to the SS16. This is a relatively quiet site, situated beside the sea, but with no direct access to it. There are 265 well defined pitches, many under green screens, and all with 3/6A electricity. Accessing the site is not difficult, but you have to pass under the coastal railway line so must use the bridge with 4 m. headroom. There is some road noise but little from the railway.

Facilities

Three sanitary blocks with free hot showers. Facilities for disabled visitors. Motorcaravan services. Laundry. Bar. Restaurant. Takeaway. Pizzeria. Shop. Swimming pools (hats must be worn) with solarium terrace. Play area and sports ground. Tennis. Bowling. WiFi (charged). Bicycle hire. Entertainment in high season. Clubs for children and teenagers. Pets restricted to assigned pitches. Bungalows to rent. Off site: Beach. Canoe and pedalo hire.

Open: 1 May - 18 October.

Directions

From north or south on A14 motorway, take exit Roseto degli Abruzzi exit. Turn onto SS150 to Roseto degli Abruzzi. Pass under 4 m. bridge below railway at south end of town, and right onto coast road. From Rome and L'Aquila on A24 motorway take Villa Vomano-Teramo exit onto SS150 (Roseto degli Abruzzi). GPS: 42.6577, 14.0353

Charges guide

Per unit incl. 2 persons and electricity	€ 19.00 - € 47.00
extra person	€ 5.00 - € 13.00

Camping Cheques accepted.

Silvi

Camping Europe Garden

Ctra Vallescura n. 10, I-64028 Silvi (Abruzzo) T: 085 930 137. E: info@europegarden.it

alanrogers.com/IT68000

This site is 13 kilometres northwest of Pescara and lies just back from the coast about 2 km. up a very steep hill from where it has pleasant views over the sea. The site predominantly consists of bungalows and chalets for hire, with around 40 spaces at the top of the site available for smaller touring units and tents. These are mainly on level terraces, but access to some may be difficult. All have 6A electricity. If installation of caravans is a problem a tractor is available to help. Cars remain with units on some of the pitches or in nearby parking spaces for the remainder. Most pitches are shaded.

Facilities

The toilet block provides a mixture of British and Turkish style WCs. Hot showers. Washing machines. Shop, bar, restaurant, takeaway (all season). Swimming pool (May-Sept. 300 sq.m; caps compulsory), small paddling pool and jacuzzi. Tennis. Playground. Entertainment programme. Free weekly excursions (15/6-8/9). Free shuttle bus service (18/5-7/9) to site's own private beach. WiFi. Dogs are not accepted. No barbecues on pitches.

Open: 18 May - 14 September.

Directions

Turn inland off SS16 coast road at km. 433 for Silvi Alta and follow site signs. From autostrada A14 take Pineto exit from north or Pescara Nord exit from the south. GPS: 42.56738, 14.09247

Charges guide

Per unit incl. 2 persons and electricity	€ 24.50 - € 49.50
extra person	€ 5.00 - € 13.00
child (3-8 yrs)	€ 4.00 - € 10.00

Baia Domizia

Baia Domizia Villaggio Camping

Via Pietre Bianche, I-81030 Baia Domizia (Campania) T: 082 393 0164. E: info@baiadomizia.it

alanrogers.com/IT68200

This large, beautifully maintained seaside site is about 70 kilometres northwest of Naples, and is within a pine forest, cleverly left in its natural state. Although it does not feel like it, there are 750 touring pitches in clearings, either of grass and sand or on hardstanding, all with electricity, 80 now also with water and waste water. Finding a pitch may take time as there are so many good ones to choose from, but staff will help in season. Most pitches are well shaded, however there are some in the sun for cooler periods. The central complex is superb with well designed buildings providing for all needs (the site is some distance from the town). A member of Leading Campings group.

Facilities

Seven new toilet blocks have hot water in washbasins (many cabins) and showers. Good access and facilities for disabled campers. Washing machines, spin dryers. Motorcaravan services. Gas supplies. Supermarket and general shop. Large bar. Restaurants, pizzeria and takeaway. Ice cream parlour. Swimming pool complex. Playground. Tennis. Windsurfing hire and school. Disco. Cinema. Gym. Excursions. Torches required in some areas. WiFi (charged). Dogs are not accepted.

Open: 18 April - 15 September.

Directions

The turn to Baia Domizia leads off the Formia-Naples road 23 km. from Formia. From Rome-Naples autostrada, take Cassino exit to Formia. Site is to the north of Baia Domizia and well signed. Site is off the coastal road that runs parallel to the SS7. GPS: 41.207222, 13.791389

Charges guide

Per unit incl. 2 persons and electricity	€ 25.00 - € 48.50
extra person	€ 6.50 - € 12.00

For latest campsite news, availability and prices visit

alanrogers.com

Massa Lubrense

Camping Nettuno

Via A Vespucci 39, Marina del Cantone, I-80061 Massa Lubrense (Campania) T: 081 808 1051.

E: info@villaggionettuno.it **alanrogers.com/IT68380**

Camping Nettuno is owned and run by the friendly Mauro family, who speak excellent English. Nestled in the bay of Marina del Cantone, it is situated in the protected area of Punta Campanella, away from the busiest tourist spots. As a result the approach roads are difficult and narrow. This tiny campsite of only 42 pitches (with 4A electricity available) is spread over three levels above the pebbly beach. Up several steps and across the road are the amenities, reception, shop, and dive centre and then above this is a restaurant with magnificent views over the bay. Pitches are informally arranged, some with a fabulous sea view (extra charge) and most with shade. Because the site is tucked into the hillside pitches are small and close together but there is plenty of cheerful assistance to find the best place.

Facilities
The single central sanitary block includes facilities for disabled campers (and access via a ramp to the beach). Washing machine. Basic motorcaravan service point. Gas supplies. Small shop. Delightful restaurant with sea views. Bar (lively at night). Dive centre. Excursions. TV in bar area. Small play area. Free tennis arranged at court next door. Fishing. Bicycle hire. Off site: Small beach (pebbles) 5 m. from bottom of site. Excellent restaurant 100 m. Amalfi Coast, Capri, nature parks, walking etc.

Open: 20 March - 2 November.

Directions
From A3 (Naples-Salerno), take Castellamare di Stabia exit onto S145. Pass Castellamare, follow signs to Meta di Sorrento via tunnel and turn off towards Positano in Meta. After 5 km. turn to Sant'Agata dei due Golfi (6.5 km) then to Nerano and Marina del Cantone. Site is well signed. GPS: 40.58389, 14.35194

Charges guide
Per unit incl. 2 persons and electricity	€ 23.00 - € 41.50
extra person	€ 5.50 - € 11.00

Lido degli Scacchi

Kawan Village Florenz

Viale Alpi Centrali 199, I-44020 Lido degli Scacchi (Emília-Romagna) T: 053 338 0193.

E: info@holidayvillageflorenz.com **alanrogers.com/IT60750**

Popular with families for over 40 years, Camping Florenz has many loyal campers who return year after year. This site is among the sand dunes and pine forest along the seafront where there are good sized, shaded and level pitches with views of the water. The gently shelving beach has fine sand and lots of chairs and umbrellas. Away from the beach area there is plenty of shade from the tall pines. The 280 touring pitches are mostly a mixture of sand and grass, of a good size and level, all with electricity (6A) and there are 200 units for hire. A large restaurant with a terrace overlooks the lively entertainment area, where lots of families were enjoying themselves when we visited.

Facilities
One excellent, new toilet block. Five mixed, mostly old sanitary blocks with half British, half Turkish style toilets and preset showers, scheduled for upgrade. Some unisex showers at beach. Good facilities for disabled campers. Motorcaravan services. Supermarket. Restaurant and bar with TV. Large outdoor pool (€ 3). Activities and children's club. Good play area. Games room. Excellent beach for swimming. New beach bar and restaurant. Bicycle hire.

Open: 28 March - 1 November.

Directions
Site is at Lido degli Scacchi just off S309 between Chioggia and Ravenna. Both Lido degli Scacchi and site are well signed from the S309 (being either Kawan or Florenz). GPS: 44.70111, 12.23806

Charges guide
Per person	€ 5.80 - € 12.00
child (3-10 yrs)	free - € 7.00
pitch	€ 12.00 - € 25.00

Camping Cheques accepted.

Lido delle Nazioni

Tahiti Camping & Terme Bungalow Park

Viale Libia 133, I-44020 Lido delle Nazioni - Comacchio (Emília-Romagna) T: 053 337 9500.

E: info@campingtahiti.com **alanrogers.com/IT60650**

Tahiti is an excellent, extremely well run, family owned site, thoughtfully laid out 800 m. from the sea (a continuous, fun road-train link is provided). An abundance of flowers and shrubs enhance its appearance. The 450 touring pitches are of varying sizes, back to back from hard roads, defined by trees with shade in most areas and all with 10A electricity. There are six types, from a basic pitch to those with kitchens plus a shower. Several languages, including English, are spoken by the friendly staff. The Thermal Oasis is luxurious and there is a 50% discount for campers.

Facilities
All toilet blocks are of a very high standard. British and Turkish style WCs. Baby room. Large supermarket, two restaurants, bar, pizzeria, takeaway, heated swimming pools. Thermal Oasis (charged). Playgrounds and miniclub. Gym. Tennis. Minigolf. Riding. Bicycle hire. Entertainment and excursions (high season). 'Disco-pub'. ATM. WiFi on part of site (charged). Free transport to beach. Archery.

Open: 30 April - 20 September.

Directions
Turn off SS309 35 km. north of Ravenna to Lido delle Nazioni (north of Lido di Pomposa) and follow site signs. GPS: 44.73457, 12.22178

Charges guide
Per unit incl. 2 persons and electricity	€ 22.70 - € 46.80
extra person	€ 5.90 - € 11.90
child (under 8 yrs)	free

FREE Alan Rogers Travel Card
Extra benefits and savings - see page 14

Savignano Mare

Camping Villaggio Rubicone

Via Matrice Destra 1, I-47039 Savignano Mare (Emília-Romagna) T: 054 134 6377.

E: info@campingrubicone.com **alanrogers.com/IT66240**

This is a sophisticated, professionally run site where the friendly owners, Sandra and Paolo Grotto are keen to fulfil your every need. Rubicone covers over 30 acres of thoughtfully landscaped, level ground by the sea. There is an amazing array of amenities on offer. The 457 touring pitches vary in size (up to 100 sq.m) and are arranged in back-to-back, double rows, most with some shade. In some areas the central pitches are a little tight for manoeuvring larger units. All the pitches are kept very neat with hedges and all have electricity, 160 with water and drainage and 20 with private sanitary facilities. Most pitches have some shade.

Facilities

Modern heated toilet blocks have hot water for showers and washbasins (half in private cabins), mainly British style toilets, baby rooms and two excellent units for disabled visitors. Washing machines. Motorcaravan services. An excellent shop and bars (all season) plus a restaurant and snack bar (26/5-9/9). Pizzeria. Swimming pools (caps mandatory; open as site). Games room with Internet. Golf (lessons available). Tennis. Solarium. Jacuzzi. Beach with lifeguard. Fishing. Sailing and windsurfing schools. Dogs are not accepted. Bicycle hire. WiFi (charged).

Open: 23 May - 16 September.

Directions

From Bologna (autostrada A14) take exit for Rimini Nord. Continue on SS16 Adriatica towards Ravenna, then exit for Savignano Mare. At roundabout go straight on to San Mauro Mare and turn left immediately after the railway. At end of street turn right to site. GPS: 44.16475, 12.441117

Charges guide

Per unit incl. 2 persons	
and electricity	€ 24.20 - € 46.80
extra person	€ 5.60 - € 11.50

No credit cards.

Tabiano di Salsomaggiore Terme

Camping Arizona

Via Tabiano 42/A, I-43039 Tabiano di Salsomaggiore Terme (Emília-Romagna) T: 052 456 5648.

E: info@camping-arizona.it **alanrogers.com/IT60900**

Camping Arizona is a green site with a zero carbon rating, set on steep slopes, and 500 m. from the pretty town of Tabiano with its thermal springs dating back to the Roman era. The focus on water is continued within this pleasant, family run site by a complex of four large pools, long water slides into a plunge pool, a jacuzzi and play area, all set in open landscaped grounds with superb views (open to the public). Camping Arizona is an expanding green site set on steep slopes and is 500 m. from the pretty town of Tabiano. The 300 level pitches with electricity (3A solar-generated on site) vary from 50-90 sq.m.

Facilities

Two modern toilet blocks provide good facilities including some for disabled visitors. Solar-heated water. Washing machines and dryers. Small, well stocked shop, bar/restaurant with patio (all 1/4-6/10). Swimming pools, slides and jacuzzi (16/5-15/9, also open to the public but free for campers). Tennis. Boules. Large play centre. WiFi throughout (charged). Off site: Woodfired pizza restaurant outside gate. Mountain bike routes. Riding 2 km. Fishing 4 km. Golf 6 km. Fidenza shopping village 8 km.

Open: 1 April - 15 October.

Directions

From autostrada A1 take exit for Fidenza and follow signs for Tabiano. The site is well marked on the left 500 m. after Tabiano town centre. GPS: 44.80621, 10.0098

Charges guide

Per unit incl. 2 persons	
and electricity	€ 20.00 - € 34.00
extra person	€ 6.00 - € 9.50
child (2-8 yrs)	€ 4.00 - € 6.50

No credit cards.

Grado

Villaggio Turistico Europa

Via Monfalcone 12, I-34073 Grado (Friuli - Venézia Giúlia) T: 043 180 877. E: info@villaggioeuropa.com

alanrogers.com/IT60050

This large, flat, high quality site is beside the sea and has 500 pitches, with 400 for touring units. They are all neat, clean and marked, most with shade and 6/10A electricity, 300 are fully serviced. The terrain is undulating and sandy in the areas nearer the sea, where cars have to be left in parking places. A huge, impressive aquatic park covers 1,500 sq.m. with two long slides, a whirlpool and many other features, including a pool bar. This is a very pleasant site with a spacious feel which families will enjoy.

Facilities

Five excellent, refurbished toilet blocks are well designed and kept very clean. Free hot water, mostly British style WCs with excellent facilities for disabled visitors. Baby showers and baths. Washing machines. Dishwashers. Freezer. Motorcaravan services. Large supermarket, small general shop. 3 bars and 2 restaurants with takeaway. Gelateria. Swimming pools (14/5-20/9). Tennis. Fishing. Bicycle hire. Playground. Full entertainment programme in season. Miniclub. Football. Basketball. Minigolf. Archery. Watersports. Dancing lessons. WiFi (charged).

Open: 23 April - 20 September.

Directions

Site is 4 km. east of Grado on road to Monfalcone. Venice-Trieste motorway exit at Reipuglia-Monfalcone, first roundabout take second exit towards airport and follow Grado signs for 13 km. Site is on the left opposite a golf course. GPS: 45.69649, 13.45595

Charges guide

Per unit incl. 2 persons	
and electricity	€ 19.90 - € 46.10
extra person	€ 5.70 - € 10.70
child (3-16 yrs)	€ 3.60 - € 9.70

For latest campsite news, availability and prices visit

alanrogers.com

Aquileia

Camping Aquileia

Via Gemina10, I-33051 Aquileia (Friuli - Venézia Giúlia) T: 043 191 042. E: info@campingaquileia.it

alanrogers.com/IT60020

Situated in former parkland, under mature trees providing plenty of welcome shade in summer, Camping Aquileia, with 115 level, grass touring pitches, is a quiet site 10 km. away from the bustling coastal beaches. The pitches, all with 4/6A electricity, are separated from the entrance, swimming pool and play areas by tall hedges, and the more peaceful part of the site with the newer sanitary block is at the rear of the site. The now small town of Aquileia, founded in 181 BC, became one of the most important Roman military and trading posts and is now a UNESCO World Heritage Site. In the basilica, only a short walk from the campsite, along the former harbour, lays one of the world's most magnificent mosaic floors. The campsite is popular with families and for those who seek a quiet base from which to visit the beaches or tour this interesting region. From reception, tours can be organised with the town's tourist office to the region's archaeological sites, and not surprisingly a weekly mosaic course is also on offer.

Facilities

Two sanitary blocks with free hot water, controllable showers and washbasins in cabins. Facilities for disabled visitors. Folding baby changing bench. Laundry facilities. Motorcaravan services. Restaurant, bar and automat for drinks and ice-cream. Large playing field with playground. Swimming and paddling pools. Bicycle hire. Mobile homes and chalets for rent. WiFi (charged). Off site: Supermarket opposite entrance. Riding 12 km. The historic towns of Trieste, Gorizia and the beach resort of Grado.

Open: Easter - 30 September.

Directions

Site is 30 km. west northwest of Trieste. From the A4 (Venice-Trieste) take exit for Palmanova and travel south for 20 km. towards Grado. Just after entering Aquileia turn left at traffic lights, signed Trieste and Goriza and site is 400 m. on the right. GPS: 45.77585, 13.37084

Charges guide

Per unit incl. 2 persons	
and electricity	€ 24.00 - € 41.00
extra person	€ 7.00 - € 8.50
child (3-11 yrs)	€ 4.00 - € 6.00
dog	€ 2.00 - € 3.00

Grado

Camping Tenuta Primero

Via Monfalcone 14, I-34073 Grado (Friuli - Venézia Giúlia) T: 043 189 6900. E: info@tenuta-primero.com

alanrogers.com/IT60065

Tenuta Primero is a large, attractive, well run, family owned site with direct access to its own private beach, marina and golf course. It offers a wealth of facilities and activities and caters for all members of the family. The 740 pitches are all level, with 6A electricity, some separating hedges and ample tree shade. The site has several restaurants and bars, and the large, elevated, flower decked Terrazza Mare overlooking the sea is great for eating and drinking whilst enjoying views over the romantic Adriatic.

Facilities

Nine traditional sanitary blocks, seven with facilities for disabled visitors. Washing machines and dryers. Motorcaravan services. Swimming pools and paddling pool. Shop, bars and restaurants, pizzeria, takeaway (all May-Sept). Beauty salon. Aerobics. Water gymnastics. Football pitch. Tennis. Boules. Skateboarding. Play areas. Windsurfing. Marina, sailing, boat launching and boat hire. Bicycle hire. Children's and family entertainment. Live music, disco, dancing. Private beach with sunshades, deck chairs and jetty. Internet corner. WiFi (free). Dogs are not accepted. Courses available for many activities.

Open: 14 April - 28 September.

Directions

Leave the A4 autostrada at the Palmanova exit and head towards Grado. In Grado, after crossing the causeway turn left towards Monfalcone on the SP19. Site is on the right after 5 km. opposite a large golf course. GPS: 45.7051, 13.4640

Charges guide

Per unit incl. 2 persons	
and electricity	€ 27.00 - € 51.00
extra person	€ 9.00 - € 13.00
child (4-15 yrs acc. to age)	free - € 11.00

FREE Alan Rogers Travel Card
Extra benefits and savings - see page 14

Lignano Sabbiadoro

Camping Sabbiadoro

Via Sabbiadoro 8, I-33054 Lignano Sabbiadoro (Friuli - Venézia Giúlia) T: 043 171 455.

E: campsab@lignano.it alanrogers.com/IT60080

Sabbiadoro is a large, top quality site that caters very well for children. It is divided into two parts with separate entrances and efficient receptions. It has 1229 pitches, 974 of which are for touring pitches and is ideal for families who like all their amenities to be close by. The level, grassy pitches vary in size, are shaded by attractive trees and have electricity (6-10A) and TV connections. The facilities are all in excellent condition and well thought out, especially the pool complex, and everything here is very modern, safe and clean. The site's private beach (with 24-hour guard) is only 250 m. away and has its own showers, toilets and baby rooms. Open in high season, the smaller and quieter part of the site with an entrance from Viale Central, is only a few metres away from the main site entrance in Via Sabbiadoro. This has four new sanitary blocks, 232 fixed pitches for touring units, an area for tents and a selection of mobile homes to rent. Shopping and nightlife can be found in the town of Sabbiadoro itself, more so in Lignano Pineta about 1.5 km. away.

Facilities

Well equipped sanitary facilities with free showers includes superb facilities for disabled visitors. Washing machines and dryers. Motorcaravan services. Huge supermarket (all season). Bazaar. Good restaurant, snack bar and takeaway. Heated outdoor pool complex with separate fun pool area, slides and fountains (all season). Heated indoor children's pool. Swimming courses. Play areas. Tennis. Fitness centre. Boat launching. Windsurfing school. Activity centre for children with well organised entertainment (high season) and language school. WiFi throughout (charged). Bicycle hire. Excursions to Venice. Off site: Shops, restaurants and bars. Riding, sailing, golf.

Open: 28 March - 4 October.

Directions

Leave A4 at Latisana exit, west of Trieste. From Latisana follow road to Lignano, then Sabbiadoro. Site is well signed as you approach the town. GPS: 45.68198, 13.12577

Charges guide

Per unit incl. 2 persons

and electricity	€ 23.80 - € 44.50
extra person	€ 6.30 - € 12.00
child (3-12 yrs)	€ 3.90 - € 6.60
dog	€ 2.70 - € 3.00

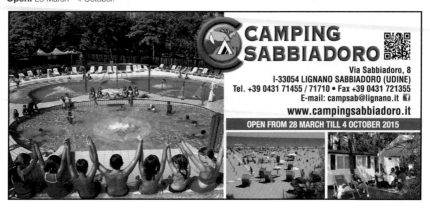

Bardolino

Camping Serenella

Localitá Mezzariva 19, I-37011 Bardolino (Lake Garda) T: 045 721 1333. E: serenella@camping-serenella.it

alanrogers.com/IT63590

Situated alongside Lake Garda, Serenella has 297 average size pitches, some with good lake views. Movement around the site may prove difficult for large units (look for the wider roads). The pitches are shaded and have 6A electricity. A long promenade with brilliant views of the mountains and lake runs the length of the campsite. It is dotted with grassy relaxation areas and beach bars where snacks are served and the atmosphere is charming. The pleasant pool complex is near a traditional style restaurant where delicious, sensibly priced food is served. There is some road noise at some of the amenities and the pool.

Facilities

Five clean, well equipped sanitary blocks include three that are more modern with laundry facilities. British style toilets, free hot water throughout. Facilities for families and disabled visitors. Washing machines and dryer. Freezer. Bar/restaurant, takeaway and shop. Watersports. Outdoor swimming pool (1/5-18/9). Entertainment and sporting programme for all in high season. Play area. Bicycle hire. WiFi on part of site (charged). Dogs are not accepted.

Open: 21 March - 25 October.

Directions

From E70/A4 Milan-Venice autostrada take Pescheria exit and follow signs to Bardolino. Site is on lakeside between Bardolino and Garda, 1 km. south of Garda. GPS: 45.55920, 10.71655

Charges guide

Per unit incl. 2 persons

and electricity	€ 18.50 - € 41.00
per person	€ 4.50 - € 10.50
child (0-5 yrs)	free - € 5.00

For latest campsite news, availability and prices visit

alanrogers.com

Bardolino

La Rocca Camp

Localitá San Pietro, I-37011 Bardolino (Lake Garda) T: 045 721 1111. E: info@campinglarocca.com

alanrogers.com/IT63600

This site was one of the first to operate on the lake and the family has a background of wine and olive oil production. La Rocca is in two areas, each side of the busy A249, the upper part being used mostly for bungalows and these have great lake views. The remaining touring pitches are on the lower part of the site, along with the main facilities. There is access between the two parts via a tunnel. The 400 pitches are mostly on terraces with shade, 10-16A electricity and access from narrow tarmac roads. Sixteen pitches are available with full services.

Facilities
Four toilet blocks, two on each side of the site. Mixed British and Turkish style WCs and controllable showers. Facilities for disabled visitors. Children's facilities. Washing machines. Motorcaravan services. Shop and bakery. Restaurant, bar and takeaway with large terrace. Swimming and paddling pools (lifeguard). Whirlpool. Pool bar. Play area. Entertainment in season. Miniclub. Internet. Bicycle hire. Games room. Watersports. WiFi over site (charged). Torches useful. Gas barbecues only, communal area provided. Off site: Public transport at gate.

Open: 1 April - 15 October.

Directions
Site is on east side of Lake Garda, on lake ring road 249. From A4 take Pescheria exit and 249 north for Garda (many signs for Gardaland). Site is well signed approaching Bardolino. GPS: 45.5645, 10.7129

Charges guide
Per unit incl. 2 persons	
and electricity	€ 20.80 - € 45.70
extra person	€ 4.90 - € 10.90
child (2-10 yrs)	free - € 9.70

No credit cards.

Cisano di Bardolino

Campings Cisano & San Vito

Via Peschiera 48, I-37011 Cisano di Bardolino (Lake Garda) T: 045 622 9098. E: cisano@camping-cisano.it

alanrogers.com/IT63570

This is a combination of two sites, each with its own reception. Some of the 700 touring pitches have superb locations along the 1 km. of shaded lakeside in Cisano. Some are on sloping ground and most are shaded, but the San Vito pitches have no lake views. Both sites are family orientated and considerable effort has been taken in the landscaping to provide maximum comfort, even for the largest units. San Vito is the smaller and more peaceful location, and shares many of the facilities of Cisano. A security fence separates the pitches from the beach, so access involves a short walk. Visitors with disabilities should select their pitch carefully to ensure an area appropriate to all their needs (there are some slopes in Cisano). On the San Vito site there is a pleasant family style restaurant (some road noise) which also sells takeaway food. San Vito is accessed through a tunnel under the road. Excellent pools and play equipment, along with a children's club and entertainment in high season are all here. The friendly, efficient staff at both sites speak English.

Facilities
Plentiful, good quality sanitary facilities are provided in both sites (nine blocks at Cisano and two at San Vito). Facilities for disabled visitors. Baby room. Washing machines. Fridge hire. Shop, two bar/restaurants and takeaway. Swimming pool (May-Sept). Whirlpool. Play area. Fishing and sailing. Free windsurfing and canoeing. Archery. Football. Minigolf. Boat launching. WiFi (charged). Car wash. Dogs are not accepted. Motorcycles not allowed on site (parking provided). No electric barbecues. Off site: Indoor pool, bicycle hire and tennis 2 km.

Open: 29 March - 12 October.

Directions
Leave A4 autoroute at Pescheria exit and head north towards Garda on lakeside road. Pass Lazise and site is signed (small sign) on left halfway to Bardolina. Site is 12 km. beyond the Gardaland theme park. GPS: 45.52290, 10.72760

Charges guide
Per unit incl. 2 persons	
and electricity	€ 18.50 - € 44.00
extra person	€ 4.50 - € 11.00
motorboat	€ 11.00 - € 20.00

Camping Cheques accepted.

NEARBY BARDOLINO AND LAZISE

CARAVANING BUNGALOWS
CISANO
San Vito Camping
Via Peschiera, 48 - C.P. 126 - I - 37010 CISANO DI BARDOLINO (VR)
Tel. +39 045 6229098 - Fax +39 045 6229059
www.camping-cisano.it - cisano@camping-cisano.it

Lazise

Camping du Parc

Via Gardesana, 110, I-37017 Lazise sul Garda (Lake Garda) T: 045 758 0127.
E: duparc@campingduparc.com alanrogers.com/IT62535

Camping du Parc is a very pleasant, family owned site which resembles a Tardis, in that it extends and extends as you progress further through the site. Olive groves are interspersed with the pitch areas which gives an open and green feel. The site is set on a slope that goes down to the lakeside beach of soft sand. The 242 touring pitches are terraced and all have 5A electricity. Units above 10 m. long will be challenged by some of the corners here. Pitches are separated by trimmed hedges and some have shade, others have fine views of the lake. The restaurant is on the lower level, with a terrace to catch the sunsets, and the pizzeria also has a patio with sea views. Relax by the beach bar or in the pool whilst the children enjoy the slides and paddling pool. This is a very good site for those who prefer peace and quiet to the noisier atmosphere of the larger sites hereabouts. Buses stop by the gate to take you to Gardaland and other tourist attractions. As a site which caters for families, there is no disco or excessive noise and when we visited there were many happy customers. Entertainment takes place in the lower sports areas and is aimed mainly at children. All facilities are open the whole season. The beach, accessed through a security gate, is safe for swimming and there is a lifeguard.

Facilities

Four modern sanitary blocks are heated, well placed and have free hot water throughout. Three blocks have facilities for disabled visitors, one for children and babies. Washing machines and dryers. Motorcaravan services. Well stocked mini-market. Restaurant with lake views. Pizzeria with terrace and views. Takeaway. Beach bar. Pool bar. Outdoor heated swimming pool (1/5-31/10). Large paddling pool with slides. Children's entertainment. Baby club. Play area. Tennis. Fitness suite. Multisports court. Fishing. Free WiFi. Off site: Bicycle hire 500 m.

Open: 13 March - 8 November.

Directions

Leave A4 Venice-Milan autostrada by taking the Brennero exit to Lake Garda and then on to Lazise. At the lakeside in town turn left and follow signs for site. GPS: 45.49833, 10.7375

Charges guide

Per unit incl. 2 persons	
and electricity	€ 22.60 - € 50.00
extra person	€ 5.80 - € 11.50
child (2-6 yrs)	€ 1.50 - € 6.00

No credit cards.

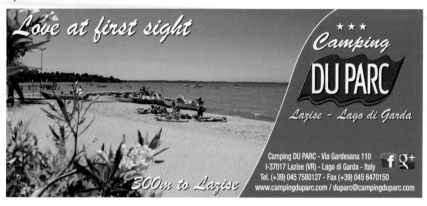

Love at first sight

★★★
Camping
DU PARC
Lazise - Lago di Garda

300m to Lazise

Camping DU PARC - Via Gardesana 110
I-37017 Lazise (VR) - Lago di Garda - Italy
Tel. (+39) 045 7580127 - Fax (+39) 045 6470150
www.campingduparc.com / duparc@campingduparc.com

Lazise

Camping Piani di Clodia

Via Fossalta 42, I-37017 Lazise (Lake Garda) T: 045 759 0456. E: info@pianidiclodia.it
alanrogers.com/IT62530

LeadingCampings

Piani di Clodia is one of the largest sites on Lake Garda and it has a positive impression of space and cleanliness. It is located on a slope between Lazise and Peschiera in the southeast corner of the lake, with lovely views across the water to Sirmione's peninsula and the mountains beyond. The site slopes (in some parts, quite steeply) down to the water's edge and has 968 pitches, all with 6/16A electricity, 290 with electricity, water and drainage, terraced where necessary and back-to-back off hard access roads. There is some shade from both mature and young trees. The pool complex is truly wonderful with a range of pools, a pleasant sunbathing area and a bar. The whole area is fenced and supervised.

Facilities

Seven modern, immaculate sanitary blocks have British and Turkish style WCs, facilities for disabled visitors and one has a baby room. Washing machines, dryers and laundry service. Motorcaravan services. Shopping complex with supermarket and general shops, two bars, self-service restaurant with takeaway. Pizzeria. Ice cream parlour. Swimming pools (28/3-10/10). Large playground. Outdoor theatre. WiFi over part of site (charged).

Open: 21 March - 11 October.

Directions

Lazise is on southeast side of Lake Garda 30 km. west of Verona. From north on A22 (Trento-Verona) take Affi exit then follow signs for Lazise and site. GPS: 45.48272, 10.72932

Charges guide

Per unit incl. 2 persons	
and electricity	€ 20.40 - € 52.90
extra person	€ 5.10 - € 13.40
child (1-9 yrs)	€ 3.20 - € 8.80

For latest campsite news, availability and prices visit
alanrogers.com

Lazise

Camping Spiaggia d'Oro

Via Sentieri 2, I-37017 Lazise (Lake Garda) T: 045 758 0007. E: info@campingspiaggiadoro.com

alanrogers.com/IT62545

Spiaggia d'Oro is a well equipped family site near Lazise on Lake Garda's eastern bank. This is a large site with 765 grassy touring pitches and a selection of chalets and mobile homes for rent. The site has its own sandy beach with a beach volleyball court. A fitness centre is a recent addition and has been developed with a good range of high specification equipment. The swimming pool complex is impressive with three pools, one for children with a slide and water games. This is a lively site in high season with a varied activity programme and a club for children.

Facilities

Five modern, suitably positioned toilet blocks provide open style washbasins and showers. Good facilities for disabled visitors. Laundry. Motorcaravan services. Supermarket. Bar. Snack bar. Swimming pools with waterslide. Separate children's pool. Fitness centre. Tennis. Playground. Children's club and entertainment programme. Direct access to beach. Mobile homes and chalets for rent. WiFi on part of site (charged).

Open: 20 March - 18 October.

Directions

Leave the A4 (Milan-Venice) autostrada at exit for Castelnuovo del Garda. Head north on the SR450. Leave this road at Ca Isidoro and join the westbound SP5 to Lazise. Site is clearly signed from here. GPS: 45.49716, 10.73806

Charges guide

Per unit incl. 2 persons	
and electricity	€ 20.00 - € 59.00
extra person	€ 5.00 - € 11.00

Lazise

Camping la Quercia

I-37017 Lazise sul Garda (Lake Garda) T: 045 647 0577. E: laquercia@laquercia.it

alanrogers.com/IT62550

La Quercia is a spacious, popular site on a slight slope leading down to Lake Garda and is decorated by palm trees and elegantly trimmed hedges. Accommodating up to 850 touring units, pitches are mostly in regular double rows between access roads, all with 6A electricity. Most are shaded by mature trees, although those furthest from the lake are more open to the sun. Much of the activity centres around the impressive pool complex with its fantastic slides and the terrace bar, restaurant and pizzeria which overlook the entertainment stage.

Facilities

Six toilet blocks are of a very high standard. Laundry. Supermarket. General shop. Bar, restaurant, self-service restaurant and pizzeria. Swimming pools (small charge). Tennis. Aerobics, judo and yoga. Scuba club. Playground with water play. Organised events (sports competitions, games, etc.) and free courses (e.g. swimming, surfboarding). Canoeing. Roller-blading. Archery. Minigolf. Evening entertainment or dancing. Babysitting service. WiFi (charged). ATM. Free weekly excursion.

Open: 29 March - 30 September.

Directions

Lazise is on the southeast side of Lake Garda 30 km. west of Verona. From north on A22 (Trento-Verona) take Affi exit then follow signs for Lazise and site. From south on A4 (Brescia-Venice) take Peschiera exit and site is 7 km. towards Lazise and Garda on SS249. GPS: 45.49318, 10.73337

Charges guide

Per unit incl. 2 persons	
and electricity	€ 24.00 - € 91.45
extra person	€ 5.65 - € 13.35

Lazise

Camping Le Palme

Via del Tronchetto, I-37017 Lazise (Lake Garda) T: 045 759 0019. E: info@lepalmecamping.it

alanrogers.com/IT63015

On the southern shore of Lake Garda, Le Palme is a quiet site on the attractive Riviera degli Olivi, yet within easy reach of numerous attractions including several theme parks. There are 133 touring pitches, all with electricity (6-10A), water and waste water connections. Trees provide some shade throughout and a few pitches have spectacular views across the lake, for which a supplement is payable. Some mobile homes and chalets are available for hire. Nearby Lazise and Peschiera del Garda are both attractive towns with plenty of history, as well as shops, bars and restaurants. The ancient city of Verona is an easy drive away.

Facilities

Three heated sanitary blocks provide hot showers, baby and laundry rooms. Motorcaravan services. Swimming pool with terrace, bar, slides and children's pool. Restaurant, pizzeria and bar with entertainment in high season. Shop with bazaar. Playground. Football. Volleyball. Rent of bicycles, fridges, private bathrooms, boat moorings and parking for boat trailers. WiFi throughout (charged). Underground car-parking available. Doctor daily in middle and high season. Direct lake access. Off site: Sailing and water sports nearby.

Open: 4 April - 27 October.

Directions

From A4 (Milano/Verona) motorway leave at exit for Peschiera and follow signs for Peschiera Centro then turn north along riverside. At roundabout take first exit and follow SR249 for Lazise. Site is signed to left 1 km. after passing Gardaland. GPS: 45.46472, 10.71476

Charges guide

Per unit incl. 2 persons	
and electricity, water and drainage	€ 17.50 - € 42.40
extra person	€ 4.50 - € 9.70
child (1-7 yrs)	€ 2.50 - € 6.00

FREE Alan Rogers Travel Card

Extra benefits and savings - see page 14

Lazise

Camping Park Delle Rose

Strada San Gaetano 20, I-37017 Lazise (Lake Garda) T: 045 647 1181. E: info@campingparkdellerose.it

alanrogers.com/IT63580

An orderly, well designed site with a feeling of spaciousness, Delle Rose is on the east side of Lake Garda, three kilometres from the attractive waterside village of Peschiera. The 455 pitches are of average size, most with grass and shade, and laid out in 30 short, terraced avenues. The ratio of recreational area to pitches is unusually high, particularly for sites at Lake Garda. Unusually, reception is located one third of the way into the site. On approach one sees the attractive restaurant, gardens and comprehensive sporting facilities including the pool complex with its stylish terraced bar and entertainment area close by.

Facilities

Five very clean, modern sanitary blocks have hot water and British style toilets, some in cabins with washbasins. Private bathrooms for hire. Good baby rooms. Facilities for disabled visitors. Washing machines. Motorcaravan services. Fridge hire. Bar/restaurant, takeaway and pool bar serving snacks. Shops. New swimming pool with flumes (mid April-Sept). Tennis. Archery. Minigolf. Play area and miniclub. Fishing (with permit). Watersports. Kayaking. Windsurfing. Beach at site. Daily medical services. Entertainment (high season). WiFi (charged).

Open: 21 April - 30 September.

Directions

From A4 Milan-Venice autostrada take exit for Pescheria, west of Verona. Travel north towards Lazise. The campsite is on the southeastern lakeside 2.5 km. north of Pescheria and well signed. GPS: 45.48300, 10.73183

Charges guide

Per unit incl. 2 persons and electricity	€ 20.00 - € 50.50
extra person	€ 5.00 - € 11.00

No credit cards.

Manerba del Garda

Camping Belvedere

Via Cavalle 5, I-25080 Manerba del Garda (Lake Garda) T: 036 555 1175. E: info@camping-belvedere.it

alanrogers.com/IT62840

Situated along a promontory reaching into Lake Garda, this friendly, traditional campsite has been terraced to give many of the 85 touring pitches wonderful views. They are mostly shaded, on gravel with 6A electricity. There is a long beach and pleasant lakeside pitches; swimming and boat launching is easy. The delightful restaurant and bar with pretty flowers is under shady trees at the water's edge. However, sanitary facilities are of a poor standard, and there are none for disabled visitors. The site is not suitable for visitors with disabilities as there are steep slopes and uneven ground. Prices are reasonable compared with others in the area.

Facilities

Five traditional sanitary blocks are basic and poorly maintained. Washing machine. Motorcaravan services. Shop selling basics. Restaurant, bar and takeaway are all open most of the season. Play area. Tennis. Music and TV in bar. Fishing. WiFi throughout (charged). Torches useful. Mobile homes to rent. Off site: Watersports nearby. Bars and restaurant a short walk away. Golf and bicycle hire 2 km. Riding 4 km. Theme parks.

Open: 4 April - 5 October.

Directions

Manerba is on western shore of Lake Garda. From A4 Milan-Venice autostrada take Desenzano exit and go north on SS572 (Saló) for 11 km. and look for site signs. Turn right off main road, right again along Via Belvedere. GPS: 45.56207, 10.56315

Charges guide

Per unit incl. 2 persons and electricity	€ 18.00 - € 37.00
extra person	€ 5.00 - € 8.50

Manerba del Garda

Camping Village Baia Verde

Via del Edera 19, I-25080 Manerba del Garda (Lake Garda) T: 036 565 1753. E: info@campingbaiaverde.com

alanrogers.com/IT62860

Baia Verde is a smart, luxurious and peaceful campsite located in the southwestern corner of Lake Garda. The 145 touring pitches are in regular rows on flat, open ground where the young trees are giving some shade. The pitches are all fully serviced (16A electricity), and 12 have superb private facilities. The remaining 46 pitches are used for mobile homes to rent and there are apartments available too. The excellent restaurant block and the building housing the other facilities are designed by an architect and it shows. A great deal of thought and loving care has gone into Baia Verde. We were impressed!

Facilities

Full range of high quality sanitary facilities in an impressive three storey building in the style of an Italian villa. Rooms for babies and children. Superb facilities for disabled visitors. Washing machines and dryers. TV lounge. Rooftop sunbathing area with jacuzzi. Entertainment and activity programme (high season). WiFi over site (charged). Only some breeds of dog accepted. Off site: Beach with fishing, swimming and boat launching 400 m. Manerba del Garda 1 km. Golf and bicycle hire 3 km. Riding 5 km.

Open: 12 April - 11 October.

Directions

Manerba is on western shore of Lake Garda at the southern end. From A4 Milan-Venice autostrada take Desenzano exit and head north on SS572 towards Saló for 12 km; then turn right following signs to site. GPS: 45.56155, 10.55352

Charges guide

Per unit incl. 2 persons and electricity	€ 26.50 - € 74.00
extra person	€ 6.00 - € 12.50
child (3-11 yrs)	€ 3.00 - € 9.50

For latest campsite news, availability and prices visit

alanrogers.com

Pacengo
Camping Lido

Via Peschiera 2, I-37017 Pacengo (Lake Garda) T: 045 759 0030. E: info@campinglido.it

alanrogers.com/IT62540

Camping Lido is one of the largest and amongst the best of the 120 campsites around Lake Garda and is situated at the southeast corner of the lake. There is quite a slope from the entrance down to the lake, so many of the 564 grass touring pitches are on terraces which give lovely views across the lake. They are of varying sizes, separated by hedges, all have 6A electrical connections and 54 are fully serviced. This is a most attractive site with tall, neatly trimmed trees standing like sentinels on either side of the broad avenue that runs from the entrance right down to the lake.

Facilities

Seven modern toilet blocks (three heated) include provision for disabled visitors and three family rooms. Washing machines and dryer. Fridge rental. Restaurant, bars, pizzeria, takeaway and well stocked supermarket (all season). Swimming pool, paddling pool and slides. Superb fitness centre. Playground. Tennis. Bicycle hire. Watersports. Fishing. Activity programme (high season). Shingle beach with landing stage and mooring for boats. Communal barbecue. WiFi (charged). Off site: Bus service 200 m. Gardaland theme park. Riding 4 km. Golf 8 km.

Open: 10 April - 12 October.

Directions

Leave A4 Milan-Venice motorway at exit for Peschiera. Head north on east side of lake on the SS249. Site entrance on left after Gardaland theme park. GPS: 45.46996, 10.72042

Charges guide

Per unit incl. 2 persons	
and electricity	€ 18.40 - € 43.50
extra person	€ 4.70 - € 10.50
child (3-7 yrs)	free - € 6.70
dog	€ 1.00 - € 6.00

Pacengo
Eurocamping Pacengo

Via Porto 13, I-37010 Pacengo di Lazise (Lake Garda) T: 045 759 0012. E: info@eurocampingpacengo.it

alanrogers.com/IT63010

Eurocamping is at the southeast corner of Lake Garda, with direct lake access and a pleasant beach. It is a good site for launching boats as there is a little harbour/marina area adjacent. This is the best part of the site, where a pleasant restaurant terrace overlooks the lake and boats. Pacengo includes a large area of mobile homes. Most pitches (468 for touring), although quite small, have very good shade and all have 4A electrical connections. The swimming pool incorporates a jacuzzi and separate children's pool. Eurocamping's lower prices may suit some campers but it is in need of some attention and would benefit from the removal of some rather old static units.

Facilities

Two new and one old sanitary block are kept reasonably clean. Supermarket. Bar, restaurant and pizzeria (closed Tues in low season). Swimming pools (10/5-15/9). Second bar at the poolside. Large play area. Tennis. Fishing. Boat launching. Organised entertainment (July/Aug). Gas barbecues permitted. WiFi on part of site (charged). Off site: Theme parks within 1.5 km. Riding 2 km. Bicycle hire 5 km. Golf 7 km. Sailing 8 km.

Open: Easter - 24 September.

Directions

From north on A22 (Trento-Verona) autostrada take Affi exit then follow signs for Lazise and site. At traffic lights in Pacengo, turn towards lake and follow road for 500 m. GPS: 45.46772, 10.71654

Charges guide

Per unit incl. 2 persons	
and electricity	€ 17.00 - € 31.50
extra person	€ 4.00 - € 7.00

No credit cards.

Rivoltella
Camping Village San Francesco

Strada Vicinale San Francesco, I-25015 Rivoltella (Lake Garda) T: 030 911 0245.

E: moreinfo@campingsanfrancesco.com **alanrogers.com/IT62520**

San Francesco is a large, very well organised site situated to the west of the Simione peninsula on the southeast shores of Lake Garda. The 323 touring pitches are generally on flat gravel and sand and enjoy shade from mature trees. There are three choices of pitch of different sizes with 6A electricity; 76 are fully serviced. They are marked by stones but there is no division between them. A wooded beach area of about 400 m. on the lake is used for watersports and there is a jetty for boating. There are delightful lake views from the restaurant and terrace.

Facilities

Sanitary facilities are in two large, modern, centrally located buildings. Spotlessly clean and well equipped. Excellent facilities for disabled campers. Shop (sells gluten-free products). Restaurant. Bar. Pool bar. Pizzeria. Takeaway and snacks. In a separate area across the road: swimming pools (26/4-14/9; disability hoist) and jacuzzi, sports centre and tennis. Entertainment, activities and excursions. Playground. Bicycle hire arranged. Torches required in some areas. WiFi (charged).

Open: 1 April - 30 September.

Directions

From autostrada A4, between Brescia and Verona, exit towards Simione and follow signs to Simione and site. GPS: 45.46565, 10.59443

Charges guide

Per unit incl. 2 persons	
and electricity	€ 25.00 - € 62.00
extra person	€ 6.50 - € 13.50
child (0-10 yrs)	free - € 9.70
dog	free

Camping Cheques accepted.

FREE Alan Rogers Travel Card
Extra benefits and savings - see page 14

Peschiera del Garda

Camping Bella Italia

Via Bella Italia 2, I-37019 Peschiera del Garda (Lake Garda) T: 045 640 0688. E: info@camping-bellaitalia.it

alanrogers.com/IT62630

Peschiera is a picturesque village on the southern shore of Lake Garda, and Camping Bella Italia is a very attractive, large, well organised and very busy site in the grounds of a former farm, just west of the centre of the village. Half of the 1,200 pitches are occupied by the site's own mobile homes and chalets and by tour operators; there are some 330 touring pitches, most towards the lakeside and reasonably level on grass under trees. All have 16A electricity, water and waste water and are separated by shrubs. There are some fine views across the lake to the mountains beyond. A superb promenade allows direct access to the town. Bella Italia collaborates with Cisano/San Vito (IT63570) and Butterfly (IT62520). The site slopes gently down to the lake with access to the water for watersports and swimming. A feature of the site is the group of pools of varying shapes and sizes with an entertainment area and varied sports provision nearby. A range of supervised activities is organised. Regulations are in place to ensure that the site is peaceful. English and Dutch are spoken by the friendly staff. Although large, this site has not lost its personal touch, and their sixty years of experience has been wisely used.

Facilities

Six modern toilet blocks have British style toilets, washbasins and showers. Baby rooms and facilities for disabled visitors. Washing machines. Motorcaravan services. Infirmary. Shops. Gelateria. Bars. Waiter service restaurant and terrace and two other restaurants (one in the old farm building). Swimming pools. Tennis. Archery. Playgrounds (small). Games room. Watersports. Fishing. Bicycle hire. Organised activities and entertainment. Mini club. WiFi over part of site (charged). ATMs. Dogs are not accepted. Off site: Fishing 1 km. Golf 2.5 km. Riding 3 km. Gardaland, Italy's most popular theme park, is about 2 km. east of Peschiera, with others nearby. Verona 40 minutes.

Open: 29 March - 26 October.

Directions

Peschiera is 32 km. west of Verona. From A4 take exit for Peschiera del Garda and follow SS11 towards Brescia. Site is at the large junction at the western entrance to the village.
GPS: 45.44165, 10.67920

Charges guide

Per unit incl. 2 persons	
and electricity	€ 27.20 - € 56.50
extra person	€ 6.60 - € 15.00
child (3-5 yrs)	free - € 5.80

Four charging seasons. No credit/debit cards.

San Felice del Benaco

Camping Europa Silvella

Via Silvella 10, I-25010 San Felice del Benaco (Lake Garda) T: 036 565 1095. E: info@europasilvella.it

alanrogers.com/IT62600

This large, traditional, lakeside site is a slightly confusing merger of two different sites with the result that the 345 pitches (about 108 for touring units) appear randomly dispersed around the site. However, those alongside the lake are in small groups and close together; the main bar, restaurant and shop are also located at the lower level. The main area is at the top of a fairly steep hill on slightly sloping or terraced grass and has slightly larger pitches. There is reasonable shade in many parts and all pitches have 4A electricity. Nine new pitches of 120 sq.m. with 10A electricity have been added. An attractive swimming pool complex also has a daytime bar and a restaurant which serves lunch and is the hub of the evening entertainment programme in high season.

Facilities

Toilet blocks include washbasins in cabins, facilities for disabled visitors and a superb children's room with small showers. Laundry. Shop. Restaurant/pizzeria. Swimming pools (11/5-13/9, hats required) with bar. Tennis, volleyball and five-a-side soccer. Playground. Bowling alley. Entertainment (every night in July/Aug). Disco for children. Bicycle hire. Tournaments. Fishing and boat launching. First aid room. WiFi on part of site (charged). Off site: Golf 5 km. Sailing 10 km. Riding 15 km. Theme parks.

Open: 29 April - 21 September.

Directions

San Felice is on the western shore of Lake Garda at the southern end. From A4 Milan-Venice autostrada take Desenzano exit and head north on SS572 towards Saló for 14 km, turn right towards San Felice and follow brown tourist signs with site name (about 3 km). Enter Manerba del Garda for sat navs.
GPS: 45.574474, 10.54857

Charges guide

Per unit incl. 2 persons	
and electricity	€ 23.00 - € 48.00
child (3-10 yrs)	free - € 8.50
extra person	€ 6.50 - € 12.50
dog	free - € 5.00

No credit cards.

For latest campsite news, availability and prices visit

alanrogers.com

Bella Italia welcomes its guests in a relaxing but
eventful holiday suitable for everyone from 1 to 100 years old!
Families can enjoy a care-free time both resting poolside
while children can play in our supervised water-parks
or visiting the beautiful surroundings.
Too lazy for extensive sport facilities?
Delight yourself with the special dishes offered by
our famous restaurants.
The evening entertainment starts with our baby dance to
continue with shows and Musical.
At 23 o'clock vehicle-curfew ensures a quiet sleep
for our satisfied campers.

Via Bella Italia 2 - Peschiera del Garda (Vr)

Tel.: 0039.045.6400688 - Fax: 0039.045.6401410
GPS: 45.44167567209166, 10.67746639251709

www.camping-bellaitalia.it

San Felice del Benaco
Camping Villaggio Weekend
Via Vallone della Selva 2, I-25010 San Felice del Benaco (Lake Garda) T: 036 543 712. E: info@weekend.it
alanrogers.com/IT62800

Created among the olive groves and terraced vineyards of the Château Villa Louisa, which overlooks it, this modern, well equipped site enjoys some superb views over the small bay which forms this part of Lake Garda. On reaching the site you will pass through a most impressive pair of gates. There are 248 pitches, all with 6/10A electricity, of which 79 are used by tour operators and for mobile homes. The touring pitches are in several different areas, and many enjoy superb views. Some pitches for larger units are set in the upper terraces on steep slopes, so manoeuvring can be challenging and low olive branches may cause problems for long or high units.

Facilities
Three sanitary blocks, one below the restaurant/shop, are modern and well maintained. Mainly British style WCs, a few washbasins in cabins and facilities for disabled visitors in one. Baby room. Laundry. Shop. Bar/restaurant (waiter service). Takeaway. Supervised swimming pool and paddling pool. Entertainment programme all season. TV. Barbecues. All facilities are open throughout the season. Two playgrounds. English spoken. WiFi in some areas (charged). Off site: Windsurfing, water-skiing and tennis nearby. Beach and fishing 400 m. Golf 2 km.

Open: 12 April - 5 October.

Directions
Approach from Saló (easier when towing) and follow site signs. From Milan-Venice autostrada take Desenzano exit towards Saló and Localitá Cisano-San Felice. Watch for narrow right fork after Cunettone roundabout. Pass petrol station on left, then turn right towards San Felice for 1 km. Site is next left. GPS: 45.59318, 10.53088

Charges guide
Per unit incl. 2 persons and electricity	€ 15.50 - € 70.00
extra person	€ 4.00 - € 12.50

Bracciano
Camping Roma Flash
Via Settevene Palo km. 19,800, I-00062 Bracciano (Lazio) T: 069 980 5458. E: info@romaflash.it
alanrogers.com/IT68120

This excellent site is in a superb location with magnificent views over Lake Bracciano, the source of Rome's drinking water. When we visited, although it was busy, it was still peaceful and relaxing. There are 275 flat, shaded pitches with 6A electricity (Europlug). A pleasant, covered restaurant set alongside a lake has a large terrace, as does a small indoor area. Elide and Eduardo speak excellent English and happily go out of their way to ensure guests enjoy their holiday. Many of the visitors told us that they return year after year and some stay for 8 to 12 weeks at a time to enjoy the Lazio region.

Facilities
Two large, modern toilet blocks have free hot water throughout and fully adjustable showers. Facilities for disabled visitors and children. Laundry facilities. Gas supplies. Bar/restaurant/pizzeria, small shop (all open as site). Swimming pool (1/6-31/8, caps compulsory). Play area. Watersports. Games room. Entertainment for children in high season. WiFi throughout (charged). Excursions. Private bus daily to Roma San Pietro and return. New sports area. Off site: Riding 6 km.

Open: 1 April - 30 September.

Directions
From A1/E45 north of Roma take exit for Orte and Viterbo (SS675), Vetralla, Sutri (SS2), Trevignano Romano (SP12d) and then towards Bracciano (SP4a). GPS: 42.130113, 12.173527

Charges guide
Per unit incl. 2 persons and electricity	€ 16.00 - € 37.00
extra person	€ 7.00 - € 9.50
child (3-10 yrs)	€ 4.00 - € 6.50

Camping Cheques accepted.

Bracciano
Camping Porticciolo
Via Porticciolo, I-00062 Bracciano (Lazio) T: 069 980 3060. E: info@porticciolo.it
alanrogers.com/IT68130

This is a small, family run site. Useful for visiting Rome, it has its own private beach on the lake and is overlooked by the impressive Bracciano Castle. The 170 pitches, some with lake views, and 120 having electricity (4-6A) are level, peaceful and shaded by very green trees. The bar/restaurant/takeaway and wood-fired pizzeria have two large terraces. Alessandro and his wife, Alessandra, have worked hard to build up this basic site since 1982. They are charming and speak excellent English.

Facilities
Three sanitary units with children's toilets and showers are showing some signs of wear and tear. Hot showers. Laundry facilities. Motorcaravan services. Gas supplies. Small shop (basics). Bar. Trattoria/pizzeria/takeaway. Tennis. Play area. Bicycle hire. Fishing. Internet point and free WiFi. Torches required in some areas. Excursions. Off site: Bus service from outside the gate to central Rome. Air-conditioned train service from Bracciano (1.5 km) into city (site runs connecting bus 09.00 daily).

Open: 1 April - 30 September.

Directions
From Rome ring road (GRA) northwest side take Cassia exit to Bracciano S493 (not Cassia bis which is further northeast). 2 km. before Bracciano village, just after going under a bridge, follow site signs and turn along the lake away from Anguillara. Site is 1 km. on the SP1f and has a fairly steep entrance. GPS: 42.10582, 12.18928

Charges guide
Per unit incl. 2 persons and electricity	€ 16.00 - € 29.00
extra person	€ 5.00 - € 8.00

For latest campsite news, availability and prices visit
alanrogers.com

Roma

Camping Tiber

Via Tiberina km. 1,400, I-00188 Roma (Lazio) T: 063 361 0733. E: info@campingtiber.com

alanrogers.com/IT68090

An excellent city site with extensive facilities, which also caters for backpackers. Although a lively site, the thoughtful layout and the division of different areas with flowering shrubs makes it surprisingly peaceful. It is ideally located for visiting Rome with a shuttle bus every 30 minutes to the station and then an easy train service to Rome (20 minutes), with trams operating late at night. The 350 touring pitches (with electricity) are mostly shaded under very tall trees and many have very pleasant views over the River Tiber. This mighty river winds around two sides of the site boundary (safely fenced) providing a cooling effect for campers and it is possible to fish for carp.

Facilities

Fully equipped, very smart sanitary facilities include hot water everywhere, private cabins, a baby room and very good facilities for disabled campers. Laundry facilities. Motorcaravan services. Shop. Bar, restaurant, pizzeria and takeaway. Swimming pool (May-end Sept, hat required) and bar. Carp fishing in river. Play area. Shuttle bus (on payment) to the underground station every 15 or 30 minutes according to season. Torches useful. WiFi on part of site (charged). Off site: Restaurants and shops.

Open: 1 April - 31 October.

Directions

From Florence, exit at Rome Nord Fiano on A1 and turn south onto Via Tiberina and site is signed. From other directions on Rome ring road (GRA) take exit 6 northbound on S3 Via Flaminia following signs to Tiberina. GPS: 42.0095, 12.50233

Charges guide

Per unit incl. 2 persons and electricity	€ 29.50 - € 35.50
extra person	€ 9.50 - € 10.50
child (3-12 yrs)	€ 6.50 - € 7.50

Roma

Happy Village & Camping

Via del Prato della Corte, 1915, I-00123 Roma (Lazio) T: 063 362 6401. E: info@happycamping.net

alanrogers.com/IT68095

Happy Village and Camping is a smart, pleasant site set on a hillside, with great views from the upper reaches where the hub of the site is situated. There is a choice of shaded pitches (6A electricity), flat in the lower section or terraced in the upper area. The restaurant and bar have large terraces overlooking the pools and countryside. Dining here at night is a delight. Everything is neat and clean. Most visitors will wish to visit Rome and the shuttle bus to the local station some 6 km. away makes this easy.

Facilities

Two clean and modern, heated sanitary blocks with British style WCs and hot water throughout. Facilities for children and disabled visitors. Washing machines. Motorcaravan services. Small shop. Modern restaurant and bar with terraces. Swimming pool and children's pool. Picnic area with huge fridge, barbecue and preparation area. WiFi in restaurant area (charged). Torches useful in some areas. Off site: Veio Natural Park. Riding 5 km.

Open: 1 March - 1 November, Christmas - 6 January.

Directions

From Rome GRA (circular road) take SS2 to Cassia Veientana/Viterbo/Vallelunga between junctions 5 and 6. The site is well signed 2 km. along SS2. GPS: 42.003242, 12.452724

Charges guide

Per unit incl. 2 persons and electricity	€ 18.50 - € 32.50
extra person	€ 7.50 - € 10.00
child (5-15 yrs)	€ 4.80 - € 7.50
dog	free

Roma

Camping Seven Hills Village

Via Cassia 1216, I-00189 Roma (Lazio) T: 063 031 0826. E: info@sevenhills.it

alanrogers.com/IT68100

Close to Rome, this site has both quiet and lively areas on steep slopes set in a delightful, lush green valley, flanked by two of the seven hills of Rome. The 250 well tended pitches for touring units are on steep terraces, mostly shaded, with 6A electricity. Two fine restaurants and the snack bar and pizzeria/takeaway cater for everyone. The site runs a regular shuttle bus, and a daily bus to Rome. The pool (extra charge), also with bar snacks, is great for cooling off and relaxing after a day in the city.

Facilities

Three soundly constructed sanitary blocks are well situated around the site, with open washbasins, and hot water in the average sized showers. Facilities for disabled campers. Well stocked shop. Bar. Two excellent restaurants with terraces. Money exchange. Swimming pool at the bottom of the site with bar/snack bar and a room where the younger element tends to congregate (separate pool charge). Disco. Excursions. Bungalows and apartments to rent. Free WiFi. Off site: Golf 4 km. Excursions to Tivoli gardens.

Open: All year (on request).

Directions

From autostrada ring road exit 3 take Via Cassia (signed SS2 Viterbo, NOT Via Cassia Bis) and look for site signs. Turn right after 1 km. and follow small road, Via Italo Piccagli, for 1 km. to site. This narrow twisting road is heavily parked on during the day. GPS: 41.993, 12.41685

Charges guide

Per unit incl. 2 persons and car	€ 24.90 - € 32.20
extra person	€ 8.00 - € 9.50
child (5-12 yrs)	€ 6.00 - € 7.50
dog	free

FREE Alan Rogers Travel Card
Extra benefits and savings - see page 14

Trevignano Romano

Camping Internazionale Lago di Bracciano

Via del Pianoro 4, I-00069 Trevignano Romano (Lazio) T: 069 985 032. E: camping.village@gmail.com

alanrogers.com/IT67850

Lago di Bracciano, just 45 km. north of Rome, is of a size that provides excellent opportunities for watersports and is inevitably very popular with windsurfers. With some pitches alongside a little beach, the site provides 110 pitches of which about 50 are for touring units. Our pitch had a full view of the lake and the gentle breeze made the temperature at the end of June quite bearable. Some shade is provided by large trees. A bar and restaurant near the entrance are behind the site's small swimming pool and play area. The local bus has a regular service to Rome.

Facilities

Two toilet blocks are clean and have open style washbasins, preset showers and facilities for disabled visitors (key). Washing machine. Motorcaravan services. Small shop. Bar and restaurant/pizzeria. Small swimming pool (15/5-15/9). Play area. Beach volleyball court. WiFi and Internet access. Mobile homes and bungalows to rent. Off site: Lago di Bracciano.

Open: 1 April - 30 September.

Directions

From the Rome GRA take exit 5 on SS2 towards Cassia. Turn left at Trevignano exit (km. 35) and follow SP4a towards the lake where you will find the site on the left, well signed. The access road is narrow. GPS: 42.14472, 12.26865

Charges guide

Per unit incl. 2 persons and electricity	€ 22.00 - € 29.50
extra person	€ 6.00 - € 8.00

Ameglia

Camping River

Localitá Armezzone, I-19031 Ameglia (Ligúria) T: 018 765 920. E: info@campingriver.com

alanrogers.com/IT64190

Camping River is a large oblong site on the banks of the Magna river but only the swimming pool/entertainment area has river views. It provides 100 level 75-100 sq.m. touring pitches (all with 3A electricity) mostly under a canopy of tall trees with much welcome shade on hot days. They are mostly separated from the equal number of permanent pitches. It is possible to launch your boat into the Magra river from the campsite and there are good fishing opportunities further up river. A busy entertainment programme is provided from mid June until September. Camping River has something for all the family; we saw fishermen setting off for the afternoon, families playing in the pool, and small children enjoying the large play area while their parents relaxed with a cup of coffee on the terrace. This is a wonderful area to explore with the Cinque Terre nearby, its beautiful coastline and interesting hill top villages. Ligúria is also a well known wine growing area.

Facilities

Two unisex sanitary blocks provide toilets (some Turkish style), washbasins and showers. Facilities for disabled visitors. Motorcaravan services. Shop, restaurant and bar, pizzeria (1/5-30/9). Swimming pool (1/5-15/9) and sun deck. Football. Hydro massage. Boat launching. Fishing. Mobile homes and bungalows to rent. Entertainment area. Beach shuttle bus. Lessons organised (scuba diving, swimming, dancing). Kayak, windsurf board, bicycle hire. WiFi (free). Off site: Tennis and riding 200 m. Archery. Sailing. Scuba diving. La Spezia. Le Cinque Terre. Golf 7 km.

Open: 1 April - 30 September.

Directions

Take Sarzana exit on the A12 (Genoa-Livorno) and follow the signs initially towards Lerici. After 3 km. follow signs to Bocca di Magra and Ameglia where the site is signed off to left. Avoid other less good sites (one claiming to be 'formerly Camping River'). The final access road is a little narrow. GPS: 44.07556, 9.96972

Charges guide

Per unit incl. 2 persons and electricity	€ 18.50 - € 43.00
extra person	€ 5.00 - € 11.00
child (2-10 yrs)	€ 2.00 - € 8.00
dog	€ 2.00

For latest campsite news, availability and prices visit

alanrogers.com

Borgio Verezzi

Camping Park Mara

via Trento Trieste, 83, I-17022 Borgio Verezzi (Ligúria) T: 019 610 479. E: info@campingparkmara.it
alanrogers.com/IT64055

Set into a hillside with wonderful views of the town and the rocky coastline of the Ligurian Sea, roughly halfway between Genoa and the French border, Park Mara is a compact site with 147 pitches. Of these, only eight are suitable for touring units up to 5.5 m, 28 are for tents and the remainder are occupied by seasonal caravans and rental chalets. The touring pitches are on the small side (40-70 sq.m) with steep access roads. All have 4A Europlugs and nearby water points. Park Mara is not suitable for campers with mobility problems. The shingle beach is just a 400-metre walk down the hill, whilst the shops, bars and restaurants of Borgio and Borgio Verezzi are also within easy reach.

Facilities
The sanitary blocks provide a mixture of British and Turkish style WCs, and hot water (payment card). Washing machines, dryers and ironing facilities. Small shop for basics. Bar. Restaurant and takeaway (Apr-Sept). Bread available. Swimming pool and children's pool. Games room. Playground. Children's Club and organised activities and entertainment (high season). Fridge hire. Safes. WiFi over part of site (charged). Off site: Beach 400 m. Bicycle hire 500 m. Shops within 1 km.

Open: 15 March - 31 December.

Directions
Borgio Verezzi is 78 km. west of Genoa. From west leave A10 at Pietra Ligure exit and follow signs for Viale Riviera to join SS1 east to Borgio Verezzi. Turn north across railway (traffic lights) towards village and immediately turn right then second left, following signs to site. GPS: 44.161536, 8.312659

Charges guide
Per unit incl. 3 persons and electricity	€ 21.00 - € 38.00
extra person	€ 6.00 - € 8.00

Ceriale

Camping Baciccia

Via Torino 19, I-17023 Ceriale (Ligúria) T: 018 299 0743. E: info@campingbaciccia.it
alanrogers.com/IT64030

This friendly, family run site is a popular holiday destination. Baciccia was the nickname of the owner's grandfather, who grew fruit trees and tomatoes on the site. Tall eucalyptus trees shade the 106 flat touring pitches. Laura and Mauro work tirelessly to ensure that you enjoy your stay here and we have watched the growth of a very effective campsite over the years. An informal restaurant, overlooking the swimming pool and sports area, is cheerfully and efficiently run by Flavio and Pamela who serve delightful seasonal Italian dishes.

Facilities
Two very clean and modern sanitary blocks near reception have British and Turkish style WCs and hot water throughout. Laundry. Motorcaravan services. Combined restaurant/bar/pizzeria/takeaway and shop. Swimming pool and paddling pool (1/4-31/10) and private beach. Tennis. Volleyball. Excellent play area. Wood-burning stove and barbecue. Fishing. Diving. Entertainment for children and adults in high season. Excursions. Bicycle hire. WiFi over site. Off site: Supermarket 200 m. Bus 200 m. Aquapark 500 m.

Open: 1 April - 20 October, 4 December - 10 January.

Directions
From the A10 between Imperia and Savona, take Albenga exit. Follow signs Ceriale/Savona and Aquapark Caravelle (which is 500 m. from site) and then site signs. Site is just south of Savona. GPS: 44.08165, 8.21763

Charges guide
Per unit incl. up to 3 persons (over 2 yrs) and electricity	€ 23.00 - € 51.00
extra person	€ 6.50 - € 11.00
dog	€ 3.00 - € 5.00

Deiva Marina

Villaggio Camping Valdeiva

Localitá Ronco, I-19013 Deiva Marina (Ligúria) T: 018 782 4174. E: camping@valdeiva.it
alanrogers.com/IT64120

A mature and cheerful site, 3 km. from the sea between the famous Cinque Terre and Portofino, Valdeiva is open for most of the year. The 40 touring pitches, with 3A electricity, are in a square at the bottom of the site, some with shade and views, and cars are parked separately. There are 100 permanent pitches on the upper reaches of the site. Camping Valdeiva does have a small swimming pool, which is very welcome if you do not wish to take the free bus to the beach. A small busy bar/restaurant offers food at realistic prices.

Facilities
The toilet block nearest the touring pitches provides cramped facilities. A new block is in the centre of the site. WCs are mainly Turkish, but there are some of British style. Washing machines and dryers. Shop (15/6-10/9). Bar/restaurant and takeaway with reasonable menu and pizza oven (15/6-10/9). Small swimming pool. Play area. Excursions. Free bus to the beach. Torches required. Bicycle hire. Camping gas. WiFi on part of site (charged).

Open: All year excl. 10/1-10/2 and 4/11-4/12.

Directions
Leave A12 at Deiva Marina exit and follow signs to Deiva Marina. Site signs are prominent at the first junction and site is on left 3 km. down this road. GPS: 44.22470, 9.55168

Charges guide
Per unit incl. 2 persons and electricity	€ 23.00 - € 36.00
extra person (over 6 yrs)	€ 6.50

FREE Alan Rogers Travel Card
Extra benefits and savings - see page 14

Pietra Ligure

Camping Pian dei Boschi

Viale Riviera 114, I-17027 Pietra Ligure (Ligúria) T: 019 625 425. E: info@piandeiboschi.it

alanrogers.com/IT64107

Camping Pian dei Boschi can be found on the Ligurian Riviera, 700 m. from the sea, close to the resort of Pietra Ligure. There are 215 pitches available for touring. They are well shaded and most have electrical connections (5-6A). A number of mobile homes are available for rent, as well as apartments (for 4-6 people). There is a large swimming pool surrounded by a wide sun terrace, with a paddling pool adjacent. The campsite restaurant includes a wood-fired pizza oven, and offers an enticing range of Mediterranean cuisine. Other on-site amenities include a tennis court and sports field.

Facilities

Two sanitary blocks with mainly Turkish style toilets, some hot water to open style washbasins, preset showers (token). Facilities for disabled visitors. Washing machines. Motorcaravan services. Shop. Bar/restaurant/pizzeria. Takeaway. Swimming pool (caps compulsory). Paddling pool. Play area. Tennis. Sports field. Entertainment and activity programme. Mobile homes and apartments for rent. Off site: Nearest beach 700 m. Golf. Watersports.

Open: Easter - end September.

Directions

From France (Menton) on A10 motorway, leave at the exit to Pietra Ligure and head south on Viale Riviera towards the town centre, from where the site is well signed. GPS: 44.14906, 8.26856

Charges guide

Per unit incl. 3 persons and electricity	€ 26.00 - € 42.00
extra person (over 2 yrs)	€ 5.20 - € 8.50
dog	€ 2.00 - € 3.50

Rapallo

Camping Miraflores

Via Savagna 10, I-16035 Rapallo (Ligúria) T: 018 526 3000. E: camping.miraflores@libero.it

alanrogers.com/IT64110

Camping Miraflores is close to the famous resort of Portofino and the Cinque Terre. It is a small, uncomplicated site with a tiny restaurant and bar offering pizzas and a reasonable menu of the day. The 87 pitches are flat and arranged around the lower levels of the site with separate terraced areas for tents (small pitches). Caravans and motorcaravans are provided with electricity (6A). A small swimming pool is free to campers (hats required). Rapallo is an attractive resort in its own right with an interesting old town centre. An A12 motorway junction is very close to the site but is shielded from sight and sound.

Facilities

Single central traditional sanitary block with a small number of toilets (some Turkish style). Showers. Washing machine. Shop, restaurant/pizzeria and takeaway meals (all 1/5-10/9). Basic games room. Playground. Swimming pool (hats compulsory). Mobile homes for rent. Tours and visits booked by reception. WiFi over site (free). Off site: Golf 500 m. Tennis and riding 1 km. Nearest beach 1.5 km. Rapallo centre 1.5 km.

Open: All year.

Directions

Site is located extremely close to the Rapallo exit from the A12 motorway. From this point, follow signs to Rapallo town and immediately at first complex roundabout look for signs to site. GPS: 44.35772, 9.20964

Charges guide

Per unit incl. 2 persons and electricity	€ 29.50 - € 32.00
extra person	€ 7.00 - € 8.00

No credit cards.

San Remo

Camping Villaggio dei Fiori

Via Tiro a Volo 3, I-18038 San Remo (Ligúria) T: 0184 660 635. E: info@villaggiodeifiori.it

alanrogers.com/IT64010

Open all year round, this open and spacious site is a member of the Sunêlia group and maintains very high standards. It is ideal for exploring the Italian and French Rivieras or for just relaxing by the enjoyable, filtered seawater pools or on the private beach. Unusually, all of the pitch areas at the site are totally paved, with some extremely large pitches for large units (ask reception to open another gate for entry). Electricity (3/6A) is available (at extra cost) to all 107 pitches, as are water and drainage, and there is an outside sink and cold water for every four pitches. There is ample shade from mature trees and shrubs, which are constantly watered and cared for in summer. The gold pitches and some wonderful tent pitches are along the seafront and have great views.

Facilities

Four clean and modern toilet blocks have British and Turkish style WCs and hot water throughout. Controllable showers. Baby rooms. Facilities for disabled campers. Laundry facilities. Motorcaravan services. Gas. Bar sells limited essential supplies. Large restaurant. Pizzeria and takeaway (all year; prepaid card system). Seawater pools (small extra charge in high season) and heated whirlpool spa (June-Sept). Tennis. Excellent play area. Fishing. Satellite TV. WiFi (charged). Bicycle hire. No dogs.

Open: All year.

Directions

From SS1 (Ventimiglia-Imperia), site is on right just before San Remo. There is a very sharp right turn into site if approaching from the west. From the A10 take San Remo exit. Site is well signed. GPS: 43.80117, 7.74867

Charges guide

Per unit incl. 4 persons and electricity	€ 29.00 - € 74.00

Some charges must be paid on arrival.

For latest campsite news, availability and prices visit

alanrogers.com

Villanova d'Albenga

Camping C'era una Volta

Localitá Fasceti, I-17038 Villanova d'Albenga (Ligúria) T: 018 258 0461. E: info@villaggioceraunavolta.it

alanrogers.com/IT64050

An attractive campsite, C'era una Volta is about 6 km. back from the sea, situated on a hillside with panoramic views. The 165 touring pitches are on terraces in different sections of the site. Varying in size, most have shade from the young trees which harbour crickets with their distinctive noise. Some of the upper pitches have good views. Cars are required to park in separate areas at busy times. There are electricity connections, with water and drainage close by. Charges are high in season but the site has an enjoyable atmosphere and is a good choice for families.

Facilities

The main toilet block is modern and above average with hot water throughout. Four additional smaller blocks are spread around the site. Maintenance can be variable. Shop. Bar and pizzeria (15/5-10/9). Restaurant. Takeaway (evenings only 1/4-30/9). Disco (July/Aug). Swimming pools (15/5-20/9). Small gym. Fitness track. Miniclub. Health centre with Finnish sauna. Hydromassage bath/shower. Turkish bath. Tennis. Adventure playground. Boules. Free WiFi over part of site. Satellite TV.

Open: 1 April - 30 September.

Directions

Leave A10 at Albenga, turn left and left again at roundabout for the SS453 for Villanova. At T-junction turn left (Garlenda), turn right in 200 m. and follow signs up a long winding narrow road beyond the Stadium. GPS: 44.04433, 8.1137

Charges guide

Per unit incl. up to 3 persons	€ 28.00 - € 49.00
extra person	€ 8.00 - € 12.00

No credit cards.

Iseo

Camping del Sole

Via per Rovato 26, I-25049 Iseo (Lombardy) T: 030 980 288. E: info@campingdelsole.it

alanrogers.com/IT62610

Camping del Sole lies on the southern edge of Lake Iseo, just outside the pretty lakeside town of Iseo. The site has 306 pitches, many taken up with chalets and mobile homes. The 180 touring pitches all have 3A electricity and some have fine views of the surrounding mountains and lake. Pitches are generally flat and of a reasonable size, but cars must park in the car park. The site has a wide range of excellent leisure amenities, including a large swimming pool. There is a bar and restaurant with a pizzeria near the pool and an entertainment area, and a second bar by the lake.

Facilities

Sanitary facilities are modern and well maintained, including special facilities for disabled visitors. Washing machines and dryers. Bar, restaurant, pizzeria, snack bar and supermarket (all open all season). Motorcaravan services. Bicycle hire. Swimming pool with children's pool (21/5-10/9). Canoe and pedal boat hire. Tennis. WiFi. Dog exercise area. Entertainment in high season. Off site: Golf 5 km. Riding 6 km.

Open: 16 April - 25 September.

Directions

Lake Iseo is 50 km. west of Lake Garda. From A4 (Milan-Venice) take Rovato exit and at roundabout go north on SPX1 following signs for Lago d'Iseo for 12 km. Site is well signed to left at large roundabout. From Brescia on SS510, turn north before Iseo towards Rovato and turn right to site. GPS: 45.65708, 10.03740

Charges guide

Per unit incl. 2 persons and electricity	€ 24.90 - € 33.40
extra person	€ 6.20 - € 10.80

Camping Cheques accepted.

Baveno

Camping Tranquilla

Via Cave-Oltrefiume 2, I-28831 Baveno (Piedmont) T: 032 392 3452. E: info@campingtranquilla.it

alanrogers.com/IT62470

Tranquilla is a quiet family run site on the western slopes above Baveno, close to Lake Maggiore. The site is in two terraced sections, both with 6A electricity connections. The 55 touring pitches vary in size with trees offering plenty of shade. There is a very pleasant swimming pool with an attractive paddling pool. Reception is housed in a modern building together with a small bar and snack bar from where the Piralla family will welcome you. Some English is spoken. The site is an ideal base from which to explore this very attractive area. Boat trips to three islands are available from the quay.

Facilities

The sanitary block offers the usual facilities including those for disabled visitors. All are kept very clean. British and Turkish style WCs. Laundry. Motorcaravan services. Pizza ordering service. Swimming pool (10/5-30/9). Play area. Free WiFi over site. Off site: Restaurant 300 m. Fishing and bus service 800 m. Sailing 1.5 km. Golf and bicycle hire 3 km. Riding 3 km. Shops nearby. Excursions and boat trips from Baveno.

Open: 15 March - 15 October.

Directions

Baveno is 90 km. northwest of Milan on the western shore of Lake Maggiore, and is on the SS33 road between Arona and Verbania. Site is well signed from SS33 in the northern part of the town. Follow site signs. Do not use sat nav for final approach. GPS: 45.91172, 8.49071

Charges guide

Per unit incl. 2 persons and electricity	€ 21.50 - € 33.50
extra person	€ 5.50 - € 8.00

FREE Alan Rogers Travel Card
Extra benefits and savings - see page 14

Dormelletto

Camping Village Lago Maggiore

Via Leonardo da Vinci 7, I-28040 Dormelletto (Piedmont) T: 032 249 7193. E: info@lagomag.com

alanrogers.com/IT62435

This lively and happy site can be found on the southwestern shores of Lake Maggiore, close to the pretty town of Arona. There are 340 pitches here, the majority of which are occupied by seasonal units leaving around 60 available for touring. Pitches are all equipped with 6A electrical connections and have reasonable shade. A number of mobile homes, apartments and bungalows are available for rent. The site has direct access to the lake and a sandy beach. On-site amenities include a well stocked shop and a bar/restaurant and there are many opportunities for sports and organised activities.

Facilities

Five toilet blocks in total, of which two are for touring units and a mix of Turkish and British style (a small charge is made for hot water and showers). Private family bathrooms for rent. Motorcaravan services. Bar, restaurant/pizzeria. Shop. Games room. Adventure and play areas. Outdoor swimming pools (May-Aug). Beach bar. Children's pool. Sports field. Bicycle hire. Entertainment and activity programme (high season). Direct access to lake. Mobile homes and chalets for rent. WiFi on part of site (charged). Off site: Supermarket across road from site. Arona 3 km. Watersports. Fishing.

Open: 1 April - 30 September.

Directions

Leave the A26 motorway at the Sesto Calende exit and join the northbound SS33 as far as Dormelletto. The campsite is clearly signed from the village. GPS: 45.73333, 8.57722

Charges guide

Per unit incl. 2 persons	
and electricity	€ 24.50 - € 44.00
extra person	€ 5.50 - € 9.50
child (2-6 yrs)	€ 3.00 - € 5.00
dog	€ 5.00 - € 6.50

Credit cards (accepted in high season).

Feriolo di Baveno

Camping Orchidea

Via Quarantadue Martiri 20, I-28831 Feriolo di Baveno (Piedmont) T: 032 328 257.

E: info@campingorchidea.it **alanrogers.com/IT62465**

Camping Orchidea is an immaculate family owned site on the western bank of Lake Maggiore, 35 km. south of the Swiss border and 8 km. from Stresa. This site has direct access to the lake and the banks of the River Stronetta, and there is a sandy beach. Orchidea has a good range of modern amenities, including a shop, bar and restaurant. Watersports are understandably popular here and pedaloes and kayaks can be rented. The 234 touring pitches are grassy and generally well shaded, all with 6A electrical connections. Some pitches face the lake (a supplement is charged in mid and peak season). There are apartments and mobile homes available for rent. Stresa, nearby, is an important town with 5,000 inhabitants and has a harbour with regular boat trips to the Borromean islands, and also a cable car to the summit of Monte Mottarone, passing the stunning Giardino Botanico Alpinia, world renowned mountain gardens. This site would suit families who prefer a simple and peaceful holiday.

Facilities

Two toilet blocks are kept clean and have hot and cold water throughout. Special facilities for children and provision for disabled visitors. Laundry facilities. Shop. Restaurant. Bar. Takeaway. Direct lake access. Pedalo and kayak hire. Fishing. Boat launching. Playground. Children's club. Mobile homes for hire. Bicycle hire. WiFi on part of site (charged). Off site: Walking and cycle trails. Tennis. Golf 3 km. Stresa 5 km. Riding 15 km. Excursions.

Open: 1 April - 19 October.

Directions

Take the Baveno/Stresa exit from the A26 (autostrada dei Trafori) and head north on the Via Sempione. In Feriolo follow signs to the campsite. GPS: 45.9334, 8.4812

Charges guide

Per unit incl. 2 persons	
and electricity	€ 21.00 - € 44.50
extra person	€ 5.20 - € 9.20
child (2-12 yrs)	€ 3.60 - € 6.10
dog	€ 2.60 - € 5.50

Entracque

Camping Valle Gesso

Str. Provinciale per Valdieri, 3, I-12010 Entracque (Piedmont) T: 0171 978 247.

E: info@campingvallegesso.com alanrogers.com/IT65030

Valle Gesso is situated in Entracque, a village near Cuneo in southern Piedmont. It borders on the Parco Naturale delle Alpi Marittime, the largest protected area in Piedmont and one of the biggest in Italy. There are 137 touring pitches, 70 of these have 3-6A Europlug, water and drainage. A dedicated area accommodates up to 70 tents. Rarely do we come across a site which appeals to such a wide variety of holiday styles. Valle Gesso offers a magnificent pool, a football and volleyball field, hiking and cycling for the more active, whilst maintaining a totally natural mountain retreat for those seeking a more restful break.

Facilities
There are three sanitary blocks, one new, one below the pool and one in a utility building. All are kept very clean and offer a mixture of British and Turkish style WCs. Motorcaravan services. Laundry. Basic shop and bar (July/Aug). Three section swimming pool and whirlpool (July/Aug). Large screen TV. Videogames. Billiard table. Playground and woods for exploring. Football. Volleyball. Communal barbecue. Bicycle hire. WiFi over site (free). Off site: Buses from gate. Fishing 1 km. Via Ferrata. Skiing 1.5 km. Alpi Marittime National Park.

Open: All year.

Directions
From Turin, take A6 and A33 to Cuneo, then at Borgo S.D. turn onto S26 for Entracque. From south, use SS20 and turn at Borgo S.D. Site signposted just after Valdieri.
GPS: 44.25076, 7.38994

Charges guide
Per unit incl. 2 persons	
and electricity	€ 22.00 - € 28.80
extra person	€ 6.00 - € 7.50
child (3-11 yrs acc to age)	€ 4.50 - € 6.50
dog	€ 3.30 - € 3.80

Feriolo di Baveno

Camping Conca d'Oro

Via 42 Martiri 26, I-28835 Feriolo di Baveno (Piedmont) T: 032 328 116. E: info@concadoro.it

alanrogers.com/IT02485

Conca d'Oro is a delightful site with spectacular views across Lake Maggiore to the distant mountains. The first impression is one of spaciousness and colour. There are 21 mobile homes for rent, the rest of the 210 grass plots provide good sized touring pitches. All have 6A electrical connections, some have shade and many have spectacular views especially at night. The land slopes gently down to a fine sandy beach. An attractive terraced restaurant serves a range of regional dishes and there is a pleasant bar and pizzeria plus a well stocked shop. The owners Maurizio and Alessandra are sure to give you a warm welcome. The site is close to the lakeside town of Baveno from where boat trips are available to the three small islands on this part of Lake Maggiore. Fishing and boat launching are possible from the beach at the site, with sailing and other watersports available. There are nature reserves nearby and drives out into the surrounding mountains provide opportunities for walkers, cyclists and climbers.

Facilities
Three toilet blocks provide all necessary facilities kept in immaculate condition, including controllable showers and open style washbasins; some toilets with washbasins. En-suite unit for disabled visitors. Laundry room. Motorcaravan services. Bar, restaurant, pizzeria and shop. Swimming, fishing and boat launching from beach. Bicycle hire. Dogs must be pre-booked and are not allowed 5/7-22/8. WiFi over site (charged). Off site: Shops, bars and restaurants nearby. Riding 700 m. Golf 1 km. Sailing 7 km.

Open: 26 March - 29 September.

Directions
Baveno is 90 km. northwest of Milan on the western shore of Lake Maggiore. Site is off the SS33 road between Baveno and Fondotoce di Verbania, 1 km. south of the junction with the SS34 and is well signed. GPS: 45.93611, 8.48583

Charges guide
Per unit incl. 2 persons	
and electricity	€ 25.00 - € 43.50
extra person	€ 5.20 - € 8.84
child (6-11 yrs)	€ 3.64 - € 6.76
dog	€ 3.64 - € 5.72

The campsite is located in a quiet and green area Toce called on 800mt from the picturesque village of Feriolo and 7km to Verbania, an area of 36.000m2, directly on Lake Maggiore lake with a sandy beach, very appreciated by our "little" guests.

The friendly reception run by Maurizio and Alessandra are at your service in a clean and well organized campsite where you can completely relax amidst nature.

To our guests disposal are the following facilities; homes, mini supermarket, a bar, a cozy restaurant where you can eat delicious specialties of the region or a tasty pizza! Power and sailboat rental.

The months of July and August Animation programm.

CONCA D'ORO
C A M P I N G ✳✳✳

Via 42 Martiri, 26 - 28835 Feriolo di Baveno - ITALY TEL
+39.0323 28116 - FAX +39.0323 28538
www.concadoro.it

FREE Alan Rogers Travel Card
Extra benefits and savings - see page 14

Fondotoce di Verbania
Camping Continental Lido

Via 42 Martiri 156, I-28924 Fondotoce di Verbania (Piedmont) T: 032 349 6300.
E: info@campingcontinental.com alanrogers.com/IT62490

Continental Lido is a large, bustling site situated on the shore of the charming little Lake Mergozzo, about one kilometre from the better known Lake Maggiore. The 343 average size touring pitches are back to back in rows on grass and although a little close together, the rest of the site has a more open feel. All have 6A electricity, TV connections, water, drainage and there is some shade. There are also 287 mobile homes and 14 apartments available to rent. There is an impressive pool complex and a small sandy beach slopes gently into the lake where swimming and watersports can also be enjoyed (no powered craft may be used). A bustling entertainment programme is provided, centred around a very large amphitheatre. Pine-clad mountains and a pretty village directly opposite the beach provide a pleasing, scenic background. An unusual feature here is the nine-hole golf course. There is a busy programme of activities from May to September. Under the same ownership as Isolino Camping Village, this site is managed by the son, Gian Paolo, who speaks good English.

Facilities
Five high standard toilet blocks have free hot water. Facilities for disabled visitors. Washing machines and dryers. Mini-fridges. Well stocked shop and bar/restaurant with terrace and takeaway. Swimming pool complex (24/4-13/9) with slides, rapids and waves, plus free sun loungers and parasols. Snack bars by pool and lake. Large amphitheatre. TV. Tennis. Golf course (9 holes). Playground. Fishing. Windsurfing, pedaloes, canoes, kayaks. Games room. Bicycle hire. Entertainment and activities (mid June-mid Sept). Bus on request to Verbania. Internet access and WiFi. Off site: Riding 1 km. Sailing 5 km. 18-hole golf 12 km. Excursions.

Open: 27 March - 21 September.

Directions
Verbania is 100 km. northwest of Milan, on the western shore of Lake Maggiore. Site is off the SS34 road between Fondotoce and Gravellona, 200 m. west of junction with SS33.
GPS: 45.94960, 8.48058

Charges guide
Per unit incl. 2 or 3 persons	
and electricity	€ 22.65 - € 54.75
extra person	€ 5.95 - € 9.35
child (6-11 yrs)	€ 4.00 - € 7.70

Fondotoce di Verbania
Camping Village Isolino

Via per Feriolo 25, I-28924 Fondotoce di Verbania (Piedmont) T: 032 349 6080. E: info@isolino.com
alanrogers.com/IT62460

Lake Maggiore is one of the most attractive Italian lakes and Isolino is an impressive site and one of the largest in the region. Most of the 442 touring pitches have shade from a variety of trees. They vary in size, all have 6A electrical connections, 216 with water, drainage and satellite TV, some with lake views. The bar and restaurant terraces overlook the very large, lagoon-style swimming pool with its island sun deck area, water games and a canyon river, and stunning views across the lake to the fir-clad mountains beyond. Often the social life of the campsite is centred around the large bar/terrace which has a small stage inside, sometimes used for musical entertainment. A huge and impressive amphitheatre is where an extensive programme of activities and entertainment takes place throughout the season. The large poolside terrace outside the bar provides an ideal casual eating area for pizzas and ice cream. In the restaurant on the floor above you can enjoy an excellent menu and the magnificent views across the lake. The site is well situated for visiting the many attractions of the region which include the famous gardens on the Borromeo islands in the lake and at the Villa Taranto, Verbania. The site is owned by the friendly Manoni family who also own Camping Continental Lido at nearby Lake Mergozzo.

Facilities
Six well built toilet blocks have hot water for showers and washbasins but cold for dishwashing and laundry. Good baby room. Laundry facilities. Motorcaravan services. Supermarket, bar and takeaway (all season). Boutique. Gelateria. Swimming pool (24/4-13/9). Entertainment (2/4-12/4 and 24/4-13-9). Amphitheatre. Fishing. Watersports. Boat launching. Bicycle hire and guided mountain bike tours. Long beach. WiFi on part of site (charged). Good English is spoken. Bookings for dogs must be made in high season. Off site: Golf 2 km. Sailing 5 km. Riding 12 km. Swiss mountains and resort of Locarno.

Open: 27 March - 21 September.

Directions
Verbania is 100 km. northwest of Milan on the western shore of Lake Maggiore. From the A26 motorway, leave at exit for Stresa/Baveno, turn left towards Fondotoce. Site is well signed off the SS33 north of Baveno and 300 m. south of the junction with the SS34 at Fondotoce.
GPS: 45.93835, 8.50008

Charges guide
Per unit incl. 3 persons	
and electricity	€ 26.95 - € 54.75
extra person	€ 5.95 - € 9.10
child (6-11 yrs)	€ 4.00 - € 7.70
dog	€ 4.00 - € 9.35

For latest campsite news, availability and prices visit
alanrogers.com

Fondotoce di Verbania
Camping la Quiete

Via Turati 72, I-28040 Fondotoce di Verbania (Piedmont) T: **032 349 6013**. E: **info@campinglaquiete.it**

alanrogers.com/IT62495

La Quiete is a small site, attractively located on the shore of Lake Mergozzo, a small lake to the west of the much larger Lake Maggiore. There are 180 pitches here, mostly well shaded and with 6A electrical connections, many of which have fine views across the lake. A number of mobile homes are available for rent. On-site amenities include a shop and bar/restaurant, as well as a sports field and volleyball court. This is excellent mountain biking and walking country and the site owners will be pleased to recommend possible routes, although little English is spoken. The site does appear to be predominantly used by Italian families.

Facilities
Three small, clean and modern sanitary facilities are well placed along the length of the site. Washing machines. Bar/restaurant. Shop. Sports field. Games room. Play area. Direct access to Lake Mergozzo. WiFi on part of site (charged). Off site: Verbania. Golf and riding 1 km. Bicycle hire 5 km. Lake Maggiore. Watersports. Fishing. Motorboats are not allowed on the lake. Walking and cycle routes.

Open: Easter - 20 September.

Directions
Leave the A26 motorway at the Casale exit and join the eastbound S34 as far as Fondotoce. Head north here on SP54 and the campsite is clearly signed. GPS: 45.9535, 8.47745

Charges guide
Per unit incl. 2 persons

and electricity	€ 17.00 - € 42.00
extra person	€ 5.50 - € 9.50
child (0-12 yrs)	free - € 6.00
dog	€ 4.00 - € 6.00

Orta San Giulio
Camping Orta

Via Domodossola 28, I-28016 Orta San Giulio (Piedmont) T: **032 290 267**. E: **info@campingorta.it**

alanrogers.com/IT62420

Lake Orta is a delightful, less visited small lake just west of Lake Maggiore. The site is on a considerable slope, and most of the 90 touring pitches (all with 6A electricity) are on the top grass terrace with spectacular views across the lake to the mountains beyond. There are some superb lakeside pitches across the main road (linked by a pedestrian underpass) although there is some traffic noise here. Amenities include a large games and entertainment room and a traditional Italian bar and restaurant serving good value family meals. Some English is spoken by the Guarnori family, who take pride in maintaining their uncomplicated site to a high standard. Book ahead to enjoy the lakeside pitches. If you are anxious about towing a large caravan to the top terraces, the owner will help out with his tractor!

Facilities
Four modern sanitary blocks are clean and well maintained providing mainly British style toilets, coin operated showers and an excellent unit for disabled visitors. Laundry facilities. Motorcaravan services. Good quality shop, bar and restaurant with basic menu serving good value Italian family meals (also takeaway, all season). Playground. Large games/TV room. WiFi in reception/bar area (charged). Fishing. Bicycle hire. Boat launching. Lake swimming and watersports. Off site: Riding and sailing 4 km. Golf 10 km.

Open: 1 March - 31 December.

Directions
Lake Orta is 85 km. northwest of Milan, just west of Lake Maggiore. Site is on the SR229 between Borgomanero and Omega, 600 m. north of the turn to Orta San Giulio. Parking area for arrivals is on lake side of the road, with reception and main entrance on the opposite side. GPS: 45.80188, 8.42047

Charges guide
Per unit incl. 2 persons

and electricity	€ 23.50 - € 40.10
extra person	€ 5.75 - € 8.80
child (3-11 yrs)	€ 4.25 - € 5.75
dog	€ 3.70 - € 5.75
Low season discounts.	

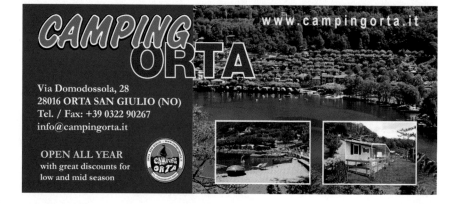

For latest campsite news, availability and prices visit
alanrogers.com

Pettenasco

Camping Royal

Via Pratolungo, 32, I-28028 Pettenasco (Piedmont) T: 0323 888 945. E: info@campingroyal.com

alanrogers.com/IT62419

It would be difficult to find a more beautiful lake than Orta, surrounded by wooded hills and mountains and fringed with ancient towns and villages. Camping Royal, family owned and run, sits on a hillside overlooking the lake. There are 60 pitches, 20 for touring, set on level terraces, each with 5A Europlug and a water point nearby. Although professionally managed, this site has maintained the typical relaxed informality for which Italy is famous. Popular with campers from all over Europe, many return year after year. Nothing seems to be too much trouble to ensure a memorable stay. A new pool was installed in 2014, which will make this site even better for family holidays, but there may be noise in high season. At other times, those seeking a relaxing holiday will enjoy sitting out overlooking the lake. The shop and bar are well stocked, and a village restaurant is 100 m. away. Bigger shopping will need a trip to Omegna. In season, the site runs a shuttle service (€2 return) to Orta San Giulio, whose history goes back to the 7th Century. The monastery and basilica on the Isola San Giulio should not be missed. Rates are very attractive, especially off peak.

Facilities

Refurbished toilet block has hot showers (20c tokens) and a mixture of British and Turkish style toilets. New wet room for disabled campers by reception. Washing machine and dryer. Laundry and dishwashing sinks. Fridges. Shop with takeaway pizzas. Bar. New swimming pool. Playground. Football field. Room with games, library, cooking hobs and TV. Children's activities (daily in July/August) and some entertainment for adults. Shuttle bus to San Giulio in season (€2 return). Bicycle, scooter and car hire arranged. Internet cabin. WiFi (charged). Off site: Restaurant 100 m. Supermarkets in Omegna. Ancient villages and towns all around the lakeshore. Medieval town of Orta and the Isola San Giulio. Ferry boats and boat cruises. Watercraft hire. Lake swimming. Fishing 3 km. Riding 6 km. Golf 15 km.

Open: 1 March - 30 November.

Directions

From A26 Autostrada, take SP229 and follow signs to Lake Orta. This road continues along eastern shore of lake to Pettenasco. Opposite a church on the left, turn right signed Camping Royal. Some sat navs miss this turn. Do not go past Pettenasco, as back road to site is extremely narrow with sharp bends. From the north, drive into village and turn left opposite church. Road up to site is steep and needs care (unsuitable for units over 7 m).
GPS: 45.82331, 8.41398

Charges guide

Per unit incl. 2 persons	
and electricity	€ 24.00 - € 34.50
extra person	€ 6.00 - € 8.50
child (2-12 yrs)	€ 4.50 - € 6.00
dog	€ 4.00 - € 5.00

BETWEEN LANDSCAPE AND NATURE

Located just a few miles from Orta San Giulio, an area of 15,000 m2 terraced, in a quiet and panoramic zone. It has 60 spacious pitches, surrounded by hedges and green areas. Open from March to November, suitable for lovers of the lake (3 km) and mountain (Mottarone 15 km), ideal for families it is also a meeting point for young people. It offers services such as a grocery shop, bar, swimming pool, soccer field, playground, meeting room with summer entertainment, internet point, library, barbecue area and bicycle hire. Restaurant and pizzeria are next door. Free bus service with Alan Rogers guide to Orta San Giulio and beaches.

Solcio di Lesa

Camping Solcio

Via al Campeggio, I-28040 Solcio di Lesa (Piedmont) T: 032 274 97. E: info@campingsolcio.com

alanrogers.com/IT62440

Camping Solcio is a family run site on the lakeside and has lovely views over the lakes and the surrounding green hills. The 105 neat touring pitches are 60-90 sq.m. with 6A electricity and mostly shaded by trees. A very pleasant restaurant and a bar back onto a large building alongside the site, and there are some views of the lake from the terraces. All manner of watersports are available here and the beach is of coarse sand. The lake is fine for safe swimming. An ambitious entertainment programme is arranged for children in high season, and there is adventure sport for the over tens.

Facilities

One main central toilet block is smart and clean. Toilets here are British style. An older block nearer reception has mixed Turkish and British style toilets. Facilities for disabled visitors. Baby room. Washing machine and dryer. Restaurant and bar with terrace. Basic shop. Full entertainment programme in season. Play areas. Baby club. Bicycle hire. Slipway for boat launching. WiFi on part of site (charged). Torches useful. Off site: Public transport 50 m. Town facilities 1 km. ATM 2 km. Riding 5 km. Golf 10 km.

Open: 9 March - 20 October.

Directions

Site is on the west side of Lake Maggiore. From A4 (Milan-Torino) take the A8 to Castelletto Sticino. Then north on SS33 towards Stresa and look for site sign in town of Lesa. Take the access road towards the lake and to the site. GPS: 45.81586, 8.54962

Charges guide

Per unit incl. 2 persons	
and electricity	€ 19.90 - € 54.90
extra person	€ 5.00 - € 8.90
child (3-13 yrs)	€ 3.80 - € 7.20
dog	€ 3.80 - € 8.70

Low season discounts.

Peschici

Centro Turistico San Nicola

Localitá San Nicola, I-71010 Peschici (Puglia) T: 088 496 4024. E: sannicola@sannicola.it

alanrogers.com/IT68450

This large site occupies a hillside position, sloping down to a cove with a 500 metre beach of fine sand – a special feature is an attractive grotto at the eastern end. Hard access roads lead to 800 terraced, sand/grass pitches (5A electricity), some with real shade. Some pitches are on the beach fringes (no extra charge) and there is a separate area for campers with animals. The infrastructure was beginning to look a little tired when we visited. Cars have to be parked away from the pitches in high season.

Facilities
Four toilet blocks of variable standards with British and Turkish style toilets, some with hot water in the washbasins and hot showers. One in the beach area had queues for showers when we visited (late June). Laundry facilities. Supermarket. Beach bar and snacks. Large bar/restaurant with terraces and pizzeria. Games room. Multisports area. Tennis. Watersports. Playground. Organised activities and entertainment for children (July/Aug). ATM. Dogs are not accepted in high season. Off site: Peschici town 1 km. Riding 6 km. Coach and boat excursions. Gargano National Park.

Open: 1 April - 15 October.

Directions
Leave autostrada A14 at exit for Poggio Imperiale, and SS693 towards Peschici and Vieste. It is a winding coast road to Peschici. Follow signs to San Nicola and follow campsite signs. Take care as there are two campsites very close to each other with virtually the same name. You want the second on the approach. The site is 1.5 hours drive from the motorway. GPS: 41.94291, 16.03493

Charges guide
Per unit incl. 2 persons and 6A electricity	€ 23.80 - € 49.40
extra person	€ 6.80 - € 13.40

Ugento

Camping Riva di Ugento

Litoranea Gallipoli, Santa Maria di Leuca, I-73059 Ugento (Puglia) T: 083 393 3600. E: info@rivadiugento.it

alanrogers.com/IT68650

There are some campsites where you can be comfortable, have all the amenities at hand and still feel you are connecting with nature. Under the pine and eucalyptus trees of the Bay of Taranto foreshore is Camping Riva di Ugento. Its 850 pitches are nestled in and around the sand dunes and the foreshore area. They have space and trees around them and the sizes differ as the environment dictates the shape of most. The sea is only a short walk from most pitches and some are at the water's edge. The site buildings resemble huge wooden umbrellas and are in sympathy with the environment.

Facilities
Twenty toilet blocks all with WCs, showers and washbasins. New bathrooms. Bar. Restaurant and takeaway. Swimming and paddling pools (10/6-15/9). Tennis. Bicycle hire. Watersports incl. windsurfing school. Cinema. TV in bar. WiFi. Entertainment for children. Dogs are not accepted. A new play area for children has been added. Beach volleyball. WiFi over site (charged). Off site: Fishing. Riding 500 m. Boat launching 4 km.

Open: 15 May - 12 October.

Directions
From Bari take the Brindisi road to Lecce, then SS101 to Gallipoli, then the SR274 towards Santa Maria di Leuca. Continue to Felline exit, and continue towards Torre San Giovanni, following the signs for Riva di Ugento. Site is well signed, turn right at traffic lights on SS19. GPS: 39.87475, 18.141117

Charges guide
Per unit incl. 2 persons, 1 child and electricity	€ 21.00 - € 47.00
extra person (over 2 yrs)	€ 5.00 - € 12.00

Camping Cheques accepted.

Vieste

Punta Lunga Camping Village

CP339, Localitá Defensola, I-71019 Vieste (Puglia) T: 088 470 6031. E: puntalunga@puntalunga.com

alanrogers.com/IT68480

Punta Lunga is located in the spectacularly beautiful Gargano region, a huge National Park, and nestles in an attractive bay. The 150 medium sized, terraced, sandy pitches (3.5-6A) are flat, mostly set on steep slopes, and some have shade. Camping along the shore is less formal and in some cases less shaded, but some pitches have spectacular views. There is a choice of restaurants. The upper one is finer dining, while the lower one is an informal beach restaurant. The site is well suited for energetic windsurfer types, but not for infirm or disabled campers. Dogs are not accepted.

Facilities
Two toilet blocks, some distance from pitches, have a mixture of unisex showers and dedicated toilets, mostly Turkish. The facilities are clean and fresh. Access difficult for infirm and disabled campers. Laundry facilities. Hairdresser. Small shop. Gas. Excellent restaurant with pleasant views. Beach bar with snacks. Gym (no instructor). Children's clubs (high season). Small play area. Bicycle hire. Windsurfing school. WiFi (€ 1/10 minutes).

Open: 15 May - 25 September.

Directions
From north take A14 exit for Poggio Imperiale, then to Vico Gargano and Vieste. From south take A14 exit Foggia, then towards Manfredonia, Mattinata and Vieste. GPS: 41.89798, 16.15047

Charges guide
Per unit incl. 2 persons and electricity	€ 20.00 - € 49.00
extra person	€ 5.00 - € 14.50
child (3-12 yrs)	€ 3.00 - € 11.00

Aglientu

Camping Baia Blu la Tortuga

Pineta di Vignola Mare, I-07020 Aglientu (Sardinia) T: 079 602 200.

E: info@campinglatortuga.com alanrogers.com/IT69550

LeadingCampings

Tortuga is named after the giant turtle-like rock off the site's beautiful beach, and is a large, professionally run campsite. The 450 sizeable touring pitches (all with 3/10A electricity) are on grass and coarse-grained sand, and shaded by tall pines with banks of colourful oleanders and wide boulevards providing easy access. This is a busy, bustling site with plenty to do, with its attractive bars and restaurants by the beach, which shelves rather steeply. The excellent play areas are cleverly placed to allow parents a break and the entertainment is first class. We were impressed by this quality family site. A member of Leading Campings group.

Facilities

Four excellent sanitary blocks (most with solar panels for hot water) with free hot showers, WCs, bidets and washbasins. Facilities for disabled campers. Quality private shower/washbasin cabins for rent. Washing machines and dryers. Motorcaravan services. Gas. Supermarket, beachside restaurant and bars, self-service restaurant, snack bar and takeaway. Gym. Doctor's surgery. Playground. Tennis. Games/TV rooms. Windsurfing and diving schools. WiFi area (charged).

Open: 28 March - 14 October.

Directions

Site is on the north coast road (SP 90) between Costa Paradiso and Santa Teresa di Gallura (18 km) at Pineta di Vignola Mare and is well signed around the 47 km. marker. GPS: 41.12436, 9.067594

Charges guide

Per unit incl. 2 persons,	
water and electricity	€ 17.20 - € 52.80
extra person	€ 5.88 - € 14.20
child (3-9 yrs)	€ 3.80 - € 12.20
dog	€ 3.50 - € 8.00

Alghero

Camping Mariposa

Via Lido 22, I-07041 Alghero (Sardinia) T: 079 950 360. E: info@lamariposa.it

alanrogers.com/IT69960

Mariposa is a sprawling beachside site with its own access to a fine sand beach, and it has a comfortable feel. The pitches are of various sizes (50-80 sq.m); those on uneven ground are best suited for tents, while those on gravel are for caravans and motorcaravans (some alongside the sea). Some pitches have shade but all have 6A electrical connections. Cars must be parked away from the pitches. There is an entertainment programme in high season. The amenities are by the site entrance and include a pizzeria, bar and restaurant with TV. The small shop is also here.

Facilities

The brightly coloured, open plan sanitary facilities are clean, with cold water to washbasins. Hot showers on payment (€ 0.50 token). Washing machines and dryer. Motorcaravan services. Shop. Restaurant and bar. Bicycle hire. Kite surfing. Diving. Windsurfing. Stand-up paddling. Sailing. Surfing. Paragliding. (Courses available at extra charge). Communal barbecue. Dogs are not accepted in August. Off site: Site-owned restaurant in town (The Kings) offers 10% discount to campers. Neptune Caves.

Open: 1 April - 15 October.

Directions

Alghero is on the northwest coast, 35 km. southwest of Sassari. Mariposa is at the north end of the town. Follow the signs on the beach road, but watch for one-way systems which you have to navigate. GPS: 40.57885, 8.31253

Charges guide

Per unit incl. 2 persons	
and electricity	€ 27.00 - € 44.00
extra person	€ 10.00 - € 13.00
child (3-12 yrs)	€ 5.00 - € 9.00

Bari Sardo

Camping l'Ultima Spiaggia

Localitá Planargia, I-08042 Bari Sardo (Sardinia) T: 078 229 363. E: info@campingultimaspiaggia.it

alanrogers.com/IT69720

L'Ultima Spiaggia (the ultimate beach) is an apt name as the beach really is extremely pleasant, although coarse grained. There are four great paddling and swimming pools, and the facilities have bright, colourful décor. The 252 pitches all have 3/6A electricity, are terraced on sand and some enjoy limited sea views. The ambitious entertainment programme can be enjoyed from the terrace of the restaurant, which offers a variety of good food, including local seafood specialities.

Facilities

Two modernised toilet units include facilities for babies and disabled campers, but are some way from the lower pitches. Washing machines and dryers. Motorcaravan services. Small supermarket. Restaurant and snack bar. Play areas. Windsurfing, diving and sailing. Aerobics. Riding. Tennis. Minigolf. Canoeing. Bicycle hire. Miniclub. Multisports area. Entertainment. WiFi (charged). Excursions. Torches useful. Off site: Restaurants, bars and shops. Fishing. Kite surfing. Free-climbing.

Open: 20 April - 30 September.

Directions

Site is on east coast of Sardinia, well signed from the main coast road, the SS125 in the village of Bari Sardo. GPS: 39.819003, 9.670484

Charges guide

Per unit incl. 2 persons	
and electricity	€ 23.50 - € 51.00
extra person	€ 7.00 - € 15.50
child (1-12 yrs acc. to age)	€ 4.50 - € 8.50
dog	€ 4.50 - € 6.50

FREE Alan Rogers Travel Card

Extra benefits and savings - see page 14

Muravera

Tiliguerta Camping Village

SP 97 km. 6 - Localitá Capo Ferrato, I-09043 Muravera (Sardinia) T: 070 991 437. E: info@tiliguerta.com

alanrogers.com/IT69750

This family site situated at Capo Ferrato changed its owners, name and direction in 2011, and the new owners have made many improvements, all of them in sympathy with the environment. The 186 reasonably sized pitches are on sand and have 3A electricity. Some have shade and views of the superb, fine beach and sea beyond. There are ten permanent pitches used by Italian units. The traditional site buildings are centrally located and contain a good quality restaurant using only fresh ingredients. This has a charming ambience with its high arched ceilings. Shaded terraces allow comfortable viewing of the ambitious entertainment programme. Cars are parked away from pitches.

Facilities

Three sanitary blocks. One is newly renovated with private bathrooms, and facilities for children and disabled visitors. The two older blocks have mixed Turkish/British style toilets. Washing machine. Motorcaravan services (extra charge). Shop, restaurant and snack bar/takeaway (10/5-30/9). Live music concerts. Dog beach. Miniclub and entertainment in high season. Tennis. Water aerobics. Sailing. Sub-aqua diving. Windsurfing school. Riding. Torches essential. Bicycle hire. WiFi over site (charged).

Open: 20 April - 12 October.

Directions

Site is in southeast corner of Sardinia in the north of the Costa Rei. From coast road SS125 or the SP97 at km. 6, take the turn to Villaggio Capo Ferrato. Site is well signed from here. GPS: 39.2923, 9.5987

Charges guide

Per unit incl. 2 persons and electricity	€ 22.50 - € 50.50
extra person	€ 5.00 - € 14.00
child (1-9 yrs acc. to age)	€ 2.00 - € 10.00
dog	€ 3.00 - € 6.00

Torre Grande

Camping Village Spinnaker

Strada Provinciale, Oristano, I-09170 Torre Grande (Sardinia) T: 078 322 074.

E: info@spinnakervacanze.com alanrogers.com/IT69900

Set on the undulating foreshore under tall pines, with beach frontage to the camping area, Spinnaker Village is a smart, purpose built, modern beach site. The 143 pitches are sandy, with 43 suitable for caravans and motorcaravans, the remainder for tents. All pitches have 6A electricity and there are plenty of water taps. Tent pitches are large and clearly marked, each with a tree to provide shade. Cars must be parked in a car park outside the site. There are many neat, white buildings on site – the restaurant, a café and the swimming pool are set around a large square, where activities for families take place. Transponders are provided for showers and for use around the site in lieu of cash.

Facilities

Toilet blocks are modern and very clean with British style toilets and facilities for disabled campers. Showers are transponder operated (€ 0.50 per shower). Washing machine. Motorcaravan services. Small shop. Restaurant and small snack bar. Swimming pool and pool bar. Play area. Bicycle hire. Miniclub and entertainment in high season. Excursions. Torches essential. WiFi over site. Off site: Riding 2 km. Golf 23 km.

Open: 1 April - 30 September.

Directions

Take SS131 Cagliari-Oristano road then minor road to Torre Grande. Just before Torre Grande village by large water tower take angled left turn back on yourself to site (signed). GPS: 39.903, 8.5301

Charges guide

Per unit incl. 2 persons and electricity	€ 19.00 - € 45.00
extra person	€ 8.00 - € 18.00

Camping Cheques accepted.

Finale di Pollina

Camping Rais Gerbi

Ctra Rais Gerbi, SS113 km. 172.9, I-90010 Finale di Pollina (Sicily) T: 092 142 6570. E: camping@raisgerbi.it

alanrogers.com/IT69350

Rais Gerbi provides very good quality camping with excellent facilities on the beautiful Tyrrhenian coast not far from Cefalu. This attractive terraced campsite is shaded by well established trees and the 189 good sized touring pitches (6A electricity) vary from informal areas under the trees near the sea, to gravel terraces and hardstandings. Most have stunning views, many with their own sinks and with some artificial shade to supplement the trees. From the mobile homes to the unusual white igloos, everything here is being established to a high quality. The large pool with its entertainment area and the restaurant, like so much of the site, overlook the beautiful rocky coastline and aquamarine sea.

Facilities

Excellent new sanitary blocks with British style toilets, free hot showers in generous cubicles. Small shop, bar, restaurant and takeaway (all 1/4-31/10). Communal barbecue. Entertainment area and pool near the sea. Tennis. WiFi over site (charged). Quality accommodation and tents for rent. Rocky beach at site. Dogs are not accepted in August. Off site: Small village of Finale 500 m. Riding 4 km. Larger historic town of Cefalu 12 km.

Open: All year.

Directions

Site is on SS113 running along northeast coast of the island, km. 172.9 just west of village of Finale (the turn into site is at end of the bridge on the edge of the village). It is 12 km. east of Cefalu and 11 km. north of Pollina. GPS: 38.02278, 14.15389

Charges guide

Per unit incl. 2 persons and electricity	€ 20.00 - € 46.00
extra person (over 3 yrs)	€ 5.00 - € 10.00

Oliveri

Camping Villaggio Marinello

Marinello, I-98060 Oliveri (Sicily) T: 094 131 3000. E: marinello@camping.it

alanrogers.com/IT69300

Camping Marinello is located alongside the sea with direct access to a lovely uncrowded sandy beach with an informal marina and natural pool areas. The 220 gravel touring pitches here are shaded by tall trees and hedges. We enjoyed a delicious traditional meal in the excellent terraced restaurant with its lovely sea views. Tours are arranged to major sightseeing destinations such as Mount Etna, Taormina and the nearby Aeolian Islands. The Greco family have been here for over 30 years and work hard to ensure that their guests enjoy a pleasant stay. There is some noise from the coastal rail line which runs along the length of the site.

Facilities

Two adequate sanitary blocks with free hot showers. Washing machines. Bazaar, market and supermarket. Bar with sea views. Restaurant and terraced eating area also with views. Electronic games. Piano bar in high season. Tennis. Basketball. Volleyball. Diving centre and windsurf school. Dogs are not accepted in July/Aug. Free WiFi on part of site. Off site: Seaside resort-style town of Oliveri.

Open: All year.

Directions

From A20 motorway take Falcone exit and follow signs to Oliveri. At the town turn north towards beach (site sign), then turn west along beach and continue 1 km. to site. Make a right turn immediately before a small narrow bridge (2.2 m. high and 2.5 m. wide). GPS: 38.13246, 15.05452

Charges guide

Per unit incl. 2 persons	
and electricity	€ 27.00 - € 46.00
extra person	€ 5.00 - € 10.00

San Croce Camerina

Camping Scarabeo

Punta Bracecetto, Santa, I-97017 San Croce Camerina (Sicily) T: 093 291 8096. E: info@scarabeocamping.it

alanrogers.com/IT69190

Camping Scarabeo is a beautiful site located in Punta Braccetto, a little fishing port in Sicily's southeast corner. It is a perfect location with exceptional facilities to match. Split into two separate sites (just 50 m. apart) with a total of 80 pitches, it is being constantly improved with care by Angela di Modica. All pitches are well shaded, some naturally and others with an artificial cane roof and have 3/6A electricity. Scarabeo lies adjacent to a sandy beach and the little village is close by. The site layout resembles a Sicilian farm courtyard and is divided into four principal areas.

Facilities

Exceptional sanitary blocks provide personal WC compartments (personal key access). Ample hot showers (free low season). Facilities for disabled visitors. Washing machine. Excellent motorcaravan service point. Takeaway. Herb garden for campers. Direct access to beach. Playground. Entertainment programme in high season. Dog washing area. Excursions arranged all year. WiFi over site (charged). Mobile homes for rent. No gas or electric barbecues. Off site: Restaurant/café 500 m. Riding 3 km..

Open: All year.

Directions

Site is 20 km. southwest of Ragusa. From Catania, take S194 towards Ragusa and, at Comiso, follow signs to San Croce Camerina, then Punta Braccetto, from where site is well signed. Use second entrance for reception. GPS: 36.81645, 14.46964

Charges guide

Per unit incl. 2 persons	
and electricity	€ 14.00 - € 36.50
child (3-6 yrs)	€ 2.00 - € 7.50

Excellent long term discounts in low season.

San Vito Lo Capo

El Bahira Camping Village

Ctra da Makari-Localitá Salinella, I-91010 San Vito Lo Capo (Sicily) T: 092 397 2577. E: info@elbahira.it

alanrogers.com/IT69140

El Bahira is a popular site in quite a remote area overlooking the Gulf of Makari toward Monte Cofano. The views are outstanding and the location is good as it is near the sea, nature reserves and ancient cities such as Segtesta and Selinunte with their awe inspiring antiquities. Partners Maurizio, Maceri, Sugameli and Michele, who speak good English, have chosen this area to develop a campsite of a high standard. The 200 fairly small pitches are on sloping gravel (chocks required), most are shady and all have electricity. There are also numerous statics which unfortunately rather spoil the look of the site.

Facilities

Three well placed sanitary blocks, showers are by token (€ 4 for 8 showers), these are unisex, in tiny cabins. Motorcaravan services. Supermarket. Restaurant and pizzeria. Swimming pool, children's pool and beach bar. Two entertainment areas. Tennis. Football/volleyball pitch. Sub-aqua facilities. Boat launching at rocky beach on site. Free WiFi on part of site. Off site: Popular resort village of San Vito Lo Capo 3 km. Riding and bicycle hire 4 km.

Open: 1 April - 4 October.

Directions

From the east follow the A19 motorway and take Castellammare del Golfo exit then follow the S187 towards Trapani. After 16 km. turn right and follow signs to San Vito Lo Capo. Site is well signed off road approaching town. GPS: 38.150707, 12.73191

Charges guide

Per unit incl. 2 persons	
and electricity	€ 24.90 - € 37.60
child (0-3 yrs)	€ 3.00

Calceranica al Lago

Camping Punta Lago

Via Lungo Lago 70, I-38050 Calceranica al Lago (Trentino - Alto Adige) T: 046 172 3229.

E: info@campingpuntalago.com alanrogers.com/IT62260

Camping Punta Lago is in a beautiful setting on Lago di Caldonazzo. This attractive family run campsite, with easy lake access across a small road, has 140 level, shaded pitches on grass. Of a good size, all have 3/6A electricity and 50 are serviced with water and drainage. The campsite first opened 45 years ago and brothers Gino and Mauro continue the friendly family tradition of ensuring you enjoy your holiday. As President of the Consortia Trentino Outdoors, Gino knows all about the range of activities available locally including fishing, lake swimming, windsurfing, sailing and canoeing.

Facilities

One central sanitary block has superb facilities with hot water throughout. Well designed bathroom and washbasin area. Excellent facilities for babies and disabled visitors. Private units for rent, some with massage baths. Washing machines and dryer. Freezer. Shop. Bar/snack bar. Fishing (with permit). Modern comprehensive play area. Entertainment programme (July/Aug). WiFi over site (charged). Cinema. TV. Off site: Bicycle hire, town and ATM 1 km. Watersports. Riding 3 km. Golf 20 km. Train 1 km. to Venice and other cities.

Open: 1 May - 15 September.

Directions

From A22 Bolzano-Trento autostrada take SS47 (Padova). After 15 km. turn for Lago di Caldonazzo and Calceranica al Lago. Approaching from west by the railway, continue along Via Donegani, turn left at Esso station into Via al Lago and right at lakeside into Via Lungo Lago. Site is on right. GPS: 46.00230, 11.25450

Charges guide

Per unit incl. 2 persons and electricity	€ 18.00 - € 40.00
extra person	€ 6.00 - € 10.00

Caldonazzo

Camping Mario Village

Via Lungolago, 4, I-38052 Caldonazzo (Trentino - Alto Adige) T: 046 172 3341.

E: direzione@campingmario.com alanrogers.com/IT62255

Camping Mario is a family site, across a small road from Lake Caldonazzo, one of the most attractive small Italian lakes where swimming, fishing and other water-based activities can be enjoyed. The 160 grassy touring pitches (80-150 sq.m) have 6/10A electricity and a further 52 also have water and drainage. Mobile homes are also available for rent. There is a large swimming pool with a new bar and pizzeria/restaurant adjacent and new play areas for children. There is also a well stocked shop. This region is popular for mountain sports, particularly mountain biking, trekking and rafting.

Facilities

Two well maintained toilet blocks provide all the usual facilities including an area for children and two rooms for disabled visitors (key access). Laundry facilities. Motorcaravan services. Well stocked shop selling fresh bread. Bar. Restaurant/pizzeria. Large swimming pool with children's pool. New play areas. Miniclub, teenage club and evening entertainment for adults in high season. Bicycle hire. Mobile homes to rent. WiFi over site (free in low season). Off site: Fishing 200 m. Bicycle hire 1.5 km.

Open: 24 April - 15 September.

Directions

Leave A22 motorway at Trento Nord, follow SS47 towards Padova. After Pergine and Valsugana, follow signs to Calceranica/Caldonazzo. After Caldonazzo railway station turn left and after level crossing, left again towards lake and the site is well signed. GPS: 46.004662, 11.260619

Charges guide

Per unit incl. 2 persons (4 persons 10/7-21/8) and electricity	€ 12.00 - € 66.00
extra person	€ 6.00 - € 10.00

Campitello di Fassa

Camping Miravalle

Streda de Greva 39, I-38031 Campitello di Fassa (Trentino - Alto Adige) T: 046 275 0502.

E: info@campingmiravalle.it alanrogers.com/IT62095

Miravalle has a wonderful mountain backdrop in a peaceful location, but unusually is within the very pretty mountain village of Campitello with all its entertainment and services. The 135 touring pitches are neat and very grassy, all with 3/6A electricity, 40 fully serviced. Some are terraced and others are at the level of the river (minimal fencing). All the site facilities are of modern construction and top quality, located in the centre of the site. We liked the clean freshness of this place and the views from anywhere on the site are fabulous.

Facilities

Excellent modern sanitary facilities are fully equipped and of a very high standard. Good provision for babies and disabled campers. Laundry facilities. Motorcaravan services. Bar, snacks and takeaway. Restaurant (July/Aug). Play area. Entertainment (15/7-25/8). Fishing. Communal barbecue. WiFi throughout (charged). Apartments for rent. Off site: Village centre 50 m. Bicycle hire 100 m. Col Rodella cable car and sports centre 200 m. (special rates for campers). Walking and cycle routes. Winter sports.

Open: 1 December - 30 March, 1 June - 30 September.

Directions

From A22 motorway, take the Egna/Ora exit and follow SS48 for 40 km. (towards Val di Fiemme). The site is clearly signed in Campitello. GPS: 46.474828, 11.740726

Charges guide

Per unit incl. 2 persons and electricity	€ 25.00 - € 37.00
extra person	€ 8.00 - € 12.50
child (2-11 yrs)	€ 5.00 - € 8.00
dog	€ 5.00

For latest campsite news, availability and prices visit

alanrogers.com

Dimaro

Dolomiti Camping Village & Wellness Resort

Via Gole 105, I-38025 Dimaro (Trentino - Alto Adige) T: 0463 974 332. E: info@campingdolomiti.com

alanrogers.com/IT61830

Dolomiti di Brenta is open for separate winter and summer seasons. It is situated at an altitude of 800 m. in an attractive, open valley surrounded by the rugged Dolomite Mountains, and is only 100 m. from the River Noce. It is an ideal base to explore this fantastic region. There are 190 level and grassy pitches, all with 4/6A electricity and some fully serviced. Young trees offer a little shade. The pitches range in size from small (25 sq.m), suitable for small tents, to large (120 sq.m), suitable for medium sized outfits. Cars must be parked away from pitches.

Facilities

Modern, heated toilet block with all necessary facilities including private bathrooms for rent. Washing machine, dryer. Motorcaravan services. Small shop (1/6-10/9). Bar, restaurant, pizzeria. Heated outdoor swimming pool (30/5-10/9). Excellent wellness centre. Large play area. Communal barbecues. Football. Volleyball. Bicycle hire. Free WiFi over site. Dogs are not accepted (July/Aug). Off site: Attractive mountain villages with their local craft shops and the Stelvio National Park. Shops, bars, restaurant and swimming pool in Malè.

Open: 5 December - 10 April and 23 May - 28 September.

Directions

Leave the A22, Brenner motorway at San Michele All'Adige, 40 km. south of Bolzano. Follow signs for SS43 through Cles, then SS42 through Malè. 19 km. after Cles turn left in Via Gole, site is on right. GPS: 46.325278, 10.863056

Charges guide

Per unit incl. 2 persons and electricity	€ 28.20 - € 42.30
extra person	€ 7.90 - € 10.90
child (2-13 yrs)	€ 5.80 - € 9.20
dog (not July-August)	€ 3.50

Laces-Latsch

Camping Latsch an der Etsch

Reichstrasse 4, via Nazionale 4, I-39021 Laces-Latsch (Trentino - Alto Adige) T: 047 362 3217.

E: info@camping-latsch.com **alanrogers.com/IT62120**

Camping Latsch an der Etsch has splendid views to the surrounding mountains. Some of the 100 shaded touring pitches are alongside the river, others are set on slopes. All have 6A electricity and 50 also have water and drainage. The site and its adjoining hotel reveal an array of amenities when explored and campers may use all the facilities of the hotel. Two interconnected swimming pools, one in the hotel, the other outside, are a great feature. Mountain walkers and anyone with adventurous ambitions will be in their element here and several chair lifts give access to higher slopes. This is an unusual site with a huge variety of thngs to do and a very pleasant ambiance.

Facilities

The sanitary block, refurbished to hotel standards in 2014, is on two floors and is heated in cool weather. Excellent private bathrooms (20 with basin, shower, toilet) for hire. Facilities for disabled visitors. Washing machine and dryer. Motorcaravan services. Shop, bar and pleasant restaurant. Attractive heated indoor pool, sauna, solarium and fitness room. Larger, irregularly shaped outdoor pool with marble surrounds. Playground. Indoor bowls. Pool room. Campers have access to all the hotel facilities.

Open: 1 January - 10 November.

Directions

Latsch/Laces is 28 km. west of Merano on the SS38 Bolzano-Silandro road. Site entrance is by the Hotel Vermoi. GPS: 46.622592, 10.864921

Charges guide

Per unit incl. 2 persons and electricity	€ 29.90 - € 36.00
extra person	€ 7.80 - € 8.80
child (3-11 yrs)	€ 6.50 - € 7.80
dog	€ 3.90 - € 5.20

Laives/Leifers

Camping-Park Steiner

J. F. Kennedy Str. 32, I-39055 Laives/Leifers (Trentino - Alto Adige) T: 047 195 0105.

E: info@campingsteiner.com **alanrogers.com/IT62100**

The very welcoming Camping Steiner is very central for touring with the whole of the Dolomite region within easy reach. With a happy atmosphere and much on-site activity, one could spend an enjoyable holiday here. The 180 individual touring pitches, mostly with good shade and hardstanding, are in rows with easy access and all have 6A electricity. There is a pleasant, family style pizzeria/restaurant with a great menu, plus indoor and outdoor pools with a sunbathing area. The Steiner Park Hotel at the entrance to the site provides another restaurant, café and full hotel facilities.

Facilities

The two sanitary blocks are equipped to a high standard. and can be heated. Facilities for disabled campers. Shop. Bar/pizzeria/restaurant with takeaway (11/4-30/10). Outdoor pool with paddling pool (11/4-30/9). Aquagym. Smaller covered heated pool (11/4-30/10). Playground. Entertainment incl. wine tastings. Dogs are not accepted in July/Aug. WiFi in some areas (free).

Open: 21 March - 31 October.

Directions

If approaching from north, at the Bolzano-Süd exit from A22 Brenner-Modena motorway follow Trento signs for 7 km. then signs for 'centre' Leifers/Laives. GPS: 46.42950, 11.3434

Charges guide

Per unit incl. 2 persons and electricity	€ 28.00 - € 36.00
extra person	€ 7.00 - € 9.00

FREE Alan Rogers Travel Card
Extra benefits and savings - see page 14

Lana

Komfortcamping Schlosshof

Feldgatterweg, I-39011 Lana (Trentino - Alto Adige) T: 0473 561 469. E: info@schlosshof.it

alanrogers.com/IT61860

Komfortcamping Schlosshof is a hotel with its own campsite of 134 pitches. The site is open from March to mid November and offers hotel standard facilities with the aim of making your stay special. The level touring pitches are between 80-130 sq.m. on either shale or grass, all with 16A electricity and many are fully serviced. The site is close to Lana, one of the largest villages in the South Tirol and famous for its Mediterranean climate. This is a German-speaking area of Italy and a good base for active families wishing to explore this region of natural beauty.

Facilities

Three well equipped sanitary blocks are all of a very high standard. Facilities for disabled visitors. Laundry facilities. Motorcaravan service point. Restaurant, bar and takeaway (all from 22/3). Bread available mornings. Indoor and outdoor swimming pools (from 22/3). Jacuzzi. Sauna. Solarium. Massage. Fenced play area. Free WiFi throughout. Off site: Bus stop 200 m. Golf and bicycle hire 2 km. Fishing 3 km. Hiking. Tennis. Cable car.

Open: 1 March - 15 November.

Directions

Leave A22 Brenner motorway at Bozen Süd. Take expressway towards Meran. At the Lana-Burgstall exit turn left. Continue across first roundabout for about 500 m. and turn right at Gasthof Tennis where site is signed. GPS: 46.61192, 11.16846

Charges guide

Per unit incl. 2 persons	
and electricity (plus meter)	€ 36.00
extra person	€ 9.00

Lana

Camping Arquin

Feldgatterweg 25, I-39011 Lana (Trentino - Alto Adige) T: 0473 561 187. E: info@camping-arquin.it

alanrogers.com/IT61865

Camping Arquin is in the South Tirol (Alto Adige) where the majority of the population speak German. It is open from early March to mid November and lies in an open valley surrounded by orchards, beyond which are high mountains. This is a region of natural beauty and is famous for its flowery meadows. The site is close to the village of Lana, one of the largest in the South Tirol and famous for its Mediterranean climate. There are 120 sunny, level, grass pitches up to 100 sq.m, all with 6A electricity and many are fully serviced.

Facilities

Modern toilet block with all necessary facilities including those for babies and disabled visitors. Motorcaravan services. Small shop (15/3-5/11). Restaurant and bar (30/3-31/10). Small heated outdoor swimming pool (1/4-30/9). Play area. WiFi throughout (free). Charcoal barbecues not permitted. Off site: Bus stop 200 m. Large swimming pool 200 m. (May onwards; free to campers). Historical town of Meran 7 km. Museums. Golf and bicycle hire 2 km. Fishing 3 km. Hiking. Paragliding. Tennis. Rock climbing. Nature parks. Cable car.

Open: 1 March - 15 November.

Directions

Leave A22 Brenner motorway at Bozen Süd. Take expressway towards Meran. At the Lana-Burgstall exit turn left. After 250 m. take first right and follow signs to site. GPS: 46.611151, 11.174434

Charges guide

Per unit incl. 2 persons	
and electricity	€ 33.00 - € 37.00
extra person	€ 7.00
child (5-10 yrs)	€ 4.00

Levico Terme

Camping Lago di Levico

Localitá Pleina, I-38056 Levico Terme (Trentino - Alto Adige) T: 046 170 6491. E: info@campinglevico.com

alanrogers.com/IT62290

Camping Lago di Levico, by a pretty lakeside in the mountains, is the result of the merging of two popular sites. An impressive new reception has efficient systems and you are soon on one of 430 mostly grassy and shaded pitches. All pitches have 6A electricity, 150 also have water and drainage and 12 have private facilities. The lakeside pitches are really quite special. Staff are welcoming and fluent in English. The swimming pool complex is popular, as is the summer family entertainment. A small shop and a minimarket are on site and it is a short distance to the local village. The restaurant, bar, pizzeria and takeaway are open all season. A steady stream of improvements continues at this site which is great for families.

Facilities

Four modern sanitary blocks provide hot water for showers, washbasins and washing. Mostly British style toilets. Single locked unit for disabled visitors. Laundry facilities. Freezer. Motorcaravan services and stopover pitches. Good shop. Bar/restaurant and takeaway. Outdoor swimming pool. Play area. Miniclub and entertainment (high season). Small zoo. Satellite TV and cartoon cinema. Watersports. Kayak hire. Fishing. Tennis. Bicycle hire. Torches useful. WiFi over site (free).

Open: 5 April - 12 October.

Directions

From A22 Verona-Bolzano road take turn for Trento on S47 to Levico Terme where campsite is very well signed. GPS: 46.00799, 11.28454

Charges guide

Per unit incl. 2 persons	
and electricity	€ 19.00 - € 52.00
extra person	€ 4.50 - € 9.90
child (3-11 yrs)	€ 4.00 - € 6.50
dog	€ 2.00 - € 5.00

For latest campsite news, availability and prices visit

alanrogers.com

Molina di Ledro

Camping Al Sole

Via Maffei 127, I-38060 Molina di Ledro (Trentino - Alto Adige) T: 046 450 8496. E: info@campingalsole.it

alanrogers.com/IT62320

Lake Ledro is only 9 km. from Lake Garda, its sparkling waters and breathtaking scenery offering a low key alternative for those who enjoy a natural setting. The drive from Lake Garda is a real pleasure and prepares you for the treat ahead. This site has been owned by the same friendly family for over 40 years and their experience shows in the layout of the site, with its mature trees and the array of facilities provided. The 180 touring pitches (70-110 sq.m) all have 6A electricity. Situated on the lake with its own sandy beach, pool and play area, the facilities include an outstanding wellness centre.

Facilities

Superb toilet block with well appointed facilities. Five private bathrooms with shower, toilet, basin and safe. Good facilities for disabled visitors. Baby room. Laundry facilities. Freezer. Motorcaravan services. Well stocked mini-market. Pleasant restaurant/pizzeria with terrace. Bar with snacks and takeaway. Sun decks and snack bar at the lake. Swimming pool. Play area. Bicycle hire. Boating, windsurfing, fishing and canoeing. Children's club. TV. WiFi over site (charged). Torches needed in some areas.

Open: Easter - 14 October.

Directions

From autostrada A22 exit for Lake Garda North to Riva del Garda. In Riva follow sign for Ledro valley. Site is well signed as you approach Lago di Ledra. GPS: 45.87805, 10.76773

Charges guide

Per unit incl. 2 persons	
and electricity	€ 24.00 - € 41.00
extra person	€ 7.50 - € 11.00
child (2-11 yrs)	€ 5.00 - € 7.00

Pergine Valsugana

Camping Punta Indiani

Valcanover, I-38057 Pergine (Trentino - Alto Adige) T: 046 154 8062. E: info@campingpuntaindiani.it

alanrogers.com/IT62310

Punta Indiani is a small peninsula on the northwestern shore of Lake Caldonazzo, one of the smaller and most easterly of the Italian lakes. This simple, family run campsite is split into three camping areas. Two are split by a railway line (the trains only run during the day – great for train spotters). There are 115 pitches here which vary in size, all with 3/4A electricity, some with shade. Many have a superb position being right on the shores of this beautiful lake. There are limited amenities on the site, but a rear gate gives access to the town which has all the usual facilities and these compensate for the site's simplicity. This site is very popular with windsurfers and offers uncomplicated camping with reasonable prices for all.

Facilities

Two modernised toilet blocks with mixed British and Turkish style toilets and hot water. Washing machine and dryer. Freezer. High season family activities including al fresco eating. Simple play area. Beach. Dogs accepted by prior arrangement only. Off site: Watersports and sailing on lake, including at Calceranica-al-Lago 3 km. Pergine Valsugana 4 km. Trento 16 km.

Open: 1 May - 30 September.

Directions

From A22 Verona-Brenner motorway, leave at Trento-Nord, follow signs for SS47 Valsugana and Padova. After Pergine Valsugana, take exit for Lago di Caldonazzo on SP1. Site is signed to left within 1 km. Watch for bridge (3.5 m) and sudden left turn into site road. GPS: 46.02773, 11.231444

Charges guide

Per unit incl. 2 persons	
and electricity	€ 20.00 - € 40.00
extra person	€ 10.00

Pozza di Fassa

Camping Vidor – Family & Wellness Resort

Strada de Ruf de Ruacia 15, I-38036 Pozza di Fassa (Trentino - Alto Adige) T: 046 276 0022.

E: info@campingvidor.it **alanrogers.com/IT62090**

This very smart, family run site is in a beautiful mountainous setting and has the most fabulous infrastructure. The 160 pitches are of average size with 16A electricity connections, some also with water, drainage and hardstanding. Vidor has excellent facilities including a super new reception, camping shop, high quality restaurant and pizzeria (serving local cuisine with special menus for children), and a café with terrace and lounge. There is a wellness centre with an indoor heated swimming pool with whirlpool etc. (charged), plus a superb beauty centre offering a large variety of modern treatments. This is a stunning site with all you need for a family holiday in the mountains. We enjoyed our visit.

Facilities

Two truly excellent, hotel standard heated sanitary blocks provide hot water and very good showers, with private bathrooms for hire. Facilities for disabled visitors. Laundry facilities. Fridge and freezer. Bar/restaurant with superb views, takeaway and shop. Heated indoor pool and gym (charged). TV room and cinema. Indoor playrooms and miniclub. Bicycle hire. Entertainment. WiFi (charged).

Open: All year except November.

Directions

From A22 Trento-Bolzano road take S48 to Pozza di Fassa. In centre of town, at roundabout take first exit towards Meida and Valle San Nicolo. Site is well signed in 2 km. GPS: 46.41987, 11.70754

Charges guide

Per unit incl. 2 persons	
and electricity	€ 19.00 - € 41.00
extra person	€ 6.00 - € 11.00

FREE Alan Rogers Travel Card
Extra benefits and savings - see page 14

Rasen

Camping Residence Corones

Niederrasen 124, I-39030 Rasen (Trentino - Alto Adige) T: 047 449 6490. E: info@corones.com

alanrogers.com/IT61990

Situated in a pine forest clearing at the foot of the attractive Antholz valley in the heart of German-speaking Südtirol, Corones is ideally situated both for winter sports enthusiasts and for walkers, cyclists, mountain bikers and those who prefer to explore the valleys and mountain roads of the Dolomites by car. There are 135 level pitches, all with 16A electricity and many also with water, drainage and satellite TV. The Residence offers luxury apartments and there are authentic Canadian log cabins for hire. The bar/restaurant and small shop are open all season. From the site you can see slopes which in winter become highly rated skiing pistes. A short drive up the broad Antholz/Anterselva valley takes you to an internationally important biathlon centre. An excellent day trip would be to drive up the valley and over the pass into Austria and then back via another pass. Back on site, a small pool and paddling pool could be very welcome. There is a regular programme of free excursions and occasional evening events are organised. Children's entertainment is provided in July and August.

Facilities

The central toilet block is traditional but well maintained and clean. Additional facilities below the Residence are of the highest quality including individual shower rooms with washbasins, washbasins with all WCs, a delightful children's unit and an excellent facility for disabled visitors. Fully equipped private shower rooms for hire. Luxurious wellness centre with saunas, solarium, jacuzzis, massage, therapy pools and heat benches. Heated outdoor swimming and paddling pools (4/5-20/10). Play area. WiFi throughout (charged). Charcoal barbecues are not permitted. Off site: Tennis 800 m. Bicycle hire 1 km. Riding and fishing 3 km. Golf (9 holes) 10 km. Canoeing/kayaking 15 km.

Open: 6 December - 7 April, 9 May - 27 October.

Directions

Rasen/Rasun is 85 km. northeast of Bolzano. From Bressanone/Brixen exit on A22 Brenner-Modena motorway, go east on SS49 for 50 km. then turn north (signed Rasen/Antholz). Turn immediately west at roundabout in Niederrasen/Rasun di Sotto to site on left in 100 m. GPS: 46.7758, 12.0367

Charges guide

Per unit incl. 2 persons, electricity on meter	€ 23.50 - € 33.80
extra person	€ 5.70 - € 8.90
child (3-15 yrs)	€ 3.20 - € 8.00
dog	€ 2.50 - € 4.50

No credit cards.

HOLIDAY IN A UNFORGETTABLE LANDSCAPE!
* camping with nice pitches
* mountain chalets and apartments with all comforts
For sports lovers, there are mountain bikes, excursions and of course, skiing fun!

Camping-Residence-Chalets
Corones ★★★★
Rasun di Sotto 124
I-39030 Rasun Anterselva | Alto Adige
Tel. +39 0474 496 490
www.corones.com | info@corones.com

Sexten

Caravan Park Sexten

Saint Josef Strasse 54, I-39030 Sexten (Trentino - Alto Adige)

T: 047 471 0444. E: info@caravanparksexten.it **alanrogers.com/IT62030**

Caravan Park Sexten is 1,520 metres above sea level and has 268 pitches, some very large and all with electricity (16A), TV connections and water and drainage in summer and winter (underground heating stops pipes freezing). Some pitches are in the open to catch the sun, others are tucked in forest clearings by the river. They are mostly gravelled to provide an ideal all year surface. It is the facilities that make this a truly remarkable site; no expense or effort has been spared to create a luxurious environment that matches that of any top class hotel. A member of Leading Campings group.

Facilities

The three main toilet blocks are remarkable in design, fixtures and fittings. Heated floors. Controllable showers. Hairdryers. Luxurious private facilities to rent. Children and baby rooms. En-suite facilities for disabled visitors. Laundry and drying room. Motorcaravan services. Shop. Bars and restaurants with entertainment 2-3 nights a week. Indoor pool. Heated outdoor pool (1/6-30/9). High quality health spa. New outdoor play area for children. Good range of activities for all. Tennis. Bicycle hire. Climbing wall. Fishing. Adventure activity packages. Internet access and WiFi (whole site). Off site: Skiing in winter (free bus to 2 ski lifts within 5 km). Walking, cycling and climbing. Fishing. Riding and golf nearby.

Open: All year.

Directions

Sexten/Sesto is 110 km. northeast of Bolzano. From Bressanone/Brixen exit on A22 Brenner-Modena motorway follow the SS49 east for 60 km. Turn south on SS52 at Innichen/San Candido and follow signs to Sexten. Site is 5 km. past village (signed). GPS: 46.66727, 12.40221

Charges guide

Per unit incl. 2 persons	€ 22.00 - € 49.00
extra person	€ 8.00 - € 13.00
child (2-14 yrs)	€ 4.50 - € 11.00
electricity (per kWh)	€ 0.70
dog	€ 3.00 - € 6.00

Tisens

Naturcaravanpark Tisens

I-39010 Tisens (Trentino - Alto Adige) T: 0473 927 131. E: info@naturcaravanpark-tisens.com

alanrogers.com/IT61844

Naturcaravanpark Tisens is a new site, open all year and located amidst orchards in tranquil Alpine surroundings. It can be found ten minutes walk from the centre of Tesimo (Tisens) and midway between Merano and Bolzano (both 14 km. distant). The 89 touring pitches are of a good size (around 90 sq.m), all with 6A electricity, water and drainage. A number of larger pitches and 'panoramic' pitches (120 sq.m) are also available. The site's 25 m. heated swimming pool and the smaller children's pool (also heated) are surrounded by meadows, ideal for sunbathing, with fine mountain views on all sides.

Facilities

Impressive, heated toilet block. En-suite facilities for disabled visitors. Small but well stocked shop, bar and restaurant with terrace and takeaway (all March-Nov). Heated swimming pool and paddling pool (April-Oct). Bicycle hire. Playground. WiFi throughout (charged). Off site: Walking and cycling. Tennis. Golf. Riding. Merano and Bolzano 14 km.

Open: All year.

Directions

Approaching from the A22 motorway and Brenner Pass, take the Merano Sud exit and follow signs to Lana. From there head towards Palade/Gampenpass as far as Tesimo/Tisens, from where the site is well signed. GPS: 46.56218, 11.17608

Charges guide

Per unit incl. 2 persons, electricity, water and waste water	€ 32.00 - € 34.00
extra person	€ 7.00

Toblach

Camping Olympia

Camping 1, I-39034 Toblach (Trentino - Alto Adige) T: 047 497 2147. E: info@camping-olympia.com

alanrogers.com/IT62000

In the Dolomite mountains, Camping Olympia continues to maintain its high standards. The 314 pitches are set out in a regular pattern and the tall pine trees, shrubs and hedges make this a very pleasant and attractive site. There are tree-clad hills on either side and craggy mountains beyond. The 238 touring pitches all have 6-16A electricity and a TV point. There are 63 fully serviced pitches with water, waste water, gas, telephone and satellite TV points. Some accommodation is available for rent, and there are 62 seasonal caravans which are mainly grouped at one end of the site.

Facilities

The toilet block is of a very high standard. Rooms with WC, washbasin and shower to rent. Baby room. Facilities for disabled visitors. Two small blocks provide further WCs and showers. Motorcaravan services. Shop. Bar, restaurant and pizzeria. Second bar with grill and terrace by pool (10/6-30/9; 20/12-Easter). Heated swimming pool (20/5-15/9). Sauna, solarium, steam bath and whirlpools. Massage and Kneipp treatments. Fishing. Bicycle hire. Play area. WiFi throughout (free). Activities and excursions. Entertainment in high season. Off site: Tennis and minigolf nearby. Riding and golf 3 km. Skiing 2 km.

Open: All year.

Directions

Toblach/Dobbiaco is 100 km. northeast of Bolzano. Site is west of town. From the A22 (Innsbruck-Bolzano), take Bressanone/Brixen exit and travel east on SS49 for 60 km. Site signed to left just after a short tunnel. From Cortina take SS48 and SS51 northwards then turn west on SS49 for 1.5 km. GPS: 46.734449, 12.194266

Charges guide

Per unit incl. 2 persons and electricity	€ 27.00 - € 37.50
extra person	€ 9.50 - € 12.50
Supplement for serviced pitch (14/7-19/8).	

Völlan

Camping Völlan

Zehentweg 6, I-39011 Völlan (Trentino - Alto Adige) T: 0473 568 056. E: info@camping-voellan.com

alanrogers.com/IT61850

A small, family campsite attractively located among orchards and woods, Camping Völlan stands on a hillside above the town of Meran/Merano in the Süd-Tirol/Alto Adige region. There are spectacular views over the surrounding valleys with mountain peaks beyond, and the area offers many opportunities for walking, cycling, mountain biking and motoring excursions visiting Alpine villages, ancient fortresses and picturesque castles. The 55 touring pitches are moderately sized (80-90 sq.m) and are generally level, although the site itself is on a slope; electricity connections are available. There is a small swimming pool and the site shop provides for 'all you need for your camping holidays'.

Facilities

One modern toilet block with showers and washbasins. Washing machine and dryer. Motorcaravan services. Shop providing basic supplies. Swimming pool with sunbathing terrace (May-Sept). Small adventure playground. TV room. Free WiFi on part of site. Off site: Shops, bars and restaurants in the village of Lana 6 km. Meran 15 km. Bozen 30 km. Museums in Völlan, Lana and Meran.

Open: 24 March - 4 November.

Directions

Völlan/Lana is 30 km. northwest of Bozen/Bolzano. Leave A22 Verona/Brenner motorway at exit for Bozen Süd and follow signs for Merano. In 20 km. take exit to Lana and then follow signs up hillside to Völlan and campsite. GPS: 46.5989, 11.14558

Charges guide

Per unit incl. 2 persons and electricity	€ 29.00 - € 34.00
extra person	€ 7.00
No credit cards.	

Völs am Schlern

Camping Seiser Alm

Saint Konstantin 16, I-39050 Völs am Schlern (Trentino - Alto Adige) T: 047 170 6459.

E: info@camping-seiseralm.com alanrogers.com/IT62040

What an amazing experience awaits you at Seiser Alm! Elisabeth and Erhard Mahlknecht have created a superb site in the magnificent Südtirol region of the Dolomite mountains. Towering peaks provide a wonderful backdrop when you dine in the charming, traditionally styled restaurant on the upper terrace. Here you will also find the bar, shop and reception. The 150 touring pitches (with 16A electricity), 150 with gas, water, drainage, satellite connection and WiFi. Guests were delighted with the site when we visited, many coming to walk or cycle, some just to enjoy the surroundings. There are countless things to see and do here, including a full entertainment programme and a brilliant new pool. Enjoy the grand 18-hole golf course alongside the site or join the organised excursions and activities. Local buses and cable cars provide an excellent service for summer visitors and skiers alike (discounts are available). In keeping with the natural setting, the majority of the luxury facilities are set into the hillside. The children's bathrooms are in a magic forest setting complete with a giant mushroom and elves! A family play park with an enclosure of animals is at the lower part of the site where goats also roam. If you wish for quiet, quality camping in a crystal clean environment, then visit this immaculate site.

Facilities

One spotless, luxury underground block is in the centre of the site. 16 private units are available. Excellent facilities for disabled visitors. Fairy tale facilities for children. Infrared sensors, underfloor heating and gently curved floors to prevent slippery surfaces. Washing machines and large drying room. Sauna. Supermarket. Quality restaurant and bar with terrace. Swimming pool (heated in cool weather). Entertainment programme six days weekly. Miniclub. Children's adventure park and play room. Rooms for ski equipment. Animal enclosure. WiFi (charged). Apartments, mobile homes and maxi-caravans for rent. Off site: Riding alongside site. 18-hole golf course and fishing 1 km. Bicycle hire and lake swimming 2 km. Paragilding. Mountain biking. Walking. Skiing in winter. Buses to cable cars and ski lifts. Horse-drawn sleigh rides.

Open: 20 December - 2 November.

Directions

From A22-E45 take Bolzano Nord exit. Take road for Prato Isarco/Blumau, then road for Fie/Völs. Road divides suddenly – if you miss the left fork as you enter a tunnel (Altopiano dello Sciliar/Schlerngebiet) you will pay a heavy price in extra kilometres. Enjoy the climb to Völs am Schlern and site is well signed. GPS: 46.53344, 11.53335

Charges guide

Per unit incl. 2 persons	€ 19.60 - € 47.00
extra person	€ 7.80 - € 11.20
child (2-16 yrs)	€ 4.40 - € 6.80
electricity (per kWh)	€ 0.60
dog	€ 3.50 - € 5.50

Albinia

Camping International Argentario

Localitá Torre Saline, I-58010 Albinia (Tuscany) T: 056 487 0302. E: info@argentariocampingvillage.com

alanrogers.com/IT66710

Argentario is split into three areas. One is a huge, brick built apartment and bungalow complex; the second is a large, flat, shaded area for motorcaravans and large caravans (4/6A electricity); the third is a separate shaded beach camping area with direct access to the dark sand. The 800 pitches and additional accommodation share facilities, so they can be very busy in high season and involve some walking. Some campers may find the long walks trying, especially as the older style facilities are tired and stressed during peak periods. The infrastructure is fairly new (2010) and elegantly designed. We see this site more for short stays than extended holidays, and as unsuitable for disabled visitors.

Facilities

Three mature blocks have mostly Turkish style toilets, a few cramped showers with hot water, and cold water at the sinks (showers are very busy at peak periods). Facilities for disabled campers but the sand surface and remoteness of some facilities are unsuitable. Washing machines. Motorcaravan services. Shop. Restaurant, bar and takeaway. Swimming pools. Tennis. Boat hire. Minigolf. ATM. Free WiFi. Cars are parked in a separate car park in high season. Torches very useful. Dogs are not accepted. Off site: Bar and restaurant on the beach.

Open: 1 April - 30 September.

Directions

Site is south of Grosseto, off the SS1 at the 150 km. mark, signed Porto San Stefano. Ignore the first 'combined' campsite sign and proceed 300 m. to the main entrance. GPS: 42.49623, 11.19413

Charges guide

Per unit incl. 2 persons and electricity	€ 24.00 - € 44.00
extra person	€ 8.00 - € 14.20
child (1-6 yrs)	€ 4.00 - € 7.00

For latest campsite news, availability and prices visit

alanrogers.com

Castiglione della Pescaia
Camping Maremma Sans Souci

Localitá Casa Mora, I-58043 Castiglione della Pescaia (Tuscany) T: 056 493 3765.

E: info@maremmasanssouci.it alanrogers.com/IT66600

This delightful seaside site has been open since 1965 and sits in natural woodland on the coast road between Follonica and Grosseto. The minimum amount of undergrowth has been cleared to provide 270 individually marked and hedged, flat touring pitches with considerable privacy. All have 6A electrical connections and 40 have a satellite TV point. Some are small and cars must be parked away from pitches in a shaded and secure car park near the entrance. There is a wide road for motorcaravans but other roads are mostly narrow and bordered by protected trees. It is a most friendly site right by the sea which should appeal to many people who like a relaxed style of camping in a comfortable woodland setting with a real personal touch.

Facilities

Five small, very clean, older style toilet blocks are well situated around the site. Free showers. Three blocks have private cabins each with WC, basin and shower. Motorcaravan services. Laundry. Shop. Excellent restaurant (half- and full-board available) and pizzeria. Bar with snacks. ATM. Bicycle hire. Diving school. Excursions organised. WiFi (free). Torches required in some areas. Off site: Excursions to the islands from Castiglione della Pescaia harbour. Sailing school 300 m.

Open: 28 March - 1 November.

Directions

Site is 2.5 km. northwest of Castiglione on road to Follonica on the S322. GPS: 42.77343, 10.84392

Charges guide

Per unit incl. 2 persons	
and electricity	€ 28.00 - € 47.00
extra person	€ 8.00 - € 14.00
child (3-5 yrs)	free - € 8.00
dog	€ 3.00 - € 4.00

Camping Cheques accepted.

Cecina Mare
Camping Village Mareblu

Via dei Campilunghi, I-57023 Cecina Mare (Tuscany) T: 058 662 9191. E: info@campingmareblu.com

alanrogers.com/IT66310

Mareblu is a well equipped family site with an impressive range of amenities, including a large swimming pool with an attractive terraced surround, and a comprehensive shopping complex. The warm welcome you receive on arrival at reception is replicated throughout the site. A 350 m. walk through a pine forest leads to a soft, sandy beach. The 360 level touring pitches have a spacious feel, are well shaded and all have 6A electrical connections. Communal barbecue areas are provided. Parking for all cars is in a dedicated area at the front of the site. A number of mobile homes and chalets are available for hire. A good, value for money site with very reasonable prices. The site's restaurant and pizzeria are very pleasant and the food served is distinctly Italian. The ambitious entertainment programme aims to include something for everyone. The site is close to Cecina Mare, a popular resort with easy access to some of Tuscany's great cities, and the island of Elba.

Facilities

Five modern toilet blocks include facilities for disabled visitors. Shopping centre. Bar, restaurant and pizzeria and takeaway. Swimming and paddling pools (April-Oct). Play area. Games field. Boules. Bicycle hire. Entertainment. Miniclub. Direct access to beach via a 350 m. track. Windsurfing and sub-aqua diving organised. Dedicated areas for barbecues. WiFi over site (charged). Dogs are not accepted in July/Aug. Off site: Boat launching 300 m. Beach 350 m. Bus 400 m. Riding 2 km. Watersports and diving. Tennis. Excursions.

Open: 28 March - 17 October.

Directions

Site is south of Livorno. From north, take A12 to Rosignano and then join the E80 to Vada, then to La Mazzanta. From here site is well signed. GPS: 43.31848, 10.47407

Charges guide

Per unit incl. 2 persons	
and electricity	€ 18.00 - € 40.00
extra person	€ 5.00 - € 9.50
child (1-7 yrs)	€ 3.50 - € 7.50

Camping Cheques accepted.

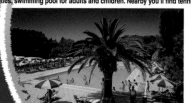

FREE Alan Rogers Travel Card
Extra benefits and savings - see page 14

Fiesole

Camping Panoramico Fiesole

Via Peramonda 1, I-50014 Fiesole (Tuscany) T: 055 599 069. E: panoramico@florencevillage.com
alanrogers.com/IT66100

This is a mature but pleasant site in a superb hilltop situation offering wonderful views over Florence. The 120 pitches, all with 5A electricity, are on terraces and steep walks to and from the various facilities could cause problems for guests with mobility problems. Pitches are separated, motorcaravans and caravans in the upper area and tents on the lower terraces. There is shade in many parts. The pool is on the upper level along with the restaurant/bar, and the views are really stunning. Some evenings you can hear music from the nearby Roman amphitheatre famous for its classical entertainment in summer.

Facilities
Two tastefully refurbished toilet blocks have mainly British style WCs, free hot water in washbasins and good showers. Washing machines and dryers. Fridges, freezer, microwaves, irons and little cookers for campers' use. Shop (1/4-31/10). Bar and restaurant (1/4-31/10). Swimming pool (1/6-30/9). Play area. Nursery. Torches required in some parts. English is spoken. Free shuttle service to Fiesole. WiFi (free). Off site: Riding 9 km. Golf 20 km. Florence with leather markets, Pitti Palace, Uffizi museum and much more.
Open: 15 March - 3 November.

Directions
From A1 take Firenze-Sud exit and follow signs to Fiesole. From Fiesole centre follow SP54 and signs for camping which should keep you out of the town centre as its roads are very narrow for large units. Take care on the last part of your journey up a steep access road to the site. Do not use sat nav. GPS: 43.8065, 11.3051

Charges guide
Per unit incl. 2 persons
and electricity   € 31.50 - € 41.00
extra person   € 9.50 - € 12.50

Firenze

Camping Internazionale

Via San Cristofano 2, Bottai, I-50029 Firenze (Tuscany) T: 055 237 4704.
E: internazionale@florencevillage.com alanrogers.com/IT66090

Camping Internazionale is set in the hills about 5 km. south of Florence. This is a well shaded, terraced site with 240 informal touring pitches set around the top of a hill. Although it is a very green site, the camping area is somewhat more open with two electricity pylons at the top of the hill and some noise from the busy motorway which is below and next to the site. It is often lively at night with many young people from tour groups. There is a small restaurant half way up the slope of the site with a resonable menu. A well located site for visiting Florence rather than for extended stays.

Facilities
Two traditional toilet blocks include free hot showers. Laundry. Some kitchen facilities. Motorcaravan services. Shop. New bar and restaurant at the lower level. Evening entertainment. Two swimming pools. Playground. WiFi over part of site (charged). Gas and electric barbecues only. Off site: 800 m. walk to bus stop. Florence 5 km. Golf 5 km. Riding and bicycle hire 10 km.
Open: 15 March - 3 November.

Directions
From A1 take Firenza Certosa exit towards Florence. Just outside Bottai turn left to the site (if you reach Galluzzo you have gone too far). From Florence take Via Senese (S2) through Galluzzo, turn right at site sign just before entering Bottai. Continue 500 m. to site. GPS: 43.72187, 11.22058

Charges guide
Per unit incl. 2 persons
and electricity   € 28.00 - € 39.00
extra person   € 7.50 - € 12.00

Gavorrano

Camping la Finoria

Via Monticello 66, I-58023 Gavorrano (Tuscany) T: 056 684 4381. E: info@campeggiolafinoria.it
alanrogers.com/IT66670

An unusual site, la Finoria is primarily set up for school groups and tents, hence the short season. Set high in the mountains with incredible views, it is a rugged site with a focus on nature. Italian school children attend education programmes here. Three motorcaravan pitches are at the top of the site for those who enjoy a challenge, with a dozen caravan pitches on lower terraces accessed by a very steep gravel track. Under huge chestnut trees there is a very pretty terraced area for tents. This has a private natural feel which some might say is what camping is all about. Electricity (3A) is available to all pitches, although long leads may be needed.

Facilities
Two mature blocks provide British and Turkish style toilets, hot showers and cold water at washbasins and sinks. Facilities for disabled campers. Washing machines and dryer. Quaint, small shop. Good restaurant and bar. Swimming pool. Tennis. Lessons on the environment. Excursions. Torches essential. Gas barbecues only. WiFi over part of site. Off site: Riding 2 km. Tennis and village 3 km. Bicycle hire 6 km. Golf 8 km. Site's private beach for relaxing and fishing 12 km.
Open: 23 June - 15 September.

Directions
From SS1 (Follonica-Grosseto) take Gavorrano exit, then Finoria road. This is a steady, steep climb for some 10 minutes. Start to descend and at junction (the only one), look left (difficult turn) downhill for a large white sign to site. Access to this site is only possible for small units. GPS: 42.9225, 10.91233

Charges guide
Per unit incl. 2 persons
and electricity   € 10.00 - € 29.00
extra person   € 3.00 - € 8.00

For latest campsite news, availability and prices visit
alanrogers.com

Limite Sull'Arno

Camping Village San Giusto

Via Castra, 71, I-50050 Capraia e Limite (Tuscany) T: 055 871 2304. E: info@campingsangiusto.it

alanrogers.com/IT66075

Camping San Giusto is a friendly, family run site in an unspoilt, typically Tuscan setting within the Montalbano National Park. There are 100 terraced touring pitches, the lower ones with 6A electricity and well shaded. Some of these pitches have superb views over the Tuscan countryside, while almost all of the upper pitches enjoy spectacular views. Amenities include a restaurant specialising in wonderful Tuscan food cooked by the father of the family owners and a pleasant, small, well stocked shop which also sells delicious homemade cakes. San Giusto will suit those looking for the peace and quiet of a traditional campsite with reasonable rates in a natural setting.

Facilities

Four sanitary blocks provide a variety of services. Most toilets are Turkish style. The small upper block is more modern. Washing machines. Bar and snack bar. Excellent restaurant. Shop. Swimming and paddling pools. Playground. Games room. WiFi (free). Communal barbecue area. Shuttle bus service. Mobile homes and chalets for rent. Off site: ATM 5 km. Bicycle hire 10 km. Walking and cycling. Florence, Siena, Vinci and Volterra. Montalbano National Park.

Open: 15 March - 5 November.

Directions

From A1 Milan-Rome autostrada take Firenze exit, then the Firenze, Pisa, Livorno road towards Empoli and Pisa. Leave at Montelupo and head towards Limite sull'Arno and on to Castra. Site is signed on the left after Castra. GPS: 43.783251, 10.988329

Charges guide

Per unit incl. 2 persons	
and electricity	€ 22.50 - € 38.00
extra person	€ 7.00 - € 9.00
child (3-12 yrs)	€ 4.00 - € 5.00

Pisa

Camping Torre Pendente

Viale delle Cascine 86, I-56122 Pisa (Tuscany) T: 050 561 704. E: info@campingtorrependente.com

alanrogers.com/IT66080

Torre Pendente is a most friendly site, efficiently run by the Signorini family who speak good English and make everyone feel welcome. It is amazingly close to the famous leaning tower of Pisa and therefore busy throughout the main season. It is a medium sized site with 220 touring pitches, all with 5A electricity, on level, grassy ground with some shade from trees and lots of artificial shade. Fifty bungalows are also available for hire. The excellent site facilities are near the entrance including a most pleasant restaurant, swimming pool complex with pool bar and a large terrace.

Facilities

Three toilet blocks are very clean and smart with British style toilets and good facilities for disabled campers. Private cabins for hire. Hot water at sinks. Washing machines. Motorcaravan services. Well stocked supermarket. Pleasant restaurant, bar and takeaway. Swimming pool with pool bar, paddling pool and spa. Playground. Boules. Entertainment in high season. WiFi over site (charged). Bungalows for hire. Off site: Bicycle hire. Bus 100 m. Railway station 300 m. Riding 3 km.

Open: 1 April - 15 October.

Directions

From A12, exit at Pisa Nord and follow for 5 km. to Pisa. Do not take first sign to town centre. Site is well signed at a later left turn (Viale delle Cascine). GPS: 43.7252, 10.3819

Charges guide

Per unit incl. 2 persons	
and electricity	€ 29.50 - € 35.00
extra person	€ 8.00 - € 10.00
child (3-10 yrs)	€ 4.50 - € 6.00

San Baronto di Lamporecchio

Camping Barco Reale

Via Nardini 11/13, I-51035 San Baronto di Lamporecchio (Tuscany) T: 057 388 332.

E: info@barcoreale.com alanrogers.com/IT66000

LeadingCampings

Just forty minutes from Florence and an hour from Pisa, this site is beautifully situated high in the Tuscan hills close to the fascinating town of Pistoia. Part of an old walled estate, there are impressive views of the surrounding countryside. It is a quiet site of 15 hectares and the 265 terraced pitches enjoy shade from mature pines and oaks. Some pitches are huge with great views and others are very private. Most are for touring units, although some have difficult access (the site provides tractor assistance). All 187 touring pitches have electricity and 40 are fully serviced. A member of Leading Campings group.

Facilities

Three modern sanitary blocks are well positioned and kept very clean. Good facilities for disabled visitors (dedicated pitches close by). Baby room. Laundry facilities. Fridge hire. Motorcaravan services. Dog shower. Shop, restaurant, bar, supervised swimming pools 10.00-18.00 caps required. Ice cream shop. Playgrounds. Bowls. Bicycle hire. Internet point. WiFi over part of site. Disco. Entertainment. Cooking lessons for Tuscan style food. Excursions. Riding. Off site: Village and shops 1 km. Markets. Fishing 8 km. Golf 15 km.

Open: 1 April - 30 September.

Directions

From Pistoia take Vinci-Empoli-Lamporecchio signs to San Baronto. From Empoli signs to Vinci and San Baronto. Final approach involves a sharp bend and a steep slope. GPS: 43.84190, 10.91130

Charges guide

Per unit incl. 2 persons	
and electricity	€ 26.60 - € 50.50
extra person	€ 7.30 - € 12.80
child (3-11 yrs)	€ 4.50 - € 8.30
dog	€ 2.00 - € 3.50

FREE Alan Rogers Travel Card

Extra benefits and savings - see page 14

San Gimignano
Camping Boschetto di Piemma

Localitá Santa Lucia 38/C, I-53037 San Gimignano (Tuscany) T: 057 790 7134.
E: info@boschettodipiemma.it alanrogers.com/IT66270

The medieval Manhattan of San Gimignano is one of Tuscany's most popular sites and this new campsite lies just 2 km. from the town. There are 100 small pitches here, all with 6A electrical connections and some with shade from mature trees. The site is in woodland surrounded by olive groves and vineyards and has been developed with much care for the environment, using rain water for irrigation and with many solar panels. Located with a sports centre, the site has use of many of the sporting amenities (tennis carries an extra charge). The swimming pool alongside the site is shared with the public, but site security is good.

Facilities
Excellent sanitary block includes facilities for disabled visitors. Cool room with fridge and freezer for campers. Shop (specialising in local produce), restaurant/pizzeria and bar (all 1/4-30/10). Heated outdoor swimming pool (1/6-15/9, small charge). Tennis (charged, lessons available). Sports centre. Playground. Entertainment and activity programme in high season. WiFi (charged). Apartments for rent. Off site: San Gimignano 2 km. Bus service to town. Cycle and walking trails. Bicycle hire 2 km. Riding 10 km. Fishing 15 km. Golf 20 km.
Open: All year.

Directions
From the Florence-Siena superstrada take exit for Poggibonsi Nord and follow signs to San Gimignano. At first roundabout follow signs to Volterra, then take first road to the left, signed Santa Lucia. Site signed close to the sports area. GPS: 43.4533, 11.0536

Charges guide
Per unit incl. 2 persons

and electricity	€ 25.00 - € 31.00
extra person	€ 8.50 - € 11.00
child (3-11 yrs)	€ 5.50 - € 6.00

San Piero a Sieve
Camping Village Mugello Verde

Via Massorondinaio 39, I-50037 San Piero a Sieve (Tuscany) T: 055 848 511.
E: mugelloverde@florencevillage.com alanrogers.com/IT66050

Mugello Verde is a country hillside site with 200 good sized pitches for motorcaravans and caravans, and smaller pitches for tents. All have 6A electricity. Some are on flat ground, others are on steep terraces where mature trees provide shade. The big attraction here is the site's proximity to the international Mugello racing track, just 5 km. away. It is used by Ferrari for practice runs and is also an international car and motorcycling track. The site has a pleasant, open feel and the accommodation for hire does not impinge on the touring area. A good site, particularly for motor racing enthusiasts.

Facilities
Two toilet blocks are well positioned and the facilities are clean with mixed British and Turkish style WCs. Hot water throughout. Facilities for disabled visitors. Laundry facilities. Shop. Restaurant/bar and pizzeria (all season). Swimming pool (31/5-14/9; no paddling pool). Play area. Tennis. Free WiFi over part of site. Off site: Riding, golf, bicycle hire and fishing all within 5 km. Mugello racing track 5 km. Barberino designer outlet 10 km.
Open: 20 March - 1 November.

Directions
From A1 autostrada take Barberino del Mugello exit and follow SS65 towards San Piero a Sieve and before town, turn left and just past Tamoil garage turn right to site. GPS: 43.96148, 11.31030

Charges guide
Per unit incl. 2 persons

and electricity	€ 24.00 - € 34.00
extra person	€ 8.00 - € 10.00
child (3-11 yrs)	free - € 6.00

San Vincenzo
Camping Park Albatros

Pineta di Torre Nuova, I-57027 San Vincenzo (Tuscany) T: 056 570 1018. E: parkalbatros@ecvacanze.it
alanrogers.com/IT66380

Camping Albatros is situated on the historic Costa Degli Etruschi and is a huge site with something for everyone. Of the 1,000 shaded pitches (6/10A electricity), the 300 for touring are in a separate area on flat ground. All have water and drainage. The top quality facilities and entertainment here are so good that you need not leave the site during your holiday. The extensive pools and water features are outstanding and the wide range of recreational facilities are superb. This is a great site for family holidays if you do not mind a few queues, and several thousand people holidaying around you.

Facilities
Two superb circular toilet blocks with hot showers and brilliant rooms for children. Facilities for disabled visitors. Washing machines. Huge air-conditioned supermarket. Bazaar. Beauty salon. Lagoon complex with five amazing pools. Two bars, two restaurants and pizzeria with large terrace with waiter service. Takeaway. Daily entertainment in season. Disco. Miniclub (4-12 yrs). Minigolf. New play areas (2013). Diving organised. Bicycle hire. No barbecues allowed. WiFi over site (charged). Train around site in high season. Off site: Beach and watersports 800 m.
Open: 18 April - 21 September.

Directions
Site is northwest of Grossetto and south of Livorno on the coast. From the SS1 take San Vincenzo exit. Site is well signed in San Vincenzo and is 6 km. south of village along the beach road. GPS: 43.04972, 10.55861

Charges guide
Per unit incl. 2 persons

and electricity	€ 26.50 - € 58.10
extra person	€ 7.50 - € 16.30
child (3-11 yrs)	free - € 11.90
dog	free

For latest campsite news, availability and prices visit
alanrogers.com

Sarteano

Parco delle Piscine

Via del Bagno Santo 29, I-53047 Sarteano (Tuscany) T: 057 826 971. E: info@parcodellepiscine.it

alanrogers.com/IT66450

Sarteano is an ancient spa town, and this large, smart site utilises that spa in its very open environs. This site is well run with an excellent infrastructure, if a little expensive. There is a friendly welcome from the English speaking staff. The 500 individual, flat pitches, (389 for touring) are all 100-150 sq.m. in size with high neat hedges giving real privacy. Electricity (6A) is available. The three unique swimming pools fed by the natural thermo-mineral springs are a novel feature here. Delle Piscine is really good as a sightseeing base or as an overnight stop from the Florence-Rome motorway (it is 6 km. from the exit).

Facilities

Two heated toilet blocks are of high quality with mainly British style WCs, many cubicles also with bidet. Gas supplies. Motorcaravan services. Restaurant/pizzeria with bar. Takeaway. Coffee bar. Swimming pools (one all season). Play area. TV room and mini-cinema with 100 seats and very large screen. Tennis. Exchange facilities. Free cookery lessons and art classes in high season. Free guided cultural tours. Free WiFi over site. No dogs. Off site: Old city 100 m. Bicycle hire 100 m.

Open: 1 April - 30 September.

Directions

From autostrada A1 take Chiusi/Chianciano exit, from where Sarteano is well signed (6 km). In Sarteano follow camping/piscine signs to site (entrance sign reads Piscine di Sarteano). GPS: 42.9885, 11.8639

Charges guide

| Per unit incl. 2 persons and electricity | € 35.00 - € 62.00 |
| extra person | € 10.00 - € 17.00 |

No credit cards.

Siena

Camping Colleverde

Strada Scacciapensieri 47, I-53100 Siena (Tuscany) T: 057 733 2545. E: info@sienacamping.com

alanrogers.com/IT66245

Camping Colleverde enjoys a panoramic setting overlooking the beautiful Tuscan city of Siena and the surrounding Chianti hills. The proprietor Andrea Sassolini and his family are on hand to ensure you have an enjoyable stay. Open for a long season, this is a great base for visiting Siena and the Chianti region. A bus stop is just 30 m. away and the railway station is 1.5 km. There are 221 touring pitches, 97 of which have 10A electricity and hardstandings and some are shaded. Smart on-site facilities include a swimming pool, a pizzeria/restaurant, bar and a shop.

Facilities

Three new top quality sanitary facilities include provision for disabled visitors. Laundry. Motorcaravan services. Shop, bar, restaurant/pizzeria (all March-Oct). Swimming and paddling pools (June-Sept). Play area. WiFi over site (charged). Mobile homes for rent. Bicycle hire. Bus tours to major attractions arranged. Off site: Railway station 1.5 km. City centre 2 km. Bicycle hire 3 km. Riding 10 km. Chianti countryside. Cycle and walking tracks.

Open: 1 March - 31 December.

Directions

Site is north of the city. Approaching from the north, leave RA3 superstrada (Florence-Siena) at Siena Nord exit. Turn right and follow signs for Hospital (Ospedale) and Camping. Site is 1 km. from the hospital and is the only campsite here, so all signs refer to Colleverde. GPS: 43.33771, 11.33048

Charges guide

| Per unit incl. 2 persons and electricity | € 32.50 - € 37.00 |
| extra person | € 9.50 - € 11.00 |

Troghi

Camping Village Il Poggetto

Via Il Poggetto 143, SP No.1 Aretina, I-50067 Troghi (Tuscany) T: 055 830 7323.

E: info@campingilpoggetto.com alanrogers.com/IT66110

This superb site has a lot to offer. It benefits from a wonderful panorama of the Colli Fiorentini hills with acres of the Zecchi family vineyards to the east adding to its appeal and is just 15 km. from Florence. The hard working owners, Marcello and Daniella, have a wine producing background and you can purchase their wines at the site's shop. Their aim is to provide an enjoyable and peaceful atmosphere for families. All 106 touring pitches are of a good size, kept neat and tidy and have 6A electricity. On arrival you are escorted to view available pitches then assisted in taking up your chosen pitch.

Facilities

Two spotless sanitary blocks with piped music offer British style WCs. Three private sanitary units for hire. Five very well equipped units for disabled visitors. Separate facilities for children and baby room. Laundry facilities. Motorcaravan services. Gas supplies. Shop. Bar. Restaurant. Swimming pools and jacuzzi (1/5-30/9). Fitness room. Bicycle and scooter hire. Playground and entertainment for children. Excursions and organised trekking. Wine and oil tastings. WiFi throughout (charged). Off site: Riding 500 m. Fishing 2 km. Golf 12 km.

Open: 1 April - 15 October.

Directions

Exit A1 at Incisa southeast of Florence and turn right on the SS69. After 4 km. turn left following signs for Pian dell Isola. At next crossing turn right towards Firenze and follow site signs. Exercise caution using your sat nav on the final approach here as you may be taken into the steep, narrow streets of the nearby village. Follow campsite signs. GPS: 43.701415, 11.405262

Charges guide

| Per unit incl. 2 persons and electricity | € 29.50 - € 35.00 |
| extra person | € 8.00 - € 10.00 |

Torre del Lago

Camping Europa

Viale dei Tigli, I-55049 Torre del Lago Puccini (Tuscany) T: 058 435 0707. E: info@europacamp.it

alanrogers.com/IT66060

Europa is a large, flat, rectangular site directly off the beach road. Inside the gate you will pass 400 permanent pitches in 17 long rows, before reaching the 200 touring pitches which occupy six rows at the far end of the site. The site's facilities including a bar, mini market, bazzar and air-conditioned restaurant. A pleasant, secluded swimming pool, jacuzzi and paddling pool are near the entrance. The touring pitches are flat, very sandy and close together (55-70 sq.m) with some shade from trees or artificial cover and 6A electricity. The site has been owned by the delightful Morescalchi family since 1967 and they are very keen that you have an enjoyable stay. The beach is a brisk 20 minute walk just 1 km. away; a bicycle would be useful. However, there is a regular site minibus service to the beach. The sand is soft and the beach shelves gently into the water. Europa is conveniently situated for visiting many of the interesting places around, such as Lucca, Pisa, Florence and the wealth of Puccini related historical items.

Facilities

Two sanitary blocks provide hot and cold showers (€ 0.50 token from reception). Toilets are mixed Turkish and British style. Facilities for disabled visitors. Laundry facilities. Cleaning goes on non-stop here. Motorcaravan services outside gate. Bar/restaurant (air conditioned), takeaway and small shop. Good swimming pool (1/5-23/9, caps required). Large play area. Entertainment. Miniclub. Bicycle hire. Satellite TV. Internet access. Dogs are not accepted (3/8-23/8). Torches useful. Electric barbecues are not permitted. WiFi over part of site (charged). Off site: Beach 1 km. Fishing. Riding 2 km. Golf 17 km.

Open: 28 March - 13 October.

Directions

From A11-12 to Pisa Nord take Marina di Torre del Lago exit following the sign 'mare' towards the sea for Marina di Torre Lago Puccini. Follow clear signs for site. GPS: 43.83115, 10.27073

Charges guide

Per unit incl. 2 persons and electricity	€ 18.00 - € 41.00
extra person	€ 4.50 - € 9.50
child (2-11 yrs)	€ 2.50 - € 4.50

Vada

Camping Tripesce

Via Cavalleggeri 88, I-57016 Vada (Tuscany) T: 058 678 8017. E: info@campingtripesce.it

alanrogers.com/IT66290

Neat and tidy, this family owned and run site has the great advantage of direct beach access through electronically controlled gates with CCTV. The beach is of fine sand and shelves gently – super for children, with watersports and a lifeguard in season. This great beach makes up for the lack of a pool on the site and the fairly small size of the 230 pitches. All have 4A electricity and 60 are serviced with water and drainage. Some shade is provided by trees and by artificial shading. The site is contained within a rectangle and bungalows for rent are discreetly placed near reception. A pleasant bar with a terrace is alongside the small restaurant and just across the road is a well stocked shop. This is a relaxing site without the razzmatazz of the larger sites along the coast and principally car-free.

Facilities

Three clean, fresh toilet blocks provide hot and cold showers (water is solar heated and free). British and Turkish style toilets. Facility for disabled visitors. Washing machines. Motorcaravan services. Bar/restaurant and takeaway. Shop. Excellent beach. Aquarobics and aerobics (high season). Play area (supervision required). Miniclub (high season). WiFi throughout (free). Fishing. Bicycle hire. Dogs are not accepted 23/5-4/9. Charcoal barbecues are not permitted. Off site: Bus service 300 m. Seaside town and ATM 1 km. Riding 5 km.

Open: 30 March - 16 October.

Directions

From S1 autostrada (free) between Livorno and Grosetto head south and take Vada exit. Site is well signed along with many others as you approach the town. GPS: 43.34301, 10.45825

Charges guide

Per unit incl. 2 persons and electricity	€ 20.00 - € 37.00
extra person	€ 5.00 - € 8.00
child (0-7 yrs)	€ 3.00 - € 5.00

No credit cards.

For latest campsite news, availability and prices visit

alanrogers.com

Castiglione del Lago
Camping Listro
Via Lungolago, I-06061 Castiglione del Lago (Umbria) T: 075 951 193. E: listro@listro.it
alanrogers.com/IT66530

This is a simple, pleasant, flat site with the best beach on Lake Trasimeno. Listro provides 110 pitches, all with 3A electricity, and many of which enjoy the shade of mature trees. Some motorcaravan pitches are on the lakeside giving stunning views out of your windows. Facilities are fairly limited with a small shop, bar and snack bar, and there is no organised entertainment. English is spoken and British guests are particularly welcome. If you enjoy the simple life and peace and quiet in camping terms then this site is for you. The campsite's beach is private and the lake has very gradually sloping beaches making it very safe for children to play and swim. This also results in very warm water, which is kept clean as fishing and tourism are the major industries hereabouts. Camping Listro is a few hundred yards north of the historic town of Castiglione which provides all the usual services and it can be seen built into the hillside above the site.

Facilities
Three sanitary blocks are kept clean. Two are rather rustic in style. British style WCs. Facilities for disabled visitors. Washing machine. Motorcaravan services. Bar. Shop. Snack bar. Play area. Fishing. Bicycle hire. Private beach. Guided tours. WiFi over part of site (charged). Off site: Bars and restaurants nearby. Good swimming pool and tennis courts (discounts using the campsite card). Town 800 m. Excursions.

Open: 1 April - 30 September.

Directions
From A1/E35 Florence-Rome autostrada take Val di Chiana exit and join the Perugia (75 bis) superstrada. After 24 km. take Castiglione exit and follow town signs. Site is clearly signed just before the town. GPS: 43.1341, 12.0448

Charges guide
Per unit incl. 2 persons and electricity	€ 14.70 - € 17.70
extra person	€ 4.90 - € 5.90
child	€ 3.90 - € 4.90

Less 10% for stays over 8 days in low season.

CAMPING LISTRO ★★
In a green setting on the shores of Lake Trasimeno • Private beach • Free hot water and electricity • Newly renovated shower and toilet facilities • Shop for essentials • Bar • Play area for children. By the site exit are: Swimming pool, Tennis courts, Athletics track, Football field, Windsurfing, Canoeing, Disco, Restaurant. Only 500 m. from the historic centre of Castiglione del Lago, the site is an ideal base for visits to Rome, Umbria and Tuscany. **GPS: N 43° 8' 5" - E 12° 2' 38"**

I-06061 Castiglione del Lago (PG) • Tel. + Fax 0039/075951193 - www.listro.it

Passignano sul Trasimeno
Camping la Spiaggia
Via Europa 22, I-06065 Passignano sul Trasimeno (Umbria) T: 075 827 246. E: info@campinglaspiaggia.it
alanrogers.com/IT66460

This site has its own beach and is pleasantly covered with pine and oak trees providing shade to most pitches. The 50 touring pitches (60-100 sq.m.) with 6/10A electricity are clearly defined and some are separated by dwarf hedges. This is an attractive, compact site which is well managed and cared for and is still being developed. A small café/restaurant has a terrace overlooking the lake and a small shop provides fresh bread to order. All sorts of activities are possible on the lake including canoeing, sailing and windsurfing and there are numerous possibilities for hiking and mountain biking in the surrounding hills. The relaxed atmosphere and easy going manner of the site make this a very restful place to visit. The town of Passignano sul Trasimeno is very close with lively bars and restaurants and a docking point for the lake steamer.

Facilities
The new toilet block is very clean and modern with free hot water. It includes facilities for disabled visitors and a baby room. Separate laundry room. Small shop for basics, bar/restaurant with terrace and takeaway (April-Sept). Lake swimming. Heated outdoor swimming pool (June-Sept). Play area. Bicycle and canoe hire. WiFi throughout (free). Beach for dogs. Off site: Restaurant across road from campsite. Tours and excursions. Riding 4 km.

Open: 1 April - 1 November.

Directions
From A1 (Firenze-Roma) take Bettolle exit towards Perugia (S326). Follow this to the Passignano exit (30 km. from the A1). Take the exit and go towards town (site signed). GPS: 43.1837, 12.1492

Charges guide
Per unit incl. 2 persons and electricity	€ 22.00 - € 28.00
extra person	€ 6.50 - € 8.50
child (2-9 yrs)	€ 5.00 - € 7.00
dog	€ 2.00

FREE Alan Rogers Travel Card
Extra benefits and savings - see page 14

Sant Arcangelo
Camping Villaggio Italgest
Via Martiri di Cefalonia, I-06063 Sant Arcangelo-Magione (Umbria) T: 075 848 238.
E: camping@italgest.com alanrogers.com/IT66520

Villaggio Italgest is a mature but pleasant site with 208 touring pitches (with 6A electricity) on level grass and plenty of shade. Cars are parked away from the pitches and the site offers a wide variety of activities with tours organised daily. The pools and restaurant are dated, but enjoyable. Directly on the shore on the south side of Lake Trasimeno, Sant Arcangelo is ideally placed for exploring Umbria and Tuscany. The area around the lake is fairly flat but has views of the distant hills and can become very hot during summer. There is some entertainment for children and adults in high season, Italian style.

Facilities
The one large and two smaller sanitary blocks have mainly British style WCs and free hot water in the washbasins and showers. Children's toilets. Baby room. Facilities for disabled visitors. Motorcaravan services. Washing machines and dryers. Well equipped campers' kitchen. Bar, restaurant, pizzeria and takeaway (all season). Shop. Recently enlarged swimming pool with flume and slides. Paddling pool. Spa. Tennis. Play area. TV (satellite) and games rooms. Disco. Films. Watersports, motorboat hire and lake swimming. Fishing. Mountain bike and scooter hire. Internet and WiFi (charged). Wide range of activities, entertainment and excursions.

Open: 1 April - 30 September.

Directions
Site is on southern shore of Lake Trasimeno. Take Magione exit from Perugia spur of Florence-Rome autostrada, proceed southwest round lake to San Arcangelo where site is signed.
GPS: 43.0881, 12.1561

Charges guide
Per unit incl. 2 persons	
and electricity	€ 18.50 - € 28.50
extra person	€ 6.00 - € 8.50
child (3-9 yrs)	€ 4.00 - € 6.50

Camping Cheques accepted.

Tuoro sul Trasimeno
Camping Village Punta Navaccia
Via Navaccia 4, I-06069 Tuoro sul Trasimeno (Umbria) T: 075 826 357. E: info@puntanavaccia.it
alanrogers.com/IT66490

Situated on the north side of Lake Trasimeno, close to two of the lake's islands, Punta Navaccia is run by the three ebullient Migliorati sisters. It is a large site with 400 flat, shaded touring pitches (with 6A electricity), mostly near the lakeside. The site is adjacent to a soft sand beach, and has a dock with facilities for mooring and launching your boat. The hub of the site is bustling with a full animation programme for children and adults. A huge amphitheatre stages entertainment, and is close to all the other services. This is a great and very Italian site, where families will have fun at reasonable prices.

Facilities
Three sanitary blocks with varied facilities are in the areas of seasonal campers. Sanitary facilities for children. Washing machine and dryer. Motorcaravan services. Heated swimming and paddling pools (1/5-30/9). Shop and bar (1/4-30/9). Restaurant and takeaway (1/4-30/9). Play area. Tennis. Covered amphitheatre. Cinema screen. Miniclub. Entertainment is organised in high season. Boat launching. Daily boat trip around island (free). Fitness room. Fishing. Bicycle hire. WiFi (charged).

Open: 15 March - 31 October.

Directions
Going south on the A1 (Florence/Firenze-Rome), take exit for Val di Chiana near Bettolle. After 15 km. take Tuoro sul Trasimeno exit. Site is well signed. GPS: 43.19191, 12.07665

Charges guide
Per unit incl. 2 persons	
and electricity	€ 21.50 - € 27.00
extra person	€ 6.50 - € 8.50
child (2-9 yrs)	€ 4.50 - € 6.50
dog	free

Bibione
Camping Capalonga
Via della Laguna 16, I-30020 Bibione-Pineda (Veneto) T: 043 143 8351. E: capalonga@bibionemare.com
alanrogers.com/IT60100

A quality site surrounded by water, Capalonga is a large site with 787 shaded touring pitches (70-90 sq.m) with 6/10A electricity, 35 fully serviced. The site is pleasantly laid out and permanent pitches are unobtrusive. The lagoon swimming pool and regular pools are excellent. Additionally, the wide, soft sand beach is very safe. Quality entertainment tops off the enjoyment here and the site has something for everyone. It has a spacious feel and bicycles are a real boon here.

Facilities
Nine toilet blocks are of a high standard and frequently cleaned. There are facilities for disabled visitors, and great children's rooms. Some washbasins in private cabins. Launderette. Dishwashers (€ 1). Motorcaravan services. Large supermarket. Bazaar. Self-service restaurant and separate bar. Two swimming pools (from 1/5). Boating (170 moorings). Fishing (sea/lagoon). Watersports, tennis and karate schools. Archery. Gym. Outdoor cinema. Volleyball. Bicycle hire. Playgrounds. Entertainment. WiFi.

Open: 24 April - 23 September.

Directions
Bibione is 80 km. east of Venice, well signed from afar on approach roads. 1 km. before Bibione turn right towards Bibione-Pineda and follow site signs.
GPS: 45.63035, 12.99450

Charges guide
Per unit incl. 2 persons	
and electricity	€ 28.00 - € 53.00
extra person	€ 7.50 - € 12.50
child (1-11 yrs acc. to age)	free - € 10.20

For latest campsite news, availability and prices visit
alanrogers.com

Bibione

Camping Lido

Via dei Ginepri 115, I-30028 Bibione-Pineda (Veneto) T: 043 143 8480. E: lido@bibionemare.com

alanrogers.com/IT60130

Camping Village Lido is a quiet, green site with direct access to the seafront in the centre of the town of Bibione-Pineda. Of 663 pitches, 388 are for touring units. Mostly shaded, there are three sizes, all with 6A electricity. There is convenient access to the long white sandy beach with its slowly shelving water, ideal for swimming/paddling. This is an impressive site with all manner of sporting and children's facilities, and an informal bar and restaurant. There are welcoming swimming pools for adults and children to relax in, although the site's main strength is the excellent beach and its central location, convenient to Bibione-Pineda's shopping area.

Facilities
Six sanitary blocks are conveniently located and are of a high standard. Car wash. Motorcaravan services. Bar, restaurant, supermarket and bazaar. Double swimming pool. Archery. Canoeing. Children's play park. Football. Volleyball. Basketball. Entertainment. Open-air cinema. Tennis and windsurfing schools. Boat mooring. Bicycle hire. WiFi (charged). Dogs and other animals are not accepted. Off site: Town of Bibione-Pineda. Marina.

Open: 12 May - 16 September.

Directions
Bibione is 80 km. east of Venice. Leave the E55 at Latisana exit and take the 354 for Bibione. Site is well signed from afar on approach roads. 1 km. before Bibione turn right towards Bibione-Pineda and follow site signs. GPS: 45.63222, 13.00132

Charges guide
Per unit incl. 2 persons and electricity	€ 18.70 - € 40.00
extra person	€ 5.10 - € 10.50

Bibione

Villaggio Turistico Internazionale

Via Colonie 2, I-30020 Bibione (Veneto) T: 043 144 2611. E: info@vti.it

alanrogers.com/IT60140

This is a large, professionally run tourist village which offers all a holiday maker could want. The Granzotto family have owned the site since the sixties and the results of their continuous improvements are very impressive. There are 300 clean pitches with electricity (10/16A), fully serviced, including TV hook-up, shaded by mature trees and mostly on flat ground. The site's large sandy beach is excellent (umbrellas and loungers are available for a small charge). All facilities are well thought out, in peak condition, and there is something for everyone. The tourist village is split by a main road (bridge for pedestrians) with the main restaurant, gym, laundry, disco, cinema and children's club, play areas and pleasant wooded spaces on the very smart chalet side.

Facilities
Seven modern toilet blocks house excellent facilities with mainly British style toilets. Excellent facilities for children and disabled campers. Private bathrooms (€ 10/day). Washing machines and dryers. Motorcaravan services. Car wash. Supermarket. Bazaar. Two good quality restaurants. Pizzeria. Snack bar. Pool complex with two large pools and a fun pool. Hydromassage. Pool bar. Fitness centre. Disco. TV. Cinema and theatre. Bicycle hire. WiFi (charged). Play areas. Tennis. Beach with bar.

Open: 28 March - 10 October.

Directions
Leave A4 east of Venice at Latisana exit on Latisana road. Then take road 354 towards Lignano, after 12 km. turn right to Bevazzana and then left to Bibione. Site is well signed on entering town. GPS: 45.6351, 13.0374

Charges guide
Per unit incl. 2 persons and electricity	€ 21.50 - € 51.00
extra person	€ 5.50 - € 13.00
child (1-9 yrs acc. to age)	free - € 10.50

Bibione

Camping Residence Il Tridente

Via Baseleghe 12, I-30028 Bibione-Pineda (Veneto) T: 043 143 9600. E: tridente@bibionemare.com

alanrogers.com/IT60150

This is an unusual site in that it has huge open spaces. Formerly a holiday centre for deprived children, it occupies a large area of woodland. It is divided into two parts by the hotel and apartment block. The 199 touring pitches (6/10A) are located among tall, shading pines in the area between the entrance and the hotel. The other section is a pleasant open area leading to the sea. It is used for many sports facilities and two excellent swimming pools.

Facilities
Three sanitary blocks, two in the main camping area and one near the sea, are of excellent quality. Mixed British and Turkish style WCs in cabins with washbasins and facilities for disabled visitors. Washing machines and dryers. Motorcaravan services. The Residence includes an excellent restaurant, pizzeria, takeaway and bar. Huge supermarket. Swimming pools. Playgrounds. 5-a-side football. Bocce. Watersports. Tennis. Gym. Fishing. WiFi (charged). Entertainment (high season). Late arrival parking with electricity. Dogs are not accepted.

Open: 12 May - 16 September.

Directions
From A4 Venice-Trieste autostrada, take Latisana exit and follow signs to Bibione and then Bibione-Pineda and site signs. GPS: 45.63476, 13.01687

Charges guide
Per unit incl. 2 persons and electricity	€ 20.00 - € 45.00
extra person	€ 6.00 - € 11.50
child (1-11 yrs acc. to age)	€ 3.60 - € 8.00

FREE Alan Rogers Travel Card
Extra benefits and savings - see page 14

Bonelli di Porto Tolle

Villaggio Barricata

Via Strada del Mare 74, I-45010 Bonelli di Porto Tolle (Veneto) T: 042 638 9198.

E: info@villaggiobarricata.com alanrogers.com/IT60590

Villaggio Barricata is a pleasant site, located within the large nature reserve at the mouth of the Po Delta. A drive through many rows of mobile homes brings you to 120 touring pitches, all with 6A electricity and water connections, and protected in the main by expensive artificial shading. On-site amenities are impressive and include a fabulous swimming pool complex, a bar/restaurant and a well stocked supermarket. A lively entertainment and activity programme is on offer during the peak season, including a children's club. A short walk leads to a long, gently shelving sandy beach.

Facilities

Heated sanitary facilities include provision for disabled visitors. Laundry. Bazaar. Bar. Restaurants. Takeaway. Shop. Swimming pools. Pool bar. Children's pool and lagoon. Wellness and spa. Aerobics. Tennis. Miniclub. Entertainment. Disco. Dancing classes. Play area. TV/games room. Bicycle hire. Riding. Archery. 5-a-side football. Canoeing. Dog beach. Accommodation and glamping. Max. one dog. WiFi on part of site (free).

Open: 24 May - 13 September.

Directions

Site is in the Parco del Delta del Po. Approaching from the A13 (Bologna-Padova), take Monselice exit and join the SP104 to Monselice Mare. Then join the SS309 Romea-Venice road to Porto Tolle exit, and follow signs to Porto Tolle then Scardovari. Site is well signed from here. GPS: 44.84613, 12.4633

Charges guide

Per unit incl. 2 persons and electricity	€ 23.00 - € 44.00

No credit cards.

Campalto

Camping Rialto

Via Orlanda 16, 30173 Campalto (Veneto) T: 041 542 0295. E: info@campingrialto.com

alanrogers.com/IT60510

Camping Rialto is a family run site with a pleasant atmosphere. Its main attraction is its close proximity to Venice, which can be reached by bus from the gate (€2.60 return). There are 89 pitches (6A Europlug) for tourers which are under mature trees and in rows between hard roads allowing easy access. They are situated further into the site past the rental accommodation and tents. A pizza restaurant/takeaway with a bar is close to the entrance along with all other administrative buildings.

Facilities

One sanitary block is offset nearer the entrance. It is of traditional design but has modern equipment and facilities for disabled visitors. Washing machines. Dryer. Motorcaravan services. Freezer for gel packs. Shop. Bar. Pizzeria and takeaway. TV at bar. Communal Barbecue area. WiFi (charged). Off site: Venice. Boat trips on the Brenta canal.

Open: 1 February - 20 October.

Directions

From Milan take Mestre Villabona exit and the A57 (Tangenziale di Mestre). Then take the Terraglio exit. At roundabout take SS13s towards Venice. At next roundabout take Campalt/Aeroporto exit (third). Site is just after Lidl store on left.
GPS: 45.48421, 12.28313

Charges guide

Per unit incl. 2 persons and electricity	€ 25.50 - € 30.50
extra person	€ 6.50 - € 8.00

Caorle

Centro Vacanze Pra' Delle Torri

Viale Altanea, 201, Localitá Pra delle Torri, I-30021 Caorle (Veneto) T: 042 129 9063. E: info@pradelletorri.it

alanrogers.com/IT60030

Pra' Delle Torri is a superb Italian Adriatic site which has just about everything! Pitches for camping, hotel accommodation and two very large, superbly equipped pool complexes, which may be rated among the best in the country. There is also a full size golf course. Of the 1,400 pitches, 800 are available for touring and are arranged in zones, with 5A electricity and shade. There is an amazing choice of quality restaurants, bars, shops and services placed strategically around an attractive square. Although a very large site, there is a great atmosphere here that families will enjoy.

Facilities

Sixteen high quality, spotless toilet blocks with excellent facilities including very attractive children's bathrooms. Units for disabled visitors. Laundry facilities. Motorcaravan services. Large supermarket and wide range of shops, restaurants, bars and takeaways. Indoor and outdoor pools. Disco with music selected by mobile phone app. Tennis. Minigolf. Fishing. Watersports. Archery. Diving. Fitness programmes and keep fit track. Crèche and supervised play area. Bowls. Mountain bike track. Wide range of organised sports and entertainment. Road train to town in high season. Dogs are not accepted.

Open: 16 April - 28 September.

Directions

From A4 Venice-Trieste motorway leave at exit for Santo Stino di Livenze and follow signs to Caorle then Santa Margherita and signs to site.
GPS: 45.57312, 12.81248

Charges guide

Per unit incl. 2 persons and electricity	€ 18.70 - € 52.50
extra person	€ 4.90 - € 10.80
child (3-11 yrs. acc. to age)	free - € 8.90

Min. stay 2 nights.

Caorle

Camping San Francesco

Via Selva Rosata, 1, I-30021 Caorle (Veneto) T: 042 129 82. E: info@villaggiosanfrancesco.com

alanrogers.com/IT60110

Camping San Francesco is a large, beachside site in a quiet location close to the coastal town of Caorle (Little Venice), known for its connection with Ernest Hemingway. Although there are over 600 mobile homes to rent, 370 level, grassy pitches are reserved for tourers. They are close to the beach, shaded, and all have electricity (10A) and fresh and waste water connections. The site has every facility for a comfortable holiday, with swimming pools, an attractive aquapark (extra charge), a good beach for swimming, a large supermarket etc. However, some touring in the area from the site and a trip to Venice are also worthwhile. The large, well organised reception is supplemented by a separate information office at the flower-decked entrance to the site. At the end of the entrance road, near the fountain, are some shops and an ice cream parlour. The shop selling Murano glass will be of particular interest, especially if you are not already acquainted with the colourful products from the islands just north of Venice. The islands and glassworks are well worth visiting. The site has three restaurants, one at the beachside pool, and during summer there are entertainment programmes for children.

Facilities

Five sanitary blocks, with all the usual facilities including free, controllable showers, washbasins in cabins, facilities for disabled visitors, children's area and baby room. Motorcaravan services. Bars, restaurants, pizzeria and ice-cream parlour. Supermarket and shopping centre plus first aid centre and a Murano glass shop. Swimming pools, paddling pools and hydromassage centre. Aquapark with waterslides (charged). Fitness centre. Solarium. Gym. Bowls. Tennis. Playground. Windsurfing school. Diving school. Games room. Entertainment and activity programme. Children's club. Excursions. Mobile homes and chalets for rent. Free WiFi throughout. Off site: Golf and riding 5 km. Venice and Caorle.

Open: 21 April - 24 September.

Directions

From A4 motorway (Venice-Trieste) take exit to Ste Stino di Livenza and follow signs to Caorle joining the P59. Site is signed from Caorle on the continuation of this road to Porto Santa Margherita. GPS: 45.56709, 12.7943

Charges guide

Per unit incl. 2 persons and electricity	€ 13.00 - € 45.00
extra person	€ 3.00 - € 10.00
child (3-6 yrs)	free - € 6.50

Camping Cheques accepted.

Cavallino-Treporti

Camping Union Lido Vacanze

Via Fausta 258, I-30013 Cavallino-Treporti (Veneto) T: 041 257 5111.

E: info@unionlido.com alanrogers.com/IT60200

This amazing site is very large, offering absolutely everything a camper could wish for. It is extremely professionally run and we were impressed with the whole organisation. It lies along a 1.2 km. long, broad sandy beach which shelves very gradually and offers a huge number of sporting activities. The site itself is regularly laid out with parallel access roads under a covering of poplars, pine and other trees. There are 2,200 pitches for touring units, all with 6/10/16A electricity and 1,969 also have water and drainage. Because of the size of the site, there is an internal road train and amenities are repeated across the site (cycling is permitted on specific roads). You do not need to leave this site during your stay – everything is here, including a smart and sophisticated wellness centre. Overnight parking is provided outside the gate with electricity, toilets and showers for those arriving after 21.00. There are two aqua parks, one with fine sandy beaches and both have swimming pools, lagoon pools for children, a whirlpool and a 160 m. 'Wild River'. Another water park is planned for 2015. A huge selection of sports and activities are offered, along with luxury amenities too numerous to list. Entertainment and fitness programmes are organised in season. The golf academy (with a professional) has a driving range, pitching green, putting green and practice bunker, and a diving centre offers lessons and open water diving. Union Lido is, above all, an orderly and clean site. This is achieved by implementing reasonable regulations to ensure peaceful, comfortable camping under good management. A member of Leading Campings group.

Facilities

Fourteen superb, fully equipped toilet blocks; 11 have facilities for disabled visitors. Launderette. Motorcaravan services. Gas supplies. Comprehensive shopping areas set around a pleasant piazza (all open till late). Eight restaurants each with a different style plus 11 pleasant and lively bars (all services open all season). Impressive aqua parks (all season). Tennis. Riding. Minigolf. Skating. Bicycle hire. Archery. Two fitness tracks in 4 ha. natural park with play area and supervised play. Golf academy. Diving centre and school. Windsurf school in season. Exhibitions. Boat excursions. Recreational events. Hairdressers. Internet cafés. ATM. Dogs are accepted in designated areas. WiFi over site (charged). Off site: Boat launching 3.5 km. Aqualandia (special rates). Excursions.

Open: 23 April - 4 October (with all services).

Directions

From Venice-Trieste autostrada leave at exit for airport or Quarto d'Altino and follow signs first for Jesolo and then Punta Sabbioni, and site will be seen just after Cavallino on the left.
GPS: 45.467883, 12.530367

Charges guide

Per unit incl. 2 persons

and electricity	€ 19.80 - € 51.70
with services	€ 22.20 - € 70.90
extra person	€ 4.90 - € 12.20
child (1-11 yrs acc. to age)	€ 2.90 - € 9.90

Three different seasons: (i) high season 29/6-31/8; (ii) mid-season 18/5-29/6 and 31/8-14/9, and (iii) off-season, outside these dates.

Cavallino-Treporti

Italy Camping Village

Via Fausta 272, I-30013 Cavallino-Treporti (Veneto) T: 041 968 090. E: info@campingitaly.it
alanrogers.com/IT60210

Italy Camping Village, under the same ownership as the better known Union Lido which it adjoins, is suggested for those who prefer a smaller, more compact site. The 180 touring pitches are on either side of sand tracks off hard access roads under a cover of trees. All have electricity connections (10A Europlug) and 126 are fully serviced. Pitches are between 60-80 sq.m. but access is impossible for large units, particularly in high season when cars are parked everywhere. A pleasant heated swimming pool (with lifeguard) has two slides, one is very long. There is direct access to a gently sloping sandy beach. A pleasant, heated, swimming pool has a slide and a whirlpool at one end, but for those who want a greater choice of activities, guests can use the facilities at Union Lido for a small additional charge. Strict regulations regarding undue noise here make this a relatively peaceful site and with lower charges than some in the area, this would be a good choice for families with young children. Advance booking is possible.

Facilities

Two high quality, fully equipped sanitary blocks include private cabins, family shower rooms and facilities for disabled visitors. Shop. Washing machines. Restaurant with TV. Bar beside beach. Heated swimming pool with flumes (May-Sept). Small playground, miniclub and children's disco. Bicycle hire. WiFi throughout (free). Only gas and electric barbecues permitted on individual pitches; charcoal only permitted in the designated area. Dogs are not accepted. Off site: Use of facilities at IT60200 Union Lido (extra charge for pool). Sports centre, golf and riding 400 m. Venice.

Open: 23 April - 27 September.

Directions

From Venice-Trieste A4 autostrada leave at exit for airport or Quarto d'Altino and follow signs for Jesolo and Punta Sabbioni. Site well signed on left after Cavallino. GPS: 45.46836, 12.53338

Charges guide

Per unit incl. 2 persons

and electricity	€ 18.10 - € 44.80
extra person	€ 4.90 - € 9.90
child (1-5 yrs)	free - € 7.10

Three charging seasons.

For latest campsite news, availability and prices visit

alanrogers.com

Cavallino-Treporti
Residence Village

Via F Baracca 47, I-30013 Cavallino-Treporti (Veneto) T: 041 968 027. E: info@residencevillage.com

alanrogers.com/IT60250

Camping Residence is a stylish site with a sandy beach directly on the Adriatic. It is well kept and has many floral displays. The 265 touring pitches are marked out with small fences or pines, and some have excellent shade. The pitches are in regular rows on level sand and vary in size (60-80 sq.m). All have 6/10A electricity connections. There are strict rules regarding noise with quiet periods required between 13.00-15.00 and no unaccompanied under 18s. A pleasant restaurant offering fine food is located in an impressive building. The beach runs the whole length of the site and shelves gradually into the sea making it safe for children. A super lagoon style pool has a large separate paddling area for children and loungers are dotted around the pool areas.

Facilities
Three large, clean and modern toilet blocks, plus a smaller one near the beach, have good facilities including British style WCs. Supermarket, separate shops for fruit and other goods. Well appointed restaurant with separate bar. Takeaway. Swimming pools with sunbathing areas. Playground. Tennis. Fitness programme. Games room. Entertainment programme. Miniclub. Bicycle hire. WiFi in some areas (charged). Dogs are not accepted.
Open: 7 May - 18 September.

Directions
From A4 Venice-Trieste autostrada take exit for airport or Quarto d'Altino. Follow signs for Jesolo, then Punta Sabbioni. Take first left after Cavallino bridge and site is 800 m. on the left.
GPS: 45.48002, 12.57395

Charges guide
Per unit incl. 2 persons and electricity	€ 21.20 - € 68.00
extra person	€ 5.40 - € 10.50

Cavallino-Treporti
Camping Vela Blu

Via Radaelli 10, I-30013 Cavallino-Treporti (Veneto) T: 041 968 068. E: info@velablu.it

alanrogers.com/IT60280

Thoughtfully landscaped within a natural wooded coastal environment, the tall pines here give shade, while attractive flowers enhance the setting and paved roads give easy access to most pitches. The 261 pitches (130 for tourers) vary in size (55-90 sq.m) and shape, but all have 10/16A electricity, water and drainage. A sister site to nos. IT60360 and IT60140, Vela Blu is a smaller family style site and a pleasant alternative to some of the other massive sites on Cavallino. It is a popular destination for Italian families, booking is essential for high season and national holidays. There is a pleasant swimming pool with a mini water park. A clean, fine sandy beach with lifeguards runs the length of one side of the site with large stone breakwaters.

Facilities
Two modern, well maintained toilet blocks include baby rooms and good facilities for disabled visitors. An attendant is on hand to maintain high standards. Laundry facilities. Motorcaravan services. Medical room. Shop. Bar. Gelateria. Restaurant and takeaway. New swimming pool complex. Games room. Satellite TV room. Pedalos. Windsurfing. Fishing. Bicycle hire. Entertainment. Charcoal barbecues are not permitted. WiFi (charged).
Open: 28 March - 26 September.

Directions
Leave A4 Venice-Trieste motorway at exit for Aeroporto and follow signs for Jesolo and Punta Sabbioni. Site is signed after village of Cavallino.
GPS: 45.45681, 12.5072

Charges guide
Per unit incl. 2 persons and all services	€ 19.90 - € 50.40
extra person	€ 4.70 - € 10.70
Camping Cheques accepted.

Cavallino-Treporti
Camping Village Cavallino

Via delle Batterie 164, I-30013 Cavallino-Treporti (Veneto) T: 041 966 133. E: info@campingcavallino.com

alanrogers.com/IT60320

This large, well ordered site is part of the Baia Holiday Group. It lies beside the sea with direct access to a superb beach of fine sand, which is very safe and has lifeguards. The site is thoughtfully laid out with the 457 large touring pitches shaded by olives and pines. All pitches have 6/10A electricity, some have water and they are generally flat and enjoy shade from mature pines. The pleasant pool, restaurant, entertainment and most other services are at the centre of the site. We enjoyed the hubbub from this area, but also the ability to find peace on the periphery. You should have a great family holiday here.

Facilities
Two remarkable new (2014) toilet blocks are well spaced and can be heated. They provide every modern requirement and include facilities for disabled campers. Launderette. Motorcaravan services. Supermarket. Bazaar. Restaurant with large terrace. Takeaway. Pizzeria. Swimming pools and whirlpool (May-Sept). Fishing. Playground. Minigolf. Bicycle hire. Entertainment. ATM. WiFi (charged). Dogs are accepted in certain areas.
Open: 24 March - 31 October.

Directions
From Venice-Trieste autostrada leave at exit for airport or Quarto d'Altino. Follow signs for Jesolo, then Punta Sabbioni. Site signs are just after Cavallino on the left. GPS: 45.45666, 12.50055

Charges guide
Per unit incl. 2 persons and electricity	€ 23.00 - € 49.90
extra person	€ 6.50 - € 12.90
child (3-9 yrs)	€ 5.50 - € 11.90

Cavallino-Treporti

Camping Village Europa

Via Fausta 332, I-30013 Cavallino-Treporti (Veneto) T: 041 968 069. E: info@campingeuropa.com

alanrogers.com/IT60410

Europa is a smart, modern site in a great position with direct access to a fine, sandy, Blue Flag beach with lifeguards. There are 450 touring pitches, all with 8A electricity, water, drainage and satellite TV connections. The site is kept beautifully clean and neat and there is an impressive array of restaurants, bars, shops and leisure amenities. These are cleverly laid out along a central avenue and include a jeweller, a doctor's surgery, Internet services and much more. All manner of leisure facilities are arranged around the site. The touring area, with some great beachside pitches, is surprisingly peaceful for a site of this size. This site would be ideal for families. A professional team provides entertainment and regular themed summer events. Some restaurant tables have pleasant sea views. Venice is easily accessible by bus and then ferry from Punta Sabbioni.

Facilities

Three toilet blocks are kept pristine and have hot water throughout. Facilities for disabled visitors. Washing machines. Large supermarket and shopping centre, bars, restaurants, cafés and pizzeria (all season; takeaway service 15/5-30/9). Excellent pool complex with slide and spa centre (all season). Tennis. Games room. Playground. Clubs for children. Entertainment programme. Direct beach access. Windsurf and pedalo hire. WiFi throughout (charged). Mobile homes, chalets and 14 eco-apartments for rent. Off site: ATM 500 m. Riding and boat launching 1 km. Golf and fishing 4 km. Walking and cycling trails.

Open: 30 March - 30 September.

Directions

From A4 autostrada (approaching from Milan) take Mestre exit and follow signs initially for Venice airport and then Jesolo. From Jesolo, follow signs to Cavallino from where site is well signed. GPS: 45.47380, 12.54903

Charges guide

Per unit incl. 2 persons	
and electricity	€ 20.00 - € 52.70
extra person	€ 5.00 - € 11.60
child (2-5 yrs)	€ 3.40 - € 10.20
dog	€ 2.70 - € 6.10

europa
CAMPING VILLAGE

www.campingeuropa.com virtual tour of our accommodation
INFO & BOOKING: info@campingeuropa.com

Cavallino-Treporti

Camping Ca'Pasquali

Via A Poerio 33, I-30013 Cavallino-Treporti (Veneto) T: 041 966 110. E: info@capasquali.it

alanrogers.com/IT60360

Situated on the attractive natural woodland coast of Cavallino with its wide, safe, sandy beach, Ca'Pasquali is a high quality holiday resort with easy access to magnificent Venice. The fine sandy beach was alive with families playing games and flying kites when we watched from the restaurant at sunset. This is a large site affiliated with nos. IT60280 and IT60140. Detail is important to the site owners and it shows everywhere. There are superb pools, a fitness area, an arena for the ambitious entertainment programme and a beachside restaurant. The 371 touring pitches (10-16A electricity) are shaded and flat (80-90 sq.m) and some have spectacular sea views. A superb site for a family holiday.

Facilities

Three spotless modern units have excellent facilities with superb amenities for disabled campers and babies. Washing machines and dryers. Motorcaravan services. Restaurant. Pizzeria. Crêperie. Cocktail bar. Snack bar. Supermarket. Bazaar. Boutique. Superb pool complex with slides, fun pool and fountains. Fitness centre. Play areas. Miniclub. Bicycle hire. Canoe hire and lessons. Entertainment. Amphitheatre. WiFi (charged). Excursion service. Caravan storage. Dogs and other animals are not accepted. Off site: Golf and riding 5 km. Sailing 20 km.

Open: 27 April - 21 September.

Directions

Leave autostrada A4 at Noventa exit in San Doná di Piave and head towards Jesolo and to Cavallino-Treporti. Site is well signed shortly after town of Cavallino. GPS: 45.45237, 12.48905

Charges guide

Per unit incl. 2 persons	
and electricity	€ 19.20 - € 52.40
extra person	€ 5.10 - € 11.40
child (1-10 yrs)	free - € 11.70
No credit cards.	

Cavallino-Treporti
Sant'Angelo Village

Via F Baracca 63, I-30013 Cavallino-Treporti (Veneto) T: 041 968 882. E: info@santangelo.it

alanrogers.com/IT60390

Sant'Angelo Village is aptly named. It is a large site, concentrated around a central square where a restaurant/pizzeria, shops, bar and an information centre with booking service for excursions can be found. The site is well planned and includes a beach snack bar with its own square, which supports the sports areas, and a fine sandy beach with lifeguards. There are 600 mostly shaded, level pitches, which are mainly around the perimeter of the site. Although large, the site has a friendly atmosphere and is ideal for families with young children and campers with mobility problems. The pool complex is impressive, as is the entertainment.

Facilities
Five modern toilet blocks provide excellent facilities with mainly British toilets and very good facilities for disabled campers and babies. Washing machines and dryers. Motorcaravan services. Restaurant and snack bar. Pizzeria. Crêperie. Gelateria. Takeaway. Supermarket. Great pool complex with water slide, pool bar and fun pool. Aerobics. Fitness centre. Play areas. Games room. Tennis. Bicycle and boat hire. Beach volleyball. Miniclub, entertainment and excursion service. WiFi (charged). Fridge box hire. Accommodation to rent. No animals.

Open: 4 May - 15 September.

Directions
Leave autostrada A4 at San Doná Noventa exit and head for San Doná di Piave, Jesolo and on to peninsula of Cavallino and Punta Sabbioni. Site is well signed shortly after Cavallino.
GPS: 45.47681, 12.55509

Charges guide
Per unit incl. 2 persons,	
electricity and water	€ 21.40 - € 48.80
extra person	€ 5.00 - € 11.00
child (3-10 yrs)	free - € 8.60
senior (over 61 yrs)	€ 3.20 - € 8.60

Cavallino-Treporti
Camping Village Garden Paradiso

Via F. Baracca 55, I-30013 Cavallino-Treporti (Veneto) T: 041 968 075. E: info@gardenparadiso.it

alanrogers.com/IT60400

Garden Paradiso is a great name for this site as it describes what it resembles. Colour from abundant flowers and attractive gardens give a very pleasant feel to this seaside site. It has three excellent, centrally situated pools with fun water features, a fitness centre, minigolf, a train to the local weekly market and many other activities for children. All 752 pitches have 6/10A electricity, satellite TV connection, water and drainage points. They are shaded by trees. A smart reception provides a professional welcome and the service that follows is impressive. The site is directly beside the sea with a beach of fine sand.

Facilities
Four smart, clean toilet blocks are fully equipped. Mixture of British and Turkish style toilets. Facilities for babies. Washing machines and dryers. Motorcaravan services. Shopping complex. Restaurant, snack bar and takeaway (all season). Pizzeria and crêperie. Aqualandia pool complex. Fitness centre. Tennis. Minigolf. Play area. Organised entertainment and excursions (high season). Bicycle hire. Windsurfing. Communal barbecue area. Caravan storage. WiFi over site (charged). No dogs.

Open: 23 April - 27 September.

Directions
Leave Venice-Trieste autostrada either by taking airport or Quarto d'Altino exits; follow signs to Jesolo and Punta Sabbioni. Take first road left after Cavallino roundabout and site is a little way on the right. GPS: 45.47897, 12.56359

Charges guide
Per unit incl. 2 persons,	
electricity, water and drainage	€ 22.00 - € 54.00
extra person	€ 5.00 - € 11.50
child (3-12 yrs) or senior (over 63)	free - € 8.95

Cavallino-Treporti
Camping Scarpiland

Via A Poerio 14, I-30013 Cavallino-Treporti (Veneto) T: 041 966 488. E: info@scarpiland.com

alanrogers.com/IT60470

Scarpiland is a family owned site which has a fine sandy beach and is directly on the Adriatic. It is a medium sized site with touring pitches under the shade of mature pines and scattered amongst mobile homes. The 147 touring pitches are level, vary in size (60-90 sq.m) and all have 6A electricity. Some are hedged and most have water. Most of the facilities are just outside the site entrance; the road is pleasant but has some traffic. The site will suit campers who prefer smaller establishments with excellent beaches and competitive prices. Excursions are organised to local attractions and into Venice.

Facilities
Two sanitary blocks, one large, clean and modern with the main site services. The second smaller unisex block has almost all Turkish style toilets. Facilities for babies in the large block plus one unit for disabled visitors. Washing machines and dryers. Fridge/freezer. Restaurant/pizzeria. Ice cream parlour. Newsagent. Supermarket. Butcher. Souvenir shop. Greengrocer and local produce (all on the main site road). Bicycle hire. Riding. WiFi (charged).

Open: 12 April - 27 September.

Directions
From Milan, take A4 to Venice and continue towards Trieste as far as A27 intersection, then follow signs to airport. At end of bypass, follow signs to Jesolo then Cavallino and Punta Sabbioni. From here site is clearly signed. GPS: 45.45507, 12.48874

Charges guide
Per unit incl. 2 persons	
and electricity	€ 15.50 - € 35.90

Minimum stay 2 nights.

For latest campsite news, availability and prices visit

alanrogers.com

Cortina d'Ampezzo

Camping Rocchetta

Via Campo 1, I-32043 Cortina d'Ampezzo (Veneto) T: 043 650 63. E: camping@sunrise.it

alanrogers.com/IT62055

Within walking distance of one of Europe's most well known winter ski and summer holiday resorts, Camping Rocchetta is an attractive, medium sized, family run site set largely under pines beside a stream. The pitches are level, on grass and all have 3A electricity and views of the surrounding mountains, some over 3,000 m. high. The site has well maintained, all-year-round facilities. English is spoken at reception and whether your interests are walking, cycling or something more strenuous, there is plenty of information available, ensuring you make the most of your stay in this beautiful region.

Facilities

Heated sanitary block, with all facilities under cover, has free, controllable showers and some washbasins in cabins. Facilities for disabled visitors. Laundry room. Motorcaravan services. Small shop. Bar with snacks. Outdoor jacuzzi. Playground. WiFi over site (charged). Off site: Cortina 1.5 km. Winter sports. Ampezzo Valley and the Dolomite mountains. Walking and cycle trails.

Open: 1 June - 20 September and 5 December - 7 April.

Directions

From the south travel north on the A27, after Belluno take exit Cadore/Cortina joining the SS51. Continue to outskirts of Cortina (passing the Olympic ski jump) site is signed to the left. GPS: 46.52262, 12.13406

Charges guide

Per unit incl. 2 persons and electricity	€ 22.00 - € 29.00
extra person	€ 7.50 - € 9.00

Eraclea Mare

Camping Village Portofelice

Viale dei Fiori 15, I-30020 Eraclea Mare (Veneto) T: 0421 66 411. E: info@portofelice.it

alanrogers.com/IT60220

Portofelice is an efficient and attractive coastal site, with a sandy beach which is a short walk through a protected pine wood. The excellent beach is very safe and has lifeguards. There are a total of 422 pitches, half of which are available for touring. These flat and shady pitches have 6/10A electricity (70 also have water, drainage and TV sockets), are well kept and cars are parked separately. Some 302 pitches are dedicated to rental accommodation. The social life of the site is centred around the stunning pool complex where the shops, pizzeria, bar, café and restaurant are also located. This is a tremendous family site. You will be spoilt for choice with the range of on-site entertainment and activities which are organised for adults and children. If you can drag yourself away from the holiday village, Venice, the Dolomites and the Italian Lakes are all within easy reach. The superb welcome pack has discounts and details of many tours and places to visit in the area. The friendly English-speaking General Manager, Maurizio Cabrelle, is always available to help make your stay special.

Facilities

Three modern sanitary blocks have the usual facilities with slightly more Turkish style toilets than British. Baby room and excellent children's block. Facilities for disabled campers. Very large supermarket and bazaar. Pizzeria and takeaway. Bar/restaurant with terraces and waiter service. American diner. Gelateria. Crêperie. Three superb pools with waterfalls, slides and an area specifically equipped for disabled guests, hydro-massage and sunbathing. Playgrounds. Go-kart track. Pedalos. Water dodgems. Tennis. 5-a-side football. Basketball. Volleyball. Sandy beach. Bicycle hire. Activities and entertainment. Miniclub. WiFi throughout (charged). Internet room. Dogs are not accepted. Off site: Bus 30 m. Riding 200 m. Fishing 5 km.

Open: 15 May - 20 September.

Directions

From A4 Venice-Trieste, exit for S Dona/Noventa. After Noventa di Piave toll booth, turn right towards S Doná di Piave. At roundabout (before town centre) keep right and follow signs to Eraclea. At Eraclea turn left (Piave river on right), and at first roundabout turn right (Eraclea Mare). Continue for 9-10 km. and turn left at roundabout just before Eraclea Mare. Site is on right in 2 km. GPS: 45.55357, 12.76752

Charges guide

Per unit incl. 2 persons and electricity	€ 16.20 - € 48.50
extra person	€ 3.80 - € 11.00
child (6-10 yrs) or senior (over 60 yrs)	€ 3.50 - € 9.90
child (2-5 yrs)	free - € 8.10

Visit our website:
www.portofelice.it
info@portofelice.it ®

PORTOFELICE
★★★★
CAMPING VILLAGE CENTRO VACANZE

Viale dei Fiori, 15
I - 30020 Eraclea Mare (VE)
Tel. +39. 0421. 66411
Fax +39. 0421. 66021

Bungalows - Mobile Homes
2 Whirlpools (20 seats)
2 Swimming pools
2 Waterslides for children
Bar - Restaurant - Pizzeria
Ice cream parlour - Take Away
Supermarket - Bazar
Internet point - Wi.Fi.
Cash dispenser - Sport centre
Playground - Entertainment
Booking pitches accepted
Ideal for families and children
Pitches with electricity,
water and waste disposal

NEW luxury Bungalow

PRICES AND SPECIAL OFFERS IN LOW SEASON

Fusina

Camping Fusina

Via Moranzani 93, I-30176 Fusina (Veneto) T: 041 547 0055. E: info@campingfusina.com

alanrogers.com/IT60530

This is traditional camping, but what fun. Choose from 500 well shaded, flat and grassy informal pitches or an unrivalled position directly by the water with amazing views over the lagoon to the towers in Saint Mark's Square. Huge ships pass within 50 metres of the site and delight the children. With water on three sides there are welcoming cool breezes. The ferry to Venice is just outside the gate, so this is an ideal site for visiting the city. As a short-stay site, there are few luxuries, but a busy bar and restaurant are at the heart of the site, along with a small shop. We enjoyed the informality here, where you are left alone to either travel to Venice or just relax watching the sunset over the lagoon from your pitch.

Facilities

Modern, well equipped facilities include units for disabled visitors, along with some existing older units. Washing machines and dryers. Motorcaravan services. Shop (15/3-31/10). Restaurant. Pizzeria and beer garden. Very lively bar. TV with satellite. Small playground. Boat hire. Marina with cranes, moorings, and maintenance facilities. Air-conditioned London cyber bus (really!). Bicycle hire. ATM. Torches useful. WiFi in some areas (charged).

Open: All year.

Directions

From SSII Padua-Venice road follow site signs on road east of Mira, turning right as signed. Site is in Fusina at end of peninsula and is well signed. Keep a keen watch for brown camping signs for Fusina and ferry terminal. GPS: 45.4195, 12.2563

Charges guide

Per unit incl. 2 persons and electricity	€ 33.00 - € 35.00
extra person	€ 9.50 - € 10.50

Lido di Jesolo

Camping Jesolo International

Viale A. da Giussano, I-30016 Lido ve Jesolo (Veneto) T: 042 197 1826. E: info@jesolointernational.it

alanrogers.com/IT60370

This is an absolutely brilliant family oriented, resort-style site that we loved, especially for its very positive value for money approach. The truly amazing array of top quality on-site activities is included in the price, some off-site attractions are free (Aqualandia, etc) and others are discounted. Jesolo International is located on a beautiful promontory with 700 m. of white sandy beach and slowly shelving waters. The 368 pitches are flat, mostly shaded and with 10/20A electricity, water and drainage, WiFi and satellite TV connection. Some have private bathrooms. The superb pool complex, where an excellent entertainment programme is presented each night, rounds off this outstanding site.

Facilities

Sanitary facilities include 72 very modern, continually cleaned bathroom units (shower, WC and basin). Rooms for babies, seniors and disabled campers. Washing machines and dryers. Dishwashers. Motorcaravan services. Supermarket. Family-style restaurant. Pizzeria. Meals and shopping delivery to pitch. Beach bar with snacks. Pool bar. Sports centre. Miniclub. Indoor gym. Tennis. Golf. Large play area. Sailing. Offshore pirate ship. Scuba diving. Language course (free). Pony riding (free). Doctor on site (free). WiFi (free). Dogs are not accepted.

Open: 24 April - 27 September.

Directions

From A4 Venice-Trieste autostrada take Dona di Piave exit and follow signs to Jesolo then Punta Sabbioni. Turn off to Lido di Jesolo just before the Cavallino bridge where the site is well signed. GPS: 45.48395, 12.58763

Charges guide

Per unit incl. 2 persons and electricity	€ 28.50 - € 61.50
extra person	€ 6.00 - € 14.50
child (1-5 yrs)	free - € 6.00

Oriago

Camping della Serenissima

Via Padana 334/a, I-30176 Mancontenta (Veneto) T: 041 921 850. E: info@campingserenissima.it

alanrogers.com/IT60500

The charming Alberti family own this delightful little site of some 155 pitches (all with 16A electricity) where one could stay for a number of days whilst visiting Venice (12 km), Padova (24 km), Lake Garda (135 km) or the Dolomites. There is a good service by bus to Venice (€ 2.60 return) and the site is situated on the Riviera del Brenta, at a section with some very large, old villas. A long, rectangular, flat site with numbered pitches on each side of a central road. There is shade in most parts with many trees, plants and grass. English is spoken and the family pride themselves on the cleanliness of their site.

Facilities

Sanitary facilities are modern and spotless and include those for disabled visitors. Additional quality toilet facilities adjacent to restaurant. Motorcaravan services. Gas supplies. Shop (all season). Bar. Restaurant and takeaway (1/6-31/10). Play area. Fishing. Bicycle hire. Local markets are well publicised. Off site: Golf and riding 3 km. Brenta canal (boat trips). Historic villas. Venice.

Open: 30 March - 6 November.

Directions

On A27 or SS309 take exit for Venezia-Mestre then signs for Ravenna, Padova and Milano. After Padova-Riviera del Brenta follow signs to Oriago. Site is well signed. GPS: 45.451769, 12.183784

Charges guide

Per unit incl. 2 persons and electricity	€ 29.00 - € 33.00
extra person	€ 7.50 - € 9.00
child (3-12 yrs)	€ 4.50 - € 5.50

Punta Sabbioni

Camping Marina di Venezia

Via Montello 6, I-30013 Punta Sabbioni (Veneto) T: **041 530 2511**. E: **camping@marinadivenezia.it**

alanrogers.com/IT60450

This is an amazingly large site (2,915 pitches) with every conceivable facility. It has a pleasant feel, with cheerful staff and no notion of being overcrowded, even when full. Marina di Venezia has the advantage of being within walking distance of the ferry to Venice. It will appeal in particular to those who enjoy an extensive range of entertainment and activities and a lively atmosphere. Individual pitches are spacious and set on sandy or grassy ground; most are separated by trees or hedges. All are equipped with 10A electricity and water. There is a special area and facilities for dog owners. The site's excellent sandy beach is one of the widest along this stretch of coast and has five pleasant beach bars.

Facilities

Nine modern toilet blocks are maintained to a very high standard with hot showers and a high proportion of British style toilets. Pleasant facilities for disabled visitors. Laundry. Range of shops. Several bars, restaurants and takeaways. Five beach bars/snack bars. Enormous swimming pool complex with slides and flumes. Several play areas. Tennis. Surfboard and catamaran hire. Wide range of organised entertainment. WiFi (charged).

Open: 1 April - 11 October.

Directions

From A4 motorway, take Jesolo exit. After Jesolo continue towards Punta Sabbioni. Site is clearly signed to the left towards the end of this road, close to the Venice ferries. GPS: 45.43750, 12.43805

Charges guide

Per unit incl. 2 persons and electricity	€ 21.90 - € 49.30
extra person	€ 4.70 - € 10.90
dog	€ 1.50 - € 5.10

Sottomarina

Camping Miramare

Via Barbarigo 103, I-30015 Sottomarina di Chioggia (Veneto) T: **041 490 610**. E: **campmir@tin.it**

alanrogers.com/IT60560

Camping Miramare is a pleasant, fairly shady site with beach access, a swimming pool and a busy entertainment programme. The site is kept beautifully clean and is divided by a road with reception on the beach side, along with most of the amenities. The other side is spacious and very peaceful with just sports amenities and a sanitary block. The 230 touring pitches are separated from the permanent units. All have 6A electricity and some have water and drainage. The beach is great, with soft sand and a lifeguard. You can hire sunshades and loungers. The restaurant offers traditional food and pizzas, which can be enjoyed on the terraces overlooking the pools. Children have several play areas and there is entertainment on site all season. The swimming and paddling pool is excellent, with two diving boards and a lifeguard. The site lies close to the ancient city of Chioggia, famous for its fishing and Venice-like construction. It is well worth a visit on a bicycle to investigate its amazing history. For those wishing to further explore the region, there are many other opportunities. An excursion to Venice naturally holds a strong appeal, but other stunning cities are also close at hand, notably Padova, Vicenza and Treviso. This is a pleasant, family oriented site which has a distinct Italian feel. English is spoken.

Facilities

Three identical, modern, very clean blocks, one in the permanent campers' area. Pushbutton hot showers and mainly Turkish style toilets. Facilities for disabled visitors. Baby room. Laundry rooms. Motorcaravan services. Pleasant bar. Restaurant, pizzeria and takeaway, smart shop (all open all season). Excellent swimming pool and separate paddling pool (9/5-21/9). Several great play areas. Multisports court. Bicycle hire. Entertainment and children's activities (high season). WiFi over site (charged). Dogs are not accepted in high season.

Open: 4 April - 21 September.

Directions

Site is off S309 south of Chioggia. Follow signs to Sottomarina, crossing the Laguna del Lusenzo, then look for site signs. Site is off Viale Mediterranneo road to the right. Site is the second of many along this narrow road. GPS: 45.19018, 12.30341

Charges guide

Per unit incl. 2 persons and electricity	€ 20.50 - € 35.50
extra person	€ 5.00 - € 8.50
child (1-6 yrs)	€ 2.50 - € 4.00

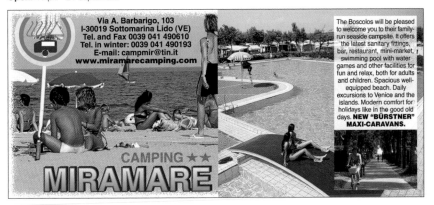

Via A. Barbarigo, 103
I-30019 Sottomarina Lido (VE)
Tel. and Fax 0039 041 490610
Tel. in winter: 0039 041 490193
E-mail: campmir@tin.it
www.miramarecamping.com

The Boscolos will be pleased to welcome you to their family-run seaside campsite. It offers the latest sanitary fittings, bar, restaurant, mini-market, swimming pool with water games and other facilities for fun and relax, both for adults and children. Spacious well-equipped beach. Daily excursions to Venice and the islands. Modern comfort for holidays like in the good old days. NEW "BÜRSTNER" MAXI-CARAVANS.

CAMPING ★★ MIRAMARE

Sottomarina

Villaggio Turistico Isamar

Isolaverde, via Isamar 9, I-30010 Chioggia (Veneto) T: 041 553 5811. E: info@villaggioisamar.com

alanrogers.com/IT60550

This is a very large, high quality site with many shops and restaurants and a huge range of leisure facilities. The camping areas are beneath pine trees and within easy reach of the two excellent pool complexes and covered entertainment centre. The pitches are arranged on either side of hard access roads and all have 6A electrical connections. There are many other areas containing well constructed chalets and holiday bungalows. The site has its own beautiful soft sand beach and is a great destination for families as it caters for all tastes. Entertainment and activity programmes are organised in several languages. It is popular with German and Dutch campers and may become crowded in high season.

Facilities

Four large, spotlessly clean sanitary blocks are arranged around the main camping area. Fully equipped and of superb quality with facilities for children and disabled visitors. Laundry. Motorcaravan services. Gas supplies. Hairdresser. Beauty centre. Supermarket and shopping centre. Ice cream shop. Pastry shop. Restaurant. Large bar/pizzeria and self-service restaurant. Swimming pools. Tennis. Gym. Playground. Games room. Riding. Volleyball. Archery. Football. Bicycle hire. Extensive entertainment and fitness programme. Supervised play for over 4s. Miniclub. ATM. Boat launching. WiFi (charged). Dogs are not accepted. Off site: Disco with bar/restaurant adjacent. Boat launching 500 m. Excursions.

Open: 16 May - 13 September.

Directions

Turn off the main 309 road towards sea just south of Adige river 10 km. south of Chioggia, and proceed 5 km. to site. GPS: 45.16236, 12.32477

Charges guide

Per unit incl. 2 persons	
and electricity	€ 24.00 - € 54.00
extra person	€ 8.00 - € 12.00
child (under 12 yrs)	free - € 10.00

Vicenza

Camping Vicenza

Strada Pelosa, I-36100 Vicenza (Veneto) T: 0444 582 311. E: info@campingvicenza.it

alanrogers.com/IT60275

This is a very pleasant site with a difference, in that it is paired with a quality hotel close to Vicenza. As such, it is able to offer use of the hotel facilities including the pool, bar/restaurant and spa (charge for spa). The 77 pitches (80 sq.m) are attractively laid out with bricked hardstandings and brick access roads, with plenty of shade from trees, and privacy from neat and mature hedges. They are smart, clean and equipped with 3/6A electricity. The hotel and site are alongside an autoroute exit, but a tall soundproofing fence along one side of the site minimises its impact. It is peaceful here despite the proximity of the autoroute, and the bus service is brilliant for visiting Vicenza.

Facilities

The single sanitary block is initially quite forbidding (concrete, post WW2 styling), but the facilities within are neat and comprehensive. Baby room with bath. Children's bathroom. Facilities for disabled visitors. Washing machine. Drying area under cover. Fridge freezer. Motorcaravan services. No shop. Restaurant and takeaway (1/4-20/9). Drinks machine. Hotel wellness centre with pool and bar. TV room. Entertainment in the hotel on Fridays. Communal barbecues. Public bus service. WiFi (free). Off site: Shops and ATM 1 km.

Open: 1 April - 30 September.

Directions

From A4 Verona - Padova autoroute take Vincenz est exit and you will immediately see campsite sign on your right as you exit the autoroute. Take a series of right turns at mini roundabouts following campsite signs bringing you to Hotel Vieste and campsite entrance. GPS: 45.518002, 11.602544

Charges guide

Per unit incl. 2 persons	
and electricity	€ 26.50 - € 34.50
extra person	€ 6.50 - € 8.50
child (3-8 yrs)	€ 3.00 - € 5.00

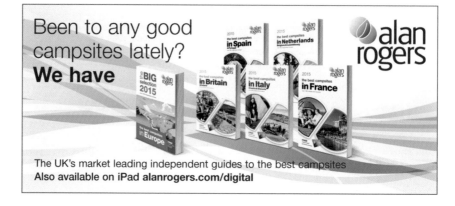

The independent Principality of Liechtenstein is the fourth smallest country in the world. Nestled between Switzerland and Austria, it has a total area of 157 square kilometres (61 square miles).

If you like clean mountain air and peaceful surroundings, then a visit to Liechtenstein would be worthwhile. The little town of Vaduz (the capital) is where you will find most points of interest, including the world famous art collection (Kunstmuseum), which holds paintings by Rembrandt and other world famous artists. Above the town of Vaduz is the restored twelfth-century castle, now owned by the prince of Liechtenstein (not open to the public). Take a walk up to the top of the hill, you can view Vaduz and the mountains stretched out below. Situated on a terrace above Vaduz is Triesenberg village, blessed with panoramic views over the Rhine Valley, a pretty village with vineyards and ancient chapels. Malbun is Liechtenstein's premier mountain resort, popular in both winter and summer, for either skiing or walking.

Triesen
Camping Mittagspitze
Sägastrasse 29, FL 9495 Triesen (Liechtenstein) T: 392 3677. E: info@campingtriesen.li
alanrogers.com/FL7580

Camping Mittagspitze is attractively and quietly situated for visiting the Principality. Set on a hillside, it has all the scenic mountain views that one could wish for. Extensive broad, level, grassed terraces on a steep slope provide unmarked pitches and electricity connections (6A) are available. Trees provide some shade, mainly along the terrace edges. Of the 240 spaces, 120 are used by seasonal caravans.

Facilities
Two good quality sanitary blocks provide all the usual facilities. Washing machine, dryer and ironing. Room where one can sit or eat. Shop (1/6-31/8; bread to order). Restaurant (all year). Small swimming pool and paddling pool (15/6-15/8), not heated but very popular in summer. Playground. TV room. Off site: Direct access to forest walks. Tennis and indoor pool nearby. Switzerland 3 km. Riding and bicycle hire 5 km. Vaduz, capital of Liechtenstein 7 km. Austria 20 km.

Open: All year.

Directions
From A3 take Trübbach exit 10 and follow road towards Balzers. Then head towards Vaduz and site is 2 km. south of Triesen on the right. Site is signed.
GPS: 47.0857, 9.5259

Charges guide
Per unit incl. 2 persons	
and electricity	€ 29.00 - € 35.00
extra person	€ 9.00
child (3-14 yrs)	€ 4.00
dog	€ 4.00

The Grand Duchy of Luxembourg is a sovereign state, lying between Belgium,

France and Germany. Divided into two areas: the spectacular Ardennes region

in the north and the rolling farmlands and woodland in the south, bordered on

the east by the wine growing area of the Moselle Valley.

Most attractions are within easy reach of Luxembourg's capital, Luxembourg-Ville, a fortress
city perched dramatically on its rocky promontory overlooking the Alzette and Petrusse Valleys.
The verdant hills and valleys of the Ardennes are a maze of hiking trails, footpaths and cycle
routes – ideal for an activity holiday. The Moselle Valley, famous for its sweet wines, is just
across the river from Germany; its charming hamlets can be discovered by bicycle or by boat.
Popular wine tasting tours take place from late spring to early autumn. Echternacht is a good
base for exploring the Mullerthal region, known as 'Little Switzerland'. Lying on the banks of the
River Sûre, its forested landscape is dotted with curious rock formations and castle ruins,
notably those at Beaufort and Larochette. The pretty Schießentümpel cascade is worth a visit.

CAPITAL: Luxembourg City

Tourist Office

Luxembourg Tourist Office

Suite 4.1, Sicilian House, Sicilian Ave,

London WC1A 2QR

Tel: 020 7434 2800

Fax: 020 7430 1773

Email: tourism@luxembourg.co.uk

Internet: www.luxembourg.co.uk

Population

537,000

Climate

A temperate climate prevails, the summer often
extending from May to late October.

Language

Letzeburgesch is the national language, with
French and German also being official languages.

Telephone

The country code is 00 352.

Money

Currency: The Euro

Banks: Mon-Fri 08.30/09.00-12.00
and 13.30-16.30.

Shops

Mon 14.00-18.30. Tues to Sat 08.30-12.00
and 14.00-18.30 (grocers and butchers close
at 15.00 on Sat).

Public Holidays

New Year; Carnival Day mid-Feb; Easter Mon;
May Day; Ascension; Whit Mon; National Day
23 June; Assumption 15 Aug; Kermesse 1 Sept;
All Saints; All Souls; Christmas 25, 26 Dec.

Motoring

Many holidaymakers travel through Luxembourg
to take advantage of the lower fuel prices, thus
creating traffic congestion at petrol stations,
especially in summer. A Blue Zone area exists
in Luxembourg City and various parts of the
country (discs from tourist offices) but meters
are also used.

see campsite map 1

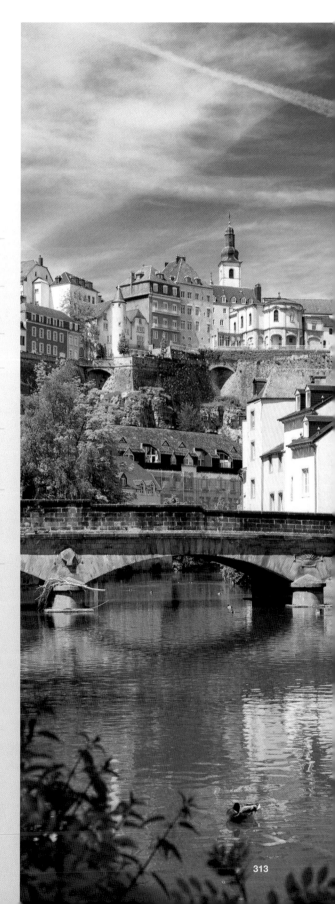

Beaufort

Camping Plage Beaufort

87 Grand-Rue, L-6310 Beaufort T: 836 099 300. E: camplage@pt.lu

alanrogers.com/LU7840

Plage Beaufort is an all-year-round site run by the Syndicat d'Initiative et du Tourisme. It is a little off the main tourist route but there is some nice countryside in the area known as Little Switzerland. The site has 312 pitches, 109 of which are taken by privately owned mobile homes and chalets, leaving around 200 for touring units. The terrain is undulating with some terracing and some pitches are hidden away in quiet corners. Pitch sizes do vary but all have 10A electricity. In summer the area provides for cycling, tennis and other sporting facilities, with the main attraction of the site being the excellent municipal swimming pool adjacent (included in price).

Facilities

Four toilet blocks, some heated, provide an interesting mixture of facilities with baby room and facilities for disabled visitors. All are spotlessly clean. Motorcaravan services. Recycling. Snack bar. Several small rather basic playgrounds. Bicycle hire. Internet access. Off site: Municipal swimming pool adjacent. The village has a variety of shops, and there is a 'buvette' serving food and drink, just outside at the far end of the site.

Open: All year.

Directions

Beaufort is midway between Diekirch and Echternach. From Reisdorf take CR128 for 5 km. and site is north of town centre, opposite the pharmacy. GPS: 49.8399, 6.28945

Charges guide

Per unit incl. 2 persons and electricity	€ 18.00 - € 22.50
extra person (from 4 yrs)	€ 5.50
dog	€ 3.00

Berdorf

Camping Bon Repos

39 rue de Consdorf, L-6551 Berdorf T: 790 631. E: irma@bonrepos.lu

alanrogers.com/LU7820

In the Petite Suisse region of Luxembourg, an area of limestone gorges which is popular with climbers and hikers, this attractive and peaceful family run site would make a good base from which to explore the eastern side of this tiny country. Located at the edge of the village of Berdorf, the site is gently sloping, with a central tarmac roadway. The 56 pitches for touring are mostly arranged in bays of four, each on a small terrace, and all have a 16A electric hook-up. Most are fairly open, a few have a little shade. A separate area is provided for tents.

Facilities

Modern and clean main sanitary building provides all the usual facilities. Smaller unit (without showers) by the tent field. Both units can be heated. Further en-suite unit. Reception (open 09.30-10.00, 19.00-20.00) sells wine, beer and soft drinks. TV and games room. Playground. Baker calls. Gas supplies. Dogs are not accepted. WiFi. Off site: Hotels for drinks and meals, and municipal sports complex with indoor swimming pool are a few minutes walk away. Bus stop 100 m. Supermarket 5 km.

Open: 1 April - 7 November.

Directions

Berdorf is 6 km. west of Echternach, the site is signed from village centre towards Consdorf. The entrance is just after a left-hand bend, take care. GPS: 49.819486, 6.347491

Charges guide

Per unit incl. 2 persons and electricity	€ 20.80
extra person	€ 6.00
child (3-13 yrs)	€ 2.00

Bourscheid

Camping Um Gritt Castlegarden

Buurschtermillen 10, L-9164 Bourscheid T: 990 449. E: umgritt@castlegarden.lu

alanrogers.com/LU7930

Camping Um Gritt is a family run campsite with friendly Dutch owners. It is located at the foot of a castle in the heart of the Ardennes, in the beautiful wooded valley of Bourscheid. It has a long season, open from April until the end of October. There are 98 reasonably level, unmarked pitches, many with little shade, including about 40 long stay pitches. All have 16A Europlug. They are laid out in a sunny, grassy meadow along the banks of the shallow River Sûre. This is an ideal place to cool off on a hot day, bathing, fishing, messing around in small boats or having a drink in the small bar/restaurant.

Facilities

There are five modern toilet blocks with all necessary facilities. Washing machine and dryer. Bread delivery. Small bar, restaurant and takeaway. Club for children and some family entertainment (July/Aug). Small playground. Volleyball. Mountain bike hire. Walking and hiking maps. WiFi throughout (charged). Off site: Lake swimming 20 minutes. Paragliding from 'point de vue Gringlay', organised from the site. Tennis and canoeing close by. Supermarket 10 mins walk. Railway stations at Ettelbruck and Diekirch, both approx. 4 km. Golf 10 km.

Open: 1 April - 31 October.

Directions

From Ettelbruck, take N7. At roundabout take second exit onto N27. Turn left onto CR308. Follow signs to Bourscheid Moulin. Cross over bridge and site is signed to left. Follow co-ordinates, not the address or postcode. GPS: 49.91015, 6.08635

Charges guide

Per unit incl. 2 persons and electricity	€ 18.50 - € 22.50
extra person	€ 4.00 - € 5.00
child (3-14 yrs)	€ 2.00 - € 2.50
dog	€ 2.00 - € 2.50

For latest campsite news, availability and prices visit

alanrogers.com

Consdorf

Camping la Pinède

33 rue Burgkapp, L-6211 Consdorf T: 790 271. E: sit.consdorf@internet.lu

alanrogers.com/LU7630

La Pinède is a pleasant municipal site in the Mullerthal region, situated adjacent to the municipal sports field. The site provides 110 individual, hedged, grassy spaces for touring units, all with 10A electricity, plus 39 pitches housing static units. There is no shop on site but all necessary shops and services are in the town within walking distance. A baker calls Monday to Saturday (not on Wednesday in low season). The immediate area is popular for cycling and hiking and the River Moselle and vineyards are an easy day trip by car. Guided walks are organised in high season.

Facilities

Sanitary facilities provide washbasins and showers in a building which can be heated in cool weather. A further small, modern unit is situated at the far end of the site. Extra facilities are to the rear of the bar. Gas supplies. Café/bar. Small adventure-style playground. Minigolf. Tennis. Football field. Bicycle hire. Internet access. Off site: Golf 6 km. Fishing 9 km. Echternach 10 km.

Open: 15 March - 15 November.

Directions

Consdorf is southwest of Echternach. From N14 Diekirch-Grevenmacher, turn left onto CR121 signed Consdorf. Site is in the town centre near sports stadium (well signed). GPS: 49.780873, 6.332062

Charges guide

Per unit incl. 2 persons and electricity	€ 18.70
extra person	€ 4.90
child	€ 2.50
dog	€ 1.90

Diekirch

Camping Bleesbrück

Bleesbrück 1, L-9359 Diekirch T: 803 134. E: info@camping-bleesbruck.lu

alanrogers.com/LU7730

Camping Bleesbrück, a family run site, is centrally located in rolling countryside, ideal for exploring the Ardennes and the Eifel. The surrounding farmland and forests lie within the Our, a natural park which can be explored on foot or by bicycle. The main site is enclosed by trees and offers 144 shaded and unshaded touring pitches with electricity (10A). There is a separate 30-pitch naturist area, screened off at the far end of the main site. The Blees flows past and offers opportunities for the angler. An entertainment programme is available for adults and children. Both electric and standard bicycles can be hired on site, and guided walks and cycle routes run past the site.

Facilities

Two sanitary units, one a separate unit for the naturist site, include washbasins in cabins, baby room and facilities with access for disabled visitors. Washing machine and dryer. Motorcaravan services. Bar. Terraced restaurant (seats 60). Takeaway (snacks). TV and games room. Sports field and large playground. Outdoor table football. Fishing. Bicycles and E-bike rental. Rental accommodation includes huts, mobile homes, apartments and chalets. WiFi (charged). Off site: Shop and petrol station at entrance. Diekirch 2 km. Vianden Castle 15 km.

Open: 1 April - 15 October.

Directions

Via Belgium: Bastogne-N15 towards Ettelbrück-Diekirch-Bleesbruck. The site is located between Diekirch and Vianden. The entrance is beside the Q8/GULF petrol station (roundabout). GPS: 49.87286, 6.18923

Charges guide

Per unit incl. 2 persons and electricity	€ 22.30
dog	€ 2.60

Eisenbach

Camping Kohnenhof

Kounenhaff 1, L-9838 Eisenbach T: 929 464. E: kohnenhof@pt.lu

alanrogers.com/LU7680

Nestling in a valley with the River Our running through it, Camping Kohnenhof offers a very agreeable location for a relaxing family holiday. From the minute you stop at the reception you are assured of a warm and friendly welcome. There are 105 pitches, 80 for touring, all with 6/16A electricity. Numerous paths cross through the wooded hillside so this could be a haven for walkers. A little bridge crosses the small river over the border to Germany. The river is shallow and safe for children (parental supervision is essential).

Facilities

Heated sanitary block with showers and washbasins in cabins. Facilities for disabled visitors. Motorcaravan services. Laundry. Bar, restaurant, takeaway (open all season). Baker calls daily. TV room. Sports field with play equipment. Boules. Bicycle hire. Golf weeks. Discounts on six local 18-hole golf courses. WiFi over site. Apartments to rent. Off site: Bus to Clervaux and Vianden stops (4 times daily) outside site entrance. Riding 5 km. Castle at Vianden 14 km. Monastery at Clervaux 14 km.

Open: 1 April - 31 October.

Directions

Take N7 north from Diekirch. At Hosingen, turn right onto the narrow and winding CR324 signed Eisenbach. Follow site signs from Eisenbach or Obereisenbach. GPS: 50.01602, 6.13600

Charges guide

Per unit incl. 2 persons and electricity	€ 19.90 - € 29.90
extra person	€ 5.00
dog	€ 3.00

Camping Cheques accepted.

FREE Alan Rogers Travel Card
Extra benefits and savings - see page 14

Enscherange

Camping Val d'Or

Um Gaertchen 2, L-9747 Enscherange T: 920 691. E: valdor@pt.lu

alanrogers.com/LU7770

Camping Val d'Or is one of those small, family run, countryside sites where you easily find yourself staying longer than planned. Set in four hectares of lush meadowland under a scattering of trees, the site is divided into two by the tree-lined Clerve river as it winds its way slowly through the site. A footbridge goes some way to joining the site together and there are two entrances for vehicles. There are 76 marked, level grass touring pitches, all with electricity (6A Europlug) and with some tree shade. Cars are parked away from the pitches. There are open views of the surrounding countryside with its wooded hills. The site's Dutch owners speak good English.

Facilities
Next to the reception is a heated sanitary block where some facilities are found, others including some showers are located under cover, outside. Showers are token operated. Laundry room. Gas supplies. Bar (all day in high season). Takeaway (high season except Sundays). Swimming and paddling in river. Three play areas (one with waterways, waterwheel and small pool). Bicycle hire. WiFi (free). Max. 1 dog. Off site: Fishing and golf 10 km.

Open: 29 March - 1 November.

Directions
From A26/E25 (Liège-Luxembourg) exit 54 travel to Bastogne. Then take N84/N15 towards Diekirch for 15 km. At crossroads turn left towards Wiltz following signs for Clervaux. Pass through Wiltz and into Weidingen, 500 m. after VW garage turn right on Wilderwiltz road. In Wilderwiltz follow signs for Enscherange where site is signed.
GPS: 50.00017, 5.99106

Charges guide
Per unit incl. 2 persons and electricity	€ 16.00 - € 22.00

No credit cards.

Ermsdorf

Camping Neumuhle

Reisdorferstrasse 27, L-9366 Ermsdorf T: 879 391. E: info@camping-neumuhle.lu

alanrogers.com/LU7810

Camping Neumuhle is located at Ermsdorf, at the heart of Luxembourg close to Diekirch. It is surrounded by the Mullerthal and some delightful countryside, known as Little Switzerland. Pitches here are spacious and all have electricity. This is great walking country and the long-distance hiking track GR5 (North Sea-Riviera) passes close to the site. Walking maps are available for loan at reception. There are 85 touring pitches all with 6A electricity and 20 chalets to rent. The site is terraced with level grass pitches separated by small hedges. The restaurant and covered terrace overlook the swimming pool and a small shop sells all basic provisions. Other on-site amenities include a large adventure playground.

Facilities
The central sanitary block is modern and clean. No facilities for disabled visitors. Restaurant with covered terrace and snack bar. Takeaway (July/Aug). Shop (July/Aug). Swimming pool (May-Aug). Adventure play area. Entertainment and activity programme. Boules. Children's club (high season). Bicycle hire. Mobile homes to rent. WiFi over site (charged). Off site: Diekirch. Luxembourg City. Walking and cycling tracks. Riding 4 km. Golf 6 km. Fishing 6 km.

Open: 15 March - 31 October.

Directions
Ermsdorf can be found northeast of the city of Luxembourg. From Diekirch, head south on CR356 and the site is well signed from Ermsdorf. From Reisdorf follow Ermsdorf road (4 km). Site is on right before village. GPS: 49.8391, 6.225

Charges guide
Per unit incl. 2 persons and electricity	€ 19.75
extra person	€ 5.50
child (1-14 yrs)	€ 3.50
dog	€ 2.00

Esch-sur-Alzette

Camping Gaalgebierg

Boite Postale 20, L-4001 Esch-sur-Alzette T: 541 069. E: gaalcamp@pt.lu

alanrogers.com/LU7700

Occupying an elevated position on the edge of town, near the French border, this site is run by the local camping and caravan club. On a hilltop and with a good variety of trees, most pitches have shade. Of the 150 grass pitches marked out by trees, 100 are for tourers, the remainder being occupied by seasonal units. There are some gravel pitches set aside for one night stays, plus four all-weather pitches for motorcaravans. All pitches have 16A electricity and TV points.

Facilities
The toilet block can be heated and includes some washbasins in cubicles, hot showers and separate facilities for disabled visitors and babies. Laundry. Key-card entry system. Motorcaravan services. Gas. Small bar, snack bar and takeaway. Playground. Bicycle hire. Boules. Entertainment and activity programme (high season). WiFi over site (charged). Off site: Restaurant within walking distance. Shops and restaurants 2 km.

Open: All year.

Directions
From motorway take exit 5 for Esch Centre but at T-junction in 1 km. avoid town centre by turning left (Schifflange) then right after railway crossing, ahead at traffic lights and follow signs to site at top of hill. GPS: 49.48492, 5.98657

Charges guide
Per unit incl. 2 persons and electricity	€ 14.95 - € 33.25
extra person	€ 2.80 - € 4.00

For latest campsite news, availability and prices visit

alanrogers.com

Ettelbruck

Camping Ettelbruck

88, Chemin du Camping 88, L-9022 Ettelbruck T: 812 185. E: eilen.ringelberg@gmx.de

alanrogers.com/LU7910

This agreeable, good value municipal site is situated on a hilltop overlooking the town. It is quietly located about 1 km. from the centre of Ettelbruck, with a nice atmosphere and well tended gardens and grass. The modern main building includes reception, an excellent restaurant and a 'salle de séjour' (with library and TV). The 136 marked pitches, 130 for touring, are accessed from tarmac roads and have electricity available (16A). Reception provides good tourist information and English is spoken. There is a welcome cup of coffee on arrival.

Facilities

A new sanitary unit using solar energy provides washbasins in cabins and hot showers. Provision for disabled campers. Laundry. Dishwasher. Motorcaravan services. Restaurant. Snack bar and takeaway (evenings). Breakfasts can also be served. Baker calls daily (order day before). Playground. Entertainment in season. Baking sessions for children. Electric car hire. WiFi (charged). Off site: Ettelbruck 1 km. Easy access to Luxembourg city by train. Hossingen swimming pools. Bicycle hire 2 km.

Open: 1 April - 15 October.

Directions

Site is signed on the western outskirts of Ettelbruck off the N15 and approached via a short one-way system. GPS: 49.846073, 6.082022

Charges guide

Per unit incl. 2 persons and electricity	€ 26.40
extra person	€ 7.50
child (8-12 yrs)	€ 3.50

Heiderscheid

Camping Fuussekaul

4 Fuussekaul, L-9156 Heiderscheid T: 268 8881. E: info@fuussekaul.lu

alanrogers.com/LU7850

This site lies in the rolling wooded hills of central Luxembourg, not far from the lakes of the Sûre river dam. Of the 370 pitches, 220 of varying sizes are for touring units, all with a 6/16A electricity connection. There are some super pitches with private electricity and water. The site consists of winding roads, some sloping, along which the pitches are set in shaded areas. The touring area (separate from the chalets and seasonal pitches) is well equipped with modern facilities, although there is no provision for visitors with disabilities. Children who visit Fuussekaul (the name means fox hole) won't want to leave.

Facilities

Four excellent sanitary blocks provide showers (token € 1), washbasins (in cabins and communal) and children and baby rooms with small toilets, washbasins and showers. Laundry. Well stocked shop. Bar. Restaurant and takeaway. Swimming pool (1/5-1/10). Beauty salon. Playgrounds. Cross-country skiing when snow permits. Bicycle hire. Children's club. WiFi over most of site (charged). Off site: Bus stops outside site entrance. Riding 500 m. Bowling 1 km. Fishing 3 km. Ettelbruckt 7 km.

Open: All year.

Directions

Take N15 from Diekirch to Heiderscheid. Site is on the left at top of hill just before reaching the village. Motorcaravan service area is signed on the right. GPS: 49.87750, 5.99283

Charges guide

Per unit incl. 2 persons and electricity	€ 20.00 - € 32.00
extra person	€ 3.00
child (under 4 yrs)	€ 1.00 - € 2.00
dog	€ 3.00

Kautenbach

Camping Kautenbach

An der Weierbach, L-9663 Kautenbach T: 950 303. E: info@campingkautenbach.lu

alanrogers.com/LU7830

Kautenbach is situated in the heart of the Luxembourg Ardennes and was established over 60 years ago. Although in an idyllic location, it is less than a mile from a railway station with regular trains to Luxembourg City to the south. There are 135 touring pitches here, mostly of a good size and with reasonable shade. All pitches have electrical connections (10A). This is excellent walking country with many tracks around the site. The site managers will be happy to recommend walks for all abilities. Kautenbach has an attractive bistro style restaurant, specialising in local cuisine.

Facilities

Three toilet blocks with open style washbasins and showers, baby changing. Facilities for disabled visitors (key). Laundry. Shop for basics (1/4-31/10, bread to order). Restaurant, bar/snack bar (all season). Direct river access. Fishing. Play area. Mobile homes, safari tents and camping pods for rent. Internet café. Off site: Railway station 1 km. Caves at Consdorf. Echternach. Château de Bourscheid. Vianden. Clervaux.

Open: 1 April - 31 October.

Directions

Head south from Namur on the A4 and then join the N4 (exit 15). Continue on the N4 to Bastogne and then join the N84 towards Wiltz. Follow signs to Kautenbach on the CR331 and the site is well signed from here. GPS: 49.95387, 6.0273

Charges guide

Per unit incl. 2 persons and electricity	€ 23.80 - € 25.35
extra person	€ 6.40
child (2-12 yrs)	€ 4.20

FREE Alan Rogers Travel Card

Extra benefits and savings - see page 14

Larochette

Camping Birkelt

1 Um Birkelt, L-7633 Larochette T: 879 040. E: info@irisparc.com

alanrogers.com/LU7610

This is very much a family site, with a great range of facilities provided. It is well organised and well laid out, set in an elevated position in attractive, undulating countryside. A tarmac road runs around the site with 427 large grass pitches (280 for touring), some slightly sloping, many with a fair amount of shade, on either side of gravel access roads in straight rows and circles. Two hundred pitches have electricity, 134 serviced ones have 16A, the remainder 10A. An all-weather swimming pool complex is beside the site entrance (free for campers) and entertainment for children is arranged in high season.

Facilities

Three modern heated sanitary buildings well situated around the site include mostly open washbasins (6 cabins in one block). Baby baths. Facilities (including accommodation to rent) for wheelchair users. Washing machines and dryers. Motorcaravan services. Shops. Coffee bar. Restaurant with terrace. Swimming pool with sliding cupola (heated all season). Outdoor pool for toddlers. Play areas. Trampolines. Volleyball. Minigolf. Tennis. Bicycle hire. Riding. Internet points. Free WiFi over site. Off site: Golf 5 km. Fishing and kayaking 10 km.

Open: 27 March - 1 November.

Directions

From N7 (Diekirch-Luxembourg City), turn onto N8 (CR118) at Berschbach (just past Mersch) towards Larochette. Site is signed on the right 1.5 km. from Larochette. Approach road is fairly steep and narrow. GPS: 49.78508, 6.21033

Charges guide

Per unit incl. 2 persons	
and electricity	€ 19.50 - € 36.00
with water and drainage	€ 22.50 - € 39.00
extra person	€ 4.25

Camping Cheques accepted.

Larochette

Camping Auf Kengert

Kengert, L-7633 Larochette-Medernach T: 837186. E: info@kengert.lu

alanrogers.com/LU7640

A friendly welcome awaits you at this peacefully situated, family run site, 2 km. from Larochette, which is 24 km. northeast of Luxembourg City, providing 180 individual pitches, all with 16A electricity (Europlug). Some in a very shaded woodland setting, on a slight slope with fairly narrow access roads. There are also eight hardened pitches for motorcaravans on a flat area of grass, complete with motorcaravan service facilities. Further tent pitches are in an adjacent and more open meadow area. There are also site owned wooden chalets for rent. This site is popular in season.

Facilities

The well maintained sanitary block in two parts includes a modern, heated unit with some washbasins in cubicles, and excellent cubicles for disabled visitors. Showers, facilities for babies, additional WCs and washbasins are below the central building. Additional block planned for 2015. Shop, bar and restaurant. Motorcaravan services. Gas supplies. Indoor and outdoor play areas. Swimming pool (Easter-30/9). WiFi (free). Off site: Bicycle hire 3 km.

Open: 1 March - 8 November.

Directions

From Larochette take the CR118/N8 (Mersch) and just outside town right on CR119 Schrondweiler), site is 2 km. GPS: 49.79992, 6.19817

Charges guide

Per unit incl. 2 persons	
and electricity	€ 22.00 - € 33.00
extra person	€ 10.00 - € 15.50
child (4-17 yrs)	€ 4.00 - € 5.00
dog	€ 1.50

Lieler

Camping Trois Frontières

Hauptstrooss 12, L-9972 Lieler T: 998 608. E: info@troisfrontieres.lu

alanrogers.com/LU7880

On a clear day, it is possible to see Belgium, Germany and Luxembourg from the campsite swimming pool, hence its name: Trois Frontières. Corinne and Erwin Levering own and manage the site themselves and all visitors receive a personal welcome and immediately become part of a large, happy family. There are 112 touring pitches on slightly sloping fields divided by pine trees which give some shade. All have 6-10A electricity. Most of the facilities are close to the entrance, leaving the camping area quiet, except for the play area. The restaurant/takeaway provides good quality food served either inside or on the pleasant terrace overlooking the pool which is covered and heated. The site is ideally situated for visits to Bitburg, Germany and spa towns in Belgium. A member of the TopCamp group.

Facilities

Toilet block including suite for visitors with disabilities, plus baby bath and changing station, and family bathroom. More WCs in second building (down some steps). Laundry. Covered, heated swimming pool (1/4-31/10). Play area. Boules. Games room. Bicycle hire. WiFi (free). Off site: Shops 2.3 km. Golf 8 km. Clervaux 12 km.

Open: All year.

Directions

Take N7 northward from Diekirch. 3 km. south of Weiswampach turn right onto CR338 to Lieler (site signed here). Site is on right as you enter the village. GPS: 50.12340, 6.10517

Charges guide

Per unit incl. 2 persons	
and electricity	€ 23.00 - € 30.50
extra person	€ 4.00 - € 8.00

For latest campsite news, availability and prices visit

alanrogers.com

Camping Kockelscheuer

22 route de Bettembourg, L-1899 Luxemburg T: 471 815. E: caravani@pt.lu

alanrogers.com/LU7660

Camping Kockelscheuer is 4 km. from the centre of Luxembourg City and quietly situated (although there can be some aircraft noise at times). On a slight slope, there are 161 individual pitches of good size, either on flat ground at the bottom of the site or on wide flat terraces with easy access, all with 16A electricity. There is also a special area for tents, with picnic tables and, in the reception building, a tent campers' lounge. For children, there is a large area with modern play equipment on safety tiles and next door to the site is a sports centre. There is a friendly welcome, charges are reasonable and English is spoken. Visit Luxembourg City by bus. Here, there are shops, museums and the Grand Duke's Palace. Explore some of the 23 km. of defensive tunnels built in the Middle Ages under the city. The area south of the campsite has several old mining towns, many of which have excellent museums and walks to discover the old workings. Nearby there are two large parks – the one at Bettembourg is a fairy tale park.

Facilities

Two fully equipped, identical sanitary buildings, both very clean. Washing machines. Motorcaravan services. Shop (order bread the previous day). Snack bar. Restaurant in adjacent sports centre also with tennis, squash etc. Rest room. No entry or exit for vehicles (reception closed 12.00-14.00). WiFi (charged). Off site: Bus 200 m. every 10 minutes to Luxembourg. Golf 200 m. Swimming pool and bicycle hire 5 km. Fishing 20 km.

Open: Week before Easter - 31 October.

Directions

Site is SSW of Luxembourg City on the N31 to Bettembourg. From the south, exit A4 at junction signed Kockelscheuer onto N4. In 2 km. turn right (Kockelscheuer and campsite) and continue to follow the signs. GPS: 49.57180, 6.10900

Charges guide

Per unit incl. 2 persons and electricity	€ 17.00
extra person	€ 4.25
child (3-14 yrs)	€ 2.25

No credit cards.

Camping Kockelscheuer – Luxembourg
22, route de Bettembourg, L-1899 Luxembourg
Telephone 47 18 15 · Fax 40 12 43 · www.camp-kockelscheuer.lu

A modern campsite situated at a forest. Large pitches with electric hook-up. Comfortable campers lounge with terrace. Big children's playground, camping shop, boules and WiFi free.

Individual sanitary cabins.

Nearby: tennis, bowling, sauna, solarium restaurant, golf, ice skating rink.

Camping Woltzdal

Maison 12, L-9974 Maulusmühle T: 998 938. E: info@woltzdal-camping.lu

alanrogers.com/LU7780

Set by a stream in a valley, Camping Woltzdal is one of the many delightful sites in the Ardennes, a region of wooded hills and river valleys that crosses the borders of Belgium, France and Luxembourg. The site has 79 flat touring pitches, set on grass amongst fir trees; all with 4A electricity and 20 of which also have water and waste water. They are fairly open and have views of the surrounding wooded hills. A railway passes the site on the far side of the stream, but there are only trains during the day. This is a family run site with a small, friendly bar/restaurant.

Facilities

The site boasts a new state-of-the-art toilet block with solar-powered water heating (access is by smart key with deposit). Large family bathrooms and facilities for disabled visitors. Laundry room. Service points for motorcaravans. Reception and small shop are in the large house at the entrance where there is also a bar and a restaurant/snack bar with terrace. Children's library/activity room. WiFi throughout (charged). Play area. Boules. Mountain bike hire. Entertainment programme for children in high season. Off site: Fishing and golf 6 km. Riding 20 km.

Open: Easter - 30 October.

Directions

Site is 6 km. north of Clervaux on the CR335 road. Leave Clervaux towards Troisvierge (N18). After 1 km. take right fork to Maulusmühle on CR335. Site is signed on right just before Maulusmühle village. Steep turn onto campsite road. GPS: 50.091283, 6.027833

Charges guide

Per unit incl. 2 persons and electricity	€ 20.00 - € 23.20
extra person	€ 7.00
child (4-12 yrs)	€ 3.60
dog	€ 4.20

FREE Alan Rogers Travel Card
Extra benefits and savings - see page 14

319

Nommern

Europacamping Nommerlayen

Rue Nommerlayen, L-7465 Nommern T: 878 078. E: info@nommerlayen-ec.lu

LeadingCampings

alanrogers.com/LU7620

Situated at the end of its own road, in the lovely wooded hills of central Luxembourg, this is a top quality site with fees to match, but it has everything! A large, central building housing most of the services and amenities opens onto a terrace around an excellent swimming pool complex with a large fun pool and an imaginative water playground. The 367 individual pitches (100 sq.m) are on grassy terraces, all have access to electricity (2/16A) and water taps. Pitches are grouped beside age-appropriate play areas and the facilities throughout the campsite reflect the attention given to families in particular. Interestingly enough the superb sanitary block is called Badtemple (having been built in the style of a Greek temple). Entry to the sauna and hot water for washbasins, showers and sinks is by a pre-paid card. Sports facilities are varied and cater for all ages. There is organised entertainment for children and families in high season and public holidays, and beyond the site, numerous walking and cycle paths. Day visits to Luxembourg, Vianden castle and the Mosel Valley are easy. A member of Leading Campings group.

Facilities

A large, high quality, modern sanitary unit provides some washbasins in cubicles, facilities for disabled visitors, family and baby rooms and a sauna. Twelve private bathrooms for hire. Laundry. Motorcaravan services. Supermarket. Restaurant. Snack bar. Bar (all 1/4-1/11). Excellent swimming pool complex (1/5-15/9) and new covered and heated pool (26/4-1/11). Fitness programmes. Bowling. Playground. Large screen TV. Entertainment in season. Bicycle hire. WiFi (free over part of site). Off site: Riding 1 km. Fishing and golf 5 km.

Open: 1 March - 1 November.

Directions

Take the 118 road between Mersch and Larochette. Site is signed 3 km. north of Larochette towards the village of Nommern on the 346 road. GPS: 49.78472, 6.16519

Charges guide

Per unit incl. 2 persons and 16A electricity	€ 23.50 - € 48.50
extra person (over 2 yrs)	€ 5.50
dog	€ 3.00

Reisdorf

Camping de la Sûre

23 route de la Sûre, L-9390 Reisdorf T: 836 246. E: reisdorfcamp@gmail.com

alanrogers.com/LU7650

Camping de la Sûre is on the banks of the river that separates Luxembourg and Germany. It is a pleasant site close to Reisdorf with 120 numbered pitches (all with 10A Europlug). These are not separated but are marked with lovely beech and willow trees that provide some shade. There are caravan holiday homes in a fenced area towards the back of the site, leaving the prime pitches for touring units. The site is surrounded by trees on the hillsides and from Reisdorf visits can be made to Vianden Castle or Trier (oldest German city) just across the border.

Facilities

Modern, clean sanitary facilities have been completely refurbished and include family shower room, sanitary facilities for children and disabled visitors. Laundry. Motorcaravan services. Small shop. New bar and restaurant. Takeaway. Playground. Sports field. Canoeing. Fishing. WiFi throughout (free). Off site: Town centre within easy walking distance. Cycle ways abound. Bicycle hire 200 m. Riding 5 km. Golf 8 km.

Open: 1 April - 30 October.

Directions

From the river bridge in Reisdorf, take the road to Echternach, de la Sûre is the second campsite on the left. GPS: 49.87003, 6.26750

Charges guide

Per unit incl. 2 persons and electricity	€ 14.00 - € 20.00
extra person	€ 5.00
child (under 14 yrs)	€ 2.50
dog	€ 2.50

For latest campsite news, availability and prices visit
alanrogers.com

Looking for competitively priced insurance for your camping or caravanning holiday?

We have been entrusted with readers' campsite holidays since 1968. Choosing the right campsite is one thing; having proper, suitable travel insurance is another.

Personal Travel Insurance

Ideal for self-drive holidays in Europe, and including cover for camping equipment. Family policies are available.

* 24 hour travel advice line and multi lingual medical assistance

* Repatriation and evacuation cover

* Repatriation due to serious illness of relatives at home

Vehicle Assistance Insurance

The vehicle assistance service is provided by Allianz Global Assistance and a network of over 7,500 garages and agents. Serving 3 million people a year, they are well used to looking after the needs of campsite-based holidaymakers.

* Roadside assistance

* Vehicle repatriation (and alternative driver)

* Cover prior to departure

Get a quote and and start looking forward to your holiday with confidence!

01580 214000
alanrogers.com/insurance

With vast areas of the Netherlands reclaimed from the sea, nearly half of the country lies at or below sea level. The result is a flat, fertile landscape, criss-crossed with rivers and canals. Famous for its windmills and bulb fields, it also boasts some of the most impressive coastal dunes in Europe.

No visit to the Netherlands would be complete without experiencing its capital city, Amsterdam, with its maze of canals, bustling cafés, museums, and summer festivals. The fields and gardens of South Holland are an explosion of colour between March and May, when the world's biggest flower auction takes place at Aalsmer. The Netherlands offers all manner of holiday, from lively seaside resorts to picturesque villages, idyllic old fishing ports and areas of unspoiled landscape.

The Vecht valley and its towns of Dalfsen, Ommen and Hardenberg are best explored by bicycle, while Giethoorn, justly dubbed the 'Venice of Holland' has to be seen from a boat. The Kinderdijk windmills on the Alblasserwaard polder are a UNESCO World Heritage Site. The islands of Zeeland are home to beautiful old towns such as Middelburg, the provincial capital Zierikzee with its old harbour and the quaint old town of Veere.

CAPITAL: Amsterdam

Tourist Office

Netherlands Board of Tourism

PO Box 30783, London WC2B 6DH

Tel: 020 7539 7958

Fax: 020 7539 7953

Email: info-uk@holland.com

Internet: www.holland.com/uk

Population

16.8 million

Climate

Temperate with mild winters and warm summers.

Language

Dutch. English is very widely spoken, so is German and to some extent French. In Friesland a Germanic language, Frisian, is spoken.

Telephone

The country code is 00 31.

Money

Currency: The Euro

Banks: Mon-Fri 09.00-16.00/1700.

Shops

Mon-Fri 09.00/09.30-17.30/18.00. Sat to 16.00/17.00. Later closing hours in largor cities.

Public Holidays

New Year; April Fools Day 1 April; Good Fri; Easter Mon; Queen's Birthday 30 April; Labour Day; Remembrance Day 4 May; Liberation Day 5 May; Ascension; Whit Mon; SinterKlaas 5 Dec; Kingdom Day 15 Dec; Christmas 25, 26 Dec.

Motoring

There is a comprehensive motorway system but, due to the high density of population, all main roads can become very busy, particularly in the morning and evening rush hours. There are many bridges which can cause congestion. There are no toll roads but there are a few toll bridges and tunnels, notably the Zeeland Bridge, Europe's longest across the Oosterschelde.

see campsite map 1

Assen

Vakantiepark Witterzomer

Witterzomer 7, NL-9405 VE Assen (Drenthe) T: 0592 393 535. E: info@witterzomer.nl

alanrogers.com/NL6153

Attractively located in a century old area of woodland and fields in the province of the Hunebedden, this is an attractive, large and well organised site. The Hunebedden are prehistoric monuments, built of enormous granite boulders and older than Stonehenge. The 600 touring pitches at Witterzomer are on grass with a woodland setting, with varying degrees of shade and 4-10A electricity. Most also have water, a drain and TV connections and some have private sanitary facilities. All of the amenities here are of excellent quality and are particularly targeted at families. They include a well stocked shop and a bar/restaurant with a good menu and takeaway meals.

Facilities

Good heated toilet blocks include separate facilities for babies and disabled visitors, as well as family bathrooms. Laundry. Shop (1/4-30/9). Restaurant/bar and takeaway (1/4-28/10). Heated outdoor swimming pool (25/4-2/9). Sports field and games room. Tennis. Bicycle hire. Minigolf. Lake with beach and fishing. Internet and WiFi throughout (charged). Max. 2 dogs. Off site: Several nature parks. Assen 4 km. Golf 6 km. Groningen 30 km.

Open: All year.

Directions

Site is 4 km. southwest of Assen. From A28 exit 33 follow N371 (Balkenweg) to Assen. After 200 m. turn right (Europaweg) and again after 200 m. to the right onto Witterhoofdweg. Follow this road for 2 km. (underneath A28) to the site (well signed). GPS: 52.9802, 6.5053

Charges guide

Per unit incl. 2 persons and electricity	€ 18.50 - € 27.00
extra person	€ 4.00

No credit cards.

Ruinen

Camping Ruinen

Oude Benderseweg 11, NL-7963 PX Ruinen (Drenthe) T: 0522 471 770.

E: info@camping-ruinen.nl alanrogers.com/NL6160

Camping Ruinen, under new ownership, is a large, spacious site with 230 pitches, 197 for touring set within the woods of Drenthe. All pitches have electricity (6/10A Europlug) and include 105 serviced pitches also with water and drainage. The numbered pitches are over 100 sq.m. in size and are on large, grassy fields. They are separated by hedges and in the shade of trees. At this comfortable site you can relax by cycling or walking through the woods or over the moors, or join organised trips in groups on a regular basis. A brand new, central complex, also housing reception, includes a swimming pool, an indoor play room, a bar, restaurant and takeaway.

Facilities

Three well spaced, modern toilet blocks provide washbasins (open style and in cabins), child size toilets and baths and a baby room. Facilities for disabled visitors. Laundry. Motorcaravan services. Shop. Restaurant with children's menu. Newly opened bar. New swimming pool with retractable roof. Play areas between the pitches. Giant chess. Boules. Minigolf. Bicycle hire. entertainment in high season. WiFi on part of site.

Open: 1 April - 1 October.

Directions

From Zwolle follow A28 north and take exit 28. At the roundabout take the first exit. Turn left under the motorway. When you arrive in Ruinen follow site signs from there. GPS: 52.77492, 6.36993

Charges guide

Per unit incl. 2 persons and electricity	€ 16.20 - € 23.50
extra person	€ 4.00
dog	€ 3.50

Schipborg

Camping De Vledders

Zeegserweg 2a, NL-9469 PL Schipborg (Drenthe) T: 0504 091 489. E: info@devledders.nl

alanrogers.com/NL6130

Camping De Vledders is set in the centre of one of the most beautiful nature reserves in Holland, between the Drentse Hondsrug and the Drentsche Aa river. This attractive site is landscaped with many varieties of trees and shrubs. There are 150 touring pitches (all with 6A electricity) on rectangular, grassy fields, separated by well kept hedges. The level pitches are around 100 sq.m. in size with some shade provided at the back from mature trees and hedges. Static units and seasonal pitches are on separate fields. In one corner of the site there is an attractive lake with sandy beaches.

Facilities

Two refurbished, heated sanitary blocks with some washbasins in cabins and controllable hot showers. Family shower rooms. Baby room. En-suite facilities for disabled visitors. Motorcaravan services. Shop for basics. Snack bar. TV in reception. Lake with fishing, boating, windsurfing. Football field. Riding. Nordic walking. Playground. Some entertainment for children (high season). Bicycle hire. Torch useful. WiFi (charged).

Open: 1 April - 30 October.

Directions

From the A28 take exit 35 and continue towards Zuidlaren. Just before Zuidlaren follow signs for Schipborg and then site signs. GPS: 53.079267, 6.665617

Charges guide

Per unit incl. 2 persons and electricity	€ 19.70 - € 23.65
extra person (over 1 yr)	€ 3.35

No credit cards.

For latest campsite news, availability and prices visit

alanrogers.com

Wezuperbrug

Molecaten Park Kuierpad

Oranjekanaal NZ 10, NL-7853 TA Wezuperbrug (Drenthe) T: 0591 381 415.

alanrogers.com/NL5790

Professionally run, this all year round site is suitable as a night stop, or for longer if you wish to participate in all the activities offered in July and August. The site itself is in a woodland setting on the edge of the village. The 550 flat and grassy pitches for touring units (with 900 in total) are of reasonable size. All have 4/6/10A electricity and 45 are fully serviced with electricity, TV aerial point, water and drainage. On-site activities include canoeing, windsurfing, water chutes and the dry ski slope, which is also open during the winter so that the locals can practise before going en-masse to Austria.

Facilities

Eleven sanitary blocks, including a new one, with hot showers. Facilities for disabled visitors. Laundry. Motorcaravan services. Supermarket (1/4-15/9; bread all year). Restaurant and bar with TV. Takeaway. Indoor pool (all year). Outdoor heated pool (1/5-15/9). Whirlpool. Internet access. Dry ski slope. Play areas. Minigolf. Lake with beach. Boat rental. New High Rope Adventure Parc with 517 m. Zip wire. WiFi throughout (charged). Off site: Fishing 500 m. Riding 1 km. Golf 1.5 km.

Open: 1 April - 31 October (mobile home accommodation, all year).

Directions

From A28 take exit 31 (Beilen) onto N381. Exit Westerbork onto N374. After 2 km. turn right to Wezuperbrug. Site is on left after 2 km.
GPS: 52.84005, 6.72593

Charges guide

Per unit incl. 2 persons and electricity	€ 20.00 - € 36.20
extra person	€ 6.00
serviced pitch	€ 6.00
dog	€ 5.00

No credit cards.

Zeewolde

Erkemederstrand Camping Horeca Jachthaven & Dagrecreatie

Erkemederweg 79, NL-3896 LB Zeewolde (Flevoland) T: 0365 228 421. E: info@erkemederstrand.nl

alanrogers.com/NL6200

Erkemederstrand is a leisure park in Flevoland with direct access to the Nuldernauw where there is a sandy beach, a lake and a forest. It provides a campsite for families, a marina, an area for youngsters to camp, a camping area for groups and a recreation area for day visitors. The campsite itself is divided into two areas: one before the dyke at the waterfront and one behind the dyke. The pitches are spacious (125-150 sq.m) and most have electricity, water and drainage. The focal point of the site and marina is the De Jutter beachside restaurant. This restaurant offers a varied menu for more formal dining, as well as catering for snacks, takeaway, ice creams or a cold beer on the terrace. There is plenty to do on the campsite, including a Red Indian village for children where they can build huts, a children's farm and an extended programme of activities. Obviously, with the proximity of the lake there are many opportunities for watersports.

Facilities

Six neat, clean and heated toilet blocks (access by key; exclusively for campers). Washbasins in cabins, showers and family bathrooms (some charges for hot water). Laundry facilities. Well stocked supermarket, bar, restaurant and takeaway (all open all season). Several play areas and children's farm. Watersports facilities and lake swimming. Fishing. Football pitch. Minigolf. Bicycle hire. Extended entertainment programme. WiFi (charged). Beach and shower for dogs. Off site: Golf 9 km. Riding 10 km.

Open: 28 March - 26 October.

Directions

From A28 (Utrecht-Zwolle) take exit 9 (Nijkerk/Almere) and follow N301 to Zeewolde. Cross the bridge and turn right following signs to site. From Amsterdam/Almere, take exit 5 and follow N27 (becomes N305) to Zeewolde. Then take N301 to Nijkerk. From bridge turn right and follow signs to site. GPS: 52.27021, 5.48871

Charges guide

Per unit incl. 2 persons and electricity	€ 27.00
extra person	€ 3.25
dog	€ 2.00

FREE Alan Rogers Travel Card
Extra benefits and savings - see page 14

Biddinghuizen

Rivièra Parc

Spijkweg 15, NL-8256 RJ Biddinghuizen (Flevoland) T: 0321 331 344. E: info@riviera.nl

alanrogers.com/NL6195

This Dutch Rivièra at the Veluwe Lake is two square kilometres, with Camping Rivièra Beach beyond the dykes, close to the water and the beach, and the bigger Rivièra Parc within the dykes. This family site has 1,195 pitches, 850 for touring, all on grass and all with 4/10A electricity. There are also 450 serviced pitches (large with water, drainage and TV connection) and 12 pitches with private sanitary facilities. The site boasts a very impressive range of facilities, including a covered play area and indoor swimming pool with restaurant (all decorated with a pirate theme) in the main building behind reception. The site is perfect for children and pre-teens.

Facilities

Good heated toilet blocks with separate facilities for babies and disabled visitors. Family rooms. Restaurants. Café. Snack bar. Takeaway. Supermarket. Swimming pool with slide. Covered play area. Laser games. Bowling. Bicycle and go-kart hire. Fishing. Amusement arcade. Internet access. Around 54 mobile homes and bungalows for hire. Off site: Riding. Watersports. Walibi World theme park 2 km. Golf 10 km.

Open: 30 March - 28 October.

Directions

Site is 2 km. southwest of Elburg. From A28 take exit to Elburg (N309). At Elburg follow signs for Dronten. Cross the bridge over the Veluwe Lake and immediately turn left (N306). Site is well signed from here and is on the left after 2 km.
GPS: 52.44671, 5.79223

Charges guide

Per unit incl. vehicle, up to 4 persons and 4A electricity	€ 29.00 - € 44.00
extra person	€ 6.25

Buren

Recreatieoord Klein Vaarwater

Klein Vaarwaterweg 114, NL-9163 ME Buren (Friesland) T: 0519 542 156. E: info@kleinvaarwater.nl

alanrogers.com/NL6030

Recreatieoord Klein Vaarwater is a bustling family holiday park on the interesting island of Ameland. The site is 1 km. from the North Sea beaches and has its own indoor pool, with bars, restaurants, supermarket and party centre. Klein Vaarwater has 190 touring pitches (all with 16A electricity), of which 130 also have water, waste water and cable. Pitching is off hardcore access lanes, close to nature, on fields taking 6-10 units, on a grass and sand underground. There is some shade to the back from trees and bushes and level pitches are numbered and partly separated by young trees. Some of the pitches enjoy good views over the countryside.

Facilities

Three heated toilet blocks have open style washbasins, hot showers (free of charge) and facilities for disabled campers. Washing machines and dryers. Supermarket. Bar, restaurant, snack bar. Boutique. Indoor pools (25x15 m) with waterslide and fun paddling pool. Fitness centre. Playing field. Boules pitch. Bowling alley. Minigolf. Entertainment programme for young and old (in the holidays). WiFi (charged). No charcoal barbecues. Off site: Bicycle hire and the village of Buren 500 m.

Open: All year.

Directions

From Leeuwarden, follow the N357 all the way north to Holwerd and take the ferry to Ameland (car reservations necessary in high season). On the island, follow the signs for Buren and then site signs.
GPS: 53.45439, 5.80476

Charges guide

Per unit incl. 2 persons and electricity	€ 19.00
extra person	€ 4.75
child (under 14 yrs)	€ 3.95
car	€ 4.00

Harlingen

Camping De Zeehoeve

Westerzeedijk 45, NL-8862 PK Harlingen (Friesland) T: 0517 413 465. E: info@zeehoeve.nl

alanrogers.com/NL6080

Superbly located, directly behind the sea dyke of the Wadden Sea and just a kilometre from the harbour of Harlingen, De Zeehoeve is an attractive and spacious site. It has 300 pitches (125 for touring units), all with 16A Europlug connection and 20 with water, drainage and electricity. There are 16 hardstandings for motorcaravans and larger units. Some pitches have views over the Harlingen canal where one can moor small boats. An ideal site for rest and relaxation, for watersports or to visit the attractions of Harlingen and Friesland. After a day of activity, one can wine and dine in the site's recently modernised restaurant or at one of the many pubs in the town.

Facilities

Three sanitary blocks include open style washbasins, washbasins in cabins with hot water, controllable showers (on payment). Family showers and baby bath. Facilities for disabled visitors. Launderette. Motorcaravan services. Bar/restaurant (July/Aug). Play area. Bicycle hire. Boat launching. Pedalo and canoe hire. Fishing. Entertainment (July/Aug). B&B. Hikers' cabins. WiFi (charged).

Open: 1 April - 15 October.

Directions

From Leeuwarden take A31 southwest to Harlingen, then follow site signs. GPS: 53.16237, 5.41688

Charges guide

Per unit incl. 2 persons and electricity	€ 22.50
extra person	€ 4.25
child (4-11 yrs)	€ 3.25
dog	€ 3.50

For latest campsite news, availability and prices visit

alanrogers.com

Koudum

Camping De Kuilart

Kuilart 1, NL-8723 CG Koudum (Friesland) T: 0514 522 221. E: info@kuilart.nl

alanrogers.com/NL5760

De Kuilart is a well run, modern and partly car-free site by Friesland's largest lake. With its own marina and many facilities, it attracts many watersports enthusiasts. There are around 543 pitches, 310 for touring units, all with electricity (6/16A), water, drainage, WiFi and TV connections, and 34 new pitches with private sanitary facilities. The restaurant provides beautiful views over Lake Fluessen.

Facilities

Four modern, heated sanitary blocks well spaced around the site with showers on payment and most washbasins (half in private cabins) have only cold water. Launderette. Motorcaravan services. Gas supplies. Restaurant/bar, supermarket, indoor pool with 3 sessions daily (all open 30/3-4/11). Sauna and solarium. Sports field. Play areas. Tennis. Bicycle hire. Fishing. Animation team (high season). Internet access. Lake swimming area. Marina. Windsurfing, boat hire and boat shop. Car hire. WiFi over site (charged). Off site: Riding and golf 4 km.

Open: All year.

Directions

Site is southeast of Koudum, on the Fluessen lake. Follow the camping sign off the N359 Bolsward-Lemmer road. GPS: 52.90250, 5.46620

Charges guide

Per unit incl. 2 persons and electricity	€ 17.50 - € 37.80
extra person	€ 4.70
dog	€ 3.50

Special weekend rates at B.Hs.
Camping Cheques accepted.

Leeuwarden

Camping De Kleine Wielen

De Groene Ster 14, NL-8926 XE Leeuwarden (Friesland) T: 0511 431 660. E: info@dekleinewielen.nl

alanrogers.com/NL5750

Camping De Kleine Wielen is named after a small lake of the same name that lies in the 1,000 hectare nature and recreation area of De Groene Ster. The campsite is adjacent to the lake – possible activities include boating on the lake or cycling and walking around this beautiful area of forest, grassland and ponds. The site provides 360 pitches, of which 220 are for touring units. The remaining pitches are used for privately owned mobile homes and three for hire. All the touring pitches have 4A electricity and many have wonderful views over the water and surrounding countryside.

Facilities

Four basic toilet blocks provide washbasins in cabins and preset showers (coin operated). Maintenance is variable. Facilities for disabled visitors. Motorcaravan services. Shop and bar (all season). Café/restaurant and takeaway (all season). Playground. Sports pitch. Minigolf. Lake with beach. Fishing. Rowing boats. Surf boards. Extensive recreation programme in July/Aug. WiFi throughout (charged). Off site: Golf 1 km. Boat launching 2 km. Riding and bicycle hire 5 km.

Open: 1 April - 1 October.

Directions

From the N355 turn off east towards Leeuwarden and follow campsite signs. GPS: 53.21650, 5.88703

Charges guide

Per unit incl. 2 persons and electricity and car	€ 20.25 - € 22.75
extra person	€ 4.25 - € 4.75

Sumar

Recreatiecentrum Bergumermeer

Solcamastraat 30, NL-9262 ND Sumar (Friesland) T: 0511 461 385. E: info@bergumermeer.nl

alanrogers.com/NL6040

Recreatiecentrum Bergumermeer's location beside the Bergum lake, makes it ideal for lovers of watersports, with sailing, surfing and canoeing available, as well as swimming from two sandy beaches. There is also a large, heated indoor swimming pool with fun paddling pool and an indoor play paradise. The site provides 270 good sized, flat touring pitches for both caravans and tents, some having attractive views over the Prinses Margrietkanaal and the surrounding countryside, others with views over the lake. All pitches are fully serviced with 10A electricity, water and drainage, and there are ten large hardstandings.

Facilities

Three sanitary buildings offer private cabins, family showers, baby bath and facilities for children and disabled visitors. Launderette. Freezer. Shop. Bar/restaurant. Pancake restaurant. Heated indoor pool. Solarium. Play area. Children's farm. Tennis. Minigolf. Fishing. Sailing dinghies, motorboats and canoes for hire. Entertainment programme in high season. Club space with disco. Bicycle hire. Boat launching. Beach. WiFi over site (charged). Off site: Riding 5 km. Golf 19 km.

Open: 27 March - 31 October.

Directions

Either go north from Amsterdam via the A7/E22 through Leeuwarden towards Drachten, or east from Amsterdam via A6, onto A7 (Leeuwarden and Groningen), then onto N31 (De Haven/Drachten) and in either case onto N356 towards Bergum following site signs. GPS: 53.19127, 6.12428

Charges guide

Per unit incl. 2 persons and electricity	€ 18.00 - € 31.00
extra person	€ 6.25

FREE Alan Rogers Travel Card
Extra benefits and savings - see page 14

alan rogers
Runner up
2014 Awards

Weidum

Camping WeidumerHout

Dekemawei 9, NL-9024 BE Weidum (Friesland) T: 0582 519 888. E: welkom@weidumerhout.nl

alanrogers.com/NL5715

Camping WeidumerHout is a member of the Karaktervolle Groene Campings group, literally 'characterful green campsites'. It has a superb rural location, close to the historic village of Weidum. There are 48 well spaced pitches (150 sq.m) with 10A electricity and two with hardstanding. The owner makes sure that all visitors can enjoy the great views over either the countryside or the river that runs past the site. The site has been developed on a farm that dates back to 1867 and has a tranquil, historic atmosphere. The site's fully equipped sauna (on payment) will add to your relaxation – owner Eddy de Boer will describe the benefits of a good sauna.

Facilities

Heated sanitary block with toilets, showers and washbasins. Baby room. Washing machine and dryer. Bar and restaurant (all year). Sauna. Solarium. Library. Bicycle hire. Beach access plus fishing and boat launching. Canoe hire. WiFi throughout (free). Fitness equipment. Torch useful. Off site: Shop and bus stop 800 m. Riding 5 km. Sailing 8 km. Golf 12 km.

Open: All year, excl. Christmas - 1 January.

Directions

From Leeuwarden head south on the A32 and follow signs for Weidum. Just before entering the village, the site is on the right. GPS: 53.14906, 5.76166

Charges guide

Per unit incl. 2 persons and electricity	€ 21.50
extra person (over 2 yrs)	€ 5.75
dog	€ 2.00

Arnhem

Camping Warnsborn

Bakenbergseweg 257, NL-6816 PB Arnhem (Gelderland) T: 0264 423 469. E: info@campingwarnsborn.nl

alanrogers.com/NL5830

Camping Warnsborn is a small, well maintained site set in the grounds of an attractive estate owned by the Gelderland Trust for natural beauty. Located on the outskirts of the historical city of Arnhem and set amongst 3.5 hectares of undulating woodland, this site really has something for everyone. There are 90 hardstanding pitches for tourers (6A electricity) arranged in either open grassy fields or surrounded by trees, with a separate secluded area for backpackers and small tents. On-site facilities include a good play area with a large sandpit and guided walks through the surrounding countryside, taking in local historical points of interest. This is an ideal site for those seeking tranquillity in a delightful natural setting.

Facilities

Modern heated toilet block including facilities for babies, families and disabled visitors. Washing machines and dryers. Well stocked shop, bread to order. TV room/library. Playground with large sandpit. Bicycle hire. Boules. Hikers' cabins. WiFi over site (charged). Off site: Good restaurant within walking distance. Burgers zoo. Shops and restaurants in Arnhem. Riding 3 km. Golf 4 km. Museums and castles. Many cycle and walking tracks throughout wooded estate.

Open: 1 April - 31 October.

Directions

From Utrecht follow the A12 and take exit N224 following signs towards Arnhem Noord/Burgers zoo. Follow signs to the site. GPS: 52.0072, 5.87135

Charges guide

Per unit incl. 2 persons and electricity	€ 18.30 - € 20.80
extra person	€ 4.50 - € 5.00
child (under 13 yrs)	€ 2.45 - € 2.70
dog	€ 2.70 - € 3.00

Arnhem

DroomPark Hooge Veluwe

Koningsweg 14, NL-6816 TC Arnhem (Gelderland) T: 0264 432 272. E: info@droomparkhoogeveluwe.nl

alanrogers.com/NL5850

Its situation at the entrance to the Hoge Veluwe national park with its moors, forests, sand drifts, walking routes and cycle paths, makes this a highly desirable holiday base with great appeal for families with children of all ages. The site itself is well managed and attractively laid out with 260 touring pitches, including 120 fully serviced places of 300 sq.m. All have electricity (4-16A), are numbered and laid out in small fields which are divided by hedging. Some are traffic free which means cars must be left in a nearby car park. There is some road noise.

Facilities

Three excellent, heated sanitary blocks with all facilities, are easily identified by colourful logos. Launderette. Motorcaravan services. Gas supplies. Supermarket. Restaurant. Takeaway. All facilities open all season. TV room. Heated outdoor and indoor pools, and paddling pool. Many small play areas. Recreation hall. Large, varied activity/play area for older children and teenagers. Football pitch, table tennis tables, skateboard loop, cycle track, basketball, pool tables. Bicycle and go-kart hire. Boules pitch. Wellness and gym. Organised activities. WiFi.

Open: All year.

Directions

Leave A12 motorway at exit 25 (Oosterbeck) and follow signs for Hoge Veluwe. Site is on right in 6 km. From the A50, take exit 21 to Schaarsbergen and follow signs. GPS: 52.03102, 5.86680

Charges guide

Per unit incl. 2 persons and electricity	€ 15.00 - € 28.00
extra person	€ 3.00 - € 5.00

For latest campsite news, availability and prices visit

alanrogers.com

Ede

Bospark Ede

Zonneoordlaan 47, NL-6718 TL Ede (Gelderland) T: 0318 612 859. E: info@bosparkede.nl

alanrogers.com/NL6339

Camping Bospark Ede is situated in the centre of the Veluwe region, between the towns of Ede and idyllic Lunteen. You can rent a chalet, or a camping pitch in a green environment with water and 16A electricity to each pitch. This small site (450 pitches, 55 for touring units) will impress with its neat, family friendly facilities, and you will be delighted by the beautiful surroundings of the forests, sand sprays and heaths. This is a perfect site if you love walking and cycling or just relaxing; it makes a good base for seeing the area as Apeldoorn and Arnhem are just 30 minutes away by car.

Facilities
Two clean, well maintained and heated sanitary blocks have preset showers (token). Baby facilities in ladies' section, but no provision for disabled campers. Launderette. Motorcaravan services. Snack bar and takeaway (1/7-30/9; weekends in low season). Outdoor swimming pool and paddling pool (1/7-30/9). Play areas. Bicycle hire. Children's entertainment (up to 12 yrs; high season). WiFi over site (charged). Off site: Riding 3 km.

Open: 31 March - 30 October.

Directions
From A30 take N224 exit towards Ede. On outskirts of Ede take N304 northwest and follow signs to site. GPS: 52.06693, 5.670683

Charges guide
Per unit incl. 4 persons and electricity	€ 15.00 - € 25.00
dog	€ 5.00

Emst-Gortel

Camping De Wildhoeve

Hanendorperweg 102, NL-8166 JJ Emst-Gortel (Gelderland) T: 0578 661 324.

E: info@wildhoeve.nl alanrogers.com/NL6285

LeadingCampings

Camping De Wildhoeve is an exceptional, welcoming, privately owned site with many amenities of the type one would normally find on larger holiday camps. The well maintained site is located in woodland and has 400 pitches with 330 for tourers. Pitching is in several areas, mostly in the shade of mature conifers. Partly separated by trees and bushes, the level pitches are numbered and all have 6/10A electricity, water and drainage. Behind reception is an indoor sub-tropical pool with a large water slide and fun paddling pool. Next to reception is a water adventure playground with a small beach. A member of Leading Campings group.

Facilities
Four well placed, heated blocks with toilets, washbasins (open style and in cabins) and free, preset hot showers. Special section for children with showers, washbasins and toilets. Baby room. Family shower room. Facilities for disabled children. Laundry facilities. Shop, grand café/restaurant. Snack bar. Indoor and outdoor pools with slides and paddling pool. Water adventure playground. Bicycle hire. Tennis. Open-air theatre. WiFi over site (charged). Dogs are not accepted. Off site: Fishing 4 km. Riding 5 km. Paleis Het Loo. Wild Animal Park, Wissel.

Open: April - September.

Directions
From the A28, take exit 15 (Epe/Nunspeet). Continue east towards Epe and at traffic lights turn south towards Emst. Continue straight ahead at roundabout in Emst. Turn right at church, into Hanendorperweg. Site is on the right after 3.5 km. GPS: 52.31369, 5.92707

Charges guide
Per unit incl. 2 persons and electricity	€ 21.00 - € 37.75
extra person	€ 5.00

Camping Cheques accepted.

Heumen

Recreatiecentrum Heumens Bos

Vosseneindseweg 46, NL-6582 BR Heumen (Gelderland) T: 0243 581 481. E: info@heumensbos.nl

alanrogers.com/NL5950

Heumens Bos covers 17 hectares of woodland and grassed fields providing 165 level touring pitches arranged in groups of ten or twelve. All pitches have 6A electricity and cable connections, and cars are parked away from the units allowing plenty of recreational space. The site is situated beside miles of beautiful woods, criss-crossed by cycle paths, in a tranquil, rural setting. Heumens Bos is open over a long season for touring families and all year for bungalows. One small section for motorcaravans has some hardstandings.

Facilities
The main, good quality sanitary building, plus another new block, are modern and heated, providing showers on payment. Rooms for families and disabled visitors. Smart launderette. Motorcaravan services. Gas supplies. Shop. Bar, restaurant and snack bar. Heated outdoor pool (1/5-30/9). Bicycle hire. Tennis. Boules. Glade area with play equipment. Activity and excursion programme (high season). Wet weather room. WiFi over site (charged).

Open: All year.

Directions
From A73 (Nijmegen-Venlo) take exit 3 (4 km. south of Nijmegen) and follow site signs. GPS: 51.76915, 5.82050

Charges guide
Per unit incl. 2 persons and electricity	€ 18.00 - € 30.00
extra person (over 3 yrs)	€ 4.00
dog (max. 1)	€ 4.00

FREE Alan Rogers Travel Card
Extra benefits and savings - see page 14

Hoenderloo

Veluwecamping De Pampel

Woeste Hoefweg 35, NL-7351 TN Hoenderloo (Gelderland) T: 0553 781 760.

E: info@veluwevakantieparken.nl alanrogers.com/NL5840

Camping De Pampel has the most congenial atmosphere and caters both for families (great facilities for children) and for those seeking peace and quiet. This is enhanced by its situation deep in the forest, with nine hectares of its own woods to explore. There are 280 pitches (20 seasonal) with 6-16A electricity. You can choose to site yourself around the edge of a large, open field with volleyball in the middle, or pick one of the individual places which are numbered, divided by trees and generally quite spacious.

Facilities

Toilet facilities are excellent, and the new Sani Plaza has to be seen. Laundry. Well stocked shop (1/4-1/10). Restaurant. Snack bar (July/Aug, otherwise weekends only). Swimming pool and new fun paddling pool with water canon (heated by solar panels; open 1/4-31/10). Play area. Pets' corner. Sports area. Indoor play area. Barbecues by permission only, no open fires. Dogs are not accepted. WiFi throughout (free). Off site: Riding 1 km. Golf 10 km. Fishing 15 km.

Open: All year.

Directions

From the A50 Arnhem-Apeldoorn road exit for Hoenderloo and follow signs.
GPS: 52.11885, 5.90569

Charges guide

Per unit incl. 2 persons and electricity	€ 20.00 - € 37.00
extra person	€ 4.25 - € 5.25
child (1-11 yrs)	€ 3.25 - € 4.25

Less 20% (excl. electricity) in low seasons.

Hummelo

Camping Jena

Rozegaarderweg 7, NL-6999 DW Hummelo (Gelderland) T: 0314 381457. E: info@campingjena.nl
alanrogers.com/NL5875

Camping Jena is an attractive, rural site on the edge of the vast forests and estate of Enghuizen. There are 175 spacious pitches (min. 100 sq.m), all for touring, with 6/10A electricity. In one area they are enclosed by hedges, shrubbery and trees, providing plenty of privacy; in other areas they are more open. For younger visitors there is a sports field, a recreation room, play equipment and a BMX track. Adults will appreciate the Golden Carp (the region's oldest hotel and restaurant) in Hummelo, just 2 kilometres away. This is an exceptionally peaceful site with many cycle routes and footpaths on the doorstep.

Facilities

Two clean sanitary blocks. Facilities for disabled visitors. Laundry. Small shop with bread. Café. Takeaway. Free WiFi in café. Off site: Motorcaravan service point at entrance. Supermarket and Golden Carp hotel/restaurant in Hummelo 2 km. Walking and cycling routes. Fishing and golf 2 km. Riding 8 km.

Open: 29 March - 26 October.

Directions

From A12 junction 27 (Arnhem/Zutphen) take exit for Doesburg N338. After Angerlo turn right onto N317, then left on N314 for a short distance towards Hummelo. Site is signed on right.
GPS: 51.993182, 6.256247

Charges guide

Per unit incl. 2 persons and electricity	€ 16.35 - € 19.10
extra person	€ 3.50
child	€ 2.00
dog	€ 2.00

No credit cards.

Lathum

Recreatiepark Rhederlaagse Meren

Marsweg 2, NL-6988 BM Lathum (Gelderland) T: 0313 632 211. E: R.Stokman@succesparken.nl
alanrogers.com/NL6328

Recreatiepark Rhederlaagse Meren is situated on the shore of the Rhederlaag, a 300-acre leisure lake with sandy beaches, boating and watersports. The 500 pitches, 125 for touring (100 sq.m), are separated by hedges and are right on the lakeside; all have 10A electricity hook-up. There is an entertainment programme for both children and adults during high season. In the evening you can relax in the site's restaurant or enjoy a snack in the cafeteria. Families with young children will enjoy the beach and play areas, while teenagers can try their hand at some of the many watersports activities.

Facilities

One clean, heated sanitary block has basic but adequate facilities (none for children or disabled visitors). Outdoor heated swimming pool (1/5-1/10). Well stocked shop, bar and restaurant (weekends only out of high season). Play area. Lake swimming. Fishing. Tennis court. Watersports. Bicycle hire. WiFi over site (charged). Off site: Veluwe National Park 2 km. Riding 10 km. Golf 15 km.

Open: All year.

Directions

From A12 exit at junction 27 (Arnhem/Zutphen). Take exit Westervoort and follow signs for Doesburg (N338). Turn left just after Lathum village.
GPS: 51.994348, 6.029896

Charges guide

Per unit incl. 4 persons and electricity	€ 28.00 - € 32.00
extra person	€ 10.00
extra child (under 12 yrs)	€ 7.50

For latest campsite news, availability and prices visit

alanrogers.com

Maurik

Camping Eiland van Maurik

Eiland van Maurik 7, NL-4021 GG Maurik (Gelderland) T: 0344 691 502. E: receptie@eilandvanmaurik.nl

alanrogers.com/NL6290

Camping Eiland van Maurik is beside a lake in the centre of an extensive nature and recreation park in the Nederrijn area. These surroundings are ideal for all sorts of activities – swimming, windsurfing, water-skiing or para-sailing, relaxing on the beach or fishing. There is even an animal farm for the children. The site has 265 numbered, flat pitches, all fully serviced (10A electricity). You could enjoy pancakes in the Oudhollandse restaurant with its views over the water. There is direct access from the site to the lakeside beach.

Facilities
The three toilet blocks for tourers include washbasins (open style and in cabins), controllable showers and a baby room. Launderette with iron and board. Shop. Bar/restaurant/pizzeria (all season). Play areas (one indoors). Playing field. Tennis. Minigolf. Entertainment in high season (incl. riding). Bicycle hire. Water-skiing. Sailing and motorboat hire. Para-sailing. Go-karts. Animal farm. Max. 2 dogs. Off site: 18-hole pitch and putt 1 km.

Open: 1 April - 1 October.

Directions
From the A15 (Rotterdam-Nijmegen) take exit 33 Tiel towards Maurik and follow signs as above. GPS: 51.97656, 5.43013

Charges guide
Per unit incl. 2 persons and electricity	€ 20.00 - € 35.00
extra person	€ 5.00
dog	€ 4.50

No credit cards.
Camping Cheques accepted.

Nunspeet

Camping De Tol

Elspeterweg 61, NL-8071 PB Nunspeet (Gelderland) T: 0341 252 413. E: info@camping-detol.nl

alanrogers.com/NL6361

Camping De Tol is a very attractive family owned and run campsite in the wooded Veluwe area, close to the town of Nunspeet. Its 188 touring pitches (80-100 sq.m; all with 4-10A electricity) are arranged in groups of six around a large leisure lake with floating play equipment. The campsite is organised with families in mind, and there is a choice of lake swimming or the heated outdoor pool, and a range of organised activities in high season. In the evening, why not relax on the terrace with a drink, then enjoy an excellent meal from the restaurant.

Facilities
Three sanitary blocks with some washbasins in cubicles (hot water on payment). En-suite unit for disabled campers (key access). Bar, restaurant and takeaway (July/Aug). Large lake with floating play equipment and beach. Outdoor heated swimming pool (1/5-mid Sept). Sports field. Minigolf. Bicycle hire. WiFi over site (charged). Dogs are not accepted. Off site: Golf and riding 2 km. Beach and fishing 4 km.

Open: 29 March - 28 October.

Directions
From A28 take exit 14 on N310 towards Elspeet. Site is 1 km. on the left. GPS: 52.35571, 5.786941

Charges guide
Per unit incl. 2 persons and electricity	€ 17.00 - € 24.00
extra person (over 3 yrs)	€ 3.50

Otterlo

Droompark De Zanding

Vijverlaan 1, NL-6731 CK Otterlo (Gelderland) T: 0318 596 111. E: info@zanding.nl

alanrogers.com/NL5780

De Zanding is a highly rated, family run site that offers almost every recreational facility, either on site or nearby, that active families or couples might seek. As soon as you turn the corner to this impressive site, children will want to investigate the play equipment by the lake. There are many sporting options and organised high season programmes for all ages. There are 463 touring pitches spread around the site (all with 4/6/10A electricity), some individual and separated, others in more open spaces shaded by trees. Some serviced pitches are in small groups between long stay units and there is another area for tents. A member of the Holland Tulip Parcs group.

Facilities
First class sanitary facilities are housed in five modern blocks that are clean, well maintained and well equipped. Good provision for babies and disabled guests. Laundry. Kitchen. Motorcaravan services. Gas supplies. Supermarket. Restaurant/bar. Lake beach and swimming. Fishing. Tennis. Minigolf. Boules. Five play areas. Bicycle hire. Organised activities. WiFi over site (charged). Off site: Riding 1 km. Golf 25 km.

Open: All year.

Directions
Leave A12 Utrecht-Arnhem motorway at Oosterbeek at exit 25 and join N310 to Otterlo. Then follow camping signs to site, watching carefully for entrance. GPS: 52.09310, 5.77757

Charges guide
Per unit incl. 2 persons and electricity	€ 25.00 - € 38.00
extra person	€ 8.00

Camping Cheques accepted.

Netherlands

Otterlo

Camping Beek en Hei

Heideweg 4, NL-6731 SN Otterlo (Gelderland) T: 0318 591 483. E: info@beekenhei.nl

alanrogers.com/NL5835

Camping Beek en Hei, located in the heart of the Veluwe nature reserve, offers space, tranquillity and beautiful scenery. There are 150 pitches within four camping areas, including an open plan family field and a touring area with tall hedges and secluded pitches, all with electricity (6A). If you prefer something a little more natural, there are pitches on the edge of the campsite in the forest and an opportunity to get back to nature with wild camping in the heart of the forest. On site facilities include a play area and organised treasure hunts and games with the local ranger. A natural lake with a beach is also within walking distance.

Facilities

One clean, heated prefabricated unit in each area has showers (€ 0.50) and baby changing. Facilities for disabled visitors in some blocks. Motorcaravan services. Launderette. Shop with basics in reception. Library/TV room. Well maintained play areas. Organised children's activities (July/Aug). Bicycle hire. Winter cabins. WiFi over site (charged). Off site: Shops and restaurants in Otterlo. Walking and cycling routes Kröller-Müller museum.

Open: All year.

Directions

Take the A12 from Utrecht-Arnhem, exit at Veenendaal and continue towards Renswoude. Take the N224 towards Arnhem-Ede for 9 km, continue on the N304 for Otterlo then follow signs for the site. GPS: 52.0918, 5.77020

Charges guide

Per unit incl. 2 persons and electricty	€ 19.75
extra person	€ 4.50
child (under 12 years)	€ 3.25

Vaassen

Camping De Helfterkamp

Gortelseweg 24, NL-8171 RA Vaassen (Gelderland) T: 0578 571 839. E: info@helfterkamp.nl

alanrogers.com/NL5845

Helfterkamp is a pretty, family friendly site located between the historical royal estate of Het Loo and the Ijssel Valley. With 14 hectares of land and making good use of traditional farm buildings, it offers an appealing, natural farming environment. There are 195 sheltered, grassy touring pitches with electricity (6/16A), arranged around the edges of green fields with children's play areas in the centre of some. A barn has been refurbished to create a craft centre for children, and it also houses a TV room, table tennis and table football. There is also a small farm for children.

Facilities

Three modern, heated toilet blocks are clean and have facilities for children and disabled visitors. Laundry facilities. Motorcaravan services. Small shop with bread to order. Recreation barn including TV, table tennis, shuffleboard and organised craft sessions. Play areas. Sports field. Children's entertainment (high season). Bicycle hire. WiFi over site (charged). Off site: Vaassen, a modern town with a wide range of shops and restaurants. Julianatoren (amusement park in Apeldoorn).

Open: 16 February - 31 October.

Directions

From the A50 to Apeldoorn take exit 26 (Vaasen). Following signs to Vaasen centre, pass through traffic lights (and Cannenburgh castle to your right). Continue for 2 km, turning right into Gortelseweg. The site entrance is 500 m. to the right. GPS: 52.2908, 5.94535

Charges guide

Per unit incl. 2 persons	€ 17.50 - € 20.50
extra person	€ 4.00
electricity (per kWh)	€ 0.40
dog	€ 2.00

Winterswijk

Vakantiepark De Twee Bruggen

Meenkmolenweg 13, NL-7109-AH Winterswijk (Gelderland) T: 0543 565 366. E: info@detweebruggen.nl

alanrogers.com/NL6425

De Twee Bruggen is a spacious recreation park set in the Achterhoek countryside. The 350 touring pitches (all with 10/16A electricity) are divided between several fields of varying sizes. Although the fields are surrounded by tall trees, the ground is open and sunny. Beyond the touring area, 71 chalets set in well tended grounds, are for rent. Indoor and outdoor swimming pools can be enjoyed by children and adults. At the indoor pool there is a covered terrace and, for relaxation, a sauna and jacuzzi. Adjacent to the pool is a small, open-air theatre, where shows are staged in high season.

Facilities

Three modern, well maintained sanitary buildings include showers and washbasins in private cabins. Fourteen pitches have private sanitary facilities. Washing machines and dryers. Motorcaravan services. Supermarket. Bar, restaurant and takeaway (all year). Heated outdoor pool (30/4-15/9). Heated indoor pool (all year). Paddling pool. Sauna. Jacuzzi. Solarium. Sports field. Tennis courts. Bicycle hire. Minigolf. Bowling. Playground. Bouncy castle. Deer field. Free WiFi over site. Max. 2 dogs.

Open: All year.

Directions

From Arnhem, take the A12 then A18 towards Varsseveld which will turn onto the N18. In Varsseveld follow signs for Aalten (N318). In Aalten follow signs for Winterswijk. Drive through Aalten and site is signed after 4 km. GPS: 51.94961, 6.6477

Charges guide

Per unit incl. 2 persons and electricity	€ 18.00 - € 43.00
extra person	€ 2.00 - € 3.00
dog	€ 3.00

Bourtange

Camping 't Plathuis

Bourtangerkanaal Noord 1, NL-9545 VJ Bourtange (Groningen) T: 0599 354 383. E: info@plathuis.nl

alanrogers.com/NL6110

Camping 't Plathuis is beautifully located in the fortified village of Bourtange. This small town dates back to the times of the invasion of the Bishop of Münster in the 1600s. The site has 92 touring pitches, most on well established, grass fields with shade from the mature trees that surround the site. On the newest area at the back of the site there are 22 serviced pitches with 6-16A electricity, water and drainage, including 14 with cable TV. There are four hardstandings available for motorcaravans. There are plans to further extend the site. To the front of the site is a lake for swimming and fishing with a sandy beach.

Facilities
Single older style, but neat and adequate, heated toilet block with toilets, washbasins (open style and in cabins) and coin-operated, controllable, hot showers. Second prefabricated block in the new field. Family shower rooms. Baby room. Facilities for disabled visitors. Laundry facilities. Shopping service for basics. Bread to order. Bar. Snack bar. Lake for swimming and fishing. Canoe hire. Playground. WiFi (charged). Off site: Village of Bourtange.

Open: 1 April - 31 October.

Directions
From A7 take exit 47 for Winschoten and continue on N367 towards Vlagtwedde. In Vlagtwedde turn on N368 towards Bourtange. Site is on the right 200 m. after entering village. GPS: 53.0093, 7.1844

Charges guide
Per unit incl. 2 persons and electricity	€ 17.50 - € 21.00
extra person	€ 4.00
child (3-10 yrs)	€ 2.50
dog	€ 2.00

Groningen

Camping Stadspark

Campinglaan 6, NL-9727 KH Groningen (Groningen) T: 0505 251 624. E: info@campingstadspark.nl

alanrogers.com/NL5770

The Stadspark is a large park to the southwest of the city, well signed and with easy access. The campsite is within a park with many trees and surrounded by water. It has 200 pitches with 150 for touring units, of which 75 have 6A electricity and 30 are fully serviced with electricity, water and drainage. Several hardstandings are available for large units and motorcaravans. The separate tent area is supervised directly by the manager. The grass areas are car-free. Buses for the city leave from right outside and timetables and maps are provided at reception. Groningen is a lively city with lots to do.

Facilities
Two sanitary blocks provide hot showers, washbasins and toilets. One is new and the other has been refurbished to a good standard. Family shower and baby room. Motorcaravan services. Shop (15/3-15/10). Restaurant, café, bar and takeaway (1/4-15/9). Bicycle hire. Volleyball. Fishing. Canoeing. WiFi (free). Off site: Riding and golf 5 km. Boat launching 6 km.

Open: 15 March - 15 October.

Directions
From Assen on A28 turn left on the A7 towards Drachten. Follow signs for Stadspark and the campsite. GPS: 53.20090, 6.53570

Charges guide
Per unit incl. 2 persons and electricity	€ 21.00
extra person	€ 3.00
child (2-12 yrs)	€ 1.50
Mastercard accepted.	

Lauwersoog

Camping Lauwersoog

Strandweg 5, NL-9976 VS Lauwersoog (Groningen) T: 0519 349 133. E: info@lauwersoog.nl

alanrogers.com/NL6090

The focus at Camping Lauwersoog is very much on the sea and watersports. One can have sailing lessons or hire canoes and there is direct access to the beach from the site. There are 450 numbered pitches with 250 for tourers; 140 have water, drainage, electricity and cable connections. The pitches are on level, grassy fields (some beside the beach), partly separated by hedges and some with shade from trees (cars parked separately). A building in the marina houses a restaurant, bar, shop, laundry and an adventure playground. It also provides beautiful views over the Lauwersmeer. The site's restaurant specialises in seafood and even the entertainment programmes for all ages have a water theme.

Facilities
The two toilet blocks for touring units provide washbasins, preset showers and child size toilets. Facilities for disabled visitors. Laundry. Campers' kitchen. Ice pack service. Motorcaravan service. Shop. Restaurant (all year), bar and snack bar including takeaway service (1/4-1/10). Play area with bouncy castle. Minigolf at the beach. Sailing school. Canoe hire. Surfing lessons (July/Aug). Riding. Bicycle and go-kart hire. Boules. WiFi. Extensive entertainment programme for all ages in high season. Communal barbecue. Torch useful. Off site: Golf 7 km.

Open: All year.

Directions
Follow N361 from Groningen north to Lauwersoog and then follow site signs. GPS: 53.40205, 6.21732

Charges guide
Per unit incl. 2 persons and 10A electricity	€ 20.00 - € 34.50
with full services	€ 22.50 - € 37.50
extra person (over 1 yr)	€ 4.75
dog	€ 4.75
Camping Cheques accepted.	

Opende

Camping 't Strandheem

Parkweg 2, NL-9865 VP Opende (Groningen) T: **0594 659 555**. E: **info@strandheem.nl**

alanrogers.com/NL6120

Camping 't Strandheem has 330 quite large, numbered pitches (110 sq.m) some with hardstanding and suitable for motorcaravans. All with electricity (4/10A), there are 180 used for touring units, partly separated by low hedges but without much shade. Of these, 45 pitches have water points, drainage and cable TV connections. The Bruinewoud family will give you a warm welcome. The reception building houses an attractive bar, a full restaurant, a disco for teenagers and a shop. The site has a lot to offer, especially for youngsters with a full entertainment programme in high season with water games in the lake next to the site, a games area and an indoor pool.

Facilities

Two modern toilet buildings have washbasins, controllable showers, child size toilets and washbasins, a good baby room and fully equipped bathroom. Facilities for disabled campers. Launderette. Motorcaravan service. Shop. Restaurant and bar. Café and snack bar. Covered swimming pool (5x5 m) with separate paddling pool, slide and sun terrace. Playgrounds. Indoor play hall. Minigolf. Fishing. Bicycle hire. Boules. Lake with beach (€ 1 p/p per day). Extensive recreation programme (July/Aug). Film and card nights. Free WiFi in reception.

Open: 1 April - 1 October.

Directions

Follow A7 west from Groningen towards Heerenveen and take exit 31. Follow campsite signs from there. GPS: 53.15278, 6.19138

Charges guide

Per unit incl. 2 persons

and electricity	€ 18.50 - € 27.50
with private sanitary facility	€ 28.00 - € 37.00

Sellingen

Campingpark De Barkhoorn

Beetserweg 6, NL-9551 VE Sellingen (Groningen) T: **0599 322510**. E: **info@barkhoorn.nl**

alanrogers.com/NL6115

Camping De Barkhoorn is located in the Westerwolde, southeast of Groningen. The campsite is surrounded by vast forests and heathland interspersed with beautiful ponds. It offers camping in a tranquil setting on spacious, verdant pitches with shade to the back provided by tall trees. A car-free site, there are 152 touring pitches (including 13 comfort pitches), all with 10A electricity, and hardstandings for motorcaravans outside the gate. This is a pleasant family campsite, ideal for families with children, and for those who enjoy walking and cycling. The German border is nearby.

Facilities

Four older style, but clean sanitary buildings including one without hot water have showers, open style washbasins and preset hot showers. Private facilities to rent. Facilities for disabled visitors. Launderette. Bar/restaurant and terrace (Fri-Sun). Snack bar also sells basics. Play areas. Recreation lake with beach. Sports field. Minigolf. Tennis. Bowling and other activities. Bicycle hire. Fishing. Canoeing. WiFi over site (charged). Cabins to rent. Off site: Swimming pool with slide and toddlers' pool 200 m. Supermarket in village 1 km.

Open: 30 March - 27 October.

Directions

Follow signs from Zwolle, Hoogeveen and Emmen for Ter Apel. Sellingen is on the main road between Ter Apel and Winschoten, 2 km. from the centre of Sellingen. Follow site signs from the village. GPS: 52.946406, 7.131192

Charges guide

Per unit incl. 2 persons

and electricity	€ 15.00 - € 25.50
extra person	€ 3.50
child (from 2 yrs)	€ 3.50
dog	€ 3.00

Eijsden

Camping De Oosterdriessen

Oostweg 1a, NL-6245 LC Oost-Maarland (Limburg) T: **0434 093 215**. E: **info@oosterdriessen.nl**

alanrogers.com/NL6595

This friendly site can be found in the southern Netherlands, around 5 km. south of the city of Maastricht, and 3 km. from the village of Eijsden. The site enjoys an attractive lakeside setting on the Pieterplas, with its own private beach and with opportunities for watersports. The 230 touring pitches here are grassy and most have 6A electricity. A special area is reserved for hikers and cyclists, and a reduced charge applied (maximum two nights stay). There is also a broad, grassy area for sport and leisure. Given its lakeside situation, this is a popular site with anglers (small fee charged).

Facilities

Single traditional style toilet block with preset showers. Facilities for disabled visitors. Baby room. Laundry. Small shop, fresh bread to order. Bar with TV. Café with terrace. Adventure play area. Bicycle hire. Fishing. Sports field. Direct lake access. Activity and entertainment programme (high season). Four log cabins for rent. Free WiFi around reception. Off site: Snack bar/restaurant 100 m.

Open: 27 April - 24 September.

Directions

Approaching from the north (Maastricht) take the southbound A2 and follow signs to Oost Maarland. From here, follow signs to the lake and the site is well signed. GPS: 50.799689, 5.70636

Charges guide

Per unit incl. 2 persons

and electricity	€ 21.20 - € 23.20
extra person	€ 5.00

No credit cards.

For latest campsite news, availability and prices visit

alanrogers.com

Gulpen

Terrassencamping Gulperberg Panorama

Berghem 1, NL-6271 NP Gulpen (Limburg) T: 0434 502 330. E: info@gulperberg.nl

alanrogers.com/NL6530

Gulperberg Panorama is just three kilometres from the attractive village of Gulpen, midway between the interesting cities of Maastricht and Aachen. The 322 touring pitches are large and flat on terraces overlooking the village on one side and open countryside on the other. Many have full services. English is spoken in reception, although all written information is in Dutch (ask if you require a translation). Gulperberg Panorama is a haven for children. During the high season there is a weekly entertainment programme to keep them occupied. The site is not suitable for visitors with disabilities. Dogs are restricted to one section of the campsite. Visitors are assured of a warm welcome and if arriving (or leaving) on a Saturday are welcomed (or bade farewell) by the Aartje Twinkle.

Facilities

Four sanitary blocks have good facilities. Family shower room and baby room. Laundry. Shop (27/4-31/8). Bar. Takeaway. New restaurant with terrace. Swimming pool (29/4-15/9). Three play areas. Bouncy cushion. TV and games room. Extensive entertainment programme for children plus family entertainment. WiFi over site (charged). Off site: Golf and bicycle hire 3 km. Fishing 4 km. Riding 5 km. Beach 15 km.

Open: Easter - 31 October.

Directions

Gulpen is east of Maastricht. Take N278 Maastricht-Aachen. Site is signed just as you enter Gulpen at the traffic lights. Turn right and follow camping signs for 3 km. GPS: 50.80673, 5.89413

Charges guide

Per unit incl. 2 persons and electricity	€ 22.00 - € 32.00
extra person (over 2 yrs)	€ 3.00 - € 4.00

Camping Cheques accepted.

Gulpen

Camping Osebos

Reymerstokker dorpsstraat 1, NL-6271 PP Gulpen (Limburg) T: 0434 501 611. E: info@osebos.nl

alanrogers.com/NL6590

Family run, Camping Osebos is a quiet, attractive and well kept terraced site with a southerly aspect in the Dutch mountains. There are 215 touring pitches, all with electricity, 90 of which have fresh water, waste water and TV connections. They are level, grassed and set in rows on terraces or in groups, on the lower part of the site. From the pitches there are extensive views of the surrounding countryside with its rolling, partially tree-clad hills. There is walking and cycling directly from the site and many picturesque villages to visit in this attractive, less well known, southern part of Holland closely bordering Belgium and Germany.

Facilities

Three heated sanitary blocks contain free showers, washbasins (open and in cabins), family showers and a new, separate children's/baby facility. Laundry facilities, washing machine, dryer plus ironing. Motorcaravan services. Shop, bar/restaurant, takeaway (22/4-31/10). Outdoor swimming pool, paddling pool. Play areas. Children's entertainment in summer. Sports pitch. Bicycle hire. Max. 2 dogs. Off site: Fishing 2 km. Golf 7 km.

Open: 1 April - 28 October.

Directions

Leave E25/A2 motorway at exit 54 (Europaploin) and head east towards Aachen on N278. In 3.5 km. after Margraten, on the descent to Gulpen, turn south towards Beutenaken. After 400 m. at bottom of hill, site is to the right. GPS: 50.80669, 5.87078

Charges guide

Per unit incl. 2 persons and electricity	€ 15.00 - € 25.00
extra person	€ 2.00 - € 3.00

Roermond

Resort Marina Oolderhuuske

Oolderhuuske 1, NL-6041 TR Roermond (Limburg) T: 0475 588 686. E: info@oolderhuuske.nl

alanrogers.com/NL6515

When staying on this interesting site, which is part of a resort complex, you know you are on holiday. The site is situated at the end of a peninsula, on a low lying spit of land and overlooks wild stretches of open water and the River Maas. There are 220 pitches, 80 of which are for touring. All have electricity (6-16A) water and drainage, are level, grassed and many are waterside – no pitch lies more than 60 m. from the water. There are numerous cycling routes from the site, either directly overland or via the passenger/cycle ferry that crosses the Maas.

Facilities

One floating block and two prefabricated sanitary units provide toilets, free showers, washbasins and outside sinks. Motorcaravan services. Shop and bar (w/ends and July/Aug), restaurant with terrace, snacks and takeaway. Small indoor pool, gym, sauna, steam bath, solarium. Sports fields. Tennis. Playgrounds. Bicycle hire. Boat launching. High season entertainment. Barrier deposit € 50. WiFi throughout (charged).

Open: 1 April - 31 October.

Directions

From Maastricht on A2 (Maastricht-Eindhoven) take exit for Roermond, continue to Roermond (centrum). In Roermond follow signs for Eindhoven and, just after Muse river bridge (Maasbrug) turn right to Hatenboer/de Weerd. Follow brown signs to Marina Oolderhuuske. GPS: 51.19195, 5.94942

Charges guide

Per unit incl. up to 4 persons and electricity	€ 24.00 - € 36.00
extra person	€ 5.00

FREE Alan Rogers Travel Card
Extra benefits and savings - see page 14

Sevenum

De Schatberg

Midden Peelweg 5, NL-5975 MZ Sevenum (Limburg) T: 0774 677 777. E: info@schatberg.nl

alanrogers.com/NL6510

In a woodland setting of 96 hectares, this friendly, family run campsite is more reminiscent of a holiday village, with a superb range of activities that make it an ideal venue for families. Look out for the deer! A large site with 1,100 pitches and many mobile homes and seasonal or weekend visitors, there are 550 touring pitches. All have electricity (6/10/16A Europlug), cable, water and drainage and average 100-150 sq.m. in size. They are on rough grass terrain, mostly with shade, but not separated. Seventy two pitches have private sanitary facilities, of which 32 also have dishwashing, fridge and gas ring, and two have a sauna and jacuzzi. Road noise can be heard in parts of this large campsite. The site is well situated for visits to Germany and Belgium, and is easily accessible from the port of Zeebrugge. The surrounding countryside offers the opportunity to enjoy nature, either by cycling or walking. For those who prefer to stay on site, the location is excellent with several lakes for fishing, windsurfing and swimming, plus an extensive range of activities and a heated outdoor swimming pool.

Facilities

Five modern, fully equipped toilet blocks, supplemented by three small wooden toilet units to save night-time walks. Family shower rooms, baby baths and en-suite units for disabled visitors. Washing machines and dryers. Motorcaravan services. Supermarket. Restaurant, bar and takeaway. Pizzeria. Pancake restaurant. Indoor pool. Outdoor pool (1/5-31/8). Trampoline. Play areas. Fishing. Watersports. Bicycle hire. Games room. Bowling. Indoor playground. Entertainment weekends and high season. Water-ski track. Charcoal barbecues not permitted. WiFi over site (free). Off site: Golf 500 m.

Open: All year.

Directions

Site is 15 km. west-northwest of Venlo. Leave the A67 Eindhoven-Venlo motorway at Helden, exit 38. Travel north on the 277 for 500 m. and site is signed at new roundabout. GPS: 51.382964, 5.976147

Charges guide

Per unit incl. 2 persons	
and electricity	€ 19.60 - € 48.20
extra person	€ 4.65
dog	€ 5.50

Camping Cheques accepted.

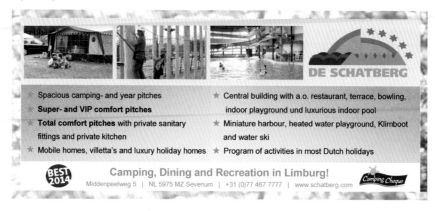

* Spacious camping- and year pitches
* **Super- and VIP comfort pitches**
* **Total comfort pitches** with private sanitary fittings and private kitchen
* Mobile homes, villetta's and luxury holiday homes
* Central building with a.o. restaurant, terrace, bowling, indoor playground und luxurious indoor pool
* Miniature harbour, heated water playground, Klimboot and water ski
* Program of activities in most Dutch holidays

Camping, Dining and Recreation in Limburg!

Middenpeelweg 5 | NL 5975 MZ Sevenum | +31 (0)77 467 7777 | www.schatberg.com

Vaals

Camping Rozenhof

Camerig 12, NL-6294 NB Vijlen-Vaals (Limburg) T: 0434 551 611. E: info@campingrozenhof.nl

alanrogers.com/NL6540

Camping Rozenhof is a friendly, family run site and its hillside location offers views over a valley that has won awards for its natural beauty. This partially wooded, hilly region is popular with countryside lovers, ramblers and cyclists. Rozenhof has 68 pitches arranged on a series of small terraced, hedged meadows. There are 61 for touring units, level and mainly on grass and all with 10A electricity. A number of mature trees afford some shade. A rustic restaurant, which can become overstretched in high season, is to the left of the wide entrance. There is a large terrace and, as the site's name suggests, roses and plants are much in evidence.

Facilities

To the rear of reception, the heated modern sanitary unit houses all the usual facilities including controllable showers (tokens), washbasins (open and in cabins). Facilities for disabled visitors. Baby room and family shower room. Washing machines and dryers. Shop. Fresh bread to order. Refurbished restaurant/bar and takeaway. Gas supplies. Playground, play room and pets' corner for children. Bicycle hire. Free WiFi over part of site.

Open: All year.

Directions

Leave A76/E314 at Knooppunt Bocholtz and follow the N281 southwest towards Vaals for 3 km. to T-junction with N278. Turn left, then first right to Vijlen. In Vijlen second road to right (Vijlen Berg) and straight on for 4 km. to T-junction at far side of forest. Turn right and continue for 300 m. to site on right. GPS: 50.77021, 5.92925

Charges guide

Per unit incl. 2 persons	
and electricity	€ 16.00 - € 25.00

For latest campsite news, availability and prices visit

alanrogers.com

Valkenburg aan de Geul

Camping Oriental

Rijksweg 6, NL-6325 PE Valkenburg aan de Geul (Limburg) T: 0436 040 075. E: info@campingoriental.nl

alanrogers.com/NL6513

Camping Oriental is an excellent family site located between Valkenburg and Maastricht. There is a mixture of 285 sunny and shaded touring pitches, all with 10A electricity and some with water, drainage and TV connections. There is also a selection of mobile homes for rent (all with TV). On-site amenities include a convivial bar, a snack bar and a well stocked shop (with fresh bread daily). There is a heated swimming pool with retractable roof, as well as a children's paddling pool. A large sports field is ideal for football, volleyball and basketball. Valkenburg has a colourful history characterised by siege and conquest. The ancient castle ruins (destroyed in 1672) can be found close to the town centre.

Facilities

Four sanitary blocks include showers and washbasins, open and in cubicles. New toilet block with facilities for disabled visitors. Baby room. Launderette. Dog shower. Shop. Bar. Snack bar. Heated and covered swimming pool. Paddling pool. Play areas. Large sports field. Zip wire. Boules. Mobile homes for rent. WiFi over part of site (charged). Off site: Shopping and restaurants in Valkenburg. Bicycle hire 5 km. Golf and riding 8 km.

Open: 17 April - 1 October.

Directions

Approaching from Maastricht, take A79 motorway eastbound and take the Valkenburg exit. The site is on Rijksweg, south of the town centre, and is well signed. GPS: 50.86005, 5.77258

Charges guide

Per unit incl. 2 persons and electricity	€ 21.00 - € 27.00
extra person (over 2 yrs)	€ 3.50

No credit cards.

Wijlre

Recreatieterrein De Gronselenput

Haasstad 3, NL-6321 PK Wijlre (Limburg) T: 0434 591 645. E: gronselenput@paasheuvelgroep.nl

alanrogers.com/NL6580

Camping Gronselenput is a small, quiet, countryside site located at the end of a narrow, tree-lined lane. It is one of five sites run by the Paasheuvel Group in Holland. Run by volunteers, it has 60 grassy level pitches, (55 for tourers, 50 with 10A electricity). With a peaceful location between a wooded hill and the River Geul (fishing allowed with a permit), it is popular with visitors with younger children and those seeking a quiet site. Cars are parked separately from the camping area, thus ensuring vehicle-free space. The site is set out in a series of small hedged meadows with pitches tending to be located around the edges. Three gravel pitches are reserved for motorcaravans.

Facilities

In the sanitary block hot water for showers is free. Entry to the toilets is directly from outside. Two baby areas. Washing machines and spin dryer. Gas supplies. Shop (excellent English spoken). Bar selling pizzas with a partly covered terrace facing one of the playgrounds. Large room used for organised children's activities (July/Aug and public holidays). WiFi over site (charged). Off site: Fishing 1 km. Bicycle hire 5 km. Riding 15 km. Golf 25 km.

Open: 2 April - 1 November.

Directions

Site is near Wijlre, 10 km. northwest of Aachen. Leave A4/E314/A76 at Knooppunt Bocholtz (not Bocholtz town). Follow N281 southwest for 5 km. and at junction turn right (northwest) to Wittem on N278. In Wittem, at lights turn right on N595 to Wijlre. GPS: 50.842167, 5.877483

Charges guide

Per unit incl. 2 persons and electricity	€ 17.00 - € 24.90
extra person	€ 2.70

Bergeijk

Camping De Paal

Paaldreef 14, NL-5571 TN Bergeijk (Noord-Brabant) T: 0497 571 977. E: info@depaal.nl

LeadingCampings

alanrogers.com/NL5970

A really first class, family run campsite, De Paal is especially suitable for families with children up to ten years old, and in low season for those seeking a quality, peaceful site. Situated in 42 hectares of woodland, it has 580 touring pitches (up to 150 sq.m). The pitches are numbered and in meadows, separated by trees, with cars parked mainly on dedicated parking areas. All have 6A electricity, TV, water, drainage and a bin. There are 60 pitches with private sanitary facilities some of which are partly underground and attractively covered with grass and flowers. Sixteen pitches have a kitchen, sleeping accommodation and sanitary facilities. Each group of pitches has a small playground; additionally, there is a large adventure playground. A member of Leading Campings group.

Facilities

High quality sanitary facilities are ultra modern, with washbasins in cabins, family rooms and baby baths. Facilities for disabled visitors. Launderette. Motorcaravan services. Underground supermarket. Restaurant (high season), bar and snack bar (all season). Indoor pool (supervised in high season). Outdoor pool (May-Sept). Tennis. Play areas. Theatre. WiFi (charged). Bicycle hire.

Open: Easter/1 April - 31 October.

Directions

From E34 Antwerpen-Eindhoven road take exit 32 (Eersel) and follow signs for Bergeijk and site (2 km. from town). GPS: 51.33635, 5.35552

Charges guide

Per unit incl. 2 persons and services	€ 31.00 - € 49.00
extra person	€ 4.00 - € 5.00
dog	€ 5.00

Eersel

Recreatiepark TerSpegelt

Postelseweg 88, NL-5521 RD Eersel (Noord-Brabant) T: 0497 512 016. E: info@terspegelt.nl

alanrogers.com/NL6630

Camping TerSpegelt is a large, attractively laid out site set around three (unsupervised) lakes used for sports, non-motorised boating, swimming and fishing. The site has 855 pitches, with 481 for touring units and tents, and 70 cabins, chalets and mobile homes for rent, plus various types of tent. All touring pitches have electricity (6-16A Europlug), and 347 also have water and drainage, and some have lakeside views. We can recommend this site to families with children (pushchairs useful) and people who like to participate in organised activities (sports and outdoor activities, campfires and themed dinners).

Facilities
Five main toilet blocks, four heated by solar panels, provide toilets, washbasins (open and in cubicles) and showers. Washbasins for children. Heated baby rooms with changing mat and bath. Facilities for disabled visitors in one block. Laundry. Motorcaravan services. Supermarket, restaurant, bar, snack bar and swimming pools (all open as site). Entertainment and activities. Watersports, climbing wall and minigolf. Bicycle and go-cart hire. Tennis. No dogs. WiFi over site (charged).

Open: 4 April - 2 November.

Directions
From Utrecht follow the A2 south towards Eindhoven, then Maastricht. Take exit for Antwerpen and follow signs for Eersel. From Eersel follow site signs. GPS: 51.33623, 5.29373

Charges guide

Per unit incl. 2 persons and electricity	€ 23.50 - € 56.50
Min. stay at some periods.	

Hilvarenbeek

Vakantiepark Beekse Bergen

Beekse Bergen 1, NL-5081 NJ Hilvarenbeek (Noord-Brabant) T: 01354 91100. E: info@libema.nl

alanrogers.com/NL5900

Centred around a large lake, Beekse Bergen campsite is part of a large leisure park complex that offers something for all the family, from the Safari Park containing over 1,000 wild animals to Speelland, which caters for children from three to eight years old. The site has 225 touring pitches, all with 4/10A electricity, 100 of which have fresh and waste water connections. They are arranged in small, level, grassy areas surrounded by hedges and mature trees. Several small sandy beaches are to be found around the lake, which can be used for, amongst other things, swimming, windsurfing and fishing.

Facilities
Sanitary facilities in the touring area include all the usual facilities including some washbasins in cabins and facilities for disabled visitors. Launderette. Supermarket. Restaurants, cafés and takeaway (weekends only in low seasons). Playgrounds. Indoor pool. Beaches and lake swimming. Watersports including rowing boats and canoe hire. Amusements. Tennis. Minigolf. Fishing. Recreation programme. Bicycle hire. Riding. Bungalows and tents to rent. WiFi (charged). Off site: Efteling amusement park.

Open: 21 March - 6 November.

Directions
From A58/E312 Tilburg-Eindhoven motorway, take exit to Hilvarenbeek on the N269 road. Follow signs to Beekse Bergen. GPS: 51.48298, 5.12800

Charges guide

Per unit incl. 2 persons and electricity	€ 15.00 - € 25.00
extra person	€ 7.00
dog	€ 4.00

Lierop

Camping De Somerense Vennen

Philipsbosweg 7, NL-5715 RE Lierop (Noord-Brabant) T: 0492 331 216. E: info@somerensevennen.nl

alanrogers.com/NL6690

De Somerense Vennen is an attractive site in lovely countryside with walking, cycling and riding trails in the Somerense heartland. A very good range of activities for children are organised here, based around the Twinkle Club, which are suitable for children of all ages. There are 125 good sized touring pitches, all with electricity (4-16A) and generally well shaded. A number of mobile homes and chalets are available for rent. There is a convivial bar/restaurant, serving the best pancakes locally! The impressive swimming pool complex (with sliding roof) includes a special children's area and a good range of games and play equipment. Reception is very welcoming and has a range of tourist information.

Facilities
Two toilet blocks, the newest (open all season) is small but clean and well equipped. Facilities for disabled visitors. Further toilet/shower by restaurant. Facilities for children in a separate, purpose built block are well decorated. Laundry. Swimming pool complex (can be covered). Bar, snack bar and restaurant. Riding centre. Play area. Children's club. Activity and entertainment programme. Free WiFi over site. Mobile homes and chalets for rent. Off site: Walking in North Brabant.

Open: 26 March - 30 October.

Directions
Use A67 Eindhoven-Venlo motorway and leave at exit 35 (Someren). In Someren head towards Lierop and then follow signs to the site. GPS: 51.400403, 5.675804

Charges guide

Per unit incl. 2 persons and electricity	€ 19.50 - € 29.50
dog	€ 4.50

For latest campsite news, availability and prices visit

alanrogers.com

Oosterhout

Camping De Katjeskelder

Katjeskelder 1, NL-4904 SG Oosterhout (Noord-Brabant) T: 0162 453 539. E: kkinfo@katjeskelder.nl

alanrogers.com/NL5540

This site is to be found in a wooded setting in a delightful area of Noord-Brabant. It is well established and offers extensive facilities with a new and impressive ultra-modern reception area. Around the 25 hectare site there are many bungalows and 102 touring pitches, all with electricity, water and waste water. Motorcaravans are now accepted (on hardstandings near the entrance), as well as tents and caravans. The site has a cat theme, hence the cat names including that of the restaurant, the Gelaarsde Kat (Puss in Boots), which is situated in the Tropikat complex.

Facilities
One heated sanitary block (looking a little tired and may be stretched in high season) provides facilities including a family shower room, baby room and provision for disabled visitors. Laundry. Supermarket. Restaurant, bar, snack bar, pizzeria (Pizzacat) and takeaway (the Hapjeskat). Indoor tropical pool. Outdoor swimming pools (all season, closed when air temperature below 8°C). Play field. Tennis. Bicycle hire. Minigolf. Several play areas for small children. Large adventure playground. Entertainment for children (all season). WiFi over site (charged).

Open: 1 April - 31 October.

Directions
From A27 Breda-Gorinchem motorway take Oosterhout Zuid exit 17 and follow signs for 7 km. to site. If using GPS, enter road as Brease Weg. GPS: 51.62901, 4.83950

Charges guide
Per unit incl. up to 5 persons and electricity, water and TV connections	€ 22.00 - € 37.00
extra person	€ 4.00

Vinkel

Vakantiepark Dierenbos

Vinkeloord 1, NL-5382 JX Vinkel (Noord-Brabant) T: 0735 343 536. E: info@libema.nl

alanrogers.com/NL5880

Run by the same group as Beekse Bergen (NL5900), Dierenbos is a large site, with motel accommodation and a bungalow park in addition to its 500 camping pitches. These are divided into several grassy areas, many in an attractive wooded setting. There are 381 for touring units, all with electrical connections (4-10A) and some with full services (water and TV connection). A small, landscaped lake has sandy beaches and is overlooked by a large, modern play area. Some of the touring pitches also overlook the water. Campers are entitled to free entry to several attractions. The varied amenities are located in and around a modern, central complex. They include heated outdoor swimming pools, an indoor sub-tropical pool with slide and jet stream, and a ten-pin bowling alley.

Facilities
Eight toilet blocks are well situated with a mixture of clean and simple facilities (some unisex) with some warm water for washing and some individual washbasins. Baby room. Supermarket. Bar. Restaurant. Snack bar/takeaway (high season). Free outdoor heated swimming pools (1/6-1/9). Indoor pool (charged). 10-pin bowling. Tennis. Minigolf. Boules. Sports field. Bicycle hire. Pedalos. Fishing. Barbecue area. Play areas on sand. Many organised activities in season. Conference facilities. Max. 1 dog.

Open: 21 March - 26 October.

Directions
Site is signed from the N50/A50 road between 's Hertogenbosch and Nijmegen, 10 km. east of 's Hertogenbosch at Vinkel. GPS: 51.70472, 5.43048

Charges guide
Per unit incl. 2 persons and electricity	€ 14.00 - € 28.00
extra person	€ 7.00
dog	€ 5.00

Alkmaar

Camping Alkmaar

Bergerweg 201, NL-1817 ML Alkmaar (Noord-Holland) T: 0725 116 924. E: info@campingalkmaar.nl

alanrogers.com/NL6705

Camping Alkmaar is a friendly, family run campsite on the outskirts of the charming town of Alkmaar and near the artisan village of Bergen. A short cycle ride will take you to the peaceful countryside of Noord-Holland with its dunes, wide sandy beaches, woods and unique polder landscape. Alternatively, a stroll along the canals in the picturesque heart of Alkmaar with its architecture, culture and cheese market may appeal. This is a tranquil site - there is no bar or restaurant and radios are not permitted. All 120 touring pitches have 6/10A electricity; 46 have hardstanding, and 21 are comfort pitches with water and drainage. A bus service runs to the town centre and the train station for connections to Amsterdam.

Facilities
New sanitary block in the touring area is clean and well maintained and has coin-operated showers and open style washbasins. Facilities for disabled visitors. Washing machine and dryer. Two motorcaravan service points. Play area. Fishing. Bicycle hire. WiFi over part of site (charged). Off site: Shops and restaurants in Alkmaar.

Open: All year.

Directions
From the western ring road of Alkmaar (N9), turn left towards Bergen (N510). After 300 m. turn left to the site. GPS: 52.6421, 4.72329

Charges guide
Per unit incl. 2 persons and electricty (5 kWh)	€ 21.00 - € 31.00
additional electricity (per kWh)	€ 0.40
extra person	€ 4.00

Amstelveen

Camping Het Amsterdamse Bos

Kleine Noorddijk 1, NL-1187 NZ Amstelveen (Noord-Holland) T: 0206 416 868.

E: info@campingamsterdam.com alanrogers.com/NL5660

Het Amsterdamse Bos is a large park to the southwest of Amsterdam, one corner of which has been specifically laid out as the city's municipal campsite and is now under family ownership. Close to Schiphol Airport (expect some noise), it is a walk/bus and a metro ride into central Amsterdam. The site is well laid out alongside a canal, with unmarked pitches on separate flat lawns mostly backing onto pleasant hedges and trees, with several areas of paved hardstandings. It takes 400 touring units, with 100 electrical connections (10A) and some with cable TV. An additional area is available for tents and groups. Some pitches can become very wet in the rain. We found the free WiFi difficult to access.

Facilities

Three new sanitary blocks are light and airy with showers (on payment). Facilities for babies and disabled visitors. Laundry facilities. Motorcaravan services. Gas supplies. Small shop with basics. Fresh bread from reception. Cooking and dining area. Play area. Bicycle hire. Internet and free WiFi over site. Twin-axle caravans not accepted. Off site: Fishing, boating, pancake restaurant in the park.

Open: 15 March - 15 December.

Directions

Amsterdamse Bos is west of Amstelveen. From the A9 motorway take exit 6 and follow N231 to site (second traffic light). GPS: 52.29357, 4.82297

Charges guide

Per unit incl. 2 persons	
and electricity	€ 20.00 - € 25.00
extra person	€ 5.00 - € 5.50
child (4-12 yrs)	€ 2.50 - € 2.75

Amsterdam

Gaasper Camping Amsterdam

Loosdrechtdreef 7, NL-1108 AZ Amsterdam (Noord-Holland) T: 0206 967 326.

alanrogers.com/NL5670

Amsterdam is probably the most popular destination for visits in the Netherlands, and Gaasper Camping is on the southeast side, a short walk from a Metro station with a direct 20 minute service to the centre. The site is well kept and neatly laid out on flat grass with attractive trees and shrubs. There are 350 touring pitches in two main areas – one more open and grassy, mainly kept for tents (30 with 10A connections), the other more formal with numbered pitches mainly divided by shallow ditches or good hedges. Areas of hardstanding are available and all caravan pitches have electrical connections.

Facilities

Three modern, clean toilet blocks (one unisex) for the tourist sections are an adequate provision. Nine new cabins with basin and shower. Hot water for showers and some dishwashing sinks on payment. Facilities for babies. Washing machine and dryer. Motorcaravan services. Gas supplies. Supermarket (1/4-1/11), café/bar/restaurant plus takeaway (1/6-1/9). Play area on grass. Off site: Riding 200 m. Fishing 1 km. Golf 4 km.

Open: 15 March - 1 November.

Directions

Take exit 1 for Gaasperplas-Weesp (S113) from the section of A9 motorway which is on the east side of the A2. Note: do not take the Gaasperdam exit (S112) which comes first if approaching from the west. GPS: 52.312222, 4.991389

Charges guide

Per unit incl. 2 persons	
and electricity	€ 19.50 - € 23.50
extra person	€ 4.75 - € 5.50

Amsterdam

Camping Vliegenbos

Meeuwenlaan 138, NL-1022 AM Amsterdam (Noord-Holland) T: 0206 368 855.

E: vliegenbos@noord.amsterdam.nl alanrogers.com/NL5675

Vliegenbos enjoys the best of both worlds with an appealing location in a large wood, ten minutes from the lively centre of Amsterdam and five minutes by bike from the countryside of the Waterland region, best known for its open expanses and picturesque towns such as Marken, Edam and Volendam. It extends over a 2.5 hectare site and has a good range of amenities including a restaurant, shop and recently renovated toilet blocks. Most of the 400 pitches are for tents, but there are 19 hardstandings (10A electricity) and a further 40 smaller hardstandings (no electricity).

Facilities

Renovated toilet blocks include facilities for disabled campers. Motorcaravan services. Bar/restaurant with takeaway. Shop (fresh bread daily). Free WiFi over part of site. Cabins for rent. Reservations are not accepted for touring pitches. Dogs accepted on request. Off site: Bus stop 200 m. Cycle tracks in the surrounding Waterland. Ferry terminal 15 minutes walk with regular free service to Amsterdam.

Open: 1 April - 26 October.

Directions

Leave the A10 Amsterdam ring road at exit S116 and follow signs to Camping Vliegenbos. GPS: 52.39055, 4.928083

Charges guide

Per unit incl. 2 persons	
and electricity	€ 28.50 - € 30.00
extra person	€ 7.70 - € 8.70
child (2-14 yrs)	€ 5.40

For latest campsite news, availability and prices visit

alanrogers.com

Amsterdam

Camping Zeeburg

Zuider IJdijk 20, NL-1095 KN Amsterdam (Noord-Holland) T: 206 944 430. E: info@campingzeeburg.nl

alanrogers.com/NL5665

Camping Zeeburg is a welcoming site attractively located to the east of Amsterdam on an island in the IJmeer and, unusually, combines a sense of nature with the advantage of being just 20 minutes (5 km) from the city centre. In a sense, Zeeburg reflects the spirit of Amsterdam, claiming to be open, friendly and tolerant. The site provides 400 pitches, 350 for tents (no electricity) and 100 pitches with 10A electricity for caravans and motorcaravans, most on hardstandings and with views over the IJmeer. Tent pitches cannot be booked in advance and the maximum duration allowed on site is 14 days. Zeeburg also offers a number of colourful eco-cabins and Romany-style wagons or 'pipowagens'. The city centre can be easily accessed by bicycle (hire available on site). On-site amenities include a busy café/restaurant. There is a shop with a bakery (which claims to bake Amsterdam's best croissants), a children's farm and a canoe rental service. A swimming pool is adjacent. The wetlands of the IJmeer are well worth exploration, extending to the Diemerpark and new city of IJburg.

Facilities

Three toilet blocks are generally simple and well used, but clean. Although adequate, facilities may be stretched at peak times. Facilities for disabled visitors (key access). Shop (all year). Café/restaurant (1/4-11/11). Very small playground. Games room. Bicycle hire. Motorcaravan services. Children's petting farm. Canoe hire. Eco-cabins and wagons to rent. Free WiFi throughout. Off site: Swimming pool. Buses and trains to city centre.

Open: All year.

Directions

Site is on the eastern side of Amsterdam. From the A10 (Amsterdam ring road) take exit S114 to Zeeburg. Then follow signs to the city centre and, before reaching the Piet Hein tunnel turn left and then right into the campsite. The site is well signed from the A10. GPS: 52.36532, 4.95871

Charges guide

Per unit incl. 2 persons and electricity	€ 15.00 - € 28.00
extra person	€ 5.00 - € 7.00
child (2-12 yrs)	€ 2.50 - € 3.50
dog	€ 2.00 - € 3.00

Bloemendaal

Kennemer Duincamping de Lakens

Zeeweg 60, NL-2051 EC Bloemendaal aan Zee (Noord-Holland) T: 0235 411 570.

E: delakens@kennemerduincampings.nl alanrogers.com/NL6870

De Lakens is beautifully located in the dunes at Bloemendaal aan Zee. This site has 900 reasonably large, flat pitches of varying sizes, whose layout makes them feel quite private - some come with a ready erected hammock! There are 410 pitches for tourers (255 with 16A electricity) separated by low hedging. This site is a true oasis of peace in a part of the Netherlands usually bustling with activity. From this site it is possible to walk straight through the dunes to the North Sea. Although there is no pool, there is the sea. The reception and management are very friendly and welcoming.

Facilities

The five new toilet blocks for tourers include controllable showers, washbasins (open style and in cabins), facilities for disabled visitors and a baby room. Launderette. Two motorcaravan service points. Bar/restaurant with terrace, pizzeria and snack bar. Supermarket. Adventure playgrounds. Basketball. Bicycle hire. Entertainment programme in high season for all. WiFi over most of site (charged). Range of glamping-style accommodation for rent. No twin-axle caravans or large motorcaravans. Dogs are not accepted. Off site: Beach within 200 m. Riding 1 km. Fishing 5 km. Golf 10 km.

Open: 27 March - 1 November.

Directions

From Amsterdam go west to Haarlem and follow the N200 from Haarlem towards Bloemendaal aan Zee. Site is on the N200, on the right hand side. GPS: 52.40563, 4.58652

Charges guide

Per unit incl. 4 persons	€ 25.60 - € 55.00
extra person	€ 5.35

Callantsoog

Camping Tempelhof

Westerweg 2, NL-1759 JD Callantsoog (Noord-Holland) T: 0224 581 522.

E: info@tempelhof.nl alanrogers.com/NL5735

LeadingCampings

This first class site on the Dutch coast has 470 pitches with 220 for touring units, the remainder used by seasonal campers, with a number of static units (mostly privately owned). All touring pitches have electricity (10/16A), water, drain and TV aerial point (70-110 sq.m. but car free). Two pitches have private sanitary facilities. The grass pitches are arranged in long rows which are separated by hedges and shrubs, with access from hardcore roads. There is hardly any shade. There are facilities for many activities, including a heated indoor pool, a fitness room and tennis courts. Tempelhof is close to the North Sea beaches (1 km). A member of Leading Campings group.

Facilities

Two modern toilet blocks include washbasins (open style and in cabins) and controllable hot showers (SEP key). Children's area and baby room. Private bathroom (charged weekly). Facilities for disabled visitors. Fully equipped laundry. Motorcaravan services. Shop, restaurant, takeaway, bar, indoor heated swimming pool with paddling pool (all 22/3-3/11). Fitness room. Recreation hall. Climbing wall. Tennis. Trim court. Play area. Entertainment programme in high season. WiFi over site (charged). Bicycle hire. Max. 2 dogs.

Open: All year.

Directions

From Alkmaar take N9 road north towards Den Helder. Turn left towards Callantsoog on the N503 road and follow site signs.
GPS: 52.846644, 4.715506

Charges guide

Per unit incl. 2 persons and electricity (plus meter)	€ 19.00 - € 39.00
extra person	€ 4.50
electricity (per kWh)	€ 0.35

Callantsoog

Camping De Nollen

Westerweg 8, NL-1759 JD Callantsoog (Noord-Holland) T: 0224 581 281. E: info@denollen.nl

alanrogers.com/NL6888

De Nollen is a comfortable, nine-hectare site, ideal for couples, seniors and families with younger children. There are a variety of pitches (60-120 sq.m) some basic, without connections, most with 10A electricity and comfort pitches with 10A electricity, water, drainage and cable TV. There is plenty to keep children occupied, with several playgrounds across the site, one with a large inflatable. The two nature reserves adjacent give the site a tranquil atmosphere. The Eetboey restaurant and snack bar offers simple meals and takeaway dishes. You can also eat outside on the terrace, and there is a play corner for younger children.

Facilities

Two modern toilet blocks with underfloor heating. Separate facilities for children. En-suite unit for disabled visitors. Launderette. Dog shower. Motorcaravan services. Microwave. Freezer. Supermarket (as site). Cafeteria/snack bar and takeaway service (Thu-Sun; daily in July/Aug). Play areas. Bouncy castle. Football. Basketball. Beach volleyball. Fishing. Fridge hire. Bicycle hire. WiFi over site (charged). Off site: Beach 2 km.

Open: 28 March - 25 October.

Directions

From the Alkmaar-Den Helder road (N9) take exit for Callantsoog. Turn right at the Het Zwanenwater nature reserve. Follow small signs to the site.
GPS: 52.841381, 4.719001

Charges guide

Per unit incl. 2 persons and electricity	€ 23.00 - € 33.00
extra person	€ 4.00
dog	€ 3.00

Castricum

Kennemer Duincamping Geversduin

Beverwijkerstraatweg 205, NL-1901 NH Castricum (Noord-Holland) T: 0251 661 095.

E: geversduin@kennemerduincampings.nl alanrogers.com/NL6862

The comfortable, family site of Geversduin lies in an area of forests and sand dunes. The site offers 614 pitches of which 221 are for touring units and 24 for accommodation to rent. They have good shade and privacy, and all pitches have 4-16A electricity connections. The pitches without electricity have a unique location and cars must be parked elsewhere. In high season, many activities are organised for youngsters including the unusual opportunity to join a forestry worker for the day. The beach is only 4 km. away and is easily accessible by bike or on foot.

Facilities

Four sanitary blocks with WCs, open style washbasins, preset hot showers and family shower rooms including baby room. Facilities for disabled visitors. Laundry with washing machines and dryers. Supermarket. Snack bar and café for meals with large terrace (weekends only in low season). Recreation area. Sports pitch. Play area. Bicycle hire. WiFi (free). Safes. Only gas barbecues are permitted. Off site: Riding 500 m. Beach and fishing 4 km.

Open: 26 March - 25 October.

Directions

On the A9 (Amsterdam-Alkmaar) take exit for the N203 and continue north towards Castricum. In Castricum follow signs to the station and from there drive south towards Heemskerk via the Beverwijkse straatweg. Site is south of Castricum and signed on the Beverwijkse straatweg. GPS: 52.53038, 4.64839

Charges guide

Per unit incl. 4 persons and electricity	€ 22.00 - € 39.50

For latest campsite news, availability and prices visit

alanrogers.com

Castricum

Kennemer Duincamping Bakkum

Zeeweg 31, NL-1901 NZ Castricum aan Zee (Noord-Holland) T: 0251 661 091.

E: bakkum@kennemerduincampings.nl alanrogers.com/NL6872

Kennemer Duincamping Bakkum lies in a wooded area in the centre of a protected dune reserve. There are 1,800 pitches of which 400 are used for touring units. These pitches are spacious and 300 are equipped with electricity (10A Europlug). Mobile homes and seasonal units use the remaining pitches in separate areas of the site. For safety and tranquillity the majority of the site is kept free of cars. Family activities and special entertainment for children are arranged in high season. The dunes are accessible from the site and offer plenty of opportunities for walking and cycling with the beach a walk of only 25 minutes. There are two areas of touring pitches, both towards the front of the site.

Facilities

Three toilet blocks for tourers with toilets, washbasins in cabins, free, controllable showers and family shower rooms. Facilities for disabled visitors. Laundry area. Excellent supermarket, baker, pizza, fish and chicken takeaways. Snack bar and restaurant. Gas supplies. Play area. Sports pitch. Tennis. Bicycle hire. Activities for children and teens. WiFi over part of site (charged). Motorbikes and dogs are not accepted.

Open: 27 March - 25 October.

Directions

On the A9 between Alkmaar and Amsterdam take exit west onto the N203. Turn left onto the Zeeweg (N513) and after a few kilometres the site is on the right. GPS: 52.5614, 4.6331

Charges guide

Per unit incl. 4 persons and electricity	€ 22.00 - € 40.45
extra person (over 2 yrs)	€ 3.50

Sint Maartenszee

Duincamping De Lepelaar

Westerduinweg 15, NL-1753 BA Sint-Maartenszee (Noord-Holland) T: 0224 56 13 51. E: info@delepelaar.nl

alanrogers.com/NL6886

De Lepelaar is perfectly situated for experiencing wild camping among the dune roses, birch, and brier bushes, in a sheltered dune valley or on top of a dune. Some of the spacious pitches have electricity and no two are the same. De Kleine Stern snack bar has a terrace and offers reasonably priced dishes. Takeaway meals are also available. There is a bus stop adjacent to the site, and from late June to early September a bus service passes the various beaches, recreation areas and villages along the coast.

Facilities

Four heated toilet blocks with all necessary facilities. Hot showers (€ 0.60) or a bucket of hot water (€ 0.20) are available. Washing machine and dryer. Small shop stocking essentials and fresh bread. Good snack bar. Freezer. Bicycle hire. WiFi in reception area (charged). Off site: Beach 1.5 km. Riding 9 km. Golf 15 km.

Open: 23 March - 22 September.

Directions

From the N9 Alkmaar-Den Helder road take the exit for Sint Maartenszee, towards the dunes. Continue straight on until you reach the dunes. At roundabout turn right and after 1.5 km. the site reception is on the left. GPS: 52.802603, 4.696484

Charges guide

Per unit incl. 2 persons and electricity	€ 20.00 - € 32.00
extra person	€ 3.00 - € 3.50
dog	€ 3.00 - € 3.50

Dalfsen

Vechtdalcamping Het Tolhuis

Het Lageveld 8, NL-7722 HV Dalfsen (Overijssel) T: 0529 458 383. E: info@tolhuis.com

alanrogers.com/NL6000

Vechtdalcamping Het Tolhuis is a pleasant, well established site with 195 pitches. Of these, 70 are for tourers, arranged on well kept, grassy lawns off paved and gravel access roads. All touring pitches have 4-10A electricity, water, waste water, cable and WiFi. Some are shaded by mature trees and bushes. The touring pitches are located apart from static units. To the rear of the site is an open-air pool (25x8 m. and heated by solar power) with a small paddling pool for toddlers with new terracing.

Facilities

Two heated toilet blocks, an immaculate new one to the front and an older one to the back, with toilets, washbasins (open style and in cabins) and controllable hot showers (key). Some rain and body showers. Special, attractive children's section. Family shower rooms. Baby room. Laundry. Small shop (bread daily). Restaurant/bar also serves snacks and drinks. Open-air pool with paddling pool. Playing field. Playground and trampoline. Entertainment team for children (high season). ATM point. WiFi over site (charged). Gas barbecues only. Dogs are not accepted in high season. Off site: Riding 3 km.

Open: 1 April - 1 October.

Directions

From the A28 take exit 21 and continue east towards Dalfsen. Site is signed in Dalfsen. GPS: 52.50228, 6.3224

Charges guide

Per unit incl. 2 persons and electricity	€ 25.00 - € 40.25
extra person	€ 3.50
dog (not high season)	€ 4.00
No credit cards.	

FREE Alan Rogers Travel Card

Extra benefits and savings - see page 14

Denekamp

Camping De Papillon

Kanaalweg 30, NL-7591 NH Denekamp (Overijssel) T: 0541 351 670.

E: info@depapillon.nl alanrogers.com/NL6470

LeadingCampings

De Papillon is perhaps one of the best and most enjoyable campsites in the Netherlands. All 245 touring pitches are spacious (120-160 sq.m), all have electricity (4/10/16A), and 220 have water and drainage. An impressive, new sanitary block has state-of-the-art equipment and uses green technology. There is a new entertainment centre with outdoor auditorium for children, and the water play area by the adventure playground and covered, heated pool is among the most imaginative and exciting we have seen. The restored heathland area offers opportunities for nature lovers; there is also a large fishing lake and a swimming lake with beach area and activities. A member of Leading Campings group.

Facilities

Two large sanitary buildings (one new 2012) with showers, toilets, washbasins in cabins, facilities for babies and for disabled visitors. Laundry room. Supermarket, restaurant, bar and takeaway. Heated pool with children's pool and sliding roof. Lake swimming with sandy beach. New modern adventure play area and smaller play areas. Pétanque. Bicycle hire. Fishing pond. Tennis. Pets to stroke. Max. 1 dog. Free WiFi over site.

Open: 29 March - 1 October.

Directions

From the A1 take exit 32 (Oldenzaal-Denekamp) and continue to Denekamp. Pass Denekamp and turn right at village of Noord-Deurningen and follow signs to site. GPS: 52.39200, 7.04900

Charges guide

Per unit incl. 2 persons and 4A electricity	€ 27.00
incl. full services	€ 30.50
extra person	€ 4.25

Hardenberg

Sprookjescamping De Vechtstreek

Grote Beltenweg 17, NL-7794 RA Rheeze-Hardenberg (Overijssel) T: 0523 261 369.

E: info@sprookjescamping.nl alanrogers.com/NL5990

It would be difficult for any child (or adult) to pass this site and not be curiously drawn to the oversized open story book which marks its entrance. From here young children turn the pages and enter the exciting world of Hannah and Bumpie, two of the nine characters around which this site's fairytale theme has been created. There are 270 touring pitches (all with 6/12A electricity) mostly laid out in small bays. Indoor and outdoor pools for children are excellent, and a new outdoor pool with terrace caters for adults and older children. There is a comprehensive daily recreation programme for children.

Facilities

Three modern, well equipped and heated toilet blocks include baby rooms, separate child sections and family showers. Two laundry rooms. Sauna, solarium and jacuzzi. Well stocked supermarket, restaurant, snack bar and takeaway (all season). Play areas. Fairytale water play park (heated). Daily activity club. Football field. Theatre. Fishing, swimming and boating recreation area at rear of site (200 m). Free WiFi over site.

Open: Easter - 30 September and last two weeks of October.

Directions

From Ommen take N34 Hardenberg road for 9 km. Turn right on N36 and proceed south for 3.5 km. Turn left at first crossroads and after 200 m. left again on local road towards Rheeze. Site is clearly signed to the left in 2 km. GPS: 52.54614, 6.57103

Charges guide

Per unit incl. 2 persons and electricity	€ 26.25 - € 44.00
extra person	€ 3.30 - € 4.75
dog	€ 6.10

Hardenberg

Vakantiepark Het Stoetenslagh

Elfde Wijk 42, NL-7797 HH Rheezerveen-Hardenberg (Overijssel) T: 0523 638 260. E: info@stoetenslagh.nl

alanrogers.com/NL6004

Arriving at Het Stoetenslagh and passing reception, you reach the pride of the campsite; a large natural lake with several little beaches. Many hours can be spent swimming, canoeing or sailing a dinghy here. There are 309 spacious grass touring pitches (120-140 sq.m) divided between several fields and arranged around clean sanitary buildings. Each field also has a small volleyball area and climbing frames. You may choose between nature pitches, standard pitches or serviced pitches with water, drainage, 10A electricity and cable connection. There are climbing frames for children, much space for playing, a children's club and, particularly popular with little ones, a small animal farm.

Facilities

Three toilet blocks include private cabins, baby facilities, family showers and facilities for disabled visitors. Beach shower. Washing machines and dryers. Motorcaravan services. Shop. Restaurant with bar. Snack bar with takeaway. Disco, bowling, curling and archery (all indoor). New indoor pool. Natural pool with sandy beaches. Canoeing. Play areas. Fishing. Bicycle hire. Activities for children and teenagers. Bouncy castle. WiFi over site.

Open: 1 April - 30 September.

Directions

From A28 take exit 22 onto the N377 towards Slagharen. Before Slagharen take N343 towards Hardenberg. Continue past Lutten exit then take first turning right. Site is 3 km. on left. GPS: 52.58694, 6.53049

Charges guide

Per serviced pitch incl. 2 persons, electricity, water and waste water	€ 22.50 - € 40.00
extra person	€ 4.50
dog	€ 3.00

For latest campsite news, availability and prices visit

alanrogers.com

Ommen

Camping De Roos

Beerzerweg 10, NL-7736 PJ Beerze-Ommen (Overijssel) T: 0523 251 234. E: info@campingderoos.nl

alanrogers.com/NL5980

De Roos is a family run site in an Area of Outstanding Natural Beauty, truly a nature lovers' campsite, immersed in an atmosphere of tranquillity. It is situated in Overijssel's Vecht Valley, a unique region set in a river dune landscape on the River Vecht. The river and its tributary wind their way unhurriedly around and through this spacious campsite. It is a natural setting that the owners of De Roos have carefully preserved. The 275 pitches and necessary amenities have been blended into the landscape with great care. Pitches, most with electricity hook-up (6A Europlug), are naturally sited, some behind blackthorn thickets, in the shadow of an old oak, or in a clearing scattered with wild flowers.

Facilities

Four well maintained sanitary blocks are kept fresh and clean. The two larger blocks are heated and include baby bath/shower and wash cabins. Launderette. Motorcaravan services. Gas supplies. Health food shop and tea room serving snacks (1/5-1/9). Bicycle hire. Boules. Several small playgrounds and field for kite flying. Sports field. Football. Volleyball. River swimming. Fishing. Internet access (charged). Dogs are not accepted. Torch useful. Bungalows for rent (all year). Off site: Riding 6 km.

Open: 11 April - 30 September.

Directions

Leave A28 at Ommen exit 21 and join N340 for 19 km. to Ommen. Turn right at traffic lights over bridge (River Vecht) and immediately left on local road towards Beerze. Site on left after 7 km. just after Beerze village sign. GPS: 52.51075, 6.515059

Charges guide

Per unit incl. 2 persons and electricity	€ 19.70 - € 22.70
extra person	€ 3.20 - € 3.90
child (under 3 yrs)	free

Ommen

Vrijetijdspark Beerze Bulten

Kampweg 1, NL-7736 PK Beerze-Ommen (Overijssel) T: 0523 251 398. E: info@beerzebulten.nl

alanrogers.com/NL5985

Beerze Bulten is a large leisure park with superb indoor and outdoor amenities, so you can enjoy yourself whatever the weather. A large, partly underground 'rabbit hole' provides a big indoor playground for children, a theatre for both indoor and outdoor shows, a buffet, a superb full wellness spa and a very large, specially designed indoor pool. Beerze Bulten has 550 pitches, mainly for touring units, but also accommodation for hire (all year). In the shade of mature woodland, all the pitches are level and numbered, and all have 10A Europlug electricity, water, drainage and TV connections. To the rear of the site is a large lake area with a sandy beach and new, exciting adventure play equipment.

Facilities

Several toilet blocks are well placed around the site, with washbasins in cabins and hot showers. Laundry. Shop. Bar and snack bar/restaurant with open-air terrace. Heated indoor and outdoor pool complex and spa centre. Multisports court. Bicycle hire. Indoor playground and theatre. Playgrounds. WiFi over site (charged). Full entertainment team in season and school holidays. Dogs only allowed on some fields.

Open: April - November (accommodation all year).

Directions

From A28, take exit 21 (Ommen) and continue east towards Ommen. From Ommen, follow N34 northeast and turn south on N36 at crossing. Site is signed from there. GPS: 52.51139, 6.54618

Charges guide

Per unit incl. 2 persons and full service pitch	€ 23.00 - € 45.30
extra person	€ 4.00 - € 5.20
dog	€ 3.50

Ommen

Camping De Koeksebelt

Zwolseweg 13, NL-7731 BC Ommen (Overijssel) T: 0529 451 378. E: info@koeksebelt.nl

alanrogers.com/NL6466

Camping De Koeksebelt is a well maintained, green site with 250 fully serviced, spacious touring pitches. All are equipped with 10A electricity, water, drainage and TV cable connections and are accessed off paved roads. Some hardstandings are available. Many of the pitches are on the banks of the river and are ideal for anglers as they can fish from their pitch. Good play areas will appeal to both children and their parents. The sanitary facilities are modern and very well maintained. The site borders a large wooded area and is within walking distance of the town of Ommen.

Facilities

Three modern toilet blocks with toilets, washbasins in cabins and controllable hot showers. Free bathroom. Baby room. Toilet for disabled visitors. Laundry with washing machines, dryers, spin dryer, iron and board. Small shop for basics. Bar/restaurant and takeaway (1/4-30/9). New outdoor heated swimming pool. Playing field. Tennis. Fishing. Watersports. Boules. Free boats for fishing. Bicycle hire. WiFi (charged). Max. 2 dogs per pitch. Off site: Riding 500 m. Boat launching 900 m.

Open: 27 March - 27 October.

Directions

From A28 take exit for Ommen and continue east towards Ommen on the N340. In Ommen, go right to cross the River Vecht. After 300 m. turn right at exit r102 and site is on the right after 500 m. GPS: 52.51668, 6.41395

Charges guide

Per unit incl. 2 persons and electricity	€ 26.00 - € 37.50
extra person	€ 5.25

No credit cards.

Ootmarsum

Camping de Haer

Rossummerstraat 22, NL-7636 PL Ootmarsum (Overijssel) T: 0541 291 847. E: info@dehaer.nl

alanrogers.com/NL6489

Camping de Haer is an attractive, family owned site in the municipality of Dinkelland, in the Dutch province of Overijssel. It is close to the picturesque town of Ootmarsum with its numerous art galleries, quaint streets and restaurants. The site has been in the Brun family for many years and is now run by brothers Bryan and Niels, who are slowly modernising the facilities. There are 120 level grass touring pitches (120-130 sq.m), some shaded, all with electricity (6A), water and drainage. There are three hardstandings for motorcaravans. It is an ideal location for couples looking for a peaceful site, and for families with young children who will enjoy the excellent play equipment. A sepkey (€ 15) is required for facilities using hot water.

Facilities

One large, modern sanitary block is spotlessly clean and has washbasins in cubicles, showers (on payment) and facilities for families and disabled visitors. Launderette. Bar, restaurant and takeaway (July/Aug). Outdoor swimming pool (1/5-30/9). Play area. Minigolf. Sports field. Free WiFi over site. Off site: Fishing 1 km. Shops 2 km. Riding and bicycle hire 2 km. Golf 15 km.

Open: 1 April - 1 November.

Directions

The site is on the N736 Ootmarsum-Oldenzaal road, 1.5 km. from Ootsmarsum and is well signed. GPS: 52.39006, 6.90168

Charges guide

Per unit incl. 2 persons and electricity	€ 20.00
extra person (over 1 yr)	€ 2.50
dog (max. 2)	€ 1.50

Breskens

Droompark Schoneveld

Schoneveld 1, NL-4511 HR Breskens (Zeeland) T: 0117 383 220. E: info@droomparkschoneveld.nl

alanrogers.com/NL6930

This site is well situated within walking distance of Breskens and it has direct access to sand dunes and the beach 500 m. beyond. It has 165 touring pitches and these are kept apart from the static caravans. All have electricity and cable TV, 27 also have water and waste connections. They are laid out in fields which are entered from long avenues that run through the site. One toilet block serves the touring area. The entrance complex includes reception and information about the children's entertainment.

Facilities

One large sanitary block provides showers, wash cubicles, child size toilets and washbasins, baby room, en-suite unit for disabled visitors, laundry, dishwashing and vegetable preparation areas. Motorcaravan services. Well stocked supermarket (5/4-31/10). Bar. Restaurant and takeaway (all year). 10-pin bowling. Indoor pool with fun pool and mini-slide. Wellness area with sauna, hot tub and solarium. Tennis. Football field. Play area. Organised entertainment in July/Aug. Bicycle hire. WiFi over site (charged). Off site: Fishing, minigolf and model village 200 m. Boat launching 3 km. Golf and riding 10 km.

Open: All year.

Directions

From the east and the Terneuzen end of the Westerschelde Tunnel, take N61 west towards Breskens. At Schoondijke continue north on N676 to Breskens. Site lies 1 km. west of Breskens (signed). GPS: 51.40107, 3.53475

Charges guide

Per unit incl. 2 persons and electricity	€ 14.00 - € 35.00
extra person	€ 3.00 - € 5.00
dog	€ 4.00

Weekly tariff and various discounts available.

Camping Cheques accepted.

Groede

Strandcamping Groede

Zeeweg 1, NL-4503 PA Groede (Zeeland) T: 0117 371 384. E: info@strandcampinggroede.nl

alanrogers.com/NL5510

A warm welcome awaits you at Strandcamping Groede, which has all you need for the perfect family seaside holiday. Family run and located close to one of the cleanest sandy beaches in the Netherlands, it aims to cater for the individual needs of visitors with pitches available for all tastes. There are 870 pitches in total, 500 for tourers, the majority of these with electrical connections (4/10A). Sympathetic landscaping has taken the natural surroundings of the dunes and sand to create areas for larger groups, families, and for those who prefer peace and quiet. The seaside feel continues in the layout of the comprehensive sports and play areas and in the brasserie and other main buildings.

Facilities

Toilet facilities are excellent with a high standard of cleanliness, including some private cabins, baby baths, a family room and a dedicated unit for visitors with disabilities. Motorcaravan services. Gas supplies. Shop, restaurant and snack bar (all weekends only in low seasons). Recreation room. Trampoline. Bouncy castle. Sports area. Several play areas (bark base). Activities for children (July/Aug). Bicycle hire. Fishing. WiFi (free).

Open: 27 March - 2 November.

Directions

From Breskens take the coast road for 5 km. to site. Alternatively, the site is signed from Groede village on the more inland Breskens-Sluis road. GPS: 51.39582, 3.48772

Charges guide

Per unit incl. 2 persons and electricity	€ 19.70 - € 46.00
extra person	€ 4.00

No credit cards.

For latest campsite news, availability and prices visit

alanrogers.com

Kamperland

Camping De Molenhoek

Molenweg 69a, NL-4493 NC Kamperland (Zeeland) T: 0113 371 202. E: info@demolenhoek.com

alanrogers.com/NL5570

This rural, family run site makes a pleasant contrast to the livelier coastal sites in this popular holiday area. There is an emphasis on catering for the users of the 300 permanent or seasonal holiday caravans and 100 tourers. Eighty of these have 6A electricity, water and drainage. The site is neat and tidy with surrounding hedges and trees giving privacy and some shade, and electrical connections are available. A large outdoor pool area has ample space for swimming, children's play and sun loungers. Entertainment, including dance evenings and bingo, is organised in season.

Facilities

Two very clean and well appointed sanitary blocks include some washbasins in cabins and facilities for children. Toilet and shower facilities for disabled visitors and for babies. Laundry facilities. Motorcaravan services. Bar/restaurant with terrace and large TVs and LCD projection. Snack bar. Heated outdoor swimming pool (15/5-15/9). Playground. Bicycle hire. Pool tables. Sports field. Entertainment for children and teenagers. WiFi (free). Off site: Tennis and watersports nearby. Riding 1 km.

Open: 1 April - 27 October.

Directions

Site is west of the village of Kamperland on the island of Noord Beveland. From the N256 Goes-Zierikzee road, exit west onto the N255 Kamperland road. Site is signed south of this road.
GPS: 51.57840, 3.69642

Charges guide

Per unit incl. 2 persons and electricity	€ 21.00 - € 36.00
extra person	€ 2.00 - € 5.00
dog	€ 4.00 - € 5.00

Nieuwvliet

Vakantiepark Pannenschuur

Zeedijk 19, NL-4504 PP Nieuwvliet (Zeeland) T: 0117 372 300. E: info@pannenschuur.nl

alanrogers.com/NL5500

This is one of several coastal sites on the narrow strip of the Netherlands between Belgium and Breskens. Quickly reached from the ports of Ostend, Zeebrugge and Vlissingen, it offers the chance to enjoy the seaside and extensive network of cycle routes. A short walk across the quiet coast road and steps over the dyke brings you to the open, sandy beach. Many of the 595 pitches are taken by seasonal holiday caravans but there are separate areas for tourers in bays of four or six units surrounded by hedges, all with electricity (6A), water, drainage and cable TV connections.

Facilities

Four toilet blocks including two modern, heated buildings, provide first class facilities including children's washrooms, baby rooms and some private cubicles. Hot water is free. Launderette. Motorcaravan services. Gas supplies. Large supermarket. Restaurant, snack bar and takeaway. Swimming pool, sauna and solarium. Large games room with soft drinks bar. Playgrounds, tennis and playing field. Bicycle hire. Kids' club. Organised activities in season. WiFi over site (charged). Max. 2 dogs. Off site: Fishing 500 m. Riding 2 km. Golf 5 km.

Open: All year (all amenities closed 14/1-31/1).

Directions

At Nieuwvliet, on the Breskens-Sluis minor road, 8 km. southwest of Breskens, turn towards the sea at sign for Nieuwvliet-Bad and follow signs to site
GPS: 51.38355, 3.44052

Charges guide

Per unit (max. 5 persons) incl. electricity	€ 25.00 - € 40.00
extra person	€ 4.00

Rates available for weekly stays.

Ouwerkerk

Kampeerterrein De Vier Bannen

Weg v.d. Buitenlandse Pers A, NL-4305 RJ Ouwerkerk (Zeeland) T: 0111 642 044.
E: informatie@vierbannen.nl alanrogers.com/NL7030

De Vier Bannen is located in a beautiful forested area, with extensive stretches of water created by the flood of 1953. There are 170 spacious pitches, including 100 comfort pitches equipped with WiFi, water, drainage and electricity (4/16A). They are spread over several fields, surrounded by trees and shrubs. On-site amenities for children include a bouncy castle and a range of play equipment, as well as a nature trail and park to develop their knowledge of the environment. There is a pub/restaurant adjacent to the site. Close by is a small sandy beach from where you can swim in the Oosterschelde. The area is perfect for fishing, diving, canoeing, kayaking, hiking and cycling along the Oosterschelde.

Facilities

Single toilet block includes showers and open style washbasins. Facilities for disabled visitors. Motorcaravan services. Laundry. Play equipment. Nature trail. WiFi over part of site (charged). Mobile homes for rent. Dogs are not accepted. Off site: Pub/restaurant. Small beach and swimming in the Oosterschelde. Fishing. Watersports. Zierikzee. Flood Museum.

Open: 15 March - 31 October.

Directions

Follow the N59 Rotterdam-Zierikzee and take exit Ouwerkerk (2 km. east of Zierikzee). From there follow the ANWB camping signs.
GPS: 51.61783, 3.98668

Charges guide

Per unit incl. 2 persons and electricity	€ 18.90
extra person	€ 4.50

Renesse

Camping De Wijde Blick

Lagezoom 23, NL-4325 CP Renesse (Zeeland) T: 0111 468 888. E: wijdeblick@ardoer.com

alanrogers.com/NL5560

The Van Oost family run this neat campsite in a pleasant and personal way. It is located on the outskirts of the village of Renesse in a quiet rural spot. From May to September a free bus runs to Renesse and the beach, just 2 km. away. De Wijde Blick has 328 pitches with 218 for touring units, all with 6/10A electricity and TV connections, and 90-120 sq.m. in area. Of these, 16 have private sanitary facilities and 202 are fully serviced. There are 20 attractively arranged motorcaravan pitches with hardstanding, and ten special 'bike and hike' pitches for those touring without a car.

Facilities

Three first class, modern toilet blocks are heated, with clean facilities including washbasins in cabins, controllable showers and facilities for disabled campers. Microwave and fridge. Bath (on payment). Laundry (with pleasant waiting area). Gas supplies. Motorcaravan services. Shop. Restaurant/bar (15/3-31/10). Swimming pool (1/5-20/9; can be covered). Free WiFi over site. Good playgrounds. Air trampoline. Volleyball area. Open-air theatre. Bicycle hire. Activities for children. Hotel chalets for rent. Breakfast service available. Off site: Tennis and minigolf.

Open: All year.

Directions

Renesse is on the island of Schouwen (connected to the mainland by a bridge and three dams). On the N57 from Middelburg take the Renesse exit. After 2 km. follow road 106 to the left and then site signs. Site is on the east side of the village. GPS: 51.71843, 3.76713

Charges guide

Per unit incl. 2 persons	€ 19.00 - € 35.00
extra person	€ 5.00
dog	€ 2.00

Renesse

Strandpark De Zeeuwse Kust

Helleweg 8, NL-4326 LJ Renesse/Noordwelle (Zeeland) T: 0111 468 282.

E: info@strandparkdezeeuwsekust.nl alanrogers.com/NL6948

LeadingCampings

Whether you want relaxation, something for the children, the seaside or activities, you will find all of these at De Zeeuwse Kust, located just 250 m. from the sea with beautiful sandy beach. The outstanding, hotel standard facilities contained within the centrally located building are in a class of their own, offering a haven whatever the weather. From the open plan kitchen, the oversized wooden stools, to the open fireplace, they are all first class. This site has 218 spacious and comfortable pitches, all with electricity (16A), water, waste water and TV connections. There are 32 pitches with private sanitary provision. The modern sanitary unit is heated and includes facilities for children and disabled visitors. A member of Leading Campings group.

Facilities

Modern, first class sanitary building providing showers, washbasins, private cabins, family shower rooms and other facilities for children and disabled visitors. Launderette. Shop/mini-market. Fresh bread (all year). Heated swimming pool. Play areas (indoors and outdoors). Sports field. Motorcaravan services. Outdoor table football. Games room with Xbox stations. Small film theatre. Recreation room. Entertainment team (special holidays, weekends and July/Aug). Sauna. Whirlpool. First aid post. Free WiFi. Dogs welcome all year.

Open: All year (with most facilities).

Directions

From the A15 take exit 12 towards Middelburg. Follow the N57 through Ouddorp and then turn right on the N652. Immediately turn left for the N651 and follow to Noordwelle. Site is well signed. GPS: 51.739062, 3.802369

Charges guide

Per unit incl. 2 persons, electricity, water and waste water	€ 20.00 - € 46.00
extra person (over 2 yrs)	€ 5.75
dog	€ 4.00

No credit cards.

Renesse

Camping Julianahoeve

Hoogenboomlaan 42, NL-4325 DM Renesse (Zeeland) T: 0111 461 414. E: julianahoeve@ardoer.com

alanrogers.com/NL6952

A very large site with 1,400 pitches, mainly for mobile homes and chalets, Camping Julianahoeve still retains a few pitches for touring units and tents. You cannot get much closer to the sea, and a path leads through the dunes to the beach. All the main touring pitches are large and fully serviced. Some have individual sanitary units, and others have hardstandings. Located in the sunniest area of the Netherlands, this is an ideal site for a family holiday by the beach. A member of the Ardoer group.

Facilities

Several well appointed toilet blocks serve the site with facilities for younger children, babies and disabled visitors. Individual sanitary units available. Launderette. Supermarket. Bar. Brasserie. Café with terrace. Snack bar. Indoor pool complex with 60 m. water slide. Play areas. Entertainment for all ages. WiFi. Dogs are not accepted. Off site: Fishing 500 m. Golf and riding 1 km.

Open: 1 April - 6 November.

Directions

From the A5 take exit 12 and follow the N57 through Ouddorp, then follow signs to Renesse. Site is well signed from the town. GPS: 51.72738, 3.75897

Charges guide

Per unit incl. 2 persons and electricity	€ 20.00 - € 58.00
extra person (over 2 yrs)	€ 5.25
child (2-4 yrs)	€ 3.50

For latest campsite news, availability and prices visit

alanrogers.com

Retranchement

Camping Cassandria Bad

Strengweg 4, NL-4525 LW Retranchement (Zeeland) T: 0117 392 300. E: info@cassandriabad.nl

alanrogers.com/NL5502

Cassandria Bad was established in 1992, lying very close to the Belgian border and the resort of Cadzand Bad, just under 2 km. from the nearest North Sea beach. Pitches are grassy and spacious; some are privately let for the full season. All pitches are equipped with 10A electricity and free cable TV connections. Except for loading and unloading, cars are not allowed in the camping area, but a large parking area is provided. On-site amenities include a bar, snack bar, shop services and games room. During the peak season, a variety of activities are organised, including karaoke, bingo and sports tournaments. This part of the Netherlands, south of the Schelde, has strong contacts with Belgium and trips to Bruges and Gent are popular. Retranchement translates as bulwarks and there are still remains of vast earthen sea walls, although now this area is best known as a paradise for nature lovers and walkers. It is also the area for cycling with excellent trails from town to town along the dykes that protect the coast.

Facilities

Two clean and well maintained sanitary units with free showers, and two family bathrooms in the main block. Good laundry facilities. Small shop (fresh bread daily). Bar with LCD projector and screen. Snack bar. Sports fields with volleyball, and 2 football pitches. Games room with table football, air hockey and electronic games. Trampoline. Several well appointed and interesting play areas. Bicycle hire. WiFi over site (charged). 1 dog allowed per pitch. Off site: Nearest beach 1.7 km. Walking and cycle routes. Fishing 5 km.

Open: 23 March - 31 October.

Directions

Approaching from the west and Bruges, use the Belgian N31 and then N376 towards Knokke-Heist and then across the Dutch border to Sluis. Here take the road to Groede and turn left towards Cadzand Bad at the second crossroads. Site is well signed from here. GPS: 51.36613, 3.38583

Charges guide

Per unit incl. up to 4 persons and electricity	€ 25.50 - € 33.50
extra person	€ 4.50
dog	€ 2.50

Discounts available in low season.

Wolphaartsdijk

Camping 't Veerse Meer

Veerweg 71, NL-4471 NB Wolphaartsdijk (Zeeland) T: 0113 581 423. E: info@campingveersemeer.nl

alanrogers.com/NL6920

This well cared for, family run site is situated beside the Veerse Meer, on the island of Zuid-Beveland, in Zeeland. Emphasis at this site is on a neat and tidy appearance, quality facilities and a friendly reception. The site occupies both sides of Veerweg with one side providing seven touring pitches with individual sanitary facilities and fully serviced hardstanding pitches for motorcaravans. On the other side are the main buildings and 40 generous touring pitches, many fully serviced and separated by hedging, and a tent field. Further seasonal and static places are kept apart. A feature of this campsite is a narrow canal crossed by a bridge, leading to an area of seasonal units. Some attractive chalets are available to rent.

Facilities

The single, modern toilet block is clean and has showers (token operated), open style wash areas, two wash cabins, facilities for children, and a baby bath. Laundry with book/magazine exchange. Motorcaravan services. Bar. Play area. Trampoline. Boules. Organised events for all in high season. Bicycle hire. Fishing. Free WiFi over site. Off site: Supermarket 500 m. Bars, restaurants and minigolf at the watersports marina complex 900 m. Riding 1.5 km. Golf 6 km.

Open: 1 April - 31 October.

Directions

From N256 Goes-Zierikzee road take Wolphaartsdijk exit heading west. Turn right after 1 km. and follow signs to Veerse Meer (the lake) along Kwistenburg, bearing left on to Aardebolle-weg, right turn onto Veerweg at mini roundabout and site reception is to left in 500 m. GPS: 51.54436, 3.81242

Charges guide

Per unit incl. 2 persons and electricity	€ 15.00 - € 22.50
extra person	€ 2.50 - € 3.00
dog	€ 2.50

No credit cards.

Barendrecht
Camping De Oude Maas
Achterzeedijk 1A, NL-2991 SB Barendrecht (Zuid-Holland) T: 0786 772 445.

E: info@recreatieparkdeoudemaas.nl alanrogers.com/NL5610

This site is easily accessed from the A15 southern Rotterdam ring road and is situated right by the river, so it is well worth considering if you are visiting Rotterdam or just want a peaceful stop. The 65 touring pitches are pleasantly sited away from the residential section, all are on grass and have 10A hook-up. There is a pleasant separate touring area for 11 motorcaravans with electricity, water and waste water connections in a hedged group near the marina and river.

Facilities
One toilet block provides all necessary facilities including a unit for disabled visitors and a baby room. Launderette. Motorcravan services. Fishing. Good play area with swings, slides and climbing frames for all ages. Bicycle hire. WiFi (charged). Max. 1 dog. Off site: Swimming pool nearby. Riding 8 km. Golf 10 km. Rotterdam city centre reached by bicycle or train from Barendecht Station 4 km.

Open: All year.

Directions
Best approached from Hook/Rotterdam then A29 Rotterdam-Bergen op Zoom motorway. Leave A29 at exit 20 (Barendrecht) and follow signs for Heerjansdam and site. GPS: 51.83361, 4.55236

Charges guide
Per unit incl. 2 persons and electricity	€ 20.00
extra person	€ 4.00
child (0-12 yrs)	€ 2.50
dog	€ 2.50

Brielle
Camping De Krabbeplaat
Oude Veerdam 4, NL-3231 NC Brielle (Zuid-Holland) T: 0181 412 363. E: info@krabbeplaat.nl

alanrogers.com/NL6980

Camping De Krabbeplaat is a family run site situated near the ferry port in a wooded, recreation area next to the Brielse Meer lake. There are 448 spacious pitches, with 68 for touring units, all with 10A electricity, cable connections and a water supply nearby. A nature conservation plan exists to ensure the site fits into its natural environment. The lake and its beaches provide the perfect spot for watersports and relaxation and the site has its own harbour where you can moor your own boat. This excellent site is very convenient for the Europort ferry terminal.

Facilities
One large and two smaller heated toilet blocks in traditional style provide separate toilets, showers and washing cabins. High standards of cleanliness. Dedicated unit for disabled campers and provision for babies. Warm water is free of charge. Dishwasher (free). Launderette. Motorcaravan services. Supermarket, snack bar, restaurant and takeaway (all season). Recreation room. Youth centre. Tennis. Playground and play field. Animal farm. Bicycle and children's pedal hire. Canoe, surf, pedal boat and boat hire. Fishing. WiFi over site (charged). Six cabins to rent. Off site: Golf 3 km.

Open: 28 March - 30 September.

Directions
From the Amsterdam direction take the A4 (Europoort), then the A15 (Europoort). Take exit for Brielle on N57 and, just before Brielle, site is signed. GPS: 51.9097, 4.18536

Charges guide
Per unit incl. 2 persons and electricity	€ 19.50 - € 28.00
extra person	€ 3.45
child (under 12 yrs)	€ 2.90

Delft
Vakantiepark Delftse Hout
Korftlaan 5, NL-2616 LJ Delft (Zuid-Holland) T: 0152 130 040. E: info@delftsehout.nl

alanrogers.com/NL5600

Pleasantly situated in Delft's park and forest area on the eastern edge of the city, is this well run, modern site. It has 160 touring pitches quite formally arranged in groups of four to six and surrounded by attractive trees and hedges. All have sufficient space and electrical connections (10A Europlug). Modern buildings near the entrance house the site amenities. A good sized first floor restaurant serves snacks and full meals and has an outdoor terrace overlooking the swimming pool and pitches. Walking and cycling tours are organised and there is a recreation programme in high season.

Facilities
Modern, heated toilet facilities include a spacious family room and children's section. Facilities for disabled visitors. Laundry. Motorcaravan services. Shop for basic food and camping items (all season). Restaurant, takeaway and bar (28/3-1/10). Small outdoor swimming pool (30/4-15/9). Adventure playground. Recreation room. Bicycle hire. Gas supplies. Max. 1 dog. WiFi (free). Off site: Fishing 1 km. Riding and golf 5 km. Regular bus service to Delft centre.

Open: 28 March - 1 November.

Directions
From Rotterdam take exit 9, turn right at traffic lights towards IKEA. At IKEA roundabout turn left and drive parallel to motorway. At end of street, turn right and site is on left in 300 m. Do not follow sat nav. GPS: 52.01767, 4.37908

Charges guide
Per unit incl. 2 persons and electricity	€ 26.50 - € 36.00
extra person (3 yrs and older)	€ 3.50
dog (max. 1)	€ 3.50

For latest campsite news, availability and prices visit
alanrogers.com

Den Haag

Vakantiecentrum Kijkduinpark

Machiel Vrijenhoeklaan 450, NL-2555 NW Den Haag (Zuid-Holland) T: 0704 482 100. E: info@kijkduinpark.nl

alanrogers.com/NL5640

This is an ultra modern, all-year-round centre and family park with many chalets, villas and bungalows for rent and a large indoor swimming pool complex. The wooded touring area is immediately to the left of the entrance, with 330 pitches in shady glades of bark-covered sand. All pitches have 10A electricity, water, waste water and cable TV connections. In a paved central area are a supermarket, a snack bar and a restaurant. The main attraction here is the Meeresstrand, 500 m. from the site entrance. This is a long, wide sandy beach with flags to denote suitability for swimming. Windsurfing is popular.

Facilities
Five modern sanitary blocks. Four private cabins for rent. Launderette. Snack bar. Shop. Restaurant. Supermarket. Indoor pool. Sun beds. Tennis. Bicycle hire. Special golfing breaks. Entertainment and activities organised in summer. WiFi over site (free in restaurant). Off site: Beach, golf and fishing 500 m. Riding 5 km.

Open: All year.

Directions
Site is southwest of Den Haag on the coast and Kijkduin is well signed as an area from all round Den Haag. GPS: 52.05968, 4.21118

Charges guide
Per unit incl. 5 persons and electricity	€ 38.00 - € 74.00
extra person	€ 5.00

Hellevoetsluis

Camping Caravaning 't Weergors

Zuiddijk 2, NL-3221 LJ Hellevoetsluis (Zuid-Holland) T: 0181 312 430. E: info@weergors.nl

alanrogers.com/NL6970

A rustic style site built around old farm buildings, 't Weergors has a comfortable mature feel. At the front of the site is a well presented farmhouse which houses reception and includes the main site services. The sanitary blocks have been renewed recently as has the farm accommodating an attractive à la carte restaurant and pancake outlet. The reception has also been renewed including a new minimarket from where you can order fresh bread. There are 100 touring pitches (plus seasonal and static places), another field at the back of the site was recently developed to provide a further 70 or 80 touring places.

Facilities
Three sanitary blocks have showers (by key), washbasins, some in cabins, children's showers and toilets plus baby baths. Laundry facilities. Motorcaravan services. Small shop (1/4-31/10). Restaurant and bar (snacks) and pancakes. Tennis. Internet access. Play area. Paddling pool. Organised entertainment in high season. Fishing pond. Bicycle hire. Rally field.

Open: 1 April - 31 October.

Directions
From Rotterdam join A15 west to Rozenburg exit 12 and join N57 south for 11 km. Turn left on N497 signed Hellevoetsluis and follow site signs for 4.5 km. to roundabout. Turn right at roundabout to site 1.5 km. on right. GPS: 51.82943, 4.11618

Charges guide
Per unit incl. 2 persons and electricity	€ 20.72
extra person	€ 3.50
child (3-12 yrs)	€ 2.50
dog	€ 1.75

Camping Cheques accepted.

Katwijk

Recreatiecentrum De Noordduinen

Campingweg 1, NL-2221 EW Katwijk aan Zee (Zuid-Holland) T: 0714 025 295. E: info@noordduinen.nl

alanrogers.com/NL5680

This is a large, well managed site surrounded by dunes and sheltered partly by trees and shrubbery, which also separate the various camping areas. The 200 touring pitches are marked and numbered but not divided. All have electricity (10A) and 75 are fully serviced with electricity, water, drainage and TV connection. There are also seasonal pitches and mobile homes for rent. Entertainment is organised in high season for various age groups. A new complex with indoor and outdoor pools, restaurant, small theatre and recreation hall provides a good addition to the site's facilities. Seasonal pitches and mobile homes are placed mostly away from the touring areas and are unobtrusive.

Facilities
The three sanitary blocks are modern and clean, with washbasins in cabins, a baby room and provision for visitors with disabilities. Laundry. Motorcaravan services. Supermarket with fresh bread daily, bar, restaurant, takeaway (all 1/4-31/10). Recreation room. Swimming pool complex. Play area. Only gas barbecues are permitted. Dogs are not accepted. Off site: Riding 150 m. Beach and fishing 300 m. Golf 6 km. Katwijk within walking distance.

Open: All year.

Directions
Leave A44 at exit 8 (Leiden-Katwijk) to join N206 to Katwijk. Take Katwijk Noord exit and follow signs to site. GPS: 52.21103, 4.40978

Charges guide
Per unit incl. 2 persons and electricity	€ 23.00 - € 37.00
extra person	€ 4.50

Camping Cheques accepted.

Meerkerk

Camping De Victorie

Broekseweg 75-77, NL-4231 VD Meerkerk (Zuid-Holland) T: 0183 352 741. E: info@campingdevictorie.nl

alanrogers.com/NL5690

Within an hour's drive of the port of Rotterdam you can be pitched on this delightful, spacious site in the green heart of the Netherlands. De Victorie, a working farm and a member of an organisation of farm sites, offers an alternative to the bustling seaside sites. A modern building houses reception, an open plan office and a space with tables and chairs, where the friendly owners may well invite you to have a cup of coffee. The 100 grass pitches (100-200 sq.m) are level and have 6A electricity supply. Everything about the site is surprising and contrary to any preconceived ideas.

Facilities

The main sanitary block is kept spotlessly clean, tastefully decorated and fully equipped. Showers are on payment. Laundry room. Additional sanitary facilities are around the site. Farm shop and small bar (once a week). Play area. Trampoline. Play field. Fishing. Riding. WiFi throughout (charged). Off site: Bicycle hire 2 km.

Open: 15 March - 31 October.

Directions

From Rotterdam follow A15 to junction with the A27. Proceed 6 km. north on A27 to Noordeloos exit (no. 25) and join N214. Site is signed 200 m. after roundabout at Noordeloos. GPS: 51.93623, 4.95748

Charges guide

Per unit incl. 2 persons and electricity	€ 12.50
extra person	€ 3.00

No credit cards. Special rates for longer stays. Large units may be charged extra.

Ouddorp

Recreatiepark De Klepperstee

Vrijheidsweg 1, NL-3253 ZG Ouddorp (Zuid-Holland) T: 0187 681 511. E: info@klepperstee.com

alanrogers.com/NL6960

De Klepperstee is a good quality, family site. The site itself is peacefully located in tranquil countryside amid renowned nature reserves and just outside the village of Ouddorp in Zuid-Holland. It offers excellent recreation areas that are spread over the centre of the site giving it an attractive open parkland appearance which is enhanced by many shrubs, trees and grass areas. The 338 spacious touring pitches are in named avenues, mostly separated by hedging and spread around the perimeter, together with the seasonal and static caravans. There is a new 24-hour, drive-in motorcaravan park with 16A electricity, sanitary facilities and a service point.

Facilities

One main sanitary block and a number of WC/shower units around the touring area provide free hot showers, washbasins, some in cabins (hot water only), baby bath and shower, child size toilets and a unit for campers with disabilities. Laundry. Motorcaravan services. Supermarket. Restaurant, bar and takeaway. Play areas. Tennis. TV, pool and electronic games. Entertainment. Single sex groups are not accepted. Off site: Fishing 500 m. Beach 600 m. Riding, bicycle hire 4 km. Golf 10 km.

Open: Easter - 31 October.

Directions

From Rotterdam follow A15 west to Rozenburg exit 12 and join N57 south for 22 km. Take exit for Ouddorp and follow signs for Stranden. Site is on the left after 3 km. GPS: 51.8161, 3.89958

Charges guide

Per unit incl. up to 4 persons	€ 14.50 - € 18.00
incl. 16A electricity	€ 18.50 - € 22.50
extra person	€ 2.50

Rijnsburg

Recreatiecentrum Koningshof

Elsgeesterweg 8, NL-2231 NW Rijnsburg (Zuid-Holland) T: 0714 026 051. E: info@koningshofholland.nl

alanrogers.com/NL5630

This popular site is run in a personal and friendly way. The 200 pitches for touring units (some with hardstandings for larger units) are laid out in small groups, divided by hedges and trees and all with 10A electrical connections. Cars are mostly parked in areas around the perimeter and 100 static caravans, confined to one section of the site, are entirely unobtrusive. Reception, a pleasant, good quality restaurant, bar and a snack bar are grouped around a courtyard-style entrance which is decorated with seasonal flowers. The site has a small outdoor, heated pool (13.5x7 m) with a separate paddling pool and imaginative children's play equipment. A member of the Holland Tulip Parcs group.

Facilities

Three good toilet blocks, two with underfloor heating, with washbasins in cabins and provision for disabled visitors. Laundry facilities. Motorcaravan services. Gas supplies. Shop (1/4-15/10). Bar (1/4-1/11). Restaurant (1/4-10/9). Snacks and takeaway (1/4-1/11). Small outdoor pool (unsupervised; 15/5-15/9). Indoor pool (1/4-1/11). Adventure playground and sports area. Tennis. Fishing pond (free). Bicycle hire. Entertainment (July/Aug). Room for shows. Max. 1 dog on a limited area of the site. WiFi.

Open: 16 March - 16 November.

Directions

From N44/A44 Den Haag-Amsterdam motorway, take exit 7 for Oegstgeest and Rijnsburg. Turn towards Rijnsburg and follow site signs. GPS: 52.20012, 4.45623

Charges guide

Per unit incl. 2 persons and electricity	€ 25.00 - € 30.00
extra person	€ 3.75

Camping Cheques accepted.

For latest campsite news, availability and prices visit

alanrogers.com

Wassenaar

Holiday & Amusement Park Duinrell

Duinrell 1, NL-2242 JP Wassenaar (Zuid-Holland) T: 0705 155 255. E: info@duinrell.nl

alanrogers.com/NL5620

A very large site, Duinrell's name means 'well in the dunes' and the water theme is continued in the adjoining amusement park and in the extensive indoor pool complex. The campsite itself is very large with 750 touring places on several flat, grassy areas (60-140 sq.m) and it can become very busy in high season. As part of a continuing improvement programme, the marked pitches have electricity, water and drainage connections and some have cable TV. Amenities shared with the park include restaurants, takeaways, pancake house, supermarket and theatre. Entry to the popular pleasure park is free for campers – indeed the camping areas surround and open out from the park. There are now 400 smartly furnished bungalows to rent.

Facilities

Six heated toilet blocks serve the touring areas. Laundry facilities. Amusement park and Tiki tropical pool complex. Restaurant, cafés, pizzeria and takeaways (weekends only in winter). Supermarket. Entertainment and theatre with shows in high season. Rope Challenge trail and training circuit. Bicycle hire. Mini-bowling. All activities have extra charges. WiFi over site (charged). Off site: Beach 4 km. Golf 12 km.

Open: All year.

Directions

Site is signed from N44/A44 (Den Haag-Amsterdam), but from the south the turning is 5 km. after passing sign for start of Wassenaar town – then follow site signs. GPS: 52.14642, 4.38737

Charges guide

Per unit incl. 2 persons	
and electricity	€ 30.50 - € 38.50
extra person	€ 10.50
dog	€ 6.00

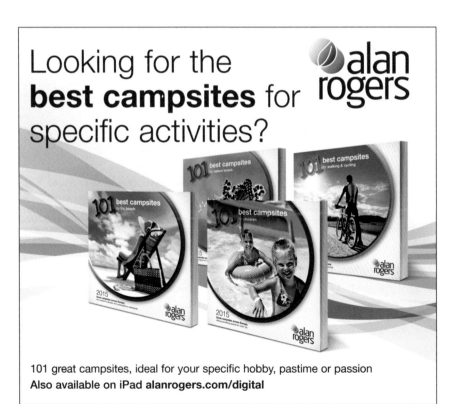

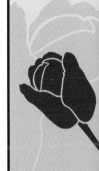

A land full of contrasts, from magnificent snow-capped mountains, dramatic fjords, vast plateaux with wild untamed tracts, to huge lakes and rich green countryside. With nearly one quarter of the land above the Arctic Circle, Norway has the lowest population density in Europe.

Norway is made up of five regions. In the heart of the eastern region, Oslo has everything one would expect from a major city, and is the oldest of the Scandinavian capitals. The west coast boasts some of the world's most beautiful fjords, with plummeting waterfalls and mountains. Trondheim, in the heart of central Norway, is a busy university town with many attractions, notably the Nidarosdomen Cathedral. The sunniest region is the south, its rugged coastline with white wooden cottages is popular with Norwegians, and ideal for swimming, sailing, scuba diving and fishing. The north is the Land of the Midnight Sun and the Northern Lights. It is home to the Sami, the indigenous people of Norway, whose traditions include fishing, hunting and reindeer herding. The scenery varies from forested valleys and narrow fjords to icy tundra, and there are several cities worth visiting including Tromsø, with the Fjellheisen cable car, Polaria aquarium with bearded seals, and the Arctic Cathedral.

CAPITAL: Oslo

Tourist Office
Norwegian Tourist Board
Charles House, 5 Lower Regent Street
London SW1Y 4LR
Tel: 020 7389 8800
Email: infouk@ntr.no
Internet: www.visitnorway.com

Population
5 million

Climate
Weather can be unpredictable, although less
extreme on the west coast. Some regions have
24 hours of daylight in summer but none in winter.

Language
Norwegian, but English is widely spoken.

Telephone
The country code is 00 47.

Money
Currency: Norwegian Krone
Banks: Mon-Fri 09.00-15.00.

Shops
Mon-Fri 09.00-16.00/17.00, Thu 09.00-
18.00/20.00 and Sat 09.00-13.00 /15.00.

Public Holidays
New Year's Day; King's Birthday 21 Feb; Holy
Thursday; Good Friday; Easter Monday; May Day;
Liberation Day 8 May; Constitution Day 17 May;
Ascension; Whit Monday; Queen's Birthday 4 July;
Saints Day 19 July; Christmas 25, 26 Dec.

Motoring
Roads are generally uncrowded around Oslo and
Bergen but be prepared for tunnels and hairpin
bends. Certain roads are forbidden to caravans or
best avoided (advisory leaflet from the Norwegian
Tourist Office). Vehicles must have sufficient road
grip and in winter it may be necessary to use
winter tyres with or without chains. Vehicles
entering Bergen on weekdays must pay a toll
and other tolls are also levied on certain roads.

see campsite map 3

Byglandsfjord
Neset Camping

N-4741 Byglandsfjord (Aust-Agder) T: 37 93 42 55. E: post@neset.no

alanrogers.com/NO2610

On a semi-promontory on the shores of the 40 km. long Byglandsfjord, Neset is a well run, friendly site ideal for spending a few active days, or as a short stop en route north from the ferry port of Kristiansand (from England or Denmark). Neset is situated on well kept grassy meadows by the lake shore, with water on three sides and the road on the fourth. There are 260 unmarked pitches with electricity and cable TV, and 40 hardstandings for motorcaravans. The main building houses reception, a small shop and a restaurant with fine views over the water. The campsite has a range of activities to keep you busy, and the excellent hardstandings for motorcaravans look out onto the lake. Byglandsfjord offers good fishing (mainly trout) and the area has marked trails for cycling, riding or walking in an area famous for its minerals. Samples of these can be found in reception, and day trips to specialist exhibitions at the Mineralparken (8 km) are possible. Walking and cycling routes abound and cycles and mountain bikes can be hired from Neset.

Facilities
Three modern, heated sanitary blocks have showers (on payment), en-suite family rooms and kitchen. Facilities for disabled campers in one block. Motorcaravan services. Restaurant and takeaway (15/6-15/8). Shop (1/5-1/10). Playground. Lake swimming, boating and fishing. Trampoline. Bouncy cushion. Outdoor fitness. Beach volleyball. Barbecue area and hot tub (winter). Boat, canoe and pedalo hire. Elk safaris arranged. Climbing, rafting and canoeing courses arranged (linked with Trollaktiv). Cross-country skiing (winter). Car wash. Free WiFi. Off site: Rock climbing wall. Marked forest trails.

Open: All year.

Directions
Site is on route 9, 2.5 km. north of the town of Byglandsfjord on the eastern shores of the lake. GPS: 58.68839, 7.80175

Charges guide
Per unit incl. 2 persons and electricity	NOK 285
extra person	NOK 10
child (5-12 yrs)	NOK 5
dog	free

Camping Cheques accepted.

Neset Camping
4741 Byglandsfjord
Aust-Agder
Norway
Tel: +47 37934050
post@neset.no
www.neset.no

Open all year

Setesdal Norway up close Photo : Anders Martinsen Fotografer

Høvåg
Sørlandets Naturistsenter Isefjærleiren

Isefjær, N-4770 Høvåg (Aust-Agder) T: 37 27 49 90. E: postmaster@isefjar.no

alanrogers.com/NO2606

Sørlandets is renowned for idyllic inlets and islands, and has a reputation as the 'Norwegian Riviera' with warm summer temperatures and sea water reaching over twenty degrees. An equally warm and enthusiastic welcome awaits naturists at Isefjær where the pitches and rental accommodation are supported by basic but comfortable facilities. The site has been lovingly developed from an ex-military recreation camp by volunteers. It is secluded with access that may prove difficult for larger units. A limited number of camping pitches enjoy views over the fjord.

Facilities
The clean sanitary blocks are typical of those found in many naturist sites, with open plan showers and washbasins. Sanitary facilities specially for children. Laundry facilities. Excellent communal kitchen and large outside barbecue area. Motorcaravan services. Restaurant with meals available three times a day. Hot tub (Sat.) Sauna. Lounge area. TV room. Fishing. Boat Launching. Fjord swimming. Diving platform. Free WiFi in lounge and reception. Accommodation to rent. Off site: Kristiansand and sightseeing along the south coast of Norway.

Open: 1 May - 1 September.

Directions
From E18 east from Kristiansand, take exit 91 (Rona) towards Høvåg on road 401. After 13 km, turn left signed Isefjær 3 km. Isefjær is at end of single track road (difficult for large units). Afternoon arrival recommended. GPS: 58.18810, 8.19991

Charges guide
Per unit incl. 2 persons and electricity	NOK 320

For latest campsite news, availability and prices visit

alanrogers.com

Rysstad

Sølvgarden Hotell og Feriesenter

N-4748 Rysstad (Aust-Agder) T: 37 93 61 30. E: post@rysstadferie.no

alanrogers.com/NO2600

Setesdal is on the upper reaches of the Otra river which runs north from Kristiansand and onwards to the southern slopes of Hardangervidda. The small village of Rysstad is named after the family that developed camping here, and later the excellent hotel and restaurant complex. The site occupies a wide tract of gently sloping woodland between the road and the river towards which it shelves gently, affording a splendid view of the valley and the towering mountains opposite. There are 50 pitches, some for tents, and 31 numbered pitches with electricity, four of which are fully serviced. They are among 22 cabins and apartments for rent.

Facilities

Modern sanitary facilities with en-suite rooms. Family and children's rooms, plus a private room (charged). Wet room for disabled visitors. Large kitchen/diner (charged). Laundry facilities. Play area and amusement hut. Sports field. Fishing, swimming and boating (boats for hire). Fitness track. Bicycle hire. Centre includes café, mini shop and restaurant. Handicraft shop. Barbecue area by river. Five-room motel and accommodation to rent. Free WiFi over site. Off site: Village within walking distance.

Open: All year.

Directions

Site is 1 km. south of the junction between route 9 (from Kristiansand) and the extended route 45 (from Stavanger). GPS: 59.09077, 7.54053

Charges guide

Per unit incl. 2 persons and electricity	NOK 335 - 430
extra person	NOK 20
child (under 5 yrs)	free

Gol

PlusCamp Gol

RV 7, N-3550 Gol (Buskerud) T: 32 07 41 44. E: gol@pluscamp.no

alanrogers.com/NO2574

Gol Campingsenter is a good overnight stop when travelling north from Oslo, although there are sufficient activities on site and nearby to merit a longer stay. There are 550 pitches in total, including 200 touring pitches all with access to 16A electricity. The site is located on both sides of the main RV7 but there is easy access to either side via a pedestrian underpass. Three well appointed sanitary blocks serve the site with all you need and hot water and showers are included. The river flowing at the edge of the campsite should encourage fishermen to choose this site.

Facilities

Three well equipped sanitary blocks have modern, en-suite facilities including family rooms, some with special extras for babies and young children. Each has well equipped kitchens/dining areas and laundries and separate rooms with access for disabled visitors. Motorcaravan services. Shop with essentials and good range of camping equipment/spares. Large outdoor swimming pool, heated with small pool with slide and an extensive area of sun loungers (extra charge). Licensed snack bar. Play areas. Licensed cafeteria. Takeaway. Football pitch. Sauna. Off site: Motorsports, ice skating, bowling and golf 12 km. Riding 10 km. Skiing 3-30 km.

Open: All year.

Directions

Approaching Gol from Hønefoss on RV 7, the site is 2.5 km. south of the centre of Gol, with reception on the left. GPS: 60.69996, 9.00471

Charges guide

Per unit incl. 2 persons and electricity	NOK 290
incl. 4 persons	NOK 330
extra person	NOK 30
dog	free

Alta

Solvang Camping

Box 1280, N-9505 Alta (Finnmark) T: 78 43 04 77. E: solvangcamp@hotmail.com

alanrogers.com/NO2435

This is a restful little site with a welcoming atmosphere. It is set well back from the main road, so there is no road noise. The site overlooks the tidal marshes of the Altafjord, which are home to a wide variety of birdlife, providing ornithologists with a grandstand view during the long summer evenings bathed by the Midnight Sun. The 30 pitches are on undulating grass amongst pine trees and shrubs, and are not marked, although there are 16 electric hook-ups (16A). The site is run by a church mission organisation. All facilities are brand new.

Facilities

New block with reception and sanitary facilities with underfloor heating, washbasins in cubicles, showers and a family room. Facilities for disabled visitors. Sauna. New kitchen with cooker, sinks and dining area. Washing machine and dryer. Large TV room. Football field. Play area. WiFi. Off site: Alta Museum. Rock carvings.

Open: 1 June - 31 August.

Directions

Site is signed off the E6, 10 km. north of Alta. GPS: 69.97968, 23.4681

Charges guide

Per unit incl. 2 persons and electricity	NOK 212

FREE Alan Rogers Travel Card
Extra benefits and savings - see page 14

Skarsvag

Kirkeporten Camping

Box 22, N-9763 Skarsvag (Finnmark) T: 78 47 52 33. E: kipo@kirkeporten.no

alanrogers.com/NO2425

This is the most northerly mainland campsite in the world (71¼ 06) and considering the climate and the wild, unspoilt location it has to be one of the best sites in Scandinavia, and also rivals the best in Europe. The 40 touring pitches, 32 with 16A electricity, are on grass or gravel hardstanding in natural tundra terrain beside a small lake, together with room for 40 tents. There are also 16 cabins to rent and five rooms in the old barn. We advise you to pack warm clothing, bedding and maybe propane for this location. Note: Although overnighting at Nordkapp Centre is permitted, it is on the very exposed gravel carpark with no electric hook-ups or showers.

Facilities
Excellent modern sanitary installations in two underfloor heated buildings. They include a sauna, two family bathrooms, baby room, and excellent unit for disabled visitors. Laundry. Kitchen with hot plates, sinks and a dining area. Motorcaravan services. Reception, restaurant and mini shop at the entrance open daily. Off site: North Cape, Kirkeporten.
Open: 1 May - 1 October.

Directions
On the island of Magerøya, from Honningsvåg take the E69 for 20 km. then fork right signed Skarsvåg. Site is on left after 3 km. just as you approach Skarsvåg. GPS: 71.11217, 25.82177

Charges guide

Per unit incl. 2 persons and electricity	€ 28.00

Alvdal

Gjelten Bru Camping

N-2560 Alvdal (Hedmark) T: 62 48 74 44. E: post@gjeltenbrucamping.no

alanrogers.com/NO2515

Located a few kilometres west of Alvdal, this peaceful little site with its traditional turf roof buildings, makes an excellent base from which to explore the area. The 40 touring pitches are on level, neatly trimmed grass, served by gravel access roads and with electricity (10A) available to all. Some pitches are in the open and others under tall pine trees spread along the river bank. There are also 13 cabins to rent. Across the bridge on the other side of the river and main road, the site owners also operate the local, well stocked supermarket and post office.

Facilities
Heated toilet facilities are clean and housed in two buildings. One unit has been refurbished and is well appointed, the other is of newer construction. There is a mix of conventional washbasins and stainless steel washing troughs, and hot showers on payment. Separate unit with WC, basin, shower and handrails for disabled visitors. Two small kitchens provide sinks, hot plates and an oven, all free of charge. Laundry facilities. Shop. TV room. Swings. Fishing. Off site: Supermarket and post office nearby. Bicycle hire 5 km.
Open: All year.

Directions
On the road 29 at Gjelten 3.5 km. west of Alvdal. Turn over the river bridge opposite village store and post office, and site is immediately on right. GPS: 62.13293, 10.57091

Charges guide

Per pitch incl. electricity	NOK 220

Granvin

Espelandsdalen Camping

N-5736 Granvin (Hordaland) T: 56 52 51 67. E: post@espelandsdalencamping.no

alanrogers.com/NO2350

If one follows Hardangerfjord on the map and considers the mighty glacier which once scooped away the land along its path, it is easy to imagine that it started life in Espelandsdalen. For generations farmers have struggled to make a living out of the narrow strip of land between water and rock. One of these farmers has converted a narrow, sloping field bisected by the road (572) into a modest lakeside campsite taking about 50 units. The grassy meadow pitches below the road run right down to the lake shore. There are 30 electrical hook-ups (10A). Campers come here for the fishing and walking, or just to marvel at the views of the valley and its towering mountain sides.

Facilities
A newly refurbished sanitary block consists of a washing trough with hot water, a shower on payment and WCs. Confectionery, ice-cream and drinks are kept in the office. Swimming, fishing and boating in lake. Pedalo hire. WiFi planned. Off site: Pleasant walk to local waterfall.
Open: 1 May - 31 August.

Directions
The northern loop of the 572 road follows Espelandsdalen and the campsite is on this road, 6 km. from its junction with route 13 at Granvin. GPS: 60.59213, 6.80671

Charges guide

Per unit incl. 2 persons and electricity	NOK 175
extra person	NOK 20
child (4-12 yrs)	NOK 15
dog	free

For latest campsite news, availability and prices visit

alanrogers.com

Kinsarvik

Ringøy Camping

N-5780 Kinsarvik (Hordaland) T: 53 66 39 17. E: torleivr@kinsarvik.net

alanrogers.com/NO2315

Although the village of Ringøy is quiet and peaceful, it lies midway between two principal crossing points of Upper Hardangerfjord, the Kinsarvik ferry and the remarkable Hardanger suspension bridge, near the junction of two key routes. Extensive landscaping has produced a series of terraces running down from the road to the tree-lined fjord, and the shore area where pitches have individual rock campfires. The owners, the Raunsgard family, are particularly proud of the site's remarkable shore-side barbecue facilities. On arrival you find a place as there is no reception – someone will call between 20:00 and 21:00. There are several sites at the popular nearby resort town of Kinsarvik, but none compares for situation or atmosphere with the small, simple Ringøy site.

Facilities
The toilet block is small and simple (with metered showers), but well designed, constructed and maintained. It is possibly inadequate during peak holiday weeks in July. Rowing boat (free). Free WiFi over site. Off site: Kinsarvik 10 km.

Open: 15 May - 15 September.

Directions
Site is on route 13, midway between Kinsarvik and Brimnes. GPS: 60.44111, 6.77988

Charges guide
Per unit incl. 2 persons and electricity	NOK 200
extra person	NOK 10
child (0-12 yrs)	NOK 5

No credit cards.

Nå

Eikhamrane Camping

N-5776 Nå (Hordaland) T: 53 66 22 48.

alanrogers.com/NO2330

For those seeking peace and quiet on the western shore of Sørfjord is Eikhamrane Camping. Arranged on a well landscaped and partly terraced field which slopes to a pebbly lakeside beach and quay. Formerly part of an orchard, which still extends on both sides of the site, there is room for 40 units on unmarked, well kept grass, 20 with electricity hook-ups (10A). There are attractive trees and good gravel roads, with areas of gravel hardstanding for poor weather. Many pitches overlook the fjord where there are also picnic benches, which afford the occasional glimpse of porpoises searching for mackerel.

Facilities
Two small timber toilet blocks, one for toilets with external access, the other for washbasins (open) and cubicles with washbasin and shower (on payment). Both are simple but very well kept. Small kitchen (hot water on payment) and laundry with sinks. Some supplies kept at reception office in the old farmhouse, home of the owner (bread and milk to order). Play area. Small quay with slipway. Motorboat hire. Watersports (sailing, canoeing and rowing), and fishing in fjord. Off site: Digranes nature reserve (birdwatching) nearby. Golf 11 km. Riding 18 km. Mountain drive to Jondal on Hardangerfjord.

Open: 1 June - 31 August.

Directions
Site is on road 550 8 km. south of the village of Nå, on the western shore of Sørfjord, 32 km. south of Utne and 16 km. north of Odda. GPS: 60.1830, 6.5517

Charges guide
Per unit incl. 2 persons and electricity	NOK 220
extra person	NOK 30
child (4-12 yrs)	NOK 20

No credit cards.

Ulvik

Ulvik Fjord Camping

Eikjeledbakkjen 2, N-5730 Ulvik (Hordaland) T: 56 52 61 70. E: post@ulvikfjord.no

alanrogers.com/NO2360

Ulvik was discovered by tourists 150 years ago when the first liners started operating to the head of Hardangerfjord. This pretty little site is 500 m. from the centre of the town. It occupies what must once have been a small orchard running down to the fjord, beside a small stream. There is room for about 80 units, 32 with electricity connections, and six cabins, all on undulating ground that slopes towards the fjord and a sheltered area for boating, fishing and barbecues. The site is linked to a hotel and campers benefit from access to its facilities.

Facilities
Reception is at the hotel opposite and campers are welcome to use the facilities here. On the site, a small wooden building houses the well kept sanitary facilities. For each sex there are two open washbasins, WCs and two modern showers on payment. Kitchen with cooker and sink. Washing machine. Boat slipway, fishing and swimming in fjord. Jetty with large barbecue area. Off site: Hotel opposite with breakfast buffet, lounges, bar and TV room. Shops and restaurants in town.

Open: 1 May - 15 September.

Directions
From the bridge carrying the Rv 7 north over Eidfjord, turn right at roundabout in the tunnel towards Ulvik on road no. 572; the site is on the southern side of the town, opposite the Ulvik Fjord Hotel. GPS: 60.56492, 6.90741

Charges guide
Per unit incl. 2 persons and electricity	NOK 235

FREE Alan Rogers Travel Card
Extra benefits and savings - see page 14

Averoy

Skjerneset Bryggecamping

Ekkilsoya, N-6530 Averoy (Møre og Romsdal) T: 71 51 18 94. E: info@skjerneset.com

alanrogers.com/NO2490

Uniquely centred around a working fishing quay set in an idyllic bay, Skjerneset Camping has been developed by the Otterlei family to give visitors an historical insight into this industry. It steps back in time in all but its facilities and offers 25 boats to hire and organised trips on a real fishing boat. Found on the tiny island of Ekkilsøya off Averøy, there is space for 30 caravans and motorcaravans on gravel hardstandings landscaped into rocks and trees, each individually shaped and sized and all having electricity connections (10/16A). There are grassy areas for tents on the upper terraces and six fully equipped cabins.

Facilities

Central unisex sanitary block has open washbasins and hot showers, a large kitchen, dining area with TV, small laundry, large drying room and several lounge areas. Additional smaller separate sex sanitary blocks. Motorcaravan services. Kitchen. Fish preparation and freezing areas. Sauna. Satellite TV. Motorboat hire. Free bicycle hire. Free WiFi. Sea fishing and sightseeing trips in owner's boat. Sales of fresh fish and prepared fish dishes for guests to heat. Off site: Golf 6 km.

Open: All year.

Directions

Site is on the little island of Ekkilsøya which is reached via a side road running west from the main Rv 64 road, 1.5 km. south of Bremsnes. GPS: 63.08114, 7.59569

Charges guide

Per unit incl. 2 persons and electricity	NOK 230
extra person	NOK 40
child	NOK 20
dog	free

No credit cards.

Bud

PlusCamp Bud

N-6340 Bud (Møre og Romsdal) T: 71 26 10 23. E: bud@pluscamp.no

alanrogers.com/NO2459

The view from Bud Camping is over the sea and this part of the coast is known for its excellent fishing. Visitors to the campsite can choose from 150 pitches on grass or hardstandings, all with 16A electricity. The facilities on site are modern and very well maintained. The site is peaceful and is a haven for fishermen and boating enthusiasts with a variety of boats for hire. The town of Bud is close with shops, bars and restaurants. You can take walks along the coast, or just relax in an atmosphere of calm which the owners actively promote.

Facilities

Central modern sanitary units with toilets and showers (extra charge) hot water available in washbasins in cubicles. Two separate communal kitchens. Washer and dryer. TV room and lounge. Boat hire. Sales of fishing and boating equipment. Motorcaravan services. Trout pond with free use of canoe. Swings. Boat launching slip. Fish preparation area and free use of freezers. Communal barbecue. Free WiFi. Off site: Petrol station, garage, post office, bank, bakery, and two grocery stores. 400 m.

Open: April - 1 October.

Directions

From Molde and the E39, travel north using Rv 64 and Rv 663 to Elnesvågen and then Rv 664 to Bud. Site is signed on left approaching town after passing football pitches on right. GPS: 62.90346, 6.927

Charges guide

Per unit incl. up to 5 persons and electricity	NOK 240
extra person	NOK 40
dog	free

Malmefjorden

Bjølstad Camping

N-6445 Malmefjorden (Møre og Romsdal) T: 71 26 56 56. E: post@bjolstad.no

alanrogers.com/NO2450

This is a delightful small, rural site, which slopes down to Malmefjorden, a sheltered arm of Fraenfjorden. Bjølstad has space for just 45 touring units on grassy, fairly level, terraces either side of the tarmac central access road. A delight for children is a large, old masted boat which provides hours of fun. At the foot of the site is a waterside barbecue area with a large, communal turfed roof area, a shallow, sandy, paddling area for children and a jetty. Both rowing and motorboats (with life jackets) can be hired and one can swim or fish in the fjord.

Facilities

The recently renovated heated sanitary unit includes coin-operated showers, en-suite family room and kitchen with sinks, cooker with hood, freezer and dining area. Laundry facilities. Playground. Rowing and motorboat hire. 9 cabins for hire. Fjord fishing including fish preparation area, and swimming. Dogs are not accepted in cabins. Communal barbecue and social gathering building at fjordside. Free WiFi near reception. Off site: Supermarket 1 km. Riding 9 km. Golf 12 km.

Open: 1 June - 30 September (maybe before on request).

Directions

Turn off Rv 64 on northern edge of Malmefjorden village towards village of Lindset. Site is signed and 1 km. on left. GPS: 62.81467, 7.22517

Charges guide

Per unit incl. 2 persons and electricity	NOK 155 - 255
extra person	NOK 10
child	NOK 5
dog	free

For latest campsite news, availability and prices visit

alanrogers.com

Åndalsnes

Trollveggen Camping

Horgheimseidet, N-6300 Åndalsnes (Møre og Romsdal) T: 71 22 37 00. E: post@trollveggen.no

alanrogers.com/NO2452

The location of this site provides a unique experience – it is set at the foot of the famous vertical cliff of Trollveggen (the Troll Wall), which is Europe's highest vertical mountain face. The site is pleasantly laid out in terraces with level grass pitches. The facility block, four cabins and reception are all very attractively built with grass roofs. Beside the river is an attractive barbecue area where barbecue parties are sometimes arranged. This site is a must for people who love nature. The site is surrounded by the Troll Peaks and the Romsdalshorn Mountains with the rapid river of Rauma flowing by. Close to Reinheimen (home of reindeer) National Park, and in the beautiful valley of Romsdalen you have the ideal starting point for trips to many outstanding attractions such as Trollstigen (The Troll Road) to Geiranger or to the Mardalsfossen waterfalls. In the mountains there are nature trails of various lengths and difficulties. The campsite owners are happy to help you with information. The town of Åndalsnes is 10 km. away and has a long tourism tradition as a place to visit. It is situated in the inner part of the beautiful Romsdalfjord and has a range of shops and restaurants.

Facilities

One heated toilet block provides washbasins, some in cubicles, and showers on payment. Family room with baby bath and changing mat, plus facilities for disabled visitors. Communal kitchen. Laundry facilities. Motorcaravan services. Car wash facility. Barbecue area (covered). Playground. Duck pond. Fishing. Free WiFi over site. Old Trollveggen Station Master's apartment for hire by arrangement. Off site: Waymarked walks from site. Climbing, glacier walking and hiking. Fjord fishing. Sightseeing trips. The Troll Road. Mardalsfossen (waterfall). Geiranger and Åndalsnes.

Open: 10 May - 20 September.

Directions

Site is located on the E136 road, 10 km. south of Åndalsnes. It is signed. GPS: 62.49444, 7.758333

Charges guide

Per unit incl. 2 persons and electricity	NOK 245
extra person (over 7 yrs)	NOK 15

Stordal

Stordal Camping

N-6250 Stordal (Møre og Romsdal) T: 47 90 64 80. E: campingstordal@gmail.com

alanrogers.com/NO2448

Stordal Camping is situated on the shores of Storfjorden where high forested valley sides open to an inlet where the Stordalselva salmon river enters the fjord. It is an ideal location for fishing and boating but also a peaceful base to explore sights like Trollstigen and Muldalfossen, the fourth highest waterfall in the world. Modern sanitary facilities housed in traditional wooden buildings with turf roofs serve 30 touring pitches, 18 with access to electricity points (16A). Passing cruise ships head for Gerainger or Ålesund and both of these popular places are easily accessed by road.

Facilities

Main modern, very clean, heated central unit has coin-operated showers and also houses a laundry. Kitchen. Facilities for disabled visitors (no shower) in reception building which also has kiosk with ice-cream and drinks. Two play areas, one featuring a galleon, sandpit and a digger. Trampolines. Boat hire. Salmon river fishing permit (charged). Fjord fishing (free). WiFi over site (charged). Off site: Supermarkets and ATM within 500 m. Valldal rafting Ålesund 55 km. Gerainger 45 km.

Open: 1 May - 15 September.

Directions

Take the main Rv 650 tourist route to Stordal. The site is clearly signed in town on a bend by supermarket. GPS: 62.378583, 6.984708

Charges guide

Per unit incl. 2 persons and electricity	NOK 250 - 270

Andenes

Andenes Camping

Storgata 53, N-8483 Andenes (Nordland) T: 41 34 03 88. E: camping@whalesafari.no

alanrogers.com/NO2428

Lying on the exposed west coast of Andøy between the quiet main road and white sandy beaches, this site has an exceptional location for the midnight sun. Extremely popular, offering mountain and ocean views, it is only three kilometres from the base of Whalesafari and Andenes town. There is space for an unspecified number of touring units and you park where you like. With only 20 places with 16A electricity connections, it is advisable to arrive by mid-afternoon. Late arrivals may pitch and pay later when reception opens. Level areas of grass with some hardstanding can be found on gently sloping ground.

Facilities

One building houses separate sex sanitary facilities, each providing two toilets, two showers (10 NOK) with curtain to keep clothes dry and three washbasins. In each, one toilet is suitable for disabled visitors and includes a washbasin. The reception building houses a kitchen, a large sitting/dining room, 2 showers, WC and washbasin. Laundry facilities. Motorcaravan services. Swings for children. WiFi (free). Off site: Well stocked supermarket 250 m.

Open: 1 June - 30 September.

Directions

Either take the scenic roads 946 and 947 on the west side of Andøy north or to the east road 82, site is on left 250 m. from where 947 rejoins the 82, 3 km. before Andenes. The scenic west route is 9 km. further. GPS: 69.30411, 16.06641

Charges guide

Per pitch incl. electricity	NOK 200
tent pitch	NOK 100
car	NOK 100

Ballangen

PlusCamp Ballangen

N-8540 Ballangen (Nordland) T: 76 92 76 90. E: post@ballangencamping.com

alanrogers.com/NO2455

Ballangen is a pleasant, lively site conveniently located on the edge of a fjord with a small sandy beach, with direct access off the main E6 road. The 150 marked pitches are mostly on sandy grass, with electricity (10/16A) available to all. There are a few hardstandings, also 54 cabins for rent. A TV room has tourist information, coffee and games machines and there is a heated outdoor pool and waterslide (charged), free fjord fishing, and boat hire. An interesting excursion is to the nearby Martinstollen mine where visitors are guided through the dimly lit Olav Shaft, 500 m. into the mountain.

Facilities

Toilet facilities include some washbasins in cubicles. Facilities for disabled visitors, sauna and solarium. Kitchen with sinks, two cookers and covered seating area. Laundry. Motorcaravan services. Well stocked shop. Café and takeaway (main season). TV/games room. Swimming pool and waterslide (charged). Minigolf. Fishing. Golf. Boat and bicycle hire. Pedal car hire. Mini zoo. Playground. Covered barbecue areas. Off site: Riding 2 km. Ballangen 4 km. has supermarket and other services. Narvik 40 km.

Open: 1 March - 31 December.

Directions

Access is off the E6, 4 km. north of Ballangen, 40 km. south of Narvik. GPS: 68.33888, 16.85780

Charges guide

Per unit incl. 2 persons and electricity	NOK 245

Kabelvag

Lyngvær Lofoten Bobilcamping

N-8313 Kleppstad (Nordland) T: 76 07 77 78. E: relorent@online.no

alanrogers.com/NO2465

This established site is very popular, with many customers returning for the well maintained facilities and easy access to fishing and boating. In the centre of Lofoten, alongside a tidal fjord with mountains all around, the setting and location is quite idyllic. Large terraces provide fine views for most of the 200 pitches, mainly grass, some with hardstanding, with electricity for 110 (10/16A). Lyngvaer provides a base to absorb the island's scenery and traditions in an area which also offers walking, ornithology and photography. The owners bake their own bread and rolls to order, with all other provisions available at a supermarket in Henningsvaer (10 km).

Facilities

Toilet facilities are spotless and cleaned regularly. Two heated sanitary units include showers in cubicles (NOK 10 for 6 mins). Well equipped motorcaravan service point. Two communal kitchens with cooking, sinks and fish freezer (free). Laundry facilities. Large sitting area with satellite TV. Play areas. Boat hire. Fishing (good fish cleaning area). WiFi (free). Off site: Henningsvaer 11 km. Kabelvag Aquarium 11 km. Golf 15 km. Lofotr Viking Museum 36 km.

Open: 1 May - 20 September.

Directions

From Svolvaer turn southwest on E10 towards Kabelvag for 5 km. Site is on left in 14 km. from Kabelvag. The site is 110 km. north on E10 from Moskenes on the right. Ferries link mainland from Skutvik to Svolvaer or from Bodø to Moskenes. GPS: 68.224812, 14.216609

Charges guide

Per unit incl. 2 persons and electricity	NOK 110 - 160
extra person	NOK 5

Eighth night free. No credit cards.

For latest campsite news, availability and prices visit

alanrogers.com

Mosjøen

PlusCamp Mosjoen

E6, N-8657 Mosjøen (Nordland) T: 75 17 79 00. E: post@mosjoenhotell.no

alanrogers.com/NO2487

This campsite off the E6 near Mosjøen, allows access to 'The World's Most Beautiful Journey'. The Kystriksveien (RV17) runs north to Bodø and south to Steinkjer, however this site offers more to the traveller than a simple stopover or change of route. Complete with six-lane, ten-pin bowling alley, games rooms, food and bar, it has both entertainment and mountain views with forested valley slopes. It has modern, well equipped sanitary facilities. Terraced pitches are level with 16A electricity, some on tarmac and gravel, and others on grass with a pleasant separate area for tents. A number of restaurants, cafés, art galleries, a museum and a public park are all within easy walking distance.

Facilities

Two heated sanitary units are linked together in the centre of the site. The newer unit offers up-to-date facilities for all, with family rooms and disabled access. Motorcaravan services (ask at reception). Kitchen and dining area. Laundry. Restaurant, café/bar. Heated outdoor swimming pool with slide. 10-pin bowling alley with bar. Pool table and video games. TV room. WiFi. Access to large ball games area. Autogas/LPG filling station off main car park. Off site: Sports area 500 m. Fishing 2 km. Skiing 8 km.

Open: All year.

Directions

When travelling north from Trondheim, 1 km. south of Mosjøen, turn left off the E6.
GPS: 65.83417, 13.22025

Charges guide

Per unit incl. electricity	NOK 250

Saltstraumen

PlusCamp Saltstraumen

Bok 33, N-8056 Saltstraumen (Nordland) T: 75 58 75 60. E: salcampi@online.no

alanrogers.com/NO2475

On a coastal route, this extremely popular site is in a very scenic location, has a magnificent backdrop, and is close to the largest Maelstrom in the world. It is an easy short walk to this outstanding phenomenon. As well as 20 cabins, the site has 60 plain touring pitches mostly on level, gravel hardstandings in rows, each with electricity (10A). A few 'softer' pitches are available for tents. The nearby fjord is renowned for the prolific numbers of coalfish and cod caught from the shore. Many try their hand at catching the evening meal. You are advised to arrive by late afternoon.

Facilities

Excellent heated sanitary facilities are clean and fully equipped. Unisex with four large individual cubicles containing a WC, shower and washbasin. Other cubicles have a toilet and washbasin. Family room. Full wet room with access for disabled visitors. Motorcaravan services. Kitchen with two full cookers. Fish cleaning area and free use of fish freezer. Laundry facilities. Playground. Minigolf. Fishing. WiFi (free). Off site: Well stocked mini supermarket and snack bar outside site entrance. Hotel and caféteria nearby. Bødo ferry 30 km.

Open: All year.

Directions

Travelling from the south: before Rognan take Rv 812 signed Saltstraumen. At junction with Rv 17 turn right. Site on left immediately after second bridge. From the north: From Rv 80 (Fauske-Bodø) turn south on Rv 17, site is 12 km. at Saltstraumen on right immediately before bridge.
GPS: 67.2355, 14.62091

Charges guide

Per unit incl. 3 persons and electricity	NOK 210 - 260
extra person	NOK 15

Storforshei

Krokstrand Camping

Krokstrand, Saltfjellveien 1573, N-8630 Storforshei (Nordland) T: 75 16 60 02.

alanrogers.com/NO2485

In a stunning location, this site is a popular resting place on the long trek to Nordkapp and is only 18 km. from the Arctic Circle and its visitor centre. There are 45 unmarked pitches set amongst birch trees with 10A electrical connections for 28 units and 15 cabins available for rent. In late spring and early summer the river alongside, headed by rapids, is impressive and there remains the possibility of the surrounding mountains being snow-capped. A reception kiosk is open 08.00-10.00 and 15.00-22.00 in high season, otherwise campers are invited to find a pitch and pay later at the hotel complex opposite.

Facilities

Modern, well maintained and clean, small sanitary unit includes two showers per sex (on payment). Laundry facilities. Small kitchen. Motorcaravan services. Play area with trampoline, well maintained. Minigolf. Fishing. Off site: Hotel with café/restaurant just outside site entrance (same ownership as the site) with good meals, snacks and very basic provisions. Souvenir shop 500 m. Caves and glacier 30 km.

Open: 1 June - 20 September.

Directions

Entrance is off E6 at Krokstrand village opposite hotel, 65 km. north of Mo I Rana and 18 km. south of the Arctic Circle. GPS: 66.46108, 15.0952

Charges guide

Per unit incl. 2 persons and electricity	NOK 240
extra person	NOK 15
child (4-12 yrs)	NOK 10

FREE Alan Rogers Travel Card
Extra benefits and savings - see page 14

Aurdal I Valdres
PlusCamp Aurdal
N-2910 Aurdal I Valdres (Oppland) T: 61 36 52 12. E: post@aurdalcamp.no

alanrogers.com/NO2556

PlusCamp Aurdal is a friendly, family run campsite in an idyllic waterside location with forested slopes on each side of the beautiful wide valley. A warm welcome awaits you and traditional grass-roofed, wooden buildings house modern, well maintained facilities. There are 240 pitches in total with 60 available for touring units, all with 10A electricity and TV points. Open all year, it offers activities that include boating, cycling, walking and skiing. The site organises weekend boat trips and the water will attract fishermen and swimmers alike, whilst a well marked hiking trail takes you to a viewpoint overlooking the campsite.

Facilities
Modern sanitary units include facilities for disabled visitors, family rooms, kitchen and dining areas with TV. Coin operated showers. Laundry. Restaurant and bar. Service to both indoor and covered outdoor terraces. Shop with basic supplies. Takeaway. Ice-cream. Trampolines. Slides. Go-kart, bicycle, canoe and boat hire complete with life jackets. Adventure playground with zip wire, football goals. Free WiFi covers site. Walking trails from site. Boat trips from site. Boat launching and 800 m. of moorings. Off site: Golf 2.5 km. Ski Centre 6 km.

Open: Open all year (full facilities April to September).

Directions
From Oslo (180 km) take the E16. On the outskirts of Aurdal turn left before the white church where the site is clearly signed. GPS: 60.91647, 9.38981

Charges guide
Per unit incl. 2 persons
and electricity   NOK 150 - 270

Oyer
PlusCamp Rustberg
Kongsvegen 691, N-2636 Oyer (Oppland) T: 61 27 77 30. E: rustberg@pluscamp.no

alanrogers.com/NO2545

Conveniently located beside the E6, 23 km. from the centre of Lillehammer, this attractive terraced site provides a comfortable base for exploring the area. Like all sites along this route it does suffer from road and train noise at times, but the site's facilities and nearby attractions more than compensate for this. There are 70 pitches with 30 available for touring units, most reasonably level and with some gravel hardstandings available for motorcaravans. There are 70 electrical connections (16A). A small open air, heated swimming pool has a water slide.

Facilities
Heated, fully equipped sanitary facilities include washbasins in cubicles, showers on payment and free saunas. Two good family bathrooms. Unit for disabled visitors. Campers' kitchen and dining room with microwave oven and double hob. Laundry. Motorcaravan services. Restaurant. Solarium (on payment). Kiosk for basics. Swimming pool and slide (1/6-31/8, weather permitting). Billiards. Golf. Playground. New reception and café. Off site: Forest walks directly from site. Fishing in the nearby river, day licence from reception. Golf 7 km.

Open: All year.

Directions
Site is well signed from the E6, 20 km. north of Lillehammer (North) exit. GPS: 61.28025, 10.36095

Charges guide
Per pitch incl. electricity   NOK 210 - 260

Trogstad
Olberg Camping
Sandsveien 4, Olberg, N-1860 Trogstad (stfold) T: 69 82 86 10. E: froesol@online.no

alanrogers.com/NO2615

Olberg is a delightful small farm site, close to Lake Øyeren and within 70 km. of Oslo. There are 35 large, level pitches and electricity connections (10-16A) are available for 28 units located on neatly tended grassy meadows with trees and shrubs. The reception building also houses a small gallery with paintings, glasswork and other crafts. A short drive down the adjacent lane takes you to the beach on Lake Øyeren, and there are many woodland walks in the surrounding area. Please bear in mind that this is a working farm. In high season fresh bread is available (except Sunday) and coffee, drinks, ices and snacks are provided. The old church and museum at Trøgstad, and Båstad church are worth visiting. Forest and elk safaris are arranged.

Facilities
Excellent, heated sanitary facilities are fully equipped and include a ramp for wheelchair access and one bathroom for families or disabled visitors. Laundry facilities. Small kitchenette with full size cooker and food preparation area. Kiosk. Snacks available. Craft gallery. Playground. Off site: Fishing 3 km. Golf, tropical pool and spa 18 km.

Open: 1 May - 1 October, other times by arrangement.

Directions
Site is signed on Rv 22, 20 km. north of Mysen on southern edge of Båstad village. GPS: 59.68837, 11.29286

Charges guide
Per unit incl. 2 persons and electricity   NOK 190

For latest campsite news, availability and prices visit
alanrogers.com

Jørpeland

Preikestolen Camping

Preikestolvegen 97, N-4100 Jørpeland (Rogaland) T: 48193950. E: info@preikestolencamping.com

alanrogers.com/NO2660

Taking its name from one of Norway's best known attractions, the Preikestolen (Pulpit Rock) cliff formation, Preikestolen Camping is situated in the beautiful region of Rogaland, surrounded by high mountains and deep fjords. This is a site where you could easily stay a few days to explore the beautiful region. The friendly owners are happy to help with maps and guidance. The site is laid out in a relaxed way with an open, level grass area where trees and bushes create little 'rooms' for your tent, caravan or motorcaravan. There are 150 pitches, 56 with electricity (10/16A), water tap and waste water drainage. In high season helicopter tours are arranged from the site (Mon - Thurs, depending on the weather).

Facilities
The modern heated sanitary block has showers, washbasins in cubicles and facilities for disabled visitors. Room with sinks but no cookers. Laundry facilities. Motorcaravan services. Freezer. Small shop and craft shop (15/5-15/9). Restaurant and takeaway (15/5-15/9). Fishing. WiFi part site. Off site: Preikestolen. Stavanger. Lysefjordsentret salmon park in Oanes. Rock carvings at Solbakk. Golf 500 m. Riding 15 km.

Open: 1 January- 31 December.

Directions
Site is on road 13, 3 km. south of Jørpeland. Follow signs to site. GPS: 58.998883, 6.092167

Charges guide

Per person	NOK 40
child	NOK 30
pitch	NOK 200
electricity	NOK 40

Brekke

Botnen Camping

N-5961 Brekke (Sogn og Fjordane) T: 57 78 54 71. E: botnen.camping@enivest.com

alanrogers.com/NO2370

For those travelling north on the E39 beyond Bergen, there are surprisingly few attractive sites until one reaches the southern shore of the mighty Sognefjord, close to the ferry crossing from Oppedal to Lavik. A left turn towards Brekke takes you to the family run Botnen Camping overlooking the fjord and with wonderful views to distant mountains. There are 70 mostly level touring pitches, all with 10A electricity, from where you may see passing cruise ships and porpoises searching for mackerel. It has its own jetty and harbour, with motorboats and canoes for hire. The motorboats for hire and the shoreline itself provide opportunities for fishermen. The access road is single track in parts, but with regular passing places.

Facilities
Toilet block with washbasins and showers (on payment). New sanitary unit for 2014 with modern facilities, kitchen, laundry and reception above. Motorcaravan services. Small shop. Trampoline. Swimming, fishing and boating in fjord. Bicycle hire. Boats and canoes for hire. WiFi over site (charged). Off site: Hiking, fishing and boating. Supermarket and gas supplies 6 km.

Open: 1 May - 30 September.

Directions
Site is on the coast road west of Brekke, 11 km. from E39. Access in places is single-track with passing places. GPS: 61.03190, 5.35124

Charges guide

Per unit incl. 2 persons and electricity	NOK 130 - 200
extra person	NOK 15

Bryggja

PlusCamp Nore Fjordsenter

N-6711 Bryggja (Sogn og Fjordane) T: 94 78 40 42. E: post@nore-fjordsenter.com

alanrogers.com/NO2394

With views across the fjord and over the mountains, ever changing in the sunlight, you can be assured of a peaceful, relaxing stay here. Although somewhat off the busy tourist routes, it is still possible to take scenic drives to popular destinations including Ålesund, Runde and Gerainger. A shorter drive takes you to the beach at Revik. The campsite has 30 pitches with electricity laid out on terraces rising from its small private harbour, beach and jetty on the edge of Nordfjord. Boats and canoes are available for hire to explore a number of inlets and islands nearby and fishing opportunities are numerous.

Facilities
Modern sanitary facilities also include a kitchen, dishwashing sinks and laundry. En-suite room with access for disabled visitors includes a shower, toilet and washbasin. Boat and canoe hire. Boat launching from sheltered harbour and quay. Playground with slide and trampoline. Fishing with cleaning and preparation area. Communal barbecue facility. Terrace seating and lounge at reception. Picnic benches. Off site: Filling station and supermarket 50 m. from site entrance.

Open: All year.

Directions
From E39 at Nordfjordeid travel west on Rv 15 for 32 km. Site is signed and on the left immediately after the filling station/supermarket and before the junction with the Rv 61. GPS: 61.94064, 5.44898

Charges guide

Per unit incl. 2 persons and electricity	NOK 255

FREE Alan Rogers Travel Card
Extra benefits and savings - see page 14

Byrkjelo
Byrkjelo Camping

N-6826 Byrkjelo (Sogn og Fjordane) T: 91 73 65 97. E: mail@byrkjelo-camping.no

alanrogers.com/NO2436

In a wide, open, sunny part of the valley, overlooked by mountains containing the largest glacier in northern Europe, this neatly laid out and well equipped small site offers 35 large marked and numbered touring pitches, all with electricity connections (10A), and 15 with gravel hardstandings. Located on the outskirts of a village, you can expect neatly mown grass, attractive trees and shrubs, and a warm welcome from the owners. Fishing is possible in the river adjacent to the site. Reception and modern facilities are housed in a traditional, turf-roofed building and there is a heated outdoor swimming pool and terrace affording views of mountain peaks.

Facilities
The well equipped, heated sanitary unit includes seven shower rooms each with washbasin, on payment. Facilities for families with babies and for disabled visitors, incorporating a WC, basin and shower with handrails. Kitchen with sinks, hot-plates and dining area. Laundry facilities. Motorcaravan services. Kiosk selling drinks, ices and confectionery. Swimming pool and children's pool (24/6-20/8), both heated (charged). Large playground. Fishing. Bicycle hire. Beach volleyball. WiFi over part of site (charged). Off site: Riding 4 km. Golf 15 km.

Open: 1 May - 20 September.

Directions
Site is beside the E39 on outskirts of the village of Byrkjelo, 19 km. east of Sandane.
GPS: 61.73055, 6.50847

Charges guide
Per unit incl. 2 persons and electricity	NOK 180 - 245
extra person	NOK 10
child	NOK 10

Gaupne
PlusCamp Sandvik

Sandvik Sor, N-6868 Gaupne (Sogn og Fjordane) T: 57 68 11 53. E: sandvik@pluscamp.no

alanrogers.com/NO2385

Sandvik is a compact, small site in Gaupne close to the Nigardsbreen Glacier and the spectacular RV55 high mountain road from Lom to Sogndal. It provides 50 touring pitches, 48 with electrical connections (8/16A), arranged in an orchard setting either side of a road. A large supermarket, post office, banks and tourist information are all within a level 500 m. stroll. A café in the reception building is open in summer for drinks and meals and the small shop sells groceries, ices, soft drinks and sweets. Fjord fishing is nearby, as are guided tours of the Nigardsbreen and Jostedalsbreen glaciers.

Facilities
The modernised, fully equipped, central sanitary unit includes en-suite units with shower (on payment), washbasin and WC. Multi-purpose unit for families, with baby changing. Separate unit for disabled campers with ramped access. Campers' kitchen with tables, chairs and TV. Laundry. Playground. Boat hire. Fishing. Bicycle hire. Free WiFi over site. Off site: New indoor swimming complex 500 m. Nigardsbreen (glacier). Sognefjellet.

Open: All year.

Directions
Signed just off Rv 55 Lom-Sogndal road on eastern outskirts of Gaupne. GPS: 61.40053, 7.30022

Charges guide
Per unit incl. up to 4 persons and electricity	NOK 170 - 210

Lærdal
Lærdal Ferie & Fritidspark

Grandavegens, N-6886 Lærdal (Sogn og Fjordane) T: 57 66 66 95. E: info@laerdalferiepark.com

alanrogers.com/NO2375

This site is beside the famous Sognefjord, the longest fjord in the world. It is ideally situated if you want to explore the glaciers, fjords and waterfalls of the region. The 100 pitches (all with 16A electricity) are level with well trimmed grass, connected by tarmac roads and are suitable for tents, caravans and motorcaravans. The fully licensed restaurant serves traditional, locally sourced meals as well as snacks and pizzas. The pretty little village of Laerdal, only 400 m. away, is well worth a visit. A walk among the old, small wooden houses is a pleasant and interesting experience. You can hire boats on the site for short trips on the fjord. Guided hiking, cycling and fishing trips are also available.

Facilities
Two modern and well decorated sanitary blocks with washbasins (some in cubicles), showers on payment, and toilets. Facilities for disabled visitors. Children's room. Washing machine and dryer. Kitchen. Motorcaravan services. Small shop, bar, restaurant and takeaway (all 1/2-20/12). TV room. Playground. Fishing. Motorboats, rowing boats, canoes, bicycles and pedal cars for hire. Go-kart sales. Free WiFi over site. Off site: Cruises on the Sognefjord 400 m. Riding 500 m. Golf 12 km.

Open: All year.

Directions
Site is on road 5 (from the Oslo-Bergen road, E16) 400 m. north of Laerdal village centre.
GPS: 61.10037, 7.46986

Charges guide
Per unit incl. 2 persons and electricity	NOK 300 - 450
extra person	NOK 50
child (4-18 yrs)	NOK 25 - 37

Camping Cheques accepted.

For latest campsite news, availability and prices visit
alanrogers.com

Sogndal

Kjørnes Camping

Kjørnes, N-6856 Sogndal (Sogn og Fjordane) T: 97 54 41 56. E: camping@kjornes.no

alanrogers.com/NO2390

Kjørnes Camping is idyllically situated on the Sognefjord, three kilometres from the centre of Sogndal. It occupies a long open meadow which is terraced down to the waterside. The site has 100 pitches for camping units (all with electricity), 14 cabins and two apartments for rent. Located at the very centre of the 'fjord kingdom' by the main no. 5 road, this site is the ideal base from which to explore the Sognefjord. You are within a short drive (maximum one hour) from all the major attractions including the Jostedal glacier, the Nærøyfjord, the Flåm Railway, the Urnes Stave Church and Sognefjellet. This site is ideal for those who enjoy peace and quiet, renowned local walks, lovely scenery or a spot of fishing with a bonus of evening sunshine. Local activities include organised guided walks on glaciers, access to several stave churches and a goat farm in the mountains. A pleasant drive takes you to Solvorn and a car park in the village from where a ferry crosses the fjord to Urnes Stave Church. From Skjolden at the head of the fjord, the Sognefjelletvegen (RV55, a national tourist road) climbs to Jotunheimen National Park and on to Lom, passing the two highest mountains (over 2,400 m) in Norway.

Facilities

A modern, high quality sanitary building has washbasins in cubicles, and a feature children's room. Baby room. Facilities for disabled visitors. Kitchen with cooking facilities, dishwasher, a dining area overlooking the fjord, and laundry facilities. Motorcaravan services. Small shop (10/6-20/8). Satellite TV, WiFi over site (free). Cabins and apartments for hire. Off site: Hiking, glacier walks, climbing, rafting, walking around Sognefjord. Details from reception. Bicycle hire 3 km.

Open: All year.

Directions

Site is off the Rv 5, 3 km. east of Sogndal, 8 km. west of Kaupanger. Access is via a short, narrow lane with passing places. GPS: 61.21157, 7.12110

Charges guide

Per unit incl. 2 persons and electricity	NOK 280
extra person	NOK 15
child (4-16 yrs)	NOK 10

Kjørnes Camping★★★★
Kjørnes - N-6856 Sogndal - Norway
Phone: 0047 975 44156
E-mail: camping@kjornes.no - http://www.kjornes.no
www.kjornes.no

Vangsnes

Tveit Camping

N-6894 Vangsnes (Sogn og Fjordane) T: 57 69 66 00. E: tveitca@online.no

alanrogers.com/NO2380

Located in the district of Vik on the south shore of Sognefjord, 4 km. from the small port of Vangsnes, Tveit Camping is part of a small working farm and it is a charming neat site. Reception and a kiosk open most of the day in high season, with a phone to summon assistance at any time. Three terraces with wonderful views of the fjord provide 35 pitches with 30 electricity connections (10A) and there are also site owned cabins. On the campsite you will find a restored Iron Age burial mound dating from 350-550 AD, whilst the statue of 'Fritjov the Intrepid' towers over the landscape at Vangsnes.

Facilities

Modern, heated sanitary facilities provide showers on payment, a unit for disabled visitors, kitchens with facilities for cooking, and laundry facilities (hot water on payment). Motorcaravan services. Kiosk (15/6-15/8). TV rooms. Playground. Trampoline. Harbour for small boats, slipway and boat/canoe hire. Fishing and fish preparation area. Free WiFi over site. Bicycle hire. Comprehensive tourist information. Off site: Walks from site. Shop, café and pub by ferry terminal in Vangsnes 4 km. Riding 15 km.

Open: 15 May - 15 September.

Directions

Site is by Rv 13 between Vik and Vangsnes, 4 km. south of Vangsnes. GPS: 61.14466, 6.6218

Charges guide

Per unit incl. 2 persons and electricity	NOK 175 - 185
extra person	NOK 10
child (under 5 yrs)	free

Vassenden

PlusCamp Jolstraholmen

Postboks 11, N-6847 Vassenden (Sogn og Fjordane) T: 95 29 78 79. E: jolstraholmen@pluscamp.no

alanrogers.com/NO2400

This family run site is situated on the E39 between Sognefjord and Nordfjord. It is 1.5 km. from the lakeside village of Vassenden, behind the family owned filling station, restaurant and supermarket complex, and by the fast-flowing Jolstra river (renowned for trout fishing). The 60 pitches (some marked) are on grass or gravel hardstanding, all with electricity (16A), and of the 15 touring pitches, ten have water, waste points and TV connections. A river tributary runs through the site forming a bathing pool and island on which some pitches are located. There are 18 cabins for hire. Guided walking tours are organised, and a riverside and woodland walk follows a 1.5 kilometre circular route from the site.

Facilities

The heated, unisex sanitary facilities have en-suite units with WC, washbasin and shower. family room. En-suite unit for disabled visitors has automatic door. Kitchen. Laundry. Large supermarket, café and takeaway. Covered barbecue area. Playground. Water slide (heated, open summer, weather permitting). Minigolf. Volleyball. Fishing with fish preparation and freezers. Guided walks. Boat hire. WiFi over site (charged; one area free). Off site: 9-hole golf course 50 m. Ski slopes within 1 km.

Open: All year.

Directions

Site is at Statoil filling station on the E39 road, 1.5 km. west of Vassenden, 18 km. east of Førde. GPS: 61.48787, 6.08432

Charges guide

Per unit incl. 1-4 persons and electricity NOK 280 - 290

Oppdal

Magalaupe Camping

Engan, N-7340 Oppdal (Sør Trøndelag) T: 72 42 46 84. E: camp@magalaupe.no

alanrogers.com/NO2505

This friendly, good value, riverside site in a sheltered position in the mountains is easily accessed from the E6. The 52 unmarked and grassy touring pitches (42 with 16A electricity) are in natural surroundings amongst birch trees and rocks and served by gravel access roads. There are also eight attractive and fully equipped site owned cabins. As the site rarely fills up, the facilities should be adequate at most times. There are a host of unusual activities in the surrounding area. These include caving, canyoning, rafting, gold panning, mineral hunting, and musk oxen, reindeer and elk safaris.

Facilities

Small, clean, heated sanitary unit fully equipped and the showers are on payment. Extra WC/washbasin units in reception building. Small kitchen with sinks, hot plate, fridge and freezer, plus a combined washing/drying machine. Motorcaravan services. Kiosk for ices, soft drinks, etc. Bar (mid June-Aug). TV lounge. Fishing. Bicycle hire. Off site: Supermarkets and other services in Oppdal 11 km. Riding and golf 12 km. Organised walking, cycling and car tours.

Open: All year.

Directions

Site is signed on E6, 11 km. south of Oppdal. Height restriction under railway bridge (3.3 m). GPS: 62.49703, 9.58535

Charges guide

Per pitch incl. 4 persons and electricity NOK 230

No credit cards.

Røros

Håneset Camping

Osloveien, N-7374 Røros (Sør Trøndelag) T: 72 41 06 00.

alanrogers.com/NO2510

At first sight Håneset Camping is unpromising, lying between the main road and the railway, with gritty sloping ground because grass has difficulty growing at this altitude. However, it is the best equipped campsite in Røros, ideal to cope with the often cold, wet weather of this 1,000 m. high plateau. You can expect a warm welcome here and in winter, a picture postcard cover of snow. All 50 unmarked touring pitches have access to electricity (10/16A), with most facilities housed in the main building complex. Walk or cycle from the site to join people from all over Europe visiting the remarkably well preserved mining town of Røros.

Facilities

Heated sanitary facilities provide three separate rooms for each sex, fully equipped with showers on payment. Washing machine and two clothes washing sinks. Huge sitting/TV room and two well equipped kitchens which the owners, the Moen family, share fully with their guests, plus nine rooms for rent. Free WiFi throughout site. Off site: Town centre 20 minutes walk. Fishing 200 m. Bicycle hire 2 km. Golf 3 km.

Open: All year.

Directions

Site is on the Rv 30 leading south from Røros to Os, 3 km. from Røros. GPS: 62.5675, 11.351944

Charges guide

Per unit incl. 2 persons and electricity NOK 200

No credit cards.

Viggja
Tråsåvika Camping

Orkanger, N-7354 Viggja (Sør Trøndelag) T: 72 86 78 22. E: post@trasavika.no

alanrogers.com/NO2500

On a headland jutting into the Trondheimfjord, some 40 km. from Trondheim, Tråsåvika commands an attractive position. For many this compensates for the extra distance into town. The 32 pitches with fjord views (some slightly sloping), all with electricity connections (10/16A), are on an open grassy field at the top of the site, or on a series of terraces below. These run down to the small sandy beach, easily accessed via a gravel service road. To one side, on a wooded bluff at the top of the site, are 19 cabins which are available all year. There are opportunities for boating and fishing from the beach on the site.

Facilities
The neat, fully equipped, sanitary unit includes two controllable hot showers per sex (on payment). Water for touring pitches is also accessed from this block. Hot water on payment in kitchen and laundry which have a hotplate, dish and clothes washing sinks, washing machine and dryer. Shop. Café (sells beer, wine and food, 20/6-30/8). TV/sitting room. Play area. Jetty and boat hire. Free fjord fishing with catches of good sized cod from the shore. Free WiFi covering touring pitches. Off site: Shopping in Orkanger 6 km.

Open: 1 May - 10 September.

Directions
Site is west of Viggja with direct access from E39 between Orkanger and Buvik, 21 km. from E6 and 40 km. west of Trondheim. Use Børsa exit from Trondheim direction off E39 to save toll charges if using Orkanger exit (6 km. detour).
GPS: 63.34686, 9.96234

Charges guide

Per pitch	NOK 190
electricity	NOK 40

Tinn Austbygd
Sandviken Camping

Austbygdevegen 111, N-3650 Tinn Austbygd (Telemark) T: 35 09 81 73. E: post@sandviken-camping.no

alanrogers.com/NO2590

Sandviken is a delightful, family run site in a scenic location, suitable for exploring Hardangervidda. Remote, yet with good access by road, it has its own shingle beach at the head of the beautiful Tinnsjo Lake. It provides 150 grassy, mostly level pitches, many with spectacular views along the lake. Most have electricity (10/16A), and there is an area for tents along the waterfront. Activities on site naturally include swimming, fishing and excellent facilities for launching boats. The modern reception building houses a small shop selling confectionery and essential supplies. Bread can be ordered daily and takeaway food is available.

Facilities
Two heated sanitary blocks include some washbasins in cubicles, showers on payment, sauna, solarium and a dual-purpose disabled/family bathroom and baby changing. Kitchen and laundry rooms (hot water on payment). New, smaller unit with kitchen, TV and dining area and en-suite family rooms adapted for disabled visitors. Motorcaravan services. Reception with kiosk, bar and takeaway snacks. Two playgrounds. TV and games room. Minigolf. Trampoline. Beach volleyball. Mini football. Fishing and watersports. Boat hire.

Open: All year.

Directions
Easiest access is via the Rv 37 from Gransherad along the western side of the lake to its position at the northern end. GPS: 59.98923, 8.81810

Charges guide

Per unit incl. 2 persons and electricity	NOK 195 - 275
extra person	NOK 20
child (4-18 yrs)	NOK 15

Harstad
Harstad Camping

Nesseveien 55, N-9411 Harstad (Troms) T: 77 07 36 62. E: postmaster@harstad-camping.no

alanrogers.com/NO2432

In a delightful setting with fine views, the campsite has space for 120 units as it slopes down to Vågsfjorden with on-site fishing and boating. This well established, popular site near Harstad, provides an excellent base on Hinnøya, the largest island in Norway. Pitches are unmarked but a flat area by the water's edge provides most of the site's 46 electricity hook-ups (16A). These pitches are sought after and a mid-afternoon arrival may gain a level pitch with electricity. Harstad Camping is ideal for those looking for a scenic view and a bustling town nearby with a variety of activities on offer.

Facilities
Two sanitary units, one modern and unisex with showers (10 NOK) and two en-suite WC with washbasins. Older unit is separate sex, each with showers (10 NOK), toilets and washbasins (some in individual cabins for ladies). Room for disabled visitors. Laundry room (token). Kitchen. Reception (08.00-23.00 high season) sells drinks, ices, postcards etc. WiFi (charged). Off site: Grottebadet waterpark 4 km. Shopping centre 2 km. Golf 4 km.

Open: All year.

Directions
Travelling north on road 83, site is well signed on right 3 km. before Harstad. After turning right, turn immediate left and site is 1 km. along tarmac road (site signed from either direction).
GPS: 68.77278, 16.57712

Charges guide

Per unit incl. 6 persons and electricity	NOK 280

FREE Alan Rogers Travel Card
Extra benefits and savings - see page 14

Portugal is the westernmost country of Europe, situated on the Iberian peninsula, bordered by Spain in the north and east, with the Atlantic coast in the south and west. In spite of its relatively small size, the country offers a tremendous variety, both in its way of life and in its history and traditions.

Every year the Algarve is the destination for some ten million sunseekers and watersports enthusiasts, who love its sheltered sandy beaches and clear Atlantic sea. In contrast, the lush hills and forests of central Portugal are home to historic buildings and monuments, in particular the capital city of Lisbon, adjacent to the estuary of the River Tagus. Lisbon's history can still be seen in the Alfama quarter, which survived the devastating earthquake of 1755; at night the city comes alive with vibrant cafés, restaurants and discos. Moving southeast of Lisbon, the land becomes rather impoverished, consisting of stretches of vast undulating plains, dominated by cork plantations. Most people head for Evora, a medieval walled town and UNESCO World Heritage Site. The Minho area in the north is said to be the most beautiful part of Portugal, home to the country's only National Park, and vineyards producing the famous Port wine.

CAPITAL: Lisbon

Tourist Office

Portuguese National Tourist Office

11 Belgrave Square, London SW1X 8PP

Tel: 020 7201 6666

E-mail: info@visitportugal.com

Internet: www.visitportugal.com

Population

10.5 million

Climate

The country enjoys a maritime climate with hot summers and mild winters with comparatively low rainfall in the south, heavy rain in the north.

Language

Portuguese

Telephone

The country code is 00 351.

Money

Currency: The Euro

Banks: Mon-Fri 08.30-11.45 and 13.00-14.45. Some large city banks operate a currency exchange 18.30-23.00.

Shops

Mon-Fri 09.00-13.00 and 15.00-19.00. Sat 09.00-13.00.

Public Holidays

New Year; Carnival (Shrove Tues); Good Fri; Liberty Day 25 Apr; Labour Day; Corpus Christi; National Day 10 June; Saints Days; Assumption 15 Aug; Republic Day 5 Oct; All Saints 1 Nov; Immaculate Conception 8 Dec; Christmas 24-26 Dec.

Motoring

The standard of roads is very variable, even some of the main roads can be very uneven. Tolls are levied on certain motorways (auto-estradas) out of Lisbon, and upon southbound traffic at the Lisbon end of the giant 25th Abril bridge over the Tagus. Parked vehicles must face the same direction as moving traffic.

see campsite map 6

Alvito
Camping Markádia

Barragem de Odivelas, Apdo 17, P-7920-999 Alvito (Beja) T: 284 763 141. E: markadia@hotmail.com

alanrogers.com/PO8350

A tranquil, lakeside site in an unspoilt setting, this will appeal most to those nature lovers who want to 'get away from it all' and to those who enjoy country pursuits such as walking, fishing and riding. There are 130 casual unmarked pitches on undulating grass and sand with ample electricity connections (16A). The site is lit but a torch is required. The friendly Dutch owner has carefully planned the site so each pitch has its own oak tree to provide shade. The open countryside and lake provide excellent views and a very pleasant environment.

Facilities
Four modern, very clean and well equipped toilet blocks are built in traditional Portuguese style with hot water throughout. Washing machines. Motorcaravan services. Bar and restaurant (1/4-30/9). Shop (all year, bread to order). Lounge. Playground. Fishing. Boat hire. Tennis. Riding. Medical post. Car wash. Dogs are not accepted in July/Aug. Facilities and amenities may be reduced outside the main season. Off site: Swimming and boating in the lake.

Open: All year.

Directions
From A2 between Setubal and the Algarve take exit 10 on IP8 (Ferreira and Beja). Take road to Torrao and 13 km. later, 1 km. north of Odivelas, turn right towards Barragem and site is 3 km. after crossing head of reservoir following small signs. GPS: 38.1812, -8.10293

Charges guide
Per unit incl. 2 persons and electricity	€ 21.00 - € 27.00
extra person	€ 6.00

No credit cards.

Beirã-Marvão
Camping Beirã-Marvão Alentejo

Estrada de Castelo de Vide, P-7330-013 Beirã-Marvão (Portalegre) T: 965 084 474.

E: info@camping-beira-marvao.com **alanrogers.com/PO8354**

Beirã-Marvão is a family run campsite close to the Spanish border, in the Serra de São Mamede National Park. This is very much rural camping and the Dutch owners' aim is that the campsite should have negligible impact on the surroundings. After the reception building, a rough track climbs to the hilltop where there are touring pitches on roughly-cut terraces between olive trees. The track then descends to an open field where there are further pitches. There is space for 20 touring units and 10 tents, with 22 electrical connections available; long cables, and possibly levelling blocks, may be needed in places.

Facilities
Modern shower block with spacious, controllable showers, open-style washbasins with cold water only (but hot tap outside). Service washes. Small bar and snack bar (1/5-30/10). Snacks from reception (winter season). Two small pre-cast, no-frills pools – parental supervision of children essential (1/1-31-12). Car hire. Powerful telescope to borrow to study night sky. Bicycle hire. Folding tents and 3 gypsy caravans for rent. Max. 1 dog. WiFi at bar (free). Off site: Riding 3 km.

Open: All year.

Directions
From north at Coimbra take A13-1 east then A13 south past Tomar. Take A23/IP6 (Abrantes) east to exit 15 (Portalegre) on N245 then N246 through Castelo de Vide to Portagem, then as above. From south at Estremoz on A6/IP7, take IP2/E802 north through Portalegre. Follow signs for Marvão and Spain and at roundabout at Portagem turn north as above. GPS: 39.42777, -7.38561

Charges guide
Per unit incl. 2 persons and electricity (6/10A)	€ 18.50
extra person	€ 4.50

Campo Maior
Camping Os Anjos

Estrada da Senhora da Saude, P-7371-909 Campo Maior (Portalegre) T: 268 688 138.

E: info@campingosanjos.com **alanrogers.com/PO8356**

This really is rural Portugal. Set in rolling countryside in a working olive grove, Os Anjos (The Angels) is an ideal spot from which to explore this lesser-known corner of the Alentejo. The white fortified town of Campo Maior is within walking distance and the historic town of Elvas, now a UNESCO World Heritage Site, is a short drive away. Solange and Joris will provide a warm welcome and as much advice as you need on where to go on foot, by bike or by car, with appropriate route sheets. The site has 30 terraced pitches accessed by a circular track, with twelve electrical connections (6A) available.

Facilities
Central toilet block has pre-set showers, some washbasins in cubicles with hot and cold water, and a unit for disabled visitors (which in winter is heated and available to all). Note: the terrain generally might cause problems for wheelchair users. Small bar with seating on terrace and in reception lounge. Small swimming pool. Boules. Bicycle hire. Barbecue evening on Fridays (BYO meat). WiFi throughout (connection fee € 2.50). Off site: Shops, bars and restaurants 1.5 km.

Open: All year.

Directions
Campo Maior is 100 km northeast of Evora. From A6/IP7 at Elvas leave at exit 11 and take N373 to Campo Maior. Then turn southeast following blue signs for 'Parque de Campismo Rural'. Site is on left in 1.5 km. From Spain via A5 at Badajoz, join A6 to exit 11 then as above. GPS: 39.008326, -7.048384

Charges guide
Per unit incl. 2 persons and electricity	€ 16.90 - € 17.20
extra person	€ 3.90

For latest campsite news, availability and prices visit
alanrogers.com

Évora

Orbitur Camping Évora

Estrada de Alcáçovas, Herdade Esparragosa, P-700-703 Évora (Evora) T: 266 705 190.

E: infoevora@orbitur.pt **alanrogers.com/PO8340**

Close to the historic former provincial capital (now a Unesco World Heritage Site), Camping Évora is well located for a short stay to explore the fascinating town and its castle. There is space for 190 touring units, most on level, sandy pitches separated by low hedges and with well developed shade; larger units can pitch on undulating ground beneath tall trees. Electrical connections (6A) are available throughout, although long cables may be needed. Being close to the motorway from Spain to Lisbon, this could also be useful as an overnight stop.

Facilities
Two traditional toilet blocks provide free hot showers, open-style washbasins and British style WCs. No facilities for disabled visitors. Laundry. Motorcaravan services. Small supermarket (Aug only). Bread to order from reception. Bar with snacks and takeaway (15/6-15/9). Swimming pool (1/4-30/9). Tennis. Play area. WiFi throughout (free). Off site: Shops, bars, restaurants, supermarkets nearby. Golf 1 km. Bicycle hire 2 km. Walled town 2 km. Riding 5 km. Fortified town of Elvas 85 km.

Open: All year.

Directions
Évora is 130 km. east of Lisbon. From A2 motorway (Lisbon/Badajoz) leave at exit 5 and take N114 to Évora. Take southern by-pass and at first roundabout turn southwest on N380 road to Alcáçovas. Site is immediately on right. GPS: 38.557294, -7.925863

Charges guide
Per unit incl 2 persons, electricity and water	€ 23.00 - € 35.00
extra person	€ 3.50 - € 5.90

Odemira

Parque de Campismo São Miguel

São Miguel, Odeceixe, P-7630-592 Odemira (Beja) T: 282 947 145. E: camping.sao.miguel@mail.telepac.pt

alanrogers.com/PO8170

Nestled in green hills near two pretty white villages, close to the beautiful Praia Odeceixe (beach) is the attractive camping park São Miguel. The site works on a maximum number of 700 campers and there are no defined pitches; you find your own place under the tall trees. There are ample 6/10A electrical points and the land slopes away gently. The impressive main building with its traditional Portuguese architecture is built around two sides of a large grassy square. There are Lisbon arcade-style verandas to sit under and enjoy a drink, coffee or meal while taking in the view across the square.

Facilities
Two traditional style toilet blocks with British style WCs and free hot showers. Unit for disabled campers but no ramp (a fairly steep step). Washing machines. Shop and self-service restaurant. Bar, snacks and pizzeria (June-Sept). Satellite TV. Playground. Tennis (charged). Swimming pool (charged). Dogs are not accepted. Torches useful. WiFi throughout (free). Off site: Bus service from gate. Numerous walking and cycling tracks in South Alentejo Nature Park. Beach and fishing 4 km.

Open: All year.

Directions
Odemira is on the Atlantic coast 75 km. north of Lagos at the southern tip. Site is south of the town on the N120 just north of the village of Odeceixe and is well signed. GPS: 37.43868, -8.75568

Charges guide
Per unit incl. 2 persons and electricity	€ 22.00 - € 34.70
extra person	€ 4.20 - € 6.75
child (5-10 yrs)	€ 2.50 - € 3.90

Odemira

Zmar Eco Campo

Herdade A de Mateus EN393/1, Sao Salvador, P-7630-011 Odemira (Beja) T: 283690010.

E: reservas@zmar.eu **alanrogers.com/PO8175**

Zmar is an exciting project which was set up in 2009. The site is located near Zambujeira do Mar, on the Alentejo coast. It is a highly ambitious initiative developed along very strict environmental lines. Renewable resources such as locally harvested timber and recycled plastic are used wherever possible and the main complex of buildings is clean-cut and impressive. A terrace overlooks an open-air pool that seems to go on for ever. The 132 pitches are 90 sq.m. and some, mainly for tents or smaller caravans and motorcaravans, benefit from artificial shade. All have 16A electricity. Caravans and wood-clad mobile homes are also available for rent.

Facilities
Eight toilet blocks provide comprehensive facilities, including for children and disabled visitors. Washing machine. Large supermarket. Bar. Restaurant. Crêperie. Takeaway. Outdoor swimming pool (April-Oct). Covered pool and wellness centre (Feb-Dec). Sports field. Games room. Play area, farm and play house. Tennis. Bicycle hire. Activities and entertainment. Mobile homes and caravans for rent. Caravan repair and servicing. The site's own debit card system is used for payment at all facilities. WiFi around central complex (free).

Open: All year (facilities all closed in January).

Directions
Odemira is on the Atlantic coast 75 km. north of Lagos at the southern tip. From the N120 (Odemira-Lagos), at roundabout 3 km. west of Odemira turn west on N393 towards Milfontes. In 6.5 km turn southwest on N393-1 towards Cabo Sardão and Zambujeira do Mar. Site is on the left in 1.6 km. GPS: 37.60422, -8.73142

Charges guide
Per unit incl. 2 or 3 persons and electricity	€ 25.00 - € 37.50

Camping Cheques accepted.

FREE Alan Rogers Travel Card
Extra benefits and savings - see page 14

Albufeira

Camping Albufeira

Estrada Das Ferreiras, P-8200-555 Albufeira (Faro) T: 289 587 629. E: geral@campingalbufeira.net

alanrogers.com/PO8210

The spacious entrance to this site will accommodate the largest of units (watch for severe speed bumps at the barrier). One of the better sites on the Algarve, it has 1,500 touring pitches on fairly flat ground with some terracing, trees and shrubs giving reasonable shade in most parts. There are some marked and numbered pitches of 50-80 sq.m. Winter stays are encouraged with the main facilities remaining open, including a pool. An attractively designed complex of traditional Portuguese-style buildings on the hill, with an unusually shaped pool and two more for children, forms the central area of the site.

Facilities

Very clean toilet blocks include hot showers. Launderette. Very large supermarket. Tabac (English papers). Waiter and self-service restaurants. Pizzeria. Bars. Swimming pools. Satellite TV. Soundproofed disco. Tennis. Playground. Bicycle hire. WiFi over part of site (charged). First aid post with doctor nearby. Car wash. ATM. Car hire. Off site: Beach and fishing 2 km. Golf 5 km.

Open: All year.

Directions

From N125 coast road or N264 (from Lisbon) at new junctions follow N395 to Albufeira. Site is 2 km. on the left. GPS: 37.10639, -8.25361

Charges guide

Per unit incl. 2 persons	€ 20.50 - € 27.00
extra person	€ 5.50
electricity	€ 3.50

Discounts for stays over 30 days (October-May).

Armação de Pêra

Parque de Campismo de Armação de Pêra

P-8365 Armação de Pêra (Faro) T: 282 312 260. E: geral@camping-armacao-pera.com

alanrogers.com/PO8410

A wide attractive entrance leads to a spacious park with a capacity of 1,200 units. You pitch on level grassy sand beneath tall trees that provide some shade, accessed from tarmac and gravel roads. Electricity (6/10A) is available for most pitches. As there are no marked pitches, the site can cater for very large units. The beach is a brisk walk away, as are the shops, bars and restaurants of the small town, and for the less energetic a bus runs from close to the entrance. There is a wide choice of beaches and resorts along this stretch of coast. Albufeira is a busy little resort just a short drive to the east, and bustling Faro and Portimão are also within easy reach.

Facilities

Three traditional sanitary blocks provide British and Turkish style WCs and showers with hot water (on payment). Facilities for disabled campers. Laundry. Supermarket. Self-service restaurant. Three bars (one all year). Swimming and paddling pools (May-Nov; charged July/Aug; no lifeguard). Games and TV rooms. Tennis. Well maintained play area. WiFi on part of site (free). Off site: Bus to town from gate. Bicycle hire 100 m. Beach, fishing and boat launching 1 km. Golf 5 km.

Open: All year.

Directions

Site is west of Albufeira. From A22 Algarve/Spain motorway leave at exit 7 (Alcantarilha) and head east on N125/IC4 to Alcantarilha, turning south on the EN269-1 towards the coast. Site on left on the third roundabout and is also known as Camping Praia de Armação de Pêra. GPS: 37.10947, -8.35329

Charges guide

Per unit incl. 2 persons and electricity	€ 14.00 - € 25.00
extra person	€ 3.00 - € 5.50

Min. stay 3 nights 1/10-31/5.

Budens

Parque de Campismo Quinta dos Carriços

Praia da Salema, Vila do Bispo, P-8650-196 Budens (Faro) T: 282 695 201. E: quintacarrico@gmail.com

alanrogers.com/PO8440

This is an attractive and peaceful valley site with a separate naturist area. A traditional tiled Portuguese-style entrance leads you down a steep incline into this excellent, well maintained site which has a village atmosphere. With continuing improvements, the site has been developed over the years by the Dutch owner. It is spread over two valleys (which are real sun traps), with many of the 500 partially terraced pitches marked and divided by trees and shrubs (oleanders and roses). Others are less well defined among trees. There are 6/16A electricity connections to 270 pitches. A small stream (sometimes dry) meanders through the site.

Facilities

Four modern, spacious sanitary blocks, well tiled with quality fittings, are spotlessly clean. Washbasins with cold water, hot water (on payment) to showers and to some washbasins in cubicles. Washing machine. Excellent facility for disabled campers. Gas supplies. Well stocked shop. Restaurant, bar and takeaway (1/3-15/10 with restricted opening in low season). TV (cable). Games room. Bicycle, scooter, moped and motorcycle hire. WiFi over part of site (charged). Off site: Bus service to town and beach from site. Fishing, golf and beach 1 km.

Open: All year.

Directions

Site is 100 km west of Faro. From A22 (Spain-Algarve) motorway exit 1 head south on N120 to Lagos and turn west following signs for Luz, then Sagres on N125. Turn south to Figuere and Salema (17 km. from Lagos) and immediately left towards Salema. Site is signed and is on right in 600 m. GPS: 37.075427, -8.831338

Charges guide

Per unit incl. 2 persons and electricity	€ 30.40 - € 34.60
extra person	€ 5.65

For latest campsite news, availability and prices visit

alanrogers.com

Lagos

Yelloh! Village Turiscampo

EN125, Espiche, Luz, P-8600-109 Lagos (Faro) T: 282 789 265. E: info@turiscampo.com

alanrogers.com/PO8202

Turiscampo is an outstanding site which has been thoughtfully refurbished and updated since it was purchased by the friendly Coll family in 2003 and the transformation is on-going. The site provides 240 pitches for touring units, mainly in rows of terraces, 197 of which have 6/10A electricity and some have shade. There are 43 deluxe pitches with water and drain. The upper terraces are occupied by 132 bungalows for rent. Just down the road is the fashionable resort of Praia de Luz, with its beach, shops, bars and restaurants. Head west and the road takes you to Sagres and the wild western tip of the Algarve. Portugal's 'Land's End' has remained unspoiled and there are numerous rocky coves and little sandy beaches to explore. The headland at Cabo de São Vicente has a working lighthouse and is well worth a visit, especially at sunset. Head east and you will come to the town of Lagos and beyond that, the whole of the Algarve with its beaches, little villages, fashionable resorts and bustling cities. This is a very good site for families, with wonderful facilities for children and plenty of activities in high season; it is equally ideal for 'snowbirds' to over-winter, with full services maintained throughout the year.

Facilities

Two heated toilet blocks provide outstanding facilities. There is a third facility beneath the pool. Spacious controllable showers. Children and baby room. Facilities for disabled visitors. Dog shower. Laundry facilities. Shop. Gas. Modern restaurant/bar with buffet and mexican-style meals. Pizza bar and takeaway. Swimming pools with terrace and jacuzzi. Aquagym. Wellness facility. Bicycle hire. Entertainment. Miniclub. Two playgrounds. Boules. Archery. Multisports court. Cable TV. Internet and WiFi (partial coverage) on payment. Bungalows to rent. Off site: Praia da Luz village 2.5 km. Beach 2.5 km.

Open: All year.

Directions

Site is 90 km west of Faro. From A22 Spain-Algarve motorway exit 1, follow N120 to Lagos then head west on N125, following signs for Luz. The impressive entrance is 3.8 km. on the right. GPS: 37.10111, -8.73278

Charges guide

Per unit incl. 2 persons and electricity	€ 21.00 - € 42.00
extra person	€ 4.00 - € 7.00
child (3-7 yrs)	free - € 4.00
dog	€ 5.00

Camping Cheques accepted.

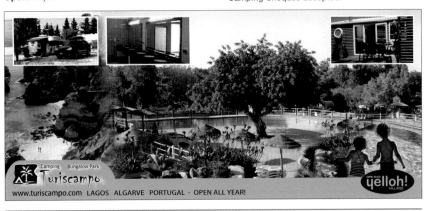

www.turiscampo.com LAGOS ALGARVE PORTUGAL - OPEN ALL YEAR!

Lagos

Orbitur Camping Valverde

Estrada da Praia da Luz, Valverde, P-8600-148 Lagos (Faro) T: 282 789 211. E: infovalverde@orbitur.pt

alanrogers.com/PO8200

Close to the village of Praia da Luz and its beach, this large, well-run site is certainly worth considering for your stay in the Algarve. It has 650 pitches of varying sizes, which are either enclosed by hedges or on open, gently sloping ground. There is good shade in most parts from established trees and shrubs and there are 6/10A electrical connections throughout. The upper terraces are occupied by chalets and mobile homes for rent. Nearby Lagos has shops, bars and restaurants, whilst a short drive away is Sagres and the western extremity of the Algarve with the lighthouse at Cabo de São Vicente.

Facilities

Six large, clean, toilet blocks have controllable hot showers but only cold water to open-style washbasins. Units for disabled campers. Laundry. Motorcaravan services. Supermarket, self-service restaurant and takeaway (1/6-30/9). Shop for basics and small bar/coffee bar in reception (1/10-31/5). Swimming pool (Easter-30/9) with paddling pool. Playground. Tennis. Lounge with TV. Games room. WiFi over part of site (free). Off site: Beach and fishing 1.5 km. Lagos 5 km.

Open: All year.

Directions

Valverde is 90 km west of Faro. From A22 Spain/Algarve motorway leave at exit 1 and follow N120 to Lagos then head west on N125, following signs for Luz. After 2 km. turn south at roundabout to Praia da Luz. Site is on right in 1.3 km. GPS: 37.09973, -8.71744

Charges guide

Per unit incl 2 persons, electricity and water	€ 25.00 - € 39.00
extra person	€ 3.90 - € 6.50

FREE Alan Rogers Travel Card
Extra benefits and savings - see page 14

Olhão

Camping Olhão

Pinheiros de Marim, P-8700 Olhão (Faro) T: 289 700 300. E: parque.campismo@sbsi.pt

alanrogers.com/PO8230

The large, sandy beaches in this area are on offshore islands reached by ferry and are, as a result, relatively quiet. This site, on the edge of town, has around 800 pitches, all with 6A electrical connections available. Its many mature trees provide good shade. The pitches are marked in rows divided by shrubs, although levelling will be necessary in places and the trees make access tricky on some. There is a separate area for tents and places for very large motorhomes. Seasonal units take up one fifth of the pitches, the touring pitches filling up quickly in July and August, so arrive early. The site has a relaxed, casual atmosphere, though there is some subdued noise in the lower area from an adjacent railway. The amenities are also very popular with the local Portuguese who have access to them in high season. The town of Olhão is close by and a bus service runs from near the site entrance to the centre for its shops, bars and restaurants and to the port from where ferries run to the islands and their beaches. Days out could include a visit to the nearby resort of Faro or a trip to Spain for a visit to the shops or a restaurant.

Facilities

Eleven sanitary blocks are adequate, kept clean even when busy and are well sited so that any pitch is close to one. Two blocks have facilities for disabled visitors. Laundry. Excellent supermarket. Kiosk. Restaurant/bar. Café and general room with cable TV. Playgrounds. Swimming pools (all year, charged in season). Tennis courts. Bicycle hire. Internet at reception. Off site: Bus service to nearest ferry at Olhão 50 m. from site. Town and port 1 km. Riding 1 km. Indoor pool, beach and fishing 2 km. Golf 7 km. Faro 12 km.

Open: All year.

Directions

From A22 (Algarve-Spain) take exit 15 for Olhão, turn west on EN125, towards town and almost immediately south into Pinheiros de Marim (site signed). Site is back off the road on the left. Look for very large, white, triangular entry arch. GPS: 37.03528, -7.8225

Charges guide

Per unit incl. 2 persons and electricity	€ 11.60 - € 21.60
extra person	€ 2.40 - € 4.20
child (5-12 yrs)	€ 1.40 - € 2.40

★★★   **Open All Year**

Camping Olhão

Tennis
Football
Bar
Swimming Pool
Restaurant
Bungalows
Mobile Homes

Algarve - Portugal   www.sbsi.pt/camping   © 351 289 700 300

Quarteira

Orbitur Camping Quarteira

Estrada da Fonte Santa, avenida Sá Cameiro, P-8125-618 Quarteira (Faro) T: 289 302 826.

E: infoquarteira@orbitur.pt **alanrogers.com/PO8220**

This is a large, busy, attractive site on undulating ground with some terracing, taking 795 units. On the outskirts of the popular Algarve resort of Quarteira, it is 600 m. from a sandy beach which stretches for a kilometre to the town centre. Many of the unmarked pitches have shade from tall trees. There are 659 electrical connections (10A on the older pitches, 16A on a group of new pitches at the far end of the site). Mobile homes are available to rent and there are others belonging to a tour operator. Like others along this coast, the site encourages long winter stays. A walk along the beach or a cycle (or bus trip) along the road takes you to the little resort of Quarteira where there are shops, bars and restaurants.

Facilities

Five toilet blocks provide British and Turkish style toilets, washbasins with cold water, hot showers plus facilities for disabled visitors. Washing machines. Motorcaravan services. Gas supplies. Supermarket. Self-service restaurant and separate takeaway (June-Sept). Swimming pools (1/3-30/9). General room with bar and satellite TV. Tennis. Open-air disco (high season). WiFi over part of site (free). Off site: Bus from gate to village and to Faro. Beach 600 m. Fishing and bicycle hire (summer) 1 km. Golf 4 km. Spanish border 90 km.

Open: All year.

Directions

Quarteira is 19 km west of Faro. From the A22 (Algarve-Spain) motorway take exit 12 for Quarteira and follow N396 to junction with N125 and turn east (Faro) then south for village of Almancil. In the village take road south to Quarteira. Site is on the left on a stretch of dual carriageway – continue to the roundabout and return. GPS: 37.0673, -8.08712

Charges guide

Per unit incl 2 persons, electricity and water	€ 25.00 - € 39.00
extra person	€ 3.90 - € 6.50

For latest campsite news, availability and prices visit

alanrogers.com

Sagres

Orbitur Camping Sagres

Cerro das Moitas, P-8650-998 Sagres (Faro) T: 282 624 371. E: infosagres@orbitur.pt

alanrogers.com/PO8430

Camping Sagres is a pleasant site at the western tip of the Algarve, close to Cabo de São Vicente, the headland at 'O Fim do Mundo' (Portugal's Lands End), in the wild and unspoilt southwest corner of the country. Tents can pitch anywhere on the lower slopes under the pine trees; higher up there are 52 marked and an unspecified number of unmarked sandy pitches, some terraced, located amongst pine trees that give good shade, including some hardstandings for motorcaravans. There are 6A electrical connections in the upper areas. Nearby are beaches, the town of Sagres and the lighthouse at the Cape.

Facilities

Three spacious toilet blocks are showing signs of wear but provide controllable showers but only cold water to washbasins and sinks. Washing machines and dryers. Motorcaravan services. Supermarket, bar and restaurant (15/6-15/9). Bread orders and basic supplies in reception in low season. TV/games room. Satellite TV in restaurant. Bicycle hire. Playground. Barbecue area. Car wash. WiFi at reception and restaurant (free). Off site: Buses from village, bars and restaurants 1 km. Beach 2.5 km. Sagres 3 km. Lighthouse 5 km. Riding 7 km. Golf 12 km.

Open: All year.

Directions

Sagres is 118 km west of Faro. From A22 (Spain-Algarve) motorway at exit 1 head south on N120 to Lagos and turn west following signs for Luz, then Sagres on N125, then south on N268, to Sagres. Turn west along coast for 2 km. Site is signed off to the right. GPS: 37.02278, -8.94583

Charges guide

Per unit incl 2 persons, electricity and water	€ 23.00 - € 35.00
extra person	€ 3.50 - € 5.90

Camping Cheques accepted.

Arganil

Camping Municipal Arganil

EN17 km. 5, Sarzedo, 3300-432 Arganil (Coimbra) T: 235 205 706. E: camping@cm-arganil.pt

alanrogers.com/PO8330

This peaceful, inland site is attractively located on the edge of the village of Sarzedo, some three kilometres from the town of Arganil. It is on a hill among pine trees above the River Alva where you can paddle, fish or canoe. A spacious and well planned site, it is of a high quality for a municipal and prices are very reasonable! There are no marked pitches but young trees define where you can park and there is space for about 150 units, mainly on a flat sandy grass terrace. There are 75 electrical connections (5-15A). Below the campsite, with gated access from the site via a steepish path and steps, is a municipal swimming pool, a tennis court and a riverside terrace/beach.

Facilities

Sanitary facilities are clean and well maintained, with Turkish and British style WCs, controllable hot showers, washbasins (mainly cold water) in semi-private partitioned cabins and a hairdressing area. Note: the block is on the edge of the top terrace and access from the lower part is via steps or a brisk walk. Shop (July-Sept). Bar. Washing machines. TV and leisure room. WiFi over part of site (free). Off site: Bus service 50 m.

Open: 1 March - 31 October.

Directions

Sarzedo is 45 km. due east of Coimbra, 55 km. by road. From IC2 north of the town take exit 8 onto IP3 Coimbra-Viseu road. Take exit 13 east onto IC6 (N17) towards Arganil and turn south in 15 km. on N324-4 to Sarzedo. Site signed to left at roundabout on village by-pass. GPS: 40.24165, 8.06772

Charges guide

Per unit incl. 2 persons and electricity	€ 10.78 - € 14.94
extra person	€ 1.80 - € 2.01

Figueira da Foz

Orbitur Camping Gala

EN 109 km. 4, Gala, P-3090-458 Figueira da Foz (Coimbra) T: 233 431 492. E: infogala@orbitur.pt

alanrogers.com/PO8090

On sandy terrain under a canopy of pine trees and close to a dune-lined beach, Gala has around 450 pitches with space for about 200 touring units and is well cared for, with plants and shrubs to welcome you. Chalets occupy the area closest to the road, and seasonal units the next; beyond that are some level marked pitches and a large pine-clad area on sloping ground nearest the sea where you choose your own spot between the trees. A short walk from there takes you to a private beach, though you should swim with caution when it is windy. Electrical connections (6/10A) are available throughout.

Facilities

The three toilet blocks have British and Turkish style toilets, washbasins (some with hot water, a few in cabins) and free hot showers. Facilities for babies, children and disabled campers. Laundry. Motorcaravan services. Gas supplies. Supermarket and bar (all year). Restaurant with terrace and takeaway (1/4-30/10). Lounge. Open-air pool (June-Sept). Playground. Tennis. TV. Doctor visits in season. Car wash area. WiFi throughout (free). Off site: Beach 400 m. Sailing 2 km. Bicycle hire 4 km.

Open: All year.

Directions

Site is 130 km south of Porto. From A1 at Coimbra or from coastal motorway A17 take A14 to Figueira da Foz and turn south on N109, cross river and site is on right in 2 km. GPS: 40.11850, -8.85683

Charges guide

Per unit incl 2 persons, electricity and water	€ 24.00 - € 38.00
extra person	€ 3.80 - € 6.40
child (5-10 yrs)	€ 2.00 - € 3.50

Camping Cheques accepted.

FREE Alan Rogers Travel Card
Extra benefits and savings - see page 14

Praia de Mira

Orbitur Camping Mira

Estrada Florestal no 1 km. 2, Dunas de Mira, P-3070-792 Praia de Mira (Coimbra) T: 231 471 234.

E: infomira@orbitur.pt **alanrogers.com/PO8070**

A small, peaceful seaside site set in pinewoods, although these have sadly been depleted by a recent storm, Camping Mira is situated to the south of Aveiro and Vagos, in a quieter and less crowded area. It fronts onto an extensive lake at the head of the Ria Barrinha. The entrance has now been moved to the rear of the site from where a track leads directly to the dunes and a wide quiet beach. The site has around 225 pitches on sandy soil, including some 40 chalets to rent. The pitches are not marked but have trees creating natural divisions. Electrical connections (6A) are available throughout.

Facilities

Two traditional toilet blocks are clean but in need of refurbishment; they provide free hot showers and open-style washbasins, some with hot water. Laundry facilities. Facilities for disabled visitors. Motorcaravan services. Shop, bar, restaurant and takeaway are franchised but should be open all season. TV room. Play area. WiFi throughout (free). Chalets to rent. Off site: Fishing 100 m. Beach 300 m. Lake 300m.

Open: 1 April - 30 September.

Directions

From A17 coastal motorway at exit 12, take the N109 south towards Figuera da Foz. At Mira turn northeast on N334 and follow signs west to Praia de Mira. Site is south of village at the southern end of the lake, on the right. GPS: 40.44519, -8.80198

Charges guide

Per unit incl 2 persons, electricity and water	€ 23.00 - € 35.00
extra person	€ 3.50 - € 5.90

Vagos

Orbitur Camping Vagueira

Rua do Parque Campismo, Gafanha da Boa Hora, P-3840-254 Vagos (Aveiro) T: 234 797 526.

E: infovagueira@orbitur.pt **alanrogers.com/PO8040**

Within easy reach of an extensive beach, hidden behind impressive dunes, Camping Vagueire is a large site shaded under tall pine trees. It can cater for a considerable number of touring units, although pitches are not numbered, on sandy soil with sparse grass; the central area is fairly level and has a large number of seasonal caravans, interspersed with touring pitches, newly marked out by young shrubs or defined by trees. Elsewhere you just find a space on the sloping ground between the trees. Electrical connections (6A) are available throughout, although long leads may be needed. Quiet at other times, the site becomes lively in high season.

Facilities

Seven modern sanitary buildings are kept clean but equipment is fairly basic; mainly British style WCs, open washbasins (some with warm water) and free showers. Facilities for disabled campers. Laundry facilities. Shop, bar/snacks and restaurant (newly franchised when we visited and not yet operating (probably March-Sept). Basic supplies from reception at other times. Outdoor disco (w/ends in high season). Games room. Playground. Tennis (charged). Satellite TV. WiFi throughout (free). Torches useful. Off site: Bus 500 m. River fishing 1 km.

Open: All year.

Directions

Site is 80 km. south of Porto. From A1 motorway, take A25 west to Aveiro. At roundabout at end of motorway turn south on EM592 through Costa Nova along river bank to Praia da Vagueira. Turn left across river and site is on left in 1 km. GPS: 40.55792, -8.74517

Charges guide

Per unit incl 2 persons, electricity and water	€ 19.00 - € 30.00
extra person	€ 2.90 - € 5.20

Cascais

Orbitur Camping Guincho

EN247, Lugar da Areia - Guincho, P-2750-053 Cascais (Lisbon) T: 214 870 450. E: infoguincho@orbitur.pt

alanrogers.com/PO8130

Attractively laid out among low pine trees, some twisted by the wind into interesting shapes, Camping Guincho is located behind sand dunes and a wide, sandy beach. With railway and motorway connection to Lisbon, the site provides a good base for combining a seaside holiday with a site-seeing visit to Portugal's fascinating capital. There is space for well over 400 touring units alongside seasonal pitches and rental accommodation. They are generally small, although larger units can be accommodated. Manoeuvring amongst the trees may be tricky, particularly when the site is full. Electrical connections (6A) are available throughout. Cascais has plenty of shops, supermarkets, bars and restaurants.

Facilities

Three sanitary blocks, one refurbished, are in the older style and could do with some refurbishment, but are clean and tidy. Open-style washbasins with cold water but hot showers. Facilities for disabled visitors. Laundry facilities. Motorcaravan services. Gas. Supermarket. Bar with excellent restaurant and takeaway. Swimming pool (5/4-30/9). General room with TV. Tennis. Playground. Entertainment in summer. WiFi on part of site (free). Chalets to rent. Off site: Riding 500 m. Beach 800 m.

Open: All year.

Directions

Cascais is 33 km. west of Lisbon. From A5 motorway exit 11 take N247 for 2 km. towards Cascais. At roundabout turn west (site signed) to site in 2.5 km. GPS: 38.72117, -9.46667

Charges guide

Per unit incl 2 persons, electricity and water	€ 25.00 - € 39.00
extra person	€ 3.90 - € 6.50
child (5-10 yrs)	€ 2.00 - € 3.50
dog	€ 1.10 - € 2.20

For latest campsite news, availability and prices visit

alanrogers.com

Costa da Caparica

Orbitur Camping Costa da Caparica

Avenida Alfonso de Albuquerque, Quinta de Ste Antonio, P-2825-450 Costa da Caparica (Setubal)

T: 212 901 366. E: infocaparica@orbitur.pt **alanrogers.com/PO8150**

With relatively easy access to Lisbon via the motorway, by bus or even by bus and ferry, this site is situated near a small resort, favoured by the Portuguese themselves, which has all the usual amenities. Of the 440 pitches, 260 are for touring units, although some can only accommodate tents; all have 6A electrical connections available. A row of pitches close to the road can accommodate larger units. In addition, there are 90 permanent caravans and 90 chalets, tents and mobile homes to rent. If you need a site by the sea from which you can visit Lisbon, then this fits the bill.

Facilities
The three toilet blocks have mostly British style toilets, washbasins with cold water and some controllable showers, although these come under pressure when the site is full. Facilities for disabled visitors. Laundry facilities. Motorcaravan services. Supermarket and bar with snacks (23/3-30/9); small shop in reception in low season. Self-service restaurant and takeaway (1/6-20/9). TV room (satellite). Playground. Gas supplies. WiFi over part of site (free). Off site: Bicycle hire 100 m. Bakery 200 m. Supermarket 600 m. Seafront and fishing 1 km.

Open: All year.

Directions
Costa da Caparica is on the coast across the Tagus bridge (toll) from Lisbon. From A2 motorway take exit 1 for Caparica and Trafaria. At 7 km. marker on IC20 turn right (signed Santo Antonio and Trafaria). Site is on the right at the second roundabout. GPS: 38.65595, -9.24107

Charges guide
Per unit incl 2 persons,
electricity and water   € 25.00 - € 39.00
extra person   € 3.90 - € 6.50
Camping Cheques accepted.

Ferreira do Zêzere

Camping Quinta da Cerejeira

Rua D. Maria Fernanda da Mota Cardoso 902, P-2240-333 Ferreira do Zêzere (Santarem) T: **249 361 756**.

E: info@cerejeira.com **alanrogers.com/PO8550**

This is a delightful, small, family-owned venture run by Gert and Teunie Verheij. It is a converted farm (quinta) which has been coaxed into a very special campsite. You pitch where you choose under fruit and olive trees on gently sloping grass below the house or on terraces beyond. There is space for 25 units with 18 electricity connections (6A). It is very peaceful with views of the surrounding green hills from the vine-covered patio above a small swimming pool. A visit to Tomar is highly recommended.

Facilities
The single rustic sanitary building has British style WCs with hot showers and pairs of washbasins in cubicles (cold water only). Washing machine. No facilities for disabled campers. Baker calls daily. Rustic room serves as reception and lounge with library and small kitchen and self-service bar (tea, coffee, soft drinks, bottled beer, wine). Swimming pool with terrace. WiFi in upper part of site (free). Three apartments to rent.

Open: 1 March - 15 October.

Directions
From Lisbon on A1 north take exit 7 onto A23 (Abrantes) then head north on A13 (Tomar) and northeast on N238 to Ferreira do Zêzere. Take N348 (Vila de Rei) and site is signed to left 1 km. from town (do not enter town). From north on A1 south of Coimbra take new A13-1 and A13 (Tomar). At exit 21 take N348 to Ferreira and then as above. GPS: 39.70075, -8.2782

Charges guide
Per unit incl. 2 persons
and electricity   € 17.50 - € 21.05
extra person   € 3.50 - € 4.50

Foz do Arelho

Orbitur Camping Foz do Arelho

Rua Maldonado Freitas, P-2500-516 Foz do Arelho (Leiria) T: **262 978 683**. E: infofozarelho@orbitur.pt

alanrogers.com/PO8480

This is a large and roomy ex-municipal site on the edge of a small seaside town and a short drive from the beach. There is space for about 40 touring units, alongside similar numbers of seasonal caravans and rentals. Pitches are generally on sandy soil, some separated by hedges, others tucked in among the trees; all have access to 6A electricity. This is quite a hilly site and since access to the central complex is uneven and there are no ramps, it is not really a site for disabled visitors. In low season it was all a bit drab, although no doubt it livens up in summer.

Facilities
Three modern sanitary buildings are kept clean but are in need of refurbishment. Seatless British and Turkish style WCs, controllable showers and hot water to some washbasins. Facilities for disabled campers. Laundry facilities. Supermarket, bar/snacks and self-service restaurant, bread to order (all 1/6-30/9). Swimming and paddling pools (1/6-30/9). Club for children (high season). Games room. Playground (supervision needed). Small amphitheatre. Torches useful. WiFi over part of site (free).

Open: All year.

Directions
Site is 100 km. north of Lisbon and 8 km. west of Caldos da Rainha. From the A8 at exit 18, take N360 to Foz do Arelho. Site is well signed and is to left after three roundabouts. GPS: 39.43067, -9.20083

Charges guide
Per unit incl 2 persons,
electricity and water   € 23.00 - € 35.00
extra person   € 3.50 - € 5.90
child (5-10 yrs)   € 2.00 - € 3.50

FREE Alan Rogers Travel Card
Extra benefits and savings - see page 14

Lisboa

Lisboa Camping & Bungalows

Estrada da Circunvalacão, P-1400-061 Lisboa (Lisbon) T: 217 628 200. E: info@lisboacamping.com

alanrogers.com/PO8140

Arriving at this large site in the suburbs of Lisbon, first impressions are good. Beyond the wide entrance with its ponds and fountains, the trees, lawns and flowering shrubs lead up to the attractive swimming pool area. Positive impressions continue: on sloping ground, the site's many terraces are well shaded by trees and shrubs and all 171 touring pitches are on concrete hardstandings with grass and a picnic table. All have 10A electricity connections, water and a drain. There is a huge separate area for tents, and 70 chalet-style bungalows are for hire. Central Lisbon is easily reached by bus with a regular service from near the gate. In the immediate vicinity there are shops, bars and restarants, but most people probably prefer to hop on a bus and go into Lisbon. There you can enjoy the vast choice of dining and retail opportunities the city has to offer, climb up to Castelo do São Jorge or join a tourist bus which enables you to hop off and on again at any of Lisbon's many historic and architectural sites A decent beach is a short drive away, with a wider choice of fine beaches further along the coast.

Facilities

Eight solar-powered toilet blocks are well equipped and kept clean, although in need of some refurbishment. Controllable showers and hot water to open-style washbasins. Facilities for disabled visitors. Launderette. Motorcaravan services. Shop, bar and self-service restaurant with takeaway (all year). Swimming and paddling pools (with lifeguard June-Sept). Tennis. Minigolf. Sports field. Playgrounds. Amphitheatre. Entertainment in high season. Games and TV rooms. Bicycle hire. Minigolf. Booking service for excursions. WiFi in restaurant area (free). Off site: Bus service from site gate to Lisbon city centre (9 km) and to airport. Sailing 5 km. Riding 7 km.

Open: All year.

Directions

Site is west of Lisbon. From A5 motorway (Estoril) leave at exit 3/4 (huge signs to Buraca and Campismo). Site is signed from all directions at these complicated junctions. Enter to the right of the fountain on the tiled road. GPS: 38.72477, -9.20737

Charges guide

Per unit incl. 2 persons and electricity	€ 24.80 - € 34.90
extra person	€ 5.95 - € 7.50
child (6-11 yrs)	€ 2.70 - € 3.80

Camping Cheques accepted.

Nazaré

Orbitur Camping Valado

Rua dos Combatentes do Ultramar 2, Valado, P-2450-148 Nazaré (Leiria) T: 262 561 111.

E: infovalado@orbitur.pt **alanrogers.com/PO8110**

Close to the old, traditional fishing port of Nazaré, which has now become something of a holiday resort with a large sandy beach sheltered by headlands providing good swimming, Valado is on undulating ground under tall pine trees. The sandy soil is soft in places, so motorcaravanners should beware. It can accommodate up to 500 units (of which 200 would be tents) and, apart from some smallish pitches with electricity and water, the bulk of the site is not marked out and can become crowded in high season. Electrical connections (6A) are available throughout, though long leads may be needed.

Facilities

The three toilet blocks have British and Turkish-style WCs, with hot water to showers and some of the open-style washbasins. All was very clean when inspected. Laundry. Motorcaravan services. Gas supplies. Supermarket and bar (15/6-31/8). Swimming pool (1/6-30/9). TV/general room. Playground. Tennis. WiFi in some areas (free). Off site: Bus service outside site. Shops, bars and restaurants, beach with fishing and marina with sailing and watersports in Nazaré 2 km. Bicycle hire 2 km.

Open: All year.

Directions

Nazaré is 130 km north of Lisbon. From A8 motorway at exit 22 head west on N8-4 towards Nazaré. Site is on right just before a new roundabout. GPS: 39.5979, -9.05626

Charges guide

| Per unit incl 2 persons, electricity and water | € 23.00 - € 35.00 |
| extra person | € 3.50 - € 5.90 |

Camping Cheques accepted.

For latest campsite news, availability and prices visit
alanrogers.com

Nazaré

Vale Paraiso Natur Park

EN242, P-2450-138 Nazaré (Leiria) T: 262 561 800. E: info@valeparaiso.com

alanrogers.com/PO8460

A pleasant, well managed site, Vale Paraiso continues to improve. Its reception and amenities buildings create a good impression and a warm welcome is offered. Occupying eight hectares of undulating pine woods, the site has 650 shady pitches, mainly in the valley and on terraces either side. Many are occupied by seasonal units, but there are around 190 marked pitches of varying size with 6/10A electricity available. Others on sandy ground are suitable for tents and there are areas occupied by chalets, canvas bungalows and tepees for rent. Twelve pitches on a terrace below the amenities area have electricity, water and waste water/chemical disposal.

Facilities

Main toilet block has controllable showers, two other blocks have push-button showers. Facilities for disabled visitors. Baby baths. All are kept very clean. Laundry facilities. Motorcaravan services. Small supermarket, restaurant and café/bar with TV. Swimming and paddling pools (1/5-30/9; adults charged in high season). Pétanque. Entertainment for children and evening entertainment in high season. WiFi in amenities area.

Open: All year excl. 20-27 December.

Directions

Nazaré is 130 km north of Lisbon. From A8 motorway exit 22, head west on IC9 to Nazaré then turn north on N242 Marinha Grande road. Site is on left and is well signed from all directions.
GPS: 39.62028, -9.05639

Charges guide

Per unit incl. 2 persons and electricity	€ 20.50 - € 32.40
extra person	€ 3.50 - € 4.95

Outeiro do Louriçal

Campismo O Tamanco

Rua do Louriçal 11, Casas Brancas, P-3105-158 Outeiro do Louriçal (Leiria) T: 236 952 551.
E: tamanco@me.com **alanrogers.com/PO8400**

O Tamanco is a peaceful countryside site, with a homely almost farmstead atmosphere; you will have chickens and geese wandering around and there is a farmyard including goats and pot-bellied pigs. The enthusiastic Dutch owners, Irene and Hans, are sure to give you a warm welcome at this delightful little site. The 65 good sized pitches are separated by cordons of all manner of fruit trees, ornamental trees and flowering shrubs, some on level grassy ground, others tucked away in glades. There is 6/10A electricity to most pitches, although long leads may be needed. Five pitches are suitable for large motorcaravans. There is some road noise on pitches at the front of the site.

Facilities

The single toilet block provides very clean and generously sized facilities including controllable showers, washbasins in cabins. Hot water to all basins and most sinks. Suite for disabled visitors can also be used for families. As facilities are limited they may be busy in peak periods. Laundry facilities. Bar with TV. Restaurant (set Portuguese meals three times weekly in low season, full menu in July/Aug). Roofed patio with fireplace. Internet access. Swimming pool. Wooden chalets and yurts for hire.

Open: 1 March - 31 October.

Directions

Outeiro do Louriçal is 170 km. north of Lisbon. From the A8/A17 (Lisboa-Porto) motorway, take exit 6 for Pombal/Carrico. Take exit for Outeiro onto N342 and O Tamanco is immediately on the left.
GPS: 39.99157, -8.78877

Charges guide

Per unit incl. 2 persons and electricity	€ 20.00 - € 25.00
extra person	€ 5.00

No credit cards.

São Pedro de Moel

Orbitur Camping São Pedro de Moel

Rua Volta do Sete, P-2430 São Pedro de Moel (Leiria) T: 244 599 168. E: infospedro@orbitur.pt

alanrogers.com/PO8100

This very attractive and well kept site is situated under tall pines on the edge of the rather select small resort of São Pedro de Moel. It is a shady and peaceful place in low season, but can be crowded in July and August. There is space for some 400 touring units, including a few small marked pitches; otherwise you choose a place between the trees in one of two large camping areas; one has plentiful 6/10A electrical connections, the other a very limited provision. A few pitches are used for permanent units and an area to one side has 120 chalets and mobile homes, mostly for hire. The sandy beach is a short walk downhill from the site (you can take the car, although parking may be difficult in the town).

Facilities

Four clean toilet blocks (not all opened in low season) have mainly British style toilets, hot showers and mainly open-style washbasins (some with hot water). Washing machines and dryer. Motorcaravan services. Gas supplies. Simple shop (1/10-31/5). Supermarket, restaurant and bar with terrace (1/6-30/9). Pool complex with paddling pool and large slide (1/6-30/9). Satellite TV. Games room. Playground. Tennis. WiFi in some areas (free).

Open: All year.

Directions

São Pedro de Moel is 140 km north of Lisbon. From A8 (auto-estrada do Oeste) at exit 24, take N242 to and through Marinha Grande; site is signed to the right on entering São Pedro de Moel.
GPS: 39.75806, -9.02588

Charges guide

Per unit incl 2 persons, electricity and water	€ 25.00 - € 39.00
extra person	€ 3.90 - € 6.50

Angeiras/Lavra
Orbitur Camping Angeiras

Rua de Angeiras, P-4455-039 Angeiras/Lavra (Porto) T: 229 27 05 71. E: infoangeiras@orbitur.pt

alanrogers.com/PO8033

A pleasant little seaside village, Angeiras has a good beach with the occasional restaurant and bar, a number of shops and a small supermarket. The campsite is close to the heart of the village and is probably the most attractive Orbitur site we have visited. It is well kept and pitches are under trees, separated by neatly trimmed hedges. Manoeuvring larger units might be tricky in places but there are areas which are not marked out where these can find a place under pine trees or in the open. There is space for some 400 touring units among the many seasonal caravans. Electrical connections (6A) available throughout. Chalets and mobile homes available to rent.

Facilities
Three toilet blocks, one recently reconstructed, a second refurbished, are kept very clean; hot water to preset showers but cold water to open-style washbasins. Baby rooms. En-suite units for disabled visitors. Laundry facilities. Motorcaravan services. Small supermarket (15/6-15/9, basic supplies in reception other times). Pleasant bar and excellent restaurant (popular with locals). Swimming and paddling pools (1/6-30/9). Tennis and multisports courts. Sports field. Minigolf. Lounge with TV. Play area. WiFi in area nearest reception (free).

Open: All year.

Directions
Angeiras is just north of Porto. From A1 motorway join A28 north (toll-free from Porto, electronic tolls from north). Leave at exit 12 (Lavra) and follow signs for Angeiras; the site is well signed from the motorway exit. GPS: 41.26718, -8.71996

Charges guide
Per unit incl 2 persons,
electricity and water   € 23.00 - € 35.00
extra person   € 3.50 - € 5.90
Camping Cheques accepted.

Caminha
Orbitur Camping Caminha

EN13 km. 90, Mata do Camarido, P-4910-180 Caminha (Viana do Costelo) T: 258 921 295.

E: infocaminha@orbitur.pt **alanrogers.com/PO8010**

In northern Portugal, close to the Spanish border, this pleasant site is just 200 m. from the beach. It has a peaceful setting in woods alongside the river estuary that marks the border with Spain and on the edge of the little town of Caminha. Of the 262 pitches, just 25 are available for touring with electricity (5/15A Europlug), the remainder are occupied by permanent units and chalets for rent. The site is shaded by tall pines with other small trees marking large sandy pitches. The main site road is surfaced but elsewhere take care not to get trapped in soft sand. Pitching and parking can be haphazard.

Facilities
The clean, well maintained toilet block is modern with British style toilets, open style washbasins and hot showers, plus beach showers. Facilities for disabled visitors and babies. Laundry facilities. Motorcaravan services. Supermarket, bar with satellite TV (1/6-30/9). Restaurant and takeaway (1/6-15/9). Bicycle hire. Entertainment in high season. Charcoal barbecues are permitted. Off site: Beach and fishing 100 m. Bus service 800 m. Kayak excursions. Birdwatching.

Open: All year.

Directions
From the north, turn off the main coast road (N13-E50) just after camping sign at end of embankment alongside estuary, 1.5 km. south of ferry. From the south on N13 turn left at Hotel Faz de Minho at start of estuary and follow for 1 km. through woods to site. GPS: 41.86635, -8.85844

Charges guide
Per unit incl. 2 persons
and electricity   € 22.60 - € 51.50
extra person   € 3.50 - € 5.90

Campo do Gerês
Parque de Campismo de Cerdeira

Rua de Cerdeira 400, P-4840 030 Campo do Gerês (Braga) T: 253 351 005. E: info@parquecerdeira.com

alanrogers.com/PO8370

Located in the Peneda-Gerês National Park, amidst spectacular mountain scenery, this excellent site offers modern facilities in a truly natural area. The national park is home to all manner of flora, fauna and wildlife, including the roebuck, wolf and wild boar. The well fenced, professional and peaceful site offers 186 good sized, unmarked, mostly level, grassy pitches in a shady woodland setting. Electricity (5/10A) is available for the touring pitches, though some long leads may be required. A very large timber complex, tastefully designed, provides a superb restaurant with a comprehensive menu.

Facilities
Three very clean sanitary blocks provide mixed style WCs, controllable showers and hot water. Good facilities for disabled visitors. Laundry. Gas supplies. Shop. Restaurant/bar. Outdoor pool (15/6-15/9). Playground. TV room (satellite). Medical post. Good tennis courts. Minigolf. Adventure park. Car wash. Barbecue areas. Torches useful. English spoken. Attractive bungalows to rent. WiFi in reception/bar area. Off site: Fishing, riding and bicycle hire 800 m.

Open: All year.

Directions
From north, N103 (Braga-Chaves), turn left at N205 (7.5 km. north of Braga). Follow N205 to Caldelas Terras de Bouro and Covide where site is signed to Campo do Gerês. An eastern approach from N103 is for the adventurous but with magnificent views over mountains and lakes. GPS: 41.7631, -8.1905

Charges guide
Per unit incl. 2 persons
and electricity   € 13.80 - € 28.00
extra person   € 3.70 - € 5.90

For latest campsite news, availability and prices visit

alanrogers.com

Póvoa de Varzim

Orbitur Camping Rio Alto

EN13 km. 13 Rio Alto-Est, Estela, P-4570-275 Póvoa de Varzim (Porto) T: 252 615 699.

E: inforioalto@orbitur.pt **alanrogers.com/PO8030**

This site makes an excellent base for visiting Porto which is some 35 km. south of Estela. It has around 700 pitches on sandy terrain and is next to what is virtually a private beach. There are some hardstandings for caravans and motorcaravans and electrical connections to most pitches (5/15A long leads may be required). The area for tents is furthest from the beach and windswept, stunted pines give some shade. There are arrangements for car parking away from camping areas in peak season. There is a quality restaurant, a snack bar and a large swimming pool across the road from reception.

Facilities

Four refurbished and well equipped toilet blocks have hot water. Laundry facilities. Facilities for disabled visitors. Gas supplies. Motorcaravan services. Car wash. Shop (1/6-15/9). Restaurant (1/6-15/9). Bar, snack bar (all year). Swimming pool (1/6-30/9). Tennis. Playground. Games room. Surfing. TV. First-aid post. Evening entertainment twice weekly in season. Bicycle hire can be arranged by reception. WiFi. Off site: Fishing 200 m. Golf 700 m.

Open: All year.

Directions

From A28 (Porto), leave at exit 18 (Fao/Apuila). At roundabout take third exit, N13 (Póvoa de Varzim) for 2.5 km. At Hotel Contriz, turn right (narrow cobbled road). Signs in 2 km. GPS: 41.44504, -8.75767

Charges guide

Per unit incl. 2 persons and electricity	€ 19.30 - € 28.50
extra person	€ 3.70 - € 6.40

Camping Cheques accepted.

Ribas

Camping Quinta Valbom

Quintã, P-4890-505 Ribas (Braga) T: 253 653 048. E: info@quintavalbom.nl

alanrogers.com/PO8377

Anyone who likes a simple, well run campsite in the depths of the countryside will love Quinta Valbom. Surrounded by wooded slopes with mountains in the distance, the site has been created from a deserted wine-producing farmstead by Dutch owners Els and Herman. It is primarily a place for campers; there are 30 pitches, all with 10A electricity available, on several terraces reached by a steep cobbled road. Those on the upper terraces are suitable only for tents. There is space for nine caravans (max. length 6 m) and one motorcaravan (Herman will meet caravanners and tow you to your pitch).

Facilities

Modern little toilet block tucked away behind a remnant of an old stone corn store; hot water to preset showers and open-style washbasins. Washing machine. Rustic bar in former adega (wine-making cellar), opening onto an attractive terrace with amazing views. Set meals which Els provides twice or three times a week (all season, subject to demand). Delightful little swimming pool. Information about excursions. Contact site about dogs (max. 3 on site). WiFi in bar and on terrace (free). Off site: Shop, bar and restaurant within about 2 km. Others and garage in Gandarela de Basto 3 km. Wide choice plus several supermarkets in Fafe 34 km. Historic Guimarães 51 km. Braga 70 km.

Open: April - September.

Directions

From west leave at exit 11, join N206 for 13 km. east to Gandarela. Just before tunnel under motorway, turn right then sharp right (Ribas). From east, take exit 12 (N206 west for 8 km). and turn left and right after going under motorway. Ignore sat nav: follow site signs. At chapel turn left to cemetery. Caravans MUST stop here and phone site to be towed. If no reply, phone: 912 715 531 or 915 135 762. Others turn left (Paço), taking right fork. In 600 m. turn left (very steep climb), pass two houses, turn right then left to site (steep slope). GPS: 41.46166, -8.01095

Charges guide

Per unit incl. 2 persons and electricity	€ 22.75 - € 26.70

Viana do Castelo

Orbitur Camping Viana do Castelo

Rua Diogo Alvares, Cabedelo, P-4900-161 Viana do Castelo (Viana do Costelo) T: 258 322 167.

E: infoviana@orbitur.pt **alanrogers.com/PO8020**

This site in northern Portugal is worth considering as it has the advantage of direct access, via a gate in the fence (locked at night), to a large and excellent soft sand beach (200 m) which is popular for windsurfing. There are 225 pitches on three wide terraces with easy access, 150 of these with electricity (long leads may be needed). Some flat, good sized pitches are numbered and reserved for caravans and motorcaravans but with little shade. The large grass area for tents has more shade. It could become crowded in July/August. A pleasant restaurant terrace overlooks the pool.

Facilities

Toilet facilities are in two blocks, both with open style washbasins and hot showers. Facilities for disabled visitors. Baby changing. Laundry. Motorcaravan services. Gas supplies. Supermarket and bar (23/3-15/9). Small restaurant with terrace and takeaway (1/6-15/9). Open-air pool (23/3-30/9). Reading room with TV, video and fireplace. Playground. Children's club (July/Aug). First-aid post. WiFi in bar area. Off site: Beach 200 m.

Open: 23 March - 30 September.

Directions

On N13 coast road driving north to south drive through Viana do Castelo and over estuary bridge. Turn immediately right off N13 (Cabedelo and the sea). Site is 3rd campsite signed, the other two are not recommended. GPS: 41.67866, -8.82637

Charges guide

Per unit incl. 2 persons and electricity	€ 25.40 - € 56.70
extra person	€ 3.90 - € 6.50

FREE Alan Rogers Travel Card
Extra benefits and savings - see page 14

Slovakia is a landlocked state in the heart of Europe, consisting of a narrow strip of land between the spectacular Tatra Mountains and the River Danube. Picturesque, there are historic castles, evergreen forests, rugged mountains, cave formations, and deep lakes and valleys.

Slovakia has much to offer the visitor, including the Tatra Mountains with their rugged peaks, deciduous forests, waterfalls and lakes. Southern and eastern Slovakia is mainly a lowland region and home to many thermal springs, Bardejov is a medieval town with a 14th-century church and a therapeutic spa nearby. There is a strong Hungarian influence in this area and much of its history and culture can be seen in Kosice with its Gothic cathedral, theatres and archaeological excavations.

Slovakia has over five thousand caves, twelve are open to the public and have their own unique characteristics. Cruises are possible through the Domica Cave, while Belianska Cave hosts summer concerts. The capital, Bratislava, spreads along both banks of the Danube and is popular with visitors, yet still retains much of its charm. The old town and castle are among the most interesting parts, and there is a wealth of galleries and museums.

CAPITAL: Bratislava

Tourist Office
Czech & Slovak Tourist Centre
16 Frognal Parade,
Finchley Road,
London NW3 5HG
Tel: 020 7794 3263 Fax: 020 7794 3265
E-mail: info@czechtravel.co.uk
Internet: www.slovakiatourism.sk

Population
5.4 million

Climate
Cold winters and mild summers. Hot summers
and some rain in the eastern lowlands.

Language
Slovak

Telephone
The country code is 00 421.

Money
Currency: The Koruna
Banks. Mon-Fri 08.00-13.00 and 14.00-17.00.

Shops
Mon-Fri 09.00-12.00 and 14.00-18.00. Some
remain open at midday. Sat 09.00-midday.

Public Holidays
New Year; Easter Mon; May Day; Liberation Day
8 May; Saints Day 5 July; Festival Day 5 July;
Constitution Day 1 Sept; All Saints 1 Nov;
Christmas 24-26 Dec.

Motoring
A full UK driving licence is acceptable. The
major route runs from Bratislava via Trencin,
Banska, Bystrica, Zilina and Poprad to Presov.
A windscreen sticker which is valid for a year
must be purchased at the border crossing for
use on certain motorways. Vehicles must be
parked on the right.

see campsite map 8

Brezno

Camping Sedliacky Dvor

Hlinik 7, SK-97701 Brezno (Banská Bystrica) T: 911078303. E: info@sedliackydvor.com

alanrogers.com/SK4949

Sedliacky Dvor, a small Dutch-owned site, is friendly and welcoming. Its six hectares only allows for 30 pitches on well kept, grassy lawns (slightly sloping), some in the shade of mature trees, and 21 with 10A electricity. From most pitches there are beautiful views over the green and hilly Slovakian countryside and since the site is compact, it is easy to connect with the welcoming owners and other camp guests. Daily activities include mushrooming and going to a local pub (by bus!). The toilet blocks are small, but were clean and fresh during our visit. This campsite is in the heart of Slovakia and an ideal base to explore the Low Tatra mountains, or make scenic day trips.

Facilities

One small, well maintained toilet block with washbasins and showers, a new second block open July/Aug. Laundry. Kitchen. Small bar. Playing field. Volleyball. Swimming pond with natural filtering. WiFi throughout (free). Off site: Fishing 1 km. Skiing 10 km. Bicycle hire 12 km. Riding and golf 15 km. Several ski resorts. National Parks. Low Tatra mountains.

Open: 15 April - 31 October (accommodation all year).

Directions

From Brezno, follow the signs towards Tisovec on road 72 (formerly 530). Drive into Rohozná and follow the campsite signs. GPS: 48.795033, 19.7287

Charges guide

Per unit incl. 2 persons	
and electricity	€ 17.00 - € 18.25
extra person	€ 3.75
child (4-15 yrs)	€ 2.75
dog	€ 1.00

Cerovo

Camping Lazy

Duchenec 163, SK-96252 Cerovo (Banská Bystrica) T: 090 859 0837. E: info@minicamping.eu

alanrogers.com/SK4955

Lazy is a real mini site of ten hectares and only 15 pitches (ten with 4/6A electricity). This means pitches are up to 300 sq.m. or more and there are panoramic views over the sloping countryside. Pitches are off one meandering, gravel access lane, some with shade to the back. Lazy is a working farm, more or less in the middle of nowhere. This makes it ideal for nature lovers (deer may be seen by day or night), with several marked and unmarked walking routes available. A great site for exploring the Slovakian countryside. Activities on site include goat milking, fishing and camp fires.

Facilities

Good, clean toilet block with washbasins and hot showers. Laundry facilities. Fridge. Drinks available. Small paddling pool for youngsters. Walking routes available. Off site: Restaurant 8 km.

Open: 1 May - 30 September.

Directions

The site is 8 km. from Cerovo. Use the 75 road and turn north towards Zvolen in Cebovce. After 9 km. there is a small wooden sign to the right. Turn left here and follow to the site. GPS: 48.251818, 19.216939

Charges guide

Per unit incl. 2 persons	
and electricity	€ 17.50 - € 21.00
extra adult	€ 2.50
child (over 6 yrs)	€ 2.00
dog	€ 0.40

Levoca

Autocamping Levocská Dolina

Kovácová vila 2, SK-05401 Levoca (Presov) T: 053 451 2705. E: rzlevoca@pobox.sk

alanrogers.com/SK4980

According to the owner, Mr Rusnák, this three-hectare campsite is one of the top ten sites in Slovakia and we agree. The site forms part of a restaurant and pension business and the good value restaurant is welcoming. The entrance is attractively landscaped with varieties of shrubs and colourful flowers and the whole site looks well cared for. There are 60 pitches for tourers, 29 with 10A electricity connections. On grassy fields with views of the mountains, there is some terracing. The main road runs steeply uphill and then continues on grass roads. This may cause larger units some difficulty in bad weather.

Facilities

Good, partly refurbished toilet block (hot water variable) with British style toilets, open washbasins and controllable, hot showers (free). Campers' kitchen. Sauna. Whirlpool. Bar/restaurant. Basic playground. WiFi in reception. Torch useful. Off site: Lake with pedalo hire 300 m. Dobsinska Ice Caves and Slovakian Paradise. Town of Levoca.

Open: All year.

Directions

From Liptovsky Mikulás, take the E50 road east towards Levoca. In Levoca follow site signs. Site is 3 km. north of the town. GPS: 49.04984, 20.58723

Charges guide

Per unit incl. 2 persons	
and electricity	€ 14.30 - € 15.45
extra person	€ 3.10
child	€ 2.00
dog	€ 1.40

For latest campsite news, availability and prices visit

alanrogers.com

Trencin

Autocamping Trencin

Na Ostrove, P.O. Box 10, SK-91101 Trencin (Trencin) T: 032 743 4013. E: autocamping.tn@mail.pvt.sk

alanrogers.com/SK4920

Trencin is an interesting town with a long history and is dominated by the partly restored castle which towers high above. The small site with room for 30 touring units (all with electricity, ten hardstandings) and rooms to let, stands on an island about one kilometre from the town centre opposite a large sports complex. Pitches occupy a grass and gravel area surrounded by bungalows, although when the site is busy, campers park between and almost on top of the bungalows. The castle is high on one side and woods and hills are on the other side, with some pitches enjoying good views of the castle. There is some rail noise. This is a friendly, neat and tidy site with German spoken during our visit.

Facilities
Toilet block is old but tiled and clean with hot water to washbasins (in cabins with curtains) and showers (doors and curtains) under cover but not enclosed. Hot water for dishwashing and laundry. Electric cookers, fridge/freezer, tables and chairs. Little shade. Bar in high season. Boating and fishing in river. Off site: Restaurants 200 m. Shops 300 m. Tennis, indoor and outdoor swimming pools within 400 m.

Open: 1 May - 15 September.

Directions
Initially follow signs for 61 Zilina and having crossed the river, bear left. Turn left at first main traffic lights, under the railway and left again. Then turn right after the stadium. Site is over the canal on the left. GPS: 48.88327, 18.04067

Charges guide
Per unit incl. 2 persons and electricity	€ 21.00
extra person	€ 5.50
child (6-12 yrs)	€ 2.70

No credit cards.

Liptovsky Trnovec

Mara Camping

SK-03222 Liptovsky Trnovec (Zilina) T: 044 559 8458. E: info@maracamping.sk

alanrogers.com/SK4915

This is a bustling Slovakian site beside the Liptovská Mara reservoir, also close to the Tatra Mountains which are popular for climbing, hiking and mountain biking. The lake can be used for sailing, surfing, boating and pedaloes, and some of this equipment may be rented on the site. Bicycles are also available for hire. There are 250 pitches, 125 for tents and 125 for touring units all with 14A electricity. With tarmac access roads, the level pitches are on a circular, grassy field and as pitching is rather haphazard, the site can become crowded in high season. Mature trees provide some shade, but in general this is an open site. English is spoken.

Facilities
Two good modern toilet blocks have British style toilets, washbasins in cabins and showers. Facilities for disabled visitors. Laundry and kitchen. Motorcaravan service. Shop. Bar with covered terrace and takeaway service. Good adventure playground. Indoor and outdoor pools. Fishing. Bicycle hire. Canoe hire, flyboard, jet ski and boat rental. Boat tours. Riding. Sailing. Games room. Beach. WiFi. Off site: Restaurant 300 m. New Tatralandia Aqua Park nearby. Walking and climbing in the Tatra Mountains.

Open: 17 April - 30 September.

Directions
From E50 road take exit for Liptovsky Mikulás and turn left towards Liptovsky Trnovec on 584 road. Continue alongside the lake to site on the left. GPS: 49.111135, 19.545946

Charges guide
Per unit incl. 2 persons and electricity	€ 22.00
extra person	€ 10.00
child (3-15 yrs)	€ 3.50
dog	€ 2.00

Martin

Autocamping Turiec

Kolonia hviezda 92, SK-03608 Martin (Zilina) T: 043 428 4215. E: recepcia@autocampingturiec.sk

alanrogers.com/SK4910

Turiec is situated in northeast Slovakia, 1.5 kilometres from the small village of Vrutky, four kilometres north of Martin, at the foot of the Lucanska Mala Fatra mountains and with castles nearby. This good site has views towards the mountains and is quiet and well maintained. Holiday activities include hiking in summer, skiing in winter, both downhill and cross-country. There is room for about 30 units on slightly sloping grass inside a circular tarmac road with some shade from tall trees. Electrical connections (6A) are available for all places. You will receive a friendly welcome from Viktor Matovcik and his wife Lydia.

Facilities
One acceptable sanitary block to the side of the camping area, but in winter the facilities in the bungalow at the entrance are used. Cooking facilities. Badminton. Rest room with TV. Small games room. Covered barbecue. WiFi. Off site: Shop outside entrance. Swimming pool 1.5 km.

Open: All year.

Directions
Site is signed from E18 road (Zilina-Martin) in the village of Vrutky, 3 km. northwest of Martin. Turn south on the bend and follow signs to Martinské Hole. GPS: 49.108492, 18.899467

Charges guide
Per unit incl. 2 persons and electricity	€ 15.20 - € 17.60
extra person	€ 4.30
child (6-10 yrs)	€ 2.60
dog	€ 0.70 - € 1.30

FREE Alan Rogers Travel Card
Extra benefits and savings - see page 14

Námestovo

Autocamping Stara Hora

Oravska Priehrada, SK-02901 Námestovo (Zilina) T: 043 552 2223. E: camp.s.hora@mail.t-com.sk

alanrogers.com/SK4905

Stara Hora has a beautiful location on the Orava artificial lake. It is in the northeast of Slovakia in the Tatra Mountains and attracts visitors from all over Europe which creates a happy and sometimes noisy atmosphere. The site has its own pebble beach with a large grass area behind it for sunbathing. Autocamping Stara Hora is on steeply sloping ground with 160 grassy pitches, all for touring units and with 10A electricity. The lower pitches are level and have good views over the lake, pitches at the top are mainly used by tents. The lake provides opportunities for fishing, boating and sailing and the area is good for hiking and cycling and in winter, it is a popular skiing area.

Facilities

The modern toilet block has British style toilets, open washbasins and controllable hot showers (free). It could be pressed in high season and hot water to the showers is only available from 07.00-10.00 and from 19.00-22.00. Shop for basics. Bar and lakeside bar. Small restaurant. Basic playground (new playground planned). Pedalo, canoe and rowing boat hire. Waterskiing. Fishing (with permit). Torch useful. Off site: Slanica Island.

Open: May - September.

Directions

From Ruzomberok take E77 road north towards Trstena. Turn left in Tvrdosin on the 520 road towards Námestovo. Site is on the right.
GPS: 49.359333, 19.555

Charges guide

Per unit incl. 2 persons	
and electricity	€ 12.00 - € 13.50
extra person	€ 3.00
child (4-10 yrs)	€ 2.00
dog	€ 1.50

Turany

Autocamping Trusalová

SK-03853 Turany (Zilina) T: 043 429 2636. E: trusalova@gmail.com

alanrogers.com/SK4900

Autocamping Trusalová is situated right on the southern edge of the Malá Fatra National Park, northeast of the historic town of Martin which has much to offer to tourists. The site is behind reception on a slight slope. Surrounded by trees with a stream rushing along one side, pitches are grass from a hard road with room for about 150 units and there are some bungalows. A quiet, orderly and pleasant campsite. Information on the area is available from reception, and this site is ideal for those wishing to explore this beautiful region. Paths from the site lead into the Park making it an ideal base for walkers and serious hikers who wish to enjoy this lovely region.

Facilities

Old, but clean and acceptable, toilet provision including hot water in washbasins, sinks and showers. Motorcaravan services. Covered barbecue area. TV lounge. Playground. Volleyball. Football. Outdoor chess board. Bicycle hire. Off site: Bar just outside site. Restaurants 500 m. and 1 km. Shops in the village 3 km.

Open: 1 June - 15 September.

Directions

Turn north between the Auto Alles car dealer and the Restaurica of the same name on road 18/E50 near the village of Turany to campsite.
GPS: 49.13833, 19.05000

Charges guide

Per unit incl. 2 persons	
and electricity	€ 14.50
extra person	€ 2.50
child	€ 1.25
dog	€ 1.60

No credit cards.

For latest campsite news, availability and prices visit

alanrogers.com

What Slovenia lacks in size it makes up for in exceptional beauty. Situated between Italy, Austria, Hungary and Croatia, it has a diverse landscape with stunning Alps, rivers, forests and the warm Adriatic coast.

Mt. Triglav is at the heart of the snow-capped Julian Alps, a paradise for lovers of the great outdoors, with opportunities for hiking, rafting and mountaineering. From the Alps down to the Adriatic coast, the Karst region is home to the famous Lipizzaner horses, vineyards, and a myriad of underground caves, including the Postojna and Skocjan caves. The tiny Adriatic coast has several bustling beach towns including Koper, Slovenia's only commercial port, whose 500 years of Venetian rule is evident in its Italianate style. Ljubljana, one of Europe's smallest capitals, with beautiful Baroque buildings, lies on the Ljubljanica river, spanned by numerous bridges, including Jože Plečnik's triple bridge. The old city and castle sit alongside a thriving commercial centre. Heading eastwards, the hilly landscape is dotted with monasteries, churches and castles, including the 13th-century Zuzemberk castle, one of Slovenia's most picturesque. The Posavje region produces cviček, a famous blend of white and red wines.

CAPITAL: Ljubljana

Tourist Office
Slovenian Tourist Board Office
10 Little College Street
London SW1P 3SH
Tel: 0870 225 5305
Fax: 020 722 5277
E-mail: london@slovenia.info
Internet: www.slovenia.info

Population
2 million

Climate
Warm summers, cold winters with snow
in the Alps.

Language
Slovene, with German often spoken
in the north and Italian in the west.

Telephone
The country code is 00 386.

Money
Currency: The Euro. Banks: Mon-Fri
08.30-16.30 with a lunch break 12.30-14.00,
plus Saturday mornings 08.30-11.30.

Public Holidays
New Year; Culture Day 8 Feb; Easter Monday;
Resistance Day 27 Apr; Labour Day 1-2 May;
National Day 25 Jun; People's Day 22 July;
Assumption; Reformation Day 31 Oct; All Saints
Day; Christmas Day; Independence Day 26 Dec.

Motoring
A small, but expanding network of motorways.
A 'vignette' system for motorway travel is in place.
The cost is around € 35 (for a six month vignette)
and they can be purchased at petrol stations
and DARS offices in Slovenia and neighbouring
countries near the border. Winter driving
equipment (winter tyres or snow chains) is
mandatory between 15 Nov and 15 March.
By law, you must have your headlights on
at all times, while driving in Slovenia. You are
also required to carry a reflective jacket, a warning
triangle and a first aid kit in the vehicle. Do not
drink and drive – any trace of alcohol in your
system will lead to prosecution.

see campsite map 4

Bled

Camping Bled

Kidriceva 10c SI, SLO-4260 Bled T: 045 752 000. E: info@camping-bled.com

alanrogers.com/SV4200

Camping Bled is situated on the western tip of Lake Bled. The waterfront here has a small public beach, immediately behind which runs a gently sloping narrow wooded valley. There are wonderful views across the lake towards its famous island. Pitches at the front, used mainly for overnighters, are now marked, separated by trees and enlarged, bringing the total number to 280. All are on gravel/grass with 16A electricity. A railway line passes close by but it is only a local line with few trains and they do not disturb the peacefulness of the site. Being on the edge of the Triglav National Park with its magnificent mountain scenery, Bled is a paradise for walking and mountain biking.

Facilities

Toilet facilities in five blocks are of a high standard (with free hot showers). Three blocks are heated. Private bathrooms for rent. Solar energy used. Laundry facilities. Motorcaravan services. Fridge hire. Supermarket. Restaurant. Play area and children's zoo. Games area. Trampolines. Organised activities in July/Aug including children's club, excursions and sporting activities. Mountain bike tours. Live entertainment. Fishing. Bicycle hire. Free WiFi over site. Off site: Riding 3 km. Golf 5 km. Within walking distance of town.
Open: 1 April - 15 October.

Directions

From the town of Bled drive along south shore of lake keeping to the right, to its western extremity (some 2 km) to the site. Site is well signed. GPS: 46.36155, 14.08075

Charges guide

Per unit incl. 2 persons	
and electricity	€ 22.30 - € 30.30
extra person	€ 9.40 - € 13.40
child (7-13 yrs)	€ 6.58 - € 9.38
dog	€ 3.00

Bohinjska Bistrica

Camping Danica Bohinj

Triglavska 60, SLO-4264 Bohinjska Bistrica T: 045 721 702. E: info@camp-danica.si

alanrogers.com/SV4250

For those wishing to visit the famous Bohinj valley, which stretches like a fjord right into the heart of the Julian Alps, Danica Bohinj is an ideal site lying in the valley 3 km. downstream of Lake Bohinjsko. It is spacious, stretching from the main road to the banks of the Sava river, on a flat meadow set in natural woodland. This excellent site has 165 pitches, 145 for touring units (all with 16A electricity), and forms an ideal base for the many sporting activities the area has to offer. Reception is well supplied with maps and tourist information as well as helpful advice as to the state of the various mountain trails.

Facilities

Three good toilet blocks with open plan washbasins and hot showers. Facilities for disabled visitors. Laundry facilities. Motorcaravan services. Bar. Café. Fresh bread (July/Aug). Tennis. Fishing. Badminton. Volleyball. Cross-country skiing from site. Bicycle hire. Free WiFi over site. Excursions in the Triglavski National Park. Off site: Shop (5 minutes walk). Four ski resorts. Riding 6 km. Canoeing, kayaking, rafting and numerous walking and mountain bike trails.
Open: All year.

Directions

Driving from Bled to Bohinj, in Bohinjska Bistrica stay on main road (it goes to the right). Site is 200 m. on the right-hand (north) side of the road. GPS: 46.27335, 13.94868

Charges guide

Per unit incl. 2 persons	
and electricity	€ 21.00 - € 29.20
extra person	€ 8.50 - € 12.60
child (7-14 yrs)	€ 6.40 - € 9.50
dog	€ 2.80

Less 10% for stays over 7 days.

Bovec

Camping Polovnik

Ledina 8, SLO-5230 Bovec T: 053 896 007. E: kamp.polovnik@siol.net

alanrogers.com/SV4280

Camping Polovnik is a small site set in a circular field with trees in the centre, providing useful shade, and an open part to one side. There are 50 unmarked pitches (45 for tourers) all with 16A electricity, off a circular, gravel access road. To the back of the site is a separate field for groups. All pitches have good views of the surrounding mountains. This site is useful as a stopover on your way to the Postojna Caves, the Slovenian Riviera or Italy, and for touring the local area with kayaking, rafting and canoeing possible. At the front of the site are a little bar and restaurant (not connected).

Facilities

One well maintained toilet block with British style toilets, open style washbasins with cold water only and preset hot showers (€ 0.50 token). Washing machine, dryer. Motorcaravan services. Play area. Free WiFi over site. Off site: Restaurant at entrance. Fishing 1 km. Bovec town. Paragliding. Zip wire. Rafting. Canyoning.
Open: 1 April - 16 October.

Directions

Bovec is 35 km. northeast of Udine (Italy). Site is south of town and well signed on the main 203 road. GPS: 46.33622, 13.55837

Charges guide

Per unit incl. 2 persons	
and electricity	€ 21.00 - € 25.00
extra person	€ 7.50 - € 8.50
child (7-14 yrs)	€ 6.00 - € 6.80

For latest campsite news, availability and prices visit

alanrogers.com

Camping Terme Catez

Topliska cesta 35, SLO-8251 Catez ob Savi T: 074 936 700. E: info@terme-catez.si

alanrogers.com/SV4415

Terme Catez is part of the modern Catez thermal spa, which includes very large and attractive indoor (31°C) and outdoor swimming complexes, both with large slides and waves. The campsite has 450 pitches, with 190 places for tourers, arranged on one large, open field, with some young trees – a real sun trap – and provides level, grass pitches which are numbered by markings on the tarmac access roads. All have 10A electricity connections. Although the site is ideally placed for an overnight stop when travelling on the E70, it is well worthwhile planning to spend some time here to take advantage of the excellent facilities that are included in the overnight camping charges.

Facilities
Two modern toilet blocks with British style toilets, washbasins in cabins, large and controllable hot showers. Child sized washbasins. Facilities for disabled visitors. Laundry facilities. Motorcaravan services. Supermarket. Kiosks for fruit, newspapers, souvenirs and tobacco. Restaurant with buffet. Bar with terrace. Large indoor and outdoor swimming complexes. Rowing boats. Jogging track. Fishing. Golf. Bicycle hire. Sauna. Solarium. Riding. Organised activities. Video games. WiFi throughout (free).

Open: All year.

Directions
Site is signed from the Ljubljana-Zagreb motorway (E70) 6 km. west of the Slovenia/Croatia border, close to Brezice. GPS: 45.89137, 15.62598

Charges guide
Per unit incl. 2 persons

and electricity	€ 40.30 - € 49.50
extra person	€ 17.90 - € 22.50
child (4-11 yrs)	€ 8.95 - € 11.25
dog	€ 4.00

Lazar Kamp

Gregorciceva, SLO-5222 Kobarid T: 053 885 333. E: edi.lazar@siol.net

alanrogers.com/SV4265

Lazar Kamp is a fairly open site with a relaxed atmosphere, from which there are good views of the surrounding mountains. Located in the countryside 40 m. above the Soca river, popular with wild watersport fans, there are plenty of walking and mountain biking opportunities directly from the site, in this attractive region of Slovenia. The site has 50 open plan grassy pitches, all with 10A electricity, arranged in large sections divided by low openwork wooden fences. The friendly, informal bar/restaurant (08.00-22.00) serves English breakfast, and in the evenings traditional Slovenian dishes including those cooked on a large grill. The site's owner and staff are most helpful.

Facilities
The sanitary block is of a very good standard and includes facilities for disabled visitors. Washing machine. Fridge. Bar. Crêperie and grill with terrace area. Internet corner. WiFi. Ranch-style clubroom. Excursions and lots of local sporting activities. Off site: Kozjak Waterfall. Mountain biking. Walking. Paragliding. Touring. Rafting. Kayaking. Canoeing.

Open: 1 April - 31 October.

Directions
Approaching Kobarid from Tolmin on 102 just before Kobarid turn right on 203 (Bovec). After 100 m. take descending slip road to right, keeping straight on to Napoléon's bridge (about 500 m), then straight on down gravel road 700 m. to site (road is unsuitable for larger units). GPS: 46.25513, 13.58626

Charges guide

Per unit incl. 2 persons and electricity	€ 24.00
extra person	€ 12.00
child (7-13 yrs)	€ 7.00

Kamp Koren Kobarid

Ladra 1b, SLO-5222 Kobarid T: 053 891 311. E: info@kamp-koren.si

alanrogers.com/SV4270

Kamp Koren, Slovenia's first ecological site, is in a quiet location above the Soca river gorge, within easy walking distance of Kobarid. The site has 90 slightly sloping pitches, all with 6/16A electricity and ample tree shade. It is deservedly very popular with those interested in outdoor sports, be it on the water, in the mountains or in the air. At the same time, its peaceful situation makes it an ideal choice for those seeking a relaxing break. There are six well equipped chalets, and a shady area mainly for tents was opened in 2014 at the top of the site.

Facilities
Two attractive and well maintained log-built toilet blocks, both recently renovated. Facilities for disabled visitors. Laundry facilities. Motorcaravan services. Shop (March-Nov). Café serves light meals, snacks and drinks apparently with flexible closing hours. Play area. Bowling. Fishing. Bicycle hire. Canoe hire. Climbing walls. Communal barbecue. WiFi. Off site: Town within walking distance. Riding 5 km. Golf 15 km. Trilav National Park.

Open: All year.

Directions
Approaching Kobarid from Tolmin on 102, just before Kobarid turn right on 203 towards Bovec and after 100 m. take descending slip road to right and keep more or less straight on to Napoléon's bridge (about 500 m). Cross bridge and site is on left in 100 m. GPS: 46.25075, 13.58658

Charges guide
Per unit incl. 2 persons

and electricity	€ 25.00 - € 28.00
extra person	€ 10.50 - € 12.00

FREE Alan Rogers Travel Card
Extra benefits and savings - see page 14

Lendava

Camping Terme Lendava

Tomsiceva ulica 2a, SLO-9220 Lendava T: 025 774 400. E: info@terme-lendava.si

alanrogers.com/SV4455

Camping Terme Lendava forms part of an important thermal resort holiday complex, located at the meeting point of Slovenia, Hungary and Croatia. This is an all-year site with 80 grassy pitches, most with electricity connections, and eight hardstandings. Lendava is an open site with views over the vineyards, although some pitches around the edge have shade from mature trees. Campers have access to a large swimming pool complex as well as the resort's various thermal facilities, including bathing in water with paraffin content, considered to be an effective treatment for rheumatic disorders. There are several good restaurants within the complex. Special facilities are also available for naturist bathers.

Facilities

Two toilet blocks, one older and one a modern prefabricated unit, have open washbasins, controllable showers and communal changing. Laundry available in hotel. Shop, bar and restaurant in hotel. Swimming pool. Thermal complex with indoor and outdoor pools. Paddling pool. Play area. Entertainment programme. WiFi (charged). Off site: Shops and restaurants. Fishing 200 m. Golf. Excursions to Hungary and Croatia.

Open: All year.

Directions

Approaching from the west (Maribor) on A5 motorway, take the exit to Lendava and follow signs to the site. GPS: 46.55167, 16.45842

Charges guide

Per person	€ 25.50 - € 28.50
child (7-13 yrs)	€ 17.85 - € 19.95

Lesce

Camping Sobec

Sobceva cesta 25, SLO-4248 Lesce T: 045 353 700. E: sobec@siol.net

alanrogers.com/SV4210

Sobec is situated in a valley between the Julian Alps and the Karavanke Mountains, in a pine grove between the Sava Dolinka river and a small lake. It is only 3 km. from Bled and 20 km. from the Karavanke Tunnel. There are 500 unmarked pitches on level, grassy fields off tarmac access roads (450 for touring units), all with 16A electricity. Shade is provided by mature pine trees and younger trees separate some pitches. Camping Sobec is surrounded by water – the Sava river borders it on three sides and on the fourth is a small, artificial lake with grassy fields for sunbathing.

Facilities

Three traditional style toilet blocks (all now refurbished) with mainly British style toilets, washbasins in cabins and controllable hot showers. Child size toilets and washbasins. Well equipped baby room. Facilities for disabled visitors. Laundry facilities. Motorcaravan services. Supermarket, bar/restaurant with stage for live performances. Playgrounds. Rafting, canyoning and kayaking organised. Miniclub. Tours to Bled and the Triglav National Park organised. WiFi throughout (free). Off site: Golf and riding 2 km.

Open: 14 April - 30 September.

Directions

Leave A2 autobahn at exit 3 and follow signs for Lesce-Bled. Go straight ahead at roundabout and site is signed to left shortly after. GPS: 46.35607, 14.14992

Charges guide

Per unit incl. 2 persons and electricity	€ 26.70 - € 32.90
extra person	€ 11.40 - € 14.50
child (7-14 yrs)	€ 8.50 - € 10.70
dog	€ 3.70

Ljubljana

Camping Ljubljana Resort

Dunajska Cesta 270, SLO-1000 Ljubljana T: 015 89 0130. E: resort@gpl.si

alanrogers.com/SV4340

Located only five kilometres north of central Ljubljana on the relatively quiet bank of the River Sava, Ljubljana Resort is an ideal city campsite. This relaxed site is attached to – but effectively separated from – the sparklingly modern Laguna swimming pool complex (open 1/6-15/9). The site has 177 pitches, largely situated between mature trees and all with electricity connections (16A). The main building and the pool complex provide several bars, restaurants and takeaways to cater for the campsite guests and day visitors. The far corner of the site offers a quick introduction to the Slovenian lifestyle, while a range of more conventional sports (tennis, beach volleyball, indoor badminton and a gym) are here as well.

Facilities

The modern toilet block includes facilities for disabled campers, a baby room and children's toilet and shower. Motorcaravan services. Laundry room. Fridge. TV lounge. Internet access in reception (free). Airport transfer service. Bicycle hire. New play area. Entertainment for children in July/Aug. Restaurant and bar with terrace. Barbecue area. Fitness centre. Spa and outdoor swimming pool (15/6-1/9). Beach volleyball. WiFi throughout (charged). Off site: Train station 800 m. Fishing and rafting on river.

Open: All year.

Directions

From either direction on the northern city ring road, take exit no. 3 for Ljubljana-Jezica north towards Crnuce for a little over 1 km. Site is signed (blue sign) on the right just before railway crossing and bridge over the river. GPS: 46.09752, 14.5187

Charges guide

Per unit incl. 2 persons and electricity	€ 22.92 - € 31.32
extra person	€ 8.70 - € 12.90
child (5-14 yrs)	€ 5.90 - € 8.50

For latest campsite news, availability and prices visit

alanrogers.com

Camping Kamne

Dovje 9, SLO-4281 Mojstrana T: 045 891 105. E: campingkamne@telemach.net

alanrogers.com/SV4150

Easily accessed from the A2/E61 autobahn this small, terraced, south facing site offers striking views of Slovenia's highest mountains which form part of the adjoining Triglav National Park. Camping Kamme has a total of 60 grass pitches for touring, 40 of which have 6/10A electrical connections. Site roads are gravel and tarmac and plenty of trees provide good shade. Ana Voga, the owner, speaks excellent English. The area is a haven for walking and mountain biking with trails of all grades against a backdrop of waterfalls, fast-flowing mountain streams and forests.

Facilities
The small excellent sanitary block is of a high quality and well maintained. New facilities for babies and disabled visitors. Motorcaravan service point. Reception/bar with TV. Small shop for essentials (25/6-10/9). Playground. Two tennis courts. Mountain bike hire. Chalets and bungalows to rent. WiFi throughout (free). Max. 2 dogs. Off site: Walking and mountain bike trails. Rock climbing. Fishing nearby (licence from reception). Riding 5 km.

Open: All year.

Directions
Site is 5.5 km. north west of the southern exit of the Karawanken tunnel which joins Villach in Austria with Slovenia. A few hundred meters from the tunnel's southern end, take exit for Kranjska Gora and at the end of the slip road left towards Kranjska Gora. After 5.5 km. at the western village sign for Dovje, site is 100 m. to the right. GPS: 46.46435, 13.95738

Charges guide
Per unit incl. 2 persons and electricity	€ 19.20 - € 25.00
extra person	€ 6.60 - € 9.00
child (5-17 yrs)	€ 4.80 - € 5.30
dog	€ 2.00

Camp Lucija

Seca 204, SLO-6320 Portoroz T: 056 90 60 00. E: camp.lucija@bernardingroup.si

alanrogers.com/SV4315

This is a long narrow site that enjoys attactive views over the bay at the western end. This part of the site is very popular and becomes quite crowded, while in the bar/restaurant area there is music playing for most of the day. The site is popular with families with young children, and a much used public cycle/pedestrian path, formally a railway line linking Triest with Porec, runs through it. There are 550 reasonably level pitches (300 for tourers) on grass/gravel, and around half have 6A electricity. There is a separate terrace for tents. There is some aircraft noise. The site is ideally placed for coastal walks. Just 300 m. from the campsite, there is a good sports centre with a range of amenities including football, tennis and minigolf. Further afield, day trips to Trieste and the Slovenian coastal towns are possible, while Venice is a longer day out. In addition, Lucija's close proximity to the Croatian border makes touring into Istria easy.

Facilities
Five sanitary blocks (one heated) have hot showers. Facilities for disabled visitors. Washing machine. Motorcaravan services. Shop. Bar/snack bar and restaurant. Playground. Fishing. Bicycle hire. WiFi (charged). Off site: Walk to Secovlje salt pans from site. Sports centre 300 m. Shops, restaurants and cafés in Portoroz. Walking and cycling routes. Watersports.

Open: 15 April - 15 October.

Directions
Approaching from the north (Koper), head south on road 111 beyond Portoroz and continue to Lucija. At bottom of hill, at traffic lights, turn right and follow camping signs. GPS: 45.501506, 13.593905

Charges guide
Per unit incl. 2 persons and electricity	€ 27.50 - € 38.50
extra person	€ 12.00 - € 17.00
child (7-14 yrs)	€ 4.00 - € 6.00
dog	€ 3.00

camp
LUCIJA
★★★
PORTOROŽ

BERNARDIN GROUP
RESORTS & HOTELS

Camp Lucija, Seča 204, Portorož, Slovenia
T +386 5 690 6000   GPS: 45 30' 6"N, 13 16' 2"E
camp.lucija@bernardingroup.si   **www.camp-lucija.si**

Moravske Toplice

Camping Terme 3000

Kranjceva ulica 12, SLO-9226 Moravske Toplice T: 025 121 200. E: recepcija.camp2@terme3000.si

alanrogers.com/SV4410

Camping Terme 3000 is a large site with 490 pitches. Three hundred are for touring units (all with 16A electricity, 30 with hardstanding), the remaining pitches being taken by seasonal campers. On a grass and gravel surface (hard tent pegs may be needed), the level, numbered pitches are of 50-100 sq.m. The site is part of an enormous thermal spa and fun pool complex (free entry to campers) under the same name. There are over 5,000 sq.m. of water activities – swimming, jet streams, waterfalls, water massages, four water slides (the longest is 170 m), and thermal baths.

Facilities
Modern and clean toilet facilities provide British style toilets, open washbasins and controllable, free hot showers. Laundry facilities. Football field. Tennis. Water gymnastics. Daily activity programme for children. Golf. WiFi (charged).

Open: All year.

Directions
From Maribor, go east to Murska Sobota. From there go north towards Martjanci and then east towards Moravske Toplice. Access to the site is on the right before the bridge. Then go through a park for a further 500 m. GPS: 46.67888, 16.22165

Charges guide
Per unit incl. 2 persons	
and electricity	€ 46.00 - € 48.50
extra person	€ 14.00 - € 18.00
child (7-13 yrs)	€ 19.60 - € 22.40

Postojna

Camping Pivka Jama

Veliki Otok 50, SLO-6230 Postojna T: 05 720 3993. E: avtokamp.pivka.jama@siol.net

alanrogers.com/SV4330

Postojna is renowned for its extraordinary limestone caves, which form one of Slovenia's prime tourist attractions. Pivka Jama is a most convenient site for the visitor, being midway between Ljubljana and Piran and only about an hour's pleasant drive from either. The 300 pitches are not clustered together but nicely segregated under trees and in small clearings, all connected by a neat network of paths and slip roads. Some level, gravel hardstandings are provided. The facilities are both excellent and extensive and run with obvious pride by enthusiastic staff. This good site is deep in what appears to be primeval forest, cleverly cleared to take advantage of the broken limestone forest bedrock. It even has its own local caves (the Pivka Jama).

Facilities
Two toilet blocks with very good facilities. Washing machines. Motorcaravan services. Campers' kitchen with hobs. Supermarket (1/6-15/9). Bar/restaurant. Swimming and paddling pools (15/6-10/9). Tennis. Bicycle hire. Day trips to Postojna Caves and other excursions organised. WiFi. Off site: Fishing 5 km. Riding and skiing 10 km. Riding and golf 30 km.

Open: 15 April - 31 October.

Directions
Site is 5 km. north of Postojna. Leave A1/E61 autobahn Postojna exit. In Postojna follow signs to Postojna Caves (Postojnska Jama) continue past caves for 4 km. where site is signed to the right. Follow road through forest 2 km. to site. GPS: 45.79068, 14.19092

Charges guide
Per person	€ 9.90 - € 11.90
child (7-14 yrs)	€ 7.90 - € 8.90
electricity	€ 3.90

Prebold

Camp Dolina Prebold

Vozlic Tomaz Dolenja vas 147, SLO-3312 Prebold T: 035 724 378. E: camp@dolina.si

alanrogers.com/SV4400

Prebold is a quiet village about 15 kilometres west of the large historic town of Celje. It is only a few kilometres from the remarkable Roman necropolis at Sempeter. Dolina is an exceptional little site where reception and bar are housed in the beautifully converted 150-year-old stable, taking 50 touring units, 25 with 10A electricity. It belongs to Tomaz and Manja Vozlic who look after the site and its guests with loving care. It has been in existence since 1960 and was one of the first private enterprises in the former Yugoslavia. Excursions are organised to the Pekel Caves and Roman remains.

Facilities
The small, heated toilet block is immaculately maintained. Washing machine and dryer. Small swimming pool (heated 30-33°C, 1/5-30/9). Play area with trampoline. Large wood-fired oven with doors for traditional cooking. Sauna. Bicycle hire. WiFi. Off site: Good supermarket and restaurant 200 m. Tennis and indoor pool within 1 km. Fishing 1.5 km.

Open: All year.

Directions
Leave E57 at Sempeter/Prebold exit. Head south, after 100 m, right at roundabout, over bridge. Follow site signs to the left after 150 m. Upon reaching Prebold, site is signed to the right down a small side street. GPS: 46.24392, 15.09108

Charges guide
Per unit incl. 2 persons and electricity	€ 22.00
extra person	€ 7.36
dog	€ 3.00

No credit cards.

For latest campsite news, availability and prices visit

alanrogers.com

Recica ob Savinji

Camping Menina

Varpolje 105, SLO-3332 Recica ob Savinji T: 035 835 027. E: info@campingmenina.com

alanrogers.com/SV4405

Camping Menina is in the heart of the 35 km. long Upper Savinja Valley, surrounded by 2,500 m. high mountains and unspoilt nature. It is being improved every year by the young, enthusiastic owner, Jurij Kolenc and has 200 pitches, all for touring units, on grassy fields under mature trees and with access from gravel roads. All have 6-10A electricity. The Savinja river runs along one side of the site, but if its water is too cold for swimming, the site also has a lake which can be used for swimming. This site is a perfect base for walking or mountain biking in the mountains and opens all year for skiing holidays.

Facilities

Two toilet blocks (one new) have modern fittings with toilets, open plan washbasins and controllable hot showers. Motorcaravan services. Bar/restaurant with open-air terrace (evenings only) and open-air kitchen. Sauna. Playing field. Play area. Fishing. Mountain bike hire. Russian bowling. Excursions (52). Live music and gatherings around the camp fire. Indian village. Hostel. Skiing in winter. Kayaking. Mobile homes to rent. Climbing wall. Rafting. Off site: Fishing 2 km. Recica and other villages with much culture and folklore are close.

Open: All year.

Directions

From Ljubljana/Celje autobahn A1. Exit at Sentupert and turn north towards Mozirje (14 km). At roundabout just before Mozirje, hard left staying on the 225 for 6 km. to Nizka then just after the circular automatic petrol station, left where site is signed. GPS: 46.31168, 14.90913

Charges guide

Per unit incl. 2 persons	
and electricity	€ 17.80 - € 23.00
extra person	€ 7.50 - € 10.00
child (5-15 yrs)	€ 3.50 - € 6.00

Smlednik

Camp Smlednik

Dragocajna 14a, SLO-1216 Smlednik T: 013 627 002. E: camp@dm-campsmlednik.si

alanrogers.com/SV4360

Camp Smlednik is relatively close to the capital, Ljubljana, yet within striking distance of Lake Bled, the Karawankes mountains and the Julian Alps. It provides a good touring base, set above the River Sava, and also provides a small, separate enclosure for those who enjoy naturism. Situated beside the peaceful tiny village of Dragocajni, in attractive countryside, the site provides 190 places for tourers each with electricity (6/10A). Although terraced, it is probably better described as a large plateau with tall pines and deciduous trees providing some shade. The naturist area measuring only some 30x100 m. accommodates 15 units adjacent to the river (INF card not required).

Facilities

Three fully equipped sanitary blocks are of varying standards, but with adequate and clean provision. In the main camping area a fairly new, solar-powered, two-storey block has free hot showers, the lower half for use within the naturist area. Normally heated showers in the old block are also free. Toilet for disabled visitors. Laundry facilities. Supermarket at entrance. Bar serves food (1/5-30/9). Two good quality clay tennis courts (charged). Swings for children. River swimming and fishing. WiFi.

Open: 1 May - 15 October.

Directions

Travelling on road no.1, both Smlednik and the site are well signed. From E61 motorway, Smlednik and site are again well signed at the Vodiice exit 11. (Watch for sharp right turn to site on bend just after camping 1 km. sign). GPS: 46.17425, 14.41628

Charges guide

Per person	€ 7.00 - € 8.00
child (7-14 yrs)	€ 3.50 - € 4.00
electricity	€ 3.00 - € 4.00

Soca

Kamp Klin

Lepena 1, SLO-5232 Soca T: 053 889 513. E: kampklin@siol.net

alanrogers.com/SV4235

With an attractive location surrounded by mountains in the Triglav National Park, Kamp Klin is next to the confluence of the Soca and Lepenca rivers, which makes it an ideal base for fishing, kayaking and rafting. The campsite has 50 pitches, all for tourers, 50 with 7A electricity, on one large, grassy field, connected by a circular, gravel access road. It is attractively landscaped with flowers and young trees, which provide some shade. Some pitches are right on the bank of the river (unfenced) and there are beautiful views of the river and the mountains.

Facilities

One modern toilet block with controllable showers. WC only for disabled visitors. Laundry with sinks. Bar/restaurant. Play area. Fishing (permit required). Torch useful. WiFi. Off site: Riding 500 m. Bicycle hire 10 km. Rambling. Rafting. Paragliding.

Open: April - October.

Directions

Site is on the main Kranjska Gora-Bovec road and is well signed 3 km. east of Soca. Access is via a sharp right turn from the main road and over a small bridge and right again. The road is winding in places with a moderate descent. GPS use co-ordinates. GPS: 46.33007, 13.644

Charges guide

Per unit incl. 2 persons	
and electricity	€ 23.00 - € 27.00
extra person	€ 11.50 - € 13.50

FREE Alan Rogers Travel Card
Extra benefits and savings - see page 14

Spain

One of the largest countries in Europe with glorious beaches, a fantastic sunshine record, vibrant towns and laid back sleepy villages, plus a diversity of landscape, culture and artistic traditions, Spain has all the ingredients for a great holiday.

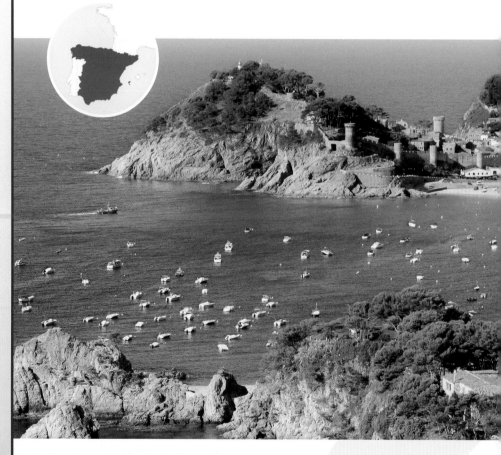

Spain's vast and diverse coastline is a magnet for visitors; glitzy, hedonistic resorts packed with bars and clubs are a foil to secluded coves backed by wooded cliffs. Yet Spain has much more to offer – the verdant north with its ancient pilgrimage routes, where the Picos de Europa sweep down to the Atlantic gems of Santander and Bilbao. Vibrant Madrid in the heart of the country boasts the Prado with works by Velázquez and Goya, the beautiful cobbled Plaza Major, plus all the attractions of a capital city. Passionate Andalucía in the south dazzles with the symbolic arts of bullfighting and flamenco beneath a scorching sun. It offers the cosmopolitan cities of Córdoba, Cádiz and Málaga, alongside magnificent examples of the past such as the Alhambra at Granada. On the Mediterranean east coast, Valencia has a wealth of monuments and cultural sites, including the magnificent City of Arts and Science.

CAPITAL: Madrid

Tourist Office

Spanish Tourist Office

6th floor, 64 North Row

London W1K 7DE

Tel: 020 7317 2011

Email: spaininfo@tourspain.es

Internet: www.tourspain.co.uk

Population

47 million

Climate

Spain has a very varied climate. The north is temperate with most of the rainfall; dry and very hot in the centre; sub-tropical along the Mediterranean.

Language

Castilian Spanish is spoken by most people with Catalan (northeast), Basque (north) and Galician (northwest) used in their respective areas.

Telephone

The country code is 00 34.

Money

Currency: The Euro

Banks: Mon-Fri 09.00-14.00. Sat 09.00-13.00.

Shops

Mon-Sat 09.00-13.00/14.00 and 15.00/16.00-19.30/20.00. Many close later.

Public Holidays

New Year; Epiphany; Saint's Day 19 Mar; Maundy Thurs; Good Fri; Easter Mon; Labour Day; Saints Day 25 July; Assumption 15 Aug; National Day 12 Oct; All Saints' Day 1 Nov; Constitution Day 6 Dec; Immaculate Conception 8 Dec; Christmas Day.

Motoring

The surface of the main roads is on the whole good, although secondary roads in some rural areas can be rough and winding. Tolls are payable on certain roads and for the Cadi Tunnel, Vallvidrera Tunnel and the Tunnel de Garraf on the A16.

see campsite map 6

Almeria

Camping la Garrofa

Ctra N340 km. 435,4, direccion a Aguadulce via Litoral, E-04002 Almería (Almería) T: 950 235 770.

E: info@lagarrofa.com **alanrogers.com/ES87650**

One of the earliest sites in Spain (dating back to 1957), la Garrofa nestles in a cove with a virtually private beach accessed only by sea or through the campsite. It is rather dramatic with the tall mountain cliffs behind. Many of the rather small 100 flat and sloping sandy pitches are shaded, with some very close to the beach and sea. Eighty have 6/10A electricity. An old fortress looks down on the campsite – you can walk to it via a valley at the back of the site and across an old Roman bridge. Other walks directly from the site include a Roman road providing fine coastal views.

Facilities

Sanitary facilities are mature but clean. Facilities for disabled campers. Shop. Restaurant/snack bar. Play area. Fishing, boat launching and a beach. Torches useful. WiFi. Off site: Town close by. Sub-aqua diving. Bicycle hire 2 km. Golf 8 km. Excursions – tickets to attractions sold. Bus stop nearby to Almeria and Aguadulce.

Open: All year.

Directions

Site is west of Almeria. Take 438 exit from the N340 and follow the Almeria/Puerto signs. Then take the Aguadulce direction, from where site is signed. GPS: 36.8257, -2.5161

Charges guide

Per unit incl. 2 persons and electricity	€ 24.50 - € 27.50
extra person	€ 6.00

Almonte

Camping la Aldea

El Rocio, E-21750 Almonte (Huelva) T: 959 442 677. E: info@campinglaaldea.com

alanrogers.com/ES88730

This site lies just on the edge of the Parque Nacional de Doñana, southwest of Sevilla on the outskirts of El Rocio. The town hosts a fiesta at the end of May with over one million people attending the local shrine. They travel for days in processions with cow-drawn or motorised vehicles to attend. If you want to stay during that weekend, book well in advance! The well planned, modern site is well set out and the 246 pitches have some natural shade from trees, or artificial shade. All have 10A electricity and 52 are serviced pitches with water and drainage.

Facilities

Two sanitary blocks provide excellent facilities including provision for disabled visitors. Motorcaravan services. Swimming pool (May-Oct). Restaurant and shop in separate new complex. Shop. Internet connection. Playground. Off site: Bus stop 5 minutes' walk. Beach 15 km. Huelva and Sevilla are about an hour's drive.

Open: All year.

Directions

From main E1/A49 Huelva-Sevilla road take exit 48 onto A483 and drive south past Almonte towards El Rocio. Site is on left just past 25 km. marker. Go down to the roundabout and back up to be on the right side of the road to turn in. GPS: 37.1428, -6.491164

Charges guide

Per unit incl. 2 persons and electricity	€ 22.30 - € 25.50
extra person	€ 4.90 - € 5.90

Cabo de Gata

Camping Cabo de Gata

Ctra Cabo de Gata s/n, E-04150 Cabo de Gata (Almería) T: 950 160 443. E: info@campingcabodegata.com

alanrogers.com/ES87630

Cabo de Gata is situated on the Gulf of Almería, a pleasant, all-year campsite offering facilities to a good standard. Popular with British visitors through the winter, and within the Cabo de Gata-Nijar Nature Park and set amongst fruit farms, it is only a 1 km. walk to a fine sandy beach. The 250 gravel pitches are level and of a reasonable size, with 6/16A electricity and limited shade from maturing trees or canopies. There are specific areas for very large units with very high canopies for shade and seven chalets for rent.

Facilities

Two, well maintained, clean toilet blocks provide all the necessary sanitary facilities, including British type WCs, washbasins and free hot showers. Facilities for disabled campers. Restaurant, bar and shop (all year). Swimming pool. Football. Pétanque. Tennis. Small playground. Library. Bicycle hire. English spoken. Entertainment programme. Internet access (charged). WiFi (free by reception). Off site: Bus from gate. Nearest beach and fishing 1 km. Golf 10 km. Riding 15 km.

Open: All year.

Directions

From A7-E15 take exit 460 or 467 and follow signs for Retamar via N344 and for Cabo de Gata. Site is on the right before village of Cabo de Gata. GPS: 36.808159, -2.232159

Charges guide

Per unit incl. 2 persons and electricity	€ 28.55 - € 32.45
extra person	€ 6.20
child (2-10 yrs)	€ 5.25
dog	€ 2.50

Special offers outside July/August.

For latest campsite news, availability and prices visit

alanrogers.com

Conil de la Frontera
Camping Roche

N340 km. 19,5, Carril de Pilahito, E-11140 Conil de la Frontera (Cádiz) T: 956 442 216.

E: info@campingroche.com **alanrogers.com/ES88590**

Camping Roche is situated in a pine forest near white sandy beaches in the lovely region of Andalucia. It is a clean, tidy and welcoming site. English is spoken but try your Spanish, German or French as the staff are very helpful. A family site, it offers a variety of facilities including a sports area and swimming pools. The restaurant has good food and a pleasant outlook over the pool. Games are organised for children. A recently built extension provides further pitches, a new toilet block and a tennis court. There are 335 pitches which include 104 bungalows to rent. The touring pitches all have electricity (10A), and 76 also have water and waste water.

Facilities
Three toilet blocks are traditional in style and provide simple, clean facilities. Washbasins have cold water only. Washing machine. Supermarket. Bar and restaurant. Swimming and paddling pools. Sports area. Tennis. Play area. Off site: Bus stops 3 times daily outside gates. Cádiz. Cape Trafalgar. Baelo Claudia archaeological site.

Open: All year.

Directions
From the N340 (Cádiz-Algeciras) turn off to site at km. 19.5 point. From Conil, take El Pradillo road. Keep following signs to site. From CA3208 road turn at km. 1 and site is 1.5 km. down this road on the right. GPS: 36.31089, -6.11268

Charges guide
Per unit incl. 2 persons and electricity	€ 18.82 - € 29.60
extra person	€ 3.71 - € 5.80

Conil de la Frontera
Camping Fuente del Gallo

Apdo 48, E-11149 Conil de la Frontera (Cádiz) T: 956 440 137. E: camping@campingfuentedelgallo.com

alanrogers.com/ES88600

Fuente del Gallo is well maintained with 184 pitches allocated to touring units. Each pitch has 6A electricity and a number of trees create shade to some pitches. Although the actual pitch areas are generally a good size, the majority are long and narrow. This could, in some cases, prevent the erection of an awning and your neighbour may feel close. In low season it is generally accepted to make additional use of an adjoining pitch. The attractive pool, restaurant and bar complex with its large, shaded terrace, are very welcoming in the height of summer. Good beaches are relatively near at 300 m.

Facilities
Two modernised and very clean sanitary blocks include excellent services for babies and disabled visitors and hot water at all facilities. Laundry room with two washing machines. Motorcaravan services. Gas supplies. Well stocked shop. Attractive bar and restaurant (breakfast served). Swimming pool (1/6-30/9 with lifeguard) with paddling pool. Play area. TV and games machines in bar area. Safety deposit boxes. Excursions. Torches useful. Picnic area with playground and games. WiFi throughout (charged). Off site: Watersports on beach. Fishing 300 m.

Open: 23 March - 30 September.

Directions
From the Cádiz-Algeciras road (N340) at km. 23.00, follow signs to Conil de la Frontera town centre, then shortly right to Fuente del Gallo and playas, following signs. GPS: 36.2961, -6.1102

Charges guide
Per unit incl. 2 persons and electricity	€ 21.00 - € 31.50
extra person	€ 5.50 - € 7.00
child (3-10 yrs)	€ 3.50 - € 5.00
dog	€ 3.00

Less 11-30% for longer stays (except Jul/Aug).

Córdoba
Camping Municipal El Brillante

Avenida del Brillante 50, E-14012 Córdoba (Córdoba) T: 957 403 836. E: elbrillante@campings.net

alanrogers.com/ES90800

Córdoba is one of the hottest places in Europe and the superb pool here is more than welcome. If you really want to stay in the city, then this large site is a good choice. It has 115 neat pitches of gravel and sand, the upper pitches covered by artificial and natural shade but the lower, newer area has little. The site becomes very crowded in high season. The entrance is narrow and may be congested so care must be exercised – there is a lay-by just outside and it is easier to walk in initially. All pitches have electricity (6/10A) plus the newer area has 32 fully serviced pitches and an area for a few large motorcaravans.

Facilities
The toilet blocks include facilities for babies and disabled visitors. Washing machine. Motorcaravan services. Gas supplies. Shop (all year). Bar (1/7-15/9). Swimming pool (1/7-Sept/Oct). Play area. Off site: Bus service to city centre from outside site. Commercial centre 300 m. (left out of site, right at traffic lights). Bicycle hire 2 km. Riding 5 km. Golf 10 km. Fishing 15 km.

Open: All year.

Directions
From Madrid (NIV/E25), take exit at km. 403 and follow signs for Mezquita/Cathedral into city centre. Pass it (on right) and turn right on main avenue. Fork right where road splits, and follow signs for site and/or white signs to left for district of El Brillante. Site is on right. GPS: 37.899975, -4.787319

Charges guide
Per unit incl. 2 persons and electricity	€ 26.50 - € 28.50
extra person	€ 7.00

No credit cards.

El Puerto de Santa Maria

Camping Playa Las Dunas

Paseo Maritimo, Playa de la Puntilla s/n, E-11500 El Puerto de Santa Maria (Cádiz) T: 956 872 210.

E: info@lasdunascamping.com **alanrogers.com/ES88650**

This site lies within the Parque Natural Bahia de Las Dunas and is adjacent to the long and gently sloping golden sands of Puntilla beach. This is a pleasant and peaceful site (though very busy in August) with some 539 separate marked pitches, 260 for touring units, with much natural shade and ample electrical connections (10A). Motorcaravans park in an area called the Oasis, which is very pretty. Tent and caravan pitches, under mature trees, are terraced and separated by low walls. This is a spacious site with a tranquil setting and it is popular with people who wish to 'winter over'. A 2 km. unshaded walk takes you into the bustling heart of Puerto Santa Maria.

Facilities

Immaculate modern sanitary facilities with separate facilities for disabled campers and a baby room. Laundry facilities are excellent. Gas supplies. Bar/restaurant (all year). Supermarket (high season). Very large swimming pool and paddling pool (July/Aug). Night security all year. Barbecues are not permitted 15/5-15/10. WiFi throughout (charged). Off site: Beach 100 m. Fishing 500 m. Bicycle hire, riding and golf 2 km. Municipal sports centre. Local buses for town and city visits and a ferry to Cádiz.

Open: All year.

Directions

Site is 5 km. north of Cádiz off N443. Take road to Puerto Santa Maria and site is well signed in town (small yellow signs). From south, turn left into town just after big bridge. Keeping sea inlet on left, follow for 1 km. to site on right. GPS: 36.5890, -6.2384

Charges guide

Per unit incl. 2 persons and electricity	€ 21.96 - € 27.11
extra person	€ 4.80 - € 5.33
child (3-10 yrs)	€ 4.10 - € 4.56

Fuente de Piedra

Espacios Rurales Fuente de Piedra

Ctra La Rábita s/n, E-29520 Fuente de Piedra (Málaga) T: 952 735 294. E: info@camping-rural.com
alanrogers.com/ES87900

In a remote area of Andalucia, this simple, tiny campsite with just 30 touring pitches looks over the salty lakes and marshes of the Laguna de Fuente. The average sized pitches are on a sloping, terraced hillside, with some having a view of the lake. With a gravel surface and fairly good shade, many pitches slope so chocks would be useful. There is a separate grassy area for tents near the pool and bungalows (cars are not permitted here). There is a municipal pool and snack bar, and a huge restaurant which serves delicious Spanish food. It is practically on site, so could be noisy at times.

Facilities

Sanitary facilities are in one block and are old fashioned and rather tired. Facilities for disabled campers. Washing machines. Shop. Restaurant. Bar with TV. Snack bar. Swimming pool. Pool bar. Electronic games. Bicycle hire. Off site: Lake with flamingos. Bicycle hire 1 km. Fishing 5 km. Riding 10 km. Golf 40 km. Excursions organised in July/Aug.

Open: All year.

Directions

Site is 20 km. northwest of Antequera. From Antequera take A92 and exit at 132 km. point and follow road to the town. Site is well signed from the town but the signs are small. GPS: 37.1292, -4.7334

Charges guide

Per unit incl. 2 persons and electricity	€ 26.40 - € 29.00
extra person	€ 5.40 - € 6.00

Granada

Camping Suspiro del Moro

Ctra Bailén-Motril km. 144, Puerto Suspiro del Moro, E-18630 Granada (Granada) T: 958 555 411.

E: campingsuspirodelmoro@yahoo.es **alanrogers.com/ES92700**

Suspiro del Moro is a small, family run site with 64 pitches, which packs a big punch with its associated Olympic-size swimming pool and huge bar and restaurant. It is cool and peaceful with great views from the site perimeter. The flat pitches (all with 5A electricity) are shaded by mature trees and there are no statics here. The whole site is neat, clean and well ordered and great for chilling out while visiting the area and the famous Alhambra (connecting buses from the gate). The large restaurant has a most extensive menu with waiter service – a pleasant and very Spanish place to enjoy a meal.

Facilities

Clean and tidy, the small toilet blocks are situated around the camping area with British style WCs and free hot showers. Laundry facilities. Small basic shop. Restaurant/bar (closed Jan). Outdoor swimming pool (15/6-7/9). Small play area on gravel. WiFi. Off site: Swimming pool and restaurant adjacent. Granada city centre 10 mins. and Granada 15 mins. by car. Public transport 50 m. from gate.

Open: All year.

Directions

Leave Granada to Motril road (E902/A44) at exit 144 (from south) or 139 (from north) and follow unnamed campsite signs. At roundabout go towards Suspiro, then left (signed after turn). Site is 600 m. on right on A4050 beside large restaurant. GPS: 37.0852, -3.6348

Charges guide

Per person	€ 5.00 - € 5.80
child (2-11 yrs)	€ 3.00 - € 4.00
pitch incl. car	€ 9.00 - € 10.50
electricity	€ 3.50 - € 3.80
Less 20% in low season.	

For latest campsite news, availability and prices visit

alanrogers.com

Granada

Camping Sierra Nevada

Avenida Juan Pablo II no. 23, E-18014 Granada (Granada) T: 958 150 062. E: campingmotel@terra.es

alanrogers.com/ES92800

This is a good site either for a night stop or for a stay of a few days while visiting Granada, especially the Alhambra, and for a city site it is surprisingly pleasant. Quite large, it has an open feel and, to encourage you to stay a little longer, a smart, irregular shape pool with a smaller children's pool open in high season. There is some traffic noise around the pool as it is on the road boundary. With 148 pitches for touring units (10/20A electricity), the site is in two connected parts with more mature trees and facilities to the northern end. Artificial shade is available throughout the site if required (but may be quite low). There is a small tour operator presence but it is not intrusive. English is spoken by the friendly staff.

Facilities
Two modern sanitary blocks, with good facilities, including cabins, very good facilities for disabled campers and babies. Washing machines. Motorcaravan services. Gas supplies. Shop. Swimming pools with lifeguards and charged (15/6-15/9). Bar/restaurant by pool. Tennis. Pétanque. Large playground. Bicycle hire. Free WiFi over part of site. Off site: Supermarket. Bus station 100 m. from site gate. Fishing 10 km. Golf 12 km. Riding 15 km.

Open: 1 March - 31 October.

Directions
Site is just outside the city to north, on road to Jaén and Madrid. From autopista, take Granada North-Almanjayar exit 123 (close to central bus station). Follow road back towards Granada and site is on the right, well signed. From other roads join the motorway to access correct exit.
GPS: 37.20402, -3.61703

Charges guide

Per unit incl. 2 persons and electricity	€ 30.00
extra person	€ 6.00

Güéjar-Sierra

Camping Las Lomas

Ctra de Sierra Nevada, E-18160 Güéjar-Sierra (Granada) T: 958 484 742. E: laslomas@campingsonline.com

alanrogers.com/ES92850

This site is high in the Sierra Nevada Natural Park and looks down on the Patano de Canales reservoir. After a scenic drive to Güéjar-Sierra, you are rewarded with a site boasting excellent facilities. It is set on a slope but the pitches have been levelled and are quite private, with high separating hedges and many mature trees giving good shade, (some pitches are fully serviced, with sinks and all but four have electricity). The large bar/restaurant complex and pools have wonderful views over the lake and a grassy sunbathing area runs down to the fence looking over the long drop below.

Facilities
Adequate sanitary blocks (heated in winter) provide clean facilities. First class facilities for disabled campers and well equipped baby room (key at reception). Motorcaravan services. Good supermarket. Restaurant/bar. Swimming pool. Play area. Minigolf. Barbecue. WiFi (charged). Torches useful. A no noise policy (including cars) is strictly enforced midnight-07.00. Off site: Buses to village and Granada (15 km). Bicycle hire 1.5 km. Fishing 3 km. Tours of The Alhambra and Granada organised. Parascending and skiing nearby.

Open: All year.

Directions
From A44/E902 (Jaén-Motril) exit 132 take A395 (Alhamba-Sierra Nevada). At 4 km, exit 5B (Sierra Nevada). At 7 km. exit right onto slip road. At junction (Cenes de la Vega-Güéjar-Sierra) turn left. In 200 m. turn right on A4026. In 1.6 km. turn left (Güéjar-Sierra) to site in 2.8 km.
GPS: 37.16073, -3.45388

Charges guide

Per person	€ 4.00 - € 6.00
pitch	€ 12.00 - € 15.00
electricity	€ 4.00

Iznate

Camping Iznate

Ctra Benamocarra-Iznate km. 2,7, E-29792 Iznate (Málaga) T: 952 535 613. E: info@campingiznate.com

alanrogers.com/ES87850

This new site is situated amid beautiful scenery 1 km. away from the picturesque village of Iznate. It is surrounded by avocado and olive trees and is on the wine route – the region is the centre of Spain's Muscadet production. The site is well thought out and immaculately maintained. The large swimming pool is an ideal spot for cooling off after a walk and the next door restaurant serves excellent food at very reasonable prices. This is a small, new site and we would recommend booking during high season. There are wonderful views all round the site and eagles, wild boar and black squirrels can be seen in the surrounding countryside.

Facilities
The modern toilet block has hot showers and facilities for disabled visitors. Laundry facilities under a covered area. Fridge hire. Small shop. Bar/restaurant with terrace adjoining the site. Swimming pool (15/5-15/9). Summer entertainment. Pétanque. Play area. TV room. WiFi. Barbecues not permitted in high season. Off site: Beach 20 minutes drive.

Open: All year.

Directions
From A7/E15 take exit 265 and head towards Cajiz and Iznate. Site is on left after Iznate.
GPS: 36.784486, -4.174556

Charges guide

Per unit incl. 2 persons and electricity	€ 15.29 - € 19.05
extra person	€ 3.80 - € 4.75
child (2-9 yrs)	€ 3.26 - € 4.07

FREE Alan Rogers Travel Card
Extra benefits and savings - see page 14

Manilva

Camping la Bella Vista

CN 340, km. 142,8, E-29691 Manilva (Málaga) T: 952 890 020. E: camping@campinglabellavista.com

alanrogers.com/ES88100

Camping la Bella Vista is a very modern campsite that uses sustainable technology. It enjoys a beach front location in San Luis de Sabanillas, a suburb of Manilva, situated in the nearby hills. The beaches are extensive with clean sand and the site boasts uninterrupted views of the sea. The pitches have water, waste, electricity (16/32A), TV and WiFi connections, and are bounded by developing trees and hedges, which as yet provide little shade or privacy. The coastline's eight kilometres of sandy beaches have reefs and coves to explore, in addition to two urban areas offering varied entertainment. The Costa del Sol enjoys 320 days of sunshine each year with an annual average temperature of 18 degrees. Manilva's history dates from the Stone Age. During the Roman period it had a thriving fishing industry, exporting products back to Rome; well preserved Roman sulphur baths and an aqueduct can be seen in the area. The main industries of the area have been fishing, agriculture and viticulture. The wine industry is currently thriving within the village and guided tours of the vineyards and wine production process are available.

Facilities

One new sanitary block has family bathrooms and facilities for disabled visitors. All areas including pool and sanitary units are accessed by stairs, lift or ramp. Washing machines and dryers. Supermarket. Restaurant with Spanish and international cuisine, with views of the Mediterranean and capable of catering for functions. Bar and lounge. Beach bar with food and drink. Feature pool, children's pool and large terrace with sea view. Play area. Medical facilities and 24-hour security patrols. Sunbeds and parasols for hire on beach. Free WiFi over site. Off site: Golf. Scuba diving. Fishing. Tennis. Paragliding. Cycling. Riding. Visits to Ronda, Casares, Antequera, Mijas, Gibraltar 35 km. and the capital Malaga 97 km. Day trips to Africa from Algerciras 30 km.

Open: All year.

Directions

From Malaga and Estepona direction take N340/E5 coast road. After Sabinillas, cross the roundabout after Duquesa golf course, continue to next roundabout, double back on dual carriageway and approach La Bella Vista from the direction of Gibraltar. GPS: 36.347211, -5.235988

Charges guide

Per unit incl. 2 persons, electricity, water and waste water	€ 29.00 - € 49.00
extra person (over 3 yrs)	€ 6.00
dog	€ 3.00

Marbella

Camping Marbella Playa

Ctra N340 km. 192,8, Eluiria, E-29600 Marbella (Málaga) T: 952 833 998.

E: recepcion@campingmarbella.com **alanrogers.com/ES88000**

This large site is 12 kilometres east of the internationally famous resort of Marbella with public transport available to the town centre and local attractions. A sandy beach is about 150 metres away with direct access. There are 430 individual pitches of up to 70 sq.m. with natural shade (additional artificial shade is provided to some), and electricity (10/20A) available throughout. Long leads may be required for some pitches, and those next to the road can experience some noise from 6 am onwards. The site is busy throughout the high season but the high staff/customer ratio and the friendly staff approach ensures a comfortable stay.

Facilities

The four rather dated sanitary blocks are fully equipped and well maintained. Three modern units for disabled visitors. Laundry service. Fridge hire. Large supermarket with butcher and fresh vegetable counter. Bar, restaurant and café (all open all year). Supervised swimming pool (free April-Sept). Playground. Children's activities. Bicycles delivered to site. WiFi over site (charged). Car wash. No charcoal barbecues (June-Oct). Torches advised. Off site: Fishing 100 m. Bus service 150 m. Beach 200 m. Golf and bicycle hire 5 km. Riding 10 km.

Open: All year.

Directions

Site is 12 km. east of Marbella with access close to the 193 km. point on the main N340 road. Signed Elviria, then follow camping signs. GPS: 36.49127, -4.76325

Charges guide

Per unit incl. 2 persons and electricity	€ 17.90 - € 35.85
extra person	€ 3.40 - € 6.00
child (1-10 yrs)	€ 2.65 - € 5.26

Reductions (up to 50%) for long stays and senior citizens outside 1/6-16/9.

For latest campsite news, availability and prices visit

alanrogers.com

Marbella

Camping Cabopino

Ctra N-340, Km.194,7, E-29604 Marbella (Málaga) T: 952 834 373. E: info@campingcabopino.com

alanrogers.com/ES88020

This large, mature site is alongside the main N340/A7 Costa del Sol coast road, 12 km. east of Marbella and 15 km. from Fuengirola. The Costa del Sol is also known as the Costa del Golf and fittingly there is a major golf course alongside the site. The site is set amongst tall pine trees which provide shade for the sandy pitches (there are some huge areas for large units). The 250 touring pitches, a mix of level and sloping (chocks advisable), all have electricity (10A), but long leads may be required for some. There is a separate area on the western side for groups of younger guests.

Facilities

Five mature but very clean sanitary blocks provide hot water throughout (may be under pressure at peak times). Washing machines. Bar/restaurant and takeaway (all year). Shop. Outdoor pool (1/5-15/9) and indoor pool (all year). Play area. Adult exercise equipment. Some evening entertainment. Excursions can be booked. ATM. Bicycle hire. Torches necessary in the more remote parts of the site. Only gas or electric barbecues are permitted. Off site: Beach 200 m. Fishing 1 km. Golf 2 km.

Open: All year.

Directions

Site is 12 km. from Marbella. Approaching Marbella from the east, leave the N340/A7 at the 194 km. marker (signed Cabopino). Site is off the roundabout at the top of the slip road. GPS: 36.49350, -4.74383

Charges guide

Per unit incl. 2 persons	
and electricity	€ 24.00 - € 36.00
extra person	€ 4.75 - € 7.20
child (2-11 yrs)	€ 3.00 - € 6.00

Camping Cheques accepted.

Marbella

Camping la Buganvilla

Ctra N340 km. 188,8, E-29600 Marbella (Málaga) T: 952 831 973. E: info@campingbuganvilla.com

alanrogers.com/ES88030

La Buganvilla is a large, straightforward site with mature trees providing shade to some of the 250 touring pitches. They all have 16A electricity and are mostly on terraces so there are some views across to the mountains and hinterland of this coastal area. The terrain is a little rugged in places and the buildings are older and in need of some attention, but all were clean when we visited. A pool complex near the bar and restaurant is ideal for cooling off after a day's sightseeing. This is an acceptable base from which to explore areas of the Costa del Sol and it is an easy drive to the picturesque Ronda Valley.

Facilities

Three painted sanitary blocks are clean and adequate. Laundry facilities (not all sinks have hot water). Outdoor pool (all year). Bar/restaurant with basic food. Well stocked small supermarket. Play area. Tennis (high season). WiFi (charged). Dogs are not accepted in July/Aug. Off site: Bus service close to site entrance. Fishing and watersports 400 m. Bicycle and scooter hire 1 km. Golf 5 km. Resort type entertainment close.

Open: All year.

Directions

Site is between Marbella and Fuengirola off the N340/A7. Access at 188.8 km. marker is only possible when travelling west, i.e. from Fuengirola. From the other direction, continue to the 'cambio de sentido' signed Elviria and turn back over the dual carriageway. Site is signed. GPS: 36.5023, -4.804

Charges guide

Per unit incl. 2 persons	
and electricity	€ 17.33 - € 35.42
extra person	€ 5.60 - € 7.64
child (under 10 yrs)	€ 3.05 - € 6.11
dog (not July/Aug)	€ 2.55 - € 3.05

Motril

Camping Don Cactus

Ctra N340 km. 343, Carchuna, E-18730 Motril (Granada) T: 958 623 109. E: camping@doncactus.com

alanrogers.com/ES92950

Situated between the main N340 and the beach, this family run campsite is pleasantly surprising with clever planning and ongoing improvements. It is a comfortable site of 320 pitches (280 for touring). The flat pitches vary in size with electricity (5/12A), some providing water and satellite TV connections, and are arranged along avenues with eucalyptus trees for shade. This quieter section of the coast is beautiful with coves and access to larger towns if wished. The friendly reception staff are very helpful with tourist advice and can arrange trips for you if needed.

Facilities

The large toilet block is dated but clean and provides British style WCs, showers and plenty of washbasins. Laundry facilities. Beach showers. Well stocked shop. Bar, restaurant and takeaway (all year). Outdoor swimming pool (open all year, in high season € 1.50 per day). Tennis. Play area. Summer activities for children. Outdoor fitness centre for adults. Pets corner. ATM. Internet point. WiFi (charged; free in bar). Dogs are not accepted in July/Aug. Barbecues only in special area.

Open: All year.

Directions

From Motril-Carchuna road (N340/E15) turn towards the sea at km. 343. (site signed, but look at roof level for large green tent on the top of the building!). Travel 600 m. then turn east to site on left. GPS: 36.70066, -3.44032

Charges guide

Per person	€ 7.65
child (4-10 yrs)	€ 7.15
pitch	€ 16.95
electricity (5A)	€ 4.85 - € 6.65

FREE Alan Rogers Travel Card
Extra benefits and savings - see page 14

Pitres

Camping El Balcon de Pitres

Ctra Orgiva-Ugijar km. 51, E-18414 Pitres (Granada) T: 958 766 111. E: info@balcondepitres.com

alanrogers.com/ES92900

A simple country site perched high in the mountains of Las Alpujarras, on the south side of the Sierra Nevada, El Balcon de Pitres has its own rustic charm. Hundreds of trees planted around the site provide shade. There are stunning views from some of the 175 level grassy pitches (large units may find pitch access difficult). The garden is kept green by spring waters, which you can hear and sometimes see, tinkling away in places. The Lopez family have built this site from barren mountain top to cool oasis in the mountains in just fifteen years.

Facilities

Two toilet blocks provide adequate facilities including some for disabled campers (but the steeply sloping site is unsuitable for visitors with mobility problems). Bar/snack bar (with TV and pool table). Swimming pools (charged: € 2.40 adult, € 1.50 child). Barbecues are not permitted. Torches useful. WiFi. Off site: Fishing. Canyoning. Trekking. Parascending. Quad bikes. Sports centre for football.

Open: All year.

Directions

Site is 30 km. northeast of Motril. Heading south on A44 (E902) exit 164 (Lanjaron) onto E348 towards Orgiva. Fork left at sign (A4132) Pampaneira 8 km. Continue to Pitres (7 km). Site signed (steep and winding roads). GPS: 36.9323, -3.3334

Charges guide

Per unit incl. 2 persons and electricity	€ 19.50
extra person	€ 5.00
child	€ 4.50

Santa Elena

Camping Despeñaperros

Ctra Infanta Elena, E-23213 Santa Elena (Jaén) T: 953 664 192. E: info@campingdespenaperros.com

alanrogers.com/ES90890

This site is on the edge of Santa Elena in a natural park with shade from mature pine trees. This is a good place to stay en-route from Madrid to the Costa del Sol or to just explore the surrounding countryside. The 116 pitches are fully serviced including a satellite TV/Internet link. All rubbish must be taken to large bins outside the site gates (a long walk from the other end of the site). The site is run in a very friendly manner where nothing is too much trouble. Reception has a monitor link with tourist information and access to the region's sites of interest.

Facilities

Two traditional, central sanitary blocks have Turkish style WCs and well equipped showers. Facilities for disabled visitors. One washing machine (launderette in town). Shop. Excellent bar (all year) and charming restaurant (May-Oct). Swimming pools (15/6-15/9). Tennis. Caravan storage. Night security. Communal barbecue area. WiFi over part of site. Off site: Walking, riding and mountain sports nearby. The main road gives good access to Jaén and Valdepeñas.

Open: All year.

Directions

Travelling on A4 (E5) take exit 259 (Santa Elena). Drive through town and site is on right up steep slope (alternative entrance for tall vehicles – ask reception). GPS: 38.34307, -3.53528

Charges guide

Per unit incl. 2 persons and electricity	€ 17.50 - € 23.65
extra person	€ 4.25 - € 4.85
child	€ 3.30 - € 4.05

Tarifa

Camping Valdevaqueros

Ctra N340 km. 75,5, E-11380 Tarifa (Cádiz) T: 956 684 174. E: info@campingvaldevaqueros.com

alanrogers.com/ES88620

Camping Valdevaqueros is located at Tarifa on the Costa de la Luz. This is a friendly site with large pitches (60-80 sq.m), most of which have electrical connections. A number of chalets and mobile homes are available for rent, as well as several apartments. On-site amenities include a large swimming pool, surrounded by a grassy sunbathing area, and a tennis court. There is a friendly bar/restaurant and a takeaway food service. The modern toilet blocks are equipped with family rooms.

Facilities

Toilet blocks with facilities for babies and disabled visitors. Private bathrooms for hire. Motorcaravan services. Supermarket. Bar. Restaurant. Swimming pool. Children's pool. Tennis. Play area. Riding. Bicycle hire. Free WiFi over part of site. Mobile homes, apartments and chalets for rent. Off site: Shops and restaurants in Blanes. Golf. Fishing. Excursions to Morocco and Gibraltar.

Open: All year.

Directions

The site is to the northwest of Tarifa. Approaching from Tarifa, take the northbound N340 (towards Cadiz) and follow signs to the site. GPS: 36.069171, -5.680736

Charges guide

Per unit incl. 2 persons and electricity	€ 20.80 - € 32.00
extra person	€ 7.00
child (2-12 yrs)	€ 5.50
dog	€ 1.00

For latest campsite news, availability and prices visit

alanrogers.com

Albarracin

Camping Ciudad de Albarracin

Junto al Polideportivo, Camino de Gea, E-44100 Albarracin (Teruel) T: 978 710 197.

E: campingalbarracin5@hotmail.com **alanrogers.com/ES90950**

Albarracin, in southern Aragón, is set in the Reserva Nacional de los Montes Universales and is a much frequented, fascinating town with a Moorish castle. The old city walls towering above date from its days when it attempted to become a separate country within Spain. This neat and clean family site is set on three levels on a hillside behind the town, with a walk of 1 km. to the centre. It is very modern and has high quality facilities including a superb building for barbecuing (all materials provided). There are 100 pitches (70 for touring units), all with electricity and separated by trees. Some require cars to be parked separately.

Facilities
The two spotless, modern sanitary buildings provide British style WCs, quite large showers and hot water. Baby bath. Washing machines. Bar/restaurant. Essentials from bar. Special room for barbecues with fire and wood provided. Play area. Outdoor swimming pool (1/7-31/8). Torches required in some areas. Off site: Shops, bars and restaurants 500 m.

Open: 1 March - 15 November.

Directions
From Teruel north on the N330 for 8 km. then west onto A1512 for 30 km. From the A23 use exit 124 then the A1512, from the N235 take exit for Albarracin and the A1512. Site is well signed in the town. GPS: 40.41655, -1.43332

Charges guide
Per unit incl. 2 persons and electricity	€ 19.35
extra person	€ 4.00

Boltaña

Camping Boltaña

Ctra N260 km. 442, E-22340 Boltaña (Huesca) T: 974 502 347. E: info@campingboltana.com

alanrogers.com/ES90620

Under the innovative and charming ownership of Raquel Rodrigeuz, Camping Boltaña nestles in the Rio Ara valley, surrounded by the Pyrenees mountains. It is very pretty and thoughtfully planned to provide tranquillity and privacy. The generously sized, 220 grassy pitches (all with 10A electricity) have good shade from a variety of carefully planted trees and shrubs. A stone building houses the site's reception, a social room with computer and excellent WiFi connection and shop. Adjacent is a good restaurant, bar and takeaway with a large terrace that has views over the site to the mountains. Activities and excursions in the surrounding area can be organised at the helpful, English-speaking reception office.

Facilities
Two modern sanitary blocks include facilities for disabled visitors and children. Laundry facilities. Fridge hire. Shop, bar, restaurant and takeaway (1/4-30/11). Swimming pools (1/5-25/10). Playground. Entertainment for children (high season). Pétanque. Guided tours and information about hiking, canyoning, rafting, climbing, mountain biking and caving. Bicycle hire. Library. Communal barbecue area. Under-cover meeting area. WiFi in some areas (free). Off site: Footpaths 500 m. Fishing 1 km. Ainsa 6 km. Canoeing 6 km. Canyoning 20 km.

Open: All year.

Directions
South of the Park Nacional de Ordesa, site is 50 km. from Jaca near Ainsa. From Ainsa travel northwest on N260 toward Boltaña (near 443 km. marker) and 1 km. from Boltaña turn south toward Margudgued. Site is well signed and is 1 km. along this road. GPS: 42.43018, 0.07882

Charges guide
Per unit incl. 2 persons and electricity	€ 22.55 - € 37.20
extra person	€ 4.10 - € 6.75
Camping Cheques accepted.	

Gavín

Camping Gavín

Ctra N260 km. 503, E-22639 Gavín (Huesca) T: 974 485 090. E: info@campinggavin.com

alanrogers.com/ES90640

Camping Gavín is set on a terraced, wooded hillside and you will find a friendly welcome. The site offers 150 touring pitches of 90 sq.m. and with 10A electricity available to all. In some areas the terracing means that some pitches are quite small. The main site buildings have been constructed using natural stone. There are also 13 bungalows and 11 superb, balconied apartments. A good restaurant, bar and supermarket are open all year (except November). At about 900 m. the site is surrounded by towering peaks at the portal of the Tena Valley. One can enjoy the natural beauty of the Pyrenees and venture near or far along the great Pyrenean footpaths.

Facilities
Excellent shower and toilet facilities in three main buildings with subtle, tasteful décor include facilities for babies, children and disabled visitors. Laundry facilities. Motorcaravan services. Well stocked supermarket. Bar, restaurant and takeaway. Swimming pools (15/6-15/9) and paddling pools (all year). Tennis. Playground and indoor play area. Bicycle hire. Individual barbecues are not permitted at some times. WiFi in reception (free).

Open: All year.

Directions
Site is off the N260, 2 km. from Biescas at km. 503. From France at Col de Portalet take A136 towards Biescas. At Biescas turn east on N260 towards Broto. GPS: 42.61940, -0.30408

Charges guide
Per unit incl. 2 persons and electricity	€ 30.30 - € 36.80
extra person	€ 5.00 - € 6.90
child (2-10 yrs)	€ 4.00 - € 5.90

FREE Alan Rogers Travel Card
Extra benefits and savings - see page 14

La Puebla de Castro

Camping Lago Barasona

Ctra N123a km. 25, E-22435 La Puebla de Castro (Huesca) T: 974 545 148. E: info@lagobarasona.com

alanrogers.com/ES91250

This site, alongside its associated ten room hotel, is beautifully positioned on terraces across a road from the shores of the Lago de Barasona (a large reservoir), with views of hills and the distant Pyrenees. The very friendly, English-speaking owners are keen to please and apply very high standards throughout the site. The attractive, grassy pitches are fairly level and generally around 100 sq.m. Pitches for larger units are also available. All have 6/10A electricity, many are well shaded and most have great views of the lake and/or the mountains. Water skiing and other watersports are available in July and August.

Facilities

Two toilet blocks in modern buildings have high standards and hot water throughout including cabins (3 for women, 1 for men). Shop (all season). Bar/snack bar and a good restaurant (all season), with a second in high season. Swimming pools (1/6-30/9). Tennis. Mountain bike hire. Miniclub (high season). Maps provided for walking and cycling. Money exchange. Mini-disco. Fitness centre with sauna, jacuzzi and gym. WiFi in some areas (free).
Off site: Canoe, windsurfing, motorboat and pedalo hire.

Open: 1 March - 12 December.

Directions

Site is east of Huesca on the west bank of Lake Barasona, close to km. 25 on the N123A, 6 km. south of Graus (about 80 km. north of Lleida/Lerida). Travelling from the south, the site is on the left from a newly built roundabout and slip road. Site is accessed via a service road next to the main road. GPS: 42.14163, 0.31525

Charges guide

Per unit incl. 2 persons	
and electricity	€ 23.00 - € 36.80
extra person	€ 4.50 - € 6.90

Labuerda

Camping Peña Montañesa

Ctra Ainsa-Francia km 2, E-22360 Labuerda (Huesca) T: 974 500 032. E: info@penamontanesa.com

alanrogers.com/ES90600

A large site situated in the Pyrenees near the Ordesa National Park, Peña Montañesa is easily accessible from Ainsa or from France via the Bielsa Tunnel (steep sections on the French side). The site is divided into three sections opening progressively throughout the season and all have shade. The 288 pitches on fairly level grass are of about 75 sq.m. and 10A electricity is available on virtually all. Grouped near the entrance are the facilities that make the site so attractive, including an attractive outdoor pool and a heated, glass covered indoor pool with jacuzzi and sauna. Here too is an attractive bar/restaurant with an open fire and a terrace; a supermarket and takeaway are opposite.

Facilities

A newer toilet block, heated when necessary, has free hot showers but cold water to open plan washbasins. Facilities for disabled visitors. Small baby room. An older block in the original area has similar provision. Washing machine and dryer. Bar, restaurant, takeaway and supermarket (all 1/1-31/12). Outdoor pool (1/4-31/10). Indoor pool, sauna and jacuzzi (all year). Outdoor social area with large TV screen and stage. Tennis. Playground. Boules. Gas barbecues only. WiFi in bar area (free).

Open: All year.

Directions

Site is clearly signed and is 2 km. north of Ainsa, on the road from Ainsa to France.
GPS: 42.4352, 0.13618

Charges guide

Per unit incl. 2 persons	
and electricity	€ 15.60 - € 21.60
extra person	€ 4.95 - € 7.15
child (2-10 yrs)	€ 4.55 - € 6.75
dog	€ 3.35 - € 4.35

Caravia Alta

Camping Caravaning Arenal de Moris

A8 Salida 330, E-33344 Caravia Alta (Asturias) T: 985 853 097. E: camoris@desdeasturias.com

alanrogers.com/ES89550

This smart, well run site is close to three fine sandy beaches so gets very busy at peak times. It has a backdrop of the mountains in the nature reserve known as the Sueve which is important for a breed of short Asturian horse, the Asturcone. The site has 330 grass pitches (220 for touring units) of 40-70 sq.m. and with 180 electricity connections available (10A). There are some shady, terraced pitches while others are on an open, slightly sloping field with limited views of the sea. The restaurant with a terrace serves local dishes and overlooks the pool with hills and woods beyond.

Facilities

Three toilet blocks provide comfortable, controllable showers and vanity style washbasins, private cabins, laundry facilities and external dishwashing (cold water). Supermarket. Bar/restaurant. Swimming pool. Tennis. Play area in lemon orchard. Limited English is spoken. No electric barbecues. WiFi in restaurant area.
Off site: Beach and fishing 200 m. Bus 1 km. from gate. Bar and restaurants in village 2 km. Golf 5 km.

Open: 1 June - 17 September.

Directions

Caravia Alta is 50 km. east of Gijón. Leave A8 Santander-Oviedo motorway at 330 km. exit, turn left on N632 towards Colunga and site is signed to right in village, near 16 km. marker. Care needed upon site entry and exit. GPS: 43.47248, -5.18332

Charges guide

Per unit incl. 2 persons	
and electricity	€ 24.10 - € 34.15
extra person	€ 5.75 - € 6.75

For latest campsite news, availability and prices visit

alanrogers.com

Colunga

Camping Costa Verde

Playa de la Griega, E-33320 Colunga (Asturias) T: 985 856 373. E: info@campingcostaverde.com

alanrogers.com/ES89500

This uncomplicated coastal site has a marked Spanish flavour and is just 1.5 km. from the pleasant town of Colunga. Although little English is spoken, the cheerful owner and his helpful staff will make sure you get a warm welcome. The great advantage for many is that, 200 m. from the gate, is a spacious beach by a low tide lagoon with a recently constructed marine parade, ideal for younger children. Some of the 192 pitches are occupied on a seasonal basis, but there are 140 for touring units. These are flat but with little shade, and electricity (5/10A) is available (long leads needed in places). The site gets very busy in high season.

Facilities

The single toilet block is of a high standard with a mixture of British and Turkish style toilets (all British for ladies), large showers and free hot water throughout. Laundry. Well stocked shop. Bar/restaurant is traditional and friendly. Play area. Torches needed. No electric barbecues. Free WiFi on part of site. Off site: Fishing in river alongside site. Nearby towns of Ribadesella, Gijón and Oviedo. Excellent beaches. Bicycle hire and riding 2 km. Sailing 4 km. Golf 20 km.

Open: Easter - 1 October.

Directions

Colunga is 45 km. east of Gijón. Leave the A8 Santander-Oviedo motorway at km. 337 exit and take N632 towards Colunga. In village, turn right on As257 towards Lastres; site is on right after 1 km. marker. GPS: 43.49875, -5.26357

Charges guide

Per unit incl. 2 persons and electricity	€ 19.90 - € 20.50
extra person	€ 5.00
child (over 5 yrs)	€ 4.50

Cudillero

Camping Cudillero

Ctra Playa de Aguilar, El Pito, E-33150 Cudillero (Asturias) T: 985 590 663. E: info@campingcudillero.com

alanrogers.com/ES89530

If you need a stop en route convenient to Gijón, or are planning to explore this part of the Costa Verde, then this attractive and well cared for site should be considered. Only 2 km. from the bustling fishing village of Cudillero, it offers 135 easily accessed touring pitches, all on level grass and with 6A electricity. Pitches are numbered and separated by mature hedges and trees that provide a degree of shade if required. This is a family owned and managed site with good, clean facilities, including a shop, a very pleasant and welcoming bar with adjoining restaurant area and a small swimming pool.

Facilities

One modern and very well maintained toilet block includes hot showers. Facilities for babies and for disabled visitors (both with key entry). Washing machine and dryer. Shop. Bar/restaurant. Swimming pool. Play area. Gas and Charcoal barbecues only. WiFi throughout (small charge). 18 well equipped chalets available to rent. Off site: Fishing and beach 1 km. Cudillero with choice of shops, bars and restaurants 2 km. Bicycle hire 4 km. Riding 12 km.

Open: Easter and 29 April - 15 September.

Directions

Leave A8 auto route at exit 425 (Muros de Nalon). Take third exit at roundabout on to N632. After 3 km. turn right towards El Pito and Cudillero and follow signs to site. On no account take caravans into Cudillero. GPS: 43.55418, -6.12932

Charges guide

Per unit incl. 2 persons and electricity	€ 22.90 - € 29.00
extra person	€ 4.95 - € 5.95
No credit cards.	

Luarca

Camping Taurán

Paraje Taurán s/n, E-33700 Luarca-Valdés (Asturias) T: 985 641 272. E: tauran@campingtauran.com

alanrogers.com/ES89435

Tucked away at the end of a single track road, this small and attractive site is ideally situated for visiting the old fishing port of Luarca. Set on a level plateau above the town, the site has views over the sea and the hills beyond. The 100 level grass pitches, all with 10A electricity, are numbered and separated by mature hedges and trees giving a good amount of shade. The modern sanitary facilities are housed in a single rustic building near to the site entrance. The site owner Rosa and her family live in the building which also houses reception, a small shop, restaurant and bar and she is always available to ensure visitors have an enjoyable stay at this tranquil site.

Facilities

One older style toilet block with modern WCs, washbasins and hot showers. Baby bath with changing mats. Facilities for disabled visitors. Washing machine and dryer. Motorcaravan services. Bar/restaurant. Shop. Small swimming pool (July/Aug). Accessible beach. No barbecues on pitches (communal area provided). Free WiFi at bar area. Dogs are not accepted. Off site: Luarca 2 km. with shops, bars and excellent fish restaurants.

Open: Early April to mid October.

Directions

From A8 auto route Gijon to A Coruña, leave at exit 465. Turn right at first roundabout then take third exit at second roundabout signed El Chano and camping. Do not take road into Luarca. Follow road and signs for 3 km. to site at end of narrow approach road. GPS: 43.55109, -6.55322

Charges guide

Per unit incl. 2 persons and electricity	€ 20.50 - € 22.00
Credit cards only accepted July/August.	

FREE Alan Rogers Travel Card

Extra benefits and savings - see page 14

Ribadedeva

Camping Las Hortensias

Playa de la Franca, E-33590 Ribadedeva (Asturias) T: 985 412 442.

E: lashortensias@campinglashortensias.com **alanrogers.com/ES89570**

Open for just four months from June to September, Las Hortensias is a friendly site located on the Cantabrian coast of northern Spain. The site enjoys a fine setting on a sheltered sandy beach, adjacent to the Mirador Hotel. There are 156 pitches connected by well lit tarmac roads. Each pitch has 6-10A electricity and there are water points throughout. After a day on the beach or exploring the nearby rock pools, the bar terrace is a great spot to enjoy the sunset. Many pitches are well shaded by pine trees, in pleasant, peaceful locations.

Facilities

Two adequate sanitary blocks, one with WCs only, the other with open plan washbasins and showers. Washing machine and dryer. Basic motorcaravan services. Small supermarket. Bar with terrace overlooking beach. Basic restaurant (campers can use the hotel restaurant with 10% discount), snack bar and takeaway. TV in bar. Play area. Gas and charcoal barbecues only. WiFi. Off site: Beach with lifeguard. Salmon and trout fishing. Canoeing. Prehistoric caves and rock engravings.

Open: 1 June - 21 September.

Directions

The A8/E2 motorway heading west from Santander becomes the N634. Turn off at Playa de La Franca and the site is clearly signposted.
GPS: 43.391608, -4.575709

Charges guide

Per unit incl. 2 persons and electricity	€ 30.25 - € 34.35
extra person	€ 7.20
child (2-12 yrs)	€ 6.20

Vidiago-Llanes

Camping la Paz

Autovia del Camtabrico 285, E-33597 Vidiago-Llanes (Asturias) T: 985 411 235.

E: delfin@campinglapaz.com **alanrogers.com/ES89600**

This unusual site occupies a spectacular mountain location. The small reception building is opposite a solid rock face and many hundreds of feet below the site. The ascent to the upper part of the site is quite daunting, but staff will place your caravan for you if required, although motorcaravan drivers will have an exciting drive to the top, especially to the loftier pitches. Once there, the views are absolutely outstanding, both along the coast and inland to the Picos de Europa mountains. There are 434 pitches, all with 10/15A electricity. There is also a lower section in a shaded valley to which access is easier, if rather tight in places. The upper area is arranged on numerous terraces, many of which require you to park your car by the roadside and climb the hill to your tent. The way down to the attractive beach is quite steep; from the lower area there is an easy walk to a smaller beach. The cliff-top restaurant and bar has commanding views over the ocean and beach. The site is very popular in high season so it does get crowded.

Facilities

Four good, modern toilet blocks are well equipped with hot showers and open plan washbasins. They are kept very clean even at peak times. Baby bath. Full laundry facilities. Motorcaravan services. Restaurant and bar/snack bar with small shop (all season). Watersports. Games room. Fishing. Torches useful in some areas. Gas and charcoal barbecues only. WiFi in the restaurant. Off site: Shop, bar and restaurant in nearby village. Golf, riding, sailing and boat launching all 8 km.

Open: Easter - 15 October.

Directions

Site is signed from A8/N634 Santander-Oviedo/Gijón road near km. 285 marker. Site approach road is just east of the village of Vidiago, marked by campsite signs (not named) and flags. Cross the railway track and exercise caution on bends.
GPS: 43.39957, -4.65149

Charges guide

Per unit incl. 2 persons and electricity	€ 35.95 - € 37.10
extra person	€ 6.95
child	€ 6.10
electricity	€ 4.90

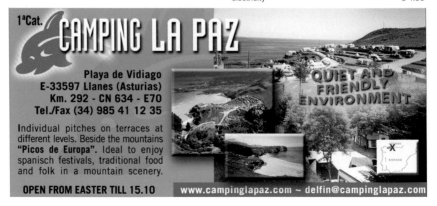

Noja

Camping Playa Joyel

Playa de Ris, E-39180 Noja (Cantabria) T: 942 630 081. E: info@playajoyel.com

alanrogers.com/ES90000

This very attractive holiday and touring site is some 40 kilometres from Santander and 80 kilometres from Bilbao. It is a busy, high quality, comprehensively equipped site by a superb beach providing 1,000 well shaded, marked and numbered pitches with 6A electricity available. These include 80 large pitches of 100 sq.m. Some 250 pitches are occupied by tour operators and seasonal units. This well managed site has a lot to offer for family holidays with much going on in high season when it gets crowded. The swimming pool complex (with lifeguard) is free to campers and the superb beaches are cleaned daily mid-June to mid-September.

Facilities
Six excellent, spacious and fully equipped toilet blocks include baby baths. Laundry. Motorcaravan services. Gas. Freezer service. Supermarket. Shop. Kiosk. Restaurant and bar. Takeaway (July/Aug). Swimming pools, bathing caps compulsory (20/5-15/9). Entertainment organised and a soundproofed pub/disco (July/Aug). Gym park. Tennis. Playground. Riding. Fishing. Nature animal park. Hairdresser (July/Aug). Medical centre. Torches necessary in some areas. Animals are not accepted. WiFi (charged).

Open: 27 March - 27 September.

Directions
From A8 (Bilbao-Santander) take km. 185 exit and N634 towards Beranga. Almost immediately turn right on CA147 to Noja. In 10 km. turn left at multiple campsite signs and go through town. At beach follow signs to site. GPS: 43.48948, -3.53700

Charges guide
Per unit incl. 2 persons	
and electricity	€ 28.90 - € 49.20
extra person	€ 4.50 - € 7.00
child (3-9 yrs)	€ 3.15 - € 5.10

Pechón

Camping Las Arenas-Pechón

Ctra Pechón-Unquera km. 2, E-39594 Pechón (Cantabria) T: 942 717 188. E: info@campinglasarenas.com

alanrogers.com/ES89700

This spacious and attractive coastal site is in a very quiet and spectacular location bordering the sea and the Tina Mayor estuary. Most pitches have stunning sea and mountain views and there is access down to two small, sandy beaches. Otherwise, enjoy the pleasant kidney shaped pool that also shares the fine views. With a capacity for 350 units, the site has many large, grassy pitches in bays or on terraces, all with 5A electricity available and connected by asphalted roads. There are some quite steep slopes to tackle – reception is at the top, as are the bar and restaurant; the latter has a terrace with fantastic views of the estuary and of the mountains beyond.

Facilities
Modern, well tiled sanitary facilities are housed in three traditional, simple style buildings. Washing machines. Well stocked supermarket. Restaurant/bar and snack bar (all season). Outdoor swimming pool and children's pool. Small playground. Riding and other activities can be arranged (collected from site). River and sea fishing. Torches helpful. English is spoken. No electric barbecues. WiFi throughout. Off site: Shops, bars and restaurants in Pechón, plus a disco/bar 1 km. Golf 28 km.

Open: 1 June - 30 September.

Directions
On A8 from Santander, take km. 272 exit for Unquera (N621). Take first exit CA380 signed Pechón and site is 2 km. on left. From Oviedo/Gijón on A8/N634 at km. 272 take N621 slip-road for Unquera (do not join motorway), then as above. GPS: 43.39093, -4.5106

Charges guide
Per unit incl. 2 persons	
and electricity	€ 27.95 - € 34.35
extra person	€ 6.90

Potes

Camping la Isla Picos de Europa

Turieno-Potes, E-39570 Potes (Cantabria) T: 942 730 896. E: campicoseuropa@terra.es

alanrogers.com/ES89620

La Isla is beside the road from Potes to Fuente Dé, with many mature trees giving good shade and glimpses of the mountains above. Established for over 25 years, a warm welcome awaits you from the owners (who speak good English) and a most relaxed and peaceful atmosphere exists here. All the campers we spoke to were delighted with the family feeling of the site. The 106 unmarked pitches are arranged around an oval gravel track under a variety of fruit and ornamental trees. Electricity (6A) is available to all pitches, although some need long leads. A brilliant small bar and restaurant are located under dense trees where you can enjoy the relaxing sound of the river which runs through the site.

Facilities
Single, clean and smart sanitary block retains the style of the site. Washbasins with cold water. Washing machine. Gas supplies. Freezer service. Small shop and restaurant/bar (1/4-30/9). Small swimming pool (caps compulsory; 1/5-30/9). Play area. Barbecue area. Fishing. Bicycle hire. Riding. Free WiFi throughout. Off site: Bus from gate in high season. Potes 2.5 km. Riding 10 km. Fuente Dé and its spectacular cable car ride 18 km.

Open: 1 April - 15 October.

Directions
From A8/N634 (Santander-Oviedo) take km. 272 exit for Unquera. Take N621 south to Panes and up spectacular gorge for 15 km. (take care if towing) to Potes. Take CA185 to Fuente Dé. Site is on right, 2.5 km. beyond Potes. GPS: 43.14999, -4.69997

Charges guide
Per unit incl. 2 persons	
and electricity	€ 18.96 - € 22.45
extra person	€ 4.18 - € 4.65

FREE Alan Rogers Travel Card

Extra benefits and savings - see page 14

Ruiloba
Camping El Helguero

Ctra Santillana-Comillas, E-39527 Ruiloba (Cantabria) T: 942 722 124. E: reservas@campingelhelguero.com

alanrogers.com/ES89610

This site, in a peaceful location surrounded by tall trees and impressive towering rock formations, caters for 240 units (of which 100 are seasonal) on slightly sloping ground. There are many marked pitches on different levels, all with access to electricity (6A), but with varying amounts of shade. There are also attractive tent and small camper sections set close in to the rocks and 22 site owned chalets. The site gets very crowded in high season, so it is best to arrive early if you have not booked. The reasonably sized swimming pool and children's pool have access lifts for disabled campers.

Facilities
Three well placed toilet blocks, although old, are clean and all include controllable showers and hot and cold water to all washbasins. Facilities for children and disabled visitors. Washing machines and dryers. Motorcaravan services. Small supermarket. Bar/snack bar plus separate more formal restaurant. Swimming pool (caps compulsory). Playground. Activities and entertainment (high season). ATM. Torches useful in some places. No electric barbecues. WiFi over site (charged by card). Off site: Bar/restaurants in village (walking distance).

Open: 1 April - 30 September.

Directions
From A8 (Santander-Oviedo) take km. 249 exit (Cabezón and Comillas) and turn north on CA135 towards Comillas. At km. 7 turn right on CA359 to Ruilobuca and Barrio la Iglesia. After village turn right up hill on CA358 to site on right. GPS: 43.38288, -4.24800

Charges guide
Per unit incl. 2 persons and electricity	€ 24.15 - € 30.15
extra person	€ 4.70 - € 5.70

Camping Cheques accepted.

San Vicente de la Barquera
Camping Caravaning Playa de Oyambre

Los Llaos, E-39547 San Vicente de la Barquera (Cantabria) T: 942 711 461. E: camping@oyambre.com

alanrogers.com/ES89710

This exceptionally well managed site is ideally positioned to use as a base to visit the spectacular Picos de Europa or one of the many sandy beaches along this northern coast. Despite its name, it is a kilometre from the beach on foot. The 120 touring pitches all have 10A electricity (long leads needed in places), ten are fully serviced. The fairly flat central area is allocated to tents while caravans are mainly sited on wide terraces (access to some could be a little tight for larger units) and there is some shade. There may be some traffic noise on the lower terraces. Some pitches are occupied by seasonal units and another 50 are taken up by chalets to let. The site is in lovely countryside (good walking and cycling country), with some views of the fabulous Picos mountains, and is near the Cacarbeno National Park. The owner's son, Pablo, and his wife Maria are assisted by Francis in providing a personal service and excellent English is spoken. The site is well lit and a guard patrols at night (high season). The site gets busy with a fairly large Spanish community in season and there can be the usual happy noise of them enjoying themselves especially at weekends.

Facilities
Good, clean sanitary facilities are in one, well kept block. Facilities for babies and disabled visitors. Washing machines. Motorcaravan services. Shop in bar. Restaurant. Takeaway. Swimming pools with lifeguard. Playground. Bicycle hire. Free WiFi over site. Off site: Bus service at entrance. Fishing and superb beach 1 km. Golf 2 km. Riding 10 km. San Vicente de la Barquera 5 km.

Open: 1 March - 28 September.

Directions
From A8 (Santander-Oviedo) take exit at km. 258 (Caviedes) and join N634. Turn towards San Vicente. Site is signed at junction to Comillas, at km. 265 on E70, 5 km. east of San Vicente. Entrance is quite steep. Another Camping La Playa within 500 m. is not recommended. GPS: 43.385268, -4.33814

Charges guide
Per unit incl. 2 persons and electricity	€ 26.75 - € 32.65
extra person	€ 5.50 - € 5.95

Camping and Caravanning Playa de Oyambre is located in the Natural Park Oyambre, one of the most beautiful places in Cantabria. A short distance from the beach (15 minute walk), in a wonderful landscape with splendid vistas of the Picos de Europa, is the ideal place to use as a basis for numerous hikes or day trips to places like The Picos de Europa, Cares route, Covadonga, etc.

Finca Peña Gerra - Los Llaos · San Vicente de la Barquera - Cantabria (Spain)
Tel. 00 34 942.71.14.61 · camping@oyambre.com · www.oyambre.com

---

Burgos

Camping Municipal Fuentes Blancas

Ctra Cartuja-Miraflores km 3,5, E-09193 Burgos (Burgos) T: 947 486 016. E: info@campingburgos.com

alanrogers.com/ES90210

Fuentes Blancas is a comfortable municipal site on the edge of the historic town of Burgos and within easy reach of the Santander ferries. There are around 350 marked pitches of 70 sq.m. on flat ground, 250 with electrical connections (6A) and there is good shade in parts. The site has a fair amount of transit trade and reservations are not possible for August, so arrive early. Burgos is an attractive city, ideally placed for an overnight stop en route to or from the south of Spain. The old part of the city around the cathedral is quite beautiful and there are pleasant walks along the riverbanks outside the site gates.

Facilities

Clean, modern style, fully equipped sanitary facilities in five blocks with controllable showers and hot and cold water to sinks (not all are always open). Facilities for babies. Washing machine/dryer. Motorcaravan services. Small shop (May-Sept). Bar/snack bar with terrace, social room with TV and DVD and restaurant (all year). Swimming pool (1/7-30/8). Playground. Entertainment for children and adults (July/Aug). WiFi over part of site, (charged). English is spoken. Off site: Fishing and river beach 200 m.

Open: All year.

Directions

From the south take the A1 Madrid to Burgos road. At Burgos follow the N623 to Santander and the site is well signed. Beware of Sat nav directions (2014). GPS: 42.34125, -3.65762

Charges guide

Per unit incl. 2 persons and electricity	€ 27.69
extra person	€ 5.19
child (2-10 yrs)	€ 3.56
dog	€ 2.44

Castrojeriz

Camping Camino de Santiago

Avenida Virgen del Manzano s/n, E-09110 Castrojeriz (Burgos) T: 947 377 255.

E: info@campingcamino.com **alanrogers.com/ES90230**

This site is located on the famous Camino de Compostela which is still walked by today's pilgrims. The path passes by the site entrance and there is an ancient pilgrims' refuge just outside the gate. It lies to the west of Burgos on the outskirts of Castrojeriz, in a superb location, almost in the shadow of the ruined castle high on the hillside. Apart from just four units to rent, the site takes only touring units. The 50 marked pitches are level, grassy and divided by hedges, with 10A electricity and mature trees providing shade. This site is also a birdwatchers' paradise – large raptors abound.

Facilities

Older style sanitary block with hot showers, washbasin with cold water. No special facilities for disabled visitors or children. Washing machine and drying room. Small shop. Gas. Safe rental. Bar/restaurant and takeaway with basic cuisine. Library. Games room. Small play area. Barbecue area. Ad hoc guided birdwatching. WiFi over site (free). Off site: Camino de Santiago and other signed footpaths from site. Castrojeriz with shops, supermarket and restaurant 0.75km.

Open: 1 March - 30 November.

Directions

From N120/A231 (Leon-Burgos), turn on Bu404 (Villasandino, Castrojeriz). Turn left at crossroads on southwest side of town, then left at site sign. From A62 (Burgos-Valladolid) turn north at Vallaquirán on Bu400/401 to Castrojeriz. Turn sharp right at filling station and follow signs. GPS: 42.2913, -4.1448

Charges guide

Per unit incl. 2 persons and electricity	€ 20.50 - € 21.75
extra person	€ 5.00 - € 5.25

Tordesillas

Kawan Village Campingred El Astral

Camino de Pollos 8, E-47100 Tordesillas (Valladolid) T: 983 770 953.

E: info@campingelastral.es **alanrogers.com/ES90290**

The site is in a prime position alongside the wide River Duero (safely fenced). It is homely and run by a charming man, Eduardo Gutierrez, who speaks excellent English and is ably assisted by brother Gustavo and sister Lola. The site is generally flat with 140 pitches separated by thin hedges. The 133 touring pitches, 132 with electricity (6/10A), six with 10A electricity, water and waste water, vary in size from 60-200 sq.m. with mature trees providing shade. The new toilet block has been designed with environmental sustainability in mind, including solar heated water. This is a friendly site ideal for exploring the area and historic Tordesillas.

Facilities

One attractive new sanitary block with fully equipped, modern facilities designed to include energy-saving measures and to be easily cleaned. Showers for children and baby room. Facilities for disabled campers. Washing machines. Motorcaravan services. Supermarket. Bar and restaurant, frequented by locals, plus a takeaway service all 1/4-30/9. Swimming pool with new disability lift, plus paddling pools (1/6-15/9). Playground. Tennis (high season). Minigolf. No charcoal barbecues. WiFi (charged).

Open: All year.

Directions

Tordesillas is 28 km. southwest of Valladolid. From all directions, leave the main road towards Tordesillas and follow signs to campsite or 'Parador' (a hotel opposite the campsite). GPS: 41.495305, -5.005222

Charges guide

Per unit incl. 2 persons and electricity	€ 16.00 - € 30.00
extra person	€ 4.60 - € 6.90
child (3-12 yrs)	€ 3.60 - € 5.70

Camping Cheques accepted.

Horcajo de Los Montes
Camping El Mirador de Cabañeros

Canada Real s/n, E-13110 Horcajo de Los Montes (Ciudad Real) T: **926 775 439**.

E: info@campingcabaneros.com **alanrogers.com/ES90960**

With panoramic views all around of the Sierra de Valdefuertes mountains, Camping El Mirador is set in the Cabañeros National Park. This is a well cared for, landscaped site with 44 terraced pitches on gravel, all with 6A electricity. Although pitches are level once sited, the approach is via a steep slope which may cause difficulties for larger units. Run by a very helpful and friendly family, this site is in a very peaceful location where you can just sit and relax or visit the many attractions that the National Park has to offer. It is an ideal base for walking and birdwatching.

Facilities
One spotlessly clean central toilet block with solar heating includes open washbasins and cubicle showers. Facilities for disabled visitors and babies. Laundry. Motorcaravan services. No shop but basics from reception. Bar and restaurant (15/6-15/9, w/ends in low season). Covered swimming pool (all year). Games room. Outside fitness area. Play areas. Off site: Bicycle hire 1 km. Fishing 5 km. Horcacio de los Montes (centre) 1.5 km. (steep walk).

Open: All year.

Directions
From Toledo take CM4013 to Las Ventas con Pena Aguilera and then CM403 to El Molinillo. Turn west onto CM4017 to Horcajo de Los Montes. Through village on CM4016 towards Alcoba de Los Montes for 2 km. and site is on left (narrow approach). GPS: 39.3219, -4.6495

Charges guide

Per unit incl. 2 persons and electricity	€ 21.90 - € 23.30
extra person	€ 5.00 - € 5.50

Camping Cheques accepted.

Molinicos
Camping Rio Mundo

Ctra Comarcal 412, km. 205, Mesones, E-02449 Molinicos (Albacete) T: **967 433 230**.

E: riomundo@campingriomundo.com **alanrogers.com/ES90980**

This uncomplicated and typically Spanish site is situated in the Sierra de Alcaraz (south of Albacete), just off the scenic route 412 between Elche de la Sierra and Valdepenas. The drive to this site is most enjoyable through beautiful scenery and from the west the main road is winding in some places. Shade is provided by mature trees for the 80 pitches, and electricity (6/10A) is supplied to 70 (long leads are useful). It is in a beautiful setting with majestic mountains and wonderful countryside to explore.

Facilities
One toilet block has been upgraded and provides clean modern facilities. Basic toilet facilities for disabled visitors. Washing machine. Small shop for basics. Outside bar serving snacks with covered seating area. Takeaway (all 15/3-12/10). Another bar by the swimming pool. Playground. Pétanque. Free WiFi over part of site. Only gas and electric barbecues permitted. Off site: Riding 7 km.

Open: 15 March - 12 October.

Directions
Site is off the 412 road which runs west to east between the A30 and 322 south of Albacete. Turn at km. 205 on the 412, 5 km. east of Riopar and west of Elche de la Sierra. From here follow signs to site. The road narrows to one lane for a few hundred yards. GPS: 38.48917, -2.34639

Charges guide

Per person	€ 4.65 - € 6.30
pitch incl. car	€ 11.60 - € 15.80
electricity (6/10A)	€ 3.90 - € 5.50

Toledo
Camping El Greco

Ctra CM4000 km. 0,7, E-45004 Toledo (Toledo) T: **925 220 090**. E: info@campingelgreco.es

alanrogers.com/ES90900

Toledo was the home of the Grecian painter, El Greco, and the site that bears his name boasts a beautiful view of the ancient city from the restaurant, bar and attractive pool and terrace area. The friendly, family owners make you welcome and are proud of their site, which is the only one in Toledo (it can get crowded). The 150 pitches are of 80 sq.m. with 10A electrical connections and shade from strategically planted trees. Most have separating hedges that give privacy, with others in herringbone layouts (long leads required in this area). The River Tajo stretches alongside the site, which has an attractive, tree-lined approach.

Facilities
Two sanitary blocks, both modernised, one with facilities for disabled campers. Laundry. Motorcaravan services. Swimming pool (15/6-15/9, charged). Small, well stocked shop in reception (all year). Restaurant/bar (1/4-30/9) with good menu and fair prices. Playgrounds. Ice machine. Communal barbecues. WiFi in bar/restaurant areas (free). Off site: Fishing in river. Bicycle hire 2 km. Golf 10 km. Riding 15 km. An hourly air-conditioned bus service runs from the gates to the city centre.

Open: All year.

Directions
Site is on C4000 road on the edge of the Toledo going west. Site signs also in city centre. From Madrid on N401, turn towards city centre then right at the roundabout at the old city gates. Site is signed. GPS: 39.865, -4.047

Charges guide

Per unit incl. 2 persons and electricity	€ 30.30
extra person	€ 6.75
child (3-10 yrs)	€ 5.75
dog	free

For latest campsite news, availability and prices visit
alanrogers.com

Albanyá

Camping Bassegoda Park

Camí Camp de l'illa, E-17733 Albanyá (Girona) T: 972 542 020. E: info@bassegodapark.com

alanrogers.com/ES80640

Surrounded by mountains alongside the Muga river, Bassegoda Park is a place to experience Spain in a natural environment but with a touch of luxury. This totally rebuilt site is just beyond Albanyá on the edge of the Alta Garrotxa National Park in an area of great beauty. In their own area, the 60 touring pitches are level and shaded, all on hardstanding and with access to electricity, water and drainage. Tents are dotted informally in the terraced forest areas. Particular care has been taken in the landscaping, layout and design of the attractive pool, bar and restaurant, the hub of the site. Regional wines and dishes are available in the reasonably priced restaurant.

Facilities
A new spacious and well equipped, main toilet building is centrally located and provides controllable showers and facilities for babies and disabled visitors. Two smaller refurbished blocks. Washing machine and dryer. Gas. Supermarket. Bar, restaurant and takeaway. Swimming pool (1/6-15/9). Playground. New leisure area (5-a-side football, volleyball, basketball). Minigolf. Activities for adults and children, plus weekend entertainment. Bicycle hire. Barbecue areas. WiFi. Torches useful.

Open: 14 March - 8 December.

Directions
From Barcelona on AP7/E15 exit 4 take the N11 towards France, then Gl510 to Llers and Gl511 to St Llorenc de la Muga and Albanyá. Site is beyond village (sharp bend), well signed. From France take exit 3 then Gl510 to Llers. There is NO exit 3 northbound on AP7/E15. GPS: 42.30654, 2.70933

Charges guide
Per unit incl. 2 persons
and electricity   € 28.30 - € 54.35
No credit cards.
Camping Cheques accepted.

Ametlla de Mar

Camping Caravanning Ametlla Village Platja

Apdo 240, Paraje Santes Creus, E-43860 Ametlla de Mar (Tarragona) T: 977 267 784.

E: info@campingametlla.com **alanrogers.com/ES85360**

Occupying a terraced hillside above colourful shingle coves and two small associated lagoons, this site falls into four areas. The central one with reception and supermarket has a group of 44 touring pitches, below this are chalets for rent and a few touring pitches on ground falling away towards the lagoons and the beach. A second larger touring section also has 54 mobile homes owned by tour operators and finally, the bar/restaurant, pool and other leisure facilities take pride of place on the hilltop, with glimpses of the sea through the trees. There is some train noise, especially in the front section.

Facilities
Two large toilet blocks, plus a smaller one. Controllable showers and open-style washbasins. Private cabins with WC and washbasin, and a few also with shower. En-suite unit for disabled visitors. Baby rooms. Motorcaravan services. Gas. Supermarket (2/4-30/9; small shop incl. bread at other times). Bar/restaurant with TV and terrace, snack menu and takeaway, pub/cocktail bar with balcony and sea views (all 2/4-30/9). Swimming pools (supervised 22/6-15/9). Children's club and play area. Fitness room. Bicycle hire. Entertainment (July/Aug). WiFi (charged).

Open: All year.

Directions
Ametlla is 50 km. south of Tarragona. From AP7/E15 (Barcelona-Valencia) at exit 39 (or from N340) follow signs for Ametlla de Mar. Bear right before village following numerous white signs and continue for 2 km. Take care on final steep bend to site. GPS: 40.8645, 0.7788

Charges guide
Per unit incl. 2 persons
and electricity   € 17.90 - € 46.40
extra person   € 3.00 - € 6.80

Amposta

Camping Eucaliptus

Platja Eucaliptus s/n, E-43870 Amposta (Tarragona) T: 977 479 046. E: eucaliptus@campingeucaliptus.com

alanrogers.com/ES85550

Ideally situated in the Parc Natural del Delta del Ebro, a unique area of wetland and a World Heritage site, Eucaliptus is close to the golden sands of Platja Eucaliptus. Arriving here is like finding an oasis after the extraordinary drive through miles of flat marshland and rice fields. There are 264 small, level, shady grass pitches, 156 for touring, all with electricity (6A). The site is very well maintained and has a pleasant bar/restaurant with a terrace that overlooks both the pool area and the campsite's own lagoon with its variety of wildlife. The pool has an attractive grassy area for sunbathing and the lagoon (fenced) replicates, in miniature, the habitat of the Delta, with helpful signs about flora and fauna.

Facilities
The single toilet block is kept very clean and includes open style washbasins and good sized shower cubicles. Baby bath. Good facilities for disabled visitors. Laundry facilities. Dog shower. Well stocked shop. Gas. Large bar with satellite TV. Good restaurant and snack bar with takeaway. Play area. Swimming pool with paddling pool (1/6-15/9). Bicycle hire. Barbecue area.

Open: 23 March - 30 September.

Directions
From AP7 take exit 41 and follow N340 south. Immediately after crossing River Ebro take exit for Els Muntells and Sant Jaume, then bear right in 4 km. on TV3405 to Els Muntells. Continue 13.5 km. to site on the right. GPS: 40.65658, 0.77978

Charges guide
Per unit incl. 2 persons
and electricity   € 25.55 - € 33.10

FREE Alan Rogers Travel Card
Extra benefits and savings - see page 14

Begur

Camping El Maset

Playa de Sa Riera, E-17255 Begur (Girona) T: 972 623 023. E: info@campingelmaset.com

alanrogers.com/ES81030

El Maset is a delightful and different family owned site in lovely wooded surroundings with views of the sea. There are 107 pitches, of which just 20 are slightly larger for caravans and motorcaravans, the remainder suitable only for tents. The site celebrated its 50th anniversary in 2011. The site entrance is steep and access to the caravan pitches can be quite tricky. However, help is available to tow your caravan to your pitch. Some of the pitches are shaded and all have electricity, 20 also have water and drainage. Tent pitches are more shaded on attractive, steep, rock-walled terraces on the hillside.

Facilities

Good sanitary facilities in three small blocks are kept very clean. Baby facilities. Washing machines and dryers. Unit for disabled campers but the ground is steep. Fridge hire. Bar/restaurant, takeaway and shop. Swimming pool. Solarium. Play area. Area for football and basketball. Excellent games room. Satellite TV. Internet (free) and WiFi (charged). Dogs are not accepted. Charcoal barbecues are not permitted. Off site: Fishing and beach 300 m. Golf and bicycle hire 1 km. Riding 2 km.

Open: 13 May - 13 October.

Directions

From the C31 Figueres-Palamos road south of Pals, north of Palafrugell, take GI653 to Begur. Site is 2 km. north of the town; follow signs for Playa de Sa Riera and site is on right (steep entrance). GPS: 41.96860, 3.21002

Charges guide

Per unit incl. 2 persons and electricity	€ 21.00 - € 30.00
extra person	€ 6.00 - € 9.00
child (1-10 yrs)	€ 3.40 - € 5.60

Begur

Camping Begur

Ctra d'Esclanya km. 2, E-17255 Begur (Girona) T: 972 623 201. E: info@campingbegur.com

alanrogers.com/ES81040

The choice of pitches on this pleasant, wooded site, just three kilometres from the coast is remarkable; some are on gently sloping grassland, others on hillside terraces or on the hilltop itself, and one steep slope has terraced tent pitches. Two hundred and thirty-two have electricity (10A), water and drainage, 30 are for tents and various corners are occupied by 45 mobile homes and chalets to rent, and by seasonal caravans. At the centre is a pleasant swimming pool with grassy terrace and a small paddling pool, overlooked by an attractive bar and snack bar. Begur has no fewer than seven beaches.

Facilities

Two modern toilet blocks are fully equipped. Each has open style washbasins, large showers, a good unit for disabled visitors. Baby room. Private bathroom for hire. Washing machines, dryers and ironing table. Motorcaravan services. Bar/snack bar. Swimming and paddling pool (all open all season). Boules. Gym (free). Play area. Large field for family activities (20/6-11/9). Children's 'huerta' (small market garden). Little farm with donkeys, goats, rabbits and chickens. WiFi.

Open: 1 April - 26 September.

Directions

From north on AP7 at exit 6 (Girona) take C66 to La Bisbal; before Palafrugell follow signs for Begur. From south on AP7 at exit 9 follow Palamós, Palafrugell, then Begur. Site is 2 km. south of Begur on minor road to Palafrugell. GPS: 41.940216, 3.200079

Charges guide

Per unit incl. 2 persons and electricity	€ 20.60 - € 43.30
extra person	€ 3.80 - € 7.40

No credit cards.

Bellver de Cerdanya

Camping Solana del Segre

Ctra N260 km. 198, E-25720 Bellver de Cerdanya (Lleida) T: 973 510 310. E: sds@solanadelsegre.com

alanrogers.com/ES91420

The Sierra del Cadi offers some spectacular scenery and the Reserva Cerdanya is very popular with Spanish skiers. This site is situated in an open, sunny lower valley beside the River Segre where the far bank is a National Park (unfenced so children will need supervision). The immediate area is ideal for walkers and offers many opportunities for outdoor activities. The site is in two sections, the lower one nearer the river being for touring units, mainly flat and grassy with 200 pitches of 100 sq.m. or more (100 for touring units), shaded by trees with 15A electricity. The upper area is taken by permanent units.

Facilities

Modern sanitary facilities are in a central building on the lower level, with extra prefabricated units (unisex toilets/showers). Facilities for disabled campers are on the upper level (wheelchair users will experience problems). Laundry facilities. Motorcaravan services. Small shop/bar/restaurant (1/7-15/9). Swimming and paddling pools (1/7-5/9). Indoor pool. Two play areas. Games room. Outdoor activity centre. Riding. Bicycle hire. River fishing. Dance area. Barbecue areas. Torches required.

Open: 1 July - 15 September.

Directions

Bellver de Cerdanya is 18 km. southwest of Puigcerdá, which is on the French border opposite Bourg-Madame. Site is on left at the 198 km. marker on the N260 from Puigcerdá to La Seu d'Urgell, well signed just beyond Bellver de Cerdanya. GPS: 42.372697, 1.760484

Charges guide

Per unit incl. 2 persons and electricity (5A)	€ 26.00 - € 32.30
extra person	€ 6.00 - € 6.40

No credit cards.

For latest campsite news, availability and prices visit

alanrogers.com

Blanes

Camping Solmar

Colom 48, E-17300 Blanes (Girona) T: 972 348 034. E: campingsolmar@campingsolmar.com

alanrogers.com/ES80220

Camping Solmar has been run by the Ribas family for over 40 years and a warm welcome awaits you. The site is located 200 m. from a sandy beach in the busy urban resort of Blanes. The accessible, shaded pitches are 65-85 sq.m. and all have 6A electricity connections. On-site amenities include an attractive restaurant, bar and terrace area, as well as a central swimming pool complex with islands and bridges. A children's club operates in peak season (4-12 years) and a fine new outdoor complex of sports facilities has just been opened. A range of fully equipped mobile homes and wooden chalets are available for rent. The site is owned and managed by Snr Ribas and his family, and has a personal and welcoming ambience as testified by a loyal British clientèle. Continual improvements have been made over the years and the facilities now provide a friendly, well resourced and well run base in the heart of the large and historic holiday resort of Blanes. Regular excursions are available in the town to all the area's main attractions, including Barcelona (65 km) and the Dalí museum in Figueres, whilst the town itself has a wide range of attractions, including some memorable firework displays.

Facilities

Four toilet blocks are clean and have open style washbasins, controllable showers in cabins and baby baths. Facilities for disabled visitors. Washing machines. Motorcaravan services. Supermarket. Restaurant. Bar. Swimming pool and terrace complex. Outdoor sports complex. Play areas. Miniclub (June onwards). Evening entertainment (high season). Tourist information and excursions. WiFi over site (charged). Mobile homes and chalets for rent. Off site: Beach and seaside amenities 200 m. Shops and restaurants in Blanes. Riding 5 km. Golf 6 km. Fishing.

Open: 23 March - 12 October.

Directions

The site is located to the south of the resort. From the outskirts of Blanes, follow signs for 'camping/hotels' then signs to site. GPS: 41.662015, 2.780429

Charges guide

Per unit incl. 2 persons	
and electricity	€ 23.20 - € 42.70
extra person	€ 4.65 - € 7.10
child (2-10 yrs)	€ 3.70 - € 5.90

FREE Alan Rogers Travel Card
Extra benefits and savings - see page 14

Blanes
Camping Bella Terra

Avenida Vila de Madrid 35-40, E-17300 Blanes (Girona) T: 972 348 017. E: info@campingbellaterra.com

alanrogers.com/ES82320

Camping Bella Terra is set in a shady pine grove facing a sandy beach on the Mediterranean coast. There are 776 pitches with 700 for touring units, the remainder taken by bungalows to rent. A Spanish caravan club takes 300 pitches between April and June. All pitches have 6A electricity and 195 are fully serviced. The site is in two sections, each with its own reception. The main reception is on the right of the road as you approach, with the swimming and paddling pools and delightful pool bar and restaurant. The other half with direct access to the beach is the older part of the site which tends to fill up first. The site is located to the much quieter south side of the town and beach and offers a more tranquil holiday experience, yet is within easy reach of all the local facilities. The whole site is divided into zones with open, accessible sandy pitches, many of which are separated. New sports facilities have been added including tennis and paddle courts. A well stocked supermarket is in the old part of the site, along with a bar in front of which activities for children and evening entertainment take place. The site has an international clientèle, including many repeat visitors throughout the season.

Facilities
The newer side of the site has new sanitary blocks with good equipment, including facilities for babies and children. The older side has blocks which are clean, but dated. Provision for disabled visitors and laundry on both sides. Shop, restaurant, bar and takeaway. Outdoor swimming and paddling pools (from May). Playground. Fishing. Bicycle hire. ATM. Internet café. WiFi over site (charged). New sports complex. Miniclub. For dogs, contact site first. Off site: Blanes town 2 km. Road train to the resort (high season). Sailing 1.5 km. Riding 8 km. Golf 25 km. Boat and coach excursions from town.

Open: 31 March - 30 September.

Directions
Site is on the southwest side of Blanes. From exit 9 on the AP7 Girona-Barcelona follow N11 to the B600 towards Blanes. Before entering Blanes turn southwest following campings/hotels signs at roundabouts, then site signs directing you away from Blanes town, which has narrow roads best avoided by large units. GPS: 41.6616, 2.77612

Charges guide
Per unit incl. 2 persons	
and electricity	€ 24.80 - € 53.70
extra person	€ 4.50 - € 6.90
child (3-10 yrs)	free - € 4.00

Camping **Bella Terra** Bungalow Park
www.campingbellaterra.com

Blanes · **Costa Brava**

Blanes
Camping Blanes

Avenida Villa de Madrid 33, Apdo 72, E-17300 Blanes (Girona) T: 972 331 591. E: info@campingblanes.com

alanrogers.com/ES82280

Camping Blanes is the first of the sites which edge the pedestrian promenade here and probably the smallest. A private gate leads to the promenade and beach. Open all year, it is family owned and run and has been in the hands of the Boix family for 50 years. With only 206 pitches and no bungalows or mobile homes, it has a comfortable family atmosphere and is popular with low season visitors. The pitches (60-80 sq.m) have 6A electricity, and shade is provided by tall pines. Care must be taken when manoeuvring large units due to low branches and the irregular shape of some of the pitches.

Facilities
Adequate sanitary block with provision for disabled visitors (by key). Baby unit. Excellent washing machines and dryers. Motorcaravan services. Shop (1/4-30/9). Bar (1/4-12/10). Restaurant & takeaway (15/6-30/9). Small swimming pool and sun terrace. Play area. No organised entertainment. Doctor visits. Bicycle hire. Beach alongside site. Car wash. WiFi over site (charged). Off site: Shops, entertainment, watersports and excursions in Blanes 500 m. Golf and riding 5 km.

Open: All year.

Directions
Site is south of the town beside the beach before Camping Bella Terra and El Pinar. Follow signs for 'campings/hotel' until individual site sign appears. GPS: 41.65918, 2.77959

Charges guide
Per unit incl. 2 persons	
and electricity	€ 15.00 - € 38.80
extra person	€ 2.50 - € 7.80
child (2-10 yrs)	€ 1.50 - € 6.70

No credit cards in winter season.

For latest campsite news, availability and prices visit
alanrogers.com

Calonge

Camping Internacional de Calonge

Ctra San Feliu/Guixols - Palamós km 7.6, E-17251 Calonge (Girona) T: 972 651 233.

E: info@intercalonge.com **alanrogers.com/ES81300**

This spacious, well laid out site has access to a fine beach via a footbridge over the coast road. Calonge is a family site with two attractive pools on different levels, a paddling pool and large sunbathing areas. A restaurant, bar and snack bar with great views are by the pool. The 466 touring pitches are on terraces and all have electricity (5A), with 84 being fully serviced. There is good shade from the tall pine trees, and some spectacular coastal views. Some access roads and steps are steep, but a road train operates in high season. The beach is accessed over the main road by 100 steps.

Facilities

Generous sanitary provision. One block is heated in winter. Laundry facilities. Motorcaravan services. Gas supplies. Shop (5/4-30/10). Restaurant (1/2-31/12). Bar, patio bar with pizzas and takeaway (5/4-24/10, weekends for the rest of the year). Swimming pools (26/3-16/10). Playground. Electronic games. Disco two nights a week (but not late) in high season. Bicycle hire. Tennis. Hairdresser. ATM. WiFi (free in hotspots). Torches necessary in some areas. Road train from the bottom of the site to the top in high season. Off site: Bus at the gate. Beach and fishing 300 m. Supermarket 500 m. Sailing 1 km. Golf 3 km. Riding 10 km.

Open: All year.

Directions

Site is on the inland side of the coast road between Palamós and Platja d'Aro. Take C31 south to 661 at Calonge. At Calonge follow signs to C253 towards Platja d'Aro and on to site, which is well signed. GPS: 41.83333, 3.08417

Charges guide

Per unit incl. 2 persons	
and electricity	€ 22.10 - € 59.55
extra person	€ 3.85 - € 8.85
child (3-10 yrs)	€ 1.90 - € 4.80
dog	€ 2.00 - € 4.70

Discounts for longer stays Oct-end May and senior citizens. No credit cards.

Calonge

Camping Cala Gogo

Avenida Andorra 13, E-17251 Calonge (Girona) T: 972 651 564. E: calagogo@calagogo.es

alanrogers.com/ES81600

Cala Gogo is a large traditional campsite with a pleasant situation on a wooded hillside with mature trees giving shade to most pitches. The 578 touring pitches, which vary in size, are in terraced rows, some with artificial shade, all have 10A electricity and water, and 200 have drainage. There may be road noise in eastern parts of the site. A few pitches are now right by the beach, the remainder are up to 800 m. uphill, but the 'Gua gua' tractor train, operating almost all season, takes people between the centre of the site and the beach and adds to the general sense of fun.

Facilities

Seven toilet blocks are of a high standard and are continuously cleaned. Some washbasins in private cabins. Two private cabins for hire. Baby rooms. Facilities for disabled visitors. Laundry room. Motorcaravan services. Gas supplies. Supermarket, shop, restaurants/takeaway and bars, two swimming pools (1 heated, lifeguards) and a paddling pool (all open all season). Playground and crèche. Sports centre. Programme of sports and entertainment. Bicycle hire. Kayaks (free). Fishing. WiFi (free in 3 hotspots). Medical service. ATM. Bus to local disco. Dogs not accepted in high season. Photo ID passes issued. Off site: Huge Aqua Park nearby with bus from site. Golf 5 km. Riding 10 km.

Open: 27 April - 15 September.

Directions

Leave the AP7/E15 at exit 6. Take C66 towards Palamós which becomes the C31. Use the C31 (Girona-Palamós) road to avoid Palamós town. Take the C253 coast road. Site is at km. 46.5, which is 4 km. south of Palamós. GPS: 41.83083, 3.08247

Charges guide

Per unit incl. 2 persons	
and electricity	€ 22.20 - € 57.60
extra person	€ 4.00 - € 8.70
child (3-12 yrs)	€ 1.40 - € 4.30
dog	€ 2.00

Discounts for longer stays and for cash payments.

FREE Alan Rogers Travel Card
Extra benefits and savings - see page 14

Cambrils

Camping Playa Cambrils Don Camilo

Ctra Cambrils-Salou km. 1,5, avenida Oleastrum, E-43850 Cambrils (Tarragona) T: 977 361 490.

E: info@playacambrils.com **alanrogers.com/ES84790**

This is a smart, well kept site with a canopy of mature shading trees, 300 m. from the beach across a busy road. There are 420 small (60 or 80 sq.m) touring pitches on flat ground, divided by hedges, all with 5A electricity. There are many permanent pitches and a quarter of the site is given up to chalet-style accommodation, which is generally separate from the touring pitches. Large units are placed in a dedicated area where the trees are higher. The very pleasant pool complex includes a smart glassed restaurant and bar with a distinct Spanish flavour reflected in the menu and tapas available throughout the day.

Facilities

Three smart, modern sanitary buildings offer sound, clean facilities with British style WCs and showers in separate buildings. Excellent facilities for disabled campers. Laundry facilities. Motorcaravan services. Supermarket, bar/snacks and separate restaurant (all April-Sept). Swimming pools (1/4-30/9). Playground. Entertainment in high season. Miniclub. Huge electronic games room. Bicycle hire. Torches useful. WiFi in reception area (free). Off site: Resort town has a wide range of shops, bars and restaurants. Boat launching 400 m. Fishing and golf 1 km.

Open: 15 March - 13 October.

Directions

Leave AP7 autopista at exit 37 and head for Cambrils and then to the beach. Turn left along beach road. Site is 1 km. east of Cambrils Playa and is well signed as you leave Cambrils marina. GPS: 41.06648, 1.08304

Charges guide

Per unit incl. 2 persons and electricity	€ 20.10 - € 45.50
extra person	€ 3.10 - € 5.75
child (under 9 yrs)	€ 2.15 - € 4.35

Camping Cheques accepted.

Camprodon

Camping Vall de Camprodon

Ctra C38 Ripoll a Camprodon, E-17867 Camprodon (Girona) T: 972 740 507. E: info@valldecamprodon.net
alanrogers.com/ES91225

This large holiday village is attractively situated in a wooded valley with cows grazing to one side, their pleasant bells often to be heard. A stream runs below the site, between it and the road. There are 200 grass and gravel pitches, some with shade, others without. Most are occupied by seasonal caravans (some rather scruffy) and private chalets interspersed with just 40 for touring units, all with 4-10A electricity. There are 26 modern chalets for rent. Only 20 km. away is the mountain and ski resort of Vallter 2000 and to the southwest is the historical town of Ripoll. Camprodon is a very pleasant old town with a magnificent ancient bridge at its centre.

Facilities

One centrally placed, fully equipped and well maintained toilet block. Large en-suite unit for disabled visitors. Baby/toddler baths. Washing machines, dryers and ironing board. Shop and bar/restaurant (July/Aug plus holiday periods and weekends in low season). Swimming and paddling pools (July/Aug). Play area. Adventure play area with zip wire. Fishing and bathing in river. Multisports court. Boules. Miniclub (July/Aug). Riding (July/Aug). WiFi (free). Motorcaravan park outside entrance (€20-26).

Open: All year.

Directions

From south on AP7 take exit 6 (Girona), then C66/A26 to Olot. From north leave AP7 at Figueres, join N11 south and turn west (Olot) to join N260/A26. At exit 84 follow signs for Camprodon on C26 via Valley of Bianya. After tunnels turn on C38 to Camprodon and site. GPS: 42.29033, 2.36242

Charges guide

Per unit incl. 2 persons and electricity	€ 35.60
extra person	€ 7.95

Camping Cheques accepted.

Canet de Mar

Camping Globo Rojo

Ctra NII km. 660.9, E-08360 Canet de Mar (Barcelona) T: 937 941 143. E: camping@globo-rojo.com
alanrogers.com/ES82430

Camping Globo Rojo is cleverly laid out in a relaxed, amphitheatre fashion. Within the various sectors, permanent campers and touring units stay alongside each other. The restaurant, which serves authentic food and tapas, is within a sensitively restored farmhouse. The site is located on the beach road (N11) so is subject to some traffic noise, but the full shading of mature trees also absorbs the noise. The 176 flat, grassy pitches include 135 touring pitches, all with 10A electricity and with an average size of 70 sq.m. An elevated pool and paddling pool are waiting for you to enjoy and the beach is close by.

Facilities

Two sanitary blocks have clean, modern equipment. Baby room. Facilities for disabled campers. Hot water throughout. Washing machines. Motorcaravan service areas. Shop. Bar. Restaurant. Takeaway. Swimming and paddling pools (with lifeguards). Miniclub. Playground. Multisports pitch. Pétanque. Electronic games. Bicycle hire. Free WiFi in restaurant area. Dog bath. Car wash.

Open: 1 April - 30 September.

Directions

Site is at 660.9 km. marker on N11. Leave C-32 autoroute at exit 20 (AP7 exit 120) and follow signs to Canet de Mar. Site is well signed on both carriageways of N11. GPS: 41.590903, 2.591951

Charges guide

Per unit incl. 2 persons and electricity	€ 21.00 - € 47.50
extra person	€ 5.00 - € 8.00

For latest campsite news, availability and prices visit

alanrogers.com

Castelló d'Empúries

Kawan Village Mas Nou

Mas Nou no. 7, E-17486 Castelló d'Empúries (Girona) T: 972 454 175. E: info@campingmasnou.com

alanrogers.com/ES80120

Some two kilometres from the sea on the Costa Brava, this is a pristine and surprisingly tranquil site in two parts, split by the access road. One part contains the pitches and toilet blocks, the other houses the impressive leisure complex. There are 450 neat, level and marked pitches on grass, a minimum of 70 sq.m. but most are 80-100 sq.m, and 300 with electricity (10A). The leisure complex is across the road from reception and features a huge L-shaped swimming pool with a children's area. A formal restaurant has an adjoining bar/café, pleasant terrace and rôtisserie under palms.

Facilities
Three absolutely excellent, fully equipped sanitary blocks include baby baths, good facilities for disabled visitors. Washing machines. Motorcaravan services. Supermarket and other shops. Baker in season. Bar/restaurant, rotisserie and takeaway. Swimming pool with lifeguard (1/5-27/9). Floodlit tennis and basketball. Minigolf. Miniclub (July/Aug). Play areas. Electronic games. Bicycle hire. Internet access and free WiFi over site. Car wash. Off site: Supermarket and shopping facilities 500 m. Public transport 500m. Riding 1.5 km. Beach 2.5 km.

Open: 28 March - 27 September.

Directions
From A7 use exit 3. Mas Nou is 2 km. east of Castelló d'Empúries, on the Roses road, 10 km. from Figueres. Do not turn left across the main road but continue to the roundabout and return. Site is clearly marked. GPS: 42.26558, 3.1025

Charges guide
Per unit incl. 2 persons and electricity	€ 23.00 - € 47.50
extra person	€ 2.65 - € 6.00
child (4-11 yrs)	free - € 3.60

Camping Cheques accepted.

Castelló d'Empúries

Camping Laguna

Platja Can Comes s/n, E-17486 Castelló d'Empúries (Girona) T: 972 450 553. E: info@campinglaguna.com

alanrogers.com/ES80150

Camping Laguna is a relaxed, spacious site on an isthmus within the Catalan National Maritime Park, on the migratory path of many different birds. It has direct access to an excellent sandy beach and the estuary of the River Muga (also a beach). The owners spend much time and effort on improvements. The 737 pitches (70 mobile homes) are shaded and clearly marked on grass and sand, all with 6/10A electricity. There are also 51 fully serviced pitches. A very attractive bar/restaurant and sitting area overlook the impressive lagoons. There are two swimming pools (one is heated in low season).

Facilities
Five superb toilet blocks, placed to avoid long walks, have solar heated water, and include facilities for children and disabled visitors. Laundry room. Bar, restaurant and takeaway. Comprehensive supermarket. Swimming pools (15/5-20/10). Football. Tennis (free in low seasons). ATM. Minigolf. Windsurfing and sailing schools (July/Aug). Fishing. Miniclub. Play areas. Bicycle hire. Riding. Entertainment programme and competitions. Doctor visits. Satellite TV. Internet access. WiFi over site (charged). Off site: Boat launching. Birdwatching (Ramsar area).

Open: 25 March - 20 October.

Directions
From AP7/E15 take exit 3 south or exit 4 north (there is no exit 3 north) and then N11 to the C260 towards Roses. At Castelló d'Empúries roundabout (there is only one) follow signs (ignore GPS from here) to Depuradora (2 km) and 'camping' for 4 km. on a hard track road to the site. GPS: 42.2374, 3.121

Charges guide
Per unit incl. 2 persons and electricity	€ 27.80 - € 62.55
extra person	€ 4.25 - € 4.65

Castelló d'Empúries

Camping Nautic Almata

Ctra GIV- 6216 km 2,3, E-17486 Castelló d'Empúries (Girona) T: 972 454 477. E: info@almata.com

alanrogers.com/ES80300

In the Bay of Roses, south of Empuriabrava and beside the Parc Natural dels Aiguamolls de l'Empordá, this is a high quality site of particular interest to nature lovers (especially birdwatchers). A large site, there are 1,109 well kept, large, numbered pitches, all with electricity and on flat, sandy ground. Beautifully laid out, it is arranged around the river and waterways, so will suit those who like to be close to water or who enjoy watersports and boating. It is also a superb beachside site. Tour operators use the site.

Facilities
Toilet blocks of a very high standard include some en-suite showers with washbasins. Good facilities for disabled visitors. Washing machines. Gas supplies. Excellent supermarket. Restaurants, pizzeria and bar. Two separate bars and snack bar by beach where discos are held in main season. Sailing, diving and windsurfing schools. 300 sq.m. swimming pool. Tennis courts. Squash. Paddle tennis. Minigolf. Games room. Riding tuition (July/Aug). Play park and miniclub. ATM. Fishing (licence required). Car, motorcycle and bicycle hire. WiFi (charged.

Open: 16 May - 20 September.

Directions
Site is signed at 26 km. marker on C252 between Castello d'Empúries and Vildemat, then 7 km. to site. Alternatively, on San Pescador-Castello d'Empúries road (GIV6261) head north and site is well signed. GPS: 42.206077, 3.10389

Charges guide
Per unit incl. 2 persons and electricity	€ 31.20 - € 62.20
extra person (over 3 yrs)	€ 3.20 - € 5.85
dog	€ 5.50 - € 7.00
boat or jet ski	€ 10.50 - € 13.70

FREE Alan Rogers Travel Card
Extra benefits and savings - see page 14

Empuriabrava

Camping Rubina Resort

Playa de la Rubina, E-17487 Empuriabrava (Girona) T: 972 450 507. E: info@rubinaresort.com

alanrogers.com/ES80200

Situated in the 'Venice of Spain', Empuriabrava is interlaced with inland waterways and canals, where many residents and holidaymakers moor their boats directly outside their expensive homes on the canal banks. Camping Rubina Resort is a large friendly site 200 m. from the wide, sandy beach, which is bordered on the east and west by the waterway canals. It is a spacious and hospitable site where people seem to make friends easily. There are 500 touring pitches of varying sizes, most enjoying some shade. All have 10A electricity and water connections. Access throughout the site is very good.

Facilities

Toilet facilities are in five fully equipped blocks with facilities for disabled campers (key in reception). Washing machines. Motorcaravan services. Supermarket, bakery and shop, bar and takeaway (all season). Restaurant (1/5-30/9) Internet café. Swimming pool (1/4-10/10). Multisports court. Watersports with windsurfing school. Organised sports activities, programmes for children and entertainment. Playgrounds. Pétanque. Bicycle hire. WiFi over site (charged). Dog shower. Apartments. Off site: Beach 200 m. Fishing 300 m.

Open: 1 April - 15 October.

Directions

Empuriabrava is north of Girona and east of Figueres on the coast. From AP7/E15 take exit 3 south or exit 4 north (note there is no exit 3 north) and then N11 to the C260 towards Roses. At Empuriabrava follow 'camping area' signs to site. GPS: 42.25267, 3.1317

Charges guide

Per unit incl. 2 persons	
and electricity	€ 20.00 - € 56.00
extra person	€ 4.00 - € 5.00
child (3-16 yrs)	€ 3.00 - € 4.00

No credit cards.

Garriguella

Camping Vell Empordà

Ctra Roses-Jonquera s/n, E-17780 Garriguella (Girona) T: 972 530 200. E: vellemporda@vellemporda.com

alanrogers.com/ES80140

Camping Vell Empordà is a friendly, family site close to the resort of Roses on the northern Costa Brava and on the outskirts of the small town of Garriguella. There are 210 touring pitches, all with 6A or 10A (extra) electricity connections. Smaller pitches are available for campers with tents. Additionally, a range of fully equipped wooden chalets are for rent. The site is terraced and well shaded. On-site amenities include a good restaurant and a well stocked supermarket. There is a convivial bar with a large terrace. The swimming pool is large and attractive and has a separate children's pool adjacent. The site has both a strong Spanish presence and also a loyal European clientèle, including some British tourists, who have been visiting for many years. Close by Garriguella is a typical small Spanish town with an interesting church, Santa Eulalia de Noves. Roses, some 7 km. away, is a smart and lively resort with a wealth of shops, cafés, restaurants and entertainment. The town is also home to a fine citadel, built by the Greeks, from where there are stunning views over the Bay of Roses and the town. This site is ideal for those who want a welcoming and authentic country location away from the larger resorts but within easy reach of local beaches and attractions.

Facilities

Two large, clean sanitary blocks have facilities for children and disabled visitors. Laundry. Motorcaravan services. Supermarket and bar (15/5-15/9), restaurant and takeaway (1/6-25/9). Large outdoor pool (15/5-15/9). Children's pool. Play area. Multisports area. Fronton court. Bicycle hire. Free WiFi over site. Chalets for rent. Off site: Shops and restaurants in Garriguella and Roses. Riding and golf 5 km. Fishing, beach and sailing 7 km.

Open: 1 February - 22 December.

Directions

Approaching from the west (Figueres) take the eastbound N260, then C252 to Garriguella then follow signs to site. GPS: 42.33888, 3.06726

Charges guide

Per unit incl. 2 persons	
and electricity	€ 18.35 - € 37.10
extra person	€ 5.10 - € 7.55
child (2-16 yrs)	€ 4.10 - € 6.15
dog	free - € 5.00

For latest campsite news, availability and prices visit

alanrogers.com

Gavá

Camping 3 Estrellas

C31 km 186,2, E-08850 Gavá (Barcelona) T: 936 330 637. E: info@camping3estrellas.com

alanrogers.com/ES83120

The name translates as the 'three stars' and this beach site lives up to its name. The 375 pitches for touring are mostly flat with 5A electricity, informally placed under trees, with no permanent units. Many pitches are along the beach front, those closer to the beach having little shade, but they are very pleasant with great views – beach access is through a security fence. Amenities, including a large pool, are in a separate area of the site, nearer to but shielded from the road, keeping noise away from the pitches. Although busy, the site has a pleasant open feel and there are 65 units for hire.

Facilities

Three traditional style toilet blocks provide clean facilities including neat facilities for disabled campers and a well equipped nursery room (key at reception). Washing machines and dryers. Motorcaravan services. Supermarket, restaurant, bar, snack bar and takeaway. Outdoor swimming pools (20/6-20/9). Play areas. Boules. Bicycle hire. Entertainment programme. ATM. Security boxes. Torches useful. WiFi throughout (charged).

Open: 15 March - 15 October.

Directions

On C31 south of Barcelona go towards Castelldefels and the site is at the 186 km. marker directly off the main road. GPS: 41.272573, 2.04254

Charges guide

Per unit incl. 2 persons	
and electricity	€ 41.90 - € 50.50
extra person	€ 6.48 - € 8.73
child (3-10 yrs)	€ 5.11 - € 5.74
dog	€ 4.00 - € 4.90

Guardiola de Berguedá

Camping El Berguedá

Ctra B400 a Saldes km. 3,5, E-08694 Guardiola de Berguedá (Barcelona) T: 938 227 432.

E: info@campingbergueda.com **alanrogers.com/ES91390**

The short scenic drive through the mountains to reach this site is breathtakingly beautiful. This attractively terraced campsite next to the Cadí-Moixeí Natural Park, is not far from the majestic Pedraforca mountain, and the area is a favourite for Catalan climbers and walkers. Access on the site is quite easy for large units, although the road from Guardiola de Berguedá is twisting. Of the 73 grass or gravel pitches there are 40 for touring, all with 6A electricity. The welcoming and helpful campsite owners will do all in their power to make your stay enjoyable.

Facilities

Two well maintained and well equipped modern toilet blocks are heated and clean. Facilities for disabled campers. Three private cabins with washbasin, toilet and bidet. Washing machines. Small shop, restaurant, bar and takeaway (w/ends only then 1/6-1/11). Outdoor pools (24/6-31/8). Play areas. Free WiFi by reception. Communal barbecues on each terrace (individual ones not permitted). Off site: Mountain biking. Walking and hiking. Snow hiking. Mountain guide service. Romanesque architecture. Artigas gardens by Gaudí. Picasso Museum. Museum of mines. Adventure park 5 km.

Open: Easter - 30 October (and weekends).

Directions

Guardiola de Berguedá is 125 km. north of Barcelona. From the C16 Manresa-Berga road 2 km. south of Guardiola de Berguedá turn west towards Saldes. Site is on right after 3.5 km. From France via Puigcerdá take the C16 (Berga/Manresa) to Guardiola de Berguedá, then as above. GPS: 42.21642, 1.83692

Charges guide

Per unit incl. 2 persons	
and electricity	€ 26.68 - € 29.00
extra person	€ 5.22 - € 5.80
child (1-10 yrs)	€ 4.18 - € 4.65

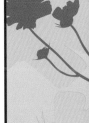

Guils de Cerdanya

Camping Pirineus

Ctra Guils de Cerdanya km. 2, E-17528 Guils de Cerdanya (Girona) T: 972 881 062. E: guils@stel.es

alanrogers.com/ES91430

On entering this well organised site close to the French border, high in the Pyrenees, you gain an immediate impression of space, green trees and grass – there is always someone watering and clearing up to maintain the high standards here. The pitches are neat, marked, of average size and organised in rows. Generally flat with some on a gentle incline, a proportion have water at their own sink on the pitch. Many trees offer shade but watch for overhanging branches if you have a high unit. From the restaurant terrace you have fine views of the mountains in the background and the pool in the foreground.

Facilities

One new, central and well equipped sanitary block of top quality and decorated with boxes of bright flowers, is kept spotlessly clean and can be heated. Good laundry facilities. Motorcaravan services. Shop, bar and restaurant (all season). Heated swimming pool and circular paddling pool. Boules. Tennis. Outdoor sports. TV and games room. Snooker. Play area and supervised clubhouse for youngsters. Excursions. Entertainment (high season). WiFi. Dogs are not accepted. Off site: Bicycle hire 2 km.

Open: 21 June - 11 September.

Directions

From Perpignan take N116 to Prades and Andorra. Exit at Piugcerdá taking N250 signed Le Seu d'Urgell and almost immediately take second right for Guils de Cerdanya. Follow for 2 km. to site on right. GPS: 42.44312, 1.90583

Charges guide

Per unit incl. 2 persons	
and electricity	€ 39.60 - € 52.60
extra person	€ 7.00
child (3-10 yrs)	€ 5.70

Hospitalet del Infante

Camping-Pension Cala d'Oques

Via Augusta s/n, E-43890 Hospitalet del Infante (Tarragona) T: 977 823 254. E: info@caladoques.com

alanrogers.com/ES85350

This peaceful and delightful, family run site has a lot going for it: its situation beside the sea with a wide beach of sand and pebbles, its amazing mountain backdrop, the views across the bay to the town and the friendly, relaxed atmosphere created by its owner of 40 years, Elisa Roller, her family and her staff. There are 152 mostly level pitches, some beside the beach, others on wide, informal terracing. Electricity (10A) is available throughout (long leads may be needed in places). Pine and olive trees are an attractive feature and provide some shade. The restaurant with its homely touches has a good local menu and a reputation extending well outside the site.

Facilities

Toilet facilities are in the central part of the main building. Clean, neat and recently refurbished with a number of en-suite units (shower, washbasin and WC). Hot water to showers by token but free to campers. New heated unit with toilets and washbasins for winter use. Unit for disabled visitors. Additional small block with toilets and washbasins at the far end of the site. Motorcaravan services. Gas. Restaurant/bar and shop (1/3-30/11). Play area. Kim's kids' club and family entertainment (high season). Fishing. Sailing. Internet and WiFi. Torches required in some areas. Mobile home and apartments to rent. Off site: Village facilities, incl. shop and restaurant 1.5 km. Bicycle hire, boat launching, golf and riding 2 km.

Open: All year.

Directions

Hospitalet del Infante is 35 km. southwest of Tarragona, accessed from the A7 (exit 38) or from the N340. From the north take first exit to Hospitalet del Infante at the 1128 km. marker. Follow 'Campings' signs before the village, then signs to site for 1.5 km. GPS: 40.97777, 0.90338

Charges guide

Per unit incl. 2 persons and electricity	€ 22.95 - € 47.90
extra person	€ 5.05 - € 8.50
child (0-10 yrs)	€ 3.00 - € 3.50
dog	€ 3.50

Discounts for seniors and for longer stays.
No credit cards.

L'Escala

Camping Lodge Neus

Cala Montgó, E-17130 L'Escala (Girona) T: 638 652 712. E: info@campingneus.com

alanrogers.com/ES80690

Camping Neus is set on the edge of the Montgri and Illes Medes Natural Park, under mature pines. There are 246 pitches arranged on sets of low terraces, all with 6/10A electricity, 40 are fully serviced. The site is peaceful at all times, especially in summer when the road beyond the site is closed to traffic. A small pool with a circular paddling pool is welcome after a hot day's sightseeing. Other amenities include a tennis court and small bar/restaurant. A new play area and a volleyball court have been added recently and gardens planted, and there is a 'wild camping' area to one side of the site.

Facilities

Renovated sanitary blocks offer sound and clean facilities with baby rooms and facilities for disabled campers. Motorcaravan services. Shop. Bar. Restaurant. Takeaway. Swimming pool. Paddling pool. Tennis. Volleyball. Play area. TV room. Entertainment and activities in peak season. Club for children. WiFi over site (charged). Bicycle hire. Fully furnished tents to rent. Only electric barbecues are permitted. Off site: Cala Montgó with beach 850 m. Fishing, kayaking, diving 850 m. L'Escala 2 km.

Open: 22 May - 20 September.

Directions

Take exit 5 from the AP7 and the GI623 to L'Escala. Continue to Cala Montgó. Site is on the right 1 km. before beach at Cala Montgó.
GPS: 42.1049, 3.15816

Charges guide

Per unit incl. 2 persons and electricity	€ 22.70 - € 50.70
extra person	€ 3.00 - € 5.00
child (4-12 yrs)	€ 1.00 - € 3.50
dog	€ 2.00

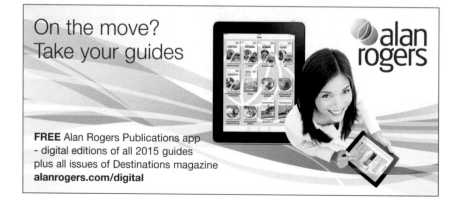
For latest campsite news, availability and prices visit
alanrogers.com

L'Escala

Camping Illa Mateua

Avenida de Montgó 260, E-17130 L'Escala (Girona) T: 972 770 200. E: info@campingillamateua.com

alanrogers.com/ES80740

If you prefer a quieter site, out of the very busy resort of L'Escala, then Illa Mateua is an excellent option. This large, family run site has a dynamic owner Marti, who speaks excellent English. The site is divided by the beach access road and has its own private accesses to the contrasting beaches - one a rocky cove and the other gentle, sandy and sloping. There are 350 pitches across both parts of the site, all with 6A electricity, some on sloping ground, although the pitches in the second part are flat. Established pine trees provide shade for most places with more coverage on the western side. A new purpose-built diving centre and club opened on the site in 2013. There are two swimming pools, the largest an 'infinity pool' enjoying an idyllic and most unusual setting on the top of a cliff overlooking the Bay of Roses. The second pool in the bar, restaurant and terrace area was scheduled for redevelopment. A CCTV system monitors the pools and general security from a purpose built centre. The new diving centre offers a comprehensive programme of training, and has a small bar and snack bar. There are bungalows to rent, including one for disabled visitors, which is normally booked well in advance.

Facilities

Very modern, fully equipped, heated sanitary blocks are kept spotlessly clean by omnipresent cleaners. Baby baths and brilliant facilities for children. Washing machines and dryers. Shop, extensive modern complex of restaurants, bars and takeaways (all open all season). Infinity pool (June onwards, lifeguard). Pool bar. Play areas. Kayak hire. Bicycle hire. Organised activities for children in high season. Diving school. Sports centre. WiFi over site (charged). ATM. Private access to beach. Off site: Road train to town centre from outside site. Cala Montgó beach 100 m. GR92 coastal path 50 m. Fishing 150 m. Riding 2 km. Golf 10 km.

Open: 11 March - 20 October.

Directions

From north on A7 take exit 3 to N11, then C31 and GI 623 signed l'Escala. From south take exit 5 from A7 signed l'Escala. Site is clearly marked from town. GPS: 42.11051, 3.16542

Charges guide

Per unit incl. 2 persons and electricity	€ 25.30 - € 53.80
extra person	€ 3.50 - € 7.10
child (3-10 yrs)	€ 2.45 - € 4.90
dog	€ 2.55 - € 4.50

No credit cards.

L'Estartit

Camping Castell Montgri

Ctra de Torroella-l'Estartit km. 4,7, E-17258 L'Estartit (Girona) T: 972 751 630.
E: cmontgri@campingparks.com alanrogers.com/ES80070

This is a very large, bustling site with all the modern paraphernalia of holiday making. A large proportion of this site is reserved for tour operators, but there are three designated areas for independent campers. These provide 590 terraced, shaded and flat pitches, all with electricity (6/10A). There are three excellent swimming complexes and a wide range of amenities and attractions. Whilst large, the site is well organised and, unlike some in this area, offers an active holiday experience for all the family – teenagers included – throughout the season. A camping pass is issued to all site residents.

Facilities
Toilet facilities are good and are being gradually upgraded, each area having its own block. Cleaning is continual (06.00-22.00) but with the numbers on site in high season, queuing and litter may be a problem. Supermarket and souvenirs. Bars and restaurants. Pizzeria. Crêperie. Takeaway. Swimming pools. Tennis. Minigolf. Playground. Disco. Entertainment. Bicycle hire. Free bus to L'Estartit. Internet and WiFi (both charged).
Open: 11 May - 29 September.

Directions
Leave AP7/E15 at exit 6 and take C66 for Palamós. Take GI642 towards Parlava and GI643 towards Torroella de Montgri, then GI641 to L'Estartit. Site is signed just north of town. GPS: 42.0511, 3.1827

Charges guide
Per person	€ 5.00 - € 5.50
child (3-10 yrs)	€ 3.50
pitch incl. car and electricity	€ 10.00 - € 61.00
dog	free

L'Estartit

Camping les Medes

Paratge Camp de l'Arbre, E-17258 l'Estartit (Girona) T: 972 751 805. E: info@campinglesmedes.com
alanrogers.com/ES80720

Les Medes is different from some of the 'all singing, all dancing' sites so popular along this coast. The friendly family of Pla-Coll are rightly proud of their innovative and award-winning site, which they have owned for almost 30 years. With just 170 pitches, the site is small enough for the owners and their staff to know their visitors, some of whom have been coming for many years. The top class facilities, along with the personal attention and activities available, make this a year-round home in the sun. The level, grassy pitches range in size from 70-80 sq.m. and are shaded. All have electricity (5/10A) and 155 also have water and drainage.

Facilities
Two modern spacious sanitary blocks can be heated and are extremely well maintained. Washbasins in cabins, top class facilities for disabled visitors. Baby baths. Washing machines and dryer. Motorcaravan services. Shop. Bar with snacks and pizza. Good value restaurant (1/4-31/10). Swimming and paddling pools (1/5-15/9). Indoor pool with sauna, solarium and massage (15/9-15/6). Play area. TV room. Entertainment, activities and excursions (July/Aug). Diving. Multisports area. Boules. Bicycle hire and self-repair shop. Internet and WiFi. Torches are useful. Dogs are not accepted in July/Aug. Off site: Riding 400 m.
Open: All year.

Directions
Site is signed from the main Torroella de Montgri-L'Estartit road GE641. Turn right after Camping Castel Montgri, at Joc's hamburger/pizzeria and follow signs. GPS: 42.048, 3.1881

Charges guide
Per unit incl. 2 persons and electricity	€ 24.50 - € 44.80
extra person	€ 4.60 - € 9.30
child (2-10 yrs)	€ 2.80 - € 6.30
No credit cards.	

L'Estartit

Camping Emporda

Ctra Toroella km. 4,8, E-17258 L'Estartit (Girona) T: 972 750 649. E: info@campingemporda.com
alanrogers.com/ES80730

Emporda is just 1 km. from the busy town and superb beach of L'Estartit. It has an open and friendly feel and is surrounded by some delightful views. There are just 250 pitches and a family atmosphere which Francesc, the director, encourages. The level, grassy pitches are 80 sq.m. in size. One area of the site is very shaded and the rest is attractively and adequately shaded by young trees. The great swimming and paddling pools are at the heart of the campsite, which has placed all the facilities neatly together. Varied entertainment is provided in high season.

Facilities
Two pleasant and very clean sanitary blocks, one with facilities for disabled campers and a baby bath. Cabins with hot and cold water, cold water at other washbasins. Washing machines and dryer. Bar. Restaurant, pizzas and takeaway. Supermarket. Large swimming pool (lifeguard in July/Aug) and paddling pool. Entertainment daily in high season; three times weekly in the evenings. Miniclub. Disco (high season). Aerobics. Two play areas. TV. Aqua gym. Bicycle hire. Chalets for rent. WiFi over site (charged).
Open: 28 March - 12 October.

Directions
From AP7 take exit 6 and follow C66 for Palamós. Then take GI642 towards Parlava and GI643 towards Torroella de Montgri. Finally, take GI641 towards L'Estartit and site is well signed on right just before entering town. GPS: 42.04907, 3.18385

Charges guide
Per unit incl. 2 persons and electricity	€ 19.40 - € 35.60
extra person	€ 3.50 - € 7.40
No credit cards.	

For latest campsite news, availability and prices visit
alanrogers.com

La Pineda

Camping La Pineda de Salou

Ctra Costa Tarragona-Salou km. 5, E-43481 La Pineda (Tarragona) T: 977 373 080.

E: info@campinglapineda.com **alanrogers.com/ES84820**

La Pineda is a clean, neat site north of Salou, just 1.5 km. from an aquapark and 2.5 km. from Port Aventura, to which there is an hourly bus service from outside the site entrance. There is some noise from the road. The site has two swimming pools; the smaller is heated. A colourful themed paddling pool and outdoor spa are also here, behind tall hedges close to the entrance. A large terrace has sun loungers, and various entertainment aimed at young people is provided in season. The 250 flat pitches for touring units (all with 5A electricity) are shaded by mature trees in attractive gardens. A further 82 are available for tents and 79 are occupied by mobile homes for rent. La Pineda is a cut above other city sites.

Facilities

Sanitary facilities have been completely refurbished and are excellent. Baby bath. Facilities for disabled visitors. Washing machines. Gas. Shop, restaurant and snacks (July/Aug). Swimming pools, themed paddling pool and outdoor spa (July/Aug). Small wellness centre with spa in private rooms. Bar (all season). New community room with satellite TV. Bicycle and road cart hire. Games room. Playground (3-12 yrs). Entertainment (July/Aug). Torches may be required. No dogs in August. WiFi throughout (charged or free with advanced booking).

Open: 1 April - 30 September.

Directions

From A7 just southwest of Tarragona take exit 35 and follow signs to La Pineda and Port Aventura then campsite signs appear.
GPS: 41.08850, 1.18233

Charges guide

Per unit incl. 2 persons and electricity (6A)	€ 30.80 - € 52.40
extra person	€ 5.70 - € 8.60
child (1-10 yrs)	€ 3.90 - € 6.40

Llafranc

Kim's Camping

Font d'en Xeco 1, E-17211 Llafranc - Palafrugell (Girona) T: 972 301 156. E: info@campingkims.com

alanrogers.com/ES81200

This attractive, terraced site, where the owner and his family have been welcoming guests for over 50 years, is arranged on the wooded slopes of a narrow valley leading to the sea. There is a strong family ethos and the site benefits from many repeat visitors. There are 325 grassy, shaded pitches (70-120 sq.m) for touring units, all with electricity (5A). Many of the larger pitches are on a plateau from which great views can be enjoyed. The terraces are connected by winding drives, which are narrow in places. The village of Llafranc and the beach are a ten minute walk.

Facilities

All sanitary facilities are spotlessly clean and include a small new block and excellent toilet facilities for disabled visitors. Laundry facilities. Gas supplies. Well stocked shop. Bar. Bakery and croissanterie. Café/restaurant (15/6-30/9). Swimming pools. Play areas and children's club. TV room. Excursions arranged – bus calls at site. Visits arranged to sub-aqua schools (high season). Bicycle hire. Torches required. WiFi over site (charged). Gas only barbecues. Communal (low season). On-site doctor.

Open: Easter - 30 September.

Directions

Llafranc is southeast of Palafrugell. Turn off the Palafrugell-Tamariu road at turn (GIV 6542) signed Llafranc. Site is on right 1 km. further on.
GPS: 41.90053, 3.18935

Charges guide

Per unit incl. 2 persons and electricity	€ 17.00 - € 46.70
extra person	€ 4.20 - € 7.15
child (3-10 yrs)	€ 2.05 - € 3.55

Discounts for long stays and for senior citizens.

Lloret de Mar

Camping Tucan

Ctra de Blanes-Lloret, E-17310 Lloret de Mar (Girona) T: 972 369 965. E: info@campingtucan.com

alanrogers.com/ES82100

Situated on the busy Costa Brava at Lloret de Mar, Camping Tucan is well placed to access all the attractions of the area and the town itself. The site has a friendly, family oriented approach, with a new children's multisports pitch, new water slides in the attractive pool area and an all season children's activity programme. It is laid out in a herringbone pattern, with 209 accessible, level touring pitches in three different sizes. They are terraced and separated by hedges, all with electricity (3/6/10A) and shade.

Facilities

Two modern toilet blocks include washbasins with hot water and facilities for children and disabled visitors, although access can be difficult. Washing machines. Gas supplies. Shop. Busy bar and good restaurant. Takeaway. Swimming pool, paddling pool, water slides and jacuzzi. Playground and fenced play area for toddlers. Multisports pitch. TV in bar. Bicycle hire. Entertainment all season. Miniclub. Internet and WiFi (charged). Only charcoal and gas barbecues permitted. Off site: Town 500 m.

Open: 1 April - 25 September.

Directions

From A7/E4, A19 or N11 Girona-Barcelona roads take an exit for Lloret de Mar. Site is 1 km. west of the town, well signed and is at the base of the hill off the roundabout. The entrance can get congested in busy periods. GPS: 41.6972, 2.8217

Charges guide

Per unit incl. 2 persons and electricity	€ 26.60 - € 68.00
extra person	€ 5.50 - € 10.00
child (3-12 yrs)	€ 3.00 - € 6.00

FREE Alan Rogers Travel Card
Extra benefits and savings - see page 14

Montroig

Playa Montroig Camping Resort

Ctra N340 km. 1136, E-43300 Montroig (Tarragona) T: 977 810 637.

E: info@playamontroig.com **alanrogers.com/ES85300**

LeadingCampings

What a superb site! Playa Montroig is about 30 kilometres beyond Tarragona set in its own tropical gardens with direct access to a very long, narrow, soft sand beach. The main part of the site lies between the sea, road and railway (as at other sites on this coast, there is some train noise) with a huge underpass. The site is divided into spacious, marked pitches with excellent shade provided by a variety of lush vegetation including very impressive palms set in wide avenues. There are 1,050 pitches, all with electricity (10A) and 564 with water and drainage. Some 47 pitches are directly alongside the beach. The site has many outstanding features: there is an excellent pool complex near the entrance, with two pools (one heated). A new Espai Grill and bar with a rock and roll disco and a pretty candlelit patio is just outside the gate. One restaurant serves good food with some Catalan fare (seats 150) and overlooks an entertainment area. A large terrace bar serves drinks or if you yearn for louder music there is a second disco with a smaller bar. There is yet another eating option in a 500-seat restaurant. Above this is the Pai-pai Caribbean cocktail bar where softer music is provided in an intimate atmosphere. Activities for children are very ambitious – there is even a ceramics kiln (multi-lingual carers). La Plaza, a spectacular open-air theatre, is an ideal setting for daily keep fit sessions and the professional entertainment provided. Several beach sports are available on the beach. This is an excellent site and there is insufficient space here to describe all the available activities. We recommend it for families with children of all ages, and there is much emphasis on providing activities outside the high season. A member of Leading Campings group.

Facilities

Very good quality sanitary buildings with washbasins in private cabins and separate WCs. Facilities for babies and disabled campers. Several launderettes. Motorcaravan services. Gas. Good shopping centre. Restaurants and bars. Fitness suite. Hairdresser. TV lounges. Beach bar. Playground. Jogging track. Sports area. Tennis. Minigolf. Organised activities including pottery. Pedalo hire. Boat mooring. Bicycle hire. Internet café. WiFi over site (charged). Dogs are not accepted. Off site: Public transport 100 m. from gate. Riding, golf and boat launching 3 km.

Open: 4 April - 26 October.

Directions

Site entrance is off main N340 nearly 30 km. southwest from Tarragona. From motorway take Cambrils exit and turn west on N340 at 1136 km. marker. GPS: 41.03345, 0.96921

Charges guide

Per unit incl. 2 persons

and electricity	€ 19.00 - € 56.00
extra person	€ 6.50 - € 8.00
child (3-10 yrs)	free - € 6.00

Discounts for longer stays and for pensioners.

Montagut

Camping Montagut

Ctra Montagut-Sadernes km. 2, E-17855 Montagut (Girona) T: 972 287 202. E: info@campingmontagut.com

alanrogers.com/ES91220

This is a delightful, small family site where everything is kept in pristine condition. Jordi and Nuria, a brother and sister team, work hard to make you welcome and maintain the superb appearance of the site. Flowers and shrubs abound, with 90 pitches on attractively landscaped and carefully constructed terraces or on flat areas overlooking the pool. All but ten are for touring units with 6A electricity available throughout. A tranquil atmosphere pervades the site and it is a delight to enjoy drinks on the pleasant restaurant terrace, or to sample the authentic menu as you enjoy the views over the Alta Garrotxa. There is much to see in the local area between the Pyrenees and the Mediterranean.

Facilities

The clean, modern sanitary block has controllable hot showers, open style washbasins, a pleasant baby room and an en-suite unit for disabled visitors. Washing and laundry facilities. Motorcaravan services. Supermarket (all season). Restaurant and bar (3/7-30/8, snacks and bar at weekends in low season). Swimming pool with sunbathing area and children's pool (1/5-30/9). Sports field. Playground. Pétanque. Barbecue area. Free WiFi over part of site. Torches are useful in some areas. Off site: Bathing in river 400 m. Shop, bar and restaurant in village 2 km. Riding 5 km. Bicycle hire 15 km. Fishing and golf 30 km. Beach 60 km.

Open: 15 April - 12 October.

Directions

From south on AP7 leave at exit 6 (Girona), take the C66/A26 towards Olot. From north leave AP7 at Figueres, join N11 south and turn west signed Olot to join N260/A26. Take exit 75, turn right towards Montagut. At end of village turn left (Sadernes) and site is on the left in 2 km. GPS: 42.2469, 2.5971

Charges guide

Per unit incl. 2 persons

and electricity	€ 20.00 - € 34.50
extra person	€ 5.35 - € 7.40
child (2-10 yrs)	€ 4.50 - € 5.90

For latest campsite news, availability and prices visit

alanrogers.com

Malgrat de Mar

Camping Els Pins

Avenida Pomareda s/n, E-08380 Malgrat de Mar (Barcelona) T: 937 653 238.
E: campingelspins@telefonica.net **alanrogers.com/ES82345**

Only the access road separates this busy campsite from a sandy beach which stretches west for over five kilometres to the resort of Malgrat de Mar and beyond. Of the 219 pitches, around 50% are devoted to holiday homes with touring pitches occupying two distinct areas. The green zone is in the heart of the resort and pitches have electricity (6A), water, drainage and TV connections and there is some shade. The blue zone has direct access to the beach and is a very quiet area with plenty of sun and little shade; pitches here are smaller and just have electrical connections.

Facilities

Sanitary block in each camping area including hot showers, cabins with shower and WC, facilities for babies and disabled visitors and laundry areas. No motorcaravan service point or chemical disposal. Bar/restaurant. Shop for basics. Swimming pool. Playgrounds. Pétanque. Activities and entertainment for children and adults (high season). Fridges for hire. Bicycle and car rental. WiFi throughout (charged). Dogs are not accepted.

Open: 15 April - 10 November.

Directions

From C32 take exit 130 to join N11 south (Malgrat de Mar). In 2 km. take exit onto B682 for Malgrat de Mar Nord. At roundabout take first exit, bear left and at next roundabout take third exit BV6001 and follow signs for Zona de Campings. At seafront turn left to site in 500 m. GPS: 41.64793, 2.77007

Charges guide

Per unit incl. 2 persons and electricity	€ 23.00 - € 42.00

Mataró

Camping Barcelona

Ctra NII km. 650, E-08304 Mataró (Barcelona) T: 937 904 720. E: info@campingbarcelona.com
alanrogers.com/ES82450

The great advantage of Camping Barcelona is the regular shuttle bus to and from Barcelona (45 mins), which is free in low season. Like other sites in this area, it is on the beach road (N11) which means it is subject to train and traffic noise. However, the 344 touring pitches, which are separated from the permanent areas, do allow you to avoid the problem. Pitches vary in size and most have electricity (6-16A Europlug). An excellent pool is provided in which to cool off and reception will assist in arranging many off site activities. There is a rocky coastline 100 m. away, but we recommend you to use the free shuttle to Mataró for serious sunning. An area containing several types of animals and fowl is on site for your enjoyment, and the management takes pride in making sure you have fun whilst staying here. Entertainment is provided in high season and both adults and children are catered for. This is a pleasant, family owned site where many languages are spoken, and where careful thought is given to catering for all holiday tastes and lifestyles. The site has a beach club and a diving club in nearby Mataró and concessions are available for the local spa facilities.

Facilities

Three clean sanitary blocks provide fine facilities; the one nearest the farm will be busy at peak periods. Baby room. Facilities for disabled campers. Washing machines. Freezer. Battery charging (free). Motorcaravan service areas. Supermarket. Bar. Restaurant. Takeaway. Pool bar. Swimming pool with lifeguard (18/5-29/9). Pétanque. Playground. Children's farm. Miniclub and entertainment (high season). Disco. Internet. WiFi (charged). Picnic area. Electronic games. Free daily bus to Barcelona (small charge, July/Aug) and regular free shuttle to the site's Mataró beach club, train station and wellness centre (concessions). Night bus from Barcelona. Bicycle hire.

Open: 1 March - 10 November.

Directions

Site is east of Mataró at the 650 km. marker on the N11. Leave the C-32 autoroute at exits 104 or 108 and follow signs for the sea and Mataró. Site is well signed on both carriageways.
GPS: 41.55055, 2.48338

Charges guide

Per unit incl. 2 persons and electricity	€ 18.00 - € 55.60
extra person	€ 3.65 - € 8.95
child (4-12 yrs)	free - € 6.45
dog	free - € 2.90

For latest campsite news, availability and prices visit
alanrogers.com

Palamós

Internacional de Palamós

E-17230 Palamós (Girona) T: **972 314 736**. E: info@internacionalpalamos.com

alanrogers.com/ES81500

This is a large, uncomplicated, comfortable site which is clean, welcoming and useful for exploring the local area from a peaceful base. Traditional in style, it is open for a long season and has a range of facilities. It might have space when others are full and has over 453 moderate sized pitches, 355 for touring. The majority are level and terraced with some less defined under pine trees on a gentle slope. Two hundred and eighteen have access to 6A electricity, and 104 have water and drainage. The sanitary facilities are excellent. The pretty beach at La Fosca is a 300 m. walk.

Facilities
Two refurbished toilet blocks and one smart new one are fully equipped with some washbasins in cabins. Facilities for disabled campers. Laundry room. Small shop. Bar and snack bar serving simple food and takeaways (all season). Swimming pool (36x16 m) with paddling pool (1/6-29/9). Small play area. Car wash. ATM. Bicycle hire. Torches necessary. WiFi over site (charged). Off site: Nearest beach and fishing 300 m. Town 1 km, hourly bus service.

Open: 28 March - 30 September.

Directions
From C31 road (direction Palamós) take exit 326 and follow signs for La Fosca and Camping Internacional Palamós (not those for another site close by called Camping Palamós). GPS: 41.85722, 3.13805

Charges guide
Per unit incl. 2 persons and electricity	€ 24.20 - € 46.90
extra person	€ 3.50 - € 5.30

No credit cards.
Camping Cheques accepted.

Pals

Camping-Resort Mas Patoxas Bungalow-Park

Ctra C31 Palafrugell-Pals km. 339, E-17256 Pals (Girona) T: **972 636 928**. E: info@campingmaspatoxas.com

alanrogers.com/ES81020

This is a mature, friendly and well laid out site for those who prefer to be apart from, but within easy travelling distance of, the beaches (5 km) and town (1 km). It has a very easy access and is set on a slight slope with wide avenues on level terraces providing 376 grassy pitches (minimum 72 sq.m). All have shared 6A electricity and water points. There are a variety of mature trees throughout the site providing welcome shade. On-site amenities include an attractive swimming pool complex with a large terrace, an air-conditioned restaurant, an ice cream parlour and a children's play area.

Facilities
Three modern sanitary blocks provide controllable hot showers, some washbasins with hot water. Baby bath and three cabins for children. Facilities for disabled campers. Laundry facilities. Fridges for rent. Gas supplies. Supermarket, restaurant/bar, ice-cream parlour, pizzeria and takeaway (limited opening in low season). Swimming pool with bar (1/5-29/9). Tennis. Entertainment and children's club (high season). Fitness area. Games areas. Massage. Disco. Bicycle hire. WiFi over site (charged).

Open: 16 January - 13 December.

Directions
Site is east of Girona and 1.5 km. south of Pals at km. 339 on the C31 Figueres-Palamós road, just north of Palafugel. GPS: 41.9568, 3.1573

Charges guide
Per unit incl. 2 persons and electricity	€ 28.30 - € 66.00
extra person	€ 4.40 - € 7.00
child (1-7 yrs)	€ 3.80 - € 5.25
dog	€ 2.70 - € 4.40

Special low season offers.

Pineda de Mar

Camping Caballo de Mar

Passeig Maritim 52-54, E-08397 Pineda de Mar (Barcelona) T: **937 671 706**. E: info@caballodemar.com

alanrogers.com/ES82380

This is definitely a site for lovers of the seaside, with direct access to a lovely, sandy beach. It is divided into two parts by the railway and dual-carriageway. The main part of the site is arranged off a central access road with plenty of shrubs and trees providing shade. In total there are 480 pitches, 380 for tourers. On the beach side of the site, the pitches are generally smaller (60-70 sq.m), all with shade; there is a bar/snack bar and a toilet block, and direct access to the beach. There are attractive new play and sports facilities for young children. There is some road and rail noise.

Facilities
Three toilet blocks, one in the main area and two in the beach area, are fully equipped and well maintained. En-suite units for hire (main side) with units for disabled visitors. Facilities for babies. Washing machines and dryer. Motorcaravan services. Shop and baker (15/6-12/9). Main bar and restaurant. Bar and snacks at the beach in high season. Swimming pool, jacuzzi and children's pool. Play area. Paddle court. Bicycle hire. Entertainment organised. Miniclub. Well equipped fitness room, massage and UVA machines. Internet. ATM. Fishing.

Open: 1 April - 30 September.

Directions
Site is off the N11 coast road, southwest of Pineda de Mar. Then leave N11 at km. 669 and following the camping signs to the road alongside the sea. Site is well signed off the beach road on southern outskirts of town. Ask at reception for directions to beach side of site to avoid low bridges. GPS: 41.61664, 2.64997

Charges guide
Per unit incl. 2 persons and electricity	€ 35.95 - € 71.75
extra person	€ 5.00 - € 9.40

Camping Cheques accepted.

Montroig
Camping La Torre del Sol

Ctra N340 km. 1136, E-43300 Montroig (Tarragona) T: 977 810 486. E: info@latorredelsol.com

alanrogers.com/ES85400

A pleasant banana tree-lined approach road gives way to avenues of palms as you arrive at Torre del Sol. This is a very large, well designed site occupying a good position in the south of Catalunya with direct access to the soft sand beach. The site is exceptionally well maintained by a large workforce. There is good shade on a high proportion of the 1,500 individual, numbered pitches (700 for touring). All have electricity and are mostly of about 90 sq.m. Strong features are 800 m. of clean beachfront, three attractive pools with two jacuzzis in the bar and restaurant area. A seawater jacuzzi and Turkish sauna were opened in 2012. Occasional train noise on some pitches. The cinema doubles as a theatre to stage shows all season. The complex of three pools, thoughtfully laid out with grass sunbathing areas and palms, has a lifeguard. There is wireless Internet access throughout the site. There is usually space for odd nights but for good places between 10/7-16/8 it is best to reserve (only taken for a stay of seven nights or more). We were impressed with the provision of season-long entertainment, giving parents a break whilst children were in the safe hands of the activities team, who ensure they enjoy the novel Happy Camp and various workshops. There is a separate area where the team will take your children to camp overnight in the Indian reservation.

Facilities
Five very well maintained, fully equipped, toilet blocks include units for disabled visitors and babies and new facilities for children. Washing machines. Gas supplies. Large supermarket, bakery and souvenir shops at entrance, open to public. Full restaurant. Takeaway. Bar with large terrace where entertainment is held daily. Beach bar. Coffee bar and ice-cream bar. Pizzeria. Open-roof cinema with permanent seating for 520. Three TV lounges. Soundproofed disco. Swimming pools (two heated). Solarium. Sauna. Two large jacuzzis. Seawater jacuzzi and Turkish sauna. Sports areas. Tennis. Squash. Language school (Spanish). Minigolf. Sub-aqua diving (first dive free). Bicycle hire. Fishing. Windsurfing school. Sailboards and pedaloes for hire. Playground, crèche and Happy Camp. Fridge hire. Library. Hairdresser. Business centre. WiFi. Car repair and car wash (pressure wash). No animals permitted. No jet skis accepted.

Open: 15 March - 31 October.

Directions
Entrance is off main N340 road by 1136 km. marker, 30 km. from Tarragona towards Valencia. From motorway take Cambrils exit and turn west on N340. GPS: 41.03707, 0.97478

Charges guide
Per unit incl. 2 persons and electricity	€ 27.50 - € 87.70
extra person	€ 3.40 - € 8.15
child (0-10 yrs)	free - € 6.10

Discounts in low season for longer stays.

Camping Cheques accepted.

Platja d'Aro
Camping Valldaro

Cami Vell 63, E-17250 Platja d'Aro (Girona) T: 972 817 515. E: info@valldaro.com

alanrogers.com/ES81700

Valldaro is a family run site, which is celebrating fifty years and is managed by the Mestres sisters who remember Alan Rogers visiting when they were young children. It is situated some 1,500 m. back from the sea at Platja d'Aro. It is a multi-national site and popular with British visitors, some of whom have been coming for many years. The site, which resembles a small village, is very well equipped with its own facilities and has been extended. A newer section with its own vehicle entrance is brought into use at peak times. It has shade and its own toilet block, as well as a medium sized swimming pool of irregular shape with a grassy sunbathing area and adjacent bar/snack bar and takeaway.

Facilities
Four sanitary blocks are of a good standard and are well maintained. Child size toilets. Washbasins (no cabins) and adjustable showers. Two supermarkets and general shops. Gas supplies. Two restaurants. Large bar. Swimming pools. Outdoor jacuzzi. Tennis. Minigolf with snack bar. Playgrounds. Sports ground. Children's club. New play area with football pitch. Organised entertainment in season. Hairdresser. Bicycle hire. Barbecue rental. WiFi over site (charged). Satellite TV. Off site: Fishing 1 km. Beach and amenities at Platja d'Aro 1.5 km. Riding 4 km. Golf 5 km.

Open: 27 March - 27 September.

Directions
From Girona on the AP7/E15 take exit 7 to Sant Feliu on C65. On C65 at km. 314 exit to Platja d'Aro (road number changes to C31). In 200 m. at roundabout take GI662 towards Platja d'Aro. Site is at km. 4. Approaching from Palamós, access via Platja d'Aro centre, and the GI662. GPS: 41.81427, 3.0437

Charges guide
Per unit incl. 2 persons and electricity	€ 30.80 - € 81.40
extra person	€ 4.60 - € 8.20
child (3-12 yrs)	€ 3.00 - € 4.60
dog	€ 4.00

Discounts in low seasons.

Camping Cheques accepted.

For latest campsite news, availability and prices visit
alanrogers.com

CAMPING BUNGALOW WELLNESS RESORT
LA TORRE DEL SOL
Cat.1 ★ ★ ★ ★

Wi-Fi ZONE

CATALUNYA

Catalunya Sud

FIRST CLASS HOLIDAYS ON THE MEDITERRANEAN

CAMPING RESORTS

soleil VILLAGE

Camping Cheque

✉ **E-43892 MIAMI PLATJA (TARRAGONA)**
Tel.: +34 977 810 486 · Fax: +34 977 811 306
www.latorredelsol.com · info@latorredelsol.com

Platja de Pals
Camping Cypsela

Ctra de Pals-Platja de Pals, E-17256 Platja de Pals (Girona) T: 972 667 696. E: info@cypsela.com

alanrogers.com/ES80900

This large and impressive, deluxe site is very efficiently run. The main part of the camping area is pinewood, with 688 clearly marked touring pitches of varying categories on sandy gravel, all with electricity and 552 with full facilities. The 267 élite pitches of 120 sq.m. are impressive. Cypsela is a busy, well administered site, only 2 km. from the sea, which we can thoroughly recommend, especially for families. The site has good quality fixtures and fittings, all kept clean and maintained to a high standard. The site has many striking features, one of which is the sumptuous complex of sports facilities and amenities near the entrance.

Facilities
Four sanitary blocks are of excellent quality with cleaning schedules and solar heating. Three have washbasins in cabins, and three have amazing rooms for children. Private sanitary facilities to rent. Superb facilities for disabled visitors. Serviced launderette. Supermarket and other shops. Restaurant, cafeteria and takeaway. Bar. Hairdresser. Swimming pools. Tennis. Squash. Minigolf. Skating rink. Fitness room. Solarium. Air conditioned social/TV room. Barbecue and party area. Comprehensive entertainment programme in season. Bicycle hire. ATM. Business centre. WiFi (charged). Dogs are not accepted.

Open: 17 May - 14 September.

Directions
From AP7/E15 at Girona take exit 6 for Palamós on C66 (road changes to C31 near La Bisbal). 7.5 km. past La Bisbal, exit to Pals on GI652. Follow signs for Platja de Pals. At El Masos take 6502 for 1 km. Main entrance is on left. GPS: 41.98608, 3.18105

Charges guide
Per unit incl. 2 persons and electricity	€ 34.10 - € 82.60
extra person	€ 6.80
child (1-10 yrs)	€ 4.50

Platja de Pals
Camping Playa Brava

Avenida del Grau 1, E-17256 Platja de Pals (Girona) T: 972 636 894. E: info@playabrava.com

alanrogers.com/ES81010

This is an attractive and efficiently run site with an open feel, having direct access to an excellent soft sand beach and a freshwater lagoon where you can enjoy watersports and launch your own boat (charged). The ground is level and grassy with shade provided for many of the 745 spacious touring pitches by a mixture of conifer and broadleaf trees. All the pitches have 10A electricity and 238 have water and drainage. The large swimming pool has an extensive grass sunbathing area and is overlooked by the terrace of the restaurant and bar. This is a clean, secure and pleasant family site, suitable for sightseeing and for those who enjoy beach and water activities. The restaurant is very pleasant and offers a most reasonable menu of the day including wine. The new inside/outside bar is open to the public. There is also a new reception building, a supermarket and a performance area. An energetic entertainment programme runs during July and August, and there is a full programme of excursions.

Facilities
Five modern, fully equipped toilet blocks include facilities for disabled visitors. Washing machines and dryers. Motorcaravan services. Supermarket. Bar/restaurant. Takeaway. Swimming pool. Tennis. Minigolf. Beach volleyball. Play area. Bicycle hire. Watersports on river and beach, including sheltered lagoon for windsurfing novices. Stage show. Internet. WiFi over site (charged). Satellite TV. Gas supplies. Torches required in some areas. Dogs are not accepted. Off site: One 18-hole golf courses (50% discount online via Playa Brava) 500 m.

Open: 17 May - 14 September.

Directions
From AP7/E15 at Girona take exit 6 towards Palamós on C66. 7.5 km. past La Bisbal, exit to Pals on GIV-6502. Follow signs for Platja de Pals-Golf Platja de Pals. Site is on left just before road ends at beach car park. GPS: 42.001130, 3.193800

Charges guide
Per unit incl. 2 persons and electricity	€ 34.00 - € 67.00
extra person	€ 2.50 - € 3.50
child (3-9 yrs)	free - € 2.50

Discounts in low season. No credit cards.

CÀMPING CARAVANING ★★★

Playa Brava

PLATJA DE PALS - COSTA BRAVA

1ª ★★★

GPS:
42.001130 N
3.193800 E

www.playabrava.com

Av. del Grau, 1 · 17256 PLATJA DE PALS (Girona) COSTA BRAVA
T. +34 972 63 68 94 · F. +34 972 63 69 52 · info@playabrava.com

For latest campsite news, availability and prices visit
alanrogers.com

Platja de Pals

Camping Inter-Pals

Avenida Mediterrania, E-17256 Platja de Pals (Girona) T: 972 636 179. E: interpals@interpals.com

alanrogers.com/ES81000

Alan Rogers visited this site in the 1970s, using it as his base in this area of the Costa Brava. Luis, the long-standing manager, still remembers his visit with affection. At that time it was described as a 'site shaded by an umbrella of pines' and it retains a very authentic Costa Brava atmosphere of tranquillity with its local stone terraces and sea views. There are 450 level, terraced pitches, most with shade and some with sea views through the trees. On-site amenities include recently renovated toilet blocks and a new supermarket. A formal restaurant with a good value menu and a bar overlook the new pool.

Facilities

Three well maintained toilet blocks include facilities for disabled campers. Motorcaravan services. Laundry facilities. Gas supplies. Fridge rental. Shops. Restaurant/bar. Pizzeria. Supermarket by entrance. Swimming pool. Jacuzzi. Playground. Bicycle hire. Organised activities and entertainment in high season. Excursions. Watersports arranged. Mini-adventure park. Medical centre. ATM. Internet access. WiFi. Some breeds of dog are excluded (check with site). Torch useful.

Open: 31 March - 25 September.

Directions

Site is on the road leading off the Torroella de Montgri-Bagur road north of Pals and going to Platja de Pals (Pals beach). Follow signs to Gran Platja and site is on right after supermarket.
GPS: 41.97533, 3.19317

Charges guide

Per unit incl. 2 persons and electricity	€ 31.60 - € 55.60
extra person	€ 4.80 - € 7.30

Camping Cheques accepted.

Poboleda

Camping Poboleda

Placa de les Casetes s/n, E-43376 Poboleda (Tarragona) T: 977 827 197. E: poboleda@campingsonline.com

alanrogers.com/ES85080

Time stands still at this unique site, watched over by La Morera de Montsant, a peak of the Serra del Montsant. Situated among olive groves, on the edge of the lovely old village of Poboleda, it is an idyllic site for tents, small caravans and motorcaravans. Large units would have problems negotiating the narrow village streets and even small caravans might find it tricky. The 151 average sized pitches (70 with 4A electricity) are set on broad grassy terraces under olive and almond trees in a peaceful haven broken only by bird song or the peal of church bells.

Facilities

One small block, open all year, is fully equipped, as is a larger block open for high season. Shower for children. Facilities for disabled visitors (key). Laundry service. Breakfast to order. Bar. Swimming pool (24/6-11/9). Tennis. Boules. Reception sells basics. WiFi area (free). Off site: Bars, restaurants and shops in village. Bicycle hire 10 km. Fishing and boat launching 12 km. Gaudí Centre in Reus 30 km. Beach and Port Aventura theme park 40 km.

Open: All year.

Directions

Poboleda is best approached from the south. From AP7 at exit 34, take T11 (Reus then Falset) and continue on N420. After Borges del Camp turn north on C242 for 18 km. over Coll d'Alforja. Take T702 west for 6 km. to Poboleda. Watch for tent signs and follow carefully through narrow village streets. Unsuitable for large units. GPS: 41.23231, 0.84316

Charges guide

Per unit incl. 2 persons and electricity	€ 32.32
extra person	€ 6.48

Roda de Bará

Camping Stel

Ctra N340 km. 1182, E-43883 Roda de Bará (Tarragona) T: 977 802 002. E: rodadebara@stel.es

alanrogers.com/ES84200

Camping Stel is situated between mountains and the sea with direct access to an excellent beach via a passage under the railway, which runs along the entire coast (so expect some rail noise, especially on the lower pitches). The 658 touring pitches are generally in rows separated by hedges, all have electricity (5A), 535 are fully serviced and many have individual sinks. In one area, radios and TVs are not allowed. The impressive central area contains a large bar/restaurant with terrace and snack bar overlooking the attractive pool complex, which includes a wonderful fun pool for children, a flume and a pleasant grass area carefully set out with palms.

Facilities

Four clean, fully equipped, sanitary blocks provide spacious controllable showers, washbasins in cabins, facilities for children and disabled visitors and eight quality private bathrooms to rent. Baby baths. Launderette. Motorcaravan services. Supermarket and tourist shop. Bar/restaurant and snack bar. Heated swimming pool with children's section, flume and jacuzzi. Sports complex. Gym. Hairdresser. Bicycle hire. Activities and excursions. Miniclub. WiFi over site. ATM. Dogs are not accepted.

Open: Week before Easter - last Sunday in September.

Directions

From east on AP7 leave at exit 31 and take motorway link to join N340 west. From west take exit 32 onto N340 east. Site is at 1182 km. marker on the N340 near Arc de Bará, between Tarragona and Vilanova. GPS: 41.16991, 1.46436

Charges guide

Per unit incl. 2 persons and electricity	€ 26.00 - € 51.00
extra person	€ 7.00 - € 9.00
child (3-10 yrs)	€ 5.00 - € 7.00

FREE Alan Rogers Travel Card
Extra benefits and savings - see page 14

Salou

Camping Resort Sangulí Salou

Passeig Miramar-Plaça Venus, Apdo 123, E-43840 Salou (Tarragona) T: 977 381 641. E: mail@sanguli.es

alanrogers.com/ES84800

Camping Resort Sangulí Salou is a superb site boasting excellent pools and entertainment. Owned, developed and managed by a local Spanish family, it has something for all the family with everything open when the site is open. There are 1,089 pitches of varying sizes (75-120 sq.m) all with electricity (7.5-10A). Mobile homes occupy 58 pitches and there are fully equipped bungalows on 147. A wonderful selection of trees, palms and shrubs provide natural shade and an ideal space for children to play. The good sandy beach is little more than 50 metres across the coast road and a small railway crossing. Although large, Sangulí has a pleasant, open feel and maintains a quality family atmosphere due to the efforts of the very keen and efficient staff. There are three very attractive themed pools, which include water slides and elephants. Amenities include a children's play park, organised activities for adults and children, a miniclub, tennis courts, table tennis, minigolf, a football pitch, volleyball, and a fitness room. Evening shows are presented in the site's magnificent amphitheatre, there is a cinema and the site's Sangulí restaurant serves Mediterranean cuisine. Located on the promenade near the centre of Salou, the site can offer the attractions of a busy resort while still being private and it is only 3 km. from Port Aventura. This is a large, professional site providing something for all the family, but still capable of providing peace and quiet for those looking for it.

Facilities

The six sanitary blocks are constantly cleaned and are always exceptional, including many individual cabins with en-suite facilities. Improvements are made each year. Some blocks have excellent facilities for babies. Launderette with service. Motorcaravan services. Car wash (charged). Gas supplies. Snack bars. Indoor and outdoor restaurants with takeaway. Swimming pools. Fitness centre. Sports complex. Fitness room (charged). Playgrounds including adventure play area. Miniclub. Minigolf. Multiple Internet options including WiFi (free). Security bracelets. Medical centre. Off site: Activities on the beach 50 m. Bus at gate. Bicycle hire 100 m. Fishing 200 m. Riding 3 km. Port Aventura 4 km. Aquopolis 5 km.

Open: 20 March - 2 November.

Directions

On west side of Salou 1 km. from the centre, site is well signed from the coast road to Cambrils and from the other town approaches.
GPS: 41.07546, 1.11651

Charges guide

Per unit incl. 2 persons and electricity	€ 29.00 - € 78.00
extra person	€ 7.00
child (4-12 yrs)	€ 5.00

Reductions outside high season for longer stays. Special long stay offers for senior citizens.

Roses

Camping Joncar Mar

Ctra Figueres s/n, E-17480 Roses (Girona) T: 972 256 702. E: info@campingjoncarmar.com

alanrogers.com/ES80080

Family owned since 1977, Joncar Mar is a mature, all-year site with limited but well maintained facilities. Its strength is its location with the beach promenade just outside the gate, and the many resort leisure facilities and local cultural attractions readily available to customers. The site is divided by a minor road and most leisure facilities are positioned on one side of the site. There are no views and the site has some apartment blocks around the periphery. The 185 pitches, 147 for touring, are small (60 sq.m) with 6A electricity, and the mobile home area in one corner of the site is cramped. Some pitches require long electricity leads. While the site offers a very basic, no-frills service, it is friendly, well organised and with a continual programme of upgrading.

Facilities

One refurbished toilet block has very good facilities with good baby room and facilities for disabled campers, the other is adequate; both are well positioned on the main side of the site and the third block on the other side is adequate. One washing machine. Small shop. Small bar and buffet restaurant. Swimming pool. Basic play area. TV in bar. Limited entertainment programme. Bicycle hire. WiFi over site (charged). Off site: Nearest beach 100 m. Public transport 600 m. Riding 3 km. Golf 20 km.

Open: All year.

Directions

Roses is north of Girona and east of Figueres on the coast. From AP7/E15 take exit 3 south or exit 4 north (no exit 3 northbound) and then the N11 to the C260 and on to Roses. Site is well signed before entering the town – follow camping signs initially.
GPS: 42.26639, 3.16355

Charges guide

Per unit incl. 2 persons and electricity	€ 14.00
extra person	€ 7.30 - € 7.50
child (2-10 yrs)	€ 4.80 - € 4.90
dog	€ 2.80 - € 3.00

Discounts for longer stays.

For latest campsite news, availability and prices visit

alanrogers.com

Salou

La Siesta Salou Camping Resort

Calle Norte 37, E-43840 Salou (Tarragona) T: 977 380 852. E: info@lasiestasalou.com

alanrogers.com/ES84700

La Siesta occupies a remarkable location close to the heart of the thriving resort of Salou, yet only two blocks from the fine sandy beach. The 300 pitches for touring, all with 10A electricity, vary in size, some suitable for larger units, others for tents. There is considerable shade from the trees and shrubs that contribute to the site's attractive appearance. Considerable recent investment has seen the creation of a pleasant, grassy play area for children and impressive new sports provision. An extensive new leisure pool complex has been built, overlooked by the existing bar/restaurant offering comprehensive and competitively priced menus, and entertainment in high season. A surprisingly large supermarket caters for most needs in season, and close by are all the shops, bars, restaurants and nightlife of Salou. The town is popular with British and Spanish holidaymakers and has just about all that a highly developed Spanish resort can offer, including miles of sandy beaches. Close by is Port Aventura, an amazing theme park, whilst days out could include a trip by train to Barcelona to see Gaudí's incredible Sagrada Familia cathedral or, in complete contrast, a drive along the coast to the Parc Natural del Delta de l'Ebre.

Facilities

One bright and clean sanitary block provides very reasonable facilities including controllable showers and open style washbasins. Unit for disabled visitors. Motorcaravan services. Supermarket (June-Sept). Various vending machines. Self-service restaurant and bar with takeaway. Extensive new pool complex. Children's club, entertainment (both June-Sept). Playground. Multisports and short tennis courts. Medical service daily in season. ATM point. Torches may be required. WiFi throughout (charged). Off site: Many shops, restaurants and bars nearby. Port Aventura is close. Bicycle hire 200 m.

Open: 1 April - 10 October.

Directions

Leave AP7 at exit 35 or A7 (toll-free) motorway at exit for Salou. Follow the Tarragona-Salou road (dual carriageway) until you pass the side of the site on the right. Site is signed (narrow turning). Follow further small signs through the one way system.
GPS: 41.0777, 1.1389

Charges guide

Per unit incl. 2 persons and electricity	€ 28.00 - € 67.50
extra person	€ 6.00 - € 9.25
child (4-9 yrs)	free - € 5.00

www.lasiestasalou.com - info@lasiestasalou.com
Tel. + 34 977 380852 - Fax. + 34 977 383191

Sant Pere Pescador

Camping Aquarius

Playa s/n, E-17470 Sant Pere Pescador (Girona) T: 972 520 101. E: reservas@aquarius.es

alanrogers.com/ES80500

This is a welcoming and organised family site approached by an attractive road flanked by orchards. Aquarius has direct access to a quiet, sandy beach that slopes gently and provides good bathing. Watersports are popular, particularly windsurfing (a school is provided). One third of the site has good shade with a park-like atmosphere. There are 430 touring pitches, all with electricity (6/16A). Markus Rupp and his wife are keen to make every visitor's experience a happy one. The site is ideal for those who really like sun and sea, with a quiet situation.

Facilities

Large, fully equipped, toilet blocks provide some cabins for each sex. Excellent facilities for disabled visitors, plus baths for children. One block has underfloor heating and family cabins. Laundry facilities. Gas. Motorcaravan services. Full size refrigerators. Supermarket. Pleasant restaurant and bar with terrace. Takeaway. Purpose built play centre (qualified attendant), playground and separate play area for toddlers. TV room. Surf Center. Minigolf. Bicycle hire. ATM. Internet. WiFi over site (charged). Dogs are accepted in one section. (Note: there is no pool).

Open: 15 March - 31 October.

Directions

Attention: sat nav suggests a different route, but easier to drive is from AP7 exit 3 (Figueres Nord) towards Roses on C-68. At roundabout Castello d'Empuries take second right to St Pere Pescador, cross town and river bridge. From there site is well signed. GPS: 42.18092, 3.09425

Charges guide

Per unit incl. 2 persons and electricity	€ 21.80 - € 46.80
extra person	€ 3.35 - € 4.70

No credit cards.

For latest campsite news, availability and prices visit

alanrogers.com

Sant Pere Pescador

Kawan Village l'Amfora

Avenida Josep Tarradellas, 2, E-17470 Sant Pere Pescador (Girona) T: 972 520 540.

E: info@campingamfora.com **alanrogers.com/ES80350**

This spacious site is family run and friendly. It is spotlessly clean and well maintained and the owner operates in an environmentally friendly way. There are 830 level, grass pitches (741 for touring units) laid out in a grid system, all with 10A electricity. Attractive trees and shrubs have been planted around each pitch. There is good shade in the more mature areas, which include 64 large pitches (180 sq.m), each with an individual sanitary unit (toilet, shower and washbasin). The newer area is more open with less shade and you can choose which you would prefer. Three excellent sanitary blocks (one heated) are fully equipped and offer free hot water, each with staff on almost permanent duty to ensure very high standards. Access around the site is generally good for disabled visitors. At the entrance, which is hard surfaced with car parking, a terraced bar and two restaurants overlook a smart pool complex with three pools for children, one with two water slides. In high season (from July) there is ambitious evening entertainment (pub, disco, shows) and an activity programme for children. Alongside the site, the magnificent sandy beach on the Bay of Roses offers good conditions for children and a choice of watersports. A bicycle is useful. Dogs are welcome and owners will appreciate the informal exercise areas.

Facilities

Three main toilet blocks, one heated, provide washbasins in cabins and roomy free showers. Baby rooms. Laundry facilities and service. Motorcaravan services. Supermarket. Terraced bar, self-service and waiter-service restaurants. Pizzeria/takeaway. Restaurant and bar on the beach with limited menu (high season). Disco bar. Swimming pools (1/5-27/9). Pétanque. Tennis. Bicycle hire. Minigolf. Play area. Miniclub. Entertainment and activities. Windsurfing. Kite surfing (low season). Boat launching and sailing. Fishing. Exchange facilities. Games and TV rooms. Internet room and WiFi over site (charged). Car wash. Torches required in beach areas. Off site: Riding 4 km. Golf 15 km.

Open: 14 April - 27 September.

Directions

From north on A17/E15 take exit 3 on N11 towards Figueres and then shortly on C260 towards Roses. At Castello d'Empúries turn right on GIV6216 to Sant Pere. From south on A17 use exit 5 (L'Escala) and turn to Sant Pere in Viladamat. Site is well signed in town. GPS: 42.18147, 3.10405

Charges guide

Per unit incl. 2 persons and electricity	€ 26.00 - € 60.00
extra person	€ 4.50 - € 6.20
child (2-9 yrs)	€ 2.50 - € 4.20
dog	€ 2.70 - € 5.20

Senior citizen specials. No credit cards.

Camping Cheques accepted.

Sant Pere Pescador

Camping la Gaviota

Ctra de la Platja s/n, E-17470 Sant Pere Pescador (Girona) T: 972 520 569. E: info@lagaviota.com

alanrogers.com/ES80310

La Gaviota is a delightful, small, family run site at the end of a cul-de-sac with direct beach access. This ensures a peaceful situation with a choice of the pleasant L-shaped pool or the fine clean beach with slowly shelving access to the water. Everything here is clean and colourful and the Gil family are very keen that you enjoy your time here. There are 157 touring pitches on flat ground with shade and 8A electricity supply. A lush green feel is given to the site by many palms and other semi-tropical trees and shrubs. The restaurant and bar are very pleasant indeed and have a distinct Spanish flavour. The cuisine is reasonably priced, perfectly prepared and served by friendly staff. All facilities are at the reception end of this rectangular site with extra washing up areas at the far end. The area is particularly well known for wind- and kite-surfing, and lessons and equipment to rent are available nearby. All facilities are open from March to October (swimming pool May to October) and a children's club operates in high season. English is spoken.

Facilities

One clean, smart toilet block is near reception, with British style WCs and excellent facilities. Superb facilities for disabled visitors. Two great family rooms plus two baby rooms. Washing machine. Gas supplies. Supermarket (fresh bread), pleasant bar, terrace and delightful restaurant (all Mar-Oct). Swimming pool (May-Oct). New playground. Games room. Organised activities for adults and children. Beach sports, kayaking, kite- and windsurfing. Torches useful. ATM. WiFi over site (charged). Off site: Boat launching 2 km. Riding 4 km. Sailing 10 km. Golf 15 km. Boat excursions. Cycling routes.

Open: 23 March - 28 October.

Directions

From the AP7/E15 take exit 3 onto the N11 north towards Figueres and then the C260 towards Roses. At Castello d'Empúries take the GIV 6216 and continue to Sant Pere Pescador. Site is well signed in the town. GPS: 42.18901, 3.10843

Charges guide

Per unit incl. 2 persons	
and electricity	€ 27.40 - € 56.20
extra person	€ 3.80 - € 5.20
child (under 10 yrs)	€ 1.00 - € 3.50
dog	€ 2.00 - € 4.50

No credit cards. Discounts for longer stays.

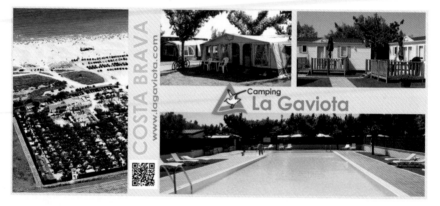

COSTA BRAVA
www.lagaviota.com
Camping La Gaviota

Santa Cristina d'Aro

Yelloh! Village Mas Sant Josep

Ctra Santa Cristina-Platja d'Aro km. 2, E-17246 Santa Cristina d'Aro (Girona) T: 972 835 108.

E: info@campingmassantjosep.com **alanrogers.com/ES81750**

This is a very large, well appointed, open site in two parts. There are 1,023 level pitches (100 sq.m) with 327 for touring units in a separate area, with shade from established trees. All have 10A electricity connections. There are wide access roads and long avenues between the zones. The main side of the site is centred around charming historic buildings, including a beautiful, but mysterious, locked and long unused chapel. Nearby is a huge, irregular lagoon-style pool with a bridge to a palm decorated island (lifeguards) and an excellent, safe paddling pool. A large complex including a bar, restaurant, takeaway and entertainment areas overlooks the pool.

Facilities

Two adequate toilet blocks for touring units (ignore block for permanent pitches). Very good facilities for disabled visitors and pleasant baby rooms. Washing machines. Dryers. Large supermarket, bars, restaurant, snack bar and takeaway. Swimming pools. Safe playgrounds. Games room. Tennis. Squash. Minigolf. 5-a-side football. Spa room and gym. Entertainment. Hairdresser. Bicycle hire. Internet. WiFi over part of site (charged). ATM.

Open: 17 April - 14 September.

Directions

From AP7 E15 (Girona-Barcelona) take exit 7 and C65 San Filiu road. At entrance to Sant Christina d'Aro take GI662 (right), then first right (Ctra De Sta Cristina). Site is 1 km. from village and signed. GPS: 41.811167, 3.018217

Charges guide

Per unit incl. 2 persons	
and electricity	€ 18.00 - € 51.00
extra person (over 7 yrs)	€ 6.00 - € 9.00

For latest campsite news, availability and prices visit

alanrogers.com

Sant Pere Pescador

Camping Las Dunas

Ctra San Marti-Sant Pere, E-17470 Sant Pere Pescador (Girona) T: 972 521 717.

E: info@campinglasdunas.com **alanrogers.com/ES80400**

LeadingCampings

Las Dunas is an extremely large, impressive and well organised resort-style site with many on-site activities and an ongoing programme of improvements. It has direct access to a superb sandy beach that stretches along the site for nearly a kilometre with a windsurfing school and beach bar. There is also a much used, huge swimming pool, plus a large double pool for children. Las Dunas is very large, with 1,700 individual hedged pitches (1,500 for touring units) of around 100 sq.m. laid out on flat ground in long, regular parallel rows. All have electricity (6/10A) and 180 also have water and drainage. Shade is available in some parts of the site. Pitches are usually available, even in the main season. Much effort has gone into planting palms and new trees here and the results are very attractive. The large restaurant and bar have spacious terraces overlooking the swimming pools or you can enjoy a very pleasant, more secluded, cavern-style pub. A magnificent disco club is close by in a soundproofed building (although people returning from this during the night can be a problem for pitches in the central area of the site). With free, quality entertainment of all types in season and positive security arrangements, this is a great site for families with teenagers. Everything is provided on site so you don't need to leave it during your stay. A popular site for British rallies. A member of Leading Campings group.

Facilities

Five excellent large toilet blocks with electronic sliding glass doors (resident cleaners 07.00-21.00). British style toilets but no seats, controllable hot showers and washbasins in cabins. Excellent facilities for youngsters, babies and disabled campers. Laundry facilities. Motorcaravan services. Extensive supermarket, boutique and other shops. Large bar with terrace. Large restaurant. Takeaway and terrace. Ice cream parlour. Beach bar in main season. Disco club. Swimming pools. Minigolf. New adventure crazy golf. Playgrounds. Tennis. Archery (occasionally). Sailing/windsurfing school and other watersports. Programme of sports, games, excursions and entertainment, partly in English (15/6-31/8). Exchange facilities. ATM. Safety deposit. Internet café. WiFi over site (charged). Dogs accepted in one section. Torches required in some areas. Off site: Resort of L'Escala 5 km. Riding and boat launching 5 km. Water park 10 km. Golf 30 km.

Open: 17 May - 19 September.

See advertisement on the back cover.

Directions

L'Escala is northeast of Girona on coast between Palamós and Roses. From A7/E15 autostrada take exit 5 towards L'Escala on GI623. Turn north 2 km. before L'Escala towards Sant Marti d'Ampúrias. Site well signed. GPS: 42.16098, 3.107774

Charges guide

Per unit incl. 2 persons	
and electricity	€ 22.50 - € 73.00
extra person	€ 3.75 - € 6.00
child (3-10 yrs)	€ 3.00 - € 3.50
dog	€ 3.50 - € 5.00

Sant Pere Pescador

Camping la Ballena Alegre

Ctra Sant Marti d'Empuries s/n, E-17470 Sant Pere Pescador (Girona) T: 972 520 302.
E: info@ballena-alegre.com **alanrogers.com/ES80600**

La Ballena Alegre is a spacious site with almost 2 km. of frontage directly onto an excellent beach of soft golden sand (which is cleaned daily). They claim that none of the 966 touring pitches is more than 100 m. from the beach. The grass pitches are individually numbered, many separated by hedges, and there is a choice of size (up to 120 sq.m). Electrical connections (5/10A) are available in all areas and there are 670 fully serviced pitches. There are several bungalow areas within the site with their own small pools and play areas, and some have shared jacuzzis. This is a great site for families. There are restaurant and bar areas beside the pleasant terraced pool complex (four pools including a pool for children). For those who wish to drink and snack late there is a pub open until 03.00. The well managed, soundproofed disco is popular with youngsters. A little train ferries people along the length of the site and a road train runs to local villages. Plenty of entertainment and activities are offered, including a well managed watersports centre, with sub-aqua, windsurfing and kite-surfing, where equipment can be hired and lessons taken. You can also use a comprehensive open-air fitness centre near the beach. A full entertainment programme is provided all season. An overflow area across the road provides additional parking and sports activities. The site has won Spanish tourist board awards and the owners are keen to promote an ecological approach through recycling, use of solar energy and the design of new buildings.

Facilities

Seven well maintained toilet blocks are of a very high standard. Facilities for children, babies and disabled campers. Launderette. Motorcaravan services. Gas supplies. A wide range of restaurants, snack bars and takeaways, including a pizzeria/trattoria, arroceria, a pub, a self-service restaurant and a beach bar in high season. Swimming pool complex. Jacuzzi. Tennis. Watersports centre. Fitness centre. Bicycle hire. Playgrounds. Soundproofed disco. Dancing twice weekly and organised activities, sports, entertainment, etc. ATM. Dogs only allowed in one zone. Internet and WiFi (charged). Torches useful in beach areas. Off site: Go-karting nearby with bus service. Fishing 300 m. Riding 2 km.

Open: 17 May - 21 September.

Directions

From A7 Figueres-Girona autopista take exit 5 to L'Escala GI623 for 18.5 km. At roundabout take sign to Sant Marti d'Empúries and follow site signs. GPS: 42.15323, 3.11248

Charges guide

Per unit incl. 2 persons and electricity	€ 27.40 - € 60.20
extra person	€ 4.20 - € 6.00
child (3-10 yrs)	€ 2.90 - € 5.00
dog	€ 2.40 - € 5.00

Discount of 10% on pitch charge for seniors all season. No credit cards.

For latest campsite news, availability and prices visit
alanrogers.com

Sitges

Camping El Garrofer

Ctra C-246a km. 39, E-08870 Sitges (Barcelona) T: 938 941 780. E: info@garroferpark.com

alanrogers.com/ES83920

This large, pine-covered site beside fields of vines is 900 m. from the beach, close to the pleasant town of Sitges. This is an attractive resort with seaside entertainments and is well worth exploring. The site has 526 pitches, many of which are occupied by seasonal caravans or chalets but are separate from the touring area. A central area on dusty, baked earth beneath the trees is devoted to touring caravans and a corner of the site has 28 pitches with water mainly used for large motorcaravans. All have 6A electricity (Europlugs). There is an open field for tents. A cosy, refurbished bar and restaurant with a small terrace offers a varied menu. Next to it are other single storey buildings including a small supermarket; these are along the site perimeter next to the road, and absorb most of the traffic noise. The restaurant has a good local reputation – the menu of the day is great value. A traditional bar is alongside and from here you can see the pretty mosaic-clad play area. An entertainment programme is organised for children in summer and a variety of family adventure activities and excursions can be organised through reception.

Facilities

One of the three sanitary blocks has been refurbished and provides roomy showers and special bright facilities for children. Separate baby room with bath. Good facilities for disabled campers. Laundry. Bar/restaurant and small supermarket. Saltwater swimming and paddling pools (1/6-31/9). Football pitch. Tennis. Play area for older children and fenced play area for toddlers. Bicycle hire. Boules. WiFi throughout (charged). Off site: Bus from outside site to Barcelona. Golf 500 m. Beach and fishing 900 m. Sailing and boat launching 2 km. Riding 4 km.

Open: 28 February - 14 December.

Directions

From north on AP7 leave at exit 29 and take C15/C158 (Sitges) to join C32 motorway east. Leave at exit 26 (Sitges). From Tarragona on AP7 leave at exit 31 to join C32 motorway; continue to exit 26. Follow signs for Sitges and site along C246a to km. 39; site is on right. GPS: 41.23352, 1.78112

Charges guide

Per unit incl. 2 persons	
and electricity	€ 30.00 - € 42.65
extra person	€ 3.60 - € 6.25
child (3-9 yrs)	€ 2.65 - € 4.90

Tarragona

Camping Tamarit Park Resort

N340a km. 1172, Tamarit, E-43008 Tarragona (Tarragona) T: 977 650 128.

E: resort@tamarit.com **alanrogers.com/ES84830**

This is a marvellous, beach-side site, attractively situated at the foot of Tamarit Castle at one end of a superb one kilometre long beach of fine sand. It is landscaped with lush Mediterranean shrubs, studded with pines and palms, and home to mischievous red squirrels. There are 470 good sized pitches for touring, all with electricity (10A), 264 of which are fully serviced with water, drainage, TV connection and electricity is 16A. Fifty pitches are virtually on the beach, so are very popular. On hard sand and grass, some are attractively separated by hedging and shaded by trees. Accommodation in the form of bungalows (156 pitches) is also available to rent. The management and staff here are very keen to please and standards are very high.

Facilities

The high quality sanitary blocks (two heated) are modern and tiled. Private bathrooms to rent. Laundry facilities. Motorcaravan services. Fridge hire. Gas. Supermarket, boutique, bars, restaurant and takeaway. Bakery. Wellness area. Swimming pool. Tennis. Pétanque. Bicycle hire. Minigolf. Playground. Sports zone. Club room with bar. Miniclub. Entertainment programme. Fishing. WiFi over site (code). Off site: Village 1.5 km. along beach.

Open: 4 April - 26 October.

Directions

From A7 take exit 32 towards Tarragona for 4.5 km. At roundabout (km. 1172) turn back towards Atafulla/Tamarit and after 200 m. turn right to Tamarit (by Caledonia Bungalow Park). Take care over railway bridge, then immediately sharp left. Site is on left after 1 km. GPS: 41.1316, 3.3610

Charges guide

Per unit incl. 2 persons	
and electricity	€ 27.00 - € 64.00

Torredembarra
Camping Clarà
Passeig Miramar, 276, E-43830 Torredembarra (Tarragona) T: 977 643 480. E: info@campingclara.es

alanrogers.com/ES84855

Camping Clarà is a small family run site with direct beach access. This ensures a peaceful situation with a fine clean beach with slowly shelving access to the water. The 125 touring pitches, on flat ground, range in size from 60-90 sq.m. All have electricity (6/10A) and some also have water and drainage. All are clearly marked in rows, but with no separation other than by the deciduous trees which provide summer shade. Additionally, a range of fully equipped mobile homes and chalets are available for rent. The restaurant and bar are very pleasant indeed and have a distinct Spanish flavour. A children's club operates in peak season (4 to 12 years).

Facilities
Sanitary facilities with spacious showers. Facilities for disabled visitors. Baby room. Washing machines and dryer. Motorcaravan services. Supermarket (fresh bread), pleasant bar and small restaurant (all season). Playground. Boules. Bicycle hire. Activities and excursions. Limited animation. WiFi over site (free). Mobile homes and chalets for rent. Torches useful. Off site: Large supermarket, bank and marina for boat launching 300 m. Beach fishing (with permit). Riding 2 km. Golf 10 km.

Open: 1 April - 30 September.

Directions
From AP7 motorway exit 32 Torredembarra and then the N340 towards Barcelona until the roundabout. At the roundabout take the first exit Torredembarra est, for about 1 km. to site. GPS: 41.14949, 1.41989

Charges guide
Per unit incl. 2 persons	
and electricity	€ 18.60 - € 36.80
extra person	€ 3.60 - € 6.00
child (3-10 yrs)	€ 2.30 - € 5.30
dog	€ 1.70 - € 2.45

CAMPING CLARÀ
camping & bungalows

Passeig Miramar, 276 · The old N-340, km 1.178
E-43830 · Torredembarra (Tarragona) Spain
Tel: + 34 977.64.34.80 · info@campingclara.es · www.campingclara.es

Torredembarra
Camping La Noria
Ctra N-340 km. 1178, E-43830 Torredembarra (Tarragona) T: 977 64 0453. E: info@camping-lanoria.com

alanrogers.com/ES84845

La Noria is just over five acres in size with over 200 level touring pitches all having access to electricity (6A). Most of the touring pitches have good shade and the motorcaravan areas have hardstanding. A central cafeteria style restaurant and small supermarket cater for most needs. Entertainment is available for young children with the multisport pitch and pétanque for those a bit older. The Mediterranean coast, with its clean sandy beaches is a short, traffic free, walk away via a dedicated tunnel under the coastal railway line. La Noria is about 70 km. south west of Barcelona making it ideally situated for day trips whilst having access to sandy beaches and tranquil Catalonia countryside. Closer to the site is Tarragona, founded in the 5th century BC, its historic centre, second century amphitheatre and picturesque squares are all worth visiting. Tarragona is now a busy town with freshly caught Mediterranean fish landed daily at the port of El Serrallo.

Facilities
Two modern toilet blocks include open style washbasins and showers. Facilities for children and disabled visitors. Laundry room. Motorcaravan services. Family restaurant. Bar. Multisport court. Play areas. Accommodation for rent. Direct beach access. Free WiFi throughout (with code). Off site: Large supermarket 700 m. Beach fishing (with permit). Boat launching and riding 2 km. Golf 10 km.

Open: Easter or 1 April - 30 September.

Directionsseco
From the Autopista de la Mediterrania take exit 32 onto the N340 eastbound. At the second roundabout take first exit to La Noria. GPS: 41.15008, 1.420964

Charges guide
Per unit incl. 2 persons	
and electricity	€ 20.95 - € 38.05
extra person	€ 3.60 - € 5.90
child (3-10 yrs)	€ 3.00 - € 5.20
No credit cards.	

For latest campsite news, availability and prices visit
alanrogers.com

Vilanova i la Geltru

Vilanova Park

Ctra de l'Arboc km. 2.5, E-08800 Vilanova i la Geltru (Barcelona) T: 938 933 402. E: info@vilanovapark.com

alanrogers.com/ES83900

Sitting on the terrace in front of the restaurant – a beautifully converted Catalan farmhouse dating from 1908 – it is difficult to believe that in 1982 this was still a farm with few trees and known as Mas Roque (Rock Farm). Since then, imaginative planting has led to there being literally thousands of trees and gloriously colourful shrubs making this large campsite most attractive. It has an impressive range of high quality amenities and facilities open all year. There are 343 marked pitches for touring units in separate areas, all with 6/10A electricity, 168 larger pitches also have water and, in some cases, drainage. They are on hard surfaces, on gently sloping ground and with plenty of shade. A further 1,000 or so pitches are mostly occupied by chalets to rent, and by tour operators. The amenities include an excellent pool with water jets and at night time a coloured, floodlit fountain, which complements the dancing and entertainment taking place in the courtyard above. Nearby is a pleasant nature park with picnic tables. A second pool higher up the site has marvellous views across the town to the sea; here also is an indoor pool and wellness complex and in high season a second, more intimate restaurant, for a special romantic dinner overlooking the twinkling evening lights.

Facilities

Excellent toilet blocks can be heated and have controllable showers and many washbasins in cabins. Baby rooms. Units for disabled visitors. Serviced and self-service laundry. Motorcaravan services. Supermarket. Souvenir shop. Restaurants. Bar with simple meals and tapas. Outdoor pools (1/4-15/10), indoor pool (all year, charged). Wellness centre including sauna, jacuzzi and gym. Play areas. Sports field. Games room. Excursions. Activity and entertainment programme for all ages. Bicycle hire. Tennis. ATM and exchange facilities. WiFi throughout (charged). Caravan storage. Off site: Golf and riding 1 km. Fishing, sailing and boat launching 3 km. Shops, restaurants and bars in Vilanova 3 km. (local buses). Excursions arranged to Barcelona, Monserrat and Bodegas Torres (wine tasting).

Open: All year.

Directions

Site is 3 km. northwest of Vilanova i la Geltru towards L'Arboc (BV2115). From Tarragona on AP7 take exit 31 onto C32, then exit 16 for Vilanova. Site is on left in 2 km. From Barcelona take AP7 exit 29, C15 Vilanova, then C31 west to km. 153, and turn north on BV2115. Site is on right.
GPS: 41.23237, 1.69092

Charges guide

Per unit incl. 2 persons	
and electricity	€ 29.90 - € 51.50
extra person	€ 6.20 - € 11.10
child (4-11 yrs)	€ 3.60 € 6.60
dog	€ 6.50 - € 13.20

No credit cards.

Camping Cheques accepted.

FREE Alan Rogers Travel Card
Extra benefits and savings - see page 14

Torroella de Montgrí
Camping El Delfin Verde

Ctra de Torroella de Montgrí, E-17257 Torroella de Montgrí (Girona) T: 972 758 454.

E: info@eldelfinverde.com **alanrogers.com/ES80800**

A popular, self-contained and high quality site in a quiet location, El Delfin Verde has its own long beach stretching along its frontage, where activities such as scuba diving are organised. There is an attractive large pool in the shape of a dolphin with a total area of 1,800 sq.m. This is a large site with 917 touring pitches and around 6,000 visitors at peak times. It is well managed by friendly staff. Level grass pitches are 100-110 sq.m. and marked, with many separated by small fences and hedging. All have electricity (6A) and access to water points.

Facilities
Six excellent large and refurbished toilet blocks plus a seventh smaller block, all with resident cleaners, have showers using desalinated water and some washbasins in cabins. Facilities for disabled visitors. Laundry facilities. Motorcaravan services. Supermarket, shops, restaurants, grills and pizzerias (all 28/4-23/9). Three bars. Swimming pools with lifeguard (from 1/5). Large sports area. 2 km. exercise track. Dancing and entertainment weekly in season. Excursions and organised activities. Bicycle hire. Minigolf. Playground. Trampolines. Beach access. WiFi.

Open: 28 April - 23 September.

Directions
From A7/E15 take exit 6 and C66 (Palafrugell). Then the GI642 east to Parlava and turn north on C31 (L'Escala). Cross River Ter and turn east on C31 (Ulla and Torroella de Montgri). Site signed off the C31 and has a long approach road. Watch for white dolphin marker. GPS: 42.01197, 3.18807

Charges guide
Per unit incl. 2 persons	
and electricity	€ 23.50 - € 61.00
extra person	€ 4.75 - € 6.00

Tossa de Mar
Camping Cala Llevadó

Ctra GI-682 de Tossa-Lloret km. 18,9, E-17320 Tossa de Mar (Girona) T: 972 340 314.

E: info@calallevado.com **alanrogers.com/ES82000**

Cala Llevado is a beautifully situated and quiet (although popular), cliff-side site, enjoying fine views of the sea and coast below. It is shaped around a wooded valley with steep access roads and terracing. High up on the site with a superb aspect is the attractive restaurant/bar with a large terrace overlooking the pleasant swimming pool directly below. There are 612 terraced, level touring pitches (489 with 10/16A electricity) on the upper levels of the two slopes, with a great many individual pitches for tents scattered around the site. Many of these pitches have fantastic settings and views. The site is unsuitable for campers with disabilities. In some areas cars may be required to park separately.

Facilities
Four very well equipped toilet blocks are immaculately maintained and well spaced around the site. Baby baths. Laundry facilities. Motorcaravan services. Gas supplies. Fridge hire. Large supermarket. Restaurant/bar, swimming and paddling pools. Three play areas. Small botanical garden. Entertainment for children and adults (July/Aug). Sports courts. Sailing, water skiing, windsurfing, diving, canoe hire. Fishing. Bicycle hire. Excursions. ATM. WiFi.

Open: 1 April - 30 September.

Directions
Leave AP7/E15 at exit 7 to C65 Sant Feliu road, then take C35 southeast to the GI681 to Tossa de Mar. Site is signed off GI682 Lloret-Tossa road at km. 18.9, 3 km. from Tossa. Route avoids difficult coastal road. GPS: 41.71292, 2.906465

Charges guide
Per unit incl. 2 persons	
and electricity (6A)	€ 26.05 - € 52.00
extra person	€ 6.35 - € 9.25

Alcossebre
Camping Playa Tropicana

Playa Tropicana, E-12579 Alcossebre (Castelló) T: 964 412 463. E: info@playatropicana.com

alanrogers.com/ES85600

Playa Tropicana is a unique site which will immediately strike visitors as being very different. It has been given a tropical theme with scores of Romanesque white statues around the site, including in the sanitary blocks. The site has 380 marked pitches separated by lines of flowering bushes under mature trees. The pitches vary in size (50-90 sq.m), most are shaded and there are electricity connections throughout (10A, some need long leads). There are 50 pitches with shared water and drainage on their boundaries. The site has a delightful position away from the main hub of tourism, alongside a good sandy beach which shelves gently into the clean waters.

Facilities
Three sanitary blocks are fully equipped and of excellent standard, with washbasins in private cabins. Baby baths and facilities for disabled visitors. Washing machine. Motorcaravan services. Gas supplies. Large supermarket. Superb restaurant and takeaway (Easter-30/9). Swimming pools (new indoor facility) and children's pool. Playground. Bicycle hire. Kayak hire. Children's club. Fishing. Torches necessary in some areas. No TVs in July/Aug. Dogs accepted in one area. WiFi over site (charged).

Open: All year.

Directions
Turn off N340 at 1018 km. marker for Alcossebre on CV142. Just before entering town turn right immediately after two sets of lights. Follow road to the coast and site is 2.5 km. Avoid other narrow, uneven route given by GPS. GPS: 40.222, 0.267

Charges guide
Per unit incl. 2 persons	
and electricity	€ 27.50 - € 63.50
extra person	€ 5.00 - € 7.00

No credit cards.

For latest campsite news, availability and prices visit

alanrogers.com

Alcossebre
Camping Ribamar

Partida Ribamar s/n, E-12579 Alcossebre (Castelló) T: 964 761 163. E: info@campingribamar.com

alanrogers.com/ES85610

Camping Ribamar is tucked away within the National Park of the Sierra de Irta, to the north of Alcossebre, and with direct access to a rugged beach. There are two grades of pitches on offer here. A number of standard pitches (30 sq.m) are available for small tents, and all have electrical connections (10A). The majority of pitches are larger (90-100 sq.m) and are classed as premium, with electricity and a water supply. A number of chalets (with air conditioning) are available for rent. Leisure facilities here include a large swimming pool plus delightful children's pool and a paddling pool. A main amenities building is adjacent and houses the site's basic bar/restaurant and shop.

Facilities

One spotlessly clean toilet block with facilities for babies and campers with disabilities. Laundry facilities. Bar. Restaurant. Shop. Swimming pool. Paddling pool. Multisports terrain. Tennis. Five-a-side football. Boules. Paddle court. Bicycle hire. Play area. Library/social room. Chalets for rent. Direct access to rocky beach. Fishing. WiFi (charged). Charcoal barbecues are not allowed. Off site: Beach 2 km. Alcossebre 3 km. Riding 10 km.

Open: All year.

Directions

Leave AP7 motorway at exit 44 and follow signs to Alcossebre using N340 and CV142. The site can be found to the north of the town. Follow signs to Sierra de Irta and then the site, which is 2.5 km. along a dusty, gravel track. GPS: 40.270282, 0.306729

Charges guide

Per unit incl. 2 persons and electricity	€ 16.50 - € 40.85
extra person	€ 3.60 - € 4.50

Benicasim
Bonterra Park

Avenida de Barcelona 47, E-12560 Benicasim (Castelló) T: 964 300 007. E: info@bonterrapark.com

alanrogers.com/ES85800

A well organised site with extensive facilitles, which is popular all year. It is a 300 m. walk to a good beach – and parking is not too difficult. The site has 320 pitches (60-90 sq.m), all with electricity (6/10A), and a variety of bungalows, some attractively built in brick. There are dedicated 'green' pitches for tents. Bonterra has a clean and neat appearance with tarmac roads, gravel covered pitches, palms, grass and trees which give good shade. Overhead sunshades are provided for the more open pitches in summer. There is a little road and rail noise.

Facilities

Three attractive, well maintained sanitary blocks provide some private cabins, some washbasins with hot water, others with cold. Baby and dog showers. Facilities for disabled campers. Laundry. Motorcaravan services. Restaurant/bar with takeaway. Shop. Swimming pool (heated Sept-June) and paddling pool. Playground (some concrete bases). Tennis. Boules. Multisports court. Small gym (charged). Disco. Bicycle hire. Miniclub. Satellite TV. WiFi over site (charged). Dogs are not accepted in July/Aug. Off site: Town facilities. Supermarket by entrance. Sandy beach and fishing 500 m.

Open: All year.

Directions

From E15/AP7 take exit 46 to N340. Site is on the quiet old main road running through Benicasim. Leave N340 at km. 987. At roundabout turn left and travel for 1.5 km. to site on left (white walls). Look for supermarkets, one 200 m. before site and a second directly opposite. GPS: 40.05708, 0.07432

Charges guide

Per unit incl. 2 persons and electricity	€ 12.85 - € 57.39
extra person	€ 2.30 - € 6.39
child (0-9 yrs)	€ 1.90 - € 5.20
dog	€ 1.02

Benidorm
Camping Villasol

Avenida Bernat de Sarria 13., E-03503 Benidorm (Alacant) T: 965 850 422. E: info@camping-villasol.com

alanrogers.com/ES86810

Benidorm is increasingly popular for winter stays and Villasol is a genuinely good, purpose built modern site. Many of the 303 well separated pitches are arranged on wide terraces which afford views of the mountains surrounding Benidorm. All pitches (80-85 sq.m) have electricity and satellite TV connections, with 160 with full services for seasonal use. Shade is mainly artificial. Reservations are only accepted for winter stays of over three months (from 1 October). There is a small indoor pool, heated for winter use, and a very attractive, large outdoor pool complex (summer only) overlooked by the bar/restaurant and attractive, elevated restaurant terrace.

Facilities

Modern toilet blocks provide free, controllable hot water to showers and washbasins and British WCs. Good facilities for disabled visitors. Laundry facilities. Good value restaurant. Bar. Shop. Swimming pools, outdoor and indoor. Satellite TV. Playground. Evening entertainment programme. Safes. Dogs are not accepted. No charcoal barbecues. Off site: Beach and bicycle hire 1.3 km.

Open: All year.

Directions

From AP7 take exit 65 (Benidorm) and turn left at 2nd set of lights. After 1 km. at more lights turn right, then right at next lights. Site is on right in 400 m. GPS: 38.538, -0.119

Charges guide

Per unit incl. 2 persons and electricity	€ 26.60 - € 36.60
extra person	€ 6.20 - € 8.00

FREE Alan Rogers Travel Card
Extra benefits and savings - see page 14

Benidorm

Camping Benisol

Avenida de la Comunidad Valenciana s/n, E-03500 Benidorm (Alacant) T: 965 851 673.

E: campingbenisol@yahoo.es **alanrogers.com/ES86830**

Camping Benisol is a well developed and peaceful site with lush, green vegetation and a mountain backdrop. Mature hedges and trees afford privacy to each pitch and some artificial shade is provided where necessary. There are 270 pitches of which around 90 are for touring units (60-80 sq.m). All have electricity hook-ups (10A) and 75 have drainage. All the connecting roads are now surfaced with tarmac. Some daytime road noise should be expected. The site has an excellent restaurant serving traditional Spanish food at great prices, with a pretty, shaded terrace overlooking the pool with its palms and thatched pool bar.

Facilities

Modern sanitary facilities, heated in winter and kept very clean, have free, solar heated water to washbasins, showers and sinks. Laundry facilities. Restaurant with terrace and bar (all year, closed 1 day a week). Swimming pool (June-Sept). Small, old style play area. Jogging track. Tennis. Golf driving range. ATM. WiFi throughout. Off site: Riding 1 km. Bicycle hire and sea fishing 3 km. Golf 14 km. Bus route.

Open: All year.

Directions

Site is northeast of Benidorm. Exit N332 at 152 km. marker and take turn signed Playa Levant. Site is 100 m. on left off the main road, well signed. GPS: 38.559, -0.097

Charges guide

Per unit incl. 2 persons and electricity	€ 20.50 - € 34.80
extra person	€ 3.65 - € 5.80
child (1-10 yrs)	€ 3.30 - € 4.85

Bocairent

Camping Mariola

Ctra Bocairent-Alcoi km 9, E-46880 Bocairent (Valencia) T: 962 135 160. E: info@campingmariola.com

alanrogers.com/ES86450

Situated high in the Sierra Mariola National Park, in a beautiful rural setting but only 12 km. from the old town of Bocairent, this is a real taste of Spain with hilltop views all around. Used mainly by the Spanish, the site is an undiscovered jewel with 170 slightly sloping pitches. These are well spaced and have shade from a mixture of young and mature trees. An orchard area well away from the main site (with no amenities close by) is used for more casual camping. A traditional, stone built restaurant is slightly elevated with views over the site. Accessed by a few steps, this attractive building is covered in roses.

Facilities

Six identical small toilet blocks offer adequate facilities with British style WCs and showers with shared changing area. Open style washbasins. Single toilet and shower for disabled visitors. Washing machine. Motorcaravan services. Small shop, bar/restaurant (all weekends only in low season). Satellite TV. Outdoor pool with separate paddling pool (July/Aug). Two multisports pitches. Play area. Communal barbecue area. Children's club and entertainment (Aug. only). WiFi (charged). Torches useful.

Open: All year.

Directions

From the CV40 exit for Ontinyent and follow the CV81. Pass Bocairent and in 2 km. look for camping sign (at textiles factory). Turn south on VV2031 to Alcoy. Turn right at first roundabout and straight on at next through small industrial estate. Persevere onwards and upwards for 10 km. and site is a turn to left. GPS: 38.753317, -0.549402

Charges guide

Per unit incl. 2 persons and electricity	€ 15.00 - € 19.00
extra person	€ 4.50 - € 5.50

Calpe

Camping Calpemar

Ctra d'Eslovenia no. 3, E-03710 Calpe (Alacant) T: 965 875 576. E: info@campingcalpemar.com

alanrogers.com/ES86790

Situated on the outskirts of Calpe, this small, quiet, well maintained site is an oasis of tranquillity. With a backdrop of mountains and a view of the spectacular Penon de Ifach Nature Reserve rising to a height of 332 metres, there are great views all around. The site has 107 fully serviced, numbered pitches (10A electricity, water and drainage). The pitches at the front of the site are divided by mature hedges and on these pitches units are sited sideways. At the rear of the site there are two separate extensions, both with 12 large, fully serviced, gravel pitches with young conifers separating each pitch. Access roads and pitches are good in the new areas. The fine sandy beach is only a 300 m. stroll from the campsite.

Facilities

Two modern toilet blocks (heated in winter), one smaller than the other. Baby room. Facilities for campers with disabilities. Washing machines and dryers. Motorcaravan service point. Bar and cafeteria (all year). Swimming pool (all year). Small play area (no safety surface). Safety deposit. Satellite TV. First aid cabin. Pet shower. Internet access (coin operated). WiFi throughout (charged). Off site: Beach 300 m. Supermarket in Calpe 300 m.

Open: All year.

Directions

On E15/A7 from Valencia take exit 63 then N332 to Benissa, Calpe/Calp for 10 km. Turn left onto Via Pa Benicolada over two roundabouts, then left onto Ave Diputacion. After two more roundabouts, at 3rd follow site signs. GPS: 38.64472, 0.05583

Charges guide

Per unit incl. 2 persons and electricity	€ 31.00 - € 41.00
extra person	€ 5.00 - € 7.00
child (2-12 yrs)	€ 3.00 - € 5.00

Campell

Camping Vall de Laguar

Calle Sant Antoni 24, la Vall de Laguar, E-03791 Campell (Alacant) T: 965 584 590.

E: info@campinglaguar.com **alanrogers.com/ES86750**

Near the pretty mountain-top village of Campell, this new site is perched high on the side of a mountain with breathtaking views of hilltop villages, the surrounding hills and distant sea. With a wholehearted welcome from the owners, the well maintained site promises a real taste of Spain. The pitches, pool, terrace and restaurant all share the views. The 68 average sized gravel pitches (30 for touring) are on terraces and all have 6A electricity and water. Trees and hedges have been planted and now give ample shade. This is a great place to get away from the coastal hustle, bustle and high rise of the beaches.

Facilities
Two sanitary blocks have excellent clean facilities including some for disabled campers. Washing machines and dryers. Restaurant with pretty terrace (closed Sept). Bar and small pool bar. Outdoor swimming pool (June-Sept). Small entertainment programme in high season. WiFi over site (free). No charcoal barbecues. Torches useful. Off site: Attractive town close by. Riding 15 km. Golf and beach 20 km.

Open: All year.

Directions
Site is 20 km. west of Xabia/Javea. From A7/E15 exit 62 head to Ondara/Valencia on the N332 and at the roundabout on the Ondara bypass head to Benidoleig/Orba. At Orba turn right and follow site signs. GPS: 38.7766, -0.105

Charges guide

Per unit incl. 2 persons and electricity	€ 22.10 - € 29.10
extra person	€ 5.25 - € 5.90

Crevillente

Marjal Costa Blanca Eco Camping Resort

Partida de las Casicas, 5, AP7 exit 730 (Catral-Crevillente), E-03330 Crevillente (Alacant) T: 965 484 945.

E: camping@marjalcostablanca.com **alanrogers.com/ES87435**

Marjal Costa Blanca is a new, fully equipped site situated 15 km. inland on the southern Alicante coast, close to the towns of Crevillente and Catral and the Parque Natural de El Hondo. The 1,432 hardstanding pitches range in size from 90-180 sq.m, and all have electricity (16A), water, drainage, TV and WiFi connections. On-site amenities include a tropical themed swimming pool complex and a modern wellness centre. There is full disabled access, including at the swimming pool and staffed gym. There is accommodation for rent, including 39 Balinese-style bungalows adapted for disabled visitors. The site is a major new initiative and ideal for both family holidays in summer and for winter sun-seekers.

Facilities
Six modern, spotlessly clean toilet blocks have washbasins and free showers in cabins. Facilities for children, babies and disabled visitors. Well equipped shop. Bar, restaurant and takeaway (all year). Swimming pool complex with outdoor pool (all year), heated indoor pool (all year), sauna and Hammam. Fully equipped gym. Wellness centre. Hairdresser. Play areas. Games rooms. Library. Multisports courts. Minigolf. Tennis. Football. Entertainment and activity programme. Business centre. Bicycle hire. Car hire service. WiFi over site (free).

Open: All year.

Directions
Take the southbound A7 coastal motorway until you reach the fork close to Elche-Crevillente. Continue on AP7 towards Cartagena and then take exit 730 (Catral) and follow signs to the site. GPS: 38.177901, -0.809504

Charges guide

Per unit incl. 2 persons and all services (plus meter)	€ 31.00 - € 45.00
extra person	€ 4.00 - € 7.00
child (4-12 yrs)	€ 3.00 - € 5.00

Camping Cheques accepted.

Guardamar del Segura

Marjal Guardamar Camping & Bungalows Resort

Ctra N332 km. 73,4, E-03140 Guardamar del Segura (Alacant) T: 966 727 070. E: camping@marjal.com

alanrogers.com/ES87430

Marjal is located beside the estuary of the Segura river, alongside the pine and eucalyptus forests of the Dunas de Guardamar Natural Park. A fine sandy beach can be reached through the forest (800 m). This is a very smart site with a huge tropical lake-style pool with bar and a superb sports complex. There are 212 pitches on this award-winning site, 162 for touring with water, electricity (16A), drainage and satellite TV points. The ground is covered with crushed marble, making the pitches clean and pleasant. There is some shade and the site has an open feel with lots of room for manoeuvring.

Facilities
Three excellent heated toilet blocks have free hot water, spacious showers and some cabins. Each block has high quality facilities for babies and disabled campers, modern laundry and dishwashing rooms. Motorcaravan services. Car wash. Well stocked supermarket. Restaurants. Bar. Large outdoor pool complex (1/4-30/9). Heated indoor pool. Jacuzzi. Sauna. Beauty salon. Superb well equipped gym. Aerobics. Physiotherapy. Play room. Minigolf. Car rental. Floodlit tennis and soccer pitch. TV room. Bicycle hire. Games room. Full entertainment programme. ATM.

Open: All year.

Directions
From the Europa highway network, follow the A-7 motorway which runs along the Mediterranean coast until you reach the Laltet exit. Then take the N-332 highway towards Cartagena to the Marjal campsite at km 73,4. GPS: 38.10933, -0.65467

Charges guide

Per unit incl. 2 persons and electricity	€ 38.00 - € 65.00
extra person	€ 7.00 - € 9.00
child (4-12 yrs)	€ 5.00 - € 6.00

Jávea

Camping Jávea

Ctra Cami de la Fontana 10, Apdo 83, E-03730 Jávea (Alacant) T: 965 791 070. E: info@camping-javea.com

alanrogers.com/ES87540

The final approach to this site emerges from the bustle of the town and is decorated with palm, orange and pine trees, the latter playing host to a colony of parakeets. English is spoken at reception. The neat, boxed hedges and palms within the site, and its backdrop of hills dotted with villas, presents an attractive setting. Three hectares provide space for 214 numbered pitches with 193 for touring units. Flat, level and rectangular in shape, the pitches vary in size (60-80 sq.m). All pitches have a granite chip surface and 8A electricity. The restaurant provides great food, way above normal campsite standards.

Facilities

Two very clean, fully equipped, sanitary blocks include two children's toilets plus a baby bath. Separate facilities for disabled campers. Two washing machines. Fridge hire. Extensive bar and restaurant with terraces where in high season you purchase bread and milk. Large swimming pool with lifeguard and sunbathing lawns. Play area. Boules. Electronic barriers (deposit for card). Caravan storage. Post. Safes. Five-a-side football. Basketball. Tennis. WiFi (free in restaurant). Car rental.

Open: All year.

Directions

Exit N332 for Jávea on A134, continue towards Port (road number changes to CV734). In town the site is well marked with large orange indicators high on posts. Watch carefully for a sudden slip road sign! GPS: 38.78333, 0.16983

Charges guide

Per unit incl. 2 persons	
and electricity	€ 25.81 - € 35.34
extra person	€ 4.88 - € 6.50
child	€ 4.09 - € 5.50

Moraira

Camping Caravanning Moraira

Camino Paellero 50, E-03724 Moraira-Teulada (Alacant) T: 965 745 249.

E: campingmoraira@campingmoraira.com **alanrogers.com/ES87550**

This neat hillside site with some views over the town and marina is quietly situated in an urban area amongst old pine trees and just 400 metres from a sheltered bay. A striking, stilted and glass-fronted reception building gives great views. Ask about the innovative building features and prepare for pleasant design surprises. Terracing provides shaded pitches of varying sizes, some small (access to some of the upper pitches may be difficult for larger units). There are 17 pitches with full services (6/10A electricity). An attractive irregularly shaped pool with a paved terrace is below the bar/restaurant and terrace. The pool has large observation windows where you can watch the swimmers and divers as this is used for sub-aqua instruction. The site runs a PADI diving school; the diving here is good and the water warm, even in winter. Buildings here have been designed by the architect owner, giving the site a stylish flair, which is very pleasing and different to mainstream campsites. A new glass fronted bar/restaurant is impressive. A sandy beach is 1.5 km. away. A large, painted water tower stands at the top of the site.

Facilities

The high quality toilet blocks, with polished granite floors and marble fittings are built to a unique and ultra-modern design. Facilities for disabled campers. Washing machines and dryers. Motorcaravan services. Bar/restaurant and shop (1/6-30/9; restaurant closed Tues). Bread and basics at the bar. Small swimming pool. Sub-aqua with instruction. Tennis. Limited entertainment for children in high season. Torches may be required. WiFi (charged in high season). Off site: Shops, bars and restaurants within walking distance. Beach and fishing 400 m. Gym and ATM 600 m. Bicycle hire 1 km. Golf 8 km.

Open: All year.

Directions

Best approach is from Teulada. From A7 exit 63 take N332 and in 3.5 km. turn right (Teulada, Moraira). In Teulada fork right to Moraira. At junction at town entrance turn right signed Calpe and in 1 km. turn right to site on bend immediately after Res. Don Julio. GPS: N38.78362, E.O.17205

Charges guide

Per unit incl. 2 persons	
and electricity	€ 18.60 - € 44.55
extra person	€ 4.60 - € 8.80
child (4-10 yrs)	€ 2.85 - € 5.50

La Marina

Camping Internacional La Marina

Ctra N332 km. 76, E-03194 La Marina (Alacant) T: 965 419 200.

E: info@campinglamarina.com alanrogers.com/ES87420

LeadingCampings

Very efficiently run by a friendly Belgian family, La Marina has 465 touring pitches of three different types and sizes ranging from 50 sq.m. to 150 sq.m. with electricity (10/16A), TV, water and drainage. Artificial shade is provided and the pitches are extremely well maintained on level, well drained ground with a special area allocated for tents in a small orchard. The huge lagoon swimming pool complex is absolutely fabulous and has something for everyone (with lifeguards). William Le Metayer, the owner, is passionate about La Marina and it shows in his search for perfection. A magnificent new, modern building which uses the latest architectural technology, houses many superb extra amenities. Facilities include a relaxed business centre with Internet access, a tapas bar decorated with amazing ceramics (handmade by the owner's mother) and a quality restaurant with a water fountain feature and great views of the lagoon. There is also a conference centre and an extensive computerised library. The whole of the lower ground floor is dedicated to children with a Marina Park play area and a 'cyber zone' for teenagers. With a further bar and a new soundproofed disco (Anima2), the building is of an exceptional, eco-friendly standard. A superb fitness centre with attentive personal trainers and a covered, heated pool (14x7 m) are incorporated. A pedestrian gate at the rear of the site gives access to the long sandy beach through the coastal pine forest that is a feature of the area. We recommend this site very highly whatever type of holidaying camper you may be. A member of Leading Campings group.

Facilities

The elegant sanitary blocks offer the very best of modern facilities and are regularly cleaned. Heated in winter, they include private cabins and facilities for disabled visitors and babies. Laundry facilities. Motorcaravan services. Gas. Supermarket. Bars. Restaurant and café. Ice-cream kiosk. Swimming pools (1/4-15/10). Indoor pool. Fitness centre. Sauna. Solarium. Jacuzzi. Play rooms. Extensive activity and entertainment programme with barbecues and swimming nights. Sports area. Tennis. Huge playgrounds. Hairdresser. Bicycle hire. Road train to beach. Exclusive area for dogs. Internet café (charged) and free WiFi. Off site: Fishing 700 m. Boat launching 5 km. Golf 7 km. Riding 15 km. Hourly bus service from outside the gate.

Open: All year.

Directions

Site is 2 km. west of La Marina. Leave N332 Guardamara de Segura-Santa Pola road at 75 km. marker if travelling north, or 78 km. marker if travelling south. Site is well signed.
GPS: 38.129649, -0.649575

Charges guide

Per unit incl. 2 persons

and all services	€ 31.00 - € 49.00
extra person	€ 6.00 - € 8.50
child (3-10 yrs)	€ 4.50 - € 6.00
dog	€ 1.10 - € 2.50

Good discounts for longer stays in low season.

FREE Alan Rogers Travel Card
Extra benefits and savings - see page 14

Moncofa

Camping Monmar

Ctra Serratelles s/n, E-12593 Moncofa (Castelló) T: 964 588 592. E: campingmonmar@terra.es

alanrogers.com/ES85900

This very neat, purpose built site is in the small town of Moncofa, just 200 metres from the sea and right beside a water park with pools and slides. There are 170 gravel based pitches arranged in rows off tarmac access roads. The 90 touring pitches all have 6A electricity, water and drainage. Hedges have been planted to separate the pitches but these are still small so there is little shade (canopies can be rented in high season). The site's facilities and amenities are all very modern but small stone reminders of the area's Roman and Arab history are used to decorate corners of the site.

Facilities

Three modern toilet blocks are well placed and provide good, clean facilities. Free hot showers and open style washbasins. Facilities and good access for disabled visitors (key). Laundry facilities. Shop (July/Aug). Bar and restaurant (weekends and high season). Swimming pool. Good play area. Boules. Library. Some entertainment in high season. WiFi over site (charged). Animals are not accepted. Off site: Beach 200 m. Water complex. Local amenities within walking distance.

Open: All year.

Directions

Turn off N340 Castellon-Valencia road on CV2250 signed Moncofa. Follow sign for tourist information office in town and then signs for site. Pass supermarket and turn left to site in 600 m. GPS: 39.80884, -0.1281

Charges guide

Per unit incl. 2 persons and electricity	€ 27.00
extra person	€ 9.00

Discounts in low season with this guide and for longer stays.

Navajas

Camping Altomira

Ctra CV-213 Navajas km. 1, E-12470 Navajas (Castelló) T: 964 713 211. E: reservas@campingaltomira.com

alanrogers.com/ES85850

Camping Altomira is a terraced site in a rural, hillside setting on the outskirts of a quiet village. It offers excellent views across the valleys and hills, a very friendly welcome and has both a Spanish and international clientèle. There are 40 touring pitches on the higher levels of the site with some shade (artificial awnings are allowed). Access roads to the gravel pitches are steep with some tight turns. All pitches have shared electricity (6A) and water points, while some have individual sinks, water and waste water disposal. There are three toilet blocks, and two designated children's facilities. In recent years, great efforts have been made to make the site accessible for campers with mobility problems.

Facilities

Three heated toilet blocks have showers in cubicles and open style washbasins. Two laundry areas. Shop. Bar/restaurant with terrace next to play area. Outdoor swimming pool (June-Sept). TV room. Bicycle hire. Kayak hire. Paintball. Zip wire. Communal barbecue areas. New BTT centre. WiFi over site (charged). Off site: Shops, bars and restaurants in the village 500 m. Station 500 m. Small Friday market. Lake beach, fishing and riding 2 km. Beach 35 km. Cycling, walking and riding on adjacent Via Verde.

Open: All year.

Directions

Site is just off the free autovia (Santander-Valencia). From A23 (Segunto-Teruel) take exit 33 (Navajes), follow CV214 to roundabout, then CV213 to site, 1 km. north of Navajas. GPS: 39.87471, -0.51051

Charges guide

Per unit incl. 2 persons and electricity	€ 18.20 - € 25.40
extra person	€ 4.80 - € 6.20

Camping Cheques accepted.

Oliva

Camping Olé

Partida Aigua Morta s/n, E-46780 Oliva (Valencia) T: 962 857 517. E: campingole@hotmail.com

alanrogers.com/ES86130

Olé is a large, flat, seaside holiday site south of Valencia and close to the modern resort of Oliva. Its entrance is only 250 m. from the pleasant sandy beach. For those who do not want to share the busy beach, a large swimming pool is opened in July and August. There are 308 small pitches of compressed gravel and with 6/10A electricity. Many are separated by hedges with pruned trees giving good shade to those away from the beach. A bar and a restaurant stand on the dunes overlooking the sea, together with a few unmarked pitches that are ideal for larger units. There are small groups of chalets and a few apartments to rent, all within their own areas.

Facilities

Three clean, well maintained sanitary blocks provide very reasonable facilities. The central one serves most of the touring pitches. Laundry facilities. Fridge rental. Well stocked supermarket (1/3-30/9). Various vending machines. Bar with TV and restaurant with daily menu, drinks and snacks (1/3-15/12). Takeaway. Swimming pool (1/7-1/9). Playground. Entertainment (July/Aug). Fishing off the beach. WiFi (charged). Off site: Bicycle hire.

Open: All year.

Directions

From the north on AP7 (Alicante-Valencia) take exit 61 on N332 through Oliva. From the south take exit 62 and turn left for Oliva. Exit at km. 213 (south) or 210 (north) signed 'urbanisation'. At roundabout take third exit, follow site signs. GPS: 38.8943, -0.0536

Charges guide

Per unit incl. 2 persons and electricity	€ 29.86 - € 43.64
extra person	€ 6.52

For latest campsite news, availability and prices visit

alanrogers.com

Oliva

Kiko Park Oliva

Ctra Assagador de Carro 2, E-46780 Oliva (Valencia) T: 962 850 905. E: kikopark@kikopark.com

alanrogers.com/ES86150

Kiko Park is a smart site nestling behind protective sand dunes alongside a Blue Flag beach. There are sets of attractively tiled steps over the dunes or a long boardwalk near the beach bar (good for prams and wheelchairs) to take you to the fine white sandy beach and the sea. From the central reception point (where good English is spoken), flat, fine gravel pitches and access roads are divided to the left and right. Backing onto one another, the 180 large pitches all have electricity and the aim is to progressively upgrade all these with full services. There are plenty of flowers, hedging and trees adding shade, privacy and colour. A pleasant, outdoor swimming pool with adjacent children's pool has a paved area with a bar in summer. The restaurant (lunchtimes only out of season) overlooks the marina, beautiful beach and sea. A wide variety of entertainment is provided all year and Spanish lessons are taught along with dance classes and aerobics during the winter. The site is run by the second generation of a family involved in camping for 30 years and their experience shows. They are brilliantly supported by a friendly, efficient team who speak many languages. The narrow roads leading to the site can be a little challenging for very large units but it is worth the effort.

Facilities

Four mature, heated sanitary blocks include facilities for babies and for disabled visitors (who will find this site flat and convenient). Laundry facilities. Motorcaravan services. Gas supplies. Supermarket (all year, closed Sundays). Restaurant. Bar with TV (high season). Beach-side bar and restaurant (lunchtimes only in low season). Swimming pools. Spa with treatments and beauty programmes (charged). Playground. Watersports facilities. Diving school in high season (from mid June). Entertainment for children (from mid June). Pétanque. WiFi (charged). Bicycle hire.

Open: All year.

Directions

From the AP7 take exit 61. From the toll turn right at T-junction and continue to lights. Turn left then at roundabout turn right. At next roundabout (fountains) take third exit signed Platja and Alicante. Follow one way system to next roundabout then site signs.
GPS: 38.9316, -0.0968

Charges guide

Per unit incl. 2 persons	€ 19.50 - € 37.10
extra person	€ 3.80 - € 7.50
child (under 10 yrs)	€ 3.10 - € 6.80
olectricity (per kWh)	€ 0.60

PLAYA OLIVA
KIKOPARK
Your holiday site awaits you at the seashore
Camping · Caravanning · Apartments · Spa · Restaurant
📞 **+ 34 96 285 09 05 www.kikopark.com**

Peñiscola

Spa Natura Resort

Ptda Villarroyos s/n, AP-7 Salida 43, E-12598 Peñiscola (Castelló) T: 964 475 480.

E: info@spanaturaresort.com **alanrogers.com/ES85590**

Set inland from the popular coastal resort of Peñiscola, Spa Natura Resort is set next to the Sierra de Irta Natura Park and Marine Reserve. This unusual development of residential and holiday park homes, designed and decorated in an environmentally friendly way, provides 110 level touring pitches, with an increase planned. All pitches have electricity (6/10A) and access to water with wide, gravel roads. Amazingly, most are set on neat, artificial grass. Some shade is provided by young palms, pines and plane trees. The pitches are separated by small wooden fences and large units can be accommodated. Pitches are set between long rows of bungalows and there are very chunky elevated roofs over some.

Facilities

Two refurbished toilet blocks include showers, open washbasins and separate toilets. Facilities for disabled visitors. Laundry facilities. Shop. Bar/restaurant. Small outdoor (June-Sept) and covered swimming pools (Oct-May). Spa centre. Gym. Indoor tennis court. Play area. Minigolf. Bicycle hire. Internet. Activity programme. No dogs in July/Aug. WiFi (charge for high speed).

Open: All year.

Directions

From A7 (Barcelona-Valencia) take exit 43 then N340 (Benicarlo). Immediately look for signs at the N340 1040 km. marker to Camping Azahar directing you down a side road. Site is visible with large elevated signs from the slip road. GPS: 40.401667, 0.381111

Charges guide

Per unit incl. 2 persons and electricity (10A)	€ 20.00 - € 47.00

Camping Cheques accepted.

Ribera de Cabanes

Camping Torre la Sal 2

Camí l'Atall, E-12595 Ribera de Cabanes (Castelló) T: 964 319 744. E: camping@torrelasal2.com

alanrogers.com/ES85700

Torre la Sal 2 is a very large site divided into two by a quiet road, with a reception on each side with friendly, helpful staff. There are three pool complexes (one can be covered in cooler weather and is heated) all of which are on the west side, whilst the beach (of shingle and sand) is on the east. Both sides have a restaurant – the one on the beach side has two air-conditioned wooden buildings and a terrace. The 530 flat pitches vary in size, some have their own sinks, and most have shade. All have 10A electricity and a few have a partial view of the sea. There are 85 bungalows around the two areas. This is a high quality site offering a great choice to campers.

Facilities

Toilet facilities are of a good standard in both sections, with British style WCs, hot water to some sinks, and facilities for disabled campers. Baby rooms. Washing machines (laundry service if required for a small charge). Motorcaravan services. Shop, bars, restaurants and takeaway. New swimming pool complex. Play park. Large disco. Sports centre. Tennis. Squash. Two football pitches. Pétanque. Outdoor gym. Games room. Bullring. Hairdresser. Activities and entertainment. WiFi (charged).

Open: All year.

Directions

From A7/E15 take exit 45 for Oropesa Del Mar on N340. Follow road to Oropesa and then the many clear signs to the site. GPS: 40.12781, 0.15894

Charges guide

Per unit incl. 2 persons and electricity	€ 23.72 - € 54.44
extra person	€ 4.11 - € 8.22
child (2-9 yrs)	€ 3.81 - € 7.62

Special prices for retired persons 1/9-30/6.

Villargordo del Cabriel

Kiko Park Rural

Ctra Embalse Contreras km. 3, E-46317 Villargordo del Cabriel (Valencia) T: 962 139 082.

E: info@kikoparkrural.com **alanrogers.com/ES86250**

Approaching Kiko Park Rural, you will see a small hilltop village set in a landscape of mountains, vines and a jewel-like lake. Kiko was a small village and farm, and the village now forms the campsite and accommodation. Amenities are contained within the architecturally authentic buildings, some old and some new. The 48 generous touring pitches (mainly hardstanding and with 6A electricity and water) have high hedges (as does the site) for privacy. Generous planting has been made, which already affords some privacy, and hundreds of trees provide shade. The restaurant serves extremely good food in a pleasant, spacious setting overlooking the pools and their surrounding immaculate lawns.

Facilities

Three toilet blocks are well equipped (but have short timers for lighting and showers), including facilities for disabled campers. Motorcaravan services. Gas. Pleasant bar. Excellent restaurant (1/6-10/9, also stocks, eggs, bread etc). Takeaway (Easter-Oct). Swimming and paddling pools. Very good playground. Bicycle hire. Entertainment in high season. Many adventure activities can be arranged, including white-water rafting, gorging, orienteering, trekking, bungee jumping and riding.

Open: All year.

Directions

From autopista A7/E15 on Valencia ring road (near airport) take A3 (E901) to the west. Villargordo del Cabriel is 80 km. towards Motilla. Take village exit 255 and follow signs through village and over hill – spot the village on a hill 2 km. away. That is the campsite! GPS: 39.552176, -1.47456

Charges guide

Per unit incl. 2 persons and electricity	€ 22.40 - € 32.90
extra person	€ 5.60 - € 6.90

Gata

Camping Sierra de Gata

Ctra Ex109 a Gata km. 4,1, E-10860 Gata (Cáceres) T: 927 672 168. E: reception@campingsierradegata.es

alanrogers.com/ES94000

This very Spanish site (some English was spoken when we visited) is owned by the local junta. It is situated 4 km. from the medieval village of Gata, south of Ciudad Rodrigo and northwest of Plasencia. Set in beautiful countryside in a National Park, a small stream runs alongside the site. The 45 touring pitches are on grass with shade from trees and artificial sails. There are 18 bungalows to sleep four to six people. A special area with huts for groups of children to stay is positioned in one corner of the site. The helpful reception staff will arrange many different kinds of activities for you from rock climbing to kayaking, birdwatching and guided walks.

Facilities

Two sanitary blocks include child size toilets. Laundry room. Medium sized shop for necessities. Restaurant/bar complex with terrace (all open in summer and w/ends in low season). Two swimming pools (15/6-15/9). Multisports court. Play area. Fishing. Bicycle and kayak hire. Wide variety of outdoor pursuits in local area can be arranged at reception. WiFi in some areas (free).
Off site: River beach 500 m. Riding 5 km. Boating 5 km.

Open: 15 January - 14 December.

Directions

Approaching from southwest from 109 Ciudad Rodrico-Coria road: where 205 meets 109 take turn 20-30 m. north (Gata 10). Travel along this road to km. 4 and follow campsite sign.
GPS: 40.21195, -6.64224

Charges guide

Per unit incl. 2 persons and electricity	€ 15.50 - € 18.00
extra person	€ 4.00 - € 4.50

For latest campsite news, availability and prices visit

alanrogers.com

Malpartida de Plasencia
Camping Parque Natural de Monfrague

Ctra Plasencia-Trujillo km. 10, E-10680 Malpartida de Plasencia (Cáceres) T: 927 459 233.

E: contacto@campingmonfrague.com **alanrogers.com/ES90270**

Situated on the edge of the Monfrague National Park, this well managed site owned by the Barrado family, has fine views to the Sierra de Mirabel and delightful surrounding countryside. Many of the 130 touring pitches are on slightly sloping, terraced ground and some have grass. Scattered trees offer a degree of shade, there are numerous water points and 10A electricity. The shop, bar and restaurant are open all season and the terrace there has pleasant views towards the National Park. Created as a National Park in 1979, Monfrague is now recognised as one of the best locations in Europe for anyone interested in birdwatching.

Facilities
Large modern toilet blocks, fully equipped, are very clean. Facilities for disabled campers and baby baths. Laundry. Motorcaravan services. Supermarket/shop. Restaurant, bar with terrace and coffee shop. TV room with recreational facilities. Swimming and paddling pools (June-Sept). Play area. Tennis court. Bicycle hire. Entertainment for children in season. Guided safaris into the Park for birdwatching. Barbecue areas. WiFi near the bar (free). Off site: Large supermarket at Plasencia 6 km.

Open: All year.

Directions
Site is 6 km. south of Plasencia on EX28. From the A1 take exit 46 to Trujillo. From A66 take exit 479 for Navalmoral de la Mata, then exit at km. 46 onto EX208. Follow signs to Parque Natural de Monfrague. Site is on left after viaduct. GPS: 39.9395, -6.084

Charges guide
Per unit incl. 2 persons and electricity	€ 20.10 - € 20.40
extra person	€ 4.20

Camping Cheques accepted.

Bayona
Camping Bayona Playa

Ctra Vigo-Bayona km. 19, E-36393 Bayona (Pontevedra) T: 986 350 035.

E: campingbayona@campingbayona.com **alanrogers.com/ES89360**

Situated on a narrow peninsula with the sea and river estuary all around it, this large and well maintained campsite is great for a relaxing break. The 450 pitches, 358 for touring, benefit from the shade of mature trees whilst still maintaining a very open feel. All have 5A electricity and 50 are fully serviced. It is busy here in high season so advance booking is recommended. Sabaris is a short walk away and Bayona is a 20 minute walk along the coast, where you can find a variety of shops, supermarkets, banks, bars and eating places. Maximum unit length is 7.5 m.

Facilities
Three well maintained modern toilet blocks (one open low season), washbasins and shower cubicles. No washing machines but site provides a service wash. Facilities for visitors with disabilities. Large well stocked supermarket and gift shop (June-Sept). Terrace bar, cafeteria, restaurant. Excellent pool complex with slide (small charge, redeemable in shop and restaurant). Play area. Organised activities July/Aug. Windsurfing school. Cash machine in reception. WiFi near reception area.

Open: All year.

Directions
From Vigo leave AG57, exit 5 (Bayona North). Follow signs to site at Sabaris, 2 km. east of Bayona. GPS: 42.113978, -8.826013

Charges guide
Per unit incl. 2 persons and electricity	€ 23.80 - € 34.80
extra person	€ 7.35
child (3-12 yrs)	€ 4.10

Santa Cruz
Camping Los Manzanos

Avenida de Emilia Pardo Bazan, E-15179 Santa Cruz (A Coruña) T: 981 614 825.

E: informacion@campinglosmanzanos.com **alanrogers.com/ES89420**

Los Manzanos has a steep access drive down to the site, which is divided by a stream into two sections linked by a bridge. Pitches for larger units are marked and numbered, 85 with electricity (12A) and, in one section, there is a fairly large, unmarked field for tents. Some aircraft noise should be expected as the site is under the flight path to A Coruña (but no aircraft at night). The site impressed us as being very clean, even when full, which it tends to be in high season. Some interesting huge stone sculptures create focal points and conversation pieces.

Facilities
One good toilet block provides modern facilities including free hot showers. Small shop with fresh produce daily (limited outside June-Sept). High quality restaurant/bar (July/Aug). Swimming pool with lifeguard, free to campers (15/6-30/9). Playground. Barbecue area. Bungalows for rent. WiFi in reception area. Off site: Bus service at end of entrance drive. Beach and fishing 1 km. Bicycle hire 2 km. Golf and riding 8 km.

Open: April - 30 September.

Directions
From the A8/A6 (A Coruña). Take exit 568 onto AP9, then exit 3. Turn left onto NV1 towards Lugo/Madrid and left again on AC173 for Santa Cruz. Site signed from roundabout. Turn right before traffic lights. Site is on the left. GPS: 43.34908, -8.33567

Charges guide
Per unit incl. 2 persons and electricity	€ 24.80 - € 31.10
extra person	€ 6.60

FREE Alan Rogers Travel Card
Extra benefits and savings - see page 14

Santiago de Compostela

Camping As Cancelas

Rue do 25 de Xullo 35, E-15704 Santiago de Compostela (A Coruña) T: 981 580 476.

E: info@campingascancelas.com **alanrogers.com/ES90240**

The beautiful city of Santiago has been the destination for European Christian pilgrims for centuries and they now follow ancient routes to this unique city, the whole of which is a national monument. The As Cancelas campsite is excellent for sharing the experiences of these pilgrims in the city and around the magnificent cathedral. It has 125 marked pitches (60-90 sq.m), arranged in terraces and divided by trees and shrubs. On a hillside overlooking the city, the views are very pleasant. The site has a steep approach road. Electrical hook-ups (5A) are available, the site is lit at night and a security guard patrols. There are many legendary festivals and processions here, the main one being on July 25th, especially in holy years (when the Saint's birthday falls on a Sunday). Examine for yourself the credibility of the fascinating story of the arrival of the bones of Saint James at Compostela (Compostela translates as 'field of stars'), and also discover why the pilgrims dutifully carry a scallop shell on their long journey. There are many pilgrims' routes, including one commencing from Fowey in Cornwall.

Facilities

Two modern toilet blocks are fully equipped, with ramped access for disabled visitors. The quality and cleanliness of the fittings and tiling is good. Laundry with service wash for a small fee. Small shop. Restaurant. Bar with TV. Well kept, unsupervised swimming pool and children's pool. Small playground. Internet access. WiFi throughout. Off site: Regular bus service into city from near football ground 200 m. Huge commercial centre (open late and handy for off season use) 20 minutes' walk downhill (uphill on the return!). Riding 3.5 km. Golf 8 km.

Open: All year.

Directions

From motorway AP9-E1 take exit 67 and follow signs for 'Casco Historico' and 'Centro Ciudad' then follow site signs. GPS: 42.88939, -8.52418

Charges guide

Per unit incl. 2 persons and electricity	€ 25.60 - € 32.60
extra person	€ 5.20 - € 6.70
child (up to 12 yrs)	€ 3.00 - € 5.10

Castañares de Rioja

Camping de La Rioja

Ctra de Haro - Sto Domingo de la Calzada, E-26240 Castañares de Rioja (La Rioja) T: 941 300 174.

E: info@campingdelarioja.es **alanrogers.com/ES92250**

This site is situated just beyond the town of Castañares de Rioja. This is a very busy site during the peak season with a huge sporting and play area and a predominantly Spanish clientele. In low season it is quieter with limited facilities available. There are 30 level, grass touring pitches, out of a total of 500 on a 5-hectare site. These are separated by hedges and trees allowing privacy. Each has their own water, drainage and electricity connection. There is one, very large sanitary block. To the rear of the site is the Oja river and there are views of the Obarenes mountains in the distance. Some noise from the main road is possible.

Facilities

The central sanitary facilities are old and traditional in style but clean. Open style washbasins and controllable showers. Laundry facilities. Shop (w/ends only in low season). Bar, restaurant, takeaway (on request). Outdoor swimming pool (20/6-20/9 supervised). Multisports court. Football. Tennis. River fishing. Children's cycle circuit. Play area. Electric or gas barbecues only. Off site: Town centre 1.5 km. Wine tasting and trails throughout the area. Bilbao (170 km). San Sebastián (210 km).

Open: 1 January - 9 December.

Directions

Heading west on N120, turn right onto LR111 signed Castañares de Rioja. Continue through town towards Haro. Site is on left, 800 m. after leaving town speed restriction. GPS: 42.52911, -2.92243

Charges guide

Per unit incl. 2 persons and electricity	€ 31.35 - € 32.55
extra person	€ 5.70 - € 6.00
child	€ 5.70 - € 6.00

For latest campsite news, availability and prices visit

alanrogers.com

Aranjuez

Camping Internacional Aranjuez

Soto del Rebollo s/n, s/n antigua NIV km 46,8, E-28300 Aranjuez (Madrid) T: 918 911 395.

E: info@campingaranjuez.com **alanrogers.com/ES90910**

Aranjuez, supposedly Spain's version of Versailles, is worthy of a visit with its beautiful palaces, leafy squares, avenues and gardens. This useful, popular and unusually well equipped site is therefore excellent for enjoying the unusual attractions or for an en route stop. It is 47 km. south of Madrid and 46 km. from Toledo. The site is alongside the River Tajo in a park-like situation with mature trees. There are 162 touring pitches, all with electricity (16A), set on flat grass amid tall trees. The site is owned by the owners of la Marina (ES87420) who have worked hard to improve the pitches and the site in general. Two tourist road trains run from the site to the palaces daily in high season with one a day (not Mondays) in low season. You can visit the huge, but slightly decaying, Royal Palace or the Casa del Labrador (translates as farmer's cottage) which is a small neo-classical palace in unusual and differing styles. They have superb gardens commissioned by Charles II. Canoes may be hired from behind the supermarket and there is a lockable moat gate to allow access to the river. There is good security, with CCTV around the river perimeter. Aranjuez is half an hour by regular train service from the centre of Madrid.

Facilities

Two of the three modern sanitary blocks are heated and all are well equipped with some washbasins in cabins. Laundry facilities. Gas supplies. Shop, bar and restaurant (all year) with attractive riverside patio (also open to the public). Takeaway. TV in bar. Swimming and paddling pools, (1/5-15/10). Tennis courts. Central play area. Pétanque. Bicycle hire. Canoe hire. Activities for children (high season). WiFi throughout (charged). Off site: Within easy walking distance of palace, gardens and museums.

Open: All year.

Directions

From Madrid on A4 take exit 37 (Aranjuez Norte). Turn left after 8 km. before Aranjuez and follow camping signs. From south take exit 52, then on through town. At last roundabout on left next to La Rana Verde follow signs. GPS: 40.0232, -3.3557

Charges guide

Per unit incl. 2 persons	
and electricity	€ 25.00 - € 33.00
extra person	€ 5.00 - € 6.50
child (3-10 yrs)	€ 3.50 - € 5.50

El Escorial

Caravanning El Escorial

ctra M600 km. 3,5, E-28280 El Escorial (Madrid) T: 902 014 900. E: info@campingelescorial.com

alanrogers.com/ES92000

El Escorial is very large and everything on site is on a grand scale – indeed a bicycle is very useful for getting around. There are 1,358 individual pitches of which 470 are for touring units, with the remainder used for permanent or seasonal units, but situated to one side of the site. The pitches are shaded (ask for a pitch without a low tree canopy if you have a 3 m. high motorcaravan). An attractive area of five hectares is set aside for 'wild camping' in tents on open fields with good shade from mature trees (long cables may be necessary for electricity). The general amenities are comprehensive and good, and include three swimming pools (unheated), plus a paddling pool.

Facilities

One large toilet block for touring pitches, and small blocks for the 'wild' camping area are all fully equipped with some washbasins in cabins. Facilities for babies and disabled campers. Large supermarket. Restaurant/bar and snack bar with takeaway (w/ends and B.Hs only in low season). Meeting rooms. Disco-bar. Swimming pools (15/5-15/9). Multisports areas. Activities for children (high season). Two well equipped playgrounds on sand. Bicycle hire. ATM. Car wash. WiFi in some areas (free).

Open: All year.

Directions

From the south go through town of El Escorial, and follow M600 Guadarrama road. Site is between the 2 and 3 km. markers north of the town on the right. From the north use A6 autopista exit 47 to M600 towards El Escorial town. Site is on the left. GPS: 40.62400, -4.099

Charges guide

Per unit incl. 2 persons	
and electricity	€ 31.30 - € 38.30
extra person	€ 6.20 - € 7.40
No credit cards.	

457

Gargantilla del Lozoya

Camping Monte Holiday

Ctra Rascafria-Lozoya km. 9, Finca El Tercio Nuevo s/n, E-28739 Gargantilla del Lozoya (Madrid)

T: 918 695 278. E: monteholiday@monteholiday.com **alanrogers.com/ES92120**

This picturesque and conservation-minded site is situated in an open, sunny lower valley in the Madrid area's only beech forest in the Parque Natural Sierre de Guadarrama. The area is ideal for walkers and nature lovers and offers many opportunities for outdoor sports enthusiasts. The site is mainly terraced and has 450 pitches, with 125 for touring units. These include a new area of 30 larger comfort pitches. All the pitches are mainly flat with grass or gravel surfaces and shade from mature trees. The upper area is taken by permanent units. An extensive new activity area includes a zip wire accessed via climbing walls. The site is part of the Campingred group.

Facilities

The modern, heated and well equipped toilet block is well maintained. Facilities for disabled visitors and babies. Laundry facilities. Motorcaravan services. Shop (basic provisions in low season). Bar and restaurant (15/6-15/9, B.Hs and weekends). TV in bar. Library. Swimming pool with lifeguard (mid June-mid Sept). Multisports court. Tennis. Beach volleyball. Play area. Gas supplies. Barbecues are not permitted 15/5-31/10. Bicycle hire. Excursions and activities (high season). WiFi in bar (free).

Open: All year.

Directions

From A1 motorway (Burgos-Madrid) take exit 69 towards Rascafria on the M604. Turn right after passing under a railway tunnel and site is on left after 800 m. GPS: 40.949917, -3.729267

Charges guide

Per unit incl. 2 persons and electricity	€ 27.10
extra person	€ 6.40
child (3-10 yrs)	€ 5.90

Camping Cheques accepted.

La Cabrera

Camping Pico de la Miel

Ctra A1, Salida 57, E-28751 La Cabrera (Madrid) T: 918 688 082. E: info@picodelamiel.com

alanrogers.com/ES92100

Pico de la Miel is a very large site 60 km. north of Madrid. Mainly a long stay site for Madrid, there are a huge number of very well established and fairly old static caravans. There is a small separate area with its own toilet block for 80 touring units, all with 8A electricity (Europlug, long cables useful). The pitches are on rather poor, sandy grass. Trees give some shade on some pitches. There are also smaller pitches for tents (the ground could be hard for pegs). The noise level from the many Spanish customers is high and you will have a chance to practise your Spanish!

Facilities

Dated but clean, heated and tiled toilet block, with some washbasins in cabins. En-suite unit with ramp for disabled visitors. Laundry. Motorcaravan services. Gas supplies. Shop. Restaurant/bar and takeaway (1/6-30/9 and w/ends and B.Hs rest of year). Excellent swimming pool complex (15/6-15/9). Tennis. Playground. Car wash. First aid. WiFi throughout. Off site: La Cabrera with bars and restaurants 500 m. Bicycle hire and riding 500 m.

Open: All year.

Directions

Site is well signed from the E5/A1. Going south or north use exit 57 and follow site signs. When at T-junction, facing a hotel, turn left. (Exit 57 is closer to the site than exit 60). GPS: 40.85797, -3.6158

Charges guide

Per unit incl. 2 persons and electricity	€ 29.60
extra person	€ 6.70
child (3-9 yrs)	€ 5.80
dog	free

Baños de Fortuna

Camping la Fuente

Camino de la Bocamina, E-30626 Baños de Fortuna (Murcia) T: 968 685 125. E: info@campingfuente.com

alanrogers.com/ES87450

Located in an area known for its thermal waters since Roman and Moorish times, and with just 88 pitches and 24 bungalows, la Fuente is a gem. Unusually, winter is high season here. The main attraction is the huge hydrotherapy centre where the water is a constant 36 degrees all year. The pool can be covered in inclement weather. The site is in two sections, one where pitches are in standard rows and the other where they are in circles around blocks. The hard, flat pitches are on shingle (rock pegs advised), have 10A electricity (Europlug) and 52 have their own mini sanitary unit. Some artificial shade has been added to 22 pitches.

Facilities

Some pitches have their own facilities, including a unit for disabled campers. Washing machines and dryers. Groceries can be ordered from reception. High quality restaurant shared with accommodation guests. Hydrotherapy centre. Snack bar by pool. Jacuzzi. Communal barbecues only. WiFi over site (charged). Off site: Spa town, massage therapies and hot pools 500 m. Fortuna with shops, bars and restaurants 3 km. Golf and riding 20 km.

Open: All year.

Directions

From A7/E15 Alicante-Murcia road take C3223 to Fortuna then follow signs to Baños de Fortuna. The site with its bright yellow walls can be easily seen from the road and is very well signed in the town. GPS: 38.20682, -1.10732

Charges guide

Per unit incl. 2 persons and electricity	€ 15.50
with individual sanitary facility	€ 17.50
extra person	€ 3.25
child (3-12 yrs)	€ 1.25

For latest campsite news, availability and prices visit

alanrogers.com

Cartagena

Camping Naturista El Portus

El Portus, E-30394 Cartagena (Murcia) T: 968 553 052. E: elportus@elportus.com

alanrogers.com/ES87520

Set in a secluded south-facing bay fringed by mountains, El Portus is a fairly large naturist site enjoying magnificent views and with direct access to a small sand and pebble beach. This part of Spain enjoys almost all-year-round sunshine. There are some 400 pitches, 300 for touring units, from 60-100 sq.m, with all but a few having electricity (6A). They are mostly on fairly level, if somewhat stony and barren ground. El Portus has a reasonable amount of shade from established trees and nearly every pitch has a view. Residential units are situated on the hillside above the site.

Facilities

Five acceptable toilet blocks, all unisex, are fully equipped with hot showers. Opened as required, they are clean and bright. Unit for disabled visitors, key from reception. Washing machines. Motorcaravan services. Well stocked shop. Bar with TV and library. Restaurants. The beach restaurant is closed in low season. Swimming pools (June-Sept). Wellness centre. Play area. Pétanque. Yoga. Tennis. Scuba-diving club (high season). Windsurfing. Fishing. Spanish lessons. Entertainment all season. Small boat moorings. WiFi over site (charged).

Open: All year.

Directions

Site is on the coast, 10 km. west of Cartagena. Follow signs to Mazarron then take E22 to Canteras. Site is well signed for 4 km. If approaching through Cartagena, exit the town on N332 following signs for Canteras. Site signed on joining the N332.
GPS: 37.585, -1.06717

Charges guide

Per unit incl. 2 persons	
and electricity	€ 26.00 - € 38.00
extra person	€ 5.00 - € 7.00
child (3-9 yrs)	€ 3.50 - € 5.50

Isla Plana

Camping Los Madriles

Ctra de la Azohia km. 4,5, E-30868 Isla Plana (Murcia) T: 968 152 151. E: camplosmadriles@forodigital.es

alanrogers.com/ES87480

An exceptional site with super facilities, Los Madriles is run by a hard working team, with constant improvements being made. Twenty kilometres west of Cartagena, the approach to the site and the surrounding area is fairly unremarkable, but the site is not. A fairly steep access road leads to the 313 flat, good to large sized terraced pitches, each having electricity, water and a waste point. Most have shade from large trees with a number benefiting from panoramic views of the sea or behind to the mountains. The site has huge rectangular and lagoon style pools with water sprays and jacuzzis.

Facilities

Four sanitary blocks and one small toilet block provide excellent facilities, including services in one block for disabled campers. Private wash cabins. Washing machines and dryers. Motorcaravan services. Car wash. Supermarket, restaurant/snack bar and bar (all open all season but hours are limited). Swimming pools with jacuzzi. Boules. Play areas. Pets are not accepted. WiFi over site (charged, or free in certain areas). Off site: Town close by. Beach and fishing (licence required) 800 m. Boat launching 3 km. Riding and bicycle hire 6 km. Golf 20 km.

Open: All year.

Directions

From E15/A7 exit 845 follow RM3 for Cartagena, Fuente Alamo and Mazarron (do not turn into Mazarron). Continue towards Puerto Mazarron and take N332 (Cartagena). On reaching coast continue on N332 (Cartagena, Alicante). At roundabout turn right towards Isla Plana and La Azohia. Site is signed and on the left in 5 km. GPS: 37.57859, -1.19558

Charges guide

Per unit incl. 2 persons and electricity	€ 26.00

Large discounts for longer stays. No credit cards.

La Manga del Mar Menor

Caravaning La Manga

Autovia Cartagena-La Manga, Salida 11, E-30386 La Manga del Mar Menor (Murcia) T: 968 563 014.

E: lamanga@caravaning.es **alanrogers.com/ES87530**

This is a very large, well equipped, holiday-style site with its own beach and both indoor and outdoor pools. With a good number of typical Spanish long stay units, the length of the site is impressive (1 km) and a bicycle is very helpful for getting about. The 800 regularly laid out, gravel touring pitches (100 or 110 sq.m) are generally separated by hedges which also provide a degree of shade. Each has a 10A electricity supply, water and the possibility of satellite TV reception. This site's excellent facilities are ideally suited for holidays in the winter when the weather is very pleasantly warm.

Facilities

Nine clean toilet blocks of standard design, well spaced around the site, include washbasins (all with hot water). Laundry. Gas supplies. Large well stocked supermarket. Restaurant. Bar. Snack bar. Swimming pool complex (April-Sept). Indoor pool, gymnasium (April-Oct), sauna, jacuzzi and massage service. Outdoor fitness for adults. Open-air family cinema (July/Aug). Tennis. Pétanque. Minigolf. Play area. Watersports school. Internet café (also WiFi). Winter activities including Spanish classes.

Open: All year.

Directions

Use exit (Salida) 11 from MU312 dual carriageway towards Cabo de Palos, signed Playa Honda (site signed also). Cross road bridge and double back. Site entrance is visible beside dual carriageway with many flags flying. GPS: 37.62445, -0.74442

Charges guide

Per unit incl. 2 persons	
and electricity	€ 20.40 - € 35.60
extra person	€ 4.20 - € 5.20

Camping Cheques accepted.

FREE Alan Rogers Travel Card
Extra benefits and savings - see page 14

Espinal

Camping Urrobi

Ctra Pamplona-Valcarlos km. 42 N135, E-31694 Espinal (Navarra) T: 948 760 200.
E: info@campingurrobi.com **alanrogers.com/ES90480**

This large site is in a beautiful location with mountain views. At the entrance is a lively bar, a reasonably priced restaurant and a well stocked shop. The site is popular with Spanish families and there are many mobile homes, so it can be busy at holiday times and weekends. However, there is plenty of room on the 150 unmarked grass pitches for touring, 82 of which have electricity points (6A) and there are plenty of water taps. Water activities of all types are catered for, with both a swimming pool and an area of the river sectioned off for safe bathing and paddling. This is a suitable site for families.

Facilities
Clean sanitary blocks include facilities for disabled visitors (key from reception). Laundry facilities. Motorcaravan services. Shop, bar and restaurant (all season). Swimming pool. Games room with TV (Spanish). Minigolf. Tennis. Playing field. Play area. Gas and charcoal barbecues only on pitches but not in Aug/Sept (communal area provided). WiFi throughout (free). Off site: Village 1 km. with shops, restaurant and bars. Forest of Irati 15 minutes. Bicycle hire 15 km. Golf and riding 40 km. Beach 70 km.

Open: 22 March - 3 November.

Directions
From Pamplona take N135 northeast for 42 km. After village of Auritzberri turn right onto NA172. Site is on the left. GPS: 42.97315, -1.351817

Charges guide
Per unit incl. 2 persons and electricity	€ 20.80 - € 31.00
extra person	€ 4.80 - € 5.25
child (2-12 yrs)	€ 3.85 - € 4.15

Etxarri-Aranatz

Camping Etxarri

Paraje Dambolintxulo s/n, E-31820 Etxarri-Aranatz (Navarra) T: 948 460 537. E: info@campingetxarri.com
alanrogers.com/ES90420

Situated in the Valle de la Burundi, this pleasant and improved site has superb views of the 1,300 m. high San-Donator Mountains. The approach is via a road lined by huge 300-year-old oak trees, which are a feature of the site. Reception is housed in the main building beside the pool with a restaurant above (access also by lift). There are 108 pitches of average size on flat ground (50 for touring units) with 6A electricity to all and water to 25. The site is well placed for fascinating walks in unspoilt countryside and is close to three recognised nature walks.

Facilities
Toilet facilities are good and include a baby bath and facilities for disabled visitors. Laundry. Motorcaravan services. Gas. Essential supplies kept in high season. Bar (1/4-30/9). Restaurant and takeaway (1/4-15/9). Swimming and paddling pools (1/6-15/9) also open to the public and can get crowded. Bicycle hire. Minigolf. Play area. Entertainment for children in high season. Tennis and squash courts. No charcoal barbecues. WiFi over site (charged). Off site: Buses and trains nearby to Pamplona. Bars, restaurants and shops 2 km.

Open: 1 March - 13 October.

Directions
Etxarri-Aranatz is 40 km. northwest of Pamplona. From A8 (San Sebastián-Bilbao) take A15 towards Pamplona, then 20 km. northwest of Pamplona, take A10 west towards Vitoria/Gasteix. At km. 19 take NA120 to and through town (site signed). Cross railway and turn left to site at end of road. GPS: 42.913031, -2.079924

Charges guide
Per unit incl. 2 persons and electricity	€ 25.50 - € 30.00
extra person	€ 5.95
child (2-10 yrs)	€ 4.95

Villafranca

Camping Bardenas

Ctra NA660 PK 13.4, E-31330 Villafranca (Navarra) T: 948 846 191. E: info@campingbardenas.com
alanrogers.com/ES90510

Camping Bardenas (sometimes signed as Camping Villafranca) is in Navarra, midway between Bilbao and Zaragoza. This site may prove useful as an en route stop, given its relative proximity to the AP68 and AP15 motorways, but it also merits longer stays. This is a new site and shade is limited at present. The 38 touring pitches are of a good size and all have electrical connections. A number of mobile homes are available for rent. On-site amenities include a swimming pool and a gym. Occasional excursions are organised to nearby vineyards, along with various other activities in peak season.

Facilities
One toilet block with excellent facilities is kept spotlessly clean. Large room for disabled visitors. Washing machine. Motorcaravan services. Shop (April-Nov). Restaurant, bar and takeaway. Outdoor swimming pool (15/6-15/9). Play area. Games room. TV in bar. Small gym. Mobile homes for rent. Communal barbecue area. Free WiFi throughout. Off site: Villafranca (shops and restaurants). Walking and mountain biking in Bardenas Reales park. Tudela.

Open: All year.

Directions
From Zaragoza on AP-15, leave at the Villafranca and Cadreita exit. By-pass Cadreita and head for Villafranca on NA-660. Shortly before reaching the town you will pass the site on your left, continue to next roundabout and perform a U-turn in order to gain site access. GPS: 42.263918, -1.738731

Charges guide
Per unit incl. 2 persons and electricity	€ 18.00 - € 26.50
extra person	€ 4.00 - € 6.00

For latest campsite news, availability and prices visit
alanrogers.com

Mendigorría
Camping El Molino de Mendigorria
E-31150 Mendigorría (Navarra) T: 948 340 604. E: info@campingelmolino.com

alanrogers.com/ES90430

This is an extensive site set by an attractive weir near the town of Mendigorría, alongside the River Arga. It takes its name from an old disused water mill (molino) close by. The site is split into separate permanent and touring sections. The touring area is a new development with 90 good sized flat pitches with electricity and water for touring units, and a separate area for tents. Many trees have been planted around the site but there is still only minimal shade. The friendly owner, Anna Beriain, will give you a warm welcome. Reception is housed in the lower part of a long building along with the bar/snack bar which has a cool shaded terrace, a separate restaurant and a supermarket. The upper floor of this building is dormitory accommodation for backpackers. The site has a sophisticated dock and boat launching facility and an ambitious watersports competition programme in season with a safety boat present at all times. There are pedaloes and canoes for hire. The site is very busy during the festival of San Fermín (bull running) in July in Pamplona (28 km). Tours of the local bodegas (groups of ten) to sample the fantastic Navarra wines can be organised by reception.

Facilities
The well equipped toilet block is very clean and well maintained, with cold water to washbasins. Facilities for children and disabled visitors. Washing machine. Large restaurant, pleasant bar. Supermarket. Superb new swimming pools for adults and children (1/6-15/9). Bicycle hire. Riverside bar. Weekly entertainment programme (July/Aug) and many sporting activities. Squash courts. River walk. Torches useful. Gas barbecues only. WiFi on part of site (charged). Off site: Bus to Pamplona 500 m. Riding 15 km. Golf 35 km.

Open: All year (excl. 23 December - 4 January).

Directions
Mendigorría is 30 km. southwest of Pamplona. From A15 San Sebastián-Zaragoza motorway, leave Pamplona bypass on A12 towards Logon. Leave at km. 23 on NA601 to hilltop town of Mendigorría. At crossroads turn right towards Larraga and downhill to site. GPS: 42.62423, -1.84259

Charges guide

Per unit incl. 2 persons and electricity	€ 25.50 - € 29.10
extra person	€ 5.40 - € 6.20
child (2-11 yrs)	€ 4.50 - € 5.20

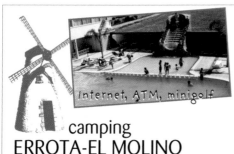
Mundaka
Camping Portuondo
Ctra Gernika-Bermeo, E-48360 Mundaka (Bizkaia) T: 946 877 701. E: recepcion@campingportuondo.com

alanrogers.com/ES90350

This site has an attractive restaurant, bar and terrace taking full advantage of the wonderful views across the ocean and estuary. Set amongst gardens, the 72 touring pitches are mainly for tents and small vans, but there are eight larger pitches at the lower levels for medium sized motorcaravans. Access to these is a little difficult as the road is very steep and there is no turning space. The site is mostly terraced, with tent pitches split, one section for your unit, the other for your car and there is some shade. Most are slightly sloping and all have 6A electricity (some may need long leads). In high season (July/August) it is essential to ring to book your space.

Facilities
Two toilet blocks include mostly British WCs and a baby room. One new block with facilities for disabled visitors. A reader reports poor cleaning and maintenance during their visit. Washing machines and dryers. Motorcaravan services. Shop (22/6-8/9). Bar and two restaurants, all open to public (28/1-15/12, closed Mon. in low season). Takeaway (22/6-8/9). Swimming pools (22/6-15/9). Free WiFi over part of site. Barbecue area. Torches useful.

Open: 23 January - 15 December.

Directions
From A8 (S Sebastián-Bilbao) take exit 18, follow signs for Gernika on BI635. Continue on BI2235 towards Bermeo. Site is on right approaching Mundaka (left turn prohibited). Take care – sharp turn with a steep access. GPS: 43.39918, -2.69610

Charges guide

Per unit incl. 2 persons and electricity	€ 32.50 - € 41.70
extra person	€ 6.90 - € 8.65
child (under 10 yrs)	€ 6.15 - € 7.85

Sweden

With giant lakes and waterways, rich forests, majestic mountains and glaciers, and vast, wide open countryside, Sweden is almost twice the size of the UK but with a fraction of the population.

Southern Sweden's unspoiled islands with their beautiful sandy beaches offer endless opportunities for boating and island hopping. The coastal cities of Gothenburg and Malmö, once centres of industry, now have an abundance of restaurants, cultural venues and attractions. With the Oresund Bridge, Malmö is just a short ride from Copenhagen. Stockholm, the capital, is a delightful place built on fourteen small islands on the eastern coast. It is an attractive, vibrant city, with magnificent architecture, fine museums and historic squares. Sparsely populated Northern Sweden is a land of forests, rivers and wilderness inhabited by moose and reindeer. Östersund, located at the shores of a lake in the heart of the country, is well known for winter sports, while Frösö Zoo, home to 700 animals and an amusement park, is a popular attraction. Today Sweden is one of the world's most developed societies, and enjoys an enviable standard of living.

CAPITAL: Stockholm

Tourist Office
Swedish Travel and Tourism Council
Sweden House, 11 Montagu Place
London W1H 2AL
Tel: 020 7870 5609
Fax: 020 7724 5872
Email: info@swetourism.org.uk
Internet: www.visitsweden.com

Population
9.6 million

Climate
Sweden enjoys a temperate climate thanks to the
Gulf Stream. There is generally less rain and more
sunshine in the summer than in Britain.

Language
Swedish. English is fairly widely spoken.

Telephone
The country code is 00 46.

Money
Currency: The Krona
Banks: Mon-Fri 09.30-15.00. Some city banks
stay open until 17.30/18.00 on Thursdays
(regions may vary).

Shops
Mon-Fri 09.00-18.00. Sat 09.00-13.00/16.00.
Some department stores remain open until
20.00/22.00.

Public Holidays
New Year; Epiphany; Easter Mon; Labour Day;
Ascension; Whit Sun; Constitution Day June 6;
Mid-summer Festival; All Saints; Christmas
Dec 24-26.

Motoring
Roads are generally much quieter than in the UK.
Dipped headlights are obligatory. Away from large
towns, petrol stations rarely open 24 hours but
most have self-service pumps (with credit card
payment). Buy diesel during working hours, it may
not be available at self-service pumps.

see campsite map 3

Mora

Mora Parkens Camping

Box 294, S-792 25 Mora (Dalarnas Län) T: 025 027 600. E: info@moraparken.se

alanrogers.com/SW2836

Mora, at the northern end of Lake Silijan, is surrounded by small localities all steeped in history and culture. On the island of Sollerön, south of Mora, is evidence of a large Viking burial ground. Traditional handicrafts are still alive in the region. Mora is lively, friendly and attractive. The campsite, which is good for family holidays, is only ten minutes walk from the town. The camping area is large, grassy, open and flat. It is bordered by clumps of trees and a stream. The staff are pleasant and helpful. Travel to Nusnäs, an old village with documents going back to the Middle Ages and see the production of the brightly coloured wooden horse. Every household should have two for luck.

Facilities

Four fully equipped toilet blocks. Campers' kitchen. Laundry. Shop. Restaurant/bar. Sauna. Fishing. Minigolf. Playground. Canoe hire. Internet access. Off site: Swimming pools. Zorn Museum. Orsa Bear Park. Dalhalla (limestone quarry) musical stage. Nusnäs.

Open: All year (full services mid June - mid August).

Directions

Follow signs to centre of town. Campsite is clearly signed from town centre and is next to Zorngården and Zorn museum. GPS: 61.008533, 14.531783

Charges guide

Per unit incl. electricity	SEK 180 - 250
tent	SEK 100 - 115

Askim

Lisebergs Camping Askim Strand

Marholmsvägen 124, S-436 45 Askim (Hallands Län) T: 031 840 200. E: askim.strand@liseberg.se

alanrogers.com/SW2706

Within easy reach of the city, this is a very pleasantly located site, close to a long gently sloping beach which is very popular for bathing. As a result the area behind the campsite is populated by many holiday homes and cabins. A very open site with very little shade, it has 200 mostly level, grassy pitches all with 10A electricity (Europlug), and two areas for tents. Many pitches are fairly compact, although there are some larger ones. The key card entry system operates the entrance barrier and access to the buildings and there is a night security guard (June-August).

Facilities

Two modern, heated sanitary buildings. Both are maintained to a high standard and provide all the usual facilities, including a good suite for small children and a unit for disabled visitors. Larger unit with recreation room and TV. Separate laundry. Kitchens with cooking facilities and washing up room with TV. Hot water is free. Motorcaravan services. Well stocked shop with fresh bread daily. Sauna. Several playgrounds. TV room. Minigolf. Free WiFi over site. Off site: Beach 300 m. Activity centre, watersports and ball games 500 m. Golf 2 km. City of Göteborg 10 km.

Open: 26 April - 25 August.

Directions

About 10 km. south of Göteborg, take exit signed Mölndal S and ports (Hamnar). Take the Rv 159 towards Frolunda, and watch for a slip road to the right. After 200 m. turn left at the roundabout, signed Askim, and follow signs to campsite. GPS: 57.62832, 11.92052

Charges guide

Per unit incl. 2 persons and electricity	SEK 255 - 440
extra person	SEK 50

Electric pitches only in high season.
Valid Camping Card required to check in.

Östersund

Östersunds Camping

Krondikesvagen 95, S-831 46 Östersund (Jämtlands Län) T: 063 144 615.

E: ostersundscamping@ostersund.se alanrogers.com/SW2850

Östersund lies on Lake Storsjön, which is Sweden's Loch Ness, with 200 sightings of the monster dating back to 1635, and more recently captured on video in 1996. Also worthy of a visit is the island of Fröson where settlements can be traced back to prehistoric times. This large site has 254 pitches, electricity (10A) and TV socket available on 131, all served by tarmac roads. There are also 41 tarmac hardstandings available, and over 220 cottages, cabins and rooms for rent. Adjacent to the site are the municipal swimming pool complex with caféteria (indoor and outdoor pools), a Scandic hotel with restaurant, minigolf, and a Statoil filling station. A large supermarket is just 500 m. from the site.

Facilities

Toilet facilities are in three units, two including controllable hot showers (on payment) with communal changing areas, suites for disabled visitors and baby changing. The third has four family bathrooms each containing WC, basin and shower. Two kitchens, each with full cookers, hobs, fridge/freezers and double sinks (all free of charge), and excellent dining rooms. Washing machines, dryers and free drying cabinet. Very good motorcaravan service point. Playground. Off site: Östersund, Fröson.

Open: All year.

Directions

Site is south of the town on the road towards Torvalla. Turn by Statoil station and site entrance is immediately on right. It is well signed from around the town. GPS: 63.15942, 14.67355

Charges guide

Per unit with electricity	€ 22.00 - € 26.00

For latest campsite news, availability and prices visit

alanrogers.com

Strömsund

Strömsunds Camping

Box 500, S-833 24 Strömsund (Jämtlands Län) T: 067 016 410. E: turism@stromsund.se

alanrogers.com/SW2857

A quiet waterside town on the north - south route 45, known as the Inlandsvägen, Strömsund is a good place to begin a journey on the Wilderness Way. This is route 342 which heads northwest towards the mountains at Gäddede and the Norwegian border. Being on the confluence of many waterways, there is a wonderful feeling of space and freedom in Strömsund. The campsite is set on a gentle grassy slope backed by forest. Another part of the site, across the road, overlooks the lake. Cabins are set in circular groups of either six or seven. The site is owned by the town council.

Facilities

Excellent facilities include two toilet blocks, one on each side of the road. Both contain showers, toilets, washbasins with dividers and underfloor heating. Facilities for disabled visitors. Laundry. Large campers' kitchen with cooking rings, microwave and sinks. Motorcaravan services. Bicycle, canoe, pedalo and boat hire. Play area. Off site: Municipal pool is next to the site. Riding 3 km.

Open: All year (full services mid June - mid August).

Directions

Site is 700 m. south of Strömsund on route 45. GPS: 63.846523, 15.534405

Charges guide

Per unit incl. 2 persons
and electricity   SEK 190 - 220

Granna

Grännastrandens Familjecamping

Box 14, S-563 21 Gränna (Jönköpings Län) T: 039 010 706. E: info@grannacamping.se

alanrogers.com/SW2670

This large, lakeside site with modern facilities and busy continental feel, is set below the old city of Gränna. Flat fields separate Gränna from the shore, one of which is occupied by the 25 acres of Grännastrandens where there are 450 numbered pitches, including a tent area and some seasonal pitches. About 210 pitches have electricity (10A). The site is flat, spacious and very regularly laid out on open ground with only a row of poplars by the lake to provide shelter, so a windbreak may prove useful against any onshore breeze. Part of the lake is walled off to form an attractive swimming area with sandy beaches, slides and islands.

Facilities

Two large, sanitary blocks of a very high standard in the centre of the site have modern, well kept facilities, some with external access, washbasins and free hot showers, some in private cubicles. Laundry facilities. Provision for disabled campers. A further small, older block is by reception. Very good cooking facilities. Motorcaravan services. Shop (15/6-20/8). TV room. Playground. Lake swimming area. Boating and fishing. Off site: Café and restaurant outside site (1/5-31/8) and town restaurants nearby. Bus stop nearby. Golf 6 km.

Open: 1 May - 30 September.

Directions

Take Gränna exit from E4 motorway (no camping sign) 40 km. north of Jönköping. Site is signed in the centre of the town, towards the harbour and ferry. GPS: 58.02762, 14.45803

Charges guide

Per unit incl. 2 persons
and electricity   SEK 180 - 350

Jönköping

Jönköping Villa Björkhagen

Friggagatan 31, S-554 54 Jönköping (Jönköpings Län) T: 036 122 863. E: info@villabjorkhagen.se

alanrogers.com/SW2665

Overlooking Lake Vättern, Villa Björkhagen is a good site, useful as a break in the journey across Sweden or visiting the city during a tour of the lakes. It is on raised ground overlooking the lake, with some shelter in parts. There are 280 pitches on well kept grass which, on one side, slopes away from reception. Some pitches on the other side of reception are flat and there are 200 electrical (10A), 100 cable TV and 40 water connections available. Jönköping is one of Sweden's oldest trading centres with a Charter dating back to 1284 and several outstanding attractions.

Facilities

Heated sanitary facilities were clean when we visited but looking rather tired. They include hot showers on payment (some in private cubicles) and a sauna, plus provision for disabled visitors and babies. Laundry. Motorcaravan services. Gas supplies. Well stocked shop (all year). Bar and restaurant (1/6-16/9). Playground. TV room. Minigolf and bicycle hire. WiFi (free). Off site: Pool complex and fishing 500 m. Beach, golf, sailing and skiing 1 km. Riding 7 km.

Open: All year (full services 1/6-16/9).

Directions

Site is well signed from the E4 road on eastern side of Jönköping. Watch carefully for exit on this fast road. GPS: 57.78702, 14.21795

Charges guide

Per unit incl. 2 persons
and electricity   € 34.00

Prices may be increased if
there is a local exhibition.

Camping Cheques accepted.

FREE Alan Rogers Travel Card

Extra benefits and savings - see page 14

Byxelkrok

Krono Camping Böda Sand

S-38773 Byxelkrok (Kalmar Län) T: 048 522 200. E: info@bodasand.se

alanrogers.com/SW2690

Krono Camping Böda Sand is beautifully situated at the northern end of the island of Öland and is one of Sweden's largest and most modern campsites. Most of the 1,200 pitches have electricity (10/16A) and TV connections, 130 have water and waste water drainage. The pitches and 165 cabins for rent are spread out in a pine forest, very close to a fabulous 10 km. long, white sand beach. Here you will also find a restaurant, kiosks, toilets and beach showers, and a relaxation centre with an indoor/outdoor pool. The reception, the toilet blocks and the services at this site are excellent and comprehensive.

Facilities

Seven heated sanitary blocks provide roomy shower cubicles, washbasins, some washbasin suites and WCs. Facilities for babies and disabled visitors (key at reception). Laundry rooms. Excellent kitchens. Motorcaravan services. Supermarket and bakery. Pizzeria, café, pub and restaurant. Takeaway. Bicycle hire, pedal cars and pedal boat hire. Minigolf. 9-hole golf course. Indoor/outdoor swimming pool (on the beach). Trim trails. Entertainment and activities for all. WiFi. Off site: Fishing 4 km.

Open: 1 May - 1 September.

Directions

From Kalmar cross Öland road bridge on road no. 137. On Öland follow road no. 136 towards Borgholm and Byxelkrok. Turn left at roundabout north of Böda and follow campsite signs to Krono Camping Böda Sand. GPS: 57.27436, 17.04851

Charges guide

Per pitch	SEK 235 - 365
incl. electricity	SEK 285 - 435

Färjestaden

Krono Camping Saxnäs

S-386 95 Färjestaden (Kalmar Län) T: 048 535 700. E: info@kcsaxnas.se

alanrogers.com/SW2680

Well placed for touring Sweden's Riviera and the fascinating and beautiful island of Öland, this family run site, part of the Krono group, has 420 marked and numbered touring pitches. Arranged in rows on open, well kept grassland dotted with a few trees, all have electricity (10/16A), 320 have TV connections and 112 also have water. An unmarked area without electricity can accommodate around 60 tents. The site has about 130 long stay units and cabins for rent. The sandy beach slopes very gently and is safe for children. Reception is efficient and friendly with good English spoken. An outdoor heated pool and a children's pool are at the entrance to the site.

Facilities

Three heated sanitary blocks provide roomy shower cubicles, washbasins, some washbasin/WC suites and WCs. Facilities for babies and disabled visitors. Laundry room. Good kitchen. Hot water is free. Gas supplies. Motorcaravan services. Shop (1/5-30/8). Pizzeria, licensed restaurant and café (all 1/5-30/8). Bar (1/7-31/7). Outdoor heated swimming pool (15/5-22/8). Playgrounds. Bouncy castle. Boules. Canoe hire. Bicycle hire. Minigolf. Family entertainment and activities. Football. Off site: Golf 500 m.

Open: 12 April - 30 September.

Directions

Cross Öland road bridge from Kalmar on road no. 137. Take exit for Öland Djurpark/Saxnäs, then follow campsite signs. Site is just north of the end of the bridge. GPS: 56.68727, 16.48182

Charges guide

Per unit incl. electricity	SEK 175 - 430

Weekend and weekly rates available.

Västervik

Camping Lysingsbadet

Lysingsvägen, S-593 53 Västervik (Kalmar Län) T: 049 088 920. E: lysingsbadet@vastervik.se

alanrogers.com/SW2675

One of the largest sites in Scandinavia, Lysingsbadet has unrivalled views of the 'Pearl of the East Coast' – Västervik and its fjords and islands. There are around 1,000 large, mostly marked and numbered pitches, spread over a vast area of rocky promontory and set on different plateaux, terraces, in valleys and woodland, or beside the water. It is a very attractive site, and one which never really looks or feels crowded even when busy. There are 83 full service pitches with TV, water and electrical connections, 163 with TV and electricity and 540 with electricity only, the remainder for tents.

Facilities

Ten modern toilet blocks of various ages house a comprehensive mix of showers, washbasins and WCs. All are kept very clean. Several kitchens. Four laundry rooms. All facilities and hot water are free. Key cards operate the barriers and gain access to sanitary blocks, pool complex and other facilities. Motorcaravan services. Supermarket (15/5-31/8). Restaurant and café/takeaway (12/6-138). Swimming pool complex (12/6-31/8). Golf. Minigolf. Bicycle and boat hire. Fishing. Entertainment and dances in high season. Playgrounds. Quick Stop service.

Open: All year.

Directions

Turn off E22 for Västervik and follow signs for Lysingsbadet. GPS: 57.738212, 16.668459

Charges guide

Per pitch	SEK 250 - 380
incl. electricity	SEK 280 - 450
incl. electricity, TV	SEK 280 - 470

For latest campsite news, availability and prices visit

alanrogers.com

Tingsryd

Tingsryds Camping

Mårdslyckesand, S-362 91 Tingsryd (Kronobergs Län) T: 047 710 554. E: info@tingsrydresort.se

alanrogers.com/SW2655

A pleasant, well managed site by Lake Tiken, Tingsryds Camping is well placed for Sweden's Glass District. The 190 large pitches are arranged in rows divided by trees and shrubs, with some along the edge of a lakeside path (public have access). All have 10/16A electricity and there is shade in parts. The facilities are housed in buildings near the site entrance, with the reception building having the restaurant, café, bar and a small shop. Adjacent to the site is a small beach, grassy lying out area, playground and lake swimming area and three tennis courts. Hire of canoes, fishing and minigolf are available on site (public access also).

Facilities

Heated sanitary facilities are in two well maintained buildings, one including showers, mostly with curtains (on payment, communal undressing), the other a campers' kitchen with sinks, hobs and dining area. Facilities for disabled visitors. Laundry with free ironing. Motorcaravan services. Shop (1/5-15/9). Restaurant and café (1/5-15/9). Minigolf. Playground. Boules. Lake swimming. Canoe hire. Fishing. Bicycle hire.

Open: All year (full services 24/5-19/8).

Directions

Site is 1 km. from Tingsryd off road no. 120, well signed around the town. GPS: 56.52872, 14.96147

Charges guide

Per unit	SEK 195 - 315
electricity	SEK 40 - 45

Arvidsjaur

Camp Gielas

Järnvägsgatan 111, S-933 34 Arvidsjaur (Norrbottens Län) T: 096 055 600. E: gielas@arvidsjaur.se

alanrogers.com/SW2865

A modern municipal site with excellent sporting facilities on the outskirts of the town, Gielas is well shielded on all sides by trees, providing a very peaceful atmosphere. The 160 pitches, 81 with electricity (16A) and satellite TV connections, are level on sparse grass and accessed by tarmac roadways. The sauna and showers, sporting, gymnasium and Internet facilities at the sports hall are free to campers. Also on site is a snackbar. The lake on the site is suitable for boating, bathing and fishing. There is a swimming pool and a 9-hole golf course nearby, and hunting trips can be arranged.

Facilities

Two modern, heated sanitary units provide controllable hot showers and a unit for disabled visitors. Well equipped kitchens (free). Washing machine and dryer. The unit by the tent area also has facilities for disabled campers and baby changing. Snack bar. Tennis. Minigolf. Play areas. Sauna. Sporting facilities. Boat and canoe hire. Pedal cars. Lake swimming. Fishing. WiFi (free). Bicycle hire.

Open: All year.

Directions

Site is on road 95, 3 km. south of town centre. GPS: 65.581798, 19.19024

Charges guide

Per unit incl. 2 persons and electricity	SEK 220 - 250

Jokkmokk

Jokkmokks Camping Center

Box 75, S-962 22 Jokkmokk (Norrbottens Län) T: 097 112 370. E: campingcenter@jokkmokk.com

alanrogers.com/SW2870

This attractive site is just 8 km. from the Arctic Circle. Large and well organised, it is bordered on one side by the river and with woodland on the other, just 3 km. from the town centre. It has 170 level, grassy pitches, with an area for tents, plus 59 cabins for rent. Electricity (10A) is available to all touring pitches. The site has a heated, open-air pool complex open in summer (no lifeguard). There are opportunities for snowmobiling, cross-country skiing in spring and ice fishing in winter. Try visiting for the famous Jokkmokk Winter Market (first Thurs-Sat in Feb) or the less chilly Autumn Market (end of August).

Facilities

Heated sanitary buildings provide mostly open washbasins and controllable showers (some are curtained with a communal changing area, a few are in cubicles with divider and seat). Baby bathroom. Suite for disabled visitors. Games room. Kitchen and launderette. A further unit with WCs, washbasins, showers plus a steam sauna, is by the pool. Shop, restaurant and bar (in summer). Takeaway (high season). Swimming pools (25x10 m. main pool with water slide, two smaller pools and paddling pool). Sauna. Bicycle hire. Playground and adventure playground. Minigolf. Football field. Games machines. Free fishing. Off site: Riding 2 km.

Open: 15 May - 15 September.

Directions

Site is 3 km. from the centre of Jokkmokk on road 97. GPS: 66.59497, 19.89270

Charges guide

Per unit incl. 2 persons and electricity	SEK 255

Örebro
Gustavsvik Camping
Sommarrovägen, S-702 30 Örebro (Örebro Län) T: 019 196 950. E: camping@gustavsvik.se
alanrogers.com/SW2780

Gustavsvik is one of the most modern and most visited camping and leisure parks in Sweden. It is ideally situated almost half way between Oslo and Stockholm or Gothenburg and Stockholm, at the junction of the E18 and E20 roads. This large campsite provides 675 marked and numbered pitches partly shaded by birch and pine trees, 494 with electrical connections and cable TV, 55 with electricity, water and waste water drainage. There are also three partly shaded areas for tents. The leisure park includes adventure golf, a mini zoo, playgrounds, pools and a water slide and a swimming lake, plus a private fishing lake.

Facilities
Three excellent heated toilet blocks including washbasins with dividers, free hot showers, family rooms, facilities for disabled visitors and children. Kitchens with free hot water. Dining area. Washing machine and dryers. Motorcaravan services. Shop. Restaurant and pub. Takeaway. TV room and playroom. Arcade with games room. WiFi. Adventure golf. Football. Swimming pool with waterslide. Swimming lake. Fishing lake. Mini zoo. Bicycle hire. Off site: Pool complex adjacent. Golf.

Open: May - October (full services 10/6-14/8).

Directions
Site is 1 km. south of Örebro town centre. Follow signs from E18/E20 or main road 50/51. GPS: 59.255382, 15.189784

Charges guide
Per unit incl. 2 persons and electricity	SEK 245 - 340

Kolmården
First Camp Kolmården
S-618 34 Kolmården (Östergötlands Län) T: 011 398 250. E: kolmarden@firstcamp.se
alanrogers.com/SW2805

This is a family site, located on Bråviken Bay on the Baltic coast 160 km. south of Stockholm. Open all year, the site is just 4 km. from Kolmården Zoo, one of Sweden's most popular family attractions. There are 300 pitches, of which 180 have electrical connections (10A). Some pitches have sea views and there is also a large beautiful wooded area for tents and 99 cabins of various standards for rent. A good range of amenities includes a 120 m. water slide and a children's playground. Adjacent to the site is a handicraft village and the Sjöstugans restaurant.

Facilities
Three sanitary blocks (two heated) provide showers, washbasins and toilets. Baby rooms and facilities for disabled visitors. Good kitchen. Hot water is free throughout. Laundry rooms. Sauna. Motorcaravan services. Well stocked shop (1/5-15/9). Snack bar. Adjacent licensed restaurant and bar. Takeaway. Playground. Bouncy castle. Water slide. Family entertainment and children's activities (high season). Minigolf. Sea fishing. WiFi. Chalets for rent.

Open: All year.

Directions
From the E4 motorway take Kolmården exit (no. 126) 23 km. north of Norrköping. Follow signs for Kolmården and site is well signed. GPS: 58.65972, 16.40065

Charges guide
Per pitch	SEK 145 - 195
electricity	SEK 45

Linköping
Glyttinge Camping
Berggärdsvägen 6, S-584 37 Linköping (Östergötlands Län) T: 013 174 928. E: glyttinge@nordiccamping.se
alanrogers.com/SW2800

Only five minutes by car from the IKEA shopping mall, Glyttinge is a site with a mix of terrain – some flat, some sloping and some woodland. It has an enthusiastic and friendly management, is maintained to a good standard, and trees and shrubs throughout create a cosy, garden-like atmosphere. There are 116 good size, mostly level pitches of which 112 have electricity (10A). Children are well catered for – the manager has laid out a fenced and very safe play area. The site is also a good stop over place halfway between Kolmården and Astrid Lindgren's World.

Facilities
The main, central toilet block (supplemented by additional smaller facilities at reception) is modern, well constructed and well equipped and maintained. It has showers in cubicles, washbasins and WC suites and hand dryers. Separate facilities for disabled visitors. Baby rooms. Laundry. Kitchen and dining/TV room, fully equipped. Motorcaravan services. Small shop (from 20/6). Playground. WiFi (free). Off site: Riding and golf 3 km. Bicycle hire 4 km. Fishing 5 km. Linköping old town.

Open: All year.

Directions
Exit E4 (Helsingborg-Stockholm) motorway north of Linköping at signs for IKEA and site. Turn right at traffic lights and camp sign and follow signs to site. GPS: 58.42135, 15.561522

Charges guide
Per unit incl. electricity	SEK 210 - 240
Low season discounts for pensioners.	

For latest campsite news, availability and prices visit
alanrogers.com

Höör

Skånes Djurparks Camping

Jularp 145, S-243 93 Höör (Skåne Län) T: 041 355 3270. E: info@grottbyn.se

alanrogers.com/SW2650

This site is probably one of the most unusual we feature. It is next to the Skånes Djurpark, a zoo park with Scandinavian species. The site is located in a sheltered valley and has 120 large, level grassy pitches for caravans and motorcaravans all with 10A electricity and a separate area for about 40 tents. The most unusual feature of the site is the sanitary block – it is underground! The fully air-conditioned building houses a superb and ample complement of facilities. Well placed for the Copenhagen - Malmo bridge or the ferries, this is also a site for discerning campers who want something distinctly different. The site also has a number of underground, caveman style, eight-bed (dormitory type) holiday units which can be rented by families or private groups (when not in use by schools on educational trips to the Stone Age Village). They open onto a circular courtyard with a barbecue and camp fire area and have access to the kitchens and dining room in the sanitary block. There are good walks through the nature park and around the lakes where one can see deer, birds and other wildlife.

Facilities

The underground block includes roomy showers, two fully equipped kitchens, laundry and separate drying room and an enormous dining/TV room. Facilities for disabled campers and baby changing. Cooking facilities. Laundry. There is a new building with a family room and baby bath. Motorcaravan services. Small shop and café (15/6-15/8). Small swimming pool (15/6-15/8) and playground for children. Off site: Fishing 1.8 km. Bicycle hire 5 km. Riding and golf 8 km.

Open: All year (full services 15/6-10/8).

Directions

Turn off no. 23 road 2 km. north of Höör (at roundabout) and follow signs for Skånes Djurpark. Campsite entrance is off the Djurpark car park. GPS: 55.96033, 13.53808

Charges guide

Per unit	SEK 180 - 200
electricity	SEK 50

Röstånga

Röstånga Camping & Bad

Blinkarpsvägen 3, S-268 68 Röstånga (Skåne Län) T: 043 591 064. E: nystrand@msn.com

alanrogers.com/SW2630

Beside the Söderåsen National Park, this scenic campsite has its own fishing lake and many activities for the whole family. There are 180 large, level, grassy pitches with electricity (10A) and a quiet area for tents with a view over the fishing lake. The tent area has its own service building and several barbecue places. A large holiday home and 21 pleasant cabins are available to rent all year round. A pool complex adjacent to the site provides a 50 m. swimming pool, three children's pools and a water slide, all heated during peak season. The friendly staff will be happy to help you to plan excursions in the area.

Facilities

Four good, heated sanitary blocks with free hot water and facilities for babies and disabled visitors. Motorcaravan services. Laundry with washing machines and dryers. Kitchen with cooking rings, oven and microwave. Small shop at reception. Bar, restaurant and takeaway. Minigolf. Tennis. Fitness trail. Fishing. Canoe hire. Children's club. WiFi (free). Off site: Swimming pool complex adjacent to site (free for campers as is a visit to the zoo). Golf 11 km. Motor racing track at Ring Knutstorp 8 km.

Open: 17 April - 20 September.

Directions

From Malmö: drive towards Lund and follow road no. 108 to Röstånga. From Stockholm: turn off at Östra Ljungby and take road no. 13 to Röstånga. In Röstånga drive through the village on road no. 108 and follow the signs. GPS: 55.996583, 13.28005

Charges guide

Per unit incl. 2 persons and electricity	€ 25.00 - € 33.00

No credit cards.

Torekov

First Camp Båstad-Torekov

Flymossa Vagen 5, S-260 93 Torekov (Skåne Län) T: 043 136 4525. E: torekov@firstcamp.se

alanrogers.com/SW2640

Part of the First Camp chain, this site is 500 m. from the fishing village of Torekov, 14 km. west of the home of the Swedish tennis WCT Open at Båstad, on the stretch of coastline between Malmö and Göteborg. Useful en route from the most southerly ports, it is a well situated site and worthy of a longer stay for relaxation. It has 535 large pitches (390 for touring units), all numbered and marked, mainly in attractive natural woodland, with some on more open ground close to the shore. Of these, 300 have electricity (10A) and cable TV, 77 also having water and drainage. The modern reception complex is also home to a good shop, a snack bar, restaurant, and pizzeria. The spacious site covers quite a large area and there is a cycle track along the shore to the bathing beach.

Facilities

Three good sanitary blocks with facilities for babies and disabled visitors. Laundry. Cooking facilities. Motorcaravan services. Bar. Restaurant, pizzeria and snack bar with takeaway (21/6-4/8). Shop and kiosk (1/6-25/8). Minigolf. Play areas and adventure park for children. Boules and outdoor chess. Bicycle and go-kart hire. TV room. Beach. Fishing. WiFi over site (charged). Off site: Games, music and entertainment in high season. Tennis close by. Golf 1 km. Riding 3 km.

Open: All year (full amenities 20 June - 5 August).

Directions

From E6 Malmö-Göteborg road take Torekov/Båstad exit and follow signs for 20 km. towards Torekov. Site is signed 1 km. before village on right. GPS: 56.43097, 12.64055

Charges guide

Per unit incl. 4 persons and electricity	SEK 190 - 305

Huddinge

Stockholm SweCamp Flottsbro

Häggstavägen, S-141 32 Huddinge (Stockholms Län) T: 085 353 2700. E: info@flottsbro.se

alanrogers.com/SW2840

Stockholm SweCamp Flottsbro is located at the south entrance to Stockholm, just 20 minutes from Stockholm city centre. The site offers 82 large numbered pitches for caravans and motorcaravans and a separate area for tents. Pitches are arranged on level terraces, 54 with electricity (10A) and TV connections. The site itself slopes down to Lake Alby and there is a good restaurant at the bottom. Flottsbro is within a large recreation area with hiking trails, beaches and other activities during the summer, and downhill and cross-country skiing during the winter. The area is also good for walking and cycling.

Facilities

Two modern sanitary facilities include free showers, a suite for disabled visitors, baby facilities and a family bathroom. Excellent campers' kitchen (inside and outside) with electric cookers, microwaves and sinks with hot water. Washing machine, dryer (charged) and sink. Shop (high season). Restaurant. Minigolf. Frisbee. Jogging tracks. Canoe hire. Playground. Beach volley and sauna raft. Off site: Large supermarket and rail station are ten minutes by car from the site. Golf and riding 15 km. Stockholm 15 km.

Open: All year (full services 15/6-15/8).

Directions

Turn off the E4-E20 at Huddinge onto road no. 259. After 2 km. turn right and follow signs to Flottsbro. GPS: 59.23043, 17.88818

Charges guide

Per unit incl. 2 persons and electricity	SEK 190 - 240

For latest campsite news, availability and prices visit

alanrogers.com

Skärholmen

Bredäng Camping Stockholm

Stora Sällskapets väg 60, S-127 31 Skärholmen (Stockholms Län) T: **089 770 71**.

E: **bredangcamping@telia.com** alanrogers.com/SW2842

Bredäng is a busy city site, with easy access to Stockholm city centre. Large and fairly level, with very little shade, there are 380 pitches, including 115 with hardstanding and 204 with electricity (10A), and a separate area for tents. Reception is open from 08.00-22.00 in the main season (12/6-20/8), reduced hours in low season, and English is spoken. A Stockholm card is available, or a three-day public transport card from the Tube station. Stockholm has many events and activities, you can take a circular tour on a free sightseeing bus, various boat and bus tours, or view the city from the Kaknäs Tower (155 m). The nearest Tube station is five minutes walk; trains run about every ten minutes between 05.00 and 02.00, and the journey takes about twenty minutes. The local shopping centre is five minutes away and a two minute walk through the woods brings you to a very attractive lake and beach.

Facilities

Four heated sanitary units of a high standard provide British style WCs, controllable hot showers, with some washbasins in cubicles. One has a baby room, a unit for disabled visitors and a first aid room. Cooking facilities are in three units around the site. Laundry facilities. Motorcaravan services and car wash. Well stocked shop, bar, takeaway and fully licensed restaurant (all 1/5-31/8). Sauna. Playground. WiFi throughout (free). Off site: Fishing 400 m. Riding 1.5 km. Bicycle hire 10 km. Golf 20 km.

Open: 13 April - 11 October.

Directions

Site is 10 km. southwest of city centre. Turn off E4/E20 at Bredängs signpost and follow clearly marked site signs. GPS: 59.29560, 17.92315

Charges guide

Per unit incl. electricity	SEK 285 - 350
1 person tent	SEK 135 - 155

Discounts for pensioners in low season.

Årjäng

Årjäng Camping & Stugor

Sommarvik, S-672 91 Årjäng (Värmlands Län) T: **057 312 060**. E: **booking@sommarvik.se**
alanrogers.com/SW2750

This is a good site in beautiful surroundings with some of the 350 pitches overlooking the clear waters of the Västra Silen lake in peaceful countryside. The numbered pitches are arranged in terraces on a hillside interspersed with pines and birches, with half set aside for static units and 20 for tents. The remaining touring pitches all have 10A electricity hook-ups and 40 also include water and drainage. The site also has 60 chalets for rent. Close to reception, a heated swimming pool with a paddling pool, terraces and sun loungers has fine views down to the lake. The lake with its sandy beach is popular and safe for children. This site makes an ideal base to explore this scenic region in summer or winter when skiing is an additional attraction.

Facilities

Five sanitary units provide shower cubicles (hot showers on payment), washbasins, toilets, family bathrooms, facilities for disabled visitors and baby changing. All are clean and acceptable but may be stretched in high season. Campers kitchens. Laundry facilities. Motorcaravan services. All activities and amenities are open 1/6-31/8. Small shop (1/5-1/10). Bar, restaurant and takeaway (15/6-20/8). Good play areas. Bicycle hire. Internet access. 'Quick stop' pitches for overnight stays. Youth hostel and conference centre. Off site: Indoor pool complex 3 km. Riding 5 km. Golf 9 km.

Open: All year (full services 19/6-22/8).

Directions

Site is well signed on road 172, 3 km. south of its junction with the E18 close to Årjäng. GPS: 59.36765, 12.13962

Charges guide

Per pitch incl. electricity	SEK 180 - 360

Kil

Frykenbadens Camping

Stubberud, S-665 91 Kil (Värmlands Län) T: 055 440 940. E: info@frykenbaden.se

alanrogers.com/SW2760

Frykenbadens Camping is in a quiet wooded area on the southern shore of Lake Fryken, taking 200 units on grassy meadows surrounded by trees. One area nearer the lake is gently sloping, the other is flat with numbered pitches arranged in rows, all with electricity (10A). Reception, a good shop, restaurant and takeaway are located in a traditional Swedish house surrounded by lawns sloping down to the shore, with minigolf, a play barn and playground, with pet area also close by. Frykenbadens Camping is a quiet, relaxing place to stay, away from the busier and more famous lakes.

Facilities

The main sanitary block is of good quality and heated in cool weather with showers on payment, open washbasins, a laundry room and room for families or disabled visitors. A further small block has good facilities. Well equipped camper's kitchen. Shop. Snack bar, restaurant and takeaway. Pub. Minigolf. Play barn and playground. Lake swimming. Canoes, rowing boats and bicycles for hire. WiFi (charged). Off site: Golf 1 km. Go-karts, riding, jogging track 4 km.

Open: All year (full services 17/6-13/8).

Directions

Site is signed from the no. 61 Karlstad-Arvika road, then 4 km. towards lake following signs. GPS: 59.54625, 13.34132

Charges guide

Per unit incl electricity	SEK 240 - 290

Stöllet

Alevi Camping

Fastnäs 53, S-680 51 Stöllet (Värmlands Län) T: 056 386 050. E: info@alevi-camping.com

alanrogers.com/SW2755

Alevi Camping is a small, welcoming site with 60 large pitches and five cabins for hire. Open all year, the site is situated on the bank of the River Klarälven, the longest river in Sweden. With its own beach this is a perfect place for swimming, fishing, canoeing and rafting. The site, which opened in 2006, offers large level pitches all with electricity (4/10A). The county of Värmland is famous for its lakes, rivers and forests. There, if you are lucky, you can see the 'big four' predators of Scandinavia – wolf, bear, wolverine and lynx.

Facilities

One new sanitary block with free hot water. Unisex toilets and showers (charged). Washbasins, both vanity style and in cubicles. Facilities for babies and disabled visitors. Family room. Good campers' kitchen with free hot water. Motorcaravan services. Reception with small shop, restaurant, takeaway. Internet at reception. TV room. Canoes and bicycle hire. River beach. Barbecue area. Sauna. Playground. Fishing. Skiing in winter. Off site: Supermarket 10 minutes by car. Husky rides and ice fishing in winter.

Open: All year.

Directions

Site is between Ekshärad and Stöllet on road no. 62, 16 km. south of Stöllet. Follow signs. GPS: 60.285267, 13.406733

Charges guide

Per unit incl. 5 persons and electricity	SEK 190 - 235

Umeå

First Camp Umeå

Nydalasjön 2, S-906 54 Umeå (Västerbotens Län) T: 090 702 600. E: umea@firstcamp.se

alanrogers.com/SW2860

An ideal stop over for those travelling the E4 coastal route, or a good base from which to explore the area, this campsite is 6 km. from the centre of this university city. It is almost adjacent to the Nydalsjön lake, which is ideal for fishing, windsurfing and bathing. There are 450 grassy pitches arranged in bays of 10-20 units, 320 with electricity (10/16A), and some are fully serviced. Outside the site, adjacent to the lake, are football pitches, an open-air swimming pool, minigolf, mini-car driving school, beach volleyball and a mini farm. There are cycle and footpaths around the area. Umeå is also a port for ferries to Vasa in Finland (4 hours).

Facilities

The new large, heated, central sanitary unit includes controllable hot showers with communal changing areas. Facilities may be stretched in high season. Kitchen. Large dining room. TV. Laundry facilities. Shop (1/6-12/8). Fully licensed restaurant, bar and takeaway (14/6-12/8). WiFi throughout (charged). Walk-on chess. Playgrounds. Bicycle hire. Rowing boat hire. Fishing in the lake. Canoes and pedal cars for hire. Adventure golf. Off site: Riding adjacent. Golf 18 km.

Open: All year (full services 25/5-12/8).

Directions

A camping sign on the E4 at a set of traffic lights 5 km. north of the town directs you to the site. Signs also indicate Holmsund and Vassa. GPS: 63.843333, 20.340556

Charges guide

Per pitch	SEK 130 - 240
incl. electricity	SEK 170 - 270

For latest campsite news, availability and prices visit

alanrogers.com

Kramfors

Flogsta Camping

S-872 80 Kramfors (Västernorrlands Län) T: **061 210 005**. E: **flogstacamping@telia.com**

alanrogers.com/SW2855

Kramfors lies just to the west of the E4, and travellers may well pass by over the new Höga Kusten bridge (one of the largest in Europe), and miss this friendly little site. This area of Ådalen and the High Coast, reaches as far as Örnsköldsvik. The attractive garden-like campsite has 50 pitches, 21 with electrical connections (10A), which are arranged on level grassy terraces, separated by shrubs and trees into bays of 2-4 units. All overlook the heated outdoor public swimming pool complex and attractive minigolf course. The non-electric pitches are on an open terrace nearer reception.

Facilities

Sanitary facilities comprise nine bathrooms, each with British style WC, basin with hand dryer, shower. Laundry facilities. More WCs and showers are in the reception building with a free sauna. New toilet block with a sauna and outside hot tub. Separate building housing a kitchen, with hot plates, fridge/freezer and TV/dining room (all free). The reception building has a small shop and snack bar. Playground. Snow mobile hire. Off site: Fishing 10 km. Golf and riding 15 km.

Open: 1 May - 30 September.

Directions

Signed from road 90 in the centre of Kramfors, the site is to the west in a rural location beyond a housing estate and by the Flogsta Bad, a municipal swimming pool complex.
GPS: 62.92562, 17.75642

Charges guide

Per pitch	SEK 160 - 200
electricity	SEK 40

Ramvik

Snibbens Camping & Stugby och Vandrarhem

Hälledal 527, S-870 16 Ramvik (Västernorrlands Län) T: **061 240 505**. E: **info@snibbenscamping.com**

alanrogers.com/SW2853

Probably, you will stop here for one night as you travel the E4 coast road and stay a week. It is a truly beautiful location in the area of 'The High Coast' listed as a World Heritage Site. During high season Snibbens is a busy, popular site but remains quiet and peaceful. Besides 30 bungalows for rent, there are 50 touring places, each with 16A electricity, set amongst delightful scenery on the shores of Lake Mörtsjön. The welcoming owners take you to your adequately sized grass pitch set amongst spacious trees. All facilities are to the highest of standards and spotlessly clean. To one end of the campsite there is a beach where the waters are suitable for swimming with a zoned area for young children.

Facilities

Excellent, spotlessly clean facilities include controllable showers and partitioned washbasins. Baby changing facilities. Two kitchens with hot plates, microwaves and a mini oven. Laundry room. Small shop (15/6-20/8). Rowing boats and pedaloes for hire. Minigolf. Free fishing. Youth hostel. Off site: Small supermarket 800 m.

Open: 30 April - 15 September.

Directions

Travelling north on the E4 and immediately prior to Höga Kusten bridge (one of the largest in Europe) take road 90 signed Kramfors. Site is directly off road 90 on left in 3 km, well signed.
GPS: 62.79896, 17.86965

Charges guide

Per pitch	SEK 180
incl. electricity	SEK 205

Arboga

Herrfallet Camping

S-732 92 Arboga (Västmanlands Län) T: **058 940 110**. E: **reception@herrfallet.se**

alanrogers.com/SW2825

Open all year, Herrfallet Camping is situated on a peninsula and designated nature reserve, on Lake Hjälmaren, one of Sweden's large lakes. There is a 1 km. long sandy beach on the site and the atmosphere is friendly and 'green'. All the 100 touring pitches have electricity hook-ups (10/16A) and the area is neatly laid out overlooking the lake where you can hire boats, canoes, pedal boats and go fishing. Fishing is free. You can explore the beautiful and peaceful surroundings by bicycle, which you can hire at reception. There are 45 large cottages of an excellent standard and five a bit smaller (for two people).

Facilities

Three sanitary blocks, one basic for the summer season, two with central heating. Open washbasins, showers (charged). Provision for disabled visitors. Fully equipped kitchen and laundry facilities. Baby room. Motorcaravan services. Sauna cottage with shower and relaxing room. Lapland hut (Sami style) for barbecue parties. Well stocked shop (high season). Restaurant and bar. Takeaway. Pedal car, pedal boat, bicycle, canoe and boat hire. Fishing (free). Minigolf. Football field. Fitness trail. Playground. Internet and WiFi. Off site: Arboga (old town with medieval festival in July) 15 km. Golf 15 km.

Open: All year (full services 27/5-28/8).

Directions

Follow signs from the E20/E18. Turn off at Sätra exit towards Arboga and cross the river. Follow signs towards Herrfallet/Västermo. 15 km. from Arboga.
GPS: 59.2814, 15.9051

Charges guide

Per unit incl. electricity (10A)	SEK 260

FREE Alan Rogers Travel Card
Extra benefits and savings - see page 14

Hallstahammar

Skantzö Bad & Camping

Sörkvarnsvägen, S-737 27 Hallstahammar (Västmanlands Län) T: 022 024 305.
E: skantzo@hallstahammar.se alanrogers.com/SW2820

A very comfortable and pleasant municipal site just off the main E18 motorway from Oslo to Stockholm, this has 200 large marked and numbered pitches, 150 of these with electricity (10A). The terrain is flat and grassy, there is good shade in parts and the site is well fenced. There are 23 alpine-style cabins for rent with window boxes of colourful flowers. Reception is very friendly. There is direct access to the towpath of the Strömsholms Kanal and nearby is the Kanal Museum. The site provides hire and transportation of canoes for longer canal tours.

Facilities

Three sanitary blocks are well maintained and equipped to a high standard, including free hot showers (in cubicles with washbasin), facilities for disabled visitors and baby changing. Another unit to the same high standards has been added and both are heated. Campers' kitchen. Good laundry facilities. Motorcaravan services. Barbecue grill area. Cafeteria and shop (27/5-31/8). Swimming pool and waterslide (21/5-22/8). Minigolf. Tennis. Playground. Bicycle hire. Fishing. Canoe hire. WiFi. Off site: Golf 6 km.

Open: 30 April - 26 September.

Directions

Turn off E18 at Hallstahammar and follow road no. 252 to west of town centre and signs to campsite. GPS: 59.61078, 16.21542

Charges guide

Per unit incl. electricity	SEK 200 - 230

Dals Långed

Laxsjöns Camping och Friluftsgård

S-660 10 Dals Långed (Västra Götalands Län) T: 053 130 010. E: office@laxsjon.se
alanrogers.com/SW2740

In the beautiful Dalsland region, Laxsjöns is an all-year-round site, catering for winter sports enthusiasts as well as summer tourists and groups. On the shores of the lake, the site is in two main areas – one flat, near the entrance, with hardstandings, and the other on attractive, sloping, grassy areas adjoining. In total there are 180 places for caravans and motorcaravans, 150 with electricity (10/16A), plus more for tents. Leisure facilities on the site include minigolf, trampolines and a playground. A restaurant is at the top of the site with a good range of dishes in high season.

Facilities

The main toilet block has hot showers (on payment), washbasins in cubicles, WCs and a hairdressing cubicle. With a further small block at the top of the site, the provision should be adequate. Facilities for disabled visitors. Laundry with drying rooms for bad weather. Cooking rooms for campers. Restaurant (high season). Shop. Minigolf. Playground. Lake for swimming, fishing and boating. Off site: Dalslands Aktiviteter, Dalslands kanal.

Open: All year (full services 22/6-15/8).

Directions

From Åmål take road no. 164 towards Bengtfors, then 172 towards Billingsfors and Dals Långed. Site is signed 5 km. south of Billingsfors, 1 km. down a good road. From the south, (Uddevalla) take road 172. GPS: 58.95296, 12.25242

Charges guide

Per pitch incl. electricity	SEK 200 - 280

Ed

Gröne Backe Camping & Stugor

Södra Moränvägen, S-668 32 Ed (Västra Götalands Län) T: 053 410 144. E: gronebackecamping@telia.com
alanrogers.com/SW2715

In the heart of the beautiful Dalsland region, this pleasant, well shaded (mostly pine) site is open all year. It is well laid out, mostly overlooking the Lilla Le lake, and there is easy access from road no. 164. There are 180 pitches for caravans and motorcaravans, most with electricity (10/16A) and special areas for tents. Also on the site are 23 cabins for rent and 40 seasonal pitches. A small shop, café and a new restaurant are at the reception building. Canoes, rowing boats and bicycles may be hired. This pleasant, friendly family site is easy to find and the location makes it ideal for a longer stay.

Facilities

Three heated toilet blocks, two in the centre, one at reception, provide washbasins both vanity type and in cubicles. Showers (on payment). Baby rooms. Facilities for disabled visitors. Laundry. Cooking facilities. Motorcaravan services. Small shop. Café and restaurant. Internet and WiFi. Playground. Minigolf. Sports field. Canoes, rowing boats, bicycles and pedal cars for hire. Beach. Sauna raft on the lake. Off site: Village services nearby. Moose ranch. Canodal (large canoe centre). Tresticklan National Park. Dalslands Aktiviteter.

Open: All year.

Directions

Site is on road no. 164 at Ed, and is well signed. GPS: 58.899417, 11.934867

Charges guide

Per unit incl. 2 persons and electricity	€ 30.60

For latest campsite news, availability and prices visit

alanrogers.com

Göteborg

Lisebergsbyn Karralund

Olbersgatan 9, S-416 55 Göteborg (Västra Götalands Län) T: 031 840 200. E: lisebergsbyn@liseberg.se

alanrogers.com/SW2705

Well positioned for visiting the city and theme park using the excellent tram system, this busy, well maintained site has 164 marked pitches. All have electricity (10A) and cable TV and there are several areas for tents. Pitches vary in size, 42 are hardstandings, some are fairly compact with no dividing hedges, and consequently units can be rather close together. Additionally there are cabins for rent, bed and breakfast facilities and a youth hostel. It can be a very busy site in the main season, which in this case means June, July and August. An advance telephone call to check for space is advisable.

Facilities

One heated sanitary building is well maintained and cleaned, and has all the usual facilities, with controllable hot showers, a good suite for small children, kitchens with cooking facilities, and a complete unit for disabled visitors. Laundry facilities near reception. Private cabins available. Motorcaravan services. Kiosk. Breakfast buffet available and fresh bread on sale. Small playground. TV room. Free WiFi over site. Off site: 30 short stay pitches for motorcaravans nearby. Riding 200 m. Supermarket 300 m. Fishing 1.5 km. Golf 3 km. Beach 8 km.

Open: All year (full services 6/5-18/8).

Directions

Site is 4 km. east of city centre. Follow signs to Lisebergsbyn and campsite symbol from E20, E6 or Rv 40. GPS: 57.70488, 12.02983

Charges guide

Per pitch	SEK 310 - 445
tent and car	SEK 195 - 345

Only pitches with electricity available in high season.

Lidköping

Lidköping KronoCamping

Läckögatan, S-531 54 Lidköping (Västra Götalands Län) T: 051 026 804. E: info@kronocamping.com

alanrogers.com/SW2710

This high quality, attractive site provides 413 pitches on flat, well kept grass. It is surrounded by some mature trees, with the lake shore as one boundary and a number of tall pines providing shade and shelter. There are 412 pitches with electricity (10A) and TV connections and 90 with water and drainage also, together with 22 cabins for rent. The site takes a fair number of seasonal units. There is a small shop (a shopping centre is very close) and a fully licensed restaurant with conservatory seating area in the reception complex. The lake is available for watersports, boating and fishing with swimming from the sandy beach or there is a swimming pool complex (free for campers) adjacent to the site.

Facilities

Excellent, modern, refurbished sanitary facilities are in two blocks with underfloor heating. Hot water is free. Make up and hairdressing areas, baby room and facilities for disabled visitors. Private cabins. Good kitchen. Motorcaravan services. Small shop. Restaurant. Minigolf. Playgrounds. TV room. Games and amusements room. Bicycle hire. Play field. Lake swimming, fishing and watersports. Sauna and jacuzzi. Internet and WiFi. Off site: Swimming pool adjacent. Riding 4 km. Golf 6 km. The castle of Läckö, Kinnekulle, Spiken's fishing harbour.

Open: All year (full services 1/6-22/8).

Directions

From Lidköping town junctions follow signs towards Läckö then pick up camping signs and continue to site. GPS: 58.513062, 13.13853

Charges guide

Per unit incl. electricity	SEK 250 - 370

Mariestad

Ekuddens Camping

Strandbadet, S-542 94 Mariestad (Västra Götalands Län) T: 050 110 637. E: info@nordiccamping.se

alanrogers.com/SW2730

Ekuddens occupies a long stretch of the eastern shore of Lake Vänern to the northwest of the town, in a mixed woodland setting, and next door to the municipal complex of heated outdoor pools and sauna. The lake, of course, is also available for swimming and boating and there are bicycles, tandems and canoes for hire at the tourist information office in town. The spacious site can take 300 units, not numbered, and there are 230 electrical hook-ups (10A). Most pitches are under the trees but some at the far end of the site are on more open ground with good views over the lake.

Facilities

Three sanitary blocks, all clean and well maintained. Free hot showers in cubicles. Facilities for disabled visitors with good access ramps. Baby rooms. Excellent kitchen with cooking and dining facilities. Laundry. Shop. Licensed bar. Takeaway (high season). Playground. Minigolf. TV room. Lake swimming, boating and fishing. Entertainment in high season. WiFi around the reception. Off site: Swimming pools adjacent. Bicycle 3 km. Golf 4 km. Riding 7 km.

Open: 1 May - 15 September (full services 15/6-15/8).

Directions

Site is 2.5 km. northwest of the town and well signed at junctions on the ring road. From the E20 motorway take exit for Mariestad S. and follow signs towards Marieholm. GPS: 58.715567, 13.794901

Charges guide

Per unit incl. 2 persons and electricity	SEK 286

FREE Alan Rogers Travel Card

Extra benefits and savings - see page 14

Strömstad

Daftö Resort

S-452 97 Strömstad (Västra Götalands Län) T: 052 626 040. E: info@dafto.se

alanrogers.com/SW2735

This extremely high quality, family campsite, with a strong pirate theme, is beautifully situated on the west coast, 5 km. south of Strömstad. A very large site, terraced in parts, has both shady and open areas. In total there are 650 pitches with 310 for touring, all with electrical hook-ups (10A, CEE plugs). In addition, there are 130 modern, very well equipped cabins of various sizes and styles. Daftö Resort, with its DaftöLand adventure park (concessions for campers), has activities for all including boating, beach volleyball, walks and yoga, and all manner of theme-based activities for children including theatre, competitions and treasure hunting. Bicycles and boats can be rented on site and boat trips and seal safaris are arranged.

Facilities

Five toilet blocks of excellent quality with washbasin cubicles, showers, family rooms, a children's bathroom, sun beds, saunas and make up rooms. Wellness centre and hairdressers. Units for disabled visitors. Kitchen with cookers, microwaves, sinks and industrial grade dishwashers. Extensive laundry facilities. Motorcaravan services. Large supermarket. Fully licensed restaurant. Heated pool (peak season). Games and TV rooms. Themed minigolf. Bicycle hire. Children's club. Boat hire, excursions and seal safaris. Internet and WiFi. Conference room. B&B. DaftöLand adventure park. Off site: Ferry to Norway (Sandefjord) from Strömstad.

Open: All year excl. 23 December - 6 January.

Directions

Daftö is 5 km. south of Strömstad on road 176. It is signed. GPS: 58.904267, 11.200117

Charges guide

Per unit incl. electricity and water   SEK 200 - 470

Tidaholm

Hökensås Camping & Holiday Village

Blåhult, S-522 91 Tidaholm (Västra Götalands Län) T: 050 223 053. E: info@hokensas.nu

alanrogers.com/SW2720

Hökensås is located just west of Lake Vättern and south of Tidaholm, in a beautiful nature reserve of wild, unspoiled scenery. This pleasant campsite is part of a holiday complex that includes wooden cabins for rent. It is relaxed and informal, with over 200 pitches either under trees or on a more open area at the far end, divided into rows by wooden rails. These are numbered and electricity (10A) is available on 135. Tents can go on the large grassy open areas by reception. This site is a find for all kinds of people who enjoy outdoor activities. The park is based on a 100 km. ridge, a glacier area with many impressive boulders and ice age debris but now thickly forested with majestic pines and silver birches, with a small, brilliant lake at every corner.

Facilities

The original sanitary block near reception is supplemented by one in the wooded area, both refurbished. Hot showers in cubicles with communal changing area are free. Separate saunas for each sex and facilities for disabled visitors and babies. Campers' kitchen at each block with cooking and laundry facilities. Small, but well stocked shop. Very good angling shop. Fully licensed restaurant with takeaway. Playground. Minigolf. Lake swimming. Fishing. Boules. Off site: The town of Tidaholm and Lake Hornborga. Fishing 2 km. Riding 10 km.

Open: All year (full services 20/6-11/8).

Directions

Approach site from no. 195 road at Brandstorp, 40 km. north of Jönköping, turn west at petrol station and camp sign signed Hökensås. Site is 9 km. up this road. GPS: 58.0982, 14.0746

Charges guide

Per unit incl. 2 persons and electricity   € 24.70

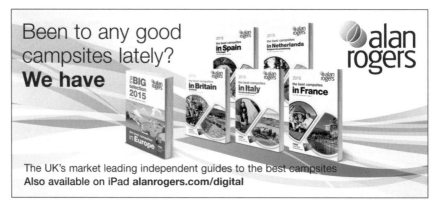

For latest campsite news, availability and prices visit

alanrogers.com

Uddevalla

Hafsten SweCamp Resort

Hafsten 120, S-451 96 Uddevalla (Västra Götalands Län) T: 052 264 4117. E: info@hafsten.se

alanrogers.com/SW2725

This privately owned site on the west coast is situated on a peninsula overlooking the magnificent coastline of Bohuslän. Open all year, it is a lovely, peaceful, terraced site with a beautiful, shallow and child friendly sandy beach and many nature trails in the vicinity. There are 220 touring pitches, all with electricity (10A), 115 of them with water and drainage. In all, there are 370 pitches including a tent area and 62 cabins of a high standard. There are plenty of activities available ranging from horse riding at the stables on the campsite's own farm to an 86 m. long water chute. Organised live music evenings with visiting performers are arranged during the summer. Almost any activity can be arranged on the site or elsewhere by the friendly owners if they are given advance notice. Amenities include two clean and well maintained service buildings, a pub, a fully licensed restaurant with wine from their own French vineyard, a well stocked shop and a takeaway. Reception is open and welcoming with natural light used to great effect, and where the new fitness and wellness facilities can be found. Modern gym and sauna equipment are installed to a high standard. The active area of the site is well away from the main campsite allowing other guests to experience a quiet, relaxed holiday.

Facilities

Two heated sanitary buildings provide the usual facilities with showers on payment. Kitchen with good cooking facilities and sinks. Dining room. Laundry facilities. Units for disabled visitors. Motorcaravan services. Shop. Restaurant, takeaway and pub. Live music evenings. TV room. Outdoor swimming pool. Relaxation centre with sauna and jacuzzi (charged). Well equipped gym. Water slide (charged). WiFi (charged). Riding. Minigolf. Tennis. Boules. Playground. Clay pigeon shooting. Boat hire (canoe, rowing, motor, pedalo). Outside gym/fitness area. WiFi over site (charged). Off site: Shopping centre and golf 13 km. Havets hus (marine museum) 30 km. Nordens Ark (animal park) 40 km.

Open: All year.

Directions

From E6, north of Uddevalla, at Torpmotet exit take 161 road towards Lysekil. At Rotviksbro roundabout take 160 road towards Orust. Exit to site is located 2 km. further on left where four flags fly. Follow signs for 4 km. along one-way road for motorcaravans and caravans. GPS: 58.31478, 11.72344

Charges guide

Per pitch incl. electricity	SEK 230 - 1395
extra person	SEK 100

Camping Cheques accepted.

A small, wealthy country, best known for its outstanding mountainous scenery, fine cheeses, delicious chocolates, Swiss bank accounts and enviable lifestyles. Centrally situated in Europe, it shares its borders with four countries: France, Austria, Germany and Italy, each one having its own cultural influence on Switzerland.

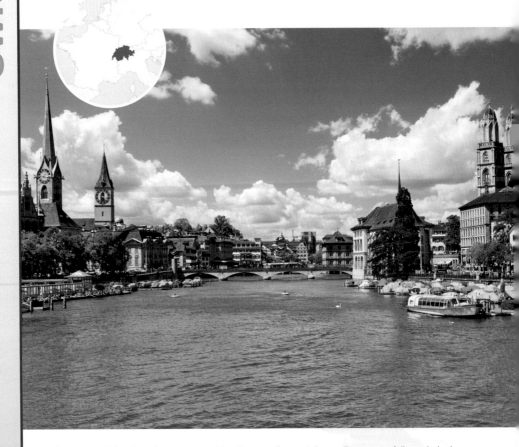

Switzerland boasts a picture postcard landscape of mountains, valleys, waterfalls and glaciers. The Bernese Oberland with its snowy peaks and rolling hills is the most popular area – Gstaad is a favourite haunt of wealthy skiers, while the mild climate and breezy conditions around Lake Thun are perfect for watersports and other outdoor activities. German-speaking Zurich is a multicultural metropolis with over 50 museums, sophisticated shops and colourful festivals, set against a breathtaking backdrop of lakes and mountains. The southeast of Switzerland has densely forested mountain slopes and the wealthy and glamorous resort of Saint Moritz. Geneva, Montreux and Lausanne on the northern shores of Lake Geneva make up the bulk of French Switzerland, with vineyards that border the lakes and medieval towns. The southernmost canton, Ticino, is home to the Italian-speaking Swiss, with the Mediterranean style lakeside resorts of Lugano and Locarno.

CAPITAL: Bern

Tourist Office
Switzerland Tourism
Switzerland Travel Centre,
30 Bedford Street, London WC2E 9ED
Tel: 020 7420 4900 Fax: 020 7845 7699
Email: info.uk@switzerland.com
Internet: www.myswitzerland.com

Population
8 million

Climate
Mild and refreshing in the northern plateau.
South of the Alps it is warmer, influenced by the
Mediterranean. The Valais is noted for its dryness.

Language
German in central and eastern areas,
French in the west and Italian in the south.
Raeto-Romansch is spoken in the southeast.
English is spoken by many.

Telephone
The country code is 00 41.

Money
Currency: Swiss Franc
Banks: Mon-Fri 08.30-16.30. Some close
for lunch.

Shops
Mon-Fri 08.00-12.00 and 14.00-18.00.
Sat 08.00-16.00. Often closed Monday mornings.

Public Holidays
New Year; Good Fri; Easter Mon; Ascension;
Whit Mon; National Day 1 Aug; Christmas 25 Dec.
Other holidays are observed in individual Cantons.

Motoring
The road network is comprehensive and well
planned. An annual road tax is levied on all cars
using Swiss motorways and the 'Vignette'
windscreen sticker must be purchased at the
border (credit cards not accepted), or in advance
from the Swiss National Tourist Office, plus
a separate one for a towed caravan or trailer.

see campsite map 4

Basel

Camping Waldhort

Heideweg 16, CH-4153 Reinach bei Basel (Basel-Land) T: 061 711 6429. E: info@camping-waldhort.ch

alanrogers.com/CH9000

This is a satisfactory site for night halts or for visits to Basel. Although there are almost twice as many static caravan pitches as spaces for touring units, this site, on the edge of a residential district, is within easy reach of the city by tram. It is flat, with 75 level pitches for touring with access from the tarmac road. The grass pitches may become muddy in very wet weather but there are gravel hardstandings for motorcaravans. All pitches have 10A electricity and young trees give some shade. Owned and run by the Camping and Caravanning Club of Basel, there is usually space available. An extra, separate camping area has been added behind the tennis club which has pleasant pitches and its own modern sanitary facilities.

Facilities

The three good quality, fully equipped sanitary blocks include facilities for babies and disabled visitors. Washing machine and dryer. Kitchen with gas rings. Freezer for ice packs. Motorcaravan services. Small shop with terrace for drinks, snacks and takeaway (all season). Play area with two small pools. No charcoal barbecues. WiFi (free). Outdoor swimming and paddling pool (1/5-30/9). Off site: Tennis courts next to site. A day ticket for travel on trams and buses throughout the Basel area can be purchased for Sfr 9 (available from reception).

Open: 1 March - 27 October.

Directions

Take Basel-Delémont motorway spur, exit for Reinach-Nord and follow site signs. Do not use the Reinach-Sud exit. GPS: 47.49973, 7.60278

Charges guide

Per unit incl. 2 persons and electricity	CHF 35.50 - 44.50
extra person	CHF 10.00
child (6-14 yrs)	CHF 6.00
dog	CHF 3.00

Bönigen

TCS Camping Bönigen-Interlaken

Campingstrasse 14, CH-3806 Bönigen (Bern) T: 033 822 1143. E: camping.boenigen@tcs.ch

alanrogers.com/CH9450

This small, quiet site, bordered on two sides by Lake Brienz, is only 1.5 kilometres from the centre of Interlaken and the autoroute exit. It is therefore a very convenient site, not only to spend time on and enjoy the lake and mountain views, but also as an ideal base to tour this picturesque region, dominated by the Eiger and Jungfrau mountains. Almost all the 120 pitches are available for touring units. On firm, level grassy ground and under tall trees, all have 6A electricity. With magnificent views over the lake, gates give direct access to a footpath and to the lake shores. Interlaken is the tourist centre of the Bernese Oberland.

Facilities

A well maintained, modern sanitary block has free showers and some washbasins in cabins. Facilities for disabled visitors. Baby room. Washing machine and dryer. Motorcaravan services. Small shop sells gas and provides essentials. Small, redesigned restaurant, snack bar and guest lounge with TV. Small solar heated swimming pool, and paddling pool. Play area. Bicycle hire. WiFi throughout. Off site: Golf 2 km. Riding 3 km. Boat trips. Cable cars. Paragliding and skydiving. Free access to adjacent municipal pool complex.

Open: 4 April - 5 October.

Directions

Site is beside the Brienzersee in the eastern suburbs of Interlaken. From A8 take exit 26 (Interlaken Ost) and follow signs for Bönigen and then site signs. Approaching from Lucerne, take exit 27 (signed Bönigen). GPS: 46.691333, 7.8935

Charges guide

Per unit incl. 2 persons and electricity	CHF 40.00 - 62.00
extra person	CHF 10.00 - 13.00
child (6-15 yrs)	CHF 5.00 - 6.50
dog	CHF 4.00

For latest campsite news, availability and prices visit

alanrogers.com

Brienz am See
Camping Aaregg
Seestrasse 28a, CH-3855 Brienz am See (Bern) T: 033 951 1843. E: mail@aaregg.ch
alanrogers.com/CH9510

Brienz, in the Bernese Oberland, is a delightful little town on the lake of the same name and the centre of the Swiss wood carving industry. Camping Aaregg is an excellent site of the highest quality situated at the eastern end of the lake with breathtaking views across the water to the surrounding mountains. Cabins for rent and seasonal pitches occupy part of the site with 180 available for touring, all with electricity (10/16A). Of these, eight lakeside pitches have been newly upgraded with full services and 18 have hardstandings, water and drainage. The trees, flowers and well tended grass make an attractive and peaceful environment.

Facilities
New, very attractive sanitary facilities built and maintained to first class standards. Showers with washbasins. Washbasins (open style and in cubicles). Children's section. Family shower rooms. Baby room. Facilities for disabled visitors. Laundry facilities. Motorcaravan services. Pleasant restaurant with café/bar and shop. Guest lounge with TV. Play area. Fishing. Bicycle hire. Boat launching. Lake swimming in clear water (unsupervised). English is spoken. WiFi in reception area. New camping pods and mini chalets for hire. Off site: Frequent train services to Interlaken and Lucerne as well as boat cruises from Brienz to Interlaken and back.

Open: 1 April - 31 October.

Directions
Site is on road B6/B11 on the east of Brienz. From the Interlaken-Luzern motorway, take Brienz exit and turn towards Brienz. Site then on left just opposite Socal petrol station. GPS: 46.7483, 8.04871

Charges guide
Per unit incl. 2 persons	
and electricity	CHF 34.00 - 74.00
extra person	CHF 7.50 - 12.00
child (6-16 yrs)	CHF 4.00 - 7.00
dog	CHF 3.00 - 4.00

Frutigen
Camping Grassi
Grassiweg 60, CH-3714 Frutigen (Bern) T: 033 671 1149. E: campinggrassi@bluewin.ch
alanrogers.com/CH9360

This is a small site with about half the pitches occupied by static caravans, used by their owners for weekends and holidays. The 70 or so places available for touring units are not marked out but are generous in size without overcrowding. Ten pitches have been upgraded to 'full comfort' and weather-resistant surfaces added to others. Most places are on level grass with two small terraces at the end of the site. There is little shade but the site is set in a river valley with trees on the hills which enclose the area. Electricity is available for all pitches but long leads may be required in parts. Camping Grassi would make a useful overnight stop en route for the Kandersteg railway terminal where cars can join the train for transportation through the Lotschberg Tunnel to the Rhône Valley and Simplon Pass, or for a longer stay to explore the Bernese Oberland, Lake Thun, Lake Brienz and Interlaken all being within easy reach. An electric car with a 70 km. range and electric bikes can now be hired.

Facilities
The well constructed, heated sanitary block is of good quality. Washing machine and dryer. Gas supplies. Motorcaravan services. Communal room with TV. Kiosk (July/Aug). Indoor and outdoor play areas and play house. Mountain bike hire. Fishing. E-bike and E-Car hire. WiFi (free). Off site: Shops and restaurants 10 minutes' walk away in village. Riding 2 km. Outdoor and indoor pools, tennis and minigolf in Frutigen. A new sauna and wellness centre has recently opened in the village. Skiing.

Open: All year.

Directions
Take Kandersteg road from Spiez and leave at Frutigen Dorf exit. Enter main street and turn left opposite Hotel Simplon from where site is signed. GPS: 46.58173, 7.64219

Charges guide
Per unit incl. 2 persons	
and electricity	CHF 24.00 - 32.00
extra person	CHF 5.80
child (1-16 yrs)	CHF 1.50 - 3.20
dog	CHF 1.50

Gampelen

TCS Camping Fanel

Sestrasse 50, CH-3236 Gampelen (Bern) T: 032 313 2333. E: camping.gampelen@tcs.ch

alanrogers.com/CH9055

This Swiss Touring Club site is particularly suited to families with children. From the terrace of the restaurant and shop there is a view of the small swimming pool and the large grass area that leads to the lake and a small wooden jetty. The site has 860 pitches (140 for touring units) making it very popular and busy, especially at weekends and holidays. The touring pitches are divided into three sections; one with large service facilities, an open grass area and another among the pine trees with little grass. This site is run in an environmentally sensitive manner and is located in a protected nature area.

Facilities

Three modern, well maintained toilet blocks with free showers and some washbasins in cabins. Facilities for disabled visitors. Baby room. Laundry facilities. Motorcaravan services. Modern self-service restaurant with takeaway. Shop. Gas supplies. Play area. Bicycle hire. Archery. Fishing and boat launching. Canoes and paddle boats for hire. Two-birth camping pods for rent. WiFi throughout (free). Off site: Boat hire and trips.

Open: 4 April - 7 October.

Directions

Site is on the northeast shore of Lake Neuchâtel. From A1 exit 29 (Murten) or exit 30 (Kerzers) travel north towards Neuchâtel as far as village of Gampelen where site is well signed. Look for TCS signs. GPS: 47.001321, 7.040568

Charges guide

Per unit incl. 2 persons and electricity	CHF 42.00 - 62.00
extra person	CHF 11.00 - 13.00

Grindelwald

Camping Gletscherdorf

Gletscherdorf 31, Locherboden strasse 29, CH-3818 Grindelwald (Bern) T: 033 853 1429.

E: info@gletscherdorf.ch **alanrogers.com/CH9480**

Set in a river valley on the edge of Grindelwald, one of Switzerland's best known winter and summer resorts, Gletscherdorf enjoys wonderful mountain views, particularly of the nearby north face of the Eiger. The new owners have made some great improvements to the grounds, pitches and facilities. There are 95 pitches in total, 33 of which are available for touring. Most are marked and have 10A electricity connections. There is space for 15 tents in an overflow field. This is, above all, a very quiet, friendly site for those who wish to enjoy the peaceful mountain air, dramatic scenery, walking and exploring or maybe mountaineering with the mountain climbing school in Grindelwald.

Facilities

Excellent small sanitary block has been refurbished and is heated. Washing machines and dryer. Motorcaravan services. Gas supplies. Coffee machine. Adapters available for Swiss electricity sockets. Community room. Torches and long leads useful. WiFi throughout (free). Dogs are not accepted in high season. Off site: Town shops and restaurants within walking distance. Bicycle hire, indoor pool and golf 1 km.

Open: 1 May - 20 October.

Directions

Just before arriving at Grindelwald, fork right at roundabout (Shell petrol) and follow road past station and coach park. Follow camping signs, passing golf course and tennis club (narrow road). Left over river bridge, then sharp left into site. Alternatively, for short units, fork left at roundabout, go through Grindelwald centre, right at Church (not before), down steep hill and sharp right into site. GPS: 46.62091, 8.04491

Charges guide

Per unit incl. 2 persons and electricity	CHF 37.00 - 40.00
extra person	CHF 7.50 - 8.00

Gwatt

TCS Camping Thunersee

CH-3770 Gwatt (Bern) T: 033 336 4067. E: camping.gwatt@bluewin.ch

alanrogers.com/CH9330

Situated on the shores of Lake Thun, Camping Thunersee is an ideal site for those who wish to explore this part of the Bernese Oberland and who would enjoy staying on a small site in a quiet area, away from the larger sites and town atmosphere of Interlaken. There are 75 numbered, but unmarked pitches for touring units, most with 4A electricity available, and about the same number of seasonal units. There are hard access roads but cars must be parked away from the pitches. Recent additions are eight premium pitches overlooking the lake and popular pods for light travellers. Although there are some trees, there is little shade in the main camping area. There is direct access to the lake for swimming and boating.

Facilities

Single, modern sanitary block, fully equipped with hot water provided for washbasins and showers. Facilities should be adequate in high season. Rooms for disabled visitors. Washing machine and dryer. Motorcaravan services. Shop. Good restaurant with terrace. Lake swimming and boating. Bicycle and pedal car hire. Internet access. WiFi throughout (free). Off site: Municipal play park adjacent. Many cycle tracks. Lakeside walks.

Open: 1 April - early October.

Directions

From Berne-Thun-Interlaken autoroute, take exit Thun-Süd for Gwatt and follow signs for Gwatt. Site is signed near town centre to the left. Coming from Spiez, the site is signed on the right, opposite a large TCS signboard. GPS: 46.72749, 7.6276

Charges guide

Per unit incl. 2 persons and electricity	CHF 42.00 - 62.00
extra person	CHF 11.00 - 13.00

For latest campsite news, availability and prices visit

alanrogers.com

Hasliberg

Camping Hofstatt-Derfli

Gässli Goldern, Hofstatt, CH-6085 Hasliberg Goldern (Bern) T: 033 971 37 07. E: welcome@derfli.ch

alanrogers.com/CH9500

This attractive site has been created by a goldsmith and her husband. Small and family run, with 45 pitches, it is in a quiet location, over 1,000 metres high at the end of a small village in the Berner Oberland. The striking metre-high mushrooms – with their white-dotted red tops they are difficult to miss - provide the electrical supply points for the 35 touring pitches and site lighting. The grass pitches are level and there are seven with gravel hardstanding for motorcaravans. The gently sloping site is partly surrounded by trees with mountain top views across the valley. English-speaking site owners.

Facilities

Well maintained all the year round, sanitary facilities are housed in the main building. Showers are controllable and free, some washbasins in cabins. Baby areas. Kitchen to rent in community room. Laundry facilities. Motorcaravan services. Small shop. Play area. Bicycle hire. Ski and snowboard room. Hot tub. WiFi throughout (charged). Off site: Shop and restaurant 300 m. in village. Lots of scenic walking in the region. Ski lifts at 1.5 and 2 km. Riding 2.5 km. Fishing 15 km.

Open: 1 June - 15 October, 25 December - 15 April.

Directions

From A8 exit 30 (Unterbach) follow signs for Luzern and Brünig Pass. At the village of Brünig (opposite Silvana Restaurant) take turning for Hasliberg. In 8 km. arrive at Hasliberg Goldern. The turn off for the site is 300 m. on the right which leads directly to the site (steep, narrow lane). GPS: 46.73687, 8.19537

Charges guide

Per unit incl. 2 persons	CHF 29.00 - 41.00
electricity (per kWh)	CHF 0.60

No credit cards.

Interlaken

Camping Lazy Rancho 4

Lehnweg 6, CH-3800 Unterseen-Interlaken (Bern) T: 033 822 8716. E: info@lazyrancho.ch

alanrogers.com/CH9430

This popular site is in a quiet location with fantastic views of the dramatic mountains of Eiger, Monch and Jungfrau. Neat, orderly and well maintained, the site is situated in a wide valley just 1 km. from Lake Thun and 1.5 km. from Interlaken. The English speaking owners, Stephane and Alina Blatter, lovingly care for the site and will endeavour to make you feel very welcome. Connected by gravel roads, the 155 pitches, of which 90 are for touring units, are on well tended level grass (7 with hardstanding, all with 10A electricity). There are also 32 pitches with water and waste water drainage, with more planned. This is a quiet, friendly site, popular with British visitors who return year after year. The owners go out of their way to advise on local trips and excursions (the Visitor Pass gives free travel on local transport). Always looking to improve their site, they have added 'igloo pods' for rent, a sauna and a hot tub and the swimming pool is being relined with the latest hygienic polymer. At Lazy Rancho you can simply sit and enjoy the scenery, or use it as a base for exploring the features of the Bernese Oberland.

Facilities

Two good sanitary blocks are both heated with free hot showers, good facilities for disabled campers and a baby room. Laundry. Campers' kitchen with microwave, cooker, fridge and utensils. Motorcaravan services. Shop. TV and games room. Play area. Small swimming pool, sauna and hot tub. Wooden igloo pods and bungalows for rent. Internet/laptop room. WiFi throughout (free). Off site: Free bus in the Interlaken area – bus stop is five minutes walk from site. Cycle trails and waymarked footpaths. Riding and bicycle hire 500 m. Golf 1 km. Fishing 1 km. Boat launching 1.5 km. Interlaken and leisure centre 2 km.

Open: 18 April - 20 October.

Directions

Site is on north side of Lake Thun. From road 8 (Thun-Interlaken) on south side of lake take exit 24 Interlaken West. Follow towards lake at roundabout then follow signs for campsites. Lazy Rancho is Camp no. 4. The last 500 m. is a little narrow but no problem. GPS: 46.68605, 7.830633

Charges guide

Per unit incl. 2 persons and electricity	CHF 37.50 - 54.50
extra person	CHF 6.00 - 8.00
child (6-15 yrs)	CHF 3.50 - 4.80

Payment also accepted in euros.

FREE Alan Rogers Travel Card
Extra benefits and savings - see page 14

Interlaken

Camping Manor Farm 1

Seestrasse 201, Unterseen, CH-3800 Interlaken-Thunersee (Bern) T: 033 822 2264. E: info@manorfarm.ch

alanrogers.com/CH9420

Manor Farm continues to be popular with British and Dutch visitors, being located in one of the traditional touring areas of Switzerland. The flat terrain is divided into 500 individual, numbered pitches, which vary considerably, both in size (40-100 sq.m) and price. There is shade in some places. There are 144 pitches with 4/13A electricity, water and drainage, and 55 also have cable TV connections. Reservations can be made, although you should find space, except perhaps in late July/early August when the best places may be taken. Around 40 per cent of the pitches are taken by permanent or letting units and four tour operators. Visitors receive the Interlaken Card which gives free local bus travel.

Facilities

Seven separate toilet blocks (heated). They include free hot water for baths and showers. Twenty private toilet units are for rent. Laundry facilities. Motorcaravan services. Shop (1/4-15/10). Site-owned restaurant adjacent (1/3-30/10). Snack bar with takeaway (1/7-20/8). TV room. Playground and paddling pool. Minigolf. Bicycle hire. Sailing school. Lake swimming. Boat hire (slipway for campers' own boats). Fishing. Excursions. Activities and entertainment in high season. Max. 1 dog. WiFi in some parts (charged). Off site: Golf (18 holes) 500 m.

Open: All year.

Directions

Site is 3 km. west of Interlaken along the road running north of the Thuner See towards Thun. From A8 (bypassing Interlaken) take exit 24 (Interlaken West) and follow signs to Camp no. 1. GPS: 46.68129, 7.81524

Charges guide

Per unit incl. 2 persons	
and electricity	CHF 35.00 - 62.00
extra person	CHF 5.00 - 10.00
child (6-15 yrs)	CHF 2.50 - 5.00

Interlaken

Camping Alpenblick

Seestrasse 130, Unterseen, CH-3800 Interlaken (Bern) T: 033 822 7757. E: info@camping-alpenblick.ch

alanrogers.com/CH9425

Alpenblick is an all-year site, located at the heart of the Bernese Oberland just 100 m. from Lake Thun. Susanne Knecht and George Zehntner took over the site in 2006 and have made many improvements, including an excellent new toilet block. The old reception building has been replaced with a new Swiss chalet housing reception, a bar, restuarant and shop. There are 100 touring pitches and a further 80 residential pitches. The touring pitches all have 10/16A electrical connections and 18 good hardstanding pitches are available for motorcaravans. Three tepees are available for rent. A larger tepee, complete with bar and indoor barbecue, is used for socialising in the evening.

Facilities

New toilet block. Laundry facilities. Shop (1/4-20/10) with daily delivery of bread. Bar, restaurant and takeaway (all year). Tepee with bar and barbecue for socialising and events. Playground. Boules. Basketball. Tepees for rent. WiFi throughout (charged). Off site: Nearest lake beach 100 m. Walking and cycle routes. Fishing. Riding. Boat trips on Lake Thun. Neuhaus lakeside restaurant and windsurfing school. Golf.

Open: All year.

Directions

Approaching from Thun and Bern on road no. 8 leave at exit 24 (Interlaken West). Head north towards Neuhaus and follow signs to Camping no. 2. GPS: 46.67999, 7.81728

Charges guide

Per unit incl. 2 persons	
and electricity	CHF 35.50 - 50.50
extra person	CHF 6.50 - 8.00
child (5-16 yrs)	CHF 3.50 - 4.00

Interlaken

TCS Camping Interlaken Ost

Brienzstrasse 24, CH-3800 Interlaken-Ost (Bern) T: 033 822 4434. E: camping.interlaken@tcs.ch

alanrogers.com/CH9435

Camping Interlaken is a member of the Touring Club Suisse and has a secluded location alongside the River Aar, on the edge of Interlaken and 500 m. from Lake Brienz (a swimming pool is 300 m. away). This is an extended site with 100 grassy, sunny pitches, some with fine views of the Oberland. Around 50 pitches are equipped with 6A electricity. Three particularly large pitches are available (extra charge) for motorcaravans with direct riverside access. Fully equipped tents and camping pods are also available for rent. Canoes, bicycles and electric cycles are all available for rent on site. Boats may be launched.

Facilities

Modern sanitary facilities include provision for disabled visitors (key access). Direct river access. Canoe and bicycle hire. Boat launching. Small shop. Fishing. Games room. Play area. Occasional activities. Rooms in new chalet complex for rent. Internet access. Free WiFi throughout. Off site: Swimming pool 300 m. Lake Brienz 500 m. Interlaken Ost station.

Open: 4 April - 7 October.

Directions

Approaching from Bern or Lucerne on A8 motorway take the Ringgenberg exit to the east of Interlaken. Follow signs to Goldswil and signs to camping Number 6. GPS: 46.692434, 7.868652

Charges guide

Per unit incl. 2 persons	
and electricity	CHF 40.00 - 60.00
extra person	CHF 11.00 - 13.00
child (6-15 yrs)	CHF 5.50 - 6.50
dog	CHF 4.00

For latest campsite news, availability and prices visit

alanrogers.com

Interlaken

Camping Jungfraublick

Gsteigstrasse 80, Matten, CH-3800 Interlaken (Bern) T: 033 822 4414. E: info@jungfraublick.ch

alanrogers.com/CH9440

The Berner Oberland is one of the most scenic and well known areas of Switzerland, with Interlaken probably the best known summer resort. Situated in the village of Matten, Jungfraublick is a delightful, medium sized site with splendid views up the Lauterbrunnen valley to the Jungfrau mountain. The 90 touring pitches (60-90 sq.m) with 6A electricity connections are in regular rows on level, well tended grass. Ten pitches now have full services and around the edge of the main touring area there are 12 hardstandings for motorcaravans. A number of fruit trees adorn but do not offer much shade. The 25 static caravans are to one side of the tourist area and do not intrude. There is some traffic noise.

Facilities
The sanitary facilities, although rather dated, are fully equipped and there is provision for disabled visitors. Showers are on payment, as is hot water for dishwashing. Laundry facilities (coin operated). Motorcaravan services. Small swimming pool (12x8 m) open mid-June-end Aug. according to the weather. Heated communal room with TV and electronic games. Barbecues must be off the ground, electric barbecues not accepted. Communal barbecue with seating. Internet corner and free WiFi on part of site. Off site: Buses into Interlaken pass the entrance every 30 mins.

Open: 1 May - 20 September.

Directions
Take the exit Nr. 25 from the N8 motorway, turn towards Interlaken. Site is within 500 m. on left. GPS: 46.67335, 7.86649

Charges guide
Per unit incl. 2 persons and electricity	CHF 28.80 - 53.20
extra person	CHF 8.80 - 10.00
child (4-16 yrs)	CHF 3.80 - 4.50
dog	CHF 3.00

Kandersteg

Camping Rendez-vous

Hubleweg, CH-3718 Kandersteg (Bern) T: 033 675 1534. E: rendez-vous.camping@bluewin.ch

alanrogers.com/CH9370

Camping Rendez-vous is an all-year site located at an altitude of 1,200 m, just outside the delightful mountain village of Kandersteg. There are 60 terraced touring pitches here and a further 20 pitches are occupied by residential caravans. Additional dormitory accommodation is available. The pitches are grassy and many have fine views over the surrounding mountain scenery. Although there are few amenities on site, Kandersteg is nearby and is an important mountain resort with a good selection of shops and restaurants, as well as a railway station and cable car service. Camping Rendez-vous is an excellent starting point for many of the area's superb walking and mountain biking opportunities, with over 500 km. of marked trails available. The site owners will be pleased to recommend routes. Adjacent to the site is the new Oeschinensee cable car which gives access to a summer toboggan run. During the winter, skiing and other winter sports are possible, with a ski school located nearby. The adjoining restaurant offers an attractive menu and terrace seating.

Facilities
Heated toilet block is adequate. Washing machines and dryers. Motorcaravan services. Small shop, bar, adjoining restaurant and takeaway service (all year) at site entrance. Communal grill. Ski equipment room. WiFi in part of site (charged). Off site: Bicycle hire, fishing and riding within 1 km. Kandersteg with a wide range of shops, restaurants and bars 1 km. Oeschinensee cable car. Railway station and cable cars. Many walking paths and cycle trails.

Open: All year.

Directions
From the north, take the N6 Bern-Spiez motorway and take the Kandersteg exit. Pass Frutigan and follow signs to Kandersteg Zentrum, then brown campsite signs. GPS: 46.49735, 7.68342

Charges guide
Per unit incl. 2 persons and electricity	CHF 34.80 - 38.80
extra person	CHF 6.60
child (1-16 yrs)	CHF 3.20
dog	CHF 2.50

Krattigen

Camping Stuhlegg

Stueleggstrasse 7, CH-3704 Krattigen (Bern) T: 033 654 2723. E: campstuhlegg@bluewin.ch

alanrogers.com/CH9410

On the outskirts of the village of Krattigen, Camping Stuhlegg is a quiet and attractive site, located well above Lake Thun and with beautiful, wide ranging views over the lake to the mountains beyond. The 60 touring pitches, all with 10/13A electricity, are arranged on grassy terraced areas with some hardstanding for motorcaravans. A central grass area serves as an overflow. A dormitory chalet has been added recently for light travellers. A few young trees provide shade. The friendly bar and bistro is also popular as a meeting point for the villagers, which adds a touch of local colour. This is a site where you can relax and enjoy the fresh mountain air and scenery.

Facilities

Two modern sanitary facilities, the one near the entrance is heated, the other at the top of the site is for summer use and unheated. They contain all the usual facilities, showers operate with either coins or tokens. Laundry room. Baby bath. Motorcaravan services. Shop, bar and bistro with takeaway (all open as site). Delightful solar heated natural swimming pool with shallow section for children. TV room and library. Play area. Communal barbecue. Internet point. WiFi throughout (free).

Open: All year excl. November.

Directions

Site is almost halfway between Spiez and Interlaken on the southern side of the Thunersee. Leave A8 at exit 20 and follow signs for Krattigen. Site is signed at top of village to the right (north). GPS: 46.657917, 7.717933

Charges guide

Per unit incl. 2 persons and electricity	CHF 28.00 - 36.00
extra person	CHF 6.00 - 7.00
child	CHF 4.60 - 5.00

Lauterbrunnen

Camping Jungfrau

CH-3822 Lauterbrunnen (Bern) T: 033 856 2010. E: info@camping-jungfrau.ch

alanrogers.com/CH9460

This friendly and ever popular site has a very imposing and dramatic situation in a steep valley with a fine view of the Jungfrau at the end. It is a busy site and, although you should usually find space, in season do not arrive too late. A fairly extensive area is made up of grass pitches and hardcore access roads. All 391 pitches (250 for touring) have shade in parts, electrical connections (13A) and 50 have water and drainage also. Over 35% of the pitches are taken by seasonal caravans, chalets to rent and two tour operators. Family owned and run by Herr and Frau Fuchs, you can be sure of a warm welcome. You can laze here amid real mountain scenery, though it does lose the sun a little early. There are many active pursuits available in the area, as well as trips on the Jungfrau railway and mountain lifts. Small chalets and a hostel over the river provide for hikers and backpackers from all over the world. Mountain meltwater cascades hundreds of feet down the sheer rock walls of the valley. In winter the site operates a free shuttle bus to the local ski lifts, and large community lounges are available for apres-ski enjoyment.

Facilities

Three fully equipped and modern sanitary blocks can be heated in winter and one provides facilities for disabled visitors. Baby baths. Laundry facilities. Motorcaravan services. Campers' kitchen. Excellent shop. Self-service restaurant with takeaway. General room with tables and chairs, TV, drinks machines, amusements. Playgrounds. Covered play area. Excursions and some entertainment in high season. Mountain bike hire. ATM. Drying room. Ski store. Free shuttle bus in winter. Internet point. WiFi throughout (free). Off site: Tourist village of Lauterbrunnen, Schilthorn (James Bond) revolving restaurant, paragliding.

Open: All year.

Directions

Go through Lauterbrunnen and fork right at far end (look for signpost) before road bends left, 100 m. before church. Final approach is not very wide but is manageable with care. GPS: 46.58807, 7.91077

Charges guide

Per person	CHF 9.90 - 11.90
child (6-15 yrs)	CHF 4.90 - 5.50
pitch incl. electricity (plus meter in winter)	CHF 25.50 - 26.50
dog	CHF 3.00

Charges are higher in winter.

For latest campsite news, availability and prices visit

alanrogers.com

Meiringen
Alpencamping
Brünigstrasse 47, CH-3860 Meiringen (Bern) T: 033 971 3676. E: info@alpencamping.ch

alanrogers.com/CH9496

Alpencamping is a small family site located close to Meiringen, an important winter sports resort and hiking centre in the summer with good road and rail links. Opened in 2007, the enthusiastic owners have developed this into a good all-year site (closed November) and continue to make steady improvements. There are 54 touring pitches which are flat and grassy and all have electrical connections. A further 32 pitches are occupied by well maintained residential units. This is a simple site with few amenities but there is a centrally located toilet block and a small shop for essentials. A supermarket is five minutes walk away. Meiringen is surrounded by stunning mountain scenery and there is a great deal to see in the area. The dramatic Reichenbach Falls are just ten minutes away, and are, of course, famous for the demise of Sherlock Holmes. Now, there is even a museum here, dedicated to the great detective! Even more dramatic are the many mountain walks in the area, many of which are easily accessible from the site. During the week some aircraft noise is possible from the nearby airbase in Spring and Autumn.

Facilities
Heated toilet block includes facilities for disabled visitors and a baby changing unit. Washing machine and dryer. Drying area for ski kit. Small shop for essentials with coffee machine. Undercover area with tables, chairs and a microwave for open-air catering. Inflatable pool (in summer). Communal barbecue. Community room with tables, easy chairs, games, TV and books. Winter sauna room. Play area. Dogs accepted (max. 2). WiFi throughout. Off site: Meiringen with a wide choice of shops, restaurants and bars 500 m. Reichenbach Falls. Brienzersee Lake. Many walking paths and cycle trails. Summer and winter skiing.

Open: All year excl. November.

Directions
From Bern take the A6 motorway towards Interlaken and Thun. At Interlaken, join the A8 towards Spiez. Continue on road 11 to Meiringen, from where the site is well signed. GPS: 46.73421, 8.17115

Charges guide

Per unit incl. 2 persons and electricity (plus meter in winter)	CHF 35.00 - 43.50
extra person	CHF 8.00 - 9.00
child (6-15 yrs)	CHF 4.50 - 5.00
dog	CHF 2.50

No credit cards.

Châtel-Saint Denis
Camping le Bivouac
Route des Paccots 21, CH-1618 Châtel-Saint Denis (Fribourg) T: 021 948 7849. E: info@le-bivouac.ch

alanrogers.com/CH9300

A pleasant little site in the forested mountains above Montreux and Vevey on Lac Leman (Lake Geneva). Le Bivouac has its own small swimming pool and children's pool. Most of the places here are taken by seasonal caravans (130) interspersed with about 30 pitches for touring units. Electrical connections (10A) are available and there are five water points. Due to access difficulties, the site is not open to tourers in winter. The active can take mountain walks in the area, or set off to explore Montreux and the lake. Others will enjoy the peace and quiet of this green hideaway. M. Fivaz, the owner, speaks excellent English and is only too happy to suggest local activities.

Facilities
The good toilet facilities in the main building include free preset hot water in washbasins, showers and sinks for laundry and dishes. Washing machine and dryer. Gas supplies. Shop (July/Aug, bread to order). Bar (1/6-30/9). Swimming and paddling pools (15/6-15/9). TV. Fishing in adjacent stream (licence from reception). Internet and WiFi. Off site: Bus to Chatel stops at the gate. Bicycle hire 3 km. Riding 10 km.

Open: 1 May - 30 September.

Directions
From motorway 12/E27 (Bern-Vevey) take Châtel-Saint Denis exit no. 2 and turn towards Les Paccots (1 km). Site is on left up hill. GPS: 46.52513, 6.91828

Charges guide

Per person	CHF 5.00 - 6.50
child (6-16 yrs)	CHF 3.00 - 4.50
pitch	CHF 15.00 - 16.50
electricity	CHF 4.50

No credit cards. Less 10% on showing this guide. Euros are accepted.

Churwalden

Camping Pradafenz

Girabodaweg 34, CH-7075 Churwalden (Graubünden) T: 81 382 19 21. E: camping@pradafenz.ch

alanrogers.com/CH9820

In the heart of the village of Churwalden on the Chur - Saint Moritz road, Pradafenz makes a convenient night stop and being amidst the mountains, is also an excellent base for walking and exploring this scenic area. At first sight, this appears to be a site for static holiday caravans but three large rectangular terraces at the front take 50 touring units. This area has a hardstanding of concrete frets with grass growing through and super pitch facilities of electricity (10A), drainage, gas and TV sockets. A flat meadow is also available for tents or as an overflow for caravans. Although the gravel road which leads to the tourers' terrace is not very steep, the very friendly German-speaking owner will tow caravans there with his tractor if required.

Facilities

New sanitary block is well appointed and heated and includes some washbasins in cabins. Family shower room. Baby room. Another two blocks are in the touring section. Washing machines, dryers and separate drying room. Motorcaravan services. Gas supplies. Small restaurant. WiFi throughout (charged). Off site: Bicycle hire 200 m. Restaurants and shops 300 m. in village. Municipal outdoor pool 500 m. Riding 3.5 km. Fishing 4 km. Golf 5 km.

Open: 25 May - 31 October to 15 December - 14 April.

Directions

Churwalden is 10 km. south of Chur. From Chur take road towards Lenzerheide. It is initially a fairly long, steep climb with one tight hairpin. In centre of Churwalden turn right in front of the tourist office towards the site. GPS: 46.77666, 9.54128

Charges guide

Per unit incl. 2 persons and electricity (winter + meter)	CHF 29.10 - 41.80
extra person	CHF 8.00 - 9.00
child (2-16 yrs)	CHF 5.00 - 6.50
dog	CHF 3.00

Davos Glaris

Camping RinerLodge

Landwasserstrasse 64, CH-7277 Davos Glaris (Graubünden) T: 081 417 0033.

E: rinerlodge@davosklosters.ch **alanrogers.com/CH9842**

Camping RinerLodge forms part of a holiday complex that has been developed at Glaris, 5 km. south of the important resort of Davos. The complex consists of a small campsite and an adjacent hotel and restaurant. The campsite offers 84 pitches, all equipped with 16A electricity. They are grassy and many have fine mountain views. A number of footpaths and cycle trails pass close to the site. The hotel restaurant is very good, and specialises in regional cuisine. There is no toilet block on site, but there are ample facilities within the hotel for use by all campers. Davos Glaris railway station, the Rinerhorn cable car and a bus stop are both very close to the site entrance, ensuring easy access to the town centre and ski slopes. The Davos Klosters Inclusive card provides free rides on local buses, trains and mountain cableways and a wide variety of other advantages. Davos, of course, is an important winter sports centre, and, thanks to the excellent transport infrastructure, this site is a good base for a skiing holiday.

Facilities

Play area. Hotel restaurant and bar adjacent. Off site: Showers and toilets in nearby hotel. Shops and restaurants in Davos and Klosters. Cable car. Indoor swimming pool. Walking and cycle trails.

Open: 13 December - 6 April, 17 May - 20 October.

Directions

The site is located at Glaris, to the south of Davos. From Davos head south on road 417 until you reach Glaris and the site is well signposted, on the right, close to the station. GPS: 46.743845, 9.779297

Charges guide

Per unit incl. 2 persons and electricity	CHF 41.30 - 42.50

For latest campsite news, availability and prices visit

alanrogers.com

Disentis

TCS Camping Fontanivas

Via Fontanivas 9, CH-7180 Disentis (Graubünden) T: 081 947 4422. E: camping.disentis@tcs.ch

alanrogers.com/CH9865

Nestled in the Surselva valley with superb views of the surrounding mountains, this is an attractive site with its own lake. Surrounded by tall pine trees, the site is owned by the Touring Club of Switzerland (the Swiss version of the AA) and provides 110 flat, level pitches, 81 with 13A electricity. There are plenty of opportunities for walks, nature trails and cycle rides, whilst the more adventurous can enjoy themselves canyoning, rafting, hang-gliding or mountain biking. For children, the playground is a challenging combination of water, rocks and bridges. Hardy souls can brave the fresh mountain waters of the lake. The Medelser Rhine near Disentis is known to be the richest place in gold in the country.

Facilities
The excellent sanitary block is well maintained with free showers and hairdryers. Facilities for disabled visitors. Baby room. Washing machine and dryer. Motorcaravan services. Shop. Restaurant/bar. Play room. Bicycle hire. Fishing. Caravans and tent bungalows to rent. WiFi throughout (charged). Off site: Disentis 2 km. Indoor pool.

Open: 20 April - 23 September.

Directions
The site is 2 km. south of Disentis. From Andermatt take the Oberalppass to Disentis. In town at T-junction turn right towards Lukmanier. Site is at bottom of hill on left, past the droopy power cables. From the east, on arriving in the town, keep left onto Lukmanier Road. GPS: 46.697, 8.85272

Charges guide
Per unit incl. 2 persons and electricity	CHF 41.80 - 67.40
extra person	CHF 10.00 - 13.00

Landquart

TCS Camping Neue Ganda

Ganda 21, CH-7302 Landquart (Graubünden) T: 081 322 3955. E: camping.landquart@tcs.ch

alanrogers.com/CH9850

Situated close to the Klosters, Davos road and the nearby town of Landquart, this deep valley campsite provides a comfortable night stop near the A13 motorway. The 80 touring pitches are not marked or separated but are all on level grass off a central gravel road through the long, narrow, wooded site. All pitches have 6/10A electricity. The many static caravans are mostly hidden from view in small alcoves. A modern, timber-clad building at the entrance houses all the necessary facilities – reception, community room and sanitary facilities. The restaurant/shop adjacent is open all year.

Facilities
The toilet block is extremely well appointed and can be heated. Facilities for disabled visitors. Baby room. Washing machine and dryer. Drying room. Motorcaravan services. Restaurant. Shop. Internet. WiFi throughout (charged). Off site: Tennis, riding and canoeing nearby. Rambling. Cycling tours. Fishing 2 km.

Open: All year excl. 27 February - 15 March and 15 October - 6 December.

Directions
From A13 motorway take Landquart exit 14 and follow road to Davos. 800 m. after crossing large bridge, take the slip road to the right (signed). At the bottom of the slope turn left under the road bridge and follow the signs to the site. Note reception is closed 11.00-16.00. GPS: 46.96900, 9.58933

Charges guide
Per unit incl. 2 persons and electricity	CHF 32.60 - 57.30
extra person	CHF 10.00 - 11.00

Le Prese

Camping Cavresc

CH-7746 Le Prese (Graubünden) T: 081 844 0259. E: info@campingcavresc.ch

alanrogers.com/CH9855

Le Prese is on the Tirano to Saint Moritz road, south of the Bernina Pass. Camping Cavresc is on grassy meadows in the Valposchiavo valley and is blessed with a southern climate, a peaceful ambience and beautiful views. It is a very good, newly built site with ultramodern sanitary facilities. For tourers there are 30 flat, level pitches, all with 10A electricity and water, plus a large area for around 50 tents. There is little shade. If the campsite reception is unmanned, walk back into town as the Sertori family, who own the site, also run the small well stocked supermarket. Le Prese is close to Italy and the Poschiavo Lake.

Facilities
The excellent toilet block is very well maintained. Showers on payment. Facilities for disabled visitors. Washing machines, dryers and iron. Motorcaravan services. Restaurant/bar (June-Oct). Small shop. Swimming pool (high season). There are plans for outdoor ice-skating to be added. Off site: Le Prese 250 m. Windsurfing, sailing and skiing.

Open: All year.

Directions
Le Prese is 6 km. south of Poschiavo. Coming from Italy on road no. 29, the site is towards the southern end of the town. Turn right towards Pagnoncini/Cantone and site is on right in 100 m. Go over a humpback bridge at the entrance. GPS: 46.2949, 10.0801

Charges guide
Per unit incl. 2 persons and electricity	CHF 36.00 - 46.00
extra person	CHF 10.00 - 13.00
child (6-16 yrs)	CHF 4.00 - 6.00

FREE Alan Rogers Travel Card

Extra benefits and savings - see page 14

Pontresina

Camping Morteratsch

Plauns 13, CH-7504 Pontresina (Graubünden) T: 081 842 6285. E: mail@camping-morteratsch.ch

alanrogers.com/CH9860

This is a mountain site in splendid scenery near Saint Moritz. Pontresina is at the mouth of the Bernina Pass road (B29) which runs from Celerina in the Swiss Engadine to Tirano in Italy. Camping Morteratsch, some 4 km. southeast of Pontresina, is situated in the floor of the valley between fir-clad mountains at 1,850 m. above sea level. There are about 250 pitches for touring units in summer, most with electricity, some in small clearings amongst tall trees and some in a larger open space. In winter the number is reduced to 60. They are neither numbered nor marked, and their size is dictated by the natural space between the trees. Four small rivers run through this long, narrow site with lovely views on each side and a larger at one end.

Facilities

Three fully equipped toilet blocks, one old and two excellent new modern ones, can be heated. Some washbasins in private cabins. Facilities for disabled visitors. Laundry facilities. Shop. Grill/snack bar for drinks or simple meals (July/Aug). TV room. WiFi. Bicycle hire. Fishing. Playground. Torch useful. Off site: Restaurant 1 km. Entertainment programme offered, winter and summer, at nearby Pontresina. Riding and skiing 4 km.

Open: 25 May - 13 October, 15 December - 15 April.

Directions

Site is on B29, the road to Tirano and Bernina Pass, 4 km. southeast of Pontresina and is well signed. GPS: 46.464075, 9.932402

Charges guide

Per unit incl. 2 persons and electricity	CHF 36.50 - 46.50
extra person	CHF 12.00
child (6-15 yrs acc. to age)	CHF 5.00 - 7.50
dog	CHF 4.00

Sent

Camping Sur En

CH-7554 Sur En/Sent (Graubünden) T: 081 866 3544. E: info@sur-en.ch

alanrogers.com/CH9830

Sur En is at the eastern end of the Engadine valley, about 10 km. from the Italian and Austrian borders. The area is perhaps better known as a skiing region, but has summer attractions as well. This level site is in an open valley with little shade. They say there is room for 120 touring units on the meadows where pitches are neither marked nor numbered; there are electricity connections for all (6A). As you approach on road 27 and spot the site way below under the shadow of a steeply rising, wooded mountain, the drop may appear daunting, but becomes less so as you proceed.

Facilities

The modern, heated sanitary block is good with some extra facilities in the main building. Washing machine and dryer. Motorcaravan services. Shop and good restaurant (all year) with covered terrace. Takeaway (high season). Outdoor heated swimming pool (June-Oct). Bicycle hire. Fishing. Entertainment (July/Aug). A symposium for sculptors is held during the second week in July. Excursions arranged in high season. New adventure ropes course in the forest. WiFi. Off site: Golf 12 km. Bus service to Scuol for train to St Moritz.

Open: All year.

Directions

Sur En is 7 km. east of Scuol. It is signed from the 27 road halfway between Scuol and Ramosch. The road is a steady, winding descent. Cross covered timber bridge (3.8 m. passable height). GPS: 46.84163, 10.33333

Charges guide

Per unit incl. 2 persons and electricity	CHF 30.25 - 36.25
extra person	CHF 6.50 - 7.50
child (6-16 yrs)	CHF 4.00 - 4.50
dog	CHF 3.00

Zernez

Camping Cul

CH-7530 Zernez (Graubünden) T: 081 856 1462. E: campingzernez@gmail.com

alanrogers.com/CH9835

Camping Cul is a friendly site in a good location on the banks of the River Inn, east of Davos. The site was established in 1952 and has remained in the same family ever since. Pitches are grassy and lightly shaded. Many have electrical connections and virtually all have fine views of the magnificent mountain scenery all around. On-site amenities include a bar, small shop and restaurant. There is a fully equipped communal kitchen. This is excellent walking and cycling country, with a number of routes possible direct from the site. The Rhätische Bahn is a superb mountain railway passing close to the site and discounted tickets are available for purchase at reception.

Facilities

Motorcaravan services. Shop, bar and restaurant (all May-Oct). Games room. Play area. Activities and entertainment programme. WiFi (charged). Off site: Covered swimming pool. Mountain railways. St Moritz, Davos and Klosters. Hiking and cycle tracks.

Open: 15 May - 25 October.

Directions

Zernez is on the B27, east of Davos. From the north, go through village and bear right on B27 with the industrial estate on your right. Signed site entrance is via the timber sawmill on the right. From the South, as you enter Zernez the entrance is on the left. GPS: 46.69686, 10.08678

Charges guide

Per unit incl. 2 persons and electricity	CHF 39.80

For latest campsite news, availability and prices visit

alanrogers.com

Montmelon

Camping Tariche

Tariche, Saint Ursanne, CH-2883 Montmelon (Jura) T: 032 433 4619. E: info@tariche.ch

alanrogers.com/CH9015

This lovely site is some 6 km. off the main road along a steep wooded valley, through which flows the Doub on its brief excursion through Switzerland from France. If you're looking for peace and tranquillity then this is a distinct possibility for a short or long stay. A very small friendly site (not suitable for large units), owned and managed by Christine Lodens, there are just 15 touring pitches. It is ideal for walking, fishing or for the more active, the possibility of kayaking along the Doub (the river is not suitable for swimming). Medieval Saint Ursanne, said to be the most beautiful village in the canton, is some 7 km.

Facilities
The modern, heated toilet block is of a high standard with free showers. Washing machine and dryer. Motorcaravan services. Good kitchen facilities include oven, hob and refrigerator. Restaurant with shaded terrace overlooking the play area so that adults can enjoy a drink and keep watch whilst enjoying the river views. Fishing. WiFi. Off site: St Ursanne 7 km.

Open: 1 March - 31 October.

Directions
From A16 exit St Ursanne (at the end of the tunnel). Turn left towards town and at roundabout turn left and go past first campsite. After 5.6 km. site is on the right next to the restaurant.
GPS: 47.33419, 7.14028

Charges guide
Per unit incl. 2 persons	
and electricity	CHF 32.00 - 42.00
extra person	CHF 9.00
child	CHF 5.00

Luzern

TCS Camping Luzern Horw

Seefeldstrasse, CH-6048 Horw-Luzern (Luzern) T: 041 340 3558. E: camping.horw@tcs.ch

alanrogers.com/CH9115

Situated in the southern suburbs of Luzern and with easy autoroute access, this site is a very convenient base for visiting what is quite deservedly a popular tourist area. The level, grassed site provides 100 touring pitches with electricity, separated into rows by trees and hedges. It is dominated by the Pilatus mountains, over 2,000 metres high. The peaks and mountain top restaurants offer fantastic views and can be reached from Alpnachstad, on the steepest cog railway in the world or by cable car from Kriens. Access to the lake from the site is over a wooden walkway which passes through a small protected nature area. The site's staff are most knowledgeable and helpful with tourist advice.

Facilities
Single, recently improved and well maintained toilet block to one end of touring area. Showers are free, some washbasins in cabins. Facilities for disabled visitors. Baby room. Washing machine and dryer. Motorcaravan services. Gas supplies. Small shop. Bar with terrace. Convenient self service restaurant with takeaway. New play area. Bicycle hire. Gas barbecues only. Free WiFi throughout. Off site: Sports ground and lake adjacent (free use for campers).

Open: 4 April - 7 October.

Directions
Site is 4 km. south of the centre of Luzern and borders the Vierwaldstatter See. Leave motorway 2 at exit 28 Luzern/Horw. Site is signed at roundabout towards Horw-Sud. GPS: 47.01185, 8.311

Charges guide
Per unit incl. 2 persons	
and electricity	CHF 39.00 - 61.00
extra person	CHF 10.00 - 13.00
child (6-15 yrs)	CHF 5.00 - 6.50
dog	CHF 4.00

Sempach

TCS Camping Sempach

Seelandstrasse 6, CH-6204 Sempach (Luzern) T: 041 460 1466. E: camping.sempach@tcs.ch

alanrogers.com/CH9110

Lucerne is a very popular city in the centre of Switzerland and Camping Sempach makes a peaceful base from which to visit the town and explore the surrounding countryside or, being a short way from the main N2 Basel - Chiasso motorway, is a convenient night stop if passing through. This neat, tidy site has 200 grass pitches for touring units, all with 6/13A electricity, a few with gravel hardstanding on either side of hard roads under trees with further places on the perimeter in the open. There are about 200 caravan holiday homes. A small river runs through the site with a connecting covered bridge.

Facilities
Four good quality sanitary blocks have the usual facilities including baby rooms and excellent facilities for disabled visitors. Washing machine and dryer. Hot plates, fridges and freezers. Motorcaravan services. Excellent self-service bar/restaurant with terrace. Play area. Shop. Children's paddling pool and playground. Lakeside beach. Bicycle hire. Free WiFi on part of site. Electric barbecues are not permitted. Bungalows for hire. Off site: Shops and restaurants in the village. Tennis courts. Minigolf and golf club. Adjacent lake swimming and beach. Fishing 300 m.

Open: 28 March - 6 October.

Directions
From the N2 take exit 21 for Sempach and follow signs for Sempach and site.
GPS: 47.12548, 8.18995

Charges guide
Per unit incl. 2 persons	
and electricity	CHF 48.40 - 72.40
extra person	CHF 11.00 - 14.00
child (6-15 yrs)	CHF 5.50 - 7.00
dog	CHF 5.00

FREE Alan Rogers Travel Card
Extra benefits and savings - see page 14

Vitznau

Camping Vitznau

CH-6354 Vitznau (Luzern) T: 041 397 1280. E: info@camping-vitznau.ch

alanrogers.com/CH9130

Camping Vitznau is situated in the small village of the same name, above and overlooking Lake Luzern, with splendid views across the water to the mountains on the other side. It is a small, neat and tidy site very close to the delightful village on the narrow, winding, lakeside road. The 90 touring pitches for caravans or motorcaravans (max length 8 m) have 15A electricity available and all have fine views. They are on level, grassy terraces with hardstanding for motorcaravans and separated by tarmac roads. There are separate places for tents. Trees provide shade in parts and this delightful site makes an excellent base for exploring around the lake, the town of Luzern and the nearby mountains.

Facilities

The single, well constructed sanitary block provides free hot showers (water heated by solar panels). No facilities for disabled visitors (steep site and access roads). Full laundry facilities. Gas supplies. Motorcaravan services. Shop and snack bar. General room for wet weather. Games room. Small heated swimming pool and children's splash pool (1/5-30/9). WiFi over site (charged). Off site: Village restaurants about five minutes walk. Watersports nearby. Fishing and bicycle hire within 1 km. Riding and bicycle hire 5 km. Golf 15 km.

Open: 31 March - 7 October.

Directions

Site is signed from the centre of Vitznau. (Swiss signs show a single black tent on a white background). GPS: 47.006666, 8.486402

Charges guide

Per unit incl. 2 persons	
and electricity	CHF 43.00 - 62.00
extra person	CHF 10.10 - 12.10
child (4-15 yrs)	CHF 4.00 - 8.50
dog	CHF 4.00 - 5.00

Le Landeron

Camping des Pêches

Route du Port 6, CH-2525 Le Landeron (Neuchâtel) T: 032 751 2900. E: info@camping-lelanderon.ch

alanrogers.com/CH9040

This recently constructed, touring campsite is on the side of Lake Biel and River Thielle, and close to the old town of Le Landeron. The site is divided into two sections, one side of the road for static caravans, and on the other is the modern campsite for tourers. The 160 touring pitches are all on level grass, numbered but not separated; a few have shade, all have 13A electricity and many conveniently placed water points. All the facilities were exceptionally well maintained and in pristine condition during our visit throughout a busy holiday weekend.

Facilities

The spacious, modern sanitary block contains all the usual facilities including a food preparation area with six cooking rings, a large freezer and refrigerator. Payment for showers is by card. Baby room. Facilities for disabled visitors. Laundry. Motorcaravan services. Community room and small café in reception building. Shop, restaurant and takeaway (all season). Playground. Bicycle hire. TV and general room. WiFi. Off site: Fishing, sailing and swimming pool 300 m. (16/5-1/9; charged). Golf and riding 7 km.

Open: 1 April - 15 October.

Directions

Le Landeron is signed from the Neuchâtel-Biel motorway, exit 10 and site is well signed from the town. GPS: 47.05254, 7.06978

Charges guide

Per unit incl. 2 persons	
and electricity	CHF 31.00 - 39.00
extra person	CHF 9.00
child (6-16 yrs)	CHF 4.00

For latest campsite news, availability and prices visit

alanrogers.com

Langwiesen

Camping Schaffhausen

Freizeitanlage Rheinwiese, Hauptstrasse, CH-8246 Langwiesen (Schaffhausen) T: 052 659 3300.

E: info@camping-schaffhausen.ch **alanrogers.com/CH9160**

Schaffhausen is a friendly site in a very pleasant setting on the banks of the Rhine, with plenty of shade from a variety of tall trees. It is level and grassy, the first half being open lawns and the rest of the touring area wooded, with numbered pitches (mostly small – up to 70 sq.m). There are many day visitors in summer as the site is ideally placed for swimming, canoeing and diving in the Rhine. Whilst here, you would not want to miss the impressive waterfalls at Schaffhausen, 150 m. wide and 25 m. high.

Facilities

For touring units there is an old, but clean, building which might be under pressure at the busiest times. Washing machine and dryer. Bar/snack bar with covered terrace for burgers etc. open daily. Bread to order, some essentials kept. Pool room also used as wet weather rest room. Two shallow paddling pools, with play area close by. Electro-bicycle hire. Dogs are not accepted at any time. Off site: Shop 500 m. Bicycle hire 2 km.

Open: 20 April - 7 October.

Directions

From Schaffhausen head east towards Kreuzlingen (road no. 13) for 2.5 km. Site is signed just before Langwiesen. If coming from the east, it is a tight turn into the site. GPS: 47.68733, 8.65583

Charges guide

Per unit incl. 2 persons	
and electricity	CHF 26.00 - 52.00
extra person	CHF 8.00 - 9.00
child (6-15 yrs)	CHF 4.00 - 4.50

Solothurn

TCS Camping Solothurn

Glutzenhofstrasse 5, CH-4500 Solothurn (Solothurn) T: 032 621 8935. E: camping.solothurn@tcs.ch

alanrogers.com/CH9010

This continues to be one of the most pleasant sites owned by the Swiss Touring Club that we have seen. It is well laid out and beautifully cared for and can be enjoyed as a base for local touring or as a restful stop en route. There are 150 level, grass pitches including 120 for touring units, all with electricity and 12 also have water and drainage. Eight pitches have hardstanding. A small marina adjoining the site is under the same ownership. The site is close to the large medieval town of Solothurn. Situated between the Aare river and farmland, the site enjoys pleasant views of the surrounding hills.

Facilities

Two extremely well maintained sanitary blocks. Facilities for disabled visitors. Washing machines and dryer. Motorcaravan services. Recently extended shop for basics plus a restaurant overlooking marina (both 3/3-30/11). Playground with bouncy castle in season. Small, unheated pool for children (1/6-15/9). Library. Games room with TV. Internet access. WiFi throughout (charged). Off site: Large municipal swimming pool 200 m. Solothurn and the River Aare. The stork colony at Altreu. River swimming, boating and canoeing. River cruises.

Open: 1 March - 1 December.

Directions

Site is on the western outskirts of Solothurn. From A5 motorway take exit Solothurn West (ouest), then follow Weststadt. The site is well signed. GPS: 47.198351, 7.523805

Charges guide

Per unit incl. 2 persons	
and electricity	CHF 44.00 - 68.00
extra person	CHF 11.00 - 14.00
child (6-15 yrs)	CHF 5.50 - 7.00
dog	CHF 5.00 - 6.00

Bad Ragaz

Camping Giessenpark

CH-7310 Bad Ragaz (St Gallen) T: 081 302 3710. E: giessenpark@bluewin.ch

alanrogers.com/CH9175

The luxury spa resort of Bad Ragaz nestles in the Rhine valley and the municipally owned Giessenpark surrounds this site, which is located in a forest. There are 86 flat, level gravel pitches of which 52 are for touring, all with access to 10A electricity. The Rhine and the extensive park and lake are within a minute's walk and add to the peaceful nature of the site. The local authority swimming pool is close to the site, which is open from mid May to mid September. A restaurant with terrace and a large children's play area are adjacent to the site.

Facilities

Good, modern toilet is well maintained with free showers. Facilities for disabled visitors. Baby room. Sinks with hot water for laundry and dishwashing. Washing machine and dryer. Motorcaravan services. Shop (limited). Restaurant. WiFi (charged). Off site: Bad Ragaz 1 km. Golf and bicycle hire 1 km. Riding 3 km.

Open: All year.

Directions

From the A13 take Bad Ragaz exit and follow Bad Ragaz signs. In town, go over small bridge and turn right immediately, then right again after 300 m. following signs towards the site. GPS: 47.00516, 9.51266

Charges guide

Per unit incl. 2 persons and electricity	CHF 38.80
extra person	CHF 8.00
child (6-16 yrs)	CHF 3.00
dog	CHF 2.00

FREE Alan Rogers Travel Card
Extra benefits and savings - see page 14

Arbón

Camping Buchhorn

Philosophenweg 17, CH-9320 Arbón (Thurgau) T: 071 446 6545. E: info@camping-arbon.ch

alanrogers.com/CH9180

This small site is directly beside Lake Bodensee in the town's parkland. The site has some shade and a few of the touring pitches are by the water's edge. A large, adjoining lawned field is used for tents and also leads to the playground and paddling pool. There are many static caravans but said to be room for 100 touring units. Pitches are on a mixture of gravel and grass, on flat areas on either side of access roads, most with 6/10A electricity. Cars may have to be parked elsewhere. A railway runs directly along one side. A single set of buildings provide all the site's amenities. There is access for boats from the campsite, but powered craft must be under a certain h.p. There are splendid views across this large, inland sea and interesting boats ply up and down between Constance and Lindau and Bregenz.

Facilities

Toilet facilities are clean and modern, and should just about suffice in high season. Washing machine, dryer and drying area. Fridge. Shop (basic supplies, drinks and snacks all season). General room. Playground. Dogs are not accepted. Off site: Tennis 150 m. Town swimming lido 400 m. Watersports and steamer trips are available on the lake; walks and marked cycle tracks around it. Nature reserve nearby.

Open: 1 April - 8 October.

Directions

On Arbon-Konstanz road 13. From Arbon, turn right at Aldi supermarket. From A1 take Arbon West exit and head towards town. Straight on at lights and turn left just after the town sign. Turn left again and head towards warehouses. Turn right, cross the railway line and follow lane to site.
GPS: 47.52470, 9.42065

Charges guide

Per person	CHF 8.00
child (6-16 yrs)	CHF 4.00
pitch	CHF 16.00
electricity	CHF 3.00

Kreuzlingen

Camping Fischerhaus

Promenadenstrasse 52, CH-8280 Kreuzlingen (Thurgau) T: 071 688 4903.

E: camping.fischerhaus@bluewin.ch **alanrogers.com/CH9185**

Camping Fischerhaus is tucked away behind the town's light industrial area and next to Lake Constance. It provides 250 pitches of which 150 are for tourers, all with 10A electricity supply. These are mainly on grass, with some long hardstandings for larger outfits, and are located towards the back of the site. The seasonal pitches are grouped together near reception and the lakeside. A small toilet block serves the touring area, with full sanitary facilities near reception. The restaurant and bar are pleasantly located by the lakeside. The town of Kreuzlingen is a short walk away along the banks of the lake past a marina.

Facilities

The main sanitary block, near reception, has WCs, showers and facilities for disabled visitors. The second block, near the area used by touring units, just has WCs. Washing machines and dryer. Small shop for basics. Hot and cold snacks available from reception. Indoor and outdoor seating areas. Restaurant and bar overlooking lake. Playground. Fishing. Communal barbecue areas. Dogs are not accepted. Off site: Swimming pool adjacent (free for campers).

Open: 20 March - 26 October.

Directions

Site is at the east side of Kreuzlingen on the banks of Lake Constance. It is well signed from all directions as is the adjoining swimming pool.
GPS: 47.64705, 9.19873

Charges guide

Per person	CHF 9.50
child (6-16 yrs)	CHF 4.50
pitch incl. electricity	CHF 17.00 - 19.50
tent pitch	CHF 8.00 - 16.00

For latest campsite news, availability and prices visit
alanrogers.com

Locarno

Camping Delta

Via Respini 7, CH-6600 Locarno (Ticino) T: 091 751 6081. E: info@campingdelta.com

alanrogers.com/CH9900

Camping Delta is an easy 800 m. walk or cycle ride from the centre of the lovely lakeside town of Locarno. It has a prime position right by the lake, with bathing direct from the site between 07.00 and 22.00, and is next to the municipal lido and sports field. The site has some moorings on an inlet at one side, with a jetty. It has 240 level touring pitches (50-100 sq.m). They are marked out at the rear but with no other demarcation, giving an informal mix of all kinds of camper. Waterside pitches are premium priced. Campers have access to the municipally owned beach and lakeside gardens.

Facilities

The single toilet block is some distance from the more expensive pitches. Facilities for disabled visitors (key). Washing machines and dryers. Motorcaravan services. Large shop. Restaurant/bar with terrace and limited menu. Fitness area. Two playgrounds. Babysitting. Badminton. Amusements. Club room with TV, library and electronic games. Entertainment and excursions. Children's entertainment. WiFi (charged). Kayak hire. Bicycle hire (incl. electric). Shuttle to Locarno. No dogs.

Open: 1 March - 31 October.

Directions

From central Locarno follow signs to Camping Delta, Lido or Stadio along the lake. Beware that approaching from south there are also Delta signs which lead you to Albergo Delta in quite the wrong place. GPS: 46.15556, 8.80027

Charges guide

Per unit incl. 2 persons and electricity	CHF 52.00 - 102.00
extra person	CHF 13.00 - 20.00
child (9-15 yrs)	CHF 6.00

Meride

TCS Camping Meride-Mendrisio

CH-6866 Meride (Ticino) T: 091 646 4330. E: camping.meride@tcs.ch

alanrogers.com/CH9970

Meride is a small village in the extreme south of Switzerland close to the Italian border, and not far from the A2/N2 motorway. Parco al Sole is on a slight slope 1 km. from the village. There is space for 65 small touring units with 13A electricity connections available for all (long leads required). The pitches are not numbered or marked out, but are level on terraces, mostly among tall trees. When the site is busy, units could be crowded, it is therefore requested that towing cars are parked outside. This site would make a good stop over, with a refreshing dip in the pool welcome at the end of a long journey.

Facilities

A good quality sanitary block with the usual facilities, free hot water and a baby room. Additional toilets by reception. Grotto Café with log fire in cool weather serving drinks and simple evening meals. Basic food supplies. Refurbished, heated swimming pool (1/6-30/8) and paddling pool. Playground. Some entertainment is organised in high season. Bouncy castle. TV and videos (in café). Tented club room for entertainment and groups. WiFi over site (free). Off site: Bicycle hire 7 km.

Open: 19 April - 22 September.

Directions

From N2/A2 motorway take exit 52 for Mendrisio towards Stabio, Varese. Head to Rancate then Basazio, Arzo and Meride. Site signed (6 km. from motorway exit). Road to site is narrow. GPS: 45.88887, 8.94883

Charges guide

Per unit incl. 2 persons and electricity	CHF 38.00 - 56.00
extra person	CHF 10.00 - 11.00
child (6-15 yrs)	CHF 5.00 - 5.50

Muzzano

TCS Camping Lugano

Via alla Foce 14, CH-6933 Muzzano (Ticino) T: 091 994 7788. E: camping.muzzano@tcs.ch

alanrogers.com/CH9950

Camping Lugano, a modernised site facing south onto Lake Lugano, must rank as one of the better sites in Switzerland for a complete family holiday. There are 250 numbered pitches (200 for touring units) all with 10A Europlug, and 26 have water and drainage. Trees in most parts of the site offer shade to those who prefer less direct sunshine. Cars must be left in the car park, which makes the site less cluttered and safer for children. The site is only a short distance from the airport, so there will be some daytime aircraft noise. Roads have been re-laid and a marina has been built giving full access for watersports.

Facilities

The original refurbished toilet block and a splendid new one which includes a baby room and an excellent suite for disabled visitors, are heated in cool weather. Laundry facilities. Motorcaravan services. Gas supplies. Shop. Bar/restaurant with pleasant terrace (Mar-Nov). Swimming pools (May-mid Oct). Day and TV rooms. Playground. Children's train (in season). Games room. Tennis. Volleyball. Football pitch. Fridge hire. Multisports area. Marina. Raft with slide on the lake. WiFi over site (free). Accommodation for rent. Off site: Sailing 2 km.

Open: All year.

Directions

TCS Camping Lugano is on the Bellinzona-Ponte Tresa road; take motorway exit 49 Lugano-Nord for Ponte Tresa and turn left at T-junction in Agno. Follow signs for Piodella or TCS at roundabout. Cross the bridge and turn very sharp right at the Suzuki garage and follow the lane. GPS: 45.99592, 8.90838

Charges guide

| Per unit incl. 2 persons and electricity | CHF 51.00 - 74.00 |
| per person | CHF 13.00 - 16.00 |

FREE Alan Rogers Travel Card
Extra benefits and savings - see page 14

Tenero

Camping Campofelice

Via alle Brere 7, CH-6598 Tenero (Ticino) T: 091 745 1417. E: camping@campofelice.ch

alanrogers.com/CH9890

Considered by many to be the best family campsite in Switzerland, Campofelice is bordered on the front by Lake Maggiore and on one side by the Verzasca estuary, where the site has its own marina. It is divided into rows, with 721 generously sized touring pitches on flat grass on either side of hard access roads. Mostly well shaded, all pitches have electricity connections (10-13A, 360 Europlug) and 410 also have water, drainage and TV connections. Pitches near the lake cost more (these are not available for motorcaravans until September) and a special area is reserved for small tents. A little more expensive than other sites in the area, but excellent value for the range and quality of the facilities. Sporting facilities are good and there are cycle paths in the area, including into Locarno. A free shuttle bus runs to Locarno ferry terminal. The beach by the lake is sandy, long and wider than the usual lakeside ones, and has now been extended, with well kept lawns for sunbathing. It shelves gently so that bathing is safe for children. Within a demarcated area are floating trampolines and rafts, and a specially marked section for toddlers. A slipway may be used for small boats and dinghies, with canoe and pedalo hire on site. A giant marquee caters for entertainments of all kinds and is used as a playground in wet weather.

Facilities

The six toilet blocks (three heated) are of exemplary quality. Washing machines and dryers. Motorcaravan services. Gas supplies. Supermarket, restaurant, bar and takeaway (all season). Snack kiosk at beach. Lifeguards on duty. Tennis. Minigolf. Bicycle hire. Canoe and pedalo hire. Boat launching. Playgrounds. Doctor calls. Dogs are not accepted. New chalet for disabled visitors. Camping accessories shop. Car hire. Car wash. WiFi (charged). Off site: Fishing 500 m. Water-skiing and windsurfing 1 km. Riding 5 km. Golf 8 km. Boatyard with maintenance facilities.

Open: 27 March - 31 October.

Directions

On the Bellinzona-Locarno road 13, exit Tenero. Site is signed at Co-op roundabout. Coming from the south, enter Tenero and follow signs to site. GPS: 46.16895, 8.85592

Charges guide

| Per unit incl. 2 persons and electricity | CHF 39.00 - 90.00 |
| extra person | CHF 9.00 - 11.00 |

Some pitches have min. stay regulations. Discounts for stays over 10 days and for seniors.

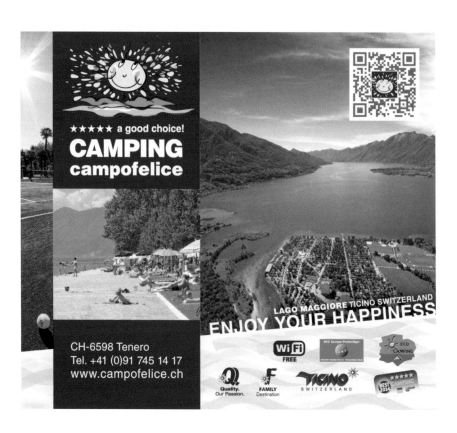

For latest campsite news, availability and prices visit

alanrogers.com

Tenero

Camping Lido Mappo

Via Mappo, CH-6598 Tenero (Ticino) T: 091 745 1437. E: camping@lidomappo.ch

alanrogers.com/CH9880

Lido Mappo lies on the lakeside at the northeast tip of Lake Maggiore, about 5 km. from Locarno, and has views of the surrounding mountains and hills across the lake. The site is attractively laid out in rows of individual, numbered pitches, mostly demarcated by access roads or hedges. Mature trees provide plenty of shade. The pitches (357 for touring) are occupied by a mixture of tents, caravans and motorcaravans; they vary in size, those by the lake cost more and must be booked by the week. Electricity (10-16A Europlug; long leads useful) is available on all pitches. With helpful, English-speaking staff, this is a quiet site with its own narrow, mainly sandy beach.

Facilities
The five recently renovated toilet blocks are well placed throughout the site with good access and facilities for disabled visitors. They include individual washbasins, all in cabins for women and some for men. Baby changing area. Washing machines and dryers. Cooking facilities and communal barbecue. Refrigerated compartments for hire. Motorcaravan services. Excellent supermarket. Restaurant/bar. Takeaway. TV room. Large playground. Volleyball. Lake swimming. Fishing. First aid post. Dogs are not accepted. Internet room and WiFi (free). Off site: Bicycle hire nearby. Riding 3 km. Golf 5 km.

Open: 1 April - 30 October.

Directions
On Bellinzona-Locarno road 13, exit Tenero. Site is signed at Co-op roundabout. From Locarno, enter Tenero and follow signs. There are several campsites, so watch for the names. GPS: 46.17706, 8.84251

Charges guide
Per unit incl. 2 persons and electricity	CHF 36.00 - 93.00
extra person	CHF 7.00

Less 5% for stays over 14 days (all season) and 10% over 21 days (low season).

Engelberg

Camping Eienwäldli

Wasserfallstrasse 108, CH-6390 Engelberg (Unterwalden) T: 041 637 1949. E: info@eienwaeldli.ch

alanrogers.com/CH9570

Idyllically situated near the beautiful village of Engelberg, surrounded by mountains, 3,500 feet above sea level, this all-year site must be one of the very best in Switzerland. The comprehensive range of facilities would be hard to beat. Half of the site is taken up by static caravans which are grouped together at one side. The camping area is in two parts – nearest the entrance there are 57 hardstandings for caravans and motorcaravans, all with electricity (metered), and beyond this is a flat meadow for about 70 tents. Reception can be found in the very modern foyer of the Eienwäldli Hotel which also houses the indoor pool, health complex, excellent shop and café/bar. The area is famous as a winter sports region and summer tourist resort.

Facilities
The main toilet block, heated in cool weather, is situated at the rear of the hotel and has free hot water in washbasins (in cabins) and charged for showers (CHF 1.00). A new modern toilet block has been added near the top of the site. Washing machines and dryers. Shop. Café/bar. New restaurant. Small lounge with kitchen, TV/DVD and library. Indoor pool complex with spa facilities. Physiotherapy suite. Ski facilities including a drying room. Refurbished play area with a rafting pool fed by fresh water from the mountain stream. Free shuttle bus. Torches useful. WiFi (charged). Off site: Golf driving range and 18-hole course nearby. Fishing 1 km.

Open: All year.

Directions
From N2 Gotthard motorway, leave at exit 33 Stans-Sud and follow signs to Engelberg. Turn right at T-junction on edge of town and follow signs to 'Wasserfall' and site. GPS: 46.80940, 8.42367

Charges guide
Per person	CHF 9.00 - 11.00
child (6-15 yrs)	CHF 4.50 - 5.50
pitch incl. electricity (plus meter)	CHF 15.00 - 17.00
dog	CHF 3.00

Credit cards accepted (surcharge).

Sarnen

Camping Seefeld Sarnen

Seestrasse 20, CH-6060 Sarnen (Unterwalden) T: 041 666 5788. E: welcome@seefeldpark.ch

alanrogers.com/CH9540

One of the finest sites we have seen, Camping Seefeld Sarnen was completely rebuilt with all the features demanded by discerning campers and reopened in 2011. The location alongside Lake Sarnen is breathtaking, with views across the water to lush meadows, wooded hills and mountains topped with snow for most of the year. The seasonal pitches are immaculately maintained on their own area. There are 94 touring pitches arranged on almost level grass, each with 13A electricity and its own water tap. There is some shade from young trees which will increase as time goes on. The site not only offers active family holidays on land and on the water, but is ideally placed for exploring this beautiful part of Switzerland. Leave the motorways and discover the enduring charm of centuries old agricultural life, centred on the welfare of the typical grey/brown cattle and the 'white gold' of milk. Within easy reach are Lake Lucerne, Brienz and its cog railway and the ever-popular Interlaken. From Stansstad, the mountain railway runs to the summit of the renowned Mount Pilatus. Hikers and cyclists can enjoy the many trails available. In summer there is a discount card for local transport.

Facilities

Heated sanitary facilities are in the main building supplemented by unheated facilities in the centre block. Baby room and cubicles for children. Facilities for disabled visitors. Washing machines and dryers. Shop, bar and restaurant with large terrace (Easter-Oct). Campers' lounge with kitchen, TV/DVD, tables and chairs. Two swimming pools with lifeguards (20/4-15/9). Two playgrounds. Watersports. Tennis. Bicycle hire. Dog bath; dogs not accepted in high season. WiFi throughout (free). Off site: Nature reserve adjacent. Luzern. Winter sports. Sports complex next door. Lake steamer trips. Easy runs to Lucerne and Interlaken. Cog railway from Brienz.

Open: All year.

Directions

Approaching from Luzern (A8), leave at Sarnen's southern junction. Pass through the town in the direction of Interlaken and Sachseln. Follow Camping Seefeld signs to the site. GPS: 46.88390, 8.24413

Charges guide

Per unit incl. 2 persons and electricity	CHF 31.00 - 59.00
dog	CHF 3.00 - 4.00

Camping Seefeld***** – for a stay to remember

- Picturesque location in the heart of Switzerland with a wealth of places to visit
- Spacious plots with own electricity and water supplies
- Up-to-date, top-quality infrastructure complete with restaurant and camping shop
- Swimming pool with beach
- Plenty of sporting and leisure activities

Camping Seefeld
Seestrasse 20
CH-6060 Sarnen
Tel. +41 (0)41 666 57 88
www.seefeldpark.ch
welcome@seefeldpark.ch

Bouveret

Camping Rive-Bleue

Camping de Passage, Chemin drie Vieilles Chenevieres, CH-1897 Bouveret (Valais) T: 024 481 2161.

E: info@camping-rive-bleue.ch **alanrogers.com/CH9600**

At the eastern end of Lac Léman (Lake Geneva) with mountain and lakeside views, Camping Rive-Bleue is an excellent destination for family holidays whilst affording quiet relaxation. The car-free camping area is a level 300 m. from the related hotel, restaurant and lido complex with free entry to campers. It has an excellent pool and paddling pool, with beautiful lawns leading down to the sandy lakeside beach. There are pedalos and canoes for hire, and a sailing school. The site has 220 marked touring pitches on well tended flat grass, with some shade from maturing trees and 150 of these have 8-12A Europlugs.

Facilities

Two newly refurbished toilet blocks are well equipped and offer all the usual facilities including spacious rooms for disabled visitors. Washing machine and dryer. Covered area with electric rings, barbecue, sinks, table and chairs, electronic games and a TV. Motorcaravan services (Euro-relais). Shop, restaurant by beach. Outdoor swimming pool (heated Jun-Aug). Fishing. WiFi (30 mins. free). Off site: Bicycle hire (first 2 hours free) 500 m.

Open: 1 April - 16 October.

Directions

Leave motorway A9/N9, south of Montreux, at exit 16 (Villeneuve) and follow signs for Evian. Just after passing town sign for Bouveret, turn right at roundabout and follow Aquaparc and site signs. GPS: 46.38657, 6.86017

Charges guide

Per unit incl. 2 persons and electricity	CHF 33.90 - 41.60
extra person	CHF 8.70 - 10.90

La Fouly
Camping des Glaciers
CH-1944 La Fouly (Valais) T: 027 783 1826. E: info@camping-glaciers.ch

alanrogers.com/CH9660

Camping des Glaciers is set amidst magnificent mountain scenery in a peaceful location in the beautiful Ferret Valley, almost 5,000 feet above sea level. The site offers generous pitches in an open, undulating meadow and the rest are level, individual plots of varying sizes in small clearings, between bushes and shrubs or under tall pines. Most of the 220 pitches have 10A electricity (long leads useful). M. Alain Darbellay has meticulously maintained the family's determination to keep the site unspoilt and in keeping with its mountain environment. He intends to maintain the strong family interest and friendships built up over the years. Additional land has been added to increase the number of pitches available.

Facilities
Three sanitary units of exceptional quality are heated when necessary. The newest unit has super facilities for children and wide access for disabled visitors. Hot water is free in all washbasins (some in cabins), showers and sinks. Laundry facilities. Baby room. Motorcaravan services. Small shop for basics. Bread and cakes to order daily. Recreation room with TV. Playground. Mountain bike hire. Communal fire pit. WiFi (free). Torches useful.
Open: 15 May - 30 September.

Directions
Leave Martigny-Gd St Bernard road (no. 21/E27) to the right where signed Orsieres/La Fouly. Site is signed on right at end of La Fouly village. Access is fairly tight and long units should take care.
GPS: 45.93347, 7.09367

Charges guide
Per unit incl. 2 persons and electricity	CHF 28.40 - 35.50
extra person	CHF 8.00

Leuk
Camping Bella-Tola
Waldstrasse 133, CH-3952 Susten-Leuk (Valais) T: 027 473 1491. E: info@bella-tola.ch

alanrogers.com/CH9720

An attractive and popular site with good standards, Bella-Tola is on the hillside above Susten (east of Sierre) with good views over the Rhône valley. The site has been extensively terraced with sectors allocated to seasonal units, a tour operator and touring units. All of the 140 individually numbered pitches have 16A electricity connections. The fullest season is mid July - mid August when reservation is advised, but there is usually room somewhere. The site boasts a good sized, heated swimming pool and children's pool (both free to campers) which, like the restaurant and bar overlooking them, are also open to non-campers and so more crowded at weekends and holidays. The Valais region enjoys lower rainfall than the rest of the country, and locals and visitors alike make good use of the swimming pools. High in the forested hillsides, there are unlimited opportunities for walking and biking, which make the steep climb to the site worthwhile. Jagged and snowcapped peaks tower above. Newly rebuilt facilities for ladies in the central toilet block are of the highest quality, and plans are in hand for the men's section. Three new family suites for rent are planned.

Facilities
Three good, modern sanitary blocks should be quite sufficient, with some washbasins in cabins. New section for ladies. Baby room and showers for children. Facilities for disabled visitors. Laundry facilities. Motorcaravan services. Shop. Newly renovated restaurant/bar. Takeaway (July/Aug). Swimming pool (heated 29/5-20/9) paddling pool with slide and pool bar. General room with TV. Bicycle hire. Play area. Films and guided walks in July/Aug. Communal barbecue. Torches advised. WiFi in some parts (free). Off site: Riding 1 km. Golf 4 km.
Open: 18 April - 31 October.

Directions
Travelling eastwards from Sierre along main road, small site road is to the right (south) just after entering Susten (site signed).
GPS: 46.29951, 7.63564

Charges guide
Per unit incl. 2 persons and electricity	CHF 47.85 - 55.95
extra person	CHF 12.05
child (2-16 yrs acc. to age)	CHF 7.20 - 9.65
dog (max. 1)	CHF 2.70

Les Haudères

Camping de Molignon

Route de Molignon, 163, CH-1984 Les Haudères (Valais) T: 027 283 1240. E: info@molignon.ch

alanrogers.com/CH9670

Camping de Molignon, surrounded by mountains, is a peaceful haven 1,450 m. above sea level. The rushing stream at the bottom of the site and the sound of cow bells and birdsong are likely to be the only disturbing factors in summer. The 95 pitches for touring units (all with 10A electricity) are on well tended terraces leading down to the river. Six chalets are available to rent. Excellent English is spoken by the owner's son who is now running the site. He is always pleased to give information on all that is available from the campsite. The easy uphill drive from Sion in the Rhône Valley is enhanced by ancient villages and the Pyramids of Euseigne.

Facilities

Two fully equipped sanitary blocks, heated in cool weather, with free hot showers. Baby room. Washing machines and dryers. Kitchen for hikers. Motorcaravan services. Gas supplies. Shop for basics (15/6-15/9). Restaurant. Heated swimming pool with cover for cool weather (6x12 m). Outdoor paddling pool. Playground. Sitting room for games and reading. Guided walks, climbing, geological museum, winter skiing. Fishing. Internet corner. WiFi in parts of site (free). Off site: Tennis and hang-gliding nearby. Ski and sports gear hire 1 km.

Open: All year.

Directions

Leave the motorway at exit 27 and follow signs southwards from Sion for the Val d'Herens through Evolène to Les Haudères where site and restaurant is signed on the right at the beginning of the village. GPS: 46.09003, 7.50722

Charges guide

Per unit incl. 2 persons	
and electricity	CHF 23.40 - 34.40
extra person	CHF 5.80 - 7.20
child (4-16 yrs)	CHF 3.20 - 4.00

Leuk

Camping Gemmi Agarn

Briannenstrasse 8, CH-3952 Susten-Leuk (Valais) T: 027 473 1154. E: info@campgemmi.ch

alanrogers.com/CH9730

The Rhône Valley is a popular through route to Italy via the Simplon Pass and a holiday region in its own right. Gemmi is a delightful small, friendly site in a scenic location with 65 level touring pitches, all with 16A electricity, on grass amidst a variety of trees, some of which offer shade. There are 41 pitches with water, 26 with drainage as well. Some pitches have TV connections. Always well maintained, the grounds have been greatly improved by the enthusiastic new owners. Seven seasonal pitches remain, with one unit for rent. Enjoying some of the best climatic conditions in Switzerland, this valley, between two mountain regions, has less rainfall and more hours of sunshine than most of the country.

Facilities

A modern sanitary block, partly heated, is kept very clean. It includes some washbasins in cabins. Eight private bathrooms for hire on a weekly basis. Laundry facilities. Motorcaravan services. Gas supplies. Shop. Small bar/restaurant where snacks and a limited range of local dishes is served. Terrace bar and snack restaurant. Play area. TV room. Small library. WiFi throughout (charged). Off site: Swimming and walking. Golf 500 m.

Open: Easter - mid October.

Directions

From east (Visp), turn left 1 km. after sign for Agarn Feithieren. From west (Sierre), turn right 2 km. after Susten at sign for Camping Torrent and Gemmi. GPS: 46.29781, 7.65937

Charges guide

Per unit incl. 2 persons	
and electricity	CHF 36.00 - 41.00
extra person	CHF 8.00 - 9.00
child (1-15 yrs)	CHF 6.00 - 6.50

Martigny

TCS Camping les Neuvilles

Rue de Levant 68, CH-1920 Martigny (Valais) T: 027 722 4544. E: camping.martigny@tcs.ch

alanrogers.com/CH9655

Easily accessible from the autoroute (A9) and close to the town centre, this site has a total of 225 pitches. There are 185 for touring units, all with 6/10A electricity (long leads may be necessary) and most on level, grassy ground (some slope slightly). There are 18 pitches with some hardstanding for motorcaravans. A number of trees provide some shade, although the site is fairly open allowing views of the surrounding mountains. Being close to the autoroute and located near an industrial area, the site can be quite noisy at times. With its ease of access and close proximity to shops, it makes a convenient night stop when travelling along the Rhône Valley for the Saint Bernard Pass.

Facilities

Two sanitary buildings, one close to the entrance, the other at the far end. Showers are large and free, some washbasins in cabins, some with only cold water. Facilities for disabled visitors. Baby room. Cooking rings. Laundry facilities. Motorcaravan services. Bar. TV room. Play area and paddling pool. Bouncy castle. Minigolf. Boules. Bicycle hire. WiFi throughout (free). Torches useful (the touring area is unlit). Off site: Shop and restaurant nearby.

Open: 4 April - 28 October.

Directions

From A9 exit 22 (Martigny) follow signs for Expo. After leaving the autoroute, at first roundabout, site is signed. Follow signs carefully; entrance to site is at the rear, by the cemetery. GPS: 46.09703, 7.07877

Charges guide

Per unit incl. 2 persons	
and electricity	CHF 38.00 - 46.00
extra person	CHF 9.00 - 11.00
child (2-7 yrs)	CHF 5.00 - 5.50

For latest campsite news, availability and prices visit

alanrogers.com

Randa

Camping Attermenzen

CH-3928 Randa (Valais) T: 027 967 2555. E: rest.camping@rhone.ch

alanrogers.com/CH9740

Randa, a picturesque Valais village, at 1,409 m, is a beautiful location for a campsite and ideal for those wishing to visit Zermatt only 10 km. away. Reception is open from mid June to mid September, otherwise call at the restaurant (closed on Tuesdays). Unmarked pitches are on an uneven field with some areas that are fairly level and 6A electricity is within easy reach. A paradise for walking, mountaineering, climbing and mountain biking and surrounded by famous 4,000 m. peaks, such as the Dom and Weisshorn, this site also offers good modern facilities with a restaurant and bar next door.

Facilities
The sanitary block is of a good standard and well maintained with free showers. Washing machine. Shop (June-Sept). Gas supplies. Restaurant/bar and takeaway (closed Jan). Bicycle hire. WiFi over site (charged). Off site: Golf 200 m. Zermatt 10 km.

Open: All year.

Directions
From A9 at Visp turn right at roundabout (Zermatt). Go through the 3.3 km. long tunnel and follow road towards Zermatt. Go through Stalden and turn right at roundabout (Zermatt). Site is 1 km. after Randa village on the left. GPS: 46.08549, 7.781

Charges guide

Per unit incl. 2 persons and electricity	CHF 28.00 - 29.00
extra person	CHF 6.00

Raron

Camping Santa Monica

Kantonstrasse 56, CH-3942 Raron-Turtig (Valais) T: 027 934 2424. E: info@santa-monica.ch

alanrogers.com/CH9770

This extensive and busy family run site has something for everyone, from super pitches and private toilet cabins to the small tent pitches. Two heated swimming pools and two play areas make it a family destination as well as a convenient stopover. The 145 touring pitches all have 16A electricity and are gently defined by saplings and marker posts. There are three grades of pitch, from standard to fully serviced. There are also ten private toilet cabins for rent. Being alongside the main road, there can be noise at busy times. With mountain views, across the valley, Santa Monica has an air of peace and spaciousness. Two separate cable cars start near the site entrance and go to two mountain villages.

Facilities
Two heated toilet blocks have free hot water in washbasins, sinks and showers. Baby bath and changing area. Facilities for disabled visitors. Private cabins to rent by the service pitches. Laundry facilities. Motorcaravan services. Gas supplies. Bar and terrace, restaurant and shop (Easter-17/10). Small pool and children's pool (heated 1/6-30/8). Playground and play house. Ski room. Club room with library. TV room. WiFi throughout (charged). Off site: Shops and restaurants nearby. Tennis courts next door. Cable cars adjacent.

Open: Easter - 17 October (call to confirm).

Directions
From Visp take the E62/19. Approaching Raron, ignore the first campsite signs and filter. Santa Monica is another 500 m. on the left, with large arched sign, just before Renault garage and opposite the Bergheim Hotel. GPS: 46.30288, 7.80238

Charges guide

Per unit incl. 2 persons and electricity	CHF 27.00 - 41.00
extra person	CHF 6.00 - 8.00
child (6-16 yrs)	CHF 4.00 - 5.00
dog (max. 1)	CHF 3.80

Reckingen

Camping Augenstern

Postfach 16, CH-3998 Reckingen (Valais) T: 027 973 1395. E: info@campingaugenstern.ch

alanrogers.com/CH9790

The village of Reckingen is about halfway between Brig and the Furka/Grimsel passes. You can still get the train with a car/caravan or a motorcaravan from Oberwald to Andermatt to avoid the steep climbs and descents of the Furka Pass, but in doing so you will miss some exhilarating scenery. This family run site, at 1,326 m. provides 100 flat, level pitches for touring units, all with 10A electricity. There is a little shade. Water points are equipped with long hoses. It provides an excellent base for walking, climbing or cycling as well as rafting on the Rhône in the summer or skiing in the winter.

Facilities
The toilet block has recently been refitted to the highest standards. Showers on payment. Washing machine and dryer. Motorcaravan services. No facilities for campers with disabilities, due to restricted access. Shop for essentials (July/Aug). Restaurant/bar with satellite TV. Play area with inflatable pool in season. WiFi throughout (charged, but free near reception). Off site: Swimming pool complex 200 m. Bicycle hire 400 m. Reckingen 500 m. Riding 800 m. Local skiing and rafting 1.5 km.

Open: 13 May - 21 October, 15 December - 21 March.

Directions
From the no. 19 road turn south in Reckingen next to church. Go down hill, along one-way street, carefully over railway and covered bridge. Over next bridge and follow the lane past the swimming pool to the site entrance. GPS: 46.46427, 8.24472

Charges guide

Per unit incl. 2 persons and electricity	CHF 35.30 - 46.00
extra person	CHF 9.00 - 11.00
No credit cards.	

FREE Alan Rogers Travel Card
Extra benefits and savings - see page 14

Saillon

Camping de la Sarvaz

100 route de Fully, CH-1913 Saillon (Valais) T: 027 744 1389. E: info@sarvaz.ch

alanrogers.com/CH9640

The Rhône valley in Valais with its terraced vineyards and young orchards provides a beautiful setting for this site. Family owned and run, Camping de la Sarvaz provides outstanding facilities and is an ideal centre for relaxing or, for the more energetic, walking, cycling, climbing or skiing. The focal point of the site is a restaurant/bar with a delightful Chinese-style garden. There are 87 level touring pitches all with 16A electricity, 45 of which have water and drainage. Four new, 140 sq.m. pitches have private cabins containing toilet and kitchen facilities. Lovely mountain views surround the site and there are nine chalets to rent. The owners are always seeking to make improvements, and have now added a heated, half-covered swimming pool with a secure shallow end for small children, a breakfast room, dishwashing machines, a minigolf course and a new motorcaravan service point.

Facilities

Heated sanitary facilities are of a very high standards, very well maintained. Free showers. Additional toilets on the first floor. Facilities for disabled visitors. Baby room. Washing machine and dryer. Three fast dishwashers. Small communal kitchen. Motorcaravan services. First class shop. Restaurant/bar (all season, not Mon/Tues). New heated, half-covered swimming pool (May-Sept). Excellent games/play areas. Additional playroom and games room. Sitting room with TV/DVD and library. Minigolf. Bicycle hire. WiFi throughout (free). Off site: Saillon 2 km. with thermal centre and spa.

Open: 6 February - 8 January.

Directions

From the A9 take exit 23 for Saxon/Saillon. Follow signs to Saillon then turn right towards the site, which is 3 km. from the autoroute exit. GPS: 46.15988, 7.167

Charges guide

Per unit incl. 2 persons	
and electricity	CHF 41.00 - 70.00
extra person	CHF 10.00
child (6-16 yrs)	CHF 5.00
dog	CHF 4.00

Vétroz

Camping du Botza

Route du Camping 1, CH-1963 Vétroz (Valais) T: 027 346 1940. E: info@botza.ch

alanrogers.com/CH9520

Situated in the Rhône Valley just off the autoroute, this is a pleasant site with views of the surrounding mountains. It is set in a peaceful wooded location, although there is occasional aircraft noise. There are 125 individual touring pitches, ranging in size (60-155 sq.m) all with 4A electricity, many with some shade and 25 with water and drainage. Pitches are priced according to size and facilities. The reception, office, lounge, shop and restaurant have all been completely rebuilt. The conservatory-style restaurant overlooks the pool and the entertainment area. Both are open to the public but free to campers. A warm welcome is assured from the enthusiastic English-speaking owner.

Facilities

New sanitary block and another completely renovated. Some private cabins in the heated sanitary block. Washing machines and dryers. Shop. Brand new restaurant (closed Jan) and terrace. Bar. Bakery. Ice cream kiosk. Takeaway. Heated swimming pool with slides and diving board (15/5-1/9). Playground. Table football and electronic games. Tennis. Basketball. TV room with Internet corner. Entertainment stage. Multi-lingual library. WiFi over site (free). Off site: Fitness trail in woods opposite. Many walks alongside small streams nearby.

Open: All year.

Directions

From the A9/E62 between Sion and Martigny, take exit 25 Conthey/Vétroz and go south towards 'zone industrial', after 200 m. turn right to 'Camping 9.33 Botza' and follow signs. Site is 2.5 km. from autoroute exit. GPS: 46.20583, 7.27867

Charges guide

Per unit incl. 2 persons	
and electricity	CHF 25.80 - 45.70
extra person	CHF 5.00 - 8.50
child (6-16 yrs)	CHF 2.50 - 4.25
dog	CHF 3.50

For latest campsite news, availability and prices visit

alanrogers.com

Visp

Camping Schwimmbad Mühleye

CH-3930 Visp (Valais) T: 027 946 2084. E: info@camping-visp.ch

alanrogers.com/CH9775

Camping Mühleye is a popular family site located in the Valais, near the busy centre of Visp. The site has 199 grassy pitches, 160 for touring units with 10A electricity, ranging in size from 80-150 sq.m, including 20 very large (150 sq.m) pitches (with electricity, water and drainage). Although the pitches are marked and numbered, the site has a relaxed informal appearance with plenty of space between units. The valley and mountain views are typically Swiss. The town of Visp is a 15 minute walk away, from which it is easy to explore the area by bus and train. Saas Fee, Zermatt and the Matterhorn are all within reach. The site's reception, restaurant and bar have been completely rebuilt to a most attractive design. Next to the site is a magnificent heated pool complex for both adults and children, which is open from May to September. Campers are entitled to entry at reduced rates when paid with camping fees and is free between 18.00 and 19.00. There are also special package rates for weekly and monthly stays.

Facilities

New central sanitary block is modern and spacious. Facilities for disabled visitors. Washing machines and dryers. Free use of fridges and freezers. Motorcaravan services. Two children's play areas and an indoor play room if wet. Large covered sitting area with tables and chairs. Extensive information for walking, hiking and mountain biking. Internet access. WiFi throughout (free). Off site: Adjacent heated pool complex (reduced rates) served by the site's shop, bar and takeaway. Visp centre and supermarket 800 m. Saas Fee 25 km. Zermatt 36 km. Riding and bicycle hire 2 km. Golf 20 km.

Open: 3 April - 31 October.

Directions

From the direction of Brig on the E62/19, drive through the town, and turn right at the Socar station and VW garage, where Mühleye is clearly signed. Follow signs to the site. From the west, watch for the petrol station on the left. GPS: 46.29808, 7.87271

Charges guide

Per unit incl. 2 persons and electricity	CHF 26.80 - 26.30
extra person	CHF 6.10 - 6.90
child (6-16 yrs)	CHF 3.20 - 3.90
dog (max. 2)	CHF 1.50 - 2.00

Lausanne

Camping De Vidy

Chemin du Camping 3, CH-1007 Lausanne (Vaud) T: 021 622 5000. E: info@clv.ch

alanrogers.com/CH9270

The ancient city of Lausanne spills down the hillside towards Lake Geneva until it meets the peaceful park in which this site is situated. Owned by the city, the managers have enhanced its neat and tidy appearance by planting many flowers and shrubs. Hard access roads separate the site into sections for tents, caravans and motorcaravans, with 10A electrical connections in all parts, except the tent areas. Pitches are on flat grass, numbered but not marked out, with 260 (of 350) for tourers. Some large pitches near the lake are suitable for American motorhomes.

Facilities

Three excellent sanitary blocks, one heated, have mostly British and some Turkish style WCs, hot water in washbasins, sinks and showers with warm, pre-mixed water. Facilities for disabled visitors. Motorcaravan services (Euro-Relais). Gas supplies. Shop and self-service bar/restaurant (1/5-30/9). Takeaway (high season). Playground. Weekend entertainment in high season. Lake swimming. Fishing. WiFi (charged). Reception has tourist information on Lausanne. Off site: Free pass for local transport. Boat excursions on the lake.

Open: All year.

Directions

Site is 500 m. west of La Maladière. Take N1 Lausanne-Süd, exit no. 3 La Maladière, and at roundabout almost turn back on yourself following signs for CIO and camping. At traffic lights turn left, then on for site. From the south and east on N9, exit at J10 and follow signs for CIO (Olympic symbols). Site signed next to CIO HQ. GPS: 46.51600, 6.59900

Charges guide

Per unit incl. 2 persons and electricity	CHF 40.20 - 42.20
extra person	CHF 8.50

Morges
TCS Camping Morges

Promenade du Petit-Bois 15, CH-1110 Morges (Vaud) T: 021 801 1270. E: camping.morges@tcs.ch

alanrogers.com/CH9240

This excellent and busy TCS campsite is on the edge of Morges, a wine growing centre with a 13th-century castle on Lake Geneva about 8 km. west of Lausanne. Flowers, shrubs and trees adorn the site and the neat, tidy lawns make a most pleasant environment. There are 170 grass pitches for touring units, all with 6/10A electricity and laid out in a regular pattern from wide hard access roads on which cars stand. There are eight larger pitches for motorcaravans with electricity, water and drainage. Le Petit Bois is next to the municipal sports field complex with views across the lake to the mountains beyond. A fence separates the site from the lake with gates for access to the small wildlife sanctuary and the water. There may be some road and rail noise at times. The friendly manager speaks good English, and will advise on local attractions.

Facilities
Three well built, fully equipped, modern toilet blocks include hot water in half the washbasins, sinks and showers. Separate block with excellent baby room. Facilities for disabled visitors. Washing machines, dryers, irons and boards. Motorcaravan services. Restaurant and takeaway. Excellent shop. Playground. Boules. Bicycle and scooter hire. Small, but fully equipped kitchen with seating. Internet point and WiFi. Children's entertainment and bouncy castle (high season). Picnic area. Fishing. Bicycle hire. Off site: Swimming pool adjacent (free to campers). Small marina. Town centre within walking distance. Tennis. Tourist bus to town calls at site on Weds. Sat. and Sun, daily in July.

Open: 1 April - 24 October.

Directions
Leave A1 autoroute (Lausanne-Geneva) at exit 15 (Morges-ouest). Turn towards town and signs for site. GPS: 46.50457, 6.48917

Charges guide
Per unit incl. 2 persons and electricity	CHF 38.90 - 55.30
child (6-15 yrs)	CHF 3.60 - 4.90
extra person	CHF 7.20 - 9.80
dog	CHF 3.00 - 5.00

Orbe
TCS Camping Le Signal

CH-1350 Orbe (Vaud) T: 024 441 3857. E: camping.orbe@tcs.ch

alanrogers.com/CH9230

Owned by the Touring Club Suisse, Camping Le Signal is located north of Lausanne, with good access to Lake Geneva and the sandy beaches of Lake Neuchâtel. There are 110 touring pitches here, all with 6A electricity. They are grassy and shaded by conifers – some slope slightly. Three fully equipped tents are available for rent. On-site amenities include a superb swimming pool, 18-hole minigolf (both next door but free to campers), small shop, bar and children's playground. A children's club is organised in July and August. Other entertainment includes sausage evenings, occasional dances and walking excursions in the area. The site has good access to the Swiss motorway network and would be suitable for an en route stop as well as a few days quiet retreat. The resident wardens are more than helpful.

Facilities
Facilities for disabled visitors. Washing machine and dryer. Shop. Bar/snack bar and takeaway. Swimming pool and minigolf adjacent (both free to campers). Play area. Occasional activities (including a club for children). Bouncy castle. Internet point and WiFi. Tents for rent. Off site: Walking and cycling. Fly fishing. Bicycle hire. Riding.

Open: 4 April - 7 October.

Directions
Approaching from the north or south on A1/N1 motorway take exit 23 to the N9. Exit at J3 towards Orbe. Entering the town, take the left filter lane to Route du Signal – signed Pool and Campsite. Site is on left at top of hill. GPS: 46.736239, 6.532343

Charges guide
Per unit incl. 2 persons and electricity	CHF 32.20 - 40.80
extra person	CHF 6.80 - 8.40
child	CHF 3.40 - 4.20
dog (max. 2)	CHF 3.00 - 5.00

For latest campsite news, availability and prices visit
alanrogers.com

Open All Year

The following sites are understood to accept caravanners and campers all year round. It is always wise to phone the site to check as the facilities available, for example, may be reduced.

Andorra

AN7145	Valira	22

Austria

AU0098	Achensee	40
AU0035	Alpin Seefeld	50
AU0025	Arlberg Panorama	47
AU0475	Brunner am See	26
AU0090	Hells Zillertal	42
AU0070	Hofer	52
AU0502	Im Thermenland	39
AU0165	Kranebitterhof	43
AU0060	Natterer See	48
AU0267	Neunbrunnen am Waldsee	36
AU0262	Oberwötzlhof	35
AU0045	Ötztal	46
AU0220	Ötztal Arena	50
AU0085	Pitztal	43
AU0155	Prutz Tirol	48
AU0405	Ramsbacher	33
AU0380	Rutar Lido (Naturist)	26
AU0440	Schluga	28
AU0065	Seehof	44
AU0102	Stadlerhof	45
AU0100	Toni	45
AU0180	Woferlgut	37
AU0160	Zell am See	38

Belgium

BE0793	Binnenvaart	63
BE0670	Clusure	70
BE0710	Colline de Rabais	71
BE0740	Eau Rouge	61
BE0733	Festival	70
BE0650	Floreal Het Veen	59
BE0665	Floreal Kempen	58
BE0732	Floreal La Roche	69
BE0701	Gossaimont	61
BE0788	Hengelhoef	63
BE0555	Klein Strand	74
BE0655	Lilse Bergen	58
BE0560	Lombarde	74
BE0684	Officiel Arlon	66
BE0735	Petite Suisse	68
BE0675	Spineuse	70
BE0725	Val de l'Aisne	68
BE0780	Wilhelm Tell	65
BE0792	Zavelbos	65

Croatia

CR6744	Brioni	85
CR6725	Porto Sole	88
CR6855	Stobrec Split	80

Czech Republic

CZ4845	Busek Praha	98
CZ4770	Dlouhá Louka	94
CZ4590	Lisci Farma	100
CZ4850	Sokol Troja	98
CZ4815	Triocamp	97

Denmark

DK2015	Esbjerg	109
DK2255	Feddet	110
DK2140	Jesperhus	113
DK2020	Møgeltønder	112
DK2150	Nibe	108
DK2215	Odense	106

Finland

FI2840	Haapasaaren Lomakylä	116
FI2970	Nallikari	119
FI2850	Rastila	119

France

FR47110	Cabri	125
FR86040	Futuriste	167
FR74230	Giffre	174
FR88040	Lac de Bouzey	153
FR65080	Lavedan	153
FR73100	Reclus	173

Germany

DE34150	Adam	185
DE30250	Alfsee	208
DE36850	Allweglehen	197
DE34520	Alte Sägemühle	192
DE30210	Am Stadtwaldsee	203
DE36960	Arterhof	196
DE38470	Auensee	227
DE34360	Bankenhof	193
DE34450	Belchenblick	191
DE32100	Biggesee	217
DE26140	Boltenhagen	210
DE35320	Bostalsee	225
DE36300	Donau-Lech	198
DE36970	Dreiquellenbad	197
DE36720	Elbsee	195
DE38360	Erzgebirgsblick	226
DE29500	Eurocamp	216
DE34390	Freiburg	186
DE36500	Gitzenweiler	200
DE32150	Goldene Meile	223
DE32020	Grav-Insel	218
DE34550	Gugel's	190
DE38200	Havelberge	212
DE30750	Heidesee	208
DE34370	Hochschwarzwald	193
DE31490	Hof Biggen	214
DE34310	Kinzigtal	192
DE34400	Kirchzarten	188
DE34060	Kleinenzhof	184
DE30080	Klüthseecamp	229
DE32600	Knaus Bad Dürkheim	218
DE28355	Knaus Eckwarderhörne	207
DE30470	Knaus Elbtalaue	206
DE31900	Knaus Hennesee	216
DE37050	Knaus Lackenhäuser	201
DE36100	Knaus Nürnberg	194
DE32220	Moselbogen	219
DE31850	Münster	216
DE34500	Münstertal	189
DE37200	Naabtal	201

DE38550	Oberhof	230
DE34200	Oberrhein	191
DE25000	Ostsee	213
DE32470	Prümtal	221
DE30100	Röders' Park	208
DE32420	Schinderhannes	222
DE30020	Schlei-Karschau	230
DE34270	Schwarzwälder Hof	191
DE31800	Sonnenwiese	217
DE28990	Stover Strand	206
DE30700	Süd-See	209
DE32800	Teichmann	205
DE36170	Via Claudia	199
DE36860	Waging	202
DE30430	Wiesenbeker Teich	205
DE32120	Wirfttal	224
DE30030	Wulfener Hals	231

Greece

GR8590	Athens	234
GR8525	Chrissa	235
GR8695	Finikes	238
GR8685	Gythion Bay	238
GR8285	Hellas International	241
GR8330	Ionion Beach	241
GR8595	Nea Kifissia	234

Hungary

HU5150	Fortuna	248
HU5184	Helló Halló Park	248
HU5260	Jonathermál	244
HU5024	Lentri	253
HU5255	Martfü	247
HU5205	Öko-Park	247
HU5094	Sárvár	250
HU5197	Termál Tiszaujvaros	245
HU5165	Zugligeti Niche	245

Italy

IT66270	Boschetto di Piemma	294
IT64010	Dei Fiori	272
IT60530	Fusina	308
IT69300	Marinello	283
IT64110	Miraflores	272
IT61844	Naturcaravanpark Tisens	289
IT62000	Olympia	289
IT69350	Rais Gerbi	282
IT69190	Scarabeo	283
IT68100	Seven Hills	269
IT62030	Sexten	288
IT65030	Valle Gesso	275

Liechtenstein

FL7580	Mittagspitze	311

Luxembourg

LU7850	Fuussekaul	317
LU7700	Gaalgebierg	316
LU7840	Plage Beaufort	314
LU7880	Trois Frontières	318

Netherlands

NL6705	Alkmaar	339
NL5835	Beek en Hei	332
NL5620	Duinrell	353
NL5950	Heumens Bos	329
NL5850	Hooge Veluwe	328
NL5640	Kijkduinpark	351
NL6030	Klein Vaarwater	326
NL5760	Kuilart	327
NL6090	Lauwersoog	333
NL5680	Noordduinen	351
NL5610	Oude Maas	350
NL5840	Pampel	330
NL5500	Pannenschuur	347
NL6328	Rhederlaagse Meren	330
NL6540	Rozenhof	336
NL6510	Schatberg	336
NL6930	Schoneveld	346
NL5735	Tempelhof	342
NL6425	Twee Bruggen	332
NL5560	Wijde Blick	348
NL6153	Witterzomer	324
NL5780	Zanding	331
NL5665	Zeeburg	341
NL6948	Zeeuwse Kust	348

Norway

NO2556	Aurdal	364
NO2515	Gjelten Bru	358
NO2574	Gol	357
NO2510	Håneset	368
NO2432	Harstad	369
NO2400	Jolstraholmen	368
NO2390	Kjørnes	367
NO2375	Lærdal	366
NO2505	Magalaupe	368
NO2487	Mosjøen	363
NO2610	Neset	356
NO2615	Olberg	364
NO2394	PlusCamp Nore	365
NO2660	Preikestolen	365
NO2545	Rustberg	364
NO2475	Saltstraumen	363
NO2385	Sandvik	366
NO2590	Sandviken	369
NO2490	Skjerneset	360
NO2600	Sølvgarden	357

Portugal

PO8210	Albufeira	374
PO8033	Angeiras	382
PO8410	Armação-Pêra	374
PO8354	Beira-Marvao Alentejo	372
PO8010	Caminha	382
PO8150	Caparica	379
PO8370	Cerdeira	382
PO8340	Évora	373
PO8480	Foz do Arelho	379
PO8090	Gala	377
PO8130	Guincho	378
PO8140	Lisboa Monsanto	380
PO8350	Markádia	372
PO8230	Olhão	376
PO8356	Os Anjos	372
PO8220	Quarteira	376
PO8440	Quinta	374
PO8030	Rio Alto	383
PO8430	Sagres	377
PO8170	São Miguel	373
PO8100	São Pedro Moel	381
PO8202	Turiscampo	375
PO8040	Vagueira	378
PO8110	Valado	380
PO8200	Valverde	375

Slovakia

SK4980	Levocská Dolina	386
SK4910	Turiec	387

Slovenia

SV4250	Danica Bohinj	392
SV4400	Dolina Prebold	396
SV4150	Kamne	395
SV4270	Koren	393
SV4340	Ljubljana	394
SV4405	Menina	397
SV4410	Terme 3000	396
SV4415	Terme Catez	393
SV4455	Terme Lendava	394

Spain

ES88730	Aldea	400
ES85850	Altomira	452
ES85360	Ametlla	415
ES90910	Aranjuez	457
ES90240	As Cancelas	456
ES90510	Bardenas	460
ES89360	Bayona Playa	455
ES88100	Bella Vista	404
ES86830	Benisol	448
ES82280	Blanes	418
ES90620	Boltana	407
ES85800	Bonterra	447
ES88030	Buganvilla	405
ES87630	Cabo de Gata	400
ES88020	Cabopino	405
ES85350	Cala d'Oques	424
ES81300	Calonge	419
ES86790	Calpemar	448
ES90890	Despeñaperros	406
ES92950	Don Cactus	405
ES90290	El Astral	413
ES92900	El Balcon	406
ES90800	El Brillante	401
ES92000	El Escorial	457
ES90900	El Greco	414
ES87520	El Portus (Naturist)	459
ES87450	Fuente	458
ES87900	Fuente de Piedra	402
ES90210	Fuentes Blancas	413
ES87650	Garrofa	400
ES90640	Gavín	407
ES87850	Iznate	403
ES87540	Javea	450
ES80080	Joncar Mar	436
ES86150	Kiko	453
ES86250	Kiko Rural	454
ES92850	Lomas	403
ES87480	Madriles	459
ES87530	Manga	459
ES88000	Marbella Playa	404
ES87420	Marina	451
ES86450	Mariola	448
ES87435	Marjal Costa Blanca	449
ES87430	Marjal Resort	449
ES80720	Medes	426
ES90960	Mirador	414

ES90270	Monfrague	455
ES85900	Monmar	452
ES92120	Monte Holiday	458
ES87550	Moraira	450
ES86130	Olé	452
ES90600	Peña Montañesa	408
ES92100	Pico-Miel	458
ES88650	Playa Las Dunas	402
ES85600	Playa Tropicana	446
ES85080	Poboleda	435
ES85610	Ribamar	447
ES88590	Roche	401
ES85590	Spa Natura Resort	453
ES92700	Suspiro-Moro	402
ES85700	Torre la Sal 2	454
ES88620	Valdevaqueros	406
ES91225	Vall de Camprodon	420
ES86750	Vall de Laguar	449
ES83900	Vilanova Park	445
ES86810	Villasol	447

Sweden

SW2755	Alevi	472
SW2750	Årjäng	471
SW2665	Björkhagen	465
SW2840	Flottsbro	470
SW2760	Frykenbaden	472
SW2865	Gielas	467
SW2800	Glyttinge	468
SW2715	Gröne Backe	474
SW2725	Hafsten	477
SW2825	Herrfallet	473
SW2720	Hökensås	476
SW2805	Kolmårdens	468
SW2740	Laxsjons	474
SW2710	Lidköping	475
SW2705	Lisebergsbyn	475
SW2675	Lysingsbadet	466
SW2836	Mora Parkens	464
SW2850	Ostersunds	464
SW2650	Skånes	469
SW2857	Strömsund	465
SW2655	Tingsryds	467
SW2860	Umeå	472

Switzerland

CH9425	Alpenblick	484
CH9740	Attermenzen	501
CH9855	Cavresc	489
CH9520	Du Botza	502
CH9570	Eienwäldli	497
CH9175	Giessenpark	493
CH9360	Grassi	481
CH9460	Jungfrau	486
CH9950	Lugano	495
CH9420	Manor Farm 1	484
CH9670	Molignon	500
CH9370	Rendez-vous	485
CH9540	Seefeld Sarnen	498
CH9830	Sur En	490
CH9270	Vidy	503

Dogs

Many British campers and caravanners prefer to take their pets with them on holiday. However, pet travel rules changed on 1 January 2012 when the UK brought its procedures into line with the European Union. From this date all pets can enter or re-enter the UK from any country in the world without quarantine provided they meet the rules of the scheme, which will be different depending on the country or territory the pet is coming from. Please refer to the following website for full details: www.gov.uk/take-pet-abroad

For the benefit of those who want to take their dogs with them or for people who do not like dogs at the sites they visit, we list here those sites that have indicated to us that they do not accept dogs. If you are, however, planning to take your dog we do advise you to check first – there may be limits on numbers, breeds, etc. or times of the year when they are excluded.

Never – these sites do not accept dogs at any time:

Austria

AU0420	Müllerhof (Naturist)	30
AU0416	Turkwiese (Naturist)	30

Belgium

BE0680	Sud	67

Croatia

CR6736	Valdaliso	87

France

FR85210	Ecureuils	178
FR85020	Jard	179
FR64060	Pavillon Royal	124

Germany

DE31950	Hertha-See	215
DE32330	Holländischer Hof	224
DE30050	Knaus Hamburg	203

Hungary

HU5090	Füred	251

Italy

IT66710	Argentario	290
IT68200	Baia Domizia	256
IT62630	Bella Italia	266
IT60360	Ca'Pasquali	305
IT60100	Capalonga	298
IT63570	Cisano & San Vito	261
IT64010	Dei Fiori	272
IT66450	Delle Piscine	295
IT63580	Delle Rose	264
IT68000	Europe Garden	256
IT60400	Garden Paradiso	306
IT60150	Il Tridente	299
IT60550	Isamar	310
IT60210	Italy	302
IT60370	Jesolo	308
IT60130	Lido (Bibione-Pineda)	299
IT60220	Portofelice	307
IT60030	Pra' Delle Torri	300
IT68480	Punta Lunga	280
IT60250	Residence	304
IT68650	Riva di Ugento	280
IT66240	Rubicone	258
IT60390	Sant'Angelo	306
IT63590	Serenella	260
IT60065	Tenuta Primero	259

Luxembourg

LU7820	Bon Repos	314

Netherlands

NL6872	Bakkum	343
NL6361	De Tol	331
NL6952	Julianahoeve	348
NL6870	Lakens	341
NL5680	Noordduinen	351
NL5840	Pampel	330
NL5980	Roos	345
NL6630	TerSpegelt	338
NL7030	Vier Bannen	347
NL6285	Wildhoeve	329

Portugal

PO8170	São Miguel	373

Spain

ES80900	Cypsela	434
ES81030	El Maset	416
ES82345	Els Pins	430
ES87480	Madriles	459
ES85900	Monmar	452
ES91430	Pirineus	423
ES81010	Playa Brava	434
ES90000	Playa Joyel	411
ES85300	Playa Montroig	428
ES84200	Stel (Roda)	435
ES89435	Taurán	409
ES85400	Torre del Sol	432
ES86810	Villasol	447

Switzerland

CH9180	Buchhorn	494
CH9890	Campofelice	496
CH9900	Delta	495
CH9185	Fischerhaus	494
CH9880	Lido Mappo	497
CH9160	Schaffhausen	493

Dogs accepted – certain periods only or other restrictions:

Austria

AU0227	Camp Grän	42
AU0060	Natterer See	48
AU0232	Sonnenberg	55

Belgium

BE0670	Clusure	70
BE0796	Lage Kempen	63
BE0560	Lombarde	74
BE0798	Parelstrand	64
BE0735	Petite Suisse	68

France

FR45010	Bois du Bardelet	176
FR17010	Bois Soleil	168
FR85440	Brunelles	179
FR85480	Chaponnet	178
FR23010	Château Poinsouze	152
FR85495	Cyprès	180
FR83120	Domaine	143
FR85930	Forges	178
FR40250	Grands Pins	132
FR66250	Huttopia Font-Romeu	148
FR78040	Huttopia Rambouillet	161
FR37140	Huttopia Rillé	177
FR85720	Indigo Noirmoutier	179
FR30080	Mas de Reilhe	148
FR24350	Moulin de la Pique	124
FR85915	Paradis	180
FR85150	Yole	180

Germany

DE34150	Adam	185
DE32320	Family Club	221
DE36500	Gitzenweiler	200
DE34420	Herbolzheim	187
DE34280	Oase	186
DE34650	Wirthshof	188

Greece

GR8520	Delphi	235

Italy

IT60590	Barricata	300
IT62485	Conca d'Oro	275
IT61830	Dolomiti	285
IT66060	Europa (Torre del Lago)	296
IT62460	Isolino	276
IT66310	Mareblu	291
IT69300	Marinello	283
IT69960	Mariposa	281
IT60560	Miramare (Chioggia)	309
IT68130	Porticciolo	268
IT62310	Punta Indiani	287
IT69350	Rais Gerbi	282
IT68450	San Nicola	280
IT62100	Steiner	285
IT66290	Tripesce	296

Luxembourg

LU7770	Val d'Or	316

Netherlands

NL6705	Alkmaar	339
NL5600	Delftse Hout	350
NL5880	Dierenbos	339
NL5640	Kijkduinpark	351
NL5630	Koningshof	352
NL6515	Oolderhuuske	335
NL6590	Osebos	335
NL5610	Oude Maas	350
NL6470	Papillon	344
NL6000	Vechtdalcamping	343
NL5830	Warnsborn	328
NL5715	WeidumerHout	328

Norway

NO2606	Isefjærleiren (Naturist)	356

Portugal

PO8350	Markádia	372
PO8356	Os Anjos	372
PO8377	Quinta Valbom	383

Spain

ES82320	Bella Terra	418
ES85800	Bonterra	447
ES88030	Buganvilla	405
ES81600	Cala Gogo	419
ES80800	Delfin Verde	446
ES80720	Medes	426
ES84820	Pineda de Salou	427

Switzerland

CH9480	Gletscherdorf	482
CH9420	Manor Farm 1	484
CH9842	RinerLodge	488
CH9540	Seefeld Sarnen	498

Travelling in Europe

When taking your car (and caravan, tent or trailer tent) or motorcaravan to the continent you do need to plan in advance and to find out as much as possible about driving in the countries you plan to visit. Whilst European harmonisation has eliminated many of the differences between one country and another, it is well worth reading the short notes we provide in the introduction to each country in this guide, in addition to this more general summary.

Of course, the main difference from driving in the UK is that in mainland Europe you will need to drive on the right. Without taking extra time and care, especially at busy junctions and conversely when roads are empty, it is easy to forget to drive on the right. Remember that traffic approaching from the right usually has priority unless otherwise indicated by road markings and signs. Harmonisation also means that most (but not all) common road signs are the same in all countries.

Your vehicle

Book your vehicle in for a good service well before your intended departure date. This will lessen the chance of an expensive breakdown. Make sure your brakes are working efficiently and that your tyres have plenty of tread (3 mm. is recommended, particularly if you are undertaking a long journey).

Also make sure that your caravan or trailer is roadworthy and that its tyres are in good order and correctly inflated. Plan your packing and be careful not to overload your vehicle, caravan or trailer – this is unsafe and may well invalidate your insurance cover (it must not be more fully loaded than the kerb weight of the insured vehicle).

There are a number of countries that have introduced low emission zones in towns and cities, including including Germany, Czech Republic, Denmark, Italy and Sweden. For up-to-date details on low emission zones and requirements please see: www.lowemissionzones.eu

CHECK ALL THE FOLLOWING:

- GB sticker. If you do not display a sticker, you may risk an on-the-spot fine as this identifier is compulsory in all countries. Euro-plates are an acceptable alternative within the EU (but not outside). Remember to attach another sticker (or Euro-plate) to caravans and trailers. Only GB stickers (not England, Scotland, Wales or N. Ireland) stickers are valid in the EU.

- Headlights. As you will be driving on the right you must adjust your headlights so that the dipped beam does not dazzle oncoming drivers. Converter kits are readily available for most vehicles, although if your car is fitted with high intensity headlights, you should check with your motor dealer. Check that any planned extra loading does not affect the beam height.

- Seatbelts. Rules for the fitting and wearing of seatbelts throughout Europe are similar to those in the UK, but it is worth checking before you go. Rules for carrying children in the front of vehicles vary from country to country. It is best to plan not to do this if possible.

- Door/wing mirrors. To help with driving on the right, if your vehicle is not fitted with a mirror on the left hand side, we recommend you have one fitted.

- Fuel. Leaded and lead replacement petrol is increasingly difficult to find in Northern Europe.

Compulsory additional equipment

The driving laws of the countries of Europe still vary in what you are required to carry in your vehicle, although the consequences of not carrying a required piece of equipment are almost always an on-the-spot fine.

To meet these requirements you should make sure that you carry the following:

- FIRE EXTINGUISHER

- BASIC TOOL KIT

- FIRST AID KIT

- SPARE BULBS

- TWO WARNING TRIANGLES – two are required in some countries at all times, and are compulsory in most countries when towing.

- HIGH VISIBILITY VEST – now compulsory in France, Spain, Italy and Austria (and likely to become compulsory throughout the EU) in case you need to walk on a motorway.

- BREATHALYSERS – now compulsory in France. Only breathalysers that are NF-approved will meet the legal requirement. French law states that one breathalyser must be produced, but it is recommended you carry two in case you use or break one.

Insurance and Motoring Documents

Vehicle insurance

Contact your insurer well before you depart to check that your car insurance policy covers driving outside the UK. Most do, but many policies only provide minimum cover (so if you have an accident your insurance may only cover the cost of damage to the other person's property, with no cover for fire and theft).

To maintain the same level of cover abroad as you enjoy at home you need to tell your vehicle insurer. Some will automatically cover you abroad with no extra cost and no extra paperwork. Some will say you need a Green Card (which is neither green nor on card) but won't charge for it. Some will charge extra for the Green Card. Ideally you should contact your vehicle insurer 3-4 weeks before you set off, and confirm your conversation with them in writing.

Breakdown insurance

Arrange breakdown cover for your trip in good time so that if your vehicle breaks down or is involved in an accident it (and your caravan or trailer) can be repaired or returned to this country. This cover can usually be arranged as part of your travel insurance policy (see below).

Documents you must take with you

You may be asked to show your documents at any time so make sure that they are in order, up-to-date and easily accessible while you travel. These are what you need to take:

- Passports (you may also need a visa in some countries if you hold either a UK passport not issued in the UK or a passport that was issued outside the EU).

- Motor Insurance Certificate, including Green Card (or Continental Cover clause).

- DVLA Vehicle Registration Document plus, if not your own vehicle, the owner's written authority to drive.

- A full valid Driving Licence (not provisional). The new photo style licence is now mandatory in most European countries.

Personal Holiday insurance

Even though you are just travelling within Europe you must take out travel insurance. Few EU countries pay the full cost of medical treatment even under reciprocal health service arrangements. The first part of a holiday insurance policy covers people. It will include the cost of doctor, ambulance and hospital treatment if needed. If required, the better companies will even pay for English language speaking doctors and nurses and will bring a sick or injured holidaymaker home by air ambulance.

An important part of the insurance, often ignored, is cancellation (and curtailment) cover. Few things are as heartbreaking as having to cancel a holiday because a member of the family falls ill. Cancellation insurance can't take away the disappointment, but it makes sure you don't suffer financially as well. For this reason you should arrange your holiday insurance at least eight weeks before you set off.

Whichever insurance you choose we would advise reading very carefully the policies sold by the High Street travel trade. Whilst they may be good, they may not cover the specific needs of campers, caravanners and motorcaravanners.

Telephone 01580 214000 for a quote for our Camping Travel Insurance with cover arranged through leading leisure insurance providers.

Alternatively visit our website at: alanrogers.com/insurance

European Health Insurance Card (EHIC)

Make sure you apply for your EHIC before travelling in Europe. Eligible travellers from the UK are entitled to receive free or reduced-cost medical care in many European countries on production of an EHIC. This free card is available by completing a form in the booklet 'Health Advice for Travellers' from local Post Offices. One should be completed for each family member. Alternatively visit www.ehic.org.uk and apply on line. Please allow time to send your application off and have the EHIC returned to you.

The EHIC is valid in all European Community countries plus Iceland, Liechtenstein, Switzerland and Norway. If you or any of your dependants are suddenly taken ill or have an accident during a visit to any of these countries, free or reduced-cost emergency treatment is available – in most cases on production of a valid EHIC.

Only state-provided emergency treatment is covered, and you will receive treatment on the same terms as nationals of the country you are visiting. Private treatment is generally not covered, and state-provided treatment may not cover all of the things that you would expect to receive free of charge from the NHS.

Remember an EHIC does not cover you for all the medical costs that you can incur or for repatriation – it is not an alternative to travel insurance. You will still need appropriate insurance to ensure you are fully covered for all eventualities.

Travelling with children

Most countries in Europe are enforcing strict guidelines when you are travelling with children who are not your own. A minor (under the age of 18) must be accompanied by a parent or legal guardian or must carry a letter of authorisation from a parent or guardian. The letter should name the adult responsible for the minor during his or her stay. Similarly, a minor travelling with just one of his/her parents, must have a letter of authority to leave their home country from the parent staying behind. Full information is available at www.fco.gov.uk

Looking for competitively priced insurance for your camping or caravanning holiday?

We have been entrusted with readers' campsite holidays since 1968. Choosing the right campsite is one thing; having proper, suitable travel insurance is another.

Personal Travel Insurance

Ideal for self-drive holidays in Europe, and including cover for camping equipment. Family policies are available.

- 24 hour travel advice line and multi lingual medical assistance

- Repatriation and evacuation cover

- Repatriation due to serious illness of relatives at home

Vehicle Assistance Insurance

The vehicle assistance service is provided by Allianz Global Assistance and a network of over 7,500 garages and agents. Serving 3 million people a year, they are well used to looking after the needs of campsite-based holidaymakers.

- Roadside assistance

- Vehicle repatriation (and alternative driver)

- Cover prior to departure

Get a quote and and start looking forward to your holiday with confidence!

01580 214000
alanrogers.com/insurance

The Alan Rogers
Travel Card

At Alan Rogers we have a network of thousands of quality inspected and selected campsites. We also have partnerships with numerous organisations, including ferry operators and tourist attractions, all of whom can bring you benefits and save you money.

Our **FREE** Travel Card binds all this together at
alanrogers.com/travelcard

So register today...and start saving.

Benefits that add up

- Offers and benefits on many Alan Rogers campsites across Europe

- Save up to 60% in low season on over 600 campsites

- Free cardholders' magazine

- Big savings on rented accommodation and hotels at 400 locations

- Discounted ferries

- Savings on Alan Rogers guides

- Vote for your favourite campsite in the Alan Rogers Awards

Register today...
and start saving

Carry the Alan Rogers Travel Card on your travels through Europe and save money all the way.

You'll enjoy exclusive deals with ferry operators, continental partners, tourist attractions and more. Even hotels, apartments, mobile homes and other campsite accommodation.

We've teamed up with Camping Cheque, the leading low season discount scheme, to offer you the widest choice of quality campsites at unbelievable prices. Simply load your card with Cheques before you travel.

Step 1
Register at **www.alanrogers.com/travelcard**

Step 2
You'll receive your activated card, along with a Welcome email containing useful links and information.

Step 3
Start using your card to save money or to redeem benefits during your holiday.

alanrogers.com/travelcard

Getting the most from off peak touring

£14.95 night
outfit+ 2 people

There are many reasons to avoid high season, if you can. Queues are shorter, there's less traffic, a calmer atmosphere and prices are cheaper. And it's usually still nice and sunny!

And when you use Camping Cheques you'll find great quality facilities that are actually open and a welcoming conviviality.

Did you know?

Camping Cheques can be used right into mid-July and from late August on many sites. Over 90 campsites in France alone accept Camping Cheques from 20th August.

Save up to 60% with Camping Cheques

Camping Cheque is a fixed price scheme allowing you to go as you please, staying on over 600 campsites across Europe, always paying the same rate and saving you up to 60% on regular pitch fees. One Cheque gives you one night for 2 people + unit on a standard pitch, with electricity. It's as simple as that.

Special offers mean you can stay extra nights free (eg 7 nights for 6 Cheques) or even a month free for a month paid! Especially popular in Spain during the winter, these longer-term offers can effectively halve the nightly rate. See Site Directory for details.

Check out our amazing Ferry Deals!

Why should I use Camping Cheques?

- It's a proven system, recognised by all 600+ participating campsites - so no nasty surprises.

- It's flexible, allowing you to travel between campsites, and also countries, on a whim - so no need to pre-book. (It's low season, so campsites are rarely full, though advance bookings can be made).

- Stay as long as you like, where you like - so you travel in complete freedom.

- Camping Cheques are valid at least 2 years - so no pressure to use them up. (If you have a couple left over after your trip, simply keep them for the following year, or use them up in the UK).

Tell me more... (but keep it brief!)

Camping Cheques was started in 1999 and has since grown in popularity each year (nearly 2 million were used last year). That should speak for itself. There are 'copycat' schemes, but none has the same range of quality campsites that save you up to 60%.

Ask for your **FREE** continental road map, which explains how Camping Cheque works

01580 214002

Order your 2015
Directory
alanrogers.com/directory

campingcheque.co.uk

CARAVAN CAMPING & MOTORHOME SHOW 2015

17-22 February
NEC Birmingham

Start the holiday season at the **CARAVAN, CAMPING & MOTORHOME SHOW** where there's something for everyone; with the latest models, holiday inspiration and accessories.

Come and discover your next adventure here!

www.**caravan**camping**motorhome**show.co.uk

MOTORHOME & CARAVAN SHOW 2015

13-18 October
NEC Birmingham

The **UK'S NATIONAL SHOW** where you will find all the latest products for 2016 under one roof! **OVER 400 EXHIBITORS** including all the leading UK and European manufacturers.

www.**motorhome**and**caravan**show.co.uk

Organised by:  **NCC events**   Supported by: THE **CARAVAN CLUB**   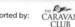 The **Camping and Caravanning Club**

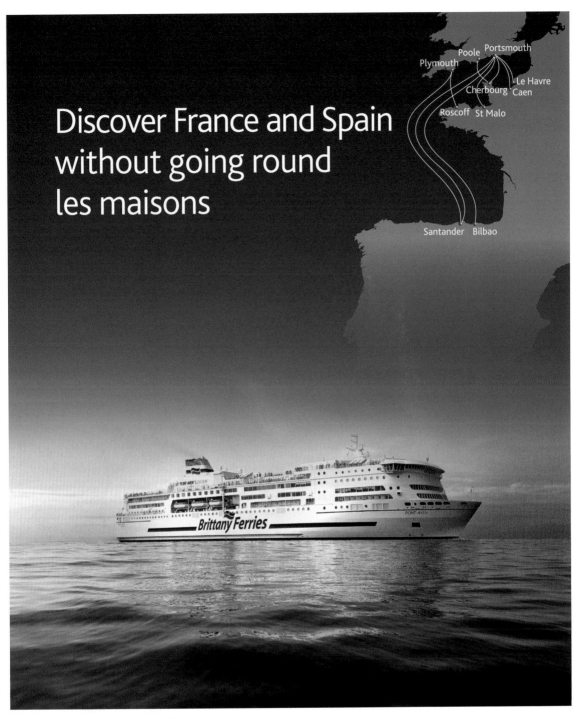

Discover France and Spain without going round les maisons

Plymouth · Poole · Portsmouth · Cherbourg · Le Havre · Caen · Roscoff · St Malo · Santander · Bilbao

any better way to save miles of driving?

Why endure a long drive through northern France when you can sail direct to the finest holiday regions of France and Spain with us? And thanks to our award-winning service and range of facilities, your holiday will start the moment you step onboard.

Visit **brittanyferries.com**
or call **0871 244 1447**

Map 1

Belgium, Luxembourg, Netherlands

0   50   100 kms

Please refer to the town index (page 532) for campsite page references

Map 2

Denmark, Germany

Please refer to the town index (page 532) for campsite page references

Map 3

Norway, Finland, Sweden

Please refer to the town index (page 532) for campsite page references

Austria, Slovenia, Switzerland

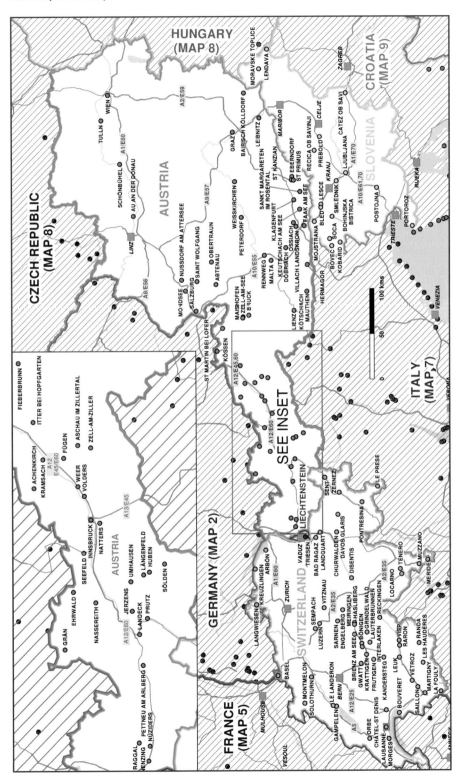

Map 4

Please refer to the town index (page 532) for campsite page references

Map 5

France (West)

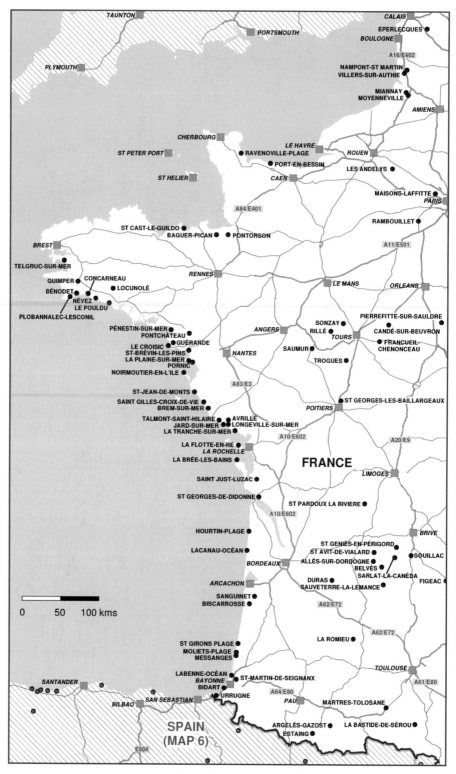

Please refer to the town index (page 532) for campsite page references

Map 5

France (East)

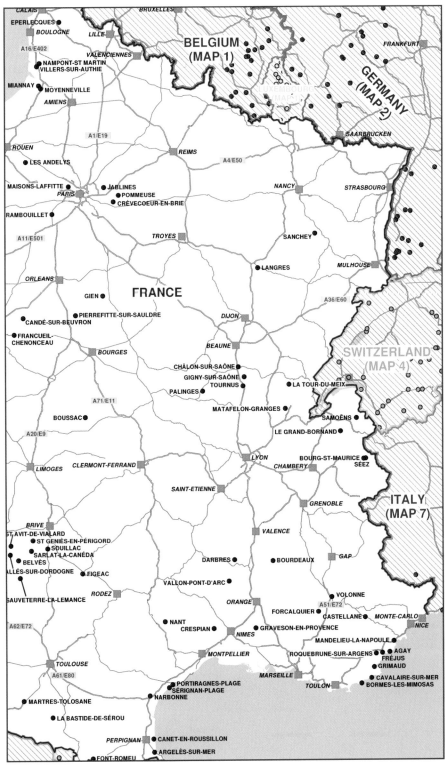

Please refer to the town index (page 532) for campsite page references

Map 6

Portugal, Spain (West)

Please refer to the town index (page 532) for campsite page references

Spain (East)

Map 6

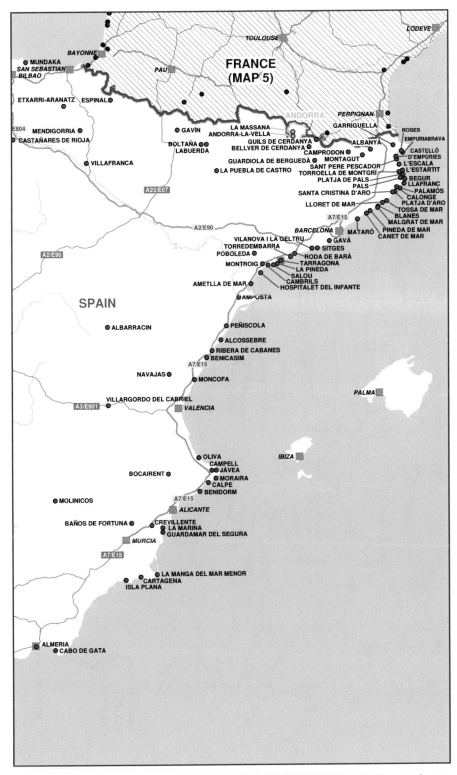

MUNDAKA
SAN SEBASTIAN
BILBAO
BAYONNE
PAU
TOULOUSE
LODEVE
FRANCE
(MAP 5)
ANDORRA
PERPIGNAN
ETXARRI-ARANATZ   ESPINAL
GAVÍN
LA MASSANA
ANDORRA-LA-VELLA
GARRIGUELLA
ROSES
E804
MENDIGORRIA
CASTAÑARES DE RIOJA
BOLTAÑA
LABUERDA
GUILS DE CERDANYA
BELLVER DE CERDANYA
ALBANYÀ
EMPURIABRAVA
VILLAFRANCA
GUARDIOLA DE BERGUEDÀ
CAMPRODON
MONTAGUT
CASTELLÓ
D'EMPÚRIES
L'ESCALA
LA PUEBLA DE CASTRO
SANT PERE PESCADOR
TORROELLA DE MONTGRÍ
L'ESTARTIT
PLATJA DE PALS
BEGUR
LLAFRANC
PALS
PALAMÓS
SANTA CRISTINA D'ARO
CALONGE
LLORET DE MAR
PLATJA D'ARO
TOSSA DE MAR
A23 E07
A7/E15
BLANES
MALGRAT DE MAR
A2/E90
BARCELONA
MATARÓ
PINEDA DE MAR
CANET DE MAR
A2/E90
VILANOVA I LA GELTRU
TORREDEMBARRA
POBOLEDA
GAVÁ
SITGES
RODA DE BARÀ
TARRAGONA
MONTROIG
LA PINEDA
SALOU
AMETLLA DE MAR
CAMBRILS
HOSPITALET DEL INFANTE
SPAIN
AMPOSTA
ALBARRACIN
PEÑISCOLA
ALCOSSEBRE
RIBERA DE CABANES
BENICASIM
A7/E15
NAVAJAS
MONCOFA
VILLARGORDO DEL CABRIEL
PALMA
A3/E901
VALENCIA
OLIVA
CAMPELL
IBIZA
BOCAIRENT
JÁVEA
MORAIRA
CALPE
MOLINICOS
BENIDORM
A7/E15
ALICANTE
BAÑOS DE FORTUNA
CREVILLENTE
LA MARINA
GUARDAMAR DEL SEGURA
MURCIA
A7/E15
LA MANGA DEL MAR MENOR
CARTAGENA
ISLA PLANA
ALMERIA
CABO DE GATA

Please refer to the town index (page 532) for campsite page references

Map 7

Italy

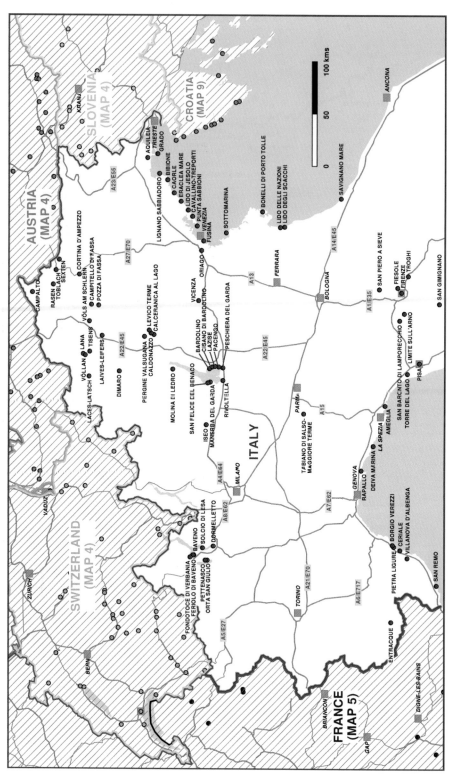

Please refer to the town index (page 532) for campsite page references

Italy

Map 7

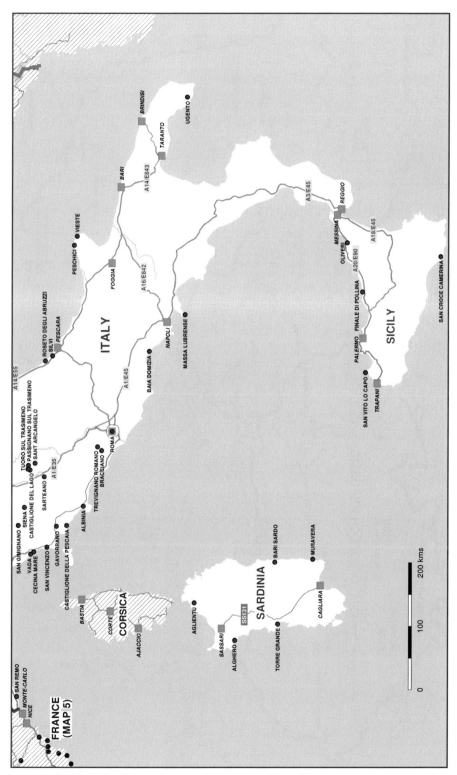

Please refer to the town index (page 532) for campsite page references

Map 8

Czech Republic, Slovakia, Hungary

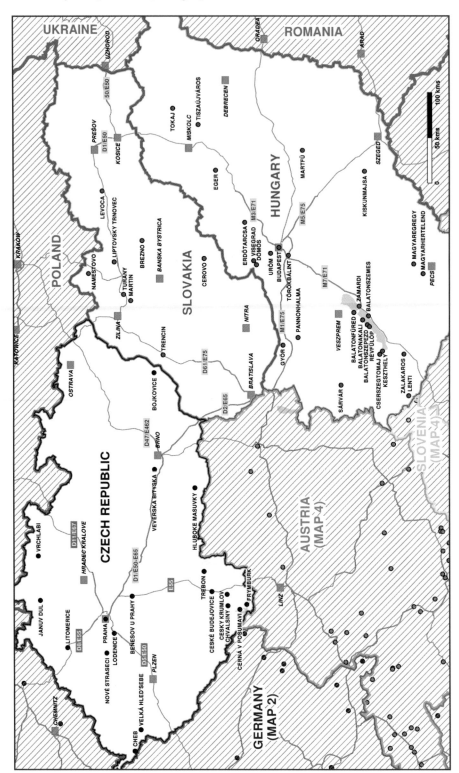

Please refer to the town index (page 532) for campsite page references

Map 9

Map 10

Croatia

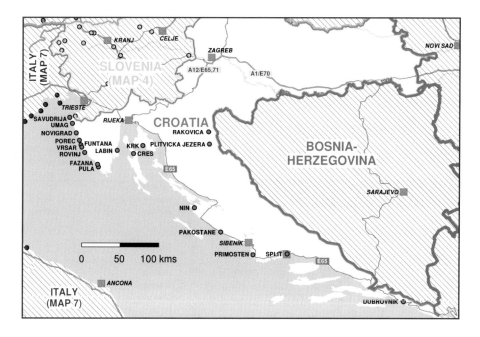

Greece

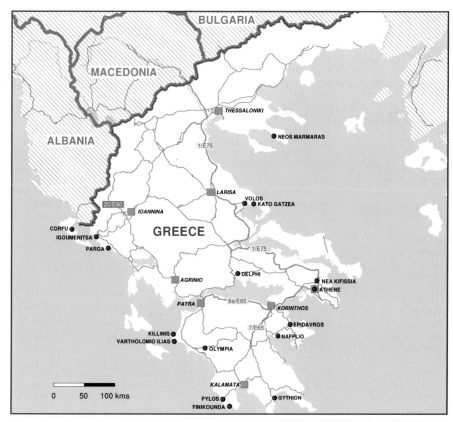

Please refer to the town index (page 532) for campsite page references

Town & Village Index

Index by Country and Campsite Name

SK4900	Trusalová	388
SK4910	Turiec	387

SV4200	Bled	392
SV4250	Danica Bohinj	392
SV4400	Dolina Prebold	396
SV4150	Kamne	395
SV4235	Klin	397
SV4270	Koren	393
SV4265	Lazar	393
SV4340	Ljubljana	394
SV4315	Lucija	395
SV4405	Menina	397
SV4330	Pivka Jama	396
SV4280	Polovnik	392
SV4360	Smlednik	397
SV4210	Sobec	394
SV4410	Terme 3000	396
SV4415	Terme Catez	393
SV4455	Terme Lendava	394

Spain

ES83120	3 Estrellas	423
ES90950	Albarracin	407
ES88730	Aldea	400
ES85850	Altomira	452
ES80200	Amberes	422
ES85360	Ametlla	415
ES80350	Amfora	439
ES80500	Aquarius	438
ES90910	Aranjuez	457
ES89550	Arenal-Moris	408
ES89700	Arenas-Pechón	411
ES90240	As Cancelas	456
ES80600	Ballena Alegre	442
ES82450	Barcelona	430
ES90510	Bardenas	460
ES80640	Bassegoda	415
ES89360	Bayona Playa	455
ES81040	Begur	416
ES82320	Bella Terra	418
ES88100	Bella Vista	404
ES86830	Benisol	448
ES91390	Berguedà	423
ES82280	Blanes	418
ES90620	Boltana	407
ES85800	Bonterra	447
ES88030	Buganvilla	405
ES82380	Caballo de Mar	431
ES87630	Cabo de Gata	400
ES88020	Cabopino	405
ES85350	Cala d'Oques	424
ES81600	Cala Gogo	419
ES82000	Cala Llevadó	446
ES81300	Calonge	419
ES86790	Calpemar	448
ES84845	Camping La Noria	444
ES80070	Castell Montgri	426
ES84855	Clara	444
ES89500	Costa Verde	409
ES89530	Cudillero	409
ES80900	Cypsela	434
ES80800	Delfin Verde	446
ES90890	Despeñaperros	406
ES92950	Don Cactus	405
ES84790	Don Camilo	420
ES80400	Dunas	441
ES90290	El Astral	413
ES92900	El Balcon	406
ES90800	El Brillante	401

ES92000	El Escorial	457
ES83920	El Garrofer	443
ES90900	El Greco	414
ES89610	El Helguero	412
ES81030	El Maset	416
ES87520	El Portus (Naturist)	459
ES82345	Els Pins	430
ES80730	Emporda	426
ES90420	Etxarri	460
ES85550	Eucaliptus	415
ES87450	Fuente	458
ES87900	Fuente de Piedra	402
ES88600	Fuente del Gallo	401
ES90210	Fuentes Blancas	413
ES87650	Garrofa	400
ES90640	Gavín	407
ES80310	Gaviota	440
ES82430	Globo Rojo	420
ES89570	Hortensias	410
ES81000	Inter-Pals	435
ES89620	Isla	411
ES87850	Iznate	403
ES87540	Javea	450
ES80080	Joncar Mar	436
ES86150	Kiko	453
ES86250	Kiko Rural	454
ES81200	Kim's	427
ES91250	Lago Barasona	408
ES80150	Laguna	421
ES80740	Illa Mateua	425
ES92850	Lomas	403
ES87480	Madriles	459
ES87530	Manga	459
ES89420	Manzanos	455
ES88000	Marbella Playa	404
ES87420	Marina	451
ES86450	Mariola	448
ES87435	Marjal Costa Blanca	449
ES87430	Marjal Resort	449
ES80120	Mas Nou	421
ES81020	Mas Patoxas	431
ES81750	Mas Sant Josep	440
ES80720	Medes	426
ES90960	Mirador	414
ES90430	Molino Mendigorria	461
ES90270	Monfrague	455
ES85900	Monmar	452
ES91220	Montagut	428
ES92120	Monte Holiday	458
ES87550	Moraira	450
ES80300	Nautic Almata	421
ES80690	Neus	424
ES86130	Olé	452
ES81500	Palamos	431
ES89600	Paz	410
ES90600	Peña Montañesa	408
ES92100	Pico-Miel	458
ES84820	Pineda de Salou	427
ES91430	Pirineus	423
ES81010	Playa Brava	434
ES90000	Playa Joyel	411
ES88650	Playa Las Dunas	402
ES85300	Playa Montroig	428
ES85600	Playa Tropicana	446
ES89710	Playa-Oyambre	412
ES85080	Poboleda	435
ES90350	Portuondo	461
ES85610	Ribamar	447
ES90980	Rio Mundo	414
ES92250	Rioja	456
ES88590	Roche	401
ES84800	Sanguli	436
ES90230	Santiago	413